www./shellgeostar.com/
route/route asp.

ALAN ROGERS'
GOOD CAMPS GUIDE

EUROPE
2000

Quality Camping and Caravanning Sites

THE ALAN ROGERS'
Good camps guide

Compiled by: Deneway Guides & Travel Ltd

Cover design: Design Section, Frome
Cover photography: 'The Algarve' – D. Hermelin

Clive Edwards, Lois Edwards & Sue Smart have asserted their rights to be identified as the authors of this work.

First published in this format 1999

© Haynes Publishing & Deneway Guides & Travel Ltd 1999

Published by: Haynes Publishing, Sparkford, Nr Yeovil, Somerset BA22 7JJ
in association with
Deneway Guides & Travel Ltd, West Bexington, Dorchester, Dorset DT2 9DG

British Library Cataloguing-in-Publication Data:
A catalogue record for this book is available from the British Library.

ISBN: 0 901586 73 0

Printed in Great Britain by J H Haynes & Co Ltd

Contents

Foreword 4

How to use the Guide 5

SELECTED AND INSPECTED CAMPSITES

ANDORRA 7   LUXEMBOURG 161

LIECHTENSTEIN 7   NETHERLANDS 166

AUSTRIA 8   NORWAY 193

BELGIUM 27   POLAND 211

CZECH REPUBLIC 35   PORTUGAL 217

DENMARK 41   SLOVAKIA 230

FINLAND 54   SLOVENIA 233

GERMANY 61   SPAIN 238

HUNGARY 94   SWEDEN 309

IRELAND 105   SWITZERLAND 323

ITALY 118

Motorsports Colour Section . . . .*between pages* 96/97

Open All Year 345

Brochure Service 346

No Dogs ! 347

Passports for Pets 348

Car Ferry Services 351

First Time Abroad 354

    Insurance 357

    Driving in Europe 358

    Getting through France 360

Motorbiking Through Europe 362

Reports by Readers 365

Naturism 366

Maps 368

Town and Village Index 378

Campsite Index 381

FOREWORD

'Independent campers and caravanners should get the Alan Rogers Good Camps Guide to inspected sites'. So said the Sunday Times, and we can think of no better endorsement of our philosophy of featuring only those sites which have been inspected by one of our experienced Site Assessors.

The Millennium Edition of our Europe Guide features reports on 694 sites in 22 countries in Europe, including Scandinavia and many countries in Eastern Europe.

However it no longer includes sites in either Britain or France as we publish separate guides for each of those popular camping and caravanning destinations. Indeed, so popular has France become in recent years that the Millennium Edition of our France Guide features 498 sites, and we have even introduced our own **Alan Rogers Travel Service** whereby readers can book many of the sites in our France Guide, and their ferry crossings, simply by telephoning our UK Travel service number.

Of course the majority of the readers of our Europe guide will travel via France en-route to their chosen destination, and we have included a few suggested routes through France from the Channel Ports, together with suggestions of names of those campsites featured in our France Guide which are particularly useful for night-stops when using these particular routes.

The introduction of our **Discount Voucher Scheme** in 1996 proved to be very successful and has been continued ever since. For 2000 we are pleased to include a two-part discount voucher in every guide which gives readers opportunities to enjoy substantial savings on travel insurance, breakdown cover and on site fees at certain sites. In many cases the potential savings can amount to more than the cost of the Guide. Full details of the 2000 Discount Voucher arrangements are to be found on page 347 and on the vouchers themselves (between pages 192/193). We would remind readers that the vouchers in this edition are valid only for use during the period 1 January - 31 December 2000.

Talking about savings, we are also pleased to draw readers attention to the **'Camping Cheques'** scheme, which is described between pages 128/129. This scheme has operated successfully in France for some time and has now been expanded to cover sites in several other European countries. These sites are identified in this guide as 'Camping Cheques' sites under their reservations details. For readers who can take their holidays avoiding the peak months of July and August this scheme offers very substantial savings.

The year 2000 sees the introduction of the **'Passports for Pets'** pilot scheme, whereby, subject to meeting all the various conditions, campers and caravanners will have the opportunity to take their dog or cat on holiday with them to mainland Europe. Full details of this scheme are shown on page 348.

It only remains for us to wish you a very happy and successful camping or caravanning New Year, and to hope that you will find this edition of our Europe guide even more useful and enjoyable than in the past.

Lois Edwards MAEd, FTS
Clive Edwards BEd, FTS
Sue Smart   Directors

The Guide's Aims and Principles

In producing all our Guides we have a number of aims and objectives designed to:

• Provide readers with the sort of factual information which, from our own extensive experiences, we would wish to know ourselves; for example, most of us want to know if a site is well maintained, if the sanitary facilities are at least adequate, sufficient and regularly cleaned, if electrical connections are available, what sort of shopping, catering and leisure facilities are provided.

• Provide some 'insight' into what a site is like – to try to convey some kind of picture in words that will give the reader an impression of the kind of atmosphere or ambience they can expect. This aspect of our reporting is the most difficult to achieve because what appeals to one person may have exactly the opposite affect on another, but the large number of readers' reports and comments we receive each year is reassuring. We make no claims to infallibility, but this feedback from readers suggests that we get it right most of the time.

• To present the factual information and our assessment of a site in a form that is easily understood, without the use of symbols. Many guides seem to rely on masses of symbols and require their readers to be expert code-breakers. Our Guides have no symbols, and therefore no 'key'.

• To provide basic information concerning tourism, particularly camping and caravanning, in each of the countries featured in the Guide.

• To report on our own experiences in respect of ferry services.

• To provide general information on camping and caravanning in Europe, the legal requirements and necessary formalities. Particularly aimed at those who have never camped abroad before but, as the information is regularly up-dated, it may also provide an 'aide-memoire' for the more experienced.

• To provide readers with the opportunity to benefit from a range of discounts through the **Camping Cheques Scheme** and through our own **Discount Vouchers**, as described elsewhere in this guide.

Quality Assurance

Having stated our objectives concerning the provision of both factual information and the more subjective aspect of 'insight', readers may be interested to know how we set about this. Firstly, we are a small organisation with only four full-time staff and a small team of part-time Site Assessors. The majority of the sites featured in our Guides have been recommended by readers initially, after which they are visited by one of our Site-Assessors before they are featured in the Guides.

Currently, our small team of dedicated part-time Site Assessors, all experienced campers or caravanners, specialising in particular countries and/or areas comprises:

Rosemary & George Boyce (Netherlands, Finland), Colin Samms & Maggie Doughty (Spain, Portugal, Italy), Gordon & Joyce Pearce (Scandinavia, Belgium, Luxembourg), Gerry Ovenden (Switzerland, Austria, Italy), Keith Smart (Germany, Eastern Europe) and Tibor Toka (Hungary).

Our thanks are due to them for the many miles they have travelled, their patience with our detailed site reports and their commitment to the philosophy of the guides.

All our 1,500 or more sites are inspected regularly every two years (occasionally every three years for the more remote ones) to monitor changes and our reports are updated accordingly. In those years when a visit is not made the sites are required to return a detailed questionnaire to us which is used to up-date factual information concerning prices, opening dates, etc. To ensure that our reports are consistent, the full-time staff also undertake a programme of site visits each year designed to monitor the situation as a whole and to make sure that there is a high degree of uniformity in terms of our assessment and reporting procedures. They also liaise directly with the sites, ferries, etc, answer the phone and readers' letters, typeset the guides, deal with advertisers and our popular breakdown insurance service and brochure distribution service, and still manage to fit in some 200/250 monitoring visits to sites throughout Europe every year.

We must also thank our readers for their reports and recommendations, particularly in terms of identifying potential new sites. The other points you raise all receive individual attention, although we cannot always respond as quickly as we would wish, particularly in the summer when site visits are a priority and in the autumn when we are literally working eighteen hours a day putting the following year's Guides together. We do follow them up and do try to let you know the outcome.

On the subject of complaints about any of our featured sites, please bear in mind the following - we are the Authors of the Guide, and we have no contractual arrangements with any of our featured sites, so we cannot actually intervene in any dispute between our readers and any featured site(s). In the event of your having a complaint about a site, ideally this should be addressed to the campsite owner in person, at the time - that way you stand the best chance of getting any problem resolved quickly. Of course we are always interested to know about any serious problems encountered by our readers in respect of a particular campsite, as these can often influence our choice of sites for the following year.

How to Use the Guide

The Guide is divided firstly by country, subsequently (in the case of larger countries) by region. These are both indicated by the page title lines which should help readers locate their area of interest fairly quickly, although for a particular area the town index provides more direct access. Regions appearing in the title lines are either defined political entities, or familiar tourist regions such as the Costas in Spain.

The index provides an invaluable source of reference, particularly when used in conjunction with the site number, grid reference and appropriate map. These maps are necessarily diagrammatic, showing the various countries and regions within them, and the approximate location of each site by reference to its site number. Their use is facilitated by dividing each map into 'grid squares', each of which is referenced by two co-ordinates in the form of letters of the alphabet (top line first). These co-ordinate letters are reproduced alongside the site name in the main index. We emphasise however that our maps are intended as a quick reference to the approximate position of sites, and not as basis for navigation.

The Title Line for each site seeks to provide the reader with a reasonably accurate idea of the campsite location on a medium-scale map, such as the Michelin Atlas. More precise details can be found in the 'How to find it' section below the individual site reviews.

Notes on information provided in the site reports

'Site' and 'Pitch' - the word site is used to describe the campsite itself (in Britain more commonly referred to as `parks), and the word pitch is used to define individual places on the campsite.

Distances - these are quoted in kilometres and metres.

Opening Dates - we give the dates when the site should be open - if we know that facilities on the site, such as restaurants, are open for a shorter period, this is mentioned. However, in some countries (Spain is a frequent culprit), site operators tend to close facilities almost at random. If there are insufficient visitors to justify keeping the pool or the restaurant open on an economic basis they will sometimes simply close it down without warning, so if you are visiting early or late in the season, it is a good idea to check with the site first if you are concerned as to whether a certain facility (or even the site itself!) will be open.

Sanitary Facilities - in years past continental sanitary facilities were by far the biggest cause of complaint from British visitors, but in recent years facilities in most European countries have improved enormously and, in many cases, are superior to those in the UK. We try to give brief details without expanding into a detailed survey. When describing WCs the word 'British' denotes the normal (pedestal) type of WC found in the UK - it may or may not have a lifting seat. Some European sites have toilets of the squatting type with a hole at ground level - nowadays these are usually known as 'Turkish' style lavatories. So far as personal washing facilities are concerned, on the plus side we say if washbasins are in private cabins, whereas on the minus side we say if only cold water is provided. Virtually all sites in this guide have at least good hot showers, sinks for washing dishes and clothes (cold/hot water). Many sites now have washing machines, dryers, etc, and mention is made of these facilities where they exist.

Charges - All charges given are per night. Some sites have fixed their prices for the following year when our Guides go to print in November, but many have not. We state to which year prices refer, except when we only have, and can thus only provide, an indication or guide to charges. Some sites accept payment by credit card, which we indicate. In general (not just at campsites) it is wise to check acceptability first, as some of these magnetic type cards are incompatible with European electronic readers.

Self-catering accommodation - e.g. mobile homes, static caravans, chalets, bungalows, apartments, hotel rooms, gites, etc. - in short any accommodation provided by the site which is available for rent. The range of accommodation and prices is far too extensive for us to describe in our individual site reviews, but we do try to mention if such accommodation is available at a site, firstly because some readers may be interested to rent this type of accommodation, and secondly because other readers prefer sites which cater exclusively, or mainly, for campers or caravanners with their own tent or caravan.

Reservations - This is an important subject, but it is difficult to describe comprehensively the various systems operated by all the individual sites. We therefore indicate in our reports whether a site accepts advance bookings or not and, if so, the most important special features of their system. It is important to distinguish between a 'booking fee' and a 'deposit'. The former is a fee payable to the site in addition to the cost of staying on the site and will always be forfeited if you cancel. A deposit, on the other hand, is a payment in advance to be deducted from your final bill. Whether or not a deposit will be refundable if you cancel is dependent on several factors and cancellation insurance is a wise precaution. In general it is best not to send money in the first instance, but rather to write to the site asking for a reservation. If they can offer what you want they will normally write asking for a deposit and/or booking fee to confirm the booking. Most sites will now accept a Eurocheque, obtainable from your bank. Several organisations, including of course the camping tour operators, such as Eurocamp Independent, Select Site Reservations, and Carefree Travel Service operate systems whereby you can book sites abroad from the UK and details are given in their respective advertisements in this Guide.

Many of our featured campsites are included on Microsoft's **Autoroute Express 2000 (Europe)** computer software as a result of our co-operation with the Microsoft Corporation, which involved us in establishing and maintaining a database of some 3,500 campsites throughout Europe on their behalf. The majority of our Alan Rogers' Inspected and Selected campsites are included on this programme, and highlighted by our logo at the end of each data-entry.

Regarding the question of when it is necessary to make a campsite reservation, the peak season in Europe generally runs from about 10 July to 20 August, with some variations between individual countries. Outside of that peak period you stand a good chance of finding space without having booked in advance, except in some particularly popular areas. Occasionally we get complaints from readers who have booked (and sometimes also paid) in advance at a particular site, but after being there for a day or two decide to leave but then have difficulty in recovering their advance payment. The only advice that we can offer in this respect is to consider very carefully the wisdom of parting with a substantial amount of money in advance unless you know the site personally and are prepared to stay for the whole of the period you have booked irrespective of the weather. Frankly the chances of a refund if you book for two weeks but leave after two days are pretty remote and certainly there is no mechanism by which we can assist in such cases.

Telephone numbers - are given for most sites, but the numbers quoted assume you are actually IN the country concerned, and are normally nine or ten digit numbers beginning with an '0' (or in Spain a '9'). If you are 'phoning from the UK remember that this '0' is usually disregarded and replaced by the appropriate Country Code - this system is currently undergoing changes, and for the latest details you should refer to an up-to-date telephone directory, or in case of difficulty, to the telephone operator.

Time - Apart from a period of about three weeks during October, the clocks in most European countries are one hour ahead of those in Britain.

ANDORRA

Andorra is situated high in the Pyrenees between France and Spain and is an independent principality covering 181 sq. miles. It is a sovereign country and the main occupations are agriculture and tourism. It is probably best known for skiing and tax free goods. The population is 55,000 (1991), density 117 per sq. km. and the capital is Andorra la Vella. The climate is temperate, with cold winters with a lot of snow and warm summers.The language is Catalan, with French and Spanish widely spoken. French francs and Spanish pesetas are both used.

UK Andorran Delegation, 63 Westover Road, London SW18 2RF Tel: 0181 874 4806
(Personal visits by appointment only, telephone morning only)

9143 Camping Xixerella, Erts, nr La Massana

All year site in attractive mountain valley.

Andorra is a country of narrow valleys and pine and birch forested mountains. Xixerella is attractively situated in just such a valley, beside a small river. The site is made up of several sections, accessed by tarmac or gravel roads. There are some terraced pitches, although generally they are not marked out and are on grass, mainly with a small degree of slope. Electricity (3A) is available for most of the 220 places. The site can be very busy from mid-July to mid-August, but otherwise it is usually quite peaceful. The main sanitary building has been refurbished to a satisfactory standard and has British WCs (no paper) with small ones for children and free hot water to the open washbasins (some private cabins), controllable showers and under-cover laundry and dishwashing facilities. There are further modern facilities down inside the round building by the pool, including a laundry, baby bath and dishwashing sinks. There is a pleasant bar with terrace, a cosy restaurant and a small shop. The swimming pool is open mid-June to mid-Sept. and is not depth-marked. Minigolf is also available and there is a well fenced children's play area. Skiing is available at Pal (6 km) or Arinsal (5 km).

How to find it: Site is 8 km. from Andorra la Vella on the road to Pal via La Massana.

General Details: Open all year, as are shop, restaurant and bar. Swimming pool (summer). Minigolf. Riding 3 km. Chemical disposal. Chalets for hire.

Charges guide: Per person Ptas 450; child 400; car 450; caravan 450; tent 450; motorcaravan 800; m/cycle 400; electricity (3A) 450; dog 250.

Reservations: Contact site. Address: Carretera de Pals, Erts (La Massana), Andorra. Tel: 836 613. FAX: 839 113.

LIECHTENSTEIN

Liechtenstein is an independent principality, bounded on the north by Switzerland and Austria, and on the south and west by Switzerland. One of the smallest independent states in the world, it has a total area of 157 sq. km. (61 sq. miles). The climate is Alpine with mild winters; average temperatures range from - 1.1° C (30° F) in January to 21.1° C (70° F) in July. Liechtenstein has a population of 29,868, of whom about one-third are resident aliens, with an overall density of about 190 people per sq.km. Native-born Liechtensteiners are descended from the Germanic Alamanni people and most still speak an Alamanni dialect of the official language, German. The country's close ties with Switzerland are also important; the Swiss franc is the official currency of Liechtenstein and the two states have operated a customs union since 1924. Liechtenstein is a constitutional monarchy governed by hereditary princes.

758 Camping Mittagsspitze, Triesen, nr Liechtenstein

Attractively and quietly situated site for visiting the Principality.

Mittagsspitze, probably the best site in the region, is on a hillside and has all the scenic views that one could wish. Extensive broad, level terraces on the steep slope provide unmarked pitches (a reader tells us that spacing causes problems in high season). Of the 185 spaces, 85 are used by seasonal caravans. A good quality sanitary block has all the usual facilities and there is an older unit near reception; both have British style WCs. The site has recently added a restaurant and there is a small swimming pool, not heated but very popular in summer. Tennis courts and an indoor pool are nearby. Liechtenstein's capital, Vaduz, is 7 km. Austria 20 km. and Switzerland 3 km.

How to find it: Site is just off the main Vaduz - Chur road 2 km. south of Triesen.

General Details: Open all year. 36,000 sq.m. Little shade. Electrical connections (6A) in many places. Shop (1/6-31/8). Swimming pool (1/6-31/8). Children's playground. Fishing. Room where one can sit or eat with cooking facilities. Washing machine, dryer and ironing. Rooms to let.

Charges 2000: Per person Sfr. 8.50; child (under 11 yrs) 4.00; car 4.00; caravan or large tent 8.00 - 10.00; small tent 5.00; dog 4.00; electricity 3.00 - 4.00; local tax 6.5%. Discounts: 8 days 5%, 15 days 10%, 21 days 15%.

Reservations: not made. Address: FL-9495 Triesen. Tel: 075/392.36.77 or 392.26.86. FAX: 075/392.36.80. E-mail: engelbert.schurte@bluewin.ch.

AUSTRIA

Centrally situated in Europe, Austria is primarily known for two contrasting attractions - its capital Vienna with its fading Imperial glories, and the variety of its Alpine hinterland. Ideally suitable for all year round visiting, either viewing the spectacular scenery and enjoying the various opportunities for winter sports or visiting the historical sites and sampling the cultural attractions. For further information contact:

Austrian National Tourist Office, 30 Saint George Street, London W1R 0AL
Tel: 020 7629 0461. Fax: 020 7499 6038. E-mail: info@anto.co.uk

Population
7,915,000 (1993), density 94.2 per sq. km.

Capital
Vienna (Wien).

Climate
Austria has a moderate Central European climate. The winter season is from December to March (in higher regions the end of May) and warm clothing, including waterproof shoes or boots, is a necessity. Even in summer the evenings in mountain resorts can be quite cool.

Language
German is the usual language but English is widely spoken and understood.

Currency
The unit of currency is the Austrian Schilling which is divided into 100 Groschen. There are bank notes to the value of 5,000, 1,000, 500, 100, 50 and 20 schillings, coins of 20, 10, 5 and 1 schillings and 50 and 10 groschen.

Banks
Banking hours are mainly 08.00 - 12.30 hrs and 13.30 - 15.00 hrs on Mon, Tues, Wed and Fri. Thurs hours are 08.00 - 12.30 and 13.30 - 17.30. Credit Cards: Most major credit cards are accepted in the larger cities and tourist areas. Travellers cheques and Eurocheques are widely accepted.

Post Offices
Offices are open Monday to Friday 08.00 -12.00 hrs and 14.00 - 18.00 hrs.

Time
GMT plus 1 (summer BST plus 1).

Telephone
To Austria from the UK the code is 0043, ignoring the '0' at the start of the area code. For calls from Austria to the UK the code is 0044.

Public Holidays
New Year; Epiphany; Easter Mon; Labour Day; Ascension; Whit Mon; Corpus Christi; Assumption, 15 Aug; National Day, 26 Oct; All Saints, 1 Nov; Immaculate Conception, 8 Dec; Christmas, 25, 26 Dec.

Shops
Shops open 08.00-18.30 hrs but many close for 2 hours at lunch and 13.00 on Sats except first Sat in every month, when they open to 17.00.

Motoring
Tolls: It is now compulsory to purchase a motorway disc. For visiting cars, motorhomes and towed caravans with a combined weight under 3.5 tons a 'weekly' disc costing 70 schillings (valid up to 10 days Thurs midnight to midnight 2 Sundays later) or 'monthly' (valid for 2 consecutive months) at 150 schillings is available.

Motorbikes can only purchase a 'monthly' at 80 schillings. They are available at major border crossings, petrol stations and post offices at present and for cash only. Fines for non-compliance are heavy. Previously levied road and tunnel tolls still apply, but a discount of 15% applies to discholders on the S16 Arlberg Tunnel, A13 Brenner - A9 Pyhon and A10 Tauern motorways.

Speed limits: For caravans and motorhomes (3.5t): 31 mph (50 kph) in built up areas, 62 mph (100 kph) other roads (including motor- ways for caravans) and 81 mph (130 kph) for motorhomes on motorways. There is a lower limit of 68 mph (110 kph) between 2200 - 0500 on the A8, A9, A10, A12, A13 and A14. A min. speed of 37 mph (60 kph) applies on roads with a rectangular blue sign showing a white car.

Towing Restrictions: The maximum overall length for car and caravan is restricted to 12 metres. It is also important that your caravan or motorhome is not overloaded.

Parking: Limited parking (blue zones) with max. parking time of 1.5-3 hrs. Parking clocks can be obtained free of charge from tobacconists (Tabak-Trafik), shops or local police stations. However in Vienna, Graz, Linz, Klagenfurt, Salzburg, Innsbruck and a few other cities there is a charge for parking vouchers which can be obtained in banks, some petrol stations and from tobacconists. They must be clearly displayed on the inside of the windscreen.

Overnighting
It is possible to park outside campsites provided permission has been obtained beforehand from the landowner. Except in Vienna and protected rural areas visitors are permitted to sleep in the camping vehicle but local restrictions can apply and campers are not allowed to set up camping equipment beside their vehicle.

Useful addresses
OCC (Osterreichischer Camping Club), Schubertring 1-3, 1010 Wien.
Tel: 01 771 99/1272. Fax: 01 711 99/1498.

OAMTC (Osterreichischer Automobil-Motorradund Touring Club), Schubertring 1-3, 1010 Wien. Tel: 01/72990.

Tirol and the West

This is the best known area of Austria as far as British visitors are concerned and the most easily accessible part of the country. It has considerable charm and a wealth of scenic, sporting and historical interest as a centre for both winter and summer tourism. Folk-lore entertainment (Tirolerabend) is on offer outdoors in summer and in Gasthof bars and Hotels in winter. Mountain paths are well marked and maintained and local authorities provide information centres in towns and lay-bys. Innsbruck is the famous capital of the region, good camp sites abound and there are many pleasant valleys to explore.

023 Camping Waldcamping, Feldkirch

Good municipal site on edge of town near borders.

Feldkirch lies near the borders with Germany, Switzerland and Liechtenstein and Waldcamping is part of the Gisingen sports stadium on the edge of the town. The Vorarlberg mountains and Bodensee (Lake Constance) are nearby and there are good sporting facilities, including a large outdoor pool with water slides, at the stadium next to the site. Set in a quiet residential suburb, about 4 km from the centre, tall trees surround the site. The 170 tourist pitches are on flat grass, either in the centre, or to the side of the hard road which runs round the camping area. In high season an overflow area may be brought into use (without electricity). There are two well constructed sanitary blocks near the entrance, one of which is open and heated in winter plus an older block at the back of the site. They have British type WCs. A neat, tidy site which caters for winter skiing and summer touring guests.

How to find it: Follow signs from centre of town for Gisingen Stadium (4 km.).

General Details: Open all year. 40,000 sq.m. Electricity connections (6A). Shop (May - Sept). Large, heated swimming pool (free for campers). Children's pool and playground. Tennis. Football. Fishing 4 km. Bicycle hire 4 km. Club room with TV and drinks machine. Bar/restaurant 1 km. Washing machines and dryers. Chemical disposal. Motorcaravan services.

Charges 1999: Per person sch. 50 - 61; child (6-14 yrs) 23 - 34; local tax 10, young person 5, child free; caravan 42 - 56, over 6 m. 56 - 70; tent 46 - 56, small tent 29 - 37; motorcaravan 66 - 84; car 33 - 46; m/cycle 25 - 33; electricity 25 (plus 4 per kw. in winter). Credit cards accepted.

Reservations: Write to site. Address: Postfach 564, 6803 Feldkirch. Tel: 05522/74308 (or mobile 0664/4321372). FAX: as phone. E-mail: kkf@montforthaus.felkirch.com.

020 Sport Camp Tirol, Landeck

Well run site with good facilities and opportunity for white water boating.

There are several medium sized sites in this area bordering the Vorarlberg and Tirol, of which this and Camping Riffler are good examples. The district is popular for winter skiing and summer watersports and mountain walking. White water sports are organised on the River Sanna which runs alongside (with access) and the River Inn. On the other side of the narrow site are fir clad mountains which, with many trees on the site, make it a very pleasant place to stop, either for one night whilst passing through, or for longer stays to explore the region. The 100 pitches, all with electricity and 70-100 sq.m, are on either side of gravel roads which run from the hard central road. The pitches are not marked out, but visitors are shown where to go. There is further space for about 20 tents at the far end of the site. As with most Austrian sites which remain open all year, the sanitary facilities are heated and of a good standard. The block for ladies is in a central position, with the men's block behind reception. There is hot water (pre-set) in the showers and sinks and about half the washbasins, British style WCs, facilities for disabled people and a children's washroom. The reception block also has a pizzeria/café and, just outside the entrance, is a shop and restaurant. Children's playground on sand base. Good English is spoken by the enthusiastic man and wife team who run the site.

How to find it: Site is on the main Vorarlberg - Tirol road by the river bridge, 1 km. west of Landeck. Signed Camping Huber and/or Sport Camp Tirol.

General Details: Open all year. 11,000 sq.m. Restaurant. Pizzeria/café. Shop. Table tennis. Children's playground. Volleyball. Programme of watersports, canyoning, rafting, kayak, etc. organised. Roller skating rink. Bicycle hire and mountain biking. Fishing. Swimming pool 1 km. Riding 1 km. Washing machine and dryer. Motorcaravan services. Bungalows and studio to let.

Charges 2000: Per adult sch. 64; child (5-15 yrs) 44; local tax (adults) 7; car 40; m/cycle 30; caravan 97; motorcaravan 117; 1 man tent 42, 2 man tent 70, family tent 97; electricity 28. Special winter rates. No credit cards.

Reservations: Write to site, no deposit or fee required. Address: Mühlkanal 1, 6500 Landeck. Tel: 05442/64636. FAX: 05442/64037. E-mail: sportcamptirol@msg.at.

AUSTRIA - Tirol and the West

015 Camping Riffler, Landeck

Small, compact site with good facilities.

This small, pretty site is almost in the centre of the small town of Landeck and, being on the main through route from the Vorarlberg to the Tirol, would serve as a good overnight stop. Square in shape, it has just 50 pitches on either side of hard access roads on level grass, with the main road on one side and the fast flowing River Samna on the other edge. Trees and flowers adorn the site giving good shade. The single toilet block has been rebuilt to an excellent standard with British WCs and hot water in washbasins, showers and sinks. There are few other amenities but a supermarket is outside the gate and other shops and restaurants about 100 m. Activities in the area include paragliding, rafting, canoeing and climbing.

How to find it: Site is at the western end of Landeck on the main no. 316 road.

General Details: Open all year except May. 3,000 sq.m. Electricity to all pitches (10A). Small general room. Restaurants and shops 100 m. in village. Children's play area. Table tennis. Fishing. Bicycle hire 500 m. Washing machine and dryer. Chemical disposal. Motorcaravan services.

Charges 2000: Per person sch. 55 - 80; child (5-14 yrs) 50 - 65; car on pitch 28 - 30; caravan or motorcaravan 90 - 105; tent 55 - 90; electricity 28 - 35; trailer 50; local taxes 17. Less 5% for stays over 10 days. Winter prices slightly more. No credit cards.

Reservations: Contact site. Address: Bruggfeldstrasse 2, 6500 Landeck. Tel: 05442/624774. FAX: 05442/624775.

022 Ötztal Arena Camp Krismer, Umhausen

Good site in quiet valley, with excellent toilet facilities.

This is a delightful site in the beautiful Ötz valley, on the edge of the village of Umhausen. On a gentle slope in an open valley, it has an air of peace and tranquillity and makes an excellent base for mountain walking, particularly in spring and autumn, skiing in winter or a relaxing holiday. The 98 pitches are all marked and numbered and have electricity; charges relate to the area available. The single, new reception building houses an attractive bar/restaurant, a TV room (with Sky) and the sanitary facilities. These are of exceptional quality with under-floor heating, British style WCs and free hot water in the washbasins (private cabins) and sinks and on payment in the showers, plus a special baby room with bath and changing area. A small toilet/wash block at the far end of the site has been refurbished for summer use. Good children's playground 300 m. The young, enthusiastic man and wife management team speak good English.

How to find it: Take Ötztal Valley exit from Imst - Innsbruck motorway, and Umhausen is 13 km. towards Solden; well signed in village.

General Details: Open all year. 6,800 sq.m. Electricity connections (12/16A). Bar/restaurant (May-Sept, Dec-April). Shops in village (200 m) – bread can be ordered at reception. Children's play area. TV room with satellite. Ski room. Fishing. Bicycle hire. Swimming pool, tennis and table tennis 100 m. Para-gliding, mountain walks and Stuiben waterfall nearby. Washing machine and dryer, iron from reception, drying room. Chemical disposal. Motorcaravan services. Caravan to rent.

Charges 2000: Per pitch sch.1 per sq.m. (65 - 85 in winter); person 70; child 50; dog 35; electricity 35 plus 10 per kw; local tax 10. No credit cards.

Reservations: Write with sch. 500 deposit. Address: 6441 Umhausen 387 (Ötztal-Tirol). Tel: 05255/5390 or 05254/8196. FAX: 05255/5390.

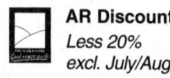

AR Discount
Less 20%
excl. July/Aug

004 Tiroler Zugspitzcamping, Ehrwald

Excellent mountain site with fine views and superb facilities.

Although Ehrwald is in Austria, it is from the entrance of Zugspitzcamping that the cable car runs to the summit of Germany's highest mountain. Standing at 1,200 feet above sea level at the foot of the mountain, the 200 pitches (120 for tourists), mainly of grass over stones, are on flat terraces with fine panoramic views in parts and all have electricity. A modern building at the entrance houses reception, shop, café and a fine restaurant with terrace which is also open to those using the cable car. There is also a hotel 100 m. away. A large modern building, heated in cool weather, has an indoor pool with sauna, whirlpool and fitness centre, as well as an outdoor pool and children's pool with slide. The two excellent sanitary facilities are also here with British style WCs and free hot water in washbasins (some cabins), showers and sinks. There are 20 private bathrooms for hire and a baby room. As well as providing a base from which to explore this interesting part of Austria by car or on foot, various activities are organised in high season.

How to find it: Follow signs in Ehrwald to Tiroler Zugspitzbahn and then signs to camp.

General Details: Open all year. 30,000 sq.m. Shop. Bar. Restaurant. Hotel. Cable-car to mountain summit. Swimming pools and fitness centre. Table tennis. Bicycle hire. Children's play area. Sports in Ehrwald. Fishing 5 km. Washing machines and dryers. Chemical disposal. Apartments to let.

Charges guide: Per person sch. 137 - 157; child (4-14 yrs) 99 - 112; pitch 75 - 103; electricity 10 per kw; local tax 9.50 - 12.50; dog 28; private bathroom 75 - 80. Special seasonal weekly offers. No credit cards.

Reservations: Write with deposit (1,000 sch.) Address: 6632 Ehrwald. Tel: 05673/2745. FAX: 05673/230951.

003 Caravan-Park Leutasch, Leutasch, nr Seefeld

Well developed site in mountain setting north of Seefeld.

This site was formerly known as Holiday Camping. Being away from the main routes (particularly for caravans), it is not for single night stops but is well suited for those who want to spend a few days, or longer, in a mountain area in a quiet setting (no groups are accepted) with opportunities for walking, climbing or touring. Although there are mountains on either side, the site itself is level and offers fine views. Additionally there is an excellent indoor heated swimming pool with sauna, steam bath, whirlpool and sun beds. Trees decorate the site (but not much shade) and it has a pleasant appearance with plants and shrubs. There are 145 level, numbered pitches of grass on stones, all with electricity, water, drainage and TV sockets. Two modern, heated sanitary blocks have British style WCs and free hot water in all basins (mainly in cabins), showers and sinks with two well equipped baby rooms and one for disabled visitors. The site works closely with the local tourist board to offer a variety of excursions, walking, mountain biking and games for children. A baby sitting service is available. Games room with pool, table tennis, etc. Good English is spoken by the friendly owners.

How to find it: Site is 4 km north of Leutasch; caravans should approach either from Seefeld from the north or via Telfs - Mosern - Seefeld from the south as Littenwald - Leutasch and Zirlerberg on the Innsbruck to Seefeld road are banned to trailers.

General Details: Open all year except Nov. 26,000 sq.m. Electricity connections (6/12A). Mini-market. Good restaurant with music twice weekly in high season. Children's playground. Bicycle hire. Fishing. Tennis. Activities and excursions. Golf 12 km. Riding 5 km. Washing machines, dryers, irons. Exchange facilities. Motorcaravan services. Apartments and rooms for rent.

Charges 2000: Per pitch incl. electricity, TV, water and drainage 80 sq.m. sch. 70 - 80 (winter 90 - 140), 100 sq.m. 80 - 100 (100 - 150); adult 80 - 110; child 10-15 yrs 70 - 100, 2-10 yrs 40 - 60; local tax 12-13; dog 30 - 50; electricity (6A) 25 (45 in winter). No credit cards.

Reservations: made for any length with deposit. Address: 6105 Leutasch. Tel: 05214/65700. FAX: 05214/657030. E-mail: caravan.park.leutasch@utanet.at.

010 Camping Seeblick Toni-Brantlhof, Kramsach, nr Rattenburg

Excellent, quiet site by Tirolean lake not far from Inn Valley autobahn.

Austria has some of the finest sites in Europe and Seeblick Toni-Brantlhof is one of the best. In a quiet, rural situation on the edge of the small Reintalersee lake, it is well worth considering for holidays in the Tirol with so many varied excursion possibilities nearby. Kramsach, a pleasant, busy tourist resort is some 3 km. from the site. The mountains which surround the site give scenic views and the camp has a neat and tidy appearance. The 250 level pitches (220 for tourists) are in regular rows from hard access roads and are of good size with grass and hardstandings, electricity (10A), TV connections, with 40 having telephone points also. The two heated sanitary blocks are of quite outstanding quality with free hot water in all basins (some in private cabins), sinks and good showers. The main one, part of the reception, restaurant and shop building has been extended and now includes en-suite toilet/basin/shower rooms (free) and the second one, on the opposite side of the camping area, as well as providing the usual facilities, has individual bathrooms to let. Both blocks are heated in cool weather and have baby rooms, facilities for disabled people and drying rooms. The large, well appointed restaurant has an adjoining roof-top terrace where one can enjoy a meal, drink or snack and admire the lovely scenery. The rebuilt mini-market is well stocked with food, drink and souvenirs. Path to lake for swimming, boating and sunbathing meadow. With a good solarium, sauna and fitness centre, children's playground and a kindergarten in high season, this makes for an excellent summer holiday and, with ski areas near, an excellent winter holiday also. Family run, good English is spoken and a friendly welcome is given.

How to find it: Take exit for Kramsach from A12 autobahn and follow signs 'Zu den Seen' in village. After 3 km. turn right at camp sign. Note: there are two sites side by side at the lake – ignore the first and continue through to Seeblick Toni.

General Details: Open all year. 40,000 sq.m. Electricity on all pitches. Cable TV. Restaurant. Bar. Snack kiosk. Shop. Fitness centre. Children's playground. Youth room. Fishing. Bicycle hire. Riding. Golf 2 km. Kindergarten in high season. Tepi club and organised activities for children in high season. Washing machines and dryers. Motorcaravan services. Chemical disposal.

Charges 2000: Per pitch sch. 97 - 140; person 72 - 89 + local tax 8; child (under 14 yrs) 56 - 64; dog 57 - 70; electricity 43. Credit cards accepted.
Euro: Per pitch 6.98 - 10.07; person 5.18 - 6.40 + local tax 0.58; child (under 14 yrs) 4.03 - 4.60; dog 4.10 - 5.04; electricity 3.09.

AR Discount
Low season packages - contact site

Reservations: made for min. 1 week with deposit. Address: Reintaler See, 6233 Kramsach (Tirol). Tel: 05337/63544. FAX: 05337/63544-305.

017 Camping Innsbruck-Kranebitten, Innsbruck

Site with good facilities, just outside Innsbruck.

This site is on a sloping meadow with good shade cover, in a pleasant situation. The 120 pitches are numbered, but not marked out and there are three separate terraces for caravans and motorcaravans. All pitches have electricity available, though long leads are necessary in parts. By the side of the site, with access to it, is a large open field with a good children's playground and plenty of space for ball games. Being so near to the attractive town of Innsbruck, it makes an excellent base from which to visit the ancient city and also to explore the many attractions nearby. The bar/restaurant also has an attractive terrace and there is a shop for basic supplies. The large, toilet block, although showing signs of age, is heated and has acceptable British style WCs, free hot water in washbasins (some in private cabins), pre-set showers and sinks. The 'Innsbruck-Card', available from the site, gives various discounts for attractions in the city, plus free travel on public transport (park-and-ride from the site, even if you do not stay overnight).

How to find it: From A12 Innsbruck - Arlberg motorway, take Innsbruck-Kranebitten exit from where site is well signed.

General Details: Open all year. 30,000 sq.m. Electrical connections (6A, 2 and 3 pin). Restaurant (1/4-31/10). Shop. Large play field adjoining. Games for children and barbecues in summer. Swimming pool 2 km. Bicycle hire 5 km. Riding, fishing or golf 10 km. Free ski-bus Dec - March. Washing machines and dryers. Chemical disposal. Motorcaravan services. Tents or caravans to rent.

Charges 2000: Per person sch. 68, plus local tax 7; child (4-14 yrs) 45; car 40; tent 40; caravan 45; motor caravan 60; m/cycle 25; electricity 30. Less 10% for stays over 10 days. Special offers for sporting groups. No credit cards.

Reservations: Contact site. Address: Kranebitter Allee 214, 6020 Innsbruck (Tirol). Tel: 0512/284180. FAX: as phone. E-mail: campinnsbruck@hotmail.com.

AR Discount
Less 5% for over 1 night

005 Camping Kröll, Laubühel, nr Mayrhofen

Good site in the Zillertal valley.

The pretty Zillertal valley runs south from the A12 Innsbruck-Worgl autobahn and then east over the Gerlos Pass through to the A10 Salzburg-Spittal motorway. The picturesque red narrow gauge Zillertalbahn runs along the valley following the River Ziller. Camping Kroll stands back from the main B169 road at the foot of the mountains which are on either side of the valley. Of the 200 pitches, 120 are available for tourists, and they are reasonably level with grass on gravel and all have electricity. Although there are a few trees, there is little shade but pleasant views. At the time of our visit a new building was almost complete which will house reception and shop and a small heated pool which will extend outside. The good quality heated sanitary block has British style WCs and free hot water in washbasins, showers and sinks. An extension to this building has sauna, solarium, games, TV and a children's room.

How to find it: Site is on the northern side of Mayrhofen and signed from the B169 road.

General Details: Open all year. 20,000 sq.m. Electricity connections (6A). Shop. Restaurant/bar. Children's playground. Small swimming pool. Washing machine and dryer. Rooms to let in Gasthof on site.

Charges guide: Per person sch 60; local tax 9 - 12; child (under 14) 40; car 30; tent or caravan 30; motorcaravan 60; m/cycle 20; dog 20; electricity on meter.

Reservations: are made to guarantee admission (no deposit). Address: 6290 Mayrhofen, Laubichl 127, Zillertal. Tel: 05285/62580. FAX: 05285/64877.

007 Camping Hofer, Zell am Ziller, nr Mayrhofen

Small, family run site near village and sports opportunities.

Zell am Ziller is in the heart of the Zillertal valley at the junction of the B169 and B165 Gerlos Pass road and nestles round the unusual 18th Century church noted for its paintings. Camping Hofer, owned by the same family for 50 years, is on the edge of the village just 5 minutes walk from the centre on a quiet side road. The 100 pitches, all with electricity, are on grass on gravel. A few trees decorate the site but offer little shade. The good quality heated sanitary provision is on the ground floor of the apartment building and has British style WCs and free hot water in washbasins (some in cabins), showers and sinks. A pleasant new development has a bar/restaurant, games and TV room and a small heated pool which can be covered. A mini-market is opposite site entrance. Once a week in summer the owner takes those who wish to rise at 4 am. to a nearby mountain to watch the sun rise. Activities for adults and children are organised in high season. A little road train gives a free service round the village. The pleasant owner, who speaks good English does his best to provide a friendly, family atmosphere.

How to find it: Site is well signed from the main B169 road at Zell am Ziller.

General Details: Open all year. 15,000 sq.m. Electricity connections (6/10A). Grill room with bar (closed Nov). Shop opposite. Bicycle hire. Swimming pool (1/4-30/10). Organised entertainment and activities in high season. Guided walks, cycle tours, barbecues, biking, skiing. Riding 4 km. Fishing 8 km. Ski room. Baby room. Youth room. Washing machines, dryers and irons. Gas supplies. Chemical disposal. Motorcaravan services.

Charges 2000: Per person sch 50 - 60; local tax (over 15 yrs) 12; child (under 14) 40 - 50; pitch 65 - 85; dog 20; electricity 7 + meter. Special winter packages. Credit cards accepted.

Reservations: Necessary for July/Aug and Christmas; made for any length with deposit. Address: Gerlossastr. 33, 6280 Zell am Ziller (Tirol). Tel: 05282/2248. FAX: 05282/2248-8.

012 Erlebnis-Comfort-Camping Aufenfeld, Aschau, nr Mayrhofen

Pleasantly situated site for summer or winter with good toilet block and indoor pool.

This site is attractively situated in a mountain region with fine views. The main area of the site itself is flat with pitches of 100 sq.m. on grass between made-up access roads and further pitches on terraces at the rear. Following the addition of more pitches, there are now 300 pitches (250 for touring units) including some with individual sanitary cubicles. The well kept, heated toilet block in the main building is of excellent quality and size with British style WCs, washbasins well spaced out with free hot water, several in private cabins for each sex, one with baby bath and one with full bath for ladies and good fully controllable free hot showers; also a dog shower. Additional units, some new, provide private cabins and family rooms. The site can become full mid-July until mid-August and at Christmas, but usually has space at other times. Ski lifts are nearby, one for beginners particularly close. A splendid, indoor swimming pool with whirl pool, sauna and sun-beds, has been added and there is a heated outdoor pool, paddling pool, and tennis court for summer use. Most of the site facilities are now housed in the new main building. A lake and leisure area has been created alongside the site.

How to find it: From Inntal motorway, take Zillertal exit, 32 km. northeast of Innsbruck. Follow road no. 169 to village of Aschau from which site is well signed.

General Details: Open all year except 7 Nov - 12 Dec. Electricity connections (6A). TV. Small shop. Self-service restaurant. General room. Indoor pool, sauna and sun-beds. Outdoor pool. Football field. Children's playground and Western fort. Beach volleyball and `fun court'. Tennis. Riding. Fishing. Bicycle hire. Golf 500 m. Washing machines, dryers. Chemical disposal. Motorcaravan services. Chalets and caravans for hire.

Charges 2000: Summer: per person sch. 55 - 85, plus local tax 10; child (under 13 yrs) 40 - 55; pitch incl. electricity and TV hook-up 80 - 120, with drainage and gas hook-up 100 - 140, with private sanitary cabin 200 - 270; hiker or m/cycle and tent 35 - 40; dog 40 - 50; electricity 25 - 35. Winter prices are higher. No credit cards.

Reservations: made with deposit and fee for min. 1 week - write to site. Address: Distelberg 1, 6274 Aschau (Zillertal-Tirol). Tel: 05282/29160. FAX: 05282/291611. E-mail: camping.fiegl@tirol.com.

AR Discount
Low and mid season discounts; contact site

13

AUSTRIA - Tirol and the West

025 Alpencamping, Weer, nr Schwaz

Pleasant Tirol site with activity programme, splendid views and a friendly welcome.

This is a good family site run by a family who provide not only a neat, friendly site, but also a variety of outdoor activities. Formerly a farm they now breed horses, give a free ride each day to youngsters and organise trekking/hacking days. For children and adults, Herr Mark junior (a certified alpine ski guide and ski instructor) runs courses for individuals or groups in climbing (there is a practise climbing wall on site and a new wet weather one), rafting, mountain bike riding, tracking, hiking, etc. Guided alpine tours can be arranged and there are pleasant walks up the lower slopes of the mountains directly from the site. Set in the Inn valley, between mountain ranges, the site has 96 flat, grass pitches (all for tourers apart from some tour operator tents) either side of gravel roads. Trees provide shade in some parts. The old farm buildings house a small, cheerful bar/restaurant, first class, heated sanitary facilities with hot showers and British style WCs and a room for washing dishes and clothes. There is an attractive wooden chalet where reception and the activities are administered. It could be used for a night stop when passing through from Innsbruck to Salzburg, but is even better for a longer stay for adventurous youngsters or for a holiday in the Tirol area. The Mark family would very much welcome visits by rallies in the Spring season and are happy to arrange programmes of entertainment and excursions. Good English is spoken. A chalet for children's use in wet weather has been constructed this year.

How to find it: Site is 200 m. east of the village of Weer on Wattens - Schwaz road no. B171 which runs parallel to the A12, just 10 km east of Innsbruck.

General Details: Open 1 April - 31 Oct. 20,000 sq.m. Electricity connections (6/10A). Restaurant, shop (1/5-30/9). Small heated swimming pool (1/5-30/9). Activity programme with instruction. Bicycle hire. Riding. Glacier tours. Table tennis. Large children's play area with good equipment. Fishing 2 km. Golf 20 km. Freezer. Washing machines and dryer. Chemical disposal. Motorcaravan services. Cabin and caravans can be hired (site arranges with local dealer.)

Charges 2000: Per person sch. 66; child (1-13 yrs) 44; pitch for car/caravan or motorcaravan 65; small tent 25; electricity 25; dog 15; local tax 7. Reductions for stays over 14 nights.

Reservations: Necessary for 1/7-15/8 and made without deposit. Address: Maholmhof, 6114 Weer bei Schwaz (Tirol). Tel: 05224/68146. FAX: 05224/681466.

011 Tirol Camp, Fieberbrunn, St Johann, nr Kitzbühel

Site in mountain region for summer or winter camping, with good installations.

This is one of many Tirol camps which cater equally for summer and winter (here seemingly more for winter, when reservation is essential and prices 50% higher). Tirol Camp is in a quiet and attractive mountain situation and has 307 pitches all on wide flat terraces, set on a gentle slope (220 for touring units). Marked out mainly by the electricity boxes, they are said to be 80-100 sq.m. and all have electricity, gas, water/drainage, TV and telephone connections. The excellent, original toilet block in the main building has British style WCs, washbasins with free hot water, shelf and mirror (a few in cabins) and good fully controllable, hot showers with seat and screen. There are also some private bathrooms on payment. This is supplemented by a splendid heated block at the top end of the site, with washbasins all in private cabins and spacious showers. A small, unheated swimming pool (12 x 8 m.) is open summer, with a paddling pool. For winter stays, the site is very close to a ski lift centre and a `langlauf' piste. There is a lake for fishing and a playground and small zoo for children.

How to find it: Site is on the east side of Fieberbrunn, which is on the St Johann-Saalfelden road.

General Details: Open all year. Electricity connections (6A). Self-service shop and snacks. Restaurant (closed Oct, Nov and May). Separate general room. Sauna. Tennis. Swimming pool (1/6-30/9). Fishing in lake. Riding. Bicycle hire. Outdoor chess. Children's playground and zoo. Washing machines, dryers and drying room. Chemical disposal. Motorcaravan services. Entertainment and activity programmes for adults and children (July/August) with Tepi club. Apartments to rent.

Charges 1999: Winter charges higher. Per pitch sch. 55 - 142; adult 50 - 100; child (4-15 yrs) 25 - 60; local taxes 18; dog 40 - 55; electricity connection (once only) 25 - 60 + meter; gas 120 + meter; TV/radio 60. Special weekly package deals with half-board offered in summer. No credit cards.

Reservations: made for any length (with deposit in winter only). Address: Lindau 20, 6391 Fieberbrunn (Tirol). Tel: 05354/56666. FAX: 05354/52516. E-mail: offive@tirol-camp.at. A 'Camping Cheques' site.

009 Camping Zillertal-Hell, Fügen, nr Schwaz

Small attractive site with excellent facilities.

The village of Fügen lies about 7 km. from the A12 autobahn at the start of the Zillertal, so is well placed for exploring the valley and the area around Schwaz. Camping Zillertal-Hell is easy to reach and has 127 marked pitches on flat grass, all with electricity and nine with water and drainage also. There are also hard-standings for motorcaravans. The modern heated sanitary block is of top quality with British style WCs, free hot water in washbasins (some in cabins), showers and sinks and a children's wash room. There is an attractive bar with terrace and basic food supplies are available with shops and restaurants in the village (800 m). There is a games and club room with TV. A very pleasantly landscaped, heated swimming pool with sunbathing area has been added. A programme of games and entertainment for children is offered during the summer, at Christmas and at Easter with bicycle trips and hiking for adults. The site could make a good overnight stop or for a longer stay but, being on a main road, there is some road noise.

How to find it: Site is beside the no. 169 road, 7 km. south of the exit for Gagering (also signed Zillertal) from the A12 Innsbruck - Worgl motorway.

General Details: Open all year. Many electrical connections (6/10A). Bar and small restaurant. Shop (1/5-1/11, 20/12-15/4). Swimming pool (20 x 10 m, 1/5-15/10). Good sized children's playground. Organised games, activities and entertainment. Bicycle hire. Fishing 500 m. Riding 2 km. Golf 15 km. Washing machine, dryer, iron and drying room. Car wash. Chemical disposal. Motorcaravan service point.

Charges 1999: Per person sch. 50 - 75, plus local tax 7; child (under 14 yrs) 35 - 55; pitch 60 - 90; electricity 30 - 35; water and drainage 20. Less 10% for stays over 8 days. No credit cards.

Reservations: accepted for min. 7 days, 10 days at Christmas. Address: 6263 Fügen/Zillertal (Tirol). Tel: 05288/62203. FAX: 05288/64615.

013 Terrassencamping Schlossberg Itter, Hopfgarten, nr Kitzbühel

Site with good facilities west of Kitzbühel.

With some 200 pitches, this well kept site is suitable both as a base for longer stays and also for overnight stops, as it lies right by a main road. It is on a slight slope but most of the 200 numbered pitches are on levelled terraces. All have electricity and cable TV connections, 150 have water and drainage and 25 have telephone sockets also. Space is said to be usually available. The site has two remarkable features – the large children's playground has a huge collection of most ingeniously devised fixed apparatus, and secondly, the sanitary facilities which have been added on the floor above the older provision. Both sanitary facilities are of a very high standard. The new section has a large room in which private cubicles have been placed round the walls and as free standing units. Some of these have washbasins set in flat surfaces with others having baths, one a massage type, or showers, with two slightly larger units for families, baby baths and footbaths. British style WCs; facilities for disabled visitors. Pots of artificial flowers complete the hotel-like atmosphere of 'Washland', all hot water is free and the facilities are heated in cool weather. The site has a pleasant open-air, solar heated swimming pool (16 x 8 m.) and children's paddling pool. Good walks and a wealth of excursions by car are available nearby. Free ski-lift from site in winter, especially suitable for beginners and children; also own toboggan run. Some road and rail noise.

How to find it: Site is 2 km. northwest of Hopfgarten on B170 to Worgl (not up by Schloss Itter). The entrance is on a bend opposite a Peugeot/Talbot garage and the site is hidden by trees, care is needed to spot it.

General Details: Open all year. 40,000 sq.m. Small shop, bar/restaurant (both closed Nov). Swimming pool (1/5-1/10). Sauna. Solarium. Children's playground. Tennis, fishing, riding, bicycle hire within 2 km. Refrigerator box hire. Youth room. Washing machine and dryer. Cooking facilities. Chemical disposal. Motorcaravan services.

Charges 1999: Summer: per person sch. 68; child (under 14 yrs) 44; car 45; tent or caravan 45; motorcaravan 75 - 90; m/cycle 30; dog 40; electricity 35; cable TV 48 plus 8 per night; local tax (over 14 yrs) 8. Prices higher for winter. Less 50% on pitch fee in mid-seasons. No credit cards.

Reservations: made with deposit and fee; usually min. 1 week (2 weeks at Christmas). Address: Itter, 6361 Hopfgarten. Tel: 05335/2181. FAX: 05335/2182.

AUSTRIA - Tirol and the West

006 Terrassencamping Natterer See, Natters, nr Innsbruck see colour
advert opposite

Excellent site in quiet lakeside situation above Innsbruck amid fine scenery.

Above Innsbruck, 7 km. southwest of the town, this site is in a quiet and isolated location around two small lakes. One of these is for bathing with a long 67 m. slide (free to campers, on payment to day visitors), while boats such as inflatables can be put on either lake. There are many fine mountain views and a wide variety of scenic excursions. For the more active, signed walks start from the site. The site offers about 200 individual pitches of varying, but adequate size, some on flat ground by the lake, others on higher, level, terraces. Electrical connections are available, with 28 pitches also having water, drain and telephone connections, another 14 with drain and phone. Many are reinforced by gravel (possibly tricky for tents). There are two excellent sanitary blocks with under-floor heating, British type WCs, free hot water in washbasins (some in private cabins) and showers, plus facilities for babies, children and disabled people. For winter camping the site offers ski and drying room and a free ski-bus service. A toboggan run and langlauf have been developed on the site, with ice skating, ice hockey and curling on the lake. During high season an extensive daily entertainment programme for children and adults offers different sports, competitions, amusement and excursions. Occasional services are held in the small chapel. The excellent restaurant with bar and large terrace overlooking the lake has a good menu and takeaway service. Three 'theme pavillions' overlooking the water are a new addition for special dinners (4-8 persons)Used by tour operators (50 pitches). Well appointed apartments and rooms to let. Very good English is spoken. This family run camp must rate as one of the best in Austria.

How to find it: From Inntal autobahn (A12) take Brenner autobahn (A13) as far as Innsbruck-sud/Natters exit (no. 3) without payment. From Italy, take exit for Innsbruck-Sud/Natters. Site is signed from the exit (4 km).

General Details: Open all year. Excellent bar/restaurant (20/12-10/01 and 20/03 -30/09). Good small shop (15/03-30/9). Children's playgrounds. Sports field. Basketball, beach volleyball and water polo. Table tennis. Youth room with games, pool and billiards. TV room with Sky. Electric bumper-boats and mountain bike hire. Children's activity programme with Indian 'tipi' tents. Child minding (day nursery) in high season. 'Aquapark' with water trampoline, slide and other attractions. Surf-bikes and wind-glider. Canoes and mini sailboats for rent. Tennis, minigolf nearby. Riding 6 km. Fishing or golf 12 km. Laundry facilities. Chemical disposal. Motorcaravan services and car wash. No dogs are accepted in mid and high seasons. Apartments and rooms to let.

Charges 2000: Per person sch. 74 - 95; child (under 14 yrs) 56 - 66; pitch 100 - 130; electricity (6A) 43 - 50; water and drainage plus 20; dog (not accepted 11/6-31/8) 40 - 50; local tax (adults) 8. Special weekly, winter, summer or Christmas packages. Credit cards accepted (Visa, Master and Eurocard).

Reservations: min. 7 days with deposit (sch. 500). Address: 6161 Natters bei Innsbruck (Tirol). Tel: 0512/546732. FAX: 0512/546732-16. E-mail: natterer.see@netway.at. A 'Camping Cheques' site.

AR Discount
Bottle of wine on arrival

014 Euro Camping Wilder Kaiser, Kössen, nr Kufstein see colour advert
in section opposite

Well designed site with superb facilities for summer and winter visits.

The village of Kössen lies to the south of the A8 Munich - Salzburg autobahn and east of the A12 motorway near Kufstein. It is, therefore, well situated for overnight stops but even more for longer stays. `Wilder Kaiser' is located at the foot of the Unterberg with views of the Kaisergebirge (the Emperor's mountains) and surrounded by forests. Being about 2 km. north of the village, it is a quiet place away from main roads. The well constructed main building at the entrance houses reception, a restaurant, shop and sanitary facilities. About 150 of the 250 pitches (grass over gravel) are available for tourists with electricity (6/10A), water, drainage, TV and gas points. They are of good size on either side of decorative brick paved roads. Some have shade from the attractive trees and all have good views. The heated central sanitary block is of excellent quality with British style WCs and free hot water in washbasins, generously sized showers and sinks. Very nicely tiled, it is kept exceptionally clean. There is also a baby room. The well stocked shop and very fine restaurant with terrace are open all year and in high season there is a snack bar. A large, imaginative children's playground is by the entrance and there is also a café here. In front of the restaurant is a heated swimming pool with children's pool. In high season, special staff run a Tepi club and other activities for adults and children. A weekly programme is displayed on notice boards. One of the top 10 best camps in Austria, it can be recommended without reservation.

How to find it: From the A8 autobahn (München - Salzburg), take the Grabenstatt exit and go south on B307/B176 to Kössen where site is signed. From the south go north on B176. From A93 (Rosenheim - Kufstein) autobahn take Oberaudorf exit and go east on B172 to Walchsee and Kössen.

General Details: Open all year. 52,000 sq.m. Shop. Large restaurant. Snack bar (high season). Club room with TV. Youth room. Sauna and solarium. Tennis. Large adventure playground with café. Entertainment programme (more comprehensive in high season). Washing machines and dryers. Motorcaravan service.

Charges guide: Per person sch. 58 - 74; local tax (over 14 yrs) 9; child (under 14) 35 - 45; pitch with electricity and TV 63 - 89; with all services 73 - 104; dog 37 - 47; electricity 27 - 32; gas connection 49; TV connection 55. Reductions for long off-season stays.

Reservations: made with deposit and fee for exact dates in high season; no min. stay except at Christmas (3 weeks). Address: 6345 Kössen (Tirol). Tel: 05375/6444. FAX: 05375/2113. A 'Camping Cheques' site.

Your ★★★★★ Holiday Paradise in the Tirol Alps near Innsbruck...

full of life

Natterer See

8 convincing reasons for you to spend your holiday with us:

- the **unique scenic location** in the middle of unspoilt nature
- the **well-placed situation** - also perfect when en route to the South
- the **thrilling water experience** of our own swimming lake (average 22°C)
- the **guarantee of sport, amusement, fun, animation** - ideal for all the family
- the **weekly discounted prices for senior citizens** and bargain hunters and our special mountain-bike-packages
- the comfortable **apartments and guest rooms** for friends and relatives
- the central position in the „**Olympia" ski region** Innsbruck / Seefeld / Stubaital
- the **high praise from ADAC** for the facilities at our site

Facilities • **individual terraced pitches** with electricity and telephone hook-up partly water and drainage Sat-TV • motorhome service station • top quality sanitation facilities • mini-market • restaurant with lake terrace • **comfortable guest rooms** • **holiday apartments** • mini-club • pool room • youth room • sport & games areas • streetball • beach volleyball • **swimming lake** with 66m giant waterslide • water-trampoline• windglider • surfbikes • canoes• bumper boats • children's swimming bay • archery • mountainbike and cycle hire • indian camp • tabletennis • open-air chess • **top animation programme** • attractive walks

• ski an drying room • ice skating • ice hockey • curling and tobogganing on-site • cross country skiing • „Olympia" ski region • ski bus

ADAC '99 Superplatz

We will be pleased to send you our detailed brochure.

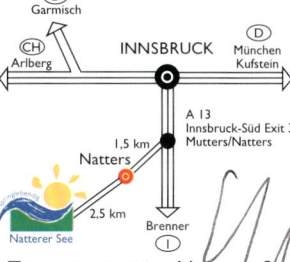

Garmisch — D
Arlberg — CH
INNSBRUCK
München Kufstein — D
A 13
Innsbruck-Süd Exit 3
Mutters/Natters
1,5 km
Natters
2,5 km
Brenner — I
Natterer See

Terrassencamping Natterer See
A-6161 Natters/Tirol/Austria

Tel. ++43(0)512/546732
Fax ++43(0)512/546732-16

email: natterer.see@netway.at
http://www.tiscover.com/natterer.see

Servus in Österreich

TOP CAMPING AUSTRIA   Tirol

MONS (Belgium)
CAMPING DU WAUX-HALL

At a short distance from the Town Centre, Camping Waux-Hall★★ invites you to stay in a quiet and restful place with clean and modern equipment (sanitary facilities, showers, washing machine), with direct access to Waux-Hall park (5 ha. of open spaces, stretches of water, tennis, children's playground, bar . . .)

75 pitches with electricity – open all year

Reservation: 00.32.65/33.55.80 (Tourist Office)
Avenue Saint-Pierre, 17, B-7000 MONS Belgium Tel: 00.32.65/33.79.23 Fax: 0032.65/36.38.48

mark hammerton
travel

family camping in france
we see things differently

We offer ready-erected, stylish 4 bedroom tents and 3 bedroom luxury mobile homes. They're brand new, state-of-the-art and come fully-equipped (down to the corkscrew). Just turn up and move in!

Our sites are small, friendly and convenient for the beaches of Brittany, the Vendee or Charentes. Most are simply not big enough for mass-market camping operators (though all are good enough to be included in this guide).

All our sites have excellent swimming pools, many with water slides, and we keep numbers low to preserve the sites' own character. But you will find mature courier couples, seasoned campers themselves, on hand to help you enjoy your holiday.

With incredibly low cross-Channel rates, total flexibility (depart any day of the week, visit as many sites as you like), a comprehensive Travel Pack and an experienced team it makes sense to see things differently in 2000.

FROM **£189**

12 nights tent holiday for 2 adults and up to 4 children starting 10th May, including return Channel crossing

See for yourself!
For full details and a virtual tour of our accommodation visit
www.markhammerton.com

make it easy on yourself

For your free brochure
01892 52 54 56
Quote AR00

e-mail: enquiries@markhammerton.com

SCHLOSS-CAMPING VOLDERS

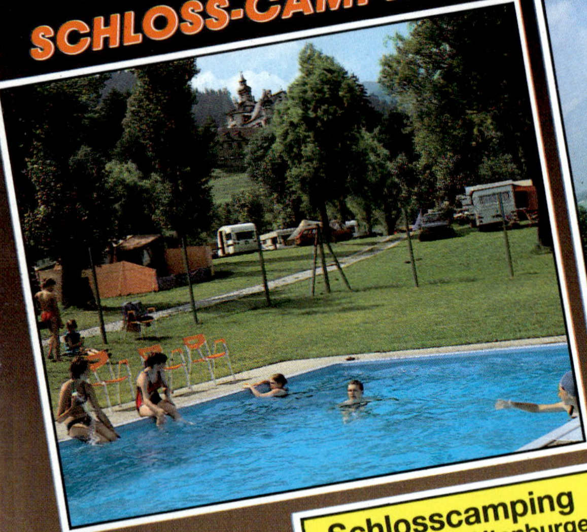

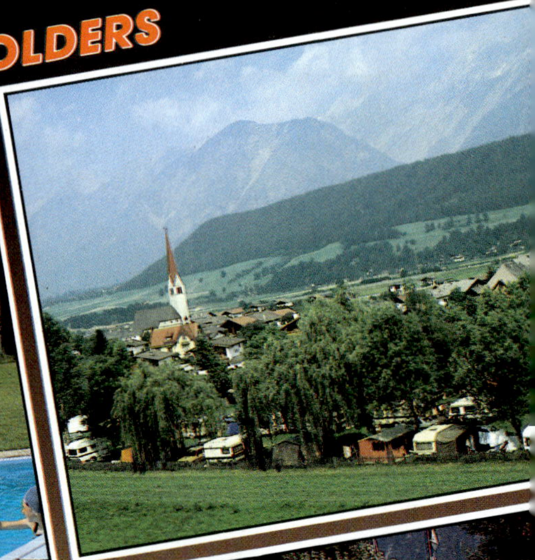

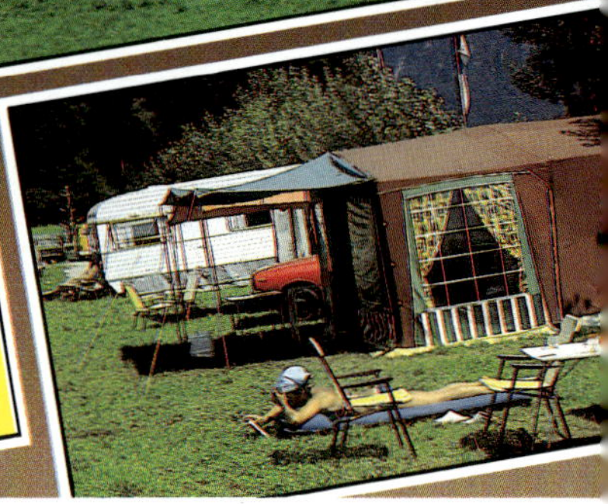

AUSTRIA

Tirol

Schlosscamping
Fam. Baron Altenburger
A-6111 Volders/Tirol
Tel/Fax. 05224/52333

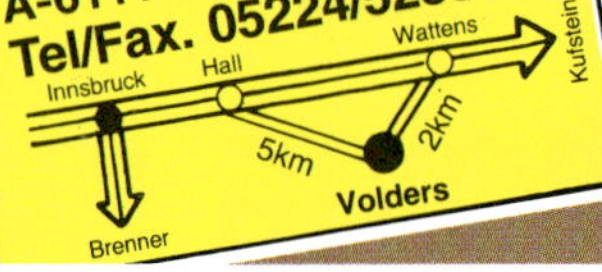

Sport Camp Woferlgut

ZellamSee Kaprun
EUROPA SPORT REGION

TOP CAMPING AUSTRIA

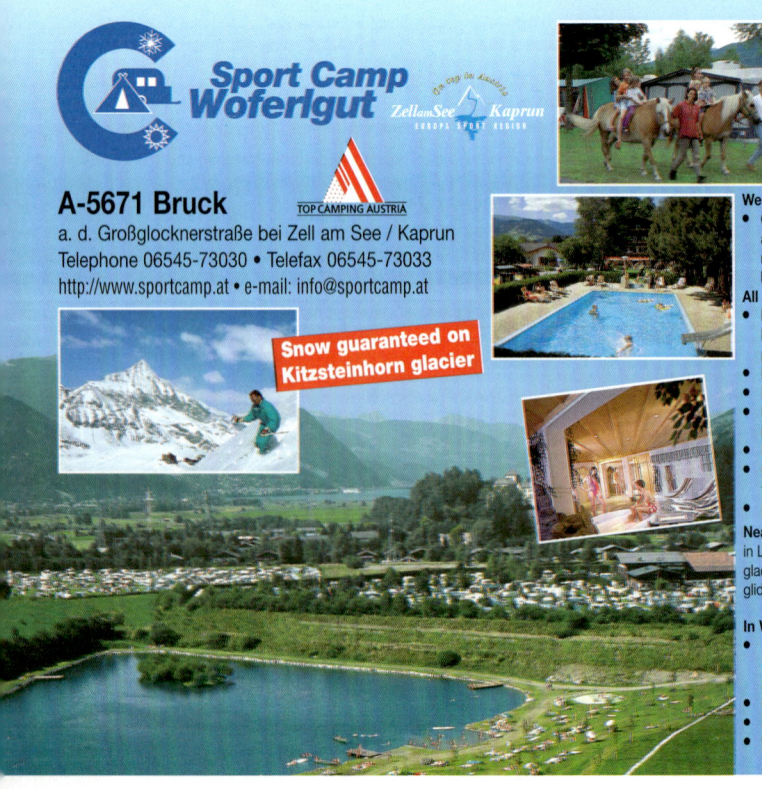

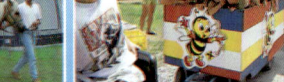

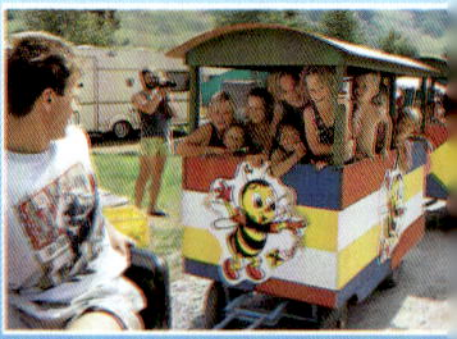

A-5671 Bruck
a. d. Großglocknerstraße bei Zell am See / Kaprun
Telephone 06545-73030 • Telefax 06545-73033
http://www.sportcamp.at • e-mail: info@sportcamp.at

Snow guaranteed on Kitzsteinhorn glacier

ADAC '99 Auszeichnu

ANWE

We offer:
- Comfortable pitches, restaurant and bar, comfortable guests rooms, appartements, caravan **hire, bicycle hire**

All inclusive sports- and leisure facilities
- **Fitness Centre** with sauna, steam bath, solarium, hydropathy pool, plunge bath, bar and massages • tennis free
- **Private Lake** / bathing and fishing
- Leisure room for the young
- Large children's playground and pets, horse riding for children, child care in summer
- Heated outdoor pool with children's pool
- Guided mountain and bicycle tours, sports programme
- Recreation room and cooking facilities

Nearby: swimming, windsurfing, sailing, waterskiin in Lake Zell, summer skiing on the Kitzsteinhorn glacier (3029 m), riding, circuit flights of the Alps, gliding, minigolf, 36-hole golf course, indoor pools.

In Winter:
- Free bus to the ski lifts of the Europa-Sport-Region (Kaprun, Zell am See and Saalbach-Hinterglemm)
- Cross country skiing cours
- Ski school and free practice lifts
- Skating rink and curling

008 Schloss-Camping, Volders, nr Innsbruck

see colour advert opposite

Pleasant Tirolean site with heated pool near Innsbruck.

The Inn valley is not only central to the Tirol, but is a very beautiful and popular part of Austria. Volders, some 15 km. from Innsbruck, is one of the little villages on the banks of the Inn and is perhaps best known for the 17th Century Baroque Servite Church and monastery. Conveniently situated here is the very pleasant Schloss-Camp which is dominated by the castle from which it gets its name which towers at the back of the site with mountains beyond. The 160 grass pitches, all with electricity, are on level or slightly sloping ground. The refurbished sanitary block near the entrance has British style WCs and free hot water in all washbasins (some in cabins), showers and sinks. Near the entrance is a nice bar/restaurant and shop with basic supplies. An animator provides games and entertainment for children in high season, when there is also a tent for groups of 30 persons. The well situated swimming pool is heated and there is a children's play area. The well laid out camping area is closely mown making this a most attractive site and the English speaking Baron who owns and runs the site gives a most friendly welcome. There are rooms to let in the castle. It is an excellent base from which to explore the region and visit Innsbruck, Salzburg, the Royal Castles at Schwangau, the Bavarian Alps and northern Italy over the Brenner Pass for day trips.

How to find it: From A12 motorway, travelling east, leave at exit for Hall, going westwards, take exit for Wattens and follow signs for Volders where site is signed.

General Details: Open 15 April - 15 October. 25,000 sq.m. Electricity connections (16A). Bar/restaurant. Shop for basics, supermarket 400 m. Snack bar with terrace. Heated swimming pool. Minigolf, Children's playground. Activity programme for children in high season.`

Charges 1999: Per person sch. 67; child (3-14 yrs) 42; car 42; m/cycle 15; caravan or tent 42; motorcaravan 84; electricity 25; dog 15; local tax 7.

Reservations: made for any length of stay with deposit and small fee. Address: 6111 Volders (Tirol). Tel: 05224/523333. FAX: as phone.

Salzburg and the Centre

There is more to Salzburg than 'The Sound of Music' and Mozart, although memorabilia of its most famous composer dominate from confectionery to souvenirs. Pasture-land, curative spas and interesting castles and monasteries abound. The Lake District, set amidst rolling hills, is near, along with salt mines to visit and music, art and drama festivals to enjoy. Salzburg has splendid gardens and ancient castles.

018 Sport Camp Woferlgut, Bruck a.d. Grossglocknerstrasse, nr Zell am See

Good, attractive, well equipped site in mountain region for summer and winter camping.

The village of Bruck lies at the junction of the B311 and the Grossglocknerstrasse in the Hohe Tauern National Park, with Salzburg to the north and Innsbruck to the northwest. Sport Camp Woferlgut, a family run site, is one of the best in Austria. Although surrounded by mountains, the site is quite flat with pleasant views. The 310 level pitches on grass are of generous size and marked out by shrubs (200 for touring units) and each has electricity connection, water, drainage, cable TV socket and gas point. Three modern sanitary blocks - the newest of which is in a class of its own - with under-floor heating and music, have excellent facilities with British type WCs, free hot showers and facilities for disabled people. The fitness centre has a fully equipped gym, whilst the other building contains a sauna and cold dip, Turkish bath, solarium (all free) massage on payment and bar. In summer there is a free activity programme, evenings with live music, club for children, weekly barbecues and guided cycle and mountain tours. The site's own lake is used for swimming and fishing, surrounded by a landscaped sunbathing area and there is a small, heated outdoor pool and child's pool near the entrance. In winter a cross-country skiing trail and toboggan run lead from the site and a free bus service is provided to nearby skiing facilities. A new restaurant has been built and there is a well stocked shop. A high grass bank has been developed between the site and the road. The management is pleased to advise on local attractions and tours, making this a splendid base for a family holiday. The site is popular with tour operators.

How to find it: Site is southwest of Bruck. From road B311, Bruck by-pass, take southern exit (Grossglockner) and site is well signed.

General Details: Open all year. 160,000 sq.m. Electricity connections (16A). Shop, restaurant (both 20/12-15/4 and 15/5-30/10). Swimming pool (15/5-30/9). Fitness centre. Two children's playgrounds. Tennis. Volleyball. Football area. Bicycle hire. Hobby room equipped with billiards, table tennis and TV. Fishing. Watersports and swimming at in the lake. Riding 2 km. Golf 3.5 km. Hiking and skiing (all year) nearby. Free programme of activities throughout the year for adults and children (Topi club) with three special staff during the summer. Collection of small animals with pony rides for young children. General room. Cooking facilities. Washing machines and dryers. Chemical disposal. Motorcaravan services. Apartments, rooms and caravans to let.

Charges 2000: Per person sch. 56 - 72, plus local tax 10; child (under 10) 46 - 62; car 50 - 66; tent or caravan 60 - 76; motorcaravan 89 - 142; m/cycle 39 - 55; cable TV (once) 100; electricity 25 plus meter. All sporting and recreational facilities are free. Special prices for senior citizens and families. No credit cards.

Reservations: Contact site. Address: 5671 Bruck a.d. Glocknerstrasse. Tel: 06545/73030. FAX: 06545/73033. E-mail: info@sportcamp.at.

see colour advert opposite

AUSTRIA - Salzburg and the Centre

016 Seecamp, Zell-am-See

Excellent lakeside site for summer and winter camping.

Zellersee, delightfully situated in the south of Salzburg province and near the start of the Grossglocknerstrasse, is ideally placed for enjoying the splendid southern Austria countryside. Seecamp is right by the water about 2 km. from the town of Zell with fine views to the south end of the lake. On entering, one is immediately struck by the order and appearance of the site, with 176 good level, mainly grass-on-gravel pitches of above average size. All have electricity (10/16A) and half have water, drainage and TV sockets. A large, modern building in the centre, houses reception, shop, restaurant (with terrace) and excellent, heated sanitary facilities which include British style WCs, a baby room and one for disabled visitors. The lake is accessible for boating and watersports, with surfing and sailing schools. In summer there is entertainment for children and a programme for adults which includes sports, rafting, canoeing, mountain biking, water ski-ing, hiking and coach excursions. Glacier ski-ing is possible in summer. All in all, a splendid site for a relaxing or active holiday amidst the mountains and green pastures.

How to find it: Follow signs for Thumersbach where site is signed.

General Details: Open all year. 28,000 sq.m. Restaurant (closed Oct-Nov). Shop (June-Aug, Dec-mid Jan). Activity programmes. Beach volleyball. Children's play area. Fishing. Bicycle hire. Riding or golf 2 km. Winter ski packages. Washing machines, dryers and irons. Chemical disposal. Motorcaravan services.

Charges 2000: Per comfort pitch sch. 130, simple pitch 105 or tent pitch 50, all less 20% in low seasons; adult 93; child (2-15 yrs) 50; dog 45; electricity, gas. TV connections 30 (once only) plus meters; local tax (over 15 yrs) 9. Special winter package prices. Credit cards accepted.

Reservations: Contact site for application form. Address: Thumersbacherstrasse 34, 5700 Zell-am-See. Tel: 06542/72115. FAX: 06542/7211515. E-mail: zell@seecamp.at.

019 Kur-Camping Erlengrund, Badgastein

Mountain site catering for summer and winter.

Although in a fairly remote area, Badgastein became popular in the last century with those `taking cures' in the waters from the hot natural springs which still fill the unique indoor swimming pool. The town is on a steep slope with the River Ache cascading down into the centre and under the main street. It also lies on the route to the south using the Tauern rail tunnel (which will take caravans) to travel between the Tirol and Carinthia. Camping Erlungrund is situated on flat ground just south of the town, surrounded by wooded mountains and provides 180 pitches (118 for touring units in summer, 90 in winter). Most of the pitches have handstanding under grass and they surround the main apartment building which houses good quality, heated, sanitary facilities. The provision includes British style WCs and free hot water to wash-basins, showers and sinks. There are family bathrooms for hire. All pitches have electricity and 60 have water, drainage and gas points as well. Basic food supplies are available and there is a restaurant just out-side the entrance. The site belongs to Hotel Europaischer Hof, campers may use the hotel's recreational facilities. There is a small heated pool in high season when a Tepi club is available for children.

How to find it: Turn off B167 road at sign 1 km before Badgastein.

General Details: Open all year. 45,000 sq. m. Electricity connections (16A). Small shop (mornings). TV room. Table tennis. Football ground. Children's playground. Washing machine and drying room. Chemical disposal.

Charges 2000: Per person sch. 61 - 68; local tax (over 15 yrs) 17; child (1-12 yrs) 47 - 52; pitch 66 - 88; small tent pitch 35 - 40; m/cycle 25; extra car 25; dog 50; electricity and gas on meter; TV connection 10.

Reservations: made for min 1 week with deposit. Address: Erlengrund Str. 6, 5640 Badgastein. Tel: 06434/2790. FAX: as phone.

021 Camping Nord-Sam, Salzburg

Neat little site in suburbs near town and autobahn.

Nord-Sam is very close to the Salzburg-Nord autobahn exit, and so makes a convenient stopover for those travelling through. It is also acceptable for a longer stay, being on the edge of the town and with its own small swimming pool. The terrain is divided into 90 marked pitches, which are not very large but are sep-arated by hedges, etc. which offer some privacy and are also attractive to wild life (including red squir-rels). Pitches are quite well shaded with about 60 electrical connections (6A). The site is well tended, with flowers and shrubs. You should find space if you arrive reasonably early. The small, heated sanitary block, below the house, is of nice quality with British toilets, individual basins with shelf, mirror and hot water, some in cabins, free hot water in showers and washing-up sinks. Salzburg is a major railway junction so you should expect some train noise at night. There is a cycle path directly to the centre.

How to find it: Site is signed from Salzburg-Nord autobahn exit and city centre; follow signs carefully.

General Details: Open 1 May - 30 Sept. 13,000 sq.m. Small shop. General room where drinks served. Swimming pool. Meals in high season. Unusual small children's play area. Bicycle hire. Washing machine and dryer. Chemical disposal. Motorcaravan services. Bus service to city (tickets from reception, change at station).

Charges guide: Per person sch. 50 - 60; child (2-14 yrs) 27 - 40; pitch 79 - 99; dog 15 - 20; electricity 25.

Reservations: Are made - contact site. Address: Samstrasse 22a, 5023 Salzburg. Tel: 0662/660494.

026 Camping Hirschenwirt, St Johann im Pongau

Small, pleasant site with first class sanitary facilities.

This small, but very pleasant site is ideally placed for those wanting a night stop when travelling on the Salzburg - Badgastein road, but could also make an excellent base for seeing this interesting area of mountains, lakes, salt mines, ice caves and famous towns. The flat, open site lies behind the Gasthof Hirschenwirt, with 40 tourist pitches on grass on either side of gravel roads. All pitches have electrical connections and sockets for satellite TV. The excellent sanitary arrangements are in the basement of the Gasthof. They have under-floor heating, British style WCs, a baby room and some private bathrooms for hire. The sauna and solarium are also here. There is a small pool for summer use. The attractive mountain area has outstanding cycle and mountain bike tracks and sporting opportunities locally include rafting, riding or paragliding. Being on a major road route there is traffic noise.

How to find it: Site is behind Gasthof Hirschenwirt at St Johann im Pongau on main B311 (Salzburg - Badgastein) road.

General Details: Open all year except Nov. 8,000 sq.m. Electricity (16A) and TV points. Bar/restaurant. Sauna and solarium. Swimming pool (June - Sept). Bicycle hire. Children's playground. Music (in restaurant) at weekends. Fishing 2 km. Riding or golf 5 km. Washing machine, dryer and drying room. Chemical disposal.

Charges 1999: Per person sch. 50 - 70; child (3-14) 20 - 30; pitch 80 - 100; electricity 6 p/kw. No credit cards.

Reservations: Write to site. Address: 5600 St Johann im Pongau. Tel: 06412/6012. FAX: 06412/6012-8. E-mail: hirschenwirt@aon.at.

AR Discount
Less 10%
after 30 days

024 Camping Appesbach, St Wolfgang, nr Salzburg

Lakeside site in an attractive region for excursions.

The situation of this site is one of its main assets, being right by the lakeside with a reasonable frontage and with a very pleasant outlook to the high hills on the opposite side. The lake can be used for all types of sailing and sail-boarding; it is possible to leave small boats by the beach and there are also some for hire. Motor boats may be used, but for restricted hours, and bathing is possible if not too cool. The site is 1 km. from the village of St Wolfgang and the many excursions possible in the area include Salzburg some 50 km. away. The site has room for about 50 permanent caravans and 150 tourists, but the pitches are not numbered or marked out. Units go on large meadows in rows and could become crowded in the main season. It can be full for July and most of August if the weather is good. There are electrical connections in most parts The two toilet blocks have British WCs, a good supply of washbasins with shelf, mirror and free hot water, but less numerous free hot showers which in one block require external undressing.

How to find it: Approaching along the no. 158 road from west, turn left at camp sign just past Ströbl and continue round lake to camp which is 1 km. before St. Wolfgang.

General Details: Open Easter - 31 Oct. Electricity connections (10A). Shop. Pleasant restaurant/bar with good food, which also serves as general room with TV. Snack bar with terrace. Small children's playground. Table tennis. Tennis nearby. Motorcaravan service point.

Charges guide: Per person sch. 56 - 63; child 33.50 - 39; pitch 40 - 130 acc. to position and size of unit; electricity 30 + meter; dog 20; boat 30; local tax: adult 9 - 12, child 4.50 - 6. Some reductions longer stays off season. Weekly inclusive package deals.

Reservations: made for min. 1 week with deposit. Address: Au 99, 5360 St. Wolfgang (Salzkammergut). Tel: 06138/2206. FAX: 06138/220633. E-mail: appesbach@aon.at

027 Seecamp-Neumarkt, Neumarkt am Wallersee

Lakeside site north of Salzburg with good facilities.

Surrounded by gentle hills and adorned with trees and flowers, Seecamp is separated from the lake by a narrow public road, although there is access to the water through the municipal bathing area. When seen in mid-week it was very quiet, but one would imagine that it is more lively during weekends in high season. The 170 grass pitches (100 for tourists, the remainder for long stay units) are on either side of gravel roads on a very gentle slope. They are not marked out or numbered but the position of electricity boxes allows sufficient space. All pitches have electricity and connections are available for TV/radio, water and drainage. Reception, a restaurant with terrace, very good sanitary facilities, heated in winter (with British type WCs, free hot water and baby room) and a first aid room are housed together in a modern, underground block near the lake. There are ramps by the steps to the toilets for disabled visitors but these are rather steep. Some facilities are used by non-camping members of the public.

How to find it: Approx. 26 km. from Salzburg, on B1/A1 Salzburg - Linz road, take turning for Neumarkt. Follow signs for Strandcamping just before the small town itself. If using motorway use Wallersee Ost exit.

General Details: Open Easter - 31 Oct. 37,000 sq.m. Electricity connections (6A). Restaurant with terrace. Shop. Minigolf. Volleyball. Children's playground. General room with TV. Bathing at lake station. Fishing. Riding 2 km. Bicycle hire 1 km. Medical/treatment room. Chemical disposal.

Charges 1999: Per pitch sch. 65 - 95; adult 65; child (2-15 yrs) 35; local tax 7; electricity 25 plus 8 per kw; TV/radio connection 60. No credit cards.

Reservations: Write to site. Address: Uferstr. 3, 5202 Neumarkt. Tel: 06216/4400. FAX: 06216/44004.

Vienna and the East

Although Vienna (Wien) is a vibrant centre for culture today, with museums, opera, famous choirs, the Spanish Riding School, well known cafés and the Danube, its glories lie in its illustrious past and the giants of music, architecture and psychology who lived and worked in the Austrian capital during its hey-day. This, coupled with its Imperial history, make it a gracious and interesting city to visit. The provinces of Lower Austria, Burgenland and Styria, land of vineyards, mountains and farmland, are off the tourist routes, although walkers are attracted to the forested hills where paths meander for hundreds of miles.

029 Donaupark Camping, Tulln a.d. Donau, nr Vienna

Good, pleasant site in quiet situation near the River Danube.

The ancient town of Tulln lies on the southern bank of the River Danube, 20 miles northwest of Vienna in the Wienerwald of Lower Austria. Vienna can be reached by train in about 30 minutes and one can sail on the river through the Wachau vineyards, orchards and charming villages viewing ruined castles and church belfries. Donaupark Camping, owned and run by the Austrian Motor Club (OAMTC), is imagina-tively laid out 'village-style' with unmarked grass pitches, grouped around six circular gravel areas which have a covered water point and drain in the centre. Other pitches are to the side of the hard road which links the circles and these include some with grill facilities for tents. 100 of the 130 tourist pitches have electricity and cable TV sockets. Tall trees surrounding the site offer shade in parts. The 140 long-stay car-avans are tucked neatly away from the tourist area at the back of the site. There are three modern, octag-onal sanitary blocks, one at reception and the other two which are linked by a cover, at the far end. These are heated, with British style WCs and free hot water in all basins, showers and sinks. Washing up and laundry rooms also have cooking rings. Two blocks have facilities for disabled visitors. There are three play areas, two for younger children and a larger one with room for ball games. The Tipi club is held here. Entry is free for campers to the park with bathing lake next to the site. Activities are organised in high season for children (with a room for wet weather) and adults with guided tours around Tulln on foot, by bike and on the river by canoe (hired from site). Steamer excursions are available. There is a half-hourly train service to Vienna and a bus service three times each week from the site in July/Aug. The restau-rant/bar with terrace keeps open quite late. This quiet location 100 m. from the Danube makes an excel-lent venue for families visiting this part of Austria. The receptionist/manager speaks good English.

How to find it: From Vienna follow south bank of the Danube on B14; from the west, leave A1 autobahn at either St Christophen or Altenbach exits and go north on B19 to Tulln. Site is on east side of Tulln, well signed.

General Details: Open 1 May - 30 Sept. 100,000 sq.m. Shop, bar and restaurant (15/5-15/9). Children's play areas. Children's club July/Aug. Tennis. Bicycle and canoe hire. Fishing 500 m. Riding 2 km. Excursions. Bus servicento city July/Aug. Washing machines and dryers. Gas supplies. Chemical disposal.

Charges 2000: Per person 60 sch; child (5-14 yrs) 40; pitch for caravan, motorcaravan or trailer tent 110 - 130; tent with car or m/cycle 40 - 50, bicycle 20 - 30; electricity 20; cable TV 20. Credit cards accepted.

Reservations: Write to camp, Address: Donaulande, 3430 Tulln an der Donau. Tel: 02272/65200. FAX: 02272/65201. E-mail: camptulln@oeamtc.at.

032 Donaupark Camping, Klosterneuburg, nr Vienna

Family site convenient for visiting Vienna.

Klosterneuburg lies just to the north of Vienna on the Danube, outside the city boundary away from the noise and bustle of the famous city but only minutes away by train. Donaupark Camping is only a few hundred metres from the river, a walk away from Klosterneuburg and its well known Baroque Abbey and the Wienerwald. The site is owned and run by the Austrian Motor Club (OAMTC) and is in a park-like situation, surrounded by trees but with little shade. The 130 pitches of varying size (some small) are on grass or hardstanding, accessed from hard roads and all with electricity (6A). Two modern sanitary facil-ities, one at reception and the other by the pitches, have British style WCs, free hot water to washbasins, showers and sinks and a unit for disabled people. There are cooking rings and a freezer for ice packs. Shop for basic supplies and a snack bar/restaurant (both May - Sept) with others a short walk away in the town. Just inside the camp is an old Vienna tram car where money can be changed. There is a small children's play area but alongside the site is 'Happyland', an amusement park which also has a large swimming pool (discounts for campers). The site organises excursions with bikes and guided sightseeing tours of Vienna. This is a good spot for families and the friendly manager speaks good English.

How to find it: Leave Vienna on the west bank of the Danube following signs for Klosterneuburg, site is signed in the town from the main road B14 and is 400 m. behind the railway station.

General Details: Open Easter - end November. 22,500 sq.m. Small shop in restaurant/snack bar. Bicycle hire. Riding 1 km. Golf 3 km. Washing machines and dryer. Chemical disposal. Motorcaravan services.

Charges 1999: Per person sch. 60; child (5-15 yrs) 40; pitch 110 - 140, small tent with car or m/cycle 40 - 60, bicycle 20 - 30; electricity 20; cable TV 20; extra car or tent 40. Credit cards accepted.

Reservations: Write to site. Address: In der Au, 3402 Klosterneuburg. Tel: 02243/25877. FAX 02243/25878. E-mail: campklosterneuburg@oeamtc.at. A 'Camping Cheques' site.

028 Camping Stumpfer, Schönbühel

Small, well appointed site between Salzburg and Vienna.

This small site with 60 pitches is directly on the River Danube, near the small town of Schönbühel, and could make a convenient night stop being near the Salzburg - Vienna autobahn. The sanitary block is part of the main building which also houses a Gasthof, with bar/restaurant of the same name, which can be used by campers. There is shade in most parts and a landing stage for boat trips on the Danube. The facilities are of good quality with British style WCs, washbasins and showers, both with hot water on payment. Special facilities for disabled visitors include ramps by the side of steps up to the washing block. There is a small shop with basic supplies. The 50 pitches for touring units are on flat grass, unmarked, with electricity connections available in all parts; the site is lit at night. This is very much a family run site with apartments for hire being added to the main building.

How to find it: Leave Salzburg - Vienna autobahn at Melk exit. Drive towards Melk, but continue towards Melk Nord. Just before bridge turn right (signed Schönbühel and St Polten), at T-junction turn right again and continue down hill. Turn right just before BP filling station (signed Schönbühel) and site is 3 km. on left with narrow entrance.

General Details: Open Easter - 31 Oct. 7,000 sq.m. Electricity connections (16A). Restaurant. Children's playground. Small shop. Fishing. Swimming pool, bicycle hire or riding within 5 km. Washing machine and dryer. Chemical disposal. Motorcaravan services.

Charges 1999: Per person sch. 45; child (6-14 yrs) 25; tent 30 - 50; caravan or motorcaravan 50 - 70; electricity 30; local tax (over 16 yrs) 10.50. Some credit cards may be accepted in 2000.

Reservations: Write to site. Address: 3392 Schönbühel 7. Tel: 02752/8510. FAX: as phone. E-mail: stumpfer.schonbuhel@aon.at.

AR Discount
Less 5%
after 7 days

030 Camping Rodaun, Wien-Sud/Vienna

Convenient city site for visiting Vienna.

This good quality site is within the city boundary and is an excellent base for visiting this old, interesting and world famous city. Just 9 km. from the centre of Vienna, there is an excellent public transport system for viewing the sights as car parking is almost impossible in the city. This is also a very pleasant camp in its own right with an excellent sanitary block (British type WCs). The site is situated in a southern suburb with a supermarket and a restaurant within 250 m. and a swimming pool, 2 km. It has space for about 100 units on flat grass pitches, neither numbered nor marked, either in the centre or outside the circular tarmac road running round the camping area. There is also a hardstanding area for motorcaravans (but no space for awnings).

How to find it: Take Pressbaum exit from Westautobahn or Vosendorf exit from Sudautobahn and follow signs. It is worth writing to the camp requesting a brochure which gives a good sketch map showing how to find the site.

General Details: Open 25 March - 15 Nov. 10,000 sq.m. Bar. Electricity connections (6A). Little shade. Washing machines, dryers and irons.

Charges guide: Per person sch. 65; child (3-13 yrs) 45; caravan 50 - 60; tent 50; motorcaravan 60; car 12; m/cycle 15; electricity 24 + meter; dog 15.

Reservations: are advised; write to site. Address: 1236 Wien-Rodaun, An der Au 2. Tel: 0222/884154.

050 Camping Fürstenfeld, Fürstenfeld, Styria

Pleasant, small site with basic facilities, near Hungarian border.

Fürstenfeld is the last village on the main route from Graz to Hungary and this site, although small with basic facilities, makes a good staging post when entering (or returning from) Lake Balaton and Budapest. The site is quietly situated on the edge of the village next to a large, well mown, play area with children's playground, space for all types of ball games and a really huge open-air swimming pool complex. This is the size of a football pitch, has a shallow end for paddling, a larger part for general swimming or pool games, an Olympic size racing pool and a diving pool with a 10 m. diving board. There are kiosks for drinks and ice creams, a cafe and changing rooms. The 50 pitches on the site are on terraces on either side of hard access roads, under a covering of trees, with electrical connections available. The single toilet block has British WCs and hot water in washbasins, showers and sinks. The provision is rather cramped and not as good as on most Austrian sites but is clean and acceptable. There is a small bar with TV, but no other facilities on site, but the village shops and restaurants are 2.5 km.

How to find it: From Graz - Vienna motorway, take Fürstenfeld exit. Site is at western end of village, signed.

General Details: Open 15 April - 15 Oct. 3,000 sq.m. Good shade. Electricity in all areas (10A). Bar. Shops and restaurants 2.5 km. Large sports park adjacent. Washing machines and dryers. Baby room.

Charges guide: Per pitch 30 - 50; person 40 - 50; child (2-14 yrs) 15 - 20; dog 10; electricity 20. Weekly package, pitch, 2 persons, electricity 600.

Reservations: Write to site. Address: Campingweg 1, 8280 Fürstenfeld. Tel: 03382/54940. FAX: 03382/51671.

AUSTRIA - Vienna and the East

031 Schlosscamping Laxenburg, Laxenburg, nr Wien/Vienna

Site with good facilities, next to swimming pool, near Vienna.

Although this campsite is a little further out (15 km.) than some of the others, it has better facilities, is in a quieter location, is easier to find - particularly if towing a caravan - and has a bus service from outside the entrance to the city. Close to the historic castle of Laxenburg, it is on the edge of the castle grounds where campers can walk in the extensive park. Adjacent to the site is a pool complex and excellent restaurant with terrace, minigolf, and children's play area. The site has a number of permanent caravans but these are in a separate place on the edge of the tourist area. The seasonal camping part has room for 320 units, all having electrical points. There are no defined pitches as such, but large flat meadows with a circular tarmac road encircling the main part and units go on each side of this road. Siting can, therefore, be a bit haphazard with a risk of crowding in high season, so arrive as early as possible. The large, single, sanitary block is of a good standard, kept clean with British type WCs and hot water in basins (some in cabins), showers and sinks. It is heated in cool weather. Well stocked shop. With an excursion programme available, this is an excellent base from which to visit the famous city or explore further afield. Parking in Vienna is no easier than any other capital or large town so it makes sense to use a site where the car can be left behind and use made of public transport. There is a bus service to the city from outside the entrance (but last return from Vienna is 9 pm) or from autobahn exit 'Vosendorf' and B17 to Liesing for P&R car park for the metro line which runs very late.

How to find it: Laxenburg is south of Vienna, take autobahn exit 'Wiener-Neudorf' to Laxenburg village. Turn right at lights in village centre and site is on left beyond village. Site signed at motorway exit through to site.

General Details: Open 30 March - 31 Oct. 50,000 sq. m. Electricity connections (4A, long leads in places). Shop (1/5-15/9). Good restaurant adjacent. Swimming pool (charge for adults). Playgrounds. Minigolf. Riding 3 km. Golf 5 km. Excursions to Vienna and Budapest (2 days) with German speaking guides. Washing machines. Chemical disposal.

Charges guide: Per person sch. 67 - 73; child (4-15 yrs) 38; pitch 62 - 69; tent 37 – 42; electricity 40; local tax 7. Credit cards accepted.

Reservations: Write to site. Address: Munchendorfer Strasse, 2361 Laxenburg. Tel: 02236/71333. FAX: 02236/713344.

Carinthia and the South

This gentle, tranquil land of some 200 lakes and mountain scenery deserves to be better known than just as a through route from Salzburg to Italy. The beautiful scenery and rural way of life make it an attractive holiday destination to those who know it. Unfortunately, few British have yet discovered its charms and those who have probably wish to keep the secret to themselves. There are few large towns, but many pleasant villages, good, often uncrowded roads and excellent sites.

033 Camping Central, Graz

Satisfactory site on outskirts of town with large swimming pool adjoining.

This appears to be the most sensible of the sites around Graz to use. It is of quite satisfactory quality and next door, with free direct access for those staying at the site, is an enormous swimming pool (120 x 90 m.) with sunbathing areas. Half of the 110 tourist pitches are individual, numbered ones on grassy strips between hedges and access roads; the other half are on a general meadow and not marked out. All have electrical connections. Four heated toilet blocks contain a good supply of washbasins (with hot water) and fewer toilets and rather unexciting, free hot showers. The city centre is about 5 km. and there is a regular bus service from nearby. The site is now open all year and plans are in hand to build a new modern sanitary block.

How to find it: In spite of its name, site is just outside the town to the southwest. From the west take 'Graz W' autobahn exit and the B70 road from Klagenfurt. From Salzburg use autobahn exit 'Graz-Sud'. Follow signs to Central and Strassgang, looking for camp sign on your right.

General Details: Open all year. 30,000 sq.m. Electricity connections (10A). In summer restaurant, either self-service or with waiter service, also serving the swimming pool and keeping some basic provisions. Tennis. Table tennis. Children's playground. Jogging track. Minigolf. Excursions organised. Riding near. Washing machines. Chemical disposal. Caravans for rent.

Charges 2000: Per unit incl. 2 persons and electricity sch. 285; 1 person and tent 155; extra adult 80; child (4-14 yrs) 50; local tax 5. No credit cards.

Reservations: probably unnecessary but will be made if you write. Address: Martinhofstr. 3, 8054 Graz. Tel: 0676/3785102. FAX: 0316/697824. E-mail: freizeit@netway.at.

N036 Rutar Lido FKK-See-Camping, Eberndorf

Secluded naturist site with indoor and outdoor pools.

This is a large (150,000 sq.m.) and very well appointed site for naturist camping and it is a member of the International Naturist Federation (FKK). Situated in the heart of the countryside and surrounded by woodland, the main feature of the site is the provision of no less than six swimming pools (four outdoor and two indoor heated ones). As if this is not enough there is also a small lake for swimming. The 365 pitches (300 for tourers) all have electrical connections and some also have water and drainage. They are on flat grass marked out by hedges with a special area for campers with dogs. Four sanitary blocks are of good quality with British type WCs, some private washcabins and free hot water to washbasins and showers and a special block for disabled visitors. There is a lake for fishing, a small chapel, table tennis, and dances are held in season. Well stocked supermarket, two bar/restaurants and two saunas adjacent to the indoor pools. The village is some distance away. Membership of the FKK or other naturist association is not obligatory but visitors are expected to comply with their rules and ideals.

How to find it: From A2 (Graz - Klagenfurt) road, take B82 south at Volkermarkt to roundabout at Ebendorf and follow signs to site.

General Details: Open all year. Some shade. Electrical connections (10/15A). Supermarket (May - Sept). Two bar/restaurants (all year). Swimming pools. Children's play area. Children's club and activities. Fitness room. Disco room. Bowling alley. Fishing. Bicycle hire or riding 2 km. Golf 5 km. Laundry facilities. Chemical disposal. Apartments to rent.

Charges 1999: Per large pitch (100 sq.m. with electricity) 140 sch; small pitch (70 sq.m.) 100; adult 80; child (3-12 yrs) 60; tax 12; pitch with water/drainage plus 20; dog 50. Less 30% in low season. Credit cards accepted. Euro: Per large pitch (100 sq.m. with electricity) 10.17; small pitch (70 sq.m.) 7.27; adult 5.81; child (3-12 yrs) 4.36; tax 0.87; pitch with water/drainage plus 1.45; dog 3.63. Less 30% in low season.

Reservations: Write to site with 50 deposit. Address: Rutar Lido, 9141 Eberndorf (Carinthia). Tel: 04236/22620. FAX: 04236/2220. E-mail: rutarlido@happynet.at.

AR Discount
Less 3%

046 Terrassen Camping Ossiachersee, Ossiach, nr Villach

Popular site of excellent quality on Lake Ossiach.

As its name implies, this modern site has been constructed with terraces, on ground which slopes gently down to the lake shore. Because of the thick growth of reeds at the water's edge, there is limited access to the lake via two small clearings. One of these has a beach for bathing and a jetty, and boats may be launched from the other. The site is protected by rising hills and enjoys lovely views across the lake to the mountains beyond. Trees, flowers, hedges and bushes abound adding atmosphere to this neat, tidy site. The 550 pitches (485 for touring units) are in rows on level grass terraces, separated by hard roads and marked by hedges, with electricity available. The site does become full in high season and although there is sufficient room on pitches, it may give the initial impression of being overcrowded. A large complex at the entrance includes a self-service restaurant and well stocked supermarket. In high season a daily 'animation' programme is organised for both children and adults, giving a wide range of sports and activities. Young people are well catered for, with their own playgrounds, games rooms and disco dancing courtyard as well as many sports facilities. The lake is available for all forms of water sports including water-skiing and windsurfing schools and there are boats for hire. Although the facilities in the five sanitary blocks vary, they are all of good quality, heated in cool weather, with British WCs and free hot water in the washbasins (some in private cabins), showers and sinks. The newest block has family washrooms. A friendly, lively site where all ages and sports inclinations are catered for in a scenic location in a very beautiful part of Austria.

How to find it: Site is directly on the lake shore just south of Ossiach village. Leave the A10 autobahn at exit for Ossiachersee, turn left onto road 94 towards Feldkirchen and shortly right to Ossiach Sud. The site is shortly after Camping Knodl, on the left.

General Details: Open 1 May - 30 Sept. 100,000 sq.m. Shade in parts. Electricity connections (4A). Restaurant (15/5-15/9). Supermarket. Children's playgrounds. Horse riding. Trampolines. Tennis, volleyball and badminton courts. Football field. Sports area. Organised entertainment. Bicycle and moped hire. Fishing. Riding. Bank. Doctor calls. Washing machines, dryers and irons. Chemical disposal. Motorcaravan service point. Car wash.

Charges 1999: Per person sch. 59 - 89; child (3-9 yrs) free low season, 40 - 59; pitch 80 - 130, acc. to location and size; small tent pitch 50 - 75; summer tax (over 18) 12.50 - 14.50; min. charge (summer) 247 - 284. No credit cards.

Reservations: Advisable 15 July-15 Aug weekends. Write with deposit (3,300 sch) and fee (100). Address: 9570 Ossiach (Kärnten). Tel: 04243/436. FAX: 04243/8171. E-mail: martinz.camping@kaernten.camping.at.

AUSTRIA - Carinthia and the South

048 Komfort-Campingpark Burgstaller, Döbriach, Millstättersee

Excellent large site close to the Millstättersee lake.

This part of Austria deserves to be better known as it is a most attractive region and has some excellent camp sites. Burgstaller is the largest of these and makes a peaceful base from which to explore Carinthia, northeast Italy and Slovenia. The site entrance is directly opposite the lawns leading to the bathing lido, to which campers have free access. There is also a heated swimming pool. The 450 pitches are on flat, well drained grass, backing onto hedges and marked out, on either side of gravel access roads. These vary in size (65-120 sq.m.), all with electricity, water and drainage and there are special pitches for motorcaravans. There are two very good quality sanitary blocks, the larger of which is part of the central complex. It has some basins in private cabins and special facilities for children and the disabled. One has underfloor heating for cool weather. There is a large, good quality restaurant with terrace, two children's play areas (one for under 6s, the other for 6-12 yrs). The games room with 3-lane bowling alley and mini bar leads off the restaurant. There is a secluded roof terrace for nude sunbathing. A covered stage and an outdoor arena provide for church services (Protestant and Catholic, in German) and folk and modern music concerts. Much activity is organised here, including games and competitions for children in summer with a winter programme of skiing, curling and skating. At Christmas, trees are gathered from the forest and there are special Easter and autumn events. This is an excellent family site for winter and summer camping with a very friendly atmosphere, particularly in the restaurant in the evenings.

How to find it: Site is well signed from around Döbriach.

General Details: Open all year. 35,000 sq.m. Electricity connections (6A). Restaurant, shop (May-Oct). Bowling alley. Disco (July/Aug). TV room. Sauna and solarium. Naturist terrace. Children's playgrounds. Beach volleyball. Basketball. Bathing and boating in lake. Fishing. Bicycle hire. Mountain bike area. Horse and pony riding. Golf 8 km. Special entrance rate for lake attractions. Comprehensive entertainment programmes. Chemical disposal. Motorcaravan services.

Charges 2000: Per person sch. 65 - 98; child (4-14 yrs) 40 - 78; local tax (over 18s) 17.50 - 18.50; pitch 50 - 130; dog 15 - 30. Discounts for retired people. No credit cards.

Reservations: Write to site. Address: 9873 Döbriach (Kärnten). Tel: 04246/7774. FAX: 04246/77744. E-mail: dieter-burgstaller@campingpark.telecom.at.

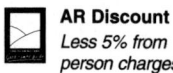

AR Discount
Less 5% from person charges

040 Camping Arneitz, Faakersee, nr Villach

Site with excellent and comprehensive facilities by a Carinthian lake.

Camping Arneitz, directly on Faakersee is one of the best in this area, central for the attractions of the region, watersports and walking. Family run, Arneitz led the way with good quality sanitary facilities. Others have caught up but Arneitz have now gone one further by adding a splendid family washroom. This large, heated, airy room has family cubicles around the walls and in the centre, washbasins at child height in a circle with a working carousel in the middle. British style WCs. There is also a hair washing salon with special basins and hairdryers. This building also houses the children's cinema. There is also a small toilet block nearer the lake. A newly built reception building at the entrance reflects the quality of the site and, apart from booking-in facilities, has a good collection of tourist literature and three desks with telephones for use by guests. The 400 level, marked pitches are mainly of gravel off hard roads, with electricity available and some having good shade from mature trees. Grass pitches are available for tents. The well stocked supermarket offers food items, wine, beer, clothes, camping and general articles. This is at the entrance of the site and includes a delightfully appointed restaurant where there is entertainment in high season. On the opposite side of the entrance road is a very well equipped children's playground with fixed climbing frames, go carts and small electric powered boats (on payment) with a large trampoline (small fee). Day trips can be made to Venice and the Postojna Caves and many other parts of northern Italy and the surrounding countryside.

How to find it: Site is southeast of Villach, southwest of Veldon. Follow signs for Faakersee and Egg rather than for Faak village.

General Details: Open 28 April - 30 Sept. 45,000 sq. m. Shade in part. Electricity connection included in price. Supermarket. Self-service restaurant, bar and terrace. General room with TV. Small cinema for children's films. Beauty salon. Large sauna/solarium. Minigolf. Children's playground. Football field. Fishing. Riding. Bicycle hire. Golf 10 km. Exchange facilities. Doctor visits. Washing machines, spin dryer, irons. Chemical disposal. Motorcaravan services.

Charges 2000: Per person sch. 88 - 96; child (under 10 yrs) 83 - 91; pitch incl. electricity 120 - 150; plus local tax. No credit cards.

Reservations: only made outside main season. Address: 9583 Faak am See (Kärnten). Tel: 04254/2137. FAX: 04254/3044 or 24535. E-mail: camping@arneitz.at.

049 Terrassencamping Maltatal, Maltatal

Site with pool and mountain view, 6 km. from autobahn, 15 from Millstättersee.

This site is good for an overnight stop but its pleasant situation and the good sized swimming pool on site encourage many to stay longer. The pool is over 300 sq.m. with a grassy lying out area and is open to all (free for campers). Many walks and excursions are available. There are 200 grassy pitches on shallow terraces (70-100 sq.m.) and mostly in rows on either side of access roads. Numbered and marked, but not separated, all have electricity and 20 also have water and drainage connections. The two toilet blocks, one with under floor heating, have British style WCs and free hot water in the washbasins (with shelf and mirror and about half in private cabins) and in the controllable showers and sinks. Six family washcabins. They should be a good supply and there are new facilities for babies and children.

How to find it: Site is 6 km. up a mountain valley from an exit at the southern end of the A10 Salzburg - Carinthia autobahn. Take autobahn exit for Gmund and Maltatal and proceed up Maltatal 6 km. to camp.

General Details: Open 8 April - 31 Oct. Electricity connections (6/10A). Only basic provisions kept (village 500 m.). Restaurant (all season). Swimming pool (20/5-15/9). Sauna. Entertainment programme for adults and children. Children's playground. Bicycle hire. Riding. Washing machines, dryers and irons. Chemical disposal. Motorcaravan services. Available from site: the Kärnten-card costing sch. 265 per adult (child 6-14 yrs sch. 130) which gives free travel on public transport and free entry to various attractions.

Charges 1999: Per person sch. 69 - 89; child (3-14 yrs) 44 - 54; local tax (over 18 yrs) 15.50; pitch 88 - 138, acc. to season and services; dog 30 - 35; electricity included . Less 5% for stays of over 11 days, 10% for 21 days. No credit cards.

Reservations: Made with deposit - contact site for details. Address: 9854 Malta 6. Tel: 04733/234. FAX: 04733/23416. E-mail: pirker-touristik@lieser-maltatal.or.at.

044 Schluga Camping, Hermagor, nr Villach

Attractive site with swimming pool and excellent facilities in rural location.

Schluga Camping, under the same ownership as Schluga Seecamping, is some 4 km. to the west of that site in a flat valley with views of the surrounding mountains. The 300 tourist pitches are of varying size, all with electrical connections and some with water and satellite TV connections. Mainly on grass covered gravel on either side of the hard surfaced access road, they are divided by shrubs and hedges. The four sanitary blocks (one splendid new one, three good older ones) are well constructed and heated in cold weather. They have British WCs, controllable free hot water to basins (some in private cabins) and to showers which have a small dressing space. Some family washrooms are available to rent. There is a heated swimming pool (12 x 7 m), fitness centre and a sauna. Entertainment in the high season includes a disco and cinema. A weekly programme sheet details events at both Schluga sites and nearby. The site is open all year, to include the winter sports season, and has a well kept tidy appearance, although it may be busy in high seasons. English spoken.

How to find it: Site is on the B111 Villach-Hermagor road (which is better quality than it appears on most maps) just east of Hermagor town.

General Details: Open all year. 50,000 sq.m. Electricity connections (6+A). Well stocked shop (1/5-30/9). Bar/restaurant with terrace (closed Nov). Kiosk for snacks/ice creams. Children's playground. Games room. Bicycle hire. Sauna. Fitness centre. Heated swimming pool (1/5-30/9). TV room. Badminton. Tennis nearby. Fishing 4 km. Riding 10 km. Kindergarten programme for small children. Washing machines and dryers. Chemical disposal. Motorcaravan services. Mobile homes, etc. to rent.

Charges 2000: Per person sch. 42.50 - 85; child (5-14 yrs) 30.50 - 61, under 5 yrs free; pitch 47.50 - 97, with electricity 76.50 - 134; supplement for water, drainage, TV connection 20 - 35; local tax (over 18) 14 - 18; dog 15 - 55. Special weekly rates for families and senior citizens. No credit cards.

Reservations: Contact site for details. Address: Obervellach 15, 9620 Hermagor-Presseggersee (Kärnten). Tel: 04282/2051 or 2760. FAX: 04282/288120. E-mail: schluga.scampingwelt@carnica.at.

AR Discount
Free guided cycle trip and walks

For a list of sites which are open all year - see page 345

AUSTRIA - Carinthia and the South

045 Naturpark Schluga Seecamping, Hermagor, nr Villach

Pleasant site in attractive out-of-the-way part of Carinthia.

This site is pleasantly situated on natural wooded hillside. The 350 pitches for touring units are individual and level, many with light shade. It is about 300 m. from a small lake with clean water, where the site has a beach of coarse sand and a large grassy meadow where inflatable boats can be kept; also a sunbathing area for naturists. Many walks and attractive car drives are available in the area. This part of Carinthia is a little off the beaten track but it still becomes full in season. The heated sanitary blocks are modern and well constructed, they are of good size with British style toilets and individual washbasins, some in cabins. There are also family washrooms available for rent. Close by is Schluga Camping, under the same ownership, which is open all year - see separate report. English is spoken.

How to find it: Site is on the B111 road (Villach-Hermagor) 6 km. east of Hermagor town.

General Details: Open 20 May - 20 Sept. 70,000 sq.m. Shade in parts. Many electrical connections (6A). Shop (20/5-10/9). Restaurant/bar by entrance where drinks or meals are served; also takeaway (all 20/5-10/9). Room for young people and children. Film room. Kiosk at beach. Surf school. Pony rides. Bicycle hire. Children's playground. Badminton and volleyball court. Fishing. Tennis (indoor and outdoor) near. Weekly activity programme with mountain walks and climbs. Washing machines and dryer. Chemical disposal. Motorcaravan services.

Charges 2000: Per person sch. 42.50 - 85; child (5-14 yrs) 30.50 - 61, under 5 yrs free; pitch 47.50 - 97, with electricity 76.50 - 134; supplement for water, drainage, TV connection 20 - 35; local tax (over 18) 14 - 18; dog 15 - 55. Special weekly rates for families and senior citizens. No credit cards.

Reservations: Contact site for details. Address: 9620 Hermagor-Presseggersee (Kärnten). Tel: 04282/2051 or 2760. FAX: 04282/288120. E-mail: schluga.scampingwelt@carnica.at.

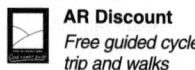

AR Discount
Free guided cycle trip and walks

047 Camping Mössler, Döbriach, nr Spittal

Friendly family site with heated swimming pool, near a Carinthian lake.

A fairly small, flat, grassy site set in very pleasant surroundings with mountain views, Mössler is close to, but not right on, the Millstättersee, a reputedly warm lake. However, as the camp has a free, well heated swimming pool of 200 sq.m., the 600 m. stroll to the lake, where campers usually have free entry to swimming and boating facilities, is not so important. It is an excellent touring area with mountain lifts and many possible excursions to lakes and mountains near at hand. The site has about 200 pitches of two different sizes but both adequate, on flat ground with connections for electricity, water, TV, telephone, gas and drainage. In high season cars stand on separate places in front of pitches. The two modern toilet blocks are of exceptional standard and quite luxurious, including under-floor heating. British type WCs. Washbasins in cabins with automatic light, free hot water, and good, free showers with full controls for hot water. Full facilities for visitors with disabilities and private bathroom facilities (with bath, shower, basin and WC) usually let by the week.

How to find it: Go to Döbriach, at east end of Millstättersee, and camp is signed.

General Details: Open 1 April - 31 Oct. 30,000 sq.m. Electricity connections (12A). Shop and restaurant (both 20/5-30/9). TV facilities. Swimming pools and children's pool. Children's playground. Sauna. Washing machine. Motorcaravan service point. Caravans for hire.

Charges guide: Per pitch sch. 85 - 160, acc. to type of unit and size of pitch; adult 71 - 91; child (6-14 yrs) 49 - 66; local tax (over 18s) 18.50. Reductions in low seasons for longer stays.

Reservations: can be made Sat. - Sat., with deposit. Address: 9873 Döbriach am Millstättersee (Kärnten). Tel: 04246/7735. FAX: 04246/773513 (summer) or 721313 (winter).

DISCOUNT VOUCHERS

Between pages 192/193 you will find two Discount Vouchers which will provide you with potential savings of more than the cost of the Guide itself! (valid 1 Jan - 31 Dec 2000 only)

Voucher A - Campsite Discount Voucher

This voucher entitles the holder to the relevant discounts or special offers at the sites in this guide that have a small Alan Rogers' logo by their entry. Retain this voucher for inspection at the campsite.

Voucher B - Travel and Breakdown Insurance

This voucher entitles the holder to a discount of 10% on Travel & Breakdown Insurance arrangements made via this Guide, as advertised between pages 160/161. To arrange cover please follow the instructions on the voucher.

BELGIUM

Belgium is a small and densely populated country divided on a federal basis into the Flemish north, Walloon south and Brussels the capital, a culturally varied city. Despite being heavily industrialised Belgium possesses some beautiful scenery, notably the great forest of the Ardennes with its rivers and gorges contrasting with the rolling plains and historic cities of Bruges and Ghent with their Flemish art and architecture and the 40 miles of coastline with safe sandy beaches.

For further information contact:

Tourism Flanders - Brussels, 31 Pepper Street, London E14 9RW
Tel: 0891 887799   Fax: 020 7458 0045   E-mail: office@flanders-tourism.org
or
Belgian Tourist Office Brussels - Ardennes, 225 Marsh Wall, London E14 9FW
Tel: 0800 9545 245 (brochure line) or 0906 302 0245 (50p per minute)   Fax: 020 7531 0393
E-mail: info@belgium-tourism.org   Internet: www.belgium-tourism.net

Population
10,040,000 (1993), density 329 per sq km.

Capital
Brussels (Bruxelles).

Climate
Belgium's temperate climate is similar to Britain but the variation between summer and winter is lessened by the effects of the Gulf Stream.

Language
There are two official languages in Belgium. French is spoken in the south and Flemish in the north; however, in the eastern provinces, German is the predominant language. Brussels is officially bi-lingual. Road signs and place names maybe written in either language or in some cases both.

Currency
The currency is the franc which is divided into 100 centimes. Notes are 100, 500, 1000 and 5000 francs, coins 0.5, 1, 5, 20 and 50 francs. Note: The Luxembourg currency is interchangeable with the same exchange rate.

Banks
Banking hours are Mon-Fri 09.00-15.30. Some banks open on Saturday mornings.
Credit Cards: Major credit cards are all widely accepted, as are travellers cheques and Eurocheques.

Post Offices
Open Mon-Fri 09.00-12.00 and 14.00-17.00, some opening on Saturday mornings.

Time
GMT plus 1 (in summer BST plus 1).

Public Holidays
New Year; Easter Mon; Labour Day; Ascension; Whit Mon; Flemish National Day, 21 July; Assumption, 15 Aug; All Saints, 1 Nov; Armistice Day, 11 Nov; Christmas, 25 Dec.

Telephone
From the UK the code is 00 32. For calls within Belgium use the local code followed by the number. For calls to the UK the code is 0044 followed by the local STD code omitting initial 0. Telephone cards available from newsagents, post offices and train stations for Fr. 100 or Fr. 500.

Shops
Shops open from 09.00-17.30/18.00 hrs - later on Thursday and Friday evenings but a little earlier on Saturdays. Some close for two hours at midday.

Motoring
For cars with a caravan or trailer: motorways are toll free except for the Liefenshoek Tunnel in Antwerp. The maximum permitted overall length of vehicle/trailer or caravan combination is 18 m.

Speed Limits: Caravans and motorhomes (7.5 tons): 31 mph (50 kph) in built up areas, 56 mph (90 kph) on other roads and 75 mph (120 kph) 4 lane roads and motorways. Minimum speed on motorways on straight level stretches is 43 mph (70 kph).

Parking: Blue Zone parking areas exist in Brussels, Ostend, Bruges, Liège, Antwerp and Gent. Parking discs can be obtained from police stations, garages, some shops and offices of the RACB - Royal Automobile Club de Belgique.

Overnighting
Only generally permitted at motorway rest areas.

For guidance on taking your dog on holiday to Europe, see page 348
For a list of sites where dogs are not accepted, see page 347

BELGIUM

055 IC-Camping, Nieuwpoort, nr Ostend/Oostende

Large holiday site 4 km. from beach with many on-site amenities.

This large site with 887 pitches caters particularly for families. On site is a heated pool complex with two pools, children's pool and a waterslide, many sporting activities, restaurants, takeaway, supermarket, children's farm and playground. The numbered pitches, all with electricity, are in regular rows on flat grass and, with 400 seasonal units, the site becomes full in July/Aug. A network of footpaths links all areas of the site and gates to the rear lead to a reservoir reserved for sailing and windsurfing (boards for hire) during certain hours only. The site is well fenced, with card operated barrier and a night guard. The seven functional sanitary units are clean and well maintained, providing British WCs, washbasins in cubicles, showers with dividers, dishwashing and laundry facilities. Hot water is free throughout and the units are accessible to disabled people. The nearest village is 2 km.

How to find it: From E40 take exit 4 (Middelkerke-Diksmuide). Turn towards Diksmuide following signs to Nieuwport. Pass through Sint-Joris and IC-Camping is on the right.

General Details: Open 31 March - 12 Nov. Supermarket. Restaurant. Cafe/bar (weekends and BHs outside July/Aug). Swimming pools with waterslide and pool games (20/5-17/9). Laundry. Tennis. Football. Adventure playground. Minigolf. Sports and show hall (volleyball, table tennis, stage shows, films). Entertainment programme July/Aug. Fishing and bicycle hire within 500 m. Riding 3 km. Golf driving range 5 km. Chemical disposal. Motorcaravan services. Caravans to rent.

Charges 2000: Per family unit (max. 6 persons) Bfr. 1,010 in July/Aug. and B.H.s, otherwise 705; electricity 50. Largest unit accepted 2½ x 8 m. Less 10% with camping carnet. No credit cards.

Reservations: made with deposit (Bfr 3,000). Address: Brugsesteenweg 49, 8620 Nieuwpoort. Tel: 058/23 60 37. FAX: 058/23 26 82. E-mail: nieuwpoort@ic-camping.be.

056 Camping De Lombarde, Middelkerke-Lombardsijde

Modern, spacious, good value holiday site, 400 m. from sea in popular resort.

Located between Lombardsijde and the coast, this site has a pleasant atmosphere and modern buildings. The 360 pitches are set out in level, grassy bays surrounded by shrubs, all with electricity (16A, long leads may be needed). Vehicles are parked in separate car parks. There are many seasonal units and 20 holiday homes to rent, leaving 180 tourist pitches. The three modern sanitary units are heated, clean and of an acceptable standard, with British style WCs, washbasins (some in cubicles), showers with hooks, dividers or curtains, facilities for disabled people, dishwashing and laundry sinks. Hot water is free throughout. Other facilities include a restaurant/bar and takeaway, shop and a large laundry. The children's adventure playground is in the centre of the site. Other activities are listed below and there is an entertainment programme in season. Torches are useful. This is a popular holiday area and the site becomes full at peak times. A pleasant stroll takes you into Lombardsijde or you can catch the tram to the town or beach.

How to find it: From traffic lights in Lombarsijde, fork left (towards sea) at next junction, follow tram-lines left into Zeelaan. Continue following tram-lines until crossroads and tram stop, turn right into Elisabethlaan. Site is on right after 200 m.

General Details: Open all year. Shop, restaurant/bar and takeaway (July/Aug plus weekends and holidays 21/3-11/11). Laundry. Tennis. Table tennis. Basketball. Boules. Fishing lake. Bicycle hire 1 km. Riding and golf 500 m. TV lounge. Children's playground. Entertainment in season. Chemical disposal. Motorcaravan services. Bungalows for rent.

Charges 2000: Per unit including electricity BFr. 425 - 875. No credit cards.

Reservations: Write or fax for details. Address: Elisabethlaan 4, 8434 Middelkerke-Lombardsijde. Tel: 058/23 68 39. FAX: 058/23 99 08. E-mail: de.lombarde@flanderscoast.be.

058 Camping Memling, Sint-Kruis, Brugge

Traditional site, ideal for visiting Brugge, conveniently located in town suburbs.

Located behind a bistro in a quiet suburb, this site is within walking distance of local shops and super-markets. The 80 unmarked pitches (60 for tourists) are on slightly undulating grass, with gravel roads, a few trees and hedgerows providing some shade, and electricity available to 45 pitches. There is a separate field for tents. The sanitary facilities are in older style but are well decorated, heated, clean and tidy, with British style WCs and washbasins (no plugs). The refurbished hot showers are on payment (Bfr 20). There are dishwashing sinks (H&C), a laundry and a freezer for campers' use. The bistro has a terrace and offers snacks or takeaway meals at reasonable prices, but there is no shop on site (supermarket 250 m, hyper-market 1 km). There is a tiny playground and bicycles can be hired. The municipal swimming pool and a park are nearby. The Maldegem Steam Centre and narrow gauge railway are 12 km. Brugge itself has a network of cycleways and for those on foot a bus runs into the centre from nearby.

How to find it: From R30 Brugge ring road take exit 6 onto N9 towards Maldegem. At Sint-Kruis turn right at traffic lights, where site signed (close to garage and supermarket).

General Details: Open all year. Electricity connections (5A). Bistro/grill and takeaway (1/4-30/9). Children's playground. Bicycle hire. Autobank exchange machine. Chemical disposal. Bungalows to rent.

Charges 2000: Per adult BFr. 110; child (under 12) 65; car 130; caravan 135; motorcaravan 225; tent 100 - 130; electricity 70; local tax 25 (once only). Credit cards accepted (Visa, Mastercard).

Reservations: Write or fax for details. Address: Veltemweg 109, 8310 Sint Kruis, Brugge. Tel: 050/35 58 45 FAX: as phone. E-mail: memling@club.innet.be.

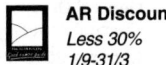

AR Discount
Less 30%
1/9-31/3

057 Camping Jeugstadion, Ieper (Ypres)

Small municipal site close to historic old town.

This is a developing site for tourists with only 21 pitches at present, some on hardstandings, all with elec-tricity, plus a separate area for tents. The barrier key also operates the lock for the modern, heated but fairly basic sanitary unit. This provides British style WCs, washbasins (cold water only) and hot showers on payment. Outside are three sinks for dishwashing with hot and cold water plus a chemical disposal point. The adjacent sports complex has courts for volleyball and squash, whilst indoor and outdoor swimming pools are only 500 m. away, and there is a very large comprehensive children's playground. At the end of Leopold III Laan is the 'Menin Gate' built in 1927, which bears the names of British and Commonwealth soldiers who lost their lives between 1914-1918. The last post is sounded beneath the gate at 8 pm. every evening in their honour. The new interactive museum entitled `The Flanders Experience' in the Cloth Hall is a moving experience. The Commonwealth War Graves Commission is a little further away in Elver-dingestraat. In mid August each year there is a festival for young people in the town, when the campsite is usually fully booked. During school holidays the sporting facilities and playgrounds in this complex are extensively used by the local children and can therefore be fairly busy and lively.

How to find it: Approaching the city from Lille turn right at roundabout in front of Lille Gate, then take second left, then left again into site access lane where site is signed. Park by barrier and walk through campsite to reception office at the 'Kantine', where they will issue a barrier key (BFr 1,000 or £20 deposit).

General Details: Open 16 March - 31 October. Electricity connections (16A). Bicycle hire.

Charges guide: Per caravan BFr. 150; tent 50; adult 75; child (under 6-12 yrs) 25.

Reservations: Contact site. Address: Leopold III Laan 16, 8900 Ieper. Tel: 057/21 72 82. FAX: 057/21 61 21.

063 Camping Grimbergen, Grimbergen, nr Brussels

Useful base from which to visit the city.

This popular little municipal site has a friendly atmosphere with 100 pitches on fairly level grass, of which around 50 have electricity. Sanitary facilities are in the older style, acceptable but not luxurious, and cleaning can be variable at times. The unit can be heated in colder months and provides British style WCs, open washbasins, and basic showers, with free hot water throughout. In addition there are three sinks under cover outside for dishwashing and separate facilities for disabled people have now been installed. The site is well placed for visiting Brussels. The bus station is by the traffic lights at the junction of N202 and N211 and buses run into the city centre every 15 minutes. In Grimbergen itself visit Norbertine Abbey, St Servaas church, and the Sunday morning market. Also worth a visit are the nearby towns of Lier and Mechelen, and the botanical gardens at Meise.

How to find it: From Brussels ring road take exit 7 (N202) to Grimbergen, turn right at traffic lights on N211 towards Vilvoorde (site is signed), then left by church (slightly oblique turn).

General Details: Open 15 March - 31 October. Electricity connections (10A). Fishing 800 m. Chemical disposal. Motorcaravan services.

Charges 1999: Per adult BFr. 100; child 40; caravan 100; car 50; motorcaravan 150; electricity 50, local tax 25. No credit cards.

Reservations: Write for details. Address: Veldkantstraat 64, 1850 Grimbergen. Tel/Fax: 02 270 9597.

BELGIUM

060 Camping Groeneveld, Bachte-Maria-Leerne, Deinze, nr Gent (Gand)

Traditional, quiet site, in a small village, within easy reach of Gent.

Although this site has 115 pitches, there are a fair number of seasonal units, leaving around 50 large tourist pitches with electricity (8A), most on an open grassy area with gravel access roads, plus an area for tents. The site has a friendly atmosphere, is quietly located and is also open over a long season. There are two clean sanitary units of differing age and design, which provide British style WCs, washbasins (cold water in one unit, H&C in the other), and free hot showers. The reception office is adjacent to a cafe/bar (open all day in July/Aug, weekends only off season) with a good range of snacks, and a comprehensive range of speciality and local beers. Also on site is a small coarse fishing lake (not fully fenced), a 3 lane floodlit petanque court (both free for campers), plus an adventure style children's play area. The range of family entertainment and activities organised in high season includes themed, musical or karaoke evenings, barbecues, petanque matches, etc. The village of Bachte-Maria-Leerne has a butcher, general store, café and bar, chemist, two restaurants, baker, plus a newsagent and tabac. The site has produced a location map of these for guests. The city of Gent is just 15 km. north of the site and 5 km. to the south is the pleasant town of Deinze.

How to find it: Deinze is southwest of Gent, between the E40 and E17. The village of Bachte-Maria-Leerne is 5 km. northeast of Deinze towards Gent via the N466. Follow signs to the Ooidonk Castle.

General Details: Open 26 March - 12 November. Shops and restaurants nearby. Hikers' cabins for rent. Chemical disposal. Motorcaravan services.

Charges 2000: Per unit incl. electricity BFr. 515 - 655, acc. to season. No credit cards.

Reservations: Write to site for details. Address: Groenevelddreeef, 9800 Deinze (Bachte-Maria-Leerne). Tel: 09/380 1014. FAX: 09/380 1760.

061 Camping Blaarmeersen, Gent (Ghent/Gand)

Comfortable, well managed site on west side of city.

This relaxed municipal site adjoins a sports complex and a fair-sized lake which provide facilities for a variety of watersports, tennis, squash, minigolf, football, athletics track, roller skating and a playground. The 224 individual, flat, grassy pitches are separated by tall hedges and mostly arranged in circular groups; with electricity to all, 26 hardstandings for motorcaravans, plus a separate area for tents with barbecue facility. There could be some road noise as the the city's ring road is close. The four sanitary units vary in size but are of a decent standard, now with hot water to all washbasins. Most of the 20 free hot showers are in one block and there are showers and toilets for disabled people. The café/bar which serves a good range of snacks and meals is open from 10 am. and the shop from 8 am. (both daily March - Oct). In Gent, tour the markets, free of charge, with the Town Crier (May-Sept, Sunday 10.30). Central Gent is 3 km – the bus stop is 150 m. and buses run every 20 minutes to the city centre. There are also good networks of paths and cycle routes around the city.

How to find it: From the E40/A10 exit 13, turn towards Gent-West, follow dual carriageway for 5 km. Look for Blaarmeersen sign, turning sharp right and following signs to leisure complex. In city avoid overpasses - most signs are on the lower levels.

General Details: Open 1 March - 15 Oct. Electricity connections (10A). Shop. Café/bar. Takeaway. Sports facilities. Sauna. Playground. Fishing on site in winter, otherwise 500 m. Bicycle hire 5 km. Riding and golf 10 km. Bottle bank. Laundry. Chemical disposal. Motorcaravan services.

Charges 2000: Per person Bfr. 110 - 130; child (5-12 yrs) 55 - 60; car 60 - 70; caravan or tent 120 - 140; motorcaravan 180 - 200; electricity 30; litter bag 10. Payment accepted in Belgian francs, by credit card or by Eurocheque only.

Reservations: most advisable in main season; made for any period (no deposit) and kept until 5 pm. Address: Zuiderlaan 12, 9000 Gent. Tel: 09/221.53.99. FAX: 09/222.41.84. E-mail: camping.blaarmeersen@gent.be.

**The sites in BELGIUM featured in this guide
are shown on the BENELUX map on page 369**

053 Camping du Waux-Hall, Mons (Bergen)

see colour advert between pages 16/17

Convenient, well laid out municipal site, close to town centre and E42 motorway.
This is a useful site for a longer look at historic Mons and the surrounding area. The 75 pitches, all with electricity (10A), are arranged on either side of an oval roadway, on grass and divided by beds of small shrubs; the landscape maintenance is excellent. The single, central sanitary unit is in older style, basic but clean, with British WCs, washbasins with H&C (most in cubicles for ladies) and free hot showers with dividers and hooks. Dishwashing and laundry sinks (H&C) are outside but under cover. There is no shop on site, only a soft drinks machine, ice creams and free tourist information available. Restaurants and shops are within easy walking distance. A large public park with refreshment bar, tennis, children's playground and lake is adjacent, with direct access from the site. Places to visit include the house of Van Gogh, the Fine Art Museum, Decorative Arts, Prehistory and Stamp Museums.

How to find it: From Mons inner ring road, follow signs for Charleroi, La Louviere, Binche, Beaumont. When turning off ring road, keep to right lane, turn for site is immediately first right. (signed Waux-Hall and camping).

General Details: Open all year. Public park adjacent. Shops and restaurants near. Fishing 300 m. Riding 2 km. Golf 4 km. Public telephone. Bottle bank. Chemical disposal.

Charges 1999: Per tent/caravan and car plus 1 adult BFr. 245; motorhome plus 1 adult 225; tent and m/cycle plus 1 adult 235; extra adult 135; child (under 12) 85; electricity more than 2 nights 6 p/kw. No credit cards.

Reservations: Write or phone for details. Address: Avenue Saint-Pierre 17, 7000 Mons (Bergen). Tel: 065/33.79.23. FAX: 065/36.38.48.

054 Camping de L'Orient, Tournai (Doornik)

Attractive site in quiet green location, close to historic town, convenient for E42.
An excellent, quality municipal site, L'Orient is immaculately kept by the manager and his wife. The 51 level, grassy, individual pitches (all for tourists) are separated by laurel hedges and have shade in some parts and electricity. Two modern sanitary units are of high quality, spotlessly clean and heated in cool weather. They have British WCs, washbasins (some in cubicles) and roomy hot showers with curtains (on payment). Facilities for laundry, dishwashing and the disabled. Adjoining the site is an attractive restaurant and bar (10 am.- 10 pm. in season) with a superb terrace overlooking the lake where campers can fish and hire pedaloes. Beside the lake are picnic and barbecue areas, a lakeside walk and a children's playground. There is also a new, high quality swimming pool complex (50% discount for campers) with cafeteria, indoor pool with spectator seating, outdoor pool with waterslide, plus all the usual changing rooms, lockers. etc. Basic provisions are available from reception. Tournai has the oldest belfry in Europe and you can also see the cathedral and museums dedicated to decorative arts, folklore, tapestry and military history. There is a good network of cycleways and footpaths around the town.

How to find it: From E32, exit 32, take N7 towards Tournai centre. Turn left at first traffic lights (site signed), left at small roundabout and site entrance is immediately on the left.

General Details: Open all year. Electricity connections (16A). Cafeteria. Bar. Laundry. Swimming pool and waterslide complex. Lake with barbecues, fishing, pedaloes for hire and children's playground.

Charges 1999: Per adult BFr 85; child (6-12 yrs) 65; caravan 100; car 80; motorcaravan 180; m/cycle 60; electricity 8 p/kw.

Reservations: Write or phone for details. Address: Vieux Chemin de Mons, 7500 Tournai. Tel: 069/22 26 35.

059 Provincial Domein De Gavers, Geraardsbergen

Modern, organised holiday site, in a peaceful location, with a large sports complex.
Adjacent to a large sports complex, with good security and a card operated barrier, about 5 km. outside Geraardsbergen, this can be a busy site in season. There are 448 grassy, level pitches, many taken by seasonal units but with 86 for tourists. Arranged on either side of surfaced access roads with some hedges and trees to provide shade in parts, electricity (5/10A) is available to most. The five sanitary buildings are modern and well equipped, providing British style WCs, hot showers with dividers (on payment), and washbasins (H&C). Facilities include a modern laundry and rooms for disabled people and babies. Within the complex there is also a shop, cafeteria, restaurant, takeaway and bars. The site offers extensive sporting activities, an excellent children's playground and a full entertainment programme over a long season.

How to find it: From E429/A8 exit 26 towards Edingen, take N255 and N495 to Geraardsbergen. Down a steep hill, then left at camp sign towards Onkerzele, through village and turn north to site.

General Details: Open all year. Shop (July/Aug). Restaurant, bar and takeaway (daily April - Sept, otherwise weekends). Tennis. Volleyball. Basketball. Mini-football. Boules. 'Midget' golf. Fishing. Canoes, windsurfers, pedaloes, yachts and row boats for hire. Bicycle hire. Tourist train. Swimming and beach area. Climbing. Entertainment in season. Launderette. Chemical disposal. Bungalows and chalets to rent.

Charges 1999: Per unit BFr. 400 - 500; tent incl. 1 person 210, 2 persons 310. Discounts of 5-30% for longer stays. Credit cards accepted.

Reservations: Write or fax for details. Address: Onkerzelestraat 280, 9500 Geraardsbergen. Tel: 054/416324. FAX: 054/410388. E-mail: gavers@oost-vlaanderen.be.

BELGIUM

067 Parc La Clusure, Bure-Tellin, nr Rochefort

Agreeable site in the popular Lhomme Valley touring area, with swimming pool.

Set in a river valley in the lovely wooded uplands of the Ardennes, this site is close to the area's best tourist attractions. The 425 large marked, grassy pitches (300 for touring units) have access to electricity (16A), cable TV and water taps and are mostly in avenues off a central, tarmac road. The three sanitary units (one heated in winter) have free hot water and provide British WCs, washbasins (some in cubicles), showers with dividers/hooks, and facilities for babies. Dishwashing and laundry facilities may be stretched at times. There is a very pleasant, well lit riverside walk (the river is shallow in summer and popular for children to play in), a heated swimming pool and children's pool with pool-side bar/terrace plus a well stocked shop, snack-bar, tennis courts, restaurant and takeaway. An organised activity programme includes courses in canoeing, mountain biking and climbing. Used by a tour operator (10 pitches). The nearby main Brussels - Luxembourg railway line, though not visually intrusive, can be noisy. The famous Grottoes of Han are nearby.

How to find it: Site is signed north off the N803 Rochefort - St Hubert road at Bure, 8 km. southeast of Rochefort with a steepish, winding descent to site.

General Details: Open all year. Shop. Restaurant. Bars. Snack bar. Takeaway. Bicycle hire. Tennis. Badminton. Volleyball. Swimming pools (1/5-15/9). Playgrounds. Activity programme (July/Aug). Fishing (license essential) and riding nearby. Bungalows and tents for hire. Laundry. Motorcaravan services. Barrier card deposit 500.

Charges 1999: Per pitch incl. 2 persons Bfr. 640; extra person 140; electricity (16A) 80; local tax 20. Credit cards accepted.

Reservations: Advisable for Easter, Whitsun and for July - mid-Aug. Made with deposit and fee (Bfr. 500). Address: Chemin de la Clusure 30, 6927 Bure-Tellin. Tel: 084/36 60 80. FAX: 084/36 67 77.

065 Camping Floréal Club Het Veen, Sint Job In't Goor, nr Antwerpen

Top quality, good value site with many sports facilities, in woodland area.

A modern site with good security and efficient reception, the 319 marked pitches (60 for tourists) are on level grass, most with some shade and electricity (10A, long leads in some places). There are also 7 hardstandings for motorcaravans. The four sanitary units are modern and spacious, with free hot water, British style WCs, washbasins (a few in cubicles) with mixer taps set in marbled surfaces, and roomy hot showers with dividers and hooks (now free). Well equipped facilities for disabled people and dishwashing and laundry facilities complete the installations. The restaurant and bar opens both day and evening during July/Aug. (weekends only other times). The well stocked shop and takeaway open daily in high season, at weekends in low seasons. There is an indoor sports hall (charged Bfr 200 per hour) and courts for tennis (150 per hour), football, basketball and softball are outside. Children's entertainment in season, plus good, safe and exciting playgrounds. Antwerp is only 20 km. and there is good cycling and walking available in the area. English is spoken.

How to find it: From Brecht (exit 4 from E19/A1) follow road to St Job In't Goor, straight on at traffic lights and immediately after canal bridge turn left at campsite sign. Continue straight on for about 1.5 km.

General Details: Open Easter - 30 Sept. Shop. Restaurant, bar, café and takeaway (daily July/Aug. weekends only at other times). Tennis. Badminton. Volleyball. Softball. Basketball. Football. Table tennis. Boules. Children's playground. Entertainment in season. Fishing. Canoeing. Bicycle hire. Riding or golf 8 km. First aid post. Laundry. Chemical disposal. Motorcaravan services.

Charges 2000: Per unit incl. electricity BFr. 575. No credit cards.

Reservations: Write or fax site. Address: Eekhoornlaan 1, 2960 Sint Job In't Goor. Tel: 03/636 13 27. FAX: 03/636 20 30.

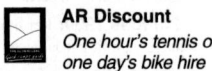

AR Discount
One hour's tennis or one day's bike hire

072 Camping Tonny, Amberloup (Ste Ode)

Family campsite with friendly atmosphere, in pleasant valley by the River Ourthe.

An attractive small site with 75 grassy touring pitches, the wooden chalet buildings here give a Tyrolean feel. The pitches (80-100 sq.m.) are separated by small shrubs and fir trees and electricity (4 or 6A) is available. Cars are parked away from the units and there is a separate meadow for tents. Surrounded by natural woodland, Camping Tonny is an ideal base for walking, cycling, fishing, canoeing and, in winter, cross-country ski-ing. The main chalet has a cafe/bar and open fireplace, small shop, TV lounge/library with a nice shady terrace for relaxing outside and is open all year (acc. to demand). There are two sanitary units (both can be heated in cool weather) which provide British style WCs, washbasins and showers with curtains, dishwashing and laundry sinks (all hot water on payment), freezer for campers use, laundry and a baby changing area. Nearby St Hubert has a Basilica, the St Michel Furnace Industrial Museum and a wildlife park, with wild boar, deer and other native species – all worth a visit.

How to find it: From N4 take exit for Libramont (N826), then to Amberloup (4 km.) where site is signed.

General Details: Open all year excl. 15 Nov - 5 Jan. Shop. Cafe/bar. TV lounge and library. Sports field. Boules. Games room. Children's playgrounds. Skittle alley. Bicycle hire. Fishing. Canoeing. Cross country skiing. Laundry. Chemical disposal. Six mobile homes and two chalets for rent.

Charges 2000: Pitch with electricity BFr. 320; without electricity 260; person 90; dog 60; electricity (6A) 6 p/kw. Off season discounts for over 55's and longer stays.

Reservations: Essential for high season. Contact site for details. Address: Tonny 35, 6680 Amberloup (St Ode). Tel: 061/688285. FAX: as phone.

073 Camping Moulin de Malempré, Manhay

Attractive site with swimming pools, very close to the E25.

This pleasant countryside site is well worth a visit and the Dutch owners will make you very welcome. The reception building houses the office and a small shop (basic provisions only), above which is an attractive restaurant and bar. The 120 marked tourist pitches are separated by small shrubs and gravel roads on sloping terrain. All have electricity (6/10A), 40 have water and drainage as well and the site is well lit. The stars of this site are the sanitary units – the existing ultra modern, two storey Scandinavian style unit is now joined by a new unisex unit which also boasts a family shower room among its heated and comfortable facilities. There are British style WCs, washbasins (some in cubicles), large pre-set showers with seats, family bathrooms on payment, a unit for disabled people with automatic taps, hoists and rails, a baby room, dishwashing sinks and laundry. Other amenities include the recently refurbished heated swimming pool, children's pools (one with mushroom fountain), a terrace for sunbathing, children's playground and trampoline. There is a little traffic noise from the adjacent E25 (not too intrusive). Nearby are the Hotton Grottoes, one of the prettiest Belgian caves (open daily Apr-Oct). English is spoken.

How to find it: From E25/A26 (Liege-Bastogne) exit 49, turn towards Lierneux on N822, follow signs to Malempré and site.

General Details: Open 1 April - 31 October. Shop (1/7-31/8). Restaurant (15/5-15/9). Bar (15/5-15/9 and weekends). Heated swimming pools (15/5-15/9). TV. Table tennis. Pool table. Boules. Children's playground. Bicycle hire 3 km. Riding 6 km. Fishing 10 km. Laundry. Chemical disposal. Motorcaravan services.

Charges 1999: Per unit incl. 2 adults BFr. 650 - 750, acc. to size; extra adult 140; child (3-11 yrs) 100; dog 90; electricity 90; family bathroom 250 per hour (plus deposit).
Euro: Per unit incl. 2 adults 16.25 - 18.75, acc. to size; extra adult 3.50; child (3-11 yrs) 2.50; dog 2.25; electricity 2.25; family bathroom 6.25 per hour (plus deposit).
Less 10% in low seasons. No credit cards.

Reservations: Made with deposit (12.50) - write or fax for details. Address: 1 Malempré, 6960 Manhay. Tel: 086/455504 or 455384. FAX: 086/455674. A 'Camping Cheques' site.

BELGIUM

074 Domaine de L'Eau Rouge, Stavelot

Attractively located, lively site close to Spa and Grand Prix circuit.

In a sheltered valley location, this popular site has a fair number of permanent units but there is usually space for tourists: The main building houses the busy reception, shop, café, bar and the main sanitary facilities. A smaller sanitary unit serves the touring area. These provide good numbers of British WCs, mostly open washbasins, but rather fewer hot showers on payment - which could be stretched at times. However, some additional facilities should be available in the near future. Hot water is also on payment for dishwashing and laundry. There are 140 grassy pitches of 110 sq.m. on sloping ground either side of a central road with speed bumps. Baker calls 9.30 am. daily in season. There are plenty of sporting activities available in the area including skiing and luge in winter, and free archery lessons on site 10 am. daily in high season. The site is close to the motor race circuit at Spa Francorchamps and is within walking distance for the fit. The site's new Dutch family owners are not only embarking on a 3-5 year programme upgrading the infrastructure, but also have other ideas in the pipeline. So, for those who regularly visit this site at Grand Prix time, things can only get better.

How to find it: Site signed from A640 Francorchamps - Stavelot road (Stavelot 3 km, Francorchamps 5 km).

General Details: Open all year except 10 Dec - 31 Jan. Shop, Café. Bar. Football. Boules. Table tennis. Archery. Barbecues. Children's playground. Entertainment in season.

Charges 1999: Per unit BFr. 400; adult 90; child (4-12 yrs) 80; extra tent 100; electricity (10A) 80.

Reservations: Write to site. Address: Cheneux 25, 4970 Stavelot. Tel: 080/86 30 75. FAX: as phone.

066 Camping Baalse Hei, Turnhout

Friendly forest site peacefully situated close to city.

The 'Campine' is an area covering three-quarters of the Province of Antwerp, noted for its nature reserves, pine forests, meadows and streams and is ideal for walking and cycling, while Turnhout itself is an interesting old town. Baalse Hei is a long-established site and has recently added a separate touring area of 55 large pitches (all with 16A electricity and TV connections and shared water point) on a large grass field which has been thoughtfully developed with young trees and bushes planted. Dishwashing facilities (hot water Bfr. 5), chemical disposal and waste bins are close to the pitches, off the hard access road. Cars are parked away from the pitches. It is 100 m. from the edge of the field to the modern, heated, sanitary building. This provides hot showers on payment, some washbasins in private cabins, British WCs (no paper) and facilities for disabled visitors. Upstairs is a club/TV room. Close to reception is a café/restaurant with bar (July-Sept, then weekends, closed mid Nov-end Jan). There is no shop but bread can be ordered in high season. There is a small lake for swimming with a beach, a boating lake and a large fishing lake (on payment). Other activities include basketball, football pitch, table tennis, 2 hard tennis courts, boules, volleyball and an adventure play area for children on sand. Entertainment and activities are organised July/Aug. Walk in the woods and you will undoubtedly come across some of the many red squirrels or take the pleasant 1.5 km. riverside walk to the next village.

How to find it: Site is northeast of Turnhout off the N119. Approaching from Antwerp on E34/A12 go onto Turnhout ring road to the end (not a complete ring) and turn right. There is a small site sign to right in 1.5 km. then country lane.

General Details: Open all year. Café/restaurant (with breakfast in high season). Lake swimming. Fishing. Tennis. Table tennis. Boules. Volleyball. Basketball. Football. Children's play equipment. Entertainment. Bicycle hire. Riding or golf 1.5 km. Launderette. Motorcaravan services. Hikers' cabins to rent. Arrival after 4 pm. departure by 10 am.

Charges 2000: Per unit all incl. Bfr. 490 - 650; electricity 30. No credit cards.

Reservations: Contact site. Address: Roodhuisstraat 10, 2300 Turnhout. Tel: 014/42 19 31. FAX: 014/42 08 53. E-mail: info@baalsehei.be.

AR Discount
Less 10%

Baalše Hei
't Groene Caravanpark

Baalse Hei offers a calm and quiet environment, boarding a nature reserve north of Turnhout. There are several lakes used for swimming, fishing and rowing, a large football field, volley- basket- and tennis facilities. There are a lot of cycling routes in the area of which maps are available. A pleasant riverside walk brings you to a small village or to the interesting town of Turnhout. Baalse Hei is a perfect location from which you can visit the art city of Antwerp. Caravans, Hikers' cabins and bicycle hire. Via E34/A12 Eindhoven-Antwerpen, exit no 24 direction Turnhout/Breda.

info@baalsehei.be
//www.baalsehei.be

Roodhuisstraat 10 - 2300 Turnhout (Belgium)
Tel. 0032 (0)14 42 19 31 - Fax 0032 (0)14 42 08 53

CZECH REPUBLIC

Although the country we have known as Czechoslovakia has a long and distinguished past, it has a chequered history. The combined country of Czechoslovakia only appeared under that name on maps after the Treaty of Versailles in 1918. The latest event in its turbulent history was the split in December 1992 into its two component parts - the Czech Republic in the west and the Slovak Republic in the east (see page 272). The Czech Republic shares frontiers with Germany, Poland, Austria and the Slovak Republic. It is picturesque and hilly, with attractive lakes and valleys, and with many spa towns. The two main regions are Bohemia, including the Giant Mountains (skiing in winter) and Moravia.

Campsites, previously state-owned and run, are being progressively privatised and modernised and are gradually offering facilities more in line with those expected in Western Europe. All the sites we have included have acceptable, if not luxurious, sanitary arrangements. We found them all to be clean with British style WCs and hot water in all washbasins, sinks and showers. However, many shower facilities have no private dressing spaces and, even in the best blocks, often no divider or curtain with just a communal dressing area.

Information about the Czech Republic can be obtained from:

The Czech Tourist Authority, 95 Great Portland Strret, London W1N 5RA
Tel: 09063 640 641. E-mail: gillespie@london.czech.cz

Population
10,323,690 (93) , density 131 per sq km.

Capital
Prague (Praha)

Climate
A continental climate with four distinct seasons, average temperatures in summer (July) are 19°C - 30°C max. and in winter (January) 1-15°C.

Language
The official language is Czech. In hotels and restaurants English or German may be spoken.

Currency
Koruna abbreviated to Kc. One Koruna is divided into 100 hellers.

Banks
Open 0830-1630 Mon-Fri. Only notes are exchanged at most border change offices.

Credit cards: The major cards can be used to obtain currency and in some hotels, restaurants, shops and some filling stations. Travellers and Eurocheques are widely accepted.

Post Offices
Offices are open Mon-Sat 08.00-16.00.

Telephone
The code for the Czech Republic is 0042.

Time
GMT plus one hour. Summer BST + 1.

Public Holidays
New Year; Easter Mon; May Day; National Day, 8 May; Saints Day, 5 July; Festival Day, 6 July; Independence Day, 28 Oct; Christmas, 24, 25, 26 Dec.

Shops
Shops are open Mon-Fri 09.00-12.00 and 14.00-18.00. Some shops remain open midday . Sat: 09.00 until midday.

Motoring
There is a good and well signposted road network throughout the Republic and, although stretches of cobbles still exist in parts, surfaces are generally good. There is a motorway from Bratislava (Slovakia) to Prague and others, radiating from the capital, are being expanded with the section to Pilsen nearing completion. New filling stations with well stocked shops (some with snack bars) are replacing the old, rather scarce, ones all over the Republic.

An annual road tax is levied on all vehicles using Czech motorways and express roads. There are three categories: motor vehicle up to 3.5 tons including trailer; with total weight between 3.5 and 12 tons and above 12 tons. The label, which must be fixed to the windscreen, can be purchased at border crossings, post offices and filling stations. The leaflet giving details of this tax shows the designated roads. Anyone driving a vehicle on a toll road without an affixed label is likely to be fined.

Seat belts are compulsory. Full UK licences are acceptable. Drinking and driving is prohibited. Infringing traffic regulations is subject to on-the-spot fines and speed traps abound.

Speed Restrictions: The max. speed limit for cars is 37 mph (60 kph) in built up areas, 56 mph (90 kph) outside them and 69 mph (110 kph) on expressways.

Parking: Cars may be parked only on the right of the road. In Prague, parking is limited and in Wenceslas Square a charge is made.

Overnighting:
Camping is forbidden in places which are not reserved for that purpose.

Useful Addresses
Motoring Organisation:
Ustredi Automotoklub CR (UAMK), FIA & AIT. Information Service for Motorists: Autoturist, Na Rybnicku 16, 120 76 Praha 2. Tel: 249 11830.

CZECH REPUBLIC

465 Autokamping Luxor, Velká Hled'sebe, nr Mariánské Lánzé (Marianbad)

Orderly site near German border for visiting Marianbad.

This site, like some others in the Czech Republic, has now come under the management of a local hotel. Located on the edge of the small village of Velká Hled'sebe, 4 km. from Marianbad, by a small lake, this is a very quiet situation. The 100 pitches (60 for touring units) are in the open on one side of the entrance road (cars stand on a tarmac park opposite the caravans) or in a clearing under tall trees away from the road. All pitches have access to electricity (10A) but connection in the clearings section may require long leads. The good sanitary block also serves the bungalows (for rent) which occupy one side of the site. There is little to do here but it is good for a night stop or for visiting the spa town of Marianbad. A restaurant with self-service terrace is open all season and a very good motel restaurant is in the village (500 m). A separate block houses a rest room, kitchen and dining room.

How to find it: Site is directly by the Stribo-Cheb road no. 21, 500 m. south of Velká Hled'sebe.

General Details: Open 1 May - 30 Sept. 30,000 sq.m. Restaurant. Motel with restaurant and shops 500 m. Small children's playground. Rest room with TV, kitchen and dining area. Fishing. Bicycle hire. Riding 5 km. Golf 8 km. Chemical disposal.

Charges 1999: Per unit incl. 2 adults and electricity Kcs. 380. No credit cards or Eurocheques.

Reservations: For information write to Interhotel Cristal Palace, 353 44 Mariánské Lánzé or phone 0165/2056-7. FAX: 0165/2058. Site address: 354 71 Velká Hled'sebe. Tel: 0165/3504.

466 Autocamping Amerika, Frantiskovy Lázné (Franzensbad)

Site near lake outside spa town.

Goethe described this small spa town as 'paradise on earth', although other writers have dismissed it as of little historical interest. However, it has a reputation as a spa centre for the treatment of female ailments and has pleasant parks and leafy streets. Camping Amerika is to the southwest, just outside the town and could make an acceptable night stop when entering West Bohemia from Bayreuth, to explore West Bohemia or to `take the waters'. The site is in an open position with slopes in places and, although there are tall trees at one edge, there is little shade in the camping area. There is room for about 50 caravans on a grass area enclosed by hard access roads and 100 tents in another area. There are electricity points for about two-thirds of the pitches, which are neither numbered nor marked out. The single sanitary block is showing signs of age but some refurbishment has been done and it is acceptable. Swimming and boating are possible on the lake. There is a restaurant with terrace, a snack bar and a kiosk for basic food supplies.

How to find it: Site is signed from the edge of the town on little Lake Amerika.

General Details: Open Easter - 15 Oct. 12,000 sq.m. Restaurant. Bar. Kiosk. Lake for swimming and boating. Children's playground. Bicycle hire. Fishing 5 km. Riding 2 or 5 km. Chemical disposal. Bungalows for hire.

Charges 1999: Per person Kcs. 60; child (6-15 yrs) 40; pitch 80; electricity 80; local tax 15. No credit cards.

Reservations: Write to site. Address: 35101 Frantiskovy Lázné. Tel: 0166/542 518. FAX: 0166/542 843.

467 Autocamping Karlovy Vary-Brezova, Karlovy-Vary (Karlsbad)

Good site by historic and famous spa.

Karlovy Vary, known throughout the West as Karlsbad is, after Prague, the most popular tourist town in the Czech Republic. Dvorak's New World symphony had its premier here and each year a Dvorak Music Festival is held. The curative waters and 19/20th century architecture draw visitors from all over the world and it can become crowded in the tourist season. This site makes an excellent base for exploring the town or taking the waters, being in a quiet location outside the town with an electric bus to take campers into the town where other vehicles are banned. The town can also be reached on foot (2 km) by walking through the woods. The site is in a natural bowl surrounded by hills and tall trees. It is said that there is room for 150 units but, as the pitches of grass on small stones are neither marked nor numbered, placing is rather haphazard and can become crowded. Camping areas are accessed from hard roads and, although there are sufficient electric sockets (10A), long leads are required in some parts. The central sanitary block is of reasonable quality with British WCs, pre-mixed warm water from push-button taps in washbasins and showers. An outside trough with cold water is provided for dishwashing. Excellent heated pool with entrance half price for campers. There are some motel rooms and two restaurants and a coffee bar. A kiosk supplies drinks and some food items. A very pleasant site where good English is spoken at reception.

How to find it: From Cheb on the Cheb-Karlovy Vary road 6/E48/E49, turn onto road 20/E49 towards Plzen. After about 7 km. fork left leaving the main road where it crosses a dam for camp after 2 km. on the right.

General Details: Open 1 April - end October. 25,000 sq.m. Restaurants. Snack-bar. Kiosk. Heated pool (on payment). Children's play area. Rooms for hire. Cooking stoves.

Charges guide: Per person Kcs. 70; child (5-16 yrs) 40; car 90; caravan 90; motorcaravan 170; m/cycle 60; electricity 30.

Reservations: Write to camp. Address: 36021 Karlovy Vary, Slovenska 9. Tel: 017/3225101 or 3225224. FAX: 017/3225225.

468 Autocamping Druhy Mlyn, Chomutov

Small, pleasant site in tranquil setting.

This very pleasant little site on level ground, enclosed by trees and nearby hills, is a world away from the devastation around Chomutov and Most caused by opencast mining. Following the one sign on the edge of town along a narrow, tree lined road, one does begin to wonder where the camp is, but patience is rewarded after about 6 km. The entrance is not too promising but behind the restaurant and car repair shop, over a bridge, it opens out into a level clearing with a circular area for camping. Pitches are neither marked nor numbered but there is room for about 50 units on grass with a clear stream running through. In the centre is a low stone circle for a wood fire with wooden benches around. Sanitary arrangements are in a brick built block which also has four rooms to rent and a kitchen with electric rings. The toilet (British), washbasin and shower areas are tiled. There is a Gasthof (closed Mondays) and a small shop. Druhy Mlyn is an oasis of peace in a noisy world with walks and hill climbing from the camp.

How to find it: From the main Karlovy Vary - Most road no. 13/E442, take the main exit into town, pass a small castle on the left and follow sign at beginning of road to camp.

General Details: Open all year. Restaurant. Small shop. Kitchen. Rooms to hire. 12 electrical connections.

Charges: Not available.

Reservations: Not made. Address: P.O. Box 131, 430 01 Chomutov. Tel: 0396/25918.

469 Camping Slunce, Zandov, nr Ceské Lipy

Pleasant site in rural situation near German border.

Away from larger towns, near the border with the old East Germany this is pleasant rural country with a wealth of Gothic and Renaissance castles. Zandov has nothing of particular interest but Camping Slunce is a popular camp with local Czechs. There is room for about 50 units on the level, circular camping area which has a hard road running round. Outside this circle are wooden bungalows for hire and tall trees. At the camp entrance, but under separate management, is a restaurant (open all year) where live music is played during high season. The general building at the entrance houses the sanitary accommodation, reception, a large, carpeted club room for games and TV and a kitchen with electric rings, full gas cooker and fridges. There is a good outdoor swimming pool.

How to find it: Zandov is 20 km. from Decin and 12 km. from Ceske Lipa on the minor road between these two towns. Signed in the centre of Zandov village.

General Details: Open 2 May - 30 Sept. Restaurant. Kiosk for basics. 36 electrical connections. Tennis. Table tennis. Swimming pool. Volleyball. Mountain bike hire. Children's playground. Well furnished club room with TV. Kitchen with good facilities.

Charges guide: Per person Kcs. 66; child 50; car 66; m/cycle 39; motorcaravan 132; caravan or tent 66; electricity 22 plus meter; local tax 3.

Reservations: Not made. Address: 471 07 Zandov. Tel: 0425/91116.

470 Autocamping Pavlovice, Liberec

Excellent camp in north Bohemia near Polish border.

Although Liberec does not have too much to write home about, it does have a zoo, botanical garden and Renaissance château. It is set in grand countryside near the Jizera mountains and not far from the Polish town of Gorlitz. Autocamp Pavlovice is nicely situated on the edge of the town near the sports ground. Just outside the entrance are the inevitable drab multi-storey workers flats, but trees screen these from view on the site. The Jested mountain at 1,012 m. dominates the distant sky line and is accessible by cable way for winter ski-ing and summer sightseeing. There are 130 pitches, all with electricity (10A), between the excellent bungalows (for hire) and different varieties of trees which give a peaceful air to the camp. Some of the caravan pitches are divided by low hedges on the edge of the site with views across open countryside. Tarmac roads lead to the camping places. The restaurant, with café, snack bar and raised terrace, also houses reception. The single, good quality sanitary block with British style WCs also has a kitchen with electric rings. There is a good-sized, recently rebuilt, swimming pool (open June-Sept) and children's play area, with fixed apparatus, in front of the restaurant. There is a speedway track right next to the camp which could cause noise disturbance when meetings are held on Sundays. This is a neat, tidy and very pleasant camp, good for a night stop or a longer stay.

How to find it: From Decin on road no. 13/E442, turn in direction of Frydlant (road 35), 100 m. before first (and only) traffic lights, to camp on left by sports stadium and large bus stop.

General Details: Open 1 May - 30 Sept. 34,000 sq.m. Restaurant. Snack bar with terrace. Tennis. Table tennis. Swimming pool. Children's playground. Shops outside entrance. Kitchen. Quality bungalows for hire.

Charges 1999: Per person Kcs. 80; child (6-15 yrs) 50; tent 50; caravan 60; car 60; motorcaravan 80; m/cycle 20; dog 30; electricity 50; local tax 15.

Reservations: Write to site. Address: Autokempink Automotoklubu Pavlovice, 460 13 Liberec. Tel: 048/512 34 68. FAX: as phone.

CZECH REPUBLIC

474 Transkemp Hracholusky-Lodni Doprava, nr Plzen/Pilsen

Pleasant, waterside site adjacent to hotel.

Set beside the River Mzi where the Hracholusky dam has created a wide basin, Lodni Doprava enjoys a quiet location amidst gentle hills and pleasant trees. The 150 pitches here are spread along three terraces looking over the water with about half having electrical connections. The large, single sanitary block also contains a rest room with TV, kitchen and fridges for campers use. Two kiosks dispense drinks and basic supplies. There is swimming, boating and waterskiing on the lake and, during high season, a steamer makes 40 km. round trips along the river. This is a pleasant site but the presence of a large car park at the entrance may mean that it becomes crowded with day visitors in the summer.

How to find it: Site is signed on the Pilsen - Nurnberg road no. 5/E50, to the west of Pilsen.

General Details: Open all year. Restaurant. Kiosks. Watersports. Swimming. Table tennis. Boat trips. Kitchen with electric rings and fridges. Rest room with TV. Washing machines, dryers and irons. Rooms and chalets to let.

Charges guide: Per person Kcs. 20 - 24, acc. to season; child (6-15 yrs) 10 - 12; car 16 - 22; m/cycle 12 - 14; caravan or tent 65 - 90, acc. to size; motorcaravan 70 - 110, acc. to season and size; awning 30 - 40; electricity 35; local tax 5 - 10. Less 10% for stays over 30 days.

Reservations: Write to site. Address: 33034 Hracholusky. Tel: 019/7914 242 or 7914 113.

475 Camping Bílá Hora, Plzen/Pilsen

Site in peaceful location convenient for visiting Pilsen.

Even non-drinkers probably know that Pilsen is famous for its beer (Pils) and as the home of the Skoda car factory. Traffic in the town centre is heavy so, if you wish to visit the city where beer has been brewed since 1295, find a camp site and use the bus. Visits to the brewery may be arranged. Camping Bílá Hora is a suitable site and is situated amidst trees in the suburb of Bílá Hora, about 3 km. from the city centre on the edge of town. Pitches are on a gentle slope in a clearing, but level concrete tracks have been made for caravans and motorcaravans, with electricity available at each pitch. It is a pleasant, quiet site with a new sanitary block (British style WCs, bath and laundry) in the camping area, plus another with the bungalows, and its own restaurant. There are shops at 200 m. and a bus stop at the site entrance. Bungalows for rent are quite separate from the camping area.

How to find it: Site is to the north of the town on the Plzen - Zruc no. 231 road where it is signed.

General Details: Open 15 April - 30 Sept. Restaurant. Kiosk with small terrace. Shops near. Bicycle hire. Children's playground. Table tennis. Volleyball. Fishing 500 m. Swimming and tennis near. Washing machine and iron. Chemical disposal. Motorcaravan services. Kitchen. Chalets for hire.

Charges guide: Per person Kcs. 50; child (10-15 yrs) 20; car 70; m/cycle 20; caravan or tent 70; motorcaravan 140; electricity 50.

Reservations: Not necessary. Address: Ul. 28.rijna 49, 30162 Plzen. Tel: 019/534905. FAX: 019/7237252.

478 Motel Autocamping Konopiste, Benesov

Camping and motel complex with excellent facilities, south of Prague.

Benesov's chief claim to fame is the Konopiste Palace, the last home of Archduke Franz Ferdinand whose assassination in Sarajevo sparked off the First World War in 1914. Autocamp Konopiste is part of a motel complex situated in a very quiet, tranquil location. On a hillside, rows of terraces separated by hedges provide 65 grassy pitches of average size, all with electricity. One of the best Czech camps, it has many different varieties of trees and much to offer those who stay there. A fitness centre and heated swimming pool are shared with motel guests. The camp has its own bar/buffet in high season with simple meals and basic food items. The two motel restaurants are open all year. The good quality sanitary block is central to the caravan pitches and has British style WCs. The whole complex has a well tended, cared for air. It makes a good centre for visiting Prague (48 km. with public transport available) and to be enjoyed in its own right (see list of activities below). On site, near the motel, is the Stodola restaurant. Open each evening from 6 pm. until 1 am. this attractive replica of an old Czech barn is well worth a visit. With local specialities served by girls in local costume in a candle lit atmosphere and accompanied by a small, live music quartet, it is an evening to remember (booking essential).

How to find it: Site is signed near the village of Benesov at Hotel Konopiste (no connection) and Motel Konopiste on main Prague - Ceske Budejovic road no. 3/E55.

General Details: Open 1 May - 30 Sept. 6,000 sq.m. Bar/restaurant (all year). Snacks (1/6-31/8). Motel restaurants. Shop (1/6-31/8, another at 200 m). Swimming pool (1/6-31/8). Tennis. Minigolf. Volleyball. Table tennis. Bicycle hire. Badminton. Fitness centre. Children's playground. Fishing 1.5 km. Riding 5 km. Kitchen. Club room with TV. Terrace. Chateau and park. Washing machine and irons. Chemical disposal. Bungalows to let.

Charges 1999: Per person Kcs. 60 - 110; child (6-15 yrs) 30 - 50; caravan 130 - 310; large tent 120 - 250, small 70 - 120; car 100 - 120; motorcaravan 190 - 380; m/cycle 50 - 100; electricity included. Credit cards accepted.

Reservations: Contact site. Address: 256 01 Benesov u. Prahy. Tel: 0301/22732. FAX: 0301/22053. E-mail: motelk@iol.cz.

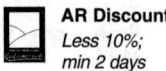

AR Discount
Less 10%;
min 2 days

477 Camping Dlouhá Louka, Céske Budejovice

Good night stop between Linz and Prague.

The medieval city of Céske Budejovice is the home of Budweiser beer and is also an industrial centre. It lies on the River Vltava with mountains and pleasant scenery nearby. Dlouhá Louka is a motel and camping complex 2 km. south of the town on the Céske Budejovice - Cesky Krumlov road. The camping part is a flat, rectangular meadow surrounded by trees which give some shade around the edges. Pitches, on grass, are not marked out or numbered so pitching can be rather haphazard. There are a few hardstandings. The single sanitary block with British style WCs is at one end making a fair walk for some. There is a very pleasant restaurant (summer only) and a small kiosk for basic food supplies. This is a useful night stop between Prague and Linz or for longer stays if this region is of interest.

How to find it: From town follow signs for Ceske Krumlov. After leaving ring road, turn right at Motel sign. Take this small road and turn right 60 m. before Camp Stromovky. Camp site name cannot be seen from the entrance - only the word Motel.

General Details: Open all year. 30,000 sq.m. Restaurant. Kiosk. Shops 200 m. Tennis. Volleyball. Table tennis. Washing machine and irons. Kitchen with electric rings. Bungalows and rooms to let.

Charges 1999: Per person Kcs. 7; child 30; car 70; tent 7; caravan 70; motorcaravan 110; m/cycle 40; dog 30; ity 80; local tax 15.

Reservations: Write to site. Address: Autocamping Motel Dlouhá Louka, Stromovka 8, 370 01 Ceské Budejovica. Tel: 038/7210601. FAX: 038/721059553141.

479 Sportcamp and 480 Caravancamp, Praha/Prague Motol

Edge of city sites for visiting Prague.

These two camps are side by side, share the same management and have a similar standard of amenities and sanitary arrangements. Both are on sloping ground with some terracing in a quiet location about 8 km. from the centre of Prague. Electricity is available for most caravan places but the grass pitches are neither numbered nor marked and it may may be crowded in high season. It is a pleasant situation with trees and a hill on one side and some shade in parts. Each site has its own restaurant and Sportcamp has a kiosk for basic food supplies with shops 200 m. distant. Caravancamp has a swimming pool. There is little to choose between these two – Caravancamp is now the larger, with room for about 200 touring units on flat pitches but is nearer the main road. Sportcamp with about 150 pitches is quieter but more hilly.

How to find them: Sites are well signed on main highway from Pilsen, road no. 5/E50, near Hotel Golf.

General Details: Both open 1 April - 31 Oct. Restaurants. Kiosk (Sportcamp). Shops 200 m. Swimming pool (Caravancamp). Tennis. Minigolf. Golf 3 km. Riding 10 km. Fishing 8 km. Chemical disposal. Motorcaravan services. Bungalows to let (Sportcamp).

Charges 1999: Per person Kcs. 120 - 140; child (6-12 yrs) 60; tent 90 - 110; car 100 - 120; caravan 120 - 150; motorcaravan 150 - 180; m/cycle 60 - 80; electricity 300. No credit cards.

Reservations: Contact sites. Sportcamp, Nad hliníkem 1202, 150 00 Praha 5, Motol. Tel: 02/57213080. FAX: 02/57215084. Caravancamp, Plzeňská 279, 150 00 Praha 5, Motol. Tel: 02/524714. FAX: 02/57215084.

481 Intercamp Kotva, Praha/Prague

Riverside city site for visiting Prague.

Kotva is pleasantly situated directly by the River Vltava, 20 minutes by public transport from the city centre. With a motorway and a railway line hidden behind the trees on the opposite bank of the river, there is traffic and train noise but the trees and a high bank otherwise give a feeling of being in the country. A train and bus terminal is a few minutes walk. It is best to use the good, cheap public transport for visiting Prague as parking is very limited and illegally parked cars are swiftly towed away (the site office sells tram tickets which can also be used on the Metro – a tram stops outside the site). The 76 pitches are on level grass with hardstanding and electricity, with a separate grass area for tents. A reader reports that drainage can be poor in wet weather. None of the pitches is marked out and it could become crowded in high season. The site is owned by a sports club and sanitary arrangements are in the main club building which also houses offices and accommodation. The heated sanitary facilities are of good quality but may be under pressure in high season. The site restaurant is in private hands and there is a shop on the left outside the gate. A well run site, English is spoken at reception and a porter is on duty at night at the entrance.

How to find it: Site is well signed on southern ring road and on main road from Pilsen or Ceske Budejovice. Follow signs for Branik.

General Details: Open all year. 12,000 sq.m. Restaurant. Shop. Fishing and boating. Tennis. Table tennis. Volleyball. Minigolf near. Golf 4 km. Exchange facilities. Chemical disposal. Bungalows, cabins and rooms to let.

Charges 2000: Per person Kcs. 100; child (6-12 yrs) 50; tent 75 - 110; car 90; m/cycle 55; caravan 180; motorcaravan 210; electricity 75. Plus local tax 17 (2 for children or students) and VAT @ 22%. No credit cards or Eurocheques (but both accepted at exchange office).

AR Discount
Less 10%

Reservations: Write to site. Address: Intercamp Kotva, U. ledáren 55, 147 00 Praha 4. Tel: 02/44461712. FAX: 02/44466110.

CZECH REPUBLIC

486 Autocamping Orlice, Kostelec

Pleasant site with good facilities in East Bohemia.

Kostelec does have an ancient castle, although not a lot else to commend it, but is a good centre from which to explore the interesting town of Hradec Kralove, East Bohemia, the Orlicke Hory and other high districts near the Polish border. Autocamping Orlice, situated on the edge of town near the swimming pool, has a river running by and is in a quiet location (except when children play in the weir!) and a pleasant appearance. The central sanitary block, one of the best we have seen in the Czech Republic, has British WCs and hot water in washbasins, sinks and excellent showers. Unlike most Czech sites, the showers have divider, space for dressing, a door that locks, and even a chair! Surrounded by tall trees, the grass pitches are of generous size although not marked or numbered, on each side of a concrete grid road which runs the length of this rectangular site. There is room for 80 units, half having electric points and with shade in parts. Limited food supplies are available in a bar/lounge during July/Aug. and there is a hotel alongside the camp but advice is to seek a better restaurant in town for meals. The friendly manageress speaks good English and will be pleased to advise on local attractions.

How to find it: Site is signed from the centre of town.

General Details: Open 15 May - 30 Sept. 30,000 sq.m. Bar/lounge. Café (15/5-30/9). Snacks (1/6-31/8). Town pool near (15/6-31/8). Tennis 100 m. Fishing 100 m. Riding 10 km. Chemical disposal. Bungalows for rent.

Charges 1999: Per person Kcs. 36 - 40; child (6-14 yrs) 16 - 20; car 50 - 60; m/cycle 26 - 36; motorcaravan 75 - 85; caravan 60 - 70; tent 50 - 60; dog 36 - 40; electricity 50; local tax 2 - 3. Credit cards accepted.

Reservations: Write to site. Address: 51741 Kostelec nad Orlici. Tel: (winter) 0444/21691 or (site) 0444/21970. FAX: as phones. E-mail: tamas@kostelec.czcom.cz.

487 Autocamping Morava, Mohelnice

Well organised camp in interesting area.

This is an interesting area of contrasts - heavy industry, fertile plains and soaring mountains, with castles, caves and cathedrals. Mohelnice itself is a small industrial town but the camp is in a peaceful setting surrounded by trees on the northern edge. It could make a useful night stop or a base for seeing the locality. The amenities on offer, particularly for children, may tempt one to stay longer. The site is roughly in two halves. The camping area is on a flat, open meadow with hard access road. Pitches are not numbered or marked so siting could be a little haphazard. Some two thirds have electricity. There is little shade but the perimeter trees should screen out road noise. There is a swimming pool and a sanitary block in this section (British style WCs). The other part of the camp is given over to a motel and bungalows with a restaurant between the two sections. An unusual feature is a tarmac driving and cycling learning area with road signs, traffic lights and road markings similar to a normal road situation. It is well set up to give youngsters a practice area without the hazard of normal traffic. Good English is spoken at reception.

How to find it: Site is signed on the western edge of town on the Olomouc - Hradec Kralove road no. 35/E442.

General Details: Open all year. 20,000 sq.m. Restaurant (all year). Kiosk/snack bar. Small shop (summer only). Live music (high season). Swimming pool. Tennis. Minigolf. Table tennis. Volleyball. Bicycle hire. Road learning track. Children's playground. TV room. Washing machine. Electric cooking rings.

Charges guide: Per person Kcs. 60; child (under 15) 30; pitch 140; electricity 60; local tax 10. No credit cards.

Reservations: Write to site. Address: 789 85 Mohelnice. Tel: 0648/430129. FAX: 0648/51011.

488 Camping Roznov, Roznov pod Radhostem

Good site with pool, on edge of resort town in North Moravia.

Roznov pod Radhostem is situated halfway up the Roznovska Becva valley amidst the Beskydy hills which extend from North Moravia into Poland in the extreme east of the Republic. It is a busy tourist centre which attracts visitors to the Wallachian open-air museum and those who enjoy hill walking. The main features of this site are the good sized, open air, swimming pool and bungalows for rent. The pitches, some of which are rather small, are on flat grass set amidst a variety of fruit and other trees. There is electricity throughout and shade in some parts. Although right by a main road with some traffic noise, the camp is surrounded by trees and hills and was reasonably quiet during our visit. The good quality central sanitary block has British WCs and hot water in basins and sinks. The rather old showers have a central rose water dispenser controlled by a chain. This block also has a large, comfortable TV lounge/meeting room. Local information is well displayed on notice boards and available from the friendly manager. Only very basic food items are available in the shop and the restaurant is not always open. A better bet is to use the restaurant at the Europlan Hotel 300 m. towards the town.

How to find it: Site is at eastern end of Roznov on main 18/E442 Zilina-Olomouc road opposite sports stadium.

General Details: Open May - September. 27,000 sq.m. Swimming pool (25 m. and heated July/Aug). Table tennis. TV lounge and meeting room. Small shop and restaurant.

Charges guide: Per person Kcs. 60; child (3-15 yrs) 50; pitch 80 - 120; electricity 50; local tax 17.

Reservations: Write to site. Address: 75661 Roznov pod Radhostem. Tel/Fax: 0651/55442.

DENMARK

Denmark is the easiest of the Scandinavian countries to visit, both in terms of cost and distance. The countryside is green and varied with flat plains, rolling hills, fertile farmland, many lakes and fjords, wild moors and long beaches, interrupted by pretty villages and towns. There are many small islands but the main land masses which make up this country are the islands of Zealand (Sjælland), Funen (Fyn) and the peninsula of Jutland (Jylland), which extends northwards from the German border at Flensburg. Copenhagen, the capital and Denmark's largest city, is on Zealand and is an exciting city with a beautiful old centre, a good array of museums and a boisterous night life. Camping in Denmark is a delight, with many sites now having facilities that rival, and sometimes even surpass, the best in other parts of Europe. Most sites now offer well designed facilities for disabled people and baby changing, and many now have private family bathrooms which generally include shower, WC and washbasin. You will find kitchens on most sites, many with hobs, ovens, microwaves and the occasional dishwasher. All these facilities are often free of extra charge. You will need either a valid International Camping Carnet, or a Danish Camping Pass (which can be purchased at the first camp you visit in Denmark). Denmark is an ideal destination for those who enjoy watersports of all types, cycling, fishing and sightseeing.

The Danish Tourist Board, 55 Sloane Street, London SW1X 9SY
Tel: 020 7259 5959. Fax: 020 7259 5955. E-mail: dtb.london@dt.dk

Population
5,162,000 (1992), density 120 per sq.km.

Capital
Copenhagen (København).

Climate
The climate can be changeable throughout the year. In general April-May is mild. June-Aug. is usually warm and sunny. Autumn is often sunny but can be unreliable and the winter months Dec-March tend to be cold, often with a little snow.

Language
The official language is Danish, but English is widely spoken.

Currency
The monetary unit is the Danish Krone (Dkr.) 1 Krone = 100 ore. Bank notes in circulation are: 1,000, 500, 100, and 50; coins are: 20, 10, 5, 2 and 1 krone, 50 and 25 ore.

Banks
In Copenhagen banks are open Mon-Wed & Fri 09.30-16.00. Thurs. to 18.00. Closed Sat. In the provinces opening hours vary from town to town. Note: Danish banks may refuse to exchange large foreign bank notes. Eurocheques and other well known traveller's cheques are cashed by banks and many hotels, restaurants and shops, which also accept most international credit cards.

Post Offices
Open Mon-Fri 09.00/10.00-17.00/17.30, Sat 09.00/10.00-12.00 (some offices in Copenhagen are closed all day on Saturdays).

Telephone
The dialling code for Denmark is 0045. from Denmark to the UK dial 0044. Phone cards available from Telecom shops (Telebutik).

Time
GMT plus 1 (summer BST plus 1).

Shops
Hours may vary in the main cities. Regular openings are Mon-Thu 09.00-17.30. Fri 09.00-19.00/20.00. Sat 09.00-13.00/14.00. First Sat in every month most shops open 09.00-16.00/ 17.00.

Food and Restaurants
The cost of food is quite high and a stock of basic supplies is useful. However, supermarket prices are now fairly similar to London prices. The price of spirits is prohibitive but for wine and beer almost acceptable! Eating out can be expensive. Try sticking to `Dagens Ret' - the day's speciality which is usually good value. The high point of Danish food culture is the cold table with a large variety of hot and cold fish and meat dishes in which `smorrebrod' (open sandwiches), the great Danish speciality, play an important part.

Motoring
Driving is much easier than at home as roads are much quieter. Driving is on the right. Parking is much easier than ours, apart from main cities, often just off pedestrianised town centres. Do not drink and drive - any quantity is liable to immediate drastic action. Dipped headlights are compulsory at all times.

Speed limits: caravans and motorhomes (3.5 tons) 31 mph (50 kph) in built up areas, 44 mph (70 kph) for caravans on all other roads, for motorhomes 50 mph (80 kph) on other roads and 69 mph (110 kph) on motorways.

Parking: In Copenhagen parking discs are required where there are no meters. Meters take 1, 2, 5, 10 and 20 Kr. coins and discs are available from post offices, banks, petrol stations, and tourist offices.

Overnighting
Overnight stays outside camp sites is not permitted without the prior permission of the respective landowner. Camping in car parks and laybys is not permitted either. Strong measures are taken against unauthorised parking in dunes and on beaches - offenders being fined on the spot.

Useful Addresses
National Motoring Organisation:
Forenede Danske Motorejere,
FDM-Huset, PO Box 500, Firskovvej 32,
2800 Lyngby. Tel: 45930800.

2020 Møgeltønder Camping, Møgeltønder, Tønder

Pleasant family run site with excellent facilities, convenient for ports.

This site is only 5 minutes walk from one of Denmark's oldest villages and 10 minutes drive from Tønder with its well preserved old buildings and magnificent pedestrian shopping street. The old town of Ribe is just 43 km. A quiet family site, it has 280 large, level, numbered pitches on grass, most with electricity (6/10A), divided up by new plantings of shrubs and small hedges. Only 25 pitches are occupied by long stay units, the remainder solely for tourists, and there are 15 cabins for rent on site. Two superb, modern, sanitary units provide good roomy showers with divider and seat (on payment), washbasins with either divider/curtain or in private cubicles, British style WCs, plus excellent bathrooms for families and the disabled. In addition there are now two kitchens with hobs and dishwashing sinks (all free), plus a laundry with sink, two washing machines and a dryer. The site also has an excellent outdoor heated swimming pool and children's pool, a good children's playground with bouncing cushion and a range of trolleys, carts and tricycles. Small shop for essentials (fresh bread can be ordered daily), TV and games rooms, minigolf, telephone and tourist information. Golf course and bicycle hire in nearby Tønder.

How to find it: Turn left off the 419 Tønder - Højer road, 4 km. from Tønder. Drive through Møgeltønder village and past the church where site is signed. Note: the main street is cobbled so drive slowly.

General Details: Open all year. Shop. Swimming pool. Children's playground. Minigolf. Kitchen and laundry facilities. Car wash. Chemical disposal. Motorcaravan services. Chalets for rent.

Charges guide: Per adult Dkr. 45; child (0-12 yrs) 25; electricity 18.

Reservations: Not normally necessary. Address: Sønderstregsvej 2, Møgeltønder, 6270 Tønder. Tel: 74.73.84.60. FAX: 74.73.80.43.

2010 Hvidbjerg Strand Camping, Blåvand, nr Esbjerg

High quality, seaside, holiday site, with indoor pools and many activities.

A family owned, 'TopCamp' holiday site, Hvidbjerg Strand is on the west coast near Blåvands Huk and is 43 km. from Esbjerg. All 650 pitches have electricity (6/10A) and 'comfort' pitches also have water, drain and satellite TV. Pitches are in rows on flat sandy grass, with areas divided by small trees and hedges. Four superb sanitary units provide WCs, washbasins (many in cubicles), roomy showers, spa baths, suites for disabled visitors, family bathrooms, kitchens and laundry facilities. The latest unit is thatched in the traditional style with a central glass covered atrium. This includes a children's bathroom which is decorated with dinosaur characters, racing car baby baths, low height WCs, basins and showers, plus 10 high quality family bathrooms, a suite for disabled visitors and an excellent kitchen with eight double hobs and sinks, two ovens and adjacent dining area. All hot water and cooking facilities are free. Some family bathrooms may be rented for exclusive use. On-site leisure facilities include an impressive, tropical style indoor pool complex with water slides, spa baths, Turkish bath and a sauna. A café/restaurant overlooks the pools. Else-where are TV rooms, solarium, outdoor barbecue areas with picnic tables, minigolf, horse riding, football, squash, badminton, fishing, many children's play areas, plus the latest indoor suite of supervised play-rooms designed for all ages with Lego, computers, video games, TV, etc. (open 09.00-16.00 daily). A Blue Flag beach and windsurfing school are adjacent to the site and the town offers a full activity programme during the main season (mid June - mid Aug). Legoland is 70 km.

How to find it: From Varde take roads 181/431 to Blåvand. Site is signed left on entering the town. (Mind speed bump on town boundary).

General Details: Open 19 March - 24 Oct. Supermarket. Café. Restaurant. Kitchen and laundry facilities. Pool complex. Comprehensive sporting and leisure facilities. Children's playgrounds. Sauna. Solarium. Dog showers. Car wash. Chemical disposal. Motorcaravan services. Cabins for rent.

Charges 1999: Per adult Dkr. 57; child (0-11 yrs) 40; pitch 38 - 63, payable high seasons and BHs only; electricity (6A) 20; 'comfort' pitch 35. Credit cards accepted.

Reservations: made without deposit. Address: Hvidbjerg Strandvej, 6857 Blåvand. Tel: 75.27.90.40. FAX: 75.27.80.28. E-mail: info@hvidbjerg.dk.

2030 Sandersvig Camping, Haderslev

Attractively laid out family site, in beautiful countryside 300 m. from beach.

This family run site offers the very best of modern facilities in a peaceful location and it is most attractively laid out. The 470 very large grassy pitches (270 for tourers) are divided up by hedges, shrubs and small trees into small enclosures, many housing only four units, most with electricity (10A). The site is well lit, very quiet at night and there are water taps close to most pitches. There are three heated sanitary blocks, one by reception, an older one (interior refitted) at the lower end of the site, and the newest at the upper end of the site. These offer British WCs, washbasins (some in private cubicles), and roomy showers (on payment). There are also suites for disabled visitors, six family bathrooms, baby rooms, excellent kitchens with ovens, electric hobs, dishwashing sinks, plus a very good laundry and a separate fish cleaning area. Cooking facilities and hot water in both kitchen and laundry are free of charge. The site also has a well stocked supermarket and fast food service with a TV lounge/dining room adjacent, an outdoor heated swimming pool which is free to campers, two artificial grass tennis courts, solarium, children's playground with trampolines and Denmark's largest bouncing cushion, games room with TV, pool table, arcade machines, telephones and tourist information. This site makes a very comfortable base for excursions. Visit the restored windmill at Sillerup 4 km. or nearby historic Kolding with its castle, museums and shops. The drive to the island of Fyn takes less than an hour, with miles of country lanes around the site for cycling and walking.

How to find it: Leave E45 at exit 66 south of Christianfeld and follow signs for Fjelstrup and Knud village, turning right 1 km. east of the village from where site is signed.

General Details: Open 27 March - 15 Sept. Supermarket (Easter-15/9). Takeaway (15/5-1/8). Swimming pool (15/5-1/9). Children's playground. Games/TV rooms. Solarium. Tennis. Beach. Riding 4 km. Bicycle hire 6 km. Fishing 7 km. Kitchen. Laundry. Chemical disposal. Motorcaravan services.

Charges 2000: Per adult Dkr. 45; child (0-11 yrs) 26; pitch 10 - 25; electricity (10A) 20. No credit cards.

Reservations: Essential for high season (15/6-15/8). Write to site. Address: Espagervej 15-17, 6100 Haderslev. Tel: 74.56.62.25. FAX: as phone. E-mail: sandersvig@dkcamp.dk.

2040 Riis Camping and Fritidscenter, Give

Quality, quiet touring site, 18 km. from Legoland and 3 km. from the Lion Park.

Riis is a friendly, family run 'TopCamp' site with 270 large touring pitches on sheltered, gently sloping, well tended lawns surrounded by trees and shrubs. Electricity (6A) is available to 220 pitches, and there are 41 cabins and 5 apartments for rent. Two excellent sanitary units provide British WCs, washbasins with divider/curtain, and controllable showers with divider and seat (on payment). There are suites for babies and the disabled, family bathrooms (one with whirlpool bath), solarium, laundry, two excellent kitchens with hobs, ovens, dishwashing sinks, a large dining room/sitting room with TV, plus a covered barbecue grill area. Cooking facilities, family bathrooms and hot water are free, but the showers and whirlpool bath are extra. The outdoor heated pool and water-slide complex (charged for in July) and the adjacent small bar which serves beer, ice cream, soft drinks and snacks are only open in main season. There is also a small, well stocked shop next to reception for necessities. Other on site amenities include a comprehensive children's play area, outdoor bowling alley, table tennis, minigolf, TV lounge and bicycle hire. More comprehensive shopping and restaurants are in nearby Give. This is a top class site suitable for long or short stays in this very attractive part of Denmark.

How to find it: Turn onto Osterhovedvej southeast of Give town centre (near Shell Garage) at signpost to Riis and site. After 4 km. turn left into gravel drive which runs through the forest to the site. Alternatively, turn off the 442 Brande-Jelling road at Riis village north of Givskud.

General Details: Open 30 April - 5 Sept. Shop. Pool complex. Cafe/bar. Kitchen and laundry facilities. Dining room. Solarium. Table tennis. Minigolf. Bowling alley. Children's playground. TV lounge. Telephone. Tourist information. Car wash. Chemical disposal. Motorcaravan services. Cabins and apartments to let.

Charges 1999: Per adult Dkr. 52; child (under 12 yrs) 34; pitch 35 (21/6-9/8 only), 'comfort' pitch plus 20; dog 10; electricity 22. Credit cards accepted.

Reservations: Site can become full in July/Aug. so reservations are advisable. Address: 7323 Give. Tel: 75.73.14.33. FAX: 75.73.58.66. E-mail: info@riis-camping.dk.

DENMARK - Jylland

2060 Birkhede Camping, Ry

Well managed site, in beautiful quiet countryside on the edge of Lake Knudso.

Birkhede has 250 marked and numbered grassy pitches on two levels, divided by trees and shrubs, all with electricity (10A). Whilst the upper level is terraced, the lower is gently sloping but more suited to larger units. Although the entrance drive is gravel, on-site access is mainly tarmac with a card operated security barrier. The two sanitary units are of excellent quality, the main block behind reception is heated and has two complete sets of facilities, only one open outside the main season. The other block serves the lower level of the site. These provide British WCs, washbasins in cubicles, controllable card operated showers with divider and seat, family bathrooms, baby room, kitchens with hobs, dishwashing and laundry sinks (hot water on payment), plus a fridge-freezer. Campers buy pre-charged cards (Dkr. 100) to obtain hot water in the kitchen, laundry, and showers. The same card operates washing machines, telephones and the entrance barrier. Other on-site amenities include a takeaway and mini-market, free heated outdoor swimming pool (9 x 25 m) with water slide and children's pool (4 x 6 m), an adventure playground, ball games area and TV lounge. The lake provides a bathing area, fishing (licences from reception) and a jetty. Good walks from the site include a climb to a viewpoint which looks out over Denmark's 'Lake District'.

How to find it: Turn off Silkeborg - Ry no. 15 road 4 km. southeast of Laven St. at Alling and campsite sign. Follow signs to site.

General Details: Open 24 April - 15 Sept. Mini-market and takeaway (May-Sept). Swimming pool (1/6-1/9). Table tennis. Bicycle, boat and canoe hire. Fishing. Windsurfing. Golf 15 km. Children's playground. TV. Kitchen. Laundry. Chemical disposal. Motorcaravan service point. Chalets and motel rooms for rent.

Charges 2000: Per adult Dkr. 54; child (0-11 yrs) 32; pitch mid June - mid Aug only 20 - 35; dog 5; electricity 14 + 2.00 per kwh. No credit cards.

Reservations: Essential in high season - contact site. Address: Lyngvej 14, 8680 Ry. Tel: 86.89.13.55. FAX: 86.89.03.13. E-mail: info@birkhede.dk.

2050 Terrassen Camping, Laven St, Silkeborg

Terraced, family run site, overlooking Lake Julso and the countryside.

Terrassen's 260 pitches are arranged on terraces with electricity (6/10A) to most. A small additional tent area (without electricity) is at the top of the site where torches may be required. There are also 29 seasonal units, 10 rental cabins, and 3 site owned caravans on site. The main sanitary unit is heated and modern and provides British WCs, washbasins (many in cubicles), controllable showers with divider and seat (on payment), 5 family bathrooms, children's bathroom, baby room, and facilities for the disabled. There is also a kitchen with 10 hobs, 2 ovens and dishwashing sinks. An older re-furbished unit contains another kitchen, plus 4 more shower cubicles with external access – despite their outward appearance they are newly re-tiled and immaculate. Cooking facilities, family bathrooms, hot water and the swimming pool are free, only showers are extra. The solar heated swimming pool (8 x 16 m, open June-end August) has a paved terrace and is well fenced. Other amenities include an adventure playground and pets corner, ball games area with basket and volleyball, a well stocked shop is adjacent to the reception office, games and TV rooms, post box, telephone, tourist information, canoe hire, car wash and motorcaravan service point. There is a restaurant just outside the site, and fishing and windsurfing are available on Lake Julso. This is a comfortable base from which to explore this area of Denmark where a warm welcome and good English will greet you. Don't forget to take a trip on Lake Julso on Hjejen, the world's oldest paddle steamer.

How to find it: From Silkeborg take the road no. 15 to Linas, turn right to Laven St. village, then right again towards Laven and follow signs to site.

General Details: Open 1 April - 12 Sept. Shop (from 1/5). Swimming pool (1/6-1/9). Kitchen. Laundry. Games/TV rooms. Children's playground. Pets corner. Canoe hire. Fishing and windsurfing on Lake Julso. Car wash. Chemical disposal. Motorcaravan services. Cabins and caravans for hire.

Charges 1999: Per adult: Dkr. 52; child (1-11 yrs) 28; pitch 10 - 30; electricity 25.

Reservations: Contact site - essential for high season. Address: Himmelbjergvej 9, Laven St, 8600 Silkeborg. Tel: 86.84.13.01. FAX: 86.84.16.55.

2080 Sølystgård Camping, Fuglsø, nr Ebeltoft

Seaside site with good views in attractive holiday location.

Located in a corner of the delightful Ebeltoft and Mols area, one of the best holiday spots in Denmark, this beach-side site is on Ebeltoft Bay, close to the Helgenæs peninsula, and surrounded by rolling countryside. The spacious site, originally a farm, is divided by hedges and trees into several well tended fields, which have varying slopes. The 280 pitches (200 for touring units) are unmarked but electricity (4/6A) is available in all areas and many places have sea views. The lovely old, thatched, white walled farm buildings form the central complex incorporating reception, a small shop and other facilities. There are two sanitary units, one a converted thatched barn solely for ladies, the other is more ordinary, with rooms for ladies and men. The former has a kitchen with hobs (on payment), dishwashing sinks (free hot water), baby room and an excellent whirlpool bathroom (on payment) at one end. Other facilities include British WCs, washbasins either in cubicles, with divider and curtain, or open, plus hot showers with divider and seat (on payment). There are facilities for disabled people, a sauna and solarium (on payment), laundry, telephone, ice pack service and tourist information. Leisure facilities include a centrally located tennis court and children's play area (with an amusing new swing), together with TV and games rooms. The beach offers good bathing with a water chute provided, and facilities for launching boats. Fishing is popular and the site has a boat to borrow without charge.

How to find it: Take road 15 from Århus to Rønde, turn right following signs to Fuglsø where you turn left towards the Helgenæs peninsula. Then left again at camp sign down a narrow lane to the site.

General Details: Open 1 April - 20 Sept. Shop. Sauna. Solarium. Whirlpool bathroom. Tennis. Billiards. Volleyball. Basketball. TV and games rooms. Children's playground. Fishing. Boat sliipway. Bicycle hire and golf 15 km. Riding 5 km. Kitchen. Laundry. Car wash. Chemical disposal. Motorcaravan services. Cabins for rent.

Charges 2000: Per adult Dkr. 52 - 60; child (under 12 yrs) 27 - 30; pitch 20 (14/6-16/8 only); electricity 22. No credit cards.

Reservations: Essential in high season – write to site. Address: Dragsmurvej 15, Fuglsø, 8420 Ebeltoft (Knebel). Tel: 86.35.12.39. FAX: as phone.

2090 Krakær Camping, Krakær, nr Ebeltoft

Sheltered, spacious forest site, with swimming pool and bistro.

Situated just north of Ebeltoft Bay in sheltered forest surroundings, but close to beaches and the ferry port of Grenå. Krakær Camping's family owners have carried out much modernisation work and the 266 marked, but not separated, pitches are mostly on level terraces or in large clearings, together with 13 cabins for rent. Access roads are good and most pitches have electrical hook-ups (10A). Newer terraces are still maturing and could be muddy in wet weather. There are two modern sanitary units, one below the reception complex, the other nearer the swimming pool, and both with heating. They provide British style WCs, washbasins in cubicles, hot showers with divider and seat (on payment), which may be pressed in main season. Other facilities include a baby room, family bathrooms, a unit for disabled people, hand dryers, free hairdryers, two kitchens with hobs and dishwashing sinks, plus a laundry with drying room. Hot water, cooking facilities and family bathrooms are free of charge, only showers are extra. A stylish refitted bistro and bar at the entrance (high season) also serves takeaway meals and has a pleasant terrace. Other amenities include a solar heated open-air swimming pool and toddlers' pool, supermarket, minigolf, TV and games room, telephone, post box and tourist information. Children have an excellent, imaginative adventure playground and pedal car track. Riding stables and tennis are nearby, and there are glorious walks all around.

How to find it: From road no. 15 at Ronde turn right to Femmøller Strand, then left towards Lyngsbæk. Site is clearly signed 2 km. along country lanes. Take care turning off main road - approach on a blind corner.

General Details: Open all year. Shop (1/4-1/9). Bistro, bar and takeaway (15/5-1/9). TV/games room. Adventure play area. Minigolf. Swimming pool (1/5-1/9). Riding 200 m. Fishing and boat slipway 3 km. Golf and bicycle hire 8 km. Kitchen. Laundry. Chemical disposal. Motorcaravan services. Cabins for hire.

Charges 2000: Per adult Dkr. 50; child (1-12 yrs) 25; pitch (high season only) 20; electricity 28 - 22. No credit cards.

Reservations: Write to site for details. Address: GL Kærvej 18, Krakær, 8400 Ebeltoft. Tel: 86.36.21.18. FAX: 86.36.21.87.

DENMARK - Jylland

2100 Blushøj Camping, Ebeltoft

Comfortable, family run touring site, with views over the Kattegat.

This is a traditional site where the owners are making a conscious effort to keep mainly to touring units – there are only 6 seasonal units and 4 rental cabins. The site has 200 pitches on levelled grassy terraces surrounded by mature hedging and shrubs. Some have glorious views of the Kattegat and others overlook peaceful rural countryside. Most pitches have electricity (10A), but long leads may be required. One sanitary unit provides British style WCs, washbasins with dividers and showers with divider and seat (on payment). The other unit has a kitchen with a mini-oven and dishwashing sinks, dining/TV room, laundry and baby facilities. A heated extension provides six very smart family bathrooms, and additional WCs and washbasins, and is adjacent to the heated and fenced swimming pool (14 x 7 m) with a water-slide and terrace. Hot water, oven, family bathrooms and the swimming pool are free, only showers are extra. Also on-site is a good children's playground, minigolf, a well stocked shop, telephone, and a motorcaravan service point. The beach below the site provides opportunities for swimming, windsurfing and sea fishing. The owners also arrange traditional entertainment – folk dancing, local choirs, and accordion music some weekends in high season. This is a fine location for a relaxed family holiday, with numerous excursion possibilities including the fine old town of Ebeltoft (4 km), with its shops and restaurants, and the world's largest wooden sailing ship, the Frigate Jylland, now fully restored and open to the public.

How to find it: From road 21 northwest of Ebeltoft turn off at junction where several sites are signed. Follow signs through the outskirts of Ebeltoft turning southeast to Elsegårde village. Turn left for Blushøj and follow camp signs.

General Details: Open from 1 April - 15 Sept. Shop. Kitchen. Laundry. Swimming pool (1/6-15/8). Minigolf. Children's playground. Beach. Fishing. Riding, bicycle hire or golf 5 km. Chemical disposal. Motorcaravan services. Cabins for rent.

Charges 1999: Per adult Dkr. 48 - 55; child 24 - 27; electricity 15. No credit cards.

Reservations: Advised for high season - contact site. Address: Elsegårdevej 53, 8400 Ebeltoft. Tel: 86.34.12.38. FAX: as phone.

2150 Sølyst Camping, Nibe

Family run site beside sheltered Limfjord, with swimming pool.

You will always be near to the water in Denmark, either open sea or, as here, alongside the more sheltered waters of a fjord. Sølyst provides 200 numbered pitches, most with electricity (6A), on gently sloping grass arranged in fairly narrow rows separated by hedges (140 for touring units). There are facilities for watersports and swimming in the fjord, the site also has a small heated swimming pool (8 x 16 m), with a children's pool and paved sunbathing area, and paddle boats can be rented. A little train provides rides for children and there is a good playground, minigolf, and TV room. The snack bar (open main season) provides takeaway meals and there are tables outside, under cover. The central sanitary unit provides British WCs, washbasins in cubicles, four family bathrooms, a baby room and facilities for disabled visitors. There is a kitchen with gas hobs, microwave, oven and dishwashing sinks, and a fully equipped laundry. A second unit provides two more family bathrooms and additional unisex WCs, basins and showers, and is located near the solarium. Hot water (except in washbasins) is charged for. The mini-market at the site entrance is open daily. Good paths have been provided for superb, easy walks in either direction, and indeed right into the nearby town of Nibe (1 km). This is a delightful example of an old Danish town with picturesque cottages and handsome 15th century church. Its harbour, once prosperous from local herring boats, is now more concerned with pleasure craft.

How to find it: Site is clearly signed from the no. 187 road west of Nibe town, with a wide entrance.

General Details: Open all year. Mini-market. Snack bar and takeaway. Swimming pool. Children's playground. TV room. Solarium. Fishing. Bicycle hire or riding 1 km. Golf 4 km. Kitchen. Laundry. Motorcaravan services. Chemical disposal. Cabins (12), rooms (3) and mobile homes (3) to rent.

Charges 1999: Per adult Dkr. 50 - 57; child (under 12 yrs) 26 - 30; pitch 20 (14/6-16/8 only); electricity 20. No credit cards.

Reservations: recommended for peak periods - write for details. Address: Løngstørvej 2, 9240 Nibe. Tel: 98.35.10.62. FAX: 98.35.34.88.

2140 Jesperhus Feriecenter, Nykøbing

Extensive, well run site with pool complex and many leisure activities, adjacent to Blomsterpark.
This large, busy and well organised 'TopCamp' site has 723 numbered pitches, mostly in rows, with some terracing, divided by shrubs and trees with shade in parts. Many pitches are taken by seasonal, tour operator or rental units, plus 70 chalets, so advance booking is advised for peak periods. Electricity (5A) is available on all pitches and water points are in all areas. Four first rate sanitary units are cleaned three times daily and the site operates a policy of regular maintenance and upgrading. Facilities include British WCs, washbasins in private cubicles or with divider/curtain, controllable showers with divider and seat, family and whirlpool bathrooms, plus suites for babies and the disabled. There are superb kitchens with full cookers and hoods, microwaves and dishwashing sinks, plus a fully equipped laundry. All hot water, cooking facilities, family bathrooms and sauna are free of charge, whirlpool bathroom and laundry are extra. The indoor and outdoor pool complex (daily charge) has three pools, diving boards, water slides with the 'Black Hole', spa pools, saunas, solarium, a café and takeaway. Elsewhere is a separate restaurant/bar and a large supermarket. Activities include a 10 lane bowling centre, 'space laser' game, minigolf, volleyball, tennis, go-carts and other outdoor sports. An indoor hall includes badminton, table tennis, and children's 'play-world'. The latest addition is a Circus every Wednesday in high season. Although it may appear to be just part of Jutland, Mors is an island in its own right surrounded by the lovely Limfjord. It is joined to the mainland by a fine 2,000 m. bridge at the end of which are signs to Blomsterpark (Northern Europe's largest flower park which also houses a Bird Zoo, Butterfly World, Terrarium and Aquarium) and the camp site - both under the same ownership. The flower park, situated well to the north of Denmark, is an incredible sight from early spring to late autumn, attracting some 4,000 visitors a day to enjoy over half a million flowering plants and magnificent landscaped gardens. With all the activities at this site an entire holiday could be spent here regardless of weather, but Jesperhus is also an excellent centre for touring a lovely area of Denmark.

How to find it: From south or north, take road no. 26 to Salling Sund bridge, site is signed Jesperhus, just north of the bridge.

General Details: Open all year. Supermarket (1/4-1/11) with gas. Restaurant. Bar. Café. Takeaway. Pool complex. Very comprehensive leisure, sporting and entertainment facilities. Children's playgrounds. Pets corner. Golf. Fishing. Riding 2 km. Bicycle hire 6 km. Kitchens. Laundry. Chemical disposal. Chalets for rent.

Charges 1999: Per adult Dkr. 55; child (1-11 yrs) 40; pitch 50 (July, BHs. and w/ends only); electricity 25. Credit cards accepted.

Reservations: Recommended for holiday periods - write for details. Address: Jesperhus Feriecenter, Legindvej 30, 7900 Nykøbing, Mors. Tel: 97.72.37.01. FAX: 97.71.02.55. E-mail: jesperhus@jesperhus.dk.

2130 Hobro Camping Gattenborg, Hobro

Imaginatively landscaped site with views over Hobro, Mariager Fjord and Vester Fjord.
This neat and very well tended site has 130 pitches on terraces arranged around a bowl shaped central activity area. Most pitches (100 for touring units) have electricity (5A) and there are many trees and shrubs. Footpaths connect the various terraces and activity areas. There are 30 seasonal units and 8 cabins for rent on site. The main heated sanitary building, towards the rear of the site, provides British style WCs, washbasins in cubicles, and controllable hot showers (on payment), plus two family bathrooms, a kitchen with hobs and dishwashing sinks, and a small laundry with a sink, washing machine and two dryers. New facilities for disabled people and a baby room have been added. A tiny unit in the centre of the site has two unisex WCs and basins (cold water only) and a small kitchen, whilst the reception building with a small shop and tourist information, has a covered picnic terrace behind, and also houses a large TV lounge and additional WC and basins. The small outdoor swimming pool with water-slide is heated, free to campers and open in high season weather permitting. Leisure facilities include a well equipped children's playground, minigolf, basketball and football ground, table tennis, billiards, giant chess, and a woodland moon-buggy track. The site is 500 m. walk from the town, close to the Viking Castle of Fyrkat and the lovely old town of Mariager.

How to find it: From E45 exit 35, take road 579 towards Hobro Centrum. Site is well signed to the right, just after railway bridge.

General Details: Open 30 March - 30 Sept. Shop (order bread before 9 pm). Swimming pool (high season). Children's play areas. Table tennis. Basketball. Football. Minigolf. Fishing 7 km. Bicycle hire near. TV lounge. Kitchen. Laundry. Chemical disposal. Motorcaravan services. Car wash.

Charges 1999: Per adult Dkr. 50 - 57; child (2-11 yrs) 26 - 30; electricity 20. No credit cards.

Reservations: Contact site. Address: Skivevej 35, 9500 Hobro. Tel: 98.52.32.88. FAX: 98.52.56.61.

DENMARK - Jylland

2170 Klim Strand Camping, Klim, Fjerritslev

Large coastal, family holiday site, with quality facilities - a paradise for children.
This privately owned 'TopCamp' site has the full complement of quality facilities, including its own fire engine and trained staff. The site has 700 numbered pitches, all with electricity (10A), laid out in rows, many divided by trees and hedges and shade in parts. Some 300 of these are 'luxury' pitches, fully serviced with electricity, water, drain and 18 channel TV hook-up. There are also 24 cabins to rent on site. The two main, centrally situated, heated sanitary buildings are very large, housing spacious showers, washbasins (some in cubicles) and British style WCs. A popular feature is the separate children's room with child size/height WCs, basins and half height shower cubicles. There are also baby rooms, bathrooms for families and disabled visitors, sauna, solariums, whirlpool bath, hairdressing rooms, fitness room, and even a dog bathroom. Two smaller sanitary units are located by reception and beach and there are well equipped kitchens and barbecue areas with dishwashing sinks, microwaves, gas hobs, and two TV lounges. All hot water, showers, cooking facilities and many family bathrooms are free of charge. On site activities include an outdoor water-slide complex, indoor heated swimming pool complex, tennis courts, pony riding (all free), numerous children's play areas, an adventure playground with aerial cable ride, roller skating area and ramp, a crèche, pizzeria and restaurant/bar (open 17.00 Mon-Fri, 12.00 Sat/Sun), supermarket, telephones and tourist information. There is live music and dancing twice a week in high season, bicycle and TV rental and an 18 hole golf course is nearby. Suggested excursions – trips to offshore islands, visits to local potteries, a brewery museum and bird watching on the Bygholm Vejle.

How to find it: Turn off Thisted-Fjerritslev no. 11 road to Klim from where site is signed.

General Details: Open 15 March - 23 Oct. (incl. all amenities). Supermarket. Pizzeria. Restaurant. Bar. Solarium and sauna. Children's playgrounds. Bicycle and TV hire. Fishing. Riding. Golf 10 km. Comprehensive leisure, sporting and entertainment facilities. Laundry. Kitchens. Chemical disposal. Motorcaravan services. Car wash. Chalets for rent.

Charges 2000: Per adult Dkr. 60; child (0-11 yrs) 42; pitch 40 (21/6-21/8 only); 'luxury' pitch 10 - 25 (acc. to season); electricity 25. Credit cards accepted.

Reservations: Essential for mid June - end August. Address: Havvejen 167, Klim, 9690 Fjerritslev. Tel: 98.22.53.40. FAX: 98.22.57.77. E-mail: ksc@klim-strand.dk.

2160 Hirtshals Camping, Hirtshals

Traditional coastal site, close to ferry port for Norway and the North Sea Centre.
This tidy, family run site is well placed for touring the tip of Jutland, and is close to the ferry port (1 km.) from which there are regular crossings to Norway. On the edge of a residential area and facing the Skagerrak (it can be a little windy) it has direct access to the beach. The 155 numbered touring pitches, all with electricity (10A) are on open, flat, sandy grass and are separated into rows by low wooden rails, with more sheltered pitches for tents behind reception, together with 10 cabins for rent. All amenities, including reception, are in a neat modern block at the entrance. They include good sanitary facilities with modern, bright fittings, including controllable hot showers (on payment), washbasins in cubicles, facilities for babies and disabled people, and a laundry with commercial machines. In high season a small `portacabin' style block provides a further shower, washbasin and WC (for each sex) by the pitches furthest from the entrance. Dishwashing sinks with free hot water, gas rings and an oven are to be found in the campers' kitchen. There is a well stocked shop (with takeaway in season), a good children's playground and a clubroom with TV. Restaurants, supermarkets and a swimming pool are to be found in the town. For the well protected or warm blooded, the main attraction of this site is the sea, with rewarding fishing and watersports. The coast from Hirtshals right up to the tip is almost one long beach with tide washed golden sand hard enough even to carry local buses - a quite memorable sight. Just north is Tversted, an ideal forest picnic spot, or 10 km. from Skagen is the fascinating buried church, or you might like to visit the remarkable Danish 'Sahara', the enormous dunes of Råbjerg Mile.

How to find it: Site is clearly signed from road nos. 13, 15 and 55. It is on the outskirts of the town.

General Details: Open 1 May - 12 Sept. Small shop, others and restaurants in the town. Club room and TV. Children's playground. Bicycle hire. Barbecue. Kitchen. Freezer. Laundry. Fish preparation sinks. Chemical disposal. Motorcaravan service point. Bus services. Cabins for hire.

Charges 1999: Per adult Dkr. 48 - 52; child (2-12 yrs) 20 - 25; electricity 20. No credit cards.

Reservations: Contact site. Address: Kystvejen 6, 9850 Hirtshals. Tel: 98.94.25.35. FAX: 98.94.33.43.

2180 Nordstrand Camping, Frederikshavn

Excellent site 2 km. from Frederikshavn and ferries to Sweden and Norway.
This is another 'TopCamp' site and provides all the comforts one could possibly need with all the attractions of the nearby beach, town and port. The 430 large pitches are attractively arranged in small enclosures of 9-13 units surrounded by hedges and trees. Many of the hedges are of flowering shrubs and this makes for a very pleasant atmosphere. 250 pitches have electricity and drainage, a further 20 have water and there are 16 on hardstandings. There are 64 seasonal units, plus 23 cabins and 3 caravans for rent. The roads are all paved and the site is well lit and fenced with the barrier locked at night. Sanitary facilities are in two very large, centrally located, modern blocks and provide spacious showers (on payment), washbasins in cubicles and British style WCs, together with some family bathrooms, rooms for disabled people and babies, and laundry with free ironing. All are spotlessly clean. Good kitchens at each block provide mini-ovens, microwaves, hobs (free of charge) and dishwashing sinks with free hot water. Leisure activities include minigolf, tennis, table tennis, billiards, chess, and fishing. The reception complex also houses a café (open in high season), with a telephone pizza service available at other times. A supermarket, tourist information, telephone and post box also on site. The beach is a level, paved 200 m. walk. An indoor swimming pool complex is 2 km. There is much to see in this area of Denmark and this site would make a very comfortable holiday base.

How to find it: Turn off the main no. 40 road 2 km. north of Frederikshavn at roundabout just north of railway bridge. Site is signed.

General Details: Open 1 April - 22 Oct. Supermarket (all season). Cafè (15/6-15/8). Pizza service. Solarium. Beach. Fishing 200 m. Bicycle hire. Children's playgrounds. Laundry. Kitchens. Car wash. Chemical disposal. Motorcaravan services. Chalets and caravans for rent.

Charges 2000: Per adult Dkr. 41 - 53; child (0-11 yrs) 27 - 34; pitch 24 - 30; dog 10; electricity 6A 25, 10A 26. Credit cards accepted.

Reservations: Essential for high season and made with deposit (Dkr. 400). Address: Apholmenvej 40, 9900 Frederikshavn. Tel: 98.42.93.50 FAX: 98.43.47.85. E-mail: nordstrand-camping@post10.tele.dk.

2215 DCU Camping Odense, Odense

Ideal base from which to explore this fairy-tale city.
Although within the confines of the city, this site is hidden away amongst mature trees and is therefore fairly quiet. The 225 pitches, of which 145 have electricity (10A), are on level grass with small hedges and shrubs dividing the area into bays. There are a number of seasonal units on site together with 14 cabins for rent. The large sanitary unit provides up to the minute facilities including British style WCs, washbasins in cubicles, controllable hot showers with divider and seat, 4 family bathrooms, hand dryers and hairdryers, a baby room, and an excellent suite for disabled visitors. In addition there is a well equipped kitchen with gas hobs, extractor hoods and dishwashing sinks, plus a laundry with washing machines and dryer. All hot water and cooking facilities are free of charge. Other on-site amenities include a shop, swimming pool complex, games marquee, TV room, large children's playground with bouncing cushion, table tennis, minigolf, ball games field and bicycle hire. A good network of cycle paths lead into the city. The Odense Adventure Pass (available at the site) allows unrestricted free travel on public transport within the city limits, free admission to the swimming baths and a free daily newspaper, with varying discounts on other attractions.

How to find it: From E20 exit 50, turn towards Odense Centrum, site entrance is 3 km. on left immediately beside the Texaco Garage.

General Details: Open 22 March - 20 October. Shop. Laundry. Kitchen. Swimming pool. Games marquee. Table tennis. TV. Children's playground. Minigolf. Bicycle hire. Tourist information. Telephone. Chemical disposal. Motorcaravan services.

Charges 1999: Per adult Dkr. 54; child 27; electricity 15 - 20.

Reservations: Contact site. Address: Odensevej 102, Odense S. Tel: 66.11.47.02. FAX: 65.91.73.43. E-mail: odense@dcu.dk.

DENMARK - Fyn

2200 Bøjden Strandcamping, nr Faaborg

Well equipped family site with beach, in the beautiful 'Garden of Denmark'.

Bøjden is located in one of the most beautiful corners of southwest Fyn (Funen in English) known as the 'Garden of Denmark'. Separated from the beach only by a hedge, many pitches have sea views as the site slopes gently down from the road. Arranged in rows on mainly level grassy terraces and divided into groups by hedges and some trees, the 300 pitches (200 for touring units) all have electricity (10A). Four special motorcaravan pitches also have water and waste points, and there is also a service point. The superb quality, heated sanitary building is centrally located and provides British style WCs, washbasins in cubicles, controllable showers with divider and seat (on payment), three family bathrooms, a baby room and excellent facilities for disabled people. Also in this building is a well appointed kitchen with hobs, oven and sinks, plus a laundry with washing machine and dryer. The older unit near reception provides more WCs, basins and showers, and a further kitchen. Cooking facilities and hot water are free, showers are extra. A swimming pool (13 x 9 m) and paddling pool (8 x 5 m.) with a sun terrace are open during suitable weather conditions. On-site amenities include a well equipped fenced toddlers playground, separate adventure playground, small aviary, games and TV rooms, solarium, fenced dog exercise area, bicycle and boat hire and a barbecue area. Restaurant and bar 100 m. from the site. Everyone will enjoy the beach (Blue Flag) for bathing, boating and water sports. The water is too shallow for shore fishing but boat trips can be arranged. Bøjden is a delightful site for an entire holiday, while remaining a very good centre for excursions.

How to find it: From Faaborg follow road no. 8 to Bøjden and site is on right 500 m. before ferry terminal (from Fynshav).

General Details: Open 1 April - 15 Sept. Shop. Takeaway. Swimming pool (15/5-25/8). Solarium. Children's adventure playgrounds. TV and games rooms. Bicycle and boat hire. Fishing. Riding. Minigolf. Golf 12 km. Kitchen. Laundry. Telephone. Tourist information, Chemical disposal. Motorcaravan services. Cabins for rent.

Charges 1999: Per adult Dkr. 52; child (under 12 yrs) 28; pitch (16/6-17/8 only) 25; electricity 20. Credit cards accepted.

Reservations: Recommended for high season - write for details. Address: Bøjden Landevej 12, 5600 Faaborg. Tel: 62.60.12.84. FAX: 62.60.12.94.

2205 Løgismosestrand Camping, Hårby

Countryside site with own beach and pool, surrounded by picturesque villages.

The owner of this site is the son of another Alan Rogers' site owner, and was the youngest campsite owner in Denmark when he purchased this site. Since that time he has refurbished the older sanitary unit, also built a new unit and, more recently, a new swimming pool (8 x 14 m) with a paddling pool (6 x 6 m), for which there will be small charge. The 200 pitches, some with a little shade, are arranged in rows and groups divided by hedges and small trees, 190 with electricity (10A). The sanitary units, heated and kept spotlessly clean, have British style WCs, washbasins in private cubicles, roomy showers with seat and divider (on payment), hairdressing and shaving areas, baby room, bathrooms for families and the disabled. The new unit also houses a very good laundry with sink, washing machine and dryer, plus an excellent fully fitted kitchen with stainless steel worktops, inset gas hobs, microwave and dishwashing sinks. Cooking facilities and hot water are free, only showers are extra. Other on-site amenities include a large undercover games room, grassy playing field, adventure playground, minigolf, table tennis, bicycle and boat hire, pony riding. There is a large well stocked shop and a snack-bar (in season) with takeaway serving burgers, hot dogs, chicken, fish and chips at reasonable prices.

How to find it: Southeast of Hårby via Sarup and Nellemose to Løgismose Skov. Site is well signed. Lanes are narrow, large outfits should take care.

General Details: Open 27 March - 18 Sept. Shop. Snackbar/takeaway. Kitchen. Laundry. Swimming pool (1/6-1/9). Beach. Minigolf. Table tennis. Bicycle and boat hire. Pony riding on site, stables 2 km. Children's playground. Golf 12 km. Telephone. Tourist information. Chemical disposal. Motorcaravan services. Cabins for rent.

Charges guide: Per adult Dkr. 44; child 22; pitch 20 (23/6-10/8 only); electricity 18.

Reservations: Essential for high season - write for details. Address: Løgismoseskov 7, 5683 Hårby. Tel: 64.77.12.50. FAX: 64.77.12.51.

2220 Billevænge Camping, Spodsbjerg, nr Rudkøbing

Quiet, family run site in a woodland near beach on island of Langeland.

Billevænge is a family owned and managed site - not pretentious, but comfortable, attractive, sheltered, and very acceptable for a quiet relaxing holiday in lovely surroundings. The central point of the site is the duck pond, animal enclosure and children's play area. The 142 pitches are on sloping grass separated into groups by mature hedges and trees, with some pitches flatter than others. Most have electrical connections. A more open area, furthest from reception and the toilet facilities, is mainly reserved for tents. Site facilities are grouped together at the entrance. The original block, which has been refurbished, is kept clean and provides roomy showers (on payment), washbasins, some with partitions and curtain, a baby room, British style WCs, and power points. A nice feature is the family shower rooms including one large and one small toilet. Dishwashing facilities (metered hot water) are provided in the campers' kitchen (gas rings) and there is a laundry. Lovely walks may be had through the surrounding woods and the beach (shallow water, safe for children) is reached by footpath direct from the site (600 m). In addition to bathing, there are facilities for windsurfing and sailing and bicycles can be hired. Boats can be hired for fishing and the site is proud of its record for really big catches. The Danes have conquered the problems of travel between the multitude of islands by an outstanding expertise in bridge building. An excellent example can be seen here when one drives past Svendborg on Funen, across the bridge to Tasinge and then the longer, handsome structure to Langeland – the 'long island'. The island also has many old windmills and castles to visit.

How to find it: From Svendborg, cross bridges to Langeland and Rudkøbing on road no. 9, cross the island to Spodsbjerg and ferry terminal (about £20 for van and 2 persons - a bridge planned, but with toll). Turn right in town following signs 1.8 km. south to site.

General Details: Open 1 April - 31 Oct. Shop. Club room. TV room. Barbecue. Minigolf. Bicycle hire. Tourist information. Telephone. Post box. Children's playground and pets corner. Beach and watersports. Fishing 2 km. Laundry and cooking facilities. Chemical disposal. Motorcaravan service point. Cabins and caravans for rent.

Charges guide: Per person Dkr. 47; child (0-11 yrs) 25; pitch fee (21/6-3/8 only, not tents) 15; electricity 18.

Reservations: Recommended for high season. Write for details. Address: Spodsbjergvej 182, 5900 Rudkøbing. Tel: 62.50.10.06. FAX: 62.50.10.46. E-mail: billevng@post5.tele.dk.

2240 Lysabildskov Camping and Feriecenter, Lysabildskov, Sydals

Small, neat, attractive coastal site on island of Als, with excellent facilities and a warm welcome.

Located in the heart of the countryside, 600 m. from a small rocky beach, this well laid out, attractive site provides all the comforts one could need for a relaxed holiday or shorter stay. The site has 192 large grassy pitches all with electricity (10A) separated into small secluded areas by mature rose and flowering shrub hedges. The centrally located sanitary block is in the older style, but has been totally refurbished inside providing roomy showers, basins with dividers/curtains and British style WCs, plus family bathrooms, facilities for disabled people and a baby room with bath. There is free hot water throughout. In addition there is a laundry and a campers' kitchen with dishwashing sinks and electric cooking hobs. These facilities are supplemented by further facilities which serve the swimming pool, apartments and reception complex and house further WCs and washbasins. The site has an outdoor heated swimming pool and children's pool (charged Dkr. 6 per day), sauna, solarium, jacuzzi (38°C), and a huge billiard room/TV lounge, tennis courts, ball games area, children's playground and playhouse. Fishing and windsurfing are possible from the beach. Well stocked shop with fast food service. The island of Als is connected to mainland Jutland by an excellent toll-free bridge. There are numerous possibilities for day trips to Søndersborg, Flensburg and Aabenra and miles of country lanes for cycling and walking surround the site.

How to find it: From Søndersborg drive towards Kegnæs on road no. 427, then towards Vibøge-Lysabild then follow the camp signs to Lysabildskov.

General Details: Open 1 April - 30 Sept. Shop. Takeaway (1/5-15/8). Swimming pool and children's pool (1/5-15/8). Sauna, solarium. and jacuzzi. Table tennis. Trampoline. Billiards. Boules. TV lounge. Barbecue area. Tennis. Ball games area. Children's playground. Fishing 600 m. Windsurfing. Telephones. Tourist information. Laundry. Cooking facilities. Chemical disposal. Motorcaravan services. Apartments and cabins for rent.

Charges 1999: Per person Dkr. 49 - 57; child 27 - 30; dog 5; electricity 20. No credit cards.

Reservations: Essential for high season (late June-mid Aug). Write to site. Address: Skovforten 4, Lysabildskov, 6470 Sydals. Tel: 74.40.43.98. FAX: 74.40.43.86. E-mail: lysabildskov@dk-camp.dk.

DENMARK - Lolland / Sjælland

2235 Sakskøbing Grøn Camping, Sakskøbing

Useful transit site within easy reach of Puttgarden - Rødby ferry.
This small, traditional style site provides a useful stop-over on the route from Germany to Sweden. There are 125 level grassy pitches, most with electricity (10A) and, although there are a fair number of seasonal units, one can usually find space. Two sanitary units provide basic, older style facilities, including push-button hot showers on payment, some curtained washbasin cubicles, a baby room, plus cooking, dish-washing and laundry facilities. There are no facilities for disabled persons. On site is a children's play-ground and the pool at the nearby sports centre is said to be the most modern in Europe. The site has a well stocked shop, which is open long hours, but the attractive town centre is semi-pedestrianised, and has good range of shops and a supermarket. The town is noted for its unusual 'smiling' water tower, which you will pass on the way to the site.

How to find it: From E47, exit 46, turn towards town on road 9. Turn right at traffic lights towards town centre (site is signed), cross railway and then turn right again, and site entrance is 250 m. on left.

General Details: Open all year. Shop. Laundry. Children's playground. Motorcaravan services. Cabins for rent.

Charges 1999: Per adult Dkr. 48; child 24; electricity 20. Credit cards accepted.

Reservations: Advised for last week June to end of July. Address: Saxes Allé 15, 4990 Sakskøbing. Tel: 54.70.47.57.

2260 DCU - Camping, Nærum, nr Copenhagen

Sheltered, friendly site with new enthusiastic management, well situated for visiting Copenhagen.
Obviously everyone arriving in Sjælland will want to visit 'wonderful, wonderful Copenhagen', but like all capital cities, it draws crowds during the holiday season and traffic to match. The site is near enough to be convenient but distant enough to afford peace and quiet (apart from the noise of nearby traffic) and a chance of relaxing after sightseeing. Nærum, one of the Danish Camping Union sites, is only 15 km. and very near a suburban railway (400 m. on foot) that takes you to the city centre. The long narrow site covers a large area alongside the ancient royal hunting forests, adjacent to the small railway line and the main road. Power lines do cross the site but there is lots of grassy open space. The 275 touring pitches are in two areas - in wooded glades taking about six units each (mostly used by tents) or on more open meadows where electrical connections (6A) are available. There are two modern toilet blocks. The one in the meadow area has been refurbished and has free, controllable hot showers, partitioned washbasins with hot water and WCs. A new, very good block at reception can be heated and also provides a laundry, dish-washing and a campers' kitchen. Good facilities are provided for babies and the disabled, and four new family bathrooms (free). General amenities include a shop, club room, TV, laundry, barbecue, playing field and playground. A full range of sporting facilities is within easy reach of the site and a café/restaurant within a few hundred metres. Nærum is a useful site to know for Copenhagen, but is also very near to the interesting friendly shopping complex of Rødøvre and the amusement park at Bakken.
Note: Should you wish to drive into the city, there is a very useful cheap car park on the quay-side. It is within easy walking distance of the centre and is located where the Kalvebød Brygge meets the Langebrø bridge (suitable for motorcaravans and caravans).

How to find it: From E55/E47, take Nærum exit (no. 14), 15 km. north of Copenhagen. Turn right at first set of traffic lights (site signed), right on road 19 at second lights, cross bridge and turn left, following signs to site.

General Details: Open early April - mid Sept. Shop. Reception and shop closed 12.00 - 14.00 and 22.00 - 07.00. Café/restaurant near. Club room and TV. Laundry and cooking facilities. Barbecue. Children's play field and adventure playground. Tourist information. Telephone. Motorcaravan service point and car wash. Train service to Copenhagen.

Charges 1999: Per adult high season Dkr. 54; child (0-11 yrs) 27; electricity 18; environmental charge 10; cabin (4 persons) 365.

Reservations: Write for details. Address: Ravnebakken, 2850 Nærum. Tel: 45.80.19.57. FAX: 45.80.11.78. E-mail: naerum@dcu.dk.

2250 Hillerød Camping, Hillerød

Neat, well run site well placed for touring Sjælland, Copenhagen and ferry to Sweden.

The northern-most corner of Sjælland is packed with interest, based not only on fascinating parts of Denmark's history but also its attractive scenery. Centrally situated, Hillerød is a hub of main roads from all directions, with this neat camp site clearly signed from the town. It has a park-like setting in a residential area with 5 acres of well kept grass and some attractive trees. There are 92 pitches of which 50 have electricity (10A) and these are marked. The site amenities are all centrally located in modern, well maintained buildings which are kept very clean. The bright, airy, heated toilet block is older in style with curtained, free hot showers, washbasins with partitions and curtain and a laundry room (free iron). Facilities for babies can also be used by disabled people. Basic supplies are kept in a small shop located with reception, adjacent to a splendid, large, comfortable club room with sofas, tables and chairs, children's corner with video and books. A campers' kitchen adjoins the facilities for dishwashing (free hot water). Tennis, golf and an indoor swimming pool are all within 1 km. The centre of Hillerød, like so many Danish towns, has been pedestrianised making shopping or outdoor refreshment a pleasure. Visit Frederiksborg Slot, a fine Renaissance Castle and home of the Museum of Danish national history. An excellent new electric train service every 10 minutes (20 mins. walk) makes a car unnecessary for a visit to Copenhagen. Hillerød, however is a fine base in itself, only 25 km. from the ferries at Helsingør and the crossing to Sweden.

How to find it: Follow road no. 6 bypassing town to south until sign at junction (signed to Frederiksborg Slot). Turn towards town and site is signed to the right.

General Details: Open Easter - 1 Oct. Small shop. Good club room with TV. Children's playground. Bicycle hire. Tennis and indoor pool near. Riding 2 km. Golf 3 km. Tourist information. Telephone. Laundry and cooking facilities. Motorcaravan services. Chemical disposal. Cabins and tents to rent.

Charges 2000: Per person Dkr. 56; child (0-11 yrs) 28; electricity 20. Credit cards accepted.

Reservations: Recommended for high season - write for details. Address: Blytækkervej, 3400 Hillerød. Tel: 48.26.48.54. FAX: as phone.

DISCOUNT VOUCHERS

Between pages 192/193 you will find two Discount Vouchers which will provide you with potential savings of more than the cost of the Guide itself!
(valid 1 Jan - 31 Dec 2000 only)

Voucher A - Campsite Discount Voucher

This voucher entitles the holder to the relevant discounts or special offers at those campsites featured in this guide which have a small Alan Rogers' logo beneath their Site Report. This section of the voucher should be retained by the holder, but made available for inspection at the campsite for the purpose of verifying your entitlement to the relevant discount or offer.

Voucher B - Travel and Breakdown Insurance

This voucher entitles the holder to a discount of 10% on Travel & Breakdown Insurance arrangements made via this Guide, as advertised between pages 160/161. To arrange cover please complete the proposal and send this, together with the appropriate premium and this voucher to: Deneway Guides & Travel Ltd., Chesil Lodge, West Bexington, Dorchester DT2 9DG. Fax 01308 898017.

A proposal form and the discount voucher will need to be completed and sent to Deneway Guides & Travel along with payment for the relevant premium in all circumstances except in very urgent cases (ie. those within seven days of departure) when we can arrange cover via telephone or (preferably) by fax .

FINLAND

Finland covers an area of 338,000 sq. km. (13,500 sq. miles) and consists of 10% water (forming 187,888 lakes), 69% forest and only 8% cultivated land. The maximum length is 1,160 km (721 miles), the maximum width is 540 km (336 miles). Being such a long country, there is a considerable difference in the type of landscape between north and south, with the gently rolling, rural landscape of the south giving way to the hills and vast forests of the north and treeless fells and peat-lands of Lapland. Forests of spruce, pine and birch are inhabited by hares, elks and occasional wolves and bears. It is well worth noting that, every few kilometres, signs depicting an elk warn motorists of the danger of these beasts dashing onto the road, with an average of 40 motorists per day being involved in accidents with this animal. If you are unfortunate enough to hit one, it must be reported to the police.

An International Camping Carnet or the Finnish Camping Card (which may be obtained from the first site you visit) are required at many sites. We have deliberately chosen the beautiful Saimaa Lake District in the southeast of the country as an introduction, due to its popularity and easy access by excellent roads. Further information can be obtained from:

The Finnish Tourist Board, 30/35 Pall Mall, London SW1Y 5LP
Tel: 020 7839 4048. Fax: 020 7321 0696

Population
5,054,982 (1993); density 15 per sq. km.

Capital
Helsinki.

Climate
Summer is warm and bright due to the close proximity to the Gulf Stream, with average temperatures in Helsinki ranging from 13.7°C in May to 20.5°C in July; winter months -0.4°C in Dec (31°F) to 6.4°C (44°F) in April.

Language
Finnish - but most young people speak English.

Currency
The Markka or Finnmark, abbreviated to FIM, and divided into 100 pennies (p). Coins are 10p, 50p, 1, 5 and 10 FIM with notes of 20, 50, 100, 500 and 1,000 FIM.

Banks
Open 09.15 - 16.15 hrs Mon - Fri. Outside normal banking hours currency can be exchanged in most hotels or large department stores, or at harbours and railway stations.
Credit cards: are widely accepted in stores, petrol stations and on some campsites.

Post Offices
Open 09.00 - 17.00 hrs, Mon - Fri.

Time
GMT plus 2 hours.

Public Holidays
New Year; Epiphany; Good Fri; Easter Mon; May Day; 1st Sat after Ascension; Whit Sat; All Saints, 1st Sat in Nov; Independence Day, 6 Dec; Christmas, 25, 26 Dec. Other holidays are Vappu Night, 30 Apr, a spring festival and `Midsummer', nearest Sat to 24 June.

Telephone
The dialling code for Finland is 00358. When calling the UK dial 99044 before the trunk number. Local calls can be made from telephone booths using 1, 5 or 10 FIM coins. Phone-card phones operate on cards purchased in advance (from Teleshops or some post offices).

Shops
Open 09.00 - 17.00 or 18.00 hrs on Mon - Fri and on Sat 09.00 - 14.00 or 15.00 hrs, although supermarkets are usually open to 20.00 hrs during the week. Department stores and shopping malls usually remain open to 18.00 hrs on Sat. The underground shopping arcade adjacent to the main railway station in Helsinki is open until 20.00 hrs every day. Butane is not available.

Motoring
Main roads in Finland are excellent and relatively uncrowded outside city limits; you can virtually have miles of dual-carriageway or motorway standard roads to yourself. The Finns are tolerant and cautious drivers and appear to adhere strictly to speed limits. You may encounter a few unsurfaced minor roads off the beaten track but these are usually quite safe for towing, providing you keep your speed down to about 30 mph.
Do not drink and drive - penalties are severe (even jail sentences) if any alcohol is detected.
Speed limits: Caravans and motorhomes (3.5 tons) 31 mph (50 kph) in built up areas, caravans 50 mph (80 kph) all other roads, motorhomes 50 - 63 mph (80 - 100 kph) on other roads and 50 - 75 mph (80 - 120 kph) on motorways. Note: there are no emergency phones on the motorway network.
Tolls: There are no toll charges on motorways.

Overnighting
Not allowed outside campsites.

The sites in FINLAND featured in this guide
are shown on the map on page 372

FINLAND

2900 Camping Kokonniemi, Porvoo

Delightful small campsite 50 km. east of Helsinki.

Convenient for the ferry if travelling along the southeast coast, the old town of Porvoo with its waterfront and old wooden houses warrants a stop. This site is 2 km. west of the town and has a garden-like appearance and a white timber reception area with hanging flower baskets. This building, the service buildings and cottages for hire are in an elevated position and backed by tall pines. At a lower level are 40 unmarked caravan pitches (32 with electricity) placed around the perimeter. These pitches are spacious and separated by a variety of shrubs and fruit bushes. Tents are pitched in the more open centre area. Sanitary facilities with white and grey decor are kept very clean and include British style WCs, hot showers (free) with seat, hooks and mat, washbasins with soap, towels, mirror and shaving points. There is a laundry area and a campers' kitchen which doubles for dishwashing. To the side of this building is the barbecue house with pine bench seating. Although beside the Kokonniemi sports centre and lake, on site there is a sauna, volleyball, badminton, bike hire and two children's play areas. Snacks and light meals are available at the café area adjoining reception and a small shop provides milk, bread, ice cream and confectionery.

How to find it: Leave no. 7/E3 Helsinki - Porvoo road at end of motorway and join road 55 for 4 km. Site is clearly signed.

General Details: Open 2 June - 20 Aug. (limited services from 14 Aug). Small shop. Café. Sauna. Bicycle hire. Badminton. Volleyball. Sports centre and lake adjacent. Barbecue house. Chemical disposal. Cottages for hire.

Charges 2000: Per unit FIM 90; tent with 1 person 45; electricity 21. Some credit cards accepted, no Eurocheques.

Reservations: May be necessary for mid-summer/July: Address: 06100 Porvoo. Tel: (0)19 581 967 or (0)9 6138 3210. FAX: (0)9 713 713. E-mail: myyntipalvelu@lomaliitto.fi.

2903 Camping Kayralampi, Kouvola

Busy southern lakeside site 5 km. from Kouvola in the Province of Kymi.

This campsite appeals to families as it is located near an amusement park which, like the campsite, is run by the Children's Day Foundation. A footbridge leads from the site to the park which is across the road and well away from the site so that no noise carries. The site itself, which is under the control of a manager, is approached by way of a short country roadway leading to reception. Centrally positioned are the timbered service buildings and café. The adequate sanitary blocks with lemon, grey and white decor were very clean when we visited and include British style WCs, facilities for the disabled, washbasins, towels, spacious showers (free) and clothes lockers. There is also a laundry and drying room and a campers' kitchen and dishwashing area. There are 160 unmarked pitches, including the tent area, and 100 have electrical connections (16A). Many pitches are placed between trees and shrubs on level but rough ground, some are in a more open area towards the lake with tents alongside. There are also 35 wooden cottages for hire. Other on site facilities include a double tennis court, minigolf, boats for hire, children's play area, two barbecue houses, 1 smoke and 4 electric saunas. Entrance to the amusement park is free for campers (a pass is given), but amusement rides are charged. Basic food such as bread and milk is sold on site with a supermarket complex within 4 km.

How to find it: Site is at junction of roads 6 and 15, 5 km. east of Kouvola and is clearly signed.

General Details: Open all year. Basic food supplies available. Tennis. Minigolf. Boat hire. Children's play area. Saunas. Barbecue huts. Amusement park. Chemical disposal. Motorcaravan services.

Charges guide: Per caravan or tent incl. 1 person FIM 45, 2-5 persons 70 (without Finnish camping card); with camping card 40 or 65; electricity 16.

Reservations: May be necessary for mid-summer/July: Address: Kanuunakuja 1, 45200 Kouvola. Tel: (0)5 321 1226. FAX: (0)5 321 1203.

FINLAND

2906 Taavetti Lomakeskus Ja Camping, Taavetti

Peaceful campsite on the shores of Lake Kivijärvi.

This campsite is situated in the commune of Luumäki, an area of natural beauty, Kivijärvi being the largest of 50 lakes. At the entrance to the site, just off road no. 6, stand red timbered buildings which house reception, shop, café and restaurant. Beyond this area a road follows the lake to the pitches, sanitary buildings and cottages for hire. There are 28 unmarked caravan pitches all with electrical connections (16A), some amongst the clearing in the trees, others nearer the lakeside. There are also 170 places for tents and 30 cottages for hire. The two sanitary blocks, one of an older design, were clean when we visited and have red decor with pine ceilings. Facilities include hot showers (free), washbasins, soap dispensers, towels, mirrors, electric points, single WCs, plus some in cabins with washbasins. Other facilities include a campers' kitchen and dishwashing area, washing machine and drying cabinet, chemical disposal and waste water point. The pleasant open style barbecue house, part of the kitchen area, has wooden bench seating. A second is at the beach. There is lake swimming, tennis court, volleyball, crazy golf, TV room, children's play area and 3 saunas. A small shop sells basic groceries such as bread and milk and soft drinks, coffee, snacks, breakfast or dinner can be ordered from the cafe/restaurant (4/6-15/8). The town of Taavetti is within 4 km, is historically interesting and has an assortment of shops, banks etc.

How to find it: Site is clearly signed, 500 m. from road no. 6 (towards Lappeenranta).

General Details: Open 5 June - 13 August. Small shop. Café (all season). Restaurant (1/6-14/8). Sports facilities as above. Fishing. Bicycle hire. Laundry facilities. Chemical disposal. Chalets to rent.

Charges 2000: Per unit FIM 80; 1 person tent 40; electricity 18. Some credit cards accepted, no Eurocheques.

Reservations: are advisable for mid-summer/July. Address: 54510 Uro, Taavetti. Tel: (0)5 425 510 or (0)9 6138 3210. FAX: (0)9 713 713. E-mail: myyntipalvelu@lomaliitto.fi.

2909 Camping Ukonniemi, Imatra

Secluded site in South Karelia near one of the highest waterfalls in Finland.

This campsite offers a tranquil location within the Imatra Leisure Centre, 3 km. from the town centre where the incredible Imatra Falls can be seen during the summer season. The Leisure Centre itself covers an area of 600 hectares on the Salpausselka ridge and has a changing terrain to suit many activities, including this 10 hectare campsite. The site is under the control of a manager and is truly 'camping in the trees' with 37 unmarked pitches, all with electrical connections (10A) and many with water points, plus 84 tent places and 35 cottages. The reception and café area is at the entrance with the sanitary block on the main avenue to the left. Kept clean and well maintained, this is a red timber building with green and white colour scheme. Facilities include free hot showers, washbasins with mirrors, shaver points and cabins with WCs, washbasins, soap dispensers and towels. Facilities for the disabled, dishwashing in a campers' kitchen, and a laundry room. There is lake swimming, sauna, fishing, lake cruising, running tracks, a lakeside restaurant, etc. all within the complex. For children, swings are located in the trees plus two play areas with slides, playhouse etc. Bread and milk are on sale at reception with shopping needs, banks, etc. in Imatra. Parts of this town are on the border zone with Russia.

How to find it: From Lappeenranta on road E18, site is clearly signed 1 km. after Imatra area sign.

General Details: Open 9 June - 13 August. Cafe. Lakeside restaurant. Bread and milk sold. Children's play areas. Lake swimming. Fishing, bicycle hire 1 km. Sauna. Chemical disposal. Chalets to rent.

Charges 2000: Per unit FIM 80; tent incl. 1 person 40; electricity 18. Some credit cards accepted, no Eurocheques.

Reservations: May be advisable for mid-summer/July. Address: Leiritie, 55420 Imatra. Tel: (0)5 472 4055 or (0)9 6138 3210. FAX: (0)9 713 713. E-mail: myyntipalvelu@lomaliitto.fi.

2912 Kultakivi Holiday Village, Punkaharju

Holiday village in forested countryside amid lakes and clearings.

This sprawling, 23 hectare holiday village offers a camping holiday to suit individual needs. You can get away from it all on a quiet secluded lakeside pitch, or participate in the many activities which suit all age groups. At the entrance and parking area stands a large elaborate building housing reception, restaurant and shop. Around this area is the tennis, minigolf, basketball and play area with water slide. The roadways lead into what is best described as a forest park environment with 135 cottages and cabins discreetly situated around the perimeter, mostly at the lakeside. There are 145 caravan pitches with electrical hook-ups (16A) in dry wooded or grassy terrain, with 500 tent places. The main sanitary block, which is well maintained, is situated towards the top of the site beside the TV room, with other WC and shower units at various points. Facilities include British style WCs, washbasins, soap dispensers, towels, mirrors, shaver points and free hot showers. There is a campers' kitchen and a dishwashing and laundry area (incl. in price). Amenities include a barbecue area, 4 family saunas, several beaches and a naturist beach. For the more active there are also jogging tracks and nature trails, fishing, boat and cycle hire. Evening entertainment can include wining, dining or dancing the night away. Although a more lively site, being placed well away from the pitches, the night-time entertainment should not disturb campers.

How to find it: Site is clearly signed off road no. 14, approx. 9 km. south of Punkaharju.

General Details: Open 30 April - 31 Aug. Barbecue area. Jogging and nature trails. Fishing. Boat and bicycle hire. Entertainment. Chemical disposal.

Charges guide: Per unit FIM 70 without camping card, 60 with; electricity 20.

Reservations: Are advisable for mid-summer/July. Address: 58550 Putikko, Punkaharju. Tel: (0)15 645 151. FAX: (0)15 645 110.

2915 Punkaharjun Lomakeskus Ja Camping, Punkaharju

Popular campsite in an area of outstanding beauty.

This campsite is part of a holiday centre and is located near the magnificent Punkaharju ridge. It stands next to the Kesamaa amusement park and enjoys a lakeside environment, making it one of the country's most popular sites. Past the entrance, which is marked by flags, is the reception area and to the right the fun park. There are 500 pitches including tent places, 130 with electrical hook-ups, also many chalets and holiday homes for hire. Some pitches are placed back from the lake, and these are in avenues and separated by shrubs and hedges. Others are by the lakeside and unmarked, with tents to the bottom of the site. The main sanitary block is towards the lake and a smaller one sits further back. Facilities, which are modern, heated and clean, include WCs, washbasins with soap, towels, hand dryer, mirrors, etc. spacious showers (free), and wash cubicles with WCs. Incorporated in the main building are individual campers' kitchens, dishwashing sinks and a laundry area. There is also a restaurant and shop with basic groceries, ice cream, etc. The fun park, which is open in the summer, belongs to the campsite but a separate entrance fee is payable. The other on site facilities are netball, tennis, lakeside beach, boats and bicycles for hire, barbecue area and four saunas. The main attractions outside the holiday centre are the Lusto Forest Museum, Retretti Art Centre and the Valtionhotelli Hotel, the oldest tourist hotel in Finland.

How to find it: Turn off at 'K' sign, 25 km. after Savonlinna on road no. 14 and site is 300 m.

General Details: Camping: 27 May - 26 August; caravans and other accommodation all year. Restaurant (15/6-15/8). Small shop (15/6-15/8). Tennis. Netball. Saunas. Boat and bicycle hire. Fishing. Riding 5 km. Golf 15 km. Fun park adjacent (5/6-12/8). Motorcaravan services. Chemical disposal.

Charges 2000: Per unit FIM 90 - 95; tent for 1 person 45 - 50; electricity 20. Credit cards accepted.

Reservations: Advisable for mid-summer/July. Address: 58450 Punkaharju 2. Tel: (0)15 739 611. FAX: (0)15 441 784.

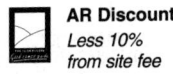

AR Discount
Less 10%
from site fee

FINLAND

2918 Camping Vuohimaki, Savonlinna

Well managed site close to East Finland's most popular resort.

The resort of Savonlinna is built on a chain of islands and is unquestionably the jewel in East Finland's crown. This campsite, on the shores of Lake Pihlajavesi, is only minutes away from the town centre. Although lacking a landscaped appearance it is distinguished by a tall, elegant wooden building, dated late 1800s, which stands to the right of the security barrier and houses reception, restaurant, shop and offices. The camping area is approached by a one way system and there are 100 unmarked pitches for caravans, all with electrical hook-ups, space for 150 tents and 12 cottages for hire. The ground is part sloped, part terraced and the pitches rough but level. This is a more open site than usual, with most of the shade and trees around the perimeter, lakeside and tent area. The two modern, heated sanitary blocks are kept spotlessly clean with grey and white decor and shiny chrome fittings. Facilities include WCs with paper, washbasins, soap and towels, free hot showers and facilities for disabled people. There is a campers' kitchen, dishwashing, barbecue and laundry area with washing machine, clothes line and free hot air dryer. Leisure amenities include volleyball, badminton, minigolf, watersports, boats and bicycle hire and two saunas. For children there are swings and slides. The restaurant serves pizzas, hamburgers, salads, etc. and the shop sells light groceries and confectionery.

How to find it: Site is signed off road no. 14, 3 km. west of Savonlinna.

General Details: Open 2 June - 27 August. Restaurant. Small shop. Volleyball. Badminton. Watersports. Boat and bicycle hire. Fishing. Children's play area. Saunas. Riding 200 m. Chemical disposal.

Charges 2000: Per unit FIM 95; 1 person 46: electricity 21. Some credit cards accepted, no Eurocheques.

Reservations: Advisable for mid-summer/July. Address: 57600 Savonlinna. Tel: (0)15 537 353 or (0)9 6138 3210. FAX: (0)9 713 713. E-mail: myyntipalvelu@lomaliitto.fi.

2922 Camping Taipale, Varkaus

Well laid out family run site alongside a lake in North Savo.

The town of Varkaus, known for its paper industry, is surrounded by water and this campsite is located 3 km. from its centre in peaceful surroundings by the water's edge. Its well kept, orderly appearance gives it instant appeal. The reception and cafe area stand to the left at the entrance and to the right are avenues of individual hardstanding pitches separated by trees and shrubs. There is a total of 90 pitches, some grass and 52 with electrical hook-ups, a large tent area and 16 cottages to hire, placed away from the camping pitches. The grey wooden sanitary block is tastefully decorated with pine interior and grey and white units, all kept spotlessly clean. Facilities include hot showers (free) with curtains, non-slip mats and clothes lockers, WCs with paper, washbasins, long bench mirror and shower for the disabled, etc. There is also a dishwashing area, laundry with drying cabinet, clothes lines, an excellent chemical disposal unit and campers kitchen. Snacks, soft drinks and beer are sold at the cafe, plus basic foodstuffs and souvenirs. On site is a barbecue house, sauna, lake swimming, beach ball, boat hire, bicycle hire, badminton. For children, wooden toys, slides, etc. are to the fore in a garden like space. To the rear of the site a gate leads to a parkland area and a bridge over the old canal, part of the Canal Museum in Varkaus.

How to find it: Site is signed from road no. 5 on road 23, approx. 3 km. from Varkaus at Canal swing bridge.

General Details: Open 25 May - 31 August. Cafe. Sauna. Lake swimming. Boat and bicycle hire. Children's play area.

Charges guide: Per unit with camping card FIM 69; without 86; family tent with card 76, 86 without; 1 person tent 45.

Reservations: Advisable for mid-summer/July. Address: Leiritie, 78250 Varkaus. Tel: (0)17 552 6644. FAX: (0)17 552 6644.

2925 Camping Rauhalahti, Kuopio

Large site on the banks of Lake Kallavesi in North Savo.

This site comes highly recommended, with a reputation for being one of the country's finest campsites. It is consistently busy, which creates a constant buzz of activity. Tubs of coloured flowers garland the forecourt and when campers arrive the flag of their country is hoisted, a welcoming touch and a colourful display when all the nations visit. Reception, which offers a 24 hour service, stands close to the entrance and from here the site is laid out in neat avenues with tarmac roads. Pitches are clearly marked and all have hardstanding. The site is level and landscaped, the exception rather than the norm in Finland. This is a more open site than usual, but it still has adequate trees and shrubs with grass areas for awnings separating each of the 237 pitches which include special ones for larger motorcaravans, all with electrical hook-ups. There are also 300 places for tents and 90 cottages for hire. The two heated, timber sanitary blocks were very clean with stainless steel washbasins, mirrors, soap dispensers, electric points, WCs, free hot showers and facilities for disabled visitors with a shower, WC, and washbasin. There is a baby room, large campers' kitchen/dishwashing, laundry service with free use of drying cabinet, and 'Ecopoints' for rubbish disposal. The restaurant offers a choice of menu serving Finnish lunch or snacks, pizzas, etc. and a mini-shop sells basic foodstuffs. This site forms part of the 80 hectare Rauhalahti recreational area and offers a beach and water sports, with equipment for hire and 3 saunas (2 electric and 1 smoke). For children there is a play room, puppet theatre, also a TV, swimming pool, tennis courts and much more. It is said Kuopio has three focal points, the Puijo Tower, Kuopio market and its harbour on the shores of the lake, all worth a visit.

How to find it: Site is clearly signed on road no. 5, 7 km. south of Kuopio.

General Details: Open 19 May - 3 September. Restaurant (all season). Mini-shop (16/6-15/8). Swimming pool (all season). Fishing. Bicycle hire. Riding. Golf 2 km. Leisure activities detailed above. Chemical disposal. Chalets to rent.

Charges 2000: Per unit FIM 95; family tent 85; electricity 20. Credit cards accepted.

Reservations: Advisable for mid-summer/July. Address: Kiviniementie, 70700 Kuopio. Tel: (0)17 361 2244. FAX: (0)17 262 4004. E-mail: rauhalahti.camping@kuopio.fi.

AR Discount
Every 5th
night free

2928 Camping Visulahti, Mikkeli

Excellent campsite and holiday centre within 4 hours drive of Helsinki.

Mikkeli is capital of the Lake District, sitting at the cross-roads of a network of lakes and the labyrinth of Saimaa islands, with more than 3,000 km. of boating routes in its region. On the shores of a Saimaa lake stands this well equipped campsite which appeals to families and varying age groups. The staff are friendly, helpful and dressed in distinctive yellow T-shirts making them easily identified throughout the complex which comprises 30 hectares of landscaped park-land. From reception, immediately beside the security barrier, tarmac roadways lead past the `Dinosauria' and water slides to the right and caravan pitches and tent places to the left. Alongside the camping area stand the restaurant, canteen, coffee pot, shop, vintage car exhibition and wax museum (the only one in Finland we are told). Beyond here the fun park continues with a motor-park and `mini Finland'. Fitting into the layout are cottages and bungalows for hire. There are around 400 pitches for caravans and tents, 200 with electrical hook-ups (16A), unmarked and laid out in avenues. Although it is an open site, shrubs and flower beds divide it into bays in places. Sanitary facilities are housed in two blocks, one facing the caravan pitches and the other by the lakeside. They are kept very clean with pine interiors and pastel colour walls. There are adequate numbers of WCs, hot showers (free), washbasins with soap, towels, mirrors, etc. and facilities for the disabled. There is also a campers' kitchen, dishwashing and laundry. Barbecue house, sauna and lake swimming. Despite the activity on site the noise level is low, with only slight road traffic during the night. Mikkeli market is worth a visit and a shopping complex with a choice of supermarkets is only minutes away.

How to find it: Site is clearly signed off road no. 5, 5 km. north of Mikkeli.

General Details: Open 18 May - 30 August (Dinosauria, etc. 18 May - 18 August). Fun park with many activities. Restaurant. Barbecue. Sauna. Lake swimming. Chemical disposal. Motorcaravan services.

Charges guide: Per unit FIM 70 without camping card, 60 with card; 1 person tent 35; electricity 17 - 25.

Reservations: Advised for mid-summer/July. Address: 50180 Mikkeli. Tel: (0)15 18 281. FAX: (0)15 176 209.

FINLAND

2930 Camping Koskenniemi, Hartola

Friendly, family run site in attractive riverside setting.

In the Eastern Hame region, 3 km. from the town of Hartola, this campsite is easily reached from Helsinki within a 2½ hour drive. It is in a delightful, quiet situation tucked in off the road and screened by trees, with a river winding its way through the 5.5 hectare site. Reception is incorporated into the attractive building which is the family home, guest house and restaurant. From here the road follows the river past 150 unmarked pitches for caravans and tents, 80 with electrical hook-ups (16A), sited mostly to the left with 10 wooden chalets spread along the river bank. The terrain is grassy, flat and open with trees interspersed and a pond towards the rear, giving it a garden-like appearance. The excellent sanitary block, adjacent to reception, is clean with modern units. A white wooden building, the heated facilities include British style WCs, washbasins with soap and towels, free hot showers, and good facilities for disabled visitors with WC, shower and bench. There is a campers' kitchen, dishwashing sinks, laundry area with machines and free drying room. River fishing is available with a licence, and there are boats to hire, minigolf, sauna and conference room, and two barbecues, (one outside, one gas under cover). For children there is a play room, a small pool table, TV, books, toys and an outdoor playhouse with sand pit. The restaurant offers a varied menu. Bread and milk can be ordered from reception.

How to find it: Site is clearly signed on left off no. 4 road, 3 km. south of Hartola.

General Details: Open all year. Restaurant. Bread and milk to order. River fishing. Boats to hire. Bicycle hire. Minigolf. Sauna. Barbecues. Play room. Golf 2 km. Chemical disposal. Motorcaravan services. Rooms and cottages to let.

Charges 2000: Per unit FIM 75 with camping card; 1 person tent 40; electricity 15. Credit cards accepted.

Reservations: May be necessary for mid-summer/July. Address: 19600 Hartola. Tel: (0)3 716 1135. FAX: (0)3 716 1086. E-mail: email@koskenniemi.com.

2932 Camping Sysmä, Sysmä

Family run site with lots of atmosphere, scenically situated on shores of Lake Päijänne.

This site is set on Finland's second largest lake, referred to as 'the pearl of the Finnish lakes' and 'the lake you can drink'. Here the air is pure with miles of countryside all around. Camping Sysmä, within walking distance of the village, has instant appeal. The reception and café area, with flower baskets and a smell of fresh coffee, stands by the entrance. The owner is friendly and smiling and the busy staff were getting the site fully operational for the season when we visited, the week after opening. There are 100 pitches for tents and 38 for caravans with electrical hook-ups (10A), plus 12 bungalows to hire. Pitches are placed amid many varieties of trees and by the water's edge, giving an overall attractive appearance. Although the various buildings of wooden construction that house all the sanitary and other site facilities look their age, even on the dilapidated side, everything inside was neat, tidy and clean. The facilities in the toilet area include British style WCs, washbasins with soap dispensers and towels, hair dryers, free hot showers with mats and bench seating. Plans are in hand to replace the buildings. There is a campers' kitchen, dishwashing sinks and laundry area. For leisure there is a TV room with comfortable chairs and log fire, table tennis, children's swimming pool and play area, water sports and boats and canoes for hire. Snacks are served at the café and there is a shop and garage at the gate, although all necessary shops, banks, etc. are to be found in Sysmä.

How to find it: Site is clearly signed 600 m. from the village of Sysmä on road no. 314.

General Details: Open 1 June - 31 Aug. Café. Shop at gate. TV room. Table tennis. Children's pool. Play area. Watersports. Boat hire. Chemical disposal. Motorcaravan services.

Charges guide: Per unit FIM 70 (with camping card 60); electricity 15.

Reservations: May be necessary for mid-summer/July. Address: Huitilantie 3, 19700 Sysmä. Tel: (0)3/7171386 or (0)4/00809133. FAX: as phone. E-mail: anne.kurvinen@sci.fi.

GERMANY

As a holiday destination it provides a rich variety of scenic and cultural interest. Although the German people are great travellers and can be found on holiday all over Europe, they nevertheless enjoy camping in their own country and good campsites can be discovered throughout the 16 'Länder'. Not only does the scenery provide great contrast - from the flat lands of the north to the mountains of the south and the forests of the west and east - but as it was only fully unified as one state in 1871, regional characteristics are a strong feature of German life and give a rich variety of folklore and customs. Medieval towns, ancient buildings and picturesque villages abound all over the country and add to the fascination of visiting Germany. Reunification may have provided many problems for politicians and people but has opened up a whole new area which was previously difficult to explore. Great strides are being made, particularly where investment has been attracted, to improve and modernise campsites.
For further information:

German National Tourist Office, Nightingale House, 65 Curzon Street, London W1Y 8NE

Tel: 0891 600100   Fax: 020 7495 6129

Population
80,767,591 (1993); density 226 per sq.km.

Capital
Berlin. After unification in 1990, the German parliament chose Berlin as the national capital and voted to move the seat of government from Bonn to Berlin over a 12 year period.

Climate
In general winters are a little colder and summers a little warmer than in the UK.

Language
German. Most Germans speak some English, but it is appreciated if you try to use any knowledge of German that you have retained.

Currency
The unit of currency is the Deutschmark which comes in notes of 10, 20, 50, 100, 200, 500 and 1,000 deutschmark and coins of DM 0.01 (one Pfennig), 0.02, 0.05, 0.10, 0.20, 0.50, 1, 2 and 5. Exchange facilities in the former GDR may be difficult but there are banks in major towns.

Banks
Banking hours are Mon-Fri 08.30-12.30 and 14.00-16.00 with late opening on Thursdays until 18.00 hrs. Closed Sat.
Credit Cards: are becoming widely accepted but only the major cards are accepted in main department stores and restaurants in the large cities. Girocheques are widely accepted.

Post Offices
Open Mon-Fri 08.00-18.00 and Sat 08.00-12.00.

Time
GMT + 1, or BST + 1 in summer.

Telephone
The code to dial Germany from the UK is 0049.

Public Holidays
New Year's Day; Good Fri; Easter Mon; Labour Day; Ascension; Whit Mon; Unification Day (3 Oct); Christmas, 25, 26 Dec; plus, in some areas, Epiphany (6 Jan), Corpus Christi (22 Jun), Assumption (15 Aug), Reformation (31 Oct) and All Saints (1 Nov).

Shops
Open Mon-Fri 08.30/09.00 to 18.00/18.30, closed Saturday 14.00 (sometimes earlier).

Motoring
An excellent network of (toll-free) motorways (Autobahns) exists in the `West' and the traffic moves fast. Remember in the `East' a lot of road building is going on amongst other works so allow plenty of time when travelling and be prepared for poor road surfaces.
Speed limits: Caravans and motorhomes (2.8 tons) 31 mph (50 kph) or 19 mph (30 kph) in built up areas, 50 mph (80 kph) all other roads for caravans, 63 mph (100 kph) other roads and 81 mph (130 kph) motorways for motorhomes. Lower limits for heavier vehicles.
Parking: Don't park on roads with Priority Road signs. Meters and parking disc zones are in use.

Overnighting
If not forbidden by local regulations, then permitted at 'Rast platz' and on streets, but not open spaces.

Miscellaneous
Recycling: By law all sites must have 5 bins: 3 for glass, 1 for paper 1 for household waste.
Signs: 'Müll' - rubbish disposal; 'Einbahnstrasse' - one-way street.
'Mittagsrühe' - Virtually all campsite receptions shut completely for two hours, usually 13.00 - 15.00 hrs, with some slight variations. Barriers are locked, sometimes for pedestrians too.
Fishing: It is compulsory to pass a test (usually available at campsites providing fishing) on recognition of fish breeds, etc. before you fish.

Useful Addresses

National Motoring Organisations:
Automobil-Club von Deutschland (AVD)
Lyoner Strasse 16, 60528 Frankfurt am Main
Tel: 069 6606-0. Office hours 08.00-17.00
Allgemeiner Deutscher Automobil-Club
(ADAC) Am Westpark 8, 81373 München.
Tel: 089 76760.

GERMANY - North West

3000 Knaus Camping-Park Wingst, Wingst, nr Bremerhaven

Site in northwest near North Sea coast and River Elbe estuary.

With an impressive landscaped entrance, a shop and restaurant to one side and reception to the other, this is a good quality site. It is a rural area with attractive villages, plenty of water and woodland, near to the interesting old port of Bremerhaven with its 29 km. of quays and maritime and fishing museums. The heart of this site is a deep set, small fishing lake and beach. Lightly wooded, pitches are accessed by circular roads on differing levels and terraced where necessary. Because of the design you don't realise that there are 410 pitches, nearly all with electricity and clearly defined by shrubs and trees (290 for touring units). There are two heated toilet blocks, one adjoining reception and one nearer the lake (access by steps from varying levels). The provision is good and well kept, with one block recently renovated. A swimming pool behind the hotel opposite is open to campers (small charge). A zoo for small animals is near, also a riding school with small, quiet Icelandic horses with a good value inclusive daily rate, including lunch.

How to find it: Wingst is on B73 Cuxhaven - Stade road, approx. 8 km. north of Henmoor.

General Details: Open all year except Nov. Restaurant. Children's playground. Minigolf. Table tennis. Fishing. Beach volleyball. Bicycle hire. Barbecue facility with roof. Riding and watersports near. Swimming pool opposite (see above). Chemical disposal. Motorcaravan services. Caravans (10) to rent on site; contact site for details.

Charges 2000: Per person DM 8.75; child (3-14 yrs) 4.50; pitch 7.50 - 12.50; small tent with m/cycle 7.50; dog 4.00; electricity 3.50. No credit cards.

Reservations: Contact site. Address: Schwimmbadallee 13, 21789 Wingst. Tel: 04778/7604. FAX: 04778/7608.

3005 Camping Schnelsen Nord, Hamburg

Good quality site for visiting Hamburg.

Situated some 15 km. from the centre of Hamburg on the northern edge of the town, Schnelsen Nord is a suitable base either for visiting this famous German city, or as a night stop before catching the Harwich ferry or travelling to Denmark. A large number of trees and shrubs offer shade and privacy. There is some traffic noise because the autobahn runs alongside (despite efforts to screen it out) and also some aircraft noise. However, the proximity of the A7 (E45) does make it easy to find. The 145 pitches are of good size (100 sq.m.), on grass with access from gravel roads. All have electricity (6A), are numbered and marked out with small trees and hedges. The single sanitary block isa well constructed modern building with good quality facilities and heated in cool weather. It has free hot water in basins (some private cabins) and on payment for showers and washing up. Only very basic supplies are stocked in reception as the site is only about 10 mins. walk from the restaurants and shops in town. There is a small children's playground, table tennis, swimming pool, tennis courts, golf and fishing within easy reach. Apart from the road traffic 'hum', this is a quiet, well laid out camp. They welcome tourists, but allow no itinerant workers to stay.

How to find it: From A7 autobahn take Schnelsen Nord exit. Stay in outside lane as you will soon need to turn back left; follow signs for Ikea store and site signs.

General Details: Open 1 April - 31 Oct. Shop (basics only). Children's playground. Facilities for the disabled. Washing machines and dryers. Sports facilities nearby.

Charges 1999: Per adult DM 7.00; child (under 13 yrs) 5.00; caravan 14.00; car 4.50; motorcaravan 18.50 - 21.50; tent 12.50 - 13.50; electricity 4.50.

Reservations: Said to be unnecessary. Address: Wunderbrunnen 2, 22457 Hamburg. Tel: 040/5594225. FAX: 040/5507334. E-mail: campingplatz-hamburg@e-online.de.

3020 Campingplatz 'Freie Hansestadt Bremen', Bremen

Small site in pleasant situation just outside the city.

Five kilometres from the city centre and in pleasant 'green belt' surroundings, near to the university, and close to a lake used for bathing and sailing, and an indoor swimming pool, this is a useful little site for visits to Bremen and district. Despite being so near the city, this site has a distinctly rural feel with quite an abundance of wildlife! There are good cycle rides and walks in the municpal woodland next door. It has 100 large pitches (75 for touring units) of at least 100 sq.m. on flat grass marked by stones on frontage, all with electricity and 12 with hardstanding for motorcaravans. The toilet block is heated and of good quality, with British style WCs, free hot water in the washbasins (four private cabins) and sinks, and free fully controllable hot showers with seat and screen. There is a unit for disabled visitors and a baby room. The site becomesvery busy and full over a long season and there is some road noise.

How to find it: From A27 northeast of Bremen take exit 19 and follow signs for University and then for site.

General Details: Open all year. Shop (March-Oct, fresh bread to order). Restaurant (March-Oct). General room. Cooking facilities. Children's playground. Bicycle hire. Barbecue area. Washing machines and dryer. Chemical disposal. Motrorcaravan services. Gas supplies.

Charges 1999: Per person DM 7.50; child (under 16) 4.50; caravan 11.00; tent 7.50 - 11.00; car on pitch 2.50; motorcaravan 15.50 - 18.00, acc. to size; m/cycle 1.00; dog 2.00. Credit cards accepted.

AR Discount
Less 10% on
person charge

Reservations: made for any length, with deposit. Address: Am Stadtwaldsee 1, 28359 Bremen. Tel: 0421/212002. FAX: 0421/219857.

3010 Kur-Camping Röders' Park, Ebsmoor, Soltau

First-class, small, award winning site, close to many amenities.

Although near to Soltau centre (1.5 km), Ebsmoor is a peaceful location, ideal for visits to the famous Luneburg Heath or as a stop on the route to Denmark. Herr and Frau Röders are a happy and dedicated couple who make their visitors most welcome and Herr Röders speaks excellent English. The central feature of the wooded site is a small lake crossed by a wooden bridge. An abundance of trees and shrubs gives a secluded setting to an already well cared for appearance. Röders' Park only offers a tranquil stay – there is no entertainment. Two modern, clean sanitary blocks (one with under-floor heating) contain all necessary facilities with a laundry room and an excellent, separate unit (including shower) for wheelchair users. There is a children's play area and a simple shop. A restaurant is planned for 2000. Many sports activities are available locally. The site has 100 pitches (75 touring), all with electricity (6A) and water, mostly with hardstanding and with reasonable privacy. Some guest rooms are available in the main building.

How to find it: From Soltau take B3 road north and turning to site is on left after 1.5 km. (opposite DCC camping sign) at yellow town boundary sign.

General Details: Open all year. Small shop and restaurant (Easter-Oct). Children's play area. Bicycle hire. Fishing and riding 1.5 km. Golf 3 km. Chemical disposal. Motorcaravan services. Gas supplies. Rooms for rent

Charges 2000: Per pitch DM 17.00; person 8.50; child 7.50; dog 3.00; electricity (6A) 1.00 per stay plus 0.80/kw. No credit cards.

Reservations: Contact site. Address: Ebsmoor 8, 29614 Soltau. Tel: 05191/2141. FAX: 05191/17952.

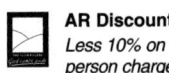

AR Discount
Less 10% on
person charge

3025 Campingpark Alfsee, Rieste, nr Osnabrück

Good modern site, 25 km. north of Osnabrück with many watersport facilities.

This is one of those inland sites which, being adjacent to lakes, has made the most of its situation to provide a wide range of watersports opportunities, and with good installations, to offer a base for enjoyable weekends or holidays. The Alfsee itself is a very large stretch of water for sailing, but even closer to the site, a short stroll from the entrance, is a small lake of 100,000 sq.m. where there is both a bathing section with sandy beach (free to campers) and a water-ski automatic tug, ski-lift style, on payment and open to all. The site has 700 pitches on flat grass (300 taken by permanent caravans). They are of irregular shape and size but mostly over 100 sq.m. with separators and there are many electrical connections. The three identical toilet blocks, heated in cool weather, are of good quality and kept clean, with British style WCs, washbasins with free hot water, shelf, mirror (some in private cabins) and hot showers with screen and seat on payment. It is a good supply, with a unit for disabled visitors. Tour operators take 5 pitches.

How to find it: From A1 north of Osnabrück take Neuenkirchen/Vörden exit. Turn left following Alfsee signs.

General Details: Open all year. Shop and restaurant (both April-Oct). Watersports (see above). Football practice field. Children's playground and entertainment. Grass tennis courts. Trampoline. Minigolf. Go-kart track. General room with amusement machines. Fishing. Bicycle hire. Riding. Golf 8 km. Washing machines and dryers. Cooking facilities. Chemical disposal. Motorcaravan services. Gas supplies. Chalets to rent.

Charges 1999: Per unit incl. 2 adults DM 22.75 - 32.50; extra adult 5.30 - 7.60; child or student 3.80 - 5.40; dog 3.00 - 5.00; electricity 3.00 (once only) plus meter.

Reservations: any length without deposit. Address: 49597 Rieste. Tel: 05464/5166. FAX: 05464/5837.

AR Discount
Less 10% on
person charge

3030 DCC Truma Campingpark, Leeden, Tecklenberg, nr Osnabrück

Large site with swimming pool and other amenities near Osnabrück.

This is a large site taking some 900 units and covers a wide area. Half the pitches (individual ones on mostly flat grassy areas but not separated) are for permanent caravans, leaving 450 for tourists and space is usually available. Many electrical connections (16A). Sanitary facilities are in four good modern blocks (heated in cool weather). They have British style WCs, washbasins, some in private cabins, with shelf and mirror, controllable hot showers; free hot water in basins, on payment in showers and in sinks for clothes and dishes - it is a good supply. Facilities are provided for disabled visitors. A new swimming pool complex and leisure area with heated pools is under construction and may be ready for 2000. Little English is spoken. There are good walks from the site with woodland not used for camping. Osnabrück is 15 km.

How to find it: From south, leave A1 at exit 73 (Tecklenburg/Lengerich). Turn right, immediately left and then right again towards Lengerich. Turn left at second traffic lights to 'Leeden-Lotte' and follow camp signs. From north take exit 72 onto E30, then take exit 14 for Lotte and Leeden.

General Details: Open all year. 300,000 sq.m. Shop (March - Oct). Restaurant/bar (closed Feb and Nov). Snacks (July/Aug). Swimming pools. Minigolf. Children's playground. Dry ski in summer. Youth room; occasional disco. Washing machines and dryers. Cooking facilities. Motorcaravan services.

Charges 1999: Per person DM 7.50; child (4-13 yrs) 5.00; pitch 12.50 - 16.50; hiker's tent 11.50; electricity 3.00 + 0.75 per kw/h; dog 2.00. Overnight stop on parking area 20.00.

Reservations: Probably unnecessary; send a card to site before arrival. Address: 49545 Tecklenburg-Leeden. Tel: 05405/1007. FAX: as phone.

3242 Country Camping Schinderhannes, Hausbay-Pfalzfeld

see colour advert opposite

Useful transit stop en-route to Black Forest, Bavaria, Austria and Switzerland.

Set in a `bowl' of land which catches the sun all day long and with trees and parkland all around, this is a very peaceful and picturesque site, very close to, but rather different from, no. 3235. There are 250 permanent caravans which are in a separate area from 90 overnight pitches on hardstanding, which are on two areas near reception. For those staying longer, the site becomes visually more attractive as you drive down into the area around the lake to a further 160 numbered pitches. These are of over 80 sq.m. on grass, some with hardstanding and all with electrical connections and with water points around. You can position yourself for shade or sun. The lake is used for swimming and inflatable boats and for fishing. The sanitary buildings, which can be heated, are of a high standard with one section, in the reception/shop building, for the overnight pitches and the remainder close to the longer stay places. They have large, free, controllable showers for the short stay area, four private cabins in total, laundry and facilities for disabled people. A pleasant large restaurant features an open fire and includes a rest area with TV and a bowling alley downstairs. English is spoken by the helpful reception staff.

How to find it: From A61 Koblenz - Ludwigshafen road, take exit 43 Pfalzfeld (30 km. south of Koblenz) and on to Hausbay where site is signed.

General Details: Open all year. Electricity connections (10A). Barrier closed 10 pm - 7 am. Restaurant with TV and bowling alley. Shop (16/3-31/10 and maybe Xmas). Tennis (on payment). Basketball. Fishing. Bicycle hire 1 km. Children's play area and fort. Laundry facilities. Chemical disposal. Rallies welcome.

Charges 1999: Per adult DM 7.00; child 5.00; pitch 14.00; dog 3.00; electricity included. No credit cards.

Reservations: For groups only, contact site. Address: 56291 Hausbay-Pfalzfeld/Hünsrück. Tel: 06746/1674 or 8470. FAX: 06746/8214. Email: schinderhannes@mir-tours.de

This site is featured out of order - it is in West Central Germany and should be listed on page 73

3450 Ferien-Campingplatz Münstertal, Münstertal, nr Freiburg

see colour advert opposite

Very impressive site with indoor and outdoor pools, just on edge of Black Forest.

On the western edge of the Black Forest just before the road starts climbing up to Todtnau, the Feldberg and Titisee, this is a site of high quality well worth consideration for your stays in the region. It has some 260 individual pitches on flat gravel, their size varying from 70-100 sq.m. Marked by trees or other means, all have electricity and 180 have waste water drains, 40 with water, TV and radio connection. The site becomes full in season and reservations, especially in July, are necessary. There are three sanitary blocks of truly first class quality, with washbasins, all in private cabins, showers with glass dividers and seat, a baby bath, a unit for visitors with disabilities and individual bathrooms for hire. All hot water is free. There is a large indoor swimming pool (14 x 7 m.) with sauna and solarium, and an outdoor pool on site. This is a very popular area for walking and winter sports.

How to find it: Münstertal is south of Freiburg. From A5 autobahn take exit 64, turn southeast via Bad Krozingen and Staufen (bypassed) and continue 5 km. to the start of Münstertal, where camp is signed from the main road.

General Details: Open all year. 40,000 sq.m. Electricity connections (16A). Shop (all year). Restaurant, particularly good and well patronised (closed Nov). Heated swimming pools, indoor all year, outdoor May-Oct. Sauna and solarium. Tennis. Minigolf. Children's playground. Games room with table tennis. Fishing. Bicycle hire. Tennis courses in summer, ski courses in winter - for children or adults. Riding 5 km. Golf 17 km. Chemical disposal. Motorcaravan services. Village amenities are near.

Charges 1999: Per person DM 11.00 - 13.50; child (2-10 yrs) 7.00 - 8.00; local tax 1.50 for over 16s; pitch 14.00 - 15.90; pitch with TV, water, drainage, radio, phone and electricity connections 21.00; electricity on meter; dog 5.00; private bathroom 15.00. No credit cards.

Reservations: are made without deposit. Address: 79244 Münstertal. Tel: 07636/7080. FAX: 07636/7448.

This site is featured out of order - it is in South West Germany and should be listed on page 77

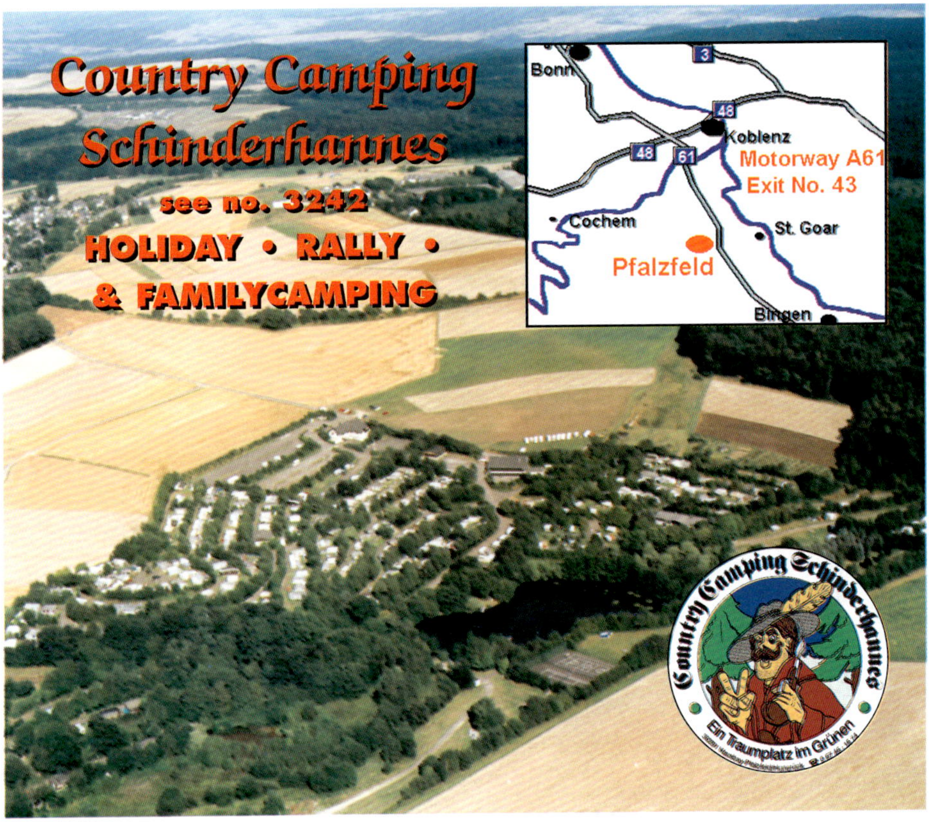

Country Camping Schinderhannes

see no. 3242

HOLIDAY · RALLY · & FAMILYCAMPING

Bonn
Koblenz
Motorway A61
Exit No. 43
Cochem
St. Goar
Pfalzfeld
Bingen

Country Camping Schinderhannes
Ein Traumplatz im Grünen

Feriencamping Münstertal

Feriencamping Münstertal
Familie Wilfried Ortlieb
D-79244 Münstertal
Phone 07636-7080 · Fax 07636-7448

Hallenbad · Tennis
Sauna · Solarium
beheiztes Freibad

This campsite is one of the best in Europe. Best ADAC rating since 1983. Pitches with electricity-, water-, telephone- and TV-connection. Tennis courts (lessons), heated covered and outdoor swimming pools, sauna, solarium, midget golf, trout fishing, winter sports in the vicinity and lots of footpaths in the surroundings.

Norway
The Direct Sea Route to the *Fjords*

Fjord Line have deep roots in passenger ferry services and following the acquisition of the Color Line service from Newcastle is proud to continue the historic link between Western Norway and Great Britain.

With up to three carefully timed sailings a week you will enjoy easy access and flexibility in travel planning.

Taking your own car to Norway with Fjord Line gives you the freedom and flexibility to go where you please. And with a population of just 4 million the roads are virtually free from traffic making Norway the ideal country for motoring tours.

Senior saver - persons aged 60 and over can save up to 50%.

Car packages - travelling as a group, car packages start from £170 for a crossing with car and up to 4 passengers.

Summer saver - save a further 25% reduction on our car package if both your outward and return sailings fall on G and H category sailings. This summer saver offer is only valid for bookings made before 29th February 2000.

Groups - 20 passengers or more are entitled to a 10% reduction on normal standard fares.

Children - save up to 50% when aged under 16 years.

Tel 0191 296 1313

from **£170** for car & up to 4 passengers

25% Summer saver

50% Child reductions for under 16s

50% Senior citizen reductions for over 60s

10% Group reductions of 20+

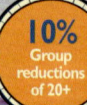

FJORDLINE

Fjord Line, Royal Quays, North Shields, Tyne & Wear NE29 6EG. Fax 0191 296 1540
www.fjordline.com e~mail fjordline.uk@fjordline.com

Sail away to the sites and delights of Denmark, Norway, Sweden & Holland.

Camping Holidays in Scandinavia and Holland are perfect for the outdoor life and great value when you sail away, in style, with Scandinavian Seaways.

One, all-inclusive price covers transportation for 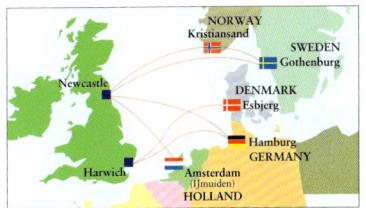 you, your family and your car aboard one of our sleek white liners plus camping vouchers to any one of a large selection of superb sites all over Sweden, Norway, Denmark or Holland. You get a lot more than you imagine, for a lot less than you think.

See your travel agent or call our 24-hour Brochure Line on 08705 333 666 (quote reference 8B153) for a copy of our 2000 Motoring Holidays Brochure.

From £110 per person for 12 nights

"The friendly sunshine paradise between the Black Forest and the Rhine, nestling on the border of Germany, France and Switzerland"

Gugel

Dreiländer Camping
79395 Neuenburg
Tel: 0049 7631 7719

Campsite with dozens of opportunities: fishing, balloon trips, swimming pool, golf, horse-riding, ski school, diving school

Beautiful setting: near Lake Constance, close to the Alps, surrounded by wonderful scenery

Perfect for camper vans: sites with own power supply, cable TV, telephone li... water supply and waste water system

Activities for kids: beach volley... adventure camp with barbecue, petting ... pony rides, disco, free entry for twins

Ideal for outings: Mainau (the "island of flowers"), fairy-tale castles, the Zeppelin Museum, Ravensburg theme park, winter sports

Open all year round

Campingpark Gitzenweiler Ho...

88131 Lindau-Oberreitnau
Germany
Tel +49 8382 94940
Fax +49 8382 949415

3455 Gugel-Drieländer Camping und Freizeitpark, Neuenburg

see colour advert opposite

Ideal night-stop near the A5 just 25 km. north of Basel.

Neuenburg is ideally placed not only for night stops when travelling from Frankfurt to Basel on the A5 autobahn, but also for enjoying and exploring the south of the Black Forest. Set in natural heath and woodland, Gugel's is an attractive site where the permanent caravans, away from the tourist area, with their well-tended gardens, enhance rather than detract from the natural beauty. There are 220 places for tourists either in small clearings in the tall trees which cover the site, in open areas or on hardstanding section used for single night stays. All have electricity connections. Opposite the entrance is a meadow where late arrivals and those who wish to depart before 7 am. may spend the night. Three good quality heated sanitary blocks have British style WCs and free hot water in washbasins (some in cabins), showers and sinks. There is one baby room and one for visitors with disabilities. Amenities include two parallel heated indoor swimming pools, a sunbathing lawn, good children's play area and another with electric cars and motorcycles (on payment). A new social room has been added with satellite TV where guests are welcomed with a glass of wine and a slide presentation of the attractions of the area. Opposite the entrance is a small lake where one can fish on daily permit. The Rhine is within walking distance. Being near the motorway, although this cannot be seen from the site, there is some road noise near the entrance. The excellent restaurant is popular with both campers and non-residents. An activity programme is offered for both children and adults at Easter and July/Aug. including sightseeing trips. The site may become crowded in high season but you should always find room. In general there is a good atmosphere and it can be recommended for both short and long stays.

How to find it: From autobahn A5 take Neuenburg exit, turn left at traffic lights, left at next junction and follow signs for 2 km. to site (called 'Neuenburg' on most signs).

General Details: Open all year. 130,000 sq.m. Electricity connections (6A). Small shop (Easter - end Oct). Restaurant (all year excl. Nov). Indoor pools (end March-early Oct). Boules. Tennis courts with racquet and ball hire. Fishing. Minigolf. Table tennis. Chess. Barbeque. Bicycle hire. Community room with TV. Activity programme with organised walks, excursions, etc. and sports and competitions for children. Golf 5 km. Riding 1.5 km. Washing machines and dryers. Chemical disposal. Motorcaravan services.

Charges 1999: Per person DM 8.90; child (2-15) 5.50; caravan or tent 9.60; small tent 6.60, car 7.60; motorcaravan 9.60 - 14.90, acc. to size; dog 3.60; electricity on meter. Discount every 10th night, persons free. No credit cards.

Reservations: made for min 2 weeks in July/Aug. with deposit. Write specifying tent or caravan. Address: 79395 Neuenburg (Oberer Wald). Tel: 07631/7719. FAX: 07635/3393.

This site is featured out of order - it is in South West Germany and should be listed on page 78

3650 Campingpark Gitzenweiler Hof, Lindau, nr Friedrichshafen

see colour advert opposite

Modernised all year site pleasantly situated near the Bodensee (Lake Constance).

A large sum of money has been invested at Gitzenweiler Hof, evident in the new reception, beautifully renovated sanitary buildings and purpose designed overnight pitches by the entrance. It is a very spacious site in a country setting and although it has about 350 permanent caravans, it can still take about 350 tourist units (although it is advisable to book for July/Aug). In the tourist section many pitches are without markings with siting left to campers, the other 200 in rows between access roads. There are 350 electricity connections and some pitches with water, drainage, telephone and TV connections. A large open-air swimming pool (33 x 25 m.) has attractive surrounds with seats (free for campers). The sanitary facilities have British style toilets, washbasins (some in cabins), free hot showers, children's bathroom, baby bath etc. Lindau is an interesting town, especially by the harbour, and possible excursions include the whole of the Bodensee, the German Alpine Road, the Austrian Vorarlberg and Switzerland. This is a pleasant, friendly, well-run site useful for overnight stops as well as longer term breaks.

How to find it: Site is signed from the B12 about 4 km. north of Lindau. Also from A96 exit 3 (Weißensberg).

General Details: Open all year. Little shade. Electrical connections (5A). Shop (limited hours in low season). Restaurant/bar (closed Feb). Swimming pool (summer). Volleyball. Children's playground and playroom with entertainment in summer. Organised activities for adults and children all year. Small zoo for children. Ground for football, etc. Free fishing in lake. Table tennis. Minigolf. Club room. Washing machines, dryers and dishwasher. Motorcaravan services. Doctor comes if needed; hospital near. Late arrivals area. American motorhomes accepted up to 10 tons.

Charges 1999: Per person DM 9.00; child 3-9 yrs 3.00, 10-15 yrs 6.00; pitch 12; tent pitches from 5-12 depending on size; electricity 4.00; dog 5.00; Discounts for stays over 14 days and in winter. Single overnight hardstandings with electricity outside camp barrier 25.00.

Reservations: made with deposit (DM 180.00) and fee (20.00). Address: 88131 Lindau-Oberreitnau. Tel: 08382/9494-0. FAX: 08382/9494-15.

This site is featured out of order - it is in South West Germany and should be listed on page 80

GERMANY - North West

3035 DCC Kur Camping Park, Bad Gandersheim

Good site, easily reached from autobahn and well placed for visiting other Harz resorts.

Attractively situated between a tree-covered hill and the B64 road, this is a well run, formal site with a stream running through the middle. It has 460 pitches of which 300 are for touring units. They are all well marked and easily accessible, divided into long and short stay areas and a section for those with animals. Open all year, the site provides good amenities for both summer walkers and winter skiers. Although on the edge of the Harz area, the excellent security at the site allows one to leave the van, etc. whilst exploring the twisty and busy roads of the main resort towns or participating in one of the organised walks. The sanitary facilities are modern and heated, with showers on payment (50 pf. coin), plus facilities for mother and baby, and child toilets. A restaurant serves snacks at lunch-time and evening meals (excl. Mondays). The pretty, old town is a 15 minute stroll.

How to find it: From autobahn A7 (E45), leave at Seesen, then road 64 to Bad Gandersheim. Site is on right, just before town and is well signed.

General Details: Open all year. Electricity connections throughout (10A). Bar/restaurant (15/3-30/10, 1/12-15/1). Shop (1/4-30/10 and 20/12-5/1). Minigolf. Table tennis. Children's play areas. Laundry facilities. Solarium. Dog shower. Tennis, riding, fishing, swimming, sailing, windsurfing all near. Chemical disposal. Motorcaravan services. Gas supplies.

Charges 1999: Per pitch DM 16.50; small tent 11.50; adult 7.50 plus local tax 1.00; child (4-13 yrs) 5.00 plus 0.50 tax; dog 2.00; electricity 0.50 plus meter. Credit cards accepted.

Reservations: Contact site. Address: Braunschweiger Str. 12, 37581 Bad Gandersheim. Tel: 05382/1595. FAX: 05382/1599.

3040 Camping Prahljust, Clausthal-Zellerfeld

Pleasant, large site in a good position to explore the Harz area.

This all year round site is well situated for both winter or summer holidays. It is a gently undulating site sloping down to a small lake. The receptionist/manager speaks good English and provides guests with an excellent information sheet in English. There are 1,000 pitches of which 350 are for permanent units, and three sanitary blocks with both private cabins and open troughs for washing. One block has a unit for wheelchair users. Amenities include a large, heated swimming pool (small charge) and a sauna. Fishing is allowed in the lake (licence essential). A bar, restaurant and a self service shop are close to reception and there is a good children's playground. Entertainment is organised in high season. Other attractions in the Harz include the highest point at Brocken (1,142 m.) with a narrow gauge steam railway and many walks.

How to find it: From autobahn A7 (E45) leave at Seesen and take route 242 for Clausthal Zellerfeld. Go through the town (direction Braunlage) and the site is 2 km. out of the town on the right, well signed. Coming from Braunlage, site is also signed `Rubezahl', on the left.

General Details: Open all year, as are bar, restaurant and shop. Electricity connections throughout (10A). Swimming pool . Sauna. Washing machines and dryers. Drying room. Children's playground. Fishing. Chemical disposal. Motorcaravan service point

Charges guide: Per pitch DM 6.75 - 8.35; adult 6.55 - 8.15; child (under 14 yrs) 5.60 - 7.35; car 3.50 - 4.20; m/cycle 2.35; electricity 1.00 plus meter; dog 4.70 - 5.00; local tax 1.50.

Reservations: Write to site. Address: 38678 Clausthal-Zellerfeld. Tel: 05323/1300. FAX: 05323/78393.

3045 Knaus Camping Walkenried, Walkenried

Woodland site in the southern Harz with indoor pool.

The southern Harz area offers much for walkers and anglers and this site organises many outings ranging from free walks to coach trips to the highest mountain in the area at Brocken (1,142 m). It also has the benefit of an indoor pool, sauna and solarium. Outdoor activities in the area include riding, watersports and tennis. There are 170 touring pitches of 80-100 sq.m. and arranged in well shaded groups on mainly slightly sloping grass and gravel. Most are separated by bushes or trees and have 4A, 2 pin electrical connections. There are some smaller hardstandings for motorhomes and a separate area for visitors with dogs. Tiled and heated sanitary facilities are satisfactory, with free hot water to 12 showers and washbasins (private cabins for ladies) and a toilet for disabled visitors, and are all in the main building by the entrance. A large children's play area is at the side of the site, also a barbecue and some seating here and by the small fishing lake. The indoor pool is free for campers (open 9-12 and 3-6, all year except 1/11-15/12).

How to find it: Walkenried is signed from B4 Erfurt-Magdeburg road just north of Nordhausen and from B243 Seesen-Nordhausen road. The site is signed in the town.

General Details: Open all year exc. Nov. Baker calls just after 8 am. Shop and restaurant (both all year). Indoor pool (closed 1/11-15/12). Sauna and solarium. Children's play area. Beach volleyball. Small fishing lake. Bicycle hire. Laundry and cooking facilities. Chemical disposal. Motorcaravan services. Caravans (10) and tents to rent.

Charges 2000: Per person DM 8.75; child (3-14 yrs) 4.50; pitch 7.50 - 12.50; tent with m/cycle 7.50; dog 4.00; electricity 3.50. No credit cards.

Reservations: Contact the site. Address: Ellricher Str. 7, 37445 Walkenried. Tel: 05525/778. FAX: 05525/2332.

3280 Camping und Ferienpark Teichmann, Vöhl-Herzhausen, Edersee

Well equipped friendly site for active holidays on the shores of the Edersee.
Situated by a 6 hectare lake with tree-covered hills all around, this well cared for site blends in attractively with its surroundings. There are facilities for windsurfing, rowing boats, pedaloes (no motor boats), swimming and fishing, all in different areas and it is also suitable for winter sports with ski runs near. There are many local walks and the opportunity exists for taking a pleasure boat trip and riding home by bicycle. Three good quality, heated sanitary blocks for tourers offer large, free hot showers, baby rooms in two and for wheelchair users. Of the 460 pitches, half are for touring units. They are mainly on flat grass, all with electricity and with some hardstandings. There is a separate area for tents. The many amenities include a mini-market and café. A good site for families, there are many activities (listed below) and a pitch can usually be found even for a one night stay. A very large open air model railway is a special attraction.

How to find it: From A44 Oberhausen - Kassel autobahn, take exit for Korbach. Site is between Korbach and Frankenberg on the B252 road, 1 km. to the south of Herzhausen, about 45 km. from the A44.

General Details: Open all year. Electricity connections (6A). Café and shop (both summer only). Restaurant all day (Feb-Dec). Watersports. Boat and bicycle hire. Lake swimming. Football. Fishing. Minigolf. Beach volleyball (high season). Tennis. Table tennis. Children's playground. Sauna and solarium. High season disco.

Charges guide: Per unit with 2 persons, electricity, water and waste water, DM 19.90 - 45.90 according to size and season. Extra person (3 -16) 3.90 - 5.90; over 16, 7.20 - 9.90.

Reservations: Made with deposit (DM 100) and fee (10); write to site. Address: 34516 Vöhl-Herzhausen. Tel: 05635/245. FAX: 05635/8145.

3270 Campingplatz Lahnaue, Marburg an der Lahn

Satisfactory site adjacent to swimming pools and within walking distance of town.
This little municipal site should make a satisfactory stop on the B3 Frankfurt-Kassel road. Situated on a long, fairly narrow strip of land between the river Lahn and the road and railway (possibly some noise), there are pleasant walks to the centre of the old university town. An adjoining sports complex includes large swimming pools, tennis courts, minigolf, a playground and general games area. The 70 pitches for touring units are all on flat grass, some at the water's edge, numbered but not separated with electricity in most areas. The small, modern sanitary block should be adequate for the usual numbers. It has hot showers on payment, one washbasin with hot water per sex, the remainder with cold, and first-class facilities for the disabled. Bread is ordered at reception the previous evening, with shops and restaurants in Marburg.

How to find it: Site is at south end of the town adjoining the ring road. Turn off ring road at 'Marburg mitte' exit then follow camping signs.

General Details: Open 1 April - 31 Oct. Electricity connections (10A). Some provisions kept. Small restaurant with breakfast served. Table tennis. Minigolf. Fishing. Bicycle hire 1 km. Riding and golf 5 km. Cooking facilities. Washing machine and dryer. Chemical disposal. Motorcaravan services. Gas supplies.

Charges 1999: Per person DM 7.00; child (2-13 yrs) 3.00; caravan 6.00; tent 5.00; car 3.00; motorcaravan 9.00; electricity 2.00 plus 2.00 per day; waste 1.00. No credit cards.

Reservations: Usually unnecessary, but site address is 35037 Marburg. Tel: 06421/21331. FAX: as phone.

3210 Campingplatz Biggesee-Sondern, Olpe-Sondern

High quality leisure complex site, on shores of large lake in Südsauerland National Park.
In an attractive setting on the shores of the Biggesee lake, this site offers many leisure opportunities, as well as high quality camping facilities. It is therefore deservedly popular, and reservation is almost always essential. Well managed, the same company also operates two other sites on the shores of the lake, where space may be available. There are 300 numbered pitches of 100 sq.m, of which about 250 are for tourists, either in rows or in circles, on terraces. There are electricity and water points throughout. The sanitary facilities are in two heated blocks of excellent quality. They have British style WCs (no paper), washbasins (many in cabins), and good showers, all with free hot water. With facilities for babies and laundry (keys from reception), the provision should be adequate. The leisure activities are numerous. Watersports on the lake include sailing and windsurfing, with a school available. You may launch your own small boat, and also swim from the shore. With roller-skating on site and tennis nearby, a playroom and playground are also available for smaller children. Skiing is possible and there are walks around the lake.

How to find it: From A45 (Siegen-Hagen) autobahn, take exit to Olpe, and turn towards Attendorn. After 6 km. turn to Bigge-Stausee. Site is signed.

General Details: Open all year. Electricity throughout (6A). Shop (closed Jan and Nov). Watersports and school. Swimming from beach. Football pitch. Table tennis. Roller-skating. Fishing. Bicycle hire. Tennis near. Riding 8 km. Golf 12 km. Children's playground and playroom. Solarium and sauna. Entertainment and excursions. Restaurant and snacks 300 m (Easter - 31/10). Cooking facilities. Laundry. Motorcaravan services.

Charges 2000: Per unit incl. electricity DM 19.00 - 25.00; person 5.50 - 7.00; child (3-15 yrs) 3.00 - 4.00; dog 4.50. No credit cards.

Reservations: Probably essential for much of the year, but phone site. Address: Erholungsanlage Biggesee-Sondern, 57462 Olpe-Sondern, Am Sonderner Kopf 3. Tel: 02761/944111. FAX: 02761/944122.

GERMANY - West Central

3215 Campingplatz Goldene Meile, Remagen, nr Bonn

Site on banks of Rhein between Bonn and Koblenz, adjacent to outdoor pool complex.

This site is beside the Rhein (boats of any type can be put onto the river) and adjacent to a large complex of open-air public swimming pools (campers pay the normal entrance). Although there is an emphasis on permanent caravans, there are about 250 pitches for tourists (from 500), 14 with water and waste water connections (more extra large ones will be ready for 2000) and 14 with waste water. They are either in the central, more mature area or in a newer area where the numbered pitches of 80-100 sq. m. are arranged around an attractively landscaped small fishing lake. They claim always to find space for odd nights, except perhaps at B.Hs. The main sanitary facilities are in the central block which is a good quality building, heated and kept clean, with British style toilets, washbasins (some in cabins), controllable hot showers with token from machine (1 DM) and facilities for wheelchair users. The shower and wash rooms are locked at 10 pm. A smart toilet block serves the newer pitches near the lake. It also has dishwashing and laundry sinks, a washing machine and dryer, chemical disposal and cooking facilities but no showers. The central buildings also house a small bar/restaurant and a small shop for basic supplies (including bread to order). This site is in a popular area and, although busy in high season, appears to be well run.

How to find it: Remagen is 23 km. south of Bonn on no. 9 road towards Koblenz. Site is on road running close to the Rhein from Remagen to Kripp and is signed from the N9 south of Remagen, which avoids the congested town (signs also for Allwetterbad). From A61 autobahn take Sinzig exit.

General Details: Open all year. Shop (April- Oct). Electricity connections in most areas (8A). Restaurant (closed Mon. low season). Children's playgrounds. Entertainment for children in July/Aug. Beach volleyball. Basketball. Football. Bicycle hire. Riding. Swiming pools adjacent (May-Sept). Chemical disposal. Motorcaravan services. Gas supplies. Main gate locked at 10 pm. (also 1-3 pm.)

Charges 1999: Per person DM 9.00; child (6-16 yrs) 7.00, under 6 free; caravan pitch 12.50; tent 6.00 - 12.50 acc. to size; dog 2.00; electricity 4.00. No credit cards.

Reservations: can be made for at least a few days. Address: 53424 Remagen/Rhein. Tel: 02642/22222. FAX: 02642/1555. E-mail: info@camping-goldene-meile.de.

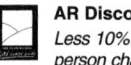 **AR Discount** *Less 10% on person charge*

http://www.camping-goldene-meile.de
e-mail: info@camping-goldene-meile.de

Campingplatz »Goldene Meile« D-53424 Remagen Tel. (0 26 42) 2 22 22

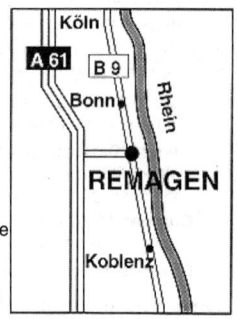

On one of the most beautiful and modern camp sites in the romantic Rhine valley between Bonn (20 km) and Koblenz (40 km) you will find ideal conditions.

For a holiday: water sports on the Rhine and in the heated all-weather pool (86m chute, sports and keep-fit (indoor and outdoor tennis courts, playing field, volleyball court, football ground), hiking in the Eifel and the Westerwald, boat trips on the Rhine and the Mosel, numerous wine festivals.

For a short stop: convenient location only 7 km from the A 61 motorway (Sinzig-Remagen exit), 2 km to the B 9. Shop, restaurant with terrace, first-class rating from ADAC for many years.

3205 Campingplatz der Stadt Köln, Köln-Poll, Köln

Convenient site beside the Rhine, very close to motorway.

The ancient city of Cologne offers much for the visitor, with many museums, art galleries, opera and open-air concerts, as well as the famous Cathedral. The 'Phantasialand' theme park is close by at Brühl and the zoo and Rhine cruises are among other attractions. The site is pleasantly situated alongside the river, with wide grass areas either side of narrow tarmac access roads and low metal barriers separating it from the public park. Of 140 unmarked, level touring pitches, 50 have electricity and there is shade for some from various mature trees. The small toilet block has fairly basic facilities, but is heated with free hot water (06.00-12.00, 17.00-23.00 hrs) in the washing troughs and regularly in token operated showers. Above is a large open-fronted room where you may cook, eat, and wash clothes and dishes (free hot water). A small shop opens in the mornings for bread and offers basic supplies and snacks in the evenings.

How to find it: Leave autobahn A4 at exit no. 13 for Köln-Poll (just to west off intersection of A3 and A4). Turn left at first traffic lights and follow site signs through a sometimes fairly narrow one-way system to the riverside, back towards the motorway bridge.

General Details: Open Easter - 15 Oct. Electricity connections (10A). Kiosk (May-Sept). Café adjacent. Cooking facilities (free). Fishing. Bicycle hire. Golf 3 km. Washing machine and dryer. Chemical disposal.

Charges 1999: Per adult DM 7.50; child (4-12 yrs) 4.50; caravan 6.00; motor-caravan 9 .00; tent 4.00 - 6.00; car 4.00; m/cycle 2.00; electricity 3.00.

Reservations: Write to site. Address: 51105 Köln 91 (Poll). Tel/Fax: 0221/831966.

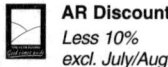 **AR Discount** *Less 10% excl. July/Aug.*

3212 Landal GreenParks Wirfttal, Stadtkyll

Site with pools and other facilities near the Belgian border between Cologne and Trier.

Peacefully set in a small valley in the heath and forest of the hills of the northern Eifel, Wirfttal has 250 pitches (150 for tourers). Mostly backing onto fences or hedges on fairly flat ground of different levels (steel pegs needed for tents and awnings), the pitches are 80 sq.m or more, and all have electricity and TV points, 17 pitches have water and waste water points. Also part of the site, but separate, is a large holiday bungalow complex. A short walk up the hill is an outdoor pool complex (discount for campers) with three pools, one heated, and minigolf. At the site entrance, is a small, free indoor pool, plus a sauna and solarium on payment, and a sports centre with outdoor tennis courts (floodlit), a super playground, bowling and an indoor tennis and squash centre. Fishing is allowed in the small lake. The site has one main toilet block (the only one open out of main season), and two small units, all heated. They have free hot water in all washbasins, showers and sinks; all ladies' washbasins and one for men in the main block are in cabins.

How to find it: Site is 1.5 km. south of Stadtkyll on road towards Schüller.

General Details: Open all year. Electricity connections (6A). Shop. Restaurant and snacks (high season). Swimming pools. Indoor pool. Tennis (indoor and outdoor). Riding. Fishing (free). Bicycle hire. Sports centre adjacent. Adventure playground. Winter sports. Bicycle hire. Animation in season. Chemical disposal.

Charges 2000: Per unit incl. 2 persons DM 19.00 - 43.00, with services 23.00 - 48.00; extra person 4.50; dog 4.50; electricity 4.50. No credit cards.

Reservations: are made (Fri.- Fri. only in high season) with 50% deposit. Address: 54589 Stadtkyll/Eifel. Tel: 06597/92920. FAX: 06597/929250. Office open 7 days/week.

3265 Campingplatz Limburg, Limburg an der Lahn, nr Koblenz

Good municipal site by Cologne-Frankfurt autobahn.

Pleasantly situated on the bank of the river Lahn between autobahn and town - both the autobahn viaduct and the cathedral are visible - this is a useful overnight stop for travellers along the Köln-Frankfurt stretch. You may, however, be tempted to stay longer as there are other attractions here, notably a very fine swimming pool complex nearby and the attractive old town of medieval buildings a gentle stroll away. The site is on level grass with 200 numbered touring pitches (out of 250 altogether) on either side of gravel tracks at right angles from the main tarmac road, which runs the length of the site. It is very popular with many nationalities and can become crowded at peak times, so arrive early. The main sanitary block near reception is rather old but improvements have been made to the facilities (showers need a token). A new, heated block at the other end of the site was completed in '99. A bar/restaurant, open during the evenings, offers drinks, simple meals and takeaway. There is a kiosk for some basic supplies. Some road and rail noise.

How to find it: Leave A3 autobahn at Limburg-Nord exit and follow road into town and then camping signs.

General Details: Open 20 April - 30 Oct. Electricity connections (140, 6A) - some need long leads. Bar/restaurant (evenings). Kiosk. Swimming pool opposite. Supermarkets and good range of shops and restaurants in town. Pleasure cruises. Fishing (permit on payment). Children's play area. Bicycle and motorcycle hire. Riding 5 km. Golf 15 km. Washing machines, dryers, cookers. Gas supplies. Chemical disposal. Motorcaravan services.

Charges 1999: Per person DM 5.80; child (3 - 14) 3.00; car 3.00; m/cycle 2.50; caravan 5.50; motorcaravan 8.50; tent 3.50 - 5.00; boat 6.00; dog 2.00; electricity 3.30; shower token 1.50; waste fee 1.20.

Reservations: Contact site. Address: 65549 Limburg a.d. Lahn. Tel: 06431/22610. FAX: 06431/92013.

3224 Campingplatz am Rhein, Rüdesheim am Rhein, nr Mainz

Relaxed, informal site, quietly located on edge of town right by the Rhein.

This is a major tourist area so it will become very busy here at certain times, but the owner says there is almost always room on the site. The 7 acre touring site (no permanent units are accepted) is flat, grassy and has quite a lot of attractive, old tall trees that offer some shade. Caravan and tent pitches are on grass (no plastic groundsheets) and the owner firmly believes in unmarked, un-numbered camping so that the grass can grow. A separate area of hardstanding is provided for motorcaravans. Electricity is available to most pitches and there are many water points. A shop and snack bar are on site and it is only 600 m. to the amenities of Rüdesheim. A public swimming pool is just outside the site and boat trips on the Rhein and many other sightseeing opportunities are available close by. Plenty of tourist information is available from reception. The satisfactory sanitary facilities are in a modernised building with token operated showers (5 mins) and almost half the washbasins in cabins.

How to find it: Site is signed in several places from the B42 in the east of Rüdesheim and is alongside the river.

General Details: Open 1 May - 30 Sept. Electrical connections (10A). Shop. Bar and snacks. Children's play area. Heated outdoor pool 100 m. Washing machines and dryer. Chemical disposal. Motorcaravan services. Gates closed to vehicles and riverside 2200 - 0800.

Charges 1999: Per person DM 7.00; child (up to 14) 4.40; caravan 7.40; awning 2.80; car 5.70; motorcaravan 11.00 - 14.00; motorbike 4.50; tent 6.40 - 8.40; electricity 4.60; dog 5.00; rubbish tax 1.40. No credit cards.

Reservations: Not made (no brochure either). Address: 65385 Rüdesheim am Rhein. Tel: 06722/2528 or 2582. FAX: 06322/8161.

GERMANY - West Central

3225 Naturpark Camping Suleika, Lorch-bei-Rudesheim

Family run site on steep hillside in Rhine-Taunus Nature Park

Approached by a narrow and steep system of lanes through the vineyards, some of which belong to the site, this situation is not for the faint hearted. Having said that, it is a popular site for caravan rallies. Once you reach the site, it is steeply arranged in small terraces up the side of the wooded hill with a stream flowing through - the water supply is direct from springs. The surroundings are most attractive, with views over the vineyards to the river below. The Riesling Walk footpath passes above the site. Of the 100 pitches, 50 are available for tourists. These are mostly on the lower terraces, in numbered groups of up to four units. There is a special area for younger campers. All have electricity and there are water points around. Cars have to be parked away from the pitches near the entrance. A central block contains a very pleasant restaurant and small shop for basics (bread to order), with sanitary facilities alongside. These are excellent, heated in cool weather and containing British style WCs, washbasins (some in cabins for each sex), free hot showers and there is also a nicely furnished baby washroom, with WC, shower and bath. With steep walks from most pitches to the facilities, this is probably not a site for visitors with disabilities; however, it is an attractive situation and reception staff are very friendly. This particular area is famous as it was briefly a 'Free State' (1919-23) and you will be able to taste and buy the site owner's wine and other items as souvenirs. There are many local attractions (as well as the Lorelei) shown on a large map, and the helpful owner speaks good English.

How to find it: There is a direct entrance road from the B42 (for cars only), between Rudesheim and Lorch, with a height limitation of 2.25 m. under a railway bridge. Higher vehicles will find the site signed on the south side of Lorch. Site is reached via a one-way system of lanes – follow the signs.

General Details: Open 1 March - 15 Nov. Site opens all day. Shade in most areas. Electricity connections (16A). Water from springs. Restaurant. Small shop. Children's playground. Some entertainment in season. Fishing 300 m. Bicycle hire. Riding 4 km. Laundry service. Chemical disposal. Motorcaravan services. Gas supplies. 10 chalets for rent.

Charges 2000: Per adult DM 8.00; child 5.00; caravan 8.00; motorcaravan 10.00 - 12.00; tent 5.00 - 8.00; car 3.00; m/cycle 1.50; dog 3.00; electricity 2.00 plus meter. No credit cards.

Reservations: made with DM 50 deposit, so only worthwhile for a longer stay. Address: Lorch-bei-Rudesheim, 65382 Rudesheim 2 (Ass). Tel: 06726/9464. FAX: 06726/9440.

AR Discount

Less 10% on person charge; welcome wine from own winery

3235 Camping am Mühlenteich, Lingerhahn, Laudert, nr Koblenz

Friendly site to west of central Rhine only 5 km. from autobahn.

Set among trees and fields in the hills at the eastern end of the Hunsrück, this site is only 15 km. from the Rhine at Oberwesel. Bingen, Boppard and Koblenz are also reached easily via the A61 autobahn. There are 100 touring pitches in addition to the 350 for permanent caravans. Some are in the main part (for longer stays), others are in a more open situation opposite (caravans and tents are mixed together) and space is usually available. The central sanitary block, in two sections, is large, heated and of good quality. With a further building for high season, there is a satisfactory supply. Washbasins have free hot water, shelf and mirror, with some private cabins for ladies in two blocks and for men in one; hot showers (fully controllable) are on payment; British style WCs. On site is an unusual pool for swimming (free of charge) fashioned from a natural basin and fed by springs. A splendid new building houses reception, a shop and café and there is very good provision for children, including some very popular children's play equipment and a video room, plus entertainment in July/August.

How to find it: From A61 autobahn take exit for Laudert. Follow signs into Lingerhahn village, between Laudert and Kastellaun. Site is signed in middle of the village.

General Details: Open all year. Electrical connections (6A). Small shop. Café (Easter-Oct and holidays). Baker calls daily at 8.30 am. Cable/satellite TV. Youth disco room. Tennis. Basketball. Table tennis. Children's adventure playground. Football field. Wagon rides in season. Bicycle hire. Riding or fishing 4 km. Golf 15 km. Barbecue. Animation in high season. Gas supplies. Chemical disposal. Motorcaravan services.

Charges 2000: Per person DM 7.00; child (under 14) 5.00; car 7.00; caravan or tent 7.00; motorcaravan 14.00; small child's tent 3.00; m/cycle 5.00; dog 3.00; electricity 3.50; cable TV 2.00. Plus local taxes. No credit cards.

Reservations: Write to site. Address: 56291 Lingerhahn. Tel: 06746/533. FAX: 06746/1566.

3220 Campingplatz Burg Lahneck, Lahnstein, nr Koblenz

Orderly, clean site with fine views over Rhein and swimming pool adjoining.

The location of this site is splendid, high up overlooking the Rhein valley and the town of Lahnstein - many of the pitches have their own super views. Adjacent is a good swimming pool with extensive grassy areas, and also the mediaeval castle Burg Lahneck (the home of the camp proprietor, which may be visited) with its smart restaurant. It is in the best part of the Rhein valley, and close to Koblenz and the Mosel. A 'Kurcentrum', under 2 km. from the site, has a thermal pool from warm springs (reduced admission to campers) with sauna and solarium. The site, which consists partly of terraces and partly of open grassy areas, has a cared for look and all is very neat and clean. One can usually find a space here, though from early July to mid-August it can become full. There are 115 individual touring pitches (out of 125 altogether) marked but not separated and mostly level, all with electricity. Campers are sited by the management. Sanitary facilities in one central, heated block are of a good standard, and are well maintained and cleaned. They have British style toilets and washbasins with shelves and mirrors, with some cabins for both sexes. Hot water is free for washbasins and washing-up sinks, showers are on payment (DM 1). Reception staff at the site are friendly and charges reasonable. There are some tour operator pitches.

How to find it: From B42 bypassing town, take Oberlahnstein exit and follow signs Kurcentrum/Burg Lahneck.

General Details: Open Easter/1 April - 31 Oct. Electricity connections (16A). Small shop. Cafe/restaurant adjoining site serves drinks, snacks, ices, etc. with some hot evening food; meals also in Burg Lahneck restaurant. Small children's playground. Town swimming pool (reduced charges for campers, 15/5-31/8). Tennis nearby. Riding 500 m. Fishing 3 km. Bicycle hire 2 km. Information about trips on the Rhein. Washing machine and dryer. Motorcaravan services. Chemical disposal. Gas supplies.

Charges 2000: Per person DM 10.50; child (3-14 yrs) 5.00; car 6.00; tent 8.50 - 10.50, acc. to size; trailer tent or caravan 10.50; motorcaravan 14.50 - 16.50; m/cycle 2.50; dog 1.00; electricity 1.00 plus meter. No credit cards.

Reservations: made without deposit for exact dates. Address: 56112 Lahnstein/Rhein, (Ortsteil Oberlahnstein). Tel: 02621/2765. FAX: 02621/18290.

3230 Campingplatz Burgen, Burgen, nr Koblenz

Pleasantly situated site on banks of the Mosel between Koblenz and Cochem.

Burgen is between the road and the river on the flat grassy bank with attractive views and, like many sites alongside the Mosel, it may occasionally be flooded at very high tide. Most of the pitches on the river's edge are occupied by permanent caravans and attendant boats, but there are 120 individual numbered hardstanding pitches for tourists, with electricity available, plus a meadow at one end. The site fills up for much of July and August but a few pitches are kept for short stay visitors. The single central sanitary block is quite good, with British style toilets, washbasins with free hot water (5 in private cabins), and 9 showers (on payment, token from reception or shop) which might be hard pressed in high season. With a railway across the water, the road and commercial boats, some noise may be expected. You can swim and fish in the Mosel (there is also a small pool on site) or just use the site as a base for visiting local attractions.

How to find it: Site is on eastern edge of town, 30 km. from Koblenz (a tight turn into the site if approaching from Koblenz).

General Details: Open 1 April - 15 Oct. 35,000 sq.m. Electricity connections (10A). Shop (essentials only all season). General room with TV and games, drinks served. Restaurant 200 m. Small swimming pool (9.5 x 6.5 m. open May-Aug.). Fishing and swimming in the Moselle. Slipway for boats. Table tennis. Children's playground. Bicycle hire 4 km. Boat trips. Washing machine and dryer. Gas supplies. Chemical disposal. Motorcaravan services.

Charges 2000: Per person DM 8.00; child (1-13 yrs) 4.00; pitch 12.00; m/cycle + tent 9.00; dog 3.00; electricity 3.00; local tax 3.00 (child 1.50). No credit cards.

Reservations: made for any length but with deposit and fee. Address: 56332 Burgen/Mosel. Tel: 02605/2396. FAX: 02605/4919.

GERMANY - West Central

3232 Family Camping Club, Mesenich bei Cochem

Developing site in peaceful area by the Mosel, near famous tourist resort.

Formerly run for long-term units, the site has recently been acquired by a progressive young family who are rapidly updating the facilities to turn it into a comfortable touring location. Situated beside the Mosel river, with views of forest and vineyard, it has the added advantage of being on a stretch of the river well away from the railway. The 50 touring pitches are among the vines, mainly level, individual ones with electricity connections, separated by bushes and the older ones with shade. On arrival there is separate parking for motorcaravans but caravans must stop on the fairly narrow site road while booking in at the main buildings back to the left. As well as reception, there is a small shop, a pleasant bar/restaurant with terrace, mini cinema, and outdoor swimming and children's pools. Also here are the well equipped heated sanitary facilities with washbasins mainly in cubicles or curtained and large showers on payment (inside). It is a popular site in July and August with many activities organised for youngsters, but they do insist on no noise after midnight.

How to find it: Mesenich is on the opposite side of the Mosel from Cochem and can be reached from the B49, crossing the river bridge at either Cochem to the north-east or Senheim to the southwest. It can also be reached from the scenic B421 Kirchberg to Zell road, turning to Senheim 15 km. after Kirchberg (rather winding and steep road at the end).

General Details: Open 15 April - 10 Oct. Electrical connections (6A). Essentials high season otherwise shop 300 m. Bar and restaurant lunch-time and evenings (not every day in low season). Swimming pools (19/6-12/9). Children's play equipment. Bicycle hire (official Mosel route for cyclists). Fishing from site. Disco-dance evenings, wine tours. Washing machines and dryer. Motorcaravan services. Fully equipped tents for hire. Good English spoken.

Charges 1999: Per unit incl. 2 persons DM 22 - 30; extra person (over 2 yrs) 5; dog 2.20; electricity 3.50. Credit cards accepted.

Reservations: Advised for July and August. Office address: Kurierweg 23, 56814 Beilstein, Mosel. Tel: 02673/1589. FAX: 02673/1751. Site address: Moselufer, 56820 Mesenich bei Cochem. Tel: 02673/4556.

3222 Camping Gülser Moselbogen, Koblenz-Güls

Well equipped all year site alongside the Mosel, just outside Koblenz.

The provision of a first class sanitary facility here, combined with the location being very convenient for sightseeing along the rivers Mosel and Rhein and the easy access to Koblenz and the A48 and A61, make this an attractive proposition for a short or longer-term stay. The site is set quite high up from the river (safe from flooding) but with no direct access to it, and has a pleasant outlook to the forested valley slopes. A large proportion of the 16 acre site is taken up by privately owned bungalows, but the touring section of 60 large individual pitches (a new less formal area is being developed for '00) is self contained and accessed by gravel paths leading off the main tiled roads. All have connections for TV and 16A electricity and there are water points in each section. Entry to the sanitary building is by a coded card that also operates the hot water to the showers (free to the washbasins, many of which are in cabins). Other rooms contain a unit for disabled visitors, dishwashing and cooking rings (charged), a laundry and chemical disposal. Bread and milk may be ordered at reception and there is a restaurant 500 m. away, with the village of Güls a farther 1.5 km.

How to find it: Site is 1.5 km. west of village of Güls, and is accessed from the B416 that runs along the north bank of the Mosel from Koblenz (where it joins the B9) towards Cochem. From the A61 take exit 38 towards Koblenz-Metternich. After 2 km. turn right towards Winningen/Flughaven/Güls (white sign) and keep on main road for Güls till the B416, turn right towards Cochem and watch for site signs in 1.5 km.

General Details: Open all year. Electrical connections (16A). Bread and milk from reception daily (order previous evening by 6 pm). Shops 1.5 km. Restaurant 500 m. Children's play area. Bicycle hire. Cooking facilities. Laundry. Motorcaravan services. Chemical disposal.

Charges 1999: Per person DM 8.50; child (3-14 yrs) 5.00; pitch 10.00; dog 3.00; electricity 3.00 plus connection 2.00; 'chip' card deposit 10.00. No credit cards.

Reservations: Not normally necessary. Address: Am Gülser Moselbogen 20, 56072 Koblenz-Güls. Tel: 0261/44474. FAX: 0261/44494.

3242 Country Camping Schinderhannes, Hausbay-Pfalzfeld

The editorial report for this site appears on page 64 next to its colour advertisement.

3245 Landal GreenParks Sonnenberg, Leiwen, nr Trier

Pleasant site with splendid indoor leisure facility on hilltop above Mosel valley.
This site is on top of a hill with attractive views over the Mosel as you climb the approach road, 4 km. from the wine village of Leiwen and the river. The site has a splendid free indoor activity pool with child's paddling pool, whirlpool, cascade and slides. Also in this building are tenpin bowling, a sauna, solarium and fitness room, tennis and badminton, plus a snack bar. Minigolf, volleyball, a football pitch and good children's play equipment are provided and make this an extremely popular place for youngsters in July and August. Combining a bungalow complex (separate) with camping, the site has 150 large, individual and numbered grassy pitches on terraces with electricity and TV connections. The single toilet block has been rebuilt with under-floor heating, British toilets, washbasins in private cabins (all for women, a couple for men) and free hot showers, and is stretched in busy times. Excursions and entertainment are organised in season, with ranger guided walks, wine-tasting, daily cruises from Leiwen to Bernkastel and coach trips to the Rhine (both May-Oct). There are two good restaurants and shop, and the site is efficiently managed with a friendly and helpful English speaking reception staff.

How to find it: From Trier-Koblenz A48/A1 take exit 129 for Schweich, Föhren and Hetzerath. Follow signs for Leiwen and in town follow signs for Ferienpark, Sonnenberg or Freibad on very winding road up hill 4 km. to site. From A1 southeast of Trier take exit 129 then above.

General Details: Open 25 Feb. - 6 Nov. 300,000 sq.m. Electrical connections (6A). Shop. Restaurant, bistro, bar and snacks (one restaurant only in low season). Disco, entertainment and excursions at busy times (not all every day). Indoor multi-purpose leisure centre with activity pool, 10 pin bowling, tennis and badminton. Volleyball. Football pitch. Minigolf. Children's playground. Bicycle hire 5 km. Fishing 10 km. Riding or golf 12 km. Laundry. Chemical disposal. Motorcaravan services. Bungalows and apartments to let.

Charges 2000: Per unit incl. 2 persons DM 28.00 - 52.00; extra person 4.50; dog 4.50; electricity (6A), satellite TV incl. 4.50. No credit cards.

Reservations: Essential mid July - end August. Write with deposit (Fri. - Fri. only in high season). Address: 54340 Leiwen. Tel: 06507/93690. FAX: 06507/936936.

3250 Landal GreenParks Warsberg, Saarburg, nr Trier

Large, well organised site with comprehensive amenities including chair lift to town.
On top of a steep hill in an attractive location, this site and the long winding approach road both offer pleasant views over the town and surrounding area. A chair lift with a terminal near the site links it to the town and is free for campers – it is well worth a ride. There are 500 numbered touring pitches of quite rea-sonable size on flat or slightly sloping ground, separated in small groups by trees and shrubs, with elec-trical connections (6A) available in most places. There are some tour operator pitches and a separate area of holiday bungalows to rent. The three toilet blocks are of very good quality, having been renewed in '99. They provide British style WCs, washbasins (most in private cabins) and showers, all with free hot water, a unit for disabled visitors, and many washing machines and dryers. There are plenty of games facilities here, a restaurant, large shop and a free heated outdoor swimming pool and children's pool close to a large area of play equipment on sand. This is a site with friendly, English speaking reception staff, which should appeal to all age groups. July is the busiest month.

How to find it: From Trier on road 51 site is well signed in the northwest outskirts of Saarburg off the Trierstrasse (signs also for 'Ferienzentrum') and from all round town. Follow signs up hill for 3 km.

General Details: Open 31 March - 5 Nov. Reception opens 9 - 12 and 2 - 5.30 (Sunday 10-12 only). Shop. Restaurant and snacks, games rooms adjacent. Swimming pools (15/5-15/9). Tennis court and `platform tennis'. Minigolf. Bicycle hire. Football field. Large children's playground. Bowling. Outdoor chess and draughts. Entertainment in season for all ages. Riding and fishing 5 km. Washing machines and dryers. Gas supplies. Chemical disposal. Motorcaravan services. Bungalows for rent (open all year).

Charges 2000: Per unit incl. 2 persons DM 23.00 - 39.00; extra person 4.50; child under 5 yrs free; dog 4.50; electricity 4.50. No credit cards.

Reservations: are made (Fri-Fri only in high season) with 50% deposit. Address: In den Urlaub, 54439 Saarburg. Tel: 06581/91460. FAX: 06581/2514.

3264 Campingplatz Büttelwoog, Dahn, Pirmasens, nr Saarbrücken

Useful night stop en-route to Black Forest, in attractive countryside

Many visitors come here for an overnight stay and then stop for longer or return on their journey home, as it is both peaceful and in an attractive area close to the border with France. In a long, narrow valley with tall trees on either side, a hard access road leads from reception and shop and the bar/restaurant to flat, numbered, grassy pitches, all of which have electricity. Some 80 long stay pitches are further along and another section behind reception gives 120 touring pitches in all. The heated sanitary facilities are quite good, here and in another block in the main part, with free hot water to showers and washbasins (a few private cabins). Torches useful at night. A pleasant site in an interesting setting with a friendly welcome.

How to find it: From Saarbrücken go towards Kaiserslauten on A6/E50 or road 423. Take Zweibrücken exit, then Pirmasens, finally turning to Dahn at Hinterweidenthal. Site is well signed in Dahn.

General Details: Open all year. Electricity connections (4A, mainly 2 pin). Small shop; café/bar for meals incl. breakfast (both 1/3-1/11). Children's playground on sand. Minigolf. Bicycle hire. Riding. Swimming pools (indoor and outdoor) 300 m. Washing machine. Chemical disposal. Town 800 m.

Charges 1999: Per adult DM 9.00; child under 12 yrs 5.00, 12-16 yrs 7.00; pitch 11.00; electricity 3.50; small dog 5.00. Less 10% from 3rd night with camping carnet. No credit cards.

Reservations: Contact site. Address: 66994 Dahn/Pfalz. Tel: 06391/5622. FAX: 06391/5326.

3260 Knaus Camping-Park Bad Dürkheim, Bad Dürkheim, nr Ludwigshafen

Site with good amenities beside lake, on edge of town.

This large site is comfortable and has some 550 pitches (about half occupied by permanent caravans) but, being the best site at this well known wine town, it is very busy in main season. However, with some emergency areas they can usually find space for everyone. The site is long with individual pitches of fair size arranged on each side of the central road, which is decorated with arches of growing vines. A lake runs along one side and bathing is possible (much of the lake has a sandy floor and there is a little beach) and non-powered boats can be launched. An activity programme offers guided tours, biking, canoeing and climbing. Three large sanitary blocks are spaced out along the central avenue. Two have been totally refurbished to a high standard (private cabins, automatic taps, etc), with the other one scheduled to be renewed within two years. They have British style toilets and free hot water in washbasins, showers and sinks and are heated in cool weather. No dogs are taken. Some noise from light aircraft, especially at weekends.

How to find it: Bad Dürkheim is on the no. 37 road west of Ludwigshafen. Site is on the eastern outskirts, signed from the Ludwigshafen road.

General Details: Open all year excl. Nov. Electrical connections. Shop (all year). Restaurant outside gates. Tennis. Beach volleyball. Sports field. Children's playground. Garden chess. Sauna . Solarium. Cooking facilities. Washing machines. Chemical disposal. Motorcaravan services. Caravans (10) and tents to rent. No dogs accepted.

Charges 2000: Per person DM 8.75; child (3-14 yrs) 4.50; pitch 7.50 - 15.00; tent and m/cycle 7.50; electricity 3.50. No credit cards.

Reservations: made for any length without deposit. Address: In den Almen 3, 67098 Bad Dürkheim. Tel: 06322/61356. FAX: 06322/8161.

3470 AZUR Campingplatz Odenwald, Kirchzell, Eberbach, nr Heidelberg

Woodland site between the rivers Neckar and Main.

In the nature reserve of the Odenwald with lots of rambling opportunities and only 7 km. from Amorbach with its Benedictine Abbey, the site gives the impression of being deep in the forest and will appeal most to those who like the peaceful attractions of hills, trees and meadows. It is by a stream in a low lying valley, away from main routes. Miltenberg is a base for pleasure cruises on the Main and a few miles down the Neckar, Bad Wimpfen is a fine example of a mediaeval town. Just over half the pitches are taken by permanent caravans but there are 120 grassy and shaded tourist pitches spread out around the site, with a separate area for tents. There is usually space but it can be full at Easter, Whitsun and late July and entertainment is organised at these times. There is a larger than usual, free, indoor pool with sauna. The sanitary facilities, in three blocks, vary from satisfactory to above average quality and are kept clean, with heating in cool weather. They have British style toilets, washbasins with some cabins and free hot water, plus a toilet and shower for disabled visitors in one.

How to find it: Site is 2 km. south of Kirchzell on the Eberbach - Amorbach road. Caravans approaching from Eberbach may choose to go on for 1 km. and turn back

General Details: Open 15 March - 15 Nov. Many electrical connections (16A). Small shop (April - Oct, at other times order bread at reception). Restaurant. Children's playground. Table tennis. Indoor swimming pool, plus sauna and solarium. Bicycle hire. Barbecue. General room with TV (satellite). Washing machines and dryer. Motorcaravan services. Gas supplies. Mobile homes for hire.

Charges 2000: Per adult DM 7.00 - 10.50; child (2-12 yrs) 5.00 - 7.50; pitch 9.00 - 13.50; small tent pitch 5.00 - 7.50; extra tent 3.00 - 4.00; dog 3.50 - 4.00; electricity 4.00.

Reservations: are made with deposit (DM 15) and fee (15); write to site for details. Address: 63931 Kirchzell-Eberbach. Tel: 09373/566. FAX: 09373/7375.

3405 Camping Bad Liebenzell, Bad Liebenzell, nr Pforzheim

Good municipal site in northeast Black Forest, adjacent to modern pool complex.
This well-run municipal site is attractively situated on the outskirts of the pleasant little spa town of Bad Liebenzell. It has direct access to an excellent, large thermal pool complex (free to campers). This includes swimming pools, a wave pool and a long slide. There is also a children's pool and grassy sunbathing area and several tennis courts. The site is often full in high season when reservation is advisable (if not arrive early). There may be some noise from the nearby roads and railway. The 235 pitches (150 for tourists) are rather small, but all have electricity and are neatly arranged in rows on flat grass between hedges, trees and good roads. Three heated sanitary blocks are well maintained with British style toilets, washbasins with free hot water (in two blocks mostly in cabins) and hot showers. There is provision for disabled visitors and babies, and enclosed washing-up sinks. This is a well run and orderly site.

How to find it: From A8 exits 43, 44 or 45 to Pforzheim then B463 road south (25 km). From A81 exit 28 to Herrenberg then B296 to Calw and B463 to Bad Liebenzell. Site is just north of town.

General Details: Open all year. 20,000 sq.m. Electricity connections (16A). Bar/restaurant with simple, good value meals. Small shop (open all year excl. Nov, but limited hours) – bread to order. Swimming pool complex (15/5-15/9). Cafe/bar by pool (closed Nov). Large room with TV and library. Tennis (instruction available at weekends). Fishing. Bicycle hire. Children's playground. Cycle tracks, nature trails, cross country skiing 8 km. Riding 5 km. Golf 2 km. Washing machines and dryers. Cooking facilities. Gas supplies. Chemical disposal. Motorcaravan services. No dogs accepted.

Charges 1999: Per person DM 10.00; child (4-16 yrs) 5.50; pitch 10.50; electricity on meter; local tax (per person, per night) 16/4-31/10 3.85, otherwise 2.85. Credit cards accepted.

Reservations: Contact site (no deposit). Address: 75378 Bad Liebenzell. Tel: 07052/40460. FAX: as phone. E-mail: bad-liebenzell@cw-net.de.

3415 Campingplatz Adam, Oberbruch, Bühl, nr Baden-Baden

Very convenient lakeside site by A5 Karlsruhe-Basle autobahn near Baden-Baden.
This site is very easily accessed from exit 52 (Bühl) on the A5 autobahn (also from the French autoroute A35 just northeast of Strasbourg) and is a useful base for the Black Forest. There is a lake that is divided into separate areas for bathing or boating and windsurfing, with a long slide – the public are admitted on payment and it attracts many on fine weekends. All the touring pitches (250 from 600) have electricity, many with waste water too, with some near the lake with water and drainage. Tents go along the lake surrounds and there are some places with paved centres to eliminate wet weather problems. At very busy times, units staying overnight only may be placed close together on a lakeside area of hardstanding. There are two heated sanitary buildings for tourers, one rebuilt in '99. They offer individual washbasins with shelf and mirror (one block having mostly private washing cabins), hot showers on payment, facilities for babies and disabled people, laundry and dishwashing. The shop and restaurant/bar remain open virtually all year (not Monday or Tuesday in low season), so this is a useful site to use out of season. In general the site has a well tended look and good English is spoken by the pleasant staff.

How to find it: Take A5/E35-52, exit 52 (Bühl), turn towards Lichtenau, go through Oberbruch and left to site. From French autoroute A35 take exits 52 or 56 onto D2 and D4 respectively then turn onto A5 as above.

General Details: Open all year. 40,000 sq.m. Many electrical connections (10A). Limited shade. Shop (31/3-30/10). Restaurant (1/3-30/10). Football. Volleyball. Tennis. Bowling alley and games room with terrace. Children's playground. Bicycle hire. Fishing. Riding or golf 5 km. Washing machine and dryer. Gas supplies. Chemical disposal. Motorcaravan services.

Charges 2000: Per person DM 9.00 - 12.00; young person (10-16 yrs) 5.50 - 6.50, child (3-10 yrs) 4.00 - 5.00; pitch 9.00 - 12.00, with services 12.00 - 15.00; electricity 3.50; dog 4.00. Credit cards accepted (4% fee).

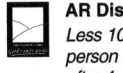

AR Discount
Less 10% on person charge after 4 nights

Reservations: Write to site. Address: 77815 Bühl-Oberbruch. Tel: 07223/23194. FAX: 07223/8982.

Camping ADAM   ADΛM

D-77815 Bühl-Oberbruch
bei Baden-Baden
Tel: (07223)23194 - Fax: (07223)8982

On the edge of the Black Forest, 20 minutes by car from Strasbourg, 15 minutes by car from the famous Spa town of Baden-Baden with Caracella thermal springs, Roman baths, casino and lots of curiosities. The surroundings offer splendid excursions; open air museum in Gutach, glass manufacture in Wolfach, the `Badische Weinstraße', the colourful nature and a big choice for wining and dining. **Open all year.**
Access: Motorway A5 Karlsruhe-Basel, Bühl exit, direction Oberbruch-Moos.

GERMANY - South West

3420 Freizeitcenter Oberrhein, Rheinmünster, nr Baden-Baden

Large well equipped holiday site near the Rhine.

This large site provides much to do and is also a good base for visiting the Black Forest. To the left of reception are a touring area and a section of hardstanding for motorcaravans. The 250 touring pitches, all with electrical connections, include 86 with water and drainage also. Two of the site lakes are for swimming (with roped-off areas for toddlers) and non-powered boating (the water was very clean when we visited), the third small one is for fishing. There are seven modern, heated sanitary buildings with free hot water and very smart fittings. Some have special rooms for children, babies and families and there are family washcabins to rent. Other facilities include a restaurant, supermarket, snack bar and small zoo. There are excellent children's play areas. This site is well worth considering for a holiday, especially for families with young and early teenage children.

How to find it: Site is signed from Rheinmünster, 16 km. southwest of Rastatt on B36. From north on A5/E35-52 take exit 51 (Baden-Baden/Iffezheim) via Hügelsheim then south onto B36; from south take exit 52 (Bühl) and via Schwarzach and Rheinmünster or exit 52 to Rheinau then north on B36 to Stollhofen.

General Details: Open all year. Electricity connections (mostly 16A, 3 pin, a few with 2 pin). Shop (1/4-31/10, local supermarket 3 km). Lakeside restaurant; snack bar (both 1/4-31/10). Modern children's play areas on sand. Tennis. Table tennis. Bicycle hire. Minigolf. Windsurf school. Swimming and boating lakes. Fishing. Riding 4 km. Golf 5 km. Chemical disposal. Motorcaravan services. Gas supplies. Chalets for hire.

Charges 2000: Per child with car DM 9.00 - 13.00; adult 8.00 - 14.00; child 7-15 yrs 6.00 - 9.00, under 6 yrs 4.00 - 7.00; dog 4.00 - 6.00; washcabin 10.00 - 14.00; electricity 3.50. Credit cards accepted.

Reservations: Made for at least a week with deposit (DM 250) and fee (25). Address: 77836 Rheinmünster. Tel: 07227/2500. FAX: 07227/2400.

3450 Ferien-Campingplatz Münstertal, Münstertal, nr Freiburg

The editorial report for this site appears on page 64 next to its colour advertisement.

3430 Schwarzwald-Camping Alisehof, Schapbach, nr Freudenstadt

Agreeable site in quiet central Black Forest situation.

This site, in a beautiful setting in a wooded valley, is for those who want to enjoy the activities of the Black Forest itself. Though very centrally situated in the Forest it is in a quiet position away from the main routes and big towns, with walks available from the site. The 180 pitches are individual numbered ones of average size in rows on terraces on a slope, steep only at the top part; there are 120 on the lower slopes available for tourists. The three sanitary blocks, two on the lower terrace, one beside reception, are first class with free hot water in most washbasins, sinks and showers. Plans are in hand to provide eight family bathrooms (for hire). There are facilities for disabled visitors and baby rooms. In high season there is an entertainment programme for children and organised walks for adults. The friendly management speak English.

How to find it: Site is 1 km. northeast of Schapbach, which is southwest from Freudenstadt. From A5 take Appelweier/Oberkirch exit towards Freudenstadt turning right to Schapbach.

General Details: Open all year. Electrical connections (16A). Shop (all year). Pleasant bar lounge in old farmhouse, open late evening (all year except when very quiet). Restaurant near. Washing machine and dryers. Children's playground. Swimming pool at Schapbach (1 km). Fishing. Minigolf close. Riding 2 km. Golf 1 km. Gas supplies. Chemical disposal. Motorcaravan services.

Charges 1999: Per person DM 8.00 - 9.00; local tax 1.30; child (under 14) 4.00 - 5.50; pitch 8.00 - 9.00; tent 2.50 - 4.50; dog 3.00; TV connection 1.00; electricity 3.00 plus meter. Less 10% on person charge for stays over 7 days. No credit cards.

Reservations: Write to site before 31 May, with deposit (DM 10) and fee (10) by Eurocheque. Address: 77776 Bad Rippoldsau-Schapbach. Tel: 07839/203. FAX: 07839/1263.

3402 Campingplatz Cannstatter Wasen, Stuttgart

Attractively modernised, well managed city municipal site.

Situated in the outskirts of the city, but only a ten minute drive from the centre and with bus and train links just 500 m. away, this is a very convenient site. Completely fenced, it is beside the river Neckar, with a walkway into the city, and is surprisingly green, with pretty flower beds, bushes and trees. Even though all 234 pitches are on hardstanding, they appear green with grass growing through the honeycomb tiles. They are unmarked, have electricity hook-ups and 25 have water and waste water also. A separate grassy area for tents is in one corner. Attractively fenced water and waste units and an area of good quality children's play equipment on bark have been thoughtfully designed. Showers and washbasins (only a couple of private cabins at present) are of quite good quality in older buildings with heating, have free hot water, and are separate from the toilets. A chemical disposal room has a hand basin, soap and paper towels and there is a modern unit for disabled visitors. Opposite here are dishwashing and laundry facilities (also with heating) and a snack-bar/restaurant with terrace open daily from 08.00 to 21.00 (good value when we stayed). A small kiosk behind reception provides basic supplies and there is plenty of tourist information.

How to find it: Site is in Bad Cannstatt close to the Daimler Benz Stadium and a large car park. It is in the east of the city signed from the B10 which can be reached from A8 exit 55 via B313, or A81 exit 17 via B327.

General Details: Open all year (1 Nov - 31 March: barrier only open 08.00-10.00 and 17.00-19.00 unless prior arrangement made). Kiosk Easter - end Oct. (bread to order). Snack bar/restaurant (closed 20 Dec - 15 Jan). Children's play area. Laundry. Chemical disposal. Motorcaravan service point (DM 5 for non-users of the site).

Charges 1999: Per person DM 8.00; child (2-14 yrs) 4.00; caravan 8.50; tent 6.00 - 8.00, acc. to size; car or m/cycle 4.00; motorcaravan 12.00; dog 4.00; electricity 3.00 connection plus 1.00 per kw; water connection 0.50.

Reservations: Not normally necessary, but contact site for details. Address: Mercedesstrasse 40, 70372 Stuttgart. Tel: 0711/556696. FAX: 0711/557454.

3440 Campingplatz Kirchzarten, Kirchzarten, nr Freiburg

Black Forest family site with excellent free swimming pools.

There are pleasant views of the Black Forest from this municipal site which is within easy reach by car of Titisee, Feldberg and Todtnau, and 8 km. from the large town of Freiburg in Breisgau. It is divided into 460 numbered pitches with electricity, 340 of which are for tourists (some used by tour operators). Most pitches, which are side by side on level ground, are of quite reasonable size and marked out at the corners, though there is nothing to separate them and there are some hardstanding motorcaravan pitches. From about late June to mid-August it does become full, and it would be advisable to reserve. The fine new swimming pool complex adjoining the site is free to campers and is a main attraction, with pools for diving, fun, swimming and children, surrounded by spacious grassy sunbathing areas and a children's play area on sand. The site's sanitary facilities are good, comprising four blocks, one for laundry, dishwashing, cooking and a heated ski-room. Two modern blocks are heated and include British style toilets, individual washbasins with mirrors and shelves, free, fully controllable hot showers, facilities for disabled visitors and a baby bath. It is only a short stroll to the village centre, which has supermarkets, restaurants, etc.

How to find it: From Freiburg take the B31 road signed Donaueschingen to Kirchzarten where site is signed (it is to the south of the village).

General Details: Open all year. 56,000 sq.m. Electricity connections (16A). Restaurant/bar. Shop. Swimming pool complex (15/5-15/9). Large children's playground. Table tennis. TV room. Adventure playground, fitness track, tennis and minigolf near. Tennis (covered court, can be booked from site). Riding. Golf 3 km. Organised recreation programme in high season. No dogs allowed. Cooking stoves, washing machines, dryers, irons, sewing machines (all on payment by meter). Chemical disposal. Caravans for hire.

Charges 1999: Per person DM 7.50 - 13.50, incl. local tax; child (4-16 yrs) 5.50 - 7.50, third child and above 3.50 - 4.50; pitch 9.00 - 11.50; electricity 2.00 plus meter. Every 15th day free. Credit cards accepted.

Reservations: made for min. 1 week without deposit. Address: Campingplatz, 79199 Kirchzarten. Tel: 07661/39375. FAX: 07661/61624.

CAMPING KIRCHZARTEN

A site in the southern Black Forest with every comfort for wonderful holidays. New heated outdoor swimming pool complex. Kurhaus with restaurant and reading room nearby. Riding, tennis, minigolf, children's playground in the wood. Fine walking country. Caravans for hire.

GERMANY - South West

3435 Terrassen-Camping Sandbank, Titisee

Pleasant, terraced lakeside site, in the Black Forest.

This satisfactory site overlooks Lake Titisee in this lovely area. There are 190 marked pitches for tourists, on gravel with electricity and on terraces with good views over the lake. Trees provide good shade in some parts. The small town of Titisee is a pleasant 20 minute walk along the lakeside and with the attractions of this part of the Forest near - Freiburg, the Rhine Falls at Schaffausen, the source of the Danube at Donaueschingen – it is ideal for a long or short stay. The large, heated sanitary block provides washbasins (many in cabins), hot showers on payment, baby room (key from management) and facilities for disabled people. There is a pleasant lakeside restaurant with terrace, which also provides takeaway food. Access to the lake is available for swimming, boating and carp fishing. Walks are organised and there is some music in high season. Reception staff are friendly and English is spoken. No motorbikes are accepted.

How to find it: From Freiburg take road 31 to Titisee. From the centre follow camping signs then signs for Bankenhof, continuing on less well made up road past this site to Sandbank.

General Details: Open 1 April - 20 Oct. Shop. Electricity connections (16A). Bar/restaurant with takeaway. Children's playground. Bicycle hire. Fishing. Organised walks. Swimming in lake. Boat excursions from Titisee. Music in season. Washing machines and dryer. Gas supplies. Chemical disposal. Motorcaravan services.

Charges 2000: Per person: DM 6.50- 8.00; child 4.50 - 5.00; pitch 10.00-12.50; electricity 2.50; dog 3.00; tax 2.00. Stay 14 days, pay for 10 outside July/Aug. Credit cards accepted.

Reservations: Not made. Address: 79822 Titisee (Hochschwarzwald). Tel: 07651/8243 or 8166. FAX: 07651/8286 or 88444.

3445 Campingplatz Belchenblick, Staufen, nr Freiburg

Quality Black Forest site with good class facilities.

The site stands at the gateway, so to speak, to the Black Forest. Not very high up itself, it is just at the start of the long road climb which leads to the top of Belchen, one of the highest summits of the forest. It is well situated for excursions by car to the best areas of the forest, e.g. the Feldberg-Titisee-Höllental circuit, and many excellent walks are available nearby. Staufen is a pleasant little place with character. The three high quality sanitary blocks are heated and have free hot water in all washbasins and fully controllable hot showers. With British style toilets; individual washbasins with shelf and mirror (6 in private cabins), there are 21 family cabins with WC, basin and shower (some on payment per night for exclusive use). Of the 210 pitches (180 for touring units), 50 have TV, water and waste water connections. A small heated indoor swimming pool is open all year and adjacent is a municipal sports complex including an open-air pool and tennis courts. Reservation is necessary from early June to late August at this popular site, which is not a cheap one. However, the charges do include free hot water and the indoor pool.

How to find it: Take autobahn exit for Bad Krozingen, south of Freiburg, and continue to Staufen. Site is southeast of the town and signed, across an unmanned local railway crossing near the entrance.

General Details: Open all year. 18,000 sq.m. Many electrical connections (10-15A). Shop (March-Nov). General room where drinks and snacks served (all year). Restaurant near. Indoor and outdoor pools. Tennis. Children's playground with barbecue section. Volleyball. Basketball. Skating. Hockey and football fields. Sauna and solarium. Bicycle hire. Fishing 500 m. Riding 2 km. Washing machine. Gas supplies. Chemical disposal. Motorcaravan services. Apartments for rent.

Charges 2000: Per person DM 11.50 - 14.00; child (2-12) 7.00; pitch 14.00; dog 4.00; electricity 1.00 p/kw hour; water connection 2.00; washcabin from 14.00. No credit cards.

Reservations: made without charge. Address: Münstertäler Str. 43, 79219 Staufen im Breisgau. Tel: 07633/7045. FAX: 07633/7908. E-mail: camping.belchenblick@t-online.de.

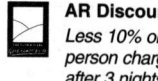

3455 Gugel-Dreiländer Camping und Freizeitpark, Neuenburg

The editorial report for this site appears on page 65 next to its colour advertisement.

3442 Terrassen Campingplatz, Herbolzheim

Useful base for Europa Park and Black Forest, near the Rhine and A5.

This well equipped campsite is in a quiet location on a wooded slope to the north of Freiburg, close to the Black Forest. It is useful as a night stop when travelling between Frankfurt and Basel, and is just 10 km. from Europa Park, only a short way from the A5 autobahn. There are 73 caravan or motorcaravan pitches available for tourists, all with electricity and with grass surfaces, on terraces linked by hard access roads. A separate meadow for tents is at the top of the site (with three cabin toilets) and some pitches are used by a tour operator. The main sanitary facilities are modern, with British style toilets, free hot water in washbasins, showers and sinks, with laundry and dishwashing. The pleasant, small bar and restaurant offers a simple menu in the evenings, with restaurants and shops in the village about 3 km. away. Activities include a small children's play area and table tennis, volleyball and football with the large open-air heated municipal swimming pool complex next door. The local market is held each Friday morning. This is good walking country and with only occasional entertainment, the site makes a very pleasant place in which to relax between daily activities, the many trees, shrubs and plants giving a pleasant, peaceful atmosphere.

How to find it: From A5 Frankfurt - Basel autobahn take exit 57, 58 or 59 and follow signs to Herbolzheim. Site is signed in south side of town near the swimming pool.

General Details: Open 1 week before Easter - 15 October. 2.5 ha. Electrical connections (10A). Small bar/restaurant (Easter - 1/10 closed Mondays). Shop for basics (order bread). Table tennis. Volleyball. Football. Heated swimming pool adjacent (1/4-15/9), other sports near. Bicycle hire 1 km. Riding 5 km. Washing machines. Chemical disposal. Motorcaravan services. Dogs not accepted 15/6-15/8.

Charges 1999: Per person DM 9.00; child (2-12 yrs) 5.00; pitch 10.00 (tents 9.00); electricity 2.00 + 1.00 p/kwh; dog (see above) 2.00. Credit cards accepted

Reservations: Contact site. Address: 79336 Herbolzheim. Tel: 07643/1460. FAX: 07643/913382. E-mail: s.hugoschmidt@t-online.de.

3452 Terrassen Camping Alte Sägemühle, Sulzburg

Pretty site beautifully situated in the southern Black Forest.

By a peaceful road leading only to a natural swimming pool and an hotel, beyond the picturesque old town of Sulzburg with its narrow streets, this attractive location is perfect for those seeking peace and quiet. In a tree-covered valley with a stream running through the centre, the site has been kept as natural as possible. Divided into terraced areas, the 50 pitches (up to 120 sq.m.) all have electrical connections, although long leads may be needed. The main building by the entrance houses reception, a small shop and the sanitary facilities which are of good quality, with showers and washbasins (two private cabins), dishwashing and a washing machine. Run by the Geuss family (Frau Geuss speaks reasonable English) the site has won an award from the state for having been kept natural, for example, no tarmac roads, no minigolf, no playgrounds, etc. Prior reservation is recommended in high season. There are opportunities for walking straight from the site into the forest, and many walks and cycle rides are shown on maps available at reception. Europa Park is less than an hour away. The tiny 500 year old Jewish Cemetery reached through the site has an interesting history. There are restaurants and other shops in Sulzburg just 1.5 km. away.

How to find it: Site is easily reached (25 minutes) from autobahn A5/E35. Take exit 64 for Bad Krozingen just south of Freiburg onto the B3 south to Heitersheim, then on through Sulzburg, or if coming from the south, exit 65 through Müllheim, Heitersheim and Sulzburg.

General Details: Open all year. Electrical connections (16A). Small shop for basics and local wines (all year). Natural, unheated swimming pool adjacent (June-Aug). Washing machine. Chemical disposal. Motorcaravan services. Bicycle hire in Sulzburg.

Charges 1999: Per person DM 8.00; child (1-15 yrs) 6.00; pitch 8.00 - 12.00; electricity 0.80 plus meter; dog 3.00; local tax (from 16 yrs) 1.00.

Reservations: Recommended - contact site. Address: 79295 Sulzburg. Tel: 07634/551181.

Terrassen Camping

Alte Sägemühle

D-79295 Sulzburg / Südl. Schwarzwald
Axel Geuß, Telefon 0 76 34 / 55 11 81

Ideal for Walking, Cycling and Excursions

25.000 m², 360-380 m. above sea level, 12 terraces, 50 pitches 80-120 m².

Idyllic forest setting in the very romantic Sulz valley. **Extremely peaceful.**

An oasis for genuine campers

Special award from Baden-Württemberg for a fine example of blending with the countryside and outstanding suitability for camping amid nature.

GERMANY - South West / South East

3410 Campingplatz Aichelberg, Aichelberg, Goppingen

Small, pleasant and friendly municipal site, near Stuttgart-München autobahn.

This is a very convenient night-stop just off the Stuttgart-München autobahn, roughly midway between Stuttgart and Ulm, and a reasonable drive from the German border at Aachen. On the edge of a wood, the shaded pitches on flat grass and hardstanding are not marked out but adequate space is allowed and all have electrical connections. There is a separate area for tents opposite the entrance. The main toilet block is well constructed and should be sufficient for the 90 static units and 36 tourist pitches. British WCs; free hot water for washbasins and sinks plus one private cabin and two showers for each sex and a family washroom. On site are a small shop and bar, a restaurant is 250 m. There is a children's playground (on sand).

How to find it: Take exit 58 from autobahn A8 just to the west of Kirchheim towards Goppingen. If coming from München turn immediately left to site, if from Stuttgart follow signs.

General Details: Open all year. Small shop all year (order bread). Village shops 4 km. Electricity (10A). Well shaded. Bar. Restaurant 250 m. Washing machine and dryer. Children's playground. Swimming pool 5 km.

Charges 1999: Per person DM 7.50; child (4-5 yrs) 3.00, (6-15 yrs) 4.00; pitch 8.00; electricity 3.00 + meter.

Reservations: Write to site (not necessary for overnight). Address: 73101 Aichelberg/Goppingen. Tel: 07164/2700. FAX: as phone.

3465 Camping Wirthshof, Markdorf, nr Friedrichshafen

Friendly site with good facilities near the Bodensee.

Lying 7 km. back from the Bodensee, 12 km. from Friedrichshafen this site could well be of interest to Britons with young children. The 324 individual touring pitches have electrical connections and are of about 80 sq.m. on well tended flat grass, joining access roads. There are now some larger pitches with water, waste water and electricity. On site is a pleasant heated outdoor swimming pool (25 x 12.5 m.) with a grassy lying-out area; it is free to campers but is also open to outsiders on payment so can be busy in season (open perhaps mid-May to mid-Sept). The three toilet blocks are being renewed in turn and provide washbasins and showers with free hot water, a unit for disabled people and children's bathroom. There is a new solar heated unit for dishwashing and laundry. No dogs are accepted in July/Aug. and there is a special section for campers with dogs at other times. Many activities are organised for children and adults over a long season.

How to find it: Site is on eastern edge of Markdorf, turn south off B33 Ravensburg road.

General Details: Open 15 March - 30 Oct. Electricity connections (10A). Shop. Restaurant/bar. Swimming pool (10/5-10/9). Sports field with goal posts. Adventure playground. Bicycle hire. Normal minigolf; also 'pit-pat', played at table height with billiard cues. Activity programme. Tennis near. Riding 8 km. Golf and fishing 10 km. Washing machines and dryers. Gas supplies. Chemical disposal. Motorcaravan services. Caravans for hire. Special one-night pitches. No dogs July/Aug.

Charges 2000: Per person DM 8.00 - 9.50; child (1-14 yrs) 5.00 - 6.50; pitch 14.00 - 16.00; serviced pitch 22.00-25.00; dog 3.00 (not allowed July/Aug); electricity 3.00. No credit cards.

Reservations: made with deposit (DM 80) and fee (20). Address: Steibensteg 12, 88677 Markdorf. Tel: 07544/2325. FAX: 07544/3982.

3665 Camping Brunnen, Brunnen, Füssen, nr Kempten

Lakeside site well placed for excursions.

Quietly situated, with mountain views, this a useful base for excursions, with Füssen and the famous castles of Neuschwanstein and Hohenschwangau close by. Right by the Forggensee, with a beach and jetty, (the water level of the reservoir can vary), it is on slightly undulating ground. The 300 pitches (230 for touring units) are all individual ones with some terracing, most have hardstanding and are from 60-120 sq.m, with electrical connections (long leads may be necessary), and there is a separate meadow for tents in summer. Excellent sanitary facilities are housed on different floors in a modern, heated building. There are several washrooms and toilet rooms (only selected ones are opened in low seasons). Hot water is free to the showers and individual washbasins, half in private cabins. Some bathrooms are for private hire and there are facilities for disabled visitors and children. Good value meals are available in the restaurant.

How to find it: At Schwangau, 3 km. northeast of Füssen on the no. 17 Munich road, turn off at crossroads in village where there are signs to Brunnen and site.

General Details: Open all year except 5 Nov - 20 Dec. 20,000 sq.m. Electricity connections (16A). Small shop. Restaurant. Children's playground. Games and TV room. Sports field. Fishing. Bicycle hire. Riding. Boat slipway 2 km. Golf 2 km. Washing machines and dryers. Drying room. Cooking facilities. Dishwasher. Gas supplies. Chemical disposal. Motorcaravan services.

Charges 2000: Per person DM 10.50 - 13.00, incl. local tax; child 2-8 yrs 5.50, 9-15 yrs 9.00; pitch 9.00 - 11.00; electricity (overnight) 2.00 otherwise 1.00 per kw; dog 5.00 extra car 4.00. Credit cards accepted.

Reservations: made for winter only, not summer, so arrive early especially when the weather is good. Address: Seestrasse 81, 87645 Schwangau-Brunnen. Tel: 08362/8273. FAX: 08362/8630. E-mail: info@camping-brunnen.de

3650 Campingpark Gitzenweiler Hof, Lindau, nr Friedrichshafen

The editorial report for this site appears on page 65 next to its colour advertisement.

3670 Internationaler Campingplatz Hopfensee, Füssen, nr Kempten

Luxury lakeside site, north of Füssen, for caravans and motorcaravans only.
This site is well placed to explore the very attractive Bavarian Alpine region which, along with the architecture and historical interest of the Royal Castles at Hohenswangau and the Baroque church at Wies, makes it a very popular holiday area. At the centre of the site is a large building with an open village-like square in the middle, adorned with cascading flowers. It houses exceptionally good, heated sanitary facilities with British style WCs, free hot water in all washbasins (some in cabins), large showers and sinks, laundry and washing-up rooms, as well as baby and children's wash rooms on the ground floor. There are some private units for hire. On the upper floors are a heated swimming pool, treatment and physiotherapy suites, a cinema, fitness centre and children's play room. A restaurant with terrace faces across the lake towards the setting sun. The 382 tourist pitches, most with shade, each have electricity, water, drain and cable TV connections. They are marked, numbered and of a good size. There is direct access to the lake for sailing, canoeing etc. and a place for parking boats. Charges are high, but include the heated indoor pool, a super new sports building, cinema etc.

How to find it: Site is 4 km. north of Füssen. Turn off the B16 to Hopfen and site is on the left through a car park. If approaching from the west on B310, turn towards Füssen at T-junction with the B16 and immediately turn right again for the road to Hopfen.

General Details: Open all year except 5 Nov - 17 Dec. 80,000 sq.m. Electricity connections (16A). Restaurant. Bar. Shop. Indoor pool and fitness centre. Supervised courses of remedial water treatments, massage, etc. Sauna, solarium and steam bath. Children's playground and kindergarten. Large new games room with table tennis, pool, etc. Bicycle hire. Tennis. Table tennis. Fishing. Riding 1 km. Ski school in winter. Motorcaravan services. No tents taken.

Charges 2000: Per person DM 13.40 - 15.25; child 2-12 yrs 7.70 - 9.30, 12-18 yrs 10.30 - 13.90; local tax (over 18) 2.40 - 3.00; pitch with cable TV & electricity 19.60 - 21.65 plus meter; dog 5.00 - 5.50; private wash cabin 15.50. No credit cards.

Reservations: made without deposit; min. 14 days 16 June-1 Sept (unless shorter time fits into charts). Address: 87629 Fussen im Königswinkel. Tel: 08362/917710. FAX: 08362/917720. E-mail: info@camping-hopfensee.com.

3680 Alpen-Caravanpark Tennsee, Krün, Garmisch-Partenkirchen

Attractive site for the active holiday with good facilities.
Tennsee is in beautiful surroundings high up (1,000 m.) in the Ammergauer Alps with super mountain views, and close to many famous places of which Innsbruck (44 km) and Oberammergau (26 km) are two of many. Mountain walks are plentiful, with several lifts close by. 139 serviced pitches have individual connections for electricity (up to 16A), gas, TV, radio, telephone, water and waste water. The other 111 pitches all have electricity and some of these are available for overnight guests at a reduced rate. The first class sanitary block has under-floor heating, British style toilets, free hot water to the washbasins in cabins and showers (private units with WC, shower, basin and bidet for rent). The unit for disabled people has the latest in flushing and warm air drying and there is a baby bath, a dog bathroom and a heated room for ski equipment (with lockers). Reception and restaurants (waiter, self service and takeaway), bar, cellar youth room and some apartments for rent and a well stocked shop are all housed in attractive buildings. Many activities and excursions are organised to local attractions by the Zick family, who run the site in a friendly and efficient manner.

How to find it: Site is just off main Garmisch-Partenkirchen/Innsbruck road between Klais and Krün, 15 km. from Garmisch.

General Details: Open all year except 12 Nov - 15 Dec. 30,000 sq.m. Shop. Restaurants with takeaway. Bar. Youth room with table tennis, amusements. Solarium. Bicycle hire. Children's playground. Fishing 400 m. Riding or golf 3 km. Organised activities and excursions. Bus service to ski slopes in winter. Cash dispenser for Euro cards. Cooking facilities. Washing machines. Free dryers and irons. Gas supplies. Chemical disposal. Motorcaravan services. Apartments to rent.

Charges 2000: Prices acc. to season: per person DM 12.50 - 13.00; 1-3 children (3-15 yrs) 6.50 - 8.50; local tax 1.95; waste 0.60 p/person; pitch 14.90 - 24.00; summer tent pitches in adjacent meadow 10.50; dog 5.50; electricity, etc. on meter. Family over-night rate on certain pitches 29.50. Easter family package 39.50. Senior citizens special rates (not winter). Credit cards accepted (Visa, Eurocard or Mastercard).

Reservations: Advised for July - Sept and Xmas and made for exact dates (no fee). Address: 82493 Klais/Krün (Bayern). Tel: 08825/17-0. FAX: 08825/17-236. E-mail: camping.tennsee@t-online.de.

GERMANY - South East

3675 Terrassen-Camping am Richterbichl, Rottenbuch, nr Peiting

Useful overnight site by the main Garmisch-Augsburg road.

This little site, beside the main B23 Garmisch-Augsburg road, has all the features required of a good transit site. About 110 pitches – 40 for permanent units and 70 for tourists – are on flat terraces in rows on either side of access roads. They are not marked out but about 80 sq.m. is allowed per unit and there is electricity in all parts (10A). There may be some road noise. The toilet block is part of the main building and is heated. It is satisfactory and provides free hot water to washbasins (four cabins) and sinks, and on payment in the showers. A little lake (quite deep with a small shallow area) on site can be used for bathing or boating with inflatables. The pleasant bar has a TV and a children's room, with table tennis, alongside.

How to find it: Site is beside the B23 road on south side of Rottenbuch (12 km. south of Schongau).

General Details: Open all year. Shop (basics kept, bread to order, shops and restaurants 5 mins walk). Bar with breakfast served. Games room. Children's playground. Bicycle hire. Fishing 4 km. Riding 5 km. Washing machine and dryer. Gas supplies. Chemical disposal. Motorcaravan services. Caravans and apartments for hire.

Charges 2000: Per person DM 8.50; local tax 1.00; child (3-14 yrs) 5.00; pitch 8.00; dog 3.00; electricity 2.00 + meter. Credit cards accepted.

Reservations: made for any period without deposit. Address: 82401 Rottenbuch. Tel: 08867/1500. FAX: 08867/8300. E-mail: christof.echtler@t-online.de.

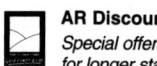
AR Discount
Special offers
for longer stays

3685 Camping Allweglehen, Berchtesgaden, nr Salzburg

All year round site with spectacular views.

Berchtesgaden is a National Park with magnificent scenery, in an area of mountains, lakes, valleys, castles and churches. Hitler built his 'Eagles Nest' on top of the Kehlstein, which is visible from the site and open to the public (bus service, no cars). The site occupies a hillside position, with spectacular mountain views. The site access road is steep (14%), particularly at the entrance, but the proprietor will use his tractor to tow caravans if requested. There are 180 pitches (160 for touring), arranged on a series of gravel terraces, separated by hedges or fir trees and all with good views and electrical connections. There is a separate area on a sloping meadow for tents. The pleasant restaurant, with terrace, offers Bavarian specialities at reasonable prices. Amenities include an outdoor heated swimming pool (16 x 8 m), a children's play area (outside site), minigolf and table tennis. The sanitary facilities are in two adjacent, heated blocks near the restaurant, with British style WCs, and free hot water to washbasins, showers and sinks.

How to find it: Easiest access is via the Austrian autobahn A10 (vignette necessary), Salzburg Sud exit and follow the B305 towards Berchtesgaden. Alternatively take the B305 from Ruhpolding (the pretty Alpenstrasse – winding and with 3.1 m. height limit), or B20 from Bad Reichenhall. Site is 4 km. northeast of Berchtesgaden.

General Details: Open all year. Electricity (16A). Restaurant. Kiosk for essentials. Children's play area. Small heated pool (small charge, 15/5-15/10). Solarium. Minigolf. Table tennis. Fishing. Excursions. Winter sports near. Bicycle hire 3 km. Riding 2 km. Laundry facilities. Gas supplies. Chemical disposal. Motorcaravan services.

Charges 1999: Per pitch DM 12.00; adult 8.50; child (6-16 yrs) 6.50; local tax 3.50 (child 1.50); waste tax 1.50; electricity 0.90 per kw. Credit cards accepted.

Reservations: Write to site (in German!). Address: 84171 Berchtesgaden. Tel: 08652/2396. FAX: 08652/63503.

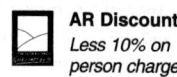
AR Discount
Less 10% on
person charge

3690 Campingplatz Wagnerhof, Bergen, nr Rosenheim

Small but excellent site close to München - Salzburg autobahn near Chiemsee.

The pretty little village of Bergen is 3 km. south of the A8 and about 10 km. from the Chiemsee, Germany's largest lake. Ringed by hills, with views of distant mountains and a large variety of trees and plants, Wagnerhof is a well organised, pleasant site in a quiet location on the edge of Bergen. Owned by two brothers, one of whom speaks excellent English, there is always a welcome here. Most of the 140 tourist pitches are part hardstanding, part grass and have electricity. Two first class heated sanitary blocks have British style WCs, free hot water in washbasins (some cabins) and sinks and on payment in showers. One block is on the ground floor of a well constructed building and the smaller one, recently refurbished, is by reception. There is a tennis court and campers who stay for more than one night may use the town swimming pool next door free of charge. No entertainment is offered on site but the village is very near. Being so close to the A8, the site makes a good night stop but you may be tempted to stay longer to explore the Chiemsee, mountains, Salzburg and other nearby attractions – or just relax.

How to find it: From A8 take exit for Bergen, follow signs to village where site is signed on the northern edge.

General Details: Open all year. 28,000 sq.m. Electricity (16A). Small shop (May - Oct). General room. Shops and restaurants in village. Swimming pool adjacent (May - Sept). Tennis. Children's playground. Bicycle hire 1 km.Fishing 8 km. Washing machine, dryer and drying room. Cooking facilities. Chemical disposal.

Charges 1999: Per person DM 7.00 - 9.50; + local tax 1.20; child (under 14 yrs) 4.50 - 5.50 + 0.60 tax; pitch 9.50 - 12.50, extra car or tent 4.75 - 6.25; electricity 4.00 (once only) + meter. No credit cards.

Reservations: made with deposit. Address: Campingstrasse 11, 83346 Bergen. Tel: 08662/8557. FAX: 08662/5924.

3635 Camping München-Obermenzing, München

Useful site for visits to city or night stops.

On the northwest edge of Munich, this site makes a good stopover for those wishing to see the city or pass the night. The flat terrain is mostly covered by mature trees. Caravan owners are best off here as they have a special section of 130 individual plots, mainly separated from each other by high hedges and opening off the hard site roads with easy access. These have electricity connections and about 30 have water and waste water connections also. About 200 tents and motorcaravans are taken on quite large, level grass areas, with an overflow section so space is usually available. The single central sanitary block is large, having been extended, and it should now be adequate in size. Cleaning appears satisfactory and there is heating in the low season. It provides British style toilets, individual washbasins with shelf and mirror, many in curtained cubicles and most with free hot water. Hot showers require tokens (DM 2) There is a shop and rest room with TV and a drinks machine (including beer). Public transport services are available to the city from very close by. By car the journey might take 20-30 minutes depending on the density of traffic. There is some road noise, but we spent a reasonably undisturbed night here.

How to find it: Site is in the northwest of the city. From Stuttgart, Nuremberg, Deggendorf or Salzburg, leave A99 at Lochhausener Strasse - site is in this road.

General Details: Open 15 March - 31 Oct. 50,000 sq.m. Electrical connections (10A). Mostly shaded. Shop (all season). TV room (April - Oct). Riding or golf 6 km. Cooking facilities on payment. Washing machine and dryers. Gas supplies. Chemical disposal. Motorcaravan services.

Charges 1999: Per person DM 7.80; child (2-14 yrs) 4.00; car 6.00; tent 7.50; caravan 9.00; motorcaravan 12.00; m/cycle 4.00; electricity 2.00 plus meter; dog 2.00 (once only). Small per person surcharge (DM 2.50) for the Beer Festival (14/9-5/10). No credit cards.

Reservations: Not made and said not to be necessary. Address: Lochhausener Str. 59, 81247 München. Tel: 089/811 22 35. FAX: 089/814 48.07.

Camping
MÜNCHEN
Obermenzing

On your way through Munich follow always the direction sign `Autobahn Stuttgart' until the beginning of the Autobahn except when approaching from the Salzburg autobahn. In this case follow `Autobahn Lindau' signs to Gräfelfing; then take Pasing exit and follow `Autobahn Stuttgart'.

A modern camping site located at the beginning of the Autobahn Munich-Stuttgart in a 57,000 sq.m. park.

Open from 15 March to 31 October.

Resident Proprietor: Andreas Blenck
Lochhausener Str. 59, 81247 München
Tel: 0049 89-811 22 35
Fax: 0049 89-814 48 07

- ✦ **Special plots for caravans.**
- ✦ **Electric supply for light and heating.**
- ✦ **First class sanitary accommodations.**
- ✦ **Hot showers, single cabins with basins.**
- ✦ **Washing machines.**
- ✦ **Dishwashing and cooking house.**
- ✦ **Self-service store for food and beverages.**
- ✦ **Tavern (Hofbräuhaus beer).**
- ✦ **Ca. 20 min. to the city by car.**
- ✦ **Good connections by bus, tram or S-train.**

Worth Remembering:

'Mittagsrühe' - In Germany, virtually all campsite receptions shut completely for two hours, usually 13.00 - 15.00 hrs, with some slight variations. Barriers are locked, sometimes for pedestrians too.

GERMANY - South East

3640 Campingplatz München-Thalkirchen, München

Reliable municipal site in river conservation area on the city outskirts.

This well run municipal site is quietly situated on the southern side of Munich in parkland formed by the River Isar conservation area, 4 km. from the city centre (there are subway and bus links). Pleasant walks may be taken in the park and the world famous Munich zoo is just 15 minutes walk along the river from the site. The large city of Munich has much to offer and the Thalkirchen site becomes very crowded during the season, when one may have much less space than one would like, particularly if only staying for one night. However, it is well equipped and clean, with a total of 550 pitches (150 for caravans, most with electricity, water and waste water; 100 for motorcaravans, mostly with electricity and a small area of hard-standing) of various sizes, marked by metal or wooden posts and rails. Like many city sites, groups are taken in one area. There are five toilet blocks, two of which can be heated, with seatless toilets, washbasins with shelf, mirror and cold water. Hot water for showers and sink is on payment. The facilities are hard pressed when the site is full. Out of the main season, when not all are open, there may be long walks from some parts. Facilities for disabled people are provided. The office, shop and snack bar open for long hours. The site is very busy (and probably noisy) during the Beer Festival (14 Sept - 5 Oct) when a daily per person surcharge of DM 7 applies.

How to find it: From autobahns follow 'Mittel' ring road to SSE of the city centre where site is signed; also follow signs for Thalkirchen or the Zoo and site is close. Well signed now from all over the City.

General Details: Open mid-March - end Oct. 40,000 sq.m. Electricity connections (10A). Some shade. Some pitches suitable for American motorhomes. Shop (7 am - 8.30 pm). Snack bar with covered terrace (7 am - 10 pm). Restaurant 200 m. Good children's playground. Tourist information, souvenirs and other services. Treatment room. Washing machines and dryers. Maximum stay 14 days. Office hours 7 am - 11 pm.

Charges guide: Per person DM 7.90; child (2-14 yrs) 2.50; tent (acc. to size) 5.50 - 7.00; car 8.50; m/cycle 4.00; caravan incl. car 19.00; motorcaravan (acc. to size) 11.00 - 13.00; electricity 3.50. Credit cards only accepted for souvenirs.

Reservations: not made except for groups - said to be room up to 4 pm. daily. Address: Zentralländstr. 49, 81379 München. Tel: 089/7231707. FAX: 089/7243177.

3630 Donau-Lech Camping, Eggelstetten, Donauwörth, nr Augsburg

Very pleasant, friendly site just off the `Romantische Strasse'.

The Haas family have developed this site well and run it very much as a family site, providing a useful information sheet in English. The lake provides swimming and wildlife for children and adults to enjoy. Alongside it are 50 marked touring pitches on flat grass arranged in rows either side of a tarred access road. With an average of 120 sq.m. per unit, electrical connections, and with water, waste water and TV connections on most pitches also, it is a comfortable site with an open feeling and developing shade. There are three separate pleasant, flat, grass areas near the entrance for people with tents (including youngsters, cyclists or motorcyclists) with unmarked pitches. Pitches for longer stay visitors are located beyond the tourers. All amenities are housed in the main building at the entrance with reception and a large bar area (with self-service machines for beer, soft drinks and microwave meals). Downstairs are a sauna and the sanitary facilities with eight controllable showers on payment (DM 1 for five minutes, slot in corridor - you can put two in and meter only runs when tap is on), toilets, washbasins with warm water and a dish-washing and laundry room, all of a satisfactory standard. Basic food supplies are kept. Suitable not only as a night stop on the way south, the site is also not far from Augsburg or Munich and the local area is very attractive; you may borrow bicycles from the proprietor.

How to find it: Turn off main B2 road about 5 km. south of Donauwörth at signs for Asbach-Bäumenheim Nord towards Eggelstetten, then follow camp signs for over 1 km. to site.

General Details: Open all year. Electricity connection (16A). Hardstanding area for winter. Shop (all year). Self service bar. General room. Youth room. Restaurants and other amenities a short drive. Table tennis. Lake for bathing on site (own risk); larger sailboarding lake 400 m. Sauna. Washing machine and dryer. Motorcaravan service point. Chemical disposal.

Charges guide: Per person DM 8.00; child (4-12 yrs) 4.70; caravan 10.00; tent 6.00 - 10.00; car 2.50; motorcaravan 12.00; electricity 4.00 or on meter; dog 3.50.

Reservations: not needed - said to be always space at present. Address: 86698 Eggelstetten. Tel: 09002/4044. FAX: 09002/4046.

3627 Azur Camping Ellwangen, Ellwangen

Good night stop or for a longer stay at developing site in an area of hills and lakes.

Situated in a quiet position on the edge of town, with the river Jagst along one side, this new six hectare site, from which you can see the large hilltop castle, has a park-like appearance with mature trees giving some shade. The 95 large, flat, grassy pitches (with one area of hardstanding to the right of the entrance) are off tarmac access roads. Electricity is available for about half the pitches from central boxes. All the facilities are in one area to the left of the site entrance in modern units, with reception, the small shop for basic supplies and a bar/restaurant with terrace open all year. More heated sanitary facilities are being added as the site develops, with some private cabins now provided in addition to showers and washbasins, all with free hot water. There are dishwashing facilities, both inside and out, a small laundry, and rooms for chemical disposal, babies and disabled visitors, plus a motorcaravan service point. Some new play equipment for children is on sand and fishing is very popular here. Very close to the site is a heated indoor municipal wave-pool, with free access for campers and there are numerous other local attractions.

How to find it: From A7 Ulm - Würzburg autobahn take exit 113 and go into Ellwangen from where site is signed on road to Rotenbach village. It is next to the Hallenbad, with a fairly tight left turn into the entrance road.

General Details: Open 15 March - 15 Nov. Electricity connections (16A). Shop. Restaurant/bar. Fishing. Children's playground. Indoor pool 200 m. Fishing. Cycle paths. Laundry facilites. Gas supplies. Chemical disposal. Motorcaravan services.

Charges 2000: Per adult DM 7.00 - 10.50; child (2-12 yrs) 5.00 - 7.50; pitch 9.00 - 13.50; small tent pitch 5.00 - 7.50; extra tent 3.00 - 4.00; dog 3.50 - 4.00; electricity 4.00. No credit cards.

Reservations: Contact site. Address: Rotenbacher Strasse, 73479 Ellwangen/Jagst. Tel: 07961/7921. FAX: 07961/562 330.

3610 Knaus-Campingpark Nürnberg, Nürnberg

Satisfactory site just outside the city.

This former municipal site (known as Camping im Volkspark Dutzendteich) is now run by the Knaus group. A perfectly acceptable, if not luxurious site, it is at its best outside the main season when it is not so busy and the tall trees make it quite attractive, as well as providing some shade. It is some 4 km. from the city centre (a 20 minute walk following signs takes you to the underground station) and 200 m. from the swimming pool and football stadium. Up to 200 units are taken on flat grass, 112 with electricity .The pitches are not marked out and the site does not like to turn people away so at the busiest times spacing might be close. The two fairly basic toilet blocks could be hard pressed in July and August. They have British style toilets, washing troughs (cold water), washbasins with hot water (some curtained cabins) and fairly small hot showers on payment (DM 2). Improvements to these sanitary facilities are in hand.

How to find it: From autobahns, take Nürnberg-Fischbach exit from A9 München-Bayreuth east of Nürnberg. Proceed 3 km. towards city then left at camp sign. From city follow 'Stadion-Messe' signs and site is well signed.

General Details: Open all year excl. Nov. Electricity connections (10A). Café. Kiosk with basic supplies. General room with pool table, amusements, where drinks from shop can be consumed. Tennis (free). Children's play area in woodland. Washing machine and dryer. Gas supplies. Chemical disposal. Motorcaravan services.

Charges 2000: Per person DM 8.75; child (3-14 yrs) 4.50; pitch 7.50 - 12.50; hiker or cyclist's tent 7.50; m/cycle 3.50; dog 4.00; electricity 3.50. No credit cards.

Reservations: not made and said to be unnecessary. Address: Hans-Kalb-Str. 56, 90471 Nürnberg 50. Tel: 09331/5521. FAX: 09331/804747.

3620 DCC-Campingpark Romantische Strasse, Dinkelsbühl, nr Ellwangen

Modern site, very close to well known town on Romantic Road.

Run by the German Camping Club (DCC), this site is by one of Germany's best known mediaeval towns, from which of course visits can be made to other places on the Romantic Road. There are 475 pitches (half of which are for touring) on broad grassy terraces overlooking a small lake. All are numbered and of about 80 sq.m., with electricity. A special area is kept for overnight stays. The lake can be used for bathing or one's own non-powered boat. The two large modern toilet blocks are of good quality and should satisfy all demands with British style toilets, washbasins with free hot water, some in private cabins, plentiful showers with hot water (DM 0.50 charge) and free hairdryers.

How to find it: Site is near road 25 and is signed in Dinkelsbühl towards Dürnwangen.

General Details: Open all year, also shop, (meals at least Easter, then May-end Sept.); 80,000 sq.m. Electrical connections (10A) and water points. Shop. General/TV room. Children's playgrounds. Minigolf. Organised daytime activities in season. Bicycle hire. Washing machines, dryers and dishwashing. Cooking facilities.

Charges guide: Per person DM 7.50; child (4-13) 5.00; (10% off these two with international camping carnet); local tax (over 4 yrs.) 1.25; pitch 16.50; dog 2.00; electricity 0.50 + meter.

Reservations: only through DCC and rather complex, costly, and usually unnecessary. Try phoning site shortly before arrival: 09851/7817. FAX: as phone.

GERMANY - South East

3605 Camping Rangau, Dechsendorf, nr Erlangen

Overnight halt close to A3 Würzburg - Nürnberg autobahn.

This site makes a convenient stopover, quickly and easily reached from the Würzburg-Nürnberg motorway and may be pleasant enough to stay a bit longer. It has 110 pitches which are mainly for tourists on flat ground, under trees, numbered and partly marked but only about 60-80 sq.m. There are also 60 permanent units. There is usually space and, in peak season, overnight visitors can often be put on adjacent football pitch. A reasonable sanitary block, heated when cold, has free hot water in well spaced washbasins with shelf and mirror, and in the controllable showers with seat, and new facilities for disabled visitors were added in '99. An older block provides WCs. A fair sized lake with direct access from the site can be used for sailing or windsurfing or for fishing on permit; boats are for hire. One can also swim here or in a swimming pool 200 m. away. The centre of Erlangen is 5 km.

How to find it: Take exit for Erlangen-West from A3 autobahn, turn towards Erlangen but after less than 1 km. at Dechsendorf turn left by camp signs and follow to site.

General Details: Open 1 April - 30 Sept. Restaurant for meals or drinks. Order bread from reception. Children's playground. Laundry facilities. Gas supplies. Chemical disposal.

Charges 2000: Per person DM 8.00; child (under 12) 3.50; pitch 8.00; dog 3.00; electricity (6A) 3.00; rubbish tax 1.00. No credit cards.

Reservations: made without deposit and kept until 6 pm. Address: Campingstrasse 44, 91056 Erlangen-Dechsendorf. Tel: 09135/8866. FAX: 09135/724743.

3615 Azur Camping Stadtsteinach, Stadtsteinach, nr Bayreuth

Friendly, well-managed site in the Franken Forest

Stadtsteinach is well placed for exploring this region with its interesting towns, forest walks and the Fichtel Mountains nearby and this is a comfortable base. Occupying a quiet position in gently undulating countryside with tree-clad hills rising to the east, there are 80 static caravans and space for 100 tourers. Brick main roads give way to hard access roads with pitches on either side, all of which have electricity. The site is on a gentle slope, pitches having been terraced where necessary and there are some hardstandings for motorcaravans. High hedges and trees separate groups of pitches in some areas giving the effect of camping in small clearings. There is a small restaurant with terrace and a shop. The two sanitary areas, one by the open field, the other part of the administration and restaurant building, are heated and of good quality. They have British WCs, free hot water to showers, sinks and washbasins (some in cabins) and facilities for disabled people. The solar heated swimming pool near the entrance is free to campers.

How to find it: Stadtsteinach is north of Bayreuth, off the A9/E51 Nürnberg-Berlin road, reached by the no. 303 road from this autobahn. The site is well signed.

General Details: Open all year. Electrical connections (16A). Restaurant and shop (Easter end Sept). Local shops 800 m. Swimming pool (high season). Children's play area. Tennis. TV. Bicycle hire 500 m. Riding 2 km. Walking. Cooking rings on payment. Laundry facilities. Gas supplies. Chemical disposal. Motorcaravan services.

Charges 2000: Per adult DM 6.00 - 9.50; child (2-12 yrs) 4.00 - 6.50; pitch 8.00 - 12.50; small tent pitch 4.50 - 6.50; extra tent 3.00 - 4.00; dog 3.50 - 4.00; electricity 4.00. No credit cards.

Reservations: Write to site with deposit (DM 20) by Eurocheque. Address: Badstrasse 5, 95346 Stadtsteinach. Tel: 09225/95401. FAX: 09225/95402.

3602 Azur Camping Romantische Strasse, Münster, nr Creglingen

Pleasant country site in good walking area.

The small village of Münster is on a scenic road just 3 km. from Creglingen and about 20 km. from the tourist town of Rothenburg which, although fascinating, is also extremely busy and commercialised. This Azur site would, therefore, be much appreciated for its peaceful situation in a wooded valley just outside Münster, with 90 grass touring pitches, many with a small degree of slope. All the pitches have electricity, water and waste water connections, either side of a stream (fenced off from a weir at the top of the site), with about 40 long stay pitches and a tent area. Basic supplies are kept and there is a pleasant bar/restaurant, a barbecue and covered sitting area and a heated indoor pool and sauna. Just 100 m. is a large lake for swimming and fishing. The main sanitary facilities have free hot water for the washbasins (two each male/female in cabins) and showers, and there is a small unit further into the site (not of the same quality).

How to find it: From the Romantische Strasse between Rothenburg and Bad Mergentheim, exit at Creglingen for Münster (3 km) and site is just beyond this village.

General Details: Open 15 March - 15 Nov. Electrical connections (16A). Shop for basics, bar/restaurant and heated indoor pool (all April - Oct). Minigolf. Children's play area. Table tennis. Lake for swimming and fishing. Bicycle hire or riding 3 km. Gas supplies. Chemical disposal. Motorcaravan services.

Charges 2000: Per adult DM 6.00 - 9.50; child (2-12 yrs) 4.00 - 6.50; pitch 8.00 - 12.50; small tent pitch 4.50 - 6.50; extra tent 3.00 - 4.00; dog 3.50 - 4.00; electricity 4.00. No credit cards.

Reservations: Advised for July/Aug. Address: 97993 Creglingen/Münster. Tel: 07933/20289. FAX: 07933/990019.

3625 Knaus Camping-Park Frickenhausen, Ochsenfurt, nr Würzburg

Pleasant riverside site just south of Würzburg.

Knaus continue to develop this site and it now has a small, heated, open-air swimming pool (for adults only at specific times), whilst on an 'island' surrounded by attractive trees alongside the gently flowing River Main is a large children's play area with modern equipment and a full size volleyball court on sand. Young trees are growing well on the site to replace the 300 lost in a violent storm a few years ago. There are 115 fair sized, numbered touring pitches on flat grass, arranged in sections leading from tarred access roads with flowers around. Most have electricity connections. About 80 long stay places are mostly separate nearer the river. All the amenities are in a long block opposite reception (Frau Hergeth speaks English). Sanitary facilities have free hot water in the quite large, fully controllable showers, the washbasins have private cabins for women), and dishwashing sinks. Soap and paper towels are provided for the toilets. Upstairs is a small shop and a restaurant with a terrace for candle-lit meals, whilst downstairs is a small café/bar. The ducks are very friendly and will invite you to feed them.

How to find it: Take exit 71 (Ochsenfurt) from the A3 autobahn at Würzburg and continue on the B13. Do not cross the Main into town but follow Frickenhausen and site signs; the site is shortly on the right.

General Details: Open all year excl. Nov. Electricity connections (6A). Restaurant, cafe/wine bar and shop (weekends only in low season). Bread to order. Club room. Small, free swimming pool, public pool 300 m. Children's play area and beach volleyball on river island. Table tennis. Bicycle hire. Fishing. Boat marina. Cooking facilities. Washing machine and dryer. Chemical disposal. Caravans (10) and tents to rent.

Charges 2000: Per person DM 8.75; child (3-14 yrs) 4.50; pitch 7.50 - 12.50; small tent and m/cycle 7.50; dog 4.00; electricity 3.50. No credit cards.

Reservations: Not made. Address: Ochsenfurter Str. 49, 97252 Frickenhausen. Tel: 09331/3171. FAX: 09331/5784.

3735 Spessart-Camping Schönrain, Gemünden-Hofstetten, nr Karlstadt

Site in attractive, peaceful woodland setting with swimming pool.

Situated a short distance from the town of Gemünden, with views of forested hills beside the river Main, this is a very friendly, family run site. Of the 200 pitches, 100 are for tourists. Some are up to 150 sq.m. in size and most have electricity, some with water and drainage also. A new area has been developed for tents. The site has an outdoor pool open from Whitsun to end Sept (weather permitting). A brand new sanitary building was under construction during our visit (now open), so facilities should be first class. A pleasant small restaurant and bar and a shop are on site with the local full-bodied Franconian wine for sale. Frau Endres welcomes British guests and speaks a little English. There are opportunities for walking and riding in the adjacent woods, excursions are organised in the main season and it is possible to hire a bicycle, ride to Würzburg and catch the pleasure boat back, or take a combined bus and cycle ride. Fishing and boating are both very popular in the locality.

How to find it: From Frankfurt - Würzburg autobahn, take Weibersbrunn-Lohr exit and then B26 to Gemünden. Turn over Main river bridge to Hofstetten. From Kassel - Wurzburg autobahn, leave at Hammelburg and take B27 to Gemünden, and as above.

General Details: Open 1 April - 30 Sept. Electrical connections (10A). Bar/restaurant (closed Tuesdays). Shop. Swimming pool. Children's playground. Table tennis. Bicycle hire. Excursions organised. Fishing 400 m. Riding 200 m. Canoeing, cycling and walking near. Gas supplies. Chemical disposal. Motorcaravan services. Caravans for hire.

Charges 2000: Per pitch 100 sq.m. DM 10.00, 150 sq.m. 15.00, small pitch for hikers or cyclists and small tent DM 8.00; person 9.00; child (under 14 yrs) 6.00; electricity 4.00. Less 10% for stays over 14 days in mid and low seasons. Credit cards accepted.

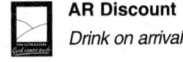

AR Discount
Drink on arrival

Reservations: Write to site. Address: 97737 Gemünden-Hofstetten. Tel: 09351/8645. FAX: 09351/8721. E-mail: info@spessart-camping.de.

GERMANY - South East

3730 Camping Park Bad Kissingen, Bad Kissingen

First class, family owned site adjacent to pretty spa town and its park.

Bad Kissingen is a very attractive town and was a favourite of Bavarian Kings, Austrian Emperors and Bismark, who lived here for a while. This quiet site is situated by the lakeside on the edge of town with direct access to the centre through the private entrance to the adjacent park. Herr Laudenbach, the friendly English-speaking owner, will greet you and personally conduct you to your pitch. A grassy, partially shaded site with a tarmac service road, there are only 99 pitches (80 with electricity, 40 with water and waste water connections), all well spaced out. Of these 20 are used by permanent units, so reservation is advisable. The exemplary sanitary block has a room for disabled people and it is kept very clean. Showers are on payment (DM 1). The laundry room has two washing machines and a dryer. A small, charming restaurant is open every evening and there is folk music to entertain you. Tennis, golf, minigolf and a swimming pool are all within easy reach and local excursions leave from the site. Gas barbecues are permitted. A large children's play area is in the adjacent park.

How to find it: Leave autobahn A7/E45 at Hammelburg. Take B287 for Bad Kissingen for 10 km. and site is on the right just before the town approach (and is signed).

General Details: Open 1 April - 15 Oct. Electrical connections (6A). Restaurant/bar (1/4-30/9). Children's play area. Aviary. Fishing. Bicycle hire and golf 1 km. Riding 3 km. Tennis, swimming pool and minigolf near. Washing machines and dryer. Chemical disposal. Motorcaravan services.

Charges 1999: Per person DM 9.50; child (under 12 yrs) 5.00; pitch for car/caravan or motorcaravan 11.00; tent 9.00; electricity 3.50; local tax 2.50; dog 2.50. No credit cards.

Reservations: Write to site. Address: Euerdorfer Str. 1, 97688 Bad Kissingen. Tel: 0971/5211. FAX: as phone.

3720 Campingplatz Naabtal, Pielenhofen bei Regensburg

Very pleasant, attractive riverside site in a beautiful tree-covered valley.

Regensburg is an ancient city on the Danube, near the Bavarian Forest which, although not as well known as the Black Forest, is a lovely area of natural beauty. Naabtal makes an excellent night stop when travelling to or from Austria or Hungary and would also make a good base for exploring this interesting part of Germany. Two-thirds of the site is taken up by static caravans used for weekends and holidays. The 130 large pitches for tourists (all with electricity) are under willow trees by the riverside or in an open field, where a new sanitary building was built in '99 (to replace a small overnight unit). There is good shade in some parts and hills covered with trees rise all around – this is good walking and mountain biking country, with marked trails. The two original toilet blocks, part of larger buildings, are heated in cool weather. They have British style WCs and free hot water in the washbasins (some in private cabins), while hot water is on payment in the showers. One of the buildings contains the shop and bar/restaurant and the other, a large meeting room with tables, catering facilities, a stage for festive occasions and a youth room with table tennis and video games. There is also a sauna and solarium, and a new, first class unit for disabled people. Alongside, under cover, are a skittle alley and next to this a tarmac curling rink. The children's playground has some imaginative fixed apparatus. Small boats can be launched on the placid river (where you may also swim at your own risk) and there are two good size tennis courts.

How to find it: Take exit 97 Nittendorf from A3 Nürnberg - Passau , and follow road to Pielenhofen (Camping Naabtal is signed from exit). Cross river and turn right to site. Site is about 11 km. from autobahn exit. From A93 exit 31 onto B8 towards Nittendorf, then B15 to Pielenhofen.

General Details: Open all year. Electricity connections (10A). Bar/restaurant (1/4-15/10 plus weekends and Xmas/New Year). Small shop (1/4-1/10, village shop 1.5 km). Tennis. Table tennis. Skittle alley. Football field. Volleyball. Curling rink. Sauna and solarium. Youth room with games. Bicycle hire. Fishing (permit required). Small boats on river. Golf 15 km. Reception will advise on local excursions, walks, cycle routes and sports. Washing machines, dryers and irons. Gas supplies. Chemical disposal. Motorcaravan services. Bungalows for hire.

Charges 2000: Per person DM 8.90; child 5.60; pitch 10.20; dog 3.50; electricity 1.00 (once only) + meter. No credit cards.

Reservations: Needed in high season; contact site. Address: 93188 Pielenhofen. Tel: 09409/373. FAX: 09409/723.

3715 Knaus Camping-Park Viechtach, nr Cham

Well managed site on the edge of the Bavarian Forest.

Although the Bavarian Forest is not as well known to the British as the Black Forest, it is an area of great natural beauty with rolling hills rising to over 1,500 m. at the highest point and ideal for those who wish to enjoy wide open spaces away from it all. The National Park near Grafenau has a 200 km. network of footpaths and a unique collection of primeval flora and fauna. Camping-Park Viechtach, although reached via a small industrial area, is a relaxing place at which to stay, well laid out in a woodland setting on the edge of the village. The various trees and shrubs give a garden effect and there is good shade in most parts. A tarmac road winds its way between the grass pitches (most terraced) which are separated by rocks and trees and marked by plaques. There are 200 pitches for touring units, all with electricity, and size varies from small for some motorcaravans to quite large for bigger units (120 sq.m.). The two heated sanitary blocks are of fair quality, one central to the touring pitches, the other at the top end of the site on the ground floor of a larger building, with a drying room. Facilities are similar, with British style WCs and free hot water to washbasins (some private cabins), sinks and showers. There is an attractive bar/restaurant with reasonable prices, a small shop for basic supplies and a camping equipment shop. A heated indoor swimming pool has a sauna and solarium, the town swimming pool and tennis courts are nearby. Whether for a night stop or for a longer stay to visit the Bavarian Forest, this site is well worth considering. English is spoken by the friendly reception staff.

How to find it: Take Viechtach exit from B85 Weiden - Passau road, and follow campsite signs.

General Details: Open all year except Nov. Electricity connections (4A). Restaurant. Shops (basics and camping equipment) Bread to order. Indoor swimming pool (free). Sauna and solarium. Large children's playground. Table tennis. Beach volleyball. Bicycle hire. Small games room. Several rooms for wet weather. Outdoor pool and tennis nearby. Washing machines, dryers and irons. Chemical disposal. Rooms in guest house, caravans (10) and tents to rent; contact site for details.

Charges 2000: Per person DM 8.75; child (3-14 yrs) 4.50; pitch 7.50 - 12.50; tent and m/cycle 7.50; dog 4.00; electricity 3.50. No credit cards.

Reservations: Write to site. Address: Waldfrieden 22, 94234 Viechtach. Tel: 09942/1095. FAX: 09942/302222.

3725 Bavaria Sport Camping Park, Eging am See, nr Passau

Modern site with good facilities, near Passau.

Eging is a Kurbad village of the type found in many parts of Germany where warm and cold water baths are used in a variety of treatments. It is located in the southwest tip of the Bavarian Forest, in good walking country and occupies an open hilltop position amidst rolling forest countryside on slightly sloping ground about 600 m. from the small lake, treatment and sports centre. Mainly level numbered pitches on terraces of grass or fine gravel are divided by bushes and saplings on either side of tarmac roads. Water and electricity points are widely spaced (long cables may be needed). There is a small bar/restaurant with terrace and another larger one by the lake. A kiosk offers basic food supplies. The single sanitary block is of good quality with free hot water in washbasins (some in private cabins) and sinks, and on payment in the showers (by slot machine door locks). Facilities for disabled people are provided. Apart from the Kur facilities, there are opportunities for a wide variety of sports nearby - swimming, tennis, table tennis, minigolf, curling, fishing, pedaloes, volleyball, electric go-karts and small motorcycles, billiards, pool, amusement machines, walking and some winter sports.

How to find it: Take exit 113 (Garham) from A3 Regensburg - Passau autobahn. Pass turn to Eging, continuing to main road and turn right, then almost immediately left. Cross level crossing and site is on left by hotel. Site is also signed in Eging.

General Details: Open all year. Electricity connections (16A). Restaurant. Variety of sports (see above). Washing machines, dryers and irons.

Charges guide: Per adult DM 7.90 - 8.90; child (3 age bands from 3-18) 4.00 - 7.90; pitch 10.50 - 11.50; dog 4.50; electricity 4.80 (includes two shower tokens); local tax 0.60; rubbish tax 1.00. Credit cards not accepted.

Reservations: Write to site. Address: Grafenauer Strasse 31, 94535 Eging am See. Tel: 08544/8089. FAX: 08544/7964.

GERMANY - South East

3695 Dreiflüsse Campingplatz, Irring bei Passau, Donautal

Good site overlooking the Danube near Passau.

Although the name of this site suggests an association with the three important rivers here, it is in fact some 9 km. from the confluence of the Danube, Inn and Ilz. Dreiflüsse Camping occupies a hillside position to the west of Passau with pitches on several rows of level terraces. The 180 places are not all marked, although electricity boxes determine where units pitch, and half have water and waste water connections. Trees and low banks separate the terraces which are of gravel with a thin covering of grass. The pleasant, Gasthof is at the entrance where the reception, shop and sanitary buildings are also located. The sanitary facilities include British type toilets and free hot water to showers and washbasins (two cabins for women, one for men). There is a small heated indoor swimming pool (charged). The energetic, jolly owner gives the site a friendly air. This is a useful en-route stop or for a longer stay to explore the delights of Passau.

How to find it: From autobahn A3, take exit 115 (Passau-Nord) from where site is signed. Follow signs from Passau on road to west of city and north bank of Danube towards Windorf and Irring.

General Details: Open 1 April - 31 Oct. 40,000 sq.m. Some shade. Electricity connections (16A). Restaurant. Shop (both all season). Indoor pool (May - 15 Sept). Play area. Table tennis. Fishing. Bicycle hire. Riding. Bus service for Passau outside site (finishes at 6 pm). Chemical disposal. Motorcaravan service point.

Charges guide: Per person DM 7.50; child (4-12) 5.00; pitch 8.50 - 12.00; dog 2.50; electricity 4.80 + per kw.

Reservations: Write to site. Address: 94113 Irring am Sonnenhang 23, Passau/Donautal. Tel: 08546/633. FAX: 08546/2686.

3700 AZUR Campingpark Bayerwald-Gottsdorf, Untergriesbach, nr Passau

Well run, quiet site with good sports facilities, in southeast Germany.

Attractively situated on high ground above, but not overlooking, the Danube (on which there is a regular boat service), this site has only 130 pitches, of which 40 are for permanent caravans. All pitches are numbered, with electricity (11-16A), and stand mostly in rows of five or six with a high hedge backing each row. The heated sanitary block provides British style WCs, free hot water in individual washbasins (mainly in cubicles), showers and sinks. Public swimming pools (a heated indoor pool and outdoor one, heated with solar panels) are just below the site (entrance charge for campers DM 6, child DM 3).

How to find it: Leave A3 (E56) Regensburg - Linz autobahn at Passau-Nord exit for the B388 towards Wegescheid. At Obernzell, turn left at Gottsdorf sign and follow to site - entrance is just before village on left.

General Details: Open all year. 120,000 sq.m. Many electrical connections (11/16A). Self-service shop. TV room. Sports field with football pitch. Volleyball. Garden chess. Minigolf. Extensive children's playground and adventure playground. Running track. Table tennis. Outdoor fitness facilities. Tennis. Children's zoo. Swimming pools nearby. Fishing 8 km. Bicycle hire 12 km. Washing machines and dryer. Cooking facilities. 40 bungalows or small houses for hire. Gas supplies. Chemical disposal. Motorcaravan services.

Charges 2000: Per adult DM 7.00 - 10.50; child (2-12 yrs) 5.00 - 7.50; pitch 9.00 - 13.50; small tent pitch 5.00 - 7.50; extra tent 3.00 - 4.00; dog 3.50 - 4.00; electricity 4.00. No credit cards.

Reservations: Advised in high seasons and made with DM 20 deposit, write to site. Address: Mitterweg 11, 94107 Untergriesbach. Tel: 08593/880. FAX: 08593/88111.

3705 Knaus Camping-Park Lackenhäuser, Neureichenau, nr Passau

Pleasant site, offering walking, skiing, fishing and an indoor pool.

This extensive site is right at the southeast tip of Germany – the border with Austria runs through one side of the site and the Czech Republic is very close too. It is a very popular site and reservations may be advisable from mid-June to Sept. Mainly on sloping ground with good views from some parts, it has 500 pitches with terracing in some areas, nearly all for tourists, and 40 chalets or caravans for hire. Electricity connections are available and water points are fed from pure springs. The many amenities include a heated indoor pool (free) with child's pool, sauna and fitness room, and an outdoor pool. The site has much winter sports trade, with its own ski lift. The three sanitary buildings are good with free hot water in washbasins (some cabins), showers and sinks, and have under floor heating. Rather off the beaten track for British campers, it is however a most pleasant site in a beautiful setting with 7 km. of walks within the camp perimeters and an attractive fishing lake. There is a friendly atmosphere with English spoken by staff.

How to find it: From Regensburg on A3 take exit 115 into Passau, then road 12 towards Freyung, turning off just before Röhrnbach for Waldkirchen and on through Jandelsbrunn to Lackenhäuser.

General Details: Open all year excl. Nov. 146,000 sq.m. Electricity connections (4A). Supermarket. Restaurant/bar. General room for young. Caravan shop. Indoor and outdoor pools (free). Sauna, fitness room and massage facilities. Small lake (ice sports in winter). Fishing. Bowling alley. Beach volleyball. Church on site. Organised activities (July/Aug. and Xmas). Cooking facilities. Baby room. Washing machines and dryers. Chemical disposal. Motorcaravan services. Bungalows and caravans to rent; contact site for details.

Charges 2000: Per person DM 8.75; child (3-14 yrs) 4.50; pitch 7.50 - 12.50; tent and m/cycle 7.50; dog 4.00; electricity 3.50. No credit cards.

Reservations: made for any period without deposit. Address: Lackenhäuser 127, 94089 Neureichenau. Tel: 08583/311. FAX: 08583/91079.

3850 Campingplatz Strandbad Aga, nr Gera

Quiet site within reach of Dresden, Leipzig and Meissen.

Now that access has become easier there is much interest in seeing the historic cities of the east and Aga is within reach of Dresden, Leipzig, Meissen, Colditz and other interesting towns. Situated in open countryside on the edge of a small lake, with individual, fenced pitches for stays of more than a couple of days, overnighters are placed on an open area. All places have electrical connections. A new sanitary building is at one side of but near to all pitches, with free hot water to the washbasins, a few of which are in private cabins and to the sinks; hot showers are on payment. These include a large (4 x 4 m.) room for wheelchair users. The restaurant/bar is also new and is open long hours. There is a small but well stocked shop and in high season a kiosk for drinks, ice creams, etc. The lake is used for swimming, boating and fishing and there is a small children's playground on one side (close to a deep part). Entertainment is organised in July and the friendly, enthusiastic owner is improving the facilities each year.

How to find it: From A4 /E40 Chemnitz - Erfurt autobahn take Gera exit (no. 58) then the B2 towards Zeitz, following Bad Köstritz signs at first then site signs.

General Details: Open 1 April - 1 Nov. Electrical connections (10A). Restaurant. Shop. Kiosk (June - Sept). Children's playground. Swimming and watersports in the lake. Entertainment in high season. Riding 1 km. Football 200 m. Washing machines and dryers. Motorcaravan service facilities. No English spoken.

Charges guide: Per adult DM 7.00; child (3-13 yrs) 3.50; motorcaravan 12.00; caravan or tent 9.00; car 3.00; m/cycle 1.00; electricity 3.00 + 0.80 per kw/h; drainage 3.00.

Reservations: Write to site. Address: Strandbad Aga, Reichenbacherstrasse 18, 07554 Aga. Tel: 036695/20209. FAX: as phone.

3847 Campingplatz Auensee, Leipzig

Impressive city site open all year.

It is unusual to find a first-class site in a city, but this large, neat and tidy site is one, with just 167 pitches of which about 140 are for short-term tourers. It is set in a mainly open area with tall trees and very attractive flower arrangements around, with some chalets and trekker huts for rent in the adjoining woodland, home to the shoe-stealing foxes. The individual, numbered, flat grassy pitches are large (100 sq.m.), all with electrical connections and five on hardstanding, arranged in several sections with a separate area for young people with tents. Three central points supply water and barbecue areas are provided. Children of all ages are well catered for with forts, an ultra-modern climbing frame all on sand, a 'super' swing and an enclosed court with tennis, football and basketball. Five sanitary buildings (all in one area), have differing mixtures of very modern equipment and offer free hot water to the washbasins (many in private cabins), although you need tokens from reception for the showers, which are smallish but have good dividers, and the hairdryers. You need a key for the well equipped rooms for mother and baby and disabled visitors. Dishwashing facilities are both open air and inside and there is also a kitchen, a laundry room and two chemical disposal rooms. All the buildings can be heated. A modern restaurant and snack bar (breakfast, lunch and supper available), plus a small shop are open all year round and there are rooms for television, billiards and children. Although public transport to the city centre goes every 10 minutes from just outside the site, it is far enough away from roads and the airport to be reasonably peaceful during the day and very quiet overnight. A popular site, it is best to arrive early.

How to find it: Site is well signed 5 km. from Leipzig centre on the B6 to Halle. From the A9 Berlin - Nurnberg take exit 17 at Schkeuditz onto the B6 towards Leipzig.

General Details: Open all year, as shop, restaurant and snack bar. Electrical connections (10A). Entertainment rooms. Several children's play areas. Bicycle hire. Fishing close by. Barbecue with seating. Kitchen. Motorcaravan service point. Chemical disposal. English usually spoken.

Charges guide: Per person DM 8.00; child 6-13 yrs 4.00, 14-18 yrs 6.00; caravan 17.00; motorcaravan 15.00; tent 10.00; small tent (under 4 sq.m.) 6.00; car 5.00; electricity 0.75 per kwh.

Reservations: Contact site. Address: Gustav-Esche Strasse 5. 04159 Leipzig. Tel: 0341/4651 600.

GERMANY - North East

3833 Camping LuxOase, Kleinröhrsdorf, nr Dresden

Developing lakeside family site.

This is a pleasantly situated new park about half an hour from the centre of Dresden, in a very peaceful location with good facilities. It is owned and run by a progressive young family. On open grassland with views across the lake (access to which is through a gate in the site fence) to the woods and low hills beyond, this is a sun-trap with little shade at present. There are 150 large touring pitches (plus 50 seasonal in a separate area), marked by bushes or posts on generally flat or slightly sloping grass. All have electricity and 100 have water and waste water facilities. At the entrance is an area of hardstanding (with electricity) for late arrivals. A brand new sanitary building (with card entry) provides modern, heated facilities with showers, bidets, washbasins and private cabins, all with free hot water, a large mother and child shower, baby changing room, units for disabled visitors and two units for hire. Also here are rooms for cooking, laundry, dishwashing and chemical disposal. More pitches are being developed and there are plans for minigolf, tennis and another sanitary building. The main entrance building contains reception, where there is a large amount of tourist information, the shop (open am. all year, pm. in high season), the bar/restaurant (all year, in high season for lunch as well) and sauna. In front of the building is some very modern children's play equipment on bark and you may swim, fish or use inflatables in the lake. There are many interesting places to visit apart from Dresden and Meissen, with the fascinating Nationalpark Sächsische Schweiz (Saxon Switzerland) on the border with the Czech Republic offering some spectacular scenery.

How to find it: From A4 (Dresden - Bautzen) take exit 85 towards Radeberg, soon following signs to site via Leppersdorf and Kleinröhrsdorf.

General Details: Open all year, as are shop, bar and restaurant. Electricity connections (10A). Bicycle hire. Lake swimming. Sports field with basketball and volleyball. Fishing. Children's play area. Sauna. Riding 1 km. Golf 11 km. Opera tickets organised at reception. Public transport to Dresden close. Gas supplies. Chemical disposal. Motorcaravan services.

Charges 1999: Per person DM 6.50 - 7.00; child (2-14 yrs) 4.00 - 4.50; motorcaravan or caravan and car 12.50 - 13.00; electricity 4.00 - 3.00; dog 3.50 - 4.00. No credit cards.

Reservations: Contact site, also for details of offers. Address: Familie Lux, Arnsdorfer Strasse 1, 01900 Kleinröhrsdorf. Tel: 035952 56666. FAX: 035952 56024.

AR Discount
Less 10% on person charge and info pack

3827 Camping Sanssouci Gaisberg, Potsdam

Peaceful lakeside site for city visits to Potsdam and Berlin with excellent facilities.

The maturing site, about 2 km. from Sanssouci Park on the banks of the Templiner See in a quiet woodland setting, is looking very attractive, reflecting the effort which has been put into its development. A new reception, shop, takeaway, restaurant and bar have been added, and all pitches now have electricity, water and waste water connections. Tall trees mark out the 150 flat, grassy tourist pitches, and access is good for large units. There is a separate area for tents by the lake. Sanitary facilities consist of one smallish toilet block of a good standard and, 50 m. further in, an excellent, very modern, heated block containing free hot showers, washbasins in private cabins with hot water, and facilities for babies, dishwashing (1 DM) and laundry, plus a very good facility for wheelchair users. Reception staff are helpful with English spoken and a useful English language information pack is available for local attractions. The pool, sauna, solarium and skittle alley at the nearby Hotel Semiramis may be used by campers. Free transport in the mornings and evenings is operated by the site to the public transport stop, saving you the long walk.

How to find it: From A10 take Potsdam exit 7, follow B1 to within 4 km. of city centre then sign to right for camp. Or A10 exit 12 on the B2 into town and follow signs for Brandenburg/Werder. Site is southwest of Sanssouci Park on the banks of the Templiner See off Zeppelinstrasse 1,200 m. along a woodland drive.

General Details: Open 1 April - 4 Nov. Electricity connections (6A). New restaurant. Shop. Rowing boats, motorboats and pedaloes for hire. Fishing. Swimming in the lake. Children's play area in central woods. Bicycle hire. Riding 3 km. Golf 10 km. Washing machine and dryer. Gas supplies. Chemical disposal. Motorcaravan services. Site closed to vehicles 13.00-15.00 hrs.

Charges 1999: Per adult DM 11.50 - 13.30; child (2-15 yrs) 1.90; pitch 12.80 - 13.60; local tax 0.90; dog 6.90; electricity 3.50. Special low season offers. No credit cards.

Reservations: Not normally necessary. Address: An der Pirschheide/Templiner See 41, 14471 Potsdam. Tel: 0331/9510988. FAX: as phone. E-mail: recra@campingweb.com.

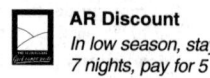

AR Discount
In low season, stay 7 nights, pay for 5

3842 Camping am Schlosspark, Lübbenau

Riverside site in delightful, woodland setting close to old town.

Situated about halfway between Berlin and Dresden, this is an attractive proposition for a short visit as well as a night stop, about 10 minutes walk from the centre of the much visited old town, on the banks of the Hauptspree. Taking 130 units (they may be rather close at very busy times), 90 have electricity. Mainly on flat grass but with a central hardstanding area for motorcaravans and a long area for tents at the end. The refurbished sanitary facilities are quite good with free hot water for washbasins (some private cabins), but showers require tokens from reception. A kitchen is provided as well as dishwashing, laundry and chemical disposal. A small shop for basics is at reception, and there are more in the adjacent town, with a `Tiergarten' café just 200 m. and the Schloßpark hotel and restaurant through the woods. You can paddle your own boat, go for a trip in a gondola, explore the Spreewald or just look round the interesting old town from this pleasant site. A public path passes between the site and the river; insect repellent is advised.

How to find it: From the A13 (Berlin - Dresden) take exit 9, turning right onto the B115 into Lübbenau then following site signs. At weekends the town is busy, requiring extra care and patience.

General Details: Open all year, as are the small shop and the café (200 m). Small children's play area. Boat and bicycle hire. Fishing. Motorcaravan service point. Huts and bungalows for hire.

Charges guide: Per person DM 7.00; child (6-14 yrs) 3.50; caravan or motorhome 14.00; tent 5.00 - 8.00, acc. to size; dog 3.00; electricity 1.50 connection plus 2.50 per day.

Reservations: Essential probably only for May Day and Whitsun weekends. Address: 03222 Lübbenau. Tel: 03542/3533. FAX: as phone.

3830 DCC Camping Am Krossinee, Schmockwitz, Berlin

Useful base for visiting Berlin.

The Deutcher Camping Club site here is efficiently run and there are daily coach tours (with tickets from reception) and public transport to the city both available from the site entrance, the journey by car to the city centre taking about 45 minutes. The Krossinsee is one of many clean lakes in the southeast of Berlin and is suitable for swimming, fishing and boating, with access by key through a gate from the woodland site. More than half the 450 pitches are for tourers. They are of varying but reasonable size, mainly on flat grass, most with electricity and a fair amount of shade. A separate area is set aside for tents. The sanitary facilities are of above average quality for a city site, situated in a modern building with plenty of private cabins, smallish showers (token from reception), hand and hair dryers, a baby room and a well equipped unit for disabled visitors. A kitchen and dishwashing room plus a separate laundry complete the provision. Near the entrance are a mini-market, a restaurant and a snack-bar which is open daily for breakfast, lunches and evening meals. A small fenced area with play equipment (mainly climbing) is on sand and earth. For visits in high season you should try to arrive as early as possible as reservations are not taken.

How to find it: From southeast Berlin on the A10 ring road take exit 19 (Niederlehme) to Wernsdorf, then follow signs to Schmockwitz and site.

General Details: Open all year. Electricity connections (10A). Shop and snack bar (Apr - Oct). Restaurant. Lake swimming, fishing, boating (hire facilities) windsurfing school and woodland walks. Kitchen and dishwashing facilities. Laundry. Bicycle hire. Berlin coach trips (all year).

Charges guide: Per adult DM 9.50; child (6-14 yrs) 4.50; pitch 12.50; hiker plus small tent 7.00; dog 3.00; electricity 2.50 plus 0.80 per kwh.

Reservations: Made for groups only. Address: Wernsdorfer Straße 45, 12527 Berlin. Tel: 030/675 8687. FAX: 030/675 9150.

3815 Azur Camping Ecktannen, Waren am Müritzsee

Large woodland site in German 'Lake District', midway between Berlin and Rostock.

Müritz is in the 'Land of 1,000 Lakes' in one of Germany's 13 National Parks. The site is at the northeast tip of the Müritzersee, although trees screen out a view of the lake, and slightly above it. There is direct access to the water with small jetties for boats, a bathing beach of sand and a lakeside restaurant. There are 300 touring pitches (all with 10A electricity) and further areas for tents. They are in undulating woodland, either under tall pines or in clearings where stumps have been left and small saplings are growing. The toilet arrangements are in two quite reasonable buildings with free hot water in the basins, the showers and for dishwashing. There is a small kiosk for basics in high season and a restaurant close by. If you are looking for a quiet (out of high season), simple site 'in the heart of nature', you may well enjoy a stay here.

How to find it: Follow B192 southeast from Waren following Azur international signs.

General Details: Open 15 March - 15 Nov. Small shop for basics in high season. Restaurant by lake just outside site. Town facilities 4km. Sailing. Fishing. Children's playground. Bicycle hire 2 km. Swimming pool 8 km. Riding 10 km. Laundry facilities. Gas supplies. Chemical disposal. Motorcaravan services.

Charges 2000: Per adult DM 6.00 - 9.50; child (2-12 yrs) 4.00 - 6.50; pitch 8.00 - 12.50; small tent pitch 4.50 - 6.50; extra tent 3.00 - 4.00; dog 3.50 - 4.00; electricity 4.00. No credit cards.

Reservations: Not necessary. Address: 17192 Waren am Müritzsee. Tel: 03991/668513. FAX: 03991/664675.

HUNGARY

There are many interesting areas of Hungary for the tourist apart from Budapest (for which you should allow at least a couple of days) and Lake Balaton (around 70% of the visitors here are German) and the British are warmly received. The Danube Bend in the northwest is justifiably popular, as is the northeast hills area (Eger and Miskolc), with the spectacular stalactites in the large cave system at the border with Slovakia in Aggtelek (north of Eger). The interesting towns of the Great Plain to the east of the Danube have a great Magyar tradition and there are many Thermal baths (often at campsites) to enjoy. There are also several notable wine areas and you can purchase quality wines at low prices. West of the Danube appears rather more advanced, while in the east and north it is still common to see agricultural workers with scythes and few tractors. There has been a rapid advance in the general standard of campsites, although the majority still have communal (single sex) changing for showers. All sites, however, have British style WCs. Most sites require payment in cash. It is advisable and convenient to use public transport when visiting Budapest. It is useful to know that the Hungarian tourist organisation (IBUSZ) has offices in most towns where you can also change money. Opening hours Mon-Sat 08.00-18.00/20.00 and 08.00-13.00 on Sundays.

For further information contact:

Hungarian National Tourist Ofice, 46 Eaton Place, London SW1X 8AL

Tel: 0891 171200 (60p per minute)

Population
10,471,000 (1995); density 113 per sq. km.

Capital
Budapest.

Climate
There are four fairly distinct seasons - hot summer (June-Aug), mild spring and autumn very cold winter with snow.

Language
The official language is Magyar, but German is widely spoken, and English and French are also spoken particularly by those engaged in the tourist industry in the west of the country.

Currency
Hungarian forints (ft) come in notes of 10, 20, 50, 100 and 500 ft. When you change cash keep receipts - necessary to convert money at the end of your visit - it is illegal to export Hungarian currency. You can change money at any IBUSZ or regional tourist office, at most large hotels or campsites. Banks can be slow and exchange rates are the same everywhere.

Banks
Open Mon-Fri 09.00-14.00, Sat 09.00-12.00.

Post Offices
Usually open Mon-Fri 08.00-17.00/18.00, Sat. 12.00-14.00/18.00, but it is quicker to buy stamps at tobacconists.

Telephone
To call from the UK the code is 0036 followed by area code less initial 0, and number. From Hungary dial 06 followed by the area code. International calls from Hungary can be dialled direct from red or grey phone boxes but it may be easier through the international operator (09).

Public Holidays
New Year; 15 March; Easter Mon; Labour Day; Whitsun; Constitution Day, 20 Aug; Republic Day, 23 Oct; Christmas, 25, 26 Dec.

Time
GMT plus 1 (summer BST plus 1).

Shopping
Open Mon-Fri 10.00-18.00, Sat 10.00-14.00. Food shops open Mon-Fri 07.00-19.00, Sat 07.00-14.00. Home produced products, including food and restaurant meals are cheap by western standards. There appears to be no shortage of goods with articles being sold by the roadside and from garages and gardens. Traditionally Hungarians take their main meal at midday so there is a better range of dishes in the restaurants at midday. All eating places display signs indicating their class from I to IV which gives some guide to comparative prices. Set menus are good value.

Motoring
Main roads are very good, as is signposting. Dipped headlights are compulsory at all times. Most of the few motorways are single carriage, single lane and care is needed.

Fuel: On motorways and in large towns petrol stations open 24 hours otherwise 06.00-20.00. Eurocard accepted at some petrol stations.

Tolls: are payable on the M1 from the Austrian border to Györ and on the full length of the M5 (Budapest - Kiskunfelegyhaza); from '99 also on the M3 (Budapest - Fuzesabony) eastward.

Speed Restrictions: Caravans and motorhomes (3.5 tons) 31 mph (50 kph) in built up areas, caravans 44 mph (70 kph) and 50 mph (80 kph) on other roads and motorways respectively, motorhomes 50 mph (80 kph) and 75 mph (120 kph) respectively.

Parking: The centre of Budapest is closed to traffic. Do not park in places where you would not park in the UK.

Overnighting
Not allowed outside campsites.

Note: Camping Gaz can be difficult to obtain.

510 Ózon Camping, Sopron

Peaceful and comfortable edge of town site close to the border.

Sopron was not over-run by the Turks or bombed in WW2, so 350 historic buildings and monuments have remained intact, making it the second major tourist centre after Budapest. It also has a music festival from mid-June to mid-July and is close to the Löverek hills. This surprisingly pleasant campsite is just over 4 km. from the centre, with the modern, chalet style reception at the entrance from where the oval site opens out into a little green valley surrounded by trees. There are also many trees within the site offering shade. The concrete access roads lead to 60 numbered grass pitches, all with electricity (6A). Some with water and waste water also are in the lower level on the left, where siting is more difficult for caravans. They are mostly flat, some with a slight slope, separated by hedges and vary from 40 sq.m. for tents up to 80 sq.m. for larger units. The sanitary facilities are in two heated buildings which are identical except that the one by reception has a laundry (free) whilst the other, near the swimming pool, has a sauna. They each have six fully controllable, curtained, hot showers (communal changing) close to the washbasins, so it could possibly be cramped here. British style WCs. Both blocks have free cookers, fridges and dish-washing. A small open air pool and paddling pool opens end May - Sept. There is a pleasant restaurant with good value meals above the friendly, helpful reception which also offers basic essentials, tourist information and money exchange. One member of staff spoke English on our last visit. Other shops at 50 and 500 m.

How to find it: From A3 south of Wien, follow roads 16 (Kingenbach) and 84 to Sopron. Site is on road to Brennerberganya, well signed in Sopron.

General Details: Open 15 April - 15 Oct. Restaurant (all season). Essentials and money exchange at reception. Shops 150 m. Swimming pool (15/5-15/9). Sauna. Tennis 2 km. Fishing 2 km. Bicycle hire 1 km. Riding 3 km. Bus service to town centre. Gas supplies. Chemical disposal. Bungalows for hire.

Charges 2000: Per unit incl. 2 persons and electricity DM 22.50; extra person 6.50; child (under 10) 4.50; dog 4.50. No credit cards.

Reservations: May be advisable in high season and are made if you write in German. Address: 9400 Sopron, Erdei Malomköz 3. Tel: 99/331-144. FAX: 99/331-145.

512 Camping-Gasthof Pihenõ, Gyõr

Small friendly site on main Budapest - Vienna road.

This privately owned site makes an excellent night stop when travelling to and from Hungary as it lies beside the main no. 10 road, near to the end of the motorway to the east of Gyõr. It is set amidst pine trees with pitches which are not numbered, but marked out by small shrubs, in a small clearing or between the trees. With space for about 25 units, all with electrical connections (6A), there are also a dozen simple, one roomed bungalows and four en-suite rooms for hire. On one side of the camp, fronting the road, are two pleasant restaurants with terrace (menu in English) and the management offer a very reasonably priced package (if desired) which includes pitch and meals. The site has added a solar heated swimming pool, with a children's pool. The single, small toilet block has free hot water in the washbasins. There are just two showers for each sex with pre-mixed hot water (10 ft for one minute) and curtained, communal dressing space. British style WCs. There is a room for washing clothes and dishes with a small cooking facility. A very friendly German speaking owner runs the site and a new restaurant with his wife who speaks a little English.

How to find it: Coming from Austria, continue through Gyõr following signs for Budapest. Continue on road no. 10 past start of motorway for 3 km. and site is on left. From Budapest, turn right onto road no. 10 at end of motorway, then as above.

General Details: Open 1 April - 30 Oct. Restaurant with good menu and reasonable prices. Swimming pool (10 x 5 m, open June -Sept). Bungalows and rooms for rent. Bread orders at reception previous evening.

Charges guide: Per pitch DM 4.00; person 2.00; electricity 1.00. Less 10% for stays over 4 days, 20% after 8.

Reservations: Write to site. Address: Oláh Ferenc, 9011 Gyõrszentivan, Kertvaros 10. Tel: 96/316 461. FAX: as phone.

HUNGARY

513 Panorama Camping, Pannonhalma, nr Györ

Very peaceful, pretty, hillside site.

In 1982 this became the first private enterprise campsite in Hungary and it offers a very pleasant outlook and peaceful stay at the start or end of your visit to this country. It is situated just 20 km. southeast of Györ, on a hillside with views across the valley to the Sokoro hills. On the edge of the village, it is just below the 1,000 year old Benedictine monastery, which has guided tours. The 75 numbered, hedged pitches (30 with 10A electricity) are on terraces, generally fairly level but reached by steepish concrete access roads, with many trees and plants around. The sanitary facilities are quite satisfactory with a small building near reception and a larger unit half-way up the site. They provide a total of 6 controllable, curtained, hot showers with curtained communal changing, 12 washbasins also with hot water and 8 British style WCs. Hot water is available for dishwashing and laundry. There are benches provided and a small, grass terrace below reception from where you can purchase beer, local wine and soft drinks, etc. Occasional big stews are cooked in high season, otherwise there is a good value restaurant 400 m. away in the village and a shop for essentials at 150 m. Hourly bus service to Györ.

How to find it: From no. 82 Györ - Veszprém road turn to Pannonhalma at Ecs. Site is well signed - the final approach road is fairly steep.

General Details: Open 1 May - 30 Sept. Bar and meals (1/6-15/9). Rest room with TV. Shops and restaurant close in village. Small children's play area. Table tennis. Fishing 4 km. Riding 3 km. Money exchange. Cooking facilities. Laundry. Chemical disposal. Rooms to let. No English spoken.

Charges guide: Per adult Forints 400; child (2-14 yrs) 200; pitch 600; dog 150; electricity 300; local tax 100.

Reservations: Advisable for high season - write in German. Address: 9090 Pannonhalma, Fenyvesalza 4/A. Tel: 96/471 240.

511 Dömös Camping, Dömös, nr Esztergom

Pleasantly situated site on the Danube Bend between river and hills.

The area of the Danube Bend is a major tourist attraction and here at Dömös is a modern, friendly, peaceful site with large pitches and easy access. The Danube is just over 50 m. away and quite fast flowing. With Budapest just 45 km, Esztergom (the ancient capital of Hungary) 15 km. and the small town of Visegrad, with its impressive cliff fortress close by, this could make an ideal base from which to explore the whole area. There are about 100 quite large pitches, of which 80 have 6A electricity, in sections on flat grass, numbered and divided by small plants and some with shade from mature trees. Opposite the smart reception which has an under-cover terrace, is a small cafe, also with a terrace, and a little further along is the modern, long, brick built sanitary building. This is tiled and has sliding doors. Beyond the laundry are very satisfactory ample, large showers with individual changing and pre-mixed hot water, open washbasins and then toilets (British style). At the top of the site is an inviting open-air swimming pool with a grass lying out area and tiny children's pool. Alongside is a large bar with pool tables and table football, beside which is a dishwashing and cooking area (free). A small children's play area on grass is here, just before seven self-contained accommodation units for hire. Sightseeing tours and horse-drawn carriage trips are arranged.

How to find it: Site is between the village and the Danube, off road 11 Esztergom - Visegrad - Szentendre.

General Details: Open 1 May - 15 Sept, as is cafe. Bar (15/5-1/9). Shop (1/6-31/8). Swimming pool ((20 x 10 m, all season). Village facilities 300 m. Fishing 50 m. Tennis adjacent. Bicycle hire 8 km. Riding 2 km. Mountain walking tours. Laundry. Chemical disposal. Motorcaravan services. English spoken.

Charges 2000: Per caravan Ft. 700; car 300; tent 450 - 650, acc. to size; motorcaravan 900; adult 600; child (2-14 yrs) 450; electricity 500; local tax 200. No credit cards (cash only).

Reservations: Not normally made, but may for British visitors for period 15/7-15/8. Address: 2027 Dömös, Duna-Part . Tel: 33/482-319. FAX: 33/414-800. (winter address: Dömös Kft, 2500 Esztergom, Bottyán J. u. 11, tel/fax: 33/414-800).

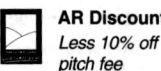

AR Discount
*Less 10% off
pitch fee*

Motorsport

A guide for campers, caravanners or motorcaravanners to some of Europe's foremost motor races.

In 1997 we decided to undertake a review, over a period of several seasons, of the most famous of Europe's motor races, including the Formula 1 grand prix, and of course the Le Mans 24 hour race, particularly from the perspective of campers and caravanners.

During the past three years we have attended Grand Prix in France, Spain, Monaco, Belgium and the UK, and the Le Mans 24 hour race, reports on all of which appear in this, our third "Motorsports Feature". We have also competed in our 1971 Lancia Fulvia 1600HF in several International Historic Rallies, including the Monte Carlo (twice) the Tulip Rally, the Rallye des Pyrenees and the Rallye de Belgique.

Of course there is a variety of specialist tour operators offering inclusive tour arrangements to many European motor races, but we really wanted to be wholly independent, and slot in attendance at some races alongside our Site Inspection Programme, and the sources of "tickets only" are fairly limited. We were therefore fortunate that, in every case we were able to obtain race tickets from "Just Tickets" who provide an excellent service (see advert in this section).

During the course of our spectating and competition motoring we have met literally hundreds of campers, caravanners and especially motorcaravanners, but rather sadly, particularly during the winter months, few of them have been British! We wonder if British caravanners and motorcaravanners actually hibernate during the winter? For example, after the Monte Carlo Rally, from our hotel bedroom window we counted over fifty motorcaravans queuing to get onto the seafront at Monte Carlo, but only one was British registered! Similarly as we were leaving Digne les Bains on the same event we overtook more than thirty motor caravans, not even one of which was British registered! OK, it was January, so what? There was plenty of snow up on the Alpine stages (–17°C at night), but the daytime temperature in Monte Carlo was +22°C, and even at 1am it was warm enough to sit outside! There's more to caravanning and motorcaravanning in the winter than just the Costa Blanca as our European neighbours seem to have discovered.

Over the course of the next few years we hope to be able to fit in visits to more Grands Prix and other motorsports events and thus to add to this motorsports feature to the point whereby it will provide a fairly comprehensive guide to European motorsports events for the independent camper, caravanner or motorcaravanner.

Clive Edwards

Spa Francorchamps (ICN UK Bureau)

Belgian Grand Prix
Spa-Francorchamps

The Spa circuit is well known as one of the most challenging of all the European Formula 1 venues. The circuit itself (which still uses some closed public roads) is longer than most, and covers quite a large area of countryside, including Francorchamps, Malmedy, Eau Rouge, and Stavelot, which happens to be the location of one of the sites featured in this guide (074 Domaine de l'Eau Rouge) which is where we stayed during our visit to the 1999 Grand Prix.

First of all it's worth mentioning that the circuit is not really based at Spa at all, but at Francorchamps, where there is direct access to the ticket office, main grandstands, pits and paddock, but it isn't by any means essential to base yourself here even if you can find a hotel or campsite with any space!

You can indeed camp at several places around the circuit, but judging from the fact that there was no camping/caravanning space left at all around the circuit when we arrived two days before the race, the fact that most of the camping areas are on a 45° slope and that there seem to be a total of about ten portaloos (mostly without any flush!) for all the camping areas, you'll need to be pretty dedicated (and self-sufficient) to consider trying to "rough camp". Frankly we weren't that brave!

Our personal strategy was to book tickets in advance through our friends at Just Tickets (see advert in this section) and similarly to book a pitch in advance at Camping Eau Rouge (No 074 in our

Guide). This proved to be a reasonably cost-effective and comfortable option, because it enables you to arrive on the Friday evening (or even on the Saturday evening) settle yourself onto your pitch and walk to the circuit either along the road or through the woods – it's about 2km to the circuit at Stavelot, where you can get a pretty good close view over two corners and a short straight, and a more distant view of the following straight, but you must get in position early – I mean really early – the circuit actually opens at 1 am on race day, and if you're not in position by 6.30am, don't bother trying! There are no stands at Stavelot, and you'll need to take your own chairs unless you're prepared to stand for ten hours. An umbrella and/or parasol is also pretty essential, as it's either very hot sunshine (34°) or torrential rain. Spa is renowned for its unpredictable weather!

Alternatively you could drive from Camping Eau Rouge to several other parts of the circuit; we chose to make the short (5 minute) drive to Les Combes this year and managed to get a very good view, even though we arrived late at the circuit having overslept! We managed to park our camper very close to the circuit, albeit on a sloping field, but at a reasonable cost (about £8 for two days).

Our decision to camp at Eau Rouge, and to book in advance was fortuitous – we arrived on the Friday evening and apart from our reserved pitch there wasn't an inch of free space anywhere on the site, which was virtually taken over by GP enthusiasts. Given the sheer numbers the site coped pretty well, but expect long queues for the few hot showers!

Similarly our decision to arrive on the Friday also proved very lucky as not only did we see the Saturday qualifying session, and the Formula 3000 race, but after that we took the camper round to Francorchamps, and thanks to our friends at Stewart GP actually managed to get an invitation to the Stewart pit during the evening – feverish activity in the pits themselves as engineers worked on the two race cars and the T car, and we even had a chance of a brief chat with Johnny Herbert, who was carrying a plate of food around – apparently his fourth meal of the day! We wished him better luck than he'd enjoyed so far during the season, but it didn't seem to make a lot of difference, as the mechanical problems which have dogged him all year put in yet another appearance, but just as we're about to go to press, we're celebrating the Stewart's first GP win (the 1999 European GP) with Johnny at the wheel!

French Grand Prix
Circuit Nevers – Magny-Cours

The Magny-Cours circuit is situated literally in the heart of the French countryside! Arriving as we did, from the east, the approach to the circuit is via a myriad of tiny country lanes, which, in the days before the GP, are well signposted.

Given our previous experience at the Spanish GP in May, in addition to our admission tickets we had also obtained a car-parking ticket from Just Tickets. This ticket was for the East car park, which was easy enough to find, but on reflection we might have done better to have parked on the verge of the approach road (a country lane) as we would have thus avoided at least some of the delay when leaving!

The Magny-Cours circuit is set in a natural bowl in the surrounding hills, and viewing from most parts is pretty good. We found "seats" on concrete terracing just before the Adelaide curve, and enjoyed a reasonable view of the straight, the curve itself and the straight beyond it.

Even so you get a still better view on TV, but of course what you don't get on TV is the atmosphere, which was wonderful. In contrast to Barcelona, the commentary, over a quite audible PA system (but also on FM radio if you prefer) was in French and English, so there was no problem keeping track of pit-stops, etc. We were also opposite an electronic "scoreboard" which

gave updated positions for the leading cars.

The only real problem was getting away afterwards – we actually sat in a queue of traffic that moved no more than ten metres in an hour! Once you do get out of the circuit the traffic is kept moving by a variety of police, gendarmes and other military personnel, but progress is still pretty slow.

So far as camping/caravanning is concerned, one option is simply to get a car-parking ticket and take your outfit into the East car park (a very large, reasonably flat, if rather muddy, field) where you can choose more or less any spot you like to pitch. There are sanitary facilities, in porta-cabins, close to the entrance from the carpark to the circuit itself, which seemed to be kept reasonably well cleaned, apart from mud – to be fair the weather had been terrible for several days prior to the race, so mud was an inevitability wherever you went.

Alternatively there are several two-star municipal campsites within about 10km of the circuit, but the one-way system operated, and strictly controlled, by the police precluded our visiting these, although we did visit the four-star municipal "le Halles" at Decize, about 20km from the circuit.

This is an attractive site, beside the river, with quite reasonably sized pitches, all with electricity, on level grass with ample shade. Unfortunately the sanitary facilities, although quite clean, were distinctly elderly, with mainly Turkish style WCs, and certainly not of a standard one would expect of a more modern four-star campsite.

If you are prepared to travel further, the very comfortable Alan Rogers inspected/selected site Camping Des Bains, (No 5801 in the Alan Rogers Good Camps Guide – France) at St.Honore les Bains, in normal conditions, should be only about an hour or so's drive from the circuit – indeed it may well only take that long to get there on race day, but you'd probably best allow about three hours to get back.

LE MANS
more than a place, more than a race

Think of Le Mans as a series of snapshots. Of Wolf Barnato's thunderous Bentley heading into the setting sun. Of the big cat Jaguars – disc brakes glowing in the dark – humbling the might of European engineering, of Steve McQueen's heartbeat as he waits for the flag to drop in the classic movie Le Mans, or the crescendo of sound as the first lap pack jostle for position on the run down to Mulsanne corner.

And above it all the gaudily lit ferris wheel slowly revolving in the night sky.

But Le Mans is more than that. It is an area of gently rolling hills and woods. An area without extremes. Of gentle summers and mild winters. Of Charolais beef cattle, and Guernseys kept for their creamy milk. Of cottage industries turning out traditional wooden furniture identical to the chairs and tables which have seen hundreds of years service in the village bars. An area never intentionally developed for commercial tourism, which annually attracts Parisians in their thousands, all of them seeking a reminder of their rural roots.

But despite the attractions of the surrounding countryside, the real magnet outside the city is the motor race circuit to the south. The first race was held in 1923 and that, like every other subsequent 24 hour race, was intended as a means of encouraging the development of road going cars.

At times the organising Automobile Club de l'Ouest may have seemed autocratic and dogmatic with their insistence of setting their own construction rules. At times the world rules governing what we should call Grande Tourisme cars seemed to be moving in a different direction to

those applying to Le Mans. But such is the lure of the race that manufacturers will support it, even if it appears they put an entire year's effort and budget in to a car which will be used once only. But invariably Le Mans has been proved right. Fans, many of whom support no other form of racing, still flock to the circuit for their annual dose of excitement. And lessons learnt at Le Mans do find their way in to the cars we drive. Jaguar proved the durability and efficiency of disc brakes at Le Mans in the mid 1950s.

The practicality of turbochargers for small petrol engines was proved at Le Mans, and today it is complex re-inforced plastics and electronics which are proved at Le Mans before finding their way in to mass production cars.

But that isn't why the fans flock there every year. They come for the atmosphere. Every June the circuit is alive and thriving like a great 24 hour family party. You could go through the entire race weekend without seeing a race car – if you wanted to. The fun fair stays open throughout the race and there are masses of stalls selling everything imaginable – and a few things you'll never understand – in the area from the Ford chicane and on towards Tetra Rouge.

Unlike many race circuits, at Le Mans you don't have to dine out exclusively on burgers and hot dogs. There are a number of good restaurants close to the track, but my favourites are La Boule d'Or, Hunaudieres and the Auberge – all of them adjacent to the Mulsanne straight.

Le Mans – grandstand night atmosphere.
A.C.O. *Guy Beaulieu*

Le Mans – refuelling a McLaren F1 GTR.   A.C.O. *Guy Beaulieu*

Those with a sense of history will head for the main gate where the Le Mans museum has been moved. Cars on display are mute reminders of how far motor racing has come since the first 24 hour race in 1923.

But even if your trip to Le Mans isn't for the 24 hour race, you have to make a visit to the circuit. Much of it is on private land, but the famous Mulsanne straight is actually a public road. The N138.

The over four miles long Mulsanne straight was always the supreme test of a car's strength. Many a leading contender suffered engine failure on Mulsanne. By the late 1980's the organisers were becoming concerned about the speed of some of the competitors on Mulsanne. Cars like the WM team's Peugeots were getting close to 250mph. In an effort to reduce speeds, two chicanes were introduced. They have reduced speeds, but some of the leading competitors are still peaking at close to 200mph.

The public road avoids the chicanes, but unfortunately you can't speed. The speed limits are reinforced by wall-to-wall Gatso speed cameras. However the real thrill doesn't come from speeding down Mulsanne, but rather by parking and soaking up the atmosphere.
Within minutes the bustle of everyday

traffic fades as your eyes follow the road down to a point on the horizon. It takes little imagination to bring to mind grainy black and white photos of Barnato's Bentley, or the works Jaguars lining up to make a victorious statement as they crossed the finish in line astern.

Famous names, perhaps known only from history books, spring to mind. The names of those who have faced the toughest challenge in motor racing. Sir Henry Birkin, Earl Howe, Lord Selsdon, Mike Hawthorn, Phil Hill, Carroll Sheby, Roy Salvadori, Jacky Ickx, Henry Pescarolo, Derek Bell, Graham Hill, Mario Andretti. The list is as long as your memory and imagination.

That is Le Mans. It is more than a place. More than a race. It is an experience which everyone should enjoy at some time in their life.

Mike Cazalet

Le Mans Fact Sheet 1

Race weekend
Traditionally the third weekend of June every year. Scrutineering is held in the city, not at the track. There is also an annual 24 hour motorcycle race usually held on the first weekend in April.

Organisers
– L'Automobile Club de l'Ouest (ACO) for tickets and other information on 'phone (+00 33) 2.43.40.24.00 or fax (+00 33) 2.43.40.24.88. Web Site: www.lemans-aco.com

Travelling times
All approximate, with caravan or motorhome:
– from Calais (via Paris 230 miles) 5½ hours + depending on traffic conditions
– from Calais (via Rouen 260 miles) 6 hours
– from Caen (94 miles) 3 hours
– from St. Malo (120 miles) 3 hours
– from Le Havre (138 miles) 3½ hours
– from Cherbourg (166 miles) 4 hours
– from Dieppe (190 miles) 4 hours

Circuit length
8.45 miles.
There is also the shorter Bugatti circuit.

Le Mans Fact Sheet 2

In the UK, Race tickets, and tickets for camping at the Circuit itself are obtainable from Just Tickets, 01304 228868 (see advertisement in this section)

Alternatively you can apply for tickets direct from:
Automobile Club de l'Ouest,
Siege Social,
Circuit des 24 Heures,
72019 Le Mans Cedex.
Tel: 02.43.40.24.24.

Bear in mind that members of the ACO get a special discount on race tickets, access to their own 'club marquee' and other goodies, as well as the benefits of all-year-round breakdown cover throughout France, so you might like to consider actually joining the ACO – full details available from their address above.

Camping at Le Mans
The Le Mans circuit itself offers racegoers several different 'campsites' usually open from the Tuesday prior to the race until the Monday after it, but early booking, or early arrival, is essential if you are not to be disappointed.

These 'sites' include Camping Houx (or Nouveau) with numbered pitches and electrical connections, and a new sanitary block with showers and WCs. This site also

has an annexe, Chemin aux Boeufs, with good access to the starting straight.

La Chapelle camping is situated in the woods on the inside of the circuit near the Dunlop Bridge, and is definitely noisy! Tertre Rouge is again close to the track, and to the funfair, whilst Camping Bleu is close to the main entrance/exit for a quick getaway. Camping Expo is also close to the entrance, and to the Museum, while Maison Blanche (also very noisy!) may allow you to get a view of the circuit from the roof of your motorhome or caravan.

Prices, in 1999, for these 'campsites' range from FFr. 180 – 450 for the whole period of the practice and the race itself, irrespective of how long you actually stay.

If you choose not to use the circuit's own camping facilities, and to stay at a 'proper' campsite, there are a fair number to choose from, including quite a few in the département of Sarthe (72) some of which are featured in the Alan Rogers Good Camps Guide to France, but bear in mind that all of these are likely to become very heavily booked-up over the weeks before, during and after the race.

Amongst the several sites within about thirty miles of the circuit are:

Camping Municipal
Bresse-sur-Braye (about 45 km. SE of Le Mans). Unusual 4-star municipal with around 60 pitches.
Tel: 02.43.35.31.13

Camping Municipal du Lac
St Calais (about 37 km. ESE of Le Mans). Fully described in the Alan Rogers Good Camps Guide for France (7202M).
Tel: 02.43.35.04.81

Camping Les Mollieres
Sille Guillaume (about 35 km. N of Le Mans). A well-shaded 3-star site with 130 pitches. Tel: 02.43.20.16.12

Camping Le Vieux Moulin
Neuville-sur-Sarthe (about 11 km. N of Le Mans). Pleasant 3-star site with about 100 pitches. Tel: 02.43.25.31.82

Camping Municipal La Route d'Or
La Fleche (about 40 km. SW of Le Mans). Fully described in the Alan Rogers Good Camps Guide for France (7201M).
Tel: 02.43.94.55.90

Castel Camping Chateau de Chanteloup

Savigne l'Eveque (15 km. NE of Le Mans). Fully described in the Alan Rogers Good Camps Guide for France (7203). Tel: 02.43.27.51.07.

Staying Alive

Judging from what we've seen in the past, some British spectators seem to bring enough food and beer with them to last the week! For those who don't have a truck-load of space there is the local Carrefour Supermarket, south of the town not far from Tertre Rouge corner – there is a bus from near the main entrance to the circuit for those who don't want to use their own transport. There is even a McDonalds next door!

Of course there are other restaurants too (this is France remember!) including three on the Mulsanne straight alone – The Hunaudieres, the Auberge and the Shangai 24 Heures.

There are at least two chemists in Le Mans, the Pharmacie Dufayet and the Pharmacie Boucret, and there is a special medical help line (02 43 40 24 24). Medical Expenses insurance cover is always advisable when travelling abroad, and don't forget to take your form E1-11 which extends your National Health cover to France.

THE MONACO GRAND PRIX

One of the good things about banking with the Midland Bank is that they are part of the Hong Kong & Shanghai Bank Corporation, who are one of Stewart GPs principal sponsors. As we'd already arranged tickets for the Monaco GP, our local Midland manager was persuaded that we were good enough customers for him to recommend that HSBC's Grand Prix Manager, Johnny Harrison, give us a tour of the paddock!

Having competed myself in the 1998 and 1999 Monte Carlo Rallyes Historique in January, I was already reasonably familiar with the Monaco circuit and it's surroundings, but the visit to the F1 paddock was a real eye-opener – first of all of course the paddock area is a long way from the temporary pits, which in any case are too small for anything other than routine servicing when the cars are out on the circuit, so everything else has to be done in the paddock, which involves a serious climb up lots of narrow stone steps – no wonder Monaco isn't the teams' favourite venue!

We were very lucky to have the paddock tour of course, which was absolutely brilliant, but there again the Monaco GP is a real "must" for any F1 enthusiast, and we were very pleasantly surprised how easy it is for the independent traveller to have a really good time here, with surprisingly little hassle.

Our original intention was to drive into Monte Carlo on the Friday prior to the race from our Alan Rogers campsite, La Vieille Ferme, (Site No 0605 in the Alan Rogers Good Camps Guide for France) at Villeneuve Loubet, suss out the situation, have our Paddock Tour, return to Villeneuve Loubet, leave our car there and use the train to travel in and out of Monte Carlo on the Saturday and Sunday.

We duly took the train on the Saturday morning – after a long queue for tickets we joined a packed, very slow, train which stopped for twenty minutes in Nice. The journey was said to take half an hour, but in fact took an hour. The return was even worse – we couldn't even get on the first two trains out of Monte Carlo, and this was only the qualifying day!

After some discussion we decided to risk the car on race day, although we were warned by some Germans on the campsite that we would need to leave really early, and to expect traffic jams, and they would be leaving Villeneuve Loubet at 5am!

We decided that a 5am start was not really on, so we left at 6.30 – to our amazement there was little traffic, and we drove straight into the first "parking for Grand Prix" car park we saw, walked about 400m to the centre of Monte Carlo and were sat down having breakfast at a local pavement bar in the Place d'Armes by 7.15am!

We'd managed to get some grandstand tickets near the swimming pool for the race, but quite frankly the extra cost of anything other than the very best stand tickets is arguably not really justified in terms of getting a good view – yes, we were close to the track, but could only see a short stretch around the back of the swimming pool, and a more distant view down to the Rascasse and the Stars and Bars. If your main interest is getting a good view of the race, you need to buy the very best stand tickets, for which most us would need a second mortgage, or watch it on TV, which is a lot cheaper.

It's not the view, or lack of it, that we like to go to GPs for, it's the atmosphere of course, and in this respect Monaco is truly exceptional – where else (after 7pm) can you walk round most of the circuit, including the tunnel, drink in the history and the Campari, eat well and at surprisingly reasonable prices, spend an hour on the beach, gawk at the mega yachts, do some sightseeing, go to the Casino (no, we didn't actually, but we could have) rub shoulders with former GP drivers to say nothing of watching the free practice, the qualifying and the race itself from a variety of situations?

Perhaps we just got lucky (and yes, we did, so far as the Paddock visit went, and many thanks to Johnny Harrison for an excellent tour) but even without that particular bonus the Monaco GP looks like becoming an annual family pilgrimage from now on.

Spanish Grand Prix
Circuit de Cataluna – Barcelona

Our visit to the Spanish Formula 1 GP was something of an eye-opener!

Although we had acquired admission tickets in advance, from Just Tickets, (see advert in this section) we were unable to get to the Saturday qualifying, so getting into the circuit on the Sunday was a new experience. Our first mistake was to take the wrong exit off the Autostrada! You'd expect that Exit 13 would be the Exit immediately after Exit 12 wouldn't you? – well, it isn't – there's another unnumbered junction between 12 and 13, which we took by mistake, and ended up driving round a deserted suburb for about half and hour, until we eventually found someone who directed us to the circuit.

Once we found the circuit the problem was to find somewhere to park – there are

plenty of numbered car-parks, but most are reserved or pre-booked, so unless you are able to attend the Saturday qualifying and buy a car parking ticket in advance, allow yourself plenty of time to find somewhere to park the car (like an hour or so!)

By chance we actually ended up in the car park next to the camping field, which involves a walk of about ten minutes to the nearest circuit gate. The camping field is reasonably flat, but the access to it isn't, and it seemed to be used exclusively by motorhomes – I wouldn't have wanted to try to manoeuvre a caravan into it, espcially in competition with several thousand cars using the entrance to the adjacent car parking field!

The camping field had several WCs and showers in porta-cabins, which would probably have been fine if it wasn't for the fact that the car park adjacent had no such facilities – this resulted in the WCs in the camping field being a tad pressed, to put it mildly! All in all the the camping facilities at the circuit might best be described in one word – primitive!

In fact our advice would be to do the same as we did and to stay on one of the many excellent sites in the Costa Brava, and drive to the circuit by car – bearing in mind that the circuit is north of Barcelona, and only about 1km off the autoroute (junction 13) it's actually within not much more than an hour or so's drive from a wide choice of good campsites.

The circuit itself is in a "bowl" in the surrounding hills, and there are good views from several vantage points – we found space on the grassy slope just above turns 1 and 2, which gave quite a good view, although not of the pits, so we tended to lose track of the situation after about 15 laps when cars started to pit – in retrospect a VHF/FM radio, preferably with headphones, would have been very useful to enable us to keep track of the pit stops, etc, via the (English language) commentary, because although we could see one of the many giant TV monitors, their commentary was all in Spanish and the picture was very faint in the strong sunlight.

Frankly you get a better all round picture of a GP from the comfort of your armchair in front of the TV at home, but, crucially, what you miss is the incredible atmosphere – next time we'll know better, get there earlier, take a walkman type radio as well as binoculars, and more by way of a picnic, but even allowing for our mistakes, this is an event not to be missed if you enjoy motorsport!

Historic Rallies

The Rallye Monte Carlo Historique

Traditionally rallying was a sport that took place on public roads, and in its heyday attracted hundreds of thousands of spectators, particularly to the more famous international rallies such as the Monte Carlo, the Tulip Rally and the Alpine Rally.

Unfortunately as the sport became more and more professional, and cars became more and more unlike their normal road-going versions, and thus quicker and quicker, the sport became the more or less the exclusive preserve of the works teams, with fewer and fewer amateurs or other private entrants.

In recent years the World Rally Championship has become an increasingly popular TV spectacle, but this has meant that the modern versions of famous events such as "The Monte" bear little relation to the original concept, and nowadays most of the action takes place in daylight over closed roads (stages) with the start and finish in Monte Carlo, and

no "concentration runs" from several starting points all over Europe, so the event has really changed out of all recognition.

In 1998 the AC de Monaco decided to resurrect the Monte in its original format, and to run it once again as a traditional road rally for "period" cars – ie those of a type which competed in the old-style Monte Carlo Rally before 1975. To an extent they were following a lead set by the organisers of the Tulip Rally, the Alpine Rally and the Rally des Pyrenees, including a number of independent rally organisers who had been doing much the same thing for several years, with significant success.

Having been a rally driver myself during the '60s, forced into retirement by the increasing cost and commercialism of "modern" rallying, we had been delighted to once more have had the opportunity to compete in international rallies on equal terms, and since 1995 we had used our 1971 Lancia Fulvia 1600HF coupé to compete on both the Rallye des Pyrenees and the Tulip Rally. When the AC de Monaco launched the 1st "Rallye Monte Carlo Historique" in 1998 we were therefore one of the first British entrants! – just as well as the event was well over-subscribed, although mainly with French, Belgian, Italian, German and Dutch competitors, so we were actually one of just seven British teams.

The Monte Carlo Rallye Historique is run on strictly traditional lines, as a regularity rally, with starts in Reims and Turin followed by Concentration Runs to Digne

Motorcaravans queueing to get on the Quay at the finish of the Monte Carlo Rally.

les Bains, a Communal Leg to Monte Carlo, followed by a night leg over closed roads in the mountains behind Monte Carlo, including the famous Col de Turini. Of course it is run in January when snow is inevitable, and timing is crucial as competitors are penalised for every second early or late at each control, and averaging exactly 50kph over tiny snow-covered roads in the Alps is no easy feat.

The French take rallying seriously, and the Reims starters enjoy a high speed run through the centre of Reims, complete with policy outriders as escorts, prior to the start which is on a huge ramp opposite the Hotel de Ville, preceded by several long speeches of course! The crowds standing out in the pouring rain to watch the start were amazing!

The night route from Reims to Chambery, in pretty horrible weather conditions consisting of a mixture of snow, sleet, rain and fog, ran via Vitry-le-Francois where the Christmas lights were on, and huge crowds lined the streets, kept back from the road by marshals and police holding blazing torches – a truly amazing sight, especially considering that this was one o'clock in the morning! Even at Langres, at an even more unearthly hour, the crowds were spectacular.

Arriving at Chambery around 7am competitors are faced with a further three hours driving around a very competitive section through the mountains of the Chartreuse before getting back to Chambery for a well-earned 18 hour rest.

The following two days saw increasing numbers of spectators in every town and village through which we passed, and even more spectators lining the minor snow-covered roads through the Ardeche where the rally returned in 1999 after several years absence. We had a gearbox problem here, but the problem was fixed by a local garage in double quick time (so quickly that we were able to make up the lost time again) and the garage point blank refused to accept any payment, even for the parts! Clearly Historic Rallying in the form of these major international events has caught the French public's imagination, even though the event had little advance publicity.

Not only has it caught the eye of the French, but of just about every other European nation as well, apart from the British apparently! During the 1999 Rallye Monte Carlo Historique, courtesy of Which Motorcaravan Magazine, we had the benefit of a Murvi Motorcaravan driven by well-known caravan photo-journalist Mike Cazalet as our support vehicle, and during his travels around France, Mike spotted literally hundreds of other motorcaravans, but not one of them sported a British registration plate. Do British motorcaravanners hibernate during the winter, or do they all emigrate to the Costa Blanca or the Algarve?

During the 1999 event, following the second night stop in an even more spectacularly lit and crowded Digne-les-Bains the route ran through the Alpes via the spectacular Lac de Serre-Poncon, Sisteron, the snow covered Col de Fontbelle and Thoard, until we found ourselves in a massive traffic jam on the approach to Entrevaux, where we were saved by the police! They stopped all the non-rally traffic, and escorted competitors down the wrong side of the road for almost six miles! Can you imagine that happening in Britain?

Both the 1998 and 1999 events followed a similar route into Monte Carlo, taking in highly competitive sections (on snow/ice covered roads closed to non-rally traffic) via Lantosque and the famous (notorious?) Col de Turini, where, this year, we had an unscheduled off-road excursion into a snow drift which cost us 23 minutes and the loss of a possible top-ten result (we had been lying 19th out of 150 at this point, and falling off the road dropped us to 80th!)

In terms of results we would have been happy just to finish, so the fact that in the 1998 event we actually came 14th overall, and third in class, was a real bonus, and even though we got a disappointing result in 1999 we'd happily have done the event just for the craic, as the Irish would say! For those interested the year 2000 Rallye Monte Carlo Historique has five starting points; Reims and Turin of course, but also Oslo, Munich and Barcelona. All the cars converge at Vals les Bains for the final stages through the Alps to Monte Carlo. The rally starts on 22nd January 2000, and finishes in Monte Carlo on 26th January.

Clive Edwards & Mervyn Brake

The MOTOR Caravanners' CLUB ™

Grand Prix Racing

Just Tickets
As the largest suppliers of **Formula One** and **Le Mans 24 Hour** spectator tickets we provide the **best range of seats in this country.**

Our **TICKET ONLY** service covers general admission, grandstand seats and parking at F.1 circuits and Le Mans. At **MONACO** we offer some of the **best viewing of all from private apartment terraces** located at the most advantageous point, and seats and hospitality at a trackside restaurant.

For **SILVERSTONE** we can book seats, hospitality marquees and helicopters.

JUST MOTORING offers inclusive self-drive arrangements with hotels at **European Formula One** events, plus for **Le Mans** ferry bookings, parking, camping and hospitality marquees.

Just Tickets
1 Charter House,
Camden Crescent,
Dover, Kent.
CT16 1LE
Tel: 01304 228866
Fax: 01304 242550
www.justtickets.co.uk

Mr/Mrs/Ms

Address

Postcode

Event

Ref GCG/98

516 Camping Zugligeti Niche, Budapest

Satisfactory, friendly site with easy access to Budapest.
Car parking is as difficult in Budapest as it is in any large town – Zugligeti Niche is the nearest campsite to the tourist centre of the town with good public transport links. The site started life as a tram terminus and when this use was discontinued, it was turned into an acceptable camping site. The narrow entrance has an old tram car on either side, one used as the reception bureau, the other for snacks and basic food supplies. The entrance road, with hardstanding caravan places on either side, passes under a road bridge to similar pitches further up. Small terrace clearings have been made amidst the trees on the steep hill to one side of the caravan area which are only suitable for small tents with parking nearby for cars. The site has made clever use of the space available. The old tram station is now an attractive restaurant. The whole situation is a quiet one near the chair lift to the summit of the Janos mountain. Sightseeing tours are organised. The sanitary arrangements are not quite up to our normal standards, although they are heated, hot water is free and toilets are British style. This is a pleasant, friendly site and the English speaking owner welcomes British guests.

How to find it: From M1 Austria - Budapest motorway, take Budakeszi exit, from where site is well signed at all junctions (look for squirrel logo). From M0 ring road take M1 exit, then through Budakeszi.

General Details: Open all year. Restaurant (all year). Kiosk with basic supplies (1/5-15/9). Supermarket 500 m. Swimming pool and other entertainment at Margarit Island, 20 mins. by public transport. Golf or riding 8 km. Gas supplies. Chemical disposal.

Charges 2000: Per person Ft. 900; child 450; car or m/cycle 550; caravan or motorcaravan 1,900; tent 550; electricity 450; local tax 50. No credit cards or Eurocheques (cash only).

Reservations: Necessary for August; write to site. Address: Camping Zugligeti Niche, Zugligeti ut. 101, 1121 Budapest. Tel: 01/200 83 46. FAX: as phone.

AR Discount
Less 10%;
welcome drink;
Stay 8 days, pay 7

515 Fortuna Camping, Törökbálint, nr Budapest

Pretty site close to bus terminal for city centre.
This pretty site lies at the foot of a hill with views of the vineyards, but Budapest is only 25 minutes away by bus (bus stop 1 km). Surrounded by mature trees, the owner, Csaba Szücs, will proudly name all 150 varieties of bushes and shrubs which edge some of the pitches. A large, modern terraced restaurant with very reasonable prices will save the weary traveller from cooking. A new, open air swimming pool will help you to cool off in summer. Concrete and gravel access roads lead to terraces where there are 120 individual pitches, all with electricity (16A, long leads may be needed), 14 with water, on slightly sloping ground. A special field area provides for group bookings, which has separate facilities. Four sanitary blocks (one with heating) provide free hot water to washbasins and showers. There are extra toilets for disabled people. Washing up facilities, plus six cookers in a sheltered area. Herr Szücs and his family will endeavour to make your stay a comfortable one and his daughter will organise tours to Budapest or the surrounding countryside, and also explain the mysteries of public transport in Budapest.

How to find it: From M1 Györ - Budapest, exit for Törökbálint following signs for town and then site. Also accessible from M7 Budapest - Balaton road.

General Details: Open all year. Restaurant and bar (all year). Shop (1/6-20/8 or essentials from reception, order bread previous day). Swimming pool (15/5-15/9). Small children's play area. Excursions organised. Washing machine. Gas supplies. Chemical disposal. Motorcaravan services. English spoken. Apartments for rent.

Charges 2000: Per person DM 6.00; child (4-14 yrs) 4.00; pitch 9.00; electricity 4.00. No credit cards.

Reservations: Recommended for high season - write to site. Address: 2045 Törökbálint. Tel: 23/335 364. FAX: 23/339 697.

AR Discount
Less 10% after
10 days; welcome
drink; info pack

The sites in HUNGARY featured in this guide
are shown on the map on page 368

HUNGARY

518 Jumbo Camping, Üröm, Budapest

Modern, thoughtfully developed site in northwest outskirts of Budapest.
On a hillside, with attractive views of the Buda hills and with public transport to the city from 500 m. away, this is a pleasant and comfortable, small site (despite the name). It is possible to park outside the short, steepish entrance which has a chain across. Reception, where you will be given a comprehensive English language information sheet, doubles as a cafe/bar area and bread orders are also taken here. The concrete and gravel access roads lead shortly to 55 terraced pitches of varying size, with hardstanding for cars and caravan wheels as well as large hardstandings for motorhomes. All pitches have 6A electricity (may require long leads) and there are some caravan pitches with water and waste water also. They are mostly divided by small hedges and the whole area is fenced. The sanitary facilities are most satisfactory, with large, controllable showers (communal changing) with free hot water also to the washbasins. British style WCs. There is also dishwashing undercover and a terrace with chairs and tables. A small open-air swimming pool is beside the small children's play area.

How to find it: Site is signed on roads to Budapest - nos. 11 from Szentendre and 10 from Komaron. It is also approachable via Györ on M1/E60 and Lake Balaton on M7/E71.

General Details: Open 1 April - 31 Oct. Cafe where bread, milk and butter available. Shop and restaurant 500 m. Barbecue area. Swimming pool (10/6-10/9). Children's play area. Riding (4 km) and tennis can be arranged. Fishing 8 km. Bus to city 500 m. every 30 minutes. Washing machine, iron and cooking facilities on payment. Chemical disposal. Motorcaravan services. English spoken and information sheet provided in English.

Charges 2000: Per pitch DM 2.50 - 8.00, acc. to size and season; adult 5.00; child (3-14 yrs) 3.00; electricity 2.00; dog 2.00; local tax 120 forints. Less 5% in low seasons. No credit cards (cash only).

Reservations: Write to site. Address: 2096 Üröm, Budakalászi ut 23-25. Tel: 26/351-251 or 60/310-901. FAX: 26/351-251.

520 Autós Caraván Camping, Eger

Large, city site in attractive touring area of northern Hungary.
The city of Eger and its surroundings (including the very attractive Bukk mountain area between Eger and Miskolc) provide much for the tourist to see, indeed far too much to list here, but reception will provide lots of information for you. Most of the city attractions are quite close together, with good public transport from close to the site, which is just 2.5 km. from the centre. The site is large, with over 180 pitches, all with electricity (10A). They are on gently sloping hardstanding with much grass, lots of shade and tarred access roads and there is a separate tent area. The quietest part is at the reception end for, at the other side of the camping area, there are many bungalows and dormitory accommodation much used by young people. However, it is quiet at night thanks to 24 hour security patrols. The sanitary facilities are rather basic, with a couple of toilets behind reception, a `portacabin' style facility to the right (nearest for many pitches) with cold water washbasins and a large block at the end of the camping area which was in need of maintenance (used by the youngsters) with dishwashing and chemical disposal facilities. However, all facilities were clean when we visited. At the far end of the park is an area with three outlets selling drinks (local wine), snacks and ices, beyond which is a large restaurant and another set in a cave. There are shops just outside the site entrance.

How to find it: Site is in the northern outskirts of the city on the west side of road no. 25. It is well signed (not usual camp signs at entrance) by a Shell station, just before the last high-rise flats.

General Details: Open 15 April - 15 October. Restaurant. Bar. Snacks. Money exchange (including travellers cheques). English spoken.

Charges guide: Per person DM 4.00, children under 6 free; caravan 8.00; motorcaravan 6.00; tent (2 person) 4.00; electricity incl. except for tents (2.00). Student card less 20%.

Reservations: Probably not necessary. Address: 3300 Eger, Rákóczi ut 79. Tel: 36/410 558. FAX: 36/411 768. E-mail: egertour@mailagria.hu.

522 Pelsőczy Camping, Tokaj, nr Nyiregyhaza

Relaxing, shady, riverside site at small town.
From the middle of June to the middle of September, this site gets quite busy, but either side of these dates it is quiet and very relaxing. Set on the banks of the wide River Tisza, the level grass pitches, about 60 in number, are close together and narrow but quite long, off a hard circular access road so siting should be quite easy. All the pitches have electricity and there is much shade. The sanitary unit has external entry WCs (British style) and curtained showers with communal undressing. Clean but basic and looking a little tired now, they are located near the entrance, where there is also the high season reception, shop and restaurant. At other times, site yourself and a gentleman will call during the evening to collect the fee. Shops for basics outside the main season are in the town over the bridge, a 600 m. walk. There may well be some day-time noise from watersports on the river but it is very quiet by night. This is a useful base for visiting northeast Hungary, not far from the Ukraine and Romania. Tokai wine is produced in this area (similar to sherry, a strong desert wine).

How to find it: Tokaj is east of Miskolc and north of Debrecen. Site is just south of the river bridge on road no. 38. (Note: beware the noisy campsite signed on the other side of the road).

General Details: Open 15 April - 10 Oct. Shop and restaurant (15/6-15/9). Town 600 m. River sports available. No English spoken (German is).

Charges: Not available - probably modest.

Reservations: Advised for high season, but in German - otherwise arrive early. Address: 3910 Tokaj, Pf.36. Tel: 47/352-626.

524 Dorcas Centre and Camping, Debrecen

Friendly, welcoming 'Christian Aid Organisation' site.
Debrecen is an interesting old town, close to the Hortobagy National Park and convenient if you are looking for a break travelling to Romania or the Ukraine. Dorcas is a Dutch Christian organisation and the campsite provides holidays for special causes – indeed, while we were there, 40 children arrived from Chernobyl for their first trip abroad. The site is about 10 km. from Debrecen in a forest location, fenced and covered with trees. The 40 flat and grassy touring pitches are off tarmac access roads, arranged in four groups. Some pitches are divided by hedges, others marked out by trees and all have electricity available (6A). There is room in the large tenting area for more units, also with electricity, if necessary. The large sanitary building is tiled and of a rather open design. It is situated between the tenting area and the main pitch areas and is of reasonable quality with free hot water to the washbasins and controllable, large, curtained showers (external changing), British WCs; also facilities for dishwashing and laundry (key at reception). There is a very pleasant restaurant and terrace offering very good value meals (with menu in English) and a shop for basics. Small swimming pool open June - Aug. and several items of children's play equipment are next to it on grass. Through the site is an area for walks and a lake for fishing.

How to find it: From Debrecen take road no. 47 south for 4 km. then left towards Hosszupalyi for 6 km. Site is signed on the right.

General Details: Open 1 May - 30 Sept. Shop. Restaurant. Swimming pool (June-Aug). Children's playgrounds. Church services (in English) fortnightly or more often if requested. Conference hall and meeting rooms. Bicycle hire. Lake nearby with fishing. Good walks. Riding 2 km. Chemical disposal. English spoken. Chalets and apartments for rent.

Charges 1999: Per unit incl. 2 adults US dollars 12.00; extra person 4.00; child (6-12 yrs) 2.00; local tax 0.50 (or HUF 120). Credit cards accepted.

Reservations: Probably unnecessary, but contact site. Address: 4002 Debrecen, Pf.146. Tel: 52/441-119. FAX: as phone.

 **For a list of sites which are open all year - see page 257**

HUNGARY

526 Jonathermal Motel-Camping, Kiskunmajsa, nr Szeged

Large, well run site with marvellous indoor and outdoor pool complex.
Situated 3 km. to the north of the town of Kiskunmajsa, a few kilometres west of road no. 5 (E75) from Budapest (140 km.) to Szeged (35 km.) this is one of the best Hungarian campsites. The camping area is large, reached by tarred access roads and the unmarked pitches are located in several areas around the motel and sanitary buildings. Some shade is available and more trees are growing. All the 120 large pitches have 4A electricity and are set on flat grass where you place the pitch number allocated to you. Reception is part of the smart bar and rest room just to the right of the entrance. A new, heated sanitary block provides first class facilities with free hot water for controllable showers and washbasins in private cabins and a unit for disabled visitors. Rubbish bins are provided and there is a separate chemical disposal facility, well marked. A kiosk sells bread (to order), fresh fruit and vegetables, groceries, stamps and postcards. The pool complex is accessed via a path through the site fence which leads firstly to the entrance to the fishing lake, then past the restaurant. Entrance to the complex costs 300 forints for adults, 200 for children (weekly tickets available) which gives you a huge 100 x 70 m. open air pool with a beach along one side, the indoor pool, children's pool, thermal, sauna and cold dip. In addition there is an open air thermal pool, a children's playground with carved wooden animals, plus swings on grass, giant chess, volleyball, tennis and minigolf plus various places to eat and drink. Massage is available on payment. This professionally run site offers the chance of relaxation but is also well placed for visiting Szeged, Csongrad or Szolnok, as well as being close to the borders with Romania and the former Yugoslavia.

How to find it: From no. 5 (E75) Budapest - Szeged road take Kiskunmajsa exit and site is well signed 3 km. north of the town.

General Details: Open all year. Kiosk on site for bread, etc. (shop opposite entrance, 120 m). Restaurant by pool complex, others near. Large swimming and thermal complex with other facilities (as above). Fishing (day permits available). Bicycle hire. Riding. Launderette. Gas supplies. Chemical disposal. Motel rooms for rent. German spoken.

Charges 2000: Per person DM 4.00 - 5.00; child (6-14 yrs) 1.00 - 2.00; caravan 2.00 - 2.50; motorcaravan 3.00 - 4.00; tent 1.50 - 2.00; car 2.00 - 2.60; electricity 4.00 - 6.00; dog 3.00; plus local tax. Less 5-10% for longer stays. Credit cards accepted.

Reservations: Possibly necessary mid-July - mid-Aug. Address: 6120 Kiskunmajsa, Kokut 26. Tel: 77/481 855. FAX: 77/481 013.

530 Kék-Duna Camping, Dunaföldvár

Pleasant site on the banks of the Danube.
Dunaföldvár is a most attractive town of 10,000 people and you are in the heart of it in just two or three minutes by foot but, as a `town site', Kék-Duna is remarkably peaceful and easily reached via the wide towpath on the west bank of the Danube. Apart from the obvious attractions of the river, with a large island opposite and pleasant walks available, the ancient town has a most interesting museum, the `Burg', with a genuine dungeon and cells, Roman relics and with a panoramic view of the town and river from its top floor. There are too many places of interest within easy reach to list here, but we thoroughly endorse our reader's recommendation of this site. It is small, fenced all round and locked at night, with flat concrete access roads to 40 pitches. All have 3A electricity, the first half being open, the remainder well shaded. The modern, tiled sanitary building has a nicely decorated ladies' section and offers 10 curtained, controllable, free showers with communal changing. British style WCs. The rest of the facilities are also of above average standard. There is a small shop and café open from mid June (otherwise it is a short walk into the town), washing machine and dishwashing (outside with cold water). A thermal swimming pool is 200 m (under the same ownership).

How to find it: From no. 6 Budapest - Pecs road take exit at Dunaföldvár for Kecskemed road no. 52, and follow until slip road on right which leads on to the riverside towpath. Site is well signed.

General Details: Open 15 April - 15 Oct. Shop and café (from mid June), town shops close. Tennis 50 m. Riding 200 m. Washing machine. Excursion information. English speaking receptionist. Bungalows for hire.

Charges guide: Per adult Forints 200 - 340; child 150 - 180; pitch 480 - 580; tent and car 290 - 390; electricity 100; dog 150.

Reservations: Advisable for July/Aug. or arrive early. Address: 7020 Dunaföldvár, Hösök Tere 12. Tel: 75/341 529.

HUNGARY

531 Sugovica Camping, Baja

Pleasant town site near Croatian and Yugoslavian borders.

If you are exploring Southern Transdanubia or en route south, then Baja is an acceptable stop, on the east banks of the Danube. The site is on a small island, quiet and relaxed, next to the hotel which owns it, where there is a small swimming pool on payment and a terraced restaurant. The 180 fair sized pitches (80 sq.m), all with 10A electricity and 7 with hardstandings for motorhomes, are on flat, grassy, firm ground, easily accessed from tarred roads and with some shade from the many trees. Behind reception are a small shop, TV room, laundry and a kitchen with fridge and freezer. The sanitary facilities are just about adequate, with British style WCs and free hot water to open washbasins and showers (communal changing), all clean when seen.

How to find it: Site is on Petoti island (sziget), well signed from just southwest of the junction of roads 51 from Budapest and 55 from Szeged, the bridge being close to a cobbled town square.

General Details: Open 1 May - 30 Sept. Shop. Restaurant 50 m. Town facilities close. Swimming pool (8 x 15 m), town 50 m. pool 100 m. away. TV room. Tennis. Table tennis. Riverside walks. Fishing. Chemical disposal. No English spoken.

Charges 1999: Per adult DM 3.00; child (6-14) 1.50; pitch 6.00; tent 4.00; electricity included; dog 1.50; local tax 1.00.

Reservations: not made. Address: 6500 Baja. Tel: 79 321 755. FAX: 79 323 155.

508 Diana Camping, Aszófö, nr Balatonfüred

Large, quiet, friendly site in forest near Lake Balaton.

This very large site of about 12 hectares was developed many years ago as a retreat for the 'party faithful'. Now just 4 hectares are used by Mr and Mrs Keller-Toth, who have leased it from the Balatontourist organisation. There is, naturally, much woodland around which you may wander. There are 27 hedged pitches of 120 sq.m. (where two 60 sq.m. ones have been joined) on grass. Many have shade from trees, as have about 65 smaller individual ones. The remainder are amongst the trees which mark them out. There is no exact number of pitches, but about 200 units are taken in all, with 150 electrical connections (2 pin, 6 or 10A) on sloping ground. The toilet facilities are admittedly old but kept very clean with chemical disposal in the men's. The shower block across the path is open 6.30-10.30 am. and 4.30-10 pm. The very smart, new ladies' section has large, push-button showers with seat, divider and private dressing, whilst the facilities for men are older (with communal changing). Washbasins, for both men and women, are older with just two with hot water for each and many with cold only, shelf, mirror and razor points. At the back of the block is the entrance to a splendid, new children's washroom (key from reception), with 3 shower/baths 2 of which are designed for handicapped children. There is a well stocked shop, with the laundry just beyond with modern machines (key from reception). A large kitchen has 6 cookers but the cold water dishwashing is probably the least attractive area. The fair-sized restaurant, open all season, has tables, benches and flowers in troughs outside. In front of this area is under cover table tennis and the play area where animation is organised in high season. There are swings, a climbing frame on grass, a sand-pit and a slide into sand.

How to find it: From road 71 on the north side of the lake, turn towards Azsófö just west of Balatonfüred, through the village and follow the signs for about 1 km. along access road (bumpy in places).

General Details: Open 26 April - 28 Sept. Shop (open 08.00-17.00 low season or 22.00 high season) Restaurant (all season). Children's play area, with animation in high season. Volleyball. Tennis. Table tennis. Post box and telephones. Many walking opportunities. Lake 3 km.

Charges guide: Per caravan, car, electricity and incl. 3 persons DM 16.00 - 20.00, acc. to season; tent 2.70 - 3.00; motorcaravan 6.20 - 7.60; person 2.60 - 3.20; child (6-14 yrs) 1.30 - 1.60; dog 1.30 - 1.60. Local tax (over 18 yrs) 0.80. Special rates for disabled persons. Eurocheques up to 23,000 Forints accepted.

Reservations: are possible - write to site. Address: 8241 Aszófö. Tel: 87/445 013. FAX: as phone.

HUNGARY

504 Autós 1 Camping, Zamárdi, nr Siófok

Large Siotour site with own direct access to Lake Balaton.

If you have young children or non-swimmers in your party, then the southern shores of the lake at this site are ideal as you can walk out for nearly 1 km. before the water rises to more than a metre in depth. It is a large site with 545 pitches, most with 6A electricity, and there must be the possibility of noise in high season, although it was peaceful during our visit in early June. There are many tall trees and the more attractive pitches are near the lakeside, some unshaded ones alongside the water. The rest, in a large central area which comprises the majority of the site, are flat, individual ones on grass. They are hedged and vary from small to quite large. A separate tent area is at the back of the site, adjacent to three very modern, tiled sanitary buildings (plus an old one on the right of the entrance). The facilities provide free hot water to push-button showers with private changing and warm to washbasins with single taps. British style WCs (no paper). Satisfactory dishwashing and laundry facilities (key from reception). Other amenities include a restaurant and a soft drinks and ice cream bar by the entrance and a bar further in, all with terraces. A shop is only 50 m. Plenty of children's wooden play equipment is on sandy grass by the lake. Next door is a large water slide area and boats for hire.

How to find it: Exit road no. 7/E71 between Balatonföldvár and Siófok towards Tihany, and site is well signed.

General Details: Open 17 May - 8 Sept. Shop adjacent. Restaurant (from June). Lake swimming, fishing and non-powered boating. Money exchange. Bath (key from reception). Chemical disposal. Table tennis.

Charges guide: Per person DM 5.10 - 7.80; child 2.55 - 3.90; pitch 11.10 - 17.00; tent and car 7.40 - 11.40; electricity 1.50; dog 5.10 - 7.80; local tax (over 18 yrs) 1.00 - 1.50.

Reservations: Write to site. Address: 8261 Zamárdi. Tel: 84/348 863 FAX: 84/348 931. When closed write to Siotour AG Hauptbüro, 8600 Siófok, Batthyány u. 2/6. Tel: 84/310 806. FAX: 84/310 803.

506 Aranypart Camping, Siófok

Large Siotour holiday park near Lake Balaton's main tourist town.

Situated right by the famous Lake, there are over 600 flat, grassy pitches available on this long site, just over half being smallish individual ones. There are many sports and entertainment facilities, with restaurants, shops and bars, making it very popular with the younger generation.

How to find it: Site is 3 km. north of Siófok. From road no. 70, exit at km. 108, cross railway and site is 200 m.

General Details: Open 30 April - 26 Sept. Electrical connections (5A). Shop. Snack bar. Restaurant. Bicycle hire. Lake swimming. Laundrette. Chemical disposal.

Charges 1999: Per person DM 4.90 - 8.00; child (2-14) 2.45 - 4.00; motorcaravan or caravan/car 6.50 - 10.50 (incl. electricity); tent/car 4.20 - 6.70; dog 4.90 - 8.00; Less 50% for students (14-18 yrs) 30/4-19/6 and 1/9-26/9.

Reservations: Contact site or Siotour (see below). Site address: 8600 Siófok. Tel: 84/352 801 or 352 519.

500 Vadvirág Camping, Balatonszemes

Very large Siotour site by Lake Balaton with many facilities.

This 14 hectare site has a beach almost one kilometre long, also used by day visitors. Just over half of the 600 touring pitches on flat grass are individual and 270 are for tents with some shade. The modern sanitary facilities have free hot water to the mainly open washbasins (some cabins) and most of the showers with a few private bathrooms for hire and facilities for disabled visitors. There are tennis courts, a water slide, all sorts of boats for hire, animation for children, as well as the attractions of the excellent swimming lake, plus a range of restaurants, shops and snack bars.

How to find it: Balatonszemes is about halfway round the southern side of Lake Balaton and the site is accessed from road 7/E71 turning towards the lake at km. 134, over the railway and then just 300 m.

General Details: Open 4 June - 5 Sept. Electrical connections 16A. Shop, snacks and restaurant. Tennis. Minigolf. Bicycle hire. Children's playground. Launderette. Chemical disposal. Motorcaravan services.

Charges 1999: Per person DM 4.90 - 8.00; child (2-14) 2.45 - 4.00; motorcaravan or caravan and car 7.50 - 11.90 (incl. electricity); tent 4.70 - 7.60; dog 4.90 - 8.00.

Reservations: Contact site or Siotour. Address: 8636 Balatonszemes. Tel: 84/360-114. FAX: as phone.

503 Panorama Camping, Cserszegtomaj, nr Hévíz

Peaceful, hillside site near west end of Lake Balaton.

Camp sites around Lake Balaton generally have the disadvantage of being close to the main road and/or the railway, as well as being extremely busy in high season. Panorama is popular too, but is essentially a quiet site and also has the benefit of extensive views from the flat, grass terraces. Only the young or very fit are recommended to take the higher levels with the best views of all. There are just 50 pitches varying in size from fairly small to quite large (100 sq.m.), all with 10A electricity, with the lower terraces having fairly easy access. The site is a sun-trap and there is not much shade from the trees. Reception is to the left of the entrance and here also is a small shop and a delightful restaurant, with terrace, offering really good value meals at lunch-time and in the evenings. A little way up the site is the very satisfactory, tiled and heated sanitary building which has free hot water to large, curtained, controllable showers (communal changing), washbasins, dishwashing and British style toilets. At the right side of the building is a ladies' hairdresser and massage room. Local attractions include Lake Balaton (7 km), whilst at Hévíz is the famous, large, thermal, warm water lake and there are castles to visit. The friendly proprietors speak no English but are keen to welcome British visitors and have a dictionary. As at many Hungarian sites, you will probably find German and or Dutch visitors who would assist if you speak no German at all.

How to find it: Site is about 2 km. north of Hévíz on the road signed to Sümeg. There is a long, hard access road with a large sign.

General Details: Open 1 April - 31 October. Shop (Mon - Sat, 07.30 - 10.00). Restaurant with bar. Washing machine. Ladies' hairdresser. Massage. Many walking and cycling opportunities. Riding and tennis 3 km.

Charges guide: Per caravan incl. 2 persons DM 17.00, tent 13.00; electricity included.

Reservations: Advisable for May and Sept (the busiet months), and made in German. Address: 8372 Cserszegtomaj, Panorama Köz 1. Tel: 83/314 412.

507 Balatontourist Camping Kristóf, Balatonalmádi, Lake Balaton

Small site with excellent toilet facilities.

This is a delightfully small site with just 33 pitches and many tall trees. Square in shape, the generously sized pitches are on either side of hard roads, on level grass with some shade and 4A electricity. The site lies between the main road and railway line and the lake. There is no direct access to the lake, but a public lakeside area adjoins the camp, and site fees include the entry price. This is a neat little site with a kiosk for breakfast and dinner (steaks, etc) drinks, bread, milk and ice cream, with village shops and supermarket just 50 m. away. The excellent toilet facility is part of the reception building, with British WCs and free hot water in the washbasins and showers (more now built and all with own changing). There is a laundry room with hot water and a washing machine (small charge), a kitchen and sitting room with TV. Balatonalmádi is at the northern end of the lake and well placed for excursions around the lake or to Budapest, and very suitable for anyone seeking a small, friendly site without the bustle of the larger camps. Good English is spoken.

How to find it: Site is on road no. 71 at Balatonalmádi, between the railway line and the lake and is signed.

General Details: Open 22 April - 20 Sept. 12,000 sq.m. Café (1/5-13/9). Children's playground. Tennis. Fishing, bicycle hire 500 m. Riding 5 km. Laundry room. Chemical disposal. Bungalows for rent.

Charges 2000: (Prices in D.Marks, payable in Forints). Per pitch DM 12.00 - 20.00; adult 4.00 - 6.00; child 2.00 - 4.00; local tax 1.10 per person over 18 yrs. Credit cards accepted.

Reservations: Essential July - 20 Aug. Write to site for booking form. Address: 8220 Balatonalmádi. Tel: 88/438-902 or 584-201. FAX: 88/338-902 or 584-202. When closed contact: Balatontourist, 8201 Veszprém, POB 128. Tel: 88/426-277. FAX: 88/426-874. E-mail: ckristof@balatontourist.hu.

HUNGARY

509 Balatontourist Camping Füred, Balatonfüred

Large, international camp on lake, with a wide range of facilities.

This is a holiday village rather than just a camping site, pleasantly decorated with flowers and shrubs, with a very wide range of shops, restaurants, fast food bars and sporting activities. Directly on the lake with 800 m. of access for boats and bathing, it has a large, grassy lying out area, a small beach area for children and various watersports are organised. Mature trees cover about two thirds of the site giving shade, with the remaining area being in the open. The 940 individual pitches of 60-120 sq.m. and all with electrical connections, are on either side of hard access roads on which pitch numbers are painted. Along the main road, which runs through the camp, are shops and kiosks, with the main bar/restaurant and terrace overlooking the lake. This building also has a 4-lane bowling alley and video games room. Close by is a street of fast food bars, about 10 in all, offering a variety of Hungarian and international dishes with attractive outdoor terraces under trees. There are other bars and restaurants dotted around the camp. There are five toilet blocks situated at various points around the site. The oldest are showing signs of age, while the two smart, modern blocks have free hot water in the showers (communal changing), with cold water only in washbasins, British style WCs and hot water for dishwashing and laundry. A wide range of sporting activities is available, the most spectacular of which is a water ski drag lift for which four towers have been erected in the lake with skiers pulled around the circuit. Windsurfing and sail boats are permitted. A swimming pool was added in '99 and new sanitary facilities. Security is good. Many coach trips and pleasure cruises are organised, details from reception. The site is part of the Balatontourist organisation.

How to find it: Site is just south of Balatonfüred, on Balatonfüred - Tihany road and is well signed. Gates closed 1-3 pm. except Sat/Sun.

General Details: Open 8 April - 16 Oct. 270,000 sq.m. Electricity connections (4/10A). Numerous bars, restaurants, cafes and food bars (1/5-15/9). Supermarket. Stalls and kiosks with wide range of goods, souvenirs, photo processing. Hairdresser. Swimming pool (1/5-30/9). Sauna and solarium. Fishing. Water ski lift. Windsurf school. Children's play area on sand. 'Bouncy castle'. Bicycle hire. Dodgem cars. Pedaloes. Tennis courts. Minigolf. Fitness centre. Video games room. Bowling alley. Riding 5 km. Post office. Money exchange. Duty free shop (hard currency). Washing machines. Gas supplies. Chemical disposal. No dogs are accepted. Wide range of bungalows for rent.

Charges 2000: (Prices in DM, payable in Forints). Per caravan pitch incl. electricity 70 sq.m. 22.00, 100 sq.m. 30.00; tent pitch (60 sq.m) 16.50; extra person (max. 6) 8.40; child (2-14 yrs) 3.40; local tax 1.60 per person over 18 yrs. Credit cards accepted.

Reservations: Write to site. Address: 8230 Balatonfüred. Tel: 87/343-823 or 580-241. FAX: 87/342-341 or 580-242. E-mail: cfured@balatontourist.hu.

DISCOUNT VOUCHERS

Between pages 192/193 you will find two Discount Vouchers which will provide you with potential savings of more than the cost of the Guide itself! (valid 1 Jan - 31 Dec 2000 only)

Voucher A - Campsite Discount Voucher

This voucher entitles the holder to the relevant discounts or special offers at those campsites featured in this guide which have a small Alan Rogers' logo beneath their Site Report. This section of the voucher should be retained by the holder, but made available for inspection at the campsite for the purpose of verifying your entitlement to the relevant discount or offer.

Voucher B - Travel and Breakdown Insurance

This voucher entitles the holder to a discount of 10% on Travel & Breakdown Insurance arrangements made via this Guide, as advertised between pages 160/161. To arrange cover please complete the proposal and send this, together with the appropriate premium and this voucher to: Deneway Guides & Travel Ltd., Chesil Lodge, West Bexington, Dorchester DT2 9DG. Fax 01308 898017.

A proposal form and the discount voucher will need to be completed and sent to Deneway Guides & Travel along with payment for the relevant premium in all circumstances except in very urgent cases (ie. those within seven days of departure) when we can arrange cover via telephone or (preferably) by fax .

IRELAND

'You're welcome' is not said lightly to the visitor who sets foot in Ireland, it is said with sincerity. On this 'Emerald Isle' you will find friendly and hospitable people, spectacular scenery and a selection of good campsites, in both north and south of the country, to suit your particular needs. Whether you choose to be sited by a lough shore, at the foothills of a mountain range or close by golden sands and mysterious rock formations, the scenery is stunning and the pace of life slow. With the help of information and maps available from both Tourist Offices you discover for yourself, not only the beauty spots, but also many historic and interesting routes to follow. For more campsites in both Northern Ireland and the Irish Republic, see the **Alan Rogers' Good Camps Guide - Britain & Ireland**.

The notes below refer to the Irish Republic. For information on travel in the North contact:

Northern Ireland Tourist Board, 59 North Street, Belfast BT1 1NB
Tel: (01232) 246609 Fax: (01232) 312424 Internet: http://www.ni-tourism.com

The Republic of Ireland

A British visitor to the Republic of Ireland does not require a passport (and one may take the dog!). British currency is accepted in most outlets although we quote charges in Irish punts (IR£), currently valued at slightly below the UK£. Travel insurance is advisable when travelling in the south (see our special discount rates for Heritage Insurance).

Bord Failte (Irish Tourist Board), 150 New Bond Street, London W1Y OAQ
Tel: 020 7518 0800. Travel Enquiries: 020 7493 3201. Fax: 020 7493 9065
E-mail: info@irishtouristboard.co.uk Internet: http:/www./ireland.travel.ie

Population
3,500,000, density 50 per sq. km.

Climate
Similar to the UK but even wetter!

Language
English. The traditional tongue Gaelic (Gaeltacht) is spoken mainly in the southwest.

Currency
The Irish pound, known as the punt, divided into 100 pence. Denominations are 1, 2, 5, 10, 20, 50 pence and IR£1, notes of IR£5, 10, 20, 50 and 100.

Banks
Open Mon-Fri 10.00-12.30 and 13.30-15.00 (Thur 13.30-17.00), but note many small country towns are served by sub-offices open only certain days.

Post Offices
Main offices open Mon-Fri 09.00-17.30 and Sat 09.00-13.00. Stamps are sometimes available in shops selling postcards.

Telephone
To call the UK dial 00 44 followed by the local STD code omitting initial 0. From the UK dial 00 353 omitting the first 0 of the code plus number.

Public Holidays
New Year; St Patrick's Day, 17 Mar; Easter; 1st Mon in June; 1st Mon in Aug; last Mon in Oct; Christmas, 25 Dec.

Shops
Open Mon-Sat 09.00-17.30 or 18.00.

Motoring
Allow plenty of time when travelling in Ireland even though the roads are relatively uncongested. Poor road surfaces, unmarked junctions and poor weather conditions can delay. Signposting or the lack of them can be a problem. A good map is a necessity. Drive on the left as in the UK. A Green Card is advised as most policies provide only minimum coverage in the Republic of Ireland

Speed Limits: On certain roads, clearly marked, the speed limits are 40 mph (65 kph) or 50 mph (80 kph) - applying to a car and trailer as well.

Parking: As in the UK. Parking meters are in use - on the spot fines can be levied for offences.

Overnighting
It is possible to camp 'free' in areas where there is no registered site except in state forests (farmers will expect a pound or two).

Outdoor Freedom Holidays.....The Green Option for the New Millennium

Ireland, one of Europe's best-kept secrets, is the Caravan and Camping destination for the discerning traveller. You take control of your holiday from start to finish, go as you please, and do as little or as much as you like. It's all on offer in Ireland, rugged coastlines, inland waterways, lakes and rivers, Celtic monuments, churches and castles, rolling hills and lush green valleys. Plus, of course, Ireland's legendary hostelries and the friendliest people you're ever likely to meet. Pick up a copy of the 2000 Caravan and Camping Annual at your local tourist office today - it's a breath of fresh air.
Alternatively contact ICC direct at: Fax: 00 353 98 28237

e-mail: info@camping-ireland.ie
Website: http//www.camping-ireland.ie
PO Box ICC, Box 4443, Dublin 2, Ireland

850 LoanEden Caravan Park, Muckross Bay, Kesh

Friendly, family owned park by the shores of Lower Lough Erne.
All caravanners who enter this exceptional park are immediately made welcome and receive the attention of the owners, Noelle and Austyn Loane. First impressions are of an overall neat and tidy appearance, with caravan holiday homes occupying the centre and left side of the park, whilst to the right stand the touring pitches. Flower beds, trees and shrubs are well maintained and an ornamental well and illuminated barbecue give added effect. What makes LoanEden special is that tourers' needs are thoughtfully catered for and not secondary to the static owners. The 24 touring and 12 long-stay pitches are level with hardstanding and water, electricity and drainage connections and a rubbish bin; also a dividing grass area on which to erect an awning. Night lighting is good. Cleanliness is utmost and the immaculate, ultra modern toilet block is completely tiled inside and houses WCs, facilities for disabled people, showers, washbasins, washing machines, dryers and sinks for dishwashing or hand washing. Nothing has been forgotten - there are soap dispensers, hand dryers, paper towels, clothes hooks and points for hairdryers and razors. Motorcaravan service point. There is a vending machine for confectionery and soft drinks plus a hot food takeaway. Children have two play areas and a games room, with plans for a third super play area. The `LoanEden Ramblers' club for 4-11 year olds provides activities each day (£1.50 per child). Young and old can enjoy pony and horse riding tuition under the supervision of the owners' daughter Victoria, an A.I. instructor, and son Andrew who is an international rider. Fishing and bicycle hire on site, golf 5 miles. Caravan storage available. An additional 30 touring pitches, a second shower and toilet block including a campers' kitchen, go-kart track and various other facilities are planned. The owners organise barbecues and barn dances in aid of charity.

How to find it: From Enniskillen take A32 Omagh road for 3½ miles and branch left on B82 Kesh road. Continue for 11 miles to village of Kesh. Cross over bridge at north end of village and turn immediately left to park in ½ mile on right.

Open: All year.

Charges 2000: Per caravan or motorcaravan incl. awning and electricity £12.00; tent £8.00; electricity £1.00.

Reservations: Advisable for high season and B.Hs. Address: Muckross Bay, Kesh, Co. Fermanagh BT93 1TX. Tel: 028 6863 1603. FAX: 028 6863 2300.

Loan Eden
Caravan Park
Muckross Bay
Co. Fermanagh
N. Ireland

Tel: 028 6863 1603
Fax: 028 6863 2300

OPEN ALL YEAR - 5✓

★ Award winning caravan park - Calor Green ★
★ Fully serviced pitches ★ Tent area ★
★ Immaculate sanitary facilities ★ Children's play areas ★
★ Quality mobile homes for sale/hire ★
★ Horse riding tuition A.I. instructor ★
★ Special on site feature - barbecue in July ★
★ Extended facilities - new toilet block, 3rd play area,
    new reception area, campers kitchen ★
★ Boat hire facilities ★ man made beach ★ Marina 5 mins walk
★ Scenic walks ★ Pony trekking ★
★ Village of Kesh - Lough Erne Hotel - Chef of the Year award ★

Ferry Services to Ireland

Irish Ferries
(01233) 211211 for brochures, etc.
or (0990) 171717 for bookings/enquiries
Holyhead - Dublin (3¼ hours), Fastcraft 109 mins
Pembroke - Rosslare (3¾ hours)

P&O European Ferries
(01581) 200276 Cairnryan - Larne:
Ferry (2¼ hours, 2 sailings daily each way)
Jet Liner (1 hour, 5 sailings daily each way)

Sea Cat Scotland
(0990) 523523
Stranraer - Belfast (1½ hours, 4 daily each way)
Heysham - Belfast (4 hours, 2 daily)
Troon - Belfast (2½ hours, 2 daily)

Swansea Cork Ferries
(01792) 456116
Swansea - Cork (10 hrs, mid-March - early Nov)

Stena Line
(0990) 707070 Frequent sailings:
Fishguard - Rosslare: Ferry (3½ hours, 2 sailings daily each way), Lynx (99 mins)
Holyhead - Dun Laoghaire: Ferry (3½ hrs), Sea Linx (110 mins) or HSS (99 mins)
Stranraer - Belfast: Ferry (3¼ hrs), HSS (105 mins)

Norse Irish Ferries
(01232) 779090
Liverpool - Belfast (8½ hrs, overnight daily, day service up to 3 weekly)

834 Drumaheglis Marina and Caravan Park, Ballymoney

Well kept site on the banks of the River Bann, convenient for the Causeway coast.

A caravan park which continually maintains a high standard, Drumaheglis is popular throughout the season. Situated on the banks of the lower Bann, approximately 4 miles from the town of Ballymoney, it appeals to watersports enthusiasts or makes an ideal base for exploring this scenic corner of Northern Ireland. The marina offers superb facilities for boat launching, water-skiing, cruising, canoeing or fishing, whilst getting out and about can take you to the Giant's Causeway, seaside resorts such as Portrush or Portstewart, the sands of Whitepark Bay, the Glens of Antrim or the picturesque villages of the Antrim coast road. For tourers only, this site instantly appeals, for it is well laid out with trees, shrubs, flower beds and tarmac roads. Electricity (5A) and water points are available on 52 pitches, of which 47 have hard-standing. The toilet blocks are modern and were spotlessly clean when we visited. They house showers which are free, individual wash cubicles, toilets and facilities for disabled visitors, plus four new family shower rooms. There are razor points, hand dryers, dishwashing sinks, washing machine and dryer and chemical disposal point. A children's play area, barbecue and picnic areas are added facilities. Ballymoney is a popular shopping town and the Riada Centre is a leading leisure establishment with a health suite which incorporates a high-tech fitness studio, sports hall, etc. Bicycle hire and golf 4 miles, riding ½ mile. There is much to see and do within this Borough and of interest is the Heritage Centre in Charlotte Street.

How to find it: From A26/B62 Portrush - Ballymoney roundabout continue for approx. 1 mile on the A26 towards Coleraine. Site is clearly signed - follow International camping signs.

Open: Easter - 1 October.

Charges guide: Per unit incl. electricity £11.00, per 7 days £66.00; unserviced £10.00, per 7 days £60.00. No credit cards.

Reservations: Essential for peak periods and weekends. Address: 36 Glenstall Road, Ballymoney, Co. Antrim BT53 7QN. Tel: 028 2766 6466. Ballymoney Borough Council: Tel: 028 2766 2280; FAX: 028 2766 7659.

REPUBLIC of IRELAND

864 Knockalla Caravan and Camping Park, Portsalon

Family run park set amidst the breathtaking scenery of Donegal.

What adds to the popularity of this site is its location, nestling between the slopes of the Knockalla Mountains and Ballymastocker Bay. The fact that the beach here has been named `the second most beautiful beach in the world' is not surprising. On entering this park, approached by an unclassified but short roadway, its elevated situation commands an immediate panoramic view of the famed Bay, Lough Swilly, Inishowen Peninsula and Dunree Head. The site is partly terraced giving an attractive, orderly layout with reception, shop and restaurant in a central position and the touring area sited to the left of reception. All 50 pitches have electrical hook-ups and hardstanding, offering a choice of solely tarmac or with adjoining grass allowing for awnings. Tents are pitched on a lower level facing reception and to the far left of the tourers. Caravan holiday homes are placed around the right hand perimeter and to the rear of the park. The main sanitary block, a white, rough cast building, is situated in the touring section. Tastefully refurbished, it is kept clean and fresh and can be heated. There are washbasins, hand dryer, hair dryer, shaver points and showers (50p token) with hooks, soap dish, curtain divider and mat. Dishwashing area and campers' kitchen with hot water. A laundry service is operated by staff. Chemical disposal and motorcaravan serice points. Gas is available. Children's play area and TV/games room. The park has a shop and café (both open July/Aug) and specialities are home made scones, apple cakes, jams, etc. plus a takeaway or table service. Full Irish breakfasts are served. Golf 3 miles, fishing, riding and bicycle hire within 10 miles.

How to find it: From Letterkenny take R245 to Rathmelton. Continue on R245 to Milford. Turn right on R246 to Kerrykeel. In village turn left towards Portsalon and at second crossroads turn right onto Portsalon/Knockalla coast road. Turn right to park at sign.

Open: 27 March - 17 September.

Charges 2000: Per motorcaravan, caravan or family tent IR£11.00; awning IR£1.50; tent for 1 or 2 persons IR£8.00; extra person IR£3.00; electricity (5A) IR£1.50. No credit cards.

Reservations: Advisable for July/Aug and B.H. w/ends; contact park. Address: Portsalon, Co. Donegal. Tel: 074 59108 or 074 53213.

REPUBLIC of IRELAND

870 Gateway Caravan and Camping Park, Ballinode, Sligo

Family run park, convenient for the beauty spots immortalised by the poet W. B. Yeats.

This is the northwest's newest park and straight away it warrants the highest accolade for its excellent design and standards set. Its situation 1.2 km. from Sligo centre means this cultural city is easily accessible, yet Gateway's off-the-road location, screened by mature trees and fencing, offers a quiet relaxing environment. After the park entrance, past the family bungalow and to the left is parking space and the reception and services block which is fronted by columns and an overhanging roof. Flower baskets add decoration and soft background music drifts through the air. Incorporated in this building are three separate rooms – one for TV, snooker and board games, the second for satellite TV and the third for selected video viewing. A passage divides the elongated building which also houses showers, WCs, washbasins with shaver points, hand-dryers and baby changing units in both the male and female areas. Showers, room for disabled visitors (with WC and shower) are entered from the outside of this block which can be heated. In an adjacent building is a dishwashing area, laundry room, fully equipped campers' kitchen plus a large indoor games room and a toddlers room with playhouses and fixed toys. An outdoor children's play area faces reception. There are 30 fully serviced touring pitches with hardstanding and satellite TV connection, 10 grass pitches with electrical hook-up for tents and 10 caravan holiday homes for hire. Touring pitches stand to the right and centre of the park, holiday homes to the left and rear, with tents pitched at the top left. Fishing or bicycle hire within 2 km, golf 8 km, riding 12 km. Evening relaxation could mean a 3 km. drive to romantic Half Moon Bay, or a drink in the fascinating surroundings of Farrells Brewery, which faces the caravan park.

How to find it: Site is 1.2 km. northeast of Sligo city, off the N16 Enniskillen - Belfast road. Approaching from the north on the N15, turn left at second traffic lights into Ash Lane, continue for 1.1 km. and turn left at traffic lights onto the N16 Sligo - Enniskillen road. Site entrance is on left in 50 m.

Open: All year.

Charges 2000: Per unit incl. 2 persons IR£8.50; adult or child in July/Aug 50p; family rate IR£8.50 - 12.50; m/cyclist incl. tent IR£8.50; hiker or cyclist incl. tent IR£5.00; electricity (10A) IR£2.00. Credit cards accepted.

Reservations: Contact site. Address: Ballinode, Sligo, Co. Sligo. Tel: 071 45618. FAX: as phone.

874 Cong Caravan and Camping Park, Cong, nr Connemara

Family run touring park and hostel in a famous and scenic location.

It would be difficult to find a more idyllic and famous spot for a Caravan Park than Cong. Situated close to the shores of Lough Corrib, Cong's scenic beauty was immortalised in the film 'The Quiet Man'. This park, which is immaculately kept, is 1.6 km. from the village of Cong, near the grounds of the magnificent and renowned Ashford Castle. The owner's house which incorporates reception, shop and the hostel, stands to the fore of the site. The 40 grass pitches, 36 with electricity, are placed at a higher level to the rear, with the tent area below and to the side - the policy on this site is for campers to 'choose a pitch' rather than have one allocated. Sanitary facilities and the holiday hostel accommodation are entered from the courtyard area. These are tastefully decorated, kept spotlessly clean and heated when necessary. Apart from the high standard of hygiene evident throughout, the toilet facilities for the campsite include hot showers with curtains, electric points, mirrors, hairdryers, washbasins, soap and hand towels. Also on site is a dishwashing area, launderette service, chemical disposal, central bin depot, barbecue, games room and extensive children's play area. Catering is also a feature. Full Irish or continental breakfast, dinner or packed lunch may be ordered, or home baked bread and scones purchased in the shop. When not spending time around the village of Cong with its picturesque river setting and Monastic relics, there is much to keep the active camper happy. Watersports, cycling, walking, climbing, caving and scenic drives can all be pursued. Riding or golf within 2 km, fishing and boat slipway 500 m. Bicycle hire on site. Not least of the 'on site' attractions at this park is a mini cinema showing 'The Quiet Man' film nightly all season.

How to find it: Leave N84 road at Ballinrobe to join R334/345 signed Cong. Turn left at end of the R345 (opposite entrance to Ashford Castle), take next road on right (approx. 300 m) and the park is on right (200 m).

Open: All year.

Charges 2000: Per pitch IR6.00; adult IR£1.50; child IR£1.00; awning IR£1.50; electricity (16A) IR£1.50; hiker/cyclist incl. tent and 1 person IR£6.50. Credit cards accepted.

Reservations: Contact park. Address: Lisloughrey, Lake Road, Cong, Connemara, Co. Mayo. Tel: 092 46089. FAX: 092 46448. E-mail: quiet.man.cong@iol.ie. Internet: www.quiet-man-cong.com.

876 Keel Sandybanks Caravan and Camping Park, Achill Island

Busy park with direct access to a Blue Flag beach on Achill Island.
This is a park offering a taste of island life and the opportunity to relax in dramatic, scenic surroundings. Achill, Ireland's largest island, is 15 miles long and 12 miles wide and is connected to the mainland by a bridge. The site is beside Keel village and approached by the R319 from the swivel bridge at Achill Sound. Although there are static holiday caravans on this site, the 42 pitches for caravans and 42 for tents are kept separate. Some with hardstanding are located at the perimeter fence overlooking the beach. Although sand based, the ground is firm and level. Roads are tarmac and there is direct access to the beach which is supervised by lifeguards. Two modern toilet blocks serve the site, one at the gate beside reception and the other in a central position. Facilities include WCs (one for disabled visitors), washbasins, hot showers (50p token), heating, hair and hand dryers, dishwashing and laundry sinks and chemical disposal. Site barrier closed 01.00 - 08.00. Play area with safety base and a TV room. Watersports enthusiasts can enjoy surfing, canoeing and board sailing on Keel Strand and Lough. Fishing trips can be arranged. Bicycle hire or golf 200 m; riding 10 km. In the village there is a food shop, takeaway, restaurants and music at night in the pubs. Occasionally a traditional music evening is organised on site. Whilst a treat in store is the natural beauty on Achill, worth seeing are Kildownet Castle, the Slievemore deserted village and the Seal Caves.

How to find it: From Achill Sound follow the R319 for 10 miles. Site is on the left before Keel village.

Open: 27 May - 9 September.

Charges 2000: Per unit IR£6.00 - 8.50; tent IR£5.00 - 6.50; electricity (13A) IR£1.00. No credit cards.

Reservations: Contact site. Address: Keel, Achill Island, Co. Mayo. Tel: 094 32054 or 098 43211.

878 Knock Caravan and Camping Park, Knock

Clean, friendly park with many local attractions including religious shrine.
This park is immediately south of the world famous shrine, which receives many visitors. Comfortable and clean, the square shaped campsite is kept very neat with tarmac roads and surrounded by clipped trees. The original pitches are of a decent size accommodating 38 caravans or motorcaravans, 20 tents and 14 holiday caravans (for hire). All pitches have hardstandings (5 doubles) and there are 52 electrical connections (13A), with an adequate number of water points. There is also an overflow field. The modern, heated sanitary block, with good facilities for disabled visitors and a nice sized rest room attached, has 4 controllable hot showers (on payment) and adequate washing and toilet facilities. A laundry and dishwashing room is also part of this building. Chemical disposal and motorcaravan service points, and gas supplies are provided. A children's playground is in the centre of the site. The park reports the addition of 36 new pitches and another sanitary block. Because of the religious connections of the area, the site is very busy in August and indeed there are unlikely to be any vacancies at all for 14 -16 August. Besides visiting the shrine and Knock Folk Museum, local activities include fishing (3 miles), golf and riding (both 7 miles). This is also a good centre for exploring scenic Co. Mayo.

How to find it: Take the N17 to the Knock site which is just south of the village. Camp site is well signed.

Open: 1 March - 31 October.

Charges 2000: Per unit IR£8.50 - 9.00; hiker/tent IR£5.50 - 6.50; electricity (13A) IR£1.50. No credit cards.

Reservations: Taken for any length, no deposit, but see editorial for August. Address: Claremorris Road, Knock, Co. Mayo. Tel: 094 88100 or 88223. FAX: 094 88295. E-mail: info@knock-shrine.ie.

879 Carra Caravan and Camping Park, Belcarra, Castlebar

Small, unpretentious park in a pretty village setting.
This is an ideal location for those seeking a real Irish village experience on a 'value for money' park. Family run, it is located in Belcarra, a regular winner of the 'Tidiest Mayo Village' award. Nestling at the foot of a wooded drumlin, it is surrounded by rolling hills and quiet roads which offer an away from it all feeling, yet Castlebar the county's largest town is only an 8 km. drive. On the pleasant 1.5 acre park, the 20 unmarked touring pitches, 14 with electric hook-up (13A), are on flat ground enclosed by ranch fencing and shaded in parts by trees. The basic sanitary block has adequate, well equipped showers (40p), etc. and there is a combined kitchen, dishwashing, laundry area with fridge/freezer, sink, table, chairs, washing machine and dryer. A comfortable lounge with TV, books and magazines is located at reception. An additional novel idea at Carra are eight horse-drawn caravans for hire. Also of interest are the talks that the owner Sean and daughter Deirdre give on the area. There are recommended walks and maps provided. In the village are shops, a post office and 'Flukies' cosy bar which serves Irish breakfast and Irish stew is a speciality. There is also a leisure centre, tennis, a free fishing area and a path to the river. Golf 8 km.

How to find it: From Castlebar take N60 Claremorris road for 8.5 km. southeast and turn right at sign for Belcarra. Continue for 4.5 km. to village and site on left at end of village.

Charges 2000: Per unit incl. all persons IR£5.00; electricity IR£1.00. No credit cards.

Open: 10 June - 23 September (bookings accepted by arrangement outside this period).

Reservations: Contact park. Address: Belcarra, Castlebar, Co. Mayo. Tel: 094 32054. FAX: 094 32351.

REPUBLIC of IRELAND

896 Lough Ree East Caravan and Camping Park, Ballykeeran, Athlone

Touring park alongside a river, screened by trees and reaching the water's edge.

Drive into the small village of Ballykeeran and this park is discretely located behind the main street. The top half of the site is in a woodland situation and after the reception and sanitary block, Lough Ree comes into view and the remaining pitches run down to the shoreline. There are 40 pitches, 20 with hardstanding and 35 with electricity. The toilet block, with partly tiled walls, is clean without being luxurious. It houses WCs, washbasins, razor and hairdryer points, mirrors and hot showers (50p). Chemical disposal. Dishwashing sinks are outside and a new laundry room has been added. A wooden chalet with accommodation and campers' kitchen is available for the use of campers and fishermen. A restaurant and singing pub are close. With fishing right on the doorstep there are boats for hire and the site has its own private mooring buoys, plus a dinghy slip and harbour. Golf or riding 4 km.

How to find it: From Athlone take the N55 in the direction of Longford for 4.8 km. Park is in the village of Ballykeeran, clearly signed.

Open: 1 April - 2 October.

Charges 1999: Per adult IR£2.50; child (under 14 yrs) IR£1.00; caravan and car IR£4.00; motorcaravan IR£3.00; family tent IR£2.00; hiker/cyclist and tent IR£3.00; awning IR£2.00; electricity IR£1.00. No credit cards.

Reservations: Contact park for details. Address: Ballykeeran, Athlone, Co. Westmeath. Tel: 0902 78561 or 0902 74414. FAX: 0902 77017. E-mail: athlonecamping@tinet.ie.

908 Forest Farm Caravan and Camping Park, Athy

Farm site with good quality facilities, off Dublin - Kilkenny road.

This new site makes an excellent stopover if travelling from Dublin to the southeast counties. It is signed on the N78 and approached by a 500 m. avenue of tall pines. Part of a working farm, the campsite spreads to the right of the modern farmhouse, which also provides B&B. The owners have cleverly utilised their land to create a site which offers 64 unmarked touring pitches on level ground. Of these, 32 are for caravans, all with electricity connections and 10 with hardstanding and 32 places are available for tents. The red brick sanitary block, heated and double glazed, occupies a central position on site. It offers quality amenities including a comfortable lounge/games room (a TV will be supplied on request). The shower and WC areas have freshly painted yellow walls and pine doors, plus top of the range fittings. Facilities include a spacious shower unit for disabled visitors and a family room with shower and WC. There is also a laundry room, with washing machine, drier and spin drier, and dishwashing sinks which are in the camper's kitchen. This is furnished with a fridge/freezer, cooker, table and chairs. Chemical disposal facilities are in a dedicated space separate from the main building. There is a basketball net, sand pit and picnic tables, also night lighting. Irish breakfasts are served at the farmhouse and farm tours available on request.

How to find it: Site is 4.8 km. northeast of Athy town off the main N78 Athy - Kilcullen road.

Open: All year.

Charges 1999: Per unit incl. 2 adults IR£9.00 - 10.00; child 50p; 1 or 2 person tent IR£3.00 - 4.00 p/person; m/cyclist, hiker or cyclist incl. tent IR£3.00 - 4.00 p/person; electricity (16A) IR£1.50.

Reservations: Contact site. Address: Dublin Road, Athy, Co. Kildare. Tel: 0507 31231 or 33070. FAX: 0507 31231. E-mail: forestfarm@tinet.ie.

914 Valley Stopover and Caravan Park, Kilmacanogue

Small, family run park located in quiet, idyllic setting and convenient for Dublin ferries.

This neat and attractive ¾ acre park in the picturesque Rocky Valley could be used either as a transit site or for a longer stay. It has appeal for those who prefer the more basic `CL' type site. There are 15 grassy pitches, 11 with electric hook-ups, 3 hardstandings, 2 water points, night lighting and a security gate. Toilet facilities, spotlessly clean when we visited, are housed in one unit and consist of 2 WCs with washbasins, mirrors, etc. and a shower (50p). There is a dishwashing/laundry sink, a spin dryer, chemical disposal point, a campers' kitchen and hot water is constantly available. A cooked full Irish breakfast is available for IR£3.50 in the family guest house. Dairy products are available and bread can be ordered. Fishing 10 miles, bicycle hire 4 miles (can be delivered), riding 2 miles, golf 4 miles. Staying put here you are only minutes from Enniskerry which lies in the glen of the Glencullen river. Here you can enjoy a delight of forest walks, or visit Powerscourt, one of the loveliest gardens in Ireland. If wanting to be at the sea, travel 6 km. to Bray and you are in one of the oldest seaside resorts in the country. Small caravan to hire.

How to find it: Turn off Dublin-Wexford N11 road at Kilmacanogue - follow signs for Glendalough. Continue for 1.6 km and take right fork signed `Waterfall'. Park is first opening on the left in approx. 200 m.

Charges 1999: Per caravan or tent with car IR£7.00; motorcaravan IR£6.00; tent with bike IR£3.00; electricity £IR1.00; awning IR£1.00. No credit cards.

Open: Easter - 31 October.

Reservations: Advised for July/Aug; contact park. Address: Valleyview, Killough, Kilmacanogue, Co. Wicklow. Tel: 01 282 9565.

910 Camac Valley Tourist Caravan and Camping Park, Dublin

Touring park with top class facilities convenient for ferry ports and Dublin city.

Opened in '96, this campsite is not only well placed for Dublin, but also offers a welcome stopover if travelling to the more southern counties from the north of the country, or vice versa. Despite its close proximity to the city, being located in the 300 acre Corkagh Park gives it a 'heart of the country' atmosphere. The site entrance and sign are distinctive and can be spotted in adequate time when approaching on the busy N7. Beyond the entrance gate and forecourt stands an attractive timber fronted building. Its design includes various roof levels and spacious interior layout, with large windows offering a view of the site. Housed here is reception, information, reading, TV and locker rooms plus heated sanitary facilities which include WCs, good sized showers (50p token) and central floor units with washbasins and mirrors. There are also shaver points, hand dryers, facilities for disabled people, baby changing room, laundry, washing up and chemical disposal. A second well designed and fitted sanitary block is operational, also a children's playground with wooden play frames and safety base. A shop and coffee bar open in June, July and August. There are 163 pitches, 48 for tents placed to the fore and the hardstandings for caravans laid out in bays and avenues with electrical connections, drainage and water points. Young trees separate pitches and roads are tarmac. There is an automatic gate and 24 hour security. Caravan storage. Dogs are not accepted in July/Aug. Fishing 8 km, bicycle hire 1.5 km, riding 9 km, golf 6 km. After a day of sightseeing in Dublin, which can be reached by bus from the site, Camac Valley offers a evening of relaxation with woodland and river walks in the park or a number of first class restaurants and pubs nearby.

How to find it: From north follow signs for West Link and M50 motorway. Exit M50 at junction 9 onto N7 Cork road. Site is on right of dual carriageway (beside Green Isle Hotel) after 2 km. and is clearly signed. At City West business park, cross over bridge and return on dual-carriageway following camp signs - site is on left after 800 m.

Open: All year.

Charges 2000: Per unit incl. 2 persons IR£10.00 - 11.00, incl. up to 4 children IR£11.00 - 13.00; extra person IR£1.00; child (under 7 yrs) 50p; motorcyclist, cyclist or hiker with tent IR£3.00 - 4.00 per person; awning IR£1.00; extra small tent IR£3.00; electricity (10A) IR£1.00. Credit cards accepted.

Reservations: Advance bookings necessary. (max. stay operates at certain times). Address: Naas Road, Clondalkin, Dublin 22. Tel: 01 464 0644. FAX: 01 464 0643. E-mail: camacmorriscastle@tinet.ie.

915 River Valley Caravan and Camping Park, Redcross Village

Friendly, family run park in small village in the heart of Co. Wicklow.

In the small country village of Redcross, which abounds with character and atmosphere, is where you will find this well run park. Although only 58 km. from Dublin, being based here you are in the heart of the countryside with beauty spots such as the Vale of Avoca, Glendalough and Powerscourt within driving distance, plus the safe beach of Brittas Bay 6 km. away. Although there are 80 caravan holiday homes on this park, the 100 touring pitches are together in a separate area. There are 80 with electrical connections (6A) and, with a choice of hardstanding or grass, you select your pitch. A luxurious new, heated sanitary block has a modern, well designed appearance which makes it a special feature at River Valley. Facilities for disabled visitors are excellent, hot water is available for dishwashing and there is a laundry area, chemical disposal and motorcaravan service points. Within this 12 acre site children can find day long amusement, whether it be Fort Apache, the adventure playground, the new 'tiny-tots' playground, or at the natural mountain stream where it is safe to paddle. They may, however, prefer to get to know the farm animals and birds in the pets corner. Other amenities include TV, games room, a tennis court, par-3 golf course and bowling green, plus a new sports complex with badminton courts and indoor football and basketball. An attractive wine and coffee bar with a conservatory is an inviting asset, or an alternative may be the cosy atmosphere of the restaurant where many home made, traditional dishes are on the menu (both 9 am-6 pm, 1/6-31/8). Gas is available. An excellent late arrivals area has electric hook-ups, water and night lighting. Rally area and caravan storage. No dogs are accepted in July/Aug. Fishing 4 miles, bicycle hire and boat launching 9 miles.

How to find it: From Dublin follow N11 Wexford road. Turn right in Rathnew and then left (under railway bridge) onto the Wexlow-Arklow road. Continue for 11 km. and turn right at Doyle's Pub. Park is in Redcross Village, under 5 km.

Open: 12 March - 23 September.

Charges 2000: Per caravan, motorcaravan or tent incl. 2 adults IR£10.00 - 11.00, small tent IR£9.00 - 10.00; extra adutl IR£3.00; child (under 15 yrs) IR£1.00; m/cyclist, cyclist or hiker and tent incl. tent IR£5.00 - 6.00; electricity IR£1.00. No credit cards.

Reservations: Made with IR£10 deposit. Address: Redcross Village, Co. Wicklow. Tel: 0404 41647. FAX: 0404 41677.

REPUBLIC of IRELAND

916 Moat Farm Caravan and Camping Park, Donard

Heart of the country experience within easy driving distance of Dublin or Rosslare.

Camping at its most idyllic is what can be enjoyed at this campsite. Here a true feel of the countryside abounds for it is part of a working farm environment and offers incredible vistas across a scenic landscape. Driving into the village of Donard in West Wicklow you little suspect that alongside the main street lies this tranquil 5 acre site. The entrance is approached by way of a short roadway where the ruins of a Medieval church sit high overlooking the forecourt and reception. Facing down the site is the sanitary block which is kept clean and includes WCs, large showers, sink units with marble effect tops, mirrors, soap dispensers and electric points. There are facilities for visitors with disabilities, a well equipped laundry room with sink, washing machine, dryer and ironing board. Next to this is a TV room with easy chairs and a long window giving a panoramic view over the site and beyond. Chemical disposal facilities are at the end of this building and a campers' kitchen with sinks, fridge and freezer with ice pack facilities is beside the farmyard buildings. Three large barbecues and a patio area are provided. There are 40 pitches for caravans and tents. The pitches with hardstanding to the right, some sheltered by tall trees, occupy both sides of a broad avenue. These are spacious and incorporate awning and car space, and all have electricity and drainage points. Tents are pitched on the grass area to the centre and left. This site makes a good base for touring or going on foot, for this is a walker's paradise with a 30 minute circular walkway around the perimeter of the site. Riding on site. There is fishing (3 km), mountain climbing or sites of archaeological interest nearby. Bicycle hire 15 km, golf 13 km. Caravan storage available.

Directions: From south on N81 turn off 14 km. north of Baltinglass at old Tollhouse pub. Site is clearly signed.

Open: All year.

Charges 1999: Per caravan, motorcaravan or family tent IR£8.00; adult IR£1.00; child 50p; tent (1 or 2 persons) IR£6.00; m/cyclist incl. tent IR£4.00; hiker or cyclist incl. tent IR£3.50; awning free; electricity (10A) IR£1.50. No credit cards.

Reservations: Contact site. Address: Donard, Co.Wicklow. Tel: 045 404727. FAX: as phone.

924 Tree Grove Caravan and Camping Park, Kilkenny

Orderly, neat and welcoming touring park within walking distance of Kilkenny.

The entrance gate to this small family run site, now into its third season, is easily spotted off the R700 road. It makes an ideal location for spending time in medieval Kilkenny, known for its elegance and famed for its beer and cats. Tree Grove has instant appeal because its young owners are friendly and have insisted on a logical layout to suit both the terrain and campers needs. It is a terraced site with the lower terrace to the right of the wide sweeping driveway laid out with 11 hardstanding pitches for caravans. All 30 pitches have electrical hook-ups (10A) and plenty of water points are to be found. On a higher level, to the left is a grass area for hikers and cyclists with further caravan and tent pitches sited near the elevated sanitary block. If needed more grass pitches face reception, which is temporarily housed in a mobile unit. Whilst there are mature trees at the entrance and around the site perimeter, many young shrubs have been planted and flower troughs effectively placed. House plants add decoration inside the toilet block giving a cared for look to this modern building. Showers are free and a family room with shower, WC and washbasin can be used by disabled people. WCs and washbasins with mirrors, shaver and hairdryer points, are in separate spacious areas. Ladies have a vanity unit with large mirror. An open, covered kitchen for campers with fridge, work-top, sink and electric kettle adjoins a comfortable games/TV room with pool table, easy chairs and magazine rack. Next to this is a laundry room with sink, washing machine, dryer and iron. Chemical disposal. On the patio there are bench seats with tables and umbrellas. Tents to rent on site. There is much to see and do around the ancient city of Kilkenny (1.5 km) with its cobbled streets and castle. Fishing, bicycle hire and riding within 2 km. Golf 3 or 15 km. County Touring Routes are worth following.

How to find it: Travelling north on the N10 Waterford/Kilkenny Road turn right at roundabout on ring road. Continue to 2nd roundabout and turn right onto R700. Site is 150 m. on right.

Open: 1 March - 15 November.

Charges 2000: Per caravan, motorcaravan or family tent incl. 2 persons IR£8.50; extra person IR£1.00; 1 man tent IR£5.00; 2 man tent IR£6.50; 4 man tent IR£7.00; car IR£1.00; awning IR£1.00; electricity (10A) IR£1.50. No credit cards.

Reservations: Contact site. Address: Danville House, Kilkenny, Co. Kilkenny. Tel: 056 70302. FAX: 056 21512. E-mail: treecc@iol.ie.

933 Casey's Caravan Park, Clonea, Dungarvan

Family run site with direct access to the beach.
Set on 20 acres of flat grass, edged by mature trees, this park offers 284 pitches which include 154 touring pitches, 118 with electrical hook-ups and 30 with hardstanding. The remainder are occupied by caravan holiday homes. The central sanitary block, operated on a key system, has good facilities kept spotlessly clean, a top priority for the owner. There are showers on payment (50p), free hot water to open style basins and washing up sinks (10p). Also housed in this block is a small laundry with machine and dryer. A further luxurious and modern block has been added with an excellent campers' kitchen, laundry room and toilet for disabled visitors. Chemical disposal. There is direct access from the park to a sandy, blue flag beach with a resident lifeguard during July/Aug. Facilities on the site include a large children's adventure play area with bark surface in its own field (not supervised by camp staff). Near the site entrance is a games room with pool table, table tennis and amusements, crazy golf and TV lounge. Gas is available. A highly recommended leisure centre is adjacent should the weather be inclement. There is no shop, but two village stores are near the beach. The park is 5½ km. from Dungarvan, a popular town for deep sea angling, from which charter boats can be hired and three 18 hole golf courses are within easy distance. Recommended drives include the scenic Vee, the Comeragh Drive and the coast road to Tramore. Dogs allowed on a lead. Full time security staff in high season.

How to find it: From Dungarvan centre follow R675 east for 3.5 km. Look for signs on the right to Clonea Bay and site. Site is approx. 1.5 km.

Open: 28 April - 10 September.

Charges 1999: Per unit IR£10.50 - 11.00; hiker or cyclist IR£4.00; electricity IR£1.00. No credit cards.

Reservations: Are made, but not between 9 July - 15 Aug; contact park. Address: Clonea, Dungarvan, Co. Waterford. Tel: 058 41919.

 # Casey's Caravan & Camping Park
Clonea, Dungarvan, Co Waterford Tel: 058 41919

Top class facilities	Two ablution blocks with laundry & kitchen
Playground	Games room and TV room
Electric sites for tents & tourers (5A)	EU Blue Flag beach
Dungarvan town 3½ miles	Two nearby shops with takeaway
Choice of scenic views to visit	Deep sea and river angling
18 hole golf course in easy reach	Adjacent hotel with 19 metre pool
	and leisure centre with bowling alley

---

938 Parsons Green Caravan and Camping Park, Clogheen

Small, family run park with excellent on-site facilities.
In a tranquil and scenic location, this open style site commands panoramic views toward the Vee Gap and Knockmealdown Mountains. Surrounded by low ranch fencing, it offers 20 pitches for caravans and motorcaravans with hardstanding and 14 on grass, all with electrical connections (6A), plus 20 pitches for tents. The sanitary facilities, to the top right of the site close to reception, are kept clean and include WCs, washbasins with mirrors and electric points, free hot showers and good facilities for disabled people (shower and toilet), plus a laundry area with washing machines, dryer and sinks, three dishwashing sinks and chemical disposal. A coffee shop is on site, ice cream, confectionery and gifts are sold and there is a takeaway. The village is within 500 m. (footpath and lighting) with shops, pubs, bank, post office, etc. The wide range of amenities on site includes a garden area, river walks, picnic area, an extensive farm museum, a pet field with selection of domestic and rare animals and birds, children's playground, minigolf, pony and trap rides, boating on the small lake and trout fishing river. TV/games room, campers' kitchen and function room. If not sitting back enjoying the scenic surroundings or participating in the many activities, there is much to see and do in this area. The manager of Parson's Green, would be more than pleased to pinpoint places of interest. Riding and golf 8 miles. Caravan holiday homes (3) and chalets (2) for hire.

How to find it: Site is in village of Clogheen, 200 m. off the R665, 24 km. west of Clonmel, 19 km. east of Mitchelstown.

Open: All year.

Charges 1999: Per caravan, family tent or motorcaravan IR£4.00; small tent IR£3.00; adult IR£2.00; child IR£1.00; awning IR£1.00; electricity IR£1.00. No credit cards.

Reservations: Contact site. Address: Clogheen, Co. Tipperary. Tel: 052 65290. FAX: 052 65504. E-mail: pjkn@tinet.ie.

REPUBLIC of IRELAND

939 Carrick-on-Suir Caravan and Camping Park, Carrick-on-Suir

Small, family run, town site in quiet and tranquil setting.

This memorable little site is not only conveniently situated off the main N24 between Waterford and Clonmel, but its owner, Frank O'Dwyer, is an excellent ambassador for his county. On his site campers are guaranteed the finest example of 'Cead Mile Failte' it is possible to encounter - personal attention and advice on where to go and what to see in the area is all part of the service. The entrance to the park is immediately past the O'Dwyers' shop, through a gate which is closed at 11 pm. The gravel drive leads past tall hedges and well kept shrubs to the right and several caravan holiday homes (for hire) to the left. The touring park lies to the rear with scenic views to the wooded hills. At present there are 30 level pitches, 23 with electricity (10A) and several with hardstanding, but this number is to be extended. There are 7 water points, chemical disposal, a motorcaravan service point and good night lighting. What makes this little site distinctive is its excellent, well designed sanitary block which has a sparkling clean freshness. Facilities include WCs, showers, washbasins with mirrors, electric points, hand dryers and plenty of hot water each morning. Laundry room with washing machine and a dishwashing area also. Camper's kitchen with TV. Basic groceries and a selection of wines available from the family shop. Gas is available. Fishing 1 km, riding 6 km, golf 3 km. Carrick town centre is a five minute walk away where there are shops, pubs, restaurants, banks, sports facilities and all services, plus a castle which is open to the public. Within a short drive is the 'magic road', the Mahon Falls, a slate quarry or a romantic river walk.

How to find it: Approaching town on N24 road, follow signs for R690 in the direction of Kilkenny. Site is north of town, clearly signed at junction with R697.

Open: All year except 20 Dec - 5 Jan.

Charges 1999: Per unit incl. 2 adults IR£9.00 - 10.00; tent IR£6.00 - 7.00; extra adult IR£1.00 - 1.50; child IR£1.00; electricity 6A IR£1.00. 10A 1.50; hiker/cyclist incl. tent IR£3.00 - 3.50. No credit cards.

Reservations: Contact site. Address: Ballyrichard, Kilkenny Road, Carrick-on-Suir, Co. Tipperary. Tel: 051 640461. E-mail: coscamping@tinet.ie.

949 Sonas Caravan and Camping Park, Ballymacoda, nr Youghal

Pleasant family run park in an unspoilt rural area.

What sells Sonas is its delightful situation, overlooking Youghal Bay with direct access to the beach and a birdwatchers' paradise. In this peaceful and quiet location, 4 km. from Ballymacoda village, it is easy to sit back and relax at this family run site. Pleasantly laid out, the 20 touring pitches are mostly to the right, with 12 pitches for caravans and motorcaravans, all with electric hook-ups (10A) and 10 with hardstanding. It is also possible to choose a more isolated spot around the perimeter where at least 20 tents can be pitched. Immediately in view is the main amenity block with 70 privately owned caravan holiday homes placed beyond. This building, which has a fresh and clean appearance, houses all the facilities which include reception and small shop (1/6-1/9) selling basic groceries, confectionery and with tourist information. There is a TV room, campers' kitchen, laundry and dishwashing area (washing machine, tumble and spin dryers, sinks) and the sanitary facilities. These are opened by key and include showers (£1), WCs, washbasins, with electric points, mirrors, etc. and were clean when we visited. To the rear of the block is a unit for disabled people. Chemical disposal. Also on site are a tennis court, volleyball and football pitch and a new adventure playground. Fishing 1 km, boat launching 2 km, golf 15 km. If not keeping fit, birdwatching, fishing or enjoying the beach, which is a mixture of shingle and sand but safe for swimming, take time to visit the area's many attractions which include the Cobh Heritage Centre and the historic walled port of Youghal.

How to find it: From Youghal turn left off the N25 to Ballymacoda. Park is 4 km. on left after village and is signed.

Charges 2000: Per unit incl. 2 adults IR£10.00 - 11.00; small tent IR£8.00; extra adult IR£1.50; child (4-14 yrs) IR£1.00; awning IR£1.00; extra car IR1.00; electricity IR£1.00; hardstanding IR£1.00. No credit cards.

Open: 1 May - 30 September.

Reservations: Contact site. Address:Ballymacoda, Co. Cork. Tel: 024 98132.

964 The Flesk Muckross Caravan and Camping Park, Killarney

Seven acre park at gateway to National Park and Lakes, near Killarney town.
This family run park has undergone extensive development and offers high quality standards. Housed in one of Europe's most modern toilet blocks are well designed, heated shower and toilet areas. Every detail has been added, including a vanity area with mirror and hair dryer and a baby bath/changing room. Pitches are well spaced and have electricity (10A), water, and drainage connections; 21 also have hardstanding with a grass area for awnings. Other on site facilities include petrol pumps, supermarket (all year), delicatessen and café (March - Oct) with extra seating on the sun terrace. There is also a laundry room, campers' kitchen with dishwashing sinks, a comfortable games room and chemical disposal point, plus night lighting and night time security checks. The grounds have been well cultivated with further shrubs, plants and an attractive barbecue and patio area. This is situated to the left of the sanitary block and is paved and sunk beneath the level roadway. Surrounded by a garden border, it has tables and chairs, making a pleasant communal meeting place which commands excellent views of Killarny's mountains. Fishing 300 m, boat launching 2 km. Winter caravan storage.

How to find it: From Killarney town centre follow the N71 and signs for Killarney National Park. Site is 1½ km on the left beside the Gleneagle Hotel.

Open: 12 March - 31 October.

Charges 2000: Per unit IR£3.00 - 3.50; adult IR£3.75; child (under 14 yrs) IR£1.00; extra car IR£1.50; small tent incl. 1 or 2 persons IR£2.50 - 3.00; m/cylist incl. tent IR£4.75 - 5.00; hiker or cyclist incl. tent IR£4.50 - 4.75; awning IR£1.50; electricity IR£1.75. Credit cards accepted.

Reservations: Advisable in peak periods, write to park. Address: Muckross Road, Killarney, Co. Kerry. Tel: 064 31704. FAX: 064 34681. E-mail: killarneylakes@tinet.ie.

FLESK MUCKROSS
CARAVAN PARK

Family run, 7 acre park, situated at the gateway to 25,000 acres of National Park and lakes.
AA award winning sanitation facilities 1994/5
Just 1 mile (1.5 km) from Killarney town on the N71 south of Kenmare,
adjacent to Gleneagle Hotel and leisure centre

MUCKROSS, KILLARNEY   **Phone: 064-31704**
CO. KERRY, IRELAND   **Prop: Johnny & Sinead Courtney**   **Fax: 064-34681**

951 Eagle Point Caravan and Camping Park, Ballylickey, Bantry Bay

Spacious, well run park on a spectacular peninsula jutting into Bantry Bay.
Midway between the towns of Bantry and Glengarriff, the peninsula of Eagle Point juts into the bay. The first impression is of a country park rather than a campsite. As far as the eye can see this 20 acre, landscaped, part-terraced park, with its vast manicured grass areas separated by mature trees, shrubs and hedges, runs parallel with the shoreline. Suitable for all ages, this is a park devoted to tourers, with campers pitched mostly towards the shore. It provides 125 pitches (60 caravans, 65 tents) thus avoiding overcrowding during peak periods. There are three toilet blocks with free hot showers, all maintained and designed well above expected standards. Other facilities include electric hook-ups, bin area, laundry and dishwashing facilities, chemical disposal and motorcaravan service points, a children's play area, tennis courts, a football field to the far right, well away from the pitches, plus a supermarket at the park entrance. A wet weather timbered building towards the water's edge houses a TV room - the brightly decorated interior is guaranteed to brighten the dullest of days. Eagle Point makes an excellent base for watersports enthusiasts - swimming is safe and there is a slipway for small craft. Fishing on site. Bicycle hire 6 km, riding 10 km, golf 2 km. No dogs are accepted.

How to find it: On coast side of the N71, 6 km. north of Bantry, 11 km. east of Glengariff. Park entrance is opposite Burmah petrol station.

Open: 28 April - 30 September.

Charges 2000: Per unit IR£10.50 - 13.50; extra adult IR£4.00; m/cyclist, hiker or cyclist IR£5.00 per person; extra car IR£2.00; electricity (6A) IR£1.00. Credit cards accepted.

Reservations: Bookings not essential. Address: Ballylickey, Bantry, West Cork. Tel: 027 50630.

REPUBLIC of IRELAND

962 Fleming's White Bridge Caravan Park, Ballycasheen, Killarney

Family run, 9 acre, woodland park on eastern outskirts of Killarney.

Once past the county border, the main road from Cork to Killarney (N22) runs down the valley of the Flesk river. On the final approach to Killarney off the N22 Cork road, the river veers away from the road to enter the Lower Lake. On this prime rural position, between the road and the river, and within comfortable walking distance of the town, is Fleming's White Bridge. The ground is flat, landscaped and generously adorned with flowers, shrubs and trees. There are now 92 pitches (46 caravans and 46 tents) which extend beyond a wooden bridge to an area surrounded by mature trees and where a new toilet block, one of three, is sited. Facilities include a shop (1/6-1/9), two TV rooms, a games room, campers' shelter for wet weather, and two laundries. Hot water is free, there are dishwashing sinks and chemical disposal facilities. This is obviously a park of which the owners are very proud. The family personally supervise the reception and grounds, maintaining high standards of hygiene, cleanliness and tidiness. There are six new luxury holiday mobile homes for hire, fishing (advice and permits provided), canoeing (own canoes), bicycle hire and woodland walks. Riding 3 km, golf 4 km. The park's convenient location, so close to Ireland's premier tourism centre does however mean that advance booking is advisable during peak summer months.

How to find it: From Cork and Mallow: at N72/N22 junction continue towards Killarney and take first turn left (signed Ballycasheen Road). Proceed for 300 m. to archway entrance on left. From Limerick: follow N22 Cork road. After passing Super Valu and Killarney Heights Hotel take first right (signed Ballycasheen Road) and continue as above. From Kenmare: On N71, pass Gleneagles Hotel and Flesk Bridge. Turn right before Shell filling station into Woodlawn Road and Ballycasheen Road for continue 2 km. to archway.

Open: 17 March - 31 October.

Charges 2000: Per unit IR£3.00 - 3.50; small tent/car or motorcaravan IR£2.50 - 3.00; adult IR£3.50; child (under 14 yrs) IR£1.00; awning IR£1.00 - 1.50; electricity (10A) IR£2.00 - 3.00; m/cyclist and tent IR£4.25 - 4.75; hiker or cyclist and tent IR£4.50 - 5.00. Credit cards accepted.

Reservations: Write to park with IR£5 non-refundable reservation fee, especially for peak periods. Address: White Bridge, Ballycasheen Road, Killarney, Co. Kerry. Tel: 064 31590. FAX: 064 37474. E-mail: fwbcamping@tinet.ie.

957 Creveen Lodge Caravan and Camping Park, Healy Pass

Immaculately run, small hill farm park, overlooking Kenmare Bay.

The address of this park is rather confusing, but Healy Pass is the well known scenic summit of the road (R574) crossing the Beara Peninsula, which lies between Kenmare Bay to the north and Bantry Bay to the south. Several kilometres inland from the north coast road (R571), the R574 starts to climb steeply southward towards the Healy Pass. Here, on the mountain foothills, is Creveen Lodge, a working hill farm with a quiet, homely atmosphere. Although not so famed as the Iveragh Peninsula, around which runs the Ring of Kerry, the northern Beara is a scenically striking area of County Kerry. Creveen Lodge, which commands views across Kenmare Bay, is divided among three gently sloping fields separated by trees. Reception is to be found in the farmhouse which also offers guests a comfortable sitting room. A small separate block, which is well appointed and immaculately maintained, has toilets and showers, plus a communal room with a fridge, freezer, TV, ironing board, fireplace, tables and chairs. Full Irish breakfast is served on request. This park is carefully tended with neat rubbish bins and rustic picnic tables informally placed, plus a children's play area with slides and swings. To allow easy access, the steep farm track is divided into a simple one-way system. There are 20 pitches in total, 16 for tents and 4 for caravans with an area of hardstanding for motorcaravans. Electrical connections are available. This is walking and climbing countryside or, of interest close by, is Derreen Gardens. Fishing 2 km, bicycle hire 9 km, boat launching 9 km. Also in the area are water sports, riding, `Seafari' cruises, shops and a restaurant.

How to find it: Park is on the Healy Pass road (R574) 1.5 km. southeast of Lauragh.

Charges 2000: Per unit IR£6.00; person IR£1.00; hiker or cyclist incl. tent IR£3.50 per person; electricity £1.00. No credit cards.

Open: Easter - 31 October.

Reservations: Write to site with an S.A.E. Address: Healy Pass, Lauragh, Co. Kerry. Tel: 064 83131. E-mail: creveen@freeocean.net.

958 Waterville Caravan and Camping Park, Waterville, Ring of Kerry

Family run park in scenic location overlooking Ballinskelligs Bay.
Drive into Waterville and immediately feel welcome - the Horgan family place emphasis on being hospitable and attentive to their guests. It is an 'away from it all' environment, picturesque and quiet. The 60 touring pitches, many with hardstanding, are located in three areas. Some are convenient for reception, whilst others are pitched to the middle and rear. There is also a sheltered corner allocated to campers, with 21 caravan holiday homes (15 for hire), unobtrusively placed around the perimeter and centre, giving the park a spacious, neatly laid out appearance. Sitting high above the bay, the view in all directions is magnificent and the well tended grounds with plants, shrubs and cordyline trees gives a tropical appearance, especially on a fine sunny day. Three sanitary blocks are all well maintained and kept clean, the newest tastefully decorated with white tiles, relieved with rows of decorative black. There are hot showers (50p token), facilities for disabled people, washing up and laundry areas, quiet room, chemical disposal facilities and a motorcaravan service point. Other facilities include a campers' kitchen, shop (with gas), takeaway (both 1/6-31/8) and TV room. As well as an outdoor children's play area and above ground swimming pool (1/6-31/8), there is a play room in an old horse drawn caravan and a timber house with toys and 'upstairs, downstairs'. Waterville is on the Ring of Kerry, convenient for all the scenic grandeur and attractions for which the area is famed. Fishing, golf and bicycle hire within 3 km. Waterville is also on the 'Kerry Way' walking route.

How to find it: Travelling south on the N70, park is 1 km. north of Waterville, 270 m. off the main road.

Open: Easter - 16 September.

Charges 2000: Per unit IR£8.00 - 8.50; adult IR£1.00; child 50p; hiker or cyclist incl. tent IR£3.75 - 4.00; m/cyclist incl. tent IR£4.25 - 4.50; electricity (6A) IR£1.00; awning IR£1.50; hardstanding or extra car IR£1.00. Credit cards accepted.

Reservations: Made with fee IR£5 plus IR£15 deposit. Address: Waterville, Ring of Kerry, Co. Kerry. Tel: 066 74191. FAX: 066 74538. E-mail: watervillecaravans@tinet.ie.

961 Mannix Point Camping and Caravan Park, Cahirciveen

Quiet and peaceful, beautifully located seashore park.
It is no exaggeration to describe Mannix Point as a nature lovers' paradise. It is situated in one of the most spectacular parts of the Ring of Kerry, overlooking the Portmagee Channel towards Valentia Island. Whilst the park is flat and open, it commands splendid views in all directions, it is right on marshland which teems with wildlife (2 acre nature reserve) and it has immediate access to the beach and seashore. The owner has planted around 500 plants with plans for around 1,000 more trees and shrubs. There are 42 pitches, 15 for tourers and 27 for tents, with electrical connections (6A) available. A charming old fisherman's cottage has been converted to provide reception. A cosy sitting room with turf fire, and 'emergency' dormitory for campers, is a feature of this site. Toilet facilities, now upgraded and immaculate, have well designed showers and free hot water. There is a modern campers' kitchen, laundry facilities, chemical disposal and motorcaravan service facilities. There is no television, but compensation comes in the form of a knowledgeable, hospitable owner who is a Bord Fáilte registered local tour guide. This park retains a wonderful air of Irish charm aided by occasional impromptu musical evenings. Watersports, bird watching, walking and photography can all be pursued here, but note that dogs are not allowed on site in June, July and August. Bicycle hire 800 m. riding 3 km, golf 14 km. Local cruises to Skelligs Rock with free transport to and from the port for walkers and cyclists. This is also an ideal resting place for people walking the Kerry Way.

How to find it: Park is 250 m. off the N70 Ring of Kerry road, 800 m. southwest of Cahirciveen (or Cahersiveen) on the road towards Waterville.

Open: 15 March - 15 October, the rest of the year also, if you write first.

Charges 1999: Per adult IR£3.25 - 3.40; child IR£1.50 - 2.00; caravan or motorcaravan IR£1.00 - 2.00; tent no charge; electricity IR£1.00; hiker/cyclist, incl. tent IR£3.25 - 3.40; m/cyclist IR£3.50 - 3.90. Book 7 nights, pay 6. Reductions for groups if pre-paid.

Reservations: Made with deposit of one night's fee. Address: Cahirciveen, Co. Kerry. Tel: 066 9472806. FAX: as phone.

REPUBLIC of IRELAND

959 Fossa Caravan and Camping Park, Killarney

Mature, well equipped park in scenic location, 5½ km. from Killarney.

A 10 minute drive from the town centre brings you to this well laid out park which is recognisable by its forecourt on which stands a distinctive building housing a roof top restaurant, reception area, shop and petrol pumps. The park is divided in two – the touring area lies to the right, tucked behind the main building, and to the left is an open grass area mainly for campers. Touring pitches, with electricity and drainage, have hardstanding and are angled between shrubs and trees in a tranquil, well cared for garden setting. To the rear at a higher level and discreetly placed are 50 caravan holiday homes (25 for hire). These are unobtrusive and sheltered by the thick foliage of the wooded slopes which climb high behind the park. The toilet facilities are modern and kept spotlessly clean. A second amenities block is placed to the far left of the grass area beside the tennis courts. Other facilities, apart from a shop (April - Sept), take-away and restaurant (5/6-26/8), include a TV lounge, campers' kitchen, laundry room, washing up area, children's play area, picnic area, games room, bicycle hire, night lighting and security patrol. Fishing or golf 2 km, riding 3 km. Not only is Fossa convenient for Killarney, it is also en-route for the famed 'Ring of Kerry', and makes an ideal base for walkers and golfers.

How to find: Park is to the right on the R562/N72, 5½ km. west of Killarney on the road to Killorglin.

Open: 1 April - 30 September.

Charges 2000: Per unit IR£3.00 - 3.50; adult IR£3.00; child (under 14 yrs) IR£1.00; electricity IR£1.50; m/cycle and tent per person IR£4.25 - 4.50; hiker or cyclist per person IR£3.50 - 4.00; awning IR£1.50; extra car IR£1.50. Credit cards accepted.

Reservations: Advisable in high season and made for min. 3 nights with IR£10 deposit. Address: Fossa, Killarney, Co. Kerry. Tel: 064 31497. FAX: 064 34459. E-mail: fossaholidays@tinet.ie.

FOSSA CARAVAN & CAMPING PARK

★ Ample hardstanding & electric hook-up ★ Separate tent area
★ Modern toilets ★ Shaving points ★ Hairdryers ★ Hot showers ★ Facilities for the disabled
★ Full laundry facilities ★ Campers kitchen ★ Free wash-up facilities
★ On site shop open 7 days Easter to Sept. ★ Restaurant (June-Aug) ★ Take away (July/Aug)
★ Children's playground ★ Tennis court ★ Games room ★ TV room ★ Bicycles for hire
★ Mobile homes for hire ★ Hostel accommodation

FOR FREE COLOUR BROCHURE WRITE TO:
Brosnan Family, Fossa Caravan & Camping Park, Fossa, Killarney, Co. Kerry, Ireland
Telephone: (064) 31497   Fax: (064) 34459

ITALY

Italy only became a unified state in 1861, hence the regional nature of the country today. There are 20 distinct regions and each one retains its own relics of an artistic tradition generally acknowledged to be the world's richest. However, the sharpest division is between north and south. The north is an advanced industrial area, relatively wealthy, whereas the south is one of the economically less developed areas of Europe. Central Italy probably represents the most commonly perceived image of the country and Tuscany, with its classic rolling countryside and the historical towns of Florence, Siena and Pisa, is one of the most visited areas. Venice is unique and as beautiful as its reputation suggests. Rome, Italy's capital, on its seven hills with its Roman legacy, is independent of both north and south. Naples, the natural heart of the south, is close to some of Italy's ancient sites such as Pompei.

Italian State Tourist Board, 1, Princes Street, London W1R 8AY
Tel: 020 7408 1254 Fax: 020 7493 6695
Brochures: 0891 600280 (60p per minute)

Population
58,000,000, density 191.7 per sq. km.

Climate
Varying considerably between north and south; the south enjoys extremely hot summers and relatively mild and fairly dry winters, whilst the mountainous regions of the north are much cooler with heavy snowfalls in winter.

Language
The language is Italian derived directly from Latin. There are several dialect forms and some German is spoken near the Austrian border.

Currency
The unit of currency is the Lira (plural Lire). Notes are 1000, 2000, 5000, 10,000, 50,000 and 100,000; coins: 50, 100, 200, 500 and 1,000.

Banks

Open Mon-Fri 08.30-13.30 and 15.00-16.00.

Post Offices

Open Mon-Sat 08.00-17.00/18.30. Smaller towns may not have a service on a Saturday. Stamps can also be bought in 'tabacchi'.

Time

GMT plus 1 (summer BST +1).

Public Holidays

New Year; Easter Mon; Liberation Day, 25 Apr; Labour Day; Assumption, 15 Aug; All Saints, 1 Nov; Immaculate Conception, 8 Dec; Christmas, 25, 26 Dec; plus some special local feast days.

Shops

Open Mon-Sat 08.30/09.00-13.00 and 16.00-19.30/20.00, with some variations in the north where the break is shorter and closing is earlier.

Food: Pizza must be sampled in Italy - thin and flat and cooked in traditional wood fired ovens. The seafood is plentiful and excellent and is rounded off nicely with the ice-cream (gelato).

Telephone

To call Italy the code is 0039. You then do need to include the `0' in the area code. To phone the UK dial 00 44 followed by the UK code minus the initial 0. As well as coins, tokens (gettone) from Tabacchi, bars and news stands are used for calls; phone cards are available.

Motoring

Driving Licence: A valid EC (pink) UK driving licence is acceptable. The older green UK licence must be accompanied by an official Italian translation (from the Italian Tourist Office or the AA). However, DVLA will exchange licences for the pink EC version with the appropriate fee.

Penalties: If you have a projection from the rear of your vehicle - such as a bicycle rack - it is obligtory to have a large 'continental' red/white hatched warning square. Fixed penalty for not having this is L. 110,000. Not wearing a seat belt will cost L. 660,000 if stopped.

Tolls: Payable on the extensive and expensive Autostrada network. If travelling distances, save time by purchasing a `Viacard' from pay booths or service areas.

Speed limits: Caravans and motorhomes (3.5 tons) 31 mph (50 kph) in built up areas, 44 mph (70 kph) and 50 mph (80 kph) for caravans on other roads and motorways respectively, 56 mph (90 kph) and 80 mph (130 kph) for motorhomes.

Fuel: Petrol stations on the Autostrada open 24 hours. Elsewhere times are 07.00-13.00 and 16.00-19.30; only 25% open on Sundays. Most motorway service stations accept credit cards, apart from American Express and Diners.

Parking: There are 'Blue Zones' in all major towns. Discs can be obtained from tourist and motoring organisations or petrol stations. In Venice use the special car parks on the mainland, linked by ferry and bus to Venice.

Breakdown: Always best to organise cover before leaving home, but if not call 116 - not a free service but they will arrange things for you.

Overnighting

Not generally allowed on open land. Special overnight parking areas are provided in the north of Italy for motorhomes. These include water facilities and services and the areas are clearly marked by blue motorhome signs. May also be permitted in rest areas and parks where local regulations allow.

Visiting Rome

It is easy to fall in love with Rome, but invariably one will depart with guilt feelings because only a fraction of the sights have been seen, or the history of this magnificent city has been barely scratched. The city is breathtaking. where magnificent Roman remains abound, and the splendour and strange secretiveness of Vatican City is totally fascinating, complete with its colourful Swiss guard. The easiest way to travel round Rome by public transport is by buying the Birg ticket, which allows you to use the metro and the buses within the city and outskirts, all for a daily rate of L. 8,500 (99 price). The choice of campsite is yours. It is possible to use to use the sites close to the city centre if you do not mind the noise and bustle normally associated with city sites. These sites include no. 6810 Camping Seven Hills. The other option is to select a site further afield which provides direct transport to the city, for example, no. 6811 Ipini Camping. This latter option gives the opportunity of a peaceful existence in cool and pleasant surroundings between forays into the extremely busy city, which can be tiring.

If you wish see Saint Peter's Square and the Basilica in all their glory we recommend arriving there at 07.00 hrs. This is before the day-trippers pour into the city and it will give the most amazing experience of virtually having the Square and the Vatican to yourself, albeit temporarily, and the opportunity of uncluttered photography. Remember, no bare knees or shoulders for some of the most appealing religious visits (a thin shawl will suffice). It is possible to arrange a Papal audience, which take place usually on Wednesdays, by sending a fax to the 'Prefettura della Casa Pontificia' (fax no. 0669/885863). There is a post office within the Vatican if you wish to send postcards with their unique postmark. Another useful tip is to enjoy an hours free tour in English of the Colosseum - after buying your ticket, look for the guides in blue uniforms inside the gates on the right. Allow as much time as you can to take in the sights of this amazing city.

ITALY - North West

6405 Camping C'era una Volta, Villanova d'Albenga, Albenga, nr Alassio

Well situated site, back from sea, with swimming pools and other amenities.

A well run, attractive site, C'era una Volta is about 8 km. back from the sea, situated on a hillside with panoramic views, and with pitches on terraces in different sections of the site. The 120 pitches for tourers (45 for tents) vary in size, most have shade, and the upper ones have views. Cars are required to park in separate areas at busy times. Pitches are equipped with electricity (6A), there is water and a drainaway close by. The main toilet block is modern, with mainly British style WCs and with hot water throughout including the free showers. Four additional smaller sanitary blocks are spread around the site. There is a charming restaurant with a large terrace, the menu is limited but good, the pizzeria and bar are of a good standard. Amenities include four swimming pools in different parts of the site open in the main season. One is large (30 m.) with a children's pool in the upper area, another, also with a children's pool is by the restaurant. A small, but modern gym is available along with a fitness track. A more concealed section at the top of the site is fenced off for naturists to sunbathe in privacy. Charges are high in season but the site is well organised with an enjoyable atmosphere. Private beach (7 km) - reduced cost to campers.

How to find it: Leave autostrada A10 at Albenga, turn left and left again at roundabout on SS453 for Villanova. Follow Villanova signs to T-junction, turn left towards Garlenda, turn right in 200 m. and follow signs to site.

General Details: Open 1 April - 30 Sept. Shade in parts, but trees mostly small. Shop. Bar, pizzeria (April - Sept). Attractive restaurant. Takeaway (high season). Disco (July/Aug). Swimming pool complex (July/Aug). 2 saunas. Tennis. Large adventure playground. Fitness track with exercise points. Small but excellent gymnasium. Riding 500 m. Golf 2 km. Programme of organised sports and other events in season, also dancing or entertainment some nights. Chemical disposal. Many bungalows for hire. No dogs accepted.

Charges 1999: Per pitch incl. up to 3 persons L.30,000 - 65,000, acc. to season and type of pitch; extra person 10,000 - 16,000; VAT and electricity included. Discounts for longer stays in low season.

Reservations: are made for min. of a few days with 30% advance payment. Address: 17038 Villanova d'Albenga (SV). Tel: 0182/580461 or 582871. FAX: 0182/582871.

The holiday village 'C'era una Volta' extends over a tree- and bush-covered area of 100,000 sq.m. It is a unique park, where the green trees and the colour and fragrance of the flowers are an essential part of the holiday. The terraced site has small Villas, Bungalows, Apartments and Pitches for Caravans and Tents. Our Sport and Recreation Centre has **4 Swimming Pools**, Tennis, Mini-Tennis, Keep-fit-Trail, Children's play area, Dancing and Musical events, Fitness-room, **Tecnogym**, Naturist Solarium, Miniclub and Animation.

SEA SUN

★ ★ ★ ★

C'ERA UNA VOLTA
CAMPING BUNGALOW CARAVAN
CENTRO TURISTICO

Camping Bungalow Caravan - Centro Turistico
C'ERA UNA VOLTA
I-17038 VILLANOVA D'ALBENGA (SV)
Riviera dei Fiori
Tel. 0039/0182580461 • Fax 0039/0182582871
Http://ceraunavolta.seasun.net/villanova/

6410 Camping Genova Est, Bogliasco, nr Genoa

Attractive, wooded site above Bogliasco just south of Genoa.

This site of 12,000 sq.m. is set on very steep slopes close to the Genoa motorways coming from the north or west and although it has very limited facilities, it is quite near the town. There is a free bus service to the beach, or if you are extremely fit a set of steep stairs will take you there in 15 minutes. The Buteros who run and own the site both speak good English and are very enthusiastic and anxious to please. The approach from the main road twists and climbs steeply with a tight final turn at the site entrance. There are 54 touring pitches. The two sanitary blocks are being refurbished for 2000. There are free hot showers and a washing machine. Men have some newer facilities which include three units with WC, washbasin and shower en suite. The small children's play area is set on a narrow terrace and in our opinion the exit from the slide is dangerous. There is a small bar which sells essential daily goods and a little restaurant with a slightly tired terrace although the views over the sea are very enjoyable. Torches are needed at night in several parts of the site. This is a site to be used for exploring Genoa rather than for extended stays.

How to find it: From autostrada A10 take Nervi exit and turn left (south) on the SS1 towards La Spezia. In Bogliasco look for a sharp left turn with a large sign for the site. Follow narrow winding road for 2 km. to site.

General Details: Open 1 March - 30 Oct. Electricty available (3/5A). Shop and bar/restaurant (both Easter - 30 Sept). Towing vehicle available. Fishing 1.5 km. Gas supplies. Chemical disposal. Motorcaravan services. Mobile home and 3 caravans to let. Not suitable for disabled people.

Charges 2000: Per person L. 9,000; child (3-10 yrs) 6,000; small tent 8,000; large tent or caravan 10,000; motorcaravan 13,000; car 5,000; electricity 3,000. Credit cards accepted.

Reservations: Contact site. Address: Via Marconi-loc Cassa, 16031 Bogliasco (GE). Tel: 010/3472053. FAX: as phone. E-mail: camping@money.it.

AR Discount
Less 10%,
all season

6401 Camping Villagio Dei Fiori, San Remo Beach, Riviera Ligure

Good quality site with pools and access to beach.

Open all year round, this open and spacious site has high standards and is ideal for exploring the Italian Riviera or for just relaxing by the enjoyable, filtered sea water pools (one for children, and both attracting a small extra charge). If you prefer unfiltered sea water, there is a path to a secluded and pleasant private beach, although bathing shoes may be required at certain tide times as there is a belt of smooth stones across part of the beach. The beach surrounds are excellent for snorkelling and fishing. Unusually this site is paved for 80% of the pitch area, with a few southern pitches on grass and sand. There is ample shade from mature trees and shrubs which are constantly watered and cared for in summer and pleasant views over the sea from the western pitches. All pitches have electricity (3A) and there is an outside sink and cold water for every four pitches. A large restaurant with pizzeria and takeaway service all year, has a large terrace and giant children's toys close by. The open area by the restaurant is used for entertainment during high season. The bar sells essential supplies only, but the shops of San Remo are just outside the campsite gates. Three clean and modern sanitary blocks are well dispersed around the site with Turkish and British type WCs and free hot water. There are facilities for disabled campers. High quality mobile homes and bungalows are for rent. The friendly management speak excellent English and will supply detailed tourist plans along with a specialised cultural visit programme produced on site. Buses run from outside the site to Monte Carlo, Nice, Cannes, Eze and many other places of interest.

How to find it: From main SS1 Ventimiglia - Imperia road, site is on right hand side of road just before town of San Remo. There is a sharp right turn if the site is approached from the west. Site is well signed.

General Details: Open all year. Restaurant/bar. Pizzeria and takeaway. Sea water swimming pools. Tennis. Table tennis. Volleyball. Children's play area. Fishing. Animation for children and adults in season. Bicycle hire. Riding 2 km. Golf 2 km. Washing machines. dryer and irons. Chemical disposal. Motorcaravan service point. No dogs or other animals are accepted.

Charges 1999: Per pitch incl. up to 4 persons: motorcaravan, caravan or large tent 44,000 - 74,000; half pitch incl. 2 persons 30-000 - 44,000; electricity 4,000. 50% of charges to be paid on arrival. Discounts for stays in excess of 7 days.

Reservations: Contact site for details. Address: Via Tiro a volo 3, 18038 Sanremo - Riviera Ligure. Tel: 0184/660635. FAX: 0184/662377. E-mail: villagiodeifiori@seasun.net.

AR Discount
Less 10% in low season

6412 Villaggio Camping Valdeiva, Deiva Marina, nr La Spezia

Small family owned site, back from sea, with small swimming pool.

A mature and peaceful site 3 km. from the sea between the famous Cinque Terre and Portofino, Valdiva is open all year. It is situated in a valley and amongst dense pines so views are restricted. Half of the 100 pitches, which are on flat ground and separated, are used as permanent pitches by Italians, the remainder shared between tourers and tents. Some of the latter are on high terraces. They are supplied with electricity (3A) and are of varying size. Cars may be required to park in a separate area depending on the pitch. The site does have a small swimming pool, which is very welcome if you do not wish to take the free bus to the beach. A small bar and restaurant offers a reasonable, but limited, menu and pizzas cooked in a traditional wood fired oven. The meal may be eaten on the terrace, which has a distinctly traditional feel with all manner of plants and decoration scattered around. Three sanitary blocks are provided for the tourers and tents, and they are all very different. One block is more modern and the others are dated, the WCs are mainly Turkish, but there are some of British style. Washbasins have hot water, soap, hairdryers and there are free hot showers. A small children's play area is available. The beach is pleasant and the surrounding village has several bars and restaurants. There are very pleasant walks and treks in the unspoilt woods of Liguria nearby or the most interesting tourist option is a visit to Cinque Terre, five villages which can only be reached by rail, boat or by cliff footpath. Their history is one of fishing but now they also specialise in wines. Unusually some of the vineyards can only be reached by boat.

How to find it: Leave autostrada A12 at Deiva Marina exit and follow signs to Deiva Marina. Signs are clear and site is on left approx. 3 km. down this road.

General Details: Open all year. Shade in most parts. Very small shop open in high season. Small swimming pool. Car wash. Chemical disposal.

Charges 1999: Per pitch 2 persons L. 25,000 - 46,000, 3 persons 30,000 - 54,000, 4 persons 35,000 - 62,000. Credit cards accepted.

Reservations: Contact site. Address: Loc. Ronco, 19013 Deiva Marina, La Spezia. Tel: 0187/824174. FAX: 0187/825352.

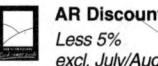

AR Discount
Less 5% excl. July/Aug.

ITALY - North West

6220 Camping Mombarone, Torre Daniele

Pleasant, scenic family run site suitable for en-route stop or an exiting climbing base.

This is a small, rustic all year site alongside the SS26 road. It has 120 pitches, of which 80 are given over to permanent chalets or caravans. The Peretto family take pride in looking after their guests and English is spoken. The site is thoughtfully laid out with trees for shade and is surrounded by very attractive mountains and wooded hills, with traditional vines bedecking the eastern slopes. If you are a keen climber this is an ideal base as the mountains in this area are extremely popular with climbers and the many famous valleys, including Valle di Champorcher and Valle di Gressony, are within easy driving distance, as is the Parco Nazionale del Gran Paradiso. There is only a small shops on site but shops and restaurants are close by in the village of Torre Daniel. There is a small framed and supported pool for children and they can paddle in the shallow river on the southern boundary. A volleyball court, table tennis and table football machine complete the range of amusements. A larger river close by provides relaxing fishing. The sanitary facilities are spotless with both British and Turkish style WCs, showers on payment (L. 2,000) and a washing machine.

How to find it: Take SS26 north from Ivrea. Site is at the 45 km. (V1) marker just before entering the town of Torre Daniele.

General Details: Open all year. Bar. Shops and restaurants in the town. Toddlers pool. Volleyball. Table tennis. Table football. Fishing. Riding 5 km. Chemical disposal. Washing machine .

Charges 1999: Per person L. 5,000; child (under 10 yrs) 4,000; caravan 5,000; car 2,000; motorcaravan 7,000; electricity 2,000. No credit cards.

Reservations: Write to site. Address: Settimo Vittone Reg. Torre Daniele (TO). Tel: 0125/757907. FAX: 0125/757396.

6240 Camping Valle Romantica, Cannobio, Lake Maggiore

Attractive site with good facilities in scenic situation.

The pretty little town of Cannobio is situated between Verbania and Locarno on the western shore of Lake Maggiore. It could make a base for exploring the Lake and its islands, although progress along the winding lakeside road, hemmed in by mountains, is slow. Serious mountain walkers are well catered for, and the Swiss resort of Locarno is not far. Steamers cross the Lake, but the only car ferry across is between Verbania and Laveno. This lovely (30,000 sq.m.) site was established about 40 years ago by the present owner's father, who planted some 20,000 plants, trees and shrubs, and there is much to interest botanists in this tree-clad mountain valley. The site has a swimming pool in a sunny position, and there is a pool in the river, where, except after heavy rain, children can play. The 130 numbered pitches for touring units are on flat grass among the trees, which provide good shade and serve to separate the pitches (but mean some narrow site roads). The three sanitary blocks have British style WCs, free hot water in the basins and showers, controlled by taps. The showers are of reasonable size, with hooks, screen and a small dressing space. Electricity (4A) is available on most pitches, although long cables are necessary in some parts. The small supermarket is well stocked, and there is a pleasant bar/restaurant with waiter service and takeaway. Entertainment (folk music) is provided one night per week in the high season. Used by tour operators (30 pitches). The owner takes a keen and active personal interest in the site, and English is spoken.

How to find it: From centre of Cannobio (where site is signed) take valley road towards Malesco; site is 1 km. on right.

General Details: Open 1 April - 30 Sept. Shop. Bar/restaurant. Swimming pool (15/5-15/9). Table tennis. Children's playground. Fishing (licence required). Bicycle hire 1 km. Fridge boxes to hire. Washing machine. Gas supplies. Chemical disposal. Motorcaravan services. Mobile homes to rent.

Charges 2000: Per person L. 10,000 - 11,500; child (1-12 yrs) 6,500 - 7,500; pitch 16,000 - 20,000; extra tent 5,000; extra car 8,000 - 10,000; dog 5,500; electricity 5,000. No credit cards.

Reservations: Made for min. 11 nights with deposit (L. 120,000) and fee (80,000). Address: 28822 Cannobio (Verbania). Tel: 0323/71249. FAX: as phone. E-mail: camping@riviera-valleromantica.com.

AR Discount
Less 10% in
low season

122

6245 Camping Riviera, Cannobio, Lake Maggiore

Good lakeside site near northern end of Lake Maggiore, with access for watersports.

Under the same active ownership as Valle Romantica, this 22,000 sq.m. site is directly on the lake with scenic views across the water and surrounding mountains. Over 250 numbered pitches, 220 with 4A electricity (long cables may be needed) are on flat grass either side of hard surfaced access roads, and are divided by trees and shrubs. The whole site has a well cared for appearance, and is certainly one of the best lakeside sites in the area. The five sanitary blocks, one new and two with facilities for disabled visitors, are of good quality with British style WCs and controllable hot water to basins and showers; these are of reasonable size, with hooks, screen and dressing area. The site shop is well stocked and the town is only a short distance away. A pleasant bar/restaurant with covered terrace, provides waiter service and a takeaway. There is a small jetty and easy access to the lake for boats, swimming and other watersports. Sailing and windsurfing regattas are organised. The site could make a suitable base for exploring the area, although progress on the busy winding road may be slow!

How to find it: Site is by the lakeside, just north of town of Cannobio. There are several sites nearby, and care should be taken not to overshoot Riviera as turning round could be difficult!

General Details: Open 1 April - 22 Oct. Shop. Bar/restaurant with takeaway. Pizzeria. Fridge boxes for hire. Fishing (licence required). Boat slipway. Sailing and windsurfing schools. Bicycle hire 500 m. Washing machines. Gas supplies. Chemical disposal. Motorcaravan services.

Charges 2000: Per person L. 10,000 - 11,500; child (1-12 yrs) 6,500 - 7,500; pitch 16,000 - 20,000; extra tent 5,000; extra car 8,000 - 10,000; dog 5,500; electricity (4A) 5,000. No credit cards.

Reservations: Made for min. 11 nights with deposit (L.120,000) and fee (80,000). Address: 28822 Cannobio (Verbania). Tel: 0323/71360. FAX: as phone. E-Mail: info@riviera-valleromantica.com.

 AR Discount
Less 10% in low season

6247 Camping Tranquilla, Baveno

Family run site close to Lake Maggiore with large restaurant and swimming pools.

Tranquilla is a family run site on the western slopes above Baveno with two small swimming pools. Reception is housed in an attractive old railway carriage from where the Luca family will make you welcome to the site with excellent English spoken. The site is in two terraced sections offering different electrical amperages (3/5A). Although on the small side, the pools are very welcome in the height of summer as the 1.5 km. walk to the lake, where swimming can be difficult, is down a steep slope, and would prove difficult for older or disabled campers. There is an unusually large restaurant with two terraces, a large menu at reasonable prices and live entertainment is provided in season. The terrace has a fountain, some views and is very popular. Pizzas are also available to eat in, or takeaway. The pitches, both permanent (55) and touring (56) are of average size and are randomly mixed, with trees offering some shade. The southern site has a two year old ladies' sanitary block, which is spotless and includes facilities for disabled campers, whilst the male side is more mature, but very clean. The northern side, which has all support facilities, has several older sanitary blocks with British and Turkish style WCs, which again are kept clean. Here you will find the washing machine, a dryer, a freezer and refrigerator for the use of campers. Tourist information is available and reception will book any of the local activities and facilities including watersports. The site is an ideal base to explore the local area which is most attractive but vehicular transport is necessary as there is no bus service.

How to find it: From Avora follow SS33 road north to Baveno, site is signed to the left in the northern part of the town. Site is approx. 1.5 km. uphill and well signed.

General Details: Open all year. Bar. Restaurant and pizzeria. Children's play area. Swimming pools in season. Table tennis. Table football. Electronic games. Camping items in adjoining store, shops nearby. Freezer and refrigerator service.

Charges 1999: Per person L. 6,500 - 7,800; child 1-3 yrs 3,800 - 4,800, 4-12 yrs 4,800 - 5,800; dog 3,500; pitch 10,500 - 13,500; electricity 3,200. No credit cards.

Reservations: Write to site. Address: Via Cave, 2. 28042 Baveno (VB). Tel/Fax: summer (0323) 923452 (winter tel/Fax: (0323) 923344).

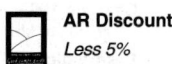 **AR Discount**
Less 5%

ITALY - North West

6248 Camping Parisi, Baveno

Quiet site on the shores of Lake Maggiore.

Camping Parisi is a small family run site on the western side of Lake Maggiore within the town of Baveno. The small and compact site has 61 pitches, all for tourers. The pitches are shaded by mature trees and there are stunning views over the lake which is this site's real strength. An early reservation would be necessary if you wish to occupy one of the lakeside pitches (extra charge). Whilst there is no swimming pool, it is possible to paddle and swim from the lake shore which is also good for sunbathing, but care must be taken with children. The site has a restaurant and bar which is accessed through a gate on the northern boundary. The public also have the use of these facilities through a separate access which is secured by night. This shared community complex also has limited fixed entertainment such as five-a-side soccer on sand, satellite TV in the bar, volleyball, table tennis, a small children's play area and a large beach area with sunbeds. Live entertainment is offered adjacent to the restaurant at weekends during high season. The site has no shop or washing machine as the town is 100 m. distant but there is a freezer for campers' use. The central sanitary facilities are clean with free hot showers and have British style WCs but, as yet, no facilities for disabled campers. These facilities are supplemented by day in the 'community area' where a modern complex offers coin slot showers, British toilets and sinks. Tourist information is available and reception will make bookings for local activities.

How to find it: From Avora follow SS33 road north to Baveno. Site is signed to the right in centre of the town on the right but a sharp eye is needed to pick out the small sign high on the wall at a narrow part of the street.

General Details: Open 1 April - 30 Sept. Community complex: Bar. TV. Restaurant. Volleyball. Five-a-side soccer. Children's play area. Table tennis. Shops nearby. Freezer service.

Charges 1999: Per person L. 8,500 - 9,500; baby (1-3 yrs) 4,000 - 4,500; child (4-12 yrs) 7,500 - 8,000; caravan 8,000 - 8,500; motorcaravan 14,000 - 15,000; tent 7,500 - 8,000; car 6,500 - 7,000; m/cycle 5,000 - 5,500; dog 2,000 - 3,000; electricity 3,500. No credit cards.

Reservations: Write to site. Address: Via Piave, 50-28831 Baveno (VB). Tel: 0323/923156 (winter: 090/9763973).

6250 Camping Au Lac du Como, Sorico, Lake Como

see colour advert between pages 128/129

Small site in scenic position on Lake Como.

Au Lac du Como is situated in a most pleasant location at the head of Lake Como in the centre of the village of Sorico facing south down the water and surrounded by wooded mountains. There is direct access to the lake for swimming, boating and other watersports with windsurfing appearing to be the most popular past-time. Static units predominate but the camping area is directly by the lake where there is said to be room for 74 touring units. However, as pitches are not marked out, pitching can be a little haphazard and the area may become crowded at times, particularly in high season when advanced booking is advised. Cars are parked just away from tents and caravans and there is further parking outside the entrance. The owner speaks good English and insists on respect for other residents so ball games, barbecues and loud music are not allowed. There is one good sanitary block in the centre of the static part and two smaller basic ones. These have mainly British WCs. Hot water in the larger block is on payment but free in the other two except for washing up and laundry. There is a hotel/restaurant at the entrance with the bar open all day, an excellent buffet breakfast service and evening meals. The site is well situated for exploring the area and nearby Switzerland via the Splugen Pass and there are marked paths and trails for walking and biking in the mountains with an interesting nature park close with a variety of flora and fauna. Although it makes a good night stop when passing this way, many visitors find it interesting and stay longer. Most guests are German and Dutch but British find their way here and are welcome.

How to find it: Easiest route is north on SS36 from Lecco to Nuovo Olonio and west on SS402 (signed Gravelona) to Sorico; site is then on the left in centre of village. Can be approached on SS340 from Como on lake-side road which is quite narrow in places but an interesting drive.

General Details: Open all year. 20,000 sq.m. Electricity connections (3A). Supermarket. Hotel bar and restaurant. Sauna and solarium. Fishing. Canoes, kayaks, bicycle hire. Washing machine and dryer. Chemical disposal. Motorcaravan service point. Bungalows, rooms and apartments to rent.

Charges 1999: Per person L. 5,000 - 10,000; child 3,500 - 7,000; pitch 7,000 - 20,000; car 6,000; m/cycle 5,000; dog or boat 3,500 - 7,000. Credit cards accepted.

Reservations: Advised for high season; write to site. Address: Via Cesare Battisti 18, 22010 Sorico (CO). Tel: 0344 84035 or 84716. FAX: 0344/84802.

6259 Camping Punta d'Oro, Lake Iseo

Pleasant, small site on Lake Iseo.

Lago d'Iseo is the fifth largest of the northern lakes and one of the least known outside Italy. However, it is a popular tourist spot for Italians and many others and therefore has not escaped exploitation. Camping Punta d'Oro, at the town of Iseo in the southeast corner of the lake, is a small, delightful campsite, which has been run by the professional Brescianini-Zatti family for the last 30 years. It slopes gently down to the lake from the railway line (they say, an infrequent local service) and there could be some road noise. The very pretty site, adorned with trees and plants, has 64 grass pitches (with just 15 static caravans) on either side of decorative brick roads. Electrical connections are available and trees at the corners define the places. Care should be taken on entry as this is tight for larger units. There are excellent views across the lake to wooded mountains on the opposite shore where small villages shelter down by the water and further mountains rise behind the site. It has a small bar/restaurant and shop with a terrace. The two small sanitary blocks have been refurbished to a high standard with a mix of British and Turkish style WCs and free hot water in washbasins, sinks and showers. All these services were immaculate when seen. There are two narrow slipways for launching boats onto the lake which are also used for swimming, along with the lakeside area on the northeast boundary, the pitches at the water's edge are more expensive. It is a good centre for exploring around the lake, Monte Isola (Italy's largest lake island) by ferry from Iseo or to ascend Monte Gugliemo (1,949 m) which is reported to take about 3½ hours. With no entertainment programme, this could well suit those looking for a very pleasant base without the activity of a larger site.

How to find it: Leave A4 (Milan-Venice) autostrada at Ospitaletto exit, go north to Rodengo and then take SS510 to Iseo. Punta d'Oro is at northern end of town - cross the railway line and turn right at corner where site is signed.

General Details: Open 1 April - 31 October. 6,000 sq.m. Electrical connections (5A). Shop. Bar/restaurant. Access to lake. Fishing. Games room. TV in bar. Bicycle hire 500 m. Riding 1.5 km. Golf 5 km. Washing machine. Chemical disposal. Motorcaravan services.

Charges 1999: Per person L. 7,000 - 9,500; child 5,500 – 7,000; pitch 14,500 - 24,000, acc. to size; electricity included; dog 3,000. Credit cards accepted.

Reservations: Write to site. Address: via Antonioli 51, 25049 Iseo (BS). Tel: 030/980084. FAX: as phone. E-mail: punta@franciacorta.it.

AR Discount
Welcome drink

6260 Camping Europa Silvella, San Felice del Benaco, Salo, nr Brescia

Site beside Lake Garda with various amenities.

This large, modern, lakeside site was formed from the merger of two different sites with the result that the 323 pitches (about 295 for tourists) are spread among a number of different sections of varying type. The chief difference between them is that the marked pitches close to the lake are in smaller groups and closer together so that one has less space. However. in the larger, very slightly sloping or terraced grassy meadows further back one can have 80 sq. m. or more instead of 50. There is reasonable shade in many parts and electricity available. All pitches have 4A electricity, 45 with water and drainage. Some areas also contain bungalows. The site has frontage to the lake in two places (with some other property in between), with beach, jetty and moorings. The private beach is most pleasant, with all manner of watersports available. There is a windsurfing school in season, along with an organised animation programme with live entertainment. A new, large modern swimming pool complex has 'hydro massage' (jacuzzi) plus a children's pool. New sanitary blocks have been completed in the last two years which include washbasins in private cabins, facilities for the disabled and a children's room with small showers, British WCs and basins. All blocks have free hot water. There is a supermarket and restaurant complex and a new children's playground. Torches may be necessary in remote parts of the site.

How to find it: From Desenzano at southerly end of Lake Garda follow S572 north towards Salo. Following signs for San Felice turn off towards lake. Then follow yellow tourist signs bearing camp name.

General Details: Open 23 April - 27 Sept. Self-service shop. Bazaar. Restaurant/bar. Laundry. Swimming pools. Tennis courts. Table tennis. Children's playground. Bowling alley. Surf boards, canoes and bicycles for hire. Animation and entertainment (every night in season). Disco. Tournaments, swimming, windsurfing and tennis lessons. First aid room. Chemical disposal. Bungalows and caravans to let.

Charges 1999: Per person L. 7,500 - 12,000; child (2-9 yrs) 6,500 - 10,000; pitch with car, electricity, water and drainage 21,500 - 31,000; pitch with electricity only 18,500 - 26,000; small tent pitch, no electricity 14,000; extra car 8,000 - 12,000; trailer 8,000 - 15,000; dog 10,000. VAT included.

Reservations: not usually necessary for caravans and tents, but will be made for min. 7 days with 30% deposit and L. 40,000 fee. Address: Via Silvella 10, 25010 S. Felice del Benaco (Brescia). Tel: 0365/651095. FAX: 0365/654395.

ITALY - North West

6280 Camping Week End, Cisano, San Felice del Benaco

Modern, well equipped site with superb views over the lake.

Created among the olive groves and terraced vineyards of the Chateau Villa Louisa, which overlooks it, this site enjoys some superb views over the small bay which forms this part of Lake Garda. Although it is some 400 m. (private path/road direct from the site) from the lake itself, for many, the views resulting from its situation on higher ground will be ample compensation for it not being an actual 'lakeside site'. Being situated above the lake, in quiet countryside, it provides an unusually tranquil environment, although even here it can become very busy in high season. The site has one good sized swimming pool and a children's pool which make up for its not actually having frontage onto the lake, and some visitors, particularly families with children, will doubtless prefer this. There are 220 pitches, all with electricity (from 3A), of which about 30% are taken by tour operators and statics. The pitches are in several different areas, many enjoying superb views. Some for larger units are on the upper terraces on steep slopes and manoeuvring can be challenging. Three modern sanitary blocks, one under the restaurant/shop, are well maintained with free hot water for large showers, washbasins (a few cabins) and washing-up. They have mainly British style WCs and facilities for disabled people. We have had reports of congestion at peak periods. There is a large attractive restaurant, with a thoughtfully laid out terrace and lawn providing waiter service and takeaway meals at reasonable prices. Children's play area with large grass area for ball games. English is spoken.

How to find it: Approach from Salo (easier when towing) and follow site signs.

General Details: Open 15 April - 23 Sept. Bar/restaurant. Shop. Swimming pools. Entertainment in season. Children's playground. Fishing 2 km. Golf 6 km. Riding 8 km. Windsurfing, water skiing and tennis near. First aid room. Washing machines and dryer. Chemical disposal. Motorcaravan services. Bungalows and caravans for hire.

Charges 2000: Per unit incl. electricity L. 18,000 - 25,000; adult 8,500 - 12,500; child (3-10) 6,500 - 9,500; extra car 6,500 - 8,500; extra m/cycle 5,500 - 6,500; dog 6,500 - 10,000. No credit cards.

Reservations: Contact site. Address: Via Vallone della Selva 10, 25010 San Felice del Benaco (Brescia). Tel: 0365/43712. FAX: 0365/42196. E-mail: cweekend@tin.it. A 'Camping Cheques' site.

...so unique!! ★★★★★

camping villaggio

WEEKEND

Quiet family site, well maintained. Modern toilet facilities. Free hot water in the showers and basins. Washing machine, bar, restaurant, pizzeria, small shop. Very scenic. 2 swimming pools, children's playing area, volleyball, table tennis, music and dancing in the evenings. Send for our brochure. Reservations accepted. Caravan, tent and bungalow for hire. New 6 person mobile-homes. Individual washing cubicles. Internet: http://www.weekend.it. e-mail: cweekend@tin.it

Via Vallone della Selva, 10 - 25010 SAN FELICE DEL BENACO (BS) ITALIA - Tel. 0039/0365 43712 Fax 0365 42196

6285 Camping Zocco, Manerba del Garda, Lake Garda

Excellent lakeside site with access for watersports.

Lake Garda is a very popular holiday area with a good number of sites well placed to explore the many attractions nearby. Camping Zocco is in a quiet, scenic location sloping gently down to the lake where there is a small jetty and good access to the water from a shingle beach. The 200 pitches for tourists, all with electricity (4A), and from 60-80 sq.m. in size, are either on slightly sloping ground from gravel roads, on terraces or around the perimeters of two open meadows. A variety of trees, including olives which provide oil and may be bought in attractive personalised bottles as a memento, give shade in some parts. The site has a very well cared for appearance. There is a bar with terrace, a new restaurant/pizzeria and a shop. The restaurant offers a variety of food at reasonable prices. Entertainment is provided for children during July/Aug. Water sports can be enjoyed on the lake, and boats may be launched from the site. Three, very clean, tiled sanitary blocks are well spaced around the site. They have mainly British style WCs, free hot water in the basins, sinks and showers, and facilities for disabled people. The Fratelli family who run this site give British visitors a warm welcome and English is spoken. Used by tour operators (20 pitches).

How to find it: From Desenzano north on 572 towards Salo, then minor road to Manerba from wheresite signed.

General Details: Open 1 April - 26 Sept. 50,000 sq m. Bar. Restuarant/pizzeria. Bar on beach (less hours in low season). Shop (1/5-15/9). Watersports. Fishing. Tennis. Football. Children's play area. Bicycle hire 1.5 km. Riding and golf 4 km. Washing machines. Chemical disposal. Motorcaravan services. Apartments and caravans for rent.

Charges 1999: Per person L. 7,200 - 9,500; child (3-11 yrs) 6,000 - 8,500; pitch incl. electricity 15,500 - 20,000; dog 3,800 - 6,500; small boat or extra car 3,800 - 6,500. Credit cards accepted.

Reservations: Made for min. 7 days with deposit (L. 150,000). Address: via del Zocco 43, 25080 Manerba (BS). Tel: 0365/551605. FAX: 0365/552053 (winter tel/fax: 0365/551036). E-mail: campzocco@tin.it.

AR Discount Less 10% on person charge, min. 7 days

6252 Camping San Francesco, Rivoltella, Lake Garda

*see colour advert
between pages 128/129*

Large well organised site on the western shores of Lake Garda.

This site is situated to the west of the peninsula of Sirmione on the southwest shores of Lake Garda. This position allows wonderful views of the lake, the most attractive Grotte di Cattulo, the far shores, Bardolini, the wooded slopes and mountains beyond. The impressive family site has 292 marked pitches which are generally on flat gravel and sand, enjoying natural shade from mature trees. The pitches are generally of average size although there were some huge units here when inspected, all have electricity (3A) and 25 have water and drainage. All have easy access. There is a private wooded beach area of approximately 400 metres which can be used for sunbathing, windsurfing, canoeing sailing and power-boating, plus a jetty for boating. The site maintains a safety watch of three men with rescue boats at all times for water activities. The site boasts its own well equipped sports centre, with three large swimming pools including one for children and a separate area for organised water activities, tennis, archery, petanque, football stadium, organised evening activities. Facilities include a bar, restaurant, pizzeria, and an entertainment programme. The sanitary facilities are in two large, identical, centrally located buildings. They were very clean when seen and offer every facility a camper could want along with free hot water at all points. The facilities for disabled campers are of the highest specification. The large, busy reception area provides security passes and tourist information on entry, and is well equipped to advise and organise any of the myriad of available internal and external sports activities, tours and ferry trips There is the possibility of some noise disturbance from an adjoining holiday complex in high season.

How to find it: From autostrada A4, between Brescia and Verona, exit towards Sirmione and take S11 to Rivoltella. Site well signed.

General Details: Open May - Sept. Electricity connections. Shop. Restaurant and snacks. Tennis. Children's playground. Chemical disposal. Fully equipped tents, caravans and mobile homes to rent.

Charges 1999: Per person L. 8,500 - 12,300; child (under 6 yrs) 7,700 - 11,200; pitch incl. electricity 18,000 - 26,200; extra car 6,500 - 9,500; m/cycle 3,400 - 4,800; boat 6,600 - 9,600. Credit cards accepted.

Reservations: Contact site. Address: Strada Vic, S. Francesco, 25010 Rivoltella (BS). Tel: 030/9110245. FAX: 030/9119464. A 'Camping Cheques' site.

AR Discount
*Less 10% in
low season*

6253 Camping Piani di Clodia, Lazise, nr Verona

Large, well organised 'all singing, all dancing' site on Lake Garda.

As might be expected in a popular area like Lake Garda, there are many camping sites and this is one of the best large sites giving a positive impression of space and cleanliness. Piani di Clodia, is a huge well-organised site located on a slope between Lazise and Peschiera in the southeast corner of the lake. It has lovely views across the water to Sirmione's peninsula and the opposite shore. You are greeted at the gate by English speaking young attendants who are keen to please. It is very close to Gardaland, one of the biggest theme parks in Europe and the huge Caneva acqua park . The rectangular site slopes down to the water's edge and has over 1,000 pitches, all with electricity (5A), terraced where necessary and back to back from hard access roads. There is some shade from mature and young trees. The swimming pool complex is truly wonderful with three pools – all large, one for 'straightforward' swimming which can be heated, another with a variety of slides and hydro-massage and the third for children. The whole area is fenced with lifeguards in attendance and a pleasant sunbathing area and bar. The shopping area is in the centre of the site with an entertainment arena in the open and another on the roof, which is covered. The quality self-service restaurant changes its menu daily and offers a takeaway service and pleasant bar. There is also a large terrace, part of which is covered. A new large upper level has been built which extends the existing restaurant and features the pizza outlet. The animation staff provide an ambitious variety of entertainment for children and adults and there are facilities for an amazing array of sports and pastimes (see below). There is a fence between the site and the lake with access points to a private beach and opportunities for a variety of watersports. Seven modern, immaculate sanitary blocks are well spaced around the site with a mix of British and Turkish style WCs and free hot water in washbasins, sinks and showers. All have facilities for disabled visitors and one has a baby room. Many tour suggestions by foot or bicycle and a wealth of tourist information are available from the reception office where English is spoken.

How to find it: Site is south of Lazise on road SS249 before Peschiera.

General Details: Open 20 March - 5 October. 220,000 sq.m. Shopping complex with supermarket, general shops for clothes etc. Two bars. Self-service restaurant with takeaway. Swimming pools. Tennis. Table tennis. Gymnastics. Bicycle hire. Riding near. Large grass space for volleyball and other ball games. Good children's playground. Outdoor theatre. Animation. Golf 12 km. Caneva acqua park, Gardaland (one of the biggest theme parks in Europe) close. Washing machines, dryers and laundry service. Motorcaravan services. Chemical disposal.

Charges 1999: Per person L. 7,300 - 13,000; child (1-9 yrs) 4,500 - 8,500; pitch with electricity 16,500 - 28,000, with water also 18,500 - 31,000.

Reservations: Contact site. Address: Loc. Bagatta, 37017 Lazise (VR). Tel: 045/7590456. FAX: 045/7590939.

ITALY - North East

6020 Camping Union Lido Vacanze, Cavallino, nr Venice/Venezia

see colour advert opposite

Superb, well organised seaside site with aqua-park and excellent facilities.

This well known site is extremely large but has first class organisation and it has been said that it sets the standard that others follow. It lies right by the sea with direct access to a long and broad beach of fine sand which fronts the camp. Shelving very gradually, the beach, which is well cleaned by the site, provides very safe bathing. The site is laid out regularly with parallel access roads under a covering of poplars and pine trees which serve also to mark out numbered pitches of adequate size (2,600 for touring units). There are separate parts for caravans, tents and motorcaravans, plus one mixed part. All have 5A electricity and 1,381 have water and drainaway also. The redesigned entrance now provides a large off-road overnight parking area with electrical connections, toilets and showers for those arriving after 9 pm. An aqua-park includes a swimming pool, lagoon pool for children, heated whirlpool and a slow flowing 160 m. long 'river' for paddling or swimming. Covering 5,000 sq.m. this is under lifeguard supervision and is open mornings and afternoons. There is also a heated pool for hotel and apartment guests, available to others on payment. The 16 sanitary blocks, which open and close progressively during the season, have free hot water in all facilities and are kept very clean. They have British style WCs, washbasins with shelf and mirror (many in cabins), hot showers, footbaths and deep sinks for washing dishes and clothes. Six blocks have facilities for disabled people. A comprehensive main shopping area set around a pleasant piazza has a wide range of shops including a large supermarket. There are seven restaurants and several pleasant and lively bars. A selection of sports is offered in the annexe across the road and fitness programmes under qualified staff are available in season. The golf 'academy' with professional in attendance, has a driving range, pitching green, putting green and practice bunker, and a new diving centre has a school and the possibilty of open water dives. There are regular entertainment and activity programmes for both adults and children. Union Lido is above all an orderly and clean site and this is achieved partly by strict adherence to regulations suiting those who like comfortable camping undisturbed by others and good management.

How to find it: From Venice-Trieste Autostrada leave at exit for airport or Quarto d'Altino and follow signs first for Jesolo and then Punta Sabbiono, and camp will be seen just after Cavallino, on the left.

General Details: Open 1 May - 30 Sept. 600,000 sq.m. Good shade in all parts. Many shops, open till late. Restaurants, bars, pizzerias. Aqua-park (from 15/5). Tennis. Riding. Table tennis. Minigolf. Skating rink. Bicycle hire. Archery. Two fitness tracks in 4 ha. natural park with children's play area and supervised play for children. Boat excursions. Recreational events for adults and children, day and evening. Italian language lessons. Golf academy. Diving centre and school. Windsurfing school in season. Church service in English in Jul/Aug. Exchange facilities and cash machine. Ladies' and gent's hairdressers. Launderette. First aid centre, doctor's surgery with treatment room and camp ambulance. Gas supplies. Motorcaravan service points. Chemical disposal. Luxury apartments, bungalows, caravans and mobile homes for hire and site owned hotel by entrance. No dogs accepted.

Charges 2000: Three different rates: (i) high season 1/7-2/9; (ii) mid-season 3/6-1/7 and 2/9-16/9, and (iii) off-season, outside these dates. Per person L. 10,000, 12,300 or 14,300; child under 3 yrs 6,000, 7,800 or 10,000, 3-12 yrs 8,500, 10,500 or 12,600; pitch incl. electricity 18,000, 21,500 or 32,500; with water and drainage 23,000, 26,500 or 37,500; extra car 5,000, 7,000, 9,000. VAT incl. Min. stay high season 1 week. Credit cards accepted.

Reservations: made for the letting units only, but site provides 'priority cards' for previous visitors. Address: 30013 Cavallino (Venezia). Tel: 041/968080 or 2575111. FAX: 041/5370355. E-mail: info@unionlido.com. UK contact: G. Ovenden, 29 Meadow Way, Heathfield, Sussex TN21 8AJ.

Visiting Venice

If you are visiting Italy a trip to Venice is a must, it is said that you will either love it or find it totally distasteful, but you will walk away, however, always enchanted. The Basilica di San Marco and the Palazzo Ducale certainly draw the largest crowds, but to itemise the other sights would be too lengthy, let alone explaining the history behind this fascinating part of Italy. We prefer to visit the city in the late afternoon, after the crowds have thinned. When looking for somewhere to eat or drink, beware of some overpriced restaurants, as Venice can be a very expensive city, try to venture away to quieter areas where it is possible to find reasonably priced menus. The specialities of Venice are fish and other seafood, and the surrounding area also produces very palatable wines.

Venice is a grouping of 117 islands, divided into 6 districts separated by 45 km. of canals. You cross the patchwork of islands and canals on a confusion of footways and attractive bridges. Be sure to allow lots of time for getting around Venice as we guarantee that you will get lost at some point. As a guide, walking directly from Saint Marco Square to the bus/train station via the Rialto Bridge will take approximately 45 minutes (without getting lost!) A good map of Venice is essential and we found a compass a real help in navigating the fascinating labyrinths of alleys, canals and bridges. There are official signs but enterprising business people here have also erected their own signs to ensure you pass their premises. This makes navigation difficult when attempting to find major features and therefore all signs which are not of the official pattern should be ignored.

Il Parco delle Vacanze

The pleasant holiday park with quality, style and atmosphere in a friendly environment right on to the Venetian Cavallino coast.
Open from 1st May to 30th September.

Camping - Caravan - Bungalow

Spacious, fitted pitches on grass under pines and poplars, for tents, caravans and motorcaravans. Many caravan pitches have water and drainage points. Caravans and mobile homes for hire, with shower and WC.
Bungalow "Lido" with kitchen-living room, 2 double bedrooms (twin beds), shower and separate WC and terrace including some for disabled guests.

Fitness - Sport - Play Park

Spacious area with games and keep-fit equipment, with trained staff, Multi-use sportsground for roller blading and other activities, volley ball, swimming instruction, wind surfing school, diving centre with school and diving excursions at sea, table tennis, minigolf, tennis and riding school. Archery and football competition. Golf Academy.
The Happy Place! Children's play area with much equipment. Climbing games and supervised play programme.

Animation - Entertainment - Activities

Amphitheatre for concerts and music shows.
Organised activities: Painting courses, artistic activities, games & recreation by trained staff.

★ ★ ★ ★

**The first campsite in Europe
to be granted UNI EN ISO 9002 certification.**

I-30013 CAVALLINO - VENEZIA
Tel. Camping 0039/041968080-0412575111
Tel. Hotel 0039/041968043-041968884
Telefax 0039/0415370355

E-mail: info@unionlido.com
Http://www.unionlido.com

Park Hotel Union Lido

3 Star hotel with 80 modern airy rooms, air conditioned and completely refurbished. Self-catering complex with 24 two-storey flatlets.
Heated swimming pool, with splash and whirlpool also available in the early and late season for our Hotel and self-catering guests.

Aqua Park

An experience! 5000 sq metres of water landscape with a gentle river, a lagoon for the children, swimming pool, whirlpools and a waterfall (15.5 - 30.9).

Scout camp for 8-12 yr olds on holiday with their parents in July-August.

camping
sanFrancesco

★★★★

New swimming pool and water games. New, first-class toilet and shower block

The camping ground is situated right at the beginning of the beautiful Sirmione peninsula, known as the 'pearl of Lake Garda'. The restaurant, pizza parlour, supermarket, two bars and sanitary facilities have just been renovated. The ground covers 100,000 m² of shady terrain reaching right down to the lake and a 300 m long beach. Our sports facilities on 35,000 m² include a big swimming pool (1,400 m²) with a lagoon for children and water games. Furthermore there is the possibility to engage in more than 10 different sports. Leaving the Milan to Venice motorway at the Sirmione exit, this ground is easy to access: and it is an ideal base for visiting the theme parks of Gardaland and Caneva nearby.

**ADAC
EREMS
Camping**

**Strada Vic. S. Francesco - I-25015 Desenzano del Garda (BS)
Tel. 0039/0309110245 - Fax 0039/0309119464
E-mail: sanfrancesco.garda@camping.it
Http: //www.camping.it/garda/sanfrancesco**

Camping Villaggio Hotel Ristorante
Au Lac de Como

**I-22010 SORICO
Tel. 0039/034484035
Fax 0039/34484802
Mobile 0039/335/216421
Internet: http://www.misterbyte.it/aulacdecomo *or*
http://www.aulacdecomo.com
E-mail: aulacdecomo@misterbyte.it *or*
info@aulacdecomo.com**

The Hotel Au Lac de Como, surrounded by the green of the Berlinghera, the natural oasis "Pian di Spagna" and the bright blue Lake, offers comfortable, modern rooms and apartments. Next to the Hotel is the Campsite with its own private beach. There are bungalows and splendid Mobile Homes for hire. In a peaceful setting, you can spend a novel and refreshing holiday and have a go at the various exciting sporting activities such as Paragliding, Hang-gliding and Outings in the surrounding forest. **New 2000: swimming pool.**

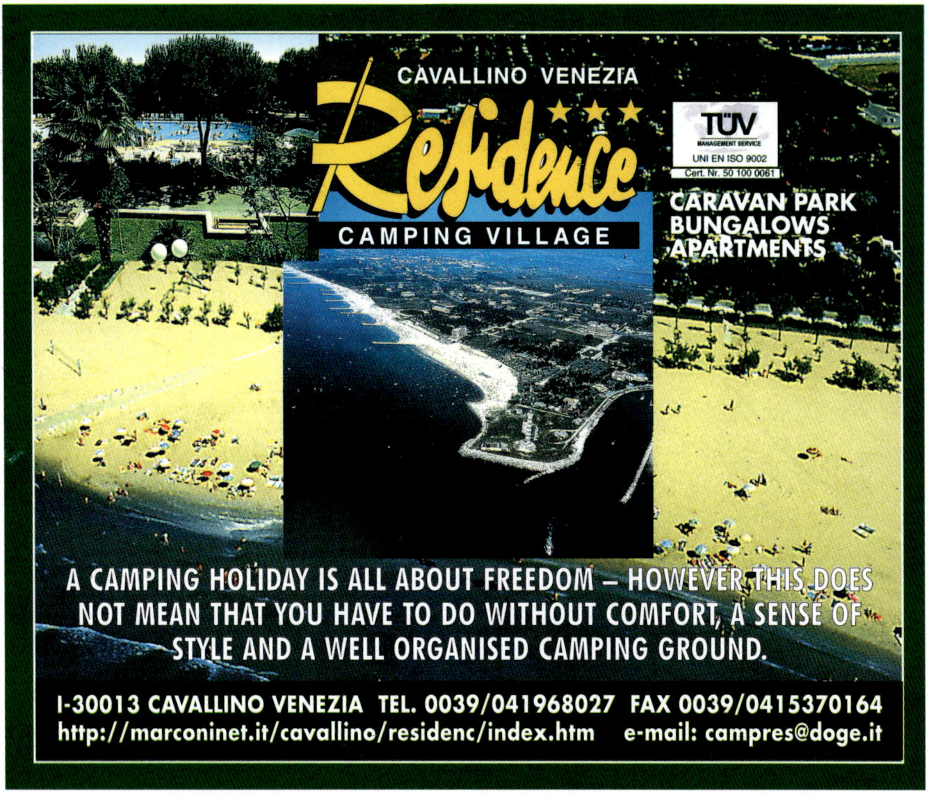

Haynes Classic Tours
Tours by Enthusiasts for Enthusiasts

Classic Car Rallies

- *Haynes Spring Classic* – For those who like to explore the performance of their classic car. Sample five different motor sport venues on one thrilling day (no race license needed).
- *Falling Leaves Classic Tours* – This is possibly your last opportunity of the year to enjoy driving your classic car in balmy autumn weather. Visiting one speed venue and many places of special interest.

Classic Tours by Coach

- Grand Tour of European Motor Museums including the Schlumpf Collection
- Essen Techno Classica Weekend
- Goodwood Festival of Speed and UK Motor Museums
- Paris and the Retro Mobile Classic Car Show
- Coys Historic Festival and UK Motor Museums
- Fly/Drive tour to Monaco, Southern France and Italy visiting seven motor museums, Venice, Pisa, Florence and the great lakes.

*For information on any of the above please call our brochure line:
Tel:01963 440804 or Fax: 01963 441004; or e-mail: mike@gmpwin.demon.co.uk*
Haynes Motor Museum Ltd, Sparkford, Yeovil, Somerset. BA22 7LH

THE LOW COST PITCH AND FERRY RESERVATION SERVICE

sites
ABROAD

TAKING YOUR OWN TENT, CARAVAN OR MOTORHOME ABROAD?

BOOKING MADE EASY
One phone call will book your whole holiday – sites, channel ferry or shuttle crossings.

VARIETY OF SITES
From 4 star sites with a full range of facilities to well-run municipal sites.

QUALITY AND SERVICE
All sites meet rigorous standards for safety and cleanliness.

VALUE FOR MONEY
A competitive package at a price you will find hard to beat.

PEACE OF MIND
A range of personal and car insurance policies to suit your needs.

For a brochure call now on
01606 787952

SAAF

BOOK FROM OVER 90 SITES IN:
FRANCE • HOLLAND • BELGIUM • GERMANY • SWITZERLAND AUSTRIA • ITALY • SPAIN • PORTUGAL • IRELAND

Camping Cheque

A great way of taking your holiday abroad outside July and August.
Pay for your site fees with Camping Cheque vouchers. Freedom and flexibility at very attractive prices.

150 Quality Sites

The majority feature in this Alan Rogers Guide (look for Camping Cheque in the text). Many of the French sites are Castels sites or Sites et Paysages sites. Key facilities open from 15 May to 15 September (minimum).

ONLY
£8.50
PER NIGHT
2 adults, pitch and electricity

Easy to Book

One phone call books your Camping Cheques, your ferry or shuttle crossings and your insurance.

Competitive Prices

Save between 10%-50% on public tariffs.

Special Offers

7 nights for 6. 14 nights for 11

FOR YOUR **FREE CATALOGUE** PHONE
01606 787953
TO FIND OUT MORE

ABTA

AITO
THE ASSOCIATION OF INDEPENDENT TOUR OPERATORS

CCARE

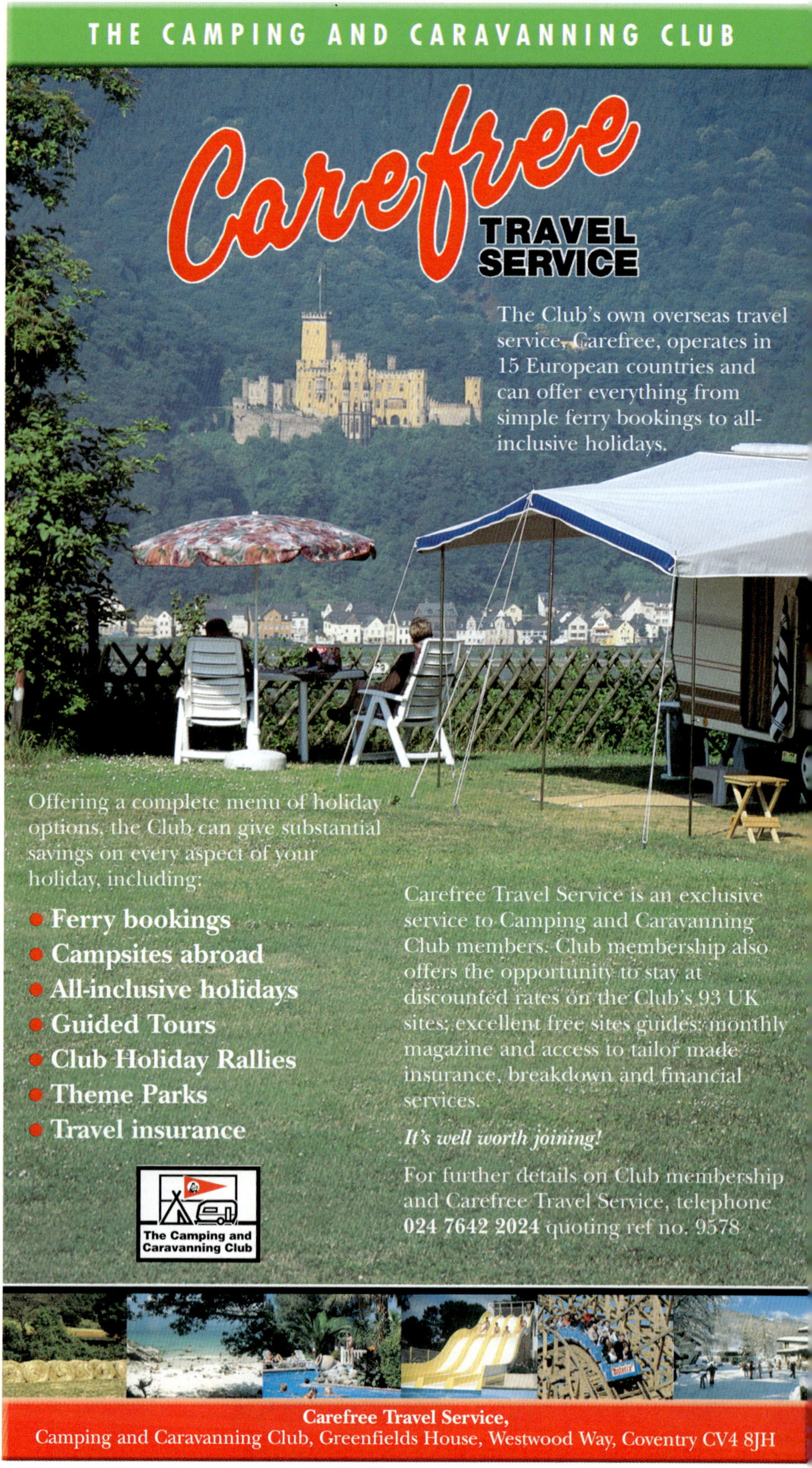

THE CAMPING AND CARAVANNING CLUB

Carefree
TRAVEL SERVICE

The Club's own overseas travel service, Carefree, operates in 15 European countries and can offer everything from simple ferry bookings to all-inclusive holidays.

Offering a complete menu of holiday options, the Club can give substantial savings on every aspect of your holiday, including:

- **Ferry bookings**
- **Campsites abroad**
- **All-inclusive holidays**
- **Guided Tours**
- **Club Holiday Rallies**
- **Theme Parks**
- **Travel insurance**

The Camping and Caravanning Club

Carefree Travel Service is an exclusive service to Camping and Caravanning Club members. Club membership also offers the opportunity to stay at discounted rates on the Club's 93 UK sites; excellent free sites guides; monthly magazine and access to tailor made insurance, breakdown and financial services.

It's well worth joining!

For further details on Club membership and Carefree Travel Service, telephone **024 7642 2024** quoting ref no. 9578

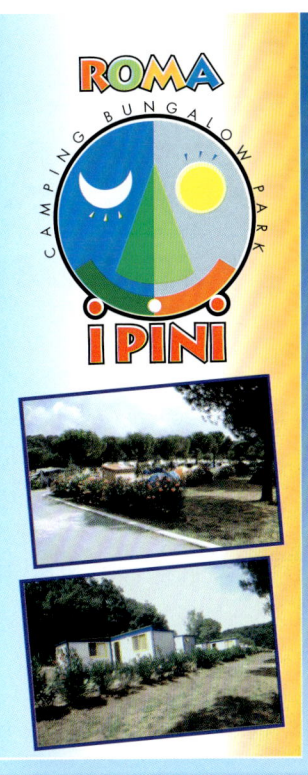

Camping "I Pini" is situated a few kilometres north of the centre of Rome, (exit autostrada A1 Roma Nord-Fiano Romano). Not only does it offer the possibility to reach the city centre with ease, it also permits our guest's various excursions locally E.G. The medieval village of Fiano Romano, or a visit to the archeological site of "Lucus Feroniae". The modern facilities offered by the campsite include bar, restaurant, mini-market, laundry, free hot showers, camper service, swimming pool and children's playground. It is also possible to go trail riding by horseback or mountain bike in the bordering Parco delle Sassete. The village area offers 20 bungalows for 2, 4 or 5 people each with it's own bathroom, kitchen and heating system.

I-00065 FIANO ROMANO ROMA
VIA DELLE SASSETE, 1/A
TEL. 0039/0765453349
FAX 0039/0765453057

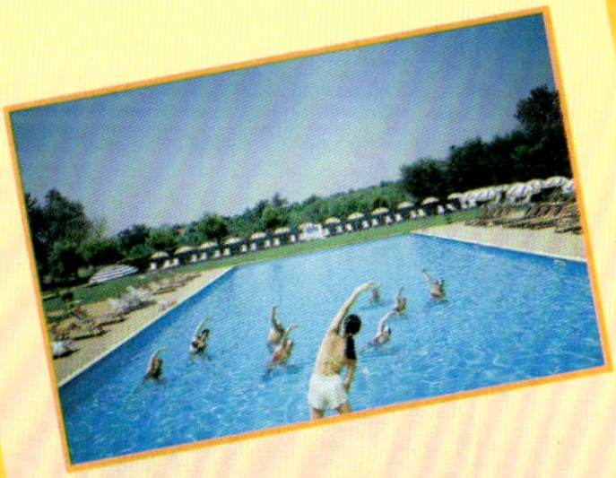

Directly by the sea
Private beach

PLEINAIR
T O U R

Our ★★★★ stars:
Special offers
for families

CAMPING ★★★★
RUBICONE VILLAGGIO

Via Matrice destra, 1 • I-47039 Savignano Mare (FO)
Tel. 0039/0541346377 - Fax 0039/0541346999
Internet: http://www.campingrubicone.com
E-mail: info@campingrubicone.com

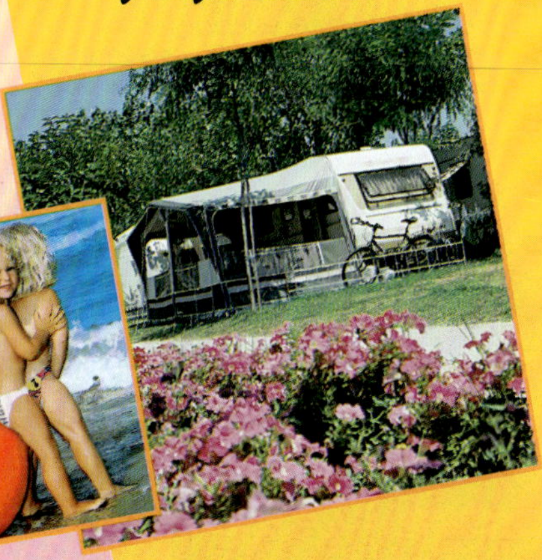

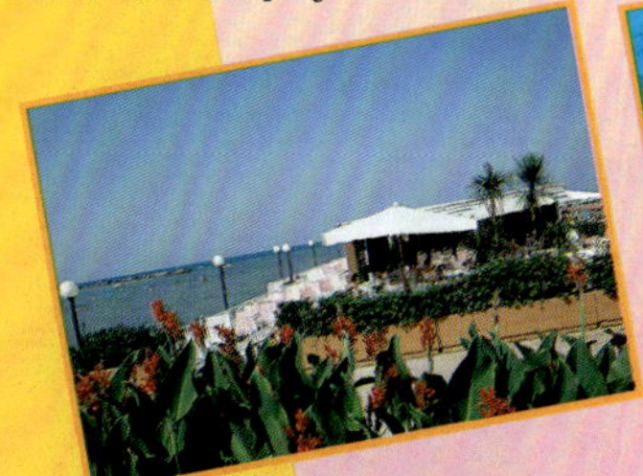

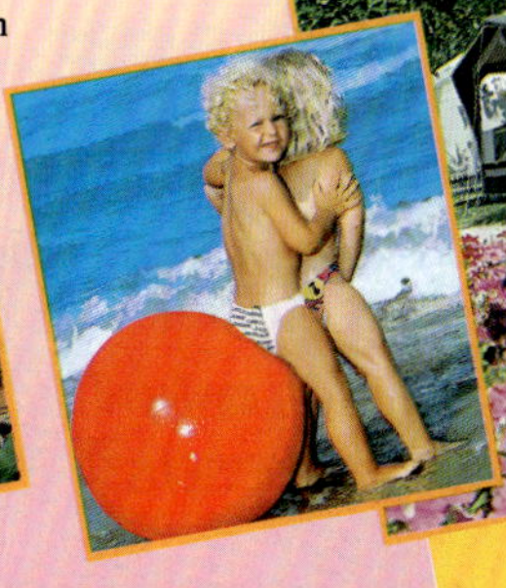

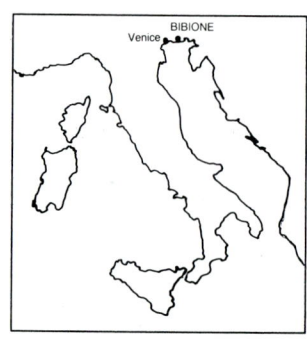

CAMPING
CAPALONGA
NATURE AT THE SEASIDE

★ PITCHES WITH MOORINGS ALONGSIDE
★ FULLY EQUIPPED CARAVANS AND MAXI-CARAVANS TO BE RENTED
★ NEW WOODEN CHALETS WITH AIR CONDITIONING. TWO WCS, ONE IN
  SHOWER ROOM AND THE SECOND IN THE BEDROOM WITH KING-SIZED BED

CAMPING CAPALONGA
I 30020 BIBIONE PINEDA (VENICE)
CALL: 0039-0431-438351

CAMPING RESIDENCE IL TRIDENTE
I 30020 BIBIONE PINEDA (VENICE) Tel: 0039-0431-439600

Camping in natural
surroundings

Like an English park

High class rooms and chalets
to rent

Fully equipped

SEA VIEWS

6010 Camping Capalonga, Bibione Pineda, nr Venice/Venezia

see colour advert opposite

Quality site with a very good beach and excellent sanitary blocks.
Capalonga is a large, well developed and cared for site, right beside the sea. The pitches are of variable size (70-90 sq.m.) and nearly all marked out. All have electrical connections (4A), some have water and drainage and there is good shade almost everywhere. The site is pleasantly laid out - roads run in arcs which avoids the 'square box' effect. Some pitches where trees define the pitch area may be tricky for large units. The beach is a very wide sandy one which is cleaned by the site and never becomes too crowded; a concrete path leads out towards the sea to avoid too much sand-walking. The sea bed shelves extremely gently and is very safe for children and the water is much cleaner here than at most places along this coast. Along the other side of the site runs a large lagoon, where boating (motor or sail) can be practised. The site provides a landing stage and moorings. There is also a swimming pool (25 x 12½ m.). The site has seven toilet blocks with hot water throughout; they are well and frequently cleaned. Two newer blocks built side by side have facilities for disabled people and very fine children's rooms with washbasins and showers at the right height. British and some Turkish style toilets, individual washbasins (some in private cabins) and a whole wall of mirrors. A large new playing field provides exercise stations, football pitch and a general area for ball games and there are play areas with equipment on the beach. A free animation programme (with an enlarged team) offers a wide range of sport, fitness and entertainment. Capalonga is an excellent site, with comprehensive facilities.

> **How to find it:** Bibione is about 80 km. east of Venice, well signed from afar on approach roads. 1 km. before Bibione turn right towards Bibione Pineda and follow camp signs.
>
> **General Details:** Open 1 May - 30 Sept. 250,000 sq.m. Electrical connections (4A). Large supermarket. General shop for campers and beach goods, cards, papers, etc. Self-service restaurant and separate bar. Swimming pool. Boating. Fishing. Launderette. Children's playground. Sports field. First-aid room. Car wash. Chemical disposal. Motorcaravan services. Dogs not accepted. Caravans and bungalows for hire.
>
> **Charges 2000:** Four charging seasons. Per person L. 10,000 - 17,000; child 1-4 yrs free - 8,000, 5-10 yrs free - 12,000; pitch with electricity 19,000 - 32,000; pitch with water and drainage also 21,000 - 34,000; extra car 4,000 - 8,000; boat 12,000 - 22,000 acc. to season and size. Credit cards accepted.
> Euro: Per person 5.16 - 8.78; child 1-4 yrs free - 4.13, 5-10 yrs free - 6.20; pitch with electricity 9.81 - 16.63; pitch with water and drainage also 10.85 - 17.56.
>
> **Reservations:** Recommended for July/Aug. and made Sat. to Sat. only, with large deposit and fee. Address: Viale della Laguna 16, 30020 Bibione Pineda (VE). Tel: 0431/438351. E-mail: capalonga@bibionemare.com.

6015 Camping Residence II Tridente, Bibione Pineda, Bibione

Natural woodland site on Adriatic, with Residence and excellent facilities.
This is an unusual site as only half the area is used for camping. Formerly a holiday centre for deprived children, it occupies a strip of woodland 200 m. wide and 400 m. long stretching from the main road to the sea. It is divided into two parts by an apartment block of first class rooms with air conditioning and full cooking and bathroom facilities which are for hire. The 250 tourist pitches are located amongst tall pines in the area between the entrance and the Residence. Pitch size varies according to the positions of the trees, but they are of sufficient size and have 4A electrical connections. The ground slopes gently from the main building to the beach of fine sand and this is used as the recreational area with two swimming pools - one 25 x 12½ m. and a smaller children's pool - tennis courts, table tennis and sitting and play places. The three sanitary blocks, two in the main camping area and one near the sea, are of excellent quality. All have similar facilities: mixed British and Turkish style WCs in cabins with washbasins, good showers, with free hot water throughout and facilities for disabled people. The Residence includes an excellent restaurant, bar and well stocked supermarket. An animation programme includes activities for children in high season. Boats may be kept at the quay on the sister site, Capalonga (no. 6010), about 1 km. away. With thick woodland on both sides, Il Tridente is a quiet, restful site with excellent facilities.

> **How to find it:** From A4 Venice - Trieste autostrada, take Latisana exit and follow signs to Bibione and then Bibione Pineda and camp signs.
>
> **General Details:** Open Easter - 30 Sept. 54,500 sq.m. Restaurant. Bar. Supermarket. Swimming pools. Children's playground. Tennis. Table tennis. Mini-football. Volleyball. Animation. Washing machines and dryers. Chemical disposal. Motorcaravan services. Caravans and wooden chalets for hire.
>
> **Charges 2000:** Four charging seasons. Per person L.10,000 - 16,000; child 1-4 yrs free - 8,000, 5-10 yrs free - 10,000; pitch 19,000 - 30,000; extra car 4,000 - 8,000. VAT included.
> Euro: Per person 5.16 - 8.26; child 1-4 yrs free - 4.13, 5-10 yrs free - 5.16; pitch 9.81 - 15.49.
>
> **Reservations:** are made; contact site for details. Address: via Baseleghe 12, 30020 Bibione Pineda. Tel: 0431/439600 (winter: 0431/438351). FAX: 0431/439193. E-mail: tridente@bibionemare.com.

6265 Villagio Turistico Camping Ideal Molino, San Felice, Salô, nr Brescia

Small Garda lakeside site with a garden-like atmosphere.

Molino is a small site with charm and character, which may appeal to those who do not like the larger and more ordered sites. A friendly family atmosphere is being maintained in the site by the daughter of the original site owners. Ingeborg is delightful and speaks perfect English. The family house, of which the charming restaurant is part, has a huge water wheel constantly turning, which was used to crush the olives from the local area. This explains the name of the campsite and the old mill equipment can still be sighted under the house although it is now disconnected. The site is mainly on fairly level ground along the lake with a hill rising quite sharply behind. It is in two main parts divided by the camp buildings, and pitches vary in character: some by the lake, some for tents on terraces, and many in rows with pergolas, flowering shrubs etc. The size of the individual plots has been increased and, although charges are not low, this attractive site should appeal to the discriminating. Caravan and some tent pitches have electricity (3A), water and drainage connections. Pitches can be reserved and in high season this is most advisable. There is a pleasant stony beach at one end; elsewhere one steps straight down into shallow water. The cleanliness of the Garda lake has been much improved by recent measures. Boats can be brought to the site and there is a floating pontoon for sunbathing, diving, boat landing. While all facilities are of good standard they are being continually updated. One of the three small sanitary blocks has been rebuilt to a very high standard and the other two are very clean. They have British style WCs, individual washbasins with free hot water and free hot showers. The site does not like radios or TVs, or any noise after 11 p.m.

How to find it: From Desenzano at southerly end of lake Garda follow S572 north towards Salô. Turn off towards lake, following signs for San Felice. Then follow yellow signs bearing camp name. Site is about 4 km. outside Salô.

General Details: Open 23 March - 30 Sept. 20,000 sq.m. Well shaded. Electricity, water and drainage connections. Shop. Restaurant/bar. Bicycle hire. Table tennis. Fishing. Water ski-ing. Free organised entertainment. Boat excursions to markets in lakeside towns. Laundry. Chemical disposal. Very well equipped bungalows for hire. No dogs accepted.

Charges 1999: Per unit incl. electricity L. 14,900 - 22,700; adult 7,400 - 11,700; child (2-9) 6,100 - 9,100; extra car 8,000 - 10,000; extra m/cycle 4,000 - 5,000; no credit cards.

Reservations: made for min 7 days from February onwards with fee and deposit; write to site. Address: via Gardiola 1, 25010 San Felice del Benaco (Brescia). Tel: 0365/62023. FAX: 0365/559395.

6270 Villaggio Turistico Camping La Gardiola, San Felice, Salo, nr Brescia

Very small, uncomplicated site with access to beach across a minor road.

If you have a large unit this site is a challenge in terms of gaining access along the long, narrow and winding beach-side access road. This applies especially on Sundays when the locals take to the beach and leave their cars parked with impunity. On arrival you discover that the site is very small, having only 40 pitches with 23 for tourers and, to save space has an innovative, small underground sanitary block with a stair lift for disabled campers. The facilities within this sanitary block are quite adequate and there is free hot water throughout. The pitches are terraced with some shading and all have electrical connections. Access to some can be interesting for large units. The shingle beach is reached across the narrow service-street. The views are stunning across the lake and the almost family atmosphere, and friendly owners give the site a very homely feel. English is spoken. However, the tiny bar only provides drinks and snacks and shopping must be done in the nearby shops or the town of San Felice. Therefore, if you enjoy small sites with an uncomplicated atmosphere and wish to mix with the locals then this could be for you but you must make a reservation with a booking fee in high season.

How to find it: Near San Felice on SS572 Salo - San Felice road, the site is well signed at San Felice.

General Details: Open 10 April - 30 Sept. 9,000 sq. m. Electrical connections on all pitches. Small kiosk on site with restaurants, shops, pizzerias, etc. nearby. Children's playground. Fishing. Chemical disposal. Caravans to rent (10).

Charges 1999: Per unit incl. electricity L. 18,000 - 31,000; adult 6,000 - 10,500; child (1-6 yrs) and over 60s 5,000 - 9,000; dog 3,000 - 6,000; extra car or m/cycle 4,500 - 6,000; VAT included.

Reservations: Contact site. Address: Via Vallone della Selva 10, 25010 San Felice del Benaco (Brescia). Tel: 0365/43712. FAX: 0365/42196.

6275 Fornella Camping, San Felice, Salo, nr Brescia

Good site with pool and access to Lake Garda.

Garda is not only the largest Italian lake, it is also one of the most beautiful and being sheltered in the north by the Dolomites enjoys a very mild climate. It is also central for exploring the many historical, architectural, artistic and cultural gems of northern Italy. Fornella Camping is another of the good sites in this region where one is spoilt for choice. The site is the sister site of Fontanelle (no. 6277) and of similar high standards. This open site is surrounded by olive and other trees with a backdrop of mountains and good views. Although there is access to the lake, this cannot be seen from all parts of the site as a tree covered hill intervenes. Of the 300 marked and numbered pitches, some 25% are used by tour operators. They are separated by access roads on flat grass and terraced where necessary, all with electricity. Mobile homes and bungalows available for renting are on the edges of the tourist site and do not intrude. Many pitches are shaded by young trees. The well appointed bar/restaurant and the shop are by the lake side with a terrace giving splendid views over the lake. The lakeside area and private beach is pebbled and pleasant. There is a pizzeria and takeaway service at certain times. The pool and children's pool are of good size and situated on the side of the site. Being well away from the main road, this is a quiet, peaceful camp. Three modern sanitary blocks are well dispersed around the site with mainly British type WCs and free hot water in washbasins (some in private cabins), showers and sinks. Facilities for disabled people. The friendly management speak excellent English.

How to find it: From main SS572 Desenzano-Salo road on the west side of the lake, head for San Felice and follow signs.

General Details: Open 1 May - 30 Sept. 70,000 sq.m. Bar/restaurant. Pizzeria and takeaway. Shop. Swimming pool. Tennis. Table tennis. Volleyball. Two children's playgrounds. Beach. Fishing. Animation for children in season. Bicycle hire 4 km. Riding 10 km. Golf 8 km. Washing machines, dryer and irons. Chemical disposal. Motorcaravan service point.

Charges 1999: Lakeside zone in brackets. Per person L. 7,500 - 11,000 (13,500); child (3-9 yrs) 6,500 - 9,000 (11,000); pitch incl. electricity (3A) 17,000 - 22.000 (26,000); extra car 7,500 - 8,500; boat, trailer 7,500 - 8,500; dog 7,500 - 8,000. Less 20% for 2 week stays in low season. No credit cards.

Reservations: Made with deposit and fee; contact site for details. Address: Via Fornella 1, 25010 San Felice del Benaco (BS). Tel: 0365/62294. FAX: 0365/559418. (Winter: tel/fax: 0365/62200). E-mail: fornella@fornella.it.

ITALY - North West

6277 Camping Fontanelle, Moniga del Garda

Good site on shores of Lake Garda with swimming pools.

Camping Fontanelle is a sister site to Fornella (no. 6275), and is near the historic village of Moniga and enjoys excellent views across the lake. The manager, Vanessa hails from Woking and gives a warm welcome. The site sits on the south-western slopes of the lake and has 200 pitches on flat and terraced ground. Approximately 25% of these are given over to tour operators but there is little impingement. All are marked and have electrical connections and there are some lakeside pitches (extra cost). Some for tents and tourers are very secluded but are distant from the campsite facilities, although small WC blocks are close by. The two main sanitary blocks are modern and clean, and offer free hot water throughout. There are facilities for disabled campers in these two blocks, plus modern washing machines and dryers. The swimming pools are in excellent order, one for adults with the children's pool alongside with a lifeguard at all times. The lakeside pitches have an access to the beach through gates in the fence. As this is a public area there is no lifeguard, although the local equivalent to the RNLI is active on the lake. We are told there is no problem with security here although the public gain access to the beach along fenced paths through the site. The site has an excellent restaurant/pizzeria where the flamboyant owner Fausto will prepare amazing pizzas (he was seventh in the world pizza making championship recently!) The attractive restaurant/bar is extremely popular. The children's play area was muddy when seen but we were told this is to be refurbished soon, there is live entertainment for adults and animation for children in season.

How to find it: From A4 or E 70 Milano/Verona road travel north on the west side of the lake to Moniga - the site is well signed.

General Details: Open 1 May - 19 September. Restaurant/bar. Shop. Swimming pools. Children's play area. Table-tennis. Tennis. TV room. Electronic games. Animation and live entertainment in season. Washing machines and dryers. Chemical disposal. Motorcaravan services.

Charges 1999: Lakeside zone in brackets. Per unit incl. electricity L. 17,000 - 22,000 (25,000); adult 7,500 - 11,000 (13,000); child (3-9 yrs) 6,500 - 9,000 (10,000); extra car 6,500 - 8,000; extra m/cycle 4,000 - 5,000; boat 7,500 - 8,000; dog 15,000 - 20,000. No credit cards.

Reservations: made for min 7 days from Feb. onwards with fee and deposit; write to site. Address: Via Magone 13, 25080 Moniga del Garda (BS). Tel: 0365/502079. FAX: 0365/503324 (when closed Tel/Fax 0365/559443).

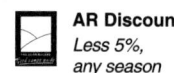

AR Discount
Less 5%,
any season

6235 Camping Monte Brione, Riva del Garda

Municipal site under new management at northern end of Lake Garda

The small resort of Riva at the head of Lake Garda shelters under a rocky escarpment and from ancient times has been an important communication and trading centre on the route between Verona and the Alps. Although it lacks the sophistication of the southern end of the lake, today it is a picturesque tourist resort and recognised as one of the European windsurfing Meccas due to a combination of strong winds with flat water. Thus, this end of the lake tends to have a younger clientele and there is a late night vibrancy which follows a day spent speeding across the lake amongst fellow windsurfers. This site is the only one to offer a swimming pool although it is possible to swim in the lake. Camping Monte Brione is situated on the edge of town at the foot of an olive covered hill, about 500 m. from the town centre and lake side. There are 99 pitches on flat, well mown grass, marked by trees and posts in groups of 4 around a water and electricity (6A) service point. Unmarked terraces on the hillside take 21 tents. Good tarmac roads dissect the site which has a neat, well tended air. Although near residential developments, there are good views of the mountains. Two sanitary blocks, which will be due for refurbishment soon, are at either end of the site and have mixed Turkish and British style WCs, free hot water in washbasins (private cabins), good sized showers and sinks and facilities for disabled people. Shop for basic supplies, snack bar, bar and covered terrace. Good sized swimming pool with a sunbathing area. Limited entertainment and animation in high season and two children's play areas. The town has many shops and restaurants and is popular with the young windsurfers.

How to find it: Leave A22 at Garda-Nord exit for Torbole and Riva. Just before Riva, through short tunnel, then turn right at camp signs.

General Details: Open Easter - early Oct. 33,000 sq.m. Electricity in all parts. Bar with terrace. Shop for basics. Snack bar. Swimming pool (1/6-30/9). Minigolf. Table tennis. Bowls. TV/video. Bicycle hire. Organised activities. Fishing 1 km. Riding 3 km. Sailing, boating and tennis near (reduced rates for campers). Chemical disposal. Motorcaravan services.

Charges 1999: Per person L. 12,500; child (3-12 yrs) 8,300; pitch 18,500; dog 6,200. Credit cards accepted.

Reservations: Write to site with 20% deposit (refundable) of anticipated bill. Address: Via Brione 32, 38066 Riva del Garda (TN). Tel: 0464/520885 or 520890. FAX: 0464/553178.

6230 Camping San Cristoforo, Pergine Valsugana, nr Trento

Quiet, mountain site near lake, with views and swimming pool.
This part of Italy is becoming better known by those wishing to spend time by a lake in splendid countryside, but away from the more crowded, better-known resorts. Lake Caldonazzo is one of the smaller
lakes, but is excellent for watersports, with lifeguards on duty in the season. Camping San Cristoforo is a
relatively new site on the edge of the small town of the same name and is separated from the lake by a
minor road, but with easy access. Owned by the friendly Oss family whose policy is to get to know their
guests and build a family atmosphere, the site has 160 pitches on flat grass on either side of hard access
roads. The pitches are of a good size, numbered in front, separated by trees and with 3A electricity. The
modern sanitary block has British style WCs, free hot water in the basins (some cabins) and showers controlled by a single tap; there are footbaths, sinks with free hot water for dishwashing and laundry and facilities for disabled people. The lake is very close offering watersports and fishing - we sighted several large
trout during our visit! There is a swimming pool (20 x 20 m.) with sunbathing area and small children's
pool. The attractive restaurant by the pool has a terrace and serves reasonably priced food. Village shops
are close, and the site has a quiet and well cared for air. English is spoken. Used by a tour operator.

How to find it: Site is southeast of Trento, just off the SS47 road; well signed from the village of San Cristoforo.

General Details: Open 25 May - 15 Sept. Electrical connections throughout. Small well stocked shop.
Bar/restaurant (all year) with waiter service and takeaway. Swimming pool and child's pool. Bicycle hire.
Minigolf. Fishing and boating 200 m. Riding 5 km. Golf 2 km. Washing machine and dryer. Chemical disposal.

Charges 1999: Per person L. 10,000 - 12,500; child 2-5 yrs 6,000 - 8,000, 6-11 yrs 7,000 - 10,000; pitch 16,000
- 17,000; extra car free - 6,000; dog 6,000. Discounts for longer stays in low season.

Reservations: Not accepted. Address: Loc. San Cristoforo, 38057 Pergine Valsugana (TN). Tel: 0461/706290.
FAX: 0461/707381.

6225 Camping Due Laghi, Levico Terme, nr Trento

Good modern site with swimming pool and mountain views, close to lake and spa town.
This modern site is close to the main road but is quiet and only 5 minutes walk from the Levico lake where
it has a small attractive private beach where one can put boats. There are 426 numbered pitches on flat
grass, in rows marked by slabs. Most are said to be approx. 80 sq.m. but there are now 60 larger pitches
(90 sq.m) with electricity, water, TV and phone connections. On site is a good swimming pool of over 300
sq.m. with a children's pool also. It is therefore suitable for a stay as well as overnight. It is said to become
full from 15/7 - 15/8 but there is always a chance of finding space. The central toilet block is both of good
quality and very large, with British and Turkish type WCs, washbasins with free hot water (some in cubicles), free screened showers with pre-set hot water and a unit for disabled people. Some private WCs may
be hired. This is a most attractive site with a variety of trees and flowers. The site supplies a comprehensive descriptive guide to the attractions of the region. English is spoken.

How to find it: Site is 20 km. southeast of Trento just off S47 road towards Padova (camp sign at turning).

General Details: Open 25 May - 15 Sept. Electrical connections (3/6A) in all parts. Shop. Sauna. Restaurant,
pizzeria and cafe/bar, with takeaway. Music weekly in high season. Children's playground. Tennis. Bicycle hire.
Fishing 500 m. Riding 2 km. Golf 5 km. Laundry. Gas supplies. Chemical disposal. Motorcaravan services.

Charges 1999: Per person L. 10,000 - 12,500; child 2-5 yrs 6,000 - 8,000, 6-11 yrs 7,000 - 10,000; pitch 14,000
- 21,000 acc. to size and facilities; extra car free - 6,000. Club card for entertainment, activities, etc. obligatory in
July/Aug. L. 10,000 per pitch/family. Discounts for longer stays in low season. No credit cards.

Reservations: made for at least 1 week in peak season, with substantial deposit and fee. Address: Loc. Costa 3,
38056 Levico Terme (Trento). Tel: 0461/706290. FAX: 0461/707381. A 'Camping Cheques' site.

6205 International Camping Dolomiti, Cortina d'Ampezzo

Family run site in mountain setting beside famous resort.
The Cortina region boasts several good sites and this is one of the nearest to the town. It is a grassy site
beside a fast flowing river in a broad flat area which is surrounded by mountain scenery – a quiet situation 3 km. from the town centre. The 390 good sized pitches are marked out by white stones on either sides
of access roads and most have electricity (4A). Half the site is well shaded. There is a heated swimming
pool on site. It makes a good centre for touring the Dolomites or for more active pursuits such as mountain walking. The main toilet block is large with Turkish style WCs, with some British, washbasins with
hot water sprinkler taps, and free controllable hot showers. A heated block has been added which has facilities for disabled visitors. With no reservations made, arrive early in the first three weeks of August.

How to find it: Site is south of Cortina, to west of main S51. There are signs from the road.

General Details: Open 15 May - 20 Sept. Small shop (open long hours) and coffee bar. Swimming pool (1/7-
31/8). Restaurant 600 m. Basic children's playground (hard base). Fishing 1 km. Bicycle hire or riding 3 km. Golf
2 km. Washing machines and ironing. Gas supplies. Chemical disposal.

Charges 1999: Per person L. 7,000 - 13,000; child (under 6) 5,000 - 8,000; pitch 11,000 - 17,000. No credit cards.
Reservations: Not made. Address: 32043 Cortina d'Ampezzo. Tel: 0436/2485. FAX: 0436/5403.

6210 Camping Steiner, Leifers/Laives, nr Bozen/Bolzano

Site with swimming pools and good facilities in central Dolomites, south of Bolzano.

Being on the main S12 which now has a motorway alternative, Camping Steiner is very central for touring with the whole of the Dolomite region within easy reach, as well as Bolzano, Merano and other attractive places. It has its share of overnight trade but is also a camp with much activity where one can spend an enjoyable holiday. It is a smallish site with part taken up by bungalows and the tourist pitches, mostly with good shade, are in rows on either side of access roads. They are all individual, most on hardstandings. The two sanitary blocks can be heated and have free hot water in washbasins, sinks and showers and British style WCs. The site is run personally by the proprietor's friendly family who speak good English. There are two swimming pools – one open air, 20 x 10 m. (May-Sept. and heated in spring), and a 12 x 6 m. enclosed pool (except July/Aug). The site has an excellent small restaurant and takeaway.

How to find it: Site is on S12 in northern part of Leifers, 8 km. south of Bolzano. From north on motorway, take Bolzano-Süd exit and follow Trento signs for 7 km; from south take Ora exit and 14 km. towards Bolzano.

General Details: Open 28 March - 7 Nov. 20,000 sq.m. Electrical connections (6A). Shop. Small restaurant, pizzeria and takeaway. Cellar bar with taped music, dancing at times. Swimming pools. General room. Children's playground and paddling pool. Table tennis. Chemical disposal. Wooden bungalows and hotel rooms for rent.

Charges 2000: Per person L. 8,000 - 10,000; child (0-6 yrs) 5,000 - 7,000; pitch incl. car and 6A electricity 18,000 - 24,000; dog 8,000; extra car 6,000. Less 5-10% after 2 weeks stay. No credit cards.

Reservations: Made for min. one week with reasonable deposit. Address: 39055 Laives (Bolzano). Tel: 0471/95 01 05. FAX: 0471/95 15 72. E-mail: steiner@dnet.it.

6200 Camping Olympia, Toblach/Dobbiaco

Dolomite Mountains site on main route with excellent facilities.

Olympia, always good, has been given a face-lift by the redesigning of the camping area and the refurbishment of the already excellent sanitary accommodation. Tall trees at each end of the site have been left, but most of those in the centre have been removed and the pitches re-laid in a regular pattern. They include 12 fully serviced with electricity, water, waste, gas and TV and phone points. Static caravans are grouped at one end leaving the centre for tourists and with a grass area at the other end for tents. The excellent sanitary provision, on two levels, is housed in the main building which also has reception, restaurant, shop and apartments. Of a very high standard, there are seven cabins with WC, washbasin and shower to rent. British style WCs and free hot water in washbasins (not in cabins but separated) showers and sinks. Two small blocks have WCs and showers. The attractive restaurant is open all day, all year, and opposite is a snack bar which also offers grill meals in high season and drinks and ices at all times. On the far side of the site, where campers can walk amidst the woods, is a little children's play area and a few animals.The small swimming pool (10 x 6 m) is open when weather permits.

How to find it: Site is between Villabassa and Toblach/Dobbiaco. From A22 Innsbruck-Bolzano autostrada, take Bressanone/Brixen exit and east on SS49 for 60 km. From Cortina SS48 and SS51 northwards then west on SS49.

General Details: Open all year. 45,000 sq.m. Restaurant. Shop. Snack bar with grill meals (not April/May or Oct/Nov). Tennis. Swimming pool. Sauna, solarium, steam bath and whirl pools. Field for games. Table tennis. Minigolf. Fishing (on payment). Bicycle hire. Children's play area. Animation programme in high season.

Charges 1999: Per person L. 12,000 - 13,000; child (3-10 yrs) 7,000 - 10,000; pitch 16,000 - 20,000; m/cycle 3,000; car 5,000 - 6,000; small tent 5,000 - 9,000.

Reservations: Write to site. Address: 39034 Toblach (Sudtirol). Tel: 0474/972147. FAX: 0474/972713. E-mail: intercamp@dnet.it.

6201 Camping Antholz, Antholz-Obertal

All year campsite in the heart of the Dolomites.

Appearances can be deceptive and this is the case with Camping Antholz. At first sight the 130 pitches (with 4A electricity), numbered, but only roughly marked out, make this a very ordinary looking site. Just inside the entrance is a pleasant looking building with reception and a smart restaurant. It is when one investigates the sanitary accommodation that one realises that this is no ordinary site, as the provision is quite superb, with under-floor heating, hair salon, cosmetics room, baby room, British style WCs and free hot water in washbasins, sinks and showers. High up in the Anterselva valley, there are splendid views of the peaks. The shop has limited supplies (village 500 m), the bar is open all day and the restaurant opens 18-22.00 hrs. This is good skiing country in winter (ski bus, ski school, ski lifts) and, with a National Park near, provides good walking in summer. Limited entertainment for children is offered in high season.

How to find it: From Bressanone exit on A22, go east on SS49 through Brunico and turn north (signed Antholz) for about 12 km. Pass Antholz village and site is on right.

General Details: Open all year. 25,000 sq.m. Restaurant (all year). Shop. Children's playground. TV room. Table tennis. Bicycle hire. Winter sports, summer walking. Washing machine and dryer. Motorcaravan services.

Charges 1999: Per unit incl. 2 persons and electricity L. 33,500 - 36,500; extra person 8,500 - 9,500; child (2-12 yrs) 6,500 - 7,500; small tent 4,500 - 5,000.

Reservations: Write to site. Address: 39030 Antholz-Obertal (BZ). Tel: 0474/492204. FAX: 0474/492444.

6000 Camping Marepineta, Sistiana, nr Trieste

Site west of Trieste with good swimming pool and sea views over Baia di Sistiana.

This site is 18 km. west of Trieste, and lies on raised ground near the sea, with views over the Sistiana Bay, Miramare Castle and the Gulf of Trieste. A pebbly beach, with car park, is about 1 km. (free bus service). Alternatively there is a large pool (unheated), on site with a terrace. Over 350 of the 500 pitches are for tourists. They are on gravel hardstandings (awnings possible) in light woodland, all with electricity (from 3A) and water nearby. No dogs or animals are allowed except in a designated area. There are six toilet blocks of varying quality, some recently modernised. They provide hot water in washbasins, with some for children and others in private cabins, and free showers. WCs of both British and Turkish style, there are facilities for disabled people and sinks for laundry and dishwashing, most with hot water. For arrivals outside office hours, a waiting area has water and toilet facilities. Used by a tour operator. It is reported that a weekend disco on the beach below the site involves noisy departures at 3 am.

How to find it: From west on A4 autostrada take Duino exit, turn left and site is 1 km; from east use S14.

General Details: Open 1 May - 30 Sept. Shop (15/5-15/9). Bars. Pizzeria. Disco. Swimming pool (1/6-15/9) with lessons. Children's playground. Football, volleyball and mini-basket. Tennis. Table tennis. Games room. Organised entertainment in season. Fishing 1 km. Bicycle hire 500 m. Riding 2 km. Golf 10 km. First aid post. Laundry with dryer and iron. Chemical disposal. New mobile homes for hire.

Charges 1999: Per pitch incl. electricity and water L. 13,000, 18,000 or 25,000, pitch with view of the bay 18,000, 22,000 or 32,000; person 6,000, 8,000 or 10,500; child (3-12 yrs) 4,000, 6,000 or 8,000. No credit cards.

Reservations: Will be made with 40% deposit and L 30.000 fee. Address: 34019 Sistiana 60/D, Duino-Aurisina (TS). Tel: 040/299264. FAX: 040/299265.

6005 Villaggio Turistico Camping Europa, Grado, nr Trieste

Large seaside site with swimming pools and other amenities.

This large flat site on the edge of the sea can take over 600 units. All pitches are marked, nearly all with good shade and there are electrical connections (4A) in all parts. The terrain is undulating and sandy in the areas nearer the sea, where cars have to be left in parking places. Dogs are taken in a special section. There is direct access to the beach but the water is shallow up to 200 m. from beach, with growing sea-weed. However, a narrow wooden jetty stretches out so one can walk along to deeper water. For those who prefer, there is a swimming pool near the sea and, on the site, a medium sized heated pool and smaller children's pool. The six toilet blocks should make up a good supply, with free hot water in all facilities, half British WCs and hot showers, as well as many washing sinks and facilities for disabled people. Not a super site perhaps, but a good honest one which, after improvements, is probably the best in the area.

How to find it: Site lies 4 km. east of Grado on road to Monfalcone. If road 35L is taken to Grado from west, continue through the town to Grado Pineta.

General Details: Open 10 April - 20 Sept. Large supermarket; small general shop (May - Sept). Large bar and self-service restaurant, with takeaway (all season). Swimming pools (May - Sept). Tennis courts. Football. Table tennis. Fishing. Bicycle hire. Children's playground. Dancing, at times, in season; organised activities July/Aug. Washing machines. Chemical disposal. Motorcaravan services. Good bungalows for hire, also some caravans.

Charges 1999: Per person L. 10,000 -15,000; child (3-10 yrs) free - 10,000; pitch incl. electricity 15,000 - 35,000, acc. to season and location. Less 10% for longer stays out of season.

Reservations: made for min. 1 week from Sat. to Sat., with deposit in high season (50% of total). Address: PO Box 129, 34073 Grado (Gorizia). Tel: 0431/80877. FAX: 0431/82284.

6037 Campeggio Giuliana Bungalow, Ca'Ballarin, Cavallino

Small site, open all year.

This camp is unique in this area in two respects, firstly it is open all year and, secondly it is 500 m. from the sea and not directly by the shore. 40 bungalows and 4 caravans (for hire) are along each side of the square shaped camp with space in the centre, under vines, for 20 units. Pitches, mainly on sand, are not marked or numbered but the resident owner tells campers where to stay. Small sanitary units have British style WCs and free hot water in basins, showers and sinks. The restaurant `Anna` is open during the summer season but, being in the village, shops and other restaurants are very close. There is musical enter-tainment in the restaurant twice weekly. Venice is a 40 minute bus/boat ride away, Lido di Jesolo about 25 minutes. The beach is some 500 m. and involves crossing a main road. Sports facilities are near. The friendly owner speaks good English and will help with information on the locality.

How to find it: From A4 Venice-Trieste autostrada take airport exit. At airport continue on SS14, follow signs for Jesolo, then Punta Sabbioni and site is at restaurant Anna in the village of Ca'Ballarin.

General Details: Open all year. Restaurant (summer only), others and shops near. Small play area. Bicycle hire. Riding and golf 1 km. Fishing 5 km. Motorcaravan services. Bungalows for hire.

Charges 1999: Per person L. 9,000 - 12,500; child under 2 free; tent and car 12,000 - 15,000; caravan and car 14,000 - 18,000. No credit cards.

Reservations: Write to site. Address: via Rialto 13, Ca'Ballarin, 30013 Cavallino (VE). Tel: 041/968039. FAX: 041/5370443. E-mail: campgiul@iol.it.

ITALY - North East

6020 Camping Union Lido Vacanze, Cavallino, Jesolo, nr Venice/Venezia

6010 Camping Capalonga, Bibione Pineda, Bibione, nr Venice/Venezia

6015 Camping Residence Il Tridente, Bibione Pineda, Bibione

These sites appear out of order on pages 128 and 129, opposite their colour advertisements.

6035 Camping Mediterraneo, Treporti, Jesolo, nr Venice/Venezia

Large site with a wide range of amenities including large swimming pools.

This big site has been considerably improved in recent years and is near Punta Sabbioni from where boats go to Venice. Mediterraneo is directly on the Adriatic Sea with a 480 m. long beach of fine sand which shelves gently and also two large pools (one for adults, the other for children) and a whirlpool. Sporting, fitness and entertainment programmes are arranged and sea swimming is supervised at designated hours by lifeguards. The 750 touring pitches, of which 500 have electricity (from 4A), water and drainaway, are partly in boxes with artificial shade, some larger without shade, with others in unmarked zones under natural woodland equipped with electric hook ups where tents must go. The eight modern sanitary blocks are good quality with British type WCs and free hot water in the washbasins, showers and sinks. The commercial centre near reception has a supermarket and other shops with a restaurant, bars and a pizzeria near the pools. Used by tour operators (145 pitches). This is an organised and efficient site.

How to find it: Site is well signed from Jesolo-Punta Sabbioni road near its end after Ca' Ballerin and before Ca' Savio. Follow camp signs, not those for Treporti as this village is some way from the site.

General Details: Open 1 May - 30 Sept. 170,000 sq.m. Shop. Large bar and snack bar by pool; full restaurant elsewhere. New playground and tennis court. Minigolf. Table tennis. Bicycle hire. Surf and swimming school. Regular monthly programme of sports, organised games, excursions etc; dancing or shows 3 times weekly in main season. Fitness programme. Riding and golf 3 km. Refrigerator hire. Washing machines. Chemical disposal. Motorcaravan services.

Charges 2000: Four rates. Per person L. 6,000 - 13,800; child (3-5 yrs) or senior (over 60 yrs) 4,300 - 11,000; pitch with electricity 11,800 - 27,700; pitch with 3 services 13,000 - 33,400; tent pitch with electricity 9,000 - 24,900. VAT included. Credit cards accepted.

Reservations: made with large deposit. Address: 30010 Cavallino-Treporti (VE). Tel: 041/966721 or 22. FAX: 041/966944. E-mail: med.camp@flashnet.it.

6025 Camping Residence, Cavallino, nr Venice/Venezia

see colour advert between pages 128/129

Pleasant, well run site by beach with first class, clean installations.

The Litorale del Cavallino has a large number of excellent sites, giving a good choice for those wishing to visit and stay in this area near Venice. Camping Residence is a very good site with a sandy beach directly on the Adriatic and is well kept, with many floral displays. Pitches are marked out with small fences or pines, which give good shade, and are laid out in regular rows on level sand. They vary in size with those for caravans larger than those for tents and all have electricity connections (6A). A medium size site (for this region) of 300 tourist pitches, it is smaller than 6020 but has the same strict rules regarding noise (no radios or dogs, quiet periods and no unaccompanied under 18s) but is less formal and more personal. The beach fronting has been enlarged and improved and the sea bed shelves gradually making it safe for children. Excellent swimming pools and sunbathing areas have been added and there is a good animation programme in high season for both children and adults. Venice can be easily reached by bus to Punta Sabbioni and ferry across the lagoon and there are organised excursions to places of interest. The three large sanitary blocks are very clean with full facilities including free hot water in basins, sinks and showers with British style WCs. Although of good quality, they are being refurbished.

How to find it: From the A4 Venice-Trieste autostrada leave at exit for Airport or Quarto D'Altino, follow signs for Jesolo and then Punta Sabbioni. Take first left after Cavallino and camp is about 800 m. on right hand side (well signed).

General Details: Open 24 March - 15 Sept. 70,000 sq m. Supermarket, separate shops for fruit and other goods. Well appointed restaurant with separate bar. Takeaway. Children's playground. swimming pools. Dancing or disco by beach until 11 pm three times weekly June-August and entertainment programme. Fitness programme. Boat moorings for hire at nearby marina. Ladies hairdresser. Car wash. Table tennis. Small tennis court. Video games room. Post office. Bureau de change. Minigolf. Doctor will call. Chemical disposal. Modern apartments for four, bungalows and maxi-caravans for hire. No dogs accepted.

Charges 1999: Per person L. 6,400 - 12,600; child (under 5 yrs) 4,100 - 9,700; pitch 13,500 - 29,200; extra car 3,200 - 7,500.

Reservations: Made for min. 1 week with L. 150,000 deposit. Address: via F.Baracca 47, 30013 Cavallino (Venezia). Tel: 041/968027 or 968127. FAX: 041/5370164.

6040 Camping Village Garden Paradiso, Cavallino, Jesolo, nr Venice

Very good medium size, seaside site with swimming pools.

There are many sites in this area and there is much competition in providing a range of facilities. Garden Paradiso has built three excellent swimming pools in the centre of the site near the restaurant and shopping complex. Compared with other sites here, this one is of medium size with 835 pitches. Most have electricity (from 6A), water and drainage points and all are marked and numbered with hard access roads, under a good cover of trees. Flowers and shrubs abound giving a pleasant and peaceful appearance. The site is directly on the sea with a beach of fine sand. There are four brick, tiled sanitary blocks around the site with a mix of British and Turkish style WCs, free hot water in the basins, showers and sinks, and facilities for babies. The restaurant, with self-service at lunch time and waiter service at night, is near the beach with a bar/snack bar in the centre of the site. Entertainment, animation and excursions are organised. Used by tour operators (35 pitches).

How to find it: Leave Venice-Trieste autostrada either by taking the airport or Quarto d'Altino exits; follow signs to Jesolo Punta Sabbioni. Take the first road on the left after Cavallino and site is a little way on the right.

General Details: Open 1 April - 30 Sept. 13,000 sq.m. Restaurant (22/4-28/9). Snack bar. Shops. Tennis. Table tennis. Minigolf. Swimming pools. Organised entertainment and excursions. Bicycle hire. Fishing 2.5 km. Riding 2 km. Children's play area. Washing machines and dryers. Chemical disposal. Motorcaravan services. Caravans and maxi-caravans for hire.

Charges 1999: Per person L. 5,500 - 12,900; junior (1-6 yrs) or senior (over 60 yrs) 3,800 - 10,100; pitch 12,000 - 31,000. Less 10% for stays over 30 days (early) 20 days (late) season. Credit cards accepted.

Reservations: Made with deposit (L. 250,000 - 300,000) - write to site for details. Address: 30013 Cavallino (VE). Tel: 041/968075. FAX: 041/5370382. E-mail: garden@vacanze-natura.com.

6030 Camping dei Fiori, Treporti, Lido del Cavallino, nr Venice

Excellent small site with swimming pools and special hydromassage pools.

The peninsula Lido del Cavallino, stretching from the outskirts of Lido del Jessolo to Punta Sabbioni, has almost 40 good camps directly on the Adriactic sea and convenient for visiting Venice and other interesting places in northeast Italy. Dei Fiori stands out amongst the other small camps in the area. As its name implies, it is aflame with colourful flowers and shrubs in summer and presents a neat and tidy appearance whilst providing a quiet atmosphere. About a quarter of the pitches are taken by static units, many for hire. The 420 pitches, with 6A electricity, are either in woodland where space varies according to the trees which have been left in their natural state, or under artificial shade where regular shaped pitches are of reasonable size. Well built bungalows for hire enhance the site and are in no way intrusive, giving a village-like effect. Shops and a restaurant are in the centre next to the swimming pools. Nearby is the hydromassage bath which is splendidly appointed and reputed to be the largest in Italy. This is under the supervision of qualified staff, as is the fitness centre. A charge is made during middle and high seasons but not in low season. The long beach is of fine sand and shelves gently into the sea. The resident animation team offer a daily programme for children and activities for adults which includes games, tournaments and entertainment. Regulations ensure the site is quiet between 11 pm. - 7.30 am. and during the afternoon siesta period. Three sanitary blocks are conveniently situated around the site and are of exceptional quality with heating, British style WCs, well equipped baby rooms, good facilities for disabled people, washing machines and dryers and free hot water in all facilities. Venice is about 40 minutes away by bus and boat and excursions are arranged from the site. The site is well maintained by friendly, English speaking management.

How to find it: Leave A4 Venice-Trieste autostrada either by taking exit for airport or Quarto d'Altino and follow signs for Jesolo and then Punta Sabbioni and camp signs just after Ca'Ballarin.

General Details: Open 5 April - 7 Oct. 10,000 sq.m. Restaurant. Snack bar (1/5-30/9). Shops. Tennis. Table tennis. Minigolf. Basketball. Swimming pools. Children's play area. Children's club. Windsurfing. Fitness centre, hydro-massage bath and programmes (1/5-30/9). Entertainment and excursions. Bicycle hire 2 km. Riding 4 km. Washing machines and dryers. Chemical disposal. Motorcaravan services. Bungalows and caravans for rent. No dogs accepted.

Charges 2000: Four seasons. Per person L. 7,300 - 14,200; child (1-5 yrs) or senior over 60 yrs 5,400 - 13,100; pitch with 3 services 15,000 - 33,500, pinewood pitch with electricity 14,000 - 29,700; tent pitch in pinewood with electricity 11,500 - 27,000. Min. stay 7 days in high season (4/7-29/8). Credit cards accepted.

Reservations: Advised for high season (incl. Whitsun) and made for min. 7 days. Write for application form as early as possible. Address: 30010 Treporti (VE). Tel: 041/966448. FAX: 041/966724. E-mail: fiori.camp@flashnet.it. A 'Camping Cheques' site.

ITALY - North East

6032 Camping Cavallino, Cavallino, nr Venice

Large seaside site with pool and extensive facilities.

This is a well ordered site run by a friendly, experienced family who have other sites in this guide. It lies by the sea with direct access to a superb beach of fine sand, which is very safe and enjoys the cover of several lifeguards. The site is thoughtfully laid out with large numbers of unusually large pitches shaded by olives and pines. All pitches have electricity (4A) and there is a 10% tour operator presence. The swimming pools are close to the restaurant, which has a large terraced area (very lively at night) and offers rapid service and takeaway. The menu is varied and reasonably priced with some excellent shell-fish and pasta dishes. An ambitious animation programme is aimed mostly at younger guests. Clean, modern toilet facilities provide a mixture of Turkish and British style WCs with facilities for disabled campers. Modern washing machines of large capacity are available, free hot water is provided in all facilities and there is constant cleaning activity in the site. A large shop provides most requirements. If you wish to visit Venice a bus service runs to the ferry at Punta Sabbioni, some 20 minutes distance. You then catch an interconnecting ferry which, after a charming journey of 40 minutes, drops you directly at St Marco Square after negotiating its way around the gondolas. A late return will mean a 2 km. walk at the end of a different bus service but the night views of Venice from the sea are wonderful. Be sure to pay independently at the ferry rather than using the supposed cheap 'all-in' tickets which in fact are more expensive.

How to find it: From Venice - Trieste autostrada leave at exit for airport or Quarto and Altino. Follow signs, first for Jesolo and then site signs will be seen just after Cavallino on the left.

General Details: Open 2 April - 10 Oct. Restaurant, bars and pizzeria. Good shop. Swimming pools. Tennis. Table tennis. Minigolf. Children's play area. Bicycle hire. Animation for adults and children, day and evening. Launderette. First aid centre. Motorcaravan services. Chemical disposal. Luxury apartments, bungalows, caravans and mobile homes for hire.

Charges 1999: Per person L. 6,000 - 11,500; child (1-6 yrs) or over 60s 5,000 - 9,500; pitch incl. electricity 15,000 - 33,000. VAT included. Min. stay in high season 1 week. No credit cards.

Reservations: Made for the letting units only, but site provides priority cards for previous visitors. Address: Via delle Batterie164, 30013 Cavallino (Venezia). Tel: 041/966133. FAX. 041/5300827.

6042 Camping Alba d'Oro, Ca,Noghera, Mestre, nr Venice

Well managed site with pool, perfectly sited for visiting Venice.

This site is ideal for visiting Venice and a private bus from the site takes you directly to the bus station on the west side of Venice (L. 2,500). There is always room here and on arrival you select your pitch. There is a separate area for backpackers and yet another for families. Of the 350 pitches, 130 have electricity (5A), they are of good size and easy to manoeuvre into. There is a good sized pool, especially welcome after a hot day spent visiting Venice. Four modern sanitary blocks have free hot water in all facilities and are kept very clean. They have British style WCs, washbasins with shelf and mirror, hot showers, footbaths and sinks for washing dishes and clothes. One block has facilities for disabled campers. The restaurant has a most pleasant terrace which overlooks the swimming pool and the lively bar is part of the same complex. The clientele changes rapidly and is very cosmopolitan, with a young backpacker element but the site is not noisy. The restaurant with its good food at reasonable prices is very busy every night. There is entertainment in season with pool parties and 'happy hours'. The east side of the site is bordered by a canal and if you wish to take your own boat to Venice it can be launched here (max. 2 m. draught) and access to Venice is gained by a charming canal journey. The site is close to the airport and pitches will hear aircraft especially to the east where you have the opportunity to view them from a grassy hill. However, as there is no night flying allowed it is worth staying here to be close to the city rather than driving to the sites in Cavallino and having the resultant long journey into Venice.

How to find it: From Venice-Trieste autostrada leave at exit for airport and follow signs for Jesolo on the SS14. Site is on right at 10 km. marker.

General Details: Open mid April - 5 Nov. Restaurant. Pizzerias. Bars. Tennis. Riding. Windsurfing school in season. Table tennis. Bicycle hire. Launderette. Motorcaravan service points. Chemical disposal. Luxury apartments, bungalows, caravans and mobile homes for rent. No dogs accepted.

Charges 1999: Per person L. 10,500 - 12,500; child (2-10 yrs) 7,000 - 8,000; pitch incl. electricity 17,000 - 19,000; tent 6,000 - 9,000. VAT included. Credit cards not accepted.

Reservations: Contact site. Address: Via Tristina, 30030 Ca,Noghera, Mestre (Venezia). Tel: 0039/0415415102. FAX: as phone.

AR Discount
Less 10%

6050 Camping Caravanning della Serenissima, Oriago, nr Venice/Venezia

Convenient site for overnight stay or for visiting Venice and other places in this region.

This is a delightful little site of some 140 pitches (all with 16A electricity) where one could stay for a number of days whilst visiting Venice (12 km), Padova (24), Verona (24), Lake Garda (135) or the Dolomites. There is a good service by bus and boat to Venice and the site is situated on the Riviera del Brenta, a section of a river with some very large old villas. The site is used mainly by Dutch and British with some Germans, and is calm and quiet. It is long, narrow and flat with numbered pitches on each side of a central road. There is good shade in most parts with many trees, plants and grass. The single sanitary block is just adequate, has been and still is being improved, with free hot water in washbasins, showers and sinks. WCs are mainly Turkish style. The management is very friendly and good English is spoken.

How to find it: From the east take road S11 at roundabout SSW of Mestre towards Padova and site is 2 km. on right. From west, leave autostrada A4 at Dolo exit, follow signs to Dolo, continue on main road through this small village and turn left at T-junction (traffic lights). Continue towards Venice on S11 for site about 6 km on left.

General Details: Open Easter - 10 Nov. Shop (all season). Restaurant and bar (June - Oct). Children's play area. Fishing. Bicycle hire. Golf or riding 3 km. Reduced price bus/boat ticket to Venice if staying for 3 days. No organised entertainment but local markets etc. well publicised. Gas supplies. Chemical disposal. Motorcaravan services. Bungalows and mobile homes to rent.

Charges 2000: Per unit L. 16,000 - 19,000; adult 11,000; child (3-12 yrs) 8,000. Credit cards accepted.

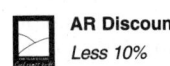

AR Discount
Less 10%

Reservations: are made. Address: 30030 Oriago (Venezia). Tel: 041/921850. FAX: 041/920286. E-mail: camping.serenissima@shineline.it.

CAMPING CARAVANNING DELLA SERENISSIMA
VENEZIA — ORIAGO S.S. 11, Km 412
ph. (041) 921.850

The ideal camping for your holidays in VENICE

Situated along the beautiful Riviera del Brenta, it is continuously linked with the historical centre of VENICE by bus. Modern services and tourist organisation assure you a quiet and comfortable stay.

6055 Villagio Turistico Isamar, S. Anna di Chioggia, nr Venice/Venezia

Seaside site south of Venice with six good swimming pools.

Many improvements have been made here over the years and these continue, making it quite difficult to itemise all the amenities. Although directly by the sea, with its own beach of fine sand, it is a fair way from the entrance to the sea. The largest camping area, which may be cramped at times, is under pines and grouped around the swimming pool, large modern sanitary block, shops, etc. near reception. There is a smaller area under artificial shade near the beach with an Olympic size, salt-water swimming pool, children's pool and four new pools. Here also are a covered entertainment section, pizzeria, bar/restaurant and small toilet block. Between these sections are well constructed bungalows available for rent. A third camping area has been developed mainly for the site's own accommodation. The pitches, on either side of hard access roads, vary in size and all have electrical connections. The site may become crowded in high season. The main toilet blocks are of good quality with British WCs (small block has only Turkish style), and free hot water in washbasins, showers and sinks. An extensive entertainment and fitness programme is offered for adults and there is supervised play for children over 4 years of age, a disco and a games room with pin tables. The site has a much higher proportion of Italian holidaymakers than many other sites and it is also popular with the Germans and Dutch.

How to find it: Turn off main 309 road towards sea just south of Adige river about 10 km. south of Chioggia, and proceed 5 km. to site.

General Details: Open 13 May - 16 Sept. Supermarket and shopping centre. Large bar/pizzeria and self-service restaurant. Tennis. Swimming pools. Children's playground. Disco. Riding. Bicycle hire. Entertainment. Fishing 500 m. Hairdresser. Fridges for hire. Gas supplies. Chemical disposal. Motorcaravan services. No dogs permitted.

Charges 1999: Four rates acc. to season (highest 22/7-19/8): Per person L. 5,000 - 14,500; child (2-5 yrs) 4,000 - 12,500; pitch with full facilities 7,000 - 34,000; tent pitch 5,000 - 15,000. Less 10% for stays over 3 weeks. Credit cards accepted (Visa, Mastercard).

Reservations: made for min. 7 days with deposit from Sat. Address: Isolaverde, 30010 S. Anna di Chioggia (VE). Tel: 041/498100. FAX: 041/490440.

6065 Camping Tahiti, Lido delle Nazioni, nr Ravenna

Superb site with swimming pools and other amenities north of Ravenna.

Tahiti is an excellent, extremely well run site, thoughtfully laid out less than a mile from the sea (the site provides a continuous small fun road train link). Flowers, shrubs, ponds and attractive wooded structures enhance its appearance and, unlike many campsites of this size, it is family owned and run. They have thought of everything here and the manager Stefano is a dynamo who seems to be everywhere, ensuring the impressive standards are maintained. The staff are smart and attentive. As well as the 25 x 12 m. swimming pool, there is a 'Atoll Beach' Caribbean style water-play fun area with palms plus a hydromassage ,bar and terrace (small extra charge for 'wet' activities). There is a large children's playground and you will find additional play areas scattered around the site, with a comprehensive mini-club and baby club complex. Here special staff organise diverse activities. There is a small outdoor theatre for summer entertainment, a hard tennis court and good minigolf. The site has a waiter service restaurant with an extensive menu, bar, pizzeria, large Spar supermarket (with trolleys!) and kiosk. A well equipped and supervised gymnasium is provided for those who wish to keep in trim. The 400 pitches are of varying size, back to back from hard roads and defined by trees with shade in most areas. There are 38 pitches with a private unit containing a WC and washbasin. Electricity (6/10A) is available throughout. One sanitary block has been rebuilt to a very high standard, the two other smaller ones refurbished and nicely decorated with plants and potted shrubs. They have a mix of British and Turkish style WCs and free hot water for washbasins, sinks and showers. The new block can be heated and has a baby room and make-up/hairdressing room. English is spoken by the friendly management, although the British have not yet really discovered this site which is popular with other European campers. The site is very busy in season with much to-ing and fro-ing, but all is always under control and it is relaxing especially for families with children. It is also keen on recycling and even has a facility for exhausted batteries. We are told that by 2000 there will be several new hardstandings with all facilities for mobile homes. Used by tour operators (40 pitches).

How to find it: Turn off the SS309 35 km. north of Ravenna to Lido delle Nazioni (north of Lido di Pomposa) and follow camp signs.

General Details: Open 20 May - 16 Sept. 80,000 sq.m. Supermarket. Self service restaurant. Pizzeria. Bar. Supermarket and shops. Swimming pools. Children's playgrounds and mini-club. Archery. Tennis. Table tennis. Minigolf. Basketball. Volleyball. Football pitch. Electronic games room. Bicycle hire. Fishing, riding 500 m. Free transport to the beach. Organised entertainment and excursions in high season. Daily medical service. Gas supplies. Chemical disposal. Motorcaravan services. Chalets and bungalows for hire. No dogs accepted.

Charges 2000: Per person L. 8,500 - 13,500; child (0-8 yrs) 6,200 - 11,000; pitch incl. electricity 16,000 - 26,900. Credit cards accepted.

Reservations: made for min. 1 week (2 weeks in high season) with deposit. Address: 44020 Lido delle Nazioni (Ferrara). Tel: 0533/399699 or 379500. FAX: 0533/379700. E-mail: info@campingtahiti.com.

6060 Camping Comunale Estense, Ferrara

Municipal site on outskirts of city.

Ferrara is an interesting and historic city, well worth a short visit. The old city, surrounded by ancient walls, is attractive and mainly pedestrianised, with several museums, a cathedral and a wealth of architectural interest, but as a result of an apparent lack of publicity, has relatively few foreign visitors. The municipal campsite on the northern outskirts offers basic facilities for all types of units and includes 50 fairly large pitches, with numerous electrical connections, and two acceptable adjacent sanitary blocks (one heated) with large free hot showers, British and Turkish style WCs, etc. The showers have no separated dressing area, the hooks are on outside walls and the tiled floors can become very slippery. Concrete portals covered in flowers around the site do brighten things up somewhat and alleviate the somewhat uncared for overall appearance. The site proved to be adequate for visiting local attractions, with a friendly reception and (for Italy) reasonable prices. However, site facilities are very limited, with just machines for snacks and cold drinks but there is an excellent trattoria within walking distance (1 km.) and a wide choice of other eating places in the city itself.

How to find it: Site is well signed from the city and is on the northern side of the ring road.

General Details: Open all year. Drinks and snacks machines. Restaurant close by. Fishing 500 m. Golf 100 m. Riding 3 km. Chemical disposal.

Charges 1999: Per person (over 8 yrs) L. 7,000; pitch 12,000; dog 3,000. No credit cards.

Reservations: Not required. Site contact address: Via Gramicia, 76, 44100 Ferrara. Tel: 0532/752396. FAX: as phone. Tourist information office: Tel: 0532/209370. FAX: 0532/212266. E-mail: infotur.comfe@fe.nettuno.it.

6602 Camping-Hotel Citta' di Bologna, Bologna

Good quality site in historic city.

This spacious site was established in '93 on the edge of the Trade Fair Centre of this ancient and historic city. The reception is impressively efficient and friendly with excellent English spoken. Although near enough to the motorway to be aware of vague traffic 'hum', the site is surrounded by fields and trees giving a peaceful atmosphere. The intention was not only to make a camp site, but to provide high quality motel-type rooms for use by those visiting trade fairs. The bungalows are self-contained, and a modern sanitary block for campers' use has been constructed in the centre of the camping area. Hot water is free in washbasins, showers and sinks. WCs, except for two in each section are Turkish style. There is excellent provision for disabled visitors (some British style WCs with free showers and alarms which ring in reception). The 150 open pitches are numbered and marked out by young trees (60-75 sq.m.) on level grass with hardstandings (open fretwork of concrete through which grass can grow) in two areas. There is a bar with adjoining terrace (completion Sept 99) where light meals are offered leading to a full menu at a later date. The manager has great plans for 2000 which include a swimming pool and fully serviced pitches. You will always find space here as there is huge over capacity. The site is excellent for an overnight stop or for longer stays to explore the most attractive and unusual city of Bologna and Emilia-Romagna.

How to find it: Site is well signed from `Fiera' exit on the autostrada on the northeast of the city.

General Details: Open all year (except 10 days at Christmas). 63,000 sq.m. Electrical connections (6A) in all areas. Bar. Soft drinks and snacks from machine. Small children's play area. Table tennis. Football. Minigolf. Volleyball. Shops and restaurant 500 m. Medical room - doctor will call. Washing machines. Chemical disposal. Motorcaravan services. Bus service to city centre from site.

Charges 2000: Per person L. 6,500 - 9.000; child (3-8 yrs) 5,000 - 6,500; pitch 14,000 - 18,000; electricity included; dog 3,000. Credit cards accepted.
Euro: Per person 3.36 - 4.65; child (3-8 yrs) 2.59 - 3.36; pitch 7.24 - 9.30; dog 1.55.

Reservations: Write to site. Address: Campeggio Citta' di Bologna, Via Romita 12/4a, 40127 Bologna. Tel: 051/325016. FAX: 051/325318. E-mail: campinghotel-bologna@iol.it.

AR Discount
Less 10%
all year

6611 Camping Il Poggetto, Troghi, nr Florence/Firenze

Excellent site with pools run by friendly family near Firenze.

This superb new site, has a lot to offer. It benefits from a wonderful panorama and on one side, a few acres of the Zecchi family vineyards adding to its charm. It is just 15 km. from Firenze. The charming and hard-working owners have a wine producing business background and you can purchase their fine wines at the site's shop. Their aim is to provide an enjoyable and peaceful atmosphere for families. The site barriers close for a daily siesta 13.00-15.00 hrs. All 90 pitches are of a good size and have electricity (7A) and there are a few in excess of 100 sq.m for larger units. On arrival you are escorted to view available pitches then assisted in taking up that position. The two spotless sanitary blocks with subtle piped music are a pleasure to use with a mix of British and Turkish style WCs, washbasins and showers. There are three private sanitary units for hire – all excellent. Five amazingly equipped units are provided for disabled campers (that is a record number!) Hot water is free throughout including for the dishwashing sinks. Washing machines, dryers, irons and clean ironing boards are available. The restaurant offers some fine Tuscan fare along with pizzas and pasta, operating a takeaway service if you require it. You can sit on the attractive large terrace overlooking the two good sized swimming pools, complemented by a hydro-massage, and enjoy the views beyond. All visitors are given a most comprehensive pack on arrival which explains everything about the site, its environs and tourist opportunities in the area, including maps and detailed information of the main attraction, Florence. A regular bus service runs directly from the site to the city. Reception sell a vastly reduced ticket for travel. There some luxury apartments for hire along with chalets and cabins.

How to find it: Leave A1 at 'Incisa Valdarno' exit and turn left and then right towards Firenze. The site is 5 km. at Troghi and is well signed.

General Details: Open 1 March - 31 Oct. Volleyball. Games room. Table tennis. Bicycle and scooter hire. Children's playground. Animation and excursions twice weekly. Tennis 100 m. Fishing or riding 2 km. Golf 12 km. Gas supplies. Chemical disposal. Motorcaravan services. Apartments, chalets and cabins to rent.

Charges 1999: Per person L. 10,500 - 12,000; child (0-12 yrs) 7,000 - 7,500; pitch 18,500 - 20,000; small tent 12,000 - 13,000. Credit cards accepted.

Reservations: Contact site. Address: Via Il Poggetto 143, 50010 Troghi (Firenze). Tel/fax: 055/8307323. E-mail: poggetto@tin.it. A 'Camping Cheques' site.

AR Discount
Less 10% excl.
June, July, Aug.

ITALY - Central

6610 Camping Panoramico, Fiesole, Florence/Firenze

Alternative site for visiting Florence with fine views.

This is a mature site in a fine hilltop situation offering enjoyable views over Florence, appreciably fresher and quieter than near the city, and with facilities of average quality, best enjoyed out of season. It can become overcrowded in main season with too many pushed in and a very steep final access on which it is difficult for caravans to restart when halted by parked cars. The final approaches to the site take you through the village of Fiesole and there are some challenging turns and tight squeezes for larger units. The site will assist with a jeep if required. Panoramico is 7 km. from the centre. There is a bus service from Fiesole to the centre of Florence (tickets from site office) but it is an extremely long uphill walk back to the campsite from the town and thus a vehicle is essential. The 120 pitches are on terraces and steep walks to and from the various facilities could cause problems for people with mobility or breathing problems. The sanitary installations are not too large but of quite good quality, with mainly British style WCs, and free hot water in washbasins and showers. At the entrance there is a large aviary which houses a mixture of sad looking birds, tortoises, pigeons and guinea pigs. There is a simple restaurant with small terraces. Torches are required in some parts of the site.

How to find it: From A1 take Firenze-Sud exit and follow signs to Fiesole (which lies NNE of central Firenze). From Fiesole centre follow camping signs out of town for approx. 1 km; the roads are very narrow both through the town and the final steep access. The site is signed on the right.

General Details: Open all year. 25,000 sq.m. Shade in many parts. Electrical connections throughout (3A). Shop (30/3-30/10). Bar (30/3-30/10). Snack bar (15/7-15/9). Motorbike rental. Fridges, irons and little cookers available for campers' use. Washing machines. Chemical disposal. Bungalows and caravans for hire.

Charges 2000: Per person L. 13,000, incl. local tax; child (3-12 yrs) 10,000; pitch 23,000; extra car 5,500. Credit cards accepted.

Reservations: Not taken and said to be unnecessary if you arrive by early afternoon. Address: Via Peramonda 1, 50014 Fiesole (Firenze). Tel: 055/599069. FAX: 055/59186. E-mail: panoramico@florencecamping.com.

6630 Camping Montescudaio, Montescudaio, nr Cecina

Well developed site, with swimming pool, south of Livorno.

This site has been fashioned out of a very extensive area of natural undulating woodland (with low trees) and has its own character. The fact that the site is cleverly divided into separate areas for families and couples, including those in tourers shows the owners desire to reduce any possibility of noise for families on site. There are 300 pitches for touring units with shade and most are good sized, plus 170 seasonal units, bungalows or large caravans, in separate clearings. Electrical connections (3A) are available in all parts. The comprehensive range of amenities includes a commercial centre with all manner of shops including a specialist winery selling high quality wines of the area. The restaurant is excellent with a Tuscan menu, pizzeria, and takeaway service. A piano bar also operates through the season. This is an attractive site which is being developed with great style. The owner is keen to please his clients and has tried to think of most camper's needs. There is a freezer for campers and an excellent laundry service. It is 4 km. from the sea at the nearest point but there is a pleasant large free swimming pool on the site with separate children's pool. A number of comprehensive children's play areas have been scattered around the site. The modern sanitary blocks are well appointed with hot water in the two main blocks. The sanitary facilities are very clean and comprehensive with British style toilets, individual washbasins with shelves, free hot water in all washbasins, showers, and baby baths. This is one of the few sites we have seen using steam cleaning as a matter of routine. Used by tour operators (25 pitches). The site has a miniature botanical garden in the centre of the site and further small gardens around the centre and pool areas.

How to find it: From new autostrada (Livorno-Grosseto) take Cecina, Guardistallo, Montescudaio exit. Follow signs to Guardistallo, not signs to Montescudaio. Site is on the Cecina-Guardistallo road, 2 km. from Cecina.

General Details: Open 12 May - 17 Sept. 250,000 sq.m. Shops. Bar. Restaurant in main season. Open-air pizzeria at one end of site with bar, many tables and small dance floor for nightly family disco from mid-June. Swimming pool. Tennis. Minigolf. Bicycle hire. Good children's playground. Table tennis. Organised events programme in main season. Medical service. Chemical disposal. Motorcaravan services. Bungalows (13) and caravans (71) for hire. E-mail and fax service.

Charges 1999: Per person (any age) 8,200 - 10,500; pitch (any unit) incl. electricity 17,800 - 24,000; dog 4,500. No credit cards.

Reservations: Write to site with L. 100,000 deposit (Euro ¦ 51.54). Address: Casella Postale no. 4, 56040 Montescudaio (Pisa). Tel: 0586/683477. FAX: 0568/630932. E-mail: mocamp@luda.livorno.it.

6600 Camping Barco Reale, San Baronto, nr Pistoia

Beautiful site in Tuscany hills, with fine views.

Just 40 minutes from Florence and an hour from Pisa, this site is beautifully situated high in the hills with fine views. Part of an old, walled estate, there are pleasant walks in the grounds. A quiet site of 10 ha, and with good shade from mature pines and oaks, there are 175 sprawling numbered pitches, some very large and private, all for tourists but not all easily accessible for towed units. All have electricity (3, 5 or 10A) and 50 have water and drainage. The two sanitary blocks, one new, the other modern, are well positioned and are kept very clean with British and Turkish type WCs, free hot water, two toilets for disabled people and a baby room. The site has an attractive bar, a very smart restaurant with terrace and a reasonably sized swimming pool which sits on the top of a hill giving stunning views to the west (on a clear day you may see the island of Capri). There is an animation programme for children in high season. A small shop is on site with others in the village (1 km). Outside the site itself but part of the estate are other leisure facilities listed below. A lake for fishing, a disco and an indoor pool are 5 km. This attractive site will appeal to those who prefer a quiet site but with plenty to do for all ages. In high season a kiosk gives tourist information. The Ferrali family take pride in their site and its high standards. It is the only site we have seen in Italy environmentally responsible enough to recycle water which is reused to service the WCs.

How to find it: From Pistoia take Vinci - Empoli - Lamporecchio signs to San Baronto. From Empoli follow signs to Vinci and San Baronto. Final approach is around a sharp bend and up a steep slope.

General Details: Open 1 April - 30 Sept. Restaurant. Bar. Disco. Small shop, other 1 km. Swimming pool (15/5-15/9). Children's playground. Table tennis. Volleyball. Football. Chess. Bowls. Bicycle hire. Golf 10 km. Fishing 8 km. Indoor pool near. Entertainment. Excursions on foot and by bus (all season). Laundry facilities. Chemical disposal. Motorcaravan services. Caravans (3) for hire. No charcoal fires are permitted.

Charges 2000: Per person L. 10,000 - 12,600; child 0-3 yrs 5,300 - 6,800, 3-12 yrs 6,300 - 8,300; tent 8,100 - 10,200; trailer tent or caravan 10,000 - 12,500; motorcaravan 15,000 - 18,400; car 5,200 - 7,100; m/cycle 3,800 - 5,500; electricity 2,500; water and drainage 2,000. Discounts for longer stays. Credit cards accepted.

AR Discount
Discounts for excursions in low seasons

Reservations: Write to site. Address: Via Nardini 11/13, 51030 San Baronto-Lamporecchio (PT). Tel/fax: 0573/88332. E-mail barcore@tin.it A 'Camping Cheques' site.

- Swimming pool
- Volleyball
- Outdoor draughts
- Skittle alley - Trekking
- Football field -"Boccia"
- Children's playground
- Supermarket
- Restaurant
- Tennis (3 Km)

The campsite lies on a hill in a pine and oak wood with a lovely panorama. The house where Leonardo da Vinci was born and the famous town of Tuscany are not far away; excursions by bus are organised. Barco Reale is an ideal site for a pleasant holiday from April to September owing to guided walks among the olive groves and wine country, the wonderful scenery, the local culture and the climate.

6608 Camping Torre Pendente, Pisa

Pisa's most central site.

Torre Pendente is a friendly site, well run by the Signorini family who speak good English and make everyone feel welcome. It is within walking distance of the famous leaning tower (but via a dimly lit underpass). Obviously its position means it is busy throughout the main season. A medium sized site, it is on level, grassy ground with tarmac or gravel access roads and some shade. There are 220 touring pitches, 160 with 5A electricity. All site facilities are near the entrance. The sanitary facilities are basic with hot showers and mainly British style toilets (cleaning may be variable) and there is a washing machine. A basic children's play area is on site. A swimming pool is planned, but meanwhile the municipal pool is near. The small shop, bar and restaurant cater for all pockets. We consider this unsophisticated site suitable for short stays to explore Pisa rather than for an extended visit. However, a visit in mid-June to coincide with the town fiesta to see the candle-lit river banks and leaning tower could be memorable.

How to find it: From autostrada A12, exit at Pisa Nord and follow signs for 5 km. to Pisa. The site is well signed at a left turn into the town centre (Viale delle Cascine) and is then a short distance on the left hand side.

General Details: Open week before Easter - 15 October. 24,000 sq.m. Shop. Bar. Restaurant. Children's playground. Boules. Bicycle hire. Chemical disposal. Motorcaravan services. Caravans and bungalows for hire.

Charges 1999: Per adult L. 11,000; child (3-10 yrs) 6,000; car 6,000; tent 10,000; 1 person tent 7,000; caravan 11,000; motorcaravan 15,000; m/cycle 3,000; dog 3,000. No credit cards.

Reservations: Contact site. Address: Viale delle Cascine 86, 56122 Pisa. Tel: 050/561704. FAX: 050/561734. E-mail: leda@mailbox.iunet.it.

6635 Camping Le Pianacce, Castagneto Carducci, nr Donoratico

Terraced site in Tuscan hills 6 km. from sea with pleasant pool; south of Livorno.

In a quiet situation 6 km. from sea at Donoratico, this site has an attractive medium-sized swimming pool and a new children's pool with water games which are overlooked by a terrace leading from the bar. The site is, however, on steeply rising ground and has 113 pitches for tourists, all with 3A electricity, in tiered rows on fairly narrow terraces. Access to most is not easy because the limited space between the small dividing hedges and the high bank of the next terrace restricts manoeuvring so installation is now made by the site's tractor. All pitches are shady. There are now three toilet blocks, including a small one at the top of the site. They have all been refurbished to a high standard; British style WCs, individual washbasins with hot water; free hot showers. The site is almost entirely for tourists, with very few seasonal units, but it is likely to be full from about mid-July to 20 Aug. Animation is provided in season for children and adults and there is a children's play area. It is a quiet site and peaceful at night. There is a nature reserve adjacent and the sandy beach is 20 km. long so there are no restrictions. Used by tour operators (40 pitches) but these are not imposing and the site has mobile homes for rent.

How to find it: Turn off main S1 just north of Donoratico in hamlet of Il Bambolo at sign to Castagneto Carducci. After 3 km. turn left at signs to Bolgheri and site, then follow camp signs. Single track final approach.

General Details: Open 1 March - 30 Oct. 80,000 sq.m. Shop. Restaurant/bar. Swimming pool and children's pool with water games (from Easter). Tennis. Minigolf. Bicycle hire. Children's playground. Information point. Free bus service to beach. Fishing or riding 6 km. Gas supplies. Motorcaravan services. Chemical disposal. New mobile homes for hire (27).

Charges 2000: Four charging seasons. Per person L. 7,000 - 14,000; child (0-10 yrs) 5,000 - 11,000; motor-caravan or caravan/tent, incl. car 12,000 - 23,000; 2 man tent incl. m/cycle 9,000 - 17,000; extra car 3,000 - 7,000; dog 5,000 - 11,000. Some special offers in low season. No credit cards.

Reservations: made with deposit; contact site. Address: Via Bolgherese, 57022 Castagneto Carducci (LI). Tel: 0565/763667. FAX: 0565/766085. E-mail: pianacce@infol.it.

6637 Camping Il Gineprino, Marina di Bibbona

New, small family run site near Mediterranean coast in Tuscany.

This is a pleasant part of Tuscany with many interesting places within visiting distance. Il Gineprino is on the edge of Bibbona but not directly on the coast. The friendly owner, Roberto was an architect and designed the entire site, which has a nice family atmosphere. When we visited there was lots of fun and dancing by the floodlit pool. Trees planted in '95 now provide shade for most of the pitches. There are 70 pitches on the main site plus a new area for 50 motorhomes, with electricity and its own sanitary block, directly across the quiet beach access road. The site has an unusually shaped pool with an associated children's pool, and the restaurant is excellent serving superb local cuisine. Cars have to be parked in a separate area opposite the site entrance. The 130 touring pitches are numbered and marked by trees at the corners and all have a water tap and electricity (4A). There is entertainment provided on two or three evenings each week in high season and excursions can be arranged. The beach is about 400 m. away and can be reached on foot through a pinewood. The three sanitary blocks, have British and Turkish style WCs, free hot water in washbasins and showers, with cold for dishwashing and laundry. Family room (on payment) with WC, washbasin and shower and facilities for disabled people. British guests are welcome and English is spoken.

How to find it: Site is signed on the approach from the main road SS1 coast road between La California and Marina di Bibbona.

General Details: Open April - end Sept. 15,000 sq.m. Shop, restaurant with terrace (both 1/5-15/9). Swimming pool with aquagym (1/5-15/9). Games room. TV room. Table tennis. Bicycle hire. Football ground. 'Bocce'. Volleyball. Fishing 500 m. Riding 1 km. Some entertainment in high season. Excursions. Chemical disposal. Motorcaravan services. New caravans (8) and bungalows (9) to rent.

Charges 1999: Per person L. 8,000 - 15,000; child (0-8 yrs) 6,500 - 10,000; tent, caravan or motorcaravan with electricity 14,000 - 20,000; extra small tent 8,000 - 10,000; dog 5,000 - 9,000. No credit cards.

Reservations: Write to site. Address: Via del Platani, 57020 Marina di Bibbona. Tel: 0586/600550. FAX: as phone. (Winter address: c/o Arch. Roberto Valori, via F.lli Rosselli 7, 57023 Cecina (LI). Tel: 0586/683500. FAX: as phone).

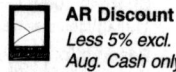

AR Discount
Less 5% excl.
Aug. Cash only.

6612 Camping Villagio Norcenni Girasole Club, Figline Valdarno, nr Firenze

Secluded site in the heart of Tuscany with many facilities and organised activities.

An excellent and busy, well run site in a picturesque, hilly situation 19 km. south of Florence, the Norcenni Girasole Club is an impressive and efficiently operated site run by the Cardini-Vannucchi family. Care has been taken in its development and the buildings and infrastructure are most attractive. Absolutely everything is to hand and guests will only need to leave the site if they wish to explore the local attractions. There are four superb swimming pools, one with a large water slide, one which can be covered and heated, and attractive smaller pools for children. A health complex provides saunas, jacuzzi, steam bath, a fitness centre, hydro-massage, Shiatzu massage or a straight massage (extra cost). The two attractive restaurants with terraces serve wonderful Tuscan food and bookings are always required. Pizzas and takeaway are also available. There are over 470 roomy pitches for tourers, all with 4A electricity and water, most shaded by well tended trees. The ground is hard and stony (tent pegs can be difficult). Tour operators occupy another 150 pitches and there are a few permanent units. Although on a fairly steep hill, pitches are on level terraces accessed from hard roads. Sanitary facilities are very good with mixed British and Turkish style WCs. Hot water is free throughout. Five family bathrooms are for hire but these need to be booked in advance. The supermarket and bazaar are extremely good, selling an array of goods which include some fine Tuscan wines. An extensive animation programme is published each week with music evenings and activities for children. A soundproof disco was built to avoid noise disturbance. Excursions are offered with one evening tour of Florence which includes a five course dinner in a historic palace. There is a daily bus direct to Florence and shuttle buses to the local railway station. An Internet Café is available for visitors and there is a professional information kiosk. Courses in the Italian language and Tuscan cooking are provided. There are many English here and all information and most of the animation is in English.

How to find it: From Florence on Rome Al/E35 autostrada take Incisa exit. Turn south on route 69 towards Arezzo. In Figline turn right for Greve and watch for Norcenni signs - site is 4 km up twisting, climbing road.

General Details: Open 1 March - 31 Oct. 110,000 sq.m. Supermarket and gift shop. Bar and restaurant with terrace. Pizzeria. Two flood-lit tennis courts. Riding. Swimming pools. Fitness centre with jacuzzi and Turkish bath. Chemical disposal. Washing machines and dryers. Excursions. Bungalows to rent. 'Bancomat'.

Charges 1999: Per person L. 11,800 - 13,400; child (2-12 yrs) 6,900 - 8,100; car 6,600 - 7,600; m/cycle 5,600 - 6,400; caravan 10,500 - 11,800; tent 9,700 - 10,800; motorcaravan 17,200 - 19,200; private toilet 15,000; daily ticket for fitness centre 11,000. No credit cards.

Reservations: Made with deposit. Address: Via Norcenni 7, 50063 Figline Valdarno (FI). Tel: 055/959666. FAX: 055/959337. E-mail: girasole@ecvacanze.it.

AR Discount
Less 10% in low season

6623 Centro Turistico San Marino, San Marino

Good modern site with swimming pool.

According to one guide book, the Republic of San Marino is 'an unashamed tourist trap which trades on its falsely preserved autonomy'. It has its own mint, postage stamps and car registration plates, has a small army and a unique E-mail address, but in all other respects, is part of Italy. However, tourists do seem to find it interesting, particularly those with patience to climb to the battlemented castles on the three highest ridges. Centro Turistico San Marino is a good 4 km. below this, at 400 m. above sea level and spreading gently down a hillside, with lovely views across to the Adriatic. It has a very attractive reception building wherein you will find the cheerful and very helpful owner Giannini who speaks excellent English and welcomes British visitors. The site has a good variety of trees offering some shade. The roomy main caravan pitches are on level terraces with hardstanding, accessed from tarmac or gravel roads, separated by hedges and with water, waste and electricity connections (5A), 10 with satellite TV connections. There are smaller pitches on lower terraces for tents. Four good sanitary blocks are kept very clean and are well spread around the site with British and Turkish style WCs and free hot water in washbasins, sinks and showers. The swimming pool has an attractive flower bedecked island, hydro-massage and solarium. Shop with limited supplies. Unusually there is a kitchen with fridge and cooker for use by campers and a room devoted to satellite TV. There is a popular restaurant with a good menu and attractive terrace overlooking the swimming pool there are pleasant views from some areas. In high season, staff organise activities for children and adults. A free bus service operates on market days and the site has a minibus for hire at competitive rates as local taxis are expensive. Used by a tour operator (30 pitches).

How to find it: Leave autostrada A14 at exit Rimini-Sud (or SS16 where signed), follow SS72 west to San Marino. Site is signed from about 15 km.

General Details: Open all year. 100,000 sq.m. Shop (all year, closed Tues. in winter). Restaurant (all year). Swimming pool (1/5-15/9). Hydro-massage. Solarium. Children's play area. Table tennis. Volleyball. Football. Archery. Boules. Tennis. Bicycle hire. Riding 5 km. Golf 10 km. Fishing 7 km. Small amphitheatre. Animation (high season). Washing machines. Gas supplies. Motorcaravan services. Chemical disposal. Bungalows for hire.

Charges 2000: Per person L. 9,000 - 15,000; child (4-10 yrs) 5,000 - 12,000; tent 6,500 - 15,000; caravan 7,500 - 18,500; car 3,500 - 8,000; motorcaravan 10,000 - 24,000; dog 2,00 - 8,500. Credit cards accepted.

Reservations: Write to site. Address: Strada San Michele 50, 47893 Repubblica di San Marino. Tel: (00 378) 0549/903964. FAX: (00 378) 0549/907120. E Mail: camping@sanmarinostde.com.

ITALY - Central

6624 Camping Villaggio Rubicone, Savignano Mare, nr Bellaria

Large and excellent site with beach, pools and extensive facilities.

This is a sophisticated, professionally run site where the very friendly owners, Sandro and Paolo Grotti are keen to fulfil your every need. The reception area is most attractive, spacious and efficient, operating an effective security system and offering a booking service for local attractions including trips to Venice, Rimini and other places of interest. Rubicone covers over 30 acres of thoughtfully landscaped, level ground by the sea and has a large beach area where guests can enjoy the facilities, including free parasols, under the watchful eyes of the lifeguard. There is shade from poplar trees for some of the 600 touring pitches which vary in size (up to 90 sq.m). The pitches are arranged in back to back double rows, in some areas the central pitches are a little tight for manoeuvring larger units. All the pitches are kept very neat and all have electrical connections (5A), 40 with water and waste water facilities, and 20 with private sanitary facilities. For the remainder, there are modern facilities with free hot water for the showers and washbasins (half in private cabins), mainly British style toilets, bidets, hairdryers, token operated irons, baby rooms and two excellent units for disabled visitors. There is a superb shop, including the best fresh meat counter we have seen. There are many bars around the site from beach bars to night club bars and the restaurant offers excellent food at very reasonable prices. The service is fast and efficient by cheerful staff members in smart uniforms. There are snack bars and a pizzeria which are open all season. The complex international animation programme for young and old is staged in a circular terraced area near the main bar. The site has an array of activities on offer (eg judo lessons) and many children's play areas. There are also many sporting opportunities including a smart double tennis court and, across the railway (via an underpass) is a huge complex including excellent swimming pools (bathing caps mandatory), solarium, jacuzzi, mini racing track, water motorbikes, 'powered' trampolines and many others.

How to find it: Site is 15 km. northwest of Rimini. From Bologna exit the A14 at Rimini north and head for the S16 to Bellaria and San Mauro a Mare; site is well signed.

General Details: Open 1 May - 30 Sept. Restaurant, snack bar and shop (from 10/5). Swimming pool (15/5). Children's play equipment. Tennis. Solarium. Jacuzzi. Mini racing track. Water motorbikes. 'Powered' trampolines. Beach showers. Fishing. Boat launching. Sailing and windsurfing schools. Bicycle hire 500 m. Riding 2 km. Golf 15 km. Washing machines. Gas supplies. Chemical disposal. Motorcaravan services. No dogs accepted.

Charges 1999: Per person L. 8,000 - 13,400; child (2-8 yrs) 6,000 - 11,800; pitch (small, medium or large) 16,500 - 25,500; pitch with WC (small or large) 53,000 - 93,000; electricity (5A) 3,500. No credit cards. Euro: Per person 4.10 - 6.87; child (2-8 yrs) 3.08 - 6.05; pitch (small, medium or large) 8.46 - 13.07; pitch with WC (small or large) 27.18 - 47.69; electricity 1.79.

Reservations: Contact site. Address: Via Matrice Destra 1, 47039 Savignano Mare (FO). Tel: 0541/346377. FAX: 0541/346999. E-mail: info@campingrubicone.com. *see colour advert between pages 128/129*

6620 Campo Norina, Pesaro

Small, seaside site with own private beach on Adriatic Riviera.

This small, rectangular site is sandwiched between mountain, road and railway and the coast. The access road is congested and Italian car parking makes the approach even more of a challenge with large units requiring care to gain access to the site and some of the pitches. The private beach of fine sand runs the 320 m. length of the site and slopes gently offering safe swimming with artificial moles running parallel to the shore, some 70 m. from it, ensuring calm water. The site could be used for visiting the attractions nearby, both inland and along the northern Adriatic coast. As with most sea-side sites in this area the site is very close to the busy inter-city railway line and could be ideal for 'spotters', although the 24 hour train noise, if you are on the western side of the site, can be a real nuisance. Pitches are arranged either side of small roads at right angles to the shore with direct access to the excellent and seemingly uncrowded beach, which is this site's strong point. The 190 pitches are marked by numbered stones and backed by hedges, all having electricity (3A). There is a small platform for dancing in high season. The site has a family atmosphere with 60% taken by Italians who provide a happy background of family noise as the touring pitches are interspersed with permanent ones. The pleasant bar/restaurant also functions as a pizzeria. The three toilet blocks are a little sad and, whilst they are kept clean, are showing signs of age. They are tiled with a mixture of British and Turkish style WCs. Cold water only in washbasins and dishwashing sinks, with hot water on payment in the showers. English is spoken by the friendly management.

How to find it: Site is mid-way between Pesaro and Fano. From autostrada, take Pesaro exit and follow signs on the SS16 for Ancona. The access road goes under the railway (high enough for motorcaravans), which it shares with Camping Marinella, and care is needed to enter Norina rather than its rival.

General Details: Open 1 April - 15 Oct, as is bar/restaurant. 25,000 sq.m. Shade in some parts. Shop and bazaar (all season). Washing machine. Chemical disposal. Electricity in all parts. Small children's playground. Dancing (July/Aug). Tennis 400 m. Riding 1 km. San Marino 40 km. and other attractions near.

Charges 1999: Per adult L. 8,000 - 12,000; child (0-6 yrs) 5,000 - 8,000; pitch incl. electricity 16,000 - 23,000, small pitch for tent 8,000 - 10,000; dog 5,000. VAT included. No credit cards.

Reservations: Necessary for August, with deposit and fee; write to site. Address: Marina Ardizia 181, 61100 Pesaro. Tel: 0721/55792. FAX: 0721/55165.

6625 Camping La Montagnola, Sovicille, nr Siena

Quiet, clean site close to Siena, Volterra and San Gimignano.

An agreeable alternative to sites closer to the centre of Siena, La Montagnola is set in secluded woodland to the north of the village of Sovicille. The owners have worked hard to provide a good basic standard of amenities. The 66 pitches are of good size (80 sq.m) and offer considerable privacy, they are clearly marked and have reasonably good shade. All are suitable for caravans and motorcaravans with electrical connections (5A). There are just three water points on the site, and the pitches furthest up the hill are arranged neatly in a circle around a central barbecue area. There is an overflow field for tents with no shade and another for sports. A single toilet block provides free hot showers and sufficient washbasins (cold water) and mainly British style toilets – not luxurious, but adequate and clean. A friendly bar/shop area offers snacks and basic provisions; a large supermarket is 6 km. (San Rocco a Philli or Rosia), a small one 6 km (Sovicille). Two restaurants are in the village. This site could make an excellent touring base for central Tuscany and is not too far from the motorway for short stays, perhaps including a visit to Siena (10 km. with an hourly bus service from the site).

> **How to find it:** From north on Firenze - Siena motorway take Siena Ovest exit, turn left on SS73, at the village Voltebass turn right following signs for Sovicille from where site is signed. From south (Grosseto) take SS223 turning at crossroads to Rosia from where site is also signed.
>
> **General Details:** Open Easter - 30 Sept. Small shop and bar. Restaurants and supermarkets near. Chemical disposal.
>
> **Charges 1999:** Per person L. 9,000; child (4-12 yrs) 6,000; pitch 10,000; electricity 2,000.
>
> **Reservations:** not really necessary. Address: 53018 Sovicille (Siena). Tel: 0577/ 314473. FAX: as phone (winter address: SS73 Ponente 190 (Siena). Tel/fax: 0577/349286).

AR Discount

Less 5%
all season

6640 Camping Pappasole, Vignale Riotorto, nr Follonica

Large, well run site on coast with many sporting activities.

This lively site offers plenty of sporting activities and is located 250 m. from its own sandy beach, facing the island of Elba. It is a large site on flat, fairly open ground offering 450 pitches of 90 sq.m. many with electricity (3A) and water, others with electricity, water and waste water connections. Some 344 of the pitches have their own cosy individual sanitary facility with WC, shower and washbasin, and next to these a compartment with 4-burner gas stove, fridge, sink with H&C water, drainer, and 5 cupboards (extra cost for this about £5 per night). Pitches are separated by bushes with some shade from mature trees and arti- ficial shade in other areas. There may be some road or rail noise in certain areas. There are three modern sanitary blocks with free hot water for the washbasins and showers and mainly Turkish but with some British style WCs. These facilities may be a fair walk from some of the pitches. Laundry facilities are pro- vided. The excellent swimming pools are a strong feature of the site. However the central focus of the site is an attractive covered area (a very tall, open marquee type structure, floodlit at night) for dancing, music and entertainment which is surrounded by the main camp buildings. The animation programme is impres- sive. There are many sporting opportunities including archery, windsurfing and sailing, tennis, and activ- ities and excursions are organised.

> **How to find it:** Site is north of Follonica just off the 'new' SS1 and well signed.
>
> **General Details:** Open 15 April - 21 Oct. Restaurant. Snacks. Bar. Shop. Swimming pools (from 27/5). Children's play area. Tennis. Table tennis. Bowls. Archery. Handball. Watersports. Minigolf. Bicycle hire. Fishing. Riding 400 m. Entertainment, activities and excursion programmes (3/6-8/9). Fridge hire. Medical services. Safety deposit boxes. Laundry facilities. Gas supplies. Chemical disposal. Motorcaravan services. Bungalows for rent.
>
> **Charges 2000:** Per person L. 7,000 - 17,000; child (3-10 yrs) 5,000 - 12,000; caravan/tent and car or motor- caravan 15,500 - 40,000, electricity included; individual sanitary facility 8,500 - 23,000; dog 4,000 - 16,000. Credit cards accepted.
>
> **Reservations:** are made for whole weeks, Sat. - Sat. Write to site. Address: Loc. Carbonifera, 57020 Vignale Riotorto (LI). Tel: 0565/20420. FAX: 0565/20346.

AR Discount

Less 10% in
low season

ITALY - Central

6641 Blucamp, Campiglia Marittima, nr Piombino

Terraced site in Tuscan hills 8 km. from sea with pleasant pool; north of Piombino.

Blucamp is a relatively new, simple site in a tranquil setting near the pretty village of Campiglia Marittima. It is owned and run by a partnership of two charming Italians who are keen to welcome British guests and good English is spoken. The famous island of Elba can be sighted from the site entrance and there are most enjoyable views over green hills and the sea from the upper pitches. The 70 pitches are terraced and on steep slopes, reception, the restaurant, bar, and pool complex being situated half-way down the main sloping road. If arriving with a large unit it is advisable to park at the top of the site and walk in to choose your pitch. There is a tractor to help if required. Cars are parked off pitches in numbered bays. In a very quiet situation, 8 km. back from sea this site has an attractive medium-sized swimming pool alongside the restaurant and bar. All pitches have young trees that provide some shade but others are more in the open, all touring pitches have 3A electricity. There is one satisfactory sanitary block with British and Turkish style WCs, individual washbasins with cold water and free hot showers. A washing machine is available. The site is entirely for tourists, with just two bungalows for rent. It is busy in high season. The small attractive restaurant is run by a separate family and offers wonderful Tuscan cuisine and specialises in fish. Service is efficient by cheerful friendly staff. After the stifling beach sites, which are dusty under huge pines, this is a most refreshing experience as there is invariably a cooling breeze. The local area has a history of Etruscan metal mining with the fascinating miner's castle of the Temperino Valley or walk in the footsteps of the Etruscan civilisation in the grotto tombs of Populonia where iron from Elba was processed. There is a ferry connection to Elba and Corsica 19 km. distant and many areas of interest in the area. This site is ideal if you enjoy small sites, wish to escape the heat and bustle of the large Riviera sites and enjoy some uncomplicated personal service in quiet surroundings. There is a siesta from 12.30 - 15.00. We are told that it will increase in size by 2000, which will include a second modern sanitary block.

How to find it: Take exit for S. Vincenzo off the main S1 road Livono to Follonica. Follow signs for Campiglia Marittima where site is signed.

General Details: Open 1 June - 15 September. Restaurant/bar. Swimming pool. Electronic games. Table tennis. Towing vehicle. Chemical disposal. Bungalows to let (2).

Charges 1999: Per person L. 8,000 - 11,500; child (0-8 yrs) 6,200 - 8,800; motorcaravan or caravan/tent incl. car 12,600 - 18,000. VAT included. Credit cards accepted.

Reservations: made with deposit; contact site. Address: Campiglia M.ma (Livorno), Castagneto Carducci (LI). Tel: 0565/838553. FAX: 0574/574272.

AR Discount
Less 5%;
cash only.

6645 Parco-Campeggio Delle Piscine, Sarteano, nr Chianciano

Site with three thermal swimming pools, 6 km. from A1 autostrada southeast of Siena.

Sarteano is situated on the spur of Monte Cetona, is a spa, and the novel feature of this site is the three unique swimming pools fed by natural thermo-mineral springs. These springs have been known since antiquity as 'del Bango Santo' which flows at a constant temperature of 24º and completely changes the pool waters every two hours. Two of these pools (one large with hydro-massage, one for children), are set in a park-like ground with picnic tables, and are free to all those staying on the whole site. This includes park visitors and tour operator clients. A third good sized pool, on the camping site itself, is opened in main season for the exclusive use of campers. Apart from the pools, the site is excellent and worth considering, either as a sightseeing base or as an overnight stop from the Florence - Rome motorway. Access to the attractive town is directly outside the site gate, and is worth exploring, especially the massive fortress with its drawbridge (straight out of a toy-box!) The views from the town are unusual, over both Umbria and Tuscany. This spacious site is well run and the infrastructure is excellent and there is lots of room to manoeuvre. There are 450 individual, flat pitches, all of good size and fully marked out with mature hedges giving considerable privacy. They claim they will always find space and reservations are not usually made. When we visited they were full and operating an additional open area with electricity (6A throughout the site) but no shade. The two heated toilet blocks are of high quality with mainly British style WCs, washbasins with free hot water, shelf, mirror; free hot showers, numerous sinks for laundry and dishwashing, with hot water. There is a friendly welcome. Dogs are not accepted.

How to find it: From autostrada A1 take Chiusi/Chianciano exit, from where Sarteano (6 km) and site signed.

General Details: Open 1 April - 30 Sept. Electrical connections (6A) all parts. Restaurant/bar. Takeaway. Newspaper kiosk. Telephones. Swimming pools (one all season). TV room, satellite TV room and mini-cinema with 100 seats and a very large screen. Tennis. Table tennis. Volleyball. Bicycle hire 500 m. Riding 3 km. Exchange facilities. Free guided cultural tours. Local market on Fridays. E-mail facility. Gas supplies. Chemical disposal. Motorcaravan services.

Charges 2000: Per adult L. 14,000 - 18,000; child (3-10 yrs) 10,000 - 12,000; car 5,000 - 7,500; tent or caravan 14,000 - 18,000; motorcaravan 19,000 - 25,500; electricity 4,500; with water and drainage plus 6,500. Credit cards accepted.

Reservations: Contact site. Address: 53047 Sarteano (Siena). Tel: 0578/26971. FAX: 0578/265889. E-mail: bagnosanto@kranet.it.

6653 Camping Listro, Castiglione del Lago

Small, unpretentious site on the western edge of Lake Trasimeno.

This is a simple, pleasant, flat site with the best beach (private to the campsite) of the lake. As the lake is very shallow with some reeds (7 m. at its deepest), it has very gradually sloping beaches making it very safe for children to play and swim. This also results in very warm water, which is kept clean as fishing and tourism are the major industries hereabouts. Camping Listro is a few hundred yards north of the historic town of Castiglione and the attractive town can be seen rising up the hillside from the site. It provides 100 pitches all with electricity (3A) with 70% of the pitches enjoying the shade of mature trees. Younger campers are in a separate area of the site, ensuring no noise disturbance and the motorcaravan area is right on the lakeside giving stunning views out of your windows. The sanitary facilities are clean and adequate with artificial shade in the washing areas, although most of the WCs are of the Turkish type. Facilities on the site are fairly limited with only a small shop and snack bar, but as the town is 800 m. away, there are many bars and restaurants near, as are sporting facilities including a good swimming pool and tennis courts (discounts using the camp-site card). There is a small children's play area on the lake shore. Dogs are accepted in the low season only. Barbecues are permitted but there is no organised entertainment. English is spoken and British guests are particularly welcome. If you enjoy the simple life and peace and quiet in camping terms then this site is for you.

How to find it: From A1/E35 Florence-Rome autostrada take Val di Chiana exit and join Perugia (75 bis) super-strada. After 24 km. take Castiglione exit and follow town signs. Site signs clearly marked just before the town.

General Details: Open 1 April - 30 Sept. Bar. Shop. Snack bar. Children's play area. Table tennis. Volleyball. Private beach. Tourist information. Motorcaravan services. Dogs are not accepted in high season.

Charges 2000: Per person (over 3 yrs) L. 6,500 - 8,000; caravan or motorcaravan 6,500 - 8,000; tent 5,000 - 8,000, acc. to season and size; car 2,000 - 3,000; m/cycle 1,500 - 2,000; electricity incl. Less 10% for stays over 8 days in low season. Credit cards accepted.

Reservations: Contact site. Address: Via Lungolago, 06061 Castiglione del Lago (PG). Tel/Fax: 075/951193.

CAMPING LISTRO ★★

In a green setting on the shore of Lake Trasimeno
Private beach ~ Free hot water and electricity
Newly renovated shower and toilet facilities
Shop for every day essentials ~ Bar ~ Play area for children
By the exit from the site are: Swimming pool, Tennis courts, Athletics track, Football field,
Windsurfing, Canoeing, Disco, Restaurant. Only 500 m. from the historical centre of Castiglione
del Lago, the site is an ideal base for visits to Rome, Umbria and Tuscany

I-06061 Castiglione del Lago (PG) Tel. & Fax 075/951193

6650 Camping Kursaal Hotel, Passignano sul Trasimeno

Well located, orderly site on north east edge of Lake Trasimeno, 1 km. from town.

Anna Posta, the charming manager of this pretty, well run site speaks English and gives a real welcome to British guests. The beach at the lakeside is popular, the lake is checked for water quality every week and there is a swimming pool (closed 13.30-16.00). All water sports are available on the lake and there are fabulous views from the site. The attractive bar and restaurant, with a wide ranging menu, are complemented by a small well stocked shop, all of which are open from 0800 -2300. daily. Part of the site is very shady with coniferous trees, and part is open with flowering trees giving a total of 160 pitches, each of 80 sq.m. but not all marked. There are plentiful electrical connections (4/6A) and no static pitches. Two sanitary blocks, well arranged and spotless, provide mainly British type toilets, free hot showers and have facilities for babies and for disabled people. A family atmosphere is encouraged on the site but this is not a place for the more uninhibited. There is an extremely pleasant 16 room hotel in the middle of the site which does require reservation.

How to find it: Take exit 'Passignano est' from Perugia spur of Florence-Rome autostrada; site then signed.

General Details: Open 25 March - 30 Oct. Bar/restaurant (live music in bar in high season). Shop - supermarket 500 m. Good swimming pool (free). Small play area for children. Fishing. Bicycle hire 500 m. Riding 2 km. Chemical disposal. Motorcaravan services. Hotel and bungalow accommodation.

Charges 1999: Per adult L. 9,000 - 10,000; child 0-3 yrs 3,000, 4-10 yrs 7,000 - 8,000; caravan or tent 11,000 - 15,000; car 3,000; motorcaravan 14,000 - 18,000; dog 2,000; electricity 2,500. Credit cards accepted.

Reservations: Accepted with 30% deposit (by Eurocheque payable to Camping Kursaal). Address: 06065 Passignano sul Trasimeno. Tel: 075/828085. FAX: 075/827182.

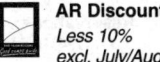

AR Discount
Less 10%
excl. July/Aug.

ITALY - Central

6654 Camping Badiaccia, Castiglione del Lago

Lakeside campsite with swimming pools.

Camping Badiaccia has excellent views of the surrounding hills and the islands of the lake. It provides a base from which to visit interesting places in this part of central Italy or as a night stop when travelling to Rome, being near the Al autostrada. Being directly on the lake gives an almost seaside atmosphere. There is a protected swimming area along the beach, with some reeded areas close by and a jetty which provides a base for fishing. The site also has a protected mooring for small boats and provides a good selection of sporting opportunities with four special staff in high season to organise activities for children and adults. Being well tended and maintained (although the children's play area was due for refurbishment when we visited) it has a pleasant appearance enhanced by a variety of plants and flowers. Some pitches are smaller than average but there is good shade in most parts. The 150 pitches for touring are numbered and separated by trees and bushes in rows from hard access roads. There is a good sized swimming pool (20 x 10 m) by the restaurant and a small one (6 x 3 m) for children in the beach area. Guided excursions to Rome and Florence are organised in high season and a list detailing local markets is displayed. Open all season are a pleasant restaurant, snack bar and a shop. The two centrally positioned sanitary blocks can be heated and have British style WCs and free hot water in washbasins, sinks and showers. English is spoken. Accommodation to rent.

How to find it: From A11 Milan-Rome autostrada take Val di Chiana exit and turn east towards Perugia on the SS75bis. Leave this at Castiglione exit and go south on SS71 to Castiglione where site is well signed.

General Details: Open 1 April - 30 Sept. 55,000 sq.m. Restaurant. Shop. Snack bar. Electricity (4A). Swimming pool and children's pool (1/6-30/9). Play area. Tennis. Table tennis. Boules. Minigolf. Volleyball. Football. Beach volleyball. Windsurfing. Watersports. Fishing. Boat hire. Riding 3 km. Golf 20 km. Entertainment and excursions in high season. Washing machines. Gas supplies. Chemical disposal. Motorcaravan services. Caravans, mobile homes and chalets for rent.

Charges 2000: Per person L. 9,000 - 11,000; child (under 10 yrs) 6,000 - 9,000; tent 9,000 - 10,000; caravan 10,000 - 11,000; motorcaravan 11,000 - 12,000; car 3,000; m/cycle 2,000; dog 3,000; electricity included. Credit cards accepted.
Euro: Per person 4.65 - 5.68; child (under 10 yrs) 3.10 - 4.65; tent 4.65 - 5.16; caravan 5.16 - 5.68; motorcaravan 5.68 - 6.20; car 1.55; m/cycle 1.03; dog 1.55.

Reservations: Write to site. Address: Via Trasimeno 1 - Voc. Badiaccia 91, 06061 Castiglione del Lago (PG). Tel: 075/9659097. FAX: 075/9659019.

6665 Camping Le Soline, Casciano di Murlo, nr Siena

Family run terraced site with pools, some 20 km. south of Siena.

A country hillside site, 800 m. from the village of Casciano, Le Soline has 100 sprawling pitches for caravans and 40 tents set on seven terraces on steep slopes, beneath the main buildings. They range in size from 36-80 sq.m, all caravan pitches have electricity (6A) most enjoying views over adjoining vineyards. The site occupies an area of 70,000 sq.m, there are many olive and other trees providing some shade for the pitches. The kind and attentive Broggini family spare no efforts in making your stay a pleasant memory and are extremely hard working to this end. The elegant restaurant has an excellent menu (we tried the seafood - it was superb!), and the terraces have fine views. An attached pizzeria is open all season, and the shop sells basic supplies. Two clean swimming pools are below the restaurant/bar complex. A good quality, heated sanitary block (recently refurbished) is on the third terrace, providing mixed British and Turkish style WCs, washbasins, hot showers, dishwashing sinks and facilities for disabled visitors. There is free hot water throughout. The site also offers a few small private sanitary units for hire. There are excellent panoramic views of the surrounding countryside and the site is well positioned to visit the many historic and cultural places in the area. There are a few bungalows for rent.

How to find it: From Siena, turn off the SS223 Siena - Grosseto road to the left to Fontazzi (about 20 km.) and keep right for Casciano, following signs.

General Details: Open all year. Restaurant, pizzeria and shop (15/3-31/10). Swimming pools (15/3-15/10). Children's playground. Volleyball. Mini-football field. Bicycle hire. Barbecue area (not allowed on pitches). Riding 600 m. Fishing 3 km. Golf 10 km. Freezer for campers use. Laundry. Car wash area. Gas supplies. Chemical disposal. Motorcaravan services. Bungalows for rent (3).

Charges 1999: Per person L.10,000; child (2-12 yrs) 7,000; car 3,000; m/cycle 2,000; caravan 10,500; tent 8,000 - 9,500; motorcaravan 11,500; dog 1,000; electricity 2,000. Credit cards accepted.

Reservations: Write to site. Address: 53010 Casciano di Murlo (Siena). Tel: 0577/817410. FAX: 0577/817415. E-mail: casoline@amiata.net.

AR Discount
Less 10% on person charge, min. 3 days

6664 Camping Toscana Colliverdi, Certaldo

Small, terraced site with very limited facilities, some 20 km. south of Siena.

Very much a 'no frills' country hillside site, 700 m. from the village of Marcialla, Toscana Colliverdi has spaces for 60 caravans and tents set on terraces. All caravan pitches have electricity (3/5A). One part of the access road is tarmac the other rough gravel - large units should use the tarmac for ease of access on the steep slopes. A small, but clean and good quality sanitary block is on the second terrace, providing only one British style WC in each block, the remainder Turkish style. The showers, exterior washbasins, dishwashing and laundry sinks all have hot water. No washing machines or facilities for disabled campers. There are excellent panoramic views of the surrounding countryside (unfortunately marred by overhead wires and a pylon supporting them sitting at the bottom of the site), however the site is well positioned to visit the many historic and cultural places of interest in the area. This includes the birthplace of Leornardo de Vinci. This site's strength is the owner, Constantino, who is there to please. You are greeted with a bottle of Chianti and a big grin. He is also an expert on the local history and culture and has an extensive array of tourist information and many fascinating snippets that are not in the guide books. Nothing is too much trouble. There are no supporting facilities but he is in close liaison with suppliers in the local village. The site is dark at night and the centre steps are a challenge as some are of differing depths – a good torch is required. If you are content to be self-supporting and want expert assistance in exploring Tuscany along with the advantage of reasonable campsite fees, then this could be for you.

How to find it: From A1 autostrada Florence - Siena, take Tavarnelle exit and head for Tavarnelle. At the village follow signs for Marcialla. Site entrance is on the left approx. 700 m. after the village of Marcialla.

General Details: Open 1 week before Easter - 30 Sept. Children's playground. No other facilities but see text.

Charges 1999: Per person L. 8,000 - 9,500; child (2-8 yrs) 5,500 - 6,000; car 3,000; m/cycle 2,500; caravan 12,500 - 15,000; motorcaravan 15,000 - 18,000; tent 8,000 - 10,000; car 3,000; electricity 3,000. No credit cards.

Reservations: Write to site. Address: Via Marcialla 349 - Loc. Marcialla, 50020 Certaldo (Firenze). Tel: 0571/669334. FAX: as phone.

The ideal stopover to Get to Know Tuscany New campsite between Florence and Siena between the green hills of the Chianti wine route. Florence 24 km – Siena 30 km – Pisa 67 km – Vinci 29 km – Certaldo 6 km – S. Gimignano 19 km – Volterra 39 km. Set amongst woods, hills and vineyards, Camping Toscana Colliverdi is very quiet and comfortable. Modern sanitary facilities with free hot showers. The pitches of 70m² are situated on more levels. Directions: Motorway Florence/Siena, exit Tavernelle and in Tavernelle follow direction Marcialla/Certaldo where site is signposted.

Camping
Toscana Colliverdi

Via Marcialla, 349 • I-50020 Certaldo (FI) • Tel. and fax 0039/0571669334 • Http://www.codekard.it/toscanacolliverdi

6660 Camping Maremma-Sans-Souci, Castigliòne della Pescaia, nr Grosseto

Seaside site on Mediterranean coast between Livorno and Rome.

This site is owned and run by the Perduca family and sits in natural woodland. The minimum amount of undergrowth has been cleared to provide 430 individually marked and hedged, flat pitches for camping enthusiasts. This offers considerable privacy in an individual settings. A positive feature of this site is that there are no seasonal pitches. Some pitches are small and cars must go to a numbered, shaded and secure car park near the entrance. An inconvenience to those who rely on the car for lighting, it does mean less vehicle movement on the site. There is a wide road for motorhomes but other roads are mostly narrow and bordered by trees (this is a protected area, and they cannot fell the trees). Therefore access to some parts is difficult for caravans and each pitch is earmarked either for caravans or for tents. A good sandy beach is less than 100 m. from one end of the site (400 m. from the other) and is used only by campers. There are five small, mature toilet blocks around the site which have lots of little extras such as hair dryers and soap dispensers. Three blocks have cabins each with WC, basin and shower, all WC's are British style. Maremma is a friendly site right by the sea which should appeal to many people who like a relaxed style.

How to find it: Site is 2.5 km. northwest of Castiglione on road to Follonica.

General Details: Open 1 April - 31 Oct. 100,000 sq.m. overall. Access not easy inside site. Electrical connections (3A) for caravan pitches. Shop. Excellent restaurant (self service in season). Bar with pizzas and other snacks. Volleyball. Washing machines. Car wash. Chemical disposal. Motorcaravan services. Excursions organised to Elba and Rome. Sailing school. Caravans for hire. English spoken. No dogs taken between 16/6-31/8.

Charges 1999: Per person L. 8,000 - 13,000; child (2-6 yrs) 7,000 - 9,000; pitch and car 11,000 - 20,000. Credit cards accepted (not Amex or Diners).

Reservations: necessary for July/Aug. and will be made for min. 1 week with deposit (L. 5,000). Address: 58043 Castiglione della Pescaia (Grosseto). Tel: 0564/933765. FAX: 0564/935759.

ITALY - Central

6661 Camping Cieloverde, Marina di Grosseto

Large site with beach and excellent facilities.

The site is situated mid-way between Marina di Grosseto and Principina a Mare. The road filter for new arrivals is very narrow but after that point there is plenty of room to manoeuvre. The impressive site has 12 circular areas with marked pitches, which are on flat gravel and sand, enjoying natural shade from mature trees. The pitches which surround their particular sanitary block rather like the layers of an onion, are generally of average size, all have electricity and many have phone sockets. All facilities are very clean and have free hot showers but note that all WCs are Turkish style. Dishwashing and laundry facilities (cold water), freezers and washing machines surround the sanitary block. Vehicles are parked in numbered bays away from the pitches. There is a regular free bus service to the private beach (1 km). There are many excellent facilities at this well kept site, with the green grass and foliage showing the care taken here. Cieloverdi is in the Maremma region of Italy and borders the National Park of Uccellina where deer, wild rams and other animals live in freedom – tours can be organised. The position of this site is in the area of the ancient Etruscan civilisation. There are ferries to the island of Elba and excursions to the other islands.

How to find it: Site is just off SS327 between Marina di Grosseto and Principina a Mare.

General Details: Open May - September. Electricity and phone connections. Restaurant and self-service snacks. Pizzeria. Bar. Ice-cream parlour. Supermarket. Tobacconist. Bazaar. Fishmonger. Tennis. Children's playground. Guarded area by beach for surf boards etc. Free bus to beach. Football. Volleyball. Basketball. Archery. Cinema. Games room. Exchange. Safe deposit. First aid centre. Chemical disposal. Dogs are not accepted in July/Aug.

Charges 1999: Per person L. 8,400 - 16,000; child (over 6 yrs) 6,300 - 12,000; pitch incl. electricity 11,500 - 22,000; half size pitch incl. electricity (2 people only) 7,300 - 15,000; m/cycle 2,800. Credit cards accepted.

Reservations: Contact site. Address: Via della Trappola, 58046 Marina di Grosseto (GR). Tel: 0564/321611 (winter 0564/30190). FAX: 0564/30178.

6656 Camping Il Collaccio, Castelvecchio di Preci

Unusual campsite with good amenities in rural Umbria.

Tuscany has grabbed the imagination and publicity, but parts of nearby Umbria are just as beautiful. Preci or, to give it its full name, Castlevecchio di Preci, is tucked away in the tranquil depths of the Umbrian countryside. The natural beauty of the Monti Sibillini National Park is near and there are walking and cycling opportunities with many marked paths and guided excursions. Historic Assisi and Perugia and the walled market town of Norcia are worth exploring and distinctive Umbrian cuisine to be enjoyed. Il Collaccio is owned and run by the Baldoni family who bought the farm over 30 years ago, rebuilt the derelict farmhouse in its original style and then decided to share it with holiday makers by developing a campsite and accommodation for hire. The farming aspect was kept, along with a unit producing salami (they run salami making courses over Easter and New Year – no preservatives!) and its products can be bought in the shop and sampled in the excellent restaurant. The camping area has been carved out of the hillside which forms a natural amphitheatre with splendid views. At first sight the narrow steep entrance seems daunting (the owner will assist) and the road which leads down to the somewhat steep camping ter- races takes one to the exit. The 90 large pitches are on level terraces with stunning views. The thousands of trees, planted to replace those cut down by the previous owner, are maturing and provide some shade. An interesting feature is a tree plantation on a lower slope where they are experimenting in cultivating truf- fles - patience is needed as the results will not be known for ten years (three to go for the Baldinis!) Three modern sanitary blocks are spaced through the site with British and Turkish style WCs, cold water in washbasins and hot, pre-mixed water in showers and sinks. An excellent, heated swimming pool (25 x 12.5 m) is by the restaurant, a children's pool, a good tennis court, volleyball, basketball, small football pitch at the lower level in the site, boules and mountain biking. With sparsely populated villages across the valley on the mountain slopes and embraced by stunning scenery, Il Collaccio and its surrounds is unusual and different. The family provide some very different excursion opportunities with small numbers doing unusual things, and there is some entertainment in high season. There is a small, but not intrusive, tour operator presence, and some attractive chalets for hire.

How to find it: From SS77 Foligno-Civitonova Marche road turn south at Muccia for Visso where Preci is signed. There is a direct route (saving a long and extremely winding approach) through a new tunnel, if the site is approached north of Eggi which is 10 km. north of Spoleto. The tunnel exit is at Sant Anatolia di Narco SS209, where turn left to Preci (when we visited there were few signs but it is worth asking for directions).

General Details: Open 7 April - 15 Oct. 100,000 sq.m. Electrical connections (6A) - long lead useful. Restaurant (all season). Shop (basics, 1/7-31/8). Swimming pools (15/5-30/9). Play area. Tennis. Volley and basket ball. Football. Table tennis. Boules. Canoeing and rafting 2 km. Fishing 10 km. Washing machine. Motorcaravan services. Chemical disposal. Dormitories for groups, chalets and rooms for hire. Money exchange.

Charges 1999: Per person 9,000 - 12,000; child (3-12 yrs) 4,500 - 6,000; tent 9,000 - 12,000; caravan or motor- caravan 11,000 - 14,000; car 3,000 - 5,000; electricity included. Credit cards accepted.

Reservations: Write to site. Address: Azienda Agricola Il Collaccio, 06047 Castelvecchio di Preci (PG). Tel: 0743/939005. FAX: 0743/939094. E-mail: collaccio@mail.caribusiness.it. A 'Camping Cheques' site.

AR Discount
Less 10% on person charge

6655 Camping Internazionale, Assisi

Modern, well equipped site with good restaurant and a fine view of the city.

Camping Internazionale is situated on the west side of Assisi and has new facilities which provide tourers with a good base to visit both St Francis' city and nearby Perugia and Lake Trasimeno. The toilet block is well appointed and clean, with free hot showers, plenty of washbasins, mainly Turkish style WCs (there are only 4 British style WCs in each block) and facilities for disabled people. The restaurant has a large garden serving reasonably priced meals, which range from pizzas to local Umbrian dishes (closed Tuesdays), and the city is lit up in the evenings to provide a beautiful backdrop from some areas in the site. The 175 pitches are large and clearly marked, on flat grass, and all have electrical connections (3A). There are plenty of water points. There is some shade which will increase as the trees reach full maturity. It can be very hot in this part of Italy and a welcome relief is the site's new large swimming pool and circular children's pool (bathing caps are mandatory and there is an extra charge L. 5,000 adult, 2,000 child). Assisi boasts one of the finest cathedrals in Christendom, among many other attractions, and a stay in this area should not be cut too short. There is a bus service into town three times daily from outside the site. This is one of the cheapest sites we have seen in Northern Italy.

How to find it: Site lies on the south side of the SS147, which branches left off SS75 Perugia - Foligno road. Follow Assisi signs and, since there are several campsite signs in the town, look for the un-named camping sign going off to the left (downhill) as you enter the city. The site is approx. 4 km. from the city. At Violi a village just before Assisi there is a warning of a low bridge of 3.3 m. - in fact it is much higher at the centre of the curved bridge and even the highest units will pass through.

General Details: Open Easter - October. Restaurant/pizzeria with self-service section. Bar with snacks. Shop. Ice cream bar. Kitchen for campers with tables and benches. Table tennis. Video games. Bicycle hire. Tennis. Volleyball. Roller skating area. Riding 2 km. Excursions to Assisi centre, local swimming pool, Rome and Siena. Bus service to city. Washing machine. Gas supplies. Chemical disposal. Motorcaravan services. Bungalows (15) and mobile homes (5) for rent.

Charges 1999: Per adult L. 9,500; child (3-10 yrs) 7,500; tent 8,500; caravan or motorcaravan 10,000; car 4,000; m/cycle 3,000; electricity included. Credit cards accepted.
Euro: Per adult 4.90; child (3-10 yrs) 3.87; tent 4.38; caravan or motorcaravan 5.16; car 2.06; m/cycle 1.54.

Reservations: made for 1 week stays in high season, but not really necessary. Address: San Giovanni in Campiglione 110, 06081 Assisi (Perugia). Tel: 075/813710 or 816816. FAX: 075/812335. E-mail: camping.assisi@edisons.it.

6800 Camping Europe Garden, Silvi Marina, nr Pescara

Site with swimming pool and views to the sea, 13 km. northwest of Pescara.

This site is somewhere decent to stay on the southeast Italian coast. It lies just back from the coast (2 km) on raised ground with views over the sea. The 204 pitches, all with 10A electricity, are nearly all on good terraces - difficulty may be experienced gaining access to some pitches; however, if installation of caravans is a problem a tractor is always available to help. When we visited the site was dry but we suspect life might become difficult on some pitches after heavy rain. Cars stand by units on over half of the pitches, in nearby parking spaces for the remainder. Most pitches are shaded. There is a good swimming pool of 300 sq.m. on site (swimming caps compulsory), jacuzzi and a small children's pool. The pool has a small bar and an entertainment programme is provided in season on a small stage and associated area within the pool boundary. A bus service is provided in July/Aug. to a private sandy beach at Silvi about 2 km. away. There are two good toilet blocks which are well cleaned and provide mixed British and Turkish style WCs, washbasins with free hot water, not fully enclosed, and free hot showers. The site is not suitable for disabled campers. Free weekly coach excursions are organised to different parts of the Province (10/7-30/8).

How to find it: Turn off inland S16 coast road at km. 433 stone for Silvi Alta and follow camp signs. From autostrada A14 take Pineto exit from north and Montesilvano exit from south. Signing is very good.

General Details: Open 1 May - 20 Sept. Electrical connections in all parts. Self-service shop. Restaurant. Bar. Tennis. Children's playground. Washing machines. Good bungalows for hire (80).

Charges 1999: Three charging seasons. Per person L. 7,000 - 11,000; child (3-8 yrs) 5,000 - 7,500; pitch 15,000 - 23,000; 2-man tent 8,000 - 13,000; electricity 3,000. Discounts for longer stays outside high season.

Reservations: made with L.150.000 deposit for first 2 weeks of August (min 2 weeks), at other times without deposit. Address: 64028 Silvi (Teramo). Tel: 085/930137 or 932844-5 (winter 085/75035). FAX: 085/932846. E-mail: egarden@camping.it or nosantar@tin.it.

ITALY - South

6805 Camping Heliopolis, Pineto

Attractive site with individual services and direct access to the beach.

Heliopolis is a well run site with a charming English speaking lady owner named Gigliola. We have included this site because it is unusually spacious for an Adriatic site, and is orderly, with clean and well maintained individual units consisting of shower, WC and kitchen unit for 120 of the 160 touring pitches. The pitches are of average size arranged in rows at right angles to the beach and most have artificial shade provided. Electrical connections (4A) are available on all and cars are parked near the entrance. The site opens directly onto a wide sand and shingle beach which shelves fairly rapidly and has lifeguards at all times. Like many Adriatic sites, it is close to the railway, and there is some noise from passing trains especially on the western side of the site. There are two excellent toilet blocks, one for men and one for women, with facilities for disabled campers. A pleasant bar, a games room, electronic games, a sizeable, attractive pool and children's pool, a good pizza restaurant with terraces, plus various beach facilities are also available. The shop offers general goods and attractive souvenirs of the Abruzzo region. The friendly reception staff can book trips to Rome, Napoli, Capri, the Republic of San Marino and other local attractions if required. Hairdresser on site in season. The site is very full in July/Aug. and the majority of guests are Italian with the live entertainment mostly in Italian. The Italians love it and the fun is contagious, also you can practice your language.

How to find it: Site is to the north of the town sharing an approach with Camping Pineto Beach; both sites are clearly signed from A14 road (exit Pineto) and SS16 (in town centre). If coming from the north, it may be worth the extra money to take the A14 if time is critical; the SS16 is busy but does offer the chance of sightseeing.

General Details: Open 1 April - 30 Sept. Bar/restaurant. Shops. Laundry facilities. Swimming pool (from June). Volleyball. Tennis and play pitches. Children's playground. Entertainment organised in high season. Doctor attends 2 hrs daily. Chemical disposal. Caravans and tents for hire.

Charges 1999: Three charging seasons. Per standard pitch L.18,000, 28,000 or 40,000; pitch with private facilities 32,000, 42,000 or 52,000; small tent pitch 8,000, 10,000 or 13,000; person 6,000, 9,000, 12,000; child (3-12 yrs) 5,000, 8,000, 10,000; electricity included; dog 3,000.

Reservations: Write to site for details. Address: Contrada Villa Fumosa 1, 64025 Pineto (TE). Tel: 085/9492720, -30 or -50. FAX: 085/9492171.

6811 Ipini Camping, Fiano Romano, nr Rome

see colour advert between pages 128/129

Excellent family site with pool, ideal for visiting Rome.

Roberto and Judy McKeever (Italian and Australian) and their partner Antonella have recently built this wonderful homely site in a quiet area 20 km. north of Rome. They spare no effort to make you welcome, ably assisted by their daughter and sons. There is one thoughtfully designed and decorated central block containing reception, restaurant, bar, snack bar and shop. It is spotless and the Italian food is wonderfully cooked, plentiful and very reasonable. The site is peaceful and well administered and the grassed terrace alongside the restaurant is busy at night with live entertainment being provided twice a week. Some of the 117 large pitches have excellent views. All have electricity (10A) and are arranged on terraces with mature trees providing some shade. The one excellent sanitary block is of hotel standard down to the decorative fittings in all cubicles. There are two extremely large and well equipped units for visitors with disabilities, new washing machines and all the supporting facilities are spotless. Hot water is free in the showers, washbasins and dishwashing sinks. The shop provides the basics and a children's play area has a baby lagoon. The new swimming pool, spa, and children's pool are superb and most welcome in the heat of summer. The site is some distance from Rome but this does ensure a tranquil existence away from the city heat and bustle. There is an air-conditioned bus service twice a day to the heart of Rome (L. 6000 return) and a free shuttle service to the local station and town. Bungalows for rent. All rates here are very competitive. The site was inspected over a weekend and was full of fun. We liked the personal touch and humour here. It is ideal for exploring Rome or the attractions close by including the medieval town of Fiano Romano or the archaeological site of 'Lucus Feronial'.

How to find it: From Rome ring road (GRA) take A1 exit to Fiano Romero. Pass through the town and follow the camping signs - there is only the one site.

General Details: Open all year. Bar. Restaurant. Shop. Snack bar. Swimming pool spa. Tennis. Children's play area. Paddle tennis. Mountain biking. Trekking. Canoeing. Washing machines. Motorcaravan services.

Charges 1999: Per person L. 10,000 - 11,000; child (3-12 yrs) 6,500 - 7,500; caravan 7,000 - 8,000; motor caravan 9,000 - 10,000; car 3,000 - 4,000; m/cycle 2,000 - 3,000; electricity included. Credit cards accepted.

AR Discount
Less 10%

Reservations: Contact site. Address: Via delle Sassete 1/A, 00065 Roma. Tel: 0765/453349. FAX: 0765/453057.

6810 Camping Seven Hills, Rome

Excellent, busy, hillside site with easy access to Rome.

A number of sites are available for visiting the 'Eternal City' and campers needs and preferences will vary. If you are looking for a very lively site which tends towards the impersonal then Seven Hills may be for you. It is in a delightful valley, flanked by two of the seven hills of Rome and is just off the autostrada ring road to the north of the city (4 km. from the centre - the site runs a bus service with frequency dictated by demand; extra charge). Arranged in two sections, the top half, near the entrance, restaurant and shop, consists of small, flat, grass terraces with two to four pitches on each, with smaller terraces for tents, all from hard access roads. Access to some pitches may be tricky. The flat section at the lower part of the site is reserved mainly for tents used by British (and one Dutch) tour operators who bring guests by coach. These tend to be younger people and the site along with its very busy pool has a distinctly youthful feel. There have been reports of some late night noise. The pool, which is at the bottom of the site has its own bar/snack bar and a room where the younger element tends to congregate along with a disco club elsewhere in the site. The site is a profusion of colour with flowering trees, plants and shrubs and a good covering of trees provides shade. An unusual feature of the site is a 'mini-zoo' and numerous peacocks strut around the terraces. The 80 pitches for tourers are not marked, but the management supervise in busy periods. The excellent central buildings house the well stocked shop and attractive restaurant and bar terrace. English is spoken and many notices are in English. Three well constructed sanitary blocks around the site have open plan washbasins, free hot water in average sized showers and British style WCs. Dishwashing under cover with cold water and facilities for disabled campers. All cash transactions on the site are made with a plastic card (similar to a BT phone card) from reception and there is a tight regime of passes and indelible ink wrist stamping at the pool (L 7,000/day 4,000 after 17.00). This is an extremely busy site with up to 10 touring buses with their occupants on the site during high season in addition to a very busy camping routine. There are bungalows, chalets and cabins to hire, all of varying standards adding to the large number of people and the feeling of constant changeover.

How to find it: Take exit 3 from autostrada ring-road on to Via Cassia (signed SS2 Viterbo - NOT Via Cassia Bis) and look for camp signs. Turn right after 1 km (13 km. stone) and follow small road for about 1 km. to site.

General Details: Open mid-March - mid-Oct. Shade in most parts. Electricity (3A) to some pitches. Shop. Bar/restaurant and terrace. Money exchange. Bus service to Rome. Table tennis. Volleyball. Swimming pool (salt water). Disco. Riding. Washing machines and irons. Chemical disposal. Excursions and cruises arranged.

Charges 1999: Per person (over 4 yrs) L. 13,000; tent 8,000; caravan 14,000; car 6,500; motorcaravan 14,000; m/cycle 4,000.

Reservations: Write to site. Address: Via Cassia 1216, 00191 Rome. Tel: 06/30310826. FAX: 06/30310039.

Camping Seven Hills - Rome

20 minutes by camp shuttle bus
from Rome centre
Supermarket • Swimming pool • Bar
Restaurant • Pizzeria • Disco

Via Cassia 1216, 00191 Roma
Tel. 06/3762751 - 30310826
Fax 06/30310039

6808 Camping La Genziana, Barrea

Unsophisticated campsite high in the Abruzzi mountains.

This is the place to get away from it all. Situated in the middle of Italy, it is well away from towns, yet only an hour or two from Rome or Pescara. This is a simple site with just adequate facilities but Sig. Pasetta makes everyone so welcome. There are 110 pitches, of which 100 have 3A electricity, with 50 more for tents. Mountain walking tracks start from the site and facilities for swimming, riding and fishing are all nearby. The site is not suitable for disabled people. The owner and his wife speak English.

How to find it: From autostrada A25, either take route 83 from Celano and site is signed 4 km. before Barrea, or route 17 from Pratola/Sulmona through Castel di Sangro. Then right to route 83 and site is 1 km. before Barrea.

General Details: Open all year. Bar and small shop but Barrea is just down the road. Motorcaravan services.

Charges 2000: Per person L. 9,000; child (under 9 yrs) 5,000; caravan 12,000; tent 11,000 - 12,000; motorcaravan 12,000; car 6,000; pet 5,000; electricity 3,000. No credit cards.

Reservations: Contact site. Address: Loc. Tre Croci, Parco Nazionale d'Abruzzo, 67030 Barrea (AQ). Tel: 0864/88101. FAX: as phone.

ITALY - South

6813 Camping Porticciolo, Rioveggio, nr Lake Bracciano

Small site with lake beach useful for visiting Rome and local historical Etruscan areas.

This is a small family run site which has its own private beach on the southwest side of Lake Brocciano. Allesandro and his wife Allesandra have worked hard to built up this site since 1982. They are charming and speak English. Allesandro is a Roman classical history expert and provides free documentary information on the local area and Rome. Unusually there is a free touring information computer terminal by reception, and a free CD will be provided to longer stay enthusiasts by Allesandro. A pleasant feature here is that the site is overlooked by the impressive castle in the village of Bracciano. There are 170 pitches (140 for tourers) split into two sections and some have lake views. The somewhat rustic, but clean, sanitary facilities are on the southern side of the site which means a little walk from the furthest pitches. Pitches are large and shaded by very green trees which are continuously watered in summer by a neat overhead watering system. All have electricity connections (3A, but 6A is available at a small extra charge). There are limited facilities here and a basic children's play area. WCs are British style with hot showers by token, washing facilities and machines. Essential provisions are offered in the shop and the bar is friendly with a large terrace. This is shared by the trattoria which opens lunch-times and the pizzeria in the evenings. The pizzas are traditional and superb, being produced in a wood fired oven. A small amount of entertainment is offered during the season and the lake is clean and great for swimming and powerboats are banned (it is Rome's drinking water! Also, separate ancient pipes directly feed the two famous fountains in St Peter's Square). Small boats, inflatables and windsurfers may be launched from the site. The site is peaceful and if you wish for an uncomplicated lakeside site away from the heat and hassle of the city then this is ideal. A bus service from outside the gate runs to central Rome (approx. 1 hour - L. 8,000 - known as a 'Birg' and equivalent to a UK all day run around ticket, used on the buses and metro and extremely good value). The site is also well placed to visit the ancient Etruscan city of Sutri, also Cerveteri which is one of the most ancient places in Italy and older than Rome itself.

How to find it: From Rome ring road (GRA) northwest side take Cassia exit to Bracciano S493 (be careful not to confuse this exit with 'Cassia bis' which is further northeast). Follow signs to village of Bracciano on southwest shore of Lago di Bracciano and site is clearly signed.

General Details: Open April - September. Shop (basic needs). Trattoria/pizzaria. Tennis. Five-a-side soccer. Small children's play area. Table tennis. Volleyball. Motorcaravan services. Tourist information.

Charges 1999: Per person L. 8,000 - 8,500; child (3-10 yrs) 6,500 - 7,000; tent, caravan or motorcaravan less than 5 m. 8,000 - 9,000, over 5 m. 10,000; small tent 6,000 - 7,000; car 2,500 - 3,000; m/cycle 2,000; electricity 3,000; dog 4,000 - 5,000. Credit cards accepted.

Reservations: Write to site. Address: Via Porticciolo, 00062 Bracciano (Roma). Tel. 06/99803060/ FAX: 06/99803030. E-mail romalake@aconet.it.

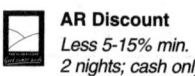

AR Discount
Less 5-15% min.
2 nights; cash only.

6815 Fondi Holiday Village, Salto di Fondi, nr Sperlonga

Picturesque seaside site with unusual cultural activity, midway between Rome and Naples.

Fondi is an attractive site, midway between Rome and Naples, 300 m. off the Terracina - Gaeta road (SS213). In a pinewood area, the carefully tended flowers and trees and the white painted buildings make it a very pleasant location. Sand dunes protect from offshore breezes. During high season there are cultural and sporting activities, a troop of ballet dancers entertain and teach, and plays, shows and films are staged in the open-air theatre. There is a wardrobe of over 400 costumes for children to use. As well as the Mediterranean beach of fine sand, there are two pools in the entertainment area near the restaurant, just back from the sea. With tennis courts, covered handball court, table tennis and a disco, there is much to offer. The 100 pitches for tourists are at the back of the site, but close to the amenities. They have some shade and are on flat grass, all with 3/5A electricity. The one large and five smaller toilet blocks are of modern construction and have some British type WCs. The showers have hot water on payment, with cold water in the washbasins and dishwashing places. Two family washrooms have hot water and facilities for disabled visitors. The large restaurant offers self service at lunch times with waiter service during the evenings serving mainly Italian and regional cuisine. A new bar, breakfast and TV rooms look out on the open, wooden fenced dance area and promenade fronting the site's private beach (250 m. wide, so there is always space). Signora Banotti, the lady owner speaks good English. All in all, an excellent site.

How to find it: Site signed on coast road SS213 between Gaeta and Terracina, 7 km. from Terracina. From Rome-Naples autostrada, depending on approach, use one of several exits between Frosinone and Ceprana.

General Details: Open all year. 40,000 sq.m. Good shade. Bar/restaurant, pizzeria, snack bar (all June-Sept). Supermarket. Greengrocer. Bazaar. Hairdresser. Main and children's swimming pools (instructor). Tennis. Table tennis. Handball. Disco. TV. Live theatre and ballet. Organised excursions possible to Rome, Capri, Naples, Pompei, Monte Cassino, etc. (with local agency).Washing machines and dryers. Gas supplies. Chemical disposal. Doctor on site daily. Dogs and pets not permitted. Bungalows for rent.

Charges 2000: Per pitch incl. 2 adults L. 30,000 - 76,000; extra person 10,000 - 22,000. No credit cards.

Reservations: Contact site. Address: Via Flacca km 6,800, 04020 Salto di Fondi (LT). Tel: 0771/555029 or 556282. FAX: 0771/555009. E-mail: holidayvillage@tiscalinet.it.

6820 Camping Baia Domizia, Baia Domizia, Mondragone, nr Napoli

Large, formal seaside site north of Naples with many amenities.

This very large site, about 70 km. north west of Naples, is largely covered by a pinewood, much of which has been left in its natural state. There are 1,200 touring pitches, often in clearings on ground which may be grassy, a bit sandy, or on a hardstanding. Finding a good pitch may take time, but staff help in season and there are many individual pitches numbered for reservation purposes. Many varieties of bushes, roses and other flowers have been added to the natural surroundings. The site is run on strict lines, with various regulations (eg. no dogs or radios) but it is not a regimented site, and the general atmosphere is quiet but easy-going. Although the site is so big, there is never very far to walk to the beach, though from the ends it may be some 300 m. to the central shops and restaurant. Near these are two good sized swimming pools, recently refurbished and a pleasant alternative to the sea on windier days, with a smaller children's pool. Seven good toilet blocks all have British style WCs, constant hot water in all washbasins (many in private cabins) and showers, and facilities for disabled people. Another super new block is under construction. A wide range of sports and other amenities is provided. Charges are undeniably high, but this site is well above average and very suitable for families with young children.

How to find it: Turning to Baia Domizia leads off Formia-Naples road 23 km. from Formia. From Rome-Naples autostrada, take Cassino exit to Formia. Site is to the north of Baia Domizia itself.

General Details: Open 29 April - 30 Sept. 450,000 sq.m. Many parts well shaded, but in full sun near beach. Electrical connections (3A) in all parts. Large supermarket and general shop. Large bar and self-service restaurant with pizzeria. Ice cream parlour. Sports ground. Children's playground. Bicycle hire. Fishing or riding 3 km. Tennis near. Excursions to Rome, Naples, Ischia, Capri. Bureau de change. Doctor on site daily. Washing machines, spin dryers. Gas supplies. Chemical disposal. Motorcaravan services. Bunglalows to rent. No dogs are accepted.

Charges 2000: Per person L. 6,000 - 16,000; child charged as adult; car or m/cycle 4,500 - 8,500; tent or caravan 11,500 - 23,000; motorcaravan 14,000 - 28,000; electricity included. Less 10% outside 24/5-4/9. Credit cards accepted.

Reservations: none, but min. 1 week stay in high season (July/Aug). Address: 81030 Baia Domizia (Caserta). Tel: 0823/930164 or 930126. FAX: 0823/930375.

6832 International Villagio I Pini, Piano di Sorrento, nr Napoli

Pleasant shady site just 3 km. before Sorrento centre.

We have selected this site because it is open all year and it is conveniently situated for public services into Sorrento, Pompei or Naples. It also avoids taking caravans into the astonishing traffic chaos of Sorrento town. There are 130 touring pitches all contained by hedges and a good swimming pool (covered in winter). Entry to this, together with all hot water and electricity, is free. There is a free bus service to a pay beach in nearby Meta. Camping I Pini is owned and operated by the Maresca family. Signora Maresca is English and they all offer you a warm welcome.

How to find it: From A3 Naples - Salerno motorway take Castellamare exit and SS145 Sorrento road. After 20 km, just past Meta town, look for large campsite sign on the right.

General Details: Open all year. Bar /restaurant. Large supermarket 200 m. Play area. Free entertainment (Aug. only). Bungalows (2-5 persons, centrally heated) to rent.

Charges 2000: (expected) Per person L. 11,000 - 14,000; caravan 11,000 - 14,000; car 5,000 - 6,000; tent: small 6,000 - 7,000, large 11,000 - 14,000.

Reservations: not usually necessary but write to Corso Italia 242, Piano di Sorrento, 80063 Naples. Tel 081/ 878689. FAX: 081/878770. E Mail: boblm@tin.it.

AR Discount
Less 10%

6835 Camping Riposo, Piano di Sorrento, nr Napoli

Small site with few facilities but reasonable charges.

Just 300 m. from the picturesque port of Piano di Sorrento is the tiny site of Camping Riposo. Simple, pretty and clean, this is only for those who just want a secluded place to park their `van whilst they explore this famous area. There are no entertainments and no pool - just a tiny bar and shop. The Scalici family offer a courteous and helpful service. The site is shaded by citrus trees and there are three excellent food shops nearby. Electrical connections are available and there is free hot water. Like most Italian sites, Riposo is very crowded in August.

How to find it: From Meta follow plentiful directions off main road SS145 (to Sorrento from autostrada at Castellamare). Access could be tricky for large units but gates can be opened wide.

General Details: Open 1 June - 30 Sept. Small bar and shop. Caravans for hire.

Charges 2000: Per person L. 9,000; child (1-6 yrs) 6,000; tent 7,500 - 10,000, acc. to size; caravan 11,000; motorcaravan 12,500; car 7,000; m/cycle 4,000; electricity and tax included.

Reservations: Write to site. Address: Via Cassano 12/14, 80063 Piano di Sorrento (NA). Tel: 081/8787374.

AR Discount
Less 15%

ITALY - South

6845 Centro Turistico San Nicola, Peschici, Gargano Peninsula

Busy, top class site on most attractive, sandy cove (but 75 km. from the autostrada).
This is a really splendid site occupying a hill-side, sloping down to a cove with a 500 m. beach of fine sand - a special feature is an attractive grotto at the eastern end. Surrounded by tree clad mountains, it is a quiet, well regulated site which is part of, but separate from, a tourist holiday complex in the same area. Hard access roads lead to spacious well constructed, grassy terraces, under shade from mature trees. Scores of pitches are on the beach fringes (no extra charge) and there is a separate area for campers with animals. There are 750 pitches of varying size, all with 5A electrical connections. Cars may have to be parked away from the pitches in high season. There are no static caravans but bungalows are available for rent. Six excellent, modern toilet blocks, two in the beach part, the others situated around the site, are of superb quality with British and Turkish style toilets and free hot water in the washbasins (some with toilets in private cabins), showers and dishwashing facilities. The shopping complex (open in high season) has a well stocked supermarket, greengrocer, hairdresser and bazaar for holiday items. There is a large bar/restaurant with terraces and a separate pizzeria. Another small shop and two small bars are by the beach. Entertainment is provided for young and old, by the restaurant in high season. The site is fairly remote with some interesting hairpins in the last 14 km. of the 75 km journey from the autostrada. With a neat, tidy appearance, the many flowerbeds provide a garden atmosphere of calm serenity, and the site prides itself in its tranquillity despite its size. The helpful staff all wear San Nicola shirts for identification. The site is popular with German campers (tannoy announcements and most notices in German only!) although English is spoken. We think this site is well worth the drive if you enjoy high quality beach sites and wish to explore the Gargano National Park.

How to find it: Leave autostrada A14 at exit for Poggio Imperiale, and proceed towards Peschici and Vieste. When signs for Peschici and Vieste diverge, follow Vieste signs keeping a sharp lookout for San Nicola. Then follow black signs for Centro Turistico San Nicola and pass Camping Baia San Nicola (on your left) just before site. It will take at least 1½ hrs from the motorway. Note: There is also a San Nicola Varano en-route which must be ignored.

General Details: Open 1 April - 15 Oct. 120,000 sq.m. Shade in main part. Electrical connections all parts (5A). Supermarket, fruit and fish shops, bazaar. Two beach bars (open 1 May). Bar/restaurant (open all season). Tennis. Watersports. Children's playground. Organised recreational activity July/Aug. Cash point. Coach and boat excursions. Washing machines and dryers. Chemical disposal. Bungalows for rent.

Charges 1999: Four charging seasons. Per adult L. 7,000 - 14,800; child (1-8 yrs) 4,800 - 10,500; tent 7,000 - 14,500; caravan or trailer tent 9,000 - 18,000; car 5,300 - 9,000; motorcaravan 12,600 - 22,000; m/cycle 4,500 - 7,800. Min. stay 7 days 18/6-3/9. No credit cards.

Reservations: Only made for site's own accommodation (min. 1 week). Address: 71010 Peschici (Foggia), Gargano. Tel: 0884/964024. FAX: 0884/964025.

6803 Camping Villagio Athena, Paestum

Compact, well run site by the sea and 2 miles from the Greek temples.
This level site, which has direct access to the beach, has most facilities to hand. Much of the site is in woodland, but sun worshippers will have no problem here. The access is easy and the staff are friendly. There are 150 pitches, of which only 20 are used for static units and these are unobtrusive. Sanitary facilities are in three blocks with mixed British and Turkish style WCs, washbasins and showers (cold water only) and hot showers on payment. There are dishwashing and laundry sinks, and toilets for disabled people. There is no disco, although there are cabaret shows provided in July/Aug. Dogs and barbecues are not permitted. The management, the Prearo brothers, aim for a pleasant and happy environment.

How to find it: Take SS18 through Paestum and, at southern end of town before the antiquities, turn right as signed and follow road straight down to sea. Site is well signed.

General Details: Open 1 April - 30 Sept. 20,000 sq.m. Shop and bar. Restaurant (open all day June - mid Sept). Riding. Tennis 1 km. Watersports. Chemical disposal. Hourly bus service. Bungalows for hire.

Charges 2000: Per person L. 7,000 - 10,000; pitch 15,000 - 25,000.

Reservations: Contact site. Address: Via Ponte di Ferro, 84063 Paestum (SA). Tel: 0828/851105 (winter 0828/724725).

6842 Camping Sant' Antonio, Seiano, Vico Equense

Peaceful base from which to explore Pompei, Herculaneum and Sorrento.

This pretty little site, just across the road from Seiano beach, would suit caravanners who like a peaceful (for Italy) location. There are only 150 pitches which are in shade offered by orange, lemon and walnut trees. The single sanitary block provides hot and cold showers, washbasins and British style WCs. Hot water is on payment. In summer (mid-June - end Sept) there is a regular 15 minute bus service to the Circumvesuviana railway which runs frequently to Sorrento, Pompei, Herculaneum and Naples - the only sensible way to travel for non-party sightseeing. English is spoken by the Maresca family who run the site.

How to find it: Take route SS163 from Castellamare to Sorrento. Just 50 m. after tunnel by-pass around Vico Equense, watch for very hard right turn for Seiano beach and follow signs down the narrow road.

General Details: Open 15 March - 15 Oct. 10, 000 sq.m. of flat, shady ground with easy access. Electricity to all pitches (3A). Small shop, bar and restaurant. Fishing and boat slipway 100 m. Bungalows for rent.

Charges 2000: Per person L. 10,000 - 12,000; child (up to 8 yrs) 8,000 - 11,000; caravan 11,000 - 13,000; motorcaravan 12,000 - 16,000; electricity included. Credit cards accepted.

Reservations: Contact site. Address: Via Marina d'Equa, Seiano, 80069 Vico Equense (NA). Tel: 081/8028570 (when closed 081/8028576). FAX: as phone.

6850 Sea World Village, San Giorgio, Bari

Seaside site in the far south of Italy.

There are few good sites in this part of Italy but Sea World Village (formerly Camping Internazionale San Giorgio) is very acceptable as a transit stop or short stay. The new owners have considerably improved the site. Bari is a busy city, but Sea World Village is on the southern edge. There are 20 tourist pitches, all with electricity, well separated from the static pitches. Access to the sea is via rocks and concrete platforms, with a small swimming pool at the water's edge, plus a separate, man-made, sandy beach which is cleaned daily. The large car park and many changing cabins means the site is crowded at weekends with day visitors. The sanitary blocks are of modern construction with mainly British style WCs and free hot showers. There are 42 bungalows, several built in the local `Trulli' style, for hire on a weekly basis.

How to find it: Take the Bari exit from autostrada A14 and follow signs for Brindisi on the dual carriageway ring road (Tangenziole). After exit 15 watch carefully for the San Giorgio exit. Turn left and site is signed 200 m. ahead, across traffic lights.

General Details: Open all year. 50,000 sq.m. Restaurant, pizzeria and market (all year). Bar (15/6-15/9). Swimming pool (15/6-15/9). Roller skating, hockey, football and tennis areas. Bowling. Disco. Watersports. Riding or golf 10 km. Fishing 5 km. Writing room. Doctor calls.

Charges 1999: Per person L.10,000 - 15,000; pitch 15,000 - 20.000; small tent with car 10,000 - 16,000 - 8,000, no car 5,000 - 10,000; electricity 3,000.

Reservations: Only for bungalows. Address: San Giorgio, ss Adriatica 78, 70126 Bari. Tel: 080/5491202.

6852 Village Camping Marina di Rossano, Rossano

Excellent site in the far south.

This is the most welcoming site we have visited in this area. Most of the staff in reception, the shops, bar and restaurant speak English with a smile. The location is not so far as it seems - it can be reached by either the west or east autostrada, without the final tortuous or very busy roads to some nearer coastal sites. It took us about four hours from Naples and it is approximately two hours from Bari. There are about 250 pitches, all under tall, shady poplar trees and cars are parked in a secure area away from the pitches. It is entirely secluded and leads directly to a large stretch of private beach. There are several toilet blocks mostly with free hot water. Dogs are only accepted with medical clearance and payment. Very suitable for disabled people, their own facilities are provided. There are many apartments and bungalows to rent. The site has an excellent swimming pool and sporting facilities, with attentive entertainment staff, at reasonable prices.

How to find it: From the north take the east coast highway (route 106 - Ionica). Leave at Rossano exit and a football stadium is immediately opposite with a site sign to its left. Follow signs for 1 km. to site. From the south, at Rossano exit turn left under road bridge. Turn left immediately before football stadium.

General Details: Open 1 April - 30 Sept. Shop. Bars. Restaurant. Swimming pools. Private beach. Tennis. Small football pitch. Basketball. Volleyball. Bicycle hire. Apartments and bungalows for hire.

Charges 1999: Per pitch L. 26,000 - 42,000; adult 7,000 - 11,500; child (3-5 yrs) 4,500 - 8,000; second car 2,500 - 4,000; dog free - 8,000; electricity incl. Credit cards accepted.

Reservations: Contact site. Address: C. da Leuca, CP98, 87069 Rossano (Cosenza). Tel: 0983/516054. FAX: 0983/512069. E-mail: sogecamp@mediterranea-net.it.

ITALY - Sardinia

The rugged coastline of Sardinia, rising from the sea of varying colour, including the incredible green of the Costa Smerelda, will amaze you. With some beaches of fine white sand, others surrounded by cliffs or rocky coves, much of the 1,300 km. of coastline is seldom visited by tourists. There are no motorways but the roads are generally quite good, apart from in the really remote areas. Petrol stations are few and far between, and close early, some even before noon. The capital, Cagliari, lies in the south of the island and has interesting architecture with some charming small resorts in the vicinity. There are regular car ferries to the islands of the north coast and to Corsica. Lobster is a speciality and the best local wine is Vernaccia, a strong amber coloured wine with a definite orange flavour. The weather is hot, dry and sunny from May to September, with a sea breeze to cool you on the beaches. We include two sites on the island. For ferry information contact: **Southern Ferries Ltd, 179 Piccadilly, London W1V 9DB. Tel: 0171 491 4968**

6860 Camping Capo d'Orso, Palau

Pretty seaside site on northern edge of Costa Smerelda.
This is a well established and decidedly pretty site on a hillside sloping down to the sea and facing Caprera Island and several beaches, 4.5 km. from the village of Palau. The terrain is fairly rocky but the 450 pitches are on level, sparsely grassed terraces, with quite good access roads. Most have 3A electricity and are of a fair size (40-80 sq.m). Cars are parked away from the pitches in July/Aug. This side of the island seems hotter and more sheltered from the wind, but there is not a lot of shade. Although the site is open May - Sept, the restaurant, bar, pizzeria, takeaway and shop are only open from 1 June, and other facilities, including the scuba-diving, sailing school and boat excursions to the nearby small islands only operate in the main season. Other facilities include tennis, an underground disco, children's and adults entertainment programme (in high season). There are pontoon moorings for boats and boat hire arrangements in high season. Sanitary facilities, in three blocks, are adequate, with hot showers (on payment in season, free at other times), open washbasins, washing-up and laundry sinks (cold water) and mainly Turkish, but with some British, type WCs. They seemed well maintained when we visited in early June, although not all the blocks were open at that time. This site could be a useful alternative to our other site on Sardinia, being somewhat cheaper, smaller and less formally organised, but with significantly less shade.

How to find it: Site is 5 km. from Palau, in the northeast of Sardinia, on the coast opposite (southwest of) Caprera Island.

General Details: Open 1 May - 30 Sept. Bar/restaurant. Pizzeria. Takeaway. Shop (all from 1/6). Tennis. Scuba diving, windsurfing, sailing (all main season). Boat hire and moorings. Disco. Entertainment programmes and excursions. Chemical disposal. Bungalows and caravans for hire.

Charges 1999: Per adult L. 7,000 - 12,000; child (6-12 yrs) 5,000 - 10,000; small tent (max. 2 persons) 7,000 - 25,000; large tent or caravan 10,000 - 35,000; motorcaravan 10,000 - 41,000; car or m/cycle free - 6,000; electricity 4,000.

Reservations: Contact site. Address: Golfe delle Saline, 07020 Palau (SS). Tel: 0789/702007. FAX: 0789/702006. E-mail: info@nuragica.it.

6855 Camping Baia Blu La Tortuga, Aglientu, nr S. Teresa di Gallura

Aptly named, large site situated on a bay of startling blue sea and golden sand.
La Tortuga is in one of the nicest corners of this island, enjoying welcome breezes and convenient for the ferry at St Teresa di Gallura (for Corsica). The site is under the same ownership as Marepineta (no. 6000) and has excellent facilities including some very modern sanitary installations. The four blocks of a similarly unusual design provide an exceptionally good ratio of facilities to pitches. The most unusual feature is the combined private shower/washbasin cabins (for rent), with controllable hot showers (on payment) and free hot water to the basins. Apart from the large number of showers, British and Turkish style WCs and washbasins, there are footbaths, basins for children, sinks for dishes and laundry (hot water am. clothes, pm. dishes) and facilities for disabled people. There are washing machines, dryers and irons. The 800 pitches (550 for touring units) all have electricity connections (3A) and are arranged in rows between tall pines, eucalyptus and shrubs with good access avenues and plenty of shade. Catering facilities include an attractive restaurant, pizzeria and takeaway and a small, pleasant bar. A large site, there is direct access to the beach and an extensive range of amenities, both on site and nearby. Used by tour operators.

How to find it: Site is on the north coast between towns of Costa Paradiso and S. Teresa di Gallura (18 km) at Pineta di Vignola Mare.

General Details: Open 15 April - 30 Sept. Bar. Restaurant, pizzeria, snack bar and takeaway (May-Sept). Supermarket. Children's playground. Tennis. Volleyball. Football. Table tennis. Games/TV rooms. Disco 50 m. Windsurfing school.Diving school. Entertainment and sports activities in season. Excursions. Riding near. Barbecue area. Gas supplies. Chemical disposal. Motorcaravan services. Mobile homes and caravans for hire.

Charges 1999: Four charging seasons. Per person L. 8,000 - 16,500; junior (under 10 yrs) or senior (over 60 yrs) 6,000 - 13,000; pitch incl. water and electricity 18,000 - 37,000, with electricity 15,000 - 33,000, tent pitch incl. electricity 12,000 - 26,000; private washcabin 5,000, with shower 11,000. No credit cards.

Reservations: made with L. 30,000 deposit. Address: Pineta di Vignola Mare, 07020 Aglientu (SS), Sardegna. Tel: 079/602060 (winter: 0365/520018). FAX: 079/602040. (winter: 0365/520690).

Heritage Classic European Rescueline

VEHICLE BREAKDOWN AND RECOVERY PLUS PERSONAL INSURANCE COVER.

Originally only available for owners of classic cars - now available to readers of The Alan Rogers Guide at a specially reduced rate including a 10% Discount
AND NO LIMIT TO THE AGE OF YOUR CAR/MOTORHOME

Exclusively arranged with Bishopsgate Insurance in association with Green Flag National Breakdown and only available from

Bishopsgate

DENEWAY GUIDES & TRAVEL LTD

Chesil Lodge, West Bexington, Dorchester, Dorset, DT2 9DG.
Telephone: 01308 897809   Facsimile: 013 08 89 80 17

"Heritage Classic European Rescueline"

If your car breaks down or you are involved in an accident, a free phone call to Green Flag National Breakdown's European Control Centre will bring rapid assistance. Their English speaking controllers will be able to pinpoint your position and brief the nearest approved garage or agent so you will soon be on your way.

Not only does Heritage Classic European Rescueline provide an excellent breakdown assistance service, but it also provides comprehensive insurance cover for you and your passengers.

Summary of Vehicle Breakdown Cover			Summary of Personal Insurance Cover		
Cover Before Commencement of Travel	To provide a replacement vehicle if your vehicle is lost through breakdown or accident up to 7 days prior to departure	Up to £750	Cancellation and Curtailment	Provides Insurance cover for holiday cancellations from the moment the premium is paid and for unused travel and accommodation not used if you have to curtail your holiday	Up to £3,000*
Roadside Assistance and Towing	Most breakdowns can be repaired quickly at the roadside although occasionally the vehicle may need to be towed to a garage	No financial limit	Medical and Other Expenses	Cover includes medical and hospital fees and additional accommodation charges. In the event of a medical emergency the National Breakdown Controller will contact Assistance International who will contact the relevant hospital and guarantee its charges. They will also arrange repatriation to the UK (including Air Ambulance) when necessary	Up to £2 million
Emergency Labour Costs	Should your vehicle need repairs to enable you to continue your journey	Up to £100	Additional Hospital Benefits	This is an addition to any amount payable under "Medical and Other Expenses"	Up to £600 (£20 per day)
Location and Despatch of Any Necessary Spare Parts	Where these are not available locally (excluding their actual cost)	No financial limit	Personal Accident	To provide compensation following an accidental bodily injury	Up to £15,000
Alternative Travel Expenses Following Loss of Use of Vehicle	The cost of transporting your party to their original destination, or repatriation to the UK, or the cost of a hire car to allow you to continue your journey	No financial limit, except £750 overall if car hire is provided	Baggage	"New for Old" cover for items less than 2 years old	Up to £1,500*
Extra Accommodation Costs	While awaiting completion of local vehicle repairs	£45 per person per day	Money and Documents	Cover for loss of travel documents and money from 72 hours prior to departure	Up to £500
Vehicle Repatriation	Cost of transporting vehicle and passengers to the UK	No financial limit	Loss of Passport	Additional travel expenses incurred in replacing lost/stolen passport	Up to £250
Vehicle Collection	The additional travelling expenses for one person to collect vehicle (once overseas repairs have been completed)	Up to £600	Additional Expenses	To cover cost of travel and accommodation if your ferry or rail transporter is delayed	Up to £200
Alternative Driver	Cost of chauffeur and additional accommodation costs should only driver become incapacitated	No financial limit	Additional Accommodation	Or tent hire costs if tent becomes uninhabitable during your holiday	Up to £100
Theft	To pay for damage to your vehicle as a result of break in	Up to £175	Delay	Compensation if your ferry crossing is delayed of £20 per 12 hours	Up to £60
Legal Expenses	To cover costs of providing legal defence or in pursuing claims against third parties following a road traffic accident	Up to £25,000	Personal Liability	If you are held to be legally liable for injury or damage to other people or their property, cover is provided to pay for damages and claimants costs and expenses	Up to £1 million
Advance of Funds/Customs Duty	An advance of funds to act as security for bail or to overcome any Customs Duty claim	Up to £4,000	Legal Expenses	To cover cost of pursuing a claim against a third party whilst on holiday	Up to £25,000
				*Excesses: The first £25 of each and every claim per insured is excluded	

Great Value Vehicle Breakdown & Recovery
plus Personal Insurance Cover

Cost of Heritage Classic European Rescueline			
Period of Cover	*Vehicle Breakdown*	*Personal Insurance Adult*	*Personal Insurance Child**
1 Day	£19.00	£6.00	£4.00
2 Days	£20.00	£7.00	£4.50
3 Days	£21.00	£8.00	£5.00
4 Days	£22.00	£9.00	£6.00
5 Days	£24.00	£10.00	£6.50
6 Days	£26.00	£12.00	£7.00
7 Days	£28.00	£13.00	£7.50
8 Days	£30.00	£14.00	£8.00
9 Days	£32.00	£15.00	£8.50
10 Days	£33.00	£16.00	£9.00
11 Days	£34.00	£17.00	£9.50
12 Days	£35.00	£18.00	£10.00
13 Days	£36.00	£19.00	£11.00
14 Days	£37.00	£21.00	£11.50
15 Days	£38.00	£22.00	£12.00
16 Days	£39.00	£23.00	£12.50
17 Days	£40.00	£24.00	£13.00
18 Days	£41.00	£25.00	£13.50
19 Days	£43.00	£26.00	£14.00
20 Days	£44.00	£27.00	£15.00
21 Days	£45.00	£28.00	£15.50
22 Days	£46.00	£29.00	£16.00
23 Days	£48.00	£30.00	£17.00
24 Days	£49.00	£31.00	£17.50
25 Days	£50.00	£32.00	£18.00
26-32 Days	£59.00	£39.00	£23.00
33-39 Days	£68.00	£46.00	£27.00
40-46 Days	£77.00	£52.00	£32.00
47-53 Days	£86.00	£59.00	£36.00
54-60 Days	£95.00	£66.00	£41.00
61-67 Days	£104.00	£72.00	£45.00
Additional Week or part	£9.00	£6.00	£4.00
Caravan/TrailerSupp.	£13.00	-	-

LESS 10% DISCOUNT

*Children from 4 up to 14 years. Children under 4 Free. Premiums include Insurance Premium Tax.

HERITAGE CLASSIC EUROPEAN RESCUELINE DEPARTURE PACK - Available free to all Heritage Classic European Rescueline policyholders - containing a GB sticker, useful tips on preparing your vehicle for the journey, details of documentation required for both vehicle and travellers, and a country guide to motoring abroad.

Please Note:
1. LIMITS OF COVER: Each Section of the insurance has an overall limit per Insured Person, but please note that other limits within the section may apply. For example, the overall limit under the Baggage Section is £1,500 but there is a single item limit of £250, and in respect of valuables as defined under this section a limit of £300 applies.
2. Heritage Classic European Rescueline contains a "7 DAY REFUND GUARANTEE". If the insurance does not meet your needs please return it to the
issuing agent within 7 days (and before your date of departure) and the premium will be refunded in full.
3. This insurance is designed to cover most hazards which may affect your holiday, but it does contain certain conditions and exclusions. These are detailed in the full policy wording.

IMPORTANT: This leaflet only gives a summary of the cover provided by Heritage Classic European Rescueline. You are strongly advised to read the full wording of this insurance as it constitutes your "contract of insurance". Full details of the policy wording are available on request but in any event will be provided when you purchase the insurance.

HOW TO APPLY

FOR IMMEDIATE COVER - TELEPHONE 01308 897809 OR FAX 013 08 89 80 17 -VISA, VISA DELTA, MASTERCARD, SWITCH AND SOLO ACCEPTED
OR COMPLETE AND RETURN THE APPLICATION FORM OVERLEAF AND SEND IT WITH YOUR CHEQUE TO:

DENEWAY GUIDES & TRAVEL LTD
CHESIL LODGE, WEST BEXINGTON, DORCHESTER, DORSET, DT2 9DG.
TELEPHONE: 01308 897809   FACSIMILE: 013 08 89 80 17

Bishopsgate

HERITAGE CLASSIC EUROPEAN RESCUELINE

APPLICATION FORM

NAME OF APPLICANT (Mr/Mrs/Miss/Ms) ....

ADDRESS...

.... Post Code ....

TEL. NO .... WORK ....

PERIOD OF TRAVEL........................... DAYS COMMENCING ON ....

NAMES OF ALL PASSENGERS IN VEHICLE (State Mr/Mrs/Miss/Ms)

AGE
(if under 16)

1   APPLICANT...   ....

2   ....

3   ....

4   ....

5   ....

6   ....

VEHICLE DETAILS

MAKE & MODEL...

REG. NO...........................EST. VALUE...YEAR...........................

MOTOR INSURERS...EXPIRY DATE...........................

ARE YOU A MEMBER OF A CAR CLUB ....

CARAVAN/TRAILER DETAILS

MAKE & MODEL ....

VALUE .... YEAR ....

COUNTRIES TO BE VISITED

....

....

COVER REQUIRED

PERSONAL TRAVEL INSURANCE   PREMIUM

.... Adults @ .... each   £ ....

.... Children @ .... each   £ ....

Vehicle Breakdown Insurance   £ ....

Caravan/Trailer (if applicable)   £ ....

Total £ ....

Less 10% Alan Rogers Guide Readers Discount

Amount Payable   Total £ ....

- Please make cheques payable to: **Deneway Guides & Travel Ltd.**
- Please debit my Visa ❑   Visa Delta ❑   Mastercard ❑   Switch ❑   Solo ❑ card (please tick)

Name that appears on card ....

Expiry date...........................Card No...Signature...............................

LUXEMBOURG

The Grand Duchy of Luxembourg is an independent sovereign state, 999 square miles in area lying between Belgium, France and Germany. Geographically, the Grand Duchy is divided into two sections: in the north the uplands of the Ardennes, a hilly and scenic region, in the south mainly rolling farmlands and woods, bordered on the east by the wine growing area of the Moselle Valley. Luxembourg City is one of the most spectacularly sited capitals in Europe and home to about one fifth of the population. Luxembourg is essentially a Roman Catholic country. For further information contact:

Luxembourg Tourist Office, 122, Regent Street, London W1R 5FE
Tel: 020 7434 2800 Fax: 020 7734 1205 E-mail: tourism@luxembourg.co.uk

Population
389,800; density 151 per sq. km.

Capital
Luxembourg City.

Climate
A temperate climate prevails, the summer often extending from May to late October.

Language
Letzeburgesch is the national language, with French and German also being official languages.

Currency
Luxembourg Franc interchangeable with the Belgium Franc. Divides into 100 centimes and comes in coins worth 5, 10, 20 and 50 francs and notes worth 100, 500, 1000 and 5000 francs.

Banks
Open 08.30/09.00-12.00 and 13.30-16.30.
Credit Cards: are widely accepted.

Post Offices
Open 08.00-12.00 and 14.00-17.00 (but those in villages often operate more restricted hours).

Time
GMT plus 1 (summer BST +1).

Telephone
For calls from Luxembourg to the UK the code is 0044 followed by the STD code omitting initial 0. To call Luxembourg from the UK the code is 00 352 followed by the number (no area codes).

Public Holidays
New Year; Carnival Day, mid-Feb; Easter Mon; May Day; Ascension; Whit Mon; National Day, 23 June; Assumption, 15 Aug; All Saints; All Souls; Christmas, 25, 26 Dec.

Shops
Open Mon 14.00-18.30. Tues to Sat 08.30-12.00 and 14.00-18.30, (grocers and butchers close at 15.00 on Sat).

Motoring
Speed Limits: Caravans and motorhomes (3.5 tons) 31 mph (50 kph) in built up areas, caravans 46 mph (75 kph) and 56 mph (90 kph) on other roads and motorways respectively, motorhomes 56 mph (90 kph) and 75 mph (120 kph).
Fuel: Visa and Eurocard are accepted.
Parking: A Blue Zone area exists in Luxembourg City (discs from ACL, police stations, tourist offices) but parking meters are also available.

Overnighting
Generally only allowed on camp sites.

Useful Addresses
Motoring Organisation:
Automobile Club du G-D de Luxembourg (ACL)
54 route de Longwy, 8007 Bertrange. Tel: 450045.
Offices hours: Mon-Fri 08.30-12.00, 13.30-18.00
Tourist Information:
Tourist Information Societies (Syndicat d'Initiative) with offices in most towns. Closed lunch time - times vary.

770 Camping Gaalgebierg, Esch-sur-Alzette

Good quality site near French border
Occupying an elevated position on the edge of town, this pleasant site is run by the local camping and caravan club. Although surrounded by hills and with a good variety of trees, not all pitches have shade. There are 150 pitches (100 for tourists) 100 sq.m., on grass, marked out by trees, some on a slight slope. All have 16A electricity and TV points. There is a small bar (on demand) with terrace, a shop for basics, plus table tennis and a children's playground. The site has an entertainment and activities programme in peak season. The sanitary units, which can be heated, provide British WCs, washbasins with free hot water (some in cubicles), hot showers on payment, excellent facilities for disabled people and babies, and dishwashing and laundry sinks. All have been recently re-furbished and have a key-card entry system. The site now operates its own minibus for visits to Luxembourg city and other excursions, free to campers. The site also provides the Luxembourg card.

How to find it: Site is well signed from the centre of Esch, but a sharp look out is needed as there are two acute right-handers on the approach to the site.

General Details: Open all year. Shop. Bar. Restaurant near. Children's playground. Volleyball. Table tennis. Boules. Badminton. Swimming pool and tennis nearby. Entertainment in season. Laundry. Chemical disposal.

Charges 1999: Per pitch LFr. 130; adult 130; child (3-12 yrs) 65; electricity (16A) 50; local tax per person 20. Less 10% for stays of 7 days, 20% for 30 days excl. July/Aug. No credit cards.

Reservations: Write to site with deposit. Address: 4001 Esch-sur-Alzette. Tel: 541069. FAX: 549630.

LUXEMBOURG

776 Camping Europe, Remich

Useful touring site by River Moselle, close to town activities.

This municipal site is the best we could find on the road which runs alongside the Moselle. Its facilities are acceptable and clean, but not luxurious, it is convenient for the town centre and is good value. We recommend that you arrive early in season as the site fills up quickly. The 110 marked pitches, all with 10A electricity, are on level grass with no static or long stay units. The municipal swimming pool and ice skating complex is at one end of the site (no direct access). The sanitary building contains British WCs, washbasins with cold water only and free hot showers. The town is a picturesque and popular resort with a tree shaded promenade along the river bank, wine cellars and facilities for wine tasting, many sporting facilities, entertainment and restaurants.

How to find it: From Rue de Moselle (running alongside river) just south of the river bridge, turn (by large car park) into Rue de Camping, and site is on left.

General Details: Open 5 April - 16 September. Chemical disposal. Within walking distance of services and attractions.

Charges guide: Per pitch LFr. 130; adult 120; child (under 15 yrs) 60; electricity 35.

Reservations: Write to site for details. Address: Rue de Camping, 5550 Remich. Tel: 698018.

775 Camping Bettembourg, Bettembourg

Small municipal site, exclusively for tourists with immaculate modern facilities.

This small site on the southern outskirts of Bettembourg is beautifully maintained. The 25 pitches, accessed from a central paved roadway, have some neatly trimmed dividing hedges and all have 16A electricity. The sanitary facilities are very good with British WCs, washbasins in cubicles, spacious showers with dividers, seat and hooks, a suite for disabled visitors, fully equipped baby room, dishwashing and laundry facilities, all with free hot water. The warden is justifiably proud of them. A cosy club room with TV and coffee bar is available should the weather be inclement. Brochures showing the local cycle path network and other tourist information may be obtained from reception. The site is near the railway station and marshalling yard so there is some noise during the day. A good value site.

How to find it: From the town centre follow camping signs, site lies to the south of the town, near the railway station, marshalling yard and Parc Municipal.

General Details: Open 15 April - 30 September. Clubroom with bar, coffee bar and TV. Bread available daily (order by 9 pm the day before). Laundry. Chemical disposal. Reception closed 12.00-14.00; barrier closed 23.00-07.00. Only French spoken.

Charges guide: Per pitch incl. electricity LFr. 150; adult 150; child (3-14 yrs) 70.

Reservations: Write to site for details. Address: Parc Jacquinot, 3241 Bettembourg. Tel: 513646. FAX: 520357.

781 Caravaning-Parc Martbusch, Berdorf

Relaxing, well tended site on edge of small town, with excellent facilities.

A municipal site adjacent to the sports facilities of an elegant small town, this site is kept neat and tidy by the parks department. The touring section is well screened from the long stay area and shaded by mature trees. The 110 grassy touring pitches (plus 50 for seasonal units) are divided by hedges, all with electricity (10A) and accessed from tarmac roadways. The sanitary facilities are housed in two good quality modern buildings which provide British WCs, washbasins (some in cubicles), spacious showers with dividers, seats and hooks (07.00-11.00 and 17.00-22.00 only), dishwashing and laundry facilities, units for babies and disabled visitors. Hot water is free throughout. There is a shop and snack bar, TV and games rooms and a 'salle de séjour'. Adjoining the site is a recreation complex which includes minigolf, tennis, indoor swimming pool (adults LFr 70; child 40; open during July/Aug), fitness centre, playgrounds, marked walks and rock climbing in the surrounding area.

How to find it: Site and recreation centre are well signed from the Consdorf - Echternach road in Berdorf centre. Follow signs to `piscine' towards Beaufort and Grundhof.

General Details: Open all year. Shop and snack bar (1/4-31/10). Children's playground. TV and games room. Fishing, bicycle hire 6 km. Riding 8 km. Golf 15 km. Bottle bank. Laundry. Chemical disposal. Recreation centre adjacent.

Charges guide: Per pitch LFr. 160; adult 160; child (3-14 yrs) 100; electricity 60. No credit cards.

Reservations: Write for details to: Tourist Info-Service CR, 7 an der Laach, 6550 Berdorf. Tel: 790643. Site address: 3 Bäim Maartbësch, 6552 Berdorf. Tel: 790545. FAX: 799182.

764 Camping Auf Kengert, Larochette

Agreeable site with good shop and restaurant, northeast of Luxembourg city.

A friendly welcome awaits you at this peacefully situated, family run site, 2 km. from Larochette, with 180 individual pitches, all with electricity (4/16A). Some are in a very shaded woodland setting, on a slight slope with fairly narrow access roads. There are six hardened pitches for motorcaravans on a flat area of grass, complete with motorcaravan service facilities. Further pitches are in an adjacent and more open meadow area. The well maintained sanitary installations are in two parts with free hot water throughout; the modern, heated unit has British style WCs, washbasins (some in cubicles), and excellent, fully equipped cubicles for disabled visitors. The showers (older in style) and a laundry room are located below the central building which houses the restaurant, large well stocked shop, etc. There is a good swimming pool for the summer months. This site is popular in season, so early arrival is advisable, or you can reserve.

How to find it: From Larochette take the CR118 (towards Mersch) and just outside town turn right on CR119 towards Schrondweiler, site is 2 km. on right.

General Details: Open 1 March - 8 Nov. Shop. Bar. Restaurant. Children's playground. Swimming pool (Easter - 30 Sept). Paddling pool. Fishing, bicycle hire, golf or riding 8 km. Laundry facilities. Gas supplies. Chemical disposal. Motorcaravan services. Bottle bank. Good English spoken.

Charges 2000: Per person LFr. 360 - 440; child (2-18 yrs) 160 - 240; electricity 80; students, walkers and cyclists less 10%. No credit cards.
Euro: per person 8.92 -10.91; child (2-18 yrs) 3.97 - 5.95; electricity 1.98.

Reservations: Write to site. Address: 7633 Larochette/Medernach. Tel: 837186. FAX: 878323. E-mail: info@kengert.lu.

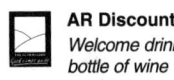 **AR Discount**
Welcome drink; bottle of wine on departure

Moien ! (which means hello in Luxembourg language)

We would like to welcome you to our family run site, peacefully set in a splendid nature. We think it is ideal for overnight stops or longer stays, perfectly situated on your way South or East.

Sanitary installations are well maintained, hot water is free and WC's are British style.

Our policy is to provide full service whole year round.

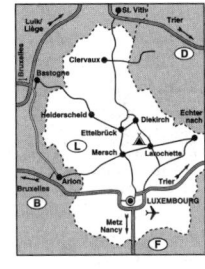

You may enjoy our solar-energy heated pool, our fine restaurant with real log-fire and our large supermarket. We can provide calor and other gas as well as unleaded petrol. For your laundry there are washing machines and dryers. Don't worry about the euro, we can exchange your Sterlings against the daily bank-rate.

We look forward to meeting you in Luxembourg !

Camping Auf Kengert

L-7633 Larochette/Medernach   Grand Duché de Luxembourg
Tel. +352-837186   fax +352-878323
www.kengert.lu   e-mail: info@kengert.lu

**The sites in LUXEMBOURG featured in this guide
are shown on the BENELUX map on page 369**

LUXEMBOURG

766 Camping Kockelscheuer, Kockelscheuer, nr Luxembourg

Neat site in quiet position close to the city.

This is a much larger site than Bettembourg (no. 775), closer to Luxembourg city (4 km. from the centre) and quietly situated (although possibly some aircraft noise). On a slight slope, there are 161 individual pitches of good size, either on flat ground at the bottom or on wide flat terraces with easy access, all with electricity. There is also a special area for tents. The two identical sanitary buildings have British WCs; washbasins with shelf, mirror and hot water (but no individual cabins), and free pre-set hot showers. For children there is a large area with modern play equipment on safety tiles and next door to the site is a sports centre. Charges are very reasonable. There is a friendly welcome from the new multi-lingual manager.

How to find it: Site is SSW of Luxembourg city on the N31 to Bettembourg.

General Details: Open Easter - 31 Oct. Electrical connections (16A). Shop (order bread the previous day). General room. Snack bar. Restaurant in adjacent sports centre also with minigolf, tennis, squash, etc. Washing machines. Rest room. Motorcaravan services. Reception closed 1200-1400 hrs.

Charges 1999: Per person Lfr. 120; child (3-14 yrs) 60; pitch 140; electricity 50 (1 or 2 days); Special weekly terms for pensioners (over 60) outside 15/6-15/9.

Reservations: are made but site says you should find space if you arrive by 5 p.m. Address: 22 Route de Bettembourg, 1899 Kockelscheuer. Tel: 471815.

761 Camping Birkelt, Larochette

Large well organised holiday site in good walking country.

This is very much a family site, with many tour operator tents and mobile homes. Set in an elevated position in attractive undulating countryside, it is well laid out. A radial tarmac road runs round the site with 400 large grass pitches, mostly sloping, many with a fair amount of shade, on either side of gravel access roads in straight rows or circles, all with electric points. As well as the swimming pool complex just outside the site entrance (free for campers), activities include table tennis, a football ground, a fitness centre with solarium and sauna, children's play areas and animation in high season. The three modern sanitary buildings are well situated around the site, with British WCs, mostly open washbasins (6 cabins in one block) and although there are no dividers in the showers, free hot water is supplied at all points. There are also dishwashers (on payment), baby baths and facilities for wheelchair users. The site is very popular with tour operators.

How to find it: From Larochette take N8 for 2 km towards Mersch where site is signed.

General Details: Open 1 April - 31 Oct. Electricity connections (6A). Restaurant with terrace. Shop. Children's playgrounds. Swimming pool. Fitness centre. Sauna. Table tennis. Minigolf. Tennis. Riding. Washing machines and dryers. Entertainment. Money exchange.

Charges 1999: Per unit incl. 2 persons Lfr. 975; extra person 150; extra car 150; electricity 85; dog 100. Less 25% in low season.

Reservations: Write to site for reservation application form. Address: B.P.31, 7601 Larochette. Tel: 879040. FAX: 879041. E-mail: camp.bir@tcp.ip.lu.

765 Camping de la Sûre, Reisdorf

Riverside site, with pleasant atmosphere, popular with fishermen.

Located on the edge of this small town, this site has 160 numbered pitches, most with electricity (16A) and arranged around a tarmac access road. Some are on the river bank (heaven for a keen fisherman - advance booking advised). They are not separated but are marked with small trees. There are some static units, but these are nearest the road in their own fenced area, leaving the prime pitches for tourists. The town centre is within easy walking distance, and cycle ways abound. The sanitary facilities are modern and clean, having been recently refitted and extended, with British WCs, some washbasins in cubicles, showers with dividers and seats, and free hot water throughout. Other services include a small shop, a café/bar with takeaway meals, a playground, minigolf and fishing.

How to find it: From the river bridge in Reisdorf, take the road to Echternach, de la Sûre is the second campsite on the left.

General Details: Open 1 April - 30 October. Small shop. Café/bar. Takeaway. Laundry. Chemical disposal. Children's playground. Minigolf. Sports field. Canoeing. Fishing.

Charges guide: Per pitch LFr. 200; adult 180; child (under 14 yrs) 80; electricity 80. Discounts for long stays and off season.

Reservations: Write to site for details. Address: 23 Rue de la Sûre, 9390 Reisdorf. Tel: 836246 or 836509. FAX: 869237.

763 Camping La Pinède, Consdorf

Pleasant municipal site in the Mullerthal region.

La Pinède is situated adjacent to the municipal sports field, with the main sanitary facilities located under the stand. These provide British style WCs, washbasins (cold water only) and controllable hot showers in a building which can be heated in cool weather. A further small, modern unit at the far end of the site is opened in July/Aug. and there are more refurbished facilities to the rear of the café/bar beside the site entrance. The site provides 109 individual, hedged, grassy spaces for tourists all with electricity (10A), plus 40 pitches housing static units. Other amenities include a small adventure-style children's playground, minigolf, football field, volleyball and tennis courts. There is no shop on site but all necessary shops and services are in the town within walking distance. The immediate area is popular for cycling and hiking and the river Moselle and vineyards are an easy day trip by car.

> **How to find it:** Consdorf is southwest of Echternach. Site is well signed from the centre of Consdorf.

> **General Detail:** Open 15 March - 15 November. Electricity connections (10A). Café/bar. Children's playground. Minigolf. Tennis. Fishing or bicycle hire 9 km. Riding 12 km. Golf 6 or 12 km. Gas supplies. Chemical disposal.

> **Charges 2000:** Per pitch LFr. 160; adult 150; child (under 14 yrs) 80; electricity 60 per day or 10 per kw; dog 60. No credit cards.

> **Reservations:** Write to site for details. Address: 33 Rue Burkapp, 6211 Consdorf. Tel: 790271. FAX: 799001.

791 Camping Kalkesdelt, Ettelbruck

Agreeable, good value site on a hilltop overlooking the town.

Quietly located about 1 km. from the centre of Ettelbruck, this municipal site has a nice atmosphere with well tended gardens and grass. The modern main building includes reception, a 'salle de séjour' (with library and TV), some excellent WCs and washbasins, a room for disabled people and a laundry. An older sanitary unit provides British style WCs, washbasins (cold water) and free hot showers with divider, shelf and hooks. It can be heated in cool weather. The 150 marked pitches are generally slightly sloping, some on terraces backed by banks and trees, others on an open area at the top of the site. All are accessed from tarmac roadways and have electricity available (16A). The restaurant, snack bar and takeaway are open each evening in season. A baker calls daily at 7.30 am. (order day before). Breakfasts can also be served. Reception has good tourist information and English is spoken. There is a small playground, table tennis and children's entertainment in high season.

> **How to find it:** Site is signed on the western outskirts of Ettelbruck off the N15 and approached via a short one-way system.

> **General Details:** Open 1 April - 31 Oct. Restaurant. Snack bar and takeaway. Bicycle hire. Playground. Table tennis. Entertainment in season. Laundry. Gas supplies. Chemical disposal. Bottle bank.

> **Charges 1999:** Per pitch LFr. 130; adult 120; child (3-14 yrs) 50; electricity 80; local `Eco' tax 20; dog free. No credit cards.

> **Reservations:** Write to site for details Address: Rue de Camping, 9022 Ettelbruck. Tel: 812185. FAX: 813186. E-mail: site@pt.lu.

767 Camping des Ardennes, Hosingen

Good value site in a very attractive small town, noted for its floral displays.

This small municipal site is located on the edge of this most attractive town with an easy level walk to all amenities and parks and floral arrangements to admire during the summer season. The 50 level, open, grassy pitches all have electricity (10A) and are arranged on either side of surfaced roadways, with a few trees providing a little shade in places. The single sanitary unit, which can be heated in winter, is well appointed, modern and very clean, with British WCs, large shower cubicles (with full screens), and open washbasins in separate men's and women's facilities. Hot water is free throughout. Dishwashing and laundry facilities with washing machine and dryer (instructions in English), also clothes lines. The site has a tiny inflatable type swimming pool principally for children, a small playground, barbecue, café/bar and boule pitch. Skis and winter sports equipment for hire. English is spoken by the Dutch wardens.

> **How to find it:** Site is off the main N7 road north of Diekirch and is signed from the centre of the town, with the sports complex.

> **General Details:** Open all year. Café/bar (opening variable). Laundry. Children's pool and playground. Boule. Barbecue. Winter sports equipment for hire. Rooms for rent (B&B). Adjacent sports complex with tennis and football, etc.

> **Charges 1999:** Per pitch LFr. 150; adult 150; child (3-12 yrs) 75; electricity 75.

> **Reservations:** Write to site for details. Address: 9809 Hosingen. Tel: 91911.

NETHERLANDS

The Netherlands offers a warm welcome to British visitors, and the general standard of campsites has improved considerably during the last few years. Consider the number of quality campsites listed for the Netherlands in this year's guide and consider also their locations throughout the country and straightaway this tells us that there is more to the Netherlands than Amsterdam and the bulb fields. Granted, both are top attractions and no visitor should miss the city of Amsterdam with its delight of bridges, canals, museums and listed buildings or miss sighting the spring-time riot of colour that adorns the fields and gardens of South Holland.

Curiosity has prompted us to venture further afield to touch on all of its twelve provinces. We discovered a country with a variety of holiday venues ranging from lively seaside resorts to picturesque villages, idyllic old fishing ports and areas where nature rules. Favourite places along the way include the Province of Overijssel, especially the Vecht valley, an area of natural beauty which centres around the town of Ommen. From here scenic routes, cycle tracks and footpaths lead to attractive hamlets and towns tucked into a woodland setting. Giethoorn, to the northwest of the province is justly dubbed the 'Venice of the North'. Another appealing spot is around Dordrecht, southeast of Rotterdam. Here the Alblasserwaard polder, a typically Dutch landscape offers time to discover the famed windmills of Kinderdijk, cheese farms and a a stork village. The lure of the islands of the Zeeland Provice is difficult to resist. These islands are joined by amazing feats of engineering, particularly the Oosterschelde storm surge barrier. Island hopping introduces lovely old towns such as Middelburg, the provincial capital Zierikzee with its old harbour or the quaint old town of Veere. For further information contact:

Netherlands Board of Tourism, PO Box 523, London SW1E 6NT

Tel: 0906 8717 777 (60p per minute) Fax: 020 7828 7941 E-mail: information@nbt.org.uk

Population
15,200,000, density 447 p/sq. km.

Climate
The sea has a great affect on the climate of the Netherlands. The average winter is mild - although a sudden cold snap in January or February will have the skaters out with a vengeance on the water- ways. Summers are warm with temperatures averaging 16-17oC centigrade in July and August. In the east and southeast winters are colder and summers warmer. Spring is the driest season.

Language
Dutch is the native tongue. English is very widely spoken, so is German and to some extent French. In Friesland a Germanic language, Frisian is spoken. The Dutch are very language- conscious partly because they are great travellers, to be found in all parts of the world - often running camp sites!

Time
GMT + 1 (summer BST + 1).

Currency
Dutch currency is the Guilder or Florin written as Dfl. or Nfl. and made up of 100 cents. Notes are 10, 25, 50, 100 and 250, coins are 5, 10, and 25 cents pieces and 1, 2.50, and 5 Nfl.

Banks
Open Mon-Fri 09.00-16.00/1700. Exchange offices (GWK) are often open longer hours.

Post Offices
Open Mon-Fri 08.30-17.00. Some offices open Sat 08.30-12.00.

Telephone
To call the Netherlands from the UK the code is 00 31, the UK from the Netherlands, 00 44.

Public Holidays
New Year; Good Fri; Easter Mon; Queen's Birthday, 30 Apr; Liberation Day, 5 May; Ascension; Whit Mon; Christmas, 25, 26 Dec.

Shops
Shops open Mon-Fri 09.00/ 09.30 -17.30/18.00. Sat. closing 16.00/ 17.00. In big cities, stores have late opening Thurs. or Fri. and close Mon. morning. The Dutch are early diners - restaurants open 17.30-22.00/23.00.

Motoring
There is a comprehensive motorway system but, due to the high density of population, all main roads can become very busy, particularly in the morning and evening rush hours. There are many bridges which can cause congestion.

Tolls: There are no toll roads but there are a few toll bridges and tunnels notably the Zeeland Bridge, Europe's longest across the Oosterschelde.

Speed Limits: Built up areas 31 mph (50 kph), other roads 50 mph (80 kph) and motorways 62 mph (100 kph) or 75 mph (120 kph). Cars towing a caravan or trailer are limited to 50 mph (80 kph) outside built-up areas.

Parking: Blue Zones exist in most towns and free parking discs are available from police stations.

Overnighting:
Prohibited outside campsites.

Useful Addresses

Motoring Organisations:
Koninklijke Nederlandsche Automobiel Club (KNAC), Westvlietweg 118, Leidschendam. Tel: (070) 399 7451. Offices hours Mon-Fri 09.00-17.00.

Koninklijke Nederlandsche Toeristenbond (ANWB), Wassenaarsweg 220, The Hague. Tel: (070) 3141420 Hours: Mon-Fri 08.00-17.30.

NETHERLANDS

550 Recreatiecentrum Pannenschuur, Nieuwvliet, nr Breskens

Seaside site near Belgian border with new indoor pool complex.

This is one of several coastal sites on the narrow strip of the Netherlands between the Belgian frontier near Knokke and the Breskens ferry. Quickly reached from the ports of Ostend, Zeebrugge and Vlissingen, it is useful for overnight stops or for a few days to enjoy the seaside. A short walk across the quiet coast road and steps over the dike bring you to the open, sandy beach. Quite a large site, most of the 595 pitches are taken by permanent or seasonal holiday caravans but there are also 165 pitches for tourists mostly in their own areas. In short rows backing onto hedges all have electricity (6A), water and drainage connections. A new, heated sanitary building provides first class facilities including a children's washroom, baby room and some private cabins (shower tokens from the supermarket). The other star attraction is the recently completed complex which provides a super indoor heated swimming pool with baby and children's sections, jacuzzi, sauna, Turkish bath and solarium. Also leading off the central café style area are a restaurant, snack bar and launderette. Overall, a very good site.

How to find it: At Nieuwvliet, on Breskens - Sluis minor road, 8 km. southwest of Breskens, turn towards the sea at sign for Nieuwvliet-Bad and follow signs to site.

General Details: Open all year. Supermarket (all year except 5/1-14/2, restricted hours in low seasons). Restaurant (all year except 4/1-7/1). Snack bar and takeaway (1/3-1/11). Swimming pool (all year). Sauna and solarium. Large games room for young with snooker, pool tables, amusement machines, soft drinks bar. Children's playground and play field. Bicycle hire. Fishing 500 m. Riding 2 km. Golf 5 km. Organised activities during season. Launderette. Gas supplies. Chemical disposal. Motorcaravan services. Bungalows and caravans for hire.

Charges 1999: Per person (over 2 yrs) Nfl. 6.50, plus tax 2.10; pitch incl. electricity 32.50; dog 7.50. Rates available for weekly stays. Credit cards accepted.

Reservations: Recommended (high season Sat.- Sat. only) and made with deposit and fee. Address: Zeedijk 19, 4504 PP Nieuwvliet-Bad (Zeeland). Tel: 0117/37 23 00. FAX: 0117/37 14 15. E-mail: info@pannenschuur.nl.

552 Vakantiepark Zeebad, Breskens

Large, friendly site near beach and ferry port.

Under the same ownership as no. 550 Pannenschuur, Camping Zeebad is just along the coast road. It is partially surrounded by small lakes and is adjacent to the beach. The established areas are well shaded but these are mainly reserved for seasonal units. However, there are 120 numbered touring pitches of 80-100 sq.m. with growing hedges. Cars are not allowed beside the pitches but alternative parking is provided. One tiled sanitary block near the entrance (some distance from the touring pitches) is supplemented by two rather cramped mobile units. Hot water is on payment and facilities at the main block include separate wash cabins, a family room and laundry facilities. British style WCs. There is an organised activity programme for children in high season. Swimming pools and minigolf are nearby and the town of Breskens is within walking distance (15 mins). An indoor pool and sports complex have been added.

How to find it: From Breskens take coast road west and site is less than 1.5 km. on the left.

General Details: Open all year. Electricity available in all parts. Restaurant with outdoor terrace. Bar. Snack bar. Supermarket. Games room. Children's playground. Activity programme for children. Weekly disco. Bicycle hire. Mobile homes for hire.

Charges guide: Per person (over 2 yrs) Nfl 5.00; pitch 25.00; dog 5.00; local tax 1.00. Less in low seasons.

Reservations: Contact site for details. Site is very busy 20/7-15/8, but some pitches are normally kept for short stays. Address: Nieuwesluisweg 5, 4510 RG Breskens. Tel: 0117/38 13 38. FAX: 0117/38 31 51.

551 Camping Groede, Groede, nr Breskens

Friendly, family run site two minutes from dunes and sandy beach.

Camping Groede is a friendly, fair sized site on the same stretch of sandy beach as no. 550. Family run, it aims to cater for the individual needs of visitors and to provide a good all-round holiday. Campers are sited as far as possible according to taste – in family areas, in larger groups or on more private pitches for those who prefer peace and quiet. In total, there are 560 pitches for tourists (with 400 seasonal units also), 275 with electrical connections (4A) and 260 with water and drainage connections also. Sanitary facilities are good with a high standard of cleanliness, British style WCs, free hot showers and some washing cabins also with hot water. A restaurant/bar provides a friendly service and there is also a snack bar (both weekends only in low season). Visitors are invited to join locals in archery and card games. Other activities include football, volleyball and plenty of activities for children in peak season. Groede is ideally sited for ferry stopovers and short stay visitors including hikers are very welcome, as well as long stay holiday makers. Run by the family van Damme who ask visitors to complete a confidential questionnaire to ensure that their site offers the best possible service and provide you with a comprehensive information booklet (in English).

How to find it: From Breskens take the coast road for 5 km. to site. Alternatively, the site is signed from Groede village on the more inland Breskens - Sluis road.

General Details: Open 27 March - 31 Oct. Shop, restaurant and snack bar (all weekends only in low seasons). Recreation room. Sports area. Several children's play areas (bark base). Bicycle hire. Fishing. Riding 1 km. Golf 11 km. Gas supplies. Chemical disposal. Motorcaravan services.

Charges 1999: Per pitch incl. 2 persons Nfl 21.50 - 31.50, with 4A electricity 25.00 - 35.00, with water and drainage also 28.00 - 38.00; extra person 4.00 (incl. taxes). No credit cards.

Reservations: Will be made (with Nfl 25 fee) but half the pitches are kept unreserved. Address: Zeeweg 1, 4503 PA Groede. Tel: 0117/37 13 84. FAX: 0117/37 22 77. A 'Camping Cheques' site.

558 Camping de Veerhoeve, Wolphaartsdijk, nr Goes

Family run site, near the shores of the Veerse Meer, ideal for families.

Situated in a popular area for watersports, this is a site well suited for sailing, windsurfing or fishing enthusiasts. As with most sites in this area there are many mature static and seasonal pitches. However, part of the friendly, relaxed site is reserved for touring units with 150 marked pitches on grassy ground, 100 with electrical connections. Sanitary facilities, in three blocks, have been well modernised with full tiling and include British style WCs. Hot showers are on payment. Other amenities include a good shop, TV, sports field and a children's playground. Slipway for launching boats and horse riding nearby.

How to find it: From N256 Goes-Zierikzee road take Wolphaartsdijk exit. Follow through village and then signs to site.

General Details: Open 3 April - 30 October. Shop (all season). Restaurant and snack bar (July/Aug. otherwise at weekends). Tennis. Children's playground. Bicycle hire. Fishing. Watersports and boat launching 1 km. Riding 1 km. Golf 7 km. Laundry facilities. Motorcaravan services. Chemical disposal. Accommodation for groups. Mobile homes and bungalows for rent.

Charges 2000: Per pitch incl. 2 persons Nfl. 32.00 - 37.50; electricity 5.00; dog 5.00. Tax included. Credit cards accepted.

Reservations: Write to site. Address: Veerweg 48, 4471 NC Wolphaartsdijk. Tel: 0113/581155. FAX: 0113/581944. A 'Camping Cheques' site.

NETHERLANDS

556 Zeeland Camping de Wijde Blick, Renesse, nr Zierikzee

Neat, well kept site in popular North Sea coast holiday area.

This site is run in a friendly and personal way by the owners, the van Oost family. Within walking distance of the village of Renesse, it is in a quiet, rural location. Laid out in a fairly formal way, with attractive trees and hedges, the site has 189 numbered tourist pitches arranged in groups of 4 to 8, all with electrical (6A) and TV connections. Cars are parked away from the pitches by the access roadways. Sanitary facilities in two blocks are very modern with first class, heated, clean facilities including washbasins in cabins, controllable showers, facilities for disabled people and a washroom for children under 6 years old. A bath is on payment. Dishwashing sinks all have free hot water and are arranged around glass roofed courtyards with seating, plants and music. The main amenities at the entrance to the site include an outdoor swimming pool with sunbathing terrace, an informal, timber clad bar/restaurant, a supermarket and a laundry (with cartoons for the children to watch). Many activities are organised for children – the campsite mascot, Billy Blick, is amusing as he welcomes the children. Very much a busy holiday area, there are restaurants and shops in the village (market on Wednesdays) and the sandy beach is 2 km. from the site.

How to find it: Renesse is on the near 'island' of Schouwen on the Haamstede - Zierikzee R106 road and site is signed to the east of the village.

General Details: Open all year. Swimming pool (1/5-15/9). Shop. Restaurant/bar (both April - Oct). Good children's play area on sand. Table tennis. Bicycle hire. Tennis and minigolf close. Riding or fishing 1.5 km. Golf 10 km. Gas supplies. Motorcaravan services. Chemical disposal. No dogs accepted. Cabins to rent.

Charges 2000: Per unit incl. 2 persons and electricity Nfl. 33.00 - 53.00; extra person 7.00; local tax included. No credit cards.

Reservations: Recommended for high season - contact site. Address: Hogezoom 112, 4325 CK Renesse (Zeeland). Tel: 0111/468888. FAX: 0111/468889. E-mail: dewijdeblick@zeelandcamping.nl.

559 Camping Rondeweibos, Rockanje

Holiday site near North Sea coastal resort.

This site is situated near the pleasant seaside resort of Rockanje, quite convenient for the North Sea ferry ports. Very much a holiday caravan site (privately owned or to let), it is large, with lines of static units separated by semi-wild hedges and trees. With 800 pitches, just 85 are available for tourers. However, these have their own pleasant area, separated from the rest of the site by the main access road. The pitches here are on grassy/sandy ground and divided into groups by more formal hedges. All have electricity and cable TV connections available with water points near. Sanitary facilities are in two blocks, one near the touring area, and which can be heated. They provide neat, clean, acceptable facilities with hot showers on payment and British style WCs. A good range of amenities (listed below) includes a popular medium sized outdoor swimming pool with a slide and whirlpool. Rockanje is situated on Voorne (which used to be an island), an area of beaches, dunes, woods and lakes. A popular area with Dutch holidaymakers, beach activities and watersports opportunities are plentiful. Rockanje's beach is a 10 minute walk.

How to find it: From N15/A15 motorway towards `Europoort' take exit marked Brielle-Hellevoetsluis onto N57 and over the bridge. After 7 km. take Rockanje exit and site is signed at next junction and in Rockanje itself.

General Details: Open: mid-March - late-Oct. Supermarket (limited hours in low seasons). Cafe, restaurant and bar (weekends only in low seasons). Tennis. Boules. Good children's playground. Swimming pool (15/5-15/9). Children's games room and organised activities in high season. Launderette. Bus service 100 m.

Charges 1999: Per person Nfl. 7.85; caravan or tent 10.00; motorcaravan 18.00; car 4.00; m/cycle 1.00; electricity 4.00; dog/cat 4.00.

Reservations: Essential in high season - contact site. Address: Schapengorsedijk 19, 3235 LA Rockanje. Tel: 0181/40 19 44. FAX: 0181/40 23 80. E-mail: rondewei@xs4all.nl.

557 Camping de Molenhoek, Kamperland, nr Middelburg

Quietly situated Zeeland site near watersports centre.

This family run site makes a pleasant contrast to the livelier coastal sites in this popular holiday area. It is rurally situated 3 km. from the Veerse Meer which is very popular for all sorts of watersports. Catering both for 300 permanent or seasonal holiday caravans and for 100 touring units, it is neat, tidy and relatively spacious. The marked touring pitches are divided into small groups with surrounding hedges and trees giving privacy and some shade, and electrical connections are available. Sanitary facilities, in one old (partly refurbished) and one newer block, include some washbasins in private cabins with free hot water and showers, dishwashing and clothes sinks with hot water on payment, British style WCs, plus toilet and shower facilities for disabled visitors and provision for babies. A large outdoor swimming pool is Molenhoek's latest attraction. Other amenities, grouped in front of a pleasant, open, grassy area with a children's paddling pool and playground, include a shop and a simple bar/restaurant with terrace and TV room. Entertainment is organised in season (dance evenings, bingo, etc.) as well as a disco for youngsters. Tennis courts are nearby. Although the site is quietly situated, there are many excursion possibilities in the area including the towns of Middelburg, Veere and Goes and the Delta Expo exhibition.

How to find it: Site is west of the village of Kamperland on the `island' of Noord Beveland. From the N256 Goes - Zierikzee road, exit west onto the N255 Kamperland road. Site is signed south of this road.

General Details: Open 29 March - 25 Oct. Restaurant/bar (high season only). Well stocked shop (all season). Swimming pool. Children's playground, pool and animals. TV room. Entertainment in high season. Bicycle hire. Fishing 2.5 km. Riding 1 km. Tennis and watersports close. Chemical disposal. Motorcaravan services. Caravans for hire.

Charges 1999: Per unit, incl. 2 persons and electricity Nfl. 41.75, 6 persons 45.75; dog 5.00. Less 25% outside high season.

Reservations: Are made - contact site. Address: Molenweg 69a, 4493 NC Kamperland. Tel: 0113/37 12 02.

Kampeer- en recreatiecentrum

DE MOLENHOEK

Only five minutes from the beach and Veerse Meer.
Quiet campsite with small fields separated by hedges.
Good restaurant and snackbar. Activity programme. Young people's room and disco. Heated swimming pool. Playground and swimming pool for children. A good campsite for the whole family for a short or long stay. Close to the "Oosterschelde" works and the "Pijlerdam".

A CAMPSITE WHERE EVERYONE IS HAPPY!

Molenweg 69A-4493 NC Kamperland Tel: (+31) 113 371202
Internet: www.xeelandnet.nl/molenhoek E-mail: molenhoek@xeelandnet.nl

560 Recreatiecentrum Delftse Hout, Delft

Well run, modern site within easy reach of Delft.

Pleasantly situated in Delft's park and forest area on the eastern edge of the city, this site is part of the Koningshof group. It has 200 tourist pitches quite formally arranged in groups of 4 to 6 and surrounded by attractive young trees and hedges. All have sufficient space and electrical connections. Modern buildings near the entrance house the site amenities. These include modern, heated toilet facilities with free hot showers and a spacious family room. A good sized first floor restaurant serves snacks or full meals and has an outdoor terrace overlooking the swimming pool and pitches. There is also a bar and recreation room. Reception provides friendly service and tourist information and also houses a shop for basic food and camping items. A small outdoor pool, volleyball, basketball and an adventure playground are in one corner. Walking and cycling tours are organised and there is a recreation programme in high season. A special package deal can be arranged including tickets to local 'royal' attractions and a visit to the Royal Delftware factory.

How to find it: Site is 1 km. east of Delft. From A13 motorway take Delft/Pijnacker (exit 9), turn towards Pijnacker and then right at first traffic lights, following camping signs through suburbs and park to site.

General Details: Open all year. Restaurant, bar and shop (all 1/4-1/10). Outdoor swimming pool (1/5-15/9). Children's playground. Table tennis. Recreation room. Bicycle hire. Fishing 1 km. Riding or golf 5 km. Bus service to Delft. Laundry. Gas supplies. Chemical disposal. Motorcaravan services. Chalets and caravans to let.

Charges 2000: Per caravan or tent plus car incl. 2 persons Nfl 43.50; extra person (3 yrs and older) 2.50; local tax 1.00; electricity (10A) 6.00; dog (1 per pitch) 4.00. Low season discounts and for senior citizens (over 55). Special packages. Credit cards accepted.

Reservations: Essential for high season (not made by telephone). Address: Korftlaan 5, 2616 LJ Delft. Tel: 015/213 00 40. FAX: 015/213 12 93. E-mail: info-delftsehout@tours.nl.

NETHERLANDS

554 Camping en Bungalowpark De Katjeskelder, Oosterhout

Well established, family run site offering extensive facilities.

This site is to be found in a wooded setting in a delightful area of Western Brabant. This is idyllic cycling and walking countryside and many known attractions such as the Efteling theme park and the Biesbosch nature park lie within a short drive. The site is immediately impressive with its new ultra-modern reception area just being completed when we visited. Around the 25 hectare site are 300 touring pitches, all with electricity and water (between two pitches), plus 13 fully serviced pitches with hardstanding for motorcaravans. Cars are prohibited alongside the pitches, but may be parked nearby. The three modern sanitary blocks are heated and provide facilities that include a family shower/wash room, controllable free showers, a baby room and provision for disabled people. The site has a 'cat' theme, hence the cat names including that of the restaurant, the 'Gelaarsde Kat' (Puss in Boots) which is situated in the 'Tropikat' complex. This tropical indoor water playground is free for campers and the site also has an outdoor swimming pool and children's pool, both supervised. The supermarket stocks fresh bread and there is a snack bar, pizzeria and takeaway (the 'Hapjeskat'). There are several play areas for small children, plus a large adventure playground and organised entertainment for children all season. Other activities include tennis, a play field, bicycle hire and minigolf.

How to find it: From A27 Breda/Gorinchem motorway take Oosterhout Zuid exit 17 and follow signs for 7 km to site.

General Details: Open 31 March - 31 Oct. Shop. Bar. Restaurant. Takeaway. Indoor tropical pool and outdoor swimming pools. Tennis. Bicycle hire. Minigolf. Adventure playground. Laundry. Chemical disposal. Motorcaravan services. Mobile homes and bungalows to rent.

Charges 1999: Per unit incl. 2 persons and electricity, water and TV connections Nfl. 39.50 - 62.50; dog 10.00.

Reservations: Necessary in high season. Address: Katjeskelder 1, 4904 SG Oosterhout. Tel: 0162/456705 (info) or 0162/453539. FAX: 0162/454090. E-Mail: kkinfo@katjeskelder.nl. A 'Camping Cheques' site.

568 Camping De Noordduinen, Katwijk

Family site within walking distance of beach and Katwijk.

This is a large, well managed site surrounded by dunes and sheltered partly by trees and shrubbery, which also separate the various camping areas. The touring pitches are marked and numbered but not divided. All have electricity (4/10A) and many are fully serviced with electricity, water, drainage and TV connection. There are also seasonal pitches and mobile homes for rent. The latter are placed mostly away from the touring areas and are unobtrusive. You are escorted to an allocated pitch and sited in a formal layout and cars are parked away from the pitches. The three sanitary blocks are modern and clean, with washbasins in cabins, a baby room and provision for people with disabilities. Hot water for showers and dishwashing is on payment. Also on site is a supermarket with fresh bread daily, a restaurant/bar which doubles as a function room and a takeaway service. Entertainment is organised in high season for various age groups, and there is a games room and children's playground. Bicycles can be hired nearby and worth a visit is Space Expo. Only gas barbecues are permitted on the pitches.

How to find it: Leave A44 at exit 8 (Leiden/Katwijk) to join N206 to Katwijk. Follow signs to site.

General Details: Open 1 April - 31 Oct. Shop. Restaurant/bar. Takeaway. Play area. Games room. Laundry. Chemical disposal. Motorcaravan services. No dogs are accepted.

Charges 1999: Per unit incl. 2 persons Nfl. 38.00 - 57.50; electricity 4.00; local tax 0.75.

Reservations: Contact site. Address: Campingweg 1, 2221 EW Katwijk. Tel: 071/4025295. FAX: 071/4033977. E-mail: info-noordduinen@tours.nl.

564 Vakantiecentrum Kijkduinpark, Den Haag

Rapidly developing park close to a long beach.

This former touring park has been transformed into an ultra-modern, all year round centre and family park, which is still developing. Many huts, villas and bungalows have been built, along with a brand new reception. The wooded touring area is immediately to the left of the entrance, with 450 pitches in shady glades of bark covered sand. There are simple pitches for tents, some pitches with electricity only and many with electricity 10A, water, waste water and cable TV connections. At present there are two modern sanitary blocks (key entry) and three 'portacabin' style units. In a paved central area stands a supermarket, snack bar and restaurant. The main attraction here is the Meeresstrand, 500 m. from the site entrance. This is a long, wide sandy beach with flags to denote suitability for swimming. It is popular with windsurfers.

How to find it: Site is southwest of Den Haag on the coast and Kijkduin is well signed as an area from all round Den Haag.

General Details: Open all year. Snack bar. Shop. Restaurant. Supermarket (all year). Bicycle hire. Special golfing breaks. Entertainment and activities organised in summer. Riding 5 km. Fishing 500 m. Launderette. Accommodation to rent.

Charges 1999: Per unit incl. 2 persons Nfl. 27.00 - 57.00, with electricity, water and drainage 35.00 - 65.00; dog (max 1) 6.00; local tax 2.20. Less 10-30% in low season. Credit cards accepted.

Reservations: Advisable for high season, write to site. Address: Machiel Vrijenhoeklaan 450, 2555 NW Den Haag. Tel: 070/4482100. FAX: 070/3232457. E-mail: info@kijkduinpark.nl.

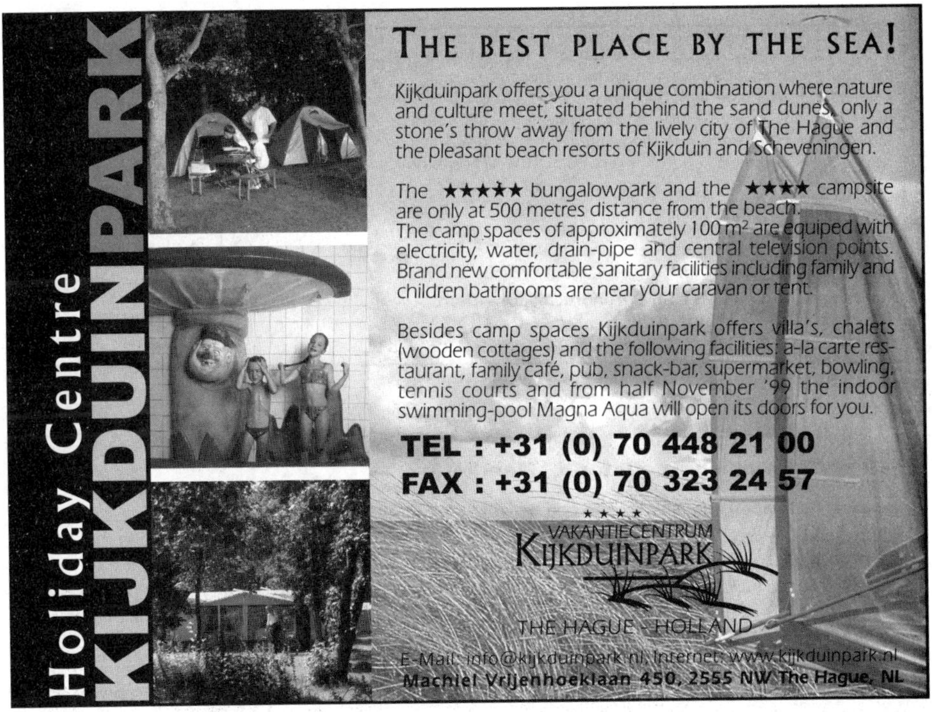

The sites in the NETHERLANDS featured in this guide
are shown on the BENELUX map on page 369

NETHERLANDS

561 Camping De Oude Maas, Barendrecht, by Rotterdam

Peaceful riverside site convenient for Rotterdam.

The entrance is the least inspiring part here and you have to drive right up to the barrier in order to activate the intercom. Once through this, you pass a long strip of mixed seasonal and touring pitches. There are two more attractive touring areas, one for 12 units with electricity, water and waste water connections in a hedged group near to the reception, shop, restaurant and river. They have their own small, mediocre sanitary building, but there is a more modern one a short walk away. This has free hot water to the showers, private cabins and washbasins, British style WCs, facilities for disabled people, a baby room and dishwashing. The third section is in a woodland setting, well back from the river on flat grass. It has a small 'portacabin' type facility but again it is not far from the main sanitary building. The site is easily accessed from the A15 southern Rotterdam ring road and is situated right by the river, so it is well worth considering if you are visiting the city or want a peaceful stop.

How to find it: From Rotterdam ring road south take exit 20 (Barendrecht) and follow signs to Achterzeedijk and Oude Maas.

General Details: Open all year. Restaurant, bar and snacks (all year). Shop (1/6-31/8, town 3 km). Fishing. Bicycle hire. Swimming pool and golf near. Launderette. Chemical disposal.

Charges 1999: Per adult Nfl. 6.15; child (under 15 yrs) 3.10; car 6.75; motorcaravan 8.10; caravan or tent 6.15; electricity (10A) 3.35; dog 3.35. Credit cards accepted.

Reservations: May be advisable high season. Write to site. Address: Achterzeedijk 1a, 2991 SB Barendrecht. Tel: 0786 77 24 45. FAX: 0786 77 30 13.

The campsite and yacht basin "De Oude Maas" is located on the banks of the Oude Maas, near Barendrecht, just a few kilometres from Rotterdam. All forms of camping are possible throughout the year. The campsite is particularly suitable for families with children. For touring campers, there are 3 fields, luxury "hikers' chalets" and a "hikers hut". The campsite has toilet facilities, a toilet and shower for the disabled, a baby washroom, a launderette, a carwash area, etc.
From the campsite, there is a beautiful view over the Oude Maas, and the immediate surroundings are ideal for activities such as sailing, swimming, golf, exercising, cycling and walking.
Achterzeedijk 1 a, 2991 SB Barendrecht/Rotterdam
Tel. +31 78 677 24 45, fax +31 78 677 30 13
Internet: www.deoudemaas.com E-mail: deoudemaas@worldonline.nl

camping en jachthaven
de oude maas

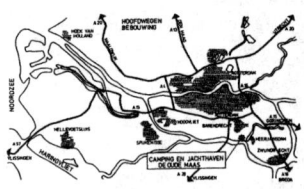

569 SVR Camping De Victorie, Meerkerk

Nature at its best on a family run site convenient to North Sea ports.

Within an hour's drive from the port of Rotterdam you can be pitched on this delightful site in the 'green heart of Holland'. De Victorie, a working farm and a member of a club of small, 'green' sites, offers an alternative to the bustling seaside sites. Everything about it is surprising and contrary to any preconceived ideas. To the left of the entrance stands a modern building which houses reception, open plan office and space with tables and chairs, where the friendly owners may well invite you to have a cup of coffee. Adjoining is the main sanitary block which is kept spotlessly clean and is tastefully decorated with grey tiled walls and floors. Facilities include British style WCs, washbasins, mirrors, etc. and showers with stool, hooks and divider (on payment). There is a dishwashing area and laundry room, plus additional sanitary facilities situated around the spacious site. The 70 grass pitches are level and generous in size with 4A electricity supply. You can choose to be pitched in the shade of one of the orchards, or in the more open meadow area. The freedom of the farmland is especially enjoyed by children. Apart from the farm animals, wildlife and tractor rides, there is a trampoline, fishing, bicycle hire and a play field for football. The farm shop sells milk, eggs, meat, cheese and ice cream.

How to find it: From Rotterdam follow A15 to junction with A27. Proceed 6 km. north on A27 to Noordeloos exit (no. 25) and join N214. Site is signed approx. 200 m. after roundabout at Noordeloos (don't enter vilage).

General Details: Open 15 March - 31 Oct. Farm shop. Children's play area. Bicycle hire. Fishing. Riding. Golf 2.5 km. Chemical disposal.

Charges 1999: Special price for SVR Club and AR readers: Per person Nfl. 2.50; caravan, tent or motorcaravan 2.50; car 1.00; large motorcaravan 3.50; electricity (4A) 2.50; local tax 0.35. No credit cards.

Reservations: Contact site. Address: Broekseweg 75-77, 4231 VD Meerkerk. Tel: 0183/352741 or 351516. FAX: 0183/351234.

NETHERLANDS

562 Camping Duinrell, Wassenaar, nr Den Haag (The Hague)

Very large site adjoining pleasure park and impressive tropical pool complex.
Duinrell means 'well in the dunes' and the water theme is continued in the adjoining amusement park and in the extensive indoor pool complex which are Duinrell's main attractions. Entry to the popular pleasure park is free for campers - indeed the camping areas surround and open out from the park. The 'Tiki' tropical pool complex has many attractions which include slides ranging from quite exciting to terrifying (according to your age!), whirlpools, saunas and many other features. There are also free outdoor pools and the centre has its own bar and cafe. Entry to the Tiki complex is at a reduced rate for campers. Duinrell is open all year and a ski school (langlauf and Alpine) with 12 artificial runs, is a winter attraction. The campsite itself is very large with 1,150 tourist pitches on several flat grassy areas and it can become very busy in high season. As part of a continuing improvement programme, 950 pitches are now marked and have electricity, cable TV, water and drainage connections. Six toilet blocks, including two very good new ones, serve the tourist areas. They have British WCs, washbasins with warm water, free hot showers and can be heated in cool weather. The amenities shared with the park include restaurants, a pizzeria and pancake house, supermarket and a theatre (shows in high season). The original 900 permanent units have been reduced to around 150, gradually being replaced with smartly furnished 'Duingalows', self catering bungalows available to rent all year. Accommodation in family rooms is also provided in the estate's old coach house.

How to find it: Site is signed from N44/A44 Den Haag-Amsterdam road, but from the south the turning is about 5 km. after passing sign for start of Wassenaar town – then follow camp signs.

General Details: Open all year. Amusement park and Tiki tropical pool complex as detailed above. Restaurant, cafes, pizzeria and takeaways (weekends only in winter). Supermarket. Entertainment and shows in season. Bicycle hire. Bowling. Winter ski school. Fishing. Laundry facilities.

Charges 1999: Per unit on 'comfort' pitch incl. electricity Nfl. 20.00, with cable TV 25.00; 'nature' pitch 17.50; person (over 3 yrs) 17.50, over 65 12.50; extra car 7.50; m/cycle 2.50; dog 10.00. Overnight stays between 17.00-10.00 hrs (when amusement park closed) less 25%. Credit cards accepted.

Reservations: Recommended in high season, Easter and Whitsun (min. 1 week), 50% payment required 6 weeks in advance plus fee (15.00). Address: Duinrell 1. 2242 JP Wassenaar. Tel. 070/515 52 57. Fax: 070/515 53 71. E-mail: info@duinrell/nl.

★ ★ ★ ★
Classificatie

Wassenaar-Holland

Enjoyment and comfort at Camping Duinrell!

* "Super" pitches from 80m² with modern facilities and new sanitary buildings providing the latest luxurious fittings and separate children's washroom
* For camping guests, a free amusement park with splashing, thrilling attractions • Tropical Tiki pool, the largest and most fun water paradise in Europe with spectacular water attractions
* In July and August a fabulous show • Spacious Sauna
* Woods and dunes, sea and beach, Den Haag and Scheveningen nearby • Luxury bungalows (4-6 p.) for hire

If you spend a night at Duinrell, you will be able to visit the funpark free of charge
Information folder:
Duinrell 1, 2242 JP Wassenaar, The Netherlands
Tel:+31 70 515 52 57 Fax: +31 70 515 53 71,
Http://www.duinrell.nl

Duinrell, It'll really cheer you up

NETHERLANDS

563 Camping Koningshof, Rijnsburg, nr Leiden

Relaxed, well run site between Den Haag and Amsterdam.

Koningshof is not far from site no. 562 but is of an entirely different type. Much smaller, it is run in a personal and friendly way with the 225 numbered pitches for touring units divided into separate small groups of four - twelve by hedges and trees. Electrical connections (4/10A) are available in all areas. Cars are parked in areas around the perimeter. There are also 145 static caravans, some for hire. Sanitary facilities are provided in three good blocks, one of which is new and has under-floor heating. They have British WCs, washbasins (some in private cabins with hot water) or in general washrooms (cold water only), free controllable hot showers and facilities for disabled visitors. The reception, a pleasant restaurant, bar and snack bar are grouped around a courtyard style entrance which is decorated with seasonal flowers. On site is a small heated swimming pool (13.5 x 7 m), with separate paddling pool and imaginative children's play equipment. It is 5 km. to a sandy beach, 15 to Den Haag and 30 to Amsterdam. The site has a number of regular British visitors from club connections and the welcome is friendly, with English spoken. Used by tour operators (25 pitches). A very useful local information booklet (in English) is provided for visitors.

How to find it: From N44/A44 Den Haag - Amsterdam motor road, take exit 7 for Oegstgeest and Rijnsburg. Turn towards Rijnsburg and follow camp signs.

General Details: Open all year. Shop (10/4-10/9). Restaurant and bar with snacks and takeaway (10/4-25/10). Small swimming pool (unsupervised, 1/5-15/9). Solarium. Adventure playground and sports area. Tennis courts. Fishing pond (free). Bicycle hire. Entertainment in high season. Room for shows. Riding and golf 5 km. Washing machines and dryers. Gas supplies. Chemical disposal. Motorcaravan services. Chalets for hire.

Charges 2000: Per pitch incl. 2 persons Nfl. 43.50; extra person (over 3 yrs) 2.50; second car (in car park) 4.00; electricity (10A) 6.00; local tax per person 1.00. Low season and senior citizen discounts; special group rates. Security barrier key deposit 25.00 (refundable). Credit cards accepted.

Reservations: Necessary for July/Aug. and made for any length with deposit and fee (payable by credit card). Address: Elsgeesterweg 8, 2231 NW Rijnsburg. Tel: 071/402 60 51. FAX: 071/402 13 36. E-mail: info-koningshof@tours.nl. A 'Camping Cheques' site.

565 Camping Club Soleil, Noordwijk, nr Den Haag

Quality site not far from Amsterdam.

The facilities here are first class, including an indoor heated swimming pool with 'massage water' and watershute, a plunge bath for children, tennis court and sun-trap terrace all free of charge. The children's play equipment is very satisfactory and they also have a play/activity room and an animal enclosure. The shop (open in high season), launderette and restaurant (Indian speciality and Dutch meal of the day) plus takeaway are all of a high standard. A 1,500 m. dune beach is 1.5 km. The site provides just over 100 pitches of 80 sq.m. plus on flat grass, mainly individual ones separated by small trees or hedges and all having (or with close access to) electricity, TV and water connections. There are some hardstandings for motorhomes. The main sanitary building is modern and has free hot water to the showers (some with external entry), washbasins, some in private cabins, baby room and dishwashing facilities. There is a secondary 'portacabin' style facility of an excellent standard (open in high season) and a chemical disposal point. Much thought has gone into the design of this park and the cars for the seasonal pitches and bungalows are parked outside the camping area. Visitors at the site during our visit were very impressed with all the facilities. There was little noise apparent from aircraft (Schipol airport).

How to find it: From A4/A44 (Amsterdam - Den Haag) take exit 3 towards Noordwijk and follow ANWB camping signs (not frequent, just keep going). Take turning to right (small sign) shortly after Camping De Wijde Blick.

General Details: Open 1 April - 31 Oct. Shop (summer). Restaurant. Takeaway. Indoor pool and tennis (both free). Animal enclosure. Launderette. Bungalows and mobile homes for hire.

Charges 1999: Per family pitch incl. TV connection, electricity and water Nfl 72.50 plus local tax 1.32 per person. Low season discounts 10-30%.

Reservations: Made for Sun.-Sun. only in high season. Write to site. Address: Kraaierslaan 7, 2204 AN Noordwijk. Tel: 0252/37 42 25. FAX: 0252/37 64 50.

567 Gaasper Camping Amsterdam, Amsterdam

Well laid out site near Metro station, southeast of Amsterdam.

As Amsterdam is probably the most popular destination for visits in the Netherlands, a second site here may be useful. Gaasper Camping is on the southeast side, a short walk from a Metro station with a direct 20 minute service to the centre. On the edge of a large park with nature areas and a lake (with sailing facilities and new swimming beaches), there are also opportunities for relaxation. The site is well kept and neatly laid out on flat grass with attractive trees and shrubs. There are 390 touring pitches in two main areas – one more open and grassy, mainly kept for tents, the other more formal with numbered pitches mainly divided by shallow ditches or good hedges. Areas of hardstanding are available and all caravan pitches have 4/10A electrical connections (20 tent pitches have 4A connections). Some 60 seasonal and permanent units have their own area. In high season the site becomes very crowded and it is necessary to arrive early to find space. The three modern, clean toilet blocks for the tourist sections should be an adequate provision. Unisex in some sections, they have washbasins (cold water), some in private cabins and pre-set hot showers with push-button. Hot water for showers and some washing-up sinks is on payment, there are British style WCs and facilities for disabled visitors. Although this is a typical, busy city site, it is better than many and there is a friendly welcome, with good English spoken.

How to find it: Take exit for Gaasperplas from the section of A9 motorway which is on the east side of the A2. Note: do not take the Gaasperdam exit which comes first if approaching from the west.

General Details: Open all year except 1/1-14/3. Small shop. Cafe/bar plus takeaway (1/4-15/10). Shopping centre and restaurant nearby. Children's play area on grass. Riding 200 m. Fishing 1 km. Golf 4 km. Washing machine and dryer. Gas supplies. Chemical disposal. Motorcaravan services.

Charges 1999: Per person Nfl. 6.75; child (4-12 yrs) 3.50; car 6.25; m/cycle 3.00; caravan 9.25; motorcaravan 11.50; tent 7.25 - 9.25, acc. to size; electricity 4.50; dog 4.00. No credit cards.

Reservations: Made for 7 days or longer by letter or fax only. Address: Loosdrechtdreef 7, 1108 AZ Amsterdam. Tel: 020/696 73 26. FAX: 020/696 93 69.

566 Camping Het Amsterdamse Bos, Aalsmeer, nr Amsterdam

Neat municipal site in large park area quite close to city.

Het Amsterdamse Bos is a very large park to the southwest of Amsterdam, one corner of which has been specially laid out as the city's municipal site. Close to Schiphol Airport (we noticed little noise), it is about 12 km. from central Amsterdam. A high season bus service runs from the site every 35 minutes during the day to the city (local services at other times are 300 m). The site is well laid out alongside a canal, with unmarked pitches on separate flat lawns mostly backing onto pleasant hedges and trees, with several areas of hardstanding. It takes 400 tourist units, with 150 electrical connections. An additional area is available for tents and groups. The four older style sanitary blocks were clean when we visited but rather let the site down, appearing somewhat small and well used. Hot water is on payment to the washbasins but there are free pre-set hot showers; British style WCs. Near the entrance are laundry and snack bar facilities.

How to find it: Amsterdamse Bos and site are west of Amstelveen. From the A9 motorway exit for either Amstelveen or Aalsmeer (easier), turn towards Aalsmeer and look out carefully for camp signs.

General Details: Open 1 April - 15 Oct. 50,000 sq.m. for camping. Small shop. Cafe/bar and snack bar. Children's sand pit. Fishing. Fishing, boating, pancake restaurant in park. Laundry facilities. Gas supplies. Chemical disposal. Motorcaravan services. Camping huts to rent.

Charges 1999: Per person Nfl 8.50; child (4-12 yrs) 4.25; car 4.25; motorcaravan 10.75; tent 5.50; caravan 6.50; m/cycle 2.25; dog 2.25; electricity 4A 3.50. Group reductions. No credit cards.

Reservations: A limited number only will be made for 'serious enquirers'. Address: Kleine Noorddijk 1, 1432 CC Aalsmeer. Tel: 020/641 68 68. FAX: 020/640 23 78.

570 Molengroet Recreatieverblijven, Noord-Sharwoude, nr Alkmaar

Pleasant site close to lake for watersports.

Whether you wish to stop over on the way to the Afsluitdijk across the top of the Ijsselmeer or partake in watersports, this is a modern site, just 40 km. from Amsterdam. The 300 touring pitches are grouped according to services provided, ranging from simple pitches with no services, to those with 10A electricity, TV, water and waste water. These pitches have the best sanitary facilities in a modern, heated building with free, pre-set hot showers. The two other buildings were renewed in '98. A large shop is open in high season, but bread and milk may be obtained at other times from reception. The bar and restaurant are open all season and there is a snack bar in high season – order snacks from the restaurant otherwise. Bicycles, surfboards and small boats may be hired and there are opportunities for tennis, squash, sauna, horse riding and swimming nearby. The nearby lake with surf school is an attractive proposition, particularly for those with teenagers. A site bus can take you to the local pool or the beach. Friendly multi-lingual staff provide local information.

How to find it: From Haarlem on A9 to Alkmaar take N245 towards Schagen. Site is southwest of Noord Sharwoude, signed to west on road to Geestermerambacht.

General Details: Open 1 April - 1 November. Shop (high season). Restaurant/bar (all season). Snack bar (high season). Fishing. Bicycle hire. Watersports close. Riding or golf 5 km. Entertainment in high season and weekends. Gas supplies. Chemical disposal. Motorcaravan services.

Charges 1999: Per unit incl. 2 persons Nfl. 33.50, with private sanitary facility 60.00. Reductions in low season and for longer stays. Credit cards accepted.

Reservations: Made with 50% deposit on booking, balance 3 weeks before arrival. Write to site. Address: Molengroet 1, Postbus 200, 1723 ZL Noord-Scharwoude. Tel: 0226/39 34 44. FAX: 0226/39 14 26. E-mail: info@molengroet.nl. A 'Camping Cheques' site.

572 Camping-Jachthaven Uitdam, Uitdam, nr Monickendam

Large waterside site for sailing and windsurfing enthusiasts, northeast of Amsterdam.

Situated beside the Markermeer which is used extensively for watersports, this large site has its own private yachting marina (320 yachts and boats). It has 350 seasonal and permanent pitches, many used by watersports enthusiasts, but also offers marked pitches on open, grassy ground overlooking the water for tourers. Electrical connections are available and amenities include a shop, TV room, tennis, children's playground and a bar/café. Sanitary facilities are rather basic in fairly open buildings with hot showers on payment and British style WCs. There is a special area for campers with bicycles. Very much dominated by the marina, this site will appeal to watersports enthusiasts, with opportunities for sailing, windsurfing and swimming, but it is also on a pretty stretch of coast, only 15 km. from Amsterdam.

How to find it: From A10, take N247 towards Volendam then Monnickendam exit south in direction of Marken, then Uitdam.

General Details: Open 1 April - 1 Nov. Shop (1/4-1/10). Bar/restaurant (weekends and high season). TV room. Tennis. Children's playground. Bicycle hire. Fishing. Yacht marina (with fuel) and slipway. Watersports facilities. Entertainment in high season. Gas supplies. Chemical disposal. Motorcaravan services.

Charges 1999: Per unit incl. 2 persons Nfl 37.50; tent 30.00, without car 23.50; extra person (over 2 yrs) 7.50; dog 6.00; boat on land 10.00, in marina 2.50 per metre, min. charge 15.00. Less 20% outside 1/5-7/9. Credit cards accepted.

Reservations: Contact site. Address: Zeedijk 2, 1154 PP Uitdam. Tel: 020/4031433. FAX: 020/4033692. E-mail: borbv@xs4all.nl.

NETHERLANDS

574 Camping Sint Maartenszee, Sint Maartenszee, nr Den Helder

Excellent family site with good facilities in North Holland.

Situated within easy travelling distance of the attractive and interesting towns of North Holland, especially Alkmaar, this family site is separated from the sea by 900 m. of grassy dunes. With the dune environment, the ground is basically sandy but grass has grown well and hedges are now established. Specialising in family holidays, unusually for the Netherlands only touring units are taken (with a bungalow park adjacent). The 300 pitches are arranged in lines backed by high hedging; 200 have electricity and 150 are fully serviced with water, drainage and cable TV connections. In low, neat buildings, all facilities are of a high standard, particularly both first class, modern sanitary blocks. Hot water for showers is free (with a fascinating panel demonstrating how solar power helps to heat the water!), and it includes wash-cabins, family shower rooms and baby bathrooms. Raised level showers for children are a nice special feature. A dishwashing and laundry room has hot water on payment with a microwave provided. Each block has a couple resident on site to clean and maintain standards throughout the day. A good restaurant/bar, with attractive terrace overlooking the minigolf, has a sitting area with open fire and board games provided. This is a pretty and interesting area of the Netherlands and Sint Maartenszee is quite near the fascinating man-made barrier built to form the Ijsselmeer which allowed the reclamation of so much land.

How to find it: From Alkmaar, take N9 northwards towards Den Helder. Site is signed after approx. 18 km. towards the sea at St-Maartensvlotbrug.

General Details: Open 31 March - 15 Oct. Restaurant/bar (all season). Supermarket (all season). Minigolf. Volleyball. Basketball. Children's play areas. Bicycle hire 200 m. Fishing 1 km. Bus service from village to Alkmaar (cheese market on Fridays April - Sept). Gas supplies. Chemical disposal. Motorcaravan services. Chalets to rent. No dogs or transistors accepted.

Charges 2000: Per unit: 60 sq.m. pitch Nfl. 15.00 - 23.50, with electricity 21.50 - 30.00; 90 sq.m. pitch with electricity 24.50 - 36.00, fully serviced 27.50 - 42.00; person 6.50, plus local tax 1.25. No credit cards.

Reservations: Made for some pitches (all with electricity) with deposit (details from site) but 40% are kept free from reservation for any length of stay. Address: Westerduinweg 30, 1753 BA Sint Maartenszee. Tel: 0224/561401. FAX: 0224/561901. E-mail: campingcsm@wxs.nl.

576 Recreatioord-Watersportcentrum De Kuilart, Koudum

Well run, modern site by Friesland's largest lake, ideal for watersports.

With its own marina and private boating facilities, De Kuilart attracts many watersports enthusiasts. The marina provides windsurfing and sailing lessons and boat hire, and there are special rates at the site for groups and sailing clubs. However, the site has an excellent indoor swimming pool as well as an area for lake swimming and on land there are sports facilities including tennis, a sauna and solarium, and woods for cycling and walking. It may also therefore appeal for a relaxing break in a pleasant area not much visited by British campers. The 450 pitches at De Kuilart are set in groups of 10 to 16 on areas of grass surrounded by well established hedges. There are 225 for touring units, some with electricity, water, waste water and TV connections. Four modern, heated sanitary blocks are well spaced around the site and are of above average quality, although showers are on payment and most washbasins (half in private cabins) have only cold water. British style WCs. The restaurant provides good views of the lake and woodland. Dogs are not accepted. A member of the Holland Tulip Parks group.

How to find it: Site is southeast of Koudum, on the Fluessen lake. Follow the camping sign off the N359 Bolsward - Lemmer road.

General Details: Open all year. Restaurant/bar (1/4-1/11). Supermarket (1/5-1/9). Indoor pool (3 sessions daily, 1/4-1/11). Sauna and solarium. Lake swimming area. Sports field. Children's playground. Bicycle hire. Fishing. Recreation team (high season). Marina (400 berth) with windsurfing, boat hire and boat shop. Garage at harbour. Riding or golf 4 km. Launderette. Gas supplies. Chemical disposal. Motorcaravan services. No dogs accepted.

Charges 1999: Per unit incl. 2 persons Nfl 27.00 - 31.00, with electricity 30.50 - 37.00; all service plus 3.00; extra person 7.00; extra car 4.00; boat on trailer 4.00; tourist tax and babies under 1 year included. Special weekend rates at B.Hs. Credit cards accepted.

Reservations: Advised as site is very popular; made from Sat. - Sat. only in peak season. Address: Kuilart 1, 8723 CG Koudum. Tel: 0514/52 22 21. FAX: 0514/52 30 10. E-mail: info@kuilart.nl. A 'Camping Cheques' site.

577 Camping Stadspark, Groningen

Woodland site for city visits or passing through night halt.

The Stadspark is a large park to the southwest of the city, well signed and with easy access. The campsite is within the park with many trees and surrounded by water. It has 200 pitches (50 seasonal), of which 130 have 4A electricity. The separate tent area is supervised directly by the manager. There are two sanitary blocks, one refurbished for '99. Hot water for showers and dishwashing is on payment. A shop is open daily, with a café April - mid-Sept. Leisure facilities include bicycle hire, fishing and canoeing. The Paterswoldse Lake is near for windsurfing, swimming or sailing. Buses to the city leave from right outside and timetables and maps are provided by Mrs Swieter, the helpful, English speaking manager.

How to find it: From Assen on the A28 turn left onto the A7. Turn onto N370 and follow site signs (Stadspark, quite close).

General Details: Open 15 March - 15 Oct. Shop. Café (1/5-15/9). Bicycle hire. Fishing. Canoeing. Riding and golf 10 km. Chemical disposal. Motorcaravan service point.

Charges 1999: Per adult Nfl. 4.75; child (2-12 yrs) 3.25; caravan or tent 7.00; car 4.50; motorcaravan 8.00 - 10.00; electricity 3.50. No credit cards.

Reservations: Contact site. Address: Campinglaan 6, 9727 KH Groningen. Tel: 050/525 1624. FAX: 050/525 0099.

579 Camping 't Kuierpadtien, Wezuperbrug, nr Emmen

Large, friendly site in northeast with its own dry-ski slope.

This all year round site is suitable as a night stop, or for longer if you wish to participate in all the activities offered in July and August (on payment). These encompass canoeing, windsurfing, water shutes and the dry-ski slope, which is also open during the winter so that the locals can practise before going en-masse to Austria. There are three opportunities for swimming with an indoor pool supplemented by a heated outdoor pool (June-Aug) and the lake itself. Sauna, solarium, whirlpool and tennis also. Children's play areas, volleyball and basketball. There are plenty of local attractions and brochures for these are available at reception. Restaurant (all year), supermarket (May-Aug, bread all year). The site itself is in a woodland setting on the edge of the village. The 450 pitches for touring units (650 total) all have electricity, are of reasonable size and are flat and grassy. There are eight quite acceptable sanitary blocks with British style WCs and free hot showers (17.30 - 10.00 in July/Aug).

How to find it: From N34 Groningen-Emmen road exit near Emmen onto N31 towards Beilen. Turn right into Schoonord where left to Wezuperbrug. Site is at beginning of village on the right.

General Details: Open all year. Electricity connections (4A). Supermarket (1/5-1/9). Restaurant (all year). Bar (1/5-1/9). Indoor and outdoor pools. Sauna. Solarium. Tennis. Volleyball. Basketball. Dry ski slope. Children's play areas. Gas supplies. Chemical disposal. Motorcaravan services.

Charges 1999: Per person (over 1 yr) Nfl. 7.60; pitch 15.75, 22.75 or 31.50, acc. to season; car 5.00. No credit cards.

Reservations: Recommended for July/Aug. and made with deposit. Address: Oranjekanaal NZ 10, 7853 TA Wezuperbrug. Tel: 0591/38 14 15. FAX: 0591/38 22 35. E-mail: info@kuierpad.nl. A 'Camping Cheques' site.

NETHERLANDS

598 Camping De Roos, Beerze-Ommen

Family run site in an area of outstanding natural beauty.

This is truly a nature lover's campsite situated in Overijssel's Vecht Valley, a unique region set in a river dune landscape on the River Vecht. The river and its tributary wends its way unhurriedly around and through this spacious site, in a natural setting which the owners have carefully preserved. Conserving the environment is paramount here and the 285 pitches and necessary amenities have been blended into the landscape with great care. Pitches, many with electricity, are naturally sited, some behind blackthorn thickets, in the shadow of an old oak, or in a clearing scattered with wild flowers. De Roos is a car-free site in peak periods – vehicles must go in the car park, except on arrival and departure. Torches are needed at night. Facilities include a pleasant reception, a health food shop and tea room. Four well maintained sanitary blocks are fresh and clean. The two larger blocks are heated and contain good sized showers, baby bath/shower and wash cabins, all with free hot water, and WCs (no paper). There are washing-up sinks and a launderette adjacent to the shop. Children have several small playgrounds and a field for kite flying. Swimming, fishing and boating is possible in the Vecht and there is a children's pool and beach area, also landing stages with steps. The enthusiastic owners have compiled walking and cycling routes (in English).

How to find it: Leave A28 at Ommen exit 21 on N340 for 19 km. to Ommen. Turn right at traffic lights over bridge and immediately left on local road towards Beerze. Site on left after 7 km. just after Beerze village sign.

General Details: Open 1 April - 29 October. Health food shop. Tea room. River swimming. Fishing. Bicycle hire. Volleyball. Basketball. Boules. Table tennis. Riding 6 km. Golf 10 km. Launderette. Gas supplies. Chemical disposal. Motorcaravan services. Chalets for hire. No dogs are accepted.

Charges 2000: Per unit incl. 2 persons Nfl. 25.00; extra person 5.75; electricity 4.00; local tax 0.85. Discounts in low season and special packages. Credit cards accepted.

Reservations: made with Nfl. 10 fee. Address: Beerzeweg 10, 7736 PJ Beerze-Ommen. Tel: 0523/251234. FAX: 0523/251903. E-mail: info@camping-de-roos.nl.

AR Discount
Less 10%

599 Camping De Vechtstreek, Rheeze-Hardenberg

Quality site with a fairy-tale theme.

It would be difficult for any child (or adult) to pass this site and not be drawn to the oversized open story book which marks its entrance. From here young children enter the exciting world of Hannah and Bumpie, two of the nine characters around which this site's fairy-tale theme has been created. The young owners of have given their park a special identity by creating this fairy tale. The colourful characters appear on finger boards and signs throughout the site. Not only is the story acted out in the restaurant at the Saturday children's buffet, the story continues in the indoor water play park which is dominated by Hannah's Castle. This is also a campsite which offers top class facilities. These include three modern heated sanitary blocks with free hot showers, baby room, family shower and outside washing-up area. There is an excellent laundry room, well stocked supermarket and restaurant. The snack bar and takeaway overlooks the water play area. The 200 touring pitches are mostly laid out in bays of around 12 units. In the centre of each is a small children's play area. There are many water points and pitches have electricity (4A). Although there are numerous static vans these are unobtrusive. The site has a mature appearance with many trees and shrubs. There is access to a fishing, swimming and boating recreation area.

How to find it: From Ommen take N34 Hardenberg road for 9 km. Turn right on N36 and proceed south for 3.5 km. Turn left at first crossroads and immediately left again on local road. Site clearly signed on left in 2 km.

General Details: Open 1 April - 25 October. Supermarket. Restaurant, snacks and takeaway. Fairy-tale water play park. Activity club. Theatre. Football field. Launderette.

Charges guide: Per unit incl. 2 persons Nfl. 29.90 - 42.70; electricity 5.00; local tax 0.60.

Reservations: Contact site: Address: Grote Beltenweg 17, 7794 RA Rheeze-Hardenberg. Tel: 0523/261369. FAX: 0523/265942.

581 Rekreatiepark De Luttenberg, Luttenberg, nr Zwolle

Large, peacefully set park with many facilities.

This woodland site is near the Sallandse Heuvelrug nature reserve in a hilly location and is well placed for relaxing walking and cycling tours. It is a large park with 120 seasonal pitches around the perimeter and 220 touring pitches (all with 4A electricity) in a central area off tarred access roads. The individual, numbered and separated, large pitches are in rows divided by hedges and trees, with easy access and on mainly gently sloping or undulating grass. A separate cluster is for dog owners. A new heated sanitary block with controllable showers gives a satisfactory overall provision together with two other blocks. All are heated and each provides pre-set hot showers on payment, open washbasins and British style WCs. Outside, under cover, are dishwashing points. There is a small shop for essentials including fresh bread, a large bar and eating area with terrace and a small, separate restaurant (low season: Tues. and Fri-Sun). Barbecue with seating. The fair-sized swimming pool and a small one for children, plus boules, football, tennis, table tennis, minigolf, volleyball and an animal enclosure provide plenty to keep younger visitors happy. Member of the Holland Tulip Parc group.

How to find it: From N35 Zwolle - Almelo turn on N348 Ommen road east of Raalte, then turn to Luttenberg and follow signs. From A1 (Amsterdam - Hengelo) take exit 23 at Deventer on N348, then as above.

General Details: Open 31 March - 1 Oct. Shop. Bar and restaurant (15/7-3/9 plus weekends). Swimming pool (15/5-15/9). Tennis. Table tennis. Volleyball. Boules. Bicycle hire. Minigolf. Fishing 1.5 km. Riding 6 km. Gas supplies. Chemical disposal. Motorcaravan services. Bungalows for rent.

Charges 2000: Per unit incl. 2 persons and electricity Nfl. 38.00, 3 persons 44.25, 4 persons 50.50; cyclists, 2 persons 26.00; extra person (over 3 yrs) 6.00. Less 15% outside 15/7-1/9. No credit cards.

Reservations: Made with fee (Nfl 10). Address: Heuvelweg 9, 8105 SZ Luttenberg. Tel: 572 30 14 05. FAX 572 30 17 57. E-mail: info@campingluttenberg.nl. A 'Camping Cheques' site.

 Rekreatiepark "De Luttenberg"

Camping de Luttenberg is situated in the part of Holland called 'Salland'. This part of the country shows a variety of nature such as woods, meadows and hay-fields. It is nice to walk and bike or to visit one of the Attraction parks or nice cities in the neighbourhood. Pitches on the park are grassy and marked with bushes, all with electricity. We also rent modern caravans. The sanitary facilities are modern, heated and clean. In high season a team of animators will fulfil your entertainment wishes.

Ask for our brochure and prices: Tel.+31.572.301405 Fax.+31.572.301757.
Recreatiepark 'De Luttenberg' Heuvelweg 9, NL-8105 SZ Luttenberg
e-mail: info@campingluttenberg.nl internet: www.campingluttenberg.nl

573 Nature Park Sikkeler, Ruurlo

Family run site and paradise for nature lovers.

This long-established park offers guests peaceful and natural surroundings with an emphasis on the fact that organised entertainment is 'taboo'. It is an award winning site surrounded by the fascinating landscape of the Achterhoek, an area tucked away in the far eastern corner of Gelderland. In a woodland setting it offers 145 touring pitches, 125 with electricity (4A) and 45 fully serviced with water, drainage, electricity and TV connection. These latter pitches are sited in a more open area, divided by shrubs and young trees. The four modern sanitary units are heated, clean and well maintained. Facilities include provision for babies and people with disabilities. Showers are free and soap is provided. There is a campers' kitchen, launderette, motorcaravan services, car wash, chemical disposal and night lighting. Adjoining reception is a pleasant bar/restaurant area and a small shop for basic groceries. Bicycles can be hired and for children there is a paddling pool, animal enclosure and play area. Sited away from the touring pitches is a number of thatched cottages and quality bungalows for hire. Nearby attractions include a castle, saw mill, cheese farm and wooden shoe factory.

How to find it: Leave A18 exit 4, on N315 towards Zelhem/Ruurlo. Site is on left 4 km. south of Ruurlo.

General Details: Open all year. Shop. Restaurant. Bicycle hire. Table tennis. Playing field. Laundry room. Motorcaravan services. Cottages and bungalows to rent.

Charges 1999: Per unit incl. 2 persons Nfl. 31.00 - 39.00; extra person 5.00; cyclist and tent 10.00; electricity 3.75; local tax 0.55; dog (1 per pitch) 5.00. Credit cards accepted.

Reservations: Not essential. Address: Sikkelerweg 8, 7261 LP Ruurlo. Tel: 0573/46.12.21. FAX: 0573/46.15.68. E-mail: info@sikkeler.nl.

NETHERLANDS

N580 Flevo-Natuur, Zeewolde

Large, well equipped naturist site in quiet forest location.

This large naturist site, set amongst the densely wooded area of the southern Flevoland polder, is well equipped and well organised. The central feature of the site is an island recreation area with a sandy beach, sunbathing lawns, children's animal enclosure, volleyball and boules areas. There are two large swimming pools, outdoor and indoor (the indoor one is open all year), and a small children's pool directly linked to the main pool. Adjacent are a sauna and solarium. A daily events programme is organised with activities for children and adults, including bingo, dancing, etc. Other amenities include tennis courts, a restaurant/bar, small snack bar with takeaway and supermarket (1/4-31/10). The 750 pitches, about half available for tourists, are mainly in groups separated by hedges. Cars must be parked on the car park at the entrance, which gives a quiet, spacious atmosphere. Visitors with motorcaravans are at a disadvantage as they are placed in a more remote area away from the centre (with inferior portacabin style sanitary facilities). The main sanitary facilities consist of three blocks, one of which can be heated for winter use. They have British style WCs, free hot showers (communal) and facilities for the disabled. This is a friendly site where naturist cards are unnecessary - entrance is open to all and day visits are possible. Nudity is obligatory in all areas when the temperature reaches 20°C.

How to find it: From the A28/E232 motorway (Amersfoort-Zwolle) take the Nijkerk exit, and turn towards Zeewolde. After 500 m. cross lifting bridge onto Flevoland then follow signs for Flevo-Natuur. From the opposite direction (ie. Almere) follow signs to Nijkerk, and then site.

General Details: Open all year. Swimming pools. Sauna and solarium. Table tennis. Minigolf. Boules. Volleyball. Entertainment programme. Supermarket. Bar. Restaurant (closed Oct - Dec). Launderette. Library. 170 bungalows for rent.

Charges guide: Per tent or caravan Nfl 12.50, with electricity 16.00; person 13.50; child (4-14 yrs) 7.00. Less outside high season. Credit cards accepted. Arrival after 15.00 hrs).

Reservations: Recommended for July - mid-Aug. and school holidays especially for electricity. Address: Wielseweg 3, 3896 LA Zeewolde. Tel: 036/552 82 41.

582 Camping de Hertshoorn, Garderen

Attractive, good quality site with woodland pitches.

Although this is quite a large site, this is not immediately apparent with its woodland location. Careful design has allowed both single pitches in little glades and groups on cleared grassy areas with plenty of gentle shade. Around 390 of the pitches are for tourists and all have electricity (10A), water and drainage. Cars must be parked on the entrance car park. Four excellent toilet blocks provide comprehensive, heated facilities with a variety of cabins and showers with free hot water (showers electronically timed), British style WCs, dishwashing facilities and freezers and one block houses a well equipped laundry. The very smart reception (more like a hotel than a campsite!) provides information packs in English, with a pleasant restaurant at the rear which the owners, the Selderijk family, call 'a living room for guests'. Well kept, small animal paddocks and stables entertain the children and there is a variety of play equipment around the site. There are indoor heated swimming and paddling pools and outdoor paddling pools. Garderen is a pretty village, 1 km. away, and the area is very suitable for cycling. Adding a new word to the camping vocabulary, the site has three 'tree-tents' for hire. These drop-shaped, canvas tents with steel frames and wooden floors are suspended from pine trees and accommodate two people (with access by ladder!) - we have yet to try them!

How to find it: From A1/E30 between Amersfoort and Apeldoorn, take Garderen exit. Cross the N344, through village and site is signed on Putten road.

General Details: Open 31 March - 30 Oct. Supermarket. Restaurant (closed Mondays). Snacks. Swimming and paddling pools. Minigolf. Children's farm. Play areas. Entertainment for children in high season. Bicycle hire. Riding 2 km. Golf 8 km. Baby equipment hire. Laundry facilities. Gas supplies. Chemical disposal. Motorcaravan services. Tree tents for rent.

Charges 2000: Per unit incl. electricity and 2 persons Nfl. 30.00 - 50.00; extra person 5.00; local tax 1.00 per person. Weekly family packages - details from site. No credit cards.

Reservations: Recommended for high season. Address: Putterweg 68-70, 3886 PG Garderen. Tel: 0577/461529. FAX: 0577/461556. E-mail: hertshoorn@vvc.nl.

583 Camping Kerkendel, Kootwijk, nr Arnhem

Friendly, family site with high quality amenities.

Kerkendel is a good quality touring site, small enough to allow friendly, personal attention from the owners, the Van Asselt family. Very suitable for families with young children, the 170 pitches are arranged in small groups with play equipment in many of the central open spaces. Cars are parked on car parks at the entrance. Hedges and attractive trees provide shade and electrical connections (4, 6 or 10A) are available on all pitches. A super new sanitary block has under-floor heating and a room with a wide range of washing and shower facilities with the emphasis on families (baby rooms, family shower rooms, low washbasins, etc). Another excellent new building with no children's facilities, is for those who prefer a quieter environment. Hot water is free throughout and entry is controlled by a card system. The adjacent fully equipped dishwashing (dishwasher!) and laundry room is of the same high standard. One small block with WCs (British style) only will be replaced within the next few years which will ensure that there are adequate facilities when the site is busy. A range of activities includes a small indoor and a heated outdoor swimming pool, tennis courts (small charge), volleyball and table tennis. There is also a children's playground, TV room, a good restaurant and snack bar, and a small supermarket. Plenty of tourist information and advice are available from reception and bicycles are available for hire to try out the network of cycle paths in the area. The site is surrounded by woodland and sandy open spaces (this is the largest sand dune in Western Europe), it is very close to two National Parks and the city of Arnhem with its Burger Zoo and Open Air Museum, and not too far from the Airborne Museum at Hartenstein-Oosterbeek.

How to find it: Kootwijk is 10 km. west of Apeldoorn. From the A1/E30 motorway, take the Kootwijk exit 18 and site is signed, 3 km. on country lanes.

General Details: Open 1 April - 1 Nov. Shop. Restaurant. Snack bar with takeaway. TV room. Indoor and outdoor swimming pools. Tennis. Bicycle hire. Volleyball. Children's playground. Laundry facilities. Animation chalet. Motorcaravan services. Simple wooden chalets to rent.

Charges 2000: Per unit incl. 2 persons NLG 33.50 - 52.00; extra person 5.75 - 6.25; dog 8.75; local tax 1.00 per person; electricity included. Credit cards accepted.

Reservations: Made free of charge - write for details. Address: Kerkendelweg 49, 3775 KM Kootwijk. Tel: 0577/45 62 24. FAX: 0577/45 65 45. E-mail: kerkendel@tref.nl. A 'Camping Cheques' site.

CAMPING KERKENDEL

Fam. Van Asselt
Kerkendelweg 49
NL-3375 KM Kootwijk

Tel.: 0031-377-45 62 24
Fax: 0031-577-45 65 45
http://www.kerkendel.nl
E-mail: kerkendel@tref.nl

HOLLAND
TULIP PARCS

ANWB *****   Camping Cheque

- Large heated pool for all the family 28° • Large heated outdoor pool 23°
- Tennis, badminton and volleyball courts, table tennis
- Restaurant, snackbar and mini-market • Activity programme for school holidays
- Situated in the heart of the Veluwe, near to the biggest sand-drift in Western Europe
- Easy to find: Motorway Amsterdam-Apeldoorn, exit Kootwijk, then follow signs

586 Camping Betuwestrand, Beesd, nr Utrecht

Pleasant, conveniently situated site for night stop or longer stay.

Just off the A2/E25 motorway (Utrecht - s'Hertogenbosch, exit 14), this is a large site with 200 places for tourers (all with 10A electricity, most with drainage) in addition to 500 well established permanent units. The touring pitches are in four distinct areas with many around an attractive lake with a large sandy beach. For families with young children there is another area away from the water. The toilet blocks are of a good standard and include British WCs, family rooms and facilities for disabled people. Hot water is on payment in both showers and washbasins in cabins. The site has a smart reception block and also a restaurant (open to the public), shop, bar, TV room and children's play area. An area of the lake is cordoned off for swimming with a slide and diving boards and it is also suitable for windsurfing. Gelderland is the part of the Netherlands between the rivers Maas and Waal, famous for fruit growing. No dogs are accepted.

How to find it: Site is 25 km. SSE of Utrecht, clearly signed from both directions on the A2/E25 road between Utrecht and s'Hertogenbosch. Take the exit 14 (Beesd) and site is 200 m.

General Details: Open 1 April - 30 Sept. Shop. Restaurant. Bar/TV room. Playground. Good lake fishing. Bicycle hire. Launderette. Tennis. Mobile homes for hire.

Charges guide: Per unit incl. up to 2 persons, electricity and tourist tax Nfl 31.00; extra person 6.00. Special weekend or weekly prices.

Reservations: Necessary in high season - contact site. Address: A. Kraalweg 40, 4153 XC Beesd. Tel: 0345/68 15 03. FAX: 0345/68 16 86.

NETHERLANDS

584 Camping De Pampel, Hoenderloo, nr Arnhem/Apeldoorn

Tranquil forest site in De Hooge Veluwe National Park.

A site with no static holiday caravans is rare in the Netherlands and this adds to the congenial atmosphere at De Pampel, which is enhanced by its situation deep in the forest, with 9 ha. of its own woods to explore. This peaceful park offers many opportunities for interesting outings with the two National Parks in the vicinity, the Kroller-Muller museum and the city of Arnhem. The area has excellent cycle paths which can be joined from a gate at the back of the site. Therre are 180 pitches (20 seasonal). You can choose to site yourself around the edge of a large open field with volleyball, etc. in the middle, or pick one of the individual places which are numbered, divided by trees and generally quite spacious. All have 4A electricity (no heaters allowed) but the furthest pitches are some distance from the sanitary facilities. The swimming pool and child's pool, heated by solar panels, are open Easter - Oct. Modern play equipment has special safety surfaces. There is just one building which houses reception, a restaurant, bar, snack bar, laundry and dishwashing, and the sanitary facilities, which are modern and a very good new addition at the end (showers on payment, British style WCs). Full catering facilities are provided in high season (6 weeks of July/Aug), otherwise at weekends only. Barbecues by permission only, no open fires.

How to find it: From the A50 Arnhem-Apeldoorn road exit for Hoenderloo and follow signs.

General Details: Open all year. Swimming pool (Easter - Oct). Restaurant. Bar. Snack bar. Shop (1/4-31/10). Children's play area. Pets corner. Sports area. Chemical disposal.

Charges 1999: Per unit incl. 2 persons Nfl. 35.00, without car 30.00; extra person 8.00; child (under 11 yrs) 6.00; dog 7.50; electricity (4A) 5.00. Less 10% 1/9-25/3.

Reservations: Made with deposit (Nfl. 100). Address: Woeste Hoefweg 33-35, 7351 TN Hoenderloo. Tel: 055/378 1760. FAX: 055/378 1992.

To tourist campers "De Pampel" is the most attractive camp-site of the Netherlands

EUROTOP
CAMPING "DE PAMPEL"

The site is the most centrally located in the "green heart" of the Netherlands, less than two kilometres from the entrance of the "Hoge Veluwe" National Park in Hoenderloo, and offers a wide diversity of tourist possibilities.
"De Pampel" is an excellent camp-site.
Come and see for yourself!

Camping "De Pampel"
Woeste Hoefweg 33-35, 7351 TN HOENDERLOO

tel. +31 55 378 1760
fax. +31 55 378 1992

---

596 Camping De Wielerbaan, Wageningen-Hoog

Family run park with an interesting history and a natural setting.

At a point where the Veluwe, the valley of Gelderland and the picturesque area of Betuwe meet, you find the Wielerbaan. Translated this name means 'cycle race-track' which still stands in the heart of this site. The present owners have utilised this area to accommodate recreation facilities which include an indoor swimming pool. Touring pitches here are divided into two areas, one in the seclusion of a forest setting with the added luxury of individual toilet cabins, the other a meadow setting where the pitches are serviced with water, electricity and drainage. There are four sanitary blocks of a reasonable standard, with another planned for 2000. They provide wash cabins, showers and a baby room. Amenities include a launderette, shop, small restaurant, takeaway and terrace. There is minigolf and boules, plus ten small play areas for children and organised entertainment in high season. Planned cycles routes are available at reception, or maps to choose your own way. It is possible to go by boat to Arnhem and worth visiting is the Burgers Zoo, the Zoo of Ouwehand or seeking out the nearby parks (discounted entrance cards are available from the site).

How to find it: Leave A12 at exit 24 towards Wageningen and follow signs to site, 1.5 km. from the town.

General Details: Open all year. Shop. Restaurant. Snacks and takeaway. Swimming pool. Minigolf. Boules. Play areas. Launderette.

Charges 2000: Per unit incl. 2 persons and electricity NFl. 26.00 - 66.00; private toilet cabin plus 8.00. Less 10% for over 55s at certain times.

Reservations: Advisable in high season; Address: Zoomweg 7-9, 6705 DM Wageningen-Hoog. Tel: 031/7 413964. FAX: 031/7420751.

KAMPEERCENTRUM ★ ★ ★ ★ ★

DE HOOGE VELUWE

Kampeercentrum De Hooge Veluwe is a campsite where many campers from different countries come to spend their holiday, because of its unique location in the green heart of the Netherlands, right in front of the entrance to the national park "De Hooge Veluwe".

Camping de Hooge Veluwe
Koningsweg 14 • 6816 TC ARNHEM
Phone (+31)- 26-443 2272 • Fax: (+31)- 26-443 68 09
E-mail hooge.veluwe@vvc.nl

585 Camping de Hooge Veluwe, Arnhem

Highly rated site in the green heart of the Netherlands.
Its situation at the entrance to the Hooge Veluwe National Park with its moors, forests, sand drifts, walking routes and cycle paths, makes this a highly desirable holiday base. The site itself is well managed and laid out in an orderly fashion. Reception is immediately to the right of the entrance and adjacent stands the recreation hall, restaurant, takeaway and supermarket. The 175 touring pitches, all with electricity (4/6A), are numbered and laid out in small fields which are divided by hedging. Some are traffic free which means cars must be left in a nearby car park. Mobile homes are discreetly placed mostly in the centre of the site, but the many trees and shrubbery make them unobtrusive, in fact many have enviable garden areas. There are five excellent, heated sanitary blocks with all facilities easily identified by colourful logos. Also on site are heated outdoor and indoor pools and a paddling pool. There is also a TV room, a number of small play areas and to the far right of the site a dedicated play ground with football pitch, tennis, cycle track, basketball, minigolf, etc. The adjacent National Park incorporates the Kroller Muller Museum and the Museonder Underground Museum. The Burgers Zoo and Safari Park and Burgers Park, are also near, all of which make interesting visits. There is some road noise and no dogs are allowed on site.

How to find it: Leave A12 motorway at exit 25 (Oosterbeck) and follow signs for Hooge Veluwe. Site is on right in approx. 6 km.

General Details: Open 31 March - 29 Oct. Supermarket. Restaurant. Takeaway. Swimming pools. Play areas. Bicycle hire. Riding 50 m. Golf 6 km. Organised activities. Launderette. Gas supplies. Chemical disposal. Motorcaravan services.

Charges 2000: Per unit incl. 2 persons and electricity Nfl. 32.50 - 49.50; extra person 6.00; tourist tax 0.75. Credit cards accepted.

Reservations: necessary in high season. Address: Koningsweg 14, 6816 TC Arnhem. Tel: 026/4432272. FAX: 026/4436809. E-mail: hooge.veluwe@vvc.nl.

De Wielerbaan
★★★★ < *WAGENINGEN-HOOG* >

Zoomweg 7-9
6705 DM Wageningen Hoog
Tel. +31 317 41 39 64
Fax +31 317 42 07 51
E-mail: wielerbaan@vvc.nl
www.wielerbaan.nl

Small, clearly laid-out campsite with a friendly atmosphere. Ideal for children. Not only families with children are welcome - we are also open for a one night stay and for senior guests. We want you to have a good night's sleep. Ideal starting point for trips by car, bicycle or on foot. All-in rates.

NETHERLANDS

595 Camping-Caravanning Heumens Bos, Heumen, nr Nijmegen

Friendly site, family run for families.

The area around Nijmegen, the oldest city in the Netherlands, has large forests for walking or cycling, nature reserves and old towns to explore, as well as being quite close to Arnhem. A warm welcome from the Grol family awaits you at this well run site. It covers 16 hectares and is open over a long season for touring families (no groups of youngsters allowed) and all year for bungalows. It offers 165 level, grass touring pitches (all with 6A hook-ups), numbered but not separated, in glades of 10 and one large field, all with easy access. Cars are parked away from the caravans. One small section for motorcaravans has some hardstandings. The main, high quality sanitary building, plus another new block, are modern and heated, providing showers on payment, British style WCs, rooms for families and disabled people and free hot water to the private cabins and other washbasins. External, covered dishwashing facilities. Another smaller building has acceptable facilities and there is a smart launderette. The restaurant, which offers a quality menu (the owners are former restaurateurs) and a new terrace, is close to the comfortable bar and there is a snack bar too as well as a large shop. An open air swimming pool with a small children's pool is maintained at 25°C by a system of heat transfer from the air. For children there is a separate glade with play equipment on sand and grass, table tennis, organised entertainment in July/Aug. and a large room for wet weather.

How to find it: From A73 (Nijmegen - Venlo) take exit 3 (4 km. south of Nijmegen) and follow site signs.

General Details: Open 1 April - 1 Nov. (bungalows all year). Shop. Bar, restaurant and snack bar (all season). Heated swimming pool (1/4-30/9). Bicycle hire. New all weather tennis courts. Boules. Table tennis. Activity and excursion programme (high season). Fishing 2 km. Golf 10 km. Launderette. Gas supplies. Chemical disposal. Motorcaravan services. Modern bungalows, caravans and tents for hire.

Charges 2000: Per pitch incl. 2 persons, caravan or tent Nfl. 28.00 - 44.00, motorcaravan 35.00 - 51.00; extra person (over 3 yrs) 6.00; electricity 4.50; dog (max 1) 6.00. Special low season weekends (incl. restaurant meal) - contact park. Credit cards accepted.

Reservations: Made without charge and advisable for July/Aug. Address: Vosseneindseweg 46, 6582 BR Heumen. Tel: 024 358 1481. FAX: 024 358 3862. E-mail: info@heumensbos.nl.

588 Vrijetijdspark Vinkeloord, Vinkel, nr s'Hertogenbosch

Large, pleasant holiday site with many amenities.

Run by the same group as Beekse Bergen (590), Vinkeloord is a large site with motel accommodation and a bungalow park in addition to its 500 camping pitches. These are divided into several grassy areas, many in an attractive wooded setting, 350 with electrical connections and also some with full services (water and TV connection). The site is a popular holiday choice with activities organised in the main seasons. The varied amenities are located in and around a modern, central complex. They include heated outdoor swimming pools, a new indoor leisure pool with slide, a ten-pin bowling alley, minigolf and tennis courts. A small, landscaped lake has sandy beaches and is overlooked by a large, modern children's play area. Some of the touring pitches also overlook the water. Campers are entitled to free entry to the adjacent 'Autotron' attraction. The eight toilet blocks are well situated for all parts of the site. The clean and simple facilities are a bit of a mixture (some unisex) with some warm water for washing, some individual washbasins and pre-set showers.

How to find it: Site is signed from the N50/A50 road between s'Hertogenbosch and Nijmegen, approx. 10 km. east of s'Hertogenbosch at Vinkel.

General Details: Open 1 April - 1 Nov. Supermarket. Bar. Modern, up-market restaurant. Snack bar/takeaway (high season only). Free outdoor heated swimming pools (May - early Sept). Indoor leisure pool (on payment). Sauna, solarium. Ten-pin bowling alley. Tennis courts. Minigolf. Table tennis. Sports field. Bicycle hire. Fishing. Barbecue area. Children's play areas on sand. Many organised activities in season. Conference facilities, motel bedrooms and bungalows for hire.

Charges 1999: Per person (from 3 yrs) Nfl. 5.00 - 9.00; pitch simple: 7.50 - 18.00, serviced (water and TV connections) 12.50 - 23.00; electricity 6.00 - 7.50. Credit cards accepted.

Reservations: Recommended for high season - write for details. Address: Vinkeloord 1, 5382 JX Vinkel (North Brabant). Tel: 073/534 35 36. FAX: 073/532 16 98. E-mail: info@autotron.nl.

587 Camping De Vergarde, Erichem, nr Tiel

Family oriented site in a quiet setting.
Situated north of s'Hertogenbosch and west of Nijmegen and Arnhem, De Vergarde has two sections on either side of a lake. Static holiday caravans are on the left, with 220 touring pitches in named sections on the right (about one third seasonal). With good access, pitches are numbered on flat grass and include 30 new ones with electricity (6A) and TV connections. There are trees all round the perimeter (but no shade on the pitches) and the site has a spacious, open feeling with the lake adding to its attractiveness. Sanitary facilities are in three blocks of an excellent standard, with British style WCs, family showers, washing machines and baby bathrooms. Most, but not all, hot water is on payment. The shop opens daily and the restaurant/bar in high season plus weekends in low season. There are heated pools for adults and children, the latter also being catered for with minigolf, pony riding, a pets corner, horse drawn wagons, large play area, volleyball and a large indoor games room for wet days. Two tennis courts. Lots of ducks and geese gather around the lake, which can be used for fishing (but not swimming).

How to find it: From A15 Dordrecht/Nijmegen road exit at Tiel West (also MacDonald's) and follow signs to Erichem village.

General Details: Open 1 March - 30 Oct. Swimming pools (1/5-1/9). Shop (1/5-1/10). Restaurant (1/5-1/10). Minigolf. Pony riding. Pets corner. Bicycle hire. Children's play area. Volleyball. Basketball. Games room. Tennis courts. Fishing. Chemical disposal. Motorcaravan services.

Charges 1999: Per unit incl. 2 adults and services (electricity, water and drainage) Nfl. 34.00 - 39.00; extra person 6.00; dog 5.00. Special weekly rates. Low season less 20%.

Reservations: Contact site. Address: Erichemseweg 84, 4117 GL Erichem. Tel: 0344/57 20 17. FAX: 0344/57 22 29. E-mail: info@devergarde.nl. A 'Camping Cheques' site.

NETHERLANDS

589 Kampeercentrum Klein Canada, Afferden, nr Nijmegen

Pretty site with good facilities in the Maas valley, close to German border.

Following the war, the family who own this site wanted to emigrate to Canada - they didn't go, but instead created this attractive site with the maple leaf theme decorating buildings, pool and play equipment. Pleasant, farm style buildings adorned with flowers house the main amenities near the entrance and the site has a sheltered atmosphere with many ornamental trees. There are three touring areas, one on an island surrounded by a landscaped moat used for fishing, the other on flat ground on the other side of the entrance. They provide 210 large, numbered pitches, all with electricity (4, 6 or 10A), water, drainage and TV connections. The newest area has 80 pitches each with its own sanitary unit and car space. Some 200 permanent and seasonal pitches form other areas. The island pitches have excellent, unisex sanitary facilities with free hot water, private cabins, controllable showers and family facilities in tiled, heated rooms alongside the bar. The other pitches are served by a good block with push-button showers. There is a small indoor pool, sauna and solarium and an outdoor pool and children's pool. A traditional looking bar has takeaway facilities tucked away behind and there is a small shop (bread to order). Cars are parked in separate areas. This is a good quality site with a lot to offer for a comfortable stay in charming surroundings.

How to find it: Afferden is on the N271 between Nijmegen and Venlo, just south of the A77/E31 motorway into Germany. Site is on the N271 and is signed.

General Details: Open all year. Bar, restaurant, snack bar, takeaway and shop (all 1/4-31/10). Outdoor pool (May - Sept). Indoor pool (all year). Sauna and solarium. Table top minigolf. Tennis. Fishing. Children's playground. Animal enclosure. Bicycle hire. Riding 5 km. Gas supplies. Chemical disposal. Motorcaravan services.

Charges 2000: Per unit incl. 4A electricity Nfl. 17.50 - 29.00, 'super comfort' pitch plus 10.00; person 6.50; child (1-12 yrs) 5.00; dog 4.00; local tax 1.25 per person. Credit cards accepted.

Reservations: made with Nfl. 20 deposit Address: Dorpsstraat 1, 5851 AG Afferden (Limburg). Tel: 0485/53 12 23. FAX: 0485/53 22 18. E-mail: info@kleincanada.nl. A 'Camping Cheques' site.

591 Vakantiecentrum De Hertenwei, Lage Mierde, nr Tilburg

Large, spacious site in southern Netherlands with swimming pools.

Set in the southwest corner of the country quite close to the Belgian border, this relaxed site covers a large area. In addition to 100 quite substantial bungalows with their own gardens (some residential, 30 to let), the site has 350 touring pitches. These are in four areas on oblong meadows surrounded by hedges and trees, with numbered pitches around the perimeters. There is a choice of pitch size (150, 100 or 64 sq.m.) and all have 4A electricity, many with water and drainage as well. The most pleasant area is probably the small one near the entrance and main buildings - these are a long walk from some of the furthest pitches. The range of amenities includes a small indoor heated swimming pool (12 x 6 m.) open all year (with admission charge), sauna, jacuzzi and solarium. Three outdoor pools, the largest 25 x 10 m. are open in summer. A modern building houses a restaurant, canteen and snack bar with a disco in the basement. Four toilet blocks of differing types but all of quite good quality are well spaced. They have British style WCs, virtually all washbasins in cabins, good, controllable showers and can be heated in cool weather. Hot water for all facilities is free. Some blocks have units for disabled people, hair washing cabins and baby baths.

How to find it: Site is by N269 Tilburg - Reusel road, 2 km. north of Lage Mierde and 16 km. south of Tilburg.

General Details: Open all year. Supermarket (Easter - end Oct, nearest 2 km). Bar by indoor pool. Outdoor pool (27/5-27/8). Restaurant, cafeteria with snack bar (all year). Disco. Two tennis courts. Children's playgrounds and play meadows. Sauna, solarium and jacuzzi. Bicycle hire. Fishing 4 km. Riding 4 km. Recreation programme in season with films, dances or disco, sports, bingo, etc. Bus service to Tilburg or Eindhoven with stop at entrance. Launderette. Gas supplies. Chemical disposal. Motorcaravan services. Chalets to rent.

Charges 2000: Per unit incl. 2 persons and electricity Nfl. 48.50 - 53.50, acc. to type; extra person 6.00; local tax 1.05; dog 6.00. Less 25-40% in low seasons. No credit cards.

Reservations: are made for min. 1 week, in summer Sat to Sat. only, with deposit. Address: Wellenseind 7-9, 5094 EG Lage Mierde. Tel: 013/509 12 95.

590 Camping Hilvarenberg and Safari Camping, Beekse Bergen Resort,
Hilvarenbeek, nr Tilburg

Large, impressive lakeside leisure complex, with many amenities.

Beekse Bergen is an impressive leisure park set around a very large, attractive lake. The park offers a range of amusements which should keep the most demanding of families happy! These include not only water based activities such as windsurfing, canoeing, jetski, rowing and fishing, but also a small amusement park, a cinema, tennis courts, minigolf and many more. The lake is bordered by sandy beaches, children's playgrounds, open-air swimming areas and water slides. Transport around and across the lake is provided by a little `train' or a sightseeing boat. These and most of the amenities are free to campers. Part of the resort is the Beekse Bergen Safari Park with reduced entry for campers, where you can see the many wild animals from either your own car, a safari bus or two safari boats, the Stanley and the Livingstone. On the far side of the lake, as well as bungalows and tents for hire, there are two distinct campsites - one on flat meadows surrounded by hedges and trees near the lake, the other in a more secluded wooded area reached by a tunnel under the nearby main road. The 600 numbered pitches are about 100 sq.m, and all have electrical connections. The lakeside area has a very good waterside restaurant, a cafe and takeaway, supermarket and indoor children's swimming pool, as well as the best sanitary facilities. The Safari Campsite has a `typical safari environment' and a viewpoint over the Safari Park (with free, unlimited entry for campers staying here). There is an independent central complex with catering, playground and launderette, plus an entertainment team. In general, the sanitary facilities are quite adequate in terms of numbers and cleanliness and include British WCs and free hot showers and some washbasins in private cabins. This is an area with many other recreational activities, including the award winning Effteling amusement park.

How to find it: From A58/E312 Tilburg - Eindhoven motorway, take exit to Hilvarenbeek on the N269 road. Park and campsite are signed Beekse Bergen.

General Details: Open 3 April - 7 Nov. Leisure park 24 April - 5 Sept. Restaurants, cafes and takeaway (weekends only in low seasons). Supermarket. Children's playgrounds and indoor pool. Beaches and lake swimming. Watersports including rowing boats (free) and canoe hire. Amusements. Tennis. Minigolf. Fishing. Recreation programme. Bicycle hire. Riding. Golf 5 km. Launderettes. Chemical disposal. Bungalows, cabins and equipped tents to rent. Twin axle caravans not accepted.

Charges guide: Per person (from 2 yrs) Nfl 6.80; pitch 19.00 - 31.00; electricity included; local tax 1.10 per person. Discounts for weekly stays, camping packages available. Credit cards accepted.

Reservations: Necessary for high season and B.Hs. Address: Leisurepark Hilvarenberg, Beekse Bergen 1, 5081 NJ Hilvarenbeek. Tel: 013/536 00 32. FAX: 013/536 67 16.

594 Vryetydspark Elfenmeer, Herkenbosch, nr Roermond

Large professionally managed site with swimming pools and other amenities.

In the southern part of the country between the borders with Germany and Belgium (both quite close), this is a big site with amenities on holiday camp scale. Situated in the Meinweg National Park, it is very popular for weekend breaks, even out of season, and the facilities are also offered on a daily basis. These include two very good outdoor heated swimming pools, both 25 x 15 m. one deep, one shallow, and a small children's pool (open about 7 May-7 Sept). Sunbathing areas extend down to the grassy surrounds of a lake used for boating and swimming. These are free to campers except for an initial fee for an identity pass. There are many permanent large caravans or seasonal tourers, but around half of the 800 pitches are available for touring units, with electrical connections (4A) in most areas. Many bungalows (for rent) are in a separate area. Pitches average about 90 sq. m. and are mostly in separate enclosures of 10 or so pitches, backing on to hedges, etc. Part is light woodland, part open grass. The new or refurbished toilet blocks are probably an adequate provision. They provide British style WCs, individual basins with shelf and cold water, pre-set free hot showers, babies' room and toilets for disabled people. There is an organised sports programme in season and a range of activities (listed below). Amenities include a supermarket, a restaurant/bar and takeaway facilities in season. Reception is large and efficient, with English spoken.

How to find it: From Roermond take Wassenberg road to southeast (to find this exit you can also follow white signs to Roerstreek industrial estate); pass turning to right to Herkenbosch after 6 km. and turn left to site about 1 km. further on.

General Details: Open 28 March - 25 Oct. Supermarket. Restaurant/bar (30/4-30/10). Takeaway. Swimming pool (30/4-31/8). Organised sports programme (July/Aug. and school holidays). Fishing lake. Large children's playground on grass and sand. Minigolf. Bowling alley. Bicycle hire. Riding or golf 1.5 km. Sailing and windsurfing courses arranged nearby. Launderette. Chemical disposal.

Charges 2000: Per person (from 2 yrs) Nfl 5.00 - 6.50; pitch (any unit) 19.50 - 34.00, acc. to season and facilities; local tax 1.10; dog 6.50. Package arrangements available. Credit cards accepted.

Reservations: made only Sat. to Sat. and recommended in peak weeks, perhaps from 7/7-10/8, with full payment in advance. Address: Meinweg 1, 6075 NA Herkenbosch (L). Tel: 0475/53 16 89. FAX: 0475/53 47 75.

NETHERLANDS

597 Camping De Paal, Bergeyk, nr Eindhoven

First class campsite, especially suitable for families with young children.

A lot of money has been invested in this touring site (no static mobile homes) in recent years, and the excellent facilities now provided mean that reservation in July/Aug. is essential. Situated in 34 hectares of woodland, there are 544 touring pitches (plus 70 seasonal pitches) offering a choice of sunshine or shade (the site map shows the choice for each pitch). All have 6A electricity, water, waste water and a bin (daily collection) and range in size up to 150 sq.m. on flat grass. Numbered and generally separated by trees in shaded areas, there is also a choice of area for parking, either on the pitch or in special car parks, affording extra safety for the children whose importance here is paramount. Each group of pitches is provided with a play area for children (31 in all) with additional facilities comprising a very large open sand-based area with adventure play equipment (with safety inspection certificate) and a large 'barn' for wet weather (also on sand) . In high season an animation team of 10 provide further entertainment. The high quality indoor heated swimming pool is open all season and consists of play pools for babies, children and a smaller, deeper one for parents, supervised in high season. The heated outdoor and toddlers pools are also shallow. Two ultra modern sanitary buildings, specifically designed with families in mind, have magnificent facilities. Toilets are separate at either side of the buildings. There are dishwashing and laundry sinks plus a spin dryer just inside the main entrance, then wash-cabins and showers with family rooms (bath, shower, washbasin), baby bathrooms, and standard showers, all with lots of space, plus 2 children's toilets. Rooms for wheelchair users are at the back. Two other older buildings are also very well fitted out. A well equipped modern laundry is just past the quite large shop (open all season, varying hours). Maps can be purchased in reception showing some of the many walking and cycling opportunities in this attractive area, whilst a short walk from the camp entrance brings you to a tennis complex with 6 indoor courts (Sept-May) with 10 outdoor all weather courts (all equipment available for hire) and a pleasant lounge bar in which to relax. Whilst catering splendidly for children, outside the high season there are many regular adult visitors to this comfortable, friendly site, very capably run by the Martens family and staff.

How to find it: From E34 Antwerpen - Eindhoven road, take exit 32 (Eersel) and follow signs for Bergeyk and site (2 km from town).

General Details: Open Easter/1 April - 31 Oct. Shop, bar and snacks (all season). Restaurant (high season). Indoor pool (all season). Outdoor pool (May - Sept). Bicycle hire. Tennis. Children's play areas. Theatre. Bicycle storage room. Laundrette. Chemical disposal. Motorcaravan services. Trekkers' huts for rent.

Charges guide: Per pitch incl. 2 persons and services Nfl 51.00; extra person (over 1 yr) 6.00; cyclist 13.50; dog 6.00. Discounts outside 5/7-16/8 daily 30%, over 7 days 35%, (over 55's 40% for more than 7 days).

Reservations: Essential for July/Aug. and made for min. 1 week Sat to Sat. Address: De Paaldreef 14, 5571 TN Bergeyk. Tel: 0497/571977. FAX: 0497/577164.

593 Camping De Dousberg, Maastricht

Spacious site in leisure park on outskirts of historic city.

Founded by the Romans, Maastricht is the Netherlands' oldest and most southern city. Situated in South Limburg, the Belgian and German borders are very close. Dousberg Parc, 4 km. from the city centre, incorporates a wide range of sporting facilities including very large outdoor and indoor swimming pools, partly 'subtropical' (free for campers), a tennis centre with indoor and outdoor courts, cycling training track, climbing wall and artificial ski slope. Camping de Dousberg, situated 300 m. up a gentle hill from the park entrance, forms part of this centre. It has 300 pitches, most with electricity (10A) and TV connections and easy access to water, arranged in hedged bays which radiate outward from the centre. Three similar toilet blocks, situated around the site, offer functional facilities of an acceptable standard. Hot water is on payment for the showers but free for dishwashing. British style WCs. There is a small shop at the centre and a cafe/bar at the entrance. It is a very busy site, with visitors of many nationalities, some of them groups of youngsters, but it is well situated for visiting a lively, interesting city.

How to find it: From north on Eindhoven - Liège motorway (A2/E25) take Maastricht/Hasselt exit and follow signs for Hasselt and then municipal signs for Dousberg. From the Liège direction follow signs for 'Centrum' and then Dousberg.

General Details: Open 26 March - 1 Nov. Small shop (5/4-15/9). Bar/restaurant (5/4-15/9). Tennis centre. Large outdoor and indoor pools (1/3-1/11). Climbing wall. Artificial ski slope, Cycling track. Children's play areas. Laundry facilities.

Charges 1999: Per person Nfl. 8.00; child (under 12 yrs) 5.75; tent or caravan 8.50; motorcaravan 12.00; car 4.00; m/cycle 3.00; electricity 4.50; local tax 1.50.

Reservations: Essential for peak season; contact site for details. Address: Dousbergweg 102, 6216 GC Maastricht. Tel: 043/343.21.71. FAX: 043/343.05.56.

This voucher entitles the holder to the relevant discount or special offer at those campsites featured in this Guide, which have a small Alan Rogers logo beneath their Site Report. This voucher should be retained by the holder for use at other campsites, but must be made available for inspection by the campsite for the purpose of verifying your entitlement to the relevant discount or special offer.

VOUCHER NUMBER
12196
E00/

Save Money!

This voucher entitles the holder to a discount of 10% on Travel & Breakdown Insurance arrangements made via this Guide, as advertised between pages 160 and 161 . To arrange cover please complete the proposal and send this, together with the appropriate premium and this voucher to: Deneway Guides & Travel Ltd., Chesil Lodge, West Bexington, Dorchester, DT2 9DG - Tel 01308-897809, Fax 01308 898017. The proposal form and the discount voucher will need to be completed and sent to Deneway Guides & Travel along with payment for the relevant premium in all circumstances **except in very urgent cases (ie those within seven days of departure) when we can arrange cover via telephone or (preferably) fax** .

VOUCHER NUMBER
12196
E00/

Save Money!

ALAN ROGERS GOOD CAMPS GUIDE (EUROPE) 2000 DISCOUNT VOUCHER

Valid 1st January 2000 - 31st December 2000

NAME:

ADDRESS:

SIGNATURE:

Save Money

ALAN ROGERS GOOD CAMPS GUIDE (EUROPE) 2000 DISCOUNT VOUCHER

Valid 1st January 2000 - 31st December 2000

NAME:

ADDRESS:

SIGNATURE:

Save Money

NORWAY

Norway has the lowest population density in Europe, which is not surprising when one realises that about one quarter of its land is above the Arctic Circle. It is a land of contrasts, from magnificent snow capped mountains, dramatic fjords, vast plateaux with wild untamed tracts, huge lakes and rich green countryside. Oslo is the oldest of the Scandinavian capitals and one of the most prettily sited, whilst Bergen is the fjord capital, Trondheim is an atmospheric city with its medieval heart intact, and Tromsø, with its stunning `Arctic Cathedral', likes to think of itself as the capital of the North. You can see the Northern Lights (Aurora Borealis) between November and February, north of the Arctic Circle, which lies between Mo i Rana and Bodø. During certain freak weather conditions it may be seen further south. The Midnight Sun is visible north of the Arctic Circle in summer - at Bodø between early June and early July, at Tromsø from late May to mid July, and at Nordkapp from mid May until late July. However you can never guarantee these experiences - it depends on meteorological conditions. Midsummer night's eve is celebrated all over the country, with thousands of bonfires along the fjords. Conservation of the environment was a practical reality in Norway long before it became a fashionable International issue. This, and the more recent improvements in the infrastructure, with many new tunnels and upgraded roads replacing some of the older more tortuous sections, explains why tourism is increasing rapidly. With main roads throughout the country now perfectly adequate for average sized caravan and motorcaravans, the most popular regions and routes do become busy during the short summer season (June - Aug). Further information from:

Norwegian Tourist Board, Charles House, 5-11 Lower Regent Street SW1Y 4LR
Tel: 020 7839 6255 Fax: 020 7839 6014 E-mail: london@nortra.no

Population
4,300,000 (1997); density 13 per sq. km.

Capital
Oslo.

Climate
The Gulf Stream follows the coast and weather is less extreme on the west coast. Generally weather in summer and winter is unpredictable (it can be very wet). Average temperatures 18.2° in Oslo, 14.5° in Bergen, 12.7° in Tromso in July. In Jan. - 3.7° in Oslo, 1.5° in Bergen, and -4.7° in Tromso. Daylight hours in Oslo are 6 hrs 3 mins in Jan. and 18 hrs 41 mins in July whilst Tromso in Jan. has no daylight and in July, 24 hours

Language
Norwegian, but English is widely spoken, particularly by the young.

Currency
The Norwegian krone, divided into 100 ore. Denominations are 10, 50, 100, 500, and 1000 kr.

Banks
Open Mon-Fri 09.00-15.00. Every largish village and town in Norway has a bank, although rural branches may have restricted opening hours.

Post Offices
Opening hours vary but are generally 08.00/08.30-16.00/ 17.00 Mon-Fri, 08.00-13.00 on Saturdays.

Time
GMT plus 1 (BST plus 1 in summer).

Telephone
To phone from the UK, the code is 0047 plus the number. From Norway to the UK, the code is 095 44, plus the number (omitting the initial 0).

Shops
Normal hours: Mon-Fri 09.00-16.00/17.00, Thu 09.00-18.00/20.00 and Sat 09.00-13.00 /15.00. There are 2,600 tax-free shops in Norway. If you buy goods for more than 308 kr make sure you get a tax refund. After deduction of a handling charge you'll get 11-18% of the buying price back in cash, at ports or major border crossings.

Food:
more expensive than in the UK, except for very good vegetables, fruit and some fish. Smoked and fresh salmon are excellent and reindeer steak very tender. A small beer in a cafe can cost £3.

Camping Gaz:
Not readily available, though some larger sites stock 904 and 907 refills. You can buy camping gaz from Statoil and AGA Progas, which have outlets throughout Norway.

Motoring
Roads are generally uncrowded around Oslo and Bergen but be prepared for tunnels and hairpin bends. Certain roads are forbidden to caravans or best avoided (advisory leaflet from the Norwegian Tourist Office). Vehicles must have sufficient road grip and in the winter it may be necessary to use winter tyres with or without studs or chains. Towed caravans up to 2.3 m. wide are permitted; if between 2.3 and 2.5 m. (max permitted width) the car towing it must be at least as wide as the caravan. Drink driving laws are extremely strict.

Tolls: Vehicles entering Bergen on weekdays must pay a toll. Vehicles up to 3.5 tonnes entering Oslo pay a toll, also to enter Kristiansand (ferry terminal). Tolls are also levied on certain roads.

Speed Limits: Caravans and motorhomes (3.5 tons) 31 mph (50 kph) in built up areas, caravans 50 mph (80 kph) on all other roads, motorhomes 50 mph (80 kph) on other roads and 56 mph (90 kph) on motorways.

Fuel: Mon-Fri petrol stations are closed between 19.00 and 05.00. At weekends stations are closed other than in closely populated areas. Major credit cards accepted in larger petrol stations.

Parking: Parking regulations in towns are very strict and subject to fines. Yellow parking meters give 1 hour, Grey -2 and Brown - 3 hours.

Overnighting
You can camp in open areas provided you are at least 150 m away from houses or cabins. Caravans may not park on laybys or picnic sites. Open fires forbidden 15 April - 15 September.

NORWAY

Camping in Norway

There are more than 1,000 campsites in Norway and you have the option to take your own tent, caravan or motorcaravan, or to use cabin (Hytte) accommodation. Camping costs for a unit incl. two persons with electricity is Nkr. 80-160 per night, whilst a cabin will cost Nkr. 200-650 per night depending on size and level of facilities. The Norwegian Public Roads Administration (Statens Vegvesen), in conjunction with local authorities, has started creating roadside campsites with basic facilities (Bobil parks). These are primarily designed for motorcaravans to overnight, some are free, others operate an honesty box system. With an ever increasing number of 'wild-campers', and these new facilities, it is not surprising that in certain areas commercial campsites are reluctant to spend money on expensive refurbishment, opting instead to increase their cabin accommodation to supplement reducing income.

So few British were going to Norway in the early 'nineties that it was an act of faith on our part to extend our guide north of Denmark. We must admit to have been heavily influenced by the arrival on the scene of Color Line who adopted a positive approach to the British camping market. More recently, the Scandinavian Seaways service to Göteborg in Sweden, has become equally popular as a entry route to Norway, for those who live closer to Harwich. In our first year entries were heavily concentrated around Bergen, this being the area traditionally favoured by British visitors, but since then we have steadily expanded our coverage. To enable the more adventurous to reach the Arctic Circle and Nordkapp, we have expanded north with a small selection of sites including the most northerly campsite in the world. The main E6 'Arctic Highway' is a good tarmac surfaced road, running some 2,000 km. from Oslo until it joins the E69 north of Alta, which then takes you the final 100 km. on to Nordkapp itself.

We continue to give low priority to the coast to the south of Stavanger/Oslo or to the valleys to the east of Oslo/Trondheim, although these are deservedly popular among Norwegian campers, they are of least interest to British campers. Norway is primarily touring country, very few campers spend more than two nights in any one camp, preferring to move on in search of wonderful scenery just around the corner. To fit in with this we have arranged our sites in a loose circuit starting at Stavanger and Haugesund, moving north via Bergen through fjordland to Trondheim. From here one can either travel north to the Arctic Circle or Nordkapp (returning through Norway or via our sites in Sweden), or turn south and continue the circuit via the eastern valleys and Oslo. Such is the attraction of the dramatic rural scenery that few campers will wish to linger long in Norway's urban gateways; we have accordingly resorted to the unusual practice of describing briefly the camping situation in each of the main gateways rather than restricting our information to one or more key sites.

There are several negatives which deserve mention. Norway can be very expensive. With few exceptions most things cost double what they cost in Britain (dependant on the exchange rate). Although it is not good normal practice, campers should buy as much food and drink as possible before leaving Britain. Norway's west coast and central mountains and fells can also be very wet; only the well equipped should consider relying entirely on tented accommodation. **Note:** Mosquitoes can be a problem in summer (from June) - go prepared.

Camping at the Gateways

Traditionally, British campers view Bergen as the usual gateway to Norway. If the visitor expects to tour only in the fjord country to the north and immediately inland then it makes sense to return to Bergen. However, looking further afield, beyond the three main fjords, there is much to be said for considering the two other west coast gateways of Stavanger and Haugesund, both well served by Fjord Line from Newcastle. Along the south coast there are several gateways served by cross-Baltic ferries from Denmark and Germany. For the long distance driver prepared to drive via Sweden, Oslo will be the obvious entry point. The following notes provide a quick guide to camping at the four main gateways.

Bergen

Unless there is little choice, we do not recommend camping in built-up Bergen. There are four sites within 10 km. of the focal old harbour:

Camping Sandviken - a congested overnight camping site for motorcaravans in the industrial harbour within walking distance of the Fjord Line quay.

Bergenshallen Camping - a small tract set aside for camping in a suburban shopping complex at Landas, 5 km. south of the town centre.

Paradis Caravan Camping - a van parking site at a suburban sports complex 7 km. south of the centre.

Midttun Motel - adjacent to a small motel in Nesttun, 9 km. south of the town centre, near the airport.

Further out of town, going inland on the main 580 highway which leads to Hardangerfjord from Nesttun, are three more attractive sites which until now we have been hesitant to recommend but which have been steadily upgraded to the point where they deserve consideration.

The first to be reached is **Grimen Camping**, a very small site just off the 580 on the shore of an attractive lake. At weekends and during the school holidays it is usually fully occupied by knowing Norwegians visiting Bergen. The owner runs a nice general store next door. He also offers a good choice of small lakeside huts at prices which are unusually low by Norwegian standards. Only a few hundred metres further on the opposite side of the 580 is another lakeside site, **Bratland Camping**, which is larger but which also tends to be fully occupied at popular times. A few miles further down the 580 is an even larger lakeside site, **Lone Camping**, which has been very sensibly developed in recent years to the point where it deserves recommendation, despite its distance (nearly 20 km) from central Bergen.

Fredrikstad

For those arriving in Norway via Gothenburg, Fredikstad is not only the obvious gateway but it is one of Norway's most interesting cities and certainly deserves at least a day or two. It has a delightful waterfront, bubbling with cheerful nautical activity. Its historic old town, across the river from the newer town, is one of the best preserved in Europe and is also bustling with life. There are many other attractions, including a choice of two good camps sites. Within walking distance of the old town, from where the new town can be reached by frequent foot ferry, is a small greenfield municipal site, **Fredrikstad Motel and Camping.** Further south, along route 107, at Torsnes is a very different proposition, **Bevo Camping**, which occupies woodland on the fjord shore, commanding a wonderful view of this very attractive stretch of coast. Although Bevo attracts many statics, there is usually space for tourers - the friendly manager likes to guide visitors to a suitable site on his bike!

Haugesund

Now served by Color Line, Haugesund is well worth considering as a departure port. It is a well preserved small town, with traditional wood buildings predominant, and a lively marine atmosphere and it has a better choice of campsites than any other major Norwegian town. About ten miles east of the town centre, just off the main route 11 leading to Oslo, there is the very large, very well equipped and imaginatively designed **Grindafjord Naturcamping** (named after its entertaining animal life!). Along the coast of the unspoilt southern half of neighbouring Karmoy island (reached by bridge) there are several rather basic but spectacularly sited waterfront sites (Karmoy deserves a visit to wander around the picturesque old fishing port of Skenshaven) but our favourite is the municipal site on the northern outskirts of the town, but only a mile from the town centre! Named **Haraldshaugen** after the neighbouring monumental obelisk - a national shrine honouring the Viking hero Harald the Fairhaired - this site is formed by a boulder strewn meadow on the shore of Haugesundfjord. It has an excellent sanitary block and a small shop.Unlike Grindafjord where statics predominate, no statics are permitted at Haraldshaugen. Another plus is the friendly atmosphere; the site is managed by the local Red Cross, run by volunteers, and all profits go into charitable medical services in the community.

    Grindafjord Naturcamping: 5570 Aksdal. Tel: 47 52 77 57 40.

    Haraldshaugen Camping: Post boks 1309, Gard, 5501 Haugesund. Tel: 52 72 80 77.

Oslo

In general, the sites in Oslo (like most major city sites) are large and very crowded. If you do need to stay in Oslo, the following sites are available, although we have received poor reports:

    Ekeberg Camping is on a hilltop with panoramic views across the city. Very busy in high season, the undulating grassy areas are unmarked. Only open 1 June - 31 Aug, it accepts about 700 units (including groups). When full the sanitary facilities are fully stretched. Site is well signed (Ekeberg) from E18 running southeast to Sweden in a suburb. Address: Ekebergvein 65, 1181 Oslo 11.

    Bogstad Camp and Turistsenter: Open all year. Follow signs from the E18 through suburbs. Also signed from 120 ring-road. Address: Ankervn 117, 0757 Oslo 7.

    Stubljan Camping: Open all year, On Oslo's southern boundary.

Stavanger

Although most British tourists head for Bergen, Stavanger is also well worth considering as a gateway. Despite its reputation as an `oil town', Stavanger is very attractive and compact and in no sense inferior to Bergen. It is well served by Fjord Line - indeed their late night departure schedules in effect offer the motorist an extra half day in Norway compared with Bergen. It is a most convenient gateway for exploring south Norway and, unlike Bergen, has a site which we can highly recommend. **Mosvangen Camping** (Henrik Ibsens grt 21, 4021 Stavanger) is only 2 km. from the centre and only just off the E18 road as it enters the town from the south. It is on the shore of the lake from which it takes its name. Gently undulating, well shaded and divided by trees, it has 200 pitches and is very well equipped.

Kristiansand

DFDS Ferries call here en-route to Gothenburg, making an alternative route by which to arrive in Norway.

NORWAY

2315 Ringoy Camping, Ringoy

Simple site by Upper Hardangerfjord.

Although the village of Ringoy is quiet and peaceful, it occupies a pivotal position, lying not only midway between two principal ferry ports of Upper Hardangerfjord (Kinsarvik and Brimnes), but also by the junction of two key roads (routes 7 and 13). There are several sites at the popular nearby resort town of Kinsarvik, but none compares for situation or atmosphere with the small, simple Ringoy site. This site is basically a steeply sloping field running down from the road to the tree-lined fjord, with flat areas for camping along the top and the bottom of the field. The toilet block is small and simple (with metered showers and British style WCs), but well designed, constructed and maintained by the Raunsgard family who are particularly proud of the site's remarkable shore-side barbecue facilities. On arrival you find a place as there is no reception - someone will call between 8 and 9 pm.

How to find it: Site is on route 13, midway between Kinsarvik and Brimnes.

General Details: Open all year. Simple facilities, possibly inadequate during peak holiday weeks in July. No shop but village mini-market and garage within a minute's walk. Rowing boat available (free).

Charges guide: Per unit Nkr. 80; electricity (10A) 15.

Reservations: Write to site. Address: 5782 Ringoy. Tel: 53.66.39.17.

2325 Sundal Camping, Mauranger

Excellent gateway site for fjordland, from either Stavanger or Bergen.

Maurangerfjord is a steep-sided arm leading off the eastern shore of the middle reaches of the Hardangerfjord. The village of Mauranger commands magnificent views across the waters. Cutting through the village is a turbulent stream, popular with those in search of trout. Its waters are ice-cold, for they descend from the nearby Folgafonn ice-cap and its renowned glacier, an hour's brisk walk from the village. Sundal Camping is divided into two sections: a wooded, waterfront site between the local road and the fjord, which combines camping with a small marina; and an open meadow site uphill of the local road. Both are served by separate well equipped toilet blocks. Sundal is not only ideally situated for Folgafonn; it is also the nearest good site to the charming small town of Rosendal, famous for the stately home of the celebrated Rosenkrantz family.

How to find it: Route 48 crosses Hardangerfjord by ferry from Gjermundshavn to Lofallstrand from where a clearly marked local road runs northeast for 16 km. along the fjord waterfront to Mauranger.

General Details: Well equipped with most facilities. Stream and lake fishing. Canoe and rowing boat hire. Small shop. Pleasant small hotel adjacent with attractive restaurant and bar.

Charges: not available.

Reservations: Contact site. address: P.O. Box 5476, Mauranger, (Hordaland). Tel: 53.48.41.86.

2320 Odda Camping, Odda

Neat, lakeside municipal site, just within walking distance of Buar glacier and the Vidfoss Falls.

Bordered by the Folgefonna glacier to the west and the Hardangervidda plateau to the east and south, Odda is an industrial town with electro-chemical enterprises based on zinc mining and hydro-electric power. At the turn of the century Odda was one of the most popular destinations for the European upper classes - the magnificent and dramatic scenery is still there, together with the added interest of the industrial impact which is well recorded at the industrial museum at Tyssedal. This municipal site has been attractively developed on the town's southern outskirts, just over a kilometre from the centre on the shores of the Sandvin lake (good salmon and trout fishing) and on the minor road leading up the Buar Valley to the Buar glacier and Folgefonna ice-cap. It is possible to walk to the ice face but in the later stages this is quite hard-going! The site is spread over 2½ acres of flat, mature woodland, which is divided into small clearings by massive boulders deposited long ago by the departing glacier. Access is by well tended tarmac roads which wind their way among the trees and boulders. There are 50 tourist pitches including many with electrical connections. A single timber building at the entrance houses the reception office (often unattended) and the simple, but clean sanitary facilities which provide, for each sex, 2 WCs, one hot shower (on payment) and 3 open washbasins. There is also a small kitchen with dishwashing facilities and a washing machine and dryer in the ladies washroom. The site fills up in the evenings and can be crowded with facilities stretched from the end of June to early August.

How to find it: Site is on the southern outskirts of Odda, signed off road to Buar, with a well marked access.

General Details: Open 1 June - 31 Aug. Town facilities close. Washing machine and dryer. Kitchen.

Charges guide: Per tent and car Nkr. 75; caravan and car 90; m/cycle 65; electricity 20.

Reservations: write to site. Address: Borsta, 5750 Odda (Hordaland). Tel: 53.64.34.10.

2330 Eikhamrane Camping, Nå, Sorfjord

Small, neat site among orchards on western shore of Sorfjord.

Sorfjord, well known for its fruit growing, has long been on a popular route for travellers across Norway via Utne (where Norway's oldest hotel is a tourist attraction in its own right) and a short ferry crossing across Hardangerfjord. Travellers are also attracted by the Folgefonn ice cap, the most accessible of the great glaciers, which lies at the head of Sorfjord. About halfway along the western shore of Sorfjord is Eikhamrane Camping. Arranged on a well landscaped and partly terraced field which slopes alongside the road to a pebbly lakeside beach, it was formerly part of an orchard which still extends on both sides of the site and uphill across the road. There is room for 50 units (about 20 caravans or motorcaravans and 30 tents) on unmarked, well kept grass with 20 electrical hook ups. There are attractive trees and good gravel roads, with areas of gravel hardstanding for poor weather. Many pitches overlook the fjord where there are also thoughtfully positioned picnic benches. There are two small timber sanitary blocks, one for toilets with external access, the other for washbasins (open) and showers (on payment). Both are simple but very well kept. There is a small kitchen with dishwashing facilities (hot water on payment) and 2 laundry sinks outside, under cover. The office (where you can order bread and where home-grown fruits are readily available) is in the old farmhouse, home of the owners, the Mage family. The site is well situated for watersports (sailing, canoeing and rowing), fishing and the nearby Digranes nature reserve (birdwatching).

How to find it: Site is on road no. 550 just outside the village of Nå, on the western shore of Sorfjord, 32 km. south of Utne and 16 km. north of Odda.

General Details: Open 1 June - 31 August only. Some supplies kept at reception office - bread and milk to order. Watersports and fishing in lake. 5 cabins to let (Nkr. 180 - 250).

Charges guide: Per person Nkr. 10; child (4-12 yrs) 5; pitch 50; extra tent 30; awning 20; electricity 10.

Reservations: write to site. Address: 5776 Nå (Hordaland). Tel: 53.66.22.48.

2370 Botnen Camping, Brekke

Good first stop for those going north from Bergen.

For those setting forth north on route 1 from Bergen there are suprisingly few attractive sites until one reaches the southern shore of mighty Sognefjord. At Brekke is a well known tourist landmark, the remarkable Breekstranda Fjord Hotel, a traditional turf-roofed complex which tourist coaches are unable to resist. A mile or two beyond the hotel, also on the shore of the fjord, is the family run Botnen Camping. An isolated, simple site which slopes steeply, it is well maintained. It has its own jetty and harbour, with rowing boats and canoes for hire, and commands a splendid view across the fjord to distant mountains.

How to find it: Site is 2 km off the coast road running west from Brekke.

General Details: Open 1 May - 1 Sept. Children's play area. Swimming, fishing and boating in fjord. Boats and canoes for hire.

Charges guide: Per person Nkr. 10; child 5; caravan 40; tent 30; electricity 15.

Reservations: Contact site. Address: 5950 Brekke. Tel: 57.78.54.71.

2340 Mo Camping, Norheimsund

Simple, well kept family site in scenic location with friendly welcome.

The main road leading inland from Bergen (route 7) is pleasant but perhaps unexciting until it reaches Norheimsund where is joins Hardangerfjord, one of the `Big Three' of Norway's spectacular fjords. Mo Camping is an attractive site on what appears to be a small lake but is actually an arm of the main fjord. At the head of this arm (within walking distance of the site, but along the side of the road) are the spectacular Steinsdals Falls which draw half a million visitors annually to view the falls from behind! This little site is part of a small working farm run by the Mo family. It has 35 unmarked touring places, with 25 electrical connections possible, on a curve of flat, well kept grass. There are also two small areas of hardstanding for poor weather. The camping area is divided from the working part of the farm by a line of charming, traditional, wooden farm buildings which include the family home, the office and the heated sanitary facilities (in a converted barn). Rather cramped, these include for each sex a shower (on payment) and two WCs with washbasins opposite. They are hard-pressed when the site is full. A laundry, plus dishwashing and drying facilities are to be added. There is a general shop at a nearby filling station (200 m). Although offering only basic facilities, this site is well looked after and is ideally situated with many good walks in the area, free fishing from the site and a two-seater canoe for hire.

How to find it: Site is by the no. 7 road just over 1 km. west of Norheimsund.

General Details: Open 1 June - 31 August only - minimal facilities, but town 1 km. and shop 200 m. Fishing. Bicycle hire 5 km. Riding 7 km. Gas supplies. Chemical disposal. Motorcaravan services.

Charges 2000: Per person Nkr. 5; child (under 12 yrs) 3; caravan, motorcaravan or tent with car 70; tent without car 40; local tax 40; electricity (16A) 20. No credit cards.

Reservations: Write to site. Address: 5601 Norheimsund, Hardaland. Tel: 56.55.17.27.

NORWAY

2350 Espelandsdalen Camping, nr Ulvik

Basic, farm campsite, but 'a glimpse of untamed Norway'.

If one follows Hardangerfjord on the map and considers the mighty glacier which once scooped away the land along its path, it is easy to imagine that it started life in Espelandsdalen. Here is the textbook upper glacial valley. Espelandsdalen runs from Granvin to Ulvik, both of which lie at the heads of their respective arms of Hardangerfjord. A minor road (route 572) links the two small towns with sharp climbs at either end (tricky for caravans). The valley bed here is occupied by a series of connected lakes, popular with canoeists. For generations farmers have struggled to make a living out of the narrow strip of land between water and rock. One of these farmers has converted a narrow, sloping field bisected by the road (572) into a modest lake-side site taking about 40 units. The section above the road has a small office, a sanitary block (washing trough with hot water, a shower on payment and WCs) and a neat row of chalets for hire. Looking down on these is the family farmstead. The grassy meadow pitches below the road run right down to the lake-shore. There are a few electrical hook ups (8-10A). Campers come here for the fishing, walking or skiing, or just to marvel at the views of the valley and its towering mountain sides.

How to find it: The northern loop of the 572 road follows Espelandsdalen and the campsite is on this road, about 6 km. from its junction with route 13 at Granvin (steep gradients - see above).

General Details: Open 1 May - 31 August. Some basic foodstuffs kept in office. Swimming, fishing and boating in lake. Boat hire. Ski track 2 km. Ten cabins to let (Nkr. 25 per night).

Charges 2000: Per unit Nkr. 60; person 10; child (4-12 yrs) 5; electricity 20. No credit cards.

Reservations: Contact site. Address: 5736 Granvin (Hordaland). Tel: 56.52.51.67. E-mail: kalsaas@online.no.

2360 Ulvik Fjord Camping, Ulvik

Small, quiet, orchard site on outskirts of Ulvik, on the fjord.

Ulvik was discovered by tourists 150 years ago when the first liners started operating to the head of Hardangerfjord, and to this day, a regular stream of cruise liners work their way into the very heartland of Norway. A century and a half of visitors has meant that Ulvik is now a well-established tourist destination, describing itself as `the pearl of Hardanger' - it even has its own conference centre - but, with only just over 1000 inhabitants, it still manages to retain an unspoilt village atmosphere. Access is by narrow, winding roads, either along the side of the fjord or up a steep road behind the town - probably not to be recommended for caravans (see How to find it). This pretty little site is 500 m. from the centre of the town. It occupies what must once have been a small orchard running down to the lake beside a small stream. There is room for about 30 units on undulating ground which slopes towards the fjord, with some flat areas and a few electrical connections. There are no facilities other than a small wooden building which houses reception, a small kitchen (with cooker and dishwashing sink) and the sanitary facilities. These are well kept and comprise, for each sex, 2 open washbasins, WCs and 2 modern showers on payment.

How to find it: Ulvik is reached by road no. 572; site is on southern side of town, opposite Ulvikfjord Pension. There is a ferry from road 7 at Brimnes. Note: Caravans can now connect with road 7 via a new tunnel.

General Details: Open 20 May - 31 Aug. Kitchen. Boat slipway, fishing and swimming in fjord. Hotel opposite, shops and restaurants in town. 10 cabins for hire.

Charges guide: Per unit Nkr. 65; hiker's or cyclist's tent 35; person 15; child (4-12 yrs) 10; electricity 20.

Reservations: write to site. Address: 5730 Ulvik. Tel: 56.52.65.77.

2380 Tveit Camping, Vik/Vangsnes

Charming, neat, family run site, ideally placed for exploring the Balestrand area.

Located in the district of Vik on the south shore of Sognefjord, 4 km. from the small port of Vangsnes, Tveit Camping is part of a small working farm. Reception and a kiosk open most of the day in high season, with a phone to summon assistance at any time. Four terraces provide 40 pitches with 30 electricity connections (10A). Modern, heated sanitary facilities provide British style WCs, washbasins (one per sex in cubicle), controllable hot showers with divider and seat (on payment), a unit for disabled visitors, kitchens with facilities for dishwashing and cooking, and a laundry with washing machine, dryer and iron (hot water on payment). Other on-site facilities include TV rooms, a fenced playground and a slipway. A shop, café, pub and post office are by the ferry terminal in Vangsnes 4 km. away. On the campsite you will find a restored Iron Age burial mound dating from 350-550AD, whilst the statue of Fritjov The 'Intrepid' towers over the landscape at Vangsnes. Visit the Kristianhus Boat and Engine Museum or see traditional Gamalost cheese making in Vik, and in Fjærland across the fjord is the Norwegian Glacier Museum.

How to find it: Site is by Rv 13 between Vik and Vangsnes, 4 km. south of Vangsnes.

General Details: Open 15 April - 15 Oct. Kiosk (15/6-15/8). TV rooms. Children's playground. Slipway and boat hire. Fishing. Laundry. Kitchen. Chemical disposal. Motorcaravan services. Cabins for rent.

Charges 2000: Per caravan Nkr. 70; motorcaravan or tent 60; person (over 5) 10; electricity 20. No credit cards.

Reservations: Write to site. Address: 6894 Vangsnes, Sogn og Fjordane. Tel: 57.69.66.00. FAX: 57.69.66.70.

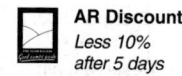
AR Discount
Less 10%
after 5 days

2385 Sandvik Camping, Gaupne

Compact, popular, small site on edge of town and close to the Nigardsbreen Glacier.
This small site has 60 touring pitches, 32 with electrical connections (8/16A), arranged on fairly level grassy terrain either side of a gravel access road, on the edge of this small town. A large supermarket, post office, banks, etc. are all within a level 500 m. stroll. The single central sanitary unit provides British style WCs, washbasins with dividers, and two hot showers per sex (on payment). In addition there is a multi-purpose unit serving the needs of families or the disabled with facilities for baby changing and a further WC, basin and shower with ramp for access. A small campers' kitchen provides dishwashing facilities, hot-plates, oven and fridge (all free of charge) together with tables, chairs and TV. The separate laundry has sinks with free hot water and a washing machine and dryer. The owner tells us that these facilities are scheduled for refurbishment, so campers can look forward to even better standards. A café in the reception building is open in summer for drinks and meals and the small shop sells ices, soft drinks, sweets, crisps, etc. This is a useful site for those using the spectacular Rv 55 high mountain road from Lom to Sogndal or for visiting the Nigardsbreen Glacier and Jostedalsbreen area of Norway.

How to find it: Signed just off Rv 55 Lom-Sogndal road on eastern outskirts of Gaupne.

General Details: Open all year. Shop and cafeteria (1/6-31/8). Kitchen. Laundry. TV. Children's playground. Chemical disposal. Cabins for rent.

Charges 1999: Per pitch Nkr. 50; tent, caravan or motorcaravan 30; adult 20; child (4-14 yrs) 10; electricity 20. Credit cards accepted.

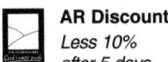 **AR Discount**
*Less 10%
after 5 days*

Reservations: Contact site. Address: 6868 Gaupne. Tel: 57.68.11.53. FAX: 57.68.16.71.

2390 Kjornes Camping, Sogndal

Simple farm site in a prime fjordside location, ideal for those on a budget.
Occupying a long open meadow which slopes down to the tree lined waterside this site is ideal for those who prefer the simple life, just enjoying the peace and quiet, the lovely scenery or a spot of fishing. Access is via a narrow lane with passing places, which drops down towards the fjord 3 km. from Sogndal. The site takes 100 touring units, but there are only 36 electrical connections (16A). There are also 8 cabins for rent but no static caravans. The sanitary unit is basic but clean, providing British style WCs, mostly open washbasins, and 2 hot showers per sex (on payment). A small kitchen has a dishwashing sink with free hot water, plus a double hot-plate and fridge (also free). The laundry is 'al fresco' with a small roof covering the sink, washing machine and dryer. A chemical disposal point completes the facilities. A scenic route (Rv 55) runs along the entire north shore of Sognefjord and the Sogndalfjord to Sogndal and then continues across the Jotunheimen mountain plateau towards Lom.

How to find it: Site is off the Rv 5, 3 km. east of Sogndal, 8 km. west of Kaupanger.

General Details: Open 1 June - end Aug. Kitchen. Laundry. Cabins for rent.

Charges guide: Per unit Nkr. 45; adult 15; child 5; small tent 30; electricity 20.

Reservations: Write to site. Address: 5800 Sogndal, Sogn og Fjordane. Tel: 57.67.45.80.

2400 Camping Jolstraholmen, Vassenden

Well presented, family run site on the E39 between Sognefjord and Nordfjord.
This attractive site is located between the road and the fast-flowing Jolstra River (renowned for its trout fishing), 1.5 km. from the lakeside village of Vassenden, and behind the Statoil filling station, restaurant and supermarket complex which is also owned and run by the site owner and his family. The 60 pitches (some marked) are on grass or gravel hardstanding all with electricity (10A) and some have water and waste points. A river tributary runs through the site and forms an island on which some additional tent pitches are located, and there are also 19 cabins. The main heated sanitary facilities, in rooms below the complex, provide British style WCs, open washbasins, controllable hot showers with divider and seat (on payment), plus one family bathroom per sex. These are supplemented by a small unit located on the island. Two small kitchens provide dishwashing and cooking facilities (free of charge) and the laundry has sinks, washing machine and dryer. Other amenities include a children's playground, 50 m. waterchute (open summer, weather permitting), minigolf, covered barbecue area, and boat hire. Ski-slopes are within 1 km., guided walking tours are organised, and a recently created riverside and woodland walk follows a 1.5 km. circular route from the site and has fishing platforms and picnic tables along the way.

How to find it: Site is beside the E39 road, 1.5 km. west of Vassenden, 18 km. east of Førde.

General Details: Open all year. Supermarket. Restaurant. Garage. Laundry. Kitchens. Barbecue area. Children's playground. Minigolf. Waterchute. Rafting. Fishing. Guided walks. Boat hire. Cabins for rent.

Charges guide: Per unit Nkr. 30 - 40; small tent 20 - 30; adult 15 - 20; child (5-15 yrs) 5 - 10; electricity 30. Credit cards accepted.

Reservations: Write to site. Address: 6840 Vassenden, Sogn og Fjordane. Tel: 57.72.71.35. FAX: 57.72.75.05.

NORWAY

2436 Byrkjelo Camping, Byrkjelo, nr Sandane

Pretty, good value site, in village location, ideal base for Nordfjord and Jostedalsbreen.

This neatly laid out and well equipped small site offers 50 large marked and numbered touring pitches, 40 with electrical connections (10A) and 15 with gravel hardstandings. At the time of inspection the owners were just completing their excellent new drive-over motorhome service point. The neatly mown grass, attractive trees and shrubs and the warm welcome from the young and enthusiastic owners make this a very pleasant place to stay. The good heated sanitary unit provides British style WCs, washbasins, and 5 shower rooms each with washbasin, changing space and seats (showers on payment). In addition, a multi-purpose unit serves the needs of families and disabled visitors, with facilities for babies and a further WC, basin and shower with handrails, etc. The campers' kitchen has dishwashing sinks, hot-plates and dining area, all free. A separate laundry provides a sink, washing machine, dryer and airing rack. Fishing is available in the river adjacent to the site. Reception and a small kiosk selling ices, sweets and soft drinks, is housed in an attractive cabin and there is a bell to summon the owners should they not be on site when you arrive. A garage, mini-market and cafe are 100 m. and the lively town of Sandane is 19 km.

How to find it: Site is beside the Rv 1 in the village of Byrkjelo, 19 km. east of Sandane.

General Details: Open 20 May - 1 Sept. Kiosk. TV room. Minigolf. Small children's playground. Fishing. Riding 4 km. Laundry. Kitchen. Motorcaravan service point. Chemical disposal. Cabins for rent.

Charges 1999: Per unit Nkr. 60; adult 10; child 5, electricity 20.

Reservations: Advisable in peak season. Address: 6867 Byrkjelo. Tel: 57.86.74.30. FAX: 57.86.71.54.

2480 Bjorkedal Camping, Volda

Interesting, excellent value, boat builder's campsite in outstanding location.

On the Rv 1 north of the Nordfjord, in Møre og Romsdal, is a lovely bowl-shaped valley famous throughout Norway for traditional boat building. Bjorkedal Camping is situated on a grassy open plateau about 300 m. off the main road and overlooking the farmland and mountains around the lake. There is space for 25 tents or vans with 10 electricity connections (16A) and also 5 cabins for rent. The small, modern and clean sanitary unit provides British style WCs, washbasins with dividers and curtains, one controllable hot shower per sex with changing space, curtain and seat (on payment), plus a unit with ramped access for disabled visitors. A kitchen with dishwashing sink and a full cooker (free), a laundry with sinks and washing machine, plus a cosy TV lounge complete the facilities. For a thousand years boats have been hand built in this valley by the Bjorkedal family. Site owner, Jakob Bjorkedal, will be pleased to show you the old water powered saw mill which he has reconstructed, and there are usually some examples of his boat building craft in the magnificent workshop with a most spectacular cathedral style timber roof. There is an extensive network of footpaths both in the valley and leading up into the surrounding circle of mountains where you can see the old cabins of the herdsmen. The site is also a convenient base from which to explore Geiranger, Runde, West Cape or Strynefjellet.

How to find it: Signed off Rv 1, midway along western side of Bjorkedal lake, 21 km. north of Nordfjordeid.

General Details: Open all year. Laundry. Kitchen. TV lounge. Small game hunting. Freshwater fishing.

Charges guide: Per unit Nkr. 40; adult 10; child 5; electricity 15.

Reservations: Write to site. Address: 6120 Folkestadbgd. Tel: 70.05.20.43.

2460 Prinsen Strandcamping, Alesund

Lively, fjordside site, just outside the attractive small town of Alesund.

Although 5 km. from the town centre, this is a more attractive option to the more crowded sites closer to town, even so, this is mainly a transit and short-stay site. Divided by trees and shrubs, and sloping gently to a small sandy beach with views down Borgundfjord, the site has 125 grassy pitches, 25 cabins and 7 rooms, 110 electricity connections (16A) and 75 cable TV hook-ups. The main heated sanitary unit, in the reception building, has British style WCs, mostly open washbasins, controllable hot showers with divider and seat (on payment), plus a sauna for each sex. A small kitchen has cooking facilities and two dishwashing sinks, the laundry has washing machines and a dryer. Further older facilities mainly serving rooms and cabins, include a bathroom for disabled visitors and families (key from reception). A hatch beside the central access road serves as the chemical disposal point and a motorcaravan service point (not drive over type). Reception shares space with the small shop (fresh bread to order). Other on-site amenities include a small children's playground, barbecue areas, slipway and boat hire, and a TV room. Alesund has lovely Art Nouveau architecture, Sunnmøre Folk Museum has 50 old houses, a boat collection and medieval and Viking artefacts, and on the island of Giske we recommend a visit to the 'Marble Church'.

How to find it: Turn off E136 at roundabout signed to Hatlane and site. Follow signs to site.

General Details: Open all year. Shop (1/6-1/9). Restaurant 800 m. Sauna. TV room. Children's playground. Slipway. Boat hire. Fishing. Bicycle hire. Kitchen. Laundry. Chemical disposal. Cabins and rooms for rent.

Charges 2000: Per unit incl. up to 6 persons Nkr. 130.00; electricity 20.00. Credit cards accepted.

Reservations: Write to site. Address: Ratvika, 6015 Alesund. Tel: 70.15.52.04. FAX: 70.15.49.96.

2470 Åndalsnes Camping and Motel, Åndalsnes

Leafy, sheltered site, close to town and the spectacular Trollstigen Mountain Road.
This attractive, popular site is situated in mature woodland beside the Rauma river 1 km. from the town centre, and close to Romsdalfjord and the breath-taking Trollstigen mountain road with its 11 giant hairpins that scale the sheer rock face. The reception, well stocked shop and cafeteria complex are on the opposite side of the road to the main touring area. The 230 grassy pitches are arranged informally between the many trees and shrubs, with 180 electric hook-ups (16A, long leads may be required). Two heated sanitary units provide British style WCs, washbasins (some in cubicles), controllable hot showers with divider and seat (tokens on payment), hairdryers, plus facilities for the disabled. Kitchens and laundries have facilities for cooking, dining, dishwashing and ironing, plus token operated washing machines and dryers. The cafeteria, which doubles as a function room/TV lounge, serves breakfast and dinner and is open daily though times vary according to demand.

How to find it: Turn off Rv 1 by the bridge to southwest of town, towards Trollstigen and Romsdalfjord. Site is signed.

General Details: Open 1 May - 15 Sept. Shop (10/5-1/9). Cafeteria (1/5-1/9). Minigolf. Bicycle hire. Canoe and boat hire. Fishing. Children's playground. Kitchen. Laundry. Chemical disposal. Chalets and cabins to rent.

Charges 2000: Per caravan or motorcaravan Nkr. 80; cyclist or m/cyclist and tent 50; extra tent 50; adult 15; child (4-12 yrs) 7.00; electricity 22. Credit cards accepted.

Reservations: Write to site. Address: 6300 Åndalsnes. Tel: 71.22.16.29. FAX: 71.22.62.16.

2450 Bjølstad Camping, Malmefjorden

Delightful rural retreat on Malmefjorden, close to the Atlantic Highway.
This small site, which slopes down to Malmefjorden, a sheltered arm of Fraenfjorden, has space for just 45 touring units on grassy, fairly level, terraces either side of the tarmac central access road. A basic, clean, heated sanitary unit provides British style WCs, one controllable hot shower with divider and shelf per sex (token on payment), plus washbasins with dividers, but one in cubicle (for ladies). A small campers' kitchen has two dishwashing sinks and a hot-plate, whilst the laundry has a washing machine and dryer. A delight for children is a large, old masted boat which provides hours of fun playing at pirates or Vikings, plus the more conventional swings, etc. At the foot of the camp is a waterside barbecue site, a special shallow paddling area for children and a jetty. Both rowing and motorboats (with lifejackets) can be hired, one can swim or fish in the fjord, and there are ten cabins for rent. No dogs accepted on site. This site is an ideal base for visiting Molde International Jazz Festival (annually mid-July), or the famous Varden viewpoint with its magnificent views over this 'Town of Roses', the fjord and 222 mountain peaks, both only 15 minutes drive from the site. Further afield, the small town of Bud is famous for its WW2 German coastal fortress, or one can drive the fantastic and scenic Atlantic Highway (now free) as it threads its way across the many islands and bridges to the west of Kristiansund.

How to find it: Turn off Rv 64 on northern edge of Malmefjorden village towards village of Lindset (lane is oil bound gravel). Site is 1 km.

General Details: Open 20 May - 31 August. Children's playground. Boat hire. Fjord fishing and swimming. Riding 9 km. Golf 12 km. Laundry. Kitchen. Cabins for rent. No dogs accepted.

Charges 2000: Per unit Nkr. 70 - 85; small tent 40; adult 10; child 5; electricity 15. Chalets 300 - 750. Credit cards accepted, but not Eurocheques.

Reservations: Write to site. Address: 6445 Malmefjorden, More og Romsdal. Tel: 71.26.56.56. FAX: 71.26.56.56.

2495 Vegset Camping, Snåsa

Pleasant site north of Snåsa, beside the E6 road.
Only 7 km. from Snåsa on the banks of Lake Snåsavatn, this site consists of 10 chalets and an extensive area for touring units, mainly on quite a slope. A new, well equipped sanitary block provides showers (Nkr. 5), plus a shower with toilet suitable for disabled people. There is a kitchen, TV room and a kiosk selling groceries. Snåsa is a centre for the South Lapp people who have their own boarding school, museum and information centre there. The Bergasen Nature Reservation is close to the village and is famous for its rare flora, especially orchids. The Gressamoen National Park is also near.

How to find it: Site is just off the E6 road, 7 km. from Snåsa.

General Details: Open Easter - 10 Oct. Kiosk. Kitchen. TV room. Swimming, fishing and boat hire.

Charges guide: Per unit Nkr. 80.

Reservations: Contact site. Address: 7760 Snåsa. Tel: 74.15.29.50.

NORWAY

2490 Skjerneset Camping, Averoy

Extraordinary island site with fishery museum near Kristiansund.

The tiny island of Ekkilsøya lies off the larger island of Averoy and is reached via a side road and bridge (no toll) from the main Rv 64 just south of Bremsnes from where the ferry crosses to Kristiansund. Although the fishing industry here is not what it used to be it is still the dominant activity and Skjerneset Camping has been developed by the Otterlei family to give visitors an insight into this industry and its history. Most of the old `Klippfisk' warehouse is now a fascinating 'fisherimuseum' and aquarium, with the remainder housing the sanitary installations, 3 small 4-bed apartments, a kitchen, laundry and lounges. There is space for 20 caravans or motorcaravans on gravel hardstandings around a rocky bluff and along the harbour's rocky frontage and all have electricity connections (16A). A small grassy area for 10 tents is under pine trees in a hollow on the top of the bluff together with the children's swings and 5 fully equipped cabins. Sanitary facilities are heated but basic, unisex, and perhaps a little quirky in their layout, but they provide British WCs, washbasins in cubicles and controllable hot showers with divider and shelf. Free hot water throughout. The kitchen provides 2 full cookers plus a hot-plate and dishwashing sinks, and the small laundry has a sink and washing machine. All were free of charge at the time of inspection. A new small sanitary unit together with a motorcaravan service point is planned for the '98 season. The small reception kiosk also has small stocks of basic packet foods, crisps, ices, sweets, postcards etc. Other on-site amenities include motor or rowing boat hire, organised sea-fishing or sightseeing trips in the owner's new sea-going boat, and for non-anglers who want a fish supper, fresh fish are always available on site. Note: this is a working harbour with deep unfenced water very close to the pitches.

How to find it: Site is on the little island of Ekkilsøya which is reached via a side road running west from the main Rv 64 road, 1.5 km. south of Bremsnes.

General Details: Open all year. Kiosk. Kitchen. Laundry. TV. Boat hire. Fishing.

Charges guide: Per unit Nkr. 90 (Less 20% outside 20/6-20/8); electricity 20.

Reservations: Write to site. Address: Ekkilsoya, 6553 Bremsnes, More og Romsdal. Tel: 71.51.18.94. FAX: 71.51.18.15.

2485 Krokstrand Camping, nr Storforshei

Cosmopolitan and popular riverside site only 18 km. from the Arctic Circle.

Attractively arranged amongst the birch trees, with a fast flowing river and waterfall alongside, and views of snow covered mountains, this site is a popular resting place for all nationalities on the long trek to Nordkapp. There are 40 unmarked pitches and electrical connections (16A) for 20 units. The well maintained, spotlessly clean, small sanitary unit provides British style WCs, open washbasins and two controllable hot showers per sex, with curtain and seat (on payment). The laundry has a washing machine and dryer, and the small kitchen a double hot-plate and dishwashing sink. There is also a chemical disposal facility and a conveniently located water tap and hose for motorcaravan tank filling. The small reception kiosk is open 16.00 - 22.00 in high season, otherwise campers are invited to find a pitch and pay later. Directions in English are given to the owner's house (within walking distance) for emergencies. An excellently maintained and brightly painted children's playground includes a trampoline, and families can enjoy a game of minigolf on the equally well tended course. Being only 18 km. drive from the Arctic Circle with its Visitor Centre, this site is in an ideal location. The small village just outside the camp entrance has a hotel with restaurant, a souvenir shop, and those interested in WW2 history will find the neatly tended grave of a Russian soldier by the site gate. The nearest town for shopping is Mo-i-Rana (60 km).

How to find it: Entrance is off E6 at Krokstrand village opposite hotel, 18 km. south of the Arctic Circle.

General Details: Open 1 June - 20 Sept. Children's playground. Minigolf. Fishing. Restaurant and souvenir shop nearby. Kitchen. Laundry. Chemical disposal. Motorcaravan services. Cabins to rent.

Charges 2000: Per unit Nkr. 70; adult 10; child 5; extra tent/hiker's tent 45; electricity 20. No credit cards.

Reservations: Write to site. Address: Krokstrand, 8630 Storforshei. Tel: 75.16.60.74.

2465 Lyngvær Lofoten Bobilcamping, Lyngvær, Lofoten Islands

Superbly positioned site by the sea on the Lofoten Islands.

This well laid out campsite, built in '91/92, has room for 200 units, half with access to electrical connections. The facilities are new, clean and good, although there are rather few of them. Showers, a little cramped, are on payment (Nkr. 10). There are extra unisex showers and toilets beside reception. A communal kitchen has cooking and washing up facilities and a large sitting area with satellite TV. There are several play areas and boat hire is available (rowing and motor boats, canoes and pedaloes). The site has its own salmon and sea trout fishing. It is a good area for walking, both by the sea and in the mountains.

How to find it: Site is signed from the ferry terminal.

General Details: Open 15 March - 31 Aug. Kitchen. TV lounge. Children's play areas. Boat hire. Fishing.

Charges guide: Per unit Nkr. 80; electricity 20. Fifth night free.

Reservations: Write to site. Address: Postboks 30, 8310 Kabelvåg. Tel: 76.07.87.81.

2475 Saltstraumen Camping, Saltstraumen

All weather site on coastal route, close to the largest Maelstrom in the world.
The site is rather ordinary but it is conveniently located within walking distance of an outstanding phenomenon, the strongest tidal current in the world, where in the course of 6 hours between 33,800 and 82,700 billion gallons of water are pressed through a narrow strait, at a rate of about 20 knots. The effect is greatest at new or full moons, check tide tables to determine the best time to visit. The 60 touring pitches are mostly level gravel hardstandings in rows, with electricity (10A) available to all, but a few 'softer' pitches are available for tents. The heated sanitary facilities are basic but clean, and provide British style WCs, open washbasins and free hot showers. The latter are just shower heads with dividers between and communal changing, although in the ladies' room there are some shower curtains. There is a kitchen with two full cookers, a laundry with washing machine and dryer. Adjacent to the site is a filling station with shop, hairdresser and nearby are a hotel and café. The site is 33 km. from Bodø and 50 km. from Fauske.

How to find it: From Rv 80 (Fauske -Bodø) turn south on Rv 17, site is 12 km. at Saltstraumen adjacent to Statoil station.

General Details: Open all year. Kitchen. Laundry. TV room. Children's playground. Minigolf. Fishing. Motorcaravan services, Chemical disposal point.

Charges guide: Per caravan Nkr. 100; motorcaravan 85; tent 75; electricity 25. Visa cards accepted.

Reservations: Write to site. Address: Boks 85, 8056 Saltstraumen. Tel: 75.58.75.60. FAX: 75.58.75.40.

2455 Ballangen Camping, Ballangen

Pleasant, lively site with small pool and waterslide, on the E6 outside of town.
This conveniently located site is on the edge of a fjord with a small rocky beach, with direct access off the main E6 road. Reception shares space with the extremely well stocked shop and takeaway (main season). The 150 marked pitches are mostly on sandy grass, with electricity (10/16A) available to 120. There are a few hardstandings, also 50 cabins for rent. The sanitary facilities are housed in a new building, with modern fittings and providing British style WCs, washbasins (some cubicles), and free, controllable hot showers with divider and seat. There are facilities for disabled visitors and a sauna and solarium. The kitchen has dishwashing sinks, a full cooker, hot-plates and a covered seating area. Other amenities include a TV room with tourist information, coffee and games machines, small outdoor pool and waterslide (charged for), tennis court, minigolf, children's playground, free fjord fishing and boat and bicycle hire. A supermarket and other services are in Ballangen 4 km. from the site. An interesting excursion is to the nearby Martinstollen Mine where visitors are guided through the dimly lit Olav Shaft 500 m. into the mountain. Narvik with it's wartime connections and museums is 40 km.

How to find it: Access is off the E6, 4 km. north of Ballangen, 40 km. south of Narvik

General Details: Open all year. Shop. Café and takeaway. Kitchen. Laundry. Sauna and solarium. TV/games room. Swimming pool and waterslide. Tennis. Minigolf. Fishing. Boat and bicycle hire. Riding 2 km. Washing machines and dryers. Car wash. Chemical disposal. Motorcaravan services. Cabins for rent (50).

Charges 2000: Per unit incl. 4 persons Nkr. 120; electricity 20; cabin 250 - 350. Credit cards accepted.

Reservations: Contact site. Address: 8540 Ballangen. Tel: 76.92.76.90. FAX: 76.92.76.92.

2435 Solvang Camping, Alta

Old-style site, with relaxed, welcoming atmosphere, on the Altafjord.
This restful little site is set well back from the main road, so there is no road noise. The site overlooks the tidal marshes of the Altafjord, which are home to a wide variety of bird-life, providing ornithologists with a grandstand view during the long summer evenings bathed by the Midnight Sun. The 30 pitches are on undulating grass amongst pine trees and shrubs, and are not marked, but there are 12 electric hook-ups (16A) available. The site also has 7 cabins and some rooms for rent. The heated sanitary facilities are basic and in a fairly old building, but provide British style WCs, mostly open washbasins and free controllable hot showers, together with a kitchen with two cookers and dishwashing sinks, plus a small laundry with a washing machine and spin dryer. In its own little kiosk outside is the modern stainless steel chemical disposal point and outside a waste water drain which, with a little ingenuity, is possible to use for draining a motorcaravan tank. The site is run by a church mission organisation, consequently only limited funds are available for repairs. However, all facilities are clean and in good order (out of season, the site provides holidays for needy children). There is a small football pitch and a playground, also a large lounge with TV. Places of interest in the area are Alta Museum with its ancient rock-carvings, and the Savco Canyon, the largest in Europe, with the controversial Alta Power Station and 100 m. dam at its upper end.

How to find it: Site is signed off the E6, 10 km. north of Alta.

General Details: Open 1 June - 10 Aug. Kitchen. Laundry. TV lounge. Football field. Children's playground. Chemical disposal. Motorcaravan services. Cabins for rent.

Charges guide: Per unit Nkr. 90; cyclist tent 70; electricity 30. Credit cards not accepted.

Reservations: Write to site. Address: Transfarelv, 9500 Alta. Tel: 78.43.04.77.

NORWAY

2445 Slettnes Fjordcamp, Oteren

Useful stopover southeast of Tromso beside the E6 road.

Beside a narrow fjord and surrounded by snowy capped mountains, this is a large site mainly for permanent caravans but with room for 20 touring units. A very well kept site, there are neat flower beds outside reception. Sanitary facilities consist of two toilets each for male and female with washbasins with mirror, etc. There are three showers each, communal but with no charge and good hot water. A kitchen houses a sink unit, full size cooker and microwave.

How to find it: Site is beside the E6 road near Oteren.

Charges guide: Per unit Nkr. 100.

Reservations: Contact site. Address: 9047 Oteren (Finnmark). Tel: 77.71.45.08.

2425 Kirkeporten Camping, Skarsvåg, Nordkapp

The most northerly campsite in the world (71° 06' 50").

This is a superb site with the most modern sanitary installations. In two under-floor heated buildings, linked by a covered timber walkway they provide British style WCs, open washbasins and free controllable hot showers with divider and seat, sauna, plus two family bathrooms, a baby room, and an excellent unit for disabled visitors. A laundry with washing machine and dryer, and a kitchen, with hot-plates, sinks and a dining area complete the facilities. All have quality fittings, excellent tiling and beautiful woodwork - the owner is a carpenter by profession. Considering the climate and the wild unspoilt location this has to be one of the best sites in Scandinavia, and also rivals the best in Europe. An added bonus is that the reindeer often come right into the campsite to graze. The 30 pitches, 22 with electricity (16A), are on grass or gravel hardstanding in natural 'tundra' terrain beside a small lake, together with 10 rental cabins and 5 rooms. The reception/cafeteria at the entrance is open daily. Sea fishing and photographic trips by boat can be arranged and buses run 4 times a day to Honningsvåg or the Nordkapp Centre. We suggest you follow the marked footpath over the hillside behind the campsite, from where you can photograph 'Nordkapp' at midnight if the weather is favourable. We also advise you pack warm clothing, bedding and maybe propane for this location. Note: Although overnighting at Nordkapp Centre is permitted, it is on the very exposed gravel car-park with no electric hook-ups or showers. Price guide: car parking and Visitor Centre Nordkapp - Nkr. 175 per person. Single ferry fare (6 m. vehicle + 2 persons) Kåfjord-Honningsvåg Nkr. 225. The ferry has been replaced by a tunnel and bridge (charge similar).

How to find it: On the island of Magerøya, from Honningsvåg take the E69 for 20 km. then fork right signed Skarsvåg. Site is on left after 3 km. just as you approach Skarsvåg.

General Details: Open 10 May - 10 Sept. Cafeteria. Kitchen. Laundry. Sauna. Good motorcaravan service point. Cabins and rooms for rent.

Charges guide: Per unit Nkr. 110; person 20; small tent 80; electricity 20. Credit cards not accepted.

Reservations: Not usually necessary. Address: 9763 Skarsvåg, Nordkapp. Tel: 78.47.52.33. FAX: 78.47.52.47.

2415 Kautokeino Fritidssenter and Camping, Suohpatjávri, Kautokeino

Newly developed, friendly, lakeside site, 8 km. south of Kautokeino.

The 30 pitches here are not marked and are generally on a firm sandy base, amongst low growing birch trees, with 20 electric hook-ups (10A) available. There are also 8 cabins and 7 motel rooms for rent and these are very attractively designed and furnished. Although the grass is trying to grow, the ground is frozen from September until May so it takes many years to establish. The sanitary building is modern, heated and well maintained, with 2 British style WCs, 2 open washbasins and 2 controllable hot showers (on payment) per sex. A small kitchen has a full cooker, dishwashing sinks and refrigerator, the laundry has washing machine, dryer and ironing facilities. A separate bathroom for the disabled also contains baby changing facilities. The site rents canoes, boats and pedalos and free fishing is available in the lake. During the season when there are enough guests, the owner arranges an evening campfire around two Sami tents, with lectures about the Sami people. There are good walks in the area to some special Sami sites, shops and other services are in Kautokeino just 8 km. away, and the site is 35 km. north of the Finnish Border.

How to find it: Site is 8 km. south of Kautokeino on the Rv 93. (Do not confuse with another site of similar name in the town)

General Details: Open 1 June - 30 Sept. Kitchen. Laundry. Chemical disposal point. Football. Volleyball. Boat hire. Fishing.

Charges guide: Per unit Nkr. 65-75; adult 10; child 5; hikers tent 45; electricity 25. Visa card accepted.

Reservations: Write to site. Address; Suohpatjávri, 9520 Kautokeino. Tel: 78.48.57.33. FAX: as phone.

2500 Trasavika Camping, Viggja, nr Orkanger

Terraced site with glorious views and sandy beach, 40 km. from Trondheim.

On a headland jutting into the Trondheimfjord and some 40 km. from Trondheim, Trasavika occupies such an attractive position that the extra distance into town is bearable. The 65 pitches are on an open grassy field at the top of the site, or on a series of terraces below which run right down to the small sandy beach, and are easily accessed via a well designed gravel service road. There are 40 electricity connections (10A). To one side, on a wooded bluff at the top of the site, are 14 rental cabins and the neat, sanitary unit. Facilities include British style WCs, open washbasins and 2 controllable hot showers per sex with divider (on payment). Hot water also on payment in the kitchen and laundry which have a hot-plate, dish and clothes washing sinks, washing machine and dryer. The reception complex also houses the small shop, licensed café and a TV/sitting room. Nobody travelling as far as mid-Norway would dream of not visiting the unusually interesting and attractive historic city of Trondheim, for long the capital of Norway.

How to find it: Site is on the edge of Viggja on the Rv 65 between Orkanger and Buvik, 17 km. from the E6 and 40 km. west of Trondheim.

General Details: Open 1 May - 30 Sept. Shop and café (20/6-31/8 only). Kitchen. Laundry. TV/sitting room. Children's playground. Jetty and boat hire. Cabins and apartments for rent.

Charges guide: Per caravan or motorcaravan Nkr. 100; tent 70 - 90; electricity 25. Credit cards accepted.

Reservations: Write to site. Address: 7354 Viggja, Sør Trondelag. Tel: 72.86.78.22.

2505 Magalaupe Camping, Oppdal

Rural, good value, riverside site, close to Dovrefjell National Park.

Lying in a sheltered position with easy access from the E6, this site offers fairly simple facilities but a host of unusual activities in the surrounding area, including caving, canyoning, rafting, gold panning, mineral hunting, and musk oxen, reindeer and elk safaris. In winter the more adventurous can also go snow-mobiling or skiing in the high Dovrefjell National Park. The 75 unmarked and grassy touring pitches, 36 with electrical connections (10/16A), are in natural surroundings amongst birch trees and rocks on several different levels and served by gravel access roads. There are also 8 attractive and fully equipped cabins for rent. The small, but very clean, heated sanitary unit provides a British style WC, three washbasins (one cubicle) and two hot showers (on payment) per sex. This is supplemented by two further WC/washbasin units in the building which also houses the reception and kiosk for ices, soft drinks, etc., the TV lounge, plus a bar which is open mid June - August. As the site rarely fills up, these simple facilities should be adequate at most times. A small kitchen has dishwashing facilities, hot-plate and freezer, plus a combined washing/drying machine. Supermarkets and other services can be found in Oppdal (11 km).

How to find it: Site is signed to western side of the E6, 11 km. south of Oppdal.

General Details: Open all year. Kiosk. Bar (mid June - Aug). TV lounge. Fishing. Bicycle hire, riding or golf 12 km. Kitchen. Laundry. Car wash. Chemical disposal. Cabins for rent.

Charges 2000: Per unit incl. 4 persons and electricity Nkr. 100; small tent without electricity 50; extra person 10. Credit cards accepted but not Eurocheques.

Reservations: Write to site. Address: Rute 5, 7340 Oppdal. Tel: 47.72.42.46.84. FAX: as phone.

2510 Håneset Camping, Roros

Acceptable, high plateau site, close to the UNESCO World Heritage town of Roros.

At first sight Håneset Camping it is not promising, lying between the main road and the railway, and nor is the gritty sloping ground of the site very imaginatively landscaped - for grass, when it grows up here, is rather coarse and lumpy. However, as we soon discovered, it is the best equipped site in the town, and ideal to cope with the often cold, wet weather of this bleak 1,000m. high plateau. The 50 unmarked touring pitches all have access to electricity (10/16A). Most facilities are housed in the main complex building. These include reception, shop and cafeteria, a huge sitting/TV room and two well equipped kitchens which the owners, the Moen family, share fully with their guests, plus 9 rooms for rent. The heated sanitary installations provide three separate rooms for each sex with British WCs, open washbasins and control-lable hot showers (on payment). A washing machine and two sinks are in one of the ladies' rooms. Outside, the only other amenities are 13 rental cabins, a children's playground, and a chemical disposal point which is in a barn near the bottom of the site. People flock from all over Europe to visit this remarkably well pre-served mining town. For over 300 years it was one of Europe's leading copper mines, and during all that time it never suffered serious fire. As a result it occupies a special place on UNESCO's world heritage list for its unique concentration of historic wooden houses. The walk to the town takes around 20 minutes.

How to find it: Site is on the Rv 30 leading south from Roros to Os, 3 km. from Roros.

General Details: Open all year. Shop and cafeteria (mid June-August). Children's playground. Kitchen. Laundry. Chemical disposal. Cabins and rooms to let.

Charges 1999: Per caravan or motorcaravan Nkr. 110 - 135; tent 90; electricity 20. No credit cards.

Reservations: Write to site. Address: 7460 Roros, Sør Trondelag. Tel: 72.41.13.72. FAX: 72.41.06.01.

NORWAY

2515 Gjelten Bru Camping, Alvdal

Cosy, village site in wooded riverside location, close to the small town of Alvdal.

Located just a few kilometres west of Alvdal, this peaceful little site with its traditional turf roof buildings, makes an excellent base from which to explore the area. The 50 touring pitches are on level neatly trimmed grass, served by gravel access roads, and with electricity (10A) available to 37. Some pitches are in the open and others under tall pine trees spread along the river bank. The heated sanitary facilities are in two buildings providing a good supply of British style WCs, a mix of conventional washbasins and stainless steel washing troughs, and controllable hot showers on payment. In addition there is a separate unit with WC, basin and shower for disabled campers. Two small kitchens, one at each block, have dishwashing facilities, hot-plates and an oven (all free). Across the bridge on the other side of the river and main road, the site owners also operate the local, well stocked mini-market and post office where you will also find a public phone. The UNESCO World Heritage town of Roros is 75 km. to the northeast of this charming little site, and the Dovrefjell National Park is also within comfortable driving distance.

How to find it: On the Rv 29 at Gjelten 3.5 km. west of Alvdal. Turn over the river bridge opposite village store and post office, and site is immediately on right.

General Details: Open all year. Kitchen. Fishing. Supermarket, post office and public telephone nearby. Children's swings. Fishing. Bicycle hire 5 km. Chemical disposal. Cabins to rent (13).

Charges 2000: Per unit incl. electricity Nkr. 110 - 125. No credit cards.

Reservations: Write to site. Address: 2560 Alvdal. Tel: 62.48.74.44. FAX: 62.78.70.20.

2555 Lom Motell and Camping, Lom

Mountain resort site, 500 m. from town and Stave Church.

This small site provides pitches for 60 touring units on slightly sloping grass on either side of a modern motel only 500 m. from the centre of this famous town and its beautiful medieval wooden Stave Church. There are 52 electrical connections (10A). The single large heated sanitary unit provides British style WCs, washbasins in cubicles, but only 2 hot showers per sex (on payment). A further free hot shower is available for those using the sauna/solarium (Nkr 30), or the very comprehensive, free gym facilities, plus a unit for families, babies or the disabled (key from reception). The small campers' kitchen provides two dishwashing sinks with free hot water, and hot-plates for cooking (also free). A separate laundry room houses washing machines, dryers and sinks again with free hot water. Also on site is a ski room, a children's playground, plus 16 cabins, apartments and motel rooms for rent. Reception shares space with the small shop, and the licensed motel cafeteria serves dinners and breakfasts (opening times vary). Besides the lovely mountain views from the site and the attractions of Lom, the site is a good base from which to explore the mountains, take a trip to see the Briksdal Glacier or visit the Norwegian Mountain Museum.

How to find it: Site is 500 m. from roundabout in centre of Lom, beside the Rv 55 towards Sogndal.

General Details: Open all year. Kiosk. Cafeteria. Kitchen. Laundry. Sauna and solarium. Gymnasium. Motorcaravan service point. Children's playground. Ski preparation room. Cabins and motel rooms for rent.

Charges guide: Per unit incl. 5 persons Nkr. 125; small motorcaravan + 2 persons 110; m/cycle and tent 90; bicycle and tent 70; electricity 25. Visa cards accepted.

Reservations: Write to site. Address: Postboks 88, 2686 Lom. Tel: 61.21.12.20. FAX: 61.12.12.23.

2545 Rustberg Hytteulerie and Camping, Øyer, nr Lillehammer

Traditional family site, convenient for visiting the 'Olympic area' of Norway.

Conveniently located beside the E6 and just 20 km. from Lillehammer, this attractive terraced site provides a comfortable base for exploring the area. Like all sites along this route it does suffer from road noise at times, but the site facilities and nearby attractions more than compensate for this. There are 90 pitches with 60 available for touring units, most reasonably level and with some gravel hardstandings for motorcaravans. There are 50 electrical connections (10A). Heated sanitary facilities provide British style WCs, washbasins (most in cubicles), and hot showers (on payment), plus two luxurious family bathrooms and a unit for the disabled each with WC, basin and shower. The campers' kitchen and dining room provides facilities for dishwashing together with a microwave and double hob (all free). A separate laundry has sinks, washing machine, dryer and drying cupboard. There is a good children's playground, an unusual billiard golf game, and a small open air swimming pool with water-slide which is open June-Aug. (weather permitting). The small reception building also houses a kiosk stocking basic foods, beer, ices, sweets, postcards and stamps. The Maihaugen Folkmuseum and Lillehammer town are 20 km, Hunderfossen (5 km.) has the Norwegian Road Museum and the more adventurous can ride the Olympic bobsleigh track.

How to find it: Site is well signed from the E6, 20 km. north of Lillehammer.

General Details: Open all year. Kiosk. Kitchen. Laundry. Swimming pool and water-slide. Billiard golf. Children's playground. Motorcaravan services.

Charges guide: Per unit Nkr. 125; small tent 110; electricity 20. Visa cards accepted.

Reservations: Write to site. Address: 2636 Øyer. Tel: 61.27.81.84. FAX: 61.27.87.05.

E01   CAMPING EL DELFIN VERDE

**Aptdo de Correos 43,
17257 Torroella de Montgri, (Gerona)**

Tel: (972) 75.84.50   Fax: (972) 76.00.70

5 MILES SOUTH EAST OF TORROELLA DE MONTGRI.

Travelling south, leave the A7 at junction 5 (north of Gerona) in the direction of L'Escala. Just before Vilademat turn right on the C252 signposted La Bisbal. After a few miles turn left towards Torroella de Montgri. At roundabout follow signs for Pals (also signposted El Delfin Verde). After approximately 3 miles you will find the site on your left before entering Pals.

5 amp electricity included in price.

GENERAL INFORMATION

There are many excursions organised by the site management including those to medieval villages, the Salvador Dali Museum, nature reserves and a handicraft centre. Horseriding, fishing, golf and all watersports are offered in the vicinity. There is a market held every day along the Costa Brava.

E04   CAMPING BALLENA ALEGRE

**Autovia Castelldefels km 12.5,
08840 Viladecans, (Barcelona)**

Tel: (93) 658.05.04   Fax: (93) 658.05.75

10 MILES SOUTH WEST OF BARCELONA.

From Barcelona take C246 dual-carriageway (signposted airport and Castelldefels). Go past campsites Filipinas and El Torro Bravo to find the site entrance on the left hand side at kilometre stone 12.5.

4 amp electricity included in price.

GENERAL INFORMATION

As this site has direct access to the beach, water sports are available. Excursions are organised from the site to Sitges, Tarragona, the monastery of Montserrat and other destinations on the Costa Brava.

Local markets are held in Barcelona daily, Gava on Tuesdays and Viladecans and Castelldefels on Wednesdays. Ask at the site office for information on all aspects of things to see and do in the area, including Port Aventura which is near Exit 35 of A7 motorway.

MUNICIPAL CAMPING MAUBEUGE P07

212 Route de Mons, 59600 Maubeuge

Tel: 03.27.62.25.48
Fax(Town Hall): 03.27.53.75.00

13 MILES SOUTH OF MONS.

From Mons head south on the N2 towards Maubeuge. The site is on the left of this road about 1 mile before you reach the town centre.

Please remember to pay for your taxe de séjour (if applicable) before leaving. 3 amp electricity included in price.

GENERAL INFORMATION

This site is an ideal base for discovering the local lakes and forests. There are local markets in Maubeuge on Monday and Saturday mornings. Fishing and canoeing are available nearby.

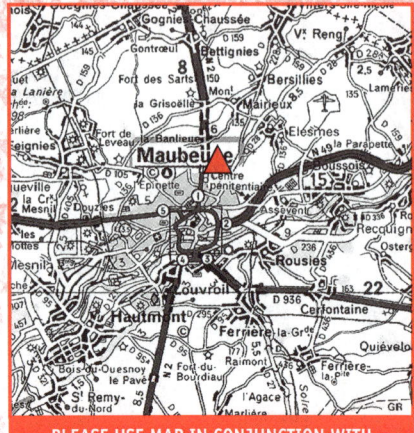

PLEASE USE MAP IN CONJUNCTION WITH MICHELIN MAP No.53

CHATEAU DE GANDSPETTE P08

62910 Eperlecques

Tel: 03.21.93.43.93   Fax: 03.21.95.74.98

18 1/2 MILES SOUTH-EAST OF CALAIS.

From Calais travel southeast on A26/E15 autoroute, leaving at junction 3 (St Omer) to join the N42 northeast towards St Omer, then N43 towards Nordausques. Turn on to D600 following signs towards Dunkerque and Watten, then just before Watten turn left at roundabout onto D207 signposted Ganspette. Site will be found on the right a short distance along this road.

Please remember to pay for your taxe de sejour 2.00FF pppd (if applicable) before leaving. 6 amp electricity included in price.

GENERAL INFORMATION

Situated in the wooded grounds of a 19th Century château, this site offers plenty of walks and a good base for visiting the Côte d'Opale and historic 2nd World War sites. Horeseriding, golf and fishing are available in the area. There are markets in Watten on Friday and St Omer on Saturdays.

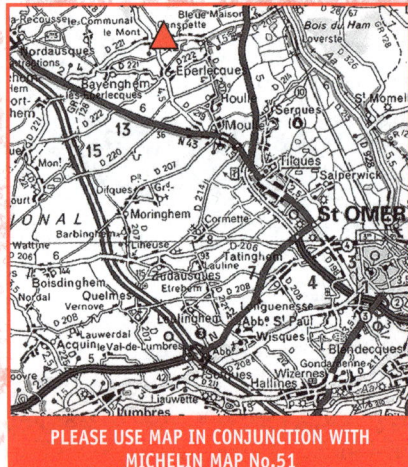

PLEASE USE MAP IN CONJUNCTION WITH MICHELIN MAP No.51

2550 Strandefjord Camping, Leira, nr Fagernes, Valdres

Mature, wooded, lakeside site in the Valdres district just outside Fagernes

Fagernes lies on the north shore of an impressive glacial lake - Strandefjorden, and just 4 km. to the south-east at Leira, on a corner of this lake, is Strandefjord Camping. This undulating, woodland site behind a light industrial estate, has 70 touring pitches, but can take up to 250 units in scattered clearings amongst the trees and beside the lake. Many pitches are only suitable for tents and only 75 have electricity (10A). Also 30 seasonal units, 31 cabins and rooms on site. The main heated, but rather basic, sanitary unit could be hard pressed in high season. It has British WCs, washbasins (some in cubicles), but only 2 hot showers per sex (on payment). Separate rooms house a small kitchen with dishwashing and cooking facilities (free of charge), and a laundry. More showers and WC's are with the saunas (equipped with TV!) under the main site complex which also houses reception, a licensed restaurant, and conference room. Other on-site facilities include a fitness track, tennis and beach volleyball courts, children's play areas, minigolf, boat hire. Fishing and swimming in the lake are possible. It is a 2 minute walk to the village mini-market.

How to find it: Turn off the E16 Oslo road onto the Rv 51, at Leira village 4 km. east of Fagernes. The site entrance is within 50m.

General Details: Open all year. Restaurant (June-Aug). Sauna. Children's play areas. Conference room. Lake swimming. Fitness track. Tennis. Beach volleyball. Minigolf. Boat hire. Laundry. Kitchen. Chemical disposal.

Charges guide: Caravan or motorcaravan Nkr. 120; tent and car 100; cycle or m/cycle and tent 85; electricity 25. Credit cards accepted.

Reservations: Write to site. Address: 2920 Leira (Oppland). Tel: 61.36.23.65. FAX: 61.36.24.80.

2570 Fossheim Hytte and Camping, nr Gol, Hallingdal

Idyllic touring site beside the Hallingdal river on the 'Adventure Road'.

Centred on the country town of Gol is one of Norway's favourite camping areas, Hallingdal. This small touring site lies just 4 km. west of the town, on the river bank, and is shaded by elegant tall birch trees. Despite being just below the main road and with a railway in the trees on the opposite side of the river, surprisingly little noise penetrates this idyllic setting. There are 50 grassy touring pitches, with electricity (10/16A) available to 40 and cable TV connections for some. Most overlook the river. In addition there are 14 cabins and 4 rooms for rent, but no static caravans are accepted. The site is well equipped, with a modern heated sanitary unit providing British style WCs, washbasins (some in cubicles), free controllable hot showers with dividers and seats, a separate unit for disabled people and a sauna. Small kitchen and laundry rooms provide cramped facilities for dishwashing and cooking (free of charge), plus sinks for clothes washing and a washing machine and dryer. Other facilities include a large, very comfortable TV lounge, a children's play area, canoe hire, and trout fishing with a specially constructed wooden walkway and platform for anglers with disabilities. A small shop is open in season with bread to order.

How to find it: Site is 4 km. west of Gol on route Rv 7 leading to Geilo. (Note: there is another site of similar name in the adjoining Hemsedal).

General Details: Open all year. Shop (1/6-31/8). TV lounge. Sauna. Children's play area. Bicycle hire. Trout fishing and canoeing. Riding 4 km. Golf 18 km. Laundry. Kitchen. Chemical disposal. Cabins and rooms for rent.

Charges 2000: Per unit incl. 2 persons and electricity Nkr. 125 - 160. Credit cards accepted (not Eurocheques).

Reservations: Write to site. Address: 3550 Gol (Buskerud). Tel: 32.02.95.80. FAX: 32.02.95.85. E-mail: foshytte@online.no.

 AR Discount
Less Nkr. 5 per night

2590 Camping Sandviken, Tinnsjo

Remote, lakeside site, in scenic location, suitable for exploring Hardangervidda.

With its own shingle beach, at the head of Tinnsjo Lake, Camping Sandviken provides 130 grassy, mostly level, pitches. In addition to the 30 seasonal units and 13 cabins, there are 80 numbered tourist pitches with electricity (5A), plus an area for tents, under trees along the waterfront. The tidy heated sanitary unit has British WCs, washbasins (some in cubicles), hot showers with dividers and seats (on payment), a sauna, solarium and a dual purpose disabled/family bathroom with ramped access and baby changing mat. Kitchen and laundry rooms provide facilities for cooking, dish and clothes washing (hot water on payment). The office/reception kiosk also sells sweets, soft drinks, ices etc. and a baker calls daily in July. A 1 km. stroll takes you to the tiny village of Tinn Austbygde which has a mini-market, bakery, café, bank, garage and post office. On-site leisure facilities include minigolf, TV and games rooms, a children's play area, watersports and fishing.

How to find it: Easiest access is via the Rv 37 from Gransherad along the western side of the lake.

General Details: Open all year. Kiosk (May-15 Sept). Kitchen. Laundry. Sauna. Solarium. Minigolf. Children's playground. Fishing. Boat hire. TV and games room. Motorcaravan services. Chemical disposal. Cabins for rent.

Charges guide: Per person Nkr. 15; child (4-18 yrs) 10; caravan or motorcaravan 70 - 85, acc. to season; tent 60 - 75; m/cycle 40 - 50; electricity 20. `Quickstop' (8 pm-9 am) 65 - 80.

Reservations: Write to site. Address: 3650 Tinn Austbygd (Telemark). Tel: 35.09.81.73.

NORWAY

2600 Rysstad Feriesenter, Setesdal

High quality site in spectacular setting within easy reach of Stavanger and Kristiansand.

Setesdal is on the upper reaches of the Otra river which runs north from the southern port of Kristiansand right up to the southern slopes of Hardangervidda. It offers a wide range of scenery, often spectacular where the valley cuts through high, steep sided mountains. It is an area famous for its colourful mining history (silver) and for its vibrant art (especially music) and folklore. Thanks to a major new hydro-electric project, a spectacular mountain road has now opened linking Setesdal with Sirdal to the west, bringing Setesdal within easy and pleasant driving range of Stavanger. At the junction of this new road and Setesdal is the small village of Rysstad, named after the family who have developed camping in this area. Trygve Rysstad now runs the Rysstad Feriesenter, founded by his father in the '50s. The site occupies a wide tract of woodland between the road and the river towards which it shelves gently, affording a splendid view of the valley and the towering mountains opposite. The site is in effect divided into two sections; one is divided by trees and hedges into numbered pitches, some occupied by chalets to hire, the other is an adjacent open field. Good modern sanitary facilities are found under the reception block with showers on payment, washbasins in cubicles, washing up sinks and cooker. There is an attractive area on the river's edge for barbecues and entertainment with an arena type setting. The little village is within walking distance.

How to find it: Site is about 1 km. south of junction between route 9 (from Kristiansand) and the extended route 45 (from Stravanger).

General Details: Open 1 May - 1 Oct. Electrical connections (20). Children's play area and amusement hut. Sports field. Fishing, swimming and boating (boats for hire). Fitness track. Bicycle hire. TV room. Laundry facilities with washing machine. Campers' kitchen. Centre includes café, shop, bank, garage and restaurant.

Charges 2000: Per person Nkr. 15; child 10; caravan or tent 120; hiker's tent 60; electricity 25. Credit cards accepted, but not Eurocheques.

Reservations: Write to site. Address: Midt i Setesdal, 4748 Rysstad. Tel: 37.93.61.30. FAX: 37.93.63.45.

2610 Neset Camping, Byglandsfjord

Modern site by lake in Otra valley, good for activity holidays in south Norway.

On a promontory on the shores of the 40 km. long Byglandsfjord, Neset is a good centre for activities or as a stop en route north from the ferry port of Kristiansand. Byglandsfjord offers good fishing (mainly trout) and the area has marked trails for cycling, riding or walking in an area famous for minerals. The site has a stone workshop where your finds can be identified and courses in stone polishing are arranged. Climbing, rafting and canoe courses (including trips to see beavers) are organised. Ski-ing is possible in the area in winter. Neset is on well kept grassy meadows by the lake shore with the water on three sides and the road on the fourth and provides 180 unmarked pitches, most with electricity available. The main building houses reception, a small shop and a restaurant with fine views over the water. There are three modern, heated sanitary blocks, two with hot showers on payment, washing up facilities (metered hot water) and a kitchen. Chalets and three caravans to hire. Barbecue area and children's play equipment around the site. This is a well run, friendly site where one could spend an active few days.

How to find it: Site is on route 39, 2½ km. north of the town of Byglandsfjord on the eastern shores of the lake.

General Details: Open all year. Restaurant. Shop. Campers' kitchen. Children's playground. Lake swimming, boating and fishing. Bicycle, canoe and pedalo hire. Courses in stone polishing, climbing, rafting and canoeing.

Charges guide: Per unit Nkr. 105; tent and m/cycle 70; adult 10; child (5-12 yrs) 5; electricity 20.

Reservations: Write to site. Address: 4680 Byglandsfjord (Aust-Agder). Tel: 37.93.42.55.

2612 Holt Camping, Tvedestrand

Useful little site on outskirts of popular small Norwegian resort.

Tvedestrand is an attractive small resort with a pretty harbour, which is very popular with the Norwegians for their own holidays. Holt Camping is quite pleasantly situated beside the main E18 road, some 3 km. from the town - there is a little noise from the road during the day but we were not disturbed when staying overnight. The campsite is part level, part sloping grassland and about half of the pitches have 16A electrical connections. There are the usual cabins for hire. The single small sanitary block has excellent, well maintained facilities including hot showers on payment (1 per sex), washbasins (H&C) and provision for dishwashing and laundry (washing machine and dryer). Serving both the touring pitches and the cabins, the facilities may well be under pressure during busy times. There is a shop and café immediately outside the site entrance. This site could be very useful en-route to Oslo from the ferry at Kristiansand or for a break in a part of Norway frequented more by the Norwegians themselves than by visitors from abroad.

How to find it: Site is beside the main E18 coast road (which actually bypasses the town), about 1 km. south of the turn off to the town itself.

General Details: Open 1 June - 31 Aug (huts all year). Shop/café outside. Laundry. Children's play area.

Charges 1999: Per unit incl. 2 persons and electricity Nkr. 100.00, without electricity 80.00.

Reservations: Contact site. Address: 4900 Tvedestrand (Aust-Agder). Tel: 37.16.02.65.

2615 Olberg Camping, Trøgstad

Peaceful, village farm site, close to Lake Øyren within 70 km. of Oslo.

A newly developed, delightful small site, Olberg Camping is located on neatly tended grassy meadow with newly planted trees and shrubs. There are 35 large, level pitches and electricity connections (16A) are available for 28 units. The excellent, heated sanitary facilities are housed in a purpose built unit, created in the end of a magnificent large, modern barn and have a ramp for wheelchair access. They provide controllable hot showers, British style WCs and washbasins, with one bathroom for families or disabled visitors. Dishwashing is outside, under cover with hot and cold water and a washing machine and ironing board are provided. A small kitchenette provides a full size cooker and food preparation area. Hot water is free throughout. The reception building also houses a small gallery with paintings, glasswork and other crafts. In high season fresh bread is available (except Sunday) and coffee, drinks, ices and pizza are now provided. A short drive down the adjacent lane takes you to the beach on Lake Øyeren, and there are many woodland walks in the surrounding area. The old church and museum at Trøgstad, and Båstad church are worth visiting. Bicycles can be hired and the local tennis court is also available. Children have a small playground with a sand-pit, trampoline, swings and climbers, but please bear in mind that this is a working farm. Forest and elk 'safaris' are arranged.

How to find it: Site is signed on Rv 22, 20 km. north of Mysen on southern edge of Båstad village.

General Details: Open all year. Kiosk. Snacks available. Craft gallery. Children's playground. Bicycle hire. Tennis nearby. Riding 2 km. Fishing 3 km. Laundry and cooking facilities. Chemical disposal. Cabins for rent.

Charges 2000: Per unit incl. 2 adults Nkr. 120; extra person (over 12) 10; electricity 20. Credit cards accepted.

Reservations: Write to site. Address: 1860 Trøgstad (Østfold). Tel: 47.69.82.86.10. FAX: 47.69.82.85.55.

AR Discount
Less 10%,
min 3 nights

The Good ArctiCamps Guide

Very few British campers are to be seen in North Norway, beyond the Arctic Circle. Except for a few enthusiasts with several weeks to spare, it is too far to drive. Yet it has much to offer.

The best way to get to North Norway is to take advantage of the special promotional fares offered by Braathens via Bergen or Oslo and then travel on by road or by ferry from Trondheim or Bodo. Car hire in North Norway is hideously expensive. However, there is an alternative: public transport. To the annoyance of taxpayers in South Norway the Norwegian government pours subsidy into North Norway and much of this goes into a remarkable network of transport services by ferry, coach and bus. These services are operated with modern vehicles to regular published timetables and all carefully interconnect. Full details are provided in a comprehensive timetable available from the Norway Tourist Board in London. This includes the amazing Hurtigruten - the 100 year old coastal 'steamer' - which links all the main coastal towns on a daily basis in each direction and which can be used for hopping from town to town starting from Bergen. Backpackers use their youth rail passes to travel by train from Oslo or Stockholm to the Arctic rail gateways of Bodo and Narvik and then explore North Norway by bicycle or public transport. However, for those who are not into lightweight camping there are two forms of camping which are unique to the Arctic and which require virtually no equipment whatsoever: rorbu camping and sjohus camping.

Arctic Norway happens to be the world's most important cod fishing coast. Every spring thousands of fishing folk pour into the coastal towns and villages to catch and process cod. Over several centuries two forms of accommodation have developed to serve this massive migration; small huts on the waterfront, like boathouses, for the fishing crew, known as rorbu, and large sheds on the quayside for the workers in the fishery, known as sjohus (sea house). The rorbu traditionally has only one or two bunk-bedrooms, plus sitting room, kitchen and washroom. The sjohus usually has three floors with cod processing on the ground floor, ample public rooms on the second floor and bunk-bedrooms on the second and third floors. In effect the rorbu is a fisherman's flat while the sjohus is a fishery hostel. Over the past twenty years, the rorbu and sjohus have been adapted for use by campers during the summer when the cod have fled elsewhere. Most are spartan, offering what might be described as bunk-house accommodation. However, some conversions (and modern versions) are in the de luxe category and charge over £100 per room per night. The normal charges range between £10 and £20 per person per night.

Although this might seem expensive by most camping standards it is very cheap by Norwegian standards and it does provide a form of camping which is highly appropriate to Arctic Norway. As a result the rorbu and sjohus tend to be heavily booked by Scandinavian visitors during the peak holiday month of July but in the months on either side of July there is usually plenty of available space (look for the sign 'ledig' for vacancy) and off-season bargains are often on offer.

For the first time camper to this area we recommend three basic options: the immediate area around Tromsø; the neighbouring island of Senja; and the offshore islands of Lofoten. These offer convenient local transport; a wide range of rorbu and sjohus accommodation; and - last but not least - a fascinating landscape which combines one of the world's most spectacular coastal mountain ranges with a thriving and picturesque fishing and sea faring community.

Tromsø Environs

There is one rather unexciting conventional campsite on the outskirts of Tromsø. If an overnight stay in the town is needed, we would recommend the central Skipperhuset, the last remaining guest house for sea captains. There is a large conventional site with a spectacular view across the fjord about 15 miles north of Tromsø; this site, Skittnelv, has a range of small plank huts for hire by the night. About 20 miles south of Tromsø there is a most unconventional site, Straumhella, where rooms are available in an outdoor museum of part-restored historic rural buildings, again in a spectacular location overlooking the turbulent sound, but to get the feel of authentic rorbu and sjohus camping one should venture forth by local Tromsbuss and ferry to either of two small islands, 35 miles north of Tromsø, Sandoy and Vannoy, each of which has one traditional fishery converted into simple camping facilities.

Senja

Easily reached either by Hurtigruten or by the faster and more frequent express ferry, Senja can be explored by bus. Scattered around the island, mostly on the wilder western shore, are almost a dozen rorbu/sjohus campsites. The tiny islet of Husoy, on the northern tip of Senja, has a particularly enchanting sjohus, famed for its fresh fish cafe. Expensive, but worth a visit just to witness the location, is Hamn, an isolated fishery now being transformed into a sjohus resort. Other good centres for Arcticamping are Mefjordvaer, Gryllerfjord and Torsken, with Hamn all on the north-west coast.

Lofoten

Separated from the mainland by the wide (and often wild) Vestfjord, the Lofoten group of islands can be reached easily by air or ferry from Tromsø, Senja or Bodo, or by road via the neighbouring Vesteralen island group. Even more dramatic than Senja, the jagged mountain backbone - long known to sailors as the Lofoten Wall - provides what must be one of the world's most spectacular camping scenes. Hugging the protected eastern shore is a series of fishing villages, where the fishing industry is still alive and well, and which offer several score sites providing rorbu and sjohus accommodation. See our selected site, no. 2465, on page 202. We were particularly impressed by the following (going down the coast from north-east to southwest):

Lofoten Rorbuferies at Kabelvag (only a few miles from the island capital of Svolvaer);

Henningsvaer Rorbuer and Giavers Sjohus at Henningsvaer;

Nusfjord Rorbu at the UNESCO - recognised village of Nusfjord;

The abundant choice of rorbu/sjohus accommodation at the picturesque adjacent villages of Reine and Hamnoy (among the best is Captain Nyboen's little establishment);

The youth hostels (Vandrerhjem) in Stamsund and Å, both in sjohus and both welcoming adults (although now both so popular among backpackers that many visitors have to be turned away).

There are also several good conventional campsites on Lofoten (see also no. 2465 on page 202). So impressive is the view from this site, Fredvang, that people travel from elsewhere in Lofoten just to stand and stare. The owners have installed several cabins for hire.

Information

There are three levels for provision of tourist information. At the national level the Norway Tourist Board (NORTRA) has offices in Britain at Charles House, Lower Regent Street, London SW1Y 4LR. At the regional level - corresponding to counties - Nordland Reiseliv, Storgaten 4A, PO Box 434, N-8001 Bodo, includes Lofoten in its territory; Troms Reiser, Storgaten 63, PO Box 1077, N 9001 Tromsø covers Tromsø, the surrounding area and Senja; and Finnmark Opplevelser, PO Box 1223, N-9501 Alta, covers the area to the north of Troms, including North Cape. Each of the three areas highlighted in this report has its own local tourist board and these can usually provide material of a much more detailed nature, including local bus timetables, large-scale local maps and accommodation guides; these are:

Tromsø Arrangements, 61/63/3 Storgaten, PO Box 312, N-9001 Tromsø;

Senja Tour, Radhusveien 1, PO Box 326, N-9301 Finnsnes and

Destination Lofoten, PO Box 210, N-8301 Svolvaer.

POLAND

The first Polish state was established about the year 1,000 and since that time has been subjected to invasions from its German, Russian and Austrian neighbours. The course of time has seen its borders reduce and expand and produced a race of rugged fighters, fierce patriots and a deeply religious nation. It was in the forefront in leading the revolt against Soviet influence with strikes and riots in the Gdansk shipyards which brought about the disintegration of communism in Eastern Europe in 1989. Now it struggles to come to terms with a free-market economy which encourages tourism to share its natural delights and historic associations. Although much of the country is flat and parts having some of the worst environment polluting industrial centres in Europe, the gentle beaches of the Baltic, the lake district in the northeast and the mountain region in the southeast have much to offer to tourists who are looking for something a little different.

For further information contact:

Poland National Tourist Office, Reno House, 310-312 Regent St, London W!R 5AJ
Tel: 020 7580 8811   E-mail: pnto@dial.pipex.com

Population
38,736,000 (1995); density 121 p/sq km.

Capital
Warsaw (Warszawa)

Climate
Cold winters, moderate summers.

Language
Polish. Some Russian, German and English.

Telephone
The code for Poland is 0048.

Time
GMT + 1 hour. BST + 1 hour in summer.

Currency
Zloty (Zl) divided into 100 groszy (gr). The New Zloty was introduced in 1995 (10,000 old Zl = 1 new Zl). The Old Zl was not valid after 1996. The import/export of Zl is prohibited.

Banks
Hours are Mon-Fri 0800 to 1800. Sat 0800 to 1400. Private banks `Kantor' 0900 to 1800 and frontier change offices will only exchange notes. Credit cards are gradually being introduced.

Public Holidays
New Year; Easter Mon; Labour Day; Constitution Day, 3 May; Corpus Christi; Assumption, 15 Aug; All Saints, 1 Nov; Independence Day, 11 Nov; Christmas, 25, 26 Dec.

Shops
Open 1000 to 1800 with some food shops from 0600 to mid afternoon.

Motoring
Wide main roads throughout. Mainly local numbers with increasing use of E numbers. Road surfaces very poor in parts, particularly in large towns often with stretches of uneven cobbles. More than 0.2% alcohol in blood illegal.

Fuel: There are frequent filling stations - diesel `NO' or `O'. There are few motorways.

Speed limits: In built-up areas 37 mph (60 kph), other roads 56 mph (90 kph), motorways 68 mph (110 kph). Caravans are limited to 44 mph (70 kph) outside built up areas.

Parking: In towns, only park in secure guarded parks.

Overnighting
Not advised outside organised camps and forbidden on sand dunes at the coast and in national parks (except on an organised campsite).

Useful Addresses
Polski Zwiazek Motorowy (PZM), FIA & AIT, 66 Kazimierzowska Street, Pl-02518 Warszawa. Tel: 22 499 361 or 212.
Office hours Mon-Fri 0745-1545.
Touring Office: Autotour ssrl, 85 Solec Street, 00950 Warszawa. Tel: 22 498 449.
Office hours Mon-Fri 0800-1600.

DISCOUNT VOUCHERS

Between pages 192/193 you will find two Discount Vouchers which will provide you with potential savings of more than the cost of the Guide itself! (valid 1 Jan - 31 Dec 2000 only)

Voucher A - Campsite Discount Voucher

This voucher entitles the holder to the relevant discounts or special offers at the sites in this guide that have a small Alan Rogers' logo by their entry. Retain this voucher for inspection at the campsite.

Voucher B - Travel and Breakdown Insurance

This voucher entitles the holder to a discount of 10% on Travel & Breakdown Insurance arrangements made via this Guide, as advertised between pages 160/161. To arrange cover please follow the instructions on the voucher.

POLAND

300 Camping Stoneczna Polana, Cieplice, nr Jelenia Góra

Well kept, secure site in southwest Poland, near the Czech border.

This is a small fenced site close to the health resort of Cieplice and the Karkonosze National Park and should provide a useful stop on your way through Poland. There are 70 individual touring pitches up to 100 sq.m. with electricity (6A) on flat grass. The sanitary facilities, which were very clean, offer free hot water to the vanity style washbasins (one cabin for ladies), showers and dishwashing. Highly recommended by a reader who found the Dutch managers most helpful, a full report will follow our inspection.

How to find it: Jelenia Góra is on road 3 (E65) about 25 km. from the Czech border. Cieplice is about 7 km. southwest of Jelenia Góra and can be accessed by turning east from road 3 onto road 366 at Piechowice and in 4.5 km. turn left at Sobieszów, site is about 3km.

General Details: Open 1 May - 30 Sept. Electrical connections 6A (some EEC connections, mainly 2 pin). Snacks (all season). Restaurant (May-Aug). Launderette. Children's play area. Satellite TV. Shop 400 m.

Charges 1999: Per person DM 4.00; child 2.00; car and caravan/tent 8.75; motorcaravan 8.50; electricity 4.50; dog 2.00; local tax 0.60

Reservations: Contact Peter or Liesbeth van Kinderen. Address: ul. Rataja 9, 58-560 Jelenia Góra - Cieplice. Tel: 075/52566.

301 Camping Lesny Nr. 52, Zielona Góra

Pleasant, quiet campsite on edge of town.

The Silesian town of Zielona Gora largely escaped damage during the war and, although without any notable sights, it has a variety of architectural styles, a population of 100,000 and has become the centre of the textile industry. The very pleasant campsite is 5 km. from the centre of town at the rear of the rather drab looking Hotel Lesny and one books in at the hotel reception which is open 24 hours. With tall trees on two sides of the square site and a small area for tents under the pines, it is a quiet site, ideal for a night stop in transit or for a longer stay if wishing to explore the southwest part of Poland. The hotel occupies one side of the camp with direct access to the 24 hour restaurant. The 200 flat tourist pitches are grass on sand between concrete access roads. They are not marked out although some are numbered and where you park is determined by electric connection boxes which have points for 4 units. The single, very good quality sanitary block is in the centre of the site. It has British WCs and hot water in washbasins, sinks and showers. There is no shop but these can be found about 10 mins walk away or in the town, together with sports facilities in the nearby stadium. With good security and surrounded by a wire fence, the gate is kept locked with keys being provided when one books in at reception.

How to find it: Site is about 5 km. north from the town centre off the no. 3/E65 road in the direction of Sulechow, near the stadium.

General Details: Open May - Oct. 14,000 sq.m. Hotel restaurant (24 hrs). Washing machine. Small play area.

Charges guide: Per person Zlts 5.00; car 2.00; caravan 5.00; motorcaravan 7.00; tent 5.00; electricity 5.00.

Reservations: Write to site. Address: 65 454 Zielona Góra, ul. Sulechowska 39. Tel: 068 254446 or 253636. FAX: 068 2704 29.

303 Motel-Camping International Nr. 111, Poznan

Popular quiet site in forest near lake.

Poznan is about half-way between Berlin and Warsaw and makes a convenient stop when travelling between these cities or on the way to the Baltic. Founded in the 9th century, this elegant city, centre of culture and learning, has grown over the centuries and is now home to some 600,000 souls and important today for its annual International Trade Fair. The Old Market Square with its beautiful Renaissance Town Hall is a great tourist attraction. Camp Nr 111 is nicely situated on the northwest outskirts of the town in a birch and pine forest near Lake Strzeszynskie, which is a popular watersports centre. The oblong site, under tall trees, has a neat, tidy air and pitches of varying sizes are grass on sand amidst the holiday bungalows. Some pitches would be difficult for very large caravans to manoeuvre but twin concrete tracks are provided to give hardstanding. There is a separate area for tents. The brick and tile sanitary block near camp entrance is old but clean with British WCs and hot water in washbasins, sinks and (small) showers. A restaurant with separate bar operates from June - Sept. and there is another by the lake with a small shop for basic food supplies in high season. Apart from watersports, where a lifeguard is on duty during high season, clay pigeon shooting is also available at this time. Other local attractions include walking and enjoying the countryside. Dutch groups rally here from time to time and English is spoken at reception.

How to find it: From Poznan centre, follow road 2/E30 towards Szczecin and then camp signs after about 7 km.

General Details: Open 1 May - 15 October. 30,000 sq.m. Restaurant. Bar. Family kitchen. Chemical disposal. Satellite TV. Swimming and watersports in nearby lake. Bungalows for hire. Motel near.

Charges guide: Per person Zlts. 2.35; tent 3.21 - 5.35; caravan 5.89 - 8.03; car 4.28; motorcaravan 14.98; electricity 6.72. Less 20% discount April/May and Sept/Oct.

Reservations: Write to site. Address: 60 480 Poznan, ul. Koszalinska. Tel: 061 848 3129. FAX: 061 848 3145.

305 Camping Tramp Nr. 33, Torun

Pleasant transit camp near river bridge.

Like so many Polish towns, Torun, once a Hanseatic trading centre, has a long, interesting and troubled history. Famous as the birth place of Copernicus, it is today a prosperous university city on the wide River Wisga with cultural and architectural interests. Camping Tramp has a pleasant appearance and lies in a basin below the level of the roads which run on both sides of the site. A variety of trees cover about half the camp where pitches with electricity mingle with holiday bungalows, with the other half being on an open meadow. Places, reached from hard access roads, are neither marked nor numbered but the position of electric boxes define where to go. The well built central sanitary block is tiled with British WCs and hot water in sinks, washbasins and showers. Like most Polish camps the showers are open (no curtains or doors) and lack dressing space. In high season a small bar/shop provides basic food supplies with shops and restaurants about 2 km. away in the town. The site is very well lit at night. The main E75 runs along one side of the camp just before a busy junction and river bridge resulting in continuous traffic noise although we did not find this too intrusive during our one night stay. Whilst not recommended as a holiday base, it makes a good night stop when travelling from between Germany and the Baltic coast.

How to find it: Site is on the south side of the main river bridge.

General Details: Open 1 May - 15 Sept. 26,000 sq.m. Small shop/snack bar.

Charges 1999: Per person Zlts 8.00; child (under 10 yrs) 4.00; caravan 20.00; tent 7.00; car 7.00; electricity 7.00. No credit cards or Eurocheques.

Reservations: Write to site. Address: ul. Kujawska 14, 87-100 Torun. Tel: 056/6547187. FAX: 056/28274.

307 Camping Lesny Nr. 21, Leba

Barely acceptable site in popular Baltic resort.

Situated at the mouth of a small river with a marina, and just north of the village of Leba, Camping Lesny is one of three which are about 500 m. from the sea and 200 m. from the village. Pleasantly situated in a quiet location with a number of mature trees, there is room for 200 units on the open meadow with pitches which are neither marked nor numbered, of grass on sand which could result in haphazard pitching when the camp is full. Although the camp is flat, the ground is uneven in places. There are two identical sanitary blocks which are rather old and, as they are not fully enclosed, rather draughty in windy weather. The facilities - British WCs and hot water in sinks, washbasins and showers - are very basic and not as good as we would normally expect, but are just about acceptable. As with so many camps in the former Warsaw Pact countries, the showers have no dressing space or place to put clothes. However, many caravanners and motor caravanners prefer to use their own provision and might like to do this here. A small bar/shop with basic supplies is open between 15 June to September with shops and restaurant in village.

How to find it: From road no. 6/E28 Koszalin-Wejherowo, turn north on the 214 at Lebork to Leba. Follow signs to camps on left on main street and continue to site.

General Details: Open 1 May - 30 Sept. 25,000 sq.m. Small bar/shop. Play area. Volleyball. Football. Table tennis. Washing machine. Community room with TV and cooking facilities.

Charges guide: Per person Zlts. 6.50; car 4.00; tent 3.00 - 4.00; caravan 10.00; motorcaravan 8.00; electricity 5.00; local tax: adult 0.60, child 0.30.

Reservations: Write to site in Polish ....! Address: 84 360 Leba, ul. Turystyczna 3. Tel: 059 661380.

309 Mister Camping Nr. 19, Sopot, nr Gdynia

Good site for visiting the Baltic coast mid-way between Gdansk and Gdynia.

Sopot is a popular seaside resort on the Gulf of Gdansk with a sandy beach, promenade and pier against a background of wooded hills. There are many attractions nearby including 'Opera-in-the-Woods' with 5,000 seats, an annual pop concert and other centres of historic interest. Camp 19 is set back from the beach and, by Polish standards, is a large site with 400 tourist pitches, some back to back on either side of concrete access roads, others in open meadows. Places are numbered but not marked out, of grass on sand and 300 pitches have electricity. With well mown grass, the site was neat and tidy. There are many tall trees around the camp although not much shade in camping areas. There are four sanitary units, two in the ground floors of adjacent hotels and two free standing blocks. Although these are old, they are clean and acceptable with British WCs and hot water in sinks, washbasins and small showers which have curtains but no dressing space. There is a small snack bar/restaurant in high season and the garage near the entrance has a good shop for basic supplies. Dutch clubs rally here and the whole camp has a pleasant quiet atmosphere, although there is some road noise near the entrance.

How to find it: Site is 2 km. north of Sopot on main road behind Shell garage.

General Details: Open 1 May - 30 Sept. 40,000 sq.m. Bar/restaurant, another at 50 m; Beach 300 m. Volleyball. Play area 300 m. Washing machine.

Charges 1999: Per unit incl. 2 adults + 1 child, with electricity Zlts. 46.00.

Reservations: Write to camp in German. Address: 81 718 Sopot, ul. Zamkowa Gora. Tel: 058/550 0445.

POLAND

311 Camping Stegna Nr. 180, Stegna, nr Gdansk

Wooded, hilly site on Baltic Sea.

With so much of Poland being very flat, it is surprising to find wooded hills so near the sea. Stegna is about 25 km. east of Gdansk in pleasant countryside and camp 180 is right by a sandy beach. The presence of a restaurant and kiosks at the camp entrance and the beach access suggest that it attracts many day visitors in summer. However, the beach stretches a long way so it should not become overcrowded. The very pleasant site has 100 terraced pitches, all with 10A electricity, on slopes under tall pines within sight and sound of the sea shore. Some of these are rather small depending on the disposition of the trees. The camp is rather let down by the state of the sanitary block. The WC sections are excellent but the parts with wash-basins and showers are very basic. However, there are three good showers at the end of the block which are kept locked with key available at reception. The site would suit those looking for a beach holiday or a respite from touring, particularly if you have your own washing facilities.

How to find it: From the no. 7/E77 Gdansk - Elbag road take the 502 at Nowy Dwor signed 'Stegna' to Stegna, turn right to enter village and then left at church signed 'Stegna Port' with camp sign.

General Details: Open 1 May - 15 Sept. 46,000 sq.m. Washing machine.

Charges guide: Per person Zlts. 6.00; child 4.50; tent 3.50 - 6.50; caravan 5.50 - 7.50; motorcaravan 10.00; awning 4.50 - 5.50; car 4.00 - 6.00; m/cycle 3.50; electricity 4.50; local tax: adult 0.50, child 0.25.

Reservations: Write to camp. Address 82 103 Stegna, ul. Morska 15. Tel: 055/478284.

313 Camping Kretowiny Nr. 247, Kretowiny, nr Morag

Excellent site on western edge of Mazurian Lake District.

Mazuria, 'land of a thousand lakes', is a very popular holiday region in the northeast corner of Poland. A sparsely populated area of thick forests, it attracts walkers, naturalists, watersports enthusiasts and campers. This, combined with much historical interest, makes it a good location for those who seek rest and relaxation away from noise and the trappings of modern tourism. Camping Kretowiny is a well organ-ised site and unusual in Poland in having individual pitches divided by hedges, rather than the over-crowding that can occur where no places are clearly defined. Scenically situated on Lake Jezioro Narie on a gentle slope, the 100 level, enclosed pitches are grass on sand, back to back between hard access roads and all have electrical connections. There is also an open lawn for about 60 tents. The two very good quality sanitary blocks are well tiled with British WCs and hot water in sinks, washbasins and on payment in the showers. There is a restaurant, bars and shops and limited entertainment in high season. The lake is used for swimming (lifeguard in summer), windsurfing, boating and fishing. Rooms and bungalows may be hired and the company who own the camp also have hotels nearby. The site has a most pleasant appear-ance with many trees, shrubs and flowers and is considered by many to be one of the most beautiful sites in the country.

How to find it: Site is signed about 7 km. south of Morag on the no. 527 Olsztyn-Morag road.

General Details: Open 1 May - 31 October. 20,000 sq.m. Restaurant, bars and shops. Watersports. Bicycle hire. Riding. Rooms and bungalows to let.

Charges 1999: Per person Zlts. 4.70; tent 4.80; caravan 6.00; car 4.70; motorcaravan 8.00; electricity 3.20.

Reservations: Write to camp. Address: 14 331 Zabi Rog, Kretowiny, Morag. Tel: 089 851618.

315 Camp Park Wilamowek, Grabowo

Quiet, isolated campsite by lake.

When you leave the hard road following signs for Camp Wilamowek along a narrow, undulating sand road, you do wonder just where you are going, but if you are looking for a restful camp on the shores of a lake amidst the forests of the Mazurian Lake District where you can fish, walk or enjoy boating, this might well suit you. The main building which houses reception, a fine restaurant with separate bar and rooms to let, is elevated above the lake with the excellent quality sanitary block nearby. The camping area is right down by the lake with a climb up to these facilities. The 55 grass on sand pitches all have elec-tricity, are neither numbered nor marked out and have little shade. There is a WC here. In winter, caravans are placed near the main building and use the toilet and cooking facilities of the apartments. The friendly owner speaks some English. Wilamowek is not for those who want bright lights and discos, but would suit those wishing to get away from it all.

How to find it: Site is signed at Sorkwty on road no. 16, 12 km. west of Mragowo.

General Details: Open all year. 80,000 sq.m. Bar. Restaurant. Basic supplies. Washing machine. Rooms to let. Watersports. Fishing. Walking.

Charges guide: Per person DM 3.00; child (6-16 yrs) 1.50; caravan 6.50; motorcaravan 9.00; tent 3.50 - 5.50; car 3.00; m/cycle 1.50; electricity 3.00; local tax 0.50.

Reservations: Write to camp. Address: 11 705 Grabowo. Tel: 089 84 8151.

POLAND

317 Hotel Camping Galindia Mazurski Eden, Jznota Bartlowo, nr Ukta

Very remote, quiet campsite with hotel on large lake.
Mazurski Eden is in the centre of the beautiful Mazurian Lake District surrounded by the interesting flora and fauna of the Piska forest. It is a quite amazing place approached by a 6 km. sand road, easily negotiable by caravans, with the entrance flanked by tall pine posts of carved figures. Wood carvings abound with statues by the waters edge, on buildings and inside the hotel. The camping area with room for 50 units, is grass on sand under tall trees which determine pitches, with electrical connection boxes topped with lamps for night illumination. The well built, wood clad, brick sanitary block stands to one side of the camping area and is an excellent provision with British WCs and hot water in sinks, washbasins and good showers. Dish and clothes washing facilities are outside but under cover. A wealth of activities is available with organised photographic safaris, canoeing and hiking trips, cycle excursions, visits to nature reserves with wolves, bison, beavers and other wild life. Sailing and other watersports are arranged and even fishing under the ice in winter. Parties, picnics and barbecues are offered with dancing and folk bands. Various national days are noted, with open air workshops for painters and sculptors and church festivals are celebrated in a family atmosphere. The Manager has a great interest in the social history of the ancient people of this area and this is reflected in the entertainment offered to group conferences being held in the hotel, to which campers are also invited.

How to find it: Turn south at Mikogajki on road no. 16 (Mragowo-Elk) and follow sign `Nw Most'. Continue on unmade road to camp.

General Details: Open all year. 80,000 sq.m. Restaurant. Grotto bar. Hotel. Watersports and entertainment.

Charges 1999: Per unit incl. 2 adults, 1 child, pitch, caravan and electricity Zlts. 49.

Reservations: Write to camp. Address: Hotel Camping Galindia Mazurski Eden, Iznota k/Mikolajek, 12 210 Ukta. Tel: 087/231669. FAX: as phone.

319 Camping Pension Kruska, Wygryny, nr Ukta

Simple campsite with excellent sanitary facilities by lake.
If looking for a cheaper option with just room for camping and no frills, this small site for about 70 units might suit. Pitches which are neither marked out nor numbered, are on slightly sloping ground between the Pension and the lake. There is no shade, units group around the electrical boxes and it could become crowded in high season. However, the brick built sanitary block is of excellent quality with British WCs and hot water in sinks, washbasins and very good showers. There is a small jetty by the lake which can be used for a variety of watersports. A separate bar and small restaurant are available in the Pension.

How to find it: Wygryny is signed from road no. 610 Ukta - Rciane-Nida.

General Details: Open all year. 12,000 sq.m. Bar. Restaurant. Shop 100 m. Swimming, fishing and watersports in lake. Rooms to rent.

Charges 1999: Per person DM 2.50; tent 3.00; caravan 5.00; car 2.00; motorcaravan 6.00; electricity 3.00.

Reservations: Write to camp in German. Address: Wygryny 52, 12 210 Ukta. Tel: 087/231597. FAX: as phone.

323 Camping Olemka Nr. 76, Czestochowa

Pleasant, leafy site near famous monastery.
Czestochowa's main claim to fame is the famous Jasna Gora monastery, one of Europe's main pilgrimage centres. The Black Madonna icon, displayed in the monastery, has attracted thousands of pilgrims for 600 years and still does today. Camp 76 is located right behind the huge monastery car and coach park, on a slight slope with level pitches of grass on sand and some hardstandings. Electricity boxes determine pitches which are otherwise not marked or numbered. There is room for about 100 units with the many mature trees which enhance the site, giving shade in some parts. The two identical toilet blocks which are quite acceptable but not luxurious, have British WCs and hot water in sinks, washbasins and rather small showers which, as with most in Poland, have no dressing space. There is a restaurant and shop in high season, with others a short distance away in the town. This site could make a useful night stop when passing through or for a day or two if visiting the monastery.

How to find it: Follow signs for 'Jasna Gora' (the monastery which being on a hill, is very obvious from most parts of town) and then camp signs.

General Details: Open all year. Bar/restaurant (main season). Shop. Washing machine. Drying room. Iron. Bungalows for rent.

Charges guide: Per caravan Zlts. 9.00; tent 5.00; car 6.00; motorcaravan 8.00; electricity 8.00 - 10.00.

Reservations: Write to camp. Address: 42 200 Czestochowa, ul. Olenki 10/50. Tel: 034 247495.

POLAND

321 Astur Camping Nr. 123, Warsaw (Warszawa)

Good city campsite in quiet location in south of town.

Camp 123 is inside the city boundary about 4 km. (20 minutes by bus) from the centre of the Polish capital. What is more, if approached from the south on roads 8/E67 or 7/E77 which merge on city outskirts, it is easy to find. Although a main road runs past the entrance, tennis courts on one side and a small park with a swimming pool on the other, along with the trees on the site, make this a very pleasant quiet base from which to explore this historic and interesting city. The site, with room for about 50 caravans and tents, is in two parts with an oblong section leading from reception and entrance and another square section beyond the sanitary provision and rented bungalows. Grass pitches on sand are on either side of concrete paved roads and all have electric connections. `Portacabin' type buildings house the toilet facilities which have British WCs and hot water in washbasins and small showers. Campers are given a key to use these as the other more open block is used by those renting bungalows where groups of children are sometimes brought to stay. There is a small hotel with a shop for basic supplies which also offers a limited menu of simple snack meals. The Vera Hotel opposite the site has a good restaurant.

How to find it: From the south on roads 7 and 8, continue into city to concrete monument in the centre of the tramway which divides carriageways. Turn left at traffic lights and camp is on left after Hotel Vera.

General Details: Open all year. 8,000 sq.m. Snack bar. Kiosk. Restaurant opposite. Shops 300 m. Tram 200 m. for city. Hotel rooms and bungalows to rent.

Charges guide: Per person Zlts. 7.00; caravan 7.00 - 8.00; tent 4.00 - 6.00; car 7.00 - 8.00; motorcaravan 12.00 - 15.00; electricity 8.50; m/cycle 5.00; cycle 1.00.

Reservations: Write to site. Address: 02 366 Warszawa (Warsaw), ul. Bitwy Warszawskiej 1920 N 15/17. Tel: 022 276778. FAX: 022 271472.

325 Auto Camping Nr. 215, Katowice

Good edge of town site for night stop.

Although the industrial complex of Katowice and the surrounding area is not a tourist centre, camp 215, being near a lake and 5 km. from the town centre in a leafy suburb, makes a good one night stop when travelling from the west to Kracow or for a few days if visiting Auschwitz. A main road runs along one corner of the camp but we did not notice undue noise during our one-night stop. Five rectangular grass lawns, separated by hard access roads provide unmarked pitches with some being under trees and some in the open and all having electricity. The well constructed, single toilet block stands to one side of the camp with British WCs and pre-mixed warm water in sinks, showers and half the washbasins. The block is heated in cool weather. There is a bar/restaurant/shop in high season, a club room with TV and a separate community room with kitchen, barbecue style grill, and tables and benches under cover. For recreation the site has a tennis court and sauna with a lake opposite for water sports.

How to find it: Site is signed at the junction of roads nos. 1 and 93 in Katowice between Czestochowa and Bielsko-Biala.

General Details: Open 1 May - 30 Sept. Restaurant. Shop. Club room (high season). Sauna. Tennis. Lake near.

Charges guide: Per person Zlts. 4.20; child (3-10 yrs) 2.10; caravan 5.00 - 8.00; car 4.00; tent 3.00; motorcaravan 7.00; m/cycle 2.00.

Reservations: Write to camp. Address: 48 266 Katowice. ul. Murchowska. Tel: 155/5388 or 156/5939.

For guidance on taking your dog on holiday to Europe, see page 348
For a list of sites where dogs are not accepted, see page 347

PORTUGAL

Portugal occupies the southwest corner of the Iberian peninsula and is a relatively small country, bordered by Spain in the north and east and the Atlantic coast in the south and west. However, for a small country it has tremendous variety both in its way of life and traditions. The Portuguese consider the Minho area in northern Portugal to be the most beautiful part of their country with its wooded mountain slopes and wild coast line, a rural and conservative region with picturesque towns. Central Portugal (the Estremadura region) with its monuments, evidence of its role in the country's history, has fertile rolling hills and adjoins the bull-breeding lands of Ribatejo (banks of the Tagus). The huge, sparsely populated plains south east of Lisbon, the cosmopolitan yet traditional capital, are dominated by vast cork plantations supplying nearly half the world's cork, but it is an impoverished area, and visitors usually head for Evora. The Algarve compensates for the dull plains south of Evora and has attracted more tourist development than the rest of the country. Portugal is therefore a land of contrasts - the sophisticated development of the Algarve as against the underdeveloped rural areas where time has stood still. There is a more liberal constitution now but the country is still poor and the cost of living generally low, although there has been a marked increase in prices in the Algarve. For British visitors, with large distances to travel, longer stays out of season are particularly attractive and most camp sites are actively encouraging this type of visitor.

ICEP Portuguese Trade & Tourism Office, 22/25a Sackville Street, London W1X 2LY
Tel: 020 7494 1441   Fax: 020 7494 1868   Brochures: 0900 1600 370 (60p per minute)

Population
9,900,000, density 106.6 per sq.km.

Capital
Lisbon (Lisboa)

Climate
The country enjoys a maritime climate with hot summers (sub-tropical in the South) and mild winters with comparatively low rainfall in the South, heavy rain in the North.

Language
Portuguese, but English is widely spoken in cities, towns and larger resorts. French can be useful.

Currency
The currency unit is the escudo, divided into 100 centavos and its symbol - the dollar sign - is written between the escudo and centavo units. Notes are issued for 5,000$00, 1,000$00, 500$00, and 50$00. Coins are issued for 50$00, 25$)), 20$00, 10$00, 5$00, 2$50, 1$00, and $50. One thousand escudos is a 'conto'.

Banks
Open Mon-Fri 08.30-11.45 and 13.00-14.45. Some large city banks operate a currency exchange service for tourists 18.30-23.00

Post Offices
Offices (Correios) normally open Mon-Fri 09.00-18.00, some larger ones on Saturday mornings.

Time
From the last Sunday in Sept to the last Sunday in March, the time in Portugal is GMT. During summer it is GMT + 1 hr (as the UK).

Telephone
To telephone Portugal from the UK dial 00 351. To the UK from Portugal dial 00 44. You need to be patient to get a line. Phone cards available (500 /1200 esc) from post offices, and tobacconists.

Public Holidays
New Year; Carnival (Shrove Tues); Good Fri; Liberty Day, 25 Apr; Labour Day; Corpus Christi; National Day, 10 June; Saints Days: Lisbon 13 June, Porto 24 June; Aassumption, 15 Aug; Republic Day 5 Oct; All Saints, 1 Nov; Immaculate Conception, 8 Dec; Christmas, 24/25//26 Dec.

Shops
Open Mon-Fri 0900-1300 and 1500-1900. Sat 0900-1300. Shopping centres are open much longer hours.

Food: Along the Atlantic coast fresh fish and shellfish are to be found on every menu - Caldeirada is a piquant mixed stew. However, Portugal is perhaps best known for Port and Maderia but don't forget the Vinho verde - marvellous with freshly caught sardines!

Motoring
The standard of roads is very variable - even some of the main roads can be very uneven. The authorities are making great efforts to improve matters, but other than on motorways or major highway routes (IP's) you should be prepared to make slow progress. Watch Portuguese drivers, as they tend to overtake when they feel like it.

Tolls: Tolls are levied on certain motorways (autoestradas) out of Lisbon, and upon southbound traffic at the Lisbon end of the giant 25th Abril bridge over the River Tagus.

Speed Limits: Car - Built-up areas 31 mph (50 kph), other roads 56 mph (90 kph), Motorways min. 25mph (40 kph) Max. 75mph (120 kph). For towing vehicles in built-up areas 31 mph (50 kph), other roads 43/50 mph (70/80 kph) and Motorways min. 25 mph (40 kph) max. 62mph (100 kph)

Fuel: Petrol stations are open from 0700-2200/2400 and some 24 hours. Credit cards are accepted but Visa is preferred. Use of a credit card incurs a surcharge of 100 esc.

Parking: Parked vehicles must face the same direction as moving traffic. Some towns have 'Blue Zones', discs available from ACP or the police.

Overnighting
Generally not allowed and fines may be imposed.

Useful Addresses

National Motoring Organisation
Automovel Club de Portugal (ACP), Rua Rosa Arauju 24-26, 1200 Lisbon. Tel: 563931. Office hours Mon-Fri 09.00-13.00, 14.00-17.00.

PORTUGAL - West Coast

801 Orbitur Camping Caminha, Mata do Camarido, nr Viana do Castelo

Pleasant site in northern Portugal close to the Spanish border.

This site is just a short 200 m. walk from the beach and has an attractive and peaceful setting in woods alongside the river estuary that marks the border with Spain. With a pleasant, open feel about it, fishing is possible in the estuary and bathing, either there or from the rather open, sandy beach. The site is partly shaded by tall pines with other small trees planted to mark the large sandy pitches, the roads throughout the site have recently been resurfaced and the water, electrical supply and lighting have been updated giving the site a much sharper image. The clean, well maintained and extended toilet block is centrally located. It has British style toilets, washbasins (cold water) with shelf, hook and mirror, and free hot showers, plus beach showers, extra dishwashing and laundry sinks (cold water). Gates locked at 11 pm.

How to find it: Turn off main coast road (N13-E50) along estuary 3 km. south of Caminha at sign to site.

General Details: Open 16 Jan - 30 Nov. Restaurant, snacks and supermarket (all May - Sept). Tennis. Children's playground. Fishing 1 km. Telephone and post box. Medical post. Laundry with ironing boards. Chemical disposal. Motorcaravan services. Bus service 800 m. English spoken.

Charges 1999: (to 31 May 2000) Per person esc. 620; child (5-10 yrs) 320; car 530; m/cycle 360; tent 490 - 850, motorcaravan 760 - 1,020, all acc. to size; boat 390; electricity 400. Off season discounts (up to 70%). Credit cards accepted.

Reservations: Contact Orbitur - Central de Reservas, Rua Diogo do Couto, 1-8o, 1100 Lisboa. Tel: 21/811 70 00 or 811 70 70. FAX: 21/814 80 45. E-mail: info@orbitur.pt.

802 Orbitur Camping Viana do Castelo, Cabdelo, nr Viana do Castelo

Site in northern Portugal with direct access to sandy beach.

This site is worth considering as it has the advantage of direct access, through a gate in the fence (locked at night), to an excellent sandy beach, popular for windsurfing. On slightly undulating, sandy ground, mostly with good shade, 225 pitches are not marked. It could be crowded in July/August. There are some hardstandings for caravans and electricity (16A) in all parts. Some pitches are very sandy. The clean, well kept sanitary facilities are in two blocks. Facilities for disabled campers have been added. Both blocks have mostly British style WCs, washbasins with cold water, but to date the second block has only cold water throughout. A pleasant restaurant overlooks the site and a ferry crosses the river to the town centre. The site is convenient for visiting the medieval town of Ponte de Lima (24 km), with its white-washed houses, towers and Roman bridge, and Viana do Castelo is famous for beautiful embroidery and festivals.

How to find it: On N13 coast road driving north to south drive through Viana do Castelo and over estuary bridge, turn immediately right off N13 towards Cabedelo and the sea. Site is the second camp signed

General Details: Open 16 Jan - 30 Nov. Supermarket, restaurant with terrace and bar (all April - Oct). Reading room with TV, video and fireplace. Children's playground. Adjacent swimming pool (open from 15/6). Tennis. Fishing 1 km. Riding 2 km. Telephone and post box. Medical post. Laundry. Gas supplies. Chemical disposal. Motorcaravan services. Bus service 200 m. English spoken. Bungalows for rent.

Charges 1999: (to 31 May 2000) Per person esc. 620; child (5-10 yrs) 310; car 530; m/cycle 360; tent 490 - 850, caravan 630 - 720, motorcaravan 760 - 1,020, all acc. to size; boat 390; electricity 400. Off season discounts (up to 70%). Credit cards accepted.

Reservations: Contact Orbitur - Central de Reservas, Rua Diogo do Couto, 1-8o, 1100 Lisboa. Tel: 21/811 70 00 or 811 70 70. FAX: 21/814 80 45. E-mail: info@orbitur.pt.

803 Orbitur Camping Rio Alto, Estela, nr Povoa de Varzim

Well managed site with good facilities adjacent to beach and golf course.

This site, which has recently been aquired by the Orbitur group, makes an excellent base for visiting Porto (by car), which is some 35 km. south of Estela. It takes around 700 units on sandy terrain, and is adjacent to what is virtually a private beach (access via a tunnel under dunes) and also to an 18 hole golf course. It has some hardstandings and electrical connections (5A) on most pitches. The area for tents is furthest from the beach and windswept, stunted pines give some shade. Four well equipped sanitary blocks have large shower cubicles including free hot water, British type WCs. The brown floors and decor give a very dark impression on entering, and there are strange, ill fitting plastic drain covers in all the showers. Washing machines and ironing facilities, plus units for disabled people. There is a restaurant, snack bar and, unusually for a seaside site, a swimming pool. The beach tunnel is open 9 am.-7 pm (lifeguard from 15 June).

How to find it: Site is reached via a cobbled road leading off EN13 towards the sea (just north of Estela), 12 km. north of Póvoa de Varzim. Travel 2.6 km. along narrow past plastic cloches (beware farm vehicles) and look right for Orbitur sign (well back). Take this right for 0.8 km. to site (beware speed bumps).

General Details: Open all year. Restaurant and snack bar, mini-market (all May - Sept). Bar (all year). Swimming pool (1/6-30/9). Tennis. Children's playground. Games room. TV. Golf 1 km. Telephone and post box. Medical post. Laundry. Car wash. Gas supplies. Chemical disposal. Entertainment in season. Bungalows to rent.

Charges 1999: (to 31 May 2000) Per person esc. 660; child (5-10 yrs) 330; car 720; m/cycle 420; tent 470 - 1,050, caravan 870 - 1,090, motorcaravan 1,130 - 1,170, all acc. to size; boat 710; electricity 380. Off season discounts (up to 70%). Credit cards accepted.

Reservations: Contact Orbitur - Central de Reservas, Rua Diogo do Couto, 1-8o, 1100 Lisboa. Tel: 21/811 70 00 or 811 70 70. FAX: 21/814 80 45. E-mail: info@orbitur.pt.

805 Orbitur Camping São Jacinto, São Jacinto

Small site in attractive location on a peninsula between sea and lagoon.

This site is in the Sao Jacinto nature reserve, on a peninsula between the Atlantic and the Barrinha, with views to the mountains beyond. The area is a weekend resort for locals and can be crowded in high season; therefore it may be difficult to find space in Jul/Aug, particularly for larger units. Swimming and fishing are both possible in the adjacent Ria, or the sea, 20 minutes walk from a guarded back gate. There is a private jetty for boats and the manager will organise hire of the 'Moliceiros' boats which are beautifully decorated and were used in days gone by to harvest seaweed for the land. It is not a large site, taking 169 units on unmarked pitches, but in most places trees help provide natural limits and shade. Two toilet blocks were spotlessly clean when inspected, and contain the usual facilities including free hot showers, dishwashing, laundry sinks, and a washing machine and ironing board in a separate part of the block. There is a small shop and a restaurant offering local food at reasonable prices and bar.

How to find it: Turn off N109 at Estarreja to Torreira and São Jacinto; bypassing Murtosa. Turn left over bridge and Sao Jacinto is further down the road on the right.

General Details: Open all year except Dec/Jan. Shop. Restaurant/bar (all May - Sept). Children's playground. Table tennis. Fishing 200 m. Bicycle hire 10 km. Telephone and post box. Laundry. Chemical disposal. Motorcaravan services. Bus service 20 m. Tourist information. Orbitur bungalows for rent.

Charges 1999: (to 31 May 2000) Per person esc. 590; child (5-10 yrs) 290; car 500; m/cycle 340; tent 470 - 820, caravan 590 - 670, motorcaravan 710 - 1,000, all acc. to size; boat 380; electricity 380. Off season discounts (up to 70%). Credit cards accepted.

Reservations: Contact Orbitur - Central de Reservas, Rua Diogo do Couto, 1-8o, 1100 Lisboa. Tel: 21/811 70 00 or 811 70 70. FAX: 21/814 80 45. E-mail: info@orbitur.pt.

807 Orbitur Camping Mira, Praia de Mira

Small well kept site on quiet inlet close to beach.

A seaside site set in pinewoods, Orbitur Camping Mira is situated to the south of Aveiro and Vagos, in a quieter and less crowded area. It fronts onto a lake at the head of the Ria de Mira, which eventually runs into the Aveiro Ria. A back gate leads directly to the sea and a wide quiet beach 300 m. away. The site has around 225 pitches which are not marked but with trees creating natural divisions. Electricity (5A) and water points are plentiful. The refurbished toilet blocks are clean, and include British style WCs, 14 free hot showers and washing machines. The site provides an inexpensive restaurant, snack bar, lounge bar and TV lounge. A medium sized supermarket is well stocked. Children's playground. The Mira Ria is fascinating with the brightly painted, decorative 'Moliceiros' mentioned above.

How to find it: Turn off N109 at Mira, about 27 km. south of Aveiro towards Praia de Mira. After about 5 km. a small sign shows a left turn which leads direct to the site. If you miss it, the site is signed from the beach resort. Make sure you ask for the Orbitur site if stuck - there are others here which are not as pleasant!

General Details: Open 1 Feb - 30 Nov. Shop and restaurant/bar (May - Sept). Snack bar. TV room. Laundry. Children's playground. Fishing 500 m. Bicycle hire or golf 1 km. Riding 5 km. Telephone and post box. Gas supplies. Chemical disposal. Motorcaravan services. Bus service 150 m. Orbitur bungalows to rent (11).

Charges 1999: (to 31 May 2000) Per person esc. 620; child (5-10 yrs) 310; car 530; m/cycle 360; tent 490 - 850, caravan 630 - 720, motorcaravan 760 - 1,020, all acc. to size; boat 390; electricity 400. Off season discounts (up to 70%). Credit cards accepted.

Reservations: Contact Orbitur - Central de Reservas, Rua Diogo do Couto, 1-8o, 1100 Lisboa. Tel: 21/811 70 00 or 811 70 70. FAX: 21/814 80 45. E-mail: info@orbitur.pt.

809 Orbitur Camping Figueira da Foz, Gala, nr Coimbra

Large site close to resort and with path to nearby private beach.

This site, for around 1,500 units, is on sandy terrain in a pinewood. Some pitches near the road may be rather noisy. One can drive or walk the 300 m. from the back of the site to a private beach; bathing needs caution when windy - the warden will advise. The site fills quickly in July/August and units may be very close together, but there should be plenty of room at other times. With 450 pitches for touring units, there are a few individual pitches with electricity and water (only 50 sq.m), the majority (70 sq.m) are unmarked with electrical connections throughout (15A). The three toilet blocks have British and Turkish style toilets, individual basins (some with hot water) and 16 free hot showers. All were clean at time of inspection despite obviously heavy usage. Besides the beach, Coimbra and nearby Roman remains are worth visiting.

How to find it: Site is 4 km. south of Figueira beyond the two rivers; turn off main road over 1 km. from bridge on southern edge of Gala, then 600 m. to site.

General Details: Open all year. Supermarket, restaurant/bar (all May - Sept). Lounge. Children's playground. Tennis. TV room. Fishing 1 km. Bicycle hire and riding 3 km. Telephone and post box. Laundry. Car wash area. Gas supplies. Chemical disposal. Motorcaravan services. Orbitur bungalows for hire (12).

Charges 1999: (to 31 May 2000) Per person esc. 620; child (5-10 yrs) 310; car 530; m/cycle 360; tent 490 - 850, caravan 630 - 720, motorcaravan 760 - 1,020, all acc. to size; boat 390; electricity 400. Off season discounts (up to 70%). Credit cards accepted.

Reservations: Contact Orbitur - Central de Reservas, Rua Diogo do Couto, 1-8o, 1100 Lisboa. Tel: 21/811 70 00 or 811 70 70. FAX: 21/814 80 45. E-mail: info@orbitur.pt.

PORTUGAL - West Coast

840 Campismo O Tamanco, nr Louriçal

Peaceful countryside site, with homely atmosphere, flowers and fruit trees.

The young Dutch owners, Irene and Hans, are sure to give you a warm welcome at this delightful little touring site. Recent additions include a new swimming pool, a bar and a restaurant (with vegetarian menu options). Courses in printing and sculpture are arranged at certain times of the year. There will also be entertainment for the children during the day. The 100 good sized pitches are separated by cordons of fruit trees, ornamental trees and flowering shrubs, on level grassy ground. There is electricity (16A) to 72 pitches and 5 pitches suitable for large motorhomes. A single sanitary block, just behind the owners house at the front of the site, provides spotlessly clean and generously sized facilities. These include British style WCs, pre-set showers and washbasins in cabins, with easy access for disabled visitors. There are dishwashing and laundry sinks outside, under cover. Hot water is free. A wide range of provisions and local produce are kept and there are bread and milk deliveries daily. The site is within walking distance of local shops and services. Market in nearby Louriçal every Sunday. One can fish or swim in a nearby lake, and the resort beaches are a short drive. Possibly some road noise on pitches at the front of the site.

How to find it: From N109/IC1 (Leira-Figuera de Foz) road, 25 km. south of Figuera in Matos de Carriço, turn on to N342 road (signed Louriçal 6 km). Site is 1.5 km. on left.

General Details: Open all year. TV room/lounge. Supermarket 800 m. Washing machine. Milk and bread deliveries daily. Bicycle hire. Chemical disposal. Bungalows for rent.

Charges 1999: Per adult Esc 350 - 400; child (up to 5 yrs) 150; tent, caravan or trailer 300; car 200; m/cycle 100; motorcaravan 500; dog 80; electricity 340. Discounts of 30% for 2 weeks, 60& for 4 weeks. No credit cards.

Reservations: Contact site. Address: O Tamanco Lda, Casas Brancas, 3100-231 Louriçal. Tel: 236/952551. FAX: as phone. E-mail: campismo.o.tamanco@mail.telepac.pt.

846 Camping-Caravanning Vale Paraiso, Nazaré

Well managed, shady site near the coast, open all year.

This pleasant campsite is by the main N242 road in 8 ha. of undulating pine woods and provides over 600 pitches, many of which are on sandy ground only suitable for tents. For other units there are around 250 individual pitches of varying size on harder ground with electrical connections (4/6/10A) available. Sanitary facilities are good, with free hot water for washbasins, showers, laundry and dishwashing sinks. Nearly all WCs are British style and there are facilities for disabled people and babies with baby baths to borrow. A range of sporting and leisure activities includes a good outdoor swimming pool with sunbathing areas and a children's playground. There is a supermarket selling a large selection of goods including camping equipment, a bar/snack bar, takeaway and a restaurant with regional cuisine. Several long beaches of white sand are 2-15 km. Animation for children, adult social events and evening entertainment are organised in season. Specific group entertainment is available on request. Nazaré is an old fishing village with narrow streets, a harbour and marina and many outdoor bars and cafés, with a lift to Sitio. There is much of historical interest in the area although the mild Atlantic climate is also conducive to just relaxing. The owners are keen to welcome British visitors and English is spoken.

How to find it: Site is 2 km. north of Nazaré, on the EN242 Marinha Grande road.

General Details: Open all year. Shop. Restaurant (March - Sept). Café/bar with TV (all year). Takeaway. Tabac. Supermarket (March - Sept). Swimming pool (March - Sept; free for children under 11 yrs). Petanque. Volleyball. Basketball. Football. Badminton. Leisure games. Amusement hall. Bicycle hire. Fishing 1.5 km. Riding 5 km. Washing machine and dryers. Safety deposit. Gas supplies. Chemical disposal. Motorcaravan services. Tourist information. E-mail and fax facilities (read free, send for a fee). Chalets and tents for rent.

Charges 1999: Per person esc.380 - 612; child (3-10 yrs) 180 - 281; tent 320 - 701; caravan 380 - 862; motorcaravan 441 - 962; car 320 - 501; m/cycle or trailer 221- 340; electricity 4A 300, 6A 400, 10A 500; pet 241 - 360; supplement for larger pitch 320 - 962. Credit cards accepted.

Reservations: Contact site. Address: EN 242, 2450-138 Nazaré. Tel: 262/561800. FAX: 262/561900. E-mail: camping.vp.nz@mail.telepac.pt.

810 Orbitur Camping Sao Pedro de Moel, nr Leira

Large and pleasant, seaside site close to small resort in central Portugal.

This quiet and attractive site is situated under tall pines, on the edge of the rather select small resort of São Pedro de Moel. The attractive, sandy beach, about 500 m. walk downhill from the site (you can take the car, although parking may be difficult in the town) is sheltered from the wind by low cliffs. The site has four clean toilet blocks with mainly British style toilets (some with bidets), individual basins (some with hot water) and free hot showers mostly in one block. The shady site can be crowded in July/Aug, when units might be rather too close for comfort, as the pitches are in blocks and unmarked. There are 500 pitches of which 400 have electrical connections (15A), a few used for permanent units. Although there are areas of soft sand, there should be no problem in finding a firm pitch. A large modern restaurant and bar are open all year, and a swimming pool was added recently.

How to find it: Site is 9 km. west of Marinha Grande, on the right as you enter São Pedro de Moel. The busy road from Marinha Grande is a combination of cobbles and very rough, badly patched surfaces - take it slowly!

General Details: Open all year. 75,000 sq.m. Supermarket, large restaurant and bar with terrace (May - Sept). Swimming pool (June - Sept). TV and games room. Children's playground. Tennis. Telephone and post box. Medical post. Laundry. Car wash. Gas supplies. Chemical disposal. Motorcaravan services. Bus service 100 m. Bungalows and mobile homes for rent.

Charges 1999: (to 31 May 2000) Per person esc. 620; child (5-10 yrs) 310; car 530; m/cycle 360; tent 490 - 850, caravan 630 - 720, motorcaravan 760 - 1,020, all acc. to size; boat 390; electricity 400. Off season discounts (up to 70%). Credit cards accepted.

Reservations: Contact Orbitur - Central de Reservas, Rua Diogo do Couto, 1-8o, 1100 Lisboa. Tel: 21/811 70 00 or 811 70 70. FAX: 21/814 80 45. E-mail: info@orbitur.pt.

845 Parque de Campismo Colina do Sol, S. Martinho do Porto

Well appointed touring site, near to beach, with own swimming pool.

Only 1 km. from the small town of S. Martinho do Porto, Colina do Sol has around 350 pitches marked by fruit and ornamental trees on grassy terraces. Electricity (6 or 10A) is available to all, although some may need long leads. The attractive entrance with its beds of bright flowers, is wide enough for even the largest of outfits. Two large, clean and modern sanitary blocks provide British style WCs (some with bidets), washbasins (some with hot water) and showers with dividers. Hot water is free throughout. Dishwashing and laundry sinks are outside but covered and ironing facilities are available. A well stocked supermarket and a restaurant, cafeteria, and bar are open May - Sept, with a delightful paved terrace beside the large clean swimming pools, one for children. The beach is at the rear of the camp, with access via a gate which is locked at night (22.00-08.00). The site is a convenient base for exploring the Costa de Prata and for excursions to old town of Leiria, with its crenellated walls towering high above the rock faces, and to the famous shrine of Fátima. Market in S. Martinho do Porto on Sunday.

How to find it: Turn from EN 242 (Caldas-Nazaré) road northeast of San Martinho do Porto. Site clearly signed.

General Details: Open all year except 15/12-15/1. Supermarket. Restaurant/cafe with bar (high season). Swimming pool. Lounge. Children's playground. Telephone and post box. Medical post. Motorcaravan services.

Charges guide: Per adult esc. 575; child (4-10 yrs) 275; small tent 495, large 585; caravan or motorcaravan 715 - 880; car 475; m/cycle 320; electricity 320.

Reservations: Contact site. Address: 2465 Sao Martinho do Porto. Tel: 262/989764. FAX: 262/989763.

811 Orbitur Camping Valado, Nazaré

Popular site close to busy resort on central west coast.

This site is on the edge of the old, traditional fishing port of Nazaré which has now become something of a holiday resort and popular with coach parties. The large beach in the town, about 2 km. downhill (steeply) from the site, is sheltered by headlands and provides good bathing. The campsite is on undulating ground under tall pine trees, takes 503 units and, although some smallish individual pitches with electricity and water can be reserved, the bulk of the site is not marked out and units could be close together especially during July/Aug. About 375 electrical connections are available. There are three toilet blocks with British and Turkish style WCs, washbasins and showers (cold water) and 17 free hot showers with seat, divider and curtain, plus dishwashing and laundry sinks under cover. All were very clean when inspected.

How to find it: Site is on the Nazaré - Alcobaca road, 2 km. east of Nazaré.

General Details: Open 1 Feb - 30 Nov. Supermarket. Bar, snack bar and restaurant with terrace (May - Sep). TV/general room. Children's playground. Tennis. Fishing and bicycle hire 2 km. Telephone and post box. Medical post. Laundry. Car wash. Gas supplies. Chemical dsposal. Motorcaravan services. English spoken. Bus service 20 m. Bungalows and mobile homes for hire.

Charges 1999: (to 31 May 2000) Per person esc. 590; child (5-10 yrs) 290; car 500; m/cycle 340; tent 470 - 820, caravan 590 - 670, motorcaravan 710 - 1,000, all acc. to size; boat 380; electricity 380. Off season discounts (up to 70%). Credit cards accepted.

Reservations: Contact Orbitur - Central de Reservas, Rua Diogo do Couto, 1-8o, 1100 Lisboa. Tel: 21/811 70 00 or 811 70 70. FAX: 21/814 80 45. E-mail: info@orbitur.pt.

PORTUGAL - West Coast

813 Orbitur Camping Guincho, Areia, nr Cascais

Large site convenient for visiting Lisbon, with nearby beach.

Although this is a popular site for permanent or long stay caravans with 1,295 pitches, it is nevertheless quite attractively laid out among low pine trees and with the new A5 autostrada connection to Lisbon (30 km), it provides a useful alternative to sites nearer the city. Located behind sand dunes and a wide, sandy but somewhat windswept beach, the site offers a wide range of facilities. These include a bar/restaurant, supermarket, general lounge with pool tables, electronic games, TV room and laundry. There is a choice of pitches (small - mainly about 50 sq.m.) mostly with electricity (15A), although siting amongst the trees may be tricky, particularly when the site is full. The three sanitary blocks are in the older style but are clean and tidy. These provide British type WCs, washbasins with cold water and all have free hot showers. There are facilities for dishwashing (cold water), washing machines, a dryer and facilities for disabled visitors.

How to find it: Approach from either direction on N247. Turn inland 6½ km. west of Cascais at camp sign. Travelling direct from Lisbon site is signed at the end of the A5 autopista.

General Details: Open all year. 70,000 sq.m. Supermarket, Restaurant, bar and terrace (March - Oct). General room with TV. Tennis. Children's playground. Entertainment in summer. Excursions. Fishing 1 km. Riding 500 m. Golf 3 km. Telephone and post box. Medical post. Laundry. Car wash. Gas uspplies. Chemical disposal. Motorcaravan services. Bungalows and mobile homes for rent.

Charges 1999: (to 31 May 2000) Per person esc. 720; child (5-10 yrs) 360; car 640; m/cycle 440; tent 600 - 980, caravan 760 - 850, motorcaravan 910 - 1,180, all acc. to size; boat 580; electricity 420. Off season discounts (up to 70%). Credit cards accepted.

Reservations: Contact Orbitur - Central de Reservas, Rua Diogo do Couto, 1-8o, 1100 Lisboa. Tel: 21/811 70 00 or 811 70 70. FAX: 21/814 80 45. E-mail: info@orbitur.pt.

814 Lisboa Camping, Parque de Campismo de Monsanto

see colour advert opposite page 224

Excellent new municipal site outside the city with outstanding amenities.

This site was rebuilt completely for Expo 98 and is without doubt the finest in Portugal. It is expensive but you get a lot for your money. The wide entrance, with ponds, fountains is impressive, with trees, lawns and flowering shrubs leading up to the swimming pool, is probably this site's most attractive feature. The site is on sloping ground with many modern terraces and is well shaded by trees and shrubs. The 170 motorcaravan pitches are on concrete hardstanding, each with its own services including a large wooden picnic table and chairs! There is a separate area for tents. The eight immaculate solar powered sanitary blocks are superb. They contain all facilities that campers, including disabled people, could wish for. The whole site is designed to be accessible to disabled campers. The two pools with a snack bar are excellent, as is the on site Roman theatre which functions in season. There is a small supermarket on site but also a Jumbo shopping centre a 5 minute walk. The site is 8 km. from central Lisbon with two bus routes giving a regular service, and 10 km. from a decent beach. It is the closest site for visiting Lisbon

How to find it: From Lisbon take the motorway towards Estoril, the camp is signed from junction 4 onto the 1C17, the site has huge signs off this road at the first exit to Buraca. The site is immediately on the right.

General Details: Open all year. 340,000 sq.m. Electrical connections. Shops and restaurants. Hairdressers. Tennis. Minigolf. Sports field. 2 Playgrounds Two swimming pools. Roman theatre General and TV rooms. Launderette. Post office. Bank. Medical post. Car wash. Organised excursions. Chalets to rent (70).

Charges 1999: Per adult esc. 560 - 800; child (6-11) 420 - 600; tent 560 - 1,000, acc. to size and season; caravan 840 - 1,200; car 350 - 500; motorcaravan 840 - 1,200; m/cycle 280 - 400.

Reservations: not made. Address: Estrada da Circunvalacao, 1400-061 Lisboa. Tel: 21/7609620/22. FAX: 21/7609633.

815 Orbitur Camping Costa da Caparica, Costa da Caparica, nr Lisbon

Site with many permanent units and small touring section at coastal resort 20 km. from Lisbon.

This is very much a site for 600 permanent caravans but it has very easy access to Lisbon (10 km.) via the motorway, by bus or even by bus and ferry if you wish. It is situated in a small resort, favoured by the Portuguese themselves, which has all the usual amenities plus a good sandy beach (200 m. from the site) and promenade walks. The small area for touring units includes some special pitches for motorcaravans. Two of the three toilet blocks have mostly British style toilets, washbasins with cold water and free hot showers. The third is older and has cold water throughout. Facilities are provided for disabled campers.

How to find it: After crossing the Tagus bridge (toll) on A2 motorway going south, immediately take turning for Caparica and Trafaria. At 7 km. marker on IC120 turn right (Orbitur sign) the site is at the second roundabout.

General Details: Open all year. Supermarket. Large bar/restaurant (Feb-Nov). Children's playground. Some organised activities and shows in season - outdoor disco/entertainment area. Excursions. Fishing 1 km. Riding 4 km. Golf 5 km. Washing machine. Treatment room; doctor calls daily in season. Gas supplies. Chemical disposal. Motorcaravan services. Bungalows and mobile homes for hire.

Charges 1999: (to 31 May 2000) Per person esc. 720; child (5-10 yrs) 360; car 640; m/cycle 440; tent 600 - 980, caravan 760 - 850, motorcaravan 910 - 1,180, all acc. to size; boat 580; electricity 420. Off season discounts (up to 70%). Credit cards accepted.

Reservations: Contact Orbitur - Central de Reservas, Rua Diogo do Couto, 1-8o, 1100 Lisboa. Tel: 21/811 70 00 or 811 70 70. FAX: 21/814 80 45. E-mail: info@orbitur.pt.

816 Parque de Campismo de Porto Covo, Porto Covo, nr Sines

Site close to fine beaches of the Costa Azul, with own pools.

This is a site in a popular seaside resort where a fairly large proportion of the pitches are occupied by Portuguese units. However, it has a sense of space as you pass the security barrier to reception which is part of an uncluttered and attractively designed square area. The pitches are somewhat small but are reasonably level, all have electricity (5/10A), some with limited shade from young trees. The sanitary blocks are clean and have free hot showers and the usual amenities plus cold outside showers, footbaths and ironing facilities. A mini-market stocks essentials and some souvenirs or a short walk to the village gives access to shops, bars and restaurants. There is recreation room with games and a TV, and a children's playground. If you do not want to venture out to the beach then the swimming pools are behind the restaurant. A jolly bar and restaurant with terrace operate on the site with a varied Portuguese menu (popular with the locals) at reasonable prices. The beaches are a short walk and feature steep cliffs.

How to find it: From E120-1 Cercal - Sines road (note: the road changes from the E120 at Tanganheira). Take left turn (southwest) to Porto Covo and site is well signed on the left.

General Details: Open all year. Restaurant/bar. Mini-market in season. Children's play area. Swimming pools. Barbecue areas. Telephones. Bungalows for rent. Bus service to Porto Covo and Lisbon from site.

Charges guide: Per adult esc. 470; child 235; tent 455 - 595; car 365; m/cycle 255; caravan 495 - 700; boat 350 - 410. All plus 7% VAT. Credit cards accepted.

Reservations: Write to site. Address: 7520-436 Porto Covo. Tel: 269/95136. FAX: 269/95239.

818 Parque de Campismo de Milfontes, Vila Nova de Milfontes

Pleasant site with good facilities, within walking distance of town and beach.

This popular site has the advantages of being open all year and being within walking distance of the town and beach. As such, it makes a perfect base for those visiting out of main season or for long winter stays. It has around 500 shady pitches on sandy terrain, which are marked out and divided by hedges and paved paths. Some pitches may be too small for caravan and car and cars may have to be parked in an internal car park. Electricity (6A) is available in all parts. The four toilet blocks are clean and well maintained and two have suites for disabled campers with ramped entrances. There is a good supply of mainly British style WCs, bidets, washbasins (some with hot water), hot and cold showers, footbaths and some children's facilities, in a mix of combinations and styles. Hot water is free. Also dishwashing and laundry sinks with cold water outside under cover. The site also has a restaurant and bar complex and a well stocked supermarket. There are opportunities for watersports fishing, canoeing and swimming from the resort beaches.

How to find it: From N120 coast road at Cercal, turn on to E390 and continue into Vila Nova de Milfontes. Turn right in town and follow camp signs. Site is on right-hand side at end of no through road. Do not confuse it with another site on left just before the entrance to Milfontes.

General Details: Open all year. Supermarket (1/4-30/9). Bar and snacks (1/4-30/9). Restaurant (June-Sept). TV room. Children's playground. Fishing and bicycle hire 1 km. Telephone. Laundry. Car wash. Chemical disposal. Motorcaravan services. Mobile homes and cabins for hire. English spoken. Dogs not permitted.

Charges guide: Per person esc 300 - 540; child (5-10 yrs) 150 - 270; tent 220 - 450; caravan or motorcaravan: small 285 - 490, large 340 - 550; car 180 - 370; m/cycle 160 - 285; electricity 300. Credit cards accepted.

Reservations: Contact site. Address: 7645 Vila Nova de Milfontes. Tel: 283/96140 or 96693. FAX: 283/96104.

819 Camping Sitava, Vila Nova de Milfontes

Large site with beach access, shaded by pines.

This is a large site with a huge entrance off the road and then a 500 m. drive through a pine forest to reception. It has good sized, level pitches, although the numerous tall pines concentrate the mind when manoeuvring. There are two large, identical sanitary blocks which are cheerful in appearance and have an array of equipment. This includes British style WCs and free hot showers. Another large building houses reception, a bar with terrace and restaurant with an unusual internal terrace. Also a TV/games area. A hundred metres into the site is a fountain in a circle of lawn, which in turn is in the centre of a covered walkway supporting blooms of vivid colours. Further into the site there is another bar and snack bar with a first floor terrace and underneath a well stocked supermarket and charcuterie. A large children's play area is opposite reception. Unusually this and other sports facilities such as tennis courts are just outside the boundary of the site. The beaches are 600 m. through a rear entrance and are gently shelving, with rocks and cliffs surrounding a fine sandy bay. Torches necessary for some pitches.

How to find it: From E201-1 Cercal - Sines road (note: road changes from the E120 at Tanganheira), take the left (southwest) to Porto Covo and follow signs (south) to Vila Nova de Milfontes. Site is well signed on the left.

General Details: Open all year. Restaurant/bar with snacks (all year). Large restaurant (summer only). Shop. Large children's play area. Table tennis. TV lounge. 5 a side soccer pitches. Tennis. Barbecue area. Telephone. First aid area. Car wash. Buses to local village and Lisbon (3 hour journey).

Charges guide: Per adult ptas 520; child 260; tent 500 - 620; car 300; caravan 620; motorcaravan 640; electricity 330. Plus 7% VAT. Credit cards accepted.

Reservations: Contact site. Address: Sitava Turismo, SA Brejo da Zimbreira, 7645 Vila Nova de Milfontes. Tel: 283/899343, 899 569, 899 or 570. FAX: 283/899571. E-mail: sitava@mail.telepac.pt.

PORTUGAL - Algarve

841 Parque de Campismo de Armação de Pêra

Modern, attractive site with excellent facilities and own pool.

This site has a wide attractive entrance with a large external parking area. The 1,200 pitches are on level grassy sand, marked by trees which provide some shade, and are easily accessed from tarmac and gravel roads. Electricity (10A) is available for most pitches. Three modern, clean and well maintained sanitary blocks, provide British and Turkish style WCs, some with bidets, washbasins, and showers with hot water on payment. There is a dedicated suite for disabled campers. The restaurant, self service café and bar, and well stocked supermarket should cater for most needs, and you can relax around the swimming pools (lifeguard in summer). The disco near to the entrance and café complex is soundproofed which should ensure a peaceful night for non-revellers. The well maintained children's play area has a safe, sandy base. The site is within easy reach of Albufeira, Portimão and is 40 km. from Faro and makes an excellent base for long or short stays in this region and for winter sun-seekers. Fishing, hunting and watersports nearby.

How to find it: Turn off EN125/ IC4 road in Alcantarilha, taking the EN269-1 towards the coast. Site is on left side before Armação de Pêra. There are other sites in the area, so be sure to find the right one.

General Details: Open all year. Supermarket. Restaurant (1/5 - 30/9). Self service café. Three bars (1/5-30/9). Kiosk. Games and TV rooms. Tennis. Children's playground. Swimming pool (all year; entrance fee July - Sept). Disco. Medical centre. Telephone and post box. Car wash. Laundry. Bungalows for hire.

Charges guide: Per adult esc. 550; child (4-10 yrs) 275; tent or awning 500 - 650, acc. to size; caravan or motorcaravan 550 - 700; m/cycle 400; electricity 400. Less 50% in low season for 3 day stay or more

Reservations: Write to site. Address: 8365 Armação de Pêra. Tel: 282/312296 or 312260. FAX 282/315379.

843 Parque de Campismo de Sagres, Sagres

Pleasant and extremely well maintained site at western tip of the Algarve.

Not very far from the lighthouse in the unspoilt southwest corner of Portugal, this site has 960 pitches for tents and 120 for tourers, they are sandy pitches and located amongst pine trees, which give good shade. There are some hardstandings with electricity (5A) throughout. The three modern, spacious sanitary blocks are excellently maintained and cleaned, providing hot and cold showers (hot showers are free), British style WCs, bidets, washbasins with cold water and footbaths. Dishwashing and laundry sinks are under cover outside the block. The restaurant, bar and cafe/grill provide reasonably priced meals including breakfast, and there is a well stocked supermarket. This is a good site for winter sun, or as a base for exploring this `Land's End' region of Portugal, away from the more crowded resorts. The beaches and the town of Sagres (the departure point of the Portuguese navigators) with its fort, are a short drive.

How to find it: Turn off road EN268, approx 2 km before Sagres, site is signed.

General Details: Open all year. Supermarket (1/4-1/11). Restaurant/bar and cafe/grill (all 1/4-30/9). TV room. Bicycle hire. Barbecue area. Children's playground. Fishing. Golf 12 km. Medical post. Washing machines and ironing boards. Car wash. Chemical disposal. Motorcaravan services. English spoken.

Charges 1999: Per adult esc. 500 - 700; child (4-10 yrs) 250 - 350; small tent or awning 400 - 600, medium 500 - 750, large 600 - 850; caravan small 500 - 750, large 600 - 850; car 250 - 450; m/cycle 150 - 250; motorcaravan small 600 - 800, large 600 - 950; electricity 250 - 350. Less 40% for 3 days or more 1/10 - 31/5.

Reservations: Write to site. Address: 8650 Vila do Bispo (Algarve). Tel: 282/624371. FAX: 282/624445.

820 Orbitur Camping Valverde, Praia da Luz, nr Lagos

Large, well run site with many individual pitches and good range of amenities.

A little over 1 km. from the village of Praia da Luz and its beach and about 7 km. from Lagos, this site is certainly worth considering for your stay in the Algarve. Taking around 675 units, it has 600 individual, numbered pitches, mostly 40-60 sq.m., some larger - up to 100 sq.m. which are enclosed by hedges. All are on flat ground or broad terraces with good shade in most parts from established trees and shrubs. Six large, clean, toilet blocks, have British style WCs, washbasins and sinks, some with cold water only, and free hot showers. Special units for disabled people. On site is a swimming pool with slide (200 sq.m) and children's pool (under 10's free, adults charged). This is an excellent site with well maintained installations and good security. There are 40 bungalows and 15 caravans for hire. It attracts a good number of long-term winter visitors, and the site is extremely well managed by Sra. Pinto, who is helpful and friendly.

How to find it: Fork left on N125 road 3 km. west of Lagos to Praia da Luz and site is under 1 km.

General Details: Open all year. 100,000 sq.m. Supermarket, shops, restaurant and bar complex with both self-service and waiter service in season (all April - Oct). Takeaway. Coffee shop. Swimming pool with water slide and children's pool (all year). Playground. Tennis court with markings for other sports. General room with TV. Excursions. Fishing and bicycle hire 3 km. Golf 10 km. Telephone and post box. Laundry. Medical post. Chemical disposal. Motorcaravan services. Bungalows, apartments and caravans to let.

Charges 1999: (to 31 May 2000) Per person esc. 750; child (5-10 yrs) 380; car 640; m/cycle 440; tent 610 - 990, caravan 780 - 860, motorcaravan 950 - 1,190, all acc. to size; boat 580; electricity 420. Off season discounts (up to 70%). Credit cards accepted.

Reservations: Contact Orbitur - Central de Reservas, Rua Diogo do Couto, 1-8o, 1100 Lisboa. Tel: 21/811 70 00 or 811 70 70. FAX: 21/814 80 45. E-mail: info@orbitur.pt.

LISBOΛCAMPING
EN BUNGALOWS

No other city has its lungs as close to its heart as Lisbon.

900 hectares of green just a stone's throw away from the city centre.

800 camping accommodation units

170 equipped lots

A forest site - totally refurbished and open all the year round.

Swimming pool, restaurant, outdoor cafés, 2 multi-purpose sport centres, mini golf, shoppingarea, and games rooms.

70 bungalows

Swimming pool

For further information please contact us at:
Estrada da Circunvalação
1500 - 171 - LISBOA
Tel: 351-21-762 31 00
Fax: 351-21-762 31 05/6

Turismo de Lisboa

Portugal

ORBITUR

The name to remember for camping in Portugal !

The most beautiful chain of 23 camping sites with 334 bungalows.
Sea, sun woodland and a mild climate.
The warmest welcome from North to South of Portugal.

1 Angeiras
2 Arganil
3 Caminha
4 Castro Daire
5 Costa de Caparica
6 Évora
7 Gala (Fig. da Foz)
8 Guarda
9 Guincho
10 Ilha de Armona
11 Luso
12 Madalena (Gaia)
13 Mira
14 Montargil
15 Portalegre
16 Quarteira
17 Rio Alto (Póvoa de Varzim)
18 São Jacinto
19 S. Pedro de Moel
20 Valado (Nazaré)
21 Valverde (Lagos)
22 Viana do Castelo
23 Viseu

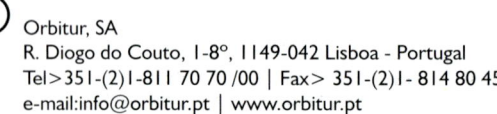

▲ *Camping*   ■ *Bungalows*   ● *Camp. + Bungalows*

ⓘ Orbitur, SA
R. Diogo do Couto, 1-8°, 1149-042 Lisboa - Portugal
Tel> 351-(2)1-811 70 70 /00 | Fax> 351-(2)1- 814 80 45
e-mail:info@orbitur.pt | www.orbitur.pt

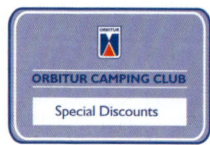

ORBITUR CAMPING CLUB
Special Discounts

821 Camping Albufeira, Albufeira, nr Faro

Attractive, high quality site, with many amenities, close to town and beaches.

The spacious entrance to this site will accommodate the largest of units (watch for severe speed bumps at the barrier!). One of the better sites on the Algarve, with installations and amenities well above the usual standard, and of which the English speaking staff are justifiably proud. The 1,500 pitches are on fairly flat ground with some terracing, trees and shrubs give reasonable shade in most parts. There are some marked and numbered pitches of 50-80 sq.m. Winter stays are encouraged, with many facilities remaining open including a heated pool. An attractively designed complex of traditional Portuguese style buildings on the hill forms the central area of the site, has pleasant views and is surrounded by a variety of flowers, shrubs, well watered lawns and there is a fountain. The waiter and self-service restaurants, a pizzeria, bars and a sound proofed disco, have views across the three swimming pools and a waterslide pool. There are five clean toilet blocks, some a little tired, and all have British style toilets, washbasins, controllable showers, laundry and dishwashing sinks with free hot water throughout. They may be hard pressed when the site is full (July/Aug) and are distant from some pitches.

How to find it: From N125 coast road or N264 (from Lisbon) at new junctions follow signs to 'Albufeira'. Site is approx. 1 km. from junctions, on left.

General Details: Open all year. Supermarket and shops. Restaurants. Bars. Disco. Swimming pool complex. Tabac. Laundry. TV room. Hairdresser. Safe deposit. ATM service. Car rental office. Children's playground. Excursions and organised entertainment. Bicycles/motorbikes for hire. Tennis. Minigolf. Sports park. Telephone and post box. Medical post. Car wash. Bus service to Albufeira (2 km). Caravans and apartments for rent.

Charges guide: Per adult Esc 795; child (4-10) 395; car 795; caravan or tent 795 - 895, acc. to size; motor-caravan 1170 - 1,790; m/cycle 530; electricity 450. (50% discount winter season).

Reservations: are made to give individual pitch, no deposit or fee. Address: 8200 Albufeira (Algarve). Tel: 289/587629. FAX: 289/587633.

823 Camping Olhão, Pinheiros de Marim, nr Olhão

Large, well laid out and acceptable site in eastern Algarve.

This site, taking around 1,000 units and open all year, has mature trees to provide reasonable shade. The pitches are marked, numbered and in rows divided by shrubs with electricity and water to all parts. Permanent and long stay units take 20% of the pitches and the tourist pitches fill up quickly June and August, so arrive early. Amenities include very pleasant swimming pools and tennis courts (fees for both), a very good restaurant/ bar (open all year), all very popular with the local Portuguese, and a café/bar with TV and games room. The eleven sanitary blocks are adeuqate and were clean when seen, with facilities for disabled campers in one block, are specifically sited to be a maximum of 50 m. from any pitch. Each has British style toilets, bidets and free hot showers. There is some noise nuisance from an adjacent railway. Mobile homes for rent. The large, sandy beaches in this area are on offshore islands reached by ferry and are, as a result, relatively quiet; some are reserved for naturists. There is a bus service to the nearest ferry at Olhao. This site can get very busy in peak periods and maintenance can be variable. It is perhaps best visited out of season.

How to find it: Just over 1 km. east of Olhão, on EN125, take turn to Pinheiros de Marim. Site is 300 m. on left.

General Details: Open all year, as are all facilities. Supermarket. Kiosk. Restaurant. Bar. Café and general room with TV. Children's playgrounds. Swimming pool (all year). Tennis. Volleyball. Bicycle hire. Fishing 2 km. Riding 1 km. Golf 20 km. Telephone and post box. Medical post. Laundry. Car wash area. Chemical disposal. Bus service 50 m. Mobile homes and caravans to hire.

Charges 2000: Per adult esc. 300 - 600; child (5-12 yrs) 150 - 300; car 250 - 500; tent 200 - 420, 300 - 600 or 500 - 1,000, acc. to size; caravan or motorcaravan 400 - 800 or 600 - 1,200; m/cycle 125 - 250; car 250 - 500; electricity 210. Less for longer winter stays. Credit cards accepted.

Reservations: Contact site. Address: 8700 Olhao (Algarve). Tel: 289/700300. FAX 289/700390. E-mail: sbsicamping@mail.telepac.pt.

PORTUGAL - Algarve / Inland

822 Orbitur Camping, Quarteira, nr Faro

Algarve site near the sea on the outskirts of Quarteira.

This is a large attractive site on undulating ground with some terracing, taking 795 units. On the outskirts of the popular Algarve resort of Quarteira, it is 600 m. from a sandy beach which stretches for 1 km. to the town centre. Many of the unmarked pitches have shade from tall trees and there are a few small individual pitches of 50 sq.m. with electricity and water for reservation. There are 680 electrical connections (15A). The five sanitary blocks provide British and Turkish style toilets, individual washbasins with cold water and free hot showers plus facilities for disabled visitors. Like others along this coast, the site encourages long winter stays. The swimming pools are excellent, with pools for adults and children, plus a water slide (high season). A large restaurant and a supermarket have separate entrances for local trade.

How to find it: Turn off N125 south towards Quarteira in Almancil (8 km west of Faro). Site is 5 km.

General Details: Open all year. Supermarket, self-service restaurant (Feb - Nov). Separate takeaway (from late May). Swimming pools (June - Sept). General room with bar and TV. Tennis. Kiosk. Open air disco. Fishing 1 km. Bicycle hire (summer) 1 km. Golf 4 km. Medical treatment room. Doctor on call. Washing machines. Gas supplies. Car wash area. Chemical disposal. Motorcaravan services. Orbitur bungalows for hire (99).

Charges 1999: (to 31 May 2000) Per person esc. 750; child (5-10 yrs) 380; car 640; m/cycle 440; tent 610 - 990, caravan 780 - 860, motorcaravan 950 - 1,190, all acc. to size; boat 580; electricity 420. Off season discounts (up to 70%). Credit cards accepted.

Reservations: Contact Orbitur - Central de Reservas, Rua Diogo do Couto, 1-8o, 1100 Lisboa. Tel: 21/811 70 00 or 811 70 70. FAX: 21/814 80 45. E-mail: info@orbitur.pt.

844 Parque de Campismo Quintos dos Carriços, Praia de Salema

Attractive, peaceful, valley site with dedicated naturist area, in unspoilt western Algarve.

A traditional tiled Portugese style entrance leads you down a steep incline into this excellent and well maintained site which has a village atmosphere. The site has been developed over the years by the Dutch owner and his family. It is spread over two valleys (which are real sun-traps), with the 300 partially terraced pitches marked and divided by trees and shrubs (oleanders and roses). A small stream meanders through the site. The more remote part of this site is dedicated to naturists. Although the site is lit torches may be useful in more remote areas. The four sanitary blocks are modern, spacious, well tiled with quality fittings, and are spotlessly clean. These provide British style WCs, washbasins with cold water, and hot showers on payment. There are dishwashing and laundry sinks and a washing machine plus an excellent facility for disabled people. Open daily (including Sundays) is a well stocked mini-market. The restaurant and bar open daily in season. A popular site for summer and winter sun-worshipper, within easy driving distance of resorts, the many fine beaches in the region provide ample opportunities for diving, swimming and fishing. Also nearby are tennis, squash, riding golf and there are excellent walks from the site.

How to find it: Turn off RN125 (Lagos-Sagres) road at junction to Salema (17 km. from Lagos); site is signed.

General Details: Open all year. Mini-market (all year). Restaurant (daily 1/3-15/10). Bar (once a week only 15/10-1/3). TV room. Telephone and post box. Bicycles, scooters and m/cycles for hire. Fishing and golf 1 km. Riding 8 km. Safety deposit. Money exchange. Laundry. Car wash. Gas supplies. Chemical disposal. Apartments and chalets for rent. Bus service from site.

Charges 2000: Per adult esc. 680; child 340; tent 680 - 880; caravan 940; car 680; m/cycle 480; motorcaravan 1,000 - 1,200; electricity 250. Discounts for long winter stays. Credit cards accepted.

Reservations: Contact site. Address: Praia de Salema, Vila de Bispo, 8650-196 Budens (Algarve). Tel: 282/695201, 695400 or 695401. FAX: 282/695122.

834 Orbitur Camping Evora, Evora

Well equipped site with swimming pool, close to historic walled town.

Situated some 1.5 km. from the historic former provincial capital, this is one of the most modern and well equipped sites in the Orbitur chain with the benefit of a good sized, new swimming pool and one for children (separate charge). A pleasantly constructed small restaurant on site is also popular with locals. The manager will organise special menus and entertainment for groups if requested. The two refurbished sanitary blocks provide free hot showers and modern British style WCs. Most of the 285 good-sized touring pitches have 15A electricity and those in the older part of the site have well developed shade. There is a children's play area and a tennis court. A small market sells essentials and a range of local specialities. It is a useful site from which to explore the town and surrounding area with its megalithic monuments.

How to find it: Site is 1½ km. southwest of the town on the N380 road to Alcacovas.

General Details: Open all year. Restaurant, bar, snack bar and shop (May - Oct). Swimming pool (June - Sept). Tennis. Children's play area. Bicycle hire 2 km. Riding or golf 5 km. Laundry. Gas supplies. Chemical disposal. Motorcaravan services. Mobile homes for rent.

Charges 1999: (to 31 May 2000) Per person esc. 620; child (5-10 yrs) 310; car 530; m/cycle 360; tent 490 - 850, caravan 630 - 720, motorcaravan 760 - 1,020, all acc. to size; boat 390; electricity 400. Off season discounts (up to 70%). Credit cards accepted.

Reservations: Contact Orbitur - Central de Reservas, Rua Diogo do Couto, 1-8o, 1100 Lisboa. Tel: 21/811 70 00 or 811 70 70. FAX: 21/814 80 45. E-mail: info@orbitur.pt.

835 Camping Markadia, Barragem de Odivelas, nr Alvito

Superb, lakeside touring site, in unspoilt setting.
This site will appeal most to those nature lovers who want to 'get away from it all' and to those who enjoy country pursuits such as walking, fishing or riding. The lake is in fact a 1,000 hectare reservoir, and more than 120 species of birds can be found in the area. The open countryside and lake provide excellent views and a very pleasant environment, albeit somewhat remote. This is an outstanding site by any standards with some of the best installations to be found on a campsite anywhere in Europe. The stellar views in the very low ambient lighting are wonderful at night, the site is lit but a torch is required. There are 130 unmarked pitches on undulating grassy ground with ample 16A electrical connections. The friendly Dutch owner has carefully planted the site so each pitch has its own oak tree to provide shade. Four very modern, very clean, and superbly equipped sanitary blocks, are built in traditional Portuguese style. They have controllable showers, British style WCs and bidets, washbasins, dishwashing and laundry sinks (open air); free hot water throughout. Washing machines and ironing boards. The bar/restaurant with terrace is open daily in season but weekends only in winter. One can swim in the reservoir (free) and rowing boats, pedaloes and windsurfers are for hire. Facilities and amenities may be reduced outside the main season.

How to find it: From N2 between Torrao and Ferreira do Alentejo, take E257 2 km. north of Odivelas for 3.5 km. Turn right towards Barragam, site is 3 km. on left after crossing head of reservoir, follow wide dirt track.

General Details: Open all year. Bar. Restaurant (Oct - March weekends only). Shop (all year). Lounge. Children's playground. Fishing. Boat hire. Bicycle hire. Tennis. Riding. Laundry. Telephone. Medical post. Car wash. Chemical disposal. Motorcaravan services. Apartments for rent. Dogs not accepted in July/Aug.

Charges 1999: Per adult esc. 720; child (5-10 yrs) 360; tent or caravan 720; car or m/cycle 720; motorcaravan 1,440; electricity 360. Discounts of 10-20% outside June - Aug, and for longer stays. No credit cards.

Reservations: are made; contact site for details. Address: Aptdo 17, Barragem de Odivelas, 7920 Alvito. Tel: 284/763141. FAX: 284/763102.

836 Parque Municipal de Campismo, Barragem de Idanha-a-Nova

Smart, good value site, with pool and quality installations, in attractive location near Castelo Branco.
This very attractive, well laid out site is unlike most municipal sites with its high level of sophistication . It is located in quiet, unspoilt countryside close to a reservoir, near the small town of Idanha-a-Nova. The site has around 500 spacious unmarked pitches on wide grassy terraces and there is a little shade from young trees. Electricity (16A) is included in the price. The four large sanitary blocks, built in the traditional Portuguese style, provide a plentiful supply of British style WCs (some with bidets), washbasins, some in private cabins, free hot showers with dividers, shelves and hooks, foot baths and facilities for the disabled. Dishwashing and laundry sinks (cold water). Amenities include tennis courts with stadium-style spectator seating and a medium sized swimming pool with child's pool, together with several playgrounds. A good supermarket, restaurant, bar and terrace complex is located centrally, open in high season.

How to find it: Approach from south using N240, turn off at Ladoeiro on N354 and follow signs to Barragem and site. Do not approach via main road.

General Details: Open all year. Supermarket (1/7-30/9). Cafe, bar and restaurant (1/7-30/9). Swimming pool. Tennis courts. TV room. Vending machines Washing machines Laundry. Telephone and post box. Medical post. Car wash. Canoe hire. Bungalows for hire.

Charges guide: Per adult esc. 250; child (4-10 yrs) 125; tent (small) 125, (large) 375; caravan 500; car 250; m/cycle 125; motorcaravan 500; electricity 120. Discounts for long stay off season.

Reservations: Write to site. Address: Barragem de Idanha-a-Nova, 6060 Idanha-a-Nova. Tel: 27/22793.

832 Orbitur Camping Guarda, Guarda

Small inland site perched on a hill-top, with a good panoramic view.
This site takes around 135 units and is just 50 km. from the Spanish frontier, on perhaps the most popular route for entering Portugal, so it makes a good transit site. The well fenced and gated site is mostly covered by mature pine trees, and is on sloping, and in places terraced ground partially surrounding a public park. There are some level pitches for caravans and the site is well lit at night. Electricity is available (long leads may be required) and plentiful water points. The two sanitary blocks give an adequate supply with British and Turkish style toilets, washbasins with cold water and three free hot showers per sex. The level of service in the restaurant/bar is tailored to demand. Guarda has some interesting historic buildings and the region is noted for its colourful markets, Serra cheese, handicrafts, religious festivals and winter sports.

How to find it: Site is 5 km. from bypass road on a hill-top on western side of town. Follow signs for centre of Guarda then camp signs.

General Details: Open 1 March - 31Oct. Mini-market, restaurant and bar (May - Sept). General room with TV. Telephone. Post box. Laundry. Gas suppplies. Chemical disposal. Motorcaravan services. Bus service 50 m.

Charges 1999: (to 31 May 2000) Per person esc. 590; child (5-10 yrs) 290; car 500; m/cycle 340; tent 470 - 820, caravan 590 - 670, motorcaravan 710 - 1,000, all acc. to size; boat 380; electricity 380. Off season discounts (up to 70%). Credit cards accepted.

Reservations: Contact Orbitur - Central de Reservas, Rua Diogo do Couto, 1-8o, 1100 Lisboa. Tel: 21/811 70 00 or 811 70 70. FAX: 21/814 80 45. E-mail: info@orbitur.pt.

PORTUGAL - Inland

831 Orbitur Camping Castro Daire, Castro Daire

Traditional small touring site beside the Carvalhal spa.

Situated in the mountains in the Dao Lafóes tourist region, between Castro Daire and Visieu, only the main road (somewhat noisy but quite well screened) separates the site from the sulphur spa and hotel complex. This has a swimming pool and tennis court (open from June). The site is small, very attractive with a garden-like atmosphere, and has two modern and clean sanitary blocks. These have free hot showers, British toilets and washbasins with cold water. There are sinks for clothes and washing up at various points through the site. The pitches are on level grass, terraced in places, with some shade from pine and oak trees. There are 60 electrical connections (15A). A small purpose built building has an open fire to barbecue food and there is a snack bar. This is a comfortable base from which one can explore the historic old spa towns and villages of this most beautiful and unspoilt mountain region.

How to find it: Site is 5 km. south of Castro Daire beside the A2 road to Visieu.

General Details: Open 1 June - 30 Sept. Bar (July/Aug). Barbecue house. Children's playground. Fishing 6 km. Telephone and post box. Laundry. Tourist information.

Charges 1999: (to 31 May 2000) Per person esc. 590; child (5-10 yrs) 290; car 500; m/cycle 340; tent 470 - 820, caravan 590 - 670, motorcaravan 710 - 1,000, all acc. to size; boat 380; electricity 380. Off season discounts (up to 70%). Credit cards accepted.

Reservations: Contact Orbitur - Central de Reservas, Rua Diogo do Couto, 1-8o, 1100 Lisboa. Tel: 21/811 70 00 or 811 70 70. FAX: 21/814 80 45. E-mail: info@orbitur.pt.

833 Orbitur Camping Arganil, Sarzedo, nr Arganil

Quiet, inland site attractively situated on the hillside above the river Alva.

The site is located in the hamlet of Sarzedo, some 2 km. from the town of Arganil. A spacious and well planned site, delightfully situated among pine trees above the River Alva where one can swim, fish, canoe and windsurf. The 150 pitches, most with electricity (15A), are of a reasonable size and are mainly on flat sandy grass terraces shaded by tall trees. The site is kept beautifully clean and neat. Access roads are tarmac. There is an excellent restaurant serving local food and an attached bar with terrace, plus a shop (closed Tuesdays) and a children's play area. Sanitary facilities are clean and well maintained, with mainly British WCs, controllable free hot showers, washbasins in semi-private partitioned cabins and hairdressing area with electric sockets. Ramped entrances make it suitable for the disabled. Laundry facilities include washing machines. The site also has five attractive timber chalets, with views over the river and countryside, for rent. There is a swimming pool in Arganil.

How to find it: From EN17 Guarda-Coimbra road, take EN342 towards Arganil. Site is signed in village of Sarzedo, about 2 km. northwest of Arganil.

General Details: Open all year. Bar and snacks (all year). Children's play area. TV room. Tennis. Fishing 6 km. Telephone and post box. Laundry. Car wash. Bus service 50 m. Bungalows for rent.

Charges 1999: (to 31 May 2000) Per person esc. 590; child (5-10 yrs) 290; car 500; m/cycle 340; tent 470 - 820, caravan 590 - 670, motorcaravan 710 - 1,000, all acc. to size; boat 380; electricity 380. Off season discounts (up to 70%). Credit cards accepted.

Reservations: Contact Orbitur - Central de Reservas, Rua Diogo do Couto, 1-8o, 1100 Lisboa. Tel: 21/811 70 00 or 811 70 70. FAX: 21/814 80 45. E-mail: info@orbitur.pt.

837 Parque Campismo de Cerdeira, Campo do Gerês

Impressive, quiet, 'away from it all' site with excellent facilities, in National Park.

Placed in the National Park of Peneda Gerês, amidst spectacular mountain scenery, this excellent modern site offers modern facilities in a truly natural area. The National Park is home to all manner of flora, fauna and wildlife, including the roebuck, weasel, badger, wolf and wild boar. The well fenced, quiet, site has some 350 good sized unmarked, mostly level, grassy pitches in a shady woodland setting. Electricity (5/10A) is available for most pitches, though some long leads may be required. Although the site is lit, a torch would be useful. There are three very clean sanitary blocks with mixed style WCs, washbasins and controllable showers. Hot water is free throughout. Dishwashing and laundry sinks under cover. A very large timber, lodge style complex which is tastefully designed and decorated near the site entrance provides a restaurant serving a full range of good value meals (including breakfasts). The restaurant was extended in '99. There is a bar and terrace, mini-market and a small playground for children. There are opportunities in the area for fishing, riding, swimming, canoeing, mountain biking and climbing.

How to find it: From N103 (Braga-Chaves road), turn left at 101 signed Vilaverde. Turn right to Terras de Bouro on road 308 and 205-3. From Terras de Bouro take 307 to Covide, turn left at campsite sign, site is 5 km.

General Details: Open all year. Mini-market. Restaurant/bar (1/4-15/10, plus weekends and holidays). Children's playground. Bicycle hire. Fishing or riding 800 m. TV room. Telephone and post box. Medical post. Laundry. Gas supplies. Chemical disposal. Tourist information. Bungalows for hire. Good English spoken.

Charges 2000: Per adult esc. 600 - 700; child (5-11 yrs) 350 - 450; tent 500 - 900; caravan 700 -1,000; car 600 - 700; m/cycle 350 - 450; motorcaravan 900 - 1,200; electricity 4A 400, 10A 600. Credit cards accepted.

Reservations: Contact site. Address: 4840 Campo do Gerês. Tel: 253/351005 or 357065. FAX: 253/353315.

838 Parque Natural de Vilar de Mouros, nr Seixas

Traditional, small and friendly site, in quiet country location, with own pool.
Located some 15 minutes walk (downhill) from the village of Vilar de Mouros and very close to the Spanish border, this small site is ideal for those looking for a more traditional campsite. The 45 marked pitches for caravans and motorcaravans, all with electricity (2 or 5A), are on slightly sloping, grassy terraces, with a separate unmarked area for tents, all set amongst trees and vines on a hillside. There are two toilet blocks, very much in the quainter, older Portuguese style, providing British style WCs (some with bidets), washbasins (cold water), and free hot showers, they also had soap and paper towel dispensers. Dishwashing and laundry sinks (cold water) under cover also a washing machine and dryer in a separate building. The site has a good range of other amenities which include a tennis court, unusual small stone swimming pool, children's pool (free to campers), and a small children's play area. There is a good cafe/bar (open 8 am.-11 pm), takeaway service, a self-service restaurant with shady terrace, and a mini-market. By far the most popular attraction is the regular Saturday evening organised gastronomic and folk-lore trips (with free mini-bus transport) to the site owners own hotel 2 km. away. There are mobile homes and hotel rooms for hire. French and a little English spoken.

How to find it: Site is signed from the N13, just north of Seixas, turn towards Vilar de Mouros. Site is on right just before village.

General Details: Open all year. Mini-market. Cafe/bar. Self-service restaurant. Swimming pool. Tennis court. TV room. Washing machine. Children's pool and playground. Telephone and post box. Medical post. Bicycle hire. Local folklore entertainment trips. Hotel rooms and mobile homes for rent.

Charges 1999: Per adult esc. 550; child 270; tent (small) 500, (large) 500; caravan 500 - 600; car 450; m/cycle 300; motorcaravan 500 - 600; electricity 400

Reservations: Contact site. Address: 4910 Vilar de Mouros. Tel: 258/727472. FAX: as phone.

THE ORBITUR CHAIN OF CAMPSITES

see colour advert
opposite page 225

Orbitur is the largest Portugese campsite chain which has sites all over Portugal and boasts a central booking agency and e-mail service which may be used to avoid disappointment at peak season. There are 22 sites which have prime camping pitches and supporting facilities along with bungalows and mobile homes for rent. The following sites have not been inspected for this guide:

Orbitur Camping Visieu   **Orbitur Camping Angeiras**

Orbitur Camping Montargil   **Orbitur Camping Portalegre**

Orbitur Camping Madalena-Gaia

Orbitur has been offering a quality camping service for over 30 years, always concentrating on quality of service. The Orbitur sites are well maintained and are in good locations. All sites strive to satisfy the needs of all campers, including handicapped people. Children's needs and playgrounds are common to all sites and entertainment is becoming the norm at all sites in summer. Orbitur also offers a vast range of sports facilities along with a programme of providing swimming pools for most sites. Health and safety is of prime importance with first aid centres being provided along with efficient and effective safety systems which comply with local control authorities.

Reservations for any of the sites should be made through the central office (not to individual sites); write to Orbitur at:

Orbitur - Central de Reservas,
Rua Diogo do Couto, 1-8o, 1149-042 Lisboa.
Tel: 21/811 70 00 or 811 70 70. FAX: 21/814 80 45.
E-mail: info@orbitur.pt. Internet: http://www.orbitur.pt.

Membership of the Orbitur Camping Club, taken either with your booking or at any site (free for pensioners) grants a 10% discount on site charges. Camp charges are reasonable and there is a general reduction of 40% to 70% (depending on length of stay) from October to March inclusive.

"Orbitur has been offering a quality camping service for over 30 years, always concentrating on quality of service. The Orbitur sites are well maintained and are in good locations. All sites strive to satisfy the needs of all campers, including handicapped people. Children's needs and playgrounds are common to all sites and entertainment is becoming the norm at all sites in summer. Orbitur also offers a vast range of sports facilities along with a programme of providing swimming pools for most sites. Health and safety is of prime importance with first aid centres being provided along with efficient and effective safety systems which comply with local control authorities."   **Colin Samms**

SLOVAKIA

Slovakia became an independent republic on 1 Jan 1993, following the split of the former Czechoslovakia into its two component parts - the Czech Republic in the west and Slovakia in the east. In central Europe, it shares boundaries with the Czech Republic, Austria, Poland, Hungary and the Ukraine. It is hilly and picturesque, with historic castles, thick forests, mountain streams, valleys and lakes, and the culture reflects a strong Hungarian influence. The Danube flows briefly into Slovakia and then along the border with Hungary. Spa towns and good skiing are winter attractions. For further information contact:

**Slovak Tourist Centre, 25 Kensington Palace Gardens, London W8 4QY
Tel: 020 7243 0803   Fax: 020 7243 0803   E-mail: skemb@netcomuk.co.uk**

Population
5,403,500 (94); density 110 per sq. km.

Capital
Bratislava

Climate
Cold winters and mild summers. Hot summers and some rain in the eastern lowlands.

Language
The official language is Slovak. Some English or German in hotels and restaurants.

Currency
Koruna or Crown (Skr) = 100 halierov. Notes are Sk. 50, 100, 200, 500 and 1000; coins are Sk. 1, 2, 5,10,20 and 50.

Banks
Hours are Mon-Fri 08.00-13.00 and 14.00-17.00; banks are closed on Sat. Only notes exchanged at most border change offices

Credit cards: The major ones can be used to obtain currency and in some hotels, restaurants shops and some petrol stations in towns and tourist areas. Travellers cheques and Eurocheques are widely accepted.

Post Offices
Offices are open Mon-Sat 08.00-16.00.

Telephones
The dialling code for Slovakia is 0042.

Time
GMT plus one hour, BST + 1 in summer.

Public Holidays
New Year; Easter Mon; May Day; Liberation Day, 8 May; Saints Day, 5 July; Festival Day, 6 July; 28 Oct; Christmas, 24, 25, 26 Dec.

Shops
Open Mon-Fri 09.00-12.00 and 14.00-18.00. Some remain open at midday. Sat: 09.00-midday.

Motoring
The major route runs from Bratislava via Trengin, Banska, Bystrica, Zilina and Poprad to Presov. A full UK driving licence is acceptable. Petrol stations on international roads and in main towns are open 24 hours.

Tolls: A windscreen sticker which is valid for a year must be purchased at the border crossing for use on certain motorways.

Speed limits: Caravans 31 mph (50 kph) in built up areas and 50 mph (80 kph) on all other roads. Motorhomes (3.5 tons) 31 mph (50 kph) in built up areas 56 mph (90 kph) other roads and 69 mph (110 kph) on motorways.

Parking: Vehicles must be parked on the right.

Overnighting
Not allowed on open land. Elsewhere permissible where a toilet is in situ.

Useful Addresses
HEPEX Ltd (the agency for tourism), P.O. 32, 94501 Komarno, Slovakia.
National Motoring Organisation: Ustredni Automotoklub SR Wolkrova ut 4, 85101 Bratislava. Tel: 07 850 911.

490 Autocamping Trusalová, Turany

Small, quiet site on edge of National Park.

Autocamping Trusalová is right on the southern edge of the Malá Fatra National Park, northeast of the historic town of Martin which has much to offer to tourists, despite being best known for the engineering works which produced most of the tanks for the Warsaw Pact countries before the recent revolution and change to a more democratic regime. Paths from the site lead into the Park making it an ideal base for walkers and serious hikers who wish to enjoy this lovely region. The site is in two halves, one on the left of entrance and the other behind reception with each having its own old, but clean and acceptable, sanitary provision of British WCs and hot water in basins, sinks and showers. Surrounded by trees with a stream rushing along one side, pitches are grass from a hard road with room for about 80 units. The area behind reception is on a slight slope. There is a bar just outside the camp and shops in the village about 3 km. away. There is a large, outdoor chess board, volleyball, table tennis and a TV lounge. Each section has a covered barbecue area with tables and chairs. Information on the area is available from reception. We received a friendly welcome from the German speaking staff. A quiet, orderly and pleasant camp.

How to find it: Turn north at Motorest Fatra on the road 18/E50 near village of Turany to camp.

General Details: Open 1 June - 15 Sept. 40,000 sq.m. Volleyball. Table tennis. TV lounge. Children's playground. Bicycle hire. Restaurants 500 m. or 1 km. Chemical disposal. Bungalows to rent.

Charges 1999: Per person Sks. 60; child (6-15 yrs) 30; tent 45 - 65; caravan 80; motorcaravan 110; car 55; m/cycle 35; electricity 60; dog 40; local tax 10. No credit cards.

Reservations: Write to site in German. Address: 03853 Turany. Tel: 0842/292636 or 292667.

495 Autocamping Zlaté piesky, Bratislava

Edge of town site by large lake.

Bratislava undoubtedly has charm, being on the Danube and having a number of interesting buildings and churches in its centre. However, industry around the city, particularly en-route to the camp from the south, presents an ugly picture and gives no hints of the hidden charms. Zlate piesky (golden sands) is part of a large, lakeside sports complex which is also used during the day in summer by local residents. The site is on the edge of town with 200 touring pitches, 120 with electrical connections, on level grass under tall trees. Twenty well equipped and many more simple bungalows for hire are spread around the site. There are two restaurants, one with waiter service, the other self service and many small snack bars around the site and the adjoining lakeside recreation area. The lake is used for swimming and watersports with pedaloes for hire and there is a fitness area in the park. There are four sanitary blocks, two for campers and two for day visitors and these may be hard pressed during high season. For a night stop or a short stay, if you are looking for a quieter site with fewer facilities, Intercamp may suit.

How to find it: Follow signs on road no. 61 for Zillina and airport and pick up signs for camp. Zlaté piesky is on the left on entering the sports area, Intercamp is on the right.

General Details: Open 1 May - 15 Oct. 90,000 sq.m. Restaurants. Snack bars. Shops. Lake for swimming and watersports with large beach area. Table tennis. Minigolf. Children's play areas. Room with billiards and electronic games. Disco. Doctor calls. Chemical disposal. Bungalows and chalets to rent.

Charges 1999: Per person Sks. 100; child (6-15 yrs) 50; caravan 90; motorcaravan 100; tent 90; dog 50; electricity 80. No credit cards.

Reservations: Write to site. Address: Senecká cesta 2, 821 04 Bratislava. Tel: 07/4425 7373 or 4445 0592. FAX: 07/4425 7373. E-mail: kempi@netax.sk.

494 Autocamping Neresnica, Zvolen

Small site on main route from Budapest to Warsaw.

If you are travelling through Slovakia from Hungary to Poland and looking for a night stop or exploring the central Slovak area, Neresnica is well situated, being on the main 66/E77 highway just to the south of the town. There could be some traffic noise but we did not notice this during our one night stay. The glories of Zvolen lie in the past rather than the present, but the camp, under private ownership, is surrounded by trees with a rushing steam along one side. The level site has room for 65 units with unmarked pitches of grass from tarmac roads and electrical connections (10A) for about 60%. The two sanitary blocks, one at either end of camp, are basic rather than luxurious but clean with British WCs, hot water in troughs and cold in cabins for washing and hot water for washing dishes under cover. Special covered areas have barbecue pits with tables and benches. The restaurant (at entrance) has an extensive menu with good value meals and sometimes provides music from a violin, cello, zither trio. Well designed bungalows for hire. Apart from Slovak, only German is spoken.

How to find it: From Zvolen centre take road 66/E77 towards Sahy. Site is signed as Neresnica at junction with 50/E571 road to Lucenec.

General Details: Open all year. 25,000 sq.m. Restaurant. Shops 200 m. Swimming pool 200 m.

Charges guide: Per person Sks. 40; child (under 10 yrs) 5; tent 50; caravan 70; car 30; motorcaravan 70; electricity 60.

Reservations: Write to site in German. Address: 96001 Zvolen. Tel: 0855/22651.

493 Autocamp Tourist Club Kosice Hamre, nr Kosice

Neat, rural site for winter and summer sports.

There is much of natural and historical interest in this part of Eastern Slovakia and T.C. Kosice is situated in beautiful mountain scenery north west of the ancient town of Kosice. Surrounded by tree clad mountains and rolling hills and by a lake, this neat, orderly site provides a quiet base for winter ski-ing (with a drag lift from the camp) and for water sports and walking in the summer. There are more simple bungalows to rent than there are pitches which are not numbered or marked out on flat grass near the lake. There are two sanitary blocks with one for campers near the lake and one for the bungalows near the restaurant. The well appointed, large restaurant also has a separate bar and terrace and a kiosk in the camping area carries basic food supplies and snacks. There is an excellent children's playground and minigolf as well as a games room with mini-bar.

How to find it: Site is signed on the Kosice - Margecarney road.

General Details: Open all year. Restaurant. Bar. Snack bar/kiosk for basics. Ski drag lift. Minigolf. Children's playground. Swimming, boating and other watersports. Games room. Bungalows for hire.

Charges guide: Per person Sks. 30; caravan or tent 40; car 40; motorcaravan 50; electricity (15A) 33.

Reservations: Contact site. Address: 04465 Kosice Hamre, Kosice. Tel: 095/961144.

SLOVAKIA

492 Autocamping Trencin, Trencin

Small, neat site on river near sports centre.

Trencin is an interesting town with a long history and dominated by the partly restored castle which towers high above. The small site with room for 30 touring units (all with electricity) and rooms to let, stands on an island about 1 km. from town centre opposite a large sports complex. Pitches occupy a grass area surrounded by bungalows, with the castle high on one side and woods and hills on the other. The sanitary block, also used by occupants of the bungalows, is old but tiled and clean with British WCs and hot water in the washbasins (in cabins with curtains) and showers (doors and curtains) under cover but not enclosed. A good sized room has electric cookers, fridge/freezer, tables and chairs. Hot water for washing clothes and dishes. There is a bar in summer with restaurant at 200 m and shops at 300 m. Tennis near, boating and fishing in river. Some road and rail noise. A very neat, tidy friendly site with English spoken during our visit.

How to find it: Site is signed in places in town, otherwise head for town sports centre.

General Details: Open 15 May - 15 Sept. 20,000 sq.m. Little shade. Bar in high season. Restaurants and shops within 500 m. Boating and fishing. Tennis, indoor and outdoor swimming pools within 400 m.

Charges 2000: Per person Sks. 100; child (6-15 yrs) 50; caravan 80; tent 70; 2 person tent 40; car 70; m/cycle 30; dog 30; electricity 90; local tax 10. No credit cards.

Reservations: Write to site. Address: na Ostrove, PO Box 10, 91101 Trencin. Tel: 0831/434013. E-mail: autocamping.tn@mail.put.sk.

491 Autocamping Turiec, Martin

Small country campsite in northeast Slovakia.

Turiec is situated 1.5 km. from the small village of Vrutky, 4 km. north of Martin, at the foot of the Lucanska Mala Fatra mountains and with castles nearby. Holiday activities include hiking in summer, skiing in winter. There is room for about 30 units on slightly sloping grass inside a circular tarmac road with shade from tall trees. Electrical connections are available for all places. A wooden chalet by the side of the camping area has a TV rest room and a small games room. Some snacks are available in season with a shop outside the entrance. There is one acceptable sanitary block to the side of the camping area, but in winter the facilities in the bungalow at the entrance are used.

How to find it: Site is signed from E18 road (Zilina - Martin) in the village of Vrutky, 3 km. north of Martin. Follow signs to Martinské Hole.

General Details: Open all year. Snack bar in summer. Badminton. Volleyball. Bicycle hire. Swimming pool 1½ km. Rest room with TV. Small games room. Laundry room with electric cooking facilities. Covered barbecue. Bungalows and rooms for hire.

Charges guide: Per caravan Sk. 55; tent 45; car 45; m/cycle 20; motorcaravan 65; electricity 50.

Reservations: Contact site. Address: 03608 Martin 8. Tel: 0842/284215.

SLOVENIA

With the collapse of former Yugoslavia in the early 'nineties we withdrew that country's sites from our guides. However, with the recovery of tourism in Slovenia we included a small section of 12 inspected sites in our '98 edition. Despite the tourism recovery very few British registered vehicles are yet to be seen in Slovenia. This is partly because the country has been concentrating its promotional efforts since becoming independent on its neighbours, in particular Germany, Austria and Italy. However, it is also because of the daunting driving distance from the UK. Whether via France or Germany, the Slovenian border is about 1,000 miles from Calais; this means that the return journey, including a tour of the country, can amount to 3,000 miles.

Nevertheless, having re-visited Slovenia, we are convinced that it fully deserves a place in our guide. The scenery almost everywhere is attractive, often spectacular; there is much of interest to enjoy; the road network is quite adequate; price levels are generally lower than Britain or mainland Europe; the people are relaxed and friendly; and last but not least, there is an ample choice of good campsites with sanitary facilities mainly on a par with those found in the more popular European destinations.

Because of difficulty in identifying and remembering Slovene place names we have arbitrarily divided the country into four quarters, with the Ljubliana area in the centre. The northwest is the quarter of prime interest to British visitors as it is not only the usual entry from Austria but it includes the awesome Julian Alps with the lakes of Bohinj and Bled to the east and the Upper Soca Valley to the west. For those with less than a week available to spend in Slovenia, there is much to be said for keeping to this alpine region. We have included six sites in this region.

The southwest quarter includes Slovenia's short stretch of Adriatic coast in which the historic port of Piran and the adjacent resort of Portoroz will be of particular interest to British visitors. Unfortunately the campsites on the coast are grossly overcrowded during the summer holiday season, mainly by Slovenes and Italians, and dominated by their static caravans.

Next the centrally situated capital Ljubljana. As the national road network radiates from Ljubljana many foreign tourists find it a convenient stop-over. Yet the old town is both interesting and attractive and fully deserves at least a full day's visit. Also deserving a visit is its historical rival, the nearby small unspoilt town of Kamnik. We include one site in each of these places.

The northeast quarter has two very different areas of attraction. The Savinja valley, in particular its upper section in the Savinja Alps, is almost as spectacular as the Julian Alps. However, it is less accessible and there is little suitable choice of campsites so we have selected only one small site in this area. The far northeast, beyond the Savinja, is a gentle rural area, largely given over to vines (home of Lutomer Riesling). We have not included any sites beyond the Savinja as this distant area is unlikely yet to attract British campers in any number.

In the pleasant rolling countryside of the southeast, the main attractions are to be found on the banks of the slow flowing Krka river. We have had no difficulty selecting a good site here as this is a popular area for those Slovenes who prefer the countryside to mountains or beaches.

For further information contact:

Slovenian Tourist Office, 49 Conduit Street, London W1R 9FB
Tel: 020 7287 7133   Fax: 020 7287 5476

Population
Just over 2 million.

Capital
Ljubljana (pop. approx 1/4 million).

Language
Slovene, with German often spoken in the north and Italian in the west. English is generally understood except by the elderly.

Currency
The basic unit is the Slovene Tolar (abbreviated as SIT) of which there are several hundred to the pound sterling (the official rate in autumn '97 was 270). Any unused Tolars should be exchanged on or soon after departure.

Banks
Now run on efficient conventional western lines. Cash machines in most towns. Banks open weekdays 8.30-16.30 with a lunch break 12.30-14.00, plus Saturday mornings 8.30-11.30. Credit cards: Main credit cards accepted, including most filling stations.

Post Offices
Opening hours as for banks.

Time
Central European Time (one hour ahead of UK).

Telephone
To call Slovenia, prefix code is 386. To call the UK prefix code is 0044. Most call boxes require a phone card. Phone system being converted from analogue to digital, therefore many numbers need to be checked.

Shops
Shops usually open by 8 in the morning, sometimes 7. Closing times vary widely.

Food: Readily available in shops and street markets. General quality a little below West European standards but rather cheaper.

Drink: Usual range readily available. Prolific choice of Slovenian wines but confusingly labelled (in Slovene) and not generally cheaper than in Britain or western Europe. Limited choice of pleasant but unexciting local beers.

Motoring
Small but expanding network of motorways radiating from Ljubljana (tolls being introduced-check with motoring organisations for latest situation). Other main roads not usually dualled and some in need of maintenance. Secondary roads often poorly maintained. Tertiary roads are often all weather graded limestone gravel (known locally as 'white roads' and shown thus on road maps).

Fuel: Filling stations readily available except in remote rural areas. Fuel is very cheap (kept at low price as an anti-inflation measure), say one-third below UK level.

Speed Limits: Driving standards mixed as privatisation of economy has resulted in presence of many high-performance cars with low-performance drivers. Overtaking on blind corners by adolescents is one result. The normal speed limit is 80 mph (130 kph), faster on motorways - slower in built up areas. Road markings and signs are generally good.

Parking: Not a problem, even in Ljubljana (except in old town). In a few towns some central streets are pedestrianised.

Overnighting
Not permitted except on private land with owners permission.

Further Information
Most towns have well marked and helpful tourist information centres. Best guidebook (very good) is Lonely Planet 'Slovenia'.

SLOVENIA

410 Spik Autocamp, nr Kransjska Gora

Large, well equipped site in spectacular setting near the Austrian border.

Most British motorists enter Slovenia on the E55 from Villach over the demanding Wurzen pass, or through the easy Karawanken tunnel. On the Slovenian side they will rejoin national route 1 and normally proceed to Kransjska Gora, this pleasant resort town being the main northern gateway for the Julian Alps. Close by the turn to Kransjska Gora is the small village of Gozd Martuljek and here, directly on route 1, is Kamp Spik, named after the peak which dominates the spectacular view from the site of the jagged Julian Alps skyline. This is the highest site in Slovenia (altitude 750 m, nearly 2,500 ft). It is large and flat, covering 8 ha of spruce woodland. The site is shared with the modern Spik Hotel and the facilities are extensive, including excellent recreational facilities. As a result of its spectacular location and its extensive facilities many of the pitches are occupied by caravans which may not be statics but which are clearly not tourers. The entire complex is now owned by the giant Petrol fuel enterprise and this could account for the somewhat impersonal manner in which the site appears to be run.

How to find it: Site is well signed on the A1 just outside Gozd Martuljek.

General Details: Open all year. All facilities expected of modern tourist complex. Swimming pool (1/7-31/8). Fishing. Bicycle hire. Climbing school. Mountaineering. Riding 6 km. Chemical disposal.

Charges 2000: Per person DM 11 - 14; child (5-12 yrs) less 30%; electricity 4; dog 3; local tax 1. Less 10% for stays over 7 days. Credit cards accepted.

Reservations: Contact site. Address: Jezerci 21, 6482 Gozd Martuljek. Tel: 064/880 120. FAX: 064/880 115. E-mail: hotelspik@petrol.si.

415 Kamp Kamne, Mojstrana

Small, friendly family-run site between Kransjska Gora and Jesenice.

For visitors proceeding down the A1 towards the prime attractions of the twin lakes of Bled and Bohinj, a delightfully informal little site is to be found just outside the village of Mojstrana. Owner Frank Voga opened the site as recently as 1989, on a small terraced orchard, immediately before the collapse of Yugoslavia. Although business was affected, he has steadily developed the facilities, a small swimming pool being added and then a tennis court ('hacked out of the rock with my own hands'). The latest addition is a set of three delightful Alpine 'bungalows' which are let. These have proved so popular that he is working on more. The little reception doubles as a local bar where locals wander up for a beer and a chat while enjoying the view across the valley of the Julian Alps. The site is particularly popular with walkers as three valleys lead west into the mountains from Mojstrana, including the trail to the ascent of Triglav, at nearly 3,000 m. the highest point of the Julian Alps. Franc's English is rather basic.

How to find it: Site is well marked on north side of the A1, just to west of exit for Mojstrana.

General Details: Open all year. Basic facilities only but of high quality and well maintained.

Charges guide: Per person SIT 720; child (7-14 yrs) less 25%; electricity 270; local tax 90.

Reservations: Contact site: Address: Dovje 9, 64281 Mojstrana. Tel: 064/891 105.

420 Kamp Zaka-Bled, Bled

Excellent site on the Bled waterfront, within walking distance of the town.

Visitors to Bled are well provided with camping facilities, there being two very large sites nearby. About 3 km. to the east of the lake, in a flat pine forest just off the main road leading from the A1 to Bled, is the heavily publicised Sobec site. Although this is very professionally managed and equipped to a very high standard, thus explaining its ranking in several guides as one of the best in Europe, the location cannot compare with that of this site which is actually on the western tip of Lake Bled. The Zaka waterfront is a small public beach immediately behind which gently runs a sloping narrow wooded valley. Unlike Sobec there is no pitch allocation, visitors being free to pitch anywhere on the grass covered 6 ha site. Unlike many other Slovenian sites the number of statics (and semi-static) appears to be carefully controlled with touring caravans, motorcaravans and tents predominating. Like many other large sites designed to accommodate over 1,000 guests, and built in the sports-orientated period of Socialist rule, the reception and toilet facilities are of a very high standard (with free hot showers), as are the extensive sports facilities. Some visitors might well be disturbed by the noise coming from above of trains as they hurtle out of a high tunnel overlooking the campsite. But this is a small price to pay for the pleasure of being in a pleasant site from which the lake, its famous little island, its castle and its town can be explored on foot or by boat.

How to find it: From town of Bled drive along south shore of lake to its western extremity (some 2 km); Bled campsite is behind the large public restaurant which faces the beach.

General Details: Open 1 April - mid-Oct. Full range of facilities. Organised entertainment in July/Aug. Fishing. Bicycle hire. Golf or riding 3 km. Fridge hire. Gas supplies. Chemical disposal. Motorcaravan services.

Charges 2000: Per person DM 10 - 13.50; child (7-14 yrs) 7 - 10; electricity 4; local tax 1. Less 10% for stays over 6 days. Credit cards accepted.

Reservations: Contact site. Address: Kidriceva 10A, 64260 Bled. Tel: 064/748 200. FAX: 064/748 202. E-mail: campingbled@s5.net.

425 Camping Danica Bohinj, Bohinj

Although not on the lake, the best site for Bohinj.

Until recently the best site for those visiting the famous Bohinj valley, which stretches like a fjord right into the heart of the Julian Alps, was the Zlatorog camp on the western tip of the lake. Appropriately named after the chamois, Zlatorog also happens to lie at the foot of a spectacular amphitheatre of Alpine peaks which rise seemingly sheer several thousand feet above the lake. However, in the wake of post-Socialist reconstruction the campsite lost much of its waterfront and the available waterfront is now so packed with Slovene campers that visitors from abroad are advised to chose the more spacious Danica site in the valley about 3 km. downstream of the lake. Danica was set up by the Bohinj Tourist Association to supplement the camping accommodation. Danica occupies a rural site originally of 2.5 ha. but recently expanded to 4 ha. which stretches from the main road leading into Bohinj from Bled to the bank of the newly formed Sava river. It is basically flat meadow, broken up by lines of natural woodland. That this is essentially a site for real campers rather than budget holiday makers is evident from the predominance of tents and touring vans and the absence of statics. There are 140 pitches, 125 for touring units.

How to find it: Driving from Bled to Bohinj, the well signed site lies just behind the village of Bohinjska Bistrica on the right-hand (north) side of the road.

General Details: Open May - Sept. Small shop. Café. Fishing. Bicycle hire. Riding 5 km.

Charges 1999: Per person SIT 800 - 1,000; child (7-14 yrs) less 25-30%; electricity 300; local tax 100. Credit cards accepted.

Reservations: Contact site. Address: 64264 Bohinjska Bistrica. Tel: 064/721 055. FAX: 064/723 330. E-mail: tdbohinj@bohinj.si.

423 Camp Soca, Soca

Family run site on the Soca river at entrance to Lepena Valley.

From Kranjska Gora an amazing road runs southwest to the upper Soca valley. This road was built by Russian prisoners of war during WW1 in order to allow Austria to move troops and supplies towards the Italian frontier. Those with large units should note that it is tough going with over 50 hairpin bends! Those who successfully negotiate the 1,600 m. summit usually drop down to the busy small town of Bovec where there are several campsites. These have little to commend them except to canoeists for the turbulent waters of the Soca in this area are world famous among kayak and raft enthusiasts. Fortunately for non-canoeists there is Camp Soca in the spectacular Lepena valley which is one end of a wonderful mountain trail, the other end of which is Bohinj. Camp Soca is just off the main road on a shelving bluff formed by a wide curve of the Soca River. The site is literally theatrical as its two upper terraces and its large lower platform form a natural amphitheatre from which the mountains at the head of the Lepena valley can be readily admired. Facilities are limited to a small but well equipped toilet block and a small reception office/shop. Those in need of a good restaurant or bar, tennis or a ride on a Lipizaner can cross the Soca on a wobbly wire and plank bridge, through the woods on the opposite bank, to a small holiday resort.

How to find it: Site is on the main road between Kranjska Gora and Bovec, between the villages of Soca and Podklanec, just to west of the side road to Lepena.

General Details: Open May - Sept. Basic services only.

Charges guide: Per person SIT 675 - 805; child (7-14 yrs) less 25%; electricity 240.

Reservations: Contact site. Address: Soca 8, 5232 Soca. Tel: 065/89 318.

427 Kamp Koren, Kobarid

Pleasant riverside site within walking distance of the rather special town of Kobarid.

British history teaches little of the terrible mountain warfare between Austria and Italy which went on in the Julian Alps throughout WW1. This macabre struggle, involving half a million casualties, is commemorated in the military museum at Kobarid and in the well-preserved fortifications and cemeteries in the neighbourhood. Kobarid itself is a pleasant country town, with easy access to nearby rivers, valleys and mountains which alone justify a visit to Camp Koren. But most British visitors will remember it for the opportunity it provides to fill that curious gap in their knowledge of European history. The campsite occupies a flat, tree-lined meadow on a wide ledge which drops down sharply to the Soca river. A small, site with just 45 pitches, it is deservedly very popular with those interested in outdoor sports, including canoeing, and this generates a pleasantly athletic atmosphere. The attractive log-built toilet block is of a standard worthy of a high class private sports club and the on-site café dispenses light meals, snacks and drinks apparently without much regard to closing hours.

How to find it: Site is on road leading east out of Kobarid, beyond so-called Napoleon's Bridge, well signed.

General Details: Open mid-March - Oct. Café. Bowling. Fishing. Bicycle and canoe hire. Riding 5 km.

Charges 1999: Per person SIT 800 - 1,200; child (7-14 yrs) less 50%; electricity 320; local tax 100.

AR Discount
Welcome drink

Reservations: Contact site. Address: 65222 Kobarid. Tel: 065/85 312 or 191 311. FAX: 065/191 310. E-mail: lidija.koren@siol.net.

SLOVENIA

430 Hotel-Camping Belvedere, Izola

Not an ideal site but the best for the Slovenian Riviera.
On paper, with the choice of no fewer than six sites, there should be no difficulty in selecting a recommended site for the Slovenian Riviera. In fact, it is very difficult, not because the sites are unsuitable, but because the sheer pressure of customers on restricted space is too heavy. Two factors exacerbate this situation. For the many Italians living in the Trieste area, and for Slovenes, the Slovenian Riviera is the nearest place for a cheap beach holiday. This is coupled with willingness by site operators to allow permanent or long seasonal letting of pitches, usually in the better positions. This not only means that touring visitors have difficulty in obtaining a satisfactory pitch, it also means that it is very difficult for site operators to maintain standards. Of the six sites the only site we can recommend happens to be the only one which is not on the waterfront. Belvedere is so named because it occupies the ridge of a high hill, half a mile's walk or drive from the sea, commanding a stunning view of the coast. During the Socialist period the site was developed into a massive leisure complex of which the camping facilities are a small part. Thanks to its inland location, it is the only coast site where the pressure on facilities is such that the management can maintain the standards we judge to be necessary.

How to find it: Follow the main A2 coast road west just beyond the Izola by-pass; the site is clearly signed but the exit is on a rather confusing summit road junction.

General Details: Open May - Oct. Limited space dedicated for tourers; very comprehensive leisure facilities including a huge swimming pool, restaurant, night club (can be very noisy late into the night) and hotel.

Charges guide: Per person SIT 600 - 1,100; child (under 10 yrs) less 30%; car 300; electricity 500; dog 200; local tax 130.

Reservations: Contact site. Address: Dobrava 1A, 6310 Izola. Tel: 066/605-100. FAX: 066/65 583.

433 Camping Pivka Jama, Postojna

Highly recommended forest site within a day-trip distance of the Riviera or Ljubljana.
Postojna is renowned for its extraordinary limestone caves which form one of Slovenia's prime tourist attractions. Among campers it is also renowned for the campsite situated in the forest only 4 km. from the caves. Deservedly recognised by the Slovenian chamber of commerce as the best campsite in the country, Pivka Jama also happens to be a most convenient site for the foreign visitor, being mid-way between Ljubljana and Piran and only about an hour's pleasant drive from either. The site is deep in what appears to be primeval forest, very cleverly cleared to take advantage of the broken limestone forest bedrock. The 300 pitches are not clustered together but nicely segregated under trees and in small clearings, all connected by a neat network of paths and slip-roads. The facilities are both excellent and extensive and run with obvious pride by enthusiastic staff. It even has its own local caves which can spare its visitors the commercialisation of Postojna.

How to find it: Take the side road leading west from Postojna (just off the trunk A10) to neighbouring Pojnska Jama and on to Pivka Jama (all well signed).

General Details: Open 1 May - 30 Sept. Extensive service and recreational facilities. Bicycle hire. Fishing 5 km. Riding 10 km. Skiing 10 km. A-frame bungalows to let (24).

Charges 1999: Per person DM 14.00; child (7-14 yrs) 10.00; electricity 4.00; local tax 1.00. Family packages available. Credit cards accepted, but not Eurocheques.

Reservations: Contact site. Address: HOT Postojna, Jamska Cesta 28, 6230 Postojna. Tel: 067/24 168. FAX: 067/24 431. E-mail: hoteli-turizem@siol.net.

435 Autocamp Jezica, Ljubljana

Convenient base for Ljubljana, only minutes by bus from the historic old town.
The Sava river slices across Slovenia from northwest to southeast, passing through the northern outskirts of Ljubljana. Jezica is actually on the south bank of the river but a thick hedge and a heavy wire fence means that many campers are unaware of the Sava's presence. The site is basically a large 3 ha. flat grass expanse, punctuated with birch trees. It has a large, modern, well designed but under managed toilet block. Ample sporting facilities are available locally, but it is essentially a convenient base for visiting or transiting Ljubljana rather than a holiday centre. The under management evident in the toilet block appears to pervade the running of the site in general, indicating a lack of direction from above. For instance, one side of the site is occupied entirely by caravans which appear to be derelict, suggesting that the dead shadow of bureaucratic socialism is still lurking here. Bearing in mind its value as a Ljubljana base we shall be surprised if action is not taken soon to raise standards.

How to find it: Follow the main road leading due north from the city, across the ring road, continuing straight ahead (not bearing right) towards Jezica suburb. Turn left immediately before the Sava bridge crossing; site is well signed.

General Details: Open all year. All basic facilities.

Charges guide: Per person SIT 860; child (7-12 yrs) less 40%; pitch 180 - 260; electricity 350; local tax 170.

Reservations: Contact site. Address: Dunajska 270, 61000 Ljubljana. Tel: 061/371 382. FAX: 061/313 649.

SLOVENIA

437 Autocamp Resnik, Kamnik

Convenient place for Kamnik, despite borderline facilities.

Nobody should visit central Slovenia without stopping off to wander around the unspoilt small country town of Kamnik which was once Ljubljana's main trade rival. The town is delightful and is only five minutes walk from the campsite. At first sight the site is rather unprepossessing, comprising a small open field with two very basic prefabricated toilet units, which are not as well serviced as they should be. However, there are compensations. Although the actual camping area is but 1 ha. it is only the edge of a much larger meadow. The site is also only part of the Kamnik sports complex which boasts a large swimming pool, and many tennis, badminton and squash courts. On the campsite is a friendly bar/café, patronised by both campers and players. On the opposite side of the road is a pleasant family inn, Pod Skalo; proprietor Michael Resnik, also runs the campsite. Ljubljana is only an easy hour's drive to the south.

How to find it: Site is 200 m. on the left along the main road leading north from Kamnik.

General Details: Open 1 May - 30 Sept. Basic facilities only. Chemical disposal.

Charges guide: Per person SIT 300; child (under 10 yrs) less 50%; pitch 200 - 400; electricity 300; dog 100; local tax 100. Credit cards accepted.

Reservations: Contact site. Address; Maistrova 15, 1240 Kamnik. Tel: 061/831 233.

440 Camp Dolina, Prebold

Tiny but perfectly run site, a good base for the Upper Savinja valley.

Prebold is a quiet village about 15 km. west of the large historic town of Celje. It is only a few kilometres from the remarkable Roman necropolis at Sempeter. To serve these two places there are two small campsites in Prebold. Our choice, Dolina, is little more than the garden of the house (taking 50 units). It belongs to Tomaz and Manja Vozlic who look after the site and its guests with loving care.The small, heated toilet block would certainly qualify for Slovenia's 'best loo' award. However, the proximity of Celje and Sempeter are not the main reason for our choice. To the south of Prebold lies some of Slovenia's best walking country and to the north lies the upper Savinja valley. It is an easy drive up the Savinja to its spectacular source in the Logar Valley; beyond its semi-circle of 2,000 m. peaks lies Austria. Although there are other campsites on the upper Savinja our preference is for Dolina.

How to find it: Site is well signed in a small side street on the northern edge of Prebold. Best reached via a signed exit on the Ljubljana - Celje motorway.

General Details: Open all year. Reception with bar. Small swimming pool (heated, 1/5-30/9). Sauna. Bicycle hire. Good supermarket and restaurant 200 m. Tennis and indoor pool within 1 km. Fishing 1.5 km. Chemical disposal. Rooms and apartments to rent.

Charges 1999: Per person SIT 1,000; electricity 300; dog 200. No credit cards.

Reservations: Contact site. Address: Dolenja vas 147, 63312 Prebold. Tel: 063/724 378. FAX: 063/724591. E-mail: dolina@email.si.

AR Discount

Welcome drink

442 Hotel Grad Otocec Camp, nr Novo Mesto

Rather exclusive site in the grounds of an ancient castle on the Krka River.

Unlike the turbulent Soca and Savinja upper rivers, the Krka flows slowly through the fertile farmland of southeast Slovenia. There are several well known campsites along its banks and, with one exception, these are part of large spa complexes which generally have little appeal to British travellers, however well equipped and well run. The exception is a quiet wooded stretch of the Krka river, immediately opposite the small island on which the 16th century fortress of Otocec is to be found. The fortress has recently been turned into a 5 star hotel and is now owned by a major leisure company. Campers have to drive or walk across the wooden bridge to register at the hotel's opulent reception desk. Once registered they are given a key which allows entry to the superior toilet block on the actual campsite. During mid-week the area is fairly quiet but at weekends the campsite and neighbouring area liven up with Slovenes attracted for canoeing, fishing, cycling and horse riding (equipment for all these can be readily hired).

How to find it: About 7 km. northeast of Novo Mesto on route 1 (E70), take the clearly signed Otocec exit on right. Cross the old road running along the north bank of the Krka river and on over the bridge to the island hotel (the campsite lies beyond on the south bank via a second bridge).

General Details: Open May - Sept. Small 2 ha. river-front site with limited but excellent essential facilities on site but with a wide range of other facilities within walking distance.

Charges guide: Per person SIT 500 - 700; child (under 7 yrs) free; tent 300; car 250; caravan 350; motorcaravan 600; electricity 450.

Reservations: Contact hotel. Address: 68222 Otocec. Tel: 068/21 830. FAX: 068/23 413.

237

SPAIN

Spain, which occupies the larger part of the Iberian peninsula, is the fourth largest country in Europe, with extremes of climate, widely contrasting geographical features and diversity of language, culture and artistic traditions. The peninsula's dominant feature is the Meseta, the immense plateau at its centre, where the summer heat is intense and the winters long and rigorous. The area to the north, with the mountains of the Pyrenees and the Asturian Picos de Europa, is the exact opposite with no extremes of temperature – green and lush. The east and south coast, protected by the Sierra ranges, enjoy a typically Mediterranean climate and in the extreme south there is virtually no winter season. In Almeria and Murcia, lack of rain as on the Meseta, gives rise to an almost desert landscape, however, the coastline has become a Mecca for those seeking sun all the year. Great monuments survive from a history affected by the Romans, Moors and the Renaissance, but modern Spain is breaking out. Already Spain has hosted the Olympics, the World Fair and Madrid has been the Cultural Capital of Europe; a long cry from the 33 year dictatorship of Franco. There is a vitality about Spain now and in the cities there is always something happening – in politics, in fashion, in the clubs, on the streets, not forgetting the more traditional fiestas. Tourism is important to Spain, as the 'Costas' have proved, but there is a new awareness of the needs of the more discerning independent traveller, a new, albeit long overdue, concern for the environment and generally a more welcoming attitude.

Spain's capital is, of course, Madrid, but the country is divided, like the USA or Germany, Austria or Switzerland, into 17 different federal states called 'autonomias', each with its own capital. For example the capital of Catalunya is Barcelona, that of Galicia is Santiago de Compostela; each federal state has its own government and parliament, and its own prime minister. The central government in Madrid retains power over the national economy and foreign affairs, for example, but other matters such as tourism are the exclusive preserve of the autonomias, which explains why there are different regulations for camping, caravanning and campsites in the various different autonomias. These differences extend to matters such as 'wild camping', 'overnighting' and even the classification (grading) of campsites.

So far as campsites are concerned, Spain has much to offer in terms of some of the best large sites in Europe, such as Playa Montroig, but it also has many attractive smaller sites which will appeal to many of our readers. There are quite a lot of sites which claim to be open all year, but services on most may well be limited to a minimum (eg. only one sanitary block operating and the shop open at weekends only). Even though all the sites featured in this guide have indicated positively that they will be open during the periods stated, we would still advise anyone contemplating a visit out of season to check first rather than rely entirely on information provided so far in advance! Readers should also bear in mind that a pitch of 80 sq.m. is considered to be large in Spain (worth remembering if you have a large outfit), although many sites, particularly in Catalunya, are now increasing pitch size to 100 sq.m. Finally we should mention that there has been a growing tendency in recent years for what we call 'Spanish weekenders' – domestic tourism, whereby the Spanish themselves take pitches for an extended period to use as a weekend holiday home – this tends to give some sites a rather strange appearance during the week when many pitches are occupied by caravans, tents, etc. but not a soul is to be seen.

For information contact:

Spanish National Tourist Office, 22/23 Manchester Square, London W1M 5AP
Tel: 020 786 8077   Fax: 020 7486 8034   Brochures: 0891 669920 (60p per minute)
Internet: http://www.tourspain.es

Population
39,000,000, density 77 per sq. km.

Capital
Madrid

Climate
Spain has a very varied climate depending where you are and the time of year. Temperate in the north, which also has most of the rainfall, dry and very hot in the centre, subtropical along the Mediterranean coast. The average winter temperature in Malaga is 57°F.

Language
Castilian Spanish is spoken by most people with Catalan (northeast), Basque (north) and Galician (northwest) also used in their respective areas.

Currency
Spanish peseta which circulates in coins of 1, 5, 10, 25, 50, 100, 200 and 500 ptas, and notes of 1000, 2000, 5000 and 10,000 ptas.

Time
GMT plus 1 (summer BST + 1).

Banks
Open Mon-Fri 09.00-14.00 Sat 09.00-13.00 (only certain towns). In tourist areas you will also find 'cases de cambio' with more convenient hours.

Post Offices
Offices (Correos) open Mon-Sat 08.00-12.00. Some open late afternoon, while some in the large cities open 08.00-15.00. Queues can be long and stamps can be bought at tobacconists (tabac).

Telephone
From the UK, the code is 00 34 followed by the internal area code, including the initial 9, and exchange number. To call the UK dial 07 44. Make international calls from 'telefone internacional' boxes or from 'Telefonica' offices.

Public Holidays

New Year; Epiphany; Saint's Day, 19 Mar; Maundy Thurs; Good Fri; Easter Mon; Labour Day; Saint's Day, 25 July; Assumption, 15 Aug; National Day, 12 Oct; All Saints Day, 1 Nov; Constitution Day, 6 Dec; Immaculate Con- cep- tion, 8 Dec; Christmas, 25 Dec.

Shops

Open Mon-Sat 09.00-13.00/14.00, afternoons 15.00/16.00-19.30/20.00. Many open longer.

Food: The Spanish in general eat much later than we do. Lunches start at 13.00 or 14.00 and evening meals 21.00-22.00, so the streets remain lively until late. You can go to a 'restaurante' for a full meal or to a 'bar' where you have a succession of 'tapas' (small snacks) or 'raciones' (larger ones). Fish stews (zarzuelas) and rice based 'paellas' are often memorable.

Motoring

The surface of the main roads is on the whole good, although secondary roads in some rural areas can be rough and winding and have slow, horse drawn traffic. In Catalan and Basque areas you will find alternative names on the signposts, for example, Gerona - Girona and San Sebastian - Donostia.

Tolls: Payable on certain roads - A1, 2, 4, 6, 7, 8, 9, 15, 18, 19, 66, 68 and for the Cadi Tunnel , the Vallvidrera Tunnel (nr. Barcelona) and the Tunnel de Garraf on the A16.

Fuel: Petrol stations on motorways often open 24 hrs. Credit cards are accepted at most stations.

Speed Limits: Built-up areas 31 mph (50 kph) or less for both car and car towing. Other roads 56/62 mph (90/100 kph). On motorways, 75 mph (120 kph). For cars towing: other roads 43/50 mph (70/80 kph), on motorways 50 mph (80 kph).

Parking: 'Blue' parking zones (zone azul) are indi- cated by signs and discs are available from hotels, the town hall and travel agencies. In the centre of some large towns there is a zone 'ora' where parking is allowed only against tickets bought in tobacconists.

Overnighting

There are different regulations in the various dif- ferent autonomias (see introduction).

Useful Addresses

Real Automovil Club de Espana (RACE), José Abascal 10, 28003 Madrid 3 . Tel: 4773200.

Costa Brava

The Costa Brava was the archetype Spanish destination in the early years of mass tourism and the tower blocks in some of the resorts are a dubious testimony to the days of the £50 package holiday. Fortunately package holiday trends changed before the developers could wreak total havoc and many villages and resorts remain very attractive and retain their charm, helped enormously by the towering cliffs and shel- tered coves which give this coast its name – the 'Wild Coast'. There are of course some distinctly lively resorts, such as Lloret, Tossa and Calella in the province of Barcelona, but also several quieter ones. The coastal scenery is often spectacular and the climate pleasant – somewhat less hot than further south – making this one of the most attractive areas for the British, particularly for those who drive through France, since it is possible to reach the Costa Brava with only one night stop en-route.

8005 Camping Cadaqués, Cadaqués

Small site with large pool and mountain views overlooking Port Lligat.

Picturesque Cadaqués is accessible by a winding road over the hills behind Roses and has an air of isola- tion. The attractive promenade is lined with restaurants and you can sit and watch the fishermen land their catches. The site is on the outskirts of Port Lligat where Salvador Dali constructed his famous home which has recently been opened to the public. It is ideal as a stopover point to see this magnificent house in a most unusual setting or to enjoy the local cuisine, beaches and watersports, and is mainly used by transit campers for short stays to visit the Dali attraction rather than for extended periods. There are 200 pitches of 60-70 sq.m, some with a slight slope, and a separate area for tents. The large swimming pool is adja- cent to the bar and restaurant with a terrace giving stunning views of the mountains, the Port of Lligat, Dali's house and the nature reserve. The site has a good, well stocked supermarket, which produces its own bread. There are few activities other than the pool and we stress that this is more a site to be used strate- gically rather than for holidays - there is no other site nearby to facilitate access to this area. The Port of Lligat is slowly being changed to accommodate the visitors to what is anticipated to become one of the most popular historic destinations in Spain.

How to find it: Leave autopista A7 (Figueres - Girona) at exit 4 and take C260 to Roses and on to Cadaqués.

General Details: Open Easter - 15 Sept. Electricity connections (5/10A). Restaurant/bar. Supermarket. Swimming pool (high season). Dogs not accepted. Laundry service and ironing. Chemical disposal.

Charges guide: Per adult ptas 535; child 410; tent 675; caravan 675; car 535; m/cycle 430; motorcaravan 980; electricity 385. Plus 7% VAT. Credit cards accepted.

Reservations: not generally necessary. Address: Ctra. de Port Lligat 17, 17488 Cadaqués (Costa Brava). Tel: 972/258126. FAX: 972/159383.

SPAIN - Costa Brava

8007 Camping Castell Montgri, L'Estartit, nr Gerona/Girona

Large holiday site with some space for 'independents'.

This is a large site with all the modern paraphernalia of holidaymaking. With around 80% of the site dedicated to catering for tour operators, it may come as a surprise that we should choose to include it in a guide for independent campers and caravanners. However, the site does include some designated areas for independent campers. These areas provide flat, well shaded pitches, all with electricity. There is a busy bar/restaurant and terrace overlooking an attractive small swimming pool with waterchute close to these areas. The remainder of the site offers a very wide range of amenities and attractions, including one further, large pool with restaurant/bar and terrace areas. There are also two independent mini-pools for toddlers around the site along with various play areas, disco, sports facilities and a live entertainment programme. The sanitary facilities are quite adequate, if not that luxurious, each area of the site having its own block, with hot showers, hot water to open plan washbasins, British style WCs, dishwashing areas (H&C) and also laundry facilities. Cleaning is on a continual basis from 6 am. to 10 pm. This site could be of interest to families with teenagers, offering the possibility for parents to rest, albeit surrounded by the tour operators tents and mobile homes, whilst the youngsters enjoy their own type of holiday within the confines of the site.

How to find it: Site is on the main Torroella de Montgri - L'Estartit road GE641, clearly signed.

General Details: Open 7 May - 8 Oct. 3 areas for tourers, all pitches with electricity. Bars and restaurants. Pizzeria. Takeaway and barbeque.Swimming pools. Supermarket and souvenirs. Football field. Tennis. Table tennis. Billiards. Volleyball. Minigolf. Children's playground. Car wash. Large screen TV and videos. Disco. Varied entertainment programme and excursions managed by English lady. Laundry facilities. Exchange and safe deposit facilities. Free site bus to L'Estartit. Riding, golf and watersports near.

Charges 2000: Per person 395 ptas; child (3-10 yrs) 340; pitch, incl. car and electricity 2,200 - 4,300; extra car or trailer 680. Prices include VAT. Minimum 7 day stay 8/7-19/8.Good discounts in low season. No credit cards.

Reservations: are made with non-returnable deposit (2,000 ptas), to guarantee admission only. Address: Ctra.de Torroella-Estartit, km.4,7, 17258 L'Estartit, (Girona). Tel: 972/75.86.30. FAX: 972/75.99.06.

AR Discount
*Less 10%
in restaurant*

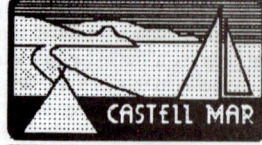

Small Pitches *Good* ✓

8010 Camping-Caravaning Castell Mar, Castelló d'Empúries, nr Figueres

Modern, seaside holiday site, suitable for families.

This is a well equipped, busy, modern site, situated only a few metres behind sand dunes of one the Gulf of Roses beaches, and within the large Aiguamolls of l'Empordà nature reserve. It is also convenient to (but quite separate from) the latest tourist development and facilities at Empuria Brava. With some 300 pitches, it is smaller than many sites in Spain and is particularly suitable for families. There is a heated outdoor swimming pool and an large open-air auditorium, where a varied entertainment programme is provided. A roof-top, terraced area with a bar and restaurant enjoys pleasant views of the surrounding area. A large stylish children's play area is close by. The pitches, most with electricity, are of a reasonable size for the Costa Brava and are on level ground - there is some man-made shade, mainly for tents, and natural shade from the trees and hedges. The large, modern sanitary block is of a high standard and is well maintained. It provides British WCs, hot showers and some washbasins in private cabins, plus facilities for the disabled and for washing up with hot water. There are opportunities for most watersports nearby and the site manager can arrange excursions by canoe through the nature reserve. Security is very good – if you want to leave before 8 am. you must make prior arrangements. There is a tour operators presence but it is not intrusive.

How to find it: From C260 Figueres - Roses road site is signed on the right (just after the turn off to the Empurio Brava complex); follow road for approx. 1.5 km.

General Details: Open 6 May - 24 Sept. Bar. Family restaurant/pizzeria. Supermarket. Large screen satellite TV/video. Children's play area. Table tennis. Swimming pools. Many organised activities and entertainments over a long season. Riding and children's donkey rides with cart. Washing machines. Exchange facilities. Telephones. Bungalows and mobile homes to rent.

Charges 2000: Per person 395 ptas; child (3-10 yrs) 340; pitch including electricity 1,950, 3,725 and 3,975 acc. to season; extra car or m/cycle 680. VAT included. Credit cards accepted.

Reservations: Necessary for July/Aug. and made with deposit (2,000 ptas) for a min. of 8 days between 9/7-15/8. Address: Platja de la Rubina, 17486 Castelló d'Empúries (Girona). Tel: 972/450822. FAX: 972/452330. Winter: 3/3221412.

1600 *5600* *4000*

£ 22p/night

possibility

8012 Camping Mas Nou, Castelló d'Empúries, nr Figueres

Pleasant rural site with swimming pool in the northern Costa Brava.

Some 2 km. from the sea, opposite the fascinating Empuria Brava development, this is a surprisingly tranquil site in surroundings not unlike English parkland – very different from the majority of Spanish sites. The site provides some 450 level, grass, pitches of a min. 70 sq.m. but most 80 -100 sq.m. They are marked and 300 have electrical connections (6/10A). There are also a few discreetly located chalets and mobile homes for hire. Although a little distance from the beach (5 minutes by car), this is compensated for by the rural setting and range of amenities and activities, which include a large L-shaped swimming pool, a tennis court, 'mini club', basketball, minigolf, bar/restaurant and takeaway (in season). These are situated some 100 m. from the pitches themselves. The site owns the supermarket on the main road at the entrance, along with a large souvenir shop. The three sanitary blocks have recently been completely renewed and provide adequate facilities, with hot showers, British WCs, washbasins with cold water only, baby bath, facilities for disabled visitors, chemical disposal, dishwashing (hot and cold water) and with washing machines and hand-washing facilities in each block. This is a site for families which has been completely renovated in the last three years. Ask the origin of the site coat of arms.

How to find it: From A7 use exit 3. Mas Nou is 2 km. east of Castelló d'Empúries, on the Roses road, some 10 km. from Figueres.

General Details: Open Easter - 30 Sept. Supermarket and other shops. Bar/restaurant. Takeaway. Swimming pool. Tennis. Minigolf. Basketball. Volleyball. Football. Mini club (July/Aug). Children's playground. Riding near. Chemical disposal. Bungalows and mobile homes for rent.

Charges 2000: Per person ptas. 490 - 720; child (4-11 yrs) 410 - 495; caravan or tent 490 - 720; car or m/cycle 490 - 675; motorcaravan 985 - 1,440; electricity 380. All plus 7% VAT.

Reservations: Write to site. Address: Ctra. Figueres - Roses, km. 38, 17486 Castelló d'Epúries (Girona). Tel: 972/45.41.75. FAX: 972/45.43.58. E-mail: masnou@intercom.es.

see colour advert between pages 320/321

SPAIN - Costa Brava

8015 Camping-Caravanning La Laguna, Empuria Brava

Unusually relaxed spacious site on isthmus, with direct access to beach and estuary.

La Laguna is aptly named, the site actually being spilt into two halves joined by a road over the lagoon. The approach to the site is by a long (4 km.), more or less, private road. This is quite an unusual site for this area, being laid out very informally among mature pine trees, in contrast to other large more formally designed sites nearby. More trees have been planted in newer areas on the other side of the lagoon. There are 750 pitches clearly marked on grass and sand, all with 6A electricity (a long lead may be useful). The facilities, particularly the sanitary installations, are quite elderly and the site's attraction is much more in terms of its informality, friendliness and value for money (particularly for long stays) than its amenities. Four toilets blocks, placed to avoid long walks, are simple in design and a little tired, but adequate, with free hot water, plenty of dishwashing sinks, well equipped laundry room and chemical disposal. An attractive bar restaurant overlooks the lagoon and a swimming pool (July/Aug), discotheque (comfortably away from main site), and riding school are on site (May-Sept), likewise a bar and shop. There is beach frontage with a sailing school. It is said to be possible to cross over to Empuria Brava when the tide is out. The river which runs along one side of the site is hidden by a high bank with a path along the top. Both the lagoon and the river are good for fishing.

How to find it: Site is signed from Castello d'Empuries bypass (C260 Figures - Roses) and is on the junction with the road for Sant Pere Pescador. Follow approach road for approx. 4 km.

Charges 1999: Per person ptas. 540 - 875; child (5-10 yrs) 460 - 720; tent or caravan 540 - 875; car 540 - 875; motorcaravan 1,015 - 1,565; m/cycle 460 - 720; electricity 440. Discounts for longer stays and pensioners. Credit cards accepted.

General Details: Open 1 March - 22 Oct. Bar. Restaurant. Shop. Swimming pool (15/5-30/9). Tennis (free in low seasons). Minigolf. Sailing school (July/Aug). Fishing. Bicycle hire. Riding. Golf 15 km. Chemical disposal. Mobile homes for hire.

Reservations: Contact site for details. Address: 17486 Castello d'Empuries (Girona). Tel: 972/45.05.53 (when closed 972/20.86.67. FAX: 972/45.07.99 (when closed 972/20.86.67). E-mail: info@campinglaguna.com.

8020 Camping-Caravaning Int. Amberes, Empuria Brava

Large, friendly site 50 m. from wide, sandy beach.

Situated in the 'Venice of Spain', Empuria Brava is interlaced with inland waterways and canals, where many residents and holiday-makers moor their boats directly outside their homes on the canal banks. Internacional Amberes is 50 m. from the wide, sandy beach, which is bordered on the east and west by the waterway canals (no access into them from the beach, only by car on the main road). The site can arrange temporary moorings for boats at Empuria Brava on request. The sea breeze here appears regularly during the afternoon so watersports are very good and hire facilities are available. Amberes is a surprisingly pretty and hospitable site where people seem to make friends easily and get to know other campers and the staff led by the manager of over 20 years, Costa Verges. There is organised sports and children's programmes. The site has 650 hedged pitches enjoying some shade from strategically placed trees, 550 with electricity and water connections, and there are pleasant views from some parts. Sanitary facilities are provided in four blocks, all recently renovated and with hot showers, British style WCs and vanity style washbasins. The restaurant and bar are located close to the site entrance and the cuisine is so popular that locals clamour to use it. The quality is amazing with special Catalunian dishes being served from platters at your table. Tables on the terrace outside add to the enjoyable atmosphere. There is a separate pizzeria and takeaway. The swimming pool is on an elevated terrace, raised out of view of most onlookers, with a small children's pool adjoining. Football and volleyball are organised by the management and a 'secret garden' style minigolf course is special to this site. Rented accommodation includes mobile homes, bungalows and apartments (with private facilities and bath) in a complex opposite the pool.

How to find it: Site is signed from main roundabout leading into Empuria Brava from Roses - Castello d'Empuries road (4 km. from Roses).

General Details: Open 15 May - 30 Sept. Supermarket. Restaurant/bar. Disco bar and restaurant. Takeaway. Watersports - windsurfing school. Boat moorings. Organised activities and entertainment. Swimming pool. Children's playgrounds (one new). Football. Table tennis. Tennis. Volleyball. Minigolf. Bicycle hire, riding or fishing 500 m. Golf 12 km. Washing machines. Chemical disposal. Motorcaravan services. Accommodation for rent.

Charges 1999: Per adult ptas. 430 - 600; child (2-12 yrs) 310 - 500; tent or caravan 760 - 1,580; car 430 - 600; m/cycle 390 - 550; motorcaravan 990 - 1,990; electricity 420. Less 20% for pensioners for stays of 15 days or over in low seasons. Credit cards accepted.

Reservations: Contact site for booking form. Address: 17487 Empuriabrava (Girona). Tel: 972/450507 (1/5-30/9). FAX: 972/671286 (all year).

8030 Camping Nautic Almata, Castelló d'Empúries, nr Figueres

Seaside site with swimming pool, boat moorings, watersports and entertainment.

Situated in the middle of the Bay of Roses, south of Empuria Brava and beside the Parc Natural dels Aiguamolls de l'Empordà, this is a site of particular interest for nature lovers (especially bird watchers). A beautifully laid out site, it is arranged around the river and waterways, so will suit those who like to camp close to water. It is worth visiting because of its unusual aspects and the feeling of being on the canals, as well as being at a high grade beach-side site. A big site with 1,109 fairly similar, large, individual, numbered pitches, all with electrical connections and on flat ground. Its name no doubt derives from the fact that boats can be tied up at a small marina within a lagoon in the site. A slipway also gives access to a river and thence to the sea, giving good opportunities for watersports. There is also direct access from one end of the site to a long sandy beach and on site there is a swimming pool of 300 sq.m. with much grassy sunbathing space. A good bar/restaurant, rotisserie and pizzeria are near the pool, with shade. The sanitary blocks are all of a high standard and recently renovated, with a new one added. They have British style toilets, washbasins with shelf or flat surface, free hot showers, fully controllable with two taps, some en-suite showers and basins and also baby baths. There are good facilities for disabled visitors and taps to draw hot water for washing-up and laundry sinks. Throughout the season there is a varied entertainment programme for both children and adults. The facilities here are impressive.

How to find it: Site is signed off C252 between Castello d'Empuries and Vildemat at end of a 1 km access road.

General Details: Open 6 May - 24 Sept. including all facilities. Excellent supermarket. Restaurant and bar. Two separate bars by beach where discos held in main season. Water-ski and windsurfing schools. Tennis, squash, volleyball, fronton all free. Minigolf. Games room with pool and table tennis. Extensive riding tuition with own stables and stud. Children's play park (near river). Car, motorcycle and bicycle hire. Hairdresser. Free car wash. Washing machines. Gas supplies. Chemical disposal. 12 bungalows and 50 self-contained rooms for hire.

Charges 1999: Per pitch ptas 1,665 - 3,900; person (over 3 yrs) 350; dog 435. Plus 7% VAT. No credit cards.

Reservations: Write to site. Address: 17486 Castelló d'Empúries (Girona). Tel: 972/454477. FAX: 972/454686. E-mail: almata@lix.intercom.es.

8035 Camping Caravaning L'Amfora, Sant Pere Pescador

see colour advert between pages 256/257

Spacious, medium sized site with direct access to the beach.

This is a friendly, colourful family site with a Greek theme to its appearance. There are 525 pitches, all with electrical connections and most with water tap, on level grass with small trees and shrubs. Of these, 64 pitches are large (180 sq.m.) for two units per pitch and have their own, individual sanitary facilities. This rare feature consists of small blocks of four units (toilet, shower and washbasin), each unit 'owned' by one pitch for their stay - virtually `en-suite' camping. The other main sanitary blocks offer free hot water, washbasins in cabins, hairdryers and baby rooms. Further new, separated pitches of 95 sq.m. have been developed with limited shade as yet. Access is good for disabled visitors. Laundry facilities are also available with washing machines, dryers and irons. There is extra provision near the pool area. An inviting terraced bar and self-service restaurant overlook two large swimming pools (one for children), which are divided by an attractive arch and fountain. Sports facilities include two tennis courts, basketball and horse riding (in season) and a doctor is attendance daily in season. Evening entertainment (pub, disco, shows) and children's animation are organised in season and watersports activities are available on the beach. Used by tour operators (25 pitches).

How to find it: From A7 motorway take exit 3 (N-11) towards Girona/Barcelona. Exit for Figueres/Roses towards Roses on C260 and, 9 km. before Roses turn right to Sant Pere Pescador. Site is signed though town.

General Details: Open 12 April - 30 Sept. Bar. Self service and waiter service restaurants. Takeaway. Pizza service. Supermarket. Swimming pools (from 15/5). Table tennis. Tennis. Windsurfing. Sailing. Bicycle hire. Riding. Minigolf. Football. Volleyball. Children's playground. Entertainment and organised activities for children. Fising 2 km. Golf 20 km. Exchange facilities. Car wash. Laundry facilities. Gas supplies. Chemical disposal. Motorcaravan services. Bungalows and mobile homes to rent.

Charges 2000: Per person ptas. 450 - 500; child (2-9 yrs) 350 - 400; pitch (100 sq.m.) 1,650 - 3,800, pitch (100 sq.m.) with individual sanitary arrangements 2,300 - 5,200, large pitch (180 sq.m.) with sanitary 2,700 - 6,100; dog 150 - 500; electricity (5A) included. Plus 7% VAT. Discounts for pensioners for longer stays. No credit cards.

Reservations: Made with deposit (ptas. 10,000) and fee (2,500) - write to site. Address: Av. Josep Tarradellas 2, 17470 Sant Pere Pescador (Girona). Tel: 972/52.05.40 or 52.05.42. FAX: 972/52.05.39. E-mail: info@campingamfora.com.

AR Discount
Less 10%
excl. 1/7-27/8

SPAIN - Costa Brava

√ Very good

No pool

8050 Camping Aquarius, Sant Pere Pescador, nr Figueres

Well run family site in quiet seaside situation suited to families and sun-lovers.

Aquarius has direct access to a quiet sandy beach with a gentle slope and good bathing, and is a site for those who really like sun and sea, with a quiet situation. One third of the site has good shade with a park-like atmosphere with the great variety of plants here being carefully labelled. An extension with less shade provided an opportunity to enlarge the pitches and they are now all at least 70-100 sq.m. which is good for Spain. A total of 447 are all numbered with 400 6A electrical connections. Attractive, large sanitary blocks are tiled with British toilets, washbasins set in flat surfaces, all with hot water (some cabins for each sex) and free hot showers, fully controllable. Facilities for disabled people are provided plus baths for children and there is also hot water in the sinks. An excellent new block has under-floor heating, so is open all season, and features family cabins with showers and basins. A large terrace area outside the bar/restaurant is unusually designed with split levels and attractive flower and water arrangements complete with fountains and large fish. The restaurant is thoughtfully decorated with local artefacts and artistic pieces. The owner has an architectural background and a wealth of knowledge on the whole Catalan area and culture. He has written a booklet of suggested tours (from reception). The whole family are justifiably proud of the site, which is strictly and efficiently run, and they continue to make improvements (a new entrance with a fountain and a stage for live performances at the restaurant). There are two 50 sq.m. areas which make up the 'play centre', open all season and with a qualified attendant and a playground near the beach. A TV room has a giant screen and ample comfortable seating. The sea here is shallow for quite a long way out. The beach bar complex with shaded terraces and minigolf has marvellous views over the Bay of Roses. The 'Surf Center' with rentals, school and shop is ideal for enthusiasts and beginners alike.

How to find it: Turn off main road by bridge south of Sant Pere Pescador and follow camp signs.

General Details: Open 31 March - 14 Oct. Supermarket with butcher. Pleasant restaurant and bar with terrace. Restaurant and bar by beach. `Surf Center'. Takeaway. Children's playground and games hall. Play centre. Table tennis. Volleyball. Minigolf. Bicycle hire. Football field. Boules. Riding 5 km. Golf 12 km. Barbecue and dance once weekly when numbers justify. Special animation for children. Security boxes. Exchange facilities. ATM. Laundry facilities. Full size refrigerators for hire. Car wash. Gas supplies. Chemical disposal. Motorcaravan services. Dogs are accepted in one section.

Charges 2000: Per adult 2.70 - 3.00; child (1-10 yrs) 2.00 - 2.30; pitch 5.20 - 22.70, acc. to season and type; animal 2.30 - 2.50; individual sanitary facility 3.00 - 8.50; electricity 2.50. All plus 7% VAT. Discounts for pensioners on longer stays. No credit cards.
Ptas: per adult 449 - 499 ptas; child (1-10 yrs) 333 - 383; pitch 865 - 3,777, acc. to season and type; animal 383 - 416; individual sanitary facility 499 - 4,114; electricity 416.

Reservations: are made for any length with £50 deposit and £15 fee. Address: 17470 Sant Pere Pescador (Girona). Tel: 872/52.00.03. FAX: 872/55.02.16. E-mail: camping@aquarius.es.

8040 Camping Las Dunas, Sant Pere Pescador, nr Figueres

see colour advert opposite page 256

Large, well organised site beside sandy beach, with pool and many on-site activities.

Las Dunas, with its caged peacocks, is right by a sandy beach (with direct access) which stretches along the site for nearly 1 km. with a windsurfing school and beach bar. There is also a much used swimming pool (30 x 14 m.) with large double children's pools. Las Dunas is a very large site with 1,500 individual pitches, now increased in size to 100 sq.m. which is good for Spain. They are laid out on flat ground in long regular parallel rows, hedged and with shade available in the older parts of the site. Space is usually available even in the main season. A special area is set aside for campers with dogs. Five excellent large sanitary blocks with resident cleaners (7-9) have British style toilets (no paper - a policy of the management), mostly controllable hot showers and washbasins in cabins. There are facilities for babies and disabled people. There is a large bar with terrace and also a pleasant, more secluded pub-type bar with slightly higher prices, a large restaurant and an ice-cream parlour. A magnificent disco club, in a sound-proof building is reputedly the biggest on the Costa Brava, although the building itself is not attractive. With free entertainment in season and good security arrangements, this site is good for families with teenagers. Torches are required in some areas of the site. Used by British tour operators.

How to find it: Use autostrada exit no. 5 towards Escala and turn north 2 km. before reaching La Escala at sign to St Martin de Ampurias.

General Details: Open 9 May - 25 Sept. Electrical connections in most parts. Large supermarket and other shops. Large restaurant. Ice-cream parlour. Takeaway. Large bar with terrace. Disco club. Beach bar in main season. Children's playgrounds. Tennis. Minigolf. Football and rugby pitches. Basketball. Volleyball. Sailing/windsurfing school and other watersports. Organised programme of events 15/6-31/8 - sports, children's games, evening shows, music and entertainment, partly in English. Laundry facilities. Motorcaravan services. Exchange facilities. Large caravans for hire. Dogs taken in only one section mid June-mid Sept.

Charges 1999: Per pitch (any unit) incl. electricity 1,700, 2,600, 3,500 or 4,100 ptas; adult 375 - 400; child (2-9 yrs) 325 - 350. All plus 7% VAT.

Reservations: made for numbered pitches with deposit and fee. Address: Apdo. de Correus 23, 17130 La Escala, Costa Brava (Girona). Tel: 872/520400 or 520401. FAX: 72/550046. E-mail dunas@dracnet.es.

8060 Camping La Ballena Alegre 2, Sant Pere Pescador, nr Figueres

Very large site in quiet position by long beach, with own swimming pool.

La Ballena Alegre 2, sister site to the Ballena Alegre south of Barcelona, is a big, relaxed site taking 1,659 units, part in a lightly wooded setting, part open, and with some 1,800 m. of frontage directly onto an excellent beach with soft golden sand. The grass pitches are individually numbered and of adequate size (over 200 are 100 sq.m.) with pitching informally arranged. Electrical connections (5A) are available in all parts and there are 70 fully serviced pitches. The site is under new management and all seven of the toilet blocks have been refurbished to a very high standard. These feature large pivoting doors for showers, wash cabins, etc, special low facilities for children, baby baths and unusual floors of slatted wood aid drainage. All looks and feels good and seems very functional. A unit for disabled people is in the block nearest reception. There are restaurant and bar areas beside the pleasant terraced swimming pool complex (four pools including a children's pool) and there is a good shop and bakery on site (with bread delivered by bike). A little train ferries people along the length of the site. Plenty of entertainment and activities are offered, including a large shop for watersports, with a windsurfing centre, where equipment can be hired and lessons taken, also a new open air fitness centre beside the beach bar! A full animation programme is provided all season with no let up at the tail end. There is an interesting security system at this site whereby number plates are photographed and stored in the computer system, which then opens the barrier auto- matically, on demand, for the duration of your stay.

How to find it: From autopista A7 Figueres -Girona take exit 5 to L'Escala CI623 for 18.5km. At the round- about take sign to San Martin d'Empúries and follow camp signs. Access has now been entirely asphalted.

General Details: Open 15 May - 27 Sept. 250,000 sq.m. Supermarket. Bar. Self-service restaurant (23/6-28/8). Takeaway (22/5-27/8). `Croissanterie' (15/6-28/8). Full restaurant (evenings all season), pizzeria and beach bar in high season. Swimming pool complex (all season). Three tennis courts. Table tennis. Watersports centre. English newspapers. Fishing 300 m. Bicycle hire. Fitness centre. Children's playgrounds. Sound proofed disco. Dancing twice weekly and organised activities, sports, entertainments, etc. in season (23/6-24/8) but generally a quiet site. Go-karting nearby with bus service. Safe deposit. Cash point. Resident doctor and site ambulance. Car wash. Dog showers. Launderette. Cash machine.Chemical disposal. Motorcaravan service point. New bungalows to rent (11).

Charges 1999: Per pitch incl. electricity (5A) ptas. 1,950, 3,500, or 3,950, acc. to season; pitch with drainage plus 300; person 375; child (3-9 yrs) 275. All plus 7% VAT. Discount of 10% on pitch charge for pensioners all season. No credit cards.

Reservations: made with deposit (ptas. 12,000), min. 10 days 10/7-10/8; contact site for details. Address: 17470 Sant Pere Pescador (Girona). Tel: 972/53.03.02 or 52.03.26. FAX: 972/52.03.32. E-mail: infb2@ballena-alegre.es. Winter address: Ave. Roma 12, 08015 Barcelona. Tel: 93/600.400.200. FAX: 93/226.65.28. E-mail: infb2@ballena-alegre.es

see colour advert between pages 256/257

8074 Camping Paradis, nr Escala

no mention of size of pitch

see colour advert between pages 256/257

Modern site with three pools and beach access

If you prefer a quieter site out of the very busy resort of L'Escala then this site is an excellent option. A large friendly family run site which is divided by the quiet beach access road. The site itself has a private access to the very safe and unspoilt beach of Cala Montgo with a charming bay of soft sand offering all manner of watersports. There are 308 pitches all with electricity, some on sloping ground but pitches them- selves tend to be flat. Established pine trees provide shade for most pitches with more coverage on the western side of the site. Non- stop maintenance ensures that all facilities at this site are always of a high standard. The modern sanitary blocks are clean with free hot showers. There are three swimming pools, the largest, completed in '98, has an idyllic setting on the top of a cliff overlooking the Bay of Roses, offering fabulous views as you enjoy the facilities provided for this large pool. The site operates its own well equipped sub-aqua diving school and campers can experience a free diving experience in the pool or more adventurous coastal diving where appropriate. A children's play area is provided and many other recreational facilities including organised activities for children in the high season. There is a 'road train' service to the local town and there are many interesting items of historic interest in the area. There is also an extensive modern complex of restaurants, bars and takeaways at the site entrance, supplemented by many local bars and restaurants all within walking distance at the very pretty local bay.

How to find it: Leave autopista A7 at exit 5 heading for Viladimat, then L'Escala. Site is well signed from the town centre.

General Details: Open 1 March - 31 Oct. Electricity connections (10A). Bars, restaurants and takeaway. Shop. Swimming pools (3). Pool bar. Beach 100 m. Children's play areas. Animation for children (high season). Basketball, volleyball and badminton. Kayak hire. Sub aqua school. Washing machines and dryers. Chemical disposal. ATM machine. Road train service to town centre from outside site. Bungalows and chalets for hire.

Charges 1999: Per adult ptas 570; child 390; pitch 2,700; electricity 475. Plus 7% VAT. Less in low seasons. No credit cards

Reservations: advisable in high season. Address: Av. de Montgó, 260, Apdo Correus 216, 17130 L'Escala (Costa Brava). Tel: 872/770200 or 771795. FAX: 872/772031. E-mail: montgoparadis@alehop.com.

SPAIN - Costa Brava

8070 Camping La Escala, La Escala

Neat and tidy, small site within walking distance of beach and town.

Under the same ownership as Las Dunas (no. 8040), but a complete contrast, this is a site with limited facilities. You can walk both to the very pleasant beach and to the centre of a modest sized, lively, yet historical popular holiday resort. Here you will find most of the usual seaside attractions. The site is not very large, but the pitches are level, marked and well shaded. They have managed to carve over 200 out of the area so they are small - just room for the car and caravan or tent - but all pitches have electricity, water and drainage. The central toilet block is basic but clean, with British style toilets (no paper), washbasins, two in cabins for ladies, free hot water and 25 free showers. Dishwashing and laundry sinks with hot water. In season there is a supermarket and a bar and restaurant offering good food with a pleasant terrace. There is some road noise despite the very high wall between the site and the busy road alongside. The site has 12 modern 2-tier bungalows to let at reasonable charges.

How to find it: On entry to La Escala at first roundabout turn right, onto Avenda Reills (heading for port), at second roundabout turn left and then continue 1 km. to site on right. Watch for gate in high wall.

General Details: Open Easter - 25 Sept. Most well shaded. Shop. Bar (open in high season). Restaurant. Good value English restaurant (Angela's) at the port area. Bungalows for hire.

Charges guide: Per person 350 ptas; child (2-9 yrs) 275; pitch incl. electricity 1,375 - 2,125; dog 350 - 450. All plus 7% VAT.

Reservations: Not necessary. Address: Apdo. Correus 23, 17130 La Escala, Costa Brava (Gerona). Tel: 872/77.00.08 or 77/00.84. FAX: 872/55.00.46.

8103 Camping El Maset, Sa Riera, Begur, nr Gerona/Girona

Little gem of a site in lovely surroundings with pool, close to beaches.

This is a delightful, tiny site with 109 pitches, of which just 14 are for caravans or motorcaravans, the remainder suitable only for tents. The owner, Sr Juan Perez is delightful, as is his secretary Josaphine, and longer staying customers may be presented with a memento of your stay. The site entrance is steep and access to the caravan pitches can be quite tricky. All these pitches have electricity, water and drainage with some shade. Access to the tent pitches, which are more shaded on attractive rock walled terraces on the mountainside (more of a hill really!) seems quite straightforward, with parking for cars not too far away – of necessity the pitches are fairly small. There are also seven traditional Catalan style 'bungalows' to rent. For such a small site the amenities are quite extensive and there is an unusual elliptical shaped swimming pool. The facilities include a bar and very homely restaurant offering excellent food, with a large terrace giving very pleasant views over the pool and towards the valley side. Takeaway service, children's games room, a modern play area thoughtfully placed on 'astroturf' and a supermarket. Sanitary facilities, in three small blocks, were clean and include free hot showers, British style WCs, soap and hot-air dryers, hot water to washbasins in two blocks and a baby bath. Under cover washing up area (H&C), washing machine and dryers. This small site provides the standard of service normally associated with the best of the larger sites. It is in the tiny resort of Sa Riera with access to the beach (300 m), in a beautiful protected bay with traditional fishing boats taking up one end of the sand. There is a a naturist beach (via a longer uphill path). Begur, with its beautiful, small, quite unspoilt bay and beach, is 10 minutes by car.

How to find it: Site is 2 km. north of Begur (Bagur). Follow signs for Playa de Sa Riera and site. Steep entrance.

General Details: Open 14 March - 24 Sept. Bar/restaurant, takeaway (all season). Shop (from May). Children's play area. Area for football and basketball. New games room. Swimming pool (all season). Solarium. Fishing 300 m. Golf, bicycle hire 1 km. Riding 8 km. Chemical disposal. Bungalows to rent. Dogs are not accepted.

Charges 2000: Per person 570 - 730 ptas; child (1-10 yrs) 430 - 570; car 560 - 720; m/cycle 400 - 500; tent 610 - 790; caravan 700 - 910; motorcaravan 770 - 980; electricity 400 (tent) or 550 (caravan). Credit cards accepted.

Reservations: Write to site. Address: Playa de Sa Riera, 17255 Begur (Gerona). Tel: 972/623023. FAX: 972/623901.

8072 Camping Les Medes, L'Estartit, nr Gerona/Girona

see colour advert between pages 256/257

Friendly, family site with pool, open all year.

Les Medes is different from some of the 'all singing, all dancing' sites so popular along this coast. The friendly owners are proud of their site. Set back from busy L'Estartit itself, it is however, only 800 m. to the nearest beach and a little train runs from near the site (June-Sept) to the town. With just 186 pitches, the site is small enough for the owners to know their visitors and being campers themselves, they have been careful in planning their facilities. The level, grassy pitches range in size from 60-80 sq.m. depending on your unit. All have electricity (10A) and the larger ones (around half) also have water and drainage. All are clearly marked in rows, but with no separation other than by the deciduous trees which provide summer shade. The two modern, spacious sanitary blocks are heated, very clean and well maintained, providing British toilets, hot and cold water in washbasins (in private cabins), good sized showers, very good facilities for disabled people and baby baths. Washing machines are provided in each block and there is hot and cold water for dishes and clothes washing. The pool area is attractively landscaped in front of the old Catalan farmhouse buildings which house reception and the small, air conditioned bar and restaurant, providing a grassy sunbathing area and an open air dance floor for twice weekly music evenings (in season). The site has well equipped apartments with central heating and TV to rent. A small indoor pool (heated) with sauna and solarium and good access for disabled people is a new addition. A diving business operates from the site and tours are organised. Torches are required in more remote parts of the site.

How to find it: Site is signed from main Torroella de Montgri - L'Estartit road GE641. Turn right after Camping Castell Montgri, at Joc's hamburger/pizzeria and follow signs.

General Details: Open all year. Electricty connections (5, 6, 10A). Bar with TV and snacks (all year). Restaurant (1/4-30/9, nearest 1 km). Shop (all year, but only basics in winter). Outdoor swimming pool (15/6-15/9). Indoor pool with sauna, solarium and masseur (15/9-15/6). Children's play area with small hut for games. Converted stables for indoor children's area and TV room. Animation and excursions in July/Aug. Large chess. Table tennis. Volleyball. Boules. Bicycle hire. Fishing 2 km. Riding 400 m. Golf 8 km. Car wash. Gas supplies. Chemical disposal. Motorcaravan services. Apartments to let (comfortable and heated). Dogs are not accepted.

Charges 2000: Per person ptas. 685; child (0-10 yrs) 500; pitch 1,500; electricity 480. All plus 7% VAT. Discounts outside high season and special offers for low season longer stays. No credit cards.

Reservations: Recommended for July/Aug. Write to site with 5,000 ptas. deposit. Address: 17258 L'Estartit (Catalunya). Tel: 972/75.18.05. FAX: 972/75.04.13. E-mail: campingslesmedes@cambrescat.es.

8080 Camping El Delfin Verde, Torroella de Montgri, nr Gerona/Girona

Large, very high quality site with friendly staff, own beach and extremely large pool.

A popular site in a quiet location, El Delfin Verde has its own long beach, which campers have to themselves, stretching along its frontage. An attractive large pool in the shape of a dolphin is a feature of the site with a total area of 1,800 sq.m. with lifeguard. There is also a children's pool. An elevated area with large bar, full restaurant and separate takeaway, which are open in the main season, gives wonderful views over the huge pool. This has water slides, two island areas, one containing a huge fountain which can be lit at night. There is a further restaurant with slightly cheaper, good value food in the main complex with an open air arena. This is a large site with nearly 6,000 persons at peak times. Level grass pitches nearer the beach are marked and many are separated by small fences and newly planted hedging. All have electricity and access to water points and a stream runs through the centre of the site. There is shade in some of the older parts and a particularly pleasant area of pine trees in the centre with pitches marked but not separated, sandy and not so level. There are five excellent large sanitary blocks and a further sixth smaller one, all with resident cleaners. All blocks have free hot water in washbasins, fully controllable showers (2 taps) of good, comfortable size with seat, plus British style toilets and some washbasins in cabins. El Delfin Verde is a large, cheerful holiday site with many good facilities, sports and a free entertainment programme in season and is well worth considering for Costa Brava holidays. Used by British tour operators.

How to find it: A very long camp approach road leads off the Torroella de Montgri - Palafrugell road (watch carefully for the sign); site is signed at the end of it.

General Details: Open 15 April - 24 Sept, including shops, one restaurant and one bar. 290,000 sq.m. Supermarket and other shops. Two restaurants, grills and pizzerias. Three bars - the one on site closes 11 pm, pool bar open until 1 am; small bar by beach open in season. 'La Vela' barbecue and party area. Sports area (football, volleyball, etc.), 8 tennis courts. 2 km. exercise track. Dancing and floor shows weekly in season. Disco. Excursions organised. General room with TV. Video room. Bicycle hire. Minigolf. Children's playground. Games room. Trampolines. Badminton. Fishing 1 km. Golf 4 km (20% discount). Hairdresser. Laundry facilities. Car repairs, servicing and washing. Gas supplies. Chemical disposal. Motorcaravan services. Apartments, mobile homes and bungalows (with own pool) to let. Dogs are not accepted in high season (8/7-12/8).

Charges 1999: Per pitch, incl. electricity 1,700, 2,600, 3,500 or 4,100 ptas; per person 375; child (2-9 yrs) 325; dog (excl. 9/7-9/8) 375; extra car 1,000 - 2,000; boat free - 375. All plus 7% VAT. Special offers on long stays in low season. No credit cards.

Reservations: Only a guarantee to admit - no specific pitch allocated. Write (all year) with deposit of ptas. 10,000. Address: Apdo Correos 43, 17257 Torroella de Montgri (Gerona). Tel: 972/758450. FAX: 972/760070. E-mail: eldelfinverde@drac.com.

see colour advert between pages 256/257

SPAIN - Costa Brava

8075 Camping Estartit, Estartit

Friendly, Belgian run site with small swimming pool, 300 m. from Estartit town.

Although facilities here are fairly limited, a short walk down the hill brings you into the heart of the extremely popular Estartit, which is very commercialised but you can find authentic tapas bars and street entertainment. Set in tall pine trees, which provide complete shade and in a narrow valley situation, this is a peaceful site with 160 pitches, all with electrical connections (2/6A), terraced and is best suited for campers with tents (there are some very steep drops between terraces). However there are two sand/gravel areas for a small number of motorcaravans and caravans (booking essential in high season), separated by a small drainage canal. The site itself is surprisingly quiet, considering its proximity to the town - there is no need to use a vehicle once on site. One modern, fully tiled sanitary block provides hot and cold showers (small fee for hot water), small laundry with washing machines and a separate baby area. On site facilities include a bar/restaurant and shop (high season). The local beaches are extremely good but if the town is too frenetic there is a very small swimming pool with a children's section and a play area next to it, plus an attractive shaded area beside the bar. Access around the site could be difficult for disabled people. Torches are necessary in the more remote parts of the site.

How to find it: Site is signed from Estartit town centre.

General Details: Open Easter/1 April - 1 Oct. Bar/restaurant and shop (1/6-15/9). Swimming pool (all season). Children's play area. Children's activities and adult social events arranged (barbecue, bingo, etc). Fishing, bicycle hire and riding within 1 km. Golf 7 km. Laundry facilities. Chemical disposal. Apartments for rent. Site is guarded day and night. No dogs 20/6-20/8.

Charges 2000: Per person 600 ptas; child (2-10 yrs) 425; car 600; caravan or family tent 650; small tent 550; motorcaravan 1,100; m/cycle 425; electricity 2A 350, 6A 425. Plus 7% VAT. Less 10-30% outside high season (10/6-31/8). No credit cards.

Reservations: Contact site. Address: 17258 Estartit. Tel: 972/758909 or 751909. FAX: 972/750991. (15/10-15/3 Vrancken Joss, Plantenstraat 74, 3500 Hasselt, Belgium).

AR Discount
Less 10%,
min. 14 nights

8120 Kim's Camping, Llafranc, nr Palafrugell

Pleasant, attractive, terraced site near the sea, with swimming pool.

Situated on the wooded slopes of a narrow valley leading to the sea, this site has a steep lower area rising to a very pleasant plateau where all facilities are provided. it has 325 grassy and partly shaded, terraced pitches, with many larger pitches on a plateau with the pool and shop. The pitches on the terraces are connected by winding driveways, narrow in places, and most have electrical connections (6A). There is adequate sanitary provision including free warm showers, British style WCs and laundry facilities. Amenities include children's playgrounds, an excellent pool area with adult and small children's pools, a bar, charming restaurant and 'al fresco' eating. All amenities are offered at a high standard of cleanliness and efficiency. The site is under 1 km. from the beach at Llafranc. This is a good place for holidays to enjoy the bustling atmosphere of Llafranc town and beach, but staying in a quieter environment. The site provides an entertainment programme in high season and diving is possible at specified times. There is an outstanding view along the coastline and of the Pyrenees from Cap Sebastian close by. Bungalows for rent. English is spoken by the very friendly management and staff.

How to find it: Turn off for Llafranc from Palafrugell - Tamariu road at turning signed 'Llafranc, Caella, Club Tenis'. Site is 1 km. on, next to the El Paraiso hotel.

General Details: Open Easter - 30 Sept. Shop. Bar. Cafe/restaurant (1/6-15/9). TV room. Swimming pools (1/6-30/9). Children's play areas. Fishing, bicycle hire 500 m. Riding 4 km. Golf 9 km. Car wash. Chemical disposal. Bungalows and mobile homes for hire.

Charges 2000: TPer person 390 - 600 ptas; child (3-10 yrs) 225 - 350; pitch incl. electricity 1,885 - 2,900. Plus 7% VAT. Discounts for long stays and for senior citizens. Credit cards accepted.

Reservations: Made with deposit (ptas. 10,000). Address: 17211 Llafranc-Palafrugell (Girona). Tel: 972/301156. FAX: 972/610894. E-mail: info@campingkims.com.

AR Discount
Welcome drink

8102 Camping Mas Patoxas, Pals, nr Gerona/Girona

Unpretentious site with satisfactory facilities in main season, set back from the coastal resorts.
This is a useful site for those who prefer to be apart from but within easy travelling distance of the beaches (5 km) and town (1 km) in high season. It has very easy access, being set on a slight slope with level terraces providing 500 grassy pitches of a minimum 72 sq.m. All have electricity (5A) and water, 150 have drainage as well. There are some pleasant views but not a lot of shade. Although there are some 70 static units, there is the impression of more as they are sited together near the entrance and pool. There are no tour operators. The three sanitary blocks are of modern construction with controllable hot showers, with dressing area, some washbasins with hot water, British style WCs, baby bath and three children's cabins with washbasin and shower. Dishwashing facilities are under cover (H&C) and five washing machines. An air-conditioned restaurant/bar provides both waiter service meals and takeaway food to order (weekends only mid Sept - April), and there is a shop (high season only). Activities include a medium sized swimming pool with sunbathing area and entertainment during the main season. Although there are no specific facilities for disabled people, access throughout the site looks to be relatively easy.

How to find it: Site is approx. 1.5 km. south of Pals on the left going towards Palafrugell on the GE650.

General Details: Open all year except 19 Dec - 14 Jan. Restaurant/bar (1/4-30/9). Pizzeria. Takeaway. Shop (1/4-30/9). Swimming pool (15/6-30/9). Tennis. Table tennis. Volleyball. Football field. Entertainment in high season. Fishing, golf 4 km. Bicycle hire, riding 2 km. Bus service from site gate. Laundry facilities. Chemical disposal. Bungalows and mobile homes to rent.

Charges 2000: Per person 500 - 700 ptas; child (1-10 yrs) 400 - 500 caravan pitch 1,500 - 2,300, tent pitch with car 1,300 - 1,800; dog 300. Plus VAT @ 7%. Special low season offers. Credit cards accepted.

Reservations: Write to site. Address: Ctra. Palafrugell-Torroella km.5, 17256 Pals (Girona). Tel: 972/636928 or 636361. FAX: 972/667349.

see colour advert between pages 256/257

8150 Camping Internacional de Palamós, Palamós, nr Gerona/Girona

Site with good swimming pool quite close to town.
As you approach this site it is unmistakable as it has a long perimeter wall with modern camping murals painted on the outside. The site has a large swimming pool, plus children's pool, with attractive palms, and has a grass sunbathing area has its own bar/terrace. There is a small snack bar/bar and a little terrace elsewhere in the site which provides a takeaway service. It is 1 km. from the town and only 400 m. to the nearest beach. It might have space when others are full and has over 500 level, terraced pitches on a gentle slope, of moderate size, with variable shade. The access roads are gravel and may suffer in the case of heavy rain. Electrical connections (6A) are available in most parts. Three toilet blocks, one of which is large and modern providing good facilities with free hot water in washbasins, pre-set showers with push-button and facilities for disabled people. The two more elderly, smaller blocks are somewhat basic, with mostly Turkish, but some British WCs and cold showers. There are some tour operator pitches. Mobile homes and bungalows to rent.

How to find it: Cars can approach site from central Palamós, but town streets are too narrow for caravans which should turn off C255 road just outside Palamós to north by Renault garage, signed to Kings Camping and La Fosca, turn right just before Kings and from there follow Internacional signs.

General Details: Open 26 March - 9 Oct. Swimming pool (36 x 16 m.), with paddling pool. Self-service shop. Restaurant and bar. Laundry room with washing machines etc. Hourly bus services to town.

Charges 1999: Per person 400 ptas; child (under 10) 300; pitch for car and tent/caravan 2,025, 2,280 or 2,590; tent pitch (m/cycle but no car) 765, 975 or 1,550; electricity 500; water/drainage 275. All plus 7% VAT.

Reservations: Write to site with 5,000 ptas deposit. Address: Apdo Correos 100, 17230 Palamos (Girona). Tel: 972/31.47.36. Office tel: 972/31.49.48 or 31.49.48. FAX: 972/31.85.11.

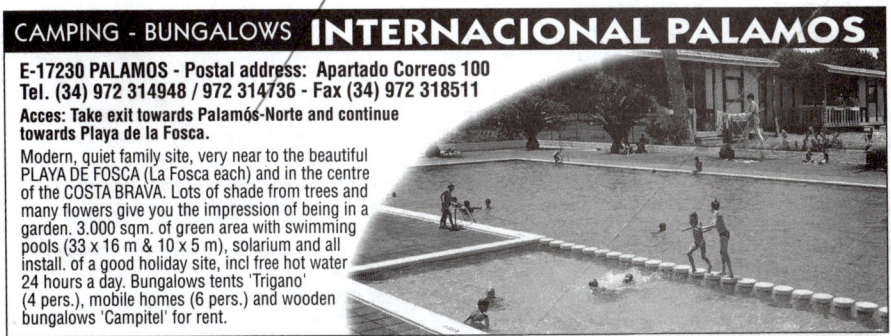

SPAIN - Costa Brava

NO

8090 Camping Caravaning Cypsela, Platja de Pals, nr Gerona/Girona

Impressive, de-luxe site, 2 km. from the sea, with many amenities.

There are many striking features in this site, one is its sumptuous complex of sport facilities and amenities near the entrance. This consists of a fine swimming pool (large for a campsite and unusually fitted with high boards), a good children's pool and playgrounds, two excellent squash courts, a tennis court, new fitness room, volleyball, table tennis, a restaurant, bar with open-air terrace and other entertainment rooms. These include a children's playroom with organised entertainment (including video screen), an amusements room with pool tables, football tables, video games, and a lounge for adult entertainment, with piano for twice weekly concerts. The bar/restaurant is very pleasant, with set course meals at low cost, as well as a full menu and takeaway service. The main part of the camping area is pinewood, with 1,061 clearly marked pitches of sandy gravel of varying sizes, some with full facilities, plus a group of new 'Elite' pitches of 120 sq.m. The newer extensions at the rear of the site have more grass and pitches are hedged with a mixture of trees. The four stylish sanitary 'houses' are of excellent quality with comprehensive cleaning schedules, providing British style toilets, three with washbasins in private cabins, free hot water and adjustable showers. Three of the four have special children's rooms with baby baths and larger ones for older children. There is also good provision for disabled people and many sinks with hot water. A comprehensive animation programme for children and adults is provided in season. Cypsela is a busy, well administered site which one can thoroughly recommend, especially for families, very efficiently run, with all fixtures and fittings of good quality and everything clean and maintained to a high standard. The gates are closed at night. Several tour operators use the site (230 pitches).

How to find it: Cypsela is on the road running from the Torroella de Montgri to Bagur down to Platja de Pals.

General Details: Open 15 May - 24 Sept. 200,000 sq.m. Access easy but care needed with trees in places. Electrical connections in all parts. Supermarket and other shops. Well appointed restaurant: or cheaper meals served in cafeteria. Bar. Lounge with drinks/snacks. Hairdressers. Swimming pools. Tennis. Squash. Table tennis. Football field. Minigolf. Fitness room. Social room/TV. Barbecue and party area. Dancing weekly in season. Organised sports and games activities in daytime. Children's playroom with organised activities. Games room with pool tables, etc. Bicycle hire, riding 150 m. Golf 6 km. Fishing 2 km. Free hourly bus service to beach. Serviced launderette. Ironing. Air conditioned telephone parlour. Doctor always on site; well equipped treatment room. Own sewage disposal plant. Car wash. Chemical disposal. Dogs are not accepted.

Charges 2000: Per person ptas. 765; child (2-10 yrs) 610; standard pitch incl. 1 vehicle 3,200; electricity 450. Contact site for details of larger pitches. All plus 7% VAT. Less 5-10% for longer stays in low season. Credit cards accepted.

Reservations: Write to site for details. Address: Ctra. Pals-Playa de Pals, km. 3, 17256 Pals (Girona). Tel: 972/667 696. FAX: 972/667 300. E-mail: info@cypsela.com.

Too Big - Time

8101 Camping Playa Brava, Platja de Pals, nr Gerona/Girona

Surprisingly 'green' and quiet, beach-side site with good facilities.

As well as having direct access to a large beach and to watersports facilities on both beach and river, this is a very grassy, level site. Shade is provided by a mixture of conifer and broad-leaf trees for most of the 500 pitches. These all have electricity (10A), a third with water and drainage also, and are of a good size ranging from 75-100 sq.m, with many large ones. There is an air of spaciousness and general tidiness. Five modern sanitary blocks have British WCs, controllable hot showers, with dressing area and hooks, washbasins with hot water, dishwashing facilities under cover and six washing machines. Facilities are provided for disabled visitors. Amenities include a medium sized pool and children's pool, with a large grass sunbathing area, two tennis courts, volleyball, children's play area on grass and an entertainment programme during July and August. There is a good golf course close by. The bar/restaurant, with terrace, provides both waiter service and takeaway meals, and there is a supermarket.

How to find it: Site is 3 km. north of village of Pals, in the direction of Platja de Pals. Follow road for 3 km. past golf course to beach; well signed.

General Details: Open 13 May - 17 Sept. Bar/restaurant. Takeaway. Supermarket. Swimming pool (from 1/6). Tennis. Volleyball. Minigolf. Children's play area. Fishing. Watersports on river and beach, including sheltered lagoon for windsurfing learners. Bicycle hire 3 km. Riding 5 km. Golf 1 km. Washing machines and driers. Chemical disposal. Dogs are not accepted.

Charges 2000: Per person ptas. 210 - 300; child (2-9 yrs) free - 250; senior (over 60 yrs) free - 300; pitch incl. electricity 75 sq.m. 2,800 - 4,000, 85 sq.m. 3,090 - 4,420. All plus 7% VAT. Discount for longer stays in low season. No credit cards.

Euros: Per person 1.26 - 1.80; child (2-9 yrs) free - 1.50; senior (over 60 yrs) free - 1.80; pitch incl. electricity 75 sq.m. 16.82 - 24.04, 85 sq.m. 18.57 - 26.56.

Reservations: Write to site. Address: Avda. del Grau s/n, 17256 Platja de Pals (Gerona). Tel: 972/636894. FAX: 972/636952. E-mail: info@playabrava.com.

0034

Dreams can not be put into picture.

If you have ever dreamed about enjoying a deserved holiday, in a privileged surrounding, near the sea, in the middle of nature, with all the comfort ...
ask for our brochure and discover how your dreams can come true*

✉ CAMPING CYPSELA - 17256 PALS (Girona) SPAIN
☎ +34 972 667 696 - Fax +34 972 667 300
e-mail: info@cypsela.com http://www.cypsela.com

*Our special offers will make it even more easy for you.

SPAIN - Costa Brava

8100 Camping Inter-Pals, Platja de Pals, nr Gerona/Girona

see colour advert between pages 256/257

Well maintained, interesting site in pinewood, close to beaches.

On sloping ground, with tall pine trees providing shade and about 500 m. from the beach, this site has 280 touring pitches and 250 for tents, on terraces and levelled plots, mostly with shade. The main entrance and its drive resembles a pretty village street as the bungalows are set on both sides of the street lined with traditional lamp-posts. There are three toilet blocks and the facilities are very clean. They have British style WCs, individual washbasins and hot showers in each block, free hot water for dishwashing and laundry, facilities for disabled campers and washing machines and dryers. Inter-Pals is set away from the busy resorts but it does provide an entertainment programme in high season and dancing takes place in a dedicated area. There is a small swimming pool of irregular shape with a pleasant grass area for sunbathing. It is on route to Platja de Pals which is a long sandy unspoilt stretch of beach, a discreet area of which is now an official naturist beach.

How to find it: Site is on the road leading off the Torroella de Montgri-Bagur road north of Pals and going to Playa de Pals - past site no. 8090.

General Details: Open 24 March - 30 Sept. Supermarket. Restaurant/bar with croissenterie. Cafe/bar by entrance. Swimming pool. Basketball, volleyball and badminton courts. Tennis. Children's playground and organised activities in high season. Washing machines and dryer.

Charges 2000: Per person 625 ptas; child (3-10 yrs) 375; pitch 2,000 -3,200; small tent and car 1,600 - 2,250. Plus 7% VAT. Discounts for long stays in low season.

Reservations: are made in sense of guarantee to admit only, no deposit. Address: 17256 Platja de Pals (Costa Brava). Tel: 972/63.61.79. FAX: 972/66.74.76. E-mail: interpals@interpals.com. A 'Camping Cheques' site.

8170 Camping Valldaro, Platja de Aro, nr Gerona/Girona

see colour advert between pages 256/257

Clean site with good swimming pool 1½ km. from a bright seaside resort.

Like a number of other large Spanish sites, Valldaro has been extended and many pitches have been made larger, bringing them up to 80 sq.m. There are 2,000 pitches with 1,300 available for tourers. The site is flat, with pitches in rows divided up by access roads. The newer section is accessed over a bridge and is brought into use at peak times. It has some shade and its own toilet block of quite good size, as well as a medium-sized swimming pool of irregular shape with grassy lying-out area and adjacent bar. You will probably find space here even at the height of the season. The original one (36 x 18 m.) is adjacent to the good Spanish-style restaurant which also offers takeaway fare. The sanitary installations at Valldaro are of reasonable standard, some with potted plants and patterned glass sink dividers. There are British style toilets, some of children's size. Individual washbasins have mirrors, shelves and hot water. About 100 free hot showers (temperature perhaps a bit variable). The camp is 600 m. back from the sea at Platja de Aro, a small resort with a long and wide beach and plenty of amusements. It is particularly pleasant out of peak weeks; it is popular with the British. There are many permanent Spanish pitches but they are in a separate area and do not impinge on the touring pitches. An animation programme is operated in high season.

How to find it: Site entrance is off the road on which you approach Platja de Aro from Girona via Castillo de Aro. You can now also approach it from the Sant Feliu - Gerona road.

General Details: Easter/1 April - 30 Sept. Electrical connections throughout. Two supermarkets and general shops. Restaurant. Large bar. Swimming pools. Tennis. Table tennis. Minigolf, with snack bar. Children's playgrounds. Sports ground with football and basketball. Organised entertainment. Hairdresser. Air conditioned telephone parlour.

Charges 2000: Per person 615 ptas; child (2-10 yrs) 365; pitch for caravan/car or motorcaravan, incl. electricity 2,000 - 3,100; pitch for tent/car or m/cycle incl. electricity 2600. All plus 7 % VAT. Less outside high season.

Reservations: are made only to guarantee admission, with deposit (4000 ptas). Address: Apdo. Correos 57, 17250 Platja de Aro (Costa Brava). Tel: 972/81.75.15. FAX: 972/81.66.62. A 'Camping Cheques' site.

8140 Camping Caravaning Treumal, Calonge, Platja d'Aro, nr Girona

Very attractive terraced site on hillside with direct access to secluded beaches.
This pretty site has been developed around the attractive gardens of a large, spectacular estate house which is close to the beach. The house is the focus of the excellent facilities of this site with a superb restaurant whose terraces overlook two tranquil beaches protected in pretty coves. The beaches are connected by a tunnel carved through solid rock through which you may safely walk. A multi-coloured, flower bedecked, and landscaped hillside leads down to the sea from the house with pretty paths and fishponds. There is a constant supply of fresh plants and flowers from the greenhouses which belonged to the house in yester-year. In summer the house area is a blaze of colour and very appealing. The site which reaches back to the road has 579 pitches on well shaded terraces. Of these 300 are accessible to tourers and there are some 50 pitches on flat ground alongside the sea – the views are stunning and you wake to the sounds of the waves. There is a small (10 m) round swimming pool in the lower areas of the gardens, if you prefer fresh water. Cars may not park by tents or caravans in high season, but must be left on car parks or roads. Electrical connections are available in all parts. The three well maintained sanitary blocks have British style toilets and free hot water in both the washbasins (with some private cabins) and the controllable showers, and a tap to draw from for the sinks. This is an excellent site for both long and short visits.

How to find it: Access to site is signed from the C253 coast road 3 km. south of Palamos.

General Details: Open 1 April - 30 Sept. Supermarket. Bar. Takeaway. Good restaurant with attractive shaded terrace (15/5-15/9). Table tennis. Fishing. Children's play area and sports area. Games room. Bicycle hire 2 km. Riding, golf 5 km. Washing machines. Car wash. Gas supplies. Chemical disposal. Motorcaravan services. Traditional Spanish-style rooms and small mobile homes to let.

Charges 2000: Per person ptas 840; child (4-10 yrs) 460; caravan, car and electricity 3,000; motorcaravan and electricity 2,500; tent, car and electricity 2,850, extra car, m/cycle or boat 930; dog 480. Plus 7% VAT. Discounts in low seasons. Credit cards accepted.

Reservations: are made to guarantee admission (needed more for caravans than for tents) with deposit. Address: Aptdo Correos 348, 17250 Playa de Aro (Girona). Tel: 972/651095. FAX: 972/651671. E-mail: info@campingtreumal.com.

8130 Camping Internacional de Calonge, Platja d'Aro, nr Gerona/Girona

Smart, spacious site with wide range of amenities, open all year.
This spacious, well laid out site has access by a footbridge over the coast road to a pretty beach. It is a family site with a two good pools (with lifeguard), plus large sunbathing area and a range of amenities which include a comfortable restaurant with large terraces and patio bar, serving good food at reasonable prices. The site is set on sloping ground and is quite large with 800 pitches, all with electricity. A large proportion are suitable for touring units, the remainder for tents, being set on attractively landscaped terraces. Access to some pitches may be a little difficult. There is good shade from the tall pine trees. Some sites which are nominally 'open all year' offer nothing but a pitch during winter, but Calonge has 167 pitches for winter use and a heated sanitary block. The generous sanitary installations in the new and renovated blocks include British style WCs, free hot showers and some washbasins in private cabins. Used by tour operators in the upper areas of the site in their own separate areas and some mobile homes similarly situated. Good security. A little road train ferries campers to the beach. There is a nature area within the site for walks or picnics. A separate area is dedicated to dogs which includes a doggie shower!

How to find it: Site is on inland side of coast road between Palamos and Platja d'Aro, just south of Sa. Calonge and 4 km. south of Palamos.

General Details: Open all year. Electricity throughout (5A). Shop (Easter-30/10, supermarket 500 m). Bar/restaurant (Easter- 30/10). Swimming pool (1/4-30/10). Children's playground on sand. Bicycle hire. Table tennis. Tennis. Volleyball. Fishing 300 m. Riding 10 km. Golf 3 km. Cash machine. Exchange. Hairdresser. Laundry. Gas supplies. Chemical disposal. Motorcaravan services. Trigano type tents and mobile homes to let.

Charges 2000: Per adult ptas. 475 - 785; child (2-10 yrs) 245 - 440; pitch for caravan or tent with car incl. electricity 1,705 - 2,730; motorcaravan incl. electricity 1,465 - 2,170. All plus 7% VAT. Discounts for longer stays Oct - end May. No credit cards.

Euro: Per adult 2.86 - 4.72; child (2-10 yrs) 1.48 - 2.64; pitch for caravan or tent with car incl. electricity 10.25 - 16.41; motorcaravan incl. electricity 8.81 - 13.04.

Reservations: Write with deposit (6,000 ptas). Address: Aptdo. Correos 272, 17251 Calonge (Girona). Tel: 972/651233. or 651464. FAX: 972/652507. E-mail: intercalonge@intercalonge.com. UK contact: Mr J Worthington, 0161-799-1274.

SPAIN - Costa Brava

8160 Camping Cala Gogo, Platja d'Aro, nr Gerona/Girona

Large, successful and vibrant site by sea with swimming pool and many amenities.

One of the best known campsites in Spain, its situation on a wooded hillside leading down to a small cove with a sandy beach is one of considerable natural beauty. In a high central position there are two good sized pools (25 x 12 m.) and children's pool – an excellent provision. Close by are shops, restaurant and a bar with adjoining terrace with views over the pools down to the beach, all open for the whole season. A second floodlit bar and takeaway are by the beach open in high season (reached via a tunnel under the main road by regular road train – there is the possibility of road noise in eastern parts of the site). The resort of Platja d'Aro is 2 km. Cala Gogo is divided into 869 individual pitches, some shaded, others with artificial shade. Pitch size ranges from 80-100 sq.m. without the car, which stands in front of or near your unit. There are now many more larger pitches and some 300 have water and drainage (including chemicals). The site is an active, bustling place, with over 3,000 campers when full. The distance from the busy beach with good bathing, depends on the position of your pitch. Some are now right by the beach, others up to 800 m. uphill, but two 'Gua gua' (South American Spanish for bus) tractor trains, operating all season, take people up and down and add to the sense of fun and energy. A programme of animation includes sports, TV and videos, tournaments, disco (until midnight only), entertainment, etc. for children and adults is free (7 nights a week), as are the sports centre facilities, plus a 'mini-club' and crèche for small ones. Also fairly close is a new aqua-park offering waterslides, wave simulation etc. with a bus from the camp. Another quieter beach is adjacent. The seven sanitary blocks are of a high standard and are continuously cleaned. They are part of an updating programme which will leave them fully tiled with British WCs, free hot water in the washbasins set in flat surfaces (some cabins), and free hot showers. The gates are closed to cars at midnight and the site is well supervised which includes video surveillance. Used by tour operators (52 pitches). An excellent site for families with children, old and young.

How to find it: Site is on the main road between Palamos and Platja d'Aro, 4.5 km. south of Palamos.

General Details: Open 15 April - 1 Oct, including amenities. 160,000 sq.m. Artificial or natural shade on most pitches. Large supermarket. General shop. Tobacconist. Restaurants and bars. Swimming pools and paddling pool. Children's playground and crèche. Sports centre. Table tennis. Sailboards and pedaloes for hire. Fishing. TV/video room. Bicycle hire 4 km. Riding 10 km. Golf 4 km. Bureau de change. Telephones. Medical service; nurse daily, doctor alternate days. Good 24 hr security service. Laundry. Gas supplies. Chemical disposal. Motorcaravan services. Bungalows, Trigano tents and mobile homes to rent. Dogs are not accepted in July/Aug.

Charges 2000: Per person 480 - 840 ptas; child (2-9 yrs) 245 - 420; car 500 - 900; tent 565 - 1,130; caravan or trailer tent 655 - 1,310; motorcaravan 815 - 1,435; electricity (5A) 515. All plus 7% VAT. No credit cards.

Reservations: are made for min. 1 week with deposit (10,000 ptas.), no fee. Address: Apdo 80, 17250 Platja d'Aro (Girona). Tel: 972/651564. FAX: 972/650553. E-mail: calagogo@calagogo.es.

AR Discount
Less 10%
excl. 21/6-31/8

8200 Camping Cala Llevadó, Tossa de Mar

see colour advert between pages 256/257

Beautifully situated cliff-side site with excellent facilities.

For splendour of position Cala Llevadó can compare with almost any in this book. Situated on steep slopes, it has fine views of the sea and coast below and is shaped something like half a bowl. There are flat terraced areas for caravans and tents on the upper levels of the two slopes and a great many individual level pitches for tents along the lower slopes leading down to the sea. There is usually a car access (may be narrow) not far from these pitches. In some areas cars may be required to park separately. Many electrical connections cover all caravan sectors and one tent area. High up in the site with a good aspect, is the attractive restaurant/bar with a large terrace overlooking the high quality children's play area and the free swimming pool (20 x 10 m) which is much frequented, plus semi-circular children's pool. There is a rather steep road leading right down to one of the four sandy or pebbly coves (one naturist) with a car park at the base. Some other pleasant little coves can also be reached by climbing down on foot (with care!). Some fairly severe climbing and descending must clearly be expected on this site and should be considered if older or disabled people are included in your party. Four very well equipped sanitary blocks are well spaced around the site and built in an attractive style, with fully controllable, free hot water in washbasins (some in cabins) and in well equipped showers, baby baths and British style toilets. The reception area has post office and telephone facilities. Cala Llevadó is luxurious and has character, with many regular clients and the atmosphere is informal and friendly. Only 150 of the 650 pitches are accessible for caravans, so reservation in season is vital. It is peacefully situated but only five minutes from the busy resort of Tossa. Torches needed at night. There are many watersports activities locally. Some tour operators.

How to find it: Cala Llevadó leads off the new Tossa-Lloret road about 3 km. from Tossa; the approach from either direction now presents no problems.

General Details: Open 1 May - 30 Sept. Large supermarket. New restaurant/bar with terrace (3/5-28/9). Swimming pools. Tennis. Three children's play areas. Entertainment for children (4-12 yrs). Sailing, water ski and windsurfing school. Fishing. Scuba diving. Bicycle hire 3 km. Post office/telephone. Washing machines and dryer. Laundry service. Gas supplies. Chemical disposal. Motorcaravan services. Tents (7) and caravans (7) for hire.

Charges 2000: Per person ptas. 630 - 930; child (3-14 yrs) 390 - 510; car or m/cycle 630 - 860; tent 630 - 930; caravan 720 - 1,000; motorcaravan 1,050 - 1,450; electricity 490; dog 440. Plus 7% VAT. Credit cards accepted. Euro: per person 3.79 - 5.59; child (3-14 yrs) 2.34 - 3.07; car or m/cycle 3.79 - 5.17; tent 3.79 - 5.59; caravan 4.33 - 6.01; motorcaravan 6.31 - 8.71; electricity 2.94; dog 2.64.

Reservations: accepted with deposit and fee. Address: Ctra. de Tossa - Lloret km. 3, 17320 Tossa de Mar (Girona). Tel: 972/340314. FAX: 972/341187. E-mail: calalleva@grn.es.

AR Discount
Less 10% on person charge

8230 Beach Camp El Pinar, Blanes, nr Gerona/Girona

see colour advert between pages 256/257

Pleasant, family orientated, smallish site adjoining good beach.

Previously named Camping El Pinar, this is essentially a family site without tour operators or mobile homes. The new name sums up the direction in which the owners are developing the site, with an emphasis on a more participatory approach to camping with an increase in the amount of activities and facilities offered – mostly directed towards sports. It is situated at the southern edge of Blanes beach, with direct access, and is about 2 km. from the town. The 690 pitches (250 on the new side), all with electricity and a minimum of 60 sq.m. are in two sections separated by the road with both sides having direct access to the beach. The older side is mostly shaded by pine or broad leaf trees the newer has young trees which do not offer a great deal of shade as yet. The newer side has its own modern sanitary block and a new large swimming pool with a generous sunbathing area, plus a children's pool which are only used in July and August. A pass is required for the pool (small deposit). The sanitary blocks are tiled, have British style WCs and controllable hot showers, including shelves and/dressing areas. There are baby baths and open plan washbasins (mostly cold water, but with hot in the ladies part of the new block). Dishwashing facilities are under cover. The sanitary facilities on the original site are beginning to look a little tired. A restaurant and takeaway service are available plus an aerobic centre with professional instructor (but no gym equipment). Beach activities and games are organised. There is a small supermarket and a secure children's play area on grass. This site will appeal particularly to families seeking easy access to a long beach (shelves quite steeply) and the attractions of a major resort. Regular bus service into the centre of Blanes.

How to find it: Site is the last going south from Blanes centre. Follow camping signs in Blanes to El Pinar sign.

General Details: Open Easter - 30 Sept. Bar/restaurant with takeaway. Small supermarket. Swimming pool. Volleyball. Table tennis. Children's playground. Activities for adults and children organised in season (2/5-16/9) including dancing, bicycle excursions, aerobics, Laundry services. Excursions. Watersports near. Gas supplies. Chemical disposal. Motorcaravan services. Bungalows and mobile homes to let.

Charges 2000: Per person 525 - 670 ptas; child 450 - 575; pitch incl. electricity 1,650 - 1,950; plus 7% VAT. Discounts for pensioners and low season longer stays. Credit cards accepted.

Reservations: Contact site (no deposit). Address: Villa de Madrid s/n, 17300 Blanes. Tel: 972/331083. FAX: 972/331100. E-mail: elpinar@mx3.redestb.es. A 'Camping Cheques' site.

AR Discount
Less 25%, min 7 days in low season

SPAIN - Costa Brava

8235 Camping Blanes, Blanes

Small campsite with direct access to beach and an elevated small pool with sun terrace.
This is a flat rectangular site between road and beach with 206 average sized pitches. It is situated in 2 hectares of a pine wood with good shade at S'Abanell beach and is about 1 km. from the centre of Blanes. All the facilities are contained in a single block near the entrance. Unusually the small pool with a sun-bathing area is atop the small and pleasant restaurant and bar and is reached by a stairway to one side of the building. The single sanitary block is close to the utility area and is clean and satisfactory with British style WCs, free hot showers, the usual washing facilities and laundry sinks with one hot tap. A baby changing surface and facilities for disabled campers complete the services. A single security gate allows access to a long public promenade and the beach of coarse sand which shelves quite steeply. A variety of watersports are available and canoes are for hire close by. This is an uncomplicated site with a bus service to and from the town which stops outside the campsite if you wish to explore the local area. Torches will be necessary in some more remote parts of the site.

How to find it: From A7 autopista, take exit 10, or the A19 to Blanes and follow general camping signs heading south from Blanes town centre, from where site is signed.

General Details: Open 1 March - 31 Oct. Bar and snack bar (1/5-15/10). Supermarket (1/6-25/9). Small pool with sunbathing terrace. Solarium. Children's playground. Electronic games. Bicycle hire 500 m. Riding 5 km. Golf 6 km. Money exchange. Security boxes for hire. Doctor on call. Laundry service. Car wash. Gas supplies. Chemical disposal. Motorcaravan services.

Charges 2000: Per pitch, including caravan, car and electricity ptas. 1,650 - 1,950; adult 525 - 670; child 450 - 575; tent and m/cycle 900 - 1,100. All plus 7% VAT. No credit cards.

Reservations: Not required. Address: Avenida Villa de Madrid 33, 17300 Blanes (when closed: Apdo 72, 17300 Blanes). Tel: 972/331591 (or 972/858021 when site is closed). FAX: 972/337063 (all year).

AR Discount
Less 10%
excl. 15/6-31/8

8240 Camping Botànic Bona Vista Kim, Calella de la Costa, nr Barcelona

Delightfully attractive, small site on hillside south of Calella de la Costa.
While Calella itself may conjure up visions of mass tourism, this site is set on a steep hillside some 3 km. out of the town. Apart from perhaps some noise from the nearby coast road and railway, it is a quite delightful setting, with an abundance of flowers, shrubs and roses (1,700 in total, all planted by the knowl-edgeable owner Kim, who has won several top Catalonian prizes for his roses). The site design success-fully marries the beautiful botanic surrounds with the attractive views of the bay. The 160 pitches, all with electricity, are 60-80 sq.m. or more and are situated on flat terraces on the slopes, with some shade. The access road is steep and many of the pitches enjoy lovely views due to the elevation. There are quite good beaches, including a naturist beach, just across the road and railway, accessible via a tunnel and crossing. The standard of work and design in the sanitary installations in three blocks is quite outstanding for a small site (indeed for any site). They include controllable, free hot showers, with dressing area, British WCs and (in the newest block) some washbasins (H&C) in cabins, a bidet in the ladies' and a baby room. Dish-washing facilities with hot water, are under cover and there are washing machines. The bar/restaurant is close to reception at the bottom of the site. It is unusual in the attractive choice of Spanish décor and in having a circular, central open-hearth fire/cooker, and serves both eat-in and takeaway meals, with two roof top terraces. The first level has a terrace with service from the restaurant and bar, above that (for over 16 year olds), is the computer controlled sauna, jacuzzi with pool sized filter, a well equipped gymnasium and a sunbathing area all enjoying views over the sea. Amenities for children include a playground by reception, satellite TV, with 2 pool tables in a separate room and a new recreation park (2,000 sq.m.) with table tennis, football, etc. The barbecue and picnic area, petanque, and recreation park are at the top of the site which is a stiff climb. On arrival, park at the restaurant and choose a pitch – Kim is most helpful with siting your van. No cycling is allowed on site due to the steep hills.

How to find it: From N11 coast road site is signed travelling south of Calella (at km. 665), and is on right hand side of road - care is needed as road is busy and sign is almost on top of turning (next to Camping Roca Grossa). Entrance is very steep. From Barcelona, after passing through Sant Pol de Mar, go into outside lane shortly after 'Camping 800 m.' sign and keep signalling left. Site entrance is just before the two lanes merge.

General Details: Open all year. Electricity throughout. Bar/restaurant, takeaway and shop (1/3-1/11). Sauna, solarium and jacuzzi. Large children's playground. Recreation park. Satellite TV. Games room. Barbecue and picnic area. Fishing 100 m. Bicycle hire 1 km. Riding, golf 3 km. Watersports near. Chemical disposal. Motorcaravan services.

Charges 2000: Per person ptas. 575; child (3-10 yrs) 500; car 575; tent or caravan 575; motorcaravan 1,150; m/cycle 500; dog 325; electricity (6A) 500. All plus 7% VAT. No credit cards.
Euros: Per person 3.45; child (3-10 yrs) 3.00; car 3.45; tent or caravan 3.45; motorcaravan 6.91; m/cycle 3.00; dog 1.95; electricity 3.00.

Reservations: Write to site. Address: Ctra. N-ll, Km.665, PO Box 38, 08370 Calella (Catalunya). Tel: 931/7692488. FAX: 931/7695804. E-mail: bonavista@redestb.es.

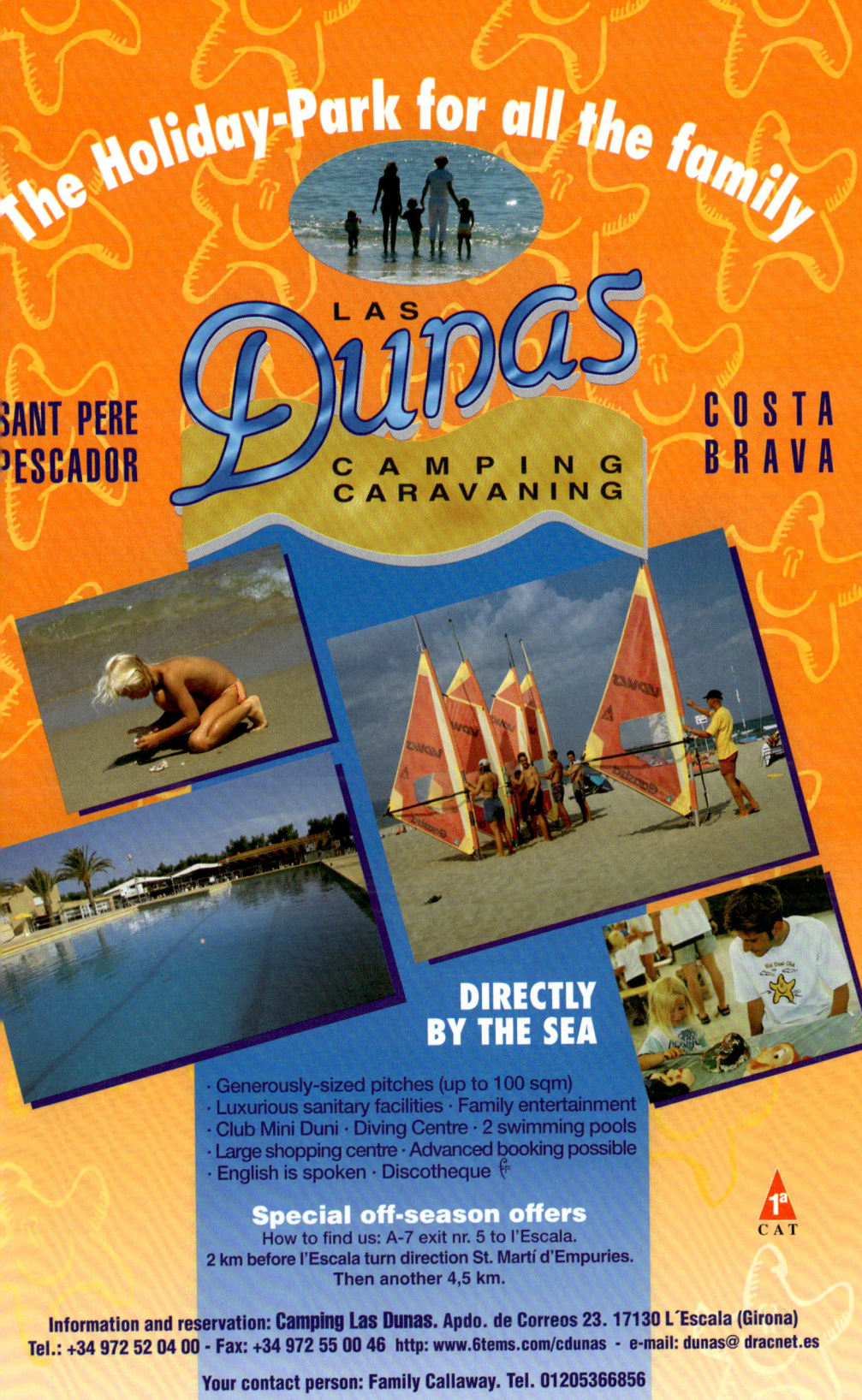

The Holiday-Park for all the family

LAS Dunas
CAMPING CARAVANING

SANT PERE PESCADOR

COSTA BRAVA

DIRECTLY BY THE SEA

· Generously-sized pitches (up to 100 sqm)
· Luxurious sanitary facilities · Family entertainment
· Club Mini Duni · Diving Centre · 2 swimming pools
· Large shopping centre · Advanced booking possible
· English is spoken · Discotheque

Special off-season offers
How to find us: A-7 exit nr. 5 to l'Escala.
2 km before l'Escala turn direction St. Martí d'Empuries.
Then another 4,5 km.

1ª
CAT

Information and reservation: Camping Las Dunas. Apdo. de Correos 23. 17130 L´Escala (Girona)
Tel.: +34 972 52 04 00 - Fax: +34 972 55 00 46 http: www.6tems.com/cdunas - e-mail: dunas@ dracnet.es

Your contact person: Family Callaway. Tel. 01205366856

Camping Caravaning

el delfin verde

Apartat de correus 43 - E-17257 TORROELLA DE MONTGRI
Tel. (34) 972 758 454 - Fax (34) 972 760 070
URL: http://www.eldelfinverde.com
E-mail: eldelfinverde@drac.com

One of the best and most beautiful holiday sites on the COSTA BRAVA

In quiet surroundings, by a magnificent wide and miles-long sand beach and with the largest fresh-water swimmpingpool of the Costa Brava. By the way, we also have the most generously-sized pitches of the region. Many green areas and groups of trees. Commercial centre. Fresh water plant.

GASTRONOMY: 3 bars, 2 restaurants, 2 grills, pizzeria, 2 snackbars and beach bar.

SPORTS: large sports area for hand-, volley-, basket- and football and badminton. 8 tennis courts, minigolf (3000 m2 - 18 holes), windsurfing school.

ACTIVITIES: Organised 'fiestas', disco 'light', dancing. Excursions, organised sports competitions and movie/video shows.

7 Modern ablution blocks with hot water everywhere, money exchange, safe, medical service, tel.

BUNGALOWS AND APPARTMENTS FOR HIRE.

Open: 15.4 – 24.9.

MOBILE HOMES, WOODEN BUNGALOWS "CAMPITEL" AND TENTBUNGALOWS "TRIGANO" FOR HIRE

Mas Patoxas

Camping Caravaning Bungalow Park

Open from 14.1 till 17.12
In summer: 1.4 till 30.9
Rest of the year only weekends.

Road Palafrugell to Pals, km 5.
Tel. (34) 972 63 69 28
    972 63 63 61
Fax (34) 972 66 73 49
E-17256 PALS (Girona)
COSTA BRAVA

Situated between the beach of Pals (5 km) and the beaches of Begur. Ideal situation near-by the sea and mountains, surrounded by forests. 500 pitches with conn. for electr., water and waste water. Modern sanitary installations with hot water in washing basins, showers and baths. Sports facilities : tennis, futball, basket, volley and table tennis.

les medes
Camping Caravaning
COSTA BRAVA

CÀMPING
les medes

Quiet, flat holiday site only 2 km from L'Estartit, surrounded by fields en inmidst of nature. At only 800m from beach, ideal f. children and watersport. All pitches are properly laid out and w. electr. conn. Modern ablution blocks (baby room, complete bath room f. disabled) w. free hot water. Swimming pool, superm., bar, restaurant, meals to take away, washing machines, car-wash w. hoover, table tennis, boules game, volley, children's playground, organised activities, bikes f. hire. **Bungalows for hire.** Familiar campsite open the whole year with heated indoor swimming-pool, solarium, sauna and heated sanitary installations. **Open throughout the year.**

Paratge Camp de l'Arbre • E-17258 L'ESTARTIT (Girona) • Tel. (34) 972 75 18 05 • Fax (34) 972 75 04 13
e-mail: campinglesmedes@cambrescat.es • http://www.campinglesmedes.com

Cala Llevadó
camping

Cala Llevadó
camping ★★★

First-class Camping and Caravanning site. **Fabulous situation** in he most beautiful part of the **Costa Brava**. Isolated and quiet. 4 beaches. Swimming pool, children's playground, bar, restaurant, supermarket, laundry service, hairdressing, medical service. **Exceptional and luxurious sanitary facilitie**s, with free hot water. Numbered pitches.
Open 1.5 - 30.9
Internet: http://www.calallevado.com

Sport and animation:
swimming-pool, tennis, windsurfing, diving, compressed air, excursions, minigolf, basket, mountain-bike.

Reservation service. Caravans and bungalows for hire. Write to:

Camping **Cala Llevadó**
Post Box 34, 17320 **Tossa de Mar**
Costa Brava - Spain
Tel (34) 972 340 314
Fax (34) 972 341 187
E-mail: calallev@grn.es

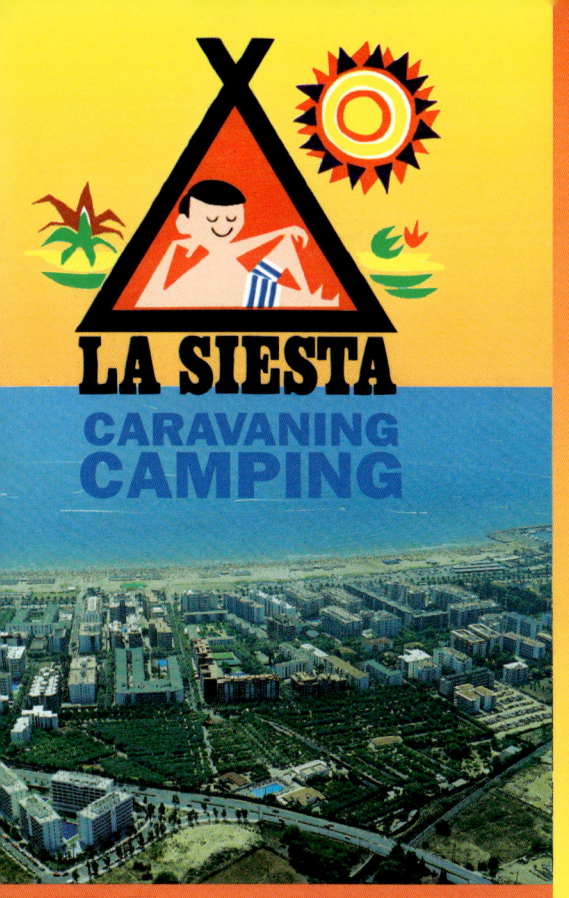

LA SIESTA
CARAVANING CAMPING

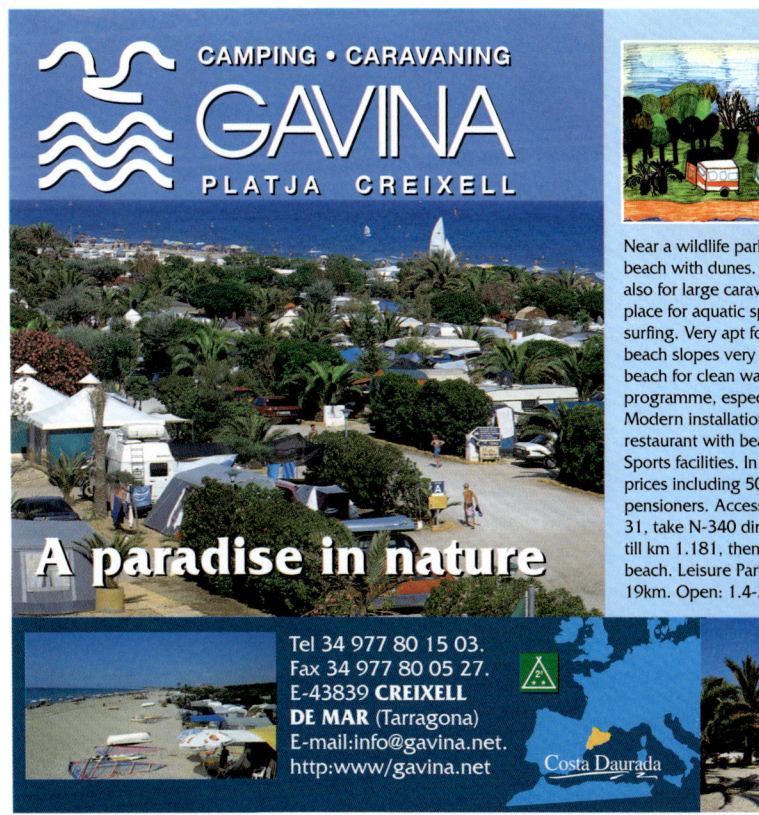

Your Holiday Park

PARC DE VACANCES

Sangulí Salou

CAMPING & BUNGALOW PARK

CAMPING & BUNGALOW PARK SANGULÍ, situated in Salou in the heart of the Costa Daurada and only 50 m from the beach, offers all amenities only a high-class camping site can offer.
• An animation programme for young and old; daily entertainment in an exceptional amphitheatre with a capacity of 2000 seats.
• 6 swimming pools, 2 supermarkets, 4 bars, 2 children's playgrounds, gift-shop, restaurant, take-away-meals, launderette, etc.
• Sports facilities, such as tennis, mini-golf, squash, indoor football, basketball, petanque, volleyball, etc.
• 6 modern ablution blocks, offering the highest level of hygiene and comfort (facilities for the disabled and babies etc.).
All this, surrounded by a unique nature and precious gardens, makes CAMPING & BUNGALOW PARK SANGULÍ your ideal holiday destination.

"This one I can recommend"

SPECIAL PRICES IN LOW SEASON
AWARDED "CAMP SITE OF THE YEAR 1988" BY THE CATALAN GOVERNMENT, "CAMP SITE OF THE YEAR 1992" BY THE ROYAL DUTCH TOURING CLUB ANWB, "CAMP SITE OF THE YEAR 1994" BY THE FRENCH MAGAZINE "CARAVANIER".

Prolongació carrer E, s/n. - Apartado de Correos 123.
43840 SALOU (Tarragona) España
Tels.: 977 38 16 41 - 977 38 16 98 - Fax: 977 38 46 16
http://www. sangulí.es   e-mail: mail@sangulí.es

Please send further information

Name ....
Street ....
Town ....
Country ....

ALAN
ROGER

Cambrils-Park
CAMPING

Ctra. Salou - Cambrils, Km. 1   43850 CAMBRILS (TARRAGONA) - España
✉ Apartado de Correos 123   43840 SALOU (Tarragona) - España
☎ 977 35 10 31 - Fax 977 35 22 10
e-mail : mail@cambrilspark.es
http://www.cambrilspark.es

The only de luxe site on the Costa Dorada.

CAMBRILS-PARK, a real holiday camping park, which you will find all types
of installations and services even for the most pretentious guests.
SWIMMING POOLS, BARS, RESTAURANT, SPORTS, SHOWS,
MINI-CLUB... and a wide and varied ANIMATION programme for young
and old. Enjoy your holidays with us, more than anywhere else.
Come to Cambrils-Park, where your dreams will come true.

Please send further information

Name ....
Street ....
Town ....
Country ....

ALAN
ROGERS

TAMARIT PARK
CAMPING BUNGALOWS

Tel. (0034) 977 65 01 28
Fax (0034) 977 65 04 51
E-43008 TARRAGONA
TAMARIT - COSTA DAURADA
internet: http://www.tamarit.com
E-Mail: tamaritpark@tamarit.com

The ideal campsite (7 km. north of Tarragona) to enjoy nature, the sun, a sloping beach (500 m. long) and all kind of water sports. The mild climate permits you to swim in the sea from April to October.

Situated in extraordinary, beautiful surroundings, beneath the ruins of the Tamarit castle. Calm and isolated site (1,2km from national road N-340 and railway track).

Only 20 km. from the exciting theme park "Universal's/Port Aventura".

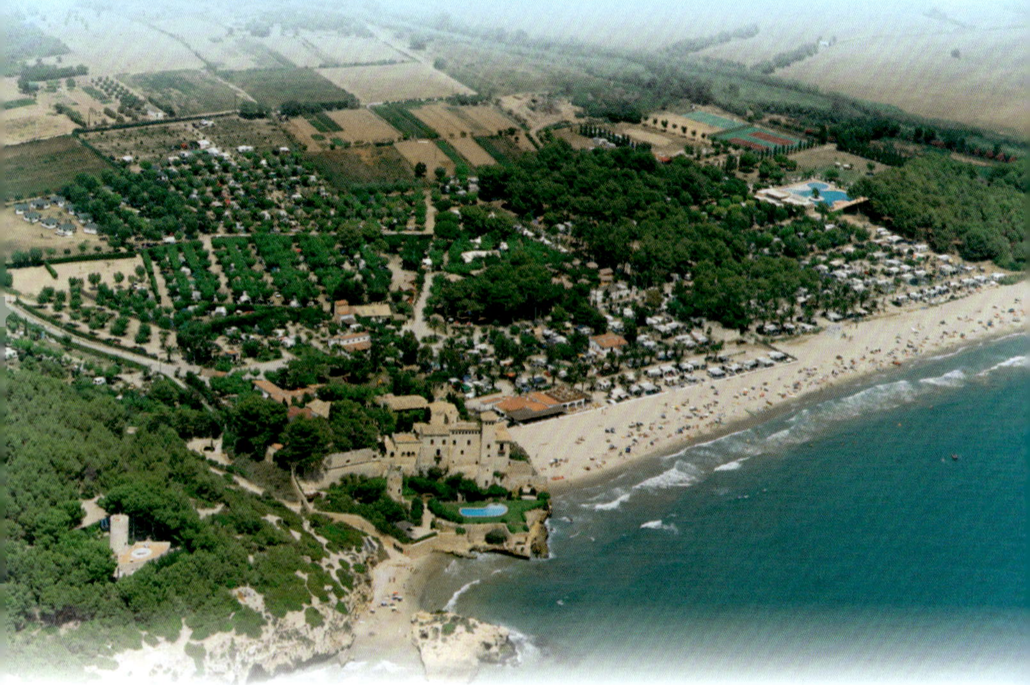

Restaurant-pizzeria directly on the beach.
Supermarket. Entertainment program for adults and children. Large sports area with two illuminated tennis courts-football-basketball-volleyball-table tennis and boccia. We are open all year round and offer special prices and 40% discount out of season for pensioners and 10 % for students with valid ID for long stays.
We speak English.

Access: A-7 until excit 32, then N-340 direction Tarragona until km. 1,172, direction beach and at the end of road, after a campsite take a LEFT.

PLAYA MONTROIG
CAMPING & BUNGALOW PARK
vacaciones VIVAS

A family holiday park equipped to the highest standards, surrounded by large tropical gardens and with a spectacular swimming pool. Situated in front of a wonderful sandy beach; PLAYA MONTROIG is a very safe and clean holiday park, that offers, among other things, the following services and installations: wide variety of leisure activities (including tournaments, shows, excursions, etc...), Hobby Centre (workshop), Sport Club tournaments and sport activities), Junior Club & Teenager Club. Sport area with basketball and football fields, skateboard track, archery, jogging track. Fitness, tennis, minigolf, a large shopping centre, restaurants, bars and discotheques.

Dream Holidays

COSTA DAURADA - MONT-ROIG - TARRAGONA
CATALUNYA · ESPAÑA

*Splendid Holidays
in contact with Nature*

Take notice of our special offers!

For further information & reservation:
Apartado de Correos 3
E-43300 Mont-roig [Tarragona] · ESPAÑA
Tel.: 34/977/81.06.37 · Fax: 34/977/81.14.11

http://www.playamontroig.com
E-mail: info@playamontroig.com

CAMPING + BUNGALOWS

PARK PLAYA BARÀ

JACUZZI

JACUZZI

SUBTROPICAL EXOTICA
ON SPAIN'S GOLDEN COAST

1ª ★★

A botanical garden,
a campers paradise

OPEN: 31.3 - 30.9

SWIMMING POOLS AND BIG JACUZZIS FREE

Spanish order for Touristic Merits and Catalan Government Tourism Diploma. Officially recommended by the leading European Automobile and Camping Clubs. ANWB Camp Site of the Year 1991. Garden like, terraced site with excellent installations.

Sand and rock beach with camp owned bar, near elegant holiday village - no high buildings, ideal for walks, not far from typical fishing village and holiday resort with many shopping possibilities. Dry, sunny climate throughout. Large, garden like pitches with conn. f. electr., water and waste water disposal, many w. own marble washing basins. The most modern sanatary install. w. free hot water, individual wash cabins, compl. children's baths, install. f. disabled, chem. toilets. Car wash. Heated swimming pool (26°), solarium. Large, compl. sports area (tennis, squash, volley, basket, large football ground, roller skating, minigolf, bicycle track, table tennis). Children's playground, medical service, safe deposit, money exchange. Bar, grill, restaurant, superm., souvenirs. Animation for all ages - Roman amphitheatre (dance, folklore, cultural progr. and many surprises). A 100% family camp with nice atmosphere for nature loving guests. Radio and tv forbidden on part of camp. Bungalows for hire. Special fees in off-season. 10% P/N reduction in main season if you stay at least 10 days. English spoken. Ask for our brochure and more inf. and/or reservation. Acces: A-7 (Barcelona-Tarragona), exit (sortida) nr. 31 (Vendrell-Coma-ruga), on the N-340 direct. Tarragona till Roman Arch, turn around arch and entrance on your right.

At only 15 min.
from the attraction park
"PORT AVENTURA"

From 31.3 - 20.6 & 31.8 - 30.9:
50% reduction P/N
90% on tennis, minigolf, surf P/N penioners.

E-43883 RODA DE BARÀ (TARRAGONA)
Tel. (34) 977 802 701 Fax (34) 977 800 456
www.barapark.es . E-mail: info@barapark.es

Only 40 km from Santander (ferry) and 70 km from Bilbao (ferry), easily and quickly reached along the magnificent, new, toll-free autovia and the coast roads.

A 25 ha. holiday site with a large (4 ha) recreation and sports area and a precious, 8 ha natural park with animals in semiliberty.

Modern, first category installations. Beautifull surroundings with direct access to wide, clean beaches. Surrounded by meadows and woods.

Service and comfort for the most exacting guests. Properly marked pitches.

English spoken. Open from Easter to 30th September.

'our beautiful holiday destination in SPAIN

CAMPING
PLAYA JOYEL

E-39180 NOJA (SANTANDER, CANTABRIA) SPAIN
Tel. (34) 942 63 00 81
Fax (34) 942 63 12 94

CAMPING
VILANOVA PARK

Apartado (postbus 64)
Tel. (34) 93 893 34 02 • Fax (34) 93 893 55 28
E-08800 Vilanova i la Geltrú (Barcelona)

An elegant site with country club atmosphere!

50 km South of Barcelona, in the wine and champagne centre of Catalonia with more than 600 palm trees. Quiet situation. Very modern sanit. install. w. hot water everywhere. Swimming pool of 1.000 sqm and children's pool with big colour fountain (lighted in the evenings). Excellent restaurant "Chaine de Rôtisseurs" in old catalan mansion. Superm., shops, English press, children's progr., activities. Large pitches w. electr. conn. Private, large ecological park of 50.000 sqm. f. beautiful walks and picnics. Access: Motorway A-7, coming fr. Barcelona: exit 29; coming fr. Tarragona: exits 30 & 31; follow indic. Vilanova i la Geltrú/Sitges.

Open throughout the year. We speak English. Special discounts for old-age pensioners from Sept. 'til June on pitches and mobile homes.

Web: www.vilanovapark.es
E-mail:
info@vilanovapark.es
reservas@vilanovapark.es

la ballena alegre

SANT PERE PESCADOR
GIRONA

Access: A-7, exit (sortida) 5, direction L'Escala. Road (Gi-623) Km 18,5 and turn of at St. Marti d'Empuries

ADAC

erkende camping
ANWB

ESPAÑA

GRAN CONFORT

In English I am called the **"Happy WHALE**. Situated next to the natural park "The Aiguamolls de l'Empordà and the Roman remains of Empuries, you will find the id spot to spend a good time w your family. The camp situated along a 1.700 long, large, sandy bea (where by the way, yo won't find any whale We offer a fantastic animation program a all facilities you need a restful holiday.

LA BALLENA ALEGRE 2
Inf.B2-AR
E-17470 Sant Pere Pescador (Girona) Spain
Tel. 34 600 400 200
and 34 972 52 03 02
Fax 34 / 972 52 03 3

Internet: http://www.ballena-alegre
E-mail: infb2@ballena-alegre.es

Costa Daurada

The 'Golden Coast' is aptly named with a fine band of pale yellow sand stretching along its length. It covers the shores of Barcelona and Tarragona provinces, from Rio Tordera to Vinaros. The section south of Barcelona includes the resorts of Sitges, Tarragona and Salou and is backed by pine-covered hills. The northern section includes Arenys and Calella, and is flatter, with a fair penetration of industry. The area is famed for its fresh vegetables and fish and in Barcelona boasts one of the most exciting cities in the world.

8310 Camping La Ballena Alegre, Vildecans, Castelldefels

Spacious, well laid out site on beach, with comprehensive shops and restaurant/bars.

La Ballena Alegre is one of the best known sites in Spain. About 16 km. from the centre of Barcelona, it has a super sandy beach more than a kilometre long and 100 m. wide, although some may prefer the new pool complex with slides and jacuzzi. It is a very large site, most of which is covered by a pinewood and divided into 1,450 pitches of about 70 sq.m. with 1,250 for touring units going on the left hand side. Space is not usually a problem, certainly outside July/Aug. The sanitary blocks are all good, although they still vary in size and type, two being new. All have free warm water in washbasins and the new blocks have some private cabins, There are free controllable hot showers with screen, mostly British style WCs and units for disabled visitors. Cleaning is good - a cleaner is on duty at each block during the day. There is an attractive bar/restaurant with entertainment in season. Although not a quiet site, with a lively atmosphere in high season and some aircraft noise, it is nevertheless well run. Used by tour operators.

How to find it: From Barcelona on N11 either turn off on C245 road to Gava and Castelldefels or take motorway A2 spur towards Castelldefels - El Prat de Llobregat and continue to Castelldefels. Entrance leads directly off C246 dual-carriageway 'Autovia Castelldefels' on coast side of the road, by a service station.

General Details: Open 1 April - 30 Sept. Large supermarket and other shops. Restaurants (24/6-30/8). Bar and snack bar. Swimming pool complex with slides and jacuzzi (25/5-25/9). Sports activities: aerobics, squash, roller skating, bicycle track, swimming, football etc. Amphitheatre with folk dances, shows etc. staged twice weekly (24/6-30/8). Soundproof disco. Children's playground. Tennis. Fishing. Bicycle hire 6 km. Riding 3 km. Golf 2 km. Garage by entrance. Hairdressers. Washing machines. Bureau de change. Treatment room with nurse; doctor daily. Gas supplies. Chemical disposal. Motorcaravan services. Chalets, bungalows and mobile homes to rent.

Charges 2000: Per person ptas. 600; child (under 10) 300; pitch incl. car and electricity 1,550, 2,500 or 3,100, m/cycle with tent 1,500, 1,600 or 2,000; dog 250. All plus 7% VAT. Credit cards accepted.

Reservations: only made in the sense of guaranteeing admission. Site address: Autovia Castelldefels km.12.5, 08840 Viladecans (Barcelona). Tel: 93/6580504. FAX: 93/6580575. E-mail: ballena1@ballena-alegre.es.

8390 Camping Vilanova Park, Vilanova i la Geltru, Sitges, nr Barcelona

Hillside site with views to sea, good quality installations and large pool complex.

This large modern site has been equipped with costly installations of good quality and is open all year. The most remarkable feature is the excellent swimming pool complex with one very large pool with water jets and a floodlit fountain. Together with a smaller children's pool, this covers an area of 1,000 sq.m. and enjoys wonderful views over the sea. In the same area is the shopping centre and large bar and restaurant, set around thoughtfully extended and refurbished old Catalan farm buildings where dancing and entertainment take place. There is an ambitious animation programme throughout the high season, and at weekends for the remainder of the year. The site is 4 km. from Vilanova town and beach (with bus service) and 11 km. from Sitges. At present there are 1,260 pitches with a very significant proportion of well separated static units. There are 460 marked pitches for touring units in separate areas of the site mostly with their own water supply. They are marked and are 70-100 sq.m. Some larger pitches (100 sq.m.) have electricity, water and drainage. The terrain, hard surfaced and mostly on very gently sloping ground, has many trees and considerable shade. Sanitary blocks are of excellent quality, can be heated and have British style WCs, washbasins (over half in cabins) with free hot water, and others with cold water. Free controllable hot showers, unusually with heaters under the seats, and hot water for washing dishes, cold for clothes. A very pleasant wildlife park is inhabited by deer and bird-life, and has picnic areas and paths. Barcelona is easily accessible - buses hourly in the main season or train from Vilanova i la Geltru every 20 minutes.

How to find it: Site lies 4 km. northwest of Vilanova i la Geltru towards L'Arboc. From Barcelona-Tarragona autopista take exit 29 and turn towards Vilanova. There is no exit at no. 29 from Tarragona direction; from here take exit 30, go into Vilafranca and turn right for Vilanova. The Vilanova bypass is now open. Alternatively from the N340 from L'Arboc directly on attractive but very winding road for 11 km. signed Vilanova i la Geltru.

General Details: Open all year. Electrical connections throughout (6A). Supermarket (Easter - 30 Sept), souvenir shop. Full restaurant and larger bar with many tables where simpler meals served (both all year). Swimming pools (Easter - 15 Oct). Bicycle hire. Tennis. Riding adjacent. Golf 5 km. Fishing 3 km. Launderette. Chemical disposal. Chalets, bungalows, caravans and cabins for rent. ATM and exchange facilities.

Charges 2000: Per person 575 - 915 ptas; child (4-12 yrs) 360 - 575; car 575 - 915; tent or caravan 575 - 915; motorcaravan 950 - 1,595; m/cycle 235 - 690; electricity (6A) 575; water connection 360. All plus 7% VAT. New tariff of excellent deals for retired people on longer stays. Credit cards accepted.

Reservations: made to guarantee to admit, with deposit. Address: Aptdo 64, 08800 Vilanova i la Geltru (Barcelona). Tel: 931/893 34 02. FAX: 931/893 55 28.

see colour advert between pages 256/257

SPAIN - Costa Daurada

8395 Camping Arc de Bara, Roda de Bara

see colour advert
between pages 256/257

Site with pool and beach access, 200 m. from Roman monument Arc de Bara.

In comparison to the gigantic sites along this coastline this site has only 300 pitches of which two-thirds are taken up with static caravans. The site is 200 m. from the impressive Roman monument, Arc de Bara, and is 60 m. from the beach. The beach is accessed by a rear gate in the site perimeter and is soft sand and shelves gently into the waves. The 100 pitches for tourers are generally shaded, are of average size (60-70 sq.m.) and set apart from the static caravans, and are closer to the beach access. The unusual feature of this site, perpetrated by one of the owners, is the modernistic design theme used on many of the camp building exteriors and interiors. The site boasts a large swimming pool and children's pool of irregular shapes which are elevated above the site's ground level and there is a small children's play area. There are three clean sanitary blocks of various designs, (one is a most unusual elevated circular building) and a fourth without showers. These offer free hot water to the washbasins (some in cabins), free controllable hot showers, British style WCs, units for disabled visitors, limited facilities for babies, dishwashing and laundry (cold water only). A facility for disabled campers has been added. The shop, bar and restaurant are open daily July-Sept. and at weekends only all other times of the year. Chalets for hire.

How to find it: From A7 autopista take exit 31 towards Tarragona. Site is on CN340 Barcelona - Tarragona road at 1182 km. marker.

General Details: Open all year Swimming pools. Bar. Restaurant. Supermarket. Washing machines and dryers. Some animation in season. Bungalows to rent.

Charges 1999: Per person 350 - 600 ptas; child (3-9 yrs) 200 - 400 ; car, tent or caravan 350 - 600; motor-caravan 600 - 1000; electricity 400. Minimum charge 3,000 per day for pitch and persons (1/7-31/8). All plus 7% VAT. Credit cards accepted.

Reservations: Contact site. Address: C.N. 340 Km. 1182, 43883 Roda de Bara (Tarragona). Tel: 977/800902. FAX: 977/801552.

8410 Park Playa Bara, Roda de Bara, nr Tarragona

see colour advert
between pages 256/257

Superbly designed site near beach, with Roman style pool complex and comprehensive amenities.

This is a most impressive site which is family owned and has been carefully developed over the years. On entry you find yourself in a beautifully sculptured, tree-lined drive with an accompanying aroma of pine and woodlands and the sound of waterfalls close by. Considering its size, with over 850 pitches, it is still a very green and relaxing site with an immense range of activities. It is well situated with a 50 m. walk to a long sandy beach via a tunnel under the railway (some noise) to a new promenade and a quality beach bar and restaurant. Much care with planning and in the use of natural stone, shrubs and flowering plants gives a most pleasing appearance to all aspects of the site. The owners have excelled themselves in the design of the new stunning, terraced Roman-style pool complex, which is the central feature of the site. This complex is really amazing. Sun-bathe on the pretty terraces or sip a drink whilst seated at the bar stools submerged inside one of the pools or enjoy the panorama over the sea from the upper Roman galley bar surrounded by stylish friezes. The heated pools boast a hydro massage and there is a jacuzzi sited at the highest point of this complex. There is a separate attractive amphitheatre which seats 2,000 and is used to stage ambitious entertainment in season. Pitches vary in size, the older ones terraced and well shaded with pine trees, the newer ones more open, with a variety of trees and bushes forming separators between them. Each pitch has electricity (5A) and a sink with water. Arrive early to find space in peak weeks (see reservations). The toilet blocks are of different sizes and types, but all extremely good with British style WCs, free hot water in washbasins and showers and in many of the sinks. There are some private cabins for both sexes in some blocks, children's baths, basins and toilets and facilities for disabled. A new feature is a selection of superb standard private sanitary facilities which may hired. The shower water is rather salty here but spring water is available from special taps. The site has an extremely well equipped gymnasium with a dedicated instructor and a massage service. Used by some British tour operators.

How to find it: Site entrance is off the main N340 just opposite the Arco de Bara Roman monument. From autopista A7, take exit 31.

General Details: Open 10 March - 30 Sept. with all amenities. Electrical connections (5A) in all parts. Supermarket. Souvenir shop. Travel agency. Full restaurant and larger bar where simpler meals and takeaway served, bars also in 3 other places, and self-service restaurant on beach. Picnic areas. Swimming pools. Jacuzzi. `Frontennis' ground and tennis courts (both floodlit). Roller skating. Football. Sports area for children. Windsurfing school. Volleyball. Basketball. Gym. Massage parlour. Petanque. Minigolf, arranged on a map of Europe. Fishing. Bicycle hire 2 km. Riding 3 km. Golf 4 km. Entertainment centre: amphitheatre with stage and dance floor, large busy room for young with pool, football, table tennis, electronic machines; bar, video room with screen and seating, satellite TV, disco room open 11 to 4 am. (weekends only outside high season). Exchange facilities and cash point machine. Hairdresser. Washing machines. Chemical disposal. Motorcaravan services.

Charges 1999: Per person 490 - 980 ptas; child (1-9 yrs) 345 - 690; car 980; large tent or caravan 980; motor-caravan 1,695; small tent 690; m/cycle 690; electricity 495. All plus 7% VAT. Less in low season for pensioners and all sports charges reduced by 90%. Credit cards accepted.

Reservations: Contact site for details. Address: 43883 Roda de Bara (Tarragona). Tel: 987/802701. FAX: 977/800456. E-mail: barapark@lix.intercom.es.

8483 Camping Caravaning Tamarit-Park, Tamarit, nr Tarragona

Modern site with direct access to beach.

This is an attractive site, beautifully situated at the foot of Tamarit castle (church service Sunday, 10 am), at one end of a superb 1 km. long beach of fine sand. It is only 9 km. from Tarragona and 16 km. from Port Aventura. The 648 pitches, some 50 of which are virtually on the beach, are marked out on hard sand and grass and some are attractively separated by a variety of Mediterranean shrubs, pines and palm trees. All have electricity (6A) and are 70, 90 or 100 sq.m. in area, with 116 suitable for winter use. Long electricity leads and metal awning pegs may be required in places but wide internal roads give good access for even the largest of units (American motorhomes accepted). Sanitary blocks (one heated) are modern and tiled, providing good facilities with British style WCs and some large shower cabins with free, controllable hot water, washbasins and dressing area. An unfortunate recent economy feature in the showers is the introduction of push-button controlled hot water with tap controlled cold, leading to a confusing mixture of temperatures. Some private bathrooms may be rented. Dishwashing facilities are under cover with hot water and laundry facilities, including washing machines, are provided. Catering includes a beach-side waiter service restaurant with superb views and the terrace has tables just a few meters from the sea. A takeaway service is available. Tamarit would be a good choice for windsurfing enthusiasts and an active family holiday by the sea. There is a tennis court and an animation programme in season. A vast, attractively designed, lagoon-type swimming pool with bar and sun terrace has recently been added. The site is approached by a long access road, rather narrow but with passing places, reached across a new bridge (6 m.) over the railway line (there is train noise on the site). This is a site with good facilities, albeit on the expensive side. Security is provided but the very low wall which is the site beach boundary must be viewed with caution. The early morning sun shining on the blue sea and the golden stone of Tamarit castle high above is a memorable sight!

How to find it: Site is 8 km. north of Tarragona, signed from N340 (km. 1171,5) towards the beach. Continue on narrow road for 1 km. to site entrance, on the left at the end of the road.

General Details: Open all year. Supermarket. Bar/restaurant. Takeaway. Swimming pool (15/5-30/9). Tennis. Volleyball. Petanque. Minigolf. Table tennis. Children's playground. Fishing. Bicycle hire 2 km. Riding 3 km. Golf 6 km. Washing machines. Exchange facilities and ATM. Car wash. Gas supplies. Chemical disposal. Motorcaravan services. Chalets, mobile homes and Trigano tents to let.

Charges 1999: Per person 625 - 825 ptas; child (1-9 yrs) 425 - 625; pitch incl. car 2,400 - 2,800; electricity 550. All plus 7% VAT. Discounts for students, pensioners, large families and longer stays in low season. Credit cards accepted.

Reservations: Write to site. Address: Platja Tamarit, 43893 Tarragona (Catalunya). Tel: 977/650128. FAX: 977/650451. E-mail: tamaritpark@tamarit.com.

see colour advert between pages 256/257

8484 Camping-Caravaning Gavina, Creixell de Mar

see colour advert between pages 256/257

Modern, friendly site with direct access to 400 m. beach.

Gavina is sister site to Camping Tamarit (no. 8483) and is a friendly beach site. It has 400 pitches (60 sq.m), of which 220 have electrical connections (6A), set on flat grass and sand, some are separated by tall hedges which provide shade. One side of the site, with large pitches for motorcaravans, is open to the beach over a very low wall. This is excellent for keen windsurfers and a range of watersports including sailing and water skiing. This beach access does have an obvious security implication. There are two sanitary buildings, both of good quality, tiled with free hot water to the showers and some washbasins. In one block, the showers have no dividers. There is a new room for babies and a unit for disabled campers in one block. Laundry facilities with washing machines. The attractive restaurant/bar has a terrace overlooking the sea and entertainment is arranged in high season. Well stocked supermarket. There is a children's play area, a tennis court and a sports area. There is a small tour operator presence.

How to find it: Take exit 32 from A7 Barcelona - Tarragona autopista and follow N340 towards Tarragona until km. 1181 sign. Take road for Creixell Platja and follow well signed road to site (by the sea).

General Details: Open Easter/1 April - 31 October. Bar/restaurant. Supermarket. Children's play area. Tennis. Table tennis. Telephones. Exchange facilities. Safe deposit boxes. Laundry facilities. Sports area. Bungalows for rent.

Charges 2000: Per person ptas 550 - 650; child (3-9 yrs) 400 - 500; pitch (any unit) 1,800 - 2,300; electricity 550. Plus 7% VAT.

Reservations: Write to site for details. Address: 43839 Creixell de Mar (Tarragona). Tel: 977/801503. FAX: 977/800527. E-mail info@gavina.net. A 'Camping Cheques' site.

SPAIN - Costa Daurada

8482 Camping La Pineda de Salou, La Pineda

Useful site for Port Aventura and Acquapark.

La Pineda is just outside Salou towards Tarragona and this site is just 300 m. from the Aquapark and 2.5 km. from Port Aventura, to which there is an hourly bus service from outside the camp entrance and there is some noise from this road. On site there is a 'no frills' medium sized swimming pool and children's pool, open from mid June, with a large lying out terrace with sun loungers, as well as various entertainments aimed at young people. The shop, restaurant and bar are open in high season and there are acceptable sanitary facilities. These include British style WCs, free hot water to the washbasins, showers, baby bath, dishwashing and laundry sinks. There are two washing machines in each block. The second building is opened in high season only. The 336 flat pitches (280 for touring) are mostly shaded and of about 70 sq.m. All have 5A electricity. The beach is only about 400 m. away. This is a plain, friendly and convenient site, without being outstanding. We believe this a site to be used for visiting Tarragona and the local area rather than for extended stays.

How to find it: From the A7 just southwest of Tarragona take exit 35 and follow signs to Port Aventura then campsite signs.

General Details: Open 31 March - 1 Oct. Shop (1/4-30/9). Restaurant, bar and snacks (15/4-15/9). Swimming pools (1/6-15/9). Five-a-side soccer pitch. Small TV room. Bicycle hire. Games room with videos and drink and snack machines. New children's playground (3-12 yrs). Entertainment (1/7-30/8). Fishing 500 m. Riding 6 km. Golf 10 km. Gas supplies. Chemical disposal. Mobile homes and chalets for hire.

Charges 2000: Per person ptas. 470 - 680; child (1-10 yrs) 340 - 530; car 440 - 720; caravan 570 - 890; motorcaravan 850 - 1,290, electricity 430 - 450; dog 150 - 310. All plus 7% VAT. Credit cards accepted.

Reservations: Made for high season (min. 7 nights) contact site. Address Ctra de la Costa Tarragona a Salou, km 5, 43480 La Pineda (Tarragona). Tel: 977/372176. FAX: 977/370620. E-mail: info@campinglapineda.com.

 AR Discount
Less 5% low season; less 5% for min. 5 days in mid-season

 **For a list of sites which are open all year - see page 257**

8470 Camping La Siesta, Salou, nr Tarragona

see colour advert between pages 256/257

Lively site in centre of Salou with swimming pool.

La Siesta is only 250 m. from the sandy beach and not very much more from all the life of the resort of Salou, which is very popular with the British and has just about all that a highly developed Spanish resort can offer. For those who do not want to walk this distance, there is a swimming pool of 300 sq.m., free of charge and open all season, on the camp itself, with filtered water. The site is divided into 470 individual pitches which are large enough and have electricity connections (10A), with smaller ones for tents. Many pitches have artificial shade provided and within some pitches there is one box for the tent or caravan, and a shared one for the car. There is also some shade from the trees and shrubs that are part of the site's atmosphere. In July/Aug. siting of campers is carried out by the management, who are friendly and helpful. There are three bright and clean sanitary blocks which provide very reasonable facilities including 48 free hot showers. Young campers are sited separately to the rear of the restaurant which has a reasonable menu and a bar with TV provided. A suprisingly large supermarket caters for most needs in season.

How to find it: Both new roads from Tarragona and Reus end at a large roundabout from where the camp is only about 200 m. and signed through a one way system in the town.

General Details: Open Easter - 31 Oct. 50,000 sq.m. Electrical connections (10A). Large supermarket. Various automatic vending machines. Swimming pool (all season). Self-service restaurant and bar with terrace overlooking pool; also cooked dishes to take away. Dancing some evenings till 11 pm. Many other shops, restaurants and dancing near. Children's playground. Fishing 500 m. Bicycle hire 200 m. Riding and golf 6 km. Medical service daily in season. Chemical disposal. Motorcaravan services. ATM point. Chalets and mobile homes for hire.

Charges 1999: Per person 510 - 695 ptas; child (4-9 yrs) 415 - 515; car 510 - 695; tent or caravan 510 - 695; motorcaravan 750 - 1,000; electricity 400. All plus 7% VAT.

Reservations: Advised 1 July - 20 Aug. and made in sense of guaranteeing a shady place, with electricity if required. Deposit required. Address: 43840 Salou (Tarragona). Tel: 977/380852. FAX: 977/383191. E-mail: siesta@tinet.fut.es.

8480 Camping Sanguli, Salou, nr Tarragona

see colour advert between pages 256/257

Quality site close to beach and town, with superb swimming pools and ambitious entertainment.

Owned, developed and managed by a local Spanish family, this exceptional site lies little more than 100 m. from the good sandy beach, across the coast road and a small railway level crossing (some train noise at times). Sister site to 8481, although large, Sanguli manages to maintain a family atmosphere due to the efforts of the very keen and efficient staff. There are three good sized, attractive pools (all with children's pools), one with grassy sunbathing area partly shaded near the entrance, and a second deep one with water chutes which forms part of the excellent sports complex with fitness centre, tennis courts, squash courts, a 'fronton', minigolf and football practice area. The third pool is the central part of the new amphitheatre area at the top of the site which includes an impressive Roman style building with huge portals, containing a bar and restaurant with terraces. The amphitheatre seats 2,000 campers and treats them to very professional free nightly entertainment (1/5-30/9). All the pools have adjacent amenity areas and bars. Amazingly the site is building another heated pool which will open for 2000. The site is also fortunate to be placed near the centre of Salou and so can offer the attractions of a busy resort while still being private. It is only 3 km. from Port Aventura. The sanitary facilities are constantly improved and are always exceptional, providing hot water in showers and basins, including many individual cabins with en-suite facilities. The showers have dividers, shelves and hooks and the WCs are British style. All are kept very clean. The site is wonderfully maintained with an expert team striving to achieve the 'Garden of Eden' which is the owners dream. There are 1,333 pitches of varying size (75-90 sq.m) and all have electricity connections (7/10A). The wonderful selection of trees, palms and shrubs provide natural shade. The site has made a real effort to cater for the young including teenagers with a 'Hop Club' (entertainment tailored for 13-17 year olds) along with a Computer Club which includes use of the Internet. This is a large, professional site providing something for all the family, but still capable of providing peace and quiet for those looking for it. The management are friendly and very efficient. Used by British tour operators (132 pitches).

How to find it: On west side of Salou about 1 km. from centre, site is well signed from the coast road to Cambrils and from the other town approaches.

General Details: Open 24 March - 29 Oct, with shop, meals and facilities available all season. 150,000 sq.m. Many electrical connections. Two supermarkets. Bars and restaurant with takeaway. Swimming pools. Sport complex with tennis, squash, football ground, etc. Children's playground. Mini club, teenagers club and computer club. Minigolf. Fishing 800 m. Bicycle hire 100 m. Riding 3 km. Golf 6 km. First-aid room. Launderette with service. Gas supplies. Chemical disposal. Motorcaravan services. Mobile homes and bungalows to rent.

Charges 2000: Three charging seasons. Per adult 650; child (3-12 yrs) 450; standard pitch (70-75 sq.m.) 2,100 - 3,800, 'special' pitch (90 sq.m.) 2,100 - 4,300, 'master' pitch (90 sq.m.) incl. water 2,300 - 4,900; extra car or m/cycle 650 - 850; electricity and dogs included. All plus 7% VAT. Less 25-35% outside high season for longer stays. Special long stay offers for senior citizens. Credit cards accepted.

Reservations: Advised for July/Aug. and made up to 1 March with sizeable booking fee; write to site. Address: Prolongacion Calle E s/n, Apdo de Correos 123, 43840 Salou (Tarragona). Tel: 977/381641. FAX: 977/384616. E-mail: mail@sanguli.es.

SPAIN - Costa Daurada

8481 Camping Cambrils Park, Salou, nr Tarragona

see colour advert between pages 256/257

Modern site with first-class facilities.

An impressive entrance drive, lined with palm trees and flowers, leads from the large very smart reception building at the entrance of this site to the pitches and facilities (sister site to 8480). It is set 500 m. back from the excellent beach in a generally quiet setting. The 706 slightly sloping, grassy pitches of around 90 sq.m. are numbered and separated by trees. All have 10A electricity, 50 also with water and waste water connections. They are served by three excellent sanitary buildings (one new). They have free hot water to the washbasins (half in cabins), showers, units for disabled visitors, dishwashing, laundry and baby bath sections. Hand and hairdryers are provided and there is also a serviced laundry. The huge supermarket, souvenir shop and 'panaderia' (fresh-baked bread and croissants) are open daily with a break from 2-4 pm. The marvellous central pool complex with water chutes is the main focus of the site with a raised wooden 'poop deck' sunbathing area with palmed surround which doubles as an entertainment stage at night. There is a huge bar/terraced area for watching the magnificent floodlit spectacles along with the use of an excellent restaurant with Mezaline design or the adjacent takeaway. By day there is a small bar at a lower level where you can enjoy a cool drink from submerged stools within the pool, a dryer version on the far side of the bar or just relax on the thick grassy sunbathing areas. There are many sporting opportunities with a football pitch (on sand), multi-games court, tennis, basketball, volleyball and petanque. Children have a large adventure fortress on sand, a most professional animation programme for young and old all through the season, pool, table football and other games. At present there is a number of tour operator pitches some with attractive thatched chalets. A new themed double pool area is planned for 2000 with a jungle flavour. It is 4 km. to Port Aventura. This is a superb family site for your camping holiday.

How to find it: Site entrance is signed about 700 m. west of Camping Sanguli, off the coast road from Salou, in Cambrils.

General Details: Open 15 April - 30 Sept, including all amenities. Restaurant. Takeaway. Supermarket. Souvenir shop. Swimming pools. Minigolf. Football. Basketball. Volleyball. Animation and entertainment all season. Mini-club. Fishing, bicycle hire 400 m. Riding 3 km. Golf 7 km. Doctor on site all season. ATM. Gas supplies. Chemical disposal. Motorcaravan services. Winter caravan storage. Bungalows for rent. No dogs are accepted.

Charges 2000: Per person ptas. 650; child (4 -12 yrs) free - 450; pitch incl. electricity 2,100 - 3,900, with water and waste water 2,300 - 4,300; all plus 7% VAT. Discounts of 25-40% outside 21/6-31/8. Credit cards accepted.

Reservations: Contact site. Address: Apdo de Correos 123, 43840 Salou (Tarragona). Tel: 977/351031. FAX: 977/352210. E-mail: mail@cambrilspark.es. A 'Camping Cheques' site.

8520 Camping Caravaning Marius, Montroig, nr Tarragona

Agreeable site with family atmosphere and personal touch, by a sandy beach.

A quiet, well tended site which is not too huge, Marius has a pleasant atmosphere. It is has one perimeter on a good sandy beach, with direct access and no roads to cross – you can almost fall out of bed and onto the beach and a large beach bar will provide resuscitation when required! The site is divided into 345 individual pitches of adequate size so it does not become too overcrowded. They are quite shady with 300 electrical connections and 8 pitches with water and drainage. Dog owners go on one half of the site which is split down the centre by a wall and large storm drain gulley (clean). Two of the sanitary blocks are dated but clean and a third is of an excellent standard. There is free hot water in the showers and half the washbasins, plus the 21 private cabins. The are British style WCs and facilities for babies and disabled campers. The use of TV sets outside your unit and the riding of bicycles on site is not permitted. The site is near nos. 8540 and 8530, and the lively fishing port of Cambrils where you can buy freshly caught fish, is about 7 km. An excellent watersports venue in high season. Some train noise and torches are required at night.

How to find it: Entrance is 28 km. from Tarragona on the Valencia road (N340).

General Details: Open 1 April - 15 Oct. 4 ha. Bar and restaurant (1/6-15/9). Supermarket (15/5-10/10). Children's club and playground. Hairdresser. Fishing. Souvenir shop. Windsurfing. Table tennis. Laundry room.Water ski and pedaloes nearby. Riding 4 km. Golf 10 km. Gas supplies. Chemical disposal. Motorcaravan services.

Charges 1999: Three charging seasons. Per person 500, 600 or 800 ptas; child (under 10) 200, 300 or 400; pitch 1,400, 1,800 or 2,300; dog 400. Plus 7% VAT. Credit cards accepted.

Reservations: Contact site. Address: 43892 Miami-Playa (Tarragona). Tel: 877/810684. FAX: 877/179658. E-mail: cmpmarius@seric.es.

8530 Camping and Bungalow Park Playa Montroig, Montroig, nr Tarragona

One of Europe's top sites with superb and innovative facilities, pool complex, entertainment and excellent sandy beach.

What a superb site! Playa Montroig is about 30 km. beyond Tarragona set in its own tropical gardens with direct access to a very long soft sand beach. Bathing, windsurfing, surfboarding two diving rafts, a diving school and many beach sports are available. The main part of the site lies between the sea, road and railway (as at other sites on this stretch of coast, there is some train noise) and there is a huge underpass. The site is divided into spacious, marked pitches with excellent shade provided by a variety of lush vegetation including very impressive palms set in wide avenues. There are 1,950 pitches, all with electricity and 330 with water and drainage connections. Some 48 pitches are directly alongside the beach – they are somewhat expensive and extremely popular. The site has many outstanding features. There is an excellent swimming pool complex near the entrance with two pools (one heated for children). There are 15 sanitary buildings, some of them small, but of very good quality with toilets and washbasins, plus really excellent, air conditioned larger buildings housing large showers, washbasins (many in private cabins) and separate WCs. There are several launderettes, special facilities for disabled campers and for babies. A 24 hour cleaning service operates. Water points around site (water said to be very pure from the site's own wells). One quality restaurant serves traditional Catalunian fare (seats 150) and overlooks an entertainment area where you may watch genuine Flamenco dancing and buffet food is served (catering for 1,000). A large terrace bar dispenses drinks or if you yearn louder music there is a disco and smaller bar inside another themed building. If you prefer international food there is yet another eating option in a very smart restaurant (seats 500). Above this is the 'Pai-pai' Carribean cocktail bar where softer music is provided in an intimate atmosphere. The 'Eurocentre', with 250 person capacity and specially equipped for entertainment and activities, large screen videos, films, shows and meetings (air conditioned). Fitness suite. Children's activities are very ambitious – there is even a ceramics kiln (multi-lingual carers). The camp theatre 'La Carpa', a spectacular open air theatre, is an ideal setting for daily keep fit sessions and the professional entertainment provided. If you are 5-11 years old you can explore the 'Tam-Tam Eco Park', a 20,000 sq.m. forest zone where experts will teach the natural life of the area. You can even camp out for a night (supervised) to study wildlife (a once weekly activity). Adults are also allowed in to separate barbecues and other evening fun. This is an excellent site and there is insufficient space here to describe all the available activities. We recommend it for families with children of all ages and there is much emphasis on providing activities outside the high season. No dogs are taken and TVs are not allowed outside your vehicle. A range of bungalow accommodation to hire.

How to find it: Site entrance is off main N340 nearly 30 km. southwest from Tarragona. From motorway take Cambrils exit and turn west on N340 at 1136 km marker.

General Details: Open 1 March - 31 Oct. About 150,000 sq.m. Good shopping centre with supermarket, greengrocer, butcher, fishmonger, tobacconist and souvenir shops. Restaurants and bars. Dancing, shows, films and videos (see Eurocentre and La Carpa above). Eco-park (see above). TV lounges (3) incl. satellite. Also beach bar. Children's playground. Free kindergarten with multi-lingual staff. Junior and teenage clubs. Fitness centre. Skateboarding. Jogging track. Activities centre with tourist information. Sports area for volleyball, football and basketball. Tennis. Minigolf. Table tennis. Organised activities for children and adults including pottery and gardening classes. Windsurfing and water skiing courses. Surfboards and pedaloes for hire. Boat mooring. Launderettes. Ladies' and men's hairdressers. Car wash. Bicycle hire. Riding or golf 3 km. Bureau de change. Safety deposit boxes. Special telephone service. Doctor always available. Gas supplies. Chemical disposal. Motorcaravan services. Mobile homes and bungalows to rent. Dogs are not accepted.

Charges 1999: Per person 450 - 800 ptas; child (under 10) 350 - 700; standard pitch B with electricity 2,300 - 4,500, standard pitch A with electricity 2,500 - 4,800, premium pitch with water also 2,700 - 5,500; premium plus pitch with electricity and water, next to the sea 3,200 - 6,500; extra car or boat 350 - 700. All plus 7% VAT. Discounts for longer stays and for pensioners. Credit cards accepted.

Reservations: are possible and made with refundable booking fee (4,000 ptas). Address: Dept. de Reservas, Apdo 3, 43300 Montroig (Tarragona). Tel: 977/810637. FAX: 977/811411. E-mail: info@playamontroig.com.

see colour advert between pages 256/257

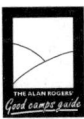

All the sites in this guide are regularly inspected by our team of experienced site assessors, but we welcome your opinion too.

See Readers' Reports - page 366

SPAIN - Costa Daurada

8540 Camping Caravaning Club La Torre del Sol, Montroig

see colour advert between pages 256/257

Large, pleasant site beside beach with good amenities and pools complex.

A member of the French Airotel chain, Torre del Sol occupies a good position with direct access to the clean, soft, sandy beach, complete with beach bar. It offers good shade on a high proportion of the 1,500 individual numbered pitches, all of which have electricity, mostly of about 70-80 sq.m. There is usually space for odd nights but for good places between 10/7-16/8 it is advisable to reserve. The site has a new complex of three swimming pools which are thoughtfully laid out with grass sunbathing areas and palms, two of which are heated. An attractive restaurant with terrace has a pleasant menu plus a pizzeria, bar, coffee bar and ice cream bar are all readily accessible near the pool. The site has very comprehensive amenities (listed below) and it offers much 'animation' with an organised programme of events, for children and adults in high season. Sub-aqua diving can be organised from the site along with parascending, safaris, boat trips and general tourist excursions. The sanitary facilities consist of four well maintained blocks giving a good provision with hot water and with some nice tiled units added on to three of the blocks comprising private cabins with washbasins and hot showers. British style toilets, units for disabled people and babies. Radios and televisions are banned outside your unit. There is a large supermarket and a bakery, you should not need to leave the site during your stay. Part of the site is between the railway and the sea so there may be occasional train noise.

How to find it: The entrance is off the main N340 road about 30 km. from Tarragona towards Valencia. From motorway take Cambrils exit and turn west on N340.

General Details: Open 15 March - 22 Oct. Large supermarket and other shops at entrance, open to public. Full restaurant. Takeaway. Bar with large terrace where shows and dancing held daily in high season. Beach bar. Pizzeria. Cinema with permanent seating for 520; 3 TV lounges (satellite TV); separate room for films or videos shown on TV. Well-soundproofed disco. Swimming pools. Solarium. Sauna. Tennis. Table tennis. Squash. Volleyball. Minigolf. Bicycle hire. Fishing. Windsurfing school; sailboards and pedaloes for hire. Children's playground and crèche. Riding 3 km. Golf 4 km. Fridge hire. Safe deposit boxes. Bureau de change. Telephone service. Medical service with treatment room. Ladies' and gents' hairdresser. Car repair and car wash (pressure wash). Washing machines. Gas supplies. Chemical disposal. Bungalows, mobile homes and tents for hire. Dogs are not accepted.

Charges 1999: Per person ptas. 400 - 950; child (under 10 yrs) 300 - 800; pitch with car, tent, caravan 1,800 - 2,800; motorcaravan and electricity 1,850 - 2,900; extra car 400 - 1,000. All plus 7% VAT. Discounts in low season for longer stays. Credit cards accepted.

Reservations: Made only for Jul/Aug. before 15 June, in sense of guaranteeing admission, with fee (3,000 ptas). Address: 43892 Miami Playa (Tarragona). Tel: 877/810486. FAX: 877/811306. A 'Camping Cheques' site.

N8537 Naturist Camping El Templo del Sol, L'Hospitalet de L'Infant

Top quality naturist site with fabulous facilities and long beaches with golden sands.

El Templo del Sol is a large, luxurious terraced naturist site with a distinctly Arabesque style and superb buildings in Moorish style. The owner has designed the magnificent main turreted building at the entrance with fountains and seven elaborate Moorish arches because to reach Paradise one is required to pass through seven doors. He has achieved it here, as all the facilities are de-luxe and quite heavenly! The three large, tiered swimming pools are wonderful with water cascading from one to the other and are part of a supporting complex nearing completion which contains a jacuzzi with views over the sea, a large bar and more luxury sanitary installations, plus a sunbathing area on the roof. The main building contains an impressive reception area and has an outstanding restaurant with an elegant mosaic central, open area with a fountain. This is for the professional entertainment provided which includes genuine Flamenco dancing. There is also a smart octagonal bar with terraces, an extremely well-stocked supermarket, a huge cinema, health food shop, souvenir shop and hairdresser. This grouping of services are said to be among the best in European naturist sites. The site has 470 pitches, mainly rather small (60/70 sq.m), but 34 fully serviced. Pitches are on terraces giving rewarding views over the sea and ready access to the idyllic beaches of soft golden sand. A separate children's pool and play area are on site. As yet there is little shade. Site lighting is provided from pleasing serpent shaped light assemblies. Sanitary blocks are amongst the best you will find in Spain providing everything you could require and extensive services for disabled campers. The site is under French management (the same as 8540 Torre del Sol) and English is spoken. There is some daytime rail noise.

How to find it: From N340 south of Tarragona, exit at km. 1123 towards L'Hopitalet and follow signs.

General Details: Open 15 May - 15 October. Tiered swimming pools and jacuzzi. Bars. Restaurants. Supermarket. Health shop. Souvenir shop. Cinema. Hairdresser. Dogs are not accepted.

Charges 1999: Per person ptas. 400 - 800; child (under 10 yrs) 300 - 650; caravan or tent incl. car and electricity 1,700 - 2,550; motorcaravan or caravan and car incl. electricity and water 1,900 - 2,800. Plus 7% VAT. Discounts for longer stays. Credit cards accepted.

Reservations: Contact site. Address: 43890 L'Hospitalet de l'Infant (Tarragona). Tel: 977/82.34.34. FAX: 977/82.34.64 (or 977/81.13.06 at Torre del Sol).

see colour advert between pages 256/257

8535 Camping-Pension Cala d'Oques, Hospitalet del Infante

Peaceful, simple site right beside the sea.

Cala d'Oques, or Goose Bay – this was where the migrant geese landed on return from wintering in South Africa. Hence the geese featured on the camp logo and the two guard geese who watch the entrance to the site. The site itself has been developed with care and dedication by Elisa Roller over 20 years or so. Part of its appeal lies in its situation beside the sea with a wide beach of sand and pebbles, its amazing mountain backdrop and the views across the bay to the town and part by the atmosphere created by Elisa, her family and staff - friendly, relaxed and comfortable. The restaurant has a reputation which extends well outside the site (the cook has been there for 15 years) and the family type entertainment is in total contrast to that provided at the larger, more fashionable sites of the Costa Daurada. In total there are 235 pitches, mostly level and laid out beside the beach, with more behind on wide, informal terracing. Odd pine and olive trees are an attractive feature but do not provide much shade. Electricity is available although long leads may necessary. Gates provide access to the beach with useful cold showers to wash the sand away. The main sanitary facilities are a rather haphazard development in part of the main building which houses the restaurant, reception, the apartments to let and the family's home. They are simple with hot water to showers (hot water on payment, a little small and no divider, and an unusual feature is that shower heads have to be collected from reception) and to just some of the washbasins. British style WCs. The far end of the site has a small block with toilets and washbasins. Dogs allowed on leads. For those interested, there is a naturist beach around the little headland just south of the site. This is an uncomplicated site which could suit those who do not need the entertainment and more sophisticated services of bigger sites.

How to find it: Hospitalet del Infante is south of Tarragona, accessed from the A7 (exit 38) or from the N340. From the north take first exit to Hospitalet del Infante at the 1128 km. marker. Follow signs in the village, site is 2 km. south, by the sea.

General Details: Open all year. Restaurant/bar and shop (1/4-30/9). Children's play area. Five-a-side soccer. Village facilities, incl. shop and restaurant 1.5 km. Fishing. Bicycle hire or riding 2 km. Gas supplies. Chemical disposal. Motorcaravan services. Rooms to let.

Charges 2000: Per person ptas. 715 - 895; child (under 10 yrs) free; tent or caravan 715 - 895; car or m/cycle 715 - 895; motorcaravan 1,250 - 1,800; dog 375 - 395; electricity 485 - 495. Discounts for stays over 2 months. No credit cards.

Reservations: Contact site. Address: Via Augusta, 43890 Hospitalet del Infante (Tarragona). Tel: 977/823254. FAX: 977/820691. E-mail: eroller@tinet.fut.es.

8392 Camping El Garrofer, Sitges

Recommended by our Spanish agent, there will be a full inspection next year of this large site. Situated just 1 km. from the beach, close to the pleasant town of Sitges, it offers over 500 individual pitches, most with electrical connections (6A). There is also a swimming pool, supermarket, bar/restaurant and laundry.

How to find it: Sitges is roughly 30 km. southwest of Barcelona and the site is accessed from the C-246 km. 39, 2 km. from town towards Vilanova i la Geltrú.

General Details: Open all year. 8 hectares. Supermarket. Bar/restaurant. Swimming pool. Car wash. Direct bus link to Barcelona. Bungalows for hire.

Charges 1999: Per person ptas.545; child (1-9) 435; pitch incl. electricity 1895; m/cycle 545; reduced prices in low seasons.

Reservations: Contact site. Address: Ctra. C.246 km.39, 08870 Sitges. Tel: 938/941780. FAX 938/110623. Email: garrofer@interplanet.es.

See advertisement on page 268

SPAIN - Costa Daurada

8536 Camping-Caravanning L'Ametlla Village Platja, L'Ametlla de Mar

New site with direct access to shingle beaches and close to a charming fishing port

The 280 pitches at this new site have been thoughtfully created on the hillside above two colourful coves with shingle beaches and two small associated lagoons. The site is environmentally correct – local planning regulations are extremely tight including the types of trees that may used and therefore it has little shade as yet. The buildings are well finished and are quality renovations of older constructions. There is a good restaurant and bar with a TV room. The amenities are also of high quality, although the current pool is small (we are told that there will be an additional larger pool in 2000). When seen there was the usual development work you would expect in a new site. We imagine that the single excellent sanitary block becomes busy at peak periods and is a brisk walk from some pitches (an additional block is also planned for 2000). There is hot water throughout, British style WCs, washbasins and some private cabins with WC and washbasin, plus others with WC, basin and shower. The showers have a system of separate push-buttons for hot and cold water. For motorcaravans wishing to spend a short period here, 25 large hardstandings are being constructed which will have electricity and water on each place. A sub-aqua diving school operates on the site in high season. This is an attractive small site in an idyllic situation near the picturesque fishing village of L'Ametlla de Mar, famous for its fish restaurants, and close to the Ebro Delta nature reserve. It is about 20 minutes from Europe's second largest theme park, Port Aventura, but as there is no bus service your own transport is required. No transit traffic is allowed within the site in high season. Used by tour operators (30 pitches). English is spoken.

How to find it: From A7 (Barcelona - Valencia) take exit 39 for L'Ametlla de Mar. Follow signs on reaching village and site is 2.5 km. south of the village along a narrow bumpy track.

General Details: Open 15 April - 31 Oct. Supermarket. Bar/restaurant. TV room. Swimming pool. Sub aqua diving. Kayaking. Fishing. Children's play area. Bicycle hire. Football. Basketball. Volleyball. Entertainment July/Aug. Barbecue area. Golf 15 km. Gas supplies. Chemical disposal. Motorcaravan services. Bungalows and mobile homes to rent.

Charges 2000: Per person ptas. 400 - 700; child (under 10 yrs) 330 - 550; car 450 - 750; tent or caravan 450 - 750; motorcaravan 800 - 1,350; m/cycle 300 - 575; electricity 575. All plus 7% VAT. Less for longer stays, especially in low season. Credit cards accepted.

Reservations: Contact site. Address: Apdo. Correus 240, Paraje Santes Creus, 43860 L'Ametlla de Mar (Tarragona). Tel: 977/267784 or 910/435781. FAX: 977/267868.

Costa del Azahar

The 'Orange Blossom' Coast runs down the east coast from Vinaros to Almanzora, with the great port of Valencia in the middle. Orange groves grow right down to the coast, particularly in the northern section and the area is rich in fresh food from land and sea. Wine, fruit and flowers play large parts in the local economy and Paella and Zarzuela are said to have originated here. Most of the best beaches are found in the area of Peñiscola or to the south of Valencia and the area is very, very sunny.

Camping-Caravaning
BONTERRA
Holiday site with luxurious installations, very near to the beach of Benicasim with its golden yellow, clean sand and to the centre of the village.
Free swimming pool. Sites with electricity, bar, restaurant, large supermarket, safe, money exchange, hot water showers, children's playground, well shaded. No dogs in July/August.
Mobile homes, wooden bungalows and bung. to rent
Special fees in off-season and for long term stays
E-12560 Benicasim (Castellón)
Tel. 964.30.00.07. Fax. 964.30.00.60

8580 Camping Bonterra, Benicasim, nr Castellón/Castelló

Appealing, Mediterranean style site by the main road.

If you are looking for a site which is not too crowded and has good facilities this site may be for you as there are few quality sites in the local area. It is not right by the edge of the sea but it is a 300 m. walk to a good, shady beach – and parking is not too difficult if you want to take the car. Good beach for scuba diving or snorkelling – hire facilities are available at Benicasim. There is also an attractive free swimming pool, plus a children's pool on the site itself, if you prefer, with palms and olive trees. A pleasantly laid out bar, restaurant and terrace which overlook the pools. The site has been extended to give a total of nearly 400 pitches at peak times, which are 70-90 sq.m. The western side of the site is mainly for tents. Bonterra has a clean and neat appearance with reddish soil, grass and a number of trees which give good shade. There is some road and rail noise. Four attractive, well maintained sanitary blocks are sensibly laid out, providing British style toilets, some private cabins and washbasins with hot water, others with cold, 56 free hot showers with solar heating and baby showers. There are also showers and WCs, for disabled campers. No dogs are accepted in Juy/Aug. A well run site useful for visiting local attractions such as the Carmelite monastery at Desierto de las Palmas, 6 km. distant or the historic town of Castillion.

How to find it: Site is east of Benicasim village, with entrance off the old main N340 road running a little back from the coast. Coming from the north, turn left at sign 'Benicasim por la costa'. On the A7 from the north use exit 45, from the south exit 46.

General Details: Open Easter - 31 Oct. 5.5 ha. Reasonable shade. All pitches have electricity. Restaurant. Bar. Snacks all season. Children's playground (some concrete bases). Disco. Adjacent supermarket. Bicycle hire. Laundry service. Chemical disposal. Motorcaravan services. Medical room. Mobile homes and chalet style bungalows to let. No dogs accepted July/Aug.

Charges 1999: Per adult ptas. 250 - 470; child (3-9 yrs) 235 - 430; car 300 - 535; m/cycle 200 - 370; caravan or tent 700 - 1,285; motorcaravan 995 - 1,830; pitch Easter, July/Aug. 1,965 - 2,460; electricity 6A 400, 10A 735. All plus 7% VAT. Special long stay rates excl. July/Aug. Credit cards accepted.

Reservations: made if you write at least a month in advance. Address: Avda. de Barcelona, Aptdo 77, 12560 Benicasim (Castelló). Tel: 964/300007. FAX: 964/300060. When closed: 964/300200.

8755 Camping-Caravanning Moraira, Moraira

Interesting smaller site with swimming pool, overlooking the town.

Quietly situated in an urban area but set amongst old pine trees and just 400 m. from a sheltered bay, this little site has been terraced to provide shaded pitches of varying size (access to the pitches is difficult for larger units). Some pitches have been provided with water and waste water facilities and a few have sea views. A high quality sanitary block with polished granite floors and marble fittings has been built to a unique and ultra-modern design. It provides extra large free hot showers and British style WCs. An attractive swimming pool with paved sunbathing terrace is another recent addition, which is also used for sub-aqua instruction. A sandy beach is 1.5 km. and shops, bars and restaurants are within walking distance.

How to find it: Site is best approached from Teulada. From A7 take exit 63 onto N332. In 3.5 km. turn right signed Teulada and Moraira. In Teulada fork right to Moraira. At junction at town entrance turn right signed Calpe and in 1 km. turn right into road to site on bend immediately after Res. Don Julio.

General Details: Open all year. Electricity connections (6/10A). Bar/restaurant and shop (main season). Swimming pool. Sub-aqua with site boat and instruction available. Tennis. Washing machine. Motorcaravan services.

Charges 1999: Per person ptas. 600; child (4-9 yrs) 450; caravan 725; tent 600; motorcaravan 950; pitch incl. car and unit 1,650. All plus 7% VAT. Less 15-60% in low seasons.

Reservations: Write to site for details. Address: Camino Paellero 50, 03724 Moraira-Teulada (Alicante). Tel: 965/745249. FAX: 965/745315.

SPAIN - Costa del Azahar

8560 Camping Playa Tropicana, Alcossebre, nr Castellón/Castelló

Unusual and pleasant themed site with pool in quiet beach situation.

Playa Tropicana is the living dream of the owners Vera and Rachid. It has been given a tropical theme with scores of 'Romanesque' white statues around the site including in the sanitary blocks. It has a delightful position away from the main hub of tourism, right by a good sandy beach which shelves gently into the clean waters. There is a shingle beach for fishing nearby and a promenade in front of the site. It is a quiet position and it is a drive rather than a walk to the centre of the village resort. The site takes 300 units on individual, marked pitches separated by lines of flowering bushes under mature trees. The pitches vary in size (50-100 sq.m), most are shaded and there are electricity connections throughout. There are 50 places for motorcaravans with water and drainage and there is a scale of charges for the different pitches. The two sanitary blocks are thoughtfully decorated in keeping with the site's theme and are of an excellent standard. They have British WCs, free hot water in well spaced washbasins, including 16 in private cabins, in the fully controllable showers (with screen) and the sinks. There are baby baths and some units with WC, basin and shower, and facilities for disabled people. A swimming pool (18 x 11 m.) and a children's pool with adjoining attractive terrace follow the theme here. The restaurant, which is part of the same complex, has a varied menu at good prices. The site has several aviaries with four enormous, colourful and voluble parrots, other various birds and two small monkeys which had just presented the owners with a great surprise – a tiny offspring.

How to find it: Alcoceber (or Alcossebre) is between Peniscola and Oropesa. Turn off N340 at 1018 km. marker towards Alcossebre on CV142. Just before entering town take right turn signed 'platjes Capicorb'. Follow road for approx. 2.5 km. turning right at beach. Site is on the right.

General Details: Open 15 March - 31 Oct. 31,000 sq.m. Large supermarket (all season). Large restaurant (Easter - late Sept). Drinks served on terrace. Swimming pool. Children's playground. Volleyball. Table tennis. Fishing. Riding 3 km. Treatment room. Washing machine. Gas supplies. Chemical disposal. Motorcaravan services. Apartments and villa to let. No TVs allowed in July/Aug. Dogs are not accepted.

Charges 2000: Per person ptas. 905; child (1-10 yrs) 715; pitch 3,135, 3,300, 3,535 or 4,500, acc. to size (50-100 sq.m); 90 sq.m. pitch with water and drainage 3,990; electricity incl. All plus 7% VAT. Discounts up to 45% out of season. Credit cards accepted.

Reservations: made for min. 15 days with substantial deposit (5,000 ptas) and fee (5,000). Address: 12579 Alcossebre (Castellón). Tel: 964/412463 or 412448. FAX: 964/412805. A 'Camping Cheques' site.

8615 Kiko Park, Playa de Oliva

Efficient, comfortable site beside Blue Flag beach and marina.

This site is located with direct access onto a spectacular, white, fine sandy beach that runs for miles - Kiko is towards the northwest end, which leads into a beautifully situated small marina and yacht club. Unfortunately the beach is not visible from the campsite itself, which is set at a lower level, behind a grassy bank. There are 200 pitches with hard surfaces, of variable size but access to them from the rather narrow internal roads could be difficult fot larger units. All pitches have electricity connections (16A, long leads may be needed) and shade and privacy is provided by deciduous trees and tall hedges. Four modern sanitary blocks are very clean and fully tiled with free hot water, large showers, washbasins (a few in cabins), British style WCs and excellent facilities for disabled visitors (who will find this site flat and convenient). There is a small bird sanctuary at the entrance, opposite the bar and supermarket. A larger beach bar is on the beach itself, which is good for swimming. The site's restaurant is also here and specialises in Valencian rice dishes and fresh fish (winning a Michelin award in '98) with entertainment in season. The yacht club also offers its facilities of swimming pool, bar, restaurant and TV room to campers at Kiko. The footpath to the marina leads into the town – a 10 minute walk. This is an excellent site for water sports enthusiasts and medium sized boats can be trolleyed onto the beach by means of a ramp. Windsurfing is reputed to be very good (details from reception) and there is a diving school from mid-June.

How to find it: From A7 north of Benidorm take exit 61 to the town and then the beach; site is at northwest end.

General Details: Open all year. Bar with TV. Beach-side bar and restaurant (all year). Supermarket (open all year, excl. Sundays). Children's playground. Watersports facilities. Entertainment for children from mid-June. Petanque. Bicycle hire. Beach volleyball. Golf 5 km. Riding 7 km. Indoor pool 1 km. Exchange facilities. Laundry facilities. Gas supplies. Chemical disposal. Motorcaravan services. Bungalows and apartments for rent.

Charges 2000: Per person ptas. 750; child (under 10 yrs) 550; pitch 1,800 - 3,500; dog 260; electricity (16A) 250 plus meter. Plus 7% VAT. Low season less 10-60% for long stays and pensioners. Credit cards accepted.

Reservations: Write to site for details. Address: Apdo. 70, 46780 Playa de Oliva (Valencia). Tel: 962/850905. FAX: 962/854320. E-mail: kikopark@interbook.net.

Costa Blanca

The Costa Blanca (the White Coast) derives its name from its 170 miles or so of silvery-white beaches along the central section of the Spanish Mediterranean coastline. There are many sheltered bays and most beaches shelve quite gently. The countryside behind the coast remains largely untouched by mass tourism and is well worth exploring, as are places such as Alicante, Cartegena and Valencia. The most popular resort is Benidorm, which has very much shed its `lager lout' image. Large sums of money have been spent building a beautifully paved promenade stretching the whole length of the beach, with palm trees at regular intervals. The beach itself is cleaned every night and the whole town presents a very well cared for image with plenty of police patrols in evidence. However, don't be too complacent as petty pilfering does occur. In the winter the town is filled with older people who never pose a problem, whilst in summer it is noisier and more boisterous with families and younger people on holiday.

8680 Camping Armanello, Benidorm

Friendly site with swimming pool just behind the town.

About 1 km. back from the eastern Benidorm beach (the one on the other side of the town is less crowded), Armanello is quietly situated just far enough away from the main coast road to avoid excessive noise. It is a natural, 'green' site, with small pitches (60 sq.m.) marked out in bays of 10 or 12 in former citrus and olive groves. There is a small and much-used swimming pool. About 103 units are taken on flat ground with electricity available throughout (16A). Two toilet blocks (arranged back to back) have washing and shower facilities with hot and cold water, British style toilets, some washbasins in cabins, hot showers and baths. Hot water also for laundry and dishwashing. Facilities near reception include a washroom, shower and WC for disabled people. The site is popular with long stay units in winter. The approach road from the main N332 is narrow and bumpy.

How to find it: From new bypass (N332) take Levante Beach road into Benidorm; watch for site signs after 1 km. directly off this road. From autopista junction 65 take Benidorm exit and at second traffic lights turn left. Site approach road is 1 km. on right.

General Details: Open all year. 25,000 sq.m. Well stocked shop (all year). Bar. No meals but restaurants near. Swimming pool. Aviary. Fishing, bicycle hire, riding or golf within 1 km. Washing machines and dryer. Gas supplies. Chemical disposal. Motorcaravan services.

Charges 1999: Per adult ptas. 600 - 700; child 500 - 600; pitch 1,800 - 2,000; car or m/cycle 600 - 700; caravan 850 - 2,000; family tent 1,200 - 2,000; small tent 600 - 700; electricity 400. Special winter prices. Plus 7% VAT. Credit cards accepted.

Reservations: contact site for details (it also has much winter trade when reservation is advisable). Address: Ave de la Comunidad Valenciana, 03500 Benidorm. Tel: 965/853190. FAX: 965/853100.

AR Discount
Less 10%

SPAIN - Costa Blanca

8681 Camping Villasol, Benidorm

Excellent, modern site with large swimming pool and views, close to town and beach.

Benidorm is increasingly popular for winter stays and Villasol is a genuinely excellent, purpose built modern site. There is a small indoor pool, heated for winter use and a very attractive, large outdoor swimming pool complex (summer only) featuring a lovely, sheltered free-form pool in a beautifully landscaped, grassy sunbathing area where palm trees and Mediterranean shrubs and flowers create a colourful and exotic atmosphere. The pool is overlooked by the bar/restaurant and restaurant terrace. The restaurant offers good value. The modern, well fitted sanitary blocks provide free, controllable hot water to the showers and washbasins and British WCs. Many of the 314 well separated pitches are arranged on wide terraces which afford views of the mountains surrounding Benidorm. All pitches (80-85 sq.m.) have electricity and satellite TV connections, with 160 with full services for seasonal use. Shade is mainly artificial as yet. The town and Levante beach are 1.3 km. within easy walking distance leaving your car on site. There is an evening entertainment programme. If you are looking for first class amenities in Benidorm, in pleasant and fairly quiet surroundings, this site would make an excellent choice. Reservation is advised even in winter.

How to find it: From the autopista take Benidorm exit (no. 65) and turn left at the second set of traffic lights. After 1 km. at another set of lights turn right, then right again at next lights. Site is on right in 400 m. From northern end of N332 bypass follow signs for Benidorm Playa Levante. In 500 m. at traffic lights turn left, then right at next lights. Site is on right after 400 m.

General Details: Open all year. Electricity throughout (5A). Satellite TV. Restaurant. Bar. Shop. Swimming pools, outdoor and indoor. Children's playground. Golf 8 km. Fishing, bicycle hire 1.3 km. Laundry facilities. No dogs accepted. A few mobile homes to rent.

Charges 1999: (to 14 April 2000). Per person ptas. 600 - 815; child (1-9 yrs) 470 - 600; car 600 - 815; small tent 625 - 875; large tent or caravan 625 - 1,390; motorcaravan 1,225 - 2,200; electricity (1,000w) 465. All plus 7% VAT. Three charging bands. Good discounts for longer stays in winter.

Reservations: Only accepted for 3 month min. stay, starting 1 Oct. Write to site. Address: Avda. Bernat de Sarriá, s/n, 03500 Benidorm (Alicante). Tel: 965/850422 or 966/800898. FAX: 966/806420.

8685 Camping Caravaning El Raco, Benidorm

Quality site with indoor and outdoor pools and views.

This purpose built site with excellent facilities and very competitive prices, originally opened in '96, has now been extended to provide 343 pitches. There is wide access from the Runcon de Loix road (no problem with access for large RVs but check with site for pitch availability before arrival). The site is fairly quietly situated 1.5 km. from the town, Levante beach and promenade. The road has both footpaths and a cycle track, making the site a good choice for motorcaravanners who may prefer to leave their unit on site. Wide tarmac roads lead to pitches of 80 sq.m. or more, surfaced in rolled grit and separated by low, clipped cypress hedging; there is not much shade as yet. Free satellite TV connections are provided to each pitch and there are 94 with all services. The whole site is on a slight downward slope away from the entrance and affords excellent views of the rugged mountains in the hinterland, although this open aspect could be a disadvantage in windy weather. The facilities are excellent. The three toilet blocks are large and well provided with showers, washbasins, laundry and dishwashing sinks (all with free hot water) and facilities for disabled people. Amenities include a well stocked shop with reasonable prices, a busy bar with TV (also open to the public) and a good value restaurant. The swimming pool is a lovely feature surrounded by a grass sunbathing area. There are no slides or diving boards - and no shade, except perhaps parasols. An indoor pool has been opened for winter use. A clean, tidy and good quality site.

How to find it: From the autopista take Benidorm exit (no. 65) and turn left at the second set of traffic lights. After 1 km. at another set of lights turn right, then straight on at next lights for 300 m. to site on right. From northern end of N332 bypass follow signs for Benidorm Playa Levante. In 500 m. at traffic lights turn left, then straight on at next lights for 300 m. to site on right.

General Details: Open all year. Electricity (5, 6, 10A) and satellite TV connections. Restaurant. Bar. Shop. Outdoor swimming pool (1/4-31/10). Indoor heated pool (1/11-31/3). Exchange facilities. Children's playground. Bicycle hire, fishing 1.5 km. Golf 8 km. Beach 1 km. Laundry facilities. Caravan storage.

Charges 1999: Per person ptas. 610 - 650; child (1-9 yrs) 425 - 460; car 610 - 650; tent 610 - 650; caravan 690 - 740; motorcaravan 990 - 1,100; m/cycle 450 - 525; electricity (220v) 435 - 450. Discounts for longer stays. VAT @ 7% incl.

Reservations: Not accepted. Address: Avda. Doctor Severo Ochoa, s/n, 03500 Benidorm (Alicante). Tel: 965/868552. FAX: 965/868544.

8683 Camping Benisol, Benidorm

Mature 'green' site with golf practice facilities.

Camping Benisol is older than the other three sites we feature in Benidorm. It is run by Jean and Brigitte Picard who provide a friendly atmosphere with a range of languages being spoken. The site is mature with well developed hedging and trees giving a good degree of privacy to each pitch. The trees are severely pruned in the winter but make tremendous growth by the summer enhanced by extra artificial shade. There are 230 of which 130 are for touring units (60-80 sq.m). All have electrical hook-ups (4/6A) and 75 have drainage also. The connecting roads are not all tarmac. The modern sanitary facilities, heated in winter and kept very clean, have free hot water to the washbasins, showers, and sinks for laundry and dishwashing. Amenities include a swimming pool with cascade and small water slides and the sports facilities listed below. The golf practice range is free to campers, although a charge is made for a bucket of balls (100 ptas for 24). Some day-time road noise should be expected.

How to find it: From autopista take Benidorm exit (no. 65), At second set of traffic lights turn left. In 1 km. at next lights continue straight on and site is on right after 500 m. From N332 at northern end of bypass follow sign for Benidorm Playa Levante and site is on left in 100 m.

General Details: Open all year. Free satellite TV link. Restaurant with terrace and bar (all year, closed 1 day a week). Shop. Swimming pool (June-Nov). Sports ground. Small children's play area. Minigolf. Table tennis. Jogging track. Tennis. Golf driving range. Bicycle hire 3 km. Fishing (sea) 3 km. Riding 1 km. Golf 14 km. Laundry facilities. Car wash. Gas supplies. Chemical disposal. Bus route. Bungalows, tents and rooms to let. Caravan storage adjacent.

Charges 1999: Per unit ptas. 1,600 - 1,800 for 60 sq.m. pitch, 1,800 - 2,000 for 70 sq.m; person 550 - 600; child (1-10 yrs) 450 - 500; extra tent or car 500 - 550; m/cycle 400 - 450; electricity (220v) 375 per kw/hr. All plus 7% VAT. Less 15-60% in low seasons. No credit cards.

Reservations: Contact site for details. Address: Avda. de la Comunidad Valenciana, s/n, 03500 Benidorm. Tel: 965/851673. FAX: 965/860895.

8686 Excalibur Medieval Camping-Caravaning, Alfaz del Pi, nr Benidorm

Superb site with excellent facilities and pools in an unusual medieval setting.

The site is new and has been built alongside a huge medieval tourist attraction 'The Castle of the Count of Alfaz' and the owner of both interests has retained that theme within the site. You will see the fairy-tale spires from the main road as you approach and the huge mythical sword of Excalibur, which is the focus of the magnificent pools and sports complex. There are 382 marked touring pitches of varying sizes on flat ground. Around 140 have artificial shade, 68 pitches are fully serviced and the remainder have electricity (16A) and connections for TV. Water and waste water points are provided in the toilet blocks. There is a huge standby generator so there will be no power cuts. The turreted sanitary blocks are of a superb standard providing hot water throughout and every other requirement including very impressive provisions for disabled campers, a policy, which is diligently maintained throughout the site. The major facilities are located in an extremely large building close to reception, and includes a series of rooms which can be converted to a banqueting room for 2000, huge bars, restaurants with terraces, games rooms and coffee rooms. The medieval décor is complete and includes wonderful French tapestries and massive chandeliers imported from England. A separate smaller building houses the supermarket, laundry and a doctor's room. The Excalibur complex is incredible, from the giant sword poised 35 m. above the huge pools with bridges, water slides, three hydro massage pools, children's pool, sunbathing areas and bars placed around the mock rock structure. Below this, with a lift for disabled people, is the luxurious heated covered pool and sports complex. This is an innovative feature – the pool has a most impressive sculpted wall with a Roman scene depicted in relief, and circular windows, which look into the depths of the outer pool. There is a gymnasium, sauna, a superb jacuzzi, which share luxurious changing facilities, showers and WCs. Back up top you can enjoy the view of the mountain backdrop from the higher levels of the rocky structure or sit on a submerged stool at the pool bar and enjoy a special medieval cocktail. Medieval banquets are held weekly, and there are discounts for customers of the site if you attend a medieval night at the nearby castle. You are just 2 km. from the beaches at Benidorm.

How to find it: From N332 (Valencia - Alicante) at 149 km. marker take road to Playa Levant and follow signs to site.

General Details: Open all year, 120,000 sq.m. Bars. Restaurant and terrace. Banqueting hall. Social room. Supermarket. Outdoor pools and hydro-massage pools. Heated indoor pool. Jacuzzi. Sauna. Gymnasium. Football. Tennis. Children's playground. Hairdresser. Laundry room. Medical room.

Charges 2000: Per person ptas. 575 - 735; child (1-9 yrs) 425 - 540; car 540 - 735; small tent 595 - 795; caravan or tent 575 - 1,250; motorcaravan 1,105 - 1,995; electricity 420. All plus 7% VAT. Discounts for long stays in low season. Credit cards accepted.

Reservations: Contact site. Address: Camino Viejo del Albir s/n, 03580 Alfaz del Pi (Alicante). Tel: 966/867139. FAX: 966/866928. E-mail: c-m@camping-medieval.com.

271

SPAIN - Costa Blanca

8687 Camping Cap Blanch, Playa del Albir, Altea

Well run site in coastal location, open all year and very popular for winter stays.

This site is immediately across the road from the pebble beach at Albir and within a few hundred yards of all Albir's shops and restaurants, so vehicles can be left on the site. Campers can join in a host of activities organised by the site, from physical ones such as tennis and walking to gentler ones such as painting or lessons in Spanish in the pleasant classroom. The site tends to be full in winter and is very popular with several nationalities, especially the Dutch. For winter stays, it would pay to get there before Christmas as January and February are the peak months. Although it is on the coast, the site is well sheltered and something of a sun-trap, the 277 pitches on flat, hard gravel being big enough to allow plenty of room for sunbeds, loungers, etc. Inland, the mountains and beautiful scenery are only a few kilometres away, with orange groves, olives and vines to see and, of course, bodegas to visit to taste the vintages. The refurbished sanitary block can be heated and provides good facilities including clean showers with adequate space, some washbasins in private cabins, British style WCs, baby facilities and a room (locked) containing facilities for disabled visitors.

Directions: Site is by the Albir - Altea coast road and can be reached from either end. From N332, north or south, watch for sign Playa del Albir and proceed through Albir until you reach the coast road. Site is on the edge of Albir, well signed.

General Details: Open all year. Electricity connections throughout (5A). Bar and restaurant, others plus shops and commercial centre close. Organised entertainment and courses. Children's playground. Tennis. Boules. Fitness centre. Telephones. Laundry. Chemical disposal. Car wash. Cabins and bungalows to rent.

Charges 1999: Per person ptas. 600; child (3-12 yrs) 500; tent 600; car 600; caravan 800; motorcaravan 1,100; m/cycle 500; electricity 500. VAT included. Less 10-35% for low season stays 7-30 days, special rates for long stays. Credit cards accepted.

Reservations: Contact site. Address: Playa Cap Blanch, 03590 Altea (Alicante). Tel: 965/845946. FAX: 965/844556.

8689 Camping Playa del Torres, Villajoyosa

Small, pleasant, family site with pool, directly on a shingle and sand beach.

Jacinto and Mercedes had recently opened this pretty site when we visited, with the lower part set under eucalyptus trees. Reception is placed in one of the site's tasteful wooden buildings close to the beach, and here the receptionist, Betty, will organise your stay (excellent English is spoken). The 85 lower pitches, some large, are on flat ground with shade from the trees, with 10 good pitches right alongside the beach fence. All have electricity, some are fully serviced and there are ample water fountains around the site along with efficient, modern lighting. A modest sized pool with a sunbathing area is situated in the centre part of the site between the bar/cafeteria/shop building and the separate sanitary block. These buildings are of a high specification as are the fittings within. The showers are excellent with free hot water and there is hot water at all sinks, the water to the washing sinks is operated by foot pedal and there is a laundry with modern machines. Some limited weekend entertainment is planned for 2000 and the upper levels of the site will be completed to include more (150) pitches with some chalets and mobile homes. Boats can be launched from the beach which is sand and shingle with weed being thrown up in places. Sub-aqua diving can be organised from the site along with other watersports. The children's play area is safe and pleasant and includes a sand-pit. Serious or recreational walking and climbing is possible approximately 20 minutes from the site – reception will assist with all tourist activities. Benidorm with its beaches is close, along with many tourist activities including the Fuentes del Algar waterfall and the huge exiting new 'Terra Mittica' theme park. If you prefer small family sites of high quality this could be for you.

How to find it: Turn left at the 140.5 km. mark on the Valencia - Alicante N332 road (watch carefully for turn).

General Details: Open all year. Swimming pool. Bar. Cafeteria. Petanque. Barbecues. Freezer.

Charges 1999: Per person ptas 550; caravan 575; motorcaravan 1,000; car 550; electricity 410 - 500. Plus 7% VAT. Less 5-50% for stays 7 days or more except Easter and July/Aug. No credit cards

Reservations: Contact site. Address: Apdo. Correos 243, 03570 Villajoyosa (Alicante).

For guidance on taking your dog on holiday to Europe, see page 348
For a list of sites where dogs are not accepted, see page 347

8741 Camping Florantilles, Torrevieja, nr Alicante

Modern site with good views, some 4 km. behind the coast, open all year.

Florantilles is a very well laid out, attractive site with good views over the top of the neighbouring citrus groves to a distant salt lake. In winter and spring the delicious scent of orange blossom fills the air, a quiet haven away from the bustle of the nearby coastal resorts. Mimosa trees provide shade for the 271 good-sized pitches (around 90 sq.m.) which are laid out on wide terraces; some very large pitches are available at extra cost. Electricity connections (10A) are provided for each pitch, together with water and a raised drain. The two main sanitary blocks provide British style WCs, controllable hot showers and laundry facilities. Several smaller blocks dotted around the site with toilets and showers but no hot water. The attractive site entrance has a large parking area with car wash facilities, with the entrance to the camping area protected by a barrier (key). There is a good size swimming pool (supervised in peak season), plus a children's pool, restaurant, bar and a well stocked shop (limited opening in low seasons). Keep fit classes, barbecues and line dancing are arranged in season. Watersports are available in nearby Torrevieja and walking clubs are popular, also bird watching, cycling and golf (discounts available). The site is very popular with British visitors, particularly in the winter months. Swiss owned and British managed.

How to find it: Leave A7 autopista at exit 77 on to recently upgraded and renumbered CV90 (formerly C3321). 1 km. south of Torrevieja turn inland (northwest) onto the C3323 signed San Miguel. In 4 km. turn right at sign `Los Montesinos' and campsite sign. Site is on left after 200 m.

General Details: Open all year. Bar (all year). Restaurant (summer only). Shop (limited hours in low seasons). Swimming pool (closed winter). Tennis. Boules. Children's playground. Golf 4 km. Fishing, bicycle hire 5 km. Watersports near. Laundry facilities. Caravan storage available.

Charges 1999: Per unit ptas 1,250; adult 550; child (1-12 yrs) 450; electricity 350. All plus 7% VAT. Special low season discounts. No credit cards.

Reservations: Write to site. Address: 03193 San Miguel de Salinas (Alicante). Tel: 965/720456. FAX: 966/723250.

8743 Camping-Caravaning Mar-jal, Guardamar del Segura

New site with huge pre-formed pool/lagoon system, superb sports complex, close to beach.

Mar-jal is located at the mouth of the Segura river next to the natural park of the Dunes of Guardamar. Reception is housed within a delicately coloured building complete with a towering Mirador, topped by a weather-vane depicting the 'Garza Real' (Heron) bird which frequents the local area and forms part of the site logo. There are 208 pitches all with water, electricity, drainage and satellite TV points, the surface covered with crushed marble and clean and pleasant. There is little shade as yet and the site has an open feel with lots of room for manoeuvring. The large restaurant has a full menu and smart waiters to serve you and it overlooks the pools and the river which leads to the sea in the near distance. This situation is shared with the Taperia and bar with large terraces fringed by trees, palms and pomegranates whilst overlooking the impressive pool/lagoon complex (1,100 sq.m). This has a water cascade, an island bar plus bridge, one part sectioned as a children's pool and a jacuzzi. There are three excellent heated sanitary blocks with British style WCs, hot water throughout and spacious showers. Within each block are high quality facilities for babies and disabled campers, modern laundry rooms with washing machines, dryers, ironing boards and dishwashing rooms (complete with drainers and paper drying rolls). A well-stocked supermarket is on site. The extensive sports area is impressive and has qualified instructors who will customise your fitness programme in conjunction with the doctor. No effort has been spared here, the quality heated indoor pool, light-exercise room, sauna, UV machines, beauty salon, fully equipped gymnasium and changing rooms, including facilities for disabled visitors, are of the highest quality. Martial arts training, aerobics and physiotherapy are also on offer. All activities are discounted for campers. A programme of entertainment is provided for adults and children in season by a professional animation team, and the beach is around 700 m.

How to find it: On the N332 40 km. south of Alicante, site is on the sea side between km. markers 73 and 74.

Charges 1999: Per person ptas. 600 - 700; child 400 - 475; caravan 625 - 900; motorcaravan 1,200 - 1,600; car 500 - 700; electricity 350, plus 35 per Kw. All plus 7% VAT. No credit cards.

General Details: Open all year: 36,000 sq.m. Supermarket. Restaurants. bar. Large outdoor pool complex. Fitness suite and gymnasium. Heated indoor pool. Sauna. Beauty salon. UV beds. Yoga. Aerobics. Soccer pitch. Volleyball. TV room. Chemical disposal. Motorcaravan service point. Mobile homes to rent.

Reservations: Contact site. Address: Ctra. Alicante - Cartagena, km. 73.4, 03140 Guardamar del Segura (Alicante). Tel: 966/725022. FAX: 966/727070. E-mail: marjal@futurnet.es.

SPAIN - Costa Blanca

8742 Camping Internacional La Marina, La Marina, nr Elche

Busy, well managed holiday site close to beach, with good facilities.

Run by a Belgian family, this site is nevertheless very popular with the Spanish themselves, with 100 of the 400 pitches taken by seasonal units. For touring units, there are four different type and size of pitch ranging from about 50 sq.m. for tents to 100 sq.m. with electricity, TV, water and drainage. Shade is available and the pitches are well maintained on fairly level, gravel ground. A special area for tents only is in a small orchard. The site has a good sized swimming pool, paddling pool and 'plunge' pool and beside the pools is a bar/restaurant with terrace (Spanish menu including tapas). These are very busy in season and tickets are required for the pool. A fitness centre and covered, heated pool (14 x 7 m.) have been added (300 ptas charge) and an elegant new central sanitary block has recently been built offering the best of modern facilities. Heated in winter, it has free controllable hot water to large shower cubicles, private washing cabins and facilities for disabled visitors. The two remaining blocks are still to be renovated, these having hot showers, but only cold water to washbasins and sinks. A gate has been created to give access to the long sandy beach through the coastal pine forest which is a feature of the area.

How to find it: Site is 2 km. west of La Marina on the seaward side of N332 Guardamara de Segura - Santa Pola road.

General Details: Open all year. Electricity connections (5A). Bar/restaurant and supermarket (all year also). Swimming pools (Easter - Oct). Indoor pool (heated Oct - Easter). Fitness centre. Sauna. Tennis. Table tennis. Children's playground. Fishing 500 m. Bicycle hire 8 km. Golf 15 km. Hairdresser. Laundry facilities incl. irons. Exchange facilities. Car wash. Gas supplies. Chemical disposal. Motorcaravan services. Chalets (5 bed) to rent.

Charges 1999: Per person ptas. 600; child (under 10 yrs) 400; pitch 1,200 (50-70 sq.m.), 1,900 (70-90 sq.m.) or 2,400 (100 sq.m.); pitch with water, sewerage 2,400; electricity 350. Plus 7% VAT. Less in low season, plus good discounts for longer stays 16/9-14/6, excluding Easter. Credit cards accepted.

Reservations: Made with deposit (5,000 ptas), min. 5 days Easter and Aug. Address: Ctra N-332 km.76, 03194 La Marina (Alicante). Tel: 965/419051. FAX: 965/419110. E-mail: lamarina@apdo.com.

N8752 Camping Naturista El Portus, Cartagena

Attractive and very friendly naturist site right beside the Mediterranean - open all year.

Set in a secluded, mountain fringed, south facing bay, El Portus is a fairly large site with direct access to a sandy beach and enjoying magnificent views. With its own micro-climate, this part of Spain enjoys all year round sunshine. Mid-day temperatures which seldom drop below 20oC and water almost always warm enough for swimming makes this an ideal site for hibernating! There are some 400 numbered pitches, ranging from 60-100 sq.m, all but a few having electricity (5/10A), mostly on fairly level, if somewhat stony, ground with a reasonable amount of shade which is gradually increasing as more trees are planted making parts very attractive. The sanitary facilities are housed in five blocks of varying style which are opened as required and are gradually being refurbished. The standard of provision and maintenance is generally good, with British style WCs, open plan hot showers, dishwashing and laundry facilities, but with only cold water to open plan washbasins. However, we suspect they may be a little hardpressed in peak season (mid July - mid Aug). Unit for disabled visitors, key from reception. Three drinking water points are clearly marked near the steps to the restaurant and non-drinking water points are well spaced around the site. There is large, supervised swimming pool and paddling pool in a sheltered, landscaped situation with grass areas for sunbathing close to the beach and a beach bar/snack bar open mid June - mid Sept. At other times there is a smaller heated pool located above the camping area, near the restaurant and close to a hillside area (known as `Beverley Hills') with a fair number of quite luxurious mobile homes. New children's play area. The restaurant with a nice relaxed atmosphere is open all year with an adjacent TV room/library, bar and shop. It enjoys superb views across the bay and of the surrounding mountains and provides a good choice of meals including a `Menu del Dia' which is also available on a half-board arrangement, including breakfast. This is a very comfortable site with welcoming, English speaking reception staff.

How to find it: Site is on the coast, 10 km. west of Cartagena, via Canteras. Follow signs to Pryca commercial centre, then turn right to Canteras. After passing through village take left turn (signed) down to El Portus.

General Details: Open all year. Restaurant. Shop. Swimming pools. Tennis. Volleyball. Table tennis. Petanque. Yoga. Scuba-diving club (July/Aug). Windsurfing. Spanish lessons. Small boat moorings. Disco and entertainment (high season). Golf (3 courses) near. Chemical disposal. Motorcaravan services. Bungalows, mobile homes and chalets to rent.

Charges 1999: Per person ptas. 775; child (3-7 yrs) 570; pitch 1,630, with electricity 2,300; extra tent 400; extra car or m/cycle 475; dog 525. Discounts for longer stays in low season (over 7, 14 or 21 days). Credit cards accepted.

Reservations: made with large deposit. Address: 30393 Cartagena. Tel: 968/553052. FAX: 968/553053. E-mail: portus@hipocom.es. UK representative: Barry Westwood, EPSOL Tours - Tel: 01296 420635 Fax: 01296 425917.

8753 Camping-Caravaning La Manga, La Manga, nr Cartagena

Impressively large, well equipped, 'holiday style' campsite with own beach and pool.

On arrival at this site, one's first impressions of the efficient reception area, etc. are very favourable, but you could easily be put off by the large number of semi-permanent mobile homes, many of which are situated beneath ugly tin roofs (for shade) which seem to dominate that part of the site which adjoins the main access road. This would be a pity, as this site has many excellent features which outweigh any negative impressions created by these rather unsightly residential units. La Manga itself seems to be largely undiscovered by the British (although our World Cup squad stayed at La Manga Club here in '98) and it is certainly an area which will appeal to those who like busy and quite smart holiday resorts. La Manga is a 22 km. long narrow strip of land, bordered by the Mediterranean on one side and by the Mar Menor on the other. There are sandy bathing beaches on both sides and considerable development in terms of hotels, apartments, restaurants, night clubs, etc. in between - shades of Miami Beach in fact!

The campsite is fairly quietly situated on the approach to `the strip' and enjoys the benefit of its own semi-private beach alongside the Mar Menor, with a sailing, canoeing and windsurfing school and the site's own, good restaurant and bar right beside the beach. The beach is dotted with impressive tall palm trees and the sea is very shallow and warm, so it is ideal for families with small children. There are some 1,000 touring pitches of two sizes (84 or 110 sq m), regularly laid out in rows on level gravel. They are separated and shaded by high hedges and all have electricity and water connections. Seven toilet blocks of standard design are well spaced around the site. They provide washbasins (with hot water in five blocks), controllable hot showers and covered cold water sinks (3 with hot water) for washing up and laundry. There is a large, supervised pool complex, with a bar/snack bar alongside, a well stocked supermarket and a wide range of activities. This site's excellent facilities are ideally suited for holidays in the winter, when the weather is said to be similar to an English summer (that could mean anything, we know, but hopefully you'll catch the drift) - November daytime temperatures, for example, are usually above 20oC. Note: the snack bar, swimming pool complex, open air cinema and medical centre are only available in season.

How to find it: Use exit 15 from MU312 dual-carriageway towards Cabo de Palos, signed Playa Honda (site signed also). Cross bridge and double back on yourself. Site entrance is clearly visible beside dual-carriageway with flags flying.

General Details: Open all year. Electricity connections (10A). Supermarket. Restaurant. Bar. Snack bar. Swimming pool complex (April - Sept). Tennis. Petanque. Open air cinema. Minigolf. Basketball. Volleyball. Football area. Children's play area. Sailing school. Golf, bicycle hire or riding 5 km. Safe deposit. Medical service. Laundry. Gas supplies. Chemical disposal. Bungalows and mobile homes to rent.

Charges 2000: Per 84 sq.m. pitch incl. 2 persons ptas. 2,600 - 3,425, 3 persons 2,900 - 3,800, 4 persons 3,225 - 4,275; per 110 sq.m. pitch incl. 2 persons 3,075 - 4,075, 3 persons 3,375 - 4,500, 4 persons 3,225 - 5,000; prices for up to 8 persons available; child under 6 yrs free; electricity included. All plus 7% VAT. Less 10, 20 or 25% for stays of more than 7, 14 or 21 days in low season. Special prices for long winter stays. Credit cards accepted.

Reservations: are made. Address: 30370 La Manga del Mar Menor (Murcia). Tel: 968/563014. FAX: 968/563426. E-mail: lamanga@caravaning.es. UK representative: Barry Westwood, EPSOL Tours - Tel: 01296 420635 Fax: 01296 425917. A 'Camping Cheques' site.

EPSOL Tours are UK agents for Camping Naturiste El Portus and Camping-Caravaning La Manga. These sites are open all year and Epsol can advise and arrange ferry tickets plus site fees, transport or car hire from Alicante or Murcia airports. Mobile homes also available to rent

EPSOL Tours - Tel: 01296 420635 Fax: 01296 425917.

DISCOUNT VOUCHERS

Between pages 192/193 you will find two Discount Vouchers which will provide you with potential savings of more than the cost of the Guide itself! (valid 1 Jan - 31 Dec 2000 only)

Voucher A - Campsite Discount Voucher

This voucher entitles the holder to the relevant discounts or special offers at the sites in this guide that have a small Alan Rogers' logo by their entry. Retain this voucher for inspection at the campsite.

Voucher B - Travel and Breakdown Insurance

This voucher entitles the holder to a discount of 10% on Travel & Breakdown Insurance arrangements made via this Guide, as advertised between pages 160/161. To arrange cover please follow the instructions on the voucher.

SPAIN - Costa Blanca

8751 Camping Cuevas Mar, Palomares, Cuevas del Almanzora

Pleasant, good quality new site in popular area, open all year.

Only opened in '95 but already gaining a reputation for its excellent, comfortable facilities and immaculate appearance, Cuevas Mar is a welcome addition in a region very popular with British visitors who appreciate its year-round dry, sunny climate. Quietly situated just back from the coast road (little or no road noise on site) and 500 m. across the road from the beach, the site offers 136 exceptionally large pitches for Spain (80-100 sq.m), all with electricity connections (6A) and firm surfaces. The pitches are screened by hedges and young trees which afford a degree of shade and have easy access from wide roads. The sheltered, tiled, oval-shaped pool (14 x 9 m) is surrounded by a grassy sunbathing area and has a thoughtfully provided long ramp to help the elderly or infirm to enter the water (other than access ramps, there are no other facilities for disabled people at present). Although unheated, the pool is kept open and clean throughout the year. Beside the pool is a free jacuzzi (also unheated), a petanque pitch and a small, shaded outdoor bar area. The central sanitary block is well designed, generous in size and adequate, providing large tiled shower cubicles, British style WCs and (rare and much appreciated) full length mirrors! Good laundry and dishwashing facilities are under cover with free hot water everywhere. There are two drinking water points on site (note: in common with many other sites in this very dry area, drinking water is supplied from tanks refilled by tanker delivery and the remainder of the water on site is non-potable).

How to find it: Site is on the landward side of the Villaricos - Garrucha road, 4 km. from Villaricos, 6 km. from Garrucha. From the N340 use exit for Cuevas del Almanzora (km. 537), and follow signs for Palomares, then site.

General Details: Open all year. Shop. Outdoor bar by pool. Restaurant 200 m.

Charges 1999: Per person ptas. 600; child 500; car 600; caravan or tent 600; motorcaravan 1,200; m/cycle 500; dog 200; electricty 500. Discounts for longer winter stays.

Reservations: Contact site. Address: 04618 Palomares, Cuevas del Almanzora (Almeria). Tel: 950/467382.

8750 Camping Los Gallardos, Los Gallardos

Friendly, English owned and managed site with all year round facilities.

Since 1991 Anthony and Shirley Jackson and their family have built this site up from barren land into the comfortable, homely site one finds today. Set in open country with views of the distinctive mountains of the region in the distance, Los Gallardos is a green oasis in which to enjoy some of the sunniest and driest winter weather to be found in mainland Europe and very many British campers do just that! There are 114 good sized, flat pitches marked by flowering trees with easy access and firm surfaces. The majority have 5/10A electricity and a few have all services with 15A electricity if required, although these new pitches have no shade as yet. The central sanitary block has good-sized showers, British style WCs and free hot water for showers and washbasins, with one hot tap to draw water for dishwashing and laundry. There are good motorcaravan service facilities. The Jacksons are keen to help visitors get the best out of their stay in Spain and organise plenty of activities all year round. The swimming pool (unheated), with sunbathing area, sunbeds and keep fit sessions, is open all year, as is the adjacent bar/restaurant (daily 9-4, 7-late) where special dish evenings, Sunday roasts, bridge mornings and games evenings are organised regularly. Excursions to Granada, local restaurants and places of interest are arranged. A good area for walking and beaches are within about 10 km. Two full sized grass lawn bowling greens have been created (temporary membership for campers). Reception and small shop with English foodstuffs and fresh bread each day. Although the site itself is quiet, some road noise from the busy nearby N340 should be expected.

How to find it: Leave CN-340 at km. 525, signed Los Gallardos and follow camp signs.

General Details: Open all year, as are shop, bar, restaurant and swimming pool. Spit roast chicken to order. English breakfasts. Swimming pool. Bowling greens. Animal farm. Boules. Bridge mornings. Spanish lessons. Exchange library, video and jigsaw puzzle hire. Golf 8 km. Riding 5 km. Excursions. Full information sheets on request. Hairdresser calls weekly. Washing machines and dryer. Gas supplies. Chemical disposal. Motorcaravan services. Caravan storage.

Charges 2000: Per person ptas. 475; child 325; car 475; caravan or tent 475; motorcaravan 950; m/cycle 375; electricity 325. Discounts for longer stays and up to 65% in winter. Credit cards accepted.

Reservations: Write to site. Address: 04280 Los Gallardos (Almeria). Tel: 950/528324. FAX: as phone. E-mail: questions@almeriaonline.com.

Costa del Sol

The Costa del Sol stretches from Gibraltar north-eastward along the Mediterranean coast for some 250 miles and, even in April and October, averages 7-8 hours of sunshine daily, with average temperatures of around 20°C. The most popular (and most commercialised) resorts are Torremolinos and Marbella, both of which have much to offer, but there are several quieter and more tranquil resorts such as Fuengirola and Nerja. For sightseeing, there are many historic towns and cities within range, including Seville, Granada, and Cordoba, as well as a host of Andalucian villages.

8760 Camping Mar Azul, El Ejido, nr Almeria

Sea-front site, on its own by beach, with good sized pitches and many sporting activities.

Right beside the sea, on flat ground and with direct access to a sandy beach, Mar Azul is in a dry and sunny area of Spain where there are not many other camping sites. The landscape is dominated by the Sierra Nevada (but is rendered somewhat unsightly behind the site by local farmers' use of acres of plastic cloches, as along most of this coast). The site normally has space as it has not yet become widely known. About 450 individual, numbered pitches are quite attractively laid out with palm trees between them and at 90 sq.m. are larger than most in Spain. Artificial shade is provided on most pitches. The four toilet blocks are of good quality with British style toilets, washbasins and free hot showers. A circular, unheated swimming pool with child's pool and a terrace and sun-beds, is near the beach, a further pool is in the centre of the site, where there is a very large area set aside for many different sports, a third pool has been added. The site lies out on its own, but the large development of Almerimar with golf course, large hotel, restaurant, some shops, etc. is little over 1 km. along the beach. El Ejido is 8 km.

How to find it: Turn off main N340/E15 road at km. 409 (El Ejido-Almerimar) exit. Site is on east side of El Ejido, from where it is signed.

General Details: Open all year. Supermarket (1/4-15/10). Bar (1/4-15/10 and winter weekends). Restaurant (1/4-15/10). Swimming pools and child's pool (1/4-15/10). Tennis. Fronton. Squash. Table tennis. Fitness centre. Boules. Volleyball. Badminton. Basketball. Riding. Archery. Bicycle hire and circuit. Roller skating. Minigolf. Football practice area. Fishing. Windsurfing school and equipment for hire. Activities organised for children. Golf 1.5 km. Washing machines. Treatment room; doctor visits in season. Chemical disposal. Motorcaravan service point. Bungalows to rent (details from site). Caravan storage.

Charges 1999: Per person 650 ptas.; child (2-10 yrs) 575; tent or caravan 650; car 650; motorcaravan 1,025; electricity 475. All plus 7% VAT. Credit cards accepted.

Reservations: are made for any length. Address: Apdo. Correos 39, 04700 El Ejido (Almeria). Tel: 950/497585 or 497505. FAX: 950/497294. E-mail: cmazul@a2000.es.

8770 Camping El Paraiso, Almuñecar

Smaller, attractive, family run site on beach with excellent restaurant.

This is a well maintained site of 80 pitches on the beach at Almuñecar Costa Tropical. It is open all year and is a useful stopping point when moving to the south coast from Granada. It is quiet and tucked away, unlike the larger sites along the coast. The owner has a penchant for blue tiles and this is evident in the various facilities on site. Imaginative use of patterned tiles brings the site to life and is most attractive under the canopy of huge trees which provide plentiful shade to most pitches. There is a variety of sanitary blocks which have been added over the years. All are clean and well maintained. A strong feature of the site is the restaurant/bar complex which has been cleverly designed and the patio area is very pretty indeed. A step out of the rear entrance past the supermarket takes you to the beach with sand of varying textures. The esplanade is attractive with many restaurants and bars. Again this is relatively peaceful, unlike the major holiday beaches on the Costas. Part of the site is on a gentle slope but the pitches are level and all are supplied with electricity. There is a free car wash and lots of covered parking on site. The site is well managed and good security is in place day and night. There are generous discounts for extended off season stays. Bus service from directly outside the site to La Herradura, a fishing resort suburb of Almuñecar. Buses also run to Granada, Nerja and Motril.

How to find it: Access from the N 340 at the 317.5 km. marker and follow campsite markers downhill towards beach - site is on the left.

General Details: Open all year. Electricity connections (4A). Very good bar/restaurant. Supermarket. Laundry facilities. Car wash. Beach. Tennis club 500 m. Walks from site.

Charges 1999: Per adult 675 ptas; child 575; tent or caravan 1,075; car 675; motorcaravan 1,075; m/cycle 475; electricity 250. All plus 7% VAT. Less 30-65% for extended stays.

Reservations: Contact site. Address: Ctra N340 km.317.5, Almuñecar (Granada). Tel/Fax: 958/632370.

SPAIN - Costa del Sol

8711 Nerja Camping, Maro-Nerja

Spectacularly situated small site with swimming pool and glorious views.

So many Spanish camp sites seem to look like local authority car parks that it is nice to be able to report on one that is about as unlike a car park as you could possibly get! Set on the lower slopes of the Sierra Almijara, some 5 km. from Nerja and 2 km. from the nearest beach, Nerja Camping is a delightful small site of 55 pitches (30 with 15A electricity) with impressive views of the surrounding mountains and nearby Mediterranean. Being situated slightly above but alongside the main coast road, it is easy to find - the price you pay is some traffic noise but this seems hardly to detract from the relaxing and almost idyllic ambience. The pitches are of reasonable size on flat terraces with mainly artificial shade, whilst the roads, although quite steep, are newly surfaced and should present little problem except perhaps to drivers of really huge motorhomes. The site also boasts a small swimming pool, a bar/restaurant serving simple fresh dishes and even large breakfasts, all cooked and served by the Irish owner Peter Kemp and his Spanish wife Make on the terrace beside their magnificent carob tree. The single sanitary block is of modern design and construction with British type WCs, some free hot showers, washbasins (1 only with hot water), dish-washing sinks (cold water) under cover and laundry facilities.

How to find it: Site is signed from main N340 coast road about 5 km. north of Nerja. If coming from Nerja, go 50 m. past site entrance to cross main road.

General Details: Open all year except Oct. Swimming pool (March - Sept). Bar/restaurant (Feb - Sept). Essentials from the bar. Pool table. Fishing 2 km. Bicycle hire or riding 5 km. Washing machines. Chemical disposal. Bus service nearby.

Charges 2000: Per person ptas. 600; child (2-10 yrs) 450; tent 600 - 750; caravan 750; car 600; motorcaravan 900; m/cycle 500; electricity 450. All plus 7% VAT. Less 20-40% outside 1/6-30/9. Special rates for long stays. No credit cards.

Reservations: Write to site for details. Address: Ctra. N340, km. 297, 28787 Maro - Nerja (Malaga). Tel: 952/529714. FAX: 952/529696.

8782 Camping-Caravaning Laguna Playa, Torre del Mar

Beach-side family run site with own swimming pool.

Laguna Playa is a modern site with very friendly staff who give a personal service. Alongside one of the Costa del Sol beaches, the site is well placed for visits to Malaga and Nerja with a regular bus service 700 m. from the site. The site organises trips to the famous Alhambra Mosque in Granada on a weekly basis. The pitches are flat, of average size and with good artificial shade supplementing that provided by the established trees on site. All pitches have electrical connections. There are attractive adults and children's swimming pools open in high season. The two sanitary blocks are modern and well equipped offering free showers. The site runs a busy restaurant offering value for money, plus a bar and supermarket, all open all year. There is a children's play area and the site organises various competitions including 'petan' in the summer. Good off peak discounts are available. A unique feature of the site is that the owners will exchange English gas cylinders for a Spanish version and the reverse if you are headed for home. This activity is registered approved by the local authorities (subject to legality of user gas cylinder stowage).

How to find it: Site is on the sea front Paseo Maritimo, at Torre del Mar on the main N340 Malaga - Nerja road.

General Details: Open all year. Electricity connections (5/10A). Bar/restaurant. Supermarket. Swimming pools. Children's play area. Laundry facilities. Car wash. Bungalows to rent.

Charges 1999: Per adult 575 ptas; child 455; tent 575; caravan 640; car 575; motorcaravan 1,175; m/cycle 460; electricity 350 (metered in winter). All plus 7% VAT. Less 10-30% in mid-season for extended stays, 20-50% in low season.

Reservations: Write to site. Address: Prolongación Paseo Marítimo s/n, 29740 Torre del Mar (Malaga). Tel: 952/540631. FAX: 952/540484.

All the sites in this guide are regularly inspected by our team of experienced site assessors, but we welcome your opinion too.

See Readers' Reports - page 366

8801 Camping La Rosaleda, Los Boliches, nr Fuengirola

Smaller family site with pool, 1 km. north of Fuengirola.

This is a small friendly site of 112 pitches tucked in the hills to the north of the fashionable resort of Fuengirola. It is convenient for visiting Torremolinos and the numerous major theme parks close by. The site enjoys some good views towards the mountains and over the town towards the sea, the beach is 1 km. There is an attractive, medium sized swimming pool with paved surround and a grass sunbathing area. The pitches are of about 60 sq.m. and on flattish, grassy/sandy ground with a good proportion having electricity (5A). Many are separated by chain link fencing, some with hedges and established trees giving natural shade for most pitches. The two sanitary blocks are dated but clean and appear to be adequate. There are free hot showers, British type WCs and dishwashing under cover. The site is very busy in July/Aug.

How to find it: For some reason the camping signs at 211.5 km. on the eastern N 340 at Fuengirola autopista direct you into the busy town centre before recrossing the autopista to gain access to the site at the end of a gravel road. However, it is a straightforward approach from the west.

General Details: Open all year. Bar/restaurant (1/6-30/9) serving mainly pizzas (to takeaway) and pastas. Small supermarket (1/7-30/9). Swimming pool with pool-side bar in main season. Fishing 800 m. Bicycle hire 500 m. Riding 2 km. Golf 5 km. Washing machines. Gas supplies. Chemical disposal.

Charges 2000: Per adult ptas. 675; child 425; caravan 850; motorcaravan 850 - 1,200; tent 750; car or m/cycle included; electricity 300. No credit cards.

AR Discount
Less 10% (if no other discounts taken)

Reservations: Write to site. Address: N-340 km. 211.5, Los Boliches, 29640 Fuengirola (Malaga). Tel: 952/460191. FAX: 952/581966.

8805 Camping Los Jarales, Mijas-Costa

Spacious, medium sized site with pool and close to attractive beaches.

This is a well maintained site on the Costa del Sol which is open all year. The site is on a slope but the pitches are level, and all are supplied with water, waste water drainage, electricity, terrestrial and satellite TV connections. Larger motorhomes are capable of `plumbing in' if required. The central sanitary block is clean and well equipped offering free showers and hot water at the sinks. There is a good size swimming pool (high season), along with a pleasant restaurant and bar which are open all year. The beaches are a few minutes walk on the far side of the N 340. Most of the pitches have natural shade from well established, attractive trees. There is a children's play area near the restaurant. The site is ideal for visiting Ronda, Marbella and the numerous theme parks close by. The staff are very friendly and will assist with bookings if required. There is a supermarket on site open in the summer but there are many supermarkets nearby, along with a myriad of bars and restaurants. Bus service from outside site to town.

How to find it: Site is well signed off the main N340 at the 197 km. marker between Fuengirola and Marbella.

General Details: Open all year. Electricity connections (5, 10 or 15A). Bar/restaurant close to beach. Supermarket. Swimming pool. Children's play area. Basketball/tennis court. Laundry facilities. Car wash.

Charges 1999: Per adult 400 - 600 ptas; child 350 - 500; tent 350 - 650; caravan 450 - 800; car 350 - 500; motorcaravan incl. 2 persons 1,450 - 2,500; m/cycle 300 - 400; electricity 350 (metered in winter). Plus 7% VAT.

Reservations: Write to site. Address: Ctra. N340 km.197, Mijas-Costa (Malaga). Tel/Fax: 952/930003.

8803 Camping La Buganvilla, nr Marbella

Large site 7 km. from Marbella with footbridge access to beach.

This site takes its name from the display of flowers native to Spain which can be seen on the restaurant/bar complex. It is large, (300 pitches) with three large sanitary blocks attractively painted powder blue. The facilities provided are more than adequate and were spotlessly clean when seen. Some of the main pitches are shaded by trees, and there are other areas for tents in heavily wooded areas (electricity provided). All other pitches have electricity and there are 20 fully serviced pitches for larger motorhomes. The site has a large bar and restaurant area, the patio of which overlooks the swimming pools. The adult pool is well maintained and free, as is the children's version. The northern part of the site is terraced with some large, additional separate pitches specifically for tour operators. There is a supermarket and modern car wash (at a cost of 200 ptas). A footbridge connects the site directly with the golden sands of the Costa del Sol beaches and, although the site is close to the N340 traffic, noise seems to be absorbed by the abundant trees on its southern edge. The tourist resort of Fuengirola is 19 km. east.

How to find it: Access is between Marbella and Fuengirola off the N340 at 188.8 km. marker. It is advisable to gain access to the site travelling from Fuengirola to Marbella otherwise you will be obliged to tackle a rough track around the rear of the site (the U-turn over the road bridge to achieve this is worthwhile). Follow campsite signs.

General Details: Open all year. Electricity connections (10A). Large bar/restaurant complex. Supermarket. Swimming pools. Children's play areas. Basketball and tennis in season. Laundry facilities. Car wash. Footbridge to beach. Regular bus service available from outside site. Good security at all times.

Charges 1998: Per adult 525 ptas; child 425; tent 750; caravan 800; car 525; motorcaravan 975; m/cycle 425; electricity 350. All plus 7% VAT.

Reservations: Contact site. Address: Ctra N340 km.188.8, 29600 Marbella (Malaga). Tel: 952/831973 or 4. FAX: 952/831974. E-mail:buganvilla@spar.es.

SPAIN - Costa del Sol

8809 Camping El Sur, Ronda

Small and interesting family owned site close to Ronda.

The generous manoeuvring area and delightfully decorated entrance to this site are a promise of something different which is fulfilled in all respects. The very friendly family who run the site have worked hard for ten years combining innovative thinking with excellent service. The single sanitary block is immaculate and the free hot showers a real treat. The average size pitches are partially shaded by carefully planted olive and almond trees. Most pitches have relaxing views of the surrounding mountains but at an elevation of 850 m. the upper pitches allow a clear view of the fascinating town of Ronda which should be visited. Most pitches have electricity and water and are terraced on sand/grass. The site's restaurant is in three large sections and is a delight, serving excellent food at reasonable prices (the owners eat there). The bar and restaurant are bedecked with very tasteful local artistry which may be purchased as a quality memento of the area and the views from the complex are enjoyable, especially at sunset. The various leisure facilities are very clean, well maintained and the personal touches of the owners are obvious which make the experience of using them more enjoyable. The kidney shaped pool is most welcome in summer as the temperatures soar. There are two children's play areas with safe activities and a minigolf course. This peaceful site also offers some attractive cabins and chalets for hire.

How to find it: Site is well signed from town centre and is off no. 341 Algeciras road, 1.5 km. south of Ronda.

General Details: Open all year. Electricity connections (5A). Bar and very large, high quality restaurant. Swimming pool. Children's playground and adventure play area. Off road bicycle hire. Laundry facilities. First aid room and doctor on call. Bungalows and chalets for hire.

Charges 1999: Per person 425 ptas; child 300; tent 400; caravan 400; car 400; m/cycle 300; motorcaravan 800; electricity 300. Plus 7% VAT

Reservations: Recommended for July/Aug. Address: Ctra Ronda - Algeciras, km. 1.5 Apartado de Correos 127, 29400 Ronda. Tel: 952/875939. FAX: 952/877054.

8810 Camping Parque Tropical, Estepona

Unusual site with all year heated indoor pool.

This is a fascinating family run site built on the site of a botanical garden and thus the pitches sit amongst exotic plants and shrubs. There are 102 pitches, all with electricity, on sloping ground although the pitches themselves tend to be flat. The modern sanitary block is clean with free hot showers and has additional facilities to service the indoor swimming pool. This is heated throughout the year and has exotic plants surrounding the inside of the pool. Floodlit by night this is a novel feature; it also has a separated children's section. An attractive restaurant and bar is open all year and the new reception block has a small shop. There is a large Spanish restaurant close by which offers Spanish entertainment and the reception staff are happy to assist with booking local excursions. The site is a few minutes from the golden sands of Estepona and the town itself which is a major tourist area but an exploration of the back streets of the old part of the town can take you back to typical Spanish settings.

How to find it: Site is well signed off N340 east of Estepona - look for the 'heated pool' camp signs.

General Details: Open all year. Electricity connections (6A). Bar/restaurant. Small shop. Indoor swimming pool. Beach 10 minutes. Bus service to town centre from outside site.

Charges 1999: Per adult ptas. 525; child 475; car 500; tent or caravan 600; motorcaravan 925; m/cycle 425; electricity 375. Reductions in low season.

Reservations: advisable in high season. Address: Ctra N340 km. 162, 29680 Estepona (Malaga). Tel: 952/93618. FAX: 952/794152.

8812 Camping Chullera 2, Sabinillas-Manilva

Peaceful site on the beach, in unspoilt area 16 km. from Estepona.

This is a peaceful site on the Costa del Sol with excellent modern sanitary blocks and an attractive 'al-fresco' type restaurant and bar. The 8 km. of sandy beach is safe and clean and a major attraction for this site. There are a number of pitches alongside the beach with electricity connections supplied. Most of the larger than average pitches have artificial or natural shade and are well cared for, some being on a gentle slope. It is ideal for visiting Marbella and Gibraltar and the staff will assist with bookings for the various local attractions if required. There is a well stocked supermarket which, like the site, is open all year round. There is a sister site, Chullera 3 offering the same standard of facilities just 1 km. away with another 250 peaceful pitches.

How to find it: Site is well signed off the main N340 at the 141.5 km. marker, 16 km. west of Estepona.

General Details: Open all year. Electricity connections (6A). Bar/café close to beach with TV. Supermarket by entrance. Children's play area. Laundry facilities. Car wash. Bus service from outside site to city.

Charges 1999: Per adult 300 - 500 ptas; child 250 - 400; tent 250 - 400 or 300 - 500; caravan 300 - 500; car 300 - 500; motorcaravan 600 - 1,000; m/cycle 250 - 400; electricity 400. All plus 7% VAT.

Reservations: Contact site. Address: Ctra. N340 km.141.5, 29692 Sabinillas-Manilva (Malaga). Tel: 952/890196. FAX: as phone.

8800 Camping-Caravaning Marbella Playa, Marbella

Large modern site on northern outskirts of Marbella, with good pool.

This site is on the outskirts of the internationally famous resort of Marbella with public transport available to the town centre. A sandy beach is about 150 m. away with direct access. There are 430 individual pitches of up to 70 sq.m. with natural shade (additional artificial shade is provided), and electricity is available throughout. A large swimming pool complex with a restaurant/bar and palm trees provides a very attractive feature. The three sanitary blocks are modern with free hot showers, 2 small baths, 2 private cabins and 16 washbasins in each. There are two fully equipped units for disabled visitors and all facilities are kept very clean. Laundry and washing up areas are modern and in good order. The supermarket is very large with its own butcher and fresh vegetable counter. The site is busy throughout the high season but the high staff/customer ratio and the friendly staff approach ensures a comfortable stay.

How to find it: Site is 12 km. east of Marbella with access close to the 193 km. point on the main N340 road.

General Details: Open all year, as are supermarket, bar, restaurant and café. Electricity connections (16/20A). Swimming pool (April-Sept). First aid centre. Children's playground (on gritty sand). Bureau de change. Large free car/van wash area.

Charges 1999: Per person 570 ptas; child (1-10 yrs) 490; car 570; caravan/tent 970; m/cycle 520; motorcaravan 1,350; electricity 400; minimum pitch fee 1,400 - 2,600. All plus 7% VAT. Reductions for long stays and senior citizens outside 16/6-31/8.

Reservations: Write to site. Address: Ctra N-340, Km. 192,800, 29600 Marbella, Costa del Sol (Malaga). Tel: 952/833998. FAX: 952/833999.

RELAX WHERE THE SUN NEVER RELAXES

CAMPING CARAVANING

Marbella playa

Because of the very good climate of the Costa del Sol, open throughout the year.

First cat. site, ideal for your holiday in winter. At the best beach of the Costa del Sol, with fine sand, clean and with clear, shallow water, ideal for fishing and watersports. Surrounded by pine tree forests and only 15 min. from PUERTO BANUS. Large supermarket, restaurant and cafeteria. First class san. install. with indiv. cabins, free hot water. Empt. point f. chem. toilets. 70 sq. sites, many with direct evacuation.

Special prices for long term stay off-season. 10% P/N discount with ICC.

E-29600 MARBELLA (Málaga) COSTA DEL SOL - Tel. (34) 952 83 39 98 Fax (34) 952 83 39 99

Some sites have supplied us with copies of their brochures

which we are pleased to forward to readers.

See our Brochure Service - page 346

SPAIN - Costa de la Luz

Costa de la Luz

This is the stretch of coast running from Gibraltar in the east to the Portuguese border in the west. Despite being even further south, it does not enjoy quite the same climate as the Costa del Sol as it borders the Atlantic rather than the Mediterranean - but this may be an advantage during high summer. The eastern end of this coast is quite attractive with many wonderful views across to Africa and we feature several sites in this area. However, the western end, apart from the Donana National Park and some large beaches, is rather different.

8850 Camping Paloma, Tarifa, nr Algeciras

Attractively situated site with beaches nearby, 12 km. northwest of Tarifa.

A spacious, neat and tidy, family orientated site, Paloma is 700 m. from the nearest beach which has good facilities for bathing and windsurfing. The site has some 380 pitches on mostly flat ground, although the westerly pitches are sloping. The pitches are of a reasonable size, separated by hedges and some are shaded by mature trees; approximately 200 pitches have electrical connections. There are two modern sanitary blocks, one of a good size, though a long walk from the southern end of the site. The other is smaller and open plan, serving the sloping areas of the site. They have mostly Turkish style WCs, some British, washbasins with cold water, (some in cubicles and with bidets for women) and 12 free controllable hot showers. Dedicated facilities for disabled visitors are provided in the smaller sanitary block with access from sloping ground, also a babies room. All sanitary facilities were very clean when seen. There is a small (free) swimming pool with a paved sunbathing area and an attractive thatched, stone bar. Paloma has a small children's play area on sand and several modern. Fully equipped bungalows to rent.

How to find it: Site is signed off the N340 Cadiz road at Punta Paloma, about 10 km. northwest of Tarifa, just west of the km 74 marker. Watch carefully for the site sign - no advance notice. Follow the signs down a sandy road for 300 m, the site is on the right.

General Details: Open all year (no electricity from Nov.- March). Electricity connections (10A), Shop. Busy bar and good restaurant. Swimming pool with adjacent bar (high season only). Children's playground. TV in bar. Excursions. Washing machine. Bungalows to rent.

Charges 1999: Per person 600 ptas; child 550; car 450; m/cycle 400; tent 450; caravan 500; motorcaravan 800; electricity 400. Plus 7% VAT. Discount of 40% from 1/11-31/3 (no electricity).

Reservations: made for one part of site, for any length and without deposit. Address: Ctra. Cadiz-Malaga Km. 70, 11380 Tarifa (Cadiz). Tel: 956/684203.

8855 Camping Tarifa, Tarifa

Attractive, family run site adjacent to 5 km. of golden beach.

The long, golden sandy beach is a good feature of this site being ideal for windsurfing. It is clean and safe for swimming, the beach being to adjacent the site with a private access. The site has a pleasant, open feel and is reasonably sheltered from any road noise. It has been thoughtfully landscaped and planted out and is remarkably clean. The 288 level pitches are of varying sizes and are surrounded by pine trees which provide shade. All have electricity and there are adequate water connections. Two modern sanitary blocks have British WCs and free, controllable hot showers. There are facilities for campers with disabilities and a baby room. All sanitary facilities were spotless when seen. The site's excellent bar/restaurant is open all year, as is the well stocked supermarket which produces its own hot bread. There is a large children's play area with safe, modern activities. The bar has been extended to include a very large patio and entertainment area, and a well designed swimming pool complex including a pool bar were added.

How to find it: Site is on main N340 Cadiz road at the 78.87 km. marker, 7.5 km. northwest of Tarifa. There are large modern signs well ahead of the site with a deceleration lane if approaching from the Tarifa direction, large gaily coloured signs mark the approach to the site.

General Details: Open all year. Electricity connections (5/10A). Bar/restaurant. Supermarket (all year). Swimming pool complex with bar. Car wash. Good security with CCTV.

Charges 1999: Per person 600 ptas; child 500; tent 450; caravan 475; car 450; m/cycle 400; motorcaravan 775; electricity 425.

Reservations: Recommended for July/Aug. Address: Ctra. N340 km. 78.87, 11380 Tarifa (Cadiz). Tel: 956/684778. FAX: as phone. E-mail: camping-tarifa@globalmail-net.

8860 Camping Fuente del Gallo, Conil de la Frontera, nr Cadiz

Well maintained small site on sloping, grassy position with excellent pool and two beaches near.
Fuente del Gallo is a clean friendly site with two nearby beaches which are suitable for bathing and water-sports. Although good beaches, access to them is down fairly steep, stony paths and may not be suitable for older or disabled persons, particularly when attempting to return to the campsite at the end of the day. The long approach roads from the village pass through a very pretty avenue of palm trees at one point. The attractive bar and restaurant facilities are of a high standard with very reasonable prices (breakfasts served). The 260 marked and numbered pitches are somewhat cramped. Nearly all have electricity and there are some trees and bushes separating them. Both of the sanitary blocks have recently been modernised. They are clean and well looked after, with hot water on payment. There are excellent facilities for disabled people and babies. A strong feature of this site is the new, well designed swimming pool area sporting a superb adult pool (entry charge), a toddlers pool, children's play area, TV room, games room and pool bar. This area is also the focus of floodlit Spanish entertainment evenings in season. The helpful staff are equipped to book discounted trips to local attractions or short tours to Africa.

How to find it: From Cadiz-Algeciras road (N340) at km. 23.00, follow signs to Conil de la Frontera town centre, then shortly right to Fuente del Gallo and 'playas' following signs.

General Details: Open week before Easter - 1 Oct, with all amenities. Electricity connections (10A). Restaurant/bar. Shop. Swimming pool (1/6-30/9). Children's playground. Watersports on beach. Fishing 300 m. Bicycle hire 2 km. Riding 1 km. Golf 5 km. Car wash area. Laundry room with two washing machines. Gas supplies. Chemical disposal. Motorcaravan services.

Charges 2000: Per person 525 ptas; child 450; tent 450; caravan 515; car 425; motorcaravan 875; electricity 425. All plus 7% VAT. Less 11-30% for longer stays. Credit cards accepted.

Reservations: Write to site. Address: Apto. 48, 11140 Conil de la Frontera. (Cadiz). Tel: 956/440137 or 442036. FAX: 956/442036.

AR Discount
Less 5-10%
acc. to season

8865 Camping Playa Las Dunas, El Puerto de Santa Maria, nr Cadiz

Large, friendly site alongside a superb beach, ideal for exploring Cadiz and Jerez.
This site lies within the Parque Natural Bahia de Les Dunes and is adjacent to the gently sloping golden sands of Puntilla beach. A 10 minute walk takes you into the bustling heart of Puerto Santa Maria Cadiz which claims to be the birthplace of the `Flamenco', along with Cadiz. This is a traditional Spanish family resort with gastronomic delights in the local port area, supplemented by an abundance of local wines and sherries produced in the immense white-washed warehouses (bodegas) which are open to visitors. Local buses will convey you to the town and cities and there is a ferry to Cadiz. This is a pleasant and peaceful site of some 400 separate marked pitches, with much natural shade and ample electrical connections. Pitches under mature trees are terraced and separated by low walls. The modern sanitary facilities are immaculate with British style WCs, free hot showers, washbasins (cold water only), separate facilities for disabled campers and a baby room. Laundry facilities are excellent. An impressive complex with a large swimming pool and toddlers' pool is open in high season, the municipal sports site very close by offers all manner of sporting activities and the beach provides additional free sports facilities such as volleyball. The site has an all year bar/restaurant facility and a well stocked supermarket which opens in high season.

How to find it: Site is 5 km. north of Cadiz off N1V. Take Puerto Santa Maria road, site signed through town.

General Details: Open all year. Electricity connections (5/10A). Bar/restaurant (all year). Supermarket (high season). Swimming pools (high season). Children's play areas. Doctor on call. Reception open 0800 - 2300 hrs. all year. Security boxes. Night security personnel all year.

Charges 1999: Per person ptas. 510 - 565; child 440 - 490; tent 510 - 610; car 440 - 485; m/cycle 355 - 395; motorcaravan 730 - 810 electricity 5A 300 -335, 10A 630 -700. All plus 7% VAT. Major credit cards accepted.

Reservations: Advised for August; contact site. Address: Paseo Maritimo Playa la Puntilla, s/m, AP 21, 11500 El Puerto de Santa Maria Cadiz. Tel: 956/872210. FAX: as phone.

SPAIN - Costa de la Luz

8872 Camping La Fontanilla, nr Mazagon

Small, unassuming site on cliff top next to superb beaches.

This quiet site is set well back from the main road on the southwest border of the Parc Nacional Coto de Danana and well is suited to those campers who prefer smaller, uncomplicated sites in 'back to nature' surroundings. The village of Mazagon is just 4 km. away and Huelva is approximately 25 km. The spectacular golden sands of the beach are a 100 m. walk from the site gate down a fairly steep slope. Beach showers are provided at the gate. There are views over the sea but the line of cliff top pitches are taken by Spanish units. The single, central sanitary block was clean and well kept when seen but the facilities may be stretched at peak periods. The site has a small bar and a very pleasant restaurant with a patio enjoying excellent sea views, also there is an attached supermarket. Close by is an attractive central, shaded children's play area. Free hot water is available throughout. A washing machine is available and separate sanitary facilities are provided for disabled campers. Some of the marked level pitches are on soft sand and most have artificial shade framing which can make parking a high unit interesting. Long leads are required in some pitches and torches are advisable close to the perimeters of the site.

How to find it: Take E01 from Sevilla to Huelva and turn south at junction 10 for Almonte. Join A483 road, then A494 for Mazagon. Site is well signed on approach to town.

General Details: Open all year. Restaurant. Bar. Supermarket (in season). Ice machine Mobile homes. Children's play area.

Charges 1999: Per adult ptas. 525; child 425; tent 525; car 525; caravan 550; m/cycle 450; motorcaravan 895; electricity 450. Credit cards accepted.

Reservations: Write to site. Address: Ctra. Huelva - Matalascanas, 21130 Mazagon (Huelva). Tel: 959/536052 or 536227. FAX: 959/526237.

8871 Camping Giralda, Isla Cristina

Large, attractive family run site close to beach and river.

The fountains at the entrance and the circular 'thatched' reception building set the tone for this very large, well managed and pleasant site which is just a few years old. The 700 pitches are spacious on sand/grass and most benefit from the attractive mature trees which abound on the site. Most pitches have electricity (there are around 700 pitches, 142 for tents). Access to the excellent beach is gained by a short stroll, crossing the minor road alongside the site and passing through attractive pine trees. The four large, modern, semi-circular `thatched' sanitary blocks are very clean and have British WCs and very good free, controllable hot showers. The site's excellent glassed bar/restaurant overlooks the river, which provides the northern site boundary and pleasant views whilst relaxing, especially at sunset. Two circular free swimming pools, one for children, are also near the restaurant, as is a resident windsurfing, canoeing and sailing school. There is also a large children's play area with safe modern activities. The many additional activities include those listed below. There is a separate area within this huge site where organised groups of children come to enjoy the activities offered within a dedicated adventure area. The accommodation and sanitary arrangements for these activities are totally separate to those provided for campers and thus there is little impingement.

How to find it: Site is off N431 Portugal - Huelva road, 10 km. east of Ayamonte. Take the Isla Cristina road, (C4117) off to the left, pass through Isla Cristina then onto La Antilla and site is 600 m. on the left - well signed.

General Details: Open all year. Electricity connections. Shop. Restaurant/bar. Snacks. Swimming pools. Basketball. Archery. Volleyball. Petan. Soccer. Mountain biking. Beach games. Table tennis. Watersports school. Children's play area. Organised activity area for children. Laundry service. Site contract security all year.

Charges 1999: Per person 675 ptas; child 500; tent 650; caravan 750; car 625; m/cycle 475; motorcaravan 1,250; electricity 500. Plus 7% VAT. Winter discounts.

Reservations: Recommended for July/Aug. Address: Ctra. Provincial 4117, Isla Cristina-La Antilla km 1.5, 21410 Isla Cristina (Huelva). Tel: 959/343318. FAX: 959/343284.

EPSOL Tours are UK agents for Camping Giralda.
The site is open all year and Epsol can advise and arrange ferry tickets plus site fees,
transport or car hire from Alicante or Murcia airports.

EPSOL Tours - Tel: 01296 420635 Fax: 01296 425917.

Central Spain

This area comprises the whole of inland Spain, south of a line just south of Burgos (Lat. 42°) excluding the coastal strip.

Extremadura is a large and sparsely populated region in the west of Spain, bordering central Portugal and consisting of two provinces, both of which bear the name of their main town. Cáceres, to the north, has a fascinating old quarter, while Plasencia and the village of Arroyo de la Luz are also worth a visit. To the south is Badajoz, the second province and the largest in Spain, with its fortified main town (it lies on the border on the historic route from Lisbon to Madrid). Also of interest are Mérida, with Roman ruins and the ruined castle at Alburquerque.

The campsites that we describe in the region are: Cáceres province - 9027 Camping Parque Natural Monfragüe and 9028 Camping Las Villuercas; Badajoz province - 9083 Camping Monesterio and 9087 Camping Merida. *See advertisement between pages 224/5.*

9280 Camping-Motel Sierra Nevada, Granada

Good site with swimming pool, useful for visiting Granada.

This is a good site either for a night stop or for a stay of a few days while visiting Granada. Quite a large site with an open feeling and, to encourage you to stay a little longer, a medium sized swimming pool of irregular shape with a smaller child's pool (admission charge 200 ptas) is open in the main season. Granada has much to offer for sightseeing, including the Alhambra; it also has some interesting shops and there are usually one or two excellent shows. The site fills up considerably each evening in the season, so the earlier you arrive, the better your chances of securing a good pitch. With 148 pitches for touring units, the site is in two connected parts with more mature trees and facilities to the northern end. There is less shade to the south but more modern facilities. Electrical connections (5A) are available. There are two main toilet blocks, one with a separate new unit with free hot showers and facilities for disabled people and babies. Extensive facilities by the pool which can be made available at peak times. They have mostly British style toilets some with bidets, individual washbasins with mirrors and free hot showers.

How to find it: Site is just north of town on Jaén/Madrid road. From autopista, take Granada North - Almanjayar exit 126 (near central bus station). Follow road back towards Granada and site is shortly on the right, well signed.

General Details: Open 1 March - 31 Oct, as are the café, bar and restaurant. About 10,000 sq.m. Shop (15/3-15/10). Swimming pool (15/6-15/9). Bar/café by pool. Rather expensive restaurant. Tennis. Children's playground (with hard surface). Fishing 10 km. Golf 12 km. Doctor lives on site. Washing machine. Car wash. Gas supplies. Chemical disposal. Motorcaravan services. Frequent bus service to city centre from outside site. Motel apartments.

Charges 2000: Per person 630 ptas; child (3-10 yrs) 525; car 630; tent 525 - 630; caravan 675; motorcaravan 1,500; electricity (5A) 450. All plus 7% VAT. Credit cards accepted.

Reservations: are made. Address: Avda. Madrid 107, 18014 Granada. Tel: 958/150062. FAX: 958/150954.

AR Discount
Stay 7 days,
have 1 free

9270 Camping Suspiro Del Moro, nr Granada

Impressive site in Sierra Nevada mountain range, useful for sightseeing.

Suspiro Del Moro is 11 km. south of Granada on the N323 Motril road or, alternatively, can be approached on the scenic mountain road from Almunecar (lots of bends this way). Many places of interest are within reasonable distance of the site, including La Alhambra, Granada and the Parador of La San Francisco. Based high in the Sierra Nevada mountain range, the area offers spectacular views from just outside the site, with trees and fences inhibiting the views inside. The site is cool, peaceful and family run, with gravel paths leading to 72 flat, grass pitches. The one main sanitary block is modern with British WCs, free hot showers (temperature can be unpredictable) and washbasins with hot water, plus good laundry and washing up facilities (cold water only). A reader reports that refurbishment is due and that maintenance can be variable. Three further small toilet blocks are around the camping area. A very attractive Olympic sized swimming pool, together with a restaurant with bar tables, umbrellas and waiter service, covers a large area behind the main camping site. The restaurant offers a large, varied menu and, like the site itself, displays a professional image. A smaller bar and TV lounge is available, and a well stocked supermarket.

How to find it: On N323 road, 11 km. from Granada on road to Motril.

General Details: Open all year. Supermarket, restaurant/bar (open acc.to occupancy). Bar. Swimming pool (high season). Small children's play area on gravel. Riding 2 km. Golf 6 km. Bicycle hire 10 km. Regular bus service from outside site to Granada. Gas supplies. Chemical disposal. Bungalows to rent. Caravan storage.

Charges 2000: Per person 475 ptas; child 375; pitch 900; electricity 300. Credit cards accepted.

Reservations: May be made for high season. Write to site. Address: N323, km. 145 (Cruce Ctra. Almunecar), 18630 Granada. Tel: 958/555411. FAX: 958/555105.

AR Discount
Less 5-10%
acc. to season

SPAIN - Central

9080 Campamento Municipal El Brillante, Cordoba

Very busy site with shaded pitches.

Cordoba is one of the hottest places in Europe – the 'frying pan' of Spain – and the pool here is more than welcome, being large and bordered by pleasant terraced gardens. If you really want to stay in the city, then this site is a good choice. It has 120 neat pitches which are attractively spaced alongside the canal which runs through the centre of the site. Most pitches are now covered by artificial and natural shade but, to get the best ones, it is essential to arrive early in any season as the site becomes very crowded. The entrance is narrow and can be congested so care must be exercised. There is a colourful aviary close to the entrance. The blocks have been renovated and an impressive new block added with facilities for babies and disabled people. The bar/restaurant has also been renovated, air conditioned and has plenty of shade. Cordoba is a fascinating town and the Mosque/Cathedral is one of the great buildings of Europe and not to be missed.

How to find it: Entering Cordoba by NIV/E25 road from Madrid, drive into city centre. After passing the Mosque/Cathedral, turn right onto the main avenue, continue and take right fork where the road splits, and follow signs for campsite and/or district of El Brillante. Keep a sharp eye out for camp signs as they are partially hidden behind foliage.

General Details: Open 1 May - 30 Sept. Bar, restaurant, shop, swimming pool, all high season only. Large supermarket 300 m. Children's play area. Aviary. Bus service to city centre from outside site. Gas supplies. Chemical disposal. Motorcaravan services.

Charges 2000: Per adult ptas. 560; child 400; car 560; tent 400 - 560, acc. to size; caravan 560; motorcaravan 875; m/cycle 300; electricity 365. No credit cards.

Reservations: are not made. It is essential to arrive early in high season. Address: Avda. del Brillante 50 (Centro), 14012 Cordoba. Tel: 957/403836. FAX: 957/282165.

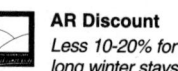
AR Discount
Less 10-20% for long winter stays

9085 Camping Carlos III, La Carlota, nr Cordoba

Good alternative site for Cordoba, 25 km. from the city.

This is a very large, busy site especially at weekends, but it has many supporting facilities including a good swimming pool for adults and separate children's pool. With the bar and catering services open all year, the site has an more open feel than the bustling municipal site in Cordoba. Unusually the site has its own hairdressing salon. The touring areas offer considerable shade for the 300 separated pitches which are canopied by trees on level, sandy ground. Around two thirds have 5A electrical connections. Sanitary facilities, in two modern blocks, have mixed British (40%) and Turkish WCs and hot showers in the block near reception. Permanent units, mobile homes and bungalows (to rent) are in a separate area, where there are sporting facilities. There may be some slight road noise.

How to find it: From N-IV Cordoba-Seville motorway take La Carlota exit at km. 429 point; site is well signed.

General Details: Open all year. Bar/restaurant, shop (all year). Swimming pools (high season). Aviary. Table tennis. Boules. Minigolf, Children's play area. Volleyball. Football. Riding 500 m. Chemical disposal. Motorcaravan services. Bus service outside site. Village 2 km.

Charges 1999: Per person ptas. 500; child (under 12 yrs) 400; car 475; m/cycle 400; tent 500; caravan 525; motorcaravan 750; electricity (5A) 375. Plus 7% VAT. Discounts (10-20%) for longer stays and outside high season. Credit cards accepted.

Reservations: Probably necessary in July/Aug. Address: Ctra. Madrid-Cadiz km. 430.5, 14100 La Carlota (Cordoba). Tel: 957/300697 or 957/300338. FAX: as phone.

9081 Camping Villsom, Dos Hermanas, nr Seville

Clean, fairly shady site with attractive pool and bar area.

This is a fine city site with an excellent new sanitary block supplementing the recently modernised existing facilities and consisting of a peaceful and attractive restaurant, bar and reception area. This, together with a new minigolf and table tennis area, has resulted in the number of pitches being reduced slightly to around 180. We are told that the oranges from the trees, which almost enclose a very pretty out-door bar area, are sold to Britain for marmalade. The site has a small shop and a most inviting small pool. Temperatures can be hotter here than almost anywhere in Spain and the pool seems essential, as are the orange trees. There is satellite TV in the bar/café. Restaurant 80 m, supermarket 400 m. Bus service from outside site to city. It is essential to book if intending to visit this site in peak weeks.

How to find it: There are many signs for Dos Hermanas - you need to be about 10 km. from Seville on NIV to Cadiz. Look for `Continente' store and sign on left and very soon afterwards turn right onto second road marked Salida dos Hermanas - Isla Menor once you have passed under a road bridge; site is immediately on right.

General Details: Open all year. Bar/café with satellite TV (open for breakfast and evening meals July/Aug). Swimming pool (June-Sept). Minigolf. Table tennis. Small shop (at reception). Laundry facilities. Children's playground. Restaurant and supermarket close.

Charges 1999: Per adult ptas. 510; child 445; tent 525; caravan 555; car 525; motorcaravan 655; m/cycle 440; electricity 330. All plus 7% VAT.

Reservations: Write to site. Address: Ctra. Sevilla-Cadiz, km. 554.8, 41700 Sevilla. Tel/Fax: 954/720828.

9083 Camping Monesterio, Monesterio

Attractive, recently constructed and conveniently located new site.
This modern site, located on the Ruta de la Plata in the Sierra de Tudia, is ideal for those travelling to or from Seville or the eastern Algarve. It has an easy access from the road and bags of space to manoeuvre for large units. The traditionally styled, modern sanitary installations include WCs, washbasins and showers with facilities for the disabled and children, plus dishwashing and laundry sinks. Hot water is free throughout. The pitches, which are spacious, all have electrical connections (16A). Also on site is a good swimming pool, launderette, supermarket and horse riding facilities. This well laid out site has shade in parts and is well fenced and lit.

How to find it: From Merida to Seville CN 630 turn right after the km. 760 marker approx 5 km. south of Monesterio. Site is well signed directly off the road

General Details: Open Easter - 15 Sept. Supermarket. Launderette. Swimming pool. Horse riding.

Charges guide: Per pitch ptas. 1,500; adult 450; child 400; tent 425 - 500; caravan 450 - 500; motorcaravan 800 - 1,500; m/cycle 350; electricity 400. All plus 7% VAT.

Reservations: Contact site. Address: CN 630, km. 726, Monesterio, Badajoz. Tel: 924/516352. FAX: 924/516316.

9087 Camping Mérida, Mérida

Attractive well maintained site, close to architecturally interesting town.
Camping Mérida is ideally located to serve both as a base to tour the local area and as an overnight stop en route when travelling either north/south or east/west. The site lies behind the restaurant, café and pool complex, beside the main road to Madrid but there is considerable noise from the busy road directly alongside the site. There are 130 good sized pitches, most with some shade and on sloping ground, with ample electricity connections (long leads may be needed). The central sanitary facility provides showers (some hot, some cold) with hooks and seat outside in a changing area, British WCs, and washbasins. Free hot water throughout. Dishwashing (H&C) and laundry sinks (cold only) are at the end of the block under cover. There is a clean medium sized swimming pool and a children's pool (with lifeguard), and a small shop for essentials. No English is spoken, but try out your Spanish. Reception is open until midnight, torches are necessary on this site. Mérida is an interesting town with a Roman amphitheatre and other ruins, a classical Theatre Festival, and a National Museum of Roman Art.

How to find it: Site is alongside road NV (Madrid-Lisbon), 5 km. east of Mérida, at km. 336.6 point.

General Details: Open all year. Shop. Restaurant/cafeteria. Bar. Swimming pool. Children's playground. Safe deposit. Money exchange. Medical post. Chemical disposal. Bungalows and group accommodation to rent. Caravan storage.

Charges 1999: Per adult ptas. 475; child 425; tent or caravan 475; car 475; motorcaravan 675; electricity 375. All plus VAT. Credit cards accepted.

Reservations: Write to site. Address Ctra. N-V Madrid-Portugal km 336, Mérida (Extremadura). Tel: 824/303453. FAX: 824/300398.

9088 Camping de Fuencaliente, Fuencaliente, nr Cuidad Real

Quiet site between Sierra Modrona and Sierra Morena with large pool.
This site nestles in an attractive valley between the Sierra Modrona and the Sierra Morena. It is ideal as a stopover if crossing Spain coast to coast, if you wish to visit the fascinating historic town of Toledo or finally if you desire a quiet 'away from it all' break. There are very few other desirable sites in this region of Castilla - la Mancha, this one is open all year round and is very peaceful with good views through pined slopes. There is a large pool with a separate children's area, which is most welcome in summer as this part of Spain gets very hot. The site is spacious with some shade from young trees but most shade is provided by artificial means. There are dedicated barbecue facilities and areas allocated for tents. The site has a good restaurant overlooking the pools. The large sanitary block is modern with excellent facilities and unusually there is no charge for electricity or use of the pool. The 91 pitches are generous at over 100 sq.m. and all have electrical connections and water. They are well maintained, as is the children's play area. Prices are very reasonable and the food was excellent when we visited. The local village of Fuencaliente is 5 km. south and provides the usual village facilities including some good Spanish restaurants and bars.

How to find it: Site is on N420 road at 105 km. marker approx. 5 km. north of Fuencaliente.

General Details: Open all year. Electrical connections (6A). Swimming pool (1/6-15/9, free). Restaurant/bar (all year). Supermarket. Children's playground. Shaded barbecue areas and dedicated seating. Laundry sinks. Chemical disposal.

Charges 1999: Per person 550 ptas; child 500; tent 475 - 550; caravan 550; car 300; m/cycle 250; motorcaravan 900; pitch incl. electricity 400. Plus 7% VAT.

Reservations: Recommended for July/Aug. Address: Km 105, N420, Cordoba - Tarragona C/Quintanilla, 23. 1° B Fuencaliente (C. Real). Tel: 926/698170 or 470381.

SPAIN - Central

9089 Camping Despeñaperros, Santa Elena (Jaén), nr Linares

New site in a strategic position with excellent facilities.

Despeñaperros is a very smart site in the heartland of La Mancha; run by a co-operative of five very friendly people who employ helpful staff. This site is an ideal break point for those travelling from Madrid towards the Costa del Sol, or those wishing to explore the local attractions including the narrow mountain Gorge of Despeñaperros (literally 'the throwing over of the dogs'); also Valdepeñas, acknowledged as the centre of the most prolific wine area of Spain. The site is located in a 30 year old pine grove which is part of the Despeñaperros nature reserve. All 116 pitches are of a good size, have natural shade from the mature pine trees and unusually have their own electricity (10A), water, TV connections and waste water drainage. The two central sanitary blocks are of a high standard and the charming restaurant and bar are excellent, sharing wonderful views of the mountains with the pools. There is year round night security.

> **How to find it:** On the N1V- E5 'Autovia de Andalucia' between Bailen and Madrid at km. 257, at the village of Santa Elena, the site is well signed.
>
> **General Details:** Open all year. Restaurant/bar. Shop. Swimming pools (15/6-15/9). Tennis. Washing machines. First aid room. Gas supplies. Chemical disposal. Motorcaravan services. Caravan storage.
>
> **Charges 2000:** Per adult 422 ptas; child 335; tent 448; car 422; caravan 448; motorcaravan 670 - 948; m/cycle 252; electricity 450. All plus 7% VAT. Credit cards accepted.
>
> **Reservations:** Contact site. Address: 23213 Santa Elena (Jaén). Tel: 953/664192.

9091 Camping Soto del Castillo, Aranjuez, nr Madrid

Useful stop-over municipal site with good facilities, south of Madrid.

Situated near the centre of the royal town of Aranjuez, worthy of a visit with its beautiful palaces, leafy avenues and gardens, and 47 km. south of Madrid, this is a useful en-route site. A little tourist train runs from the site daily. The site is close to the River Tajo in a park-like situation amid mature trees. The 225 touring pitches, all with electricity, are set on flat grass, unmarked amid tall trees. Siting is informal but places are of moderate size. The site has good facilities including a pool, small supermarket and restaurant (also open to the public) with takeaway, TV room, children's play area and volleyball. The largest sanitary block is heated in winter and well equipped with roomy hot showers, some washbasins in cabins and British WCs. Two smaller blocks are of more open design. Washing up facilities have only cold water.

> **How to find it:** Site is just north of the town centre (from where it is signed) Aranjuez is bypassed by the old NIV, so ensure you follow the signs for the town, some 47 km. south of Madrid. Watch for sign to site - a sharp left turn off the main road with little notice, at the end of a small archway of trees.
>
> **General Details:** Open all year. Bar. Restaurant. Takeaway. Small shop. Swimming pool (15/6-15/9). Children's play area. Volleyball. TV room. Bicycle hire. Laundry facilities. Gas supplies. Chemical disposal. Walking distance of palace, gardens and museums, etc. Apartments for rent.
>
> **Charges 2000:** Per person ptas. 475 - 625; child (3-10 yrs) 400 - 500; car 400 - 525; caravan 550 - 700; motorcaravan 600 - 775; tent 425 - 675, acc. to season and size; electricity 525. Discounts for groups or long stays. Credit cards accepted.
>
> **Reservations:** Write to site. Address: Soto del Rebollo s/n, 28300 Aranjuez (Madrid). Tel: 911/8911395. FAX: 911/8914197.

9090 Camping El Greco, Toledo

Quiet, spacious site with attractive pool.

Toledo was the home of the painter and the site that bears his name boasts a beautiful view of the city from the restaurant, bar and pool. The friendly, family owners make you welcome and are proud of their site. Ivy clad pergolas run down each side of the swimming pool (charged) with tables in the shade - it can be very hot here. There is an hourly air conditioned bus service to the city centre from the gates, which tours the outside of the walls first. There is always plenty of space and reservation is said to be unnecessary. There are 150 pitches of 80 sq.m. with electrical connections and shade from strategically planted trees. Access to some pitches may be tricky for caravans (narrow and at an angle). A new sanitary block was built in '98 including modern facilities for disabled campers and all the facilities are modern and kept clean. The site stretches along the river Tagus but fishing in it is a better bet than swimming. This site is worth a few days for the amazing sights of the old city of Toledo and the pool is a good feature, but it is only an hour's drive from Madrid and thus makes a good base for a longer stay.

> **How to find it:** Site is on the C502 road on the edge of the town, signed towards Puebla de Montelban; site signs also in city centre. From Madrid on the N401, turn off right towards Toledo city centre but turn right again at the gates to the old city. Site is signed from the next right turn. Don't be misled by the `Camping' signs on the road into Toledo from Madrid - these lead to an inferior site.
>
> **General Details:** Open all year. Swimming pool (1/6-5/9, charged). Restaurant/bar (all year) with good menu and fair prices. Shop in reception (all year). Volleyball. Children's playgrounds. Laundry facilities.
>
> **Charges 1999:** Per person ptas. 595; child (3-10 yrs) 495; car 550; m/cycle 480; caravan or trailer tent 635; tent 620; motorcaravan 1,170; electricity (6A) 475. Plus 7% VAT.
>
> **Reservations:** not necessary and not made. Address: Ctra. Comarcal 502, 45004 Toledo. Tel/fax: 925/220090.

Taking your own Tent, Caravan or Motorhome abroad?

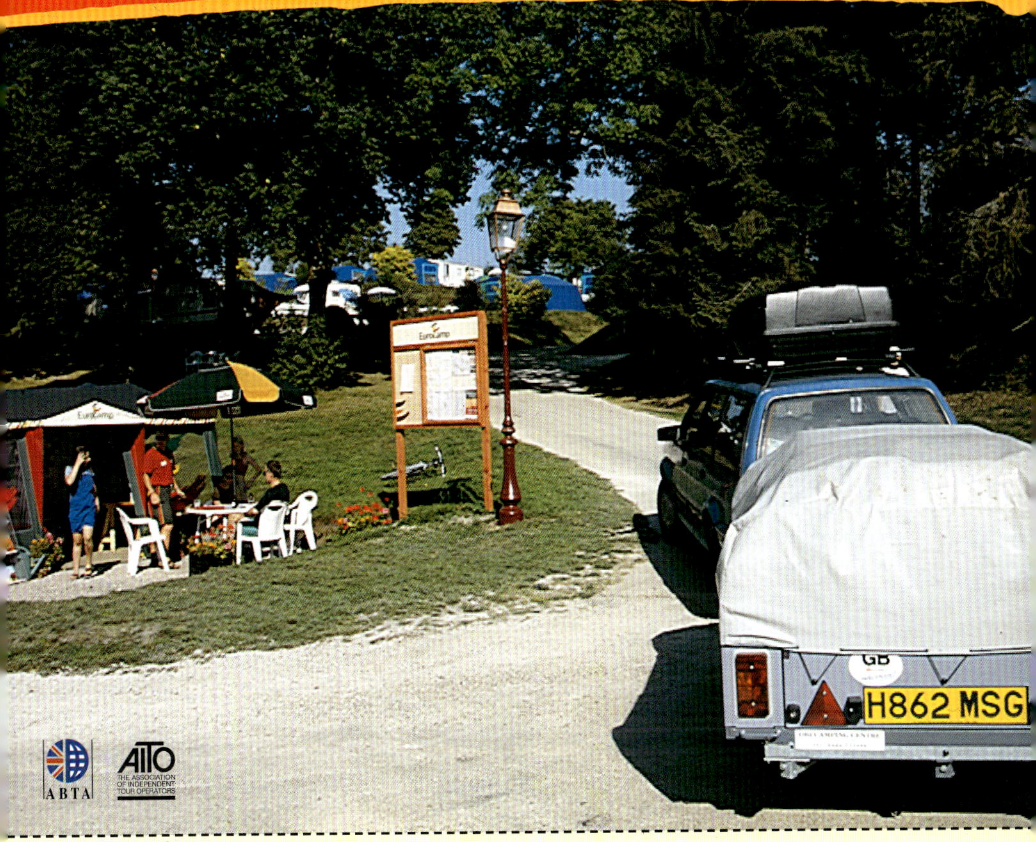

Eurocamp Independent
FREEPOST ALM 1584
Hartford Manor
NORTHWICH
Cheshire
CW8 1BF

No Stamp Required

Independent

THE EASY WAY TO TAKE YOUR OWN TENT, TRAILER TENT, CARAVAN OR MOTORHOME TO EUROPE.

One phone call will book your whole holiday

Choose from over 100 of Europe's best sites

Use of Eurocamp Couriers and Children's Couriers

Free comprehensive Travel Pack

Competitive prices

Friendly and efficient service

Never travelled abroad? Phone now for a

FIRST TIME ABROAD VIDEO

Cost £5.00
Refunded when you book

To receive your copy of the 2000 brochure, complete the attached card or call

01606 787951

Mr/Mrs/Miss _____ Initials _____

Surname _____

Address _____

_____

_____

_____ Postcode _____

How many adults are in your party? _____

If applicable what are the ages of your children? _____

Do you have a:

tent ☐   trailer tent ☐
caravan ☐   motorhome ☐

How many times have you taken your own equipment abroad? _____

Tick if you do not wish to receive direct mail from other carefully screened companies whose products or services we feel may be of interest ☐

EIARE

9028 Camping Las Villuercas, Guadalupe, Caceres

Rural touring site, with pool and excellent restaurant.

This site nestles in an attractive valley northwest of Guadalupe. The pools and restaurant are of a very high standard and the restaurant leads to a pretty patio with overhead vines and potted plants allowing elevated views of the pools. The 70 pitches are level and of a reasonable size; some are marked, although large units may experience difficulty in getting into the more central pitches. There is limited shade from young trees and a more shaded area in a spinney. A river runs alongside the site and we are told that the ground can be muddy in very wet periods. The single toilet block is in the older style but very clean, providing British type WCs, washbasins and free hot showers (although the hot water could be overwhelmed in busy periods). There are no facilities for disabled campers as yet. An ideal location for visiting the Monastery and the town of Guadalupe, an attractive historic tourist town with plenty of bars and restaurants.

How to find it: From NV/E90 Madrid - Mérida exit at Navelmoral de la Mata. Follow south to Guadalupe on CC713 (approx. 83 km). Site is 2 km. from Guadalupe, near the Monastery.

General Details: Open all year. Restaurant. Bar. Shop. Swimming pools. Tennis. Children's playground. Barbecue area. Telephone. Safe deposit. Medical post. Car wash. Hostel accommodation.

Charges 1999: Per adult ptas. 400; child 350; tent (small) 350, (large) 400; car 375; caravan 400; m/cycle 350; motorcaravan 600; electricity 350. Credit cards not accepted.

Reservations: Write to site. Address: C/Carretera Villanueva, Guadalupe (Caceres). Tel: 927/367139 or 367561.

9027 Camping Parque Natural de Monfragüe, Caceres

Excellent site with superb pool and views.

This is a well managed and excellent site with views to the Sierra de Mirabel and surrounding country-side. The site is within the Monfragüe National Park and a trip to see the buzzards, vultures and eagles is highly recommended. You will also be some 6 km. from Plasencia and close to Merida with the Roman ruins and Guadalupe's monastery and medieval village. Tours are organised by the friendly site manage-ment. There is a very good swimming pool and children's pool. The 128 marked pitches are on slightly sloping ground which was being terraced, and there is shade in parts. Everything is well maintained and water points are plentiful. The large modern toilet blocks are in superb condition and very clean, providing British style WCs, washbasins and free hot showers, and there are facilities for disabled campers. The site provides animation for children in high season and a good play area. A supermarket will provide all needs in season with a small shop in reception out of season. A large bustling, air-conditioned restaurant offers a wide and varied menu and you can eat on the veranda whilst enjoying the wonderful views. Alternatively eat more casually in the bar, or just take a drink on the patio or in the air-conditioned coffee bar. A room is also provided with TV and recreation facilities, also an attractive open fire for the cooler times.

How to find it: Plasencia is some 144 km. south of Salamanca. Take C-524 Plasencia - Trujillo road; site is on left approx. 6 km. south of Plasencia.

General Details: Open all year. Restaurant, bar and coffee shop. Supermarket/shop (April-Sept). Swimming pools (late May-Sept). Children's play area. Tennis. Basketball. Animation in season. Laundry. Telephone and post box. Safe deposit. Medical post. Car wash. English spoken. Bungalows to rent.

Charges 1999: Per adult ptas. 475; child 400; tent (small) 450, (large) 450; car 500; caravan 475; m/cycle 300; motorcaravan 700; electricity 400. Credit cards accepted.

Reservations: Write to site. Address: Apdo Correos, 36 10680 Malpartida de Plasencia, (Caceres). Tel: 927/459233 or 220. FAX: 927/459233.

9026 Camping El Burro Blanco, Miranda del Castañar, nr Salamanca

Peaceful village site in the mountains of the Sierra de Francia.

This campsite has been recommended by readers and because they were so impressed, we are taking the unusual step of entering it before it has been fully assessed by ourselves. The campsite has been devel-oped from scratch by Mr and Mrs Zegveld, a pleasant and helpful Dutch couple. It is 70 km. south of Salamanca in a delightful area next to the medieval town of Miranda del Castañar. Covering 3.5 hectares of woodland (mainly oak) there is shade for all 70 pitches of 60-70 sq.m. (no statics), of which 6 are for tents, the rest having electricity (2, 6 or 10A). Free hot water is supplied to the showers, two washbasins and a tap for dishwashing and laundry sinks. The village is 1 km. where there are several small restau-rants, bars and other shops. The attractions here are not only the situation in an area hardly touched by modern life, but also the history. It was once a centre of government and a seat of the Inquisition, and it also has its own micro-climate, July often being very hot with changeable weather at other times.

How to find it: Take C512 Salamanca - Coria road southwest for approx. 70 km. or C515 Bejar - Ciudad Rodrigo road turning south on C512. The road to Miranda del Castañar is 7 km northeast of the village of Cepeda.

General Details: Open 1 April - 1 December. Bar on site. Restaurants, bars and shops in village. Swimming pool nearby, river swimming 1.5 km. Laundrette. Chemical disposal.

Charges 2000: Per person 500 ptas; child (0-5 yrs) 450; pitch 1,400; electricity 200, 500 or 800.

Reservations: Contact site. Address: Camino de las Norias s/n, Miranda del Castañar, 37660 Prov. de Salamanca. Tel/FAX: 923/161 100. E-mail: elbb@cempresarial.com.

SPAIN - Central

9025 Camping Regio, Salamanca

Convenient, touring site, next to hotel complex with an excellent pool.

Salamanca is one of Europe's oldest university cities, and the beautiful old sandstone town has to be visited. Find the famous frog which is hidden in the fabulous University facade and discover what unusual Spanish fortune will be granted you! Or just enjoy the wonderfully accessible Salamantine architecture and the myriad of bars around the Plaza Mayor (we recommend another famous Salamantine attraction in the form of a coin juggling waiter in La Covachuela off the Plaza). This is also a useful staging post en route to the south of Spain or central Portugal. The site is some 4 km. outside the town on the road to Madrid. It is behind the Hôtel Regio and campers can take advantage of the hotel facilities which include a quality restaurant, a somewhat cheaper cafeteria and an excellent swimming pool and children's pool which were rebuilt in '97 (small charge). There is a pool bar and a shaded patio. The site itself has a small bar and restaurant and other facilities including tennis, basketball courts, and a children's playground. The 270 pitches are on slightly sloping ground, with some shade in parts. The pitches are clearly marked out with plentiful electricity points (15A) in little red-roofed towers and there are many water points with unusual taps. The large sanitary block has British style WCs, washbasins, free hot showers and washing machines in a dedicated room - all very clean. When we visited the sanitary block was undergoing a major refurbishment including the construction of marvellous facilities for disabled campers. An impressive new children's play area was also being built along with a motorcaravan service point.

How to find it: Take N501 route from Salamanca (Avila/Madrid) but follow signs from this to St Marta de Tormes (which is now bypassed). Hôtel Regio is on the old road on the right after about 4 km.

General Details: Open all year. Restaurant, cafe and swimming pool at adjoining hotel. Bar. Supermarket (June - 15 Sept). Children's play area. Tennis. Basketball. Laundry. Telephone and post box. Safe deposit. Money exchange. Medical post. Car wash. Motorcaravan service point. English spoken.

Charges 1999: Per adult ptas. 325 - 450; child 275 - 400; tent (small) 400, (large) 450; car 325 - 450; caravan 325 - 450; m/cycle 275 - 400; motorcaravan 600 - 750; electricity 325 - 450. Credit cards accepted.

Reservations: Write to site. Address: Ctra. de Madrid, km 4, 37900 Santa Marta de Tormes. Tel: 923/130888. FAX: 923/130044.

9210 Camping Pico de la Miel, La Cabrera, nr Madrid

Useful site north of Madrid, close to N1/E.

Pico de la Miel is well signed and easy to find, 2-3 km. southwest off the main road, with an amazing mountain backdrop. Whilst mainly a long-stay site for Madrid, with a variety and number of very well established, fairly old mobile homes, there is a separate area with its own toilet block for touring units. Over 60 pitches on rather poor, sandy grass, some with artificial shade, are clearly marked; others, not so level, under the odd pine tree are not marked, plus more for tents (the ground could be hard for pegs). Electricity connections are available. The tiled toilet block is good, light and airy with some washbasins in cabins and free hot water to laundry and washing up sinks. An en-suite unit with ramp is provided for people with disabilities. The excellent pool complex is supervised and the bar/restaurant and shop have a terrace overlooking a good, modern children's playground.

How to find it: Site is well signed from the N1. Going south use exit 57 or 58, going north exit 59 or 60, and follow site signs.

General Details: Open all year. Electricity connections. Shop. Restaurant. Bar. Swimming pool. Tennis. Chalets to hire. Note: amenities may not be available all year.

Charges 1999: Per person ptas. 631; child 537; car 631; tent or caravan 631; motorcaravan 1,028; electricity 375. All plus 7% VAT. Less 10-25% for longer stays.

Reservations: Contact site. Address: Ctra. N1, km. 58, 28751 La Cabrera (Madrid). Tel: 911/688082 or 698541. FAX: 911/688082.

9200 Camping Caravaning El Escorial, El Escorial, nr Madrid

Site with swimming pools and other amenities 50 km. northwest of Madrid.

There is a shortage of good sites in the central regions of Spain, but this is one, well situated for sight-seeing visits with the El Escorial monastery, the enormous civil war monument of the Valle de los Caidos is very close and Madrid and Segovia both 50 km. There are 1,358 individual pitches (some marked), of which 750 are occupied by permanent caravans. There are another 250 'wild' spaces for tourists on open fields, with improving shade (long cables may be necessary for electricity) and there should usually be space. There are three large new or refurbished toilet blocks, plus two smart, new small toilet blocks for the 'wild' camping area. British style WCs, some without seats; washbasins with free hot water, shelf and mirror (some in private cabins), hot showers with push-button but controllable temperature, baby baths and facilities for disabled campers. The blocks can be heated in cool weather. The general amenities on site are good and include three swimming pools (unheated), plus a children's pool in a central area with a bar/restaurant with terrace and plenty of grassy sitting out areas. There is a very large range of smart sports activities available and the site has a very large supermarket selling fresh meat, vegetables and fresh baked bread daily.

How to find it: From the south go through the town of El Escorial, follow the M 600 - Guadarrama road - the site is near the 8 km. marker, 3.5 km north of town on the right. If approaching from the north use the A6 autopista take exit 47 and the M600 towards El Escorial town. Site is on the left.

General Details: Open all year. Large supermarket (1/3-31/10) and souvenir shop. Restaurant/bar and snack bar (1/3-31/10). Disco-bar. Swimming pools. Three tennis courts. Two football pitches. Basketball. 'Fronton'. Two well equipped children's playgrounds on sand. Riding, golf 7 km. Chemical disposal. Caravan storage.

Charges 1999: Per person 650 ptas; child (3-9 yrs) 625; caravan or tent 650; car 650; motorcaravan 1,150; electricity 400. VAT included. Credit cards accepted.

Reservations: to guarantee admission made if you write but considered unnecessary. Address: Apdo. Correos 8, 28280 El Escoril (Madrid). Tel: 918/902412.

In the very heart of Spain

Really worth while to make a stop over on your way to the south.

CAMPING - CARAVANING

El Escorial

BUNGALOW PARK

E-28280 EL ESCORIAL (MADRID)
Gratis A-6, exit 47.
Road Guadarrama-El Escorial M-600, km 3,500
Apartado de correos nº 8
e-mail: planeta.azul@mad.servicom.es
www.campingescorial.com
Tel. (34) 918 90 24 12
Fax (34) 918 96 10 62
Open all year

Situated in the most beautiful part of Castille, 3 km from the impressive National Monument Valle de los Caidos (Valley of the Fallen) and 8 km from the monastry San Lorenzo del Escorial, pantheon of the Spanish kings. Ideal situation to visit Madrid, Segovia, Avila, Toledo, Aranjuez... 25 km from Puerto de Navacerrada and the ski-runs of Cotos and Valdesqui. Heated san. install., restaurant, supermarket, many sports facilities, large pitches, comfortable bungalows, in summer 3 swimming pools and other install.

The sites in SPAIN featured in this guide are shown on the map on page 375

SPAIN - Central

9095 Camping Ciudad de Albarracin, Albarracin, nr Teruel

Satisfactory site for visiting interesting, historic town in southern Aragon.

Albarracin is a much frequented, fascinating town with a Moorish castle and other antiquities to see, set in the 'Reserva Nacional de los Montes Universales', with some wonderful scenery around. The site is set on a hillside at the back of the town, with views of it and a walk of perhaps 1 km. to the centre. It is modern and long, set on fairly flat ground, sloping for the last third. There are 70 pitches (to be increased to 130), all with electrical connections, separated by trees and ranging in size up to 70 sq.m. The modern sanitary building is kept very clean and provides British style WCs for ladies and mixed British and Turkish for men. The vanity style washbasins have free hot water, as do the showers, which are quite large but have no divider. There is a baby bath in the ladies' and provision in between for dishwashing and laundry with one machine. No shop but essentials available from the bar. The bar/restaurant, with terrace and TV, is said to be open all season, but there are shops, bars and restaurants in the town as well. A municipal swimming pool, just 100 m. away, is open in high season and there is a small children's play area. No English spoken yet, until the owner's children gain in confidence!

How to find it: From Teruel north on N330 for about 8 km. then west on A1512 for 37 km. Well signed in town.

General Details: Open 1 April - 31 Oct, as is bar/restaurant. Essentials from bar. Town shops 500 m. Special room for barbecues with fire and wood provided.

Charges 1999: Per person ptas. 375; child (under 14) 275; car 375; caravan 400; tent 375; motorhome 675; electricity 300. Credit cards accepted.

Reservations: No English spoken; policy not known but probably not necessary. Address: Ciudad de Albarracin, Amparo Hernandez Lozano, 44100 Albarracin (Teruel). Tel: 978/710197 or 710107.

9250 Camping Costajan, Aranda de Duero

Good night stop en route to or from ferries, 75 km. south of Burgos.

This site has 225 pitches (with electricity) with around 100 available for all types of tourer. Large units may find access to the variably sized pitches a bit tricky among mixed olive and pine trees and on the slightly undulating sandy ground. Ignore the few unsightly static caravans, as this is a shady, clean and friendly spot for an overnight stop. A swimming pool complex is also open to the public (under the same management). The good, modern sanitary facilities have hot and cold water, dishwashing and laundry sinks and just one water point. New bungalows to rent - details from site. Reception opens 8 am. - 2 pm. and 6 pm. - 10 pm.

How to find it: Turn off the N1 at junction 144 signed Aranda de Duero north. Follow camping signs to site (under 1 km).

General Details: Open all year. Shop (all year). Cafe/snacks, swimming pool and bar (all 15/5-15/9). Tennis. Football. Minigolf. Fishing 3 km. Riding 2 km. Exchange facilities. Washing machine. Chemical disposal. Bungalows for rent.

Charges 1999: Per person ptas. 535; child 510; caravan 535; tent 535; car 535; motorcaravan 790; m/cycle 425; electricity 450. Credit cards accepted.

Reservations: Said to be unnecessary. Address: Ctra. no.1, km. 162, 09400 Aranda de Duero (Burgos). Tel: 947/502070. FAX: 947/511354.

9023 Camping Camino de Santiago, Castrojeriz, nr Burgos

Small countryside site with outstanding views, slightly remote with a superb location.

This site lies to the West of Burgos on the outskirts of Castrojeriz, an unspoilt original small Spanish town. In a superb location, almost in the shadow of the ruined castle high on the adjacent hillside, it will appeal to those who like perfect solitude and a true touring camp site without all the modern trimmings, at a reasonable cost. The 50 marked pitches are level, grassy, divided by hedges and shaded by trees, with electricity available to all. Sanitary facilities are adequate, with showers (two free hot showers each sex, heated by solar panels), British and Turkish style WCs, and washbasins with cold water only. All of these are in the older style, but were well maintained and clean when we visited. A further small sanitary block is next to the barbecue area. A small shop with basic necessities shares space with the bar/coffee shop and reception and there are two shady terraces outside. A games room with table football, a pool table and table tennis, and two tennis courts complete the facilities.

How to find it: From N120 (Osorno-Burgos) road, turn onto BV404 for Villasandino and Castrojeriz. Turn left at crossroads on southwest side of town and then left at campsite sign.

General Details: Open 1 May - 30 Sept. Shop (1/6-30/8). Bar, café/coffee shop with terrace (1/6-30/8). Games room. Tennis courts. Barbecue area. Mountain bike hire. Washing machines. Fishing 2 km. Riding 15 km. Safe deposit. Medical post. Chemical disposal. Caravans and tents for hire.

Charges 1999: Per person ptas. 425; child 375; tent 425; caravan 400; car 375; m/cycle 250; motorcaravan 625; electricity 425. All plus 7% VAT. Credit cards accepted.

Reservations: Write or fax site for details. Address: C/.Virgen del Manzano, s/m , 09110 Castrojeriz (Burgos). Tel: 947/377255. FAX: 983/359549.

9021 Camping Municipal Fuentes Blancas, Burgos

Comfortable, municipal site, within easy reach of Santander ferries.

Burgos is an attractive city, ideally placed for overnight stop en route to the south of Spain. The old part of the city around the cathedral is quite beautiful and there are pleasant walks along the river banks. Fuentes Blancas is a municipal site with clean, modern, sanitary facilities in five blocks, although some may not be open outside July/Aug. These include British WCs, vanity style washbasins, free hot showers and facilities for babies. There are around 350 marked pitches of 70 sq.m. on flat ground, 112 with electrical connections and there is good shade in parts. A small shop caters for most needs and the terraced snack bar is friendly without being noisy. A swimming pool is open in main season only. The site has a fair amount of transit trade and reservations are not possible for August, so arrive early. Bus service to city or a fairly shaded walk.

How to find it: From the north (Santander) follow signs for E5/N1 (E80/N620) Valladolid/Madrid on the main through road (dual-carriageway). Immediately after crossing river turn left at small camp sign and follow river east in direction of Cartuja de Miraflores. Site is approx. 3 km. on left.

General Details: Open 1 March - 30 Sept. Electricity connections (6A). Small shop (1/4-30/9). Bar/snack bar (all season). Swimming pool (15/5-15/9). Children's playground. Table tennis. Basketball. Football. Fishing 150 m. Bicycle hire 2 km. Safe deposit. Medical post. Money exchange. Washing machine. Chemical disposal. Motorcaravan service point. Information service. English spoken.

Charges 1999: Per pitch incl. caravan and electricity ptas 1,636 (package); adult 528; child (2-10 yrs) 374. Plus 7% VAT. Credit cards accepted.

Reservations: Not made. Address: Ctra. Cartuja Miraflores, 09193 Burgos. Tel: 947/486016. FAX: as phone.

Northern Spain

This area includes the Costa Verde, the Basque Coast, the Pyrenees and inland Spain north of a line between Valladolid and just north of Burgos (lat. 42°). The Costa Verde is largely unspoiled, with clean water, sandy beaches and rocky coves against a backdrop of mountains including the magnificent Picos de Europa. The beaches and countryside on the Basque Coast are rather more developed in terms of tourism and industry and tend to be very popular, particularly during July and August. Both these areas are easily accessible from the ports of Santander or Bilbao. The Pyrenees stretch from the Bay of Biscay in the west (with the highest peaks) to the Mediterranean in the east, and include two spectacular natural parks, the Ordesa in Aragon and Aigues Tortes in Catalonia. The mountain gorges and valleys remain largely unspoiled. Visitors will find much of 'Old Spain' in gastronomy and the way of life generally.

8942 Camping Los Manzanos, Santa Cruz, nr La Coruña

Large clean site with good pool well placed for visiting La Coruña.

This site is to the east of the historic port of La Coruña, not far from some ria (lagoon) beaches and with good communications to both central and north Galicia - it is only an hour and a half drive from Santiago de la Compostela, for example. The site has a steep sloping access and is divided by a stream into two main sections, linked by a wooden bridge. Some interesting sculptures create focal points and conversation pieces. The lower section is on a gentle slope. Pitches for larger units are marked and numbered, all with electricity (10A) and, in one section, there is a fairly large, unmarked field for tents. Two good toilet blocks have modern installations and free hot showers. The site impressed us as being very clean, even when full, which it tends to be in high season. The swimming pool was clean, with a lifeguard, free to campers, and stays open most of the day and evening. Small shop with fresh produce daily, and restaurant/bar serving good food and a range of wines at reasonable prices. Señor Sanjurjo speaks good English and visitors are assured of a friendly welcome. Some aircraft noise.

How to find it: From E50 motorway, do not go right into Coruña, but take the N-VI link road across the bridge, following signs towards Meiras and Lugo. Just over the bridge turn left towards Santa Cruz. Turn right at the centre of Santa Cruz and the site is signed from there.

General Details: Open Easter - 15 Sept. Swimming pool. Shop. Restaurant/bar. Children's playground. Barbecue area. Telephone and post box. Medical post.

Charges 1999: Per adult ptas 600; child 500; car 600; m/cycle 500; caravan 625; tent 600; motorcaravan 1,200; electricity 450. All plus 7% VAT.

Reservations: Write to site. Address: Ctra. Sta Cruz - Meiras, km. 0.7, La Coruña. Tel: 881/614825.

SPAIN - North

9024 Camping As Cancelas, Santiago de Compostela

Hillside site, with quality facilities, overlooking the pilgrims' city.

As Cancelas currently has 156 marked pitches (30-70 sq.m), arranged in terraces and divided by trees and shrubs, on a hillside overlooking the city. The site has a steep approach road which extends into most pitch accesses which can be difficult for large units. Electrical hook-ups (5A) are available, the site is lit at night and a security guard patrols. There is a regular bus service into the city from the bottom of the hill outside the site, and a small mini market (open late and handy for off season use) is just 5 minutes level walk away. The site has a well kept, unsupervised, swimming pool and children's pool which are free to campers. The two ultra modern, luxurious toilet blocks provide British WCs, washbasins in marble tops, hand dryers and sockets, spacious controllable showers with dividers, hooks and marble seats and a suite for disabled visitors with ramped access. The quality and cleanliness of the fittings and tiling is outstanding. In addition, there are dishwashing, laundry and chemical disposal facilities. Free hot water throughout. Lounge bar with TV (all year), restaurant and mini market (July/Aug) together with a small children's playground. No English is spoken. Santiago, with its legendary festivals and processions, is the destination for Christians, who find their way to the city across the centuries old pilgrims' routes.

How to find it: From the N550 La Coruna - Santiago road, at large roundabout (near petrol station, Repsol), take exit to Lugo (C547)/La Coruna (A9), and immediately turn left into Rua das Cancelas (site is signed), turn right at stadium, site is 800 m. on left.

General Details: Open all year. Mini market. Restaurant. Bar. Laundry. Swimming pools. Children's playground. Telephone and post box. Safe deposit. Medical post.

Charges 1999: Per adult ptas. 550 - 600; child (up to 12 yrs) 400 - 475; car 400 - 645; tent 550 - 645; caravan 550 - 665; m/cycle 400 - 500; motorcaravan 1,100 - 1,290; electricity 450 All plus VAT.

Reservations: Write to site. Address: Rue do 25 de Xulio 35, 15704 Santiago de Compostela. Tel: 981/580476 or 580266. FAX: 981/575553.

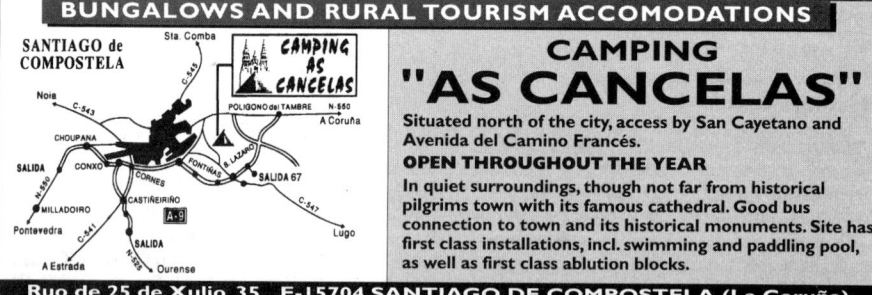

8941 Camping Valdovino, Valdovino, nr Ferrol

Friendly site with top class facilities close to supervised beach.

This site is on the edge of the village, about 300 m. from the beach. The sea here can be lively but at the back of the beach is a calm ria (lagoon) suitable for younger children. The camping area is divided into small enclosures with space for four to six large units each and takes about 150 units in all. They are well shaded by trees and surrounded by hedges of the most beautiful blue hydrangeas which flower all summer. All have access to electricity (16 or 25A), with some lighting at night. The one large toilet block is centrally positioned, and is very clean and luxurious, with baby baths, facilities for disabled people, spacious pre-set warm showers, British WCs, a good supply of washbasins, and is pleasantly decorated including many potted plants. In front of the site is a large and low priced supermarket, which also serves the villagers. An excellent restaurant and bar complex offers attractive food via waiter service, cafeteria or takeaway. Paella, tapas, sandwiches and fresh local fish feature prominently and there is a good value menu of the day. The prices in the restaurant and supermarket are very competitive and remain static throughout the season. There is also an ice-cream parlour. The owner, Señora Soto Lopez, speaks good English, and can provide information about visits in the area.

How to find it: From Pontedeume on N-VI, drive north, but at Fene branch towards Cedeira rather than Ferrol. The road meets the C646 at the coast in Valdovino itself, and site is almost opposite, down road to the beach.

General Details: Open 1 April - 30 Sept. Supermarket. Restaurant/bar. Café. Takeaway and ice-cream parlour. Children's playground. Basketball. Fronton courts. Fishing 300 m. Golf 8 km. Riding 15 km. Safe deposit. Laundry. Medical post. Gas supplies. Chemical disposal. Apartments for rent.

Charges 2000: Per adult ptas 600 - 625; child 475 - 485; tent 645 - 665; car 645 - 665; caravan 665 - 685; m/cycle 500 - 515; motorcaravan 1,290 - 1,330; electricity 450. Plus 7% VAT. Credit cards accepted.

Reservations: Write to site. Address: Apdo 104 (Ferrol), Valdoviño (La Coruña). Tel: 881/48.70.76 or 487246. FAX: 881/486131.

8945 Camping Lagos de Somiedo, Somiedo

Most unusual small site in the towering mountainous Asturias Natural Park; caravans not accepted.

Thirty-five kilometres of winding narrow roads with rock overhangs, hairpin bends and breathtaking views finally bring you to the lake and campsite at 1,600 m. A site for powerful small campervans, cars, backpackers and walkers of endurance, it is not recommended for medium or large motorhomes (caravans are not accepted). The Lana family make you welcome at their unique site, which is tailored for those who wish to explore the natural and cultural values of the Somiedo National Park without the support of `normal' campsite amenities. There are separate areas for tents and vehicles and no electricity, but in this extraordinary glacial valley you can leave reality behind in the exploration for the marvels of nature including bears, wolves and wild goats which frequent these mountains. The site has one charming wooden building which functions as reception, bar, restaurant, library and sanitary block. Stringent conservation regulations prohibit further building. There are hot showers, sinks and British style toilets within the thoughtfully decorated building, which contains many items of natural interest. A very small village within 500 m. has a small bar/restaurant set tight into the vertical rock face, offering traditional food. Here you will witness the cultural heritage of men and women living in harsh, though beautiful, surroundings. There is a cool wind here most of the time and a torch is essential at night.

How to find it: From N634 via Oviedo turn left on A515 at Cornellana for 9 km. At Longona left on AS227; at the 38 km marker, Pol de Somiedo, turn left for 3.38 km. and at Urma left again for 5.29 km. Site signed.

General Details: Open Easter - 15 Oct. Combined reception, small restaurant, bar and reference section. Telephone. Horses for hire, trekking. Lectures on flora, fauna, history and culture. Barbecue area. Group tent area. Small children's play area with novel local culture stances and games. Two small village houses for rent.

Charges 1999: Per adult ptas. 500; child 450; tent incl. 2 persons 500; tent with 3 or more persons 550; car 450; m/cycle 375; motorcaravan 950. All plus 7% VAT. Credit cards accepted.

Reservations: not necessary. Address: Valle de Lago, 33840 Somiedo (Asturias). Tel: 985/763776.

8940 Camping Los Cantiles, Luarca, nr Oviedo

Well maintained cliff-top site to west of Gijón and Oviedo.

Luarca is a picturesque little place with an inner harbour and two sandy beaches adjoining. Los Cantiles is 2 km. to the east of town on a cliff top jutting out into the sea, with good views. The site has no permanent units and is a pleasant place to stop along this coastline. The 230 pitches, 83 with electricity (3A) are mostly on level grass, divided by shrubs. You can take the car to the Laurca beaches and the small town is within walking distance downhill (remember you have to walk back up!) There is a friendly welcome from the Dutch owner who provides a room with cooking facilities for tenters. Two modern, clean sanitary blocks, one renovated and one newer and very smart, have mainly British toilets; individual basins with hot water and free hot showers. Units for disabled people and baby bathroom.

How to find it: Turn off main N634 road at Km 502.7 point east of Laurca; site is signed

General Details: Open all year. Small shop (all year). Bar with hot snacks (15/6-1/10). Lounge/reading room. Bicycle hire. Indoor pool and fitness centre 300 m. Fishing 70 m. Riding 6 km. Laundry. Freezer service. Safe deposit. Gas supplies. Chemical disposal. English spoken. Caravans and chalets for rent. Caravan storage.

Charges 2000: Per adult ptas. 450; child (4-10 yrs) 400; family tent 525; individual tent 450; caravan 550; motorcaravan 900; car 450; m/cycle 300; electricity 300. Plus 7% VAT. No credit cards.

Reservations: Advised for mid Jul - end Aug and made by post with deposit (ptas. 2,500). Address: Villar s/n, Ctra. N-634 km. 502.7, 33700 Luarca (Asturias). Tel: 985/640938. FAX: as phone. E-mail: cantiles@conectia.net.

AR Discount
Less 10%
after 3 days,
excl. 15/6-15/9

8950 Camping Costa Verde, Colunga

Busy but acceptable site by a good beach.

This site is some 1.5 km. from the town of Colunga and has adequate rather than luxurious facilities which are beginning to show signs of heavy usage. Further afield are the towns of Ribadesella, Gijón and Oviedo. The most attractive feature is a spacious, supervised beach with a low tide lagoon which is ideal for younger children. The 160 regularly laid out pitches will all be full in high season. Electricity is available throughout. A sports and play area, plus barbecues, is at the end of the site across a bridge which, although mainly fenced off, could allow children to fall into the river is so minded! The single toilet block has a mixture of British and Turkish style toilets (all British for ladies). Showers are large (without separators) but on payment. The shop is well stocked and the bar is friendly. The owner makes his own cider!

How to find it: From Santander take the N634 to Ribadesella, and continue for 21 km. along the N632 coast road towards Gijón. Take the right turn towards Lastres from the centre of Colunga.

General Details: Open Easter - early Oct. Shop. Electricity connections (6A). Bar/cafe. Sports field. Children's playground. Telephone and post box. Safe deposit. Laundry. Little English spoken.

Charges 1999: Per adult ptas 475; child (over 5 yrs) 425; tent 425 - 495; caravan 525; car 425; m/cycle 350; motorcaravan 800; electricity 325. VAT included. Credit cards accepted.

Reservations: essential for peak weeks and made for exact dates with deposit. Send for booking form. Address: 33320 Colunga (Asturias). Tel: 98/5856373.

SPAIN - North

8955 Camping Arenal de Moris, Caravia Alta, Prado

Peaceful, rural site, very close to sea and mountains.

This site is close to three fine sandy beaches and is surrounded by mountains in the natural reservation area known as the Sueve. A hunting reserve, this is important for a breed of short Asturian horses, the 'Asturcone'. The Picos de Europa are only 35 km, Covadonga and its lakes is near and Ribadesella is 12 km. It is an ideal area for sea and mountain sports, riding, walking, birdwatching and cycling. The 350 grass pitches are 40-70 sq.m, some terraced with little shade, others on an open, slightly sloping field with views of the sea. Three sanitary blocks have controllable showers (no dividers), vanity style washbasins, and external dishwashing (cold water). The restaurant serves local dishes and overlooks the pool across to hills and woods. A play area is in a lemon orchard. The beach is a short walk.

How to find it: Site is signed from the N632 Ribadesella - Gijón road at km. 14 point.

General Details: Open 1 June - 31 Aug. plus weekends in April, May and to last weekend in Sept. Electricity connections (5A). Supermarket. Restaurant. Swimming pool. Tennis. Children's play area. Laundry. Chemical disposal. Little English spoken.

Charges 1999: Per person ptas. 525; child 495; car 510; m/cycle 400; caravan 650; tent 525; motorcaravan 900; electricity 340.

Reservations: Contact site. Address: Ctra. 632, 33344 Caravia Alta (Asturias). Tel/fax: 985/853097 or 853050.

8965 Camping Picos de Europa, Avin-Onis, Cangas de Onis

New site in ideal situation to explore western end of the Picos de Europa.

It is said that, due to their proximity to the sea, the Picos (peaks) are called Europa as early navigators, on sighting them, knew they were again near the continent of Europe. Indeed, it is probably best to follow the coast to reach Cangas de Onis, the gate to the Picos, when first locating the site. Once settled you can explore these dramatic limestone mountains on foot, by bicycle, by horse, etc. Covadonga with its lakes and national park is only 13 km. On the other hand, the coast at Llanes is only 25 km. The site itself is newly developed with direct access off the AS114 in a valley situation beside a fast flowing river. Local stone has been used for the L-shaped building at the main entrance which houses reception, a restaurant and the main sanitary facilities. The bar has an unusual circular window and small terrace overlooking the river. The 140 marked, smallish pitches have been developed in three corridor type avenues, on level grass backing on to hedging and with electricity to most. The tent area is over the bridge past the fairly small, round swimming and paddling pool. Extra toilet facilities, showers, baby bath, etc are also provided here. Laundry and dishwashing facilities and chemical disposal are under cover in a separate round building. Extra pitches are being developed. Excursions can be arranged in the mountains, on horseback if wished. Canoes can be hired and the site also runs a Speleology school and has a hostel nearby with 100 beds.

How to find it: Site is 15 km. east of Cangas on AS114 road.

General Details: Open all year. Bar, restaurant and shop (open main season). Swimming pool. Excursions. Canoeing, riding and caving. Washing machine. Chemical disposal. Hostel accommodation.

Charges 1999: Per adult ptas. 500; child (under 14 yrs) 450; small tent 500; large tent or caravan 600; car 450; m/cycle 350; motorcaravan 700; electricity 350. All plus 7% VAT.

Reservations: needed for July/Aug. Address: 33556 Avin-Onis (Asturias). Tel :98/5844070. FAX: 98/5844267.

8964 Camping El Molino de Cabuérniga, Sopeña

Rural 'alpine meadow' location, close to old Spanish village.

Located in a peaceful valley with views of the mountains, beside the river Saja and only a short walk from the old and attractive village, this site is on an open, level, grassy meadow with few trees. There are 102 marked pitches, all with electricity (3A), although long leads may be needed. The site is lit at night. A single, modern sanitary block provides free hot showers in curtained cubicles, British WCs and wash-basins (cold water only). Dishwashing (H&C) and laundry sinks are outside the block. The site also has a small shop for basic needs, café, bar and barbecue area (open in main season). There is a small, but very simple, children's playground. This comfortable site is very good value and ideal for a few nights whilst you explore the Cabuérniga Valley which forms part of the Reserva Nacional del Saja. The area is great for active pursuits with opportunities for mountain biking, climbing, walking, swimming or fishing in the river, riding, hunting, paragliding and 4x4 safaris. Sopeña Fiesta is in mid-July each year.

How to find it: From N634 at Cabezon de la Sal turn on C625, continue for approx. 10 km. to km. 42 where site is signed before Valle de Cabuérniga. Turn into village (watch out for low eaves/gutters on buildings), bearing right, watching carefully for small green site signs through village.

General Details: Open all year. Shop. Café. Bar. Barbecue. Terrace. Children's playground. Fishing. Bicycle hire. Telephone and post box. Safe deposit. Money exchange. Washing machines and ironing. Tourist information. Chemical disposal. Attractive apartments to rent. No English spoken.

Charges 2000: Per adult ptas. 460; child 400; tent 460; caravan 500; car 460; m/cycle 350; motorcaravan 800; electricity 350. Plus VAT. Credit cards accepted.

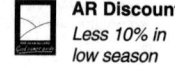

AR Discount
Less 10% in low season

Reservations: Contact site. Address: 39515 Sopeña de Cabuérniga. Tel/fax: 942/706259 or 706278. E-mail: c.cabuerniga@mx3.redestb.es.

8962 Camping La Isla - Picos de Europa, Potes

Relaxed and friendly family site, with good shade and mountain views.

La Isla is beside the road from Potes to Fuente Dé, with mountain views and good shade. Established for over 25 years, a warm welcome awaits from the lady owner, who speaks good English. The 160 unmarked pitches are arranged around an oval gravel track under a variety of fruit and ornamental trees. Electricity (3A) is available (may need long leads). The single sanitary block is clean and in the older style, but is steadily being up-graded. It provides British WCs, washbasins with cold water, and free hot showers. There is also a washing machine plus laundry and dishwashing sinks (cold water only). A small bar/cafe is by the (very clean) small river adjacent to the site, serving good value meals, local dishes and takeaway and overlooking a barbecue and picnic area under the trees beside the river. Behind reception is a small shop providing a good variety of essentials. The small swimming pool (caps compulsory) is unsupervised. Potes with its Monday market is only 4 km, whilst the monastery at Toribio is also within easy reach. There are opportunities for riding and 4x4 safaris, together with other active outdoor pursuits.

How to find it: Site is on right hand side, 4 km. outside Potes, on N621 Potes to Espinama/Fuente Dé road.

General Details: Open 1 April - 30 Oct. Small shop. Cafe/bar and terrace. Takeaway. Small swimming pool (15/5-15/10). Children's playground. Barbecue and picnic area. Fishing. Bicycle hire. Riding. Telephone and post box. Safe deposit. Laundry. Freezer service. Gas supplies. Chemical disposal. Chalets to rent.

Charges 2000: Per adult ptas. 455 - 485; child (0-10 yrs) 365 - 395; tent 420 - 455; caravan or trailer tent 485; car 455; m/cycle 285; motorcaravan 735 - 1,100; electricity 315 - 330. All plus VAT. Credit cards accepted.

Reservations: Write to site. Address: Potes - Turieno (Cantabria). Tel: 942/730896. FAX: as phone. For apartments phone/fax 942/733073.

AR Discount
Less 10% in low season

8963 Camping La Viorna, Potes

Well appointed terraced site, with magnificent mountain views in heart of Picos de Europa.

The wonderful views from the open terraces of this site make it an ideal base for a stay in this region and it is especially popular with mature couples and motorcaravanners. The 110 pitches of around 70 sq.m. are marked by young trees which will, in time, provide some shade - but not yet. There is good access for all sizes of unit and electricity to all pitches. In high season, however, tents may be placed on less accessible, steeply sloping areas. The single sanitary block is good, neat and attractive and is surrounded by beds of flowers. Its interior is clean and modern with British WCs, washbasins (cold water) with soap, and good hot showers with divider and seat. Facilities for disabled visitors double as a unit for babies (key from reception). The laundry room has plenty of sinks, a washing machine and ironing, and there is a dishwashing room (all cold water). Well stocked shop and restaurant/bar (open in season) with a terrace overlooking the excellent swimming pool and children's pool (caps compulsory). The site is only 2 km. from Potes, capital of the Picos, close to Toribio Monastery and a short, but spectacular, drive from Fuente Dé.

How to find it: Take N621 from Unquera to Potes. After town take left fork signed Toribio de Liebana and site is on right after 800 m.

General Details: Open Easter/1 April - 30 Oct. Electricity connections (3 or 6A). Shop. Restaurant/bar with terrace. Swimming pools. Children's playground. Games room. Sporting activities are arranged. Telephone and post box. Medical post. Laundry. Tourist information. Some English spoken.

Charges 1999: Per pitch ptas. 1,250 - 1,350; adult 450 - 475; child 375 - 400; car 450 - 475; m/cycle 375 - 400; electricity 3A 275, 6A 350. All plus VAT.

Reservations: Write to site. Address: Ctra Santo Toribio, Potes (Cantabria). Tel: 942/732021 or 732101. FAX: 942/732019.

8970 Camping Las Arenas, Pechon

Pleasant, green and spacious touring site, with mountain views and beach access.

This campsite is in a very quiet, but rather spectacular location bordering the sea and the Tina Mayor estuary, with views to the mountains and access to a small beach. It is a very green, 10 ha. site with lots of shade from acacias, oak and poplar trees, and is good value for your holiday budget. Taking 337 units, half of the site is divided into marked, grassy pitches (60 sq.m) in various bays or on terraces with sea and mountain views, but some up and down walking. Electrical connections are available and the roads are asphalted. The clean, and well tiled sanitary facilities are in the older style. The various blocks provide a good supply of British WCs and washbasins, with hot showers (no divider, on payment), plus dishwashing, laundry sinks and washing machines. There is a well stocked supermarket, restaurant and snack bar and there are opportunities for fishing, swimming, diving, windsurfing or cycling from the site.

How to find it: Turn off N634, Santander - Coruna road, just east of Unquera on road to Pechon. Site is 2 km.

General Details: Open 1 June - 30 Sept. Electricity connections (5A). Restaurant. Snack bar. Supermarket. Children's playground. Fishing. Windsurfer and bicycle hire. Telephone and post box. Safe deposit. Medical post. Money exchange. Laundry. English spoken. Apartments to let.

Charges 1999: Per adult ptas 565; child 480; car 565; m/cycle 410; tent 550; caravan 700; motorcaravan 945; electricity 345; All plus 7% VAT. Credit cards accepted.

Reservations: Contact site. Address: 39594 Pechon. Tel: 942/717188. FAX: as phone.

8960 Camping La Paz, Vidiago, nr Llanes

Superb and unusual terraced site, by the sea, with spectacular views.

La Paz is arranged on several terraces with sea views, with a lower area in a valley. The way down to the beach is steep but the views, both to the Picos de Europa and to seaward, from the upper terraces are impressive. There are 434 pitches of between 30-70 sq.m, quite a few only suitable for tents, and electricity (3 or 5A) is available. Because of the steep access, units are positioned on upper terraces by site staff with Landrovers. The area at beach level is more suitable for very large units. The four, first class sanitary blocks, with some interesting and unusual design features, are modern, well equipped and spotlessly clean. These have British WCs, washbasins, hot showers (tokens from reception), and baby bath. There are also full laundry and dishwashing facilities. Spring water is available from a number of taps throughout the site. There is a cliff-top café/restaurant and bar overlooking the beach, and a mini-market. It is best to book in high season since the site is deservedly popular and one of the best managed along this coast with a policy of respecting the maximum capacity. La Paz is above Vidiago beach where there are opportunities for swimming, windsurfing and fishing. It is also well placed for excursions to the eastern end of the Picos de Europa. Llanes 10 km. to the west, will appeal to inveterate shoppers.

How to find it: From Santander take the N634 towards Llanes. Site is signed from the main road at km.292, before you arrive in Vidiago.

General Details: Open 1 June - 20 Sept. Cafe/restaurant and bar. Mini market. Laundry. Lounge. Watersports. Table tennis. Games room. Fishing. Telephone and post box. Safe deposit. Medical post. Chemical disposal. Motorcaravan services. Tourist information. English spoken.

Charges 1999: Per adult ptas 555; child 495; car 575; m/cycle 475; tent 575; caravan 735; motorcaravan 975; electricity 390. All plus VAT @ 7%. Credit cards accepted.

Reservations: Recommended for peak weeks. Address: Km.292 C.N.634 Irun-Coruna, Playa de Vidiago, 33597 Vidiago-Llanes (Asturias). Tel: 985/411012. FAX: 985/411235.

Camping - Caravaning
LA PAZ

E-33597 Vidiago - LLANES (ASTURIAS)
Road N-634 (E-70), km 292.
Tel. (34) 985 41 10 12 • Tel. & fax (34) 985 41 12 35.

In extraordinary quiet, very beautiful surroundings and directly at the fantastic, very clean beach. 170.000 sqm. surface with very good installations. At only 45 km from the famous mountain chain **"PICOS DE EUROPA"**. The country side is really very beautiful; a "must" for all nature lovers.

8971 Camping Caravaning Playa de Oyambre, San Vicente de la Barquera

Excellent quality modern site with own swimming pool, near good beaches.

This exceptionally well managed site is ideally positioned to use as a base to visit the spectacular Picos de Europa or one of the many sandy beaches along this northern coast. The site is in lovely countryside (good walking and cycling country), with views of the Picos, 5 km. from San Vicente de la Barquera. The 200 marked pitches are mostly of a good size (average 80 sq.m. with the largest ones often taken by seasonal units). They are arranged on gentle wide terraces with little shade and with electricity in most places. The excellent sanitary facilities, in one central main block, are spotless with cleaners on duty all day and evening. The showers are spacious with a divider and hooks; British WCs, a good supply of washbasins and facilities for babies and disabled visitors. Hot water is free throughout. Dishwashing (H&C) and laundry sinks (cold only) and washing machines (tokens from reception) are also provided. The site is lit and a guard patrols at night. The local doctor visits 3-4 pm. daily in high season. A well stocked supermarket is open until 10 pm. and there are fresh fish deliveries 3 days a week. Good, clean and homely restaurant, and a large bar with TV and games machines. The fair sized swimming pool and a children's pool have a lifeguard. The site gets busy in season and there can be some noise.

How to find it: Site is signed at the junction to Comillas, at km. 265 on the E70, 5 km. east of San Vicente de la Barquera. The entrance is quite steep (take care with caravans).

General Details: Open Easter - 30 Sept. Electricity connections (5A). Supermarket (15/6-15/9). Restaurant. Bar/TV lounge. Games room with machines. Swimming pools (1/6-15/9). Children's playground. Basketball. Football. Fishing 1 km. Riding 5 km. Safe deposit. Medical post, doctor visits daily. Laundry. Chemical disposal. Motorcaravan service point. Hotel rooms and chalets for rent. English spoken.

Charges 1999: Per adult ptas. 500; child 450; pitch 1,050; electricity 350. All plus VAT. Credit cards accepted.

Reservations: Advised, particularly if you have a large unit. Write to site. Address: San Vicente de la Barquera, 39547 Los Llaos (Cantabria). Tel: 942/711461. FAX: 942/711530. E-mail: oyambre@ctv.es.

8961 Camping El Helguero, Ruiloba, nr Santillana del Mar

Well designed site with pool, good facilities for the disabled, close to good beaches.

Although this site is surrounded by tall trees, there is little shade for the pitches. It caters for around 240 units on slightly sloping ground, with many marked out pitches on different levels, all with access to electricity. There are also attractive tent and small camper sections amongst interesting rock formations. Two toilet blocks, although showing signs of age, are clean and cared for, with free hot water in all installations. These include British style WCs, washbasins and soap dispensers, showers with curtains, plus facilities for disabled visitors and children, dishwashing, laundry sinks and washing machine. There is a good, clean swimming pool and children's pool (bathing caps compulsory - sold on site). We were pleased to see the pool also had an access lift for visitors with disabilities. In high season a well stocked shop provides fresh food and other goods, and the bar and restaurant complex is busy and friendly - you can have a typical Spanish meal for £8. This is a good site for disabled people, in a peaceful location, and is excellent value out of main season. One can generally find space here even in high season, but arrive early. The site is used by tour operators. Santillana del Mar is 12 km.

How to find it: From the C6316 road from Santillana del Mar to Comillas, turn left at Sierra. Site is signed as 'Camping Ruiloba'.

General Details: Open Easter - 30 Sept. Electricity connections (6A). Shop (July/Aug. 9 am - 1 pm). Restaurant/bar, other restaurants n village. Swimming pool with lifeguard. Children's playground. Games machines. Activities for children and entertainment for adults. Bicycle hire. Fishing 3 km. Tourist information. Medical post. Laundry. Chemical disposal. Motorcaravan service point. Chalets to let. Caravan storage.

Charges 1999: Per adult ptas 400 - 500; child (4-10 yrs) 375 - 400; caravan or tent 400 - 500; car 400 - 500; m/cycle 250; motorcaravan 800 - 1,000; electricity 350. Credit cards accepted.

Reservations: Write to site. Address: 39527 Ruiloba (Cantabria). Tel: 942/722124. FAX: 942/721020.

9000 Camping Playa Joyel, Noja, nr Santander

see colour advert
between pages 256/257

High quality, comprehensively equipped busy site with pool, by superb beach.

This very attractive holiday and touring site is some 40 km. from Santander and 70 km. from Bilbao, with 1,000 well shaded, marked and numbered pitches (70-80 sq.m.). Electricity is available (3A with new blue Euro-sockets). There are six spacious toilet blocks which have British WCs, vanity style washbasins, large shower cubicles with bench, baby baths and dishwashing facilities, plus a large laundry. Hot water is free throughout. The swimming pool complex with lifeguard is free to campers (bathing caps compulsory). Other facilities include a superb restaurant and bar, well stocked supermarket, good value takeaway, hairdresser, kiosk, and a general shop with souvenirs, camping gaz, etc. There is no shortage of entertainment on site with a soundproof pub/disco (July-Aug), large indoor games hall with minigolf, video and table games, plus tennis courts, horse riding, an animal park, children's playgrounds, recreation area and sports field, and the superb beach which is cleaned daily 15/6-20/9. A `no cycling on site' rule operates in July/Aug. Security patrols at night. Although prices are higher, this well managed camp has a lot to offer for family holidays with much going on in high season when it gets very busy. Used by tour operators.

How to find it: From A8 (E70) toll-free motorway at Beranga (km.185) take the N634 then, almost immediately, take the S403 for Noja. Follow signs to site.

General Details: Open Easter - 30 Sept. Restaurant (July/Aug). Bar, café and snacks (all season). Takeaway (July/Aug). Supermarket (all season). General shop. Kiosk. Swimming pools (15/5-15/9). Tennis. Pub/disco (July/Aug). Games hall. Gym park. Children's playground. Pharmacy - doctors visit daily in season. Riding. Fishing. Animal park. Barbecue area. Bicycle hire 1.5 km. Golf 20 km. Laundry. Hairdresser (July/Aug). Safe deposit. Money exchange. Freezer service. Car wash. Motorcaravan service point. English spoken.

Charges 1999: Per adult ptas. 500 - 750; child (under 10) 350 - 600; pitch 1,500 - 1,600; electricity 375 - 400. All plus 7% VAT. No credit cards.

Reservations: made for 1 week or more. Early arrival or reservation is essential in high season. Address: 39108 Noja (Santander-Cantabria). Tel: 942/630081. FAX: 942/631294. A 'Camping Cheques' site.

Some sites have supplied us with copies of their brochures
which we are pleased to forward to readers.
See our Brochure Service - page 346

8980 Camping Municipal Bella Vista, Santander

Municipal site on approach to Cabo Mayor lighthouse.

An agreeable site, with a well cared for look, Bella Vista is on raised ground in a quiet location. There are good views and the site is about 300 m. from a sandy cove which is approached by flight of steps down the cliff. The long, narrow site is grassy with a tarred access road but without much shade, providing 207 marked pitches. An area under pine trees at one side, gives a degree of shelter for small tents. Electricity (6/10A) is available and some pitches with water and drainage also. A restaurant, shop and laundry are on site, together with a basketball and football court, children's playground plus minigolf and petanque. The six toilet blocks (three for men and three for women in separate buildings) have been refurbished to a good standard and are well maintained. They have some British style WCs, vanity type washbasins, controllable, free hot showers with dressing area, but no dividers, plus dishwashing and laundry sinks. Primarily a transit site with space usually available, it is an excellent stop-over for those travelling via Santander.

How to find it: Site is northeast of the town on road to Cabo Mayor lighthouse. On leaving ferry terminal turn right and follow coast road for approx. 5 km.

General Details: Open all year. Shop. Café. Children's playground. Basketball and football court. Minigolf. Petanque. Fishing 500 m. Golf 250 m. Riding 2.5 km. Safe deposit. Medical post. Money exchange. Laundrette and ironing facilities. Chemical disposal. Bus service. English spoken. Bungalows for hire. Caravan storage.

Charges 2000: Per adult ptas. 640; child 480; pitch (incl. caravan, motorcaravan or family tent) 1,600, with services 2,130; small tent 480 - 695, acc. to size; car 640; m/cycle 430; electricity 400. Credit cards accepted.

Reservations: No stated policy, but site address is Carretera del Faro S/No, 39012 Santander. Tel: 942/391530 or 391536. FAX: 942/391536.

AR Discount
Free game of minigolf

8990 Camping Los Molinos de Cantabria, Bareyo

Peaceful site with excellent views close to Cantabrian coast.

Camping Los Molinos at Bareyo is ideal for those who wish to enjoy a tranquil setting with excellent views after or before the trials of a sea crossing and for touring the local area. The site is divided into two main areas, the lower established area with a large number of permanent units on a gentle slope and with southern mountain views. The newer, upper areas are terraced and planted with young trees which will eventually offer shade. The higher the terrace the better the views (long leads may be required). The very top level is for tents at present and it has wonderful views of the mountains inland and the sea to the north. There are 500 average sized touring pitches, on level ground, and all have electricity. Modern sanitary buildings with British style WCs and free, controllable showers are kept very clean. Facilities for disabled campers have access ramps. There is a first floor restaurant and a bar with a pleasant terrace, swimming pools (with lifeguard) and a mini-market. In high season there is free bus to the beach and town.

How to find it: From autovia E70-A8 Bilbao -Santander road, take exit 185, N634 to Noja take first right S403, turn on SP 4141 for 5 km. Site signed to left on local road.

General Details: Open Easter - Sept. Shop. Restaurant/bar. Children's playground. Telephone and post box. Safe deposit. Laundry. Medical post with doctor daily in high season. Chemical disposal. Bungalows for hire.

Charges 1999: Per adult ptas 500; child 350; tent 600; car 300; caravan or motorcaravan 1,000; m/cycle 300; electricity 375. Plus 7% VAT. No credit cards.

Reservations: Write to site. Address: 39190 Bareyo (Cantabria). Tel: 942/670569. FAX: as phone.

8995 Camping Los Molinos, Noja

Site with good facilities close to an excellent beach.

Camping Los Molinos at Noja is ideally located for touring the local area and as an overnight stop en route when travelling by ferry via Bilbao or Santander. Los Molinos is close to the village of Noja on the coast of Cantabria and is 300 m. from the Playa del Ris beach which has fine sand and clear water. The site is divided into two main areas both with a large number of permanent units. There are 500 touring pitches, on level ground, but with little shade; all have electricity. A large separate area is for tents. Modern sanitary buildings have British style WCs and free controllable hot showers. Washing machines, dishwashing (H&C) and laundry sinks are under cover. Facilities for disabled campers have access ramps. Also on site are two bars (one with disco in season), a restaurant with a pleasant terrace offering reasonably priced food, a café for snacks, a pizzeria, tapas and takeaway. There are two swimming pools (with lifeguard), and a well stocked supermarket. Unusually the site has its own karting complex and many other facilities include tennis, basketball, and a children's play area. In high season there is free bus hourly to the town.

How to find it: From E70-A8 Bilbao -Santander, take exit 185, N634 to Noja take first right S403. It is 10 km. to Noja. Follow signs to Playa del Ris where site signed.

General Details: Open 12 Feb - 15 Nov. Supermarket. Restaurant/bars. Cafés. Takeaway and ice-cream parlour. Children's playground. Basketball. Telephone and post box. Safe deposit. ATM. Laundry. Medical post (doctor calls daily in high season). Chemical disposal. Car wash. Mobile homes for rent.

Charges 1999: Per adult ptas. 450 - 600; child 450 - 475; tent 550 - 700; car 300 - 350; caravan or motorcaravan 900 - 1,300; m/cycle 300 - 400; electricity 375. Plus 7% VAT. Credit cards not accepted.

Reservations: Contact site. Address: Playa del Ris, 39180 Noja. Tel: 942/630725. FAX: 942/630425.

9035 Camping Portuondo, Mundaka

Attractive terraced site suitable only for tents or small units.

This site is a good base from which to explore the local area and the old Spanish town. However, the entry to this well cared for site is steep (18%) and at an oblique angle to the road (best approached from the Bermeo direction) and the 135 pitches are not suitable for large outfits. In fact, caravans are not accepted at all between 15 July and 20 August. The site is partly terraced, with pitches marked and numbered and there is some shade in parts. Most pitches are very slightly sloped and all have electricity (5A, some may need long leads). The good quality sanitary facilities include controllable hot showers, washbasins, hand and hairdryers, mostly British WCs and a new heated baby bathroom. Dishwashing and laundry sinks are outside under cover. Hot water is free throughout. The owner also runs a restaurant (at site entrance) with a full range of meals and snacks and a takeaway service. Small shop. There is a large covered patio with tables and benches above the shower block and a barbecue area.

How to find it: From N634 or autopista (S. Sebastian-Bilbao), turn at Amorebieta onto the C6315 road to Gernika/Bermeo. Approach site from Bermeo direction due to oblique access.

General Details: Open all year. Shop (15/6-15/9). Restaurant and takeaway (1/2-15/12). Bar. Table tennis. Barbecue area. Fishing 100 m. Safe deposit. Washing machines and dryers. Chemical disposal. Bungalows for rent. Caravan storage. English spoken.

Charges 2000: Per adult ptas. 585; child (under 10 yrs) 500; pitch 1,250; pitch with electricity 1,700. All plus 7% VAT. Less 5-10% for longer stays. Credit cards accepted.

Reservations: Write to site. Address: 48630 Mundaka (Bizkaia). Tel: 94/687.77.01. FAX: as phone. E-mail: recepcion@campingportuondo.com.

AR Discount
Less 15%
excl. 16/6-14/9
(not bungalows)

9038 Camping Orio, Orio

Typical seaside site, suitable for first/last night of tour.

This site has 400 pitches, with many long stay units and privately owned statics, but there should always be adequate space for tourers. As it is only 50 m. from the beach, there is no shade. The pitches are in rows divided by tarmac roads and hedges, all with electricity (5A). The main sanitary block has recently been refurbished and provides showers (pre-set hot water) with large changing rooms, washbasins, British WCs and baby baths. Hot water is free throughout. A large kitchen is provided with additional dishwashing and laundry sinks (cold water) outside under cover. Good facilities for wheelchairs. Two additional smaller, older sanitary blocks on site are opened in the main season. Small swimming pool, children's pool (unsupervised), squash and tennis courts, with fishing in the nearby river and the sea. A cafe/bar and mini market are open in July/Aug. This site is fairly expensive in high season, with the cheaper pitches furthest from the beach, but closer to the sanitary installations. Dogs not accepted. No English spoken.

How to find it: Turn off N634 road at km. 12.5 in centre of Orio (sign is easy to miss), and follow signs to site. Take care, the streets in Orio town centre are not wide.

General Details: Open 1 Jan - 31 Oct. Cafe. Bar. Mini market. Money exchange. Swimming pools. Barbecue area. Children's playground. Squash and tennis courts. Fishing. Telephone and post box. Safe deposit. Medical post. Mobile homes for rent.

Charges 1999: Per unit incl. 2 persons ptas. 2,967; extra adult 486; child (2-10 yrs) 397. VAT included. Credit cards accepted.

Reservations: Write to site. Address: 20810 Orio (Gipuzkoa). Tel: 943/834801. FAX: 943/133433.

9030 Camping Igueldo, San Sebastian

Site on high ground just outside the town.

Igueldo has an imposing situation on top of a hill, by the side of San Sebastian, with a fine panoramic view on the land side. It is also quite a pleasant site in a part of Spain where Britons may want to find a camp and where there are not many available. Although not a luxurious one, it is a friendly place. The sanitary blocks have been extended and improved to give a much more satisfactory provision. The terrain has been divided into 289 individual pitches, though they are not very large - 70 sq.m. They are of two types, 191 with electricity (5A) and water. There are also some tiny tent pitches of 20 sq.m. San Sebastian is a large, pleasant and quite fashionable town which has all the shops, restaurants, entertainment and night life that one could want, as well as some sandy beaches, which are usually busy in the season. The nearest beach is about 5 km. from the site.

How to find it: The turning to Igueldo is on the west side of the town and is well signed from the main road.

General Details: Open all year. 33,000 sq.m. Little shade. Shop. Bar. Restaurant with takeaway food.

Charges 1999: Per unit, incl. car, 3 persons, and with services ptas. 3,100, without services 2,750; extra adult 450; child (3-10 yrs) 325; small tent pitch, incl. car, 2 adults 1,500; electricity 350. All plus 7% VAT. Special winter prices available.

Reservations: none made. Address: 20190 Igueldo. Tel: 943/214502. FAX: 943/280411.

SPAIN - North

9040 Camping de Haro, La Rioja

Friendly site with pools close to famous wine producing area.

This quiet site is on the outskirts of the village of Haro, renowned for Rioja wines. It is a family run site with excellent pools and supporting facilities. The village of Haro is within walking distance and for wine enthusiasts there are traditional Bodegas to visit and engage in tastings. There is considerable room to manoeuvre at the entrance and the modern reception provides tourist information, the cheery manager speaking excellent English. Close to the entrance are three pools and a good bar/restaurant with pleasant views. The mini market offers fresh bread in season and there are laundry facilities. There is one central modern facilities block with another planned, incorporating facilities for disabled campers, which were not available when seen. Hot showers are free. There is a possibility that these facilities may be busy at peak periods until the new block is available. All facilities were clean and well maintained when we visited. A river runs alongside the site which can provide some fishing, and there is secure fencing. The site provides animation for the children in season and there is a pleasant play area. Approximately half the good sized pitches on level ground are occupied by permanent campers as the area is very popular with Spanish holidaymakers in the summer. Electricity connections are provided, although long leads may be required on some pitches and torches are advisable close to the perimeter of the site furthest from the entrance.

How to find it: Take E804 road from Bilbao south to Logroño; enter Haro at exit 9 and the site is well signed as the town is approached.

General Details: Open all year excl. 9 Dec. - 7 Jan. Electricity connections (3 or 5A). Restaurant. Bar. Supermarket (in season). Three swimming pools. Drinks and ice machine homes. Children's play area and animation in season. Car wash.

Charges 1999: Per adult ptas. 495; child 390; tent 495; car 495; caravan 495; m/cycle 435; motorcaravan 860; electricity 310. Credit cards accepted.

Reservations: Write to site. Address: 26200 Haro (La Rioja). Tel: 941/312737. FAX: 941/312068.

9042 Camping Etxarri, Etxarri-Aranatz, nr Pamplona

This site has been recommended by our agent and will be fully inspected next year. About 40 km. west of Pamplona, the site provides a base for many routes to view the Megalithic sites that are a featureof the Navarra area. Local guide books give details of many possible routes. The campsite provides 250 pitches for tents, plus 25 for caravans which have water and electricity hook-ups. There are also rooms to let and log cabins. Activities include archery, riding and table tennis and hang-gliding, paragliding and mountain biking can be arranged. The site has a restaurant.

How to find it: The village of Etxarri-Aranatz is on the N240A between Pamplona and Vitoria.

General Details: Open Easter, then 1 June - 31 Dec. 10 hectares. Shop. Bar. Restaurant. First aid room. Laundry.

Charges 1999: Per person ptas. 425; child 375; pitch incl. electricty 1,250.

Reservations: Contact site. Address: 31820 Etxarri-Aranatz. Tel: 948/460537. FAX: as phone. E-mail: campingetxarri@navarra.net.

Some sites have supplied us with copies of their brochures which we are pleased to forward to readers.

See our Brochure Service - page 346

9070 Camping Pirineos, Santa Cilia de Jaca, nr Jaca

Pretty site with attractive swimming pool, convenient for touring in the Pyrenees.

This all year site has a quite mild climate, being near the River Aragon and not too high. Unusually for Spain the trees are mainly oak and provide reasonable shade. Although there is space for caravans, it is possibly more suited for motorcaravans, owing to the kerbs and trees to be negotiated. The large number of permanent units detracts a little from the overall impression and there is some daytime road noise along one side. However, there is an attractive swimming pool and children's pool with bar and terrace which is open from mid-June to end of August, as is the supermarket. The restaurant and bar are open all year lunch-times and evenings. One heated sanitary block is open all year, providing a quite satisfactory supply, with hot water for the showers, washbasins, dishwashing and laundry sinks. A second, very modern block is open June to August only. Both have British WCs. It is a friendly site which is also useful for off-season camping on the 250 all-electric(6A), mostly level and quite large touring pitches.

How to find it: Site is 15 km. west of Jaca on N240 (65 km. northwest of Huesca).

General Details: Open all year. Shade in parts. Restaurant and bar (open all year). Supermarket (high season, otherwise essentials kept in bar). Swimming pools (June - Aug). Two tennis courts. Table tennis. Children's playground. Petanque. Bicycle hire. Fishing 200 m. Launderette. Gas supplies. Chemical disposal. Small hotel with accommodation to let. Bungalows to rent. Dogs are not accepted in high season.

Charges 2000: Per adult 675; child (2-9 yrs) 650; car 675; caravan or tent 675; motorcaravan 1,200; electricity 575; all plus 7% VAT: Credit cards accepted.

Reservations: Contact site. Address: Centro de Vacaciones, Ctra N240 km 300, 22791 Santa Cilia de Jaca (Huesca). Tel/fax: 974/377351. A 'Camping Cheques' site.

AR Discount
Less 20%
in low season

9100 Camping Casablanca, Zaragoza

Typical small city site suitable for overnight stop.

Although not a perfect site, Casablanca is reasonable for overnight or for a short stay. On flat meadow (with little grass) there are 180 pitches with 10A electricity. It does lack shade, and it can be hot here. It has a medium sized swimming pool on site, although this is only open July/Aug. The sanitary block is basic with little hot water and could be hard-pressed at busiest times. British style WCs.

How to find it: Site is just outside town to southwest in the Val de Fierro district; access roads lead off N11 Madrid road (km. 316) or N330 Valencia road and are well signed, if a little difficult to follow.

General Details: Open 1 April - 15 Oct. Shop and restaurant/bar (from 1 June). Town shop 200 m. Many electrical connections.

Charges 1999: Per adult ptas. 615; child 500; car 615; tent/caravan 615; motorcaravan 975; electricity 455.

Reservations: can be made to Campings Betsa, C/Nov. 139, 17600 Figueras (Gerona). Tel: 976/753870. FAX: 976/753875.

9105 Camping Lago Park, Nuevalos, nr Zaragoza

Site in attractive area with many visitors for the Monasterio de Piedra.

The drawbacks here are the rather steep access, possible up and down treks to the sanitary block (which might not cope with a full site) and possible noise from the disco (although soundproofed), which doubt-less gets very busy with the many tent pitches. If you can accept all this or visit out of the main season, you will be rewarded with a site which is positioned just outside the ancient village, between lake and mountains, and which is very suitable as a base for exploring this really attractive area. On a steep hill-side, the 300 pitches (250 for tourers) are on terraces. With only a few pitches suitable for large caravans, they are numbered and marked by trees, just over 50% having electrical connections (10A). The single sanitary block is acceptable and has British style WCs (some Turkish for men), washbasins with cold water and some controllable hot showers (no dividers). Facilities on site, open for the main season, include the swimming pool and a restaurant/bar and shop. A bull-ring is now apparently used as children's play area, although the brochures show young bulls in action.

How to find it: From Zaragoza (120 km.) take fast A2/N11/E90 road and turn onto C202 road beyond Calatayud to Nuevalos (25 km). From Madrid exit A2 at Alhama de Aragon (13 km). Follow signs for Monasterio de Piedra from all directions.

General Details: Open 1 April - 30 Sept. Restaurant/bar (open June-Sept). Shop (all season). Swimming pool (late June-Sept). Fishing 300 m. Riding 2 km. Gas supplies. Chemical disposal. Chalets (4 persons) to rent.

Charges 2000: Per person ptas. 675; child (3-10 yrs) 650; car 700; m/cycle 525; caravan 750; tent 725; motor-caravan 1,300; electricity 600. Credit cards accepted.

Reservations: Contact site. Address: 50210 Nuevalos. Tel: 976/84.90.38, 84.90.48 or 84.90.57.

AR Discount
Less 15%
after 7 days

SPAIN - North

9125 Camping Lago de Barasona, La Puebla de Castro, nr Huesca

Hillside site by lake in the pre-Pyrenees.

This site is beautifully positioned in terraces by the shores of the Lago de Barasona (a large reservoir), with views of hills and the distant Pyrenees. The local administration has put together some excellent tourist information (in English) and a brochure detailing the local way-marked walks and the owner has matched this with his own quality brochure. The recently discovered Roman town of Labitolosa, just 1.5 km. away on foot, direct from the site, is best seen in high summer when further excavations take place. The site has its own canoes for hire and waterskiing is available also in July and August. You may also swim and fish in the lake which has a very shallow area extending for 20 m. or so. If you prefer, the site offers its own outdoor pool, open from as early as April when the weather is often quite warm. The very friendly, English speaking owner would welcome more British visitors, especially in the spring, when the area is very attractive. The grassy, fairly level pitches are up to 100 sq.m. in size for larger units and all have 6A electricity connections. Many are well shaded and views of the lake and/or hills are available. Some up and down walking is necessary to the shop (July/Aug), bar/restaurant, swimming pool and the two sanitary units. The lower, recently modernised building is nicely presented, although hot water is only available in the cabins (3 for ladies, 1 for men) and the smallish showers (no divider), and some dish-washing and laundry sinks. Volleyball, football and a new children's play area were all under construction. A pleasant and peaceful site in a lovely area.

How to find it: Site is on the west bank of the lake, close to km. 25 on the N123, 4.5 km. south of Graus (approx. 80 km. north of Lleida/Lerida).

General Details: Open 1 April - 30 Sept. Bar/snack bar and restaurant (all season). Shop (15/5-15/9). Swimming pool (15/5-15/9). Tennis. Table tennis. Mountain bike hire. Canoe, motor boat and pedaloes for hire. Lake swimming, fishing, canoeing etc. Walking (maps provided). Riding 4 km. Money exchange. Mobile homes and bungalows to let.

Charges 1999: Per person ptas. 450 - 590; child (2-10 yrs) 375 - 485; car 500 - 675; caravan or tent 500 - 675; motorcaravan 800 - 1,100; electricity 485. Plus VAT @ 7%. Credit cards accepted.

Reservations: Not needed outside mid-July - mid-August. Address: Ctra N-123a, km. 25, 22435 La Puebla de Castro (Huesca). Tel: 974/54 51 48. FAX: as phone. E-mail: camping-lago-barasona@spicom.es. A 'Camping Cheques' site.

9142 Camping Solana del Segre, Bellver de Cerdanya, nr Puigcerda

Rustic site with mountain views in scenic area, for outdoor sports enthusiasts.

The Sierra del Cadi offers some spectacular scenery and the Reserva Cerdanya is very popular with Spanish skiers. This site is situated in an open sunny lower valley beside the River Segré where the trout fishing is reputed to be very good (permits from Bellver village). The immediate area is ideal for walkers and offers many opportunities for outdoor sports enthusiasts; riding, golf, hang-gliding, canoeing and rock climbing are all available and can be arranged with reception. The superb Olympic watersports facility in the interesting old town of Le Seu (25 km, market on Tuesdays), boasts an impressive man-made white water canoeing course where tuition is provided for the brave-hearted. The site is in two sections, the lower one nearer the river being the main tourist one, mainly flat and grassy with pitches of 70 sq.m. or more, mostly marked out by trees and all with 6A electricity and quite easy access. There are 300 pitches in total, 150 suitable for winter use. The sanitary facilities are in three sections and are of satisfactory quality, with free hot water. The showers are of fair size with seats outside. The shop and bar/restaurant open Easter - mid Sept. and Christmas, otherwise at weekends only, but the town is very close. The fair-sized swimming pool is open from June and there is a children's play area, games room/disco, volleyball and petanque. There is a large number of local seasonal units in the summer season and the site is very busy at weekends.

How to find it: On the N260 from Puigcerda, the site is just beyond Bellver de Cerdanya towards La Seu (Seo).

General Details: Open all year except 14 Sept - 10 Oct. Shop, Bar/restaurant (see text). Children's play area. Games room. Swimming pool. Golf 8 or 18 km. Skiing 10 km. Many other sports in area. Chemical disposal. Motorcaravan services. Chalets and apartments (basic) to rent.

Charges 1999: Per person 631; child (under 10) 584; tent, caravan, car all 631; motorcaravan 1,300; electricity 600. Credit cards accepted.

Reservations: Generally only necessary at weekends in high season. Address: Ctra N-260, Km 198. 25720 Bellver de Cerdanya (Lleida). Tel: 873/510310. FAX: 873/510698.

9060 Camping Peña Montañesa, Labuerda, nr Ainsa

Large, riverside site by the Ordesa National Park in the Pyrenees.

Although situated quite high up in the Pyrenees, Pena Montanesa is easily accessible from Ainsa or from France via the Bielsa Tunnel, and is ideally situated for exploring the beautiful Pyrenees. The site is essentially divided into three sections opening progressively throughout the season and providing progressively less shade as the trees in the newer section grow. The 288 pitches on fairly level grass are of approximately 75 sq.m. and 10A electricity is available on virtually all of them. The newer pitches (open in the main season) have the benefit of a brand new sanitary block, heated when necessary. It has free hot water for the showers, cold for open plan washbasins, facilities for disabled visitors, a small baby bathroom and British style WCs. The older pitches are served by an older sanitary block of nevertheless satisfactory standard, with similar provision. This is quite a large site which has grown very quickly and as such may at times be a little hard pressed. Near the entrance are grouped the facilities that make the site so attractive. Apart from a fair sized outdoor pool and children's pool, there is a heated indoor pool with jacuzzi and sauna (open all year) and an attractive bar, restaurant (with open fire) and terrace. The supermarket and takeaway are opposite.

How to find it: Site is 2 km. from Ainsa, on the road from Ainsa to France.

General Details: Open all year. 80,000 sq.m. Bar. Restaurant. Takeaway. Supermarket. Outdoor swimming pool and children's pool (March - Oct). Indoor pool with jacuzzi and sauna (all year). Children's playground. Boules. Minigolf. Table tennis. Bicycle hire. Riding. Fishing 100 m. Canoeing near. Washing machine. Chemical disposal. Bungalows and caravans to rent. Caravan storage.

Charges 2000: Per person ptas. 680; child (1-9 yrs) 580; pitch 2,050; dog 350; electricity 560. All plus 7% VAT. Credit cards accepted.

Reservations: are made for camping with ptas. 10,000 deposit by visa, giro or eurocheque (25,000 ptas. for a bungalow). Address: Ctra. Ainsa-Francia km.2, 22360 Labuerda-Ainsa (Huesca). Tel/fax: 974/500032. E-mail: info@penamontanesa.com.

AR Discount
Welcome drink in low season

Camping Caravanning Bungalows
Peña Montañesa

Road Ainsa - France, 2 km from Ainsa
E-22369 Labuerda - Ainsa (Prov. Huesca)
Tel: (34) 974 500032

In amidst the beautiful landscape of the Pyrenees near the Nature Reserve Ordesa and Monte Perdido.

On the border of the river CINCA, ideal for canoeing and kayak-sports - and only 2 km from a lake. Spacious sanitary installations with free hot water in showers. Restaurant, snack bar, supermarket, telephone, postal service, money exchange, tourist information, swimming pools, children's playground, boules game and table tennis. Leisure programme for children & adults. We Speak English.

A friendly camp site in very quiet surroundings.

OPEN THROUGHOUT THE YEAR
BUNGALOWS FOR HIRE
OFF-SEASON REDUCTION

Web: www.penamontanesa.com
info@penamontanesa.com

 **For a list of sites which are open all year - see page 257**

9122 Camping Montagut, Montagut

Small, pretty, family site in Alta Garrotxa with pool and good facilities, open all year.

This is a most pleasant family site where everything is kept in pristine condition. Jordi and Nuria are a brother and sister team who work hard to make you welcome and maintain the superb appearance of the site. Flowers and shrubs abound, with pitches on attractively landscaped and carefully constructed terraces or on flat areas overlooking the attractive pool. A tranquil atmosphere pervades the site and drinks on the pleasant restaurant terrace are recommended, along with sampling the authentic menu provided, as you enjoy the views over the Alta Garrotxa. The site is surrounded by farmland and there is a very large play area on the lower levels of the site if you wish to take part in sports which include soccer, petanque, and volleyball. The medium sized pool is neat and clean, as are the associated children's pool and play areas. There is a modern sanitary block with free hot showers, washing and laundry facilities plus a modern section for babies and disabled campers; everything was spotless when seen. A barbecue area is provided and a motorcaravan service point. There is much to see in the local area between the Pyrenees and the Mediterranean Sea, and we particularly recommend a trip to the stunning village of Castellfollit de la Roca perched seemingly precariously on a precipice 60 m. above the Fluvia river. Or, on a different scale, the pretty 'El pont romantic d'oix' which is a bridge in a most pleasant setting which the site has chosen to use on their logo. You will need you own transport at this site as there is no bus service. Torches are required in some areas and long leads would be useful in the upper terraces. This is a superb all year site for relaxing and enjoying the peaceful situation and wonderful scenery. Torches may be needed in the more remote parts of site.

How to find it: Going west from Figueres on N260 Ripoll road, approx. 10 km. past Besalu, towards Castellfollit de la Roca, turn right towards Sardernes. On reaching Montagut still follow the road to Sardernes and the site entrance is at the 2 km. marker.

Charges 2000: Per person ptas 525 - 625; child 425 - 525; caravan or tent 575 - 675; motorcaravan 875 - 1025; car 525 - 625; electricity 475. Plus 7% VAT. No credit cards.

General Details: Open all year. Swimming pools. Restaurant and bar. Supermarket. Laundry facilities. Children's playground. Soccer. Petanque. Volleyball.

Reservations: Contact site. Address: Ctra. de Montagut a Sadernes, km 2. 17855 Montagut (Girona). Tel: 972/287202. FAX: 972/ 287201. E-mail:camp.montgut@mx3.redestb.es.

9121 Camping de la Vall d'Ager, Ager, nr Lleida

Very peaceful all year round site in lovely setting.

Ager is not on a through-route to anywhere, so if you are coming here it is for a specific reason, hence the peaceful situation. One of the main reasons for being here is that it is a hang glider's paradise, the Montsec mountain (1,677 m.) overlooking the site in the Catalan pre-Pyrenees, being the launch point. When you also consider that climbing, walking, mountain biking, canoeing and other water sports are all available in the vicinity, you may well wish to visit this pleasant site. There are 180 touring pitches on slightly sloping ground, marked out by trees and with some shade. Electricity (10A) is available to all. The central sanitary building provides good facilities, with soap and paper towels in the toilet sections and free hot water in the washbasins and large showers (with divider and lots of room to change). The building also houses separate rooms for the disabled, dishwashing (hot) and laundry (cold) facilities, plus a washing machine and dryer downstairs. There is a large bar with snack area and a restaurant which opens all year. The small shop is open April - Sept. only, but the village is only 3/400 m. away. The swimming pool is open in high season and there is a well provisioned area of children's play equipment.

How to find it: The site is on the edge of the village, which is on the L904, either direct from Balaguer (which is 28 km. NNE of Lleida) or from the C147 Balaguer/Tremp road. Either way, the L904 (which is being modernised) has old, narrow sections requiring caution.

General Details: Open all year, as are the bar, snack bar and restaurant. Shop (main season only). Bicycle hire. Delta-wing store. Swimming pools. Children's play equipment. Chemical disposal. Accommodation to let.

Charges 1999: Per person ptas. 561; child (under 10 yrs) 514; tent or caravan 561; motorcaravan 1,122; electricity (10A) 561. Credit cards accepted.

Reservations: Unlikely to be needed. Address: 25691 Ager, La Noguera (Lleida). Tel: 973/455200 or 201. FAX: 973/455202.

9123 Camping El Solsones, Solsona

Useful night-stop in a peaceful situation.

Situated on a hillside, 2 km. from Solsona with pleasant views of the hills on three sides and an open feeling, this all year site would make for a pleasant short stop, with all facilities open. There are many weekend units here, but still room for 100 vans and 100 tents out of the total of 312 pitches. These are slightly sloping, with some shade available and 4, 6 or 10A electricity. The modern sanitary facilities are in two buildings, with free hot water to the showers, washbasins, laundry and dishwashing sinks. There is a swimming pool for the high season, a small aviary and children's play equipment. For winter visitors, the Ski Port del Conte is 18 km. and there are facilities for riding, golf and walking in the vicinity. A friendly welcome is provided by the owner who has no English, but good French.

How to find it: Solsona is at the junction of the L301, C1410 and C149 in Lleida, 45 km. northwest of Manresa. The site is 2 km out of town on the LV4241 signed to Sant Llorenc de Morunys and Ski Port del Comte.

General Details: Open all year as are shop, restaurant and bar. Swimming pools. Bicycle hire. Children's play area. Petanque. Fronton. Aviary. Golf, riding and skiing nearby. Motorcaravan service point. Chemical disposal.

Charges 1999: Per person ptas. 600; child (2-10 yrs) 550; car 600; m/cycle 550; caravan or tent 600; motorcaravan 1,100; electricity (4A) 300: Plus 7% VAT. Credit cards accepted.

Reservations: Contact site for high season (in French). Address: Ctra Sant Llorenc, Km 2. 25280 Solsona. (Lleida). Tel: 873/482861. FAX: 873/481300.

8506 Camping-Caravaning Serra de Prades, Vilanova de Prades, nr Reus

Tranquil site on edge of village, nestling in granite foothills.

On the edge of the village of Vilanova, on the lower mountain slopes with good views (950 m), this is a welcoming and peaceful site. The 215 pitches are on terraces formed with natural stone and with good access from resurfaced roads; 90% have electrical connections (176 with 6A, 13 with 10A). The planting of hedges and trees continues, to separate pitches and provide a green environment and shade. All facilities are at the entrance to the site and include a modern, very well maintained sanitary block with British style WCs and are heated. Solar power is used to ecologically supplement the hot water supply and there recycling bins for rubbish. The bar/restaurant offers a wide range of meals including regional dishes. There is plenty to do on the site and in the area and the site has facilities for horse riding (with guided treks) and for the hire of 4x4 vehicles. The helpful staff will give you many leaflets and brochures to guide you to interesting visits, including the attractive, old village itself. Organised activities for children and adults. The village swimming pool is 100 m. and is free for campers.

How to find it: From autopista A2 take exit 8 (L'Albi) and follow signs to El Vilosell, Vallclara, then Vilanova de Prades. Alternatively from exit 9 (Montblanc) and turn right on N-240 towards Vimbodi, turn left on T-7004 to Vallclara, Vilanova de Prades and site.

General Details: Open all year. Shop. Bar/restaurant. Satellite TV. Archery. Basketball. Volleyball. Tennis. Riding with guided treks. 4x4 vehicle hire. Entertainment in season. Swimming pool 100 m. Laundry facilities. Safety deposit. Exchange facilities. Chemical disposal. Motorcravan service point. Bungalows (5) to rent.

Charges 1999: Per person ptas. 595; child (under 10 yrs) 495; tent 595; caravan 595; car 595; m/cycle 495; motorcaravan 1,190; m/cycle 495; electricity 495. Plus 7% VAT. Credit cards accepted.

Reservations: Write to site. Address: c/Sant Antoni s/n, 43439 Vilanova de Prades (Tarragona). Tel: 877/869050. FAX: as phone. E-mail: serraprades@svt.es.

Why camp in Menorca?

Menorca, steeped in history and blanketed by mystery, is an enchanting island waiting to be explored. Roughly 270 square miles in area, you can easily trek, bike or drive round the island in no time. The building of leisure facilities is now heavily taxed by the regional government and the proceeds used to buy land for National Parks and Nature Reserves, thereby protecting the island for future generations.

The C721 highway provides the back-bone to the island, connecting modest market towns to Mahon (the main town) in the east and Ciutadella in the west. Mahon's classic Georgian style buildings, complete with sash windows, will endear them to the British traveller. Its impressive harbour was captured by the British in 1708 during the Spanish War of Succession. In complete contrast, Ciutadella has a more Gothic feel to it. A labyrinth of tiny streets entwine the 'little city', most of which can only be accessed on foot. Monte Toro stands proudly at the centre of the island surveying all. To the south a greener lush terrain exists with long, luxurious beaches, while to the north a giant rockery erupts riddled with caves and prehistoric finds. Fishermen still put to sea in double ended boats directly descended from the Arab designs. Crude stone memorials (tavla) litter the landscape with dry stone walls (tanca) and olive groves standing tribute to the generations of arduous Menorcans.

SPAIN - Menorca

Why camp in Menorca?

Fishing, walking, sailing, golfing, snorkelling, bird watching, shopping and cheese making or simply sun-bathing are just a handful of examples of what is on offer in Menorca. As my seven year old said 'It's too hard to write about Menorca because its too good'.
So why camp in Menorca? Because you can and it's a super relaxed way of discovering and enjoying this marvellous, unspoilt Spanish island.

8000 Camping Son Bou, Son Bou, Menorca

Modern campsite with attractive pool and terrace on the beautiful island of Menorca.
When the owner of Camping Son Bou originally asked us to visit with a view to the site being included in the Europe Guide, we did not think it was worth following up being on a small island in the middle of the Mediterranean. However, we are glad that we did and the site is more than happy to arrange the overnight ferry crossing from Barcelona or Valencia with a 25% discount in low season and 15% in the high season. Yes, it is expensive and you would need to stay for a decent length of time to make it worth while (you do also get 10% discount on your site fees) but this beautiful island cries out to be explored. It is peaceful and tranquil, with its characteristic dry stone walls, its low white buildings with terracotta tiled roof, its beautiful coastline, ancient monuments and pretty villages with their cycle of fiestas of religious origin with the noble horse as the central element.
The site itself only opened in July 1996 and has been purpose built in local style with a large irregular shaped pool with marvellous view across to the `mountain', Monte Toro, and overlooked by a pine cov-ered terrace for shade with bar and restaurant. The 216 large pitches are arranged in circles radiating out from the main facilities and clearly edged with stones. Natural pine tree shade covers most but the outer ring and drinking water and refuse points are well placed. Electricity is available on nearly all pitches. The ground is hard and devoid of grass except where special sprinklers operate, then its very green! The toilet block is well planned and of good quality, open plan in places. Controllable hot showers are well equipped, with some washbasins in cabins, others in vanity style with large mirrors. Separate room with two baby baths. En-suite facilities for handicapped visitors are complimented by ramped access to all other facili-ties on most of the site. Washing up and laundry sinks all with cold water as have the washbasins. No washing machines but serviced wash available. Shop on site open from 15 June - 15 Sept. All other facil-ities open when the site opens. The 'menu of the day' is good value and in the high season there is an open air cinema most evenings, and a barbecue with guitarist some evenings. Bicycle hire can be arranged by the day or week. The site gets very busy with Spanish from the mainland in high season. Earlier in the year it is quieter and greener. If you do not fancy the ferry crossings the site has some neat wooden chalets and ready erected Trigano tents (which you see in France) for hire fully equipped for four persons. Epsol Tours are the UK agents.The village of Son Bou itself is 0.75 km. away and very much a small tourist centre. The sandy beach is the longest in the island, well organised with life guards, snack bars, sun beds and umbrellas to hire. Note: there is a naturist section at the far end.

How to find it: From Mahon (Mao) follow the main road to Ciutadella. Go past the town of Alaior (bypassed), for a further km. approx. Watch for restaurant on left and road sign for San Jaime /Son Bou. Turn left on this road (the surface is not as good as the main road). Continue for 3.5 km.and site on right.

General Details: Open 15 May - 30 September. 65,000 sq. m. Shop. Bar. Restaurant. Large outdoor pool. Tennis court. Petanque. Football. Basketball. Volleyball. Children's play area. Chemical disposal. English spoken. The site also has access to a comprehensive activity programme covering birdwatching, walking, mountain biking, canoeing, diving, windsurfing, water skiing and various excursions.

Charges 1999: Per adult 720 - 900 ptas; child (3-13 yrs) 520 - 650; tent for one person 400 - 500; tent for two persons 800 - 1,000; car 480 - 600; m/cycle 360 - 450; motorhome 1,280 - 1,600; electricity 500; ready erected tent 6,000 - 9,000.

Reservations: Contact site. Address: Ctra. de San Jaime km. 3.5, Apdo. de Correos 85, Alaior 07730, Menorca. Tel/fax 971/377605. E-mail: sonbou@infotelecom.es. The site can also arrange the ferries from Spain. A UK contact for ferries, reservations and possible cheap flights is Epsol Tours - see below.

AR Discount
Less 10%

EPSOL Tours are UK agents for Camping Son Bou.
Epsol can advise and arrange ferry tickets plus site fees, transport
or car hire from the airport. Wooden chalets and Trigano tents available to rent
EPSOL Tours - Tel: 01296 420635 Fax: 01296 425917.

SWEDEN

Sweden covers an area almost twice that of the UK but has a population only one seventh of ours, with over half the land surface covered by forests and lakes. Stretching from north of the Arctic circle for 1,000 miles to a southern limit about level with Glasgow, inevitably the roads are quiet and almost traffic free with a range of scenery varying from the vast, wild open spaces of Lapland to the rich forests of the south and a choice of climate to match. The very beautiful southwest region, the 'Swedish Lake and Glass country', makes a perfect introduction to this fascinating land. It is easily reached, either by a wide choice of ferries or overland from Norway. The area is dominated by the two great lakes, Vänern (2,000 sq. miles) and Vättern (750 sq. miles), Europe's second and third largest lakes. Stockholm, the capital, is a delightful place built on a series of fourteen small islands, housing monumental architecture and fine museums giving it an ageing, lived-in atmosphere and providing the country's most active culture and night life. Today Sweden enjoys one of the highest standards of living in the world and a quality of life to go with it. For further information contact:

Swedish Travel and Tourism Council, 11 Montague Place, London W1H 2AL
Tel: 020 7870 5600   Fax: 020 7724 5872   Brochures: 01476 578811
E-mail: sttc-info@swedish-tourism.org.uk

Population
8,700,000, density 19.3 per sq. km.

Capital
Stockholm

Climate
Sweden enjoys a temperate climate thanks to the Gulf Stream. The weather is similar to Britain's, apart from the fact that there is generally less rain and more sunshine in the summer.

Language
English is fairly widely spoken but a phrase book is advised.

Currency
Swedish currency is the Krona (plural Kronor) made up of 100 öre. It comes in coins of 50 öre, 1 kr, 5 kr and 10 kr, and notes of 20, 50, 100, 500, 1,000 and 10,000 kr.

Banks
Open Mon-Fri 09.30-15.00. Some city banks stay open til 17.30/18.00. All are closed on Sats.

Post Offices
Open 09.00-18.00 on weekdays and 09.00/10.00 - 13.00 on Saturdays. You can also buy stamps at stationers and tobacconists.

Telephone
To dial Sweden from the UK, dial 00 46 followed by the area code (omitting the initial zero) followed by number. For Britain dial 009 44.

Time
GMT plus 1 (summer BST +1).

Public Holidays
New Year; Epiphany; Good Fri; Easter Mon; Labour Day; Ascension; Whit Sun/Mon; Midsummer, Sat between 20-26 June; All Saints, Sat between 31 Oct-6 Nov; Christmas, 24-26 Dec.

Shops
Open Mon-Fri 09.00-18.00. Sat 09.00-13.00/ 16.00. In some large towns department stores remain open until 20.00/22.00.

Food: The Swedes generally eat fairly early. Lunch can start at 11.00, the evening meal at 18.00. A typical Swedish 'Smorgasbord' can be enjoyed all over the country.

Motoring
Roads are much quieter than in the UK. Secondary roads may be gravel surfaced but are still good. Dipped headlights are obligatory.

Speed Limits: Caravans and motorhomes (3.5 tons) 31 mph (50 kph) in built up areas; 50 mph (80 kph) on other roads for caravans. Motorhomes 44 - 56 mph (70 - 90 kph) on other roads and 56 - 69 mph (90 - 110 kph) on motorways.

Fuel: Away from large towns, petrol stations rarely open 24 hrs. Buy diesel during working hours, it is rarely available at self service pumps. Credit cards generally accepted except in some 24 hr stations where payment must be made in 20/100 kr notes.

Parking: Meters are in use in several larger towns.

Overnighting
Allowed in most areas, with the permission of the landowner.

Note: Mosquitos can be a problem in summer (from June) - go prepared.

Useful Addresses
National Motoring Organisations:
Motormannens Riksforbund (M),AIT, Sturegatan 32, Stockholm. Tel: 08 7823800.
Kungl Automobil Klubben (KAK)FIA, Gyllenstiernsgatan 4, 11526, Stockholm. Tel: 0860 0055.

The sites in SWEDEN featured in this guide
are shown on the SCANDINAVIA map on page 376

SWEDEN - South

2640 Krono Camping Båstad-Torekov, Torekov, nr Båstad (Skåne)

Good quality site in woodland edging the sea on western Swedish coast north of Helsingborg.
This Krono camp is 500 m. from the fishing village of Torekov, 14 km. west of the home of the Swedish tennis WCT Open at Båstad on the stretch of coastline between Malmö and Göteborg. Useful en route from the most southerly ports, it is a very good site and worthy of a longer stay for relaxation. It has 525 large pitches (325 for touring units), all numbered and marked, mainly in attractive natural woodland (mostly pine and birch), with some on more open ground close to the shore. Of these, 350 have electricity and cable TV, 77 also having water and drainage. Three very good sanitary blocks include a modern one of high quality and two refurbished older blocks. Hot water is free throughout and there are facilities in each block for cooking, dishwashing, babies and disabled visitors. A laundry is at the reception complex. This modern complex is professionally run and is also home for a good shop, two small boutiques, a snack bar with takeaway, restaurant, pizzeria, minigolf, and a fishermen's style bar (Zorba's), open until 1 am. The spacious site covers quite a large area and there is a cycle track along the shore to the beach with bathing. Several good children's play areas (games organised in high season) and an outdoor stage for musical entertainment and dancing (also in high season). This well run site is a pleasant place to stay.

How to find it: From E6 Malmö - Göteborg road take Torekov/Båstad exit and follow signs for 20 km. towards Torekov. Site is signed 1 km. before village on right.

General Details: Open 16 April - 17 Sept. Restaurant, pizzeria and snack bar with takeaway (7/6-15/8). Bar. Shop and kiosk. Minigolf. Sports fields. Children's play areas. Bicycle hire. TV room. Beach. Fishing. Tennis close. Golf 1 km. Riding 3 km. Games, music and entertainment in high season. Laundry. Cooking facilities. Chemical disposal. Motorcaravan service point. Bungalows, tents and cabins for hire.

Charges 1999: Per unit Skr. 130 -170; electricity/TV connection 35. Credit cards accepted, not Eurocheques.

Reservations: Advised in high season, contact site for details. Address: 260 93 Torekov. Tel: 0431/364525. FAX: 0431/364625. E-mail: info@kronocamping.se.

2650 Skånes Djurparks Camping, Jularp, Höör (Skåne)

Unique, small, friendly, family run site in conservation area with unusual features and attractions.
This site is probably one of the most unusual we feature. It is adjacent to the Skånes Djurpark - a zoo park with Scandinavian species - and has on site a reconstructed Stone Age Village. The site is located in a sheltered valley and has some 90 large, level grassy pitches for caravans and motorhomes all with 10A electricity, a few with waste water drain, and a separate area for tents. There is a small, heated, family swimming pool behind reception, a mini shop for essentials and a children's playground. A restaurant is just outside the camp entrance. The most unusual feature of the site is the sanitary block - it is underground! The fully air-conditioned building houses a superb and ample complement of facilities including roomy showers in private cubicles, washbasins and British style WCs, two fully equipped kitchens, laundry and separate drying room and an enormous dining/TV room. Facilities for disabled people and baby changing. Hot water is free throughout. The site also has a number of underground, caveman style, 8 bed (dormitory type) holiday units which can be rented by families or private groups (when not in use by schools on educational trips to the Stone Age Village). They open onto a circular courtyard with barbecue/camp fire area and have access to the kitchens and dining room in the sanitary block. There are good walks through the nature park and around the lakes, where one can see deer, birds and other wildlife. Well placed for the new Copenhagen - Malmo bridge or the ferries, this is also a site for discerning campers who want something distinctly different.

How to find it: Turn off no. 23 road 2 km. north of Höör (at roundabout) and follow signs for Skånes Djurpark. Campsite entrance is off the Djurpark car park.

General Details: Open all year. Mini-shop (April - Oct). Café (June - Aug). Swimming pool (June - Aug). Restaurant nearby. Children's playground. Stone Age Village. Fishing 1.8 km. Riding and golf 8 km. Bicycle hire 3 km. Telephone. Tourist information. Cooking facilities. Laundry. Chemical disposal. Apartments for hire.

Charges 2000: Per unit Skr. 120; electricity 25 (summer) - 35 (winter). Credit cards accepted, but not Eurocheques.

Reservations: Recommended for high season (July/Aug). Address: Jularp, 243 93 Höör. Tel: 0413/553270. FAX: 0413/200 61. E-mail: info@grottbyn.com.

2655 Tingsryds Camping, Tingsryd (Småland)

Pleasant, well managed municipal site by Lake Tiken, well placed for Sweden's Glass District.
Tingsryds' 129 large pitches are arranged in rows divided by trees and shrubs, with some along the edge of a lakeside path (public have access). All have access to electricity (10A) and there is shade in parts. Access is from a tarmac perimeter road and the facilities are housed in buildings near the site entrance, with the reception building having the restaurant, cafe, bar and a small shop. The heated sanitary installations are in two buildings, one housing showers mostly with curtains (on payment, communal undressing), washbasins with mirrors, hand dryers, shaver/hairdryer sockets and British style WCs, the other a campers' kitchen with hobs and dining area, plus dishwashing sinks with further sinks outside under cover (hot water from separate tap), laundry with free ironing, facilities for disabled people and a family room. All are well maintained and very clean. The site is well lit at night. Adjacent to the site is a small beach, grassy lying out area, children's playground and lake swimming area and three tennis courts. Hire of canoes, fishing and minigolf are available on site (public access also). There are two large supermarkets, a heated indoor 'Waterworld', bowling alley, and further shops and restaurants in the town (1 km), which can be reached via a level footpath/cycle track directly from the site. The town hosts a Folk Festival and market in July each year. This site is an ideal place from which to explore the factories and shops of the 'Kingdom of Crystal'.

How to find it: Site is 1 km. from Tingsryd off road no. 120, well signed around the town.

General Details: Open 1 April - 20 Oct. Shop (1/5-15/9). Restaurant, cafe, bar (1/5-15/9). Tennis. Minigolf. Children's playground. Boules. Lake swimming. Beach volleyball. Canoe hire. Fishing. Bicycle hire 1 km. Golf 15 km. Telephones. Tourist information. Laundry. Cooking facilities. Chemical disposal. Motorcaravan services. Cabins for rent.

Charges 2000: Per unit Skr. 130; electricity 20. Credit cards accepted, but not Eurocheques.

Reservations: Recommended for high season. Write to site. Address: 362 32 Tingsryd. Tel: 0477/10554 (season) or 0477/11825 (off-season). FAX: 0477/31825.

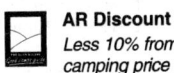

AR Discount
Less 10% from camping price

2680 Krono Camping Saxnäs, Färjestaden (Öland)

Large site well placed for touring Sweden's Riviera - fascinating and beautiful island of Öland.
This family-run site, part of the Krono group, has 420 marked and numbered touring pitches arranged in rows on open, well kept grassland dotted with a few trees, all with electricity (10A). A further unmarked area without electricity can accommodate around 60 tents. 320 of these pitches also have TV connections and a further 116 also have water connections. The site has about 130 long stay units and cabins for rent. Reception is efficient and friendly with good English spoken, and the site has a comprehensive tourist information bureau. There are now three heated sanitary blocks which provide a good supply of roomy private showers, washbasins, some washbasin/WC suites and WCs. There are facilities for babies and disabled visitors, good, well equipped laundry room and good campers' kitchen facilities with cookers, microwaves and dishwasher (free), together with dishwashing sinks. Hot water is free throughout. The site has a licensed restaurant, pizzeria, café, shop, minigolf, volleyball and football field together with two good children's playground. In high season children's games are organised and a crèche also operates. Dances are held twice weekly in season with other activities on other evenings. The beach is sandy, slopes very gently and is very safe for children. Nearby attractions include the 7 km. long Öland road bridge, Kalmar and its castle, museums and old town on the mainland, Eketorp prehistoric fortified village, Öland Djurpark and many old windmills.

How to find it: Cross Öland road bridge from Kalmar on road no. 137. Take exit for Öland Djurpark/Saxnäs, then follow campsite signs. Site is just north of the end of the bridge.

General Details: Open 15 April - 23 Sept. Shop (1/5-30/8). Pizzeria, licensed restaurant and café (all 1/5-30/8). Bar (1/7-31/7). Children's playground and crèche. Boules. Beach with volleyball. Fishing. Bicycle hire. Minigolf. Football. Riding 2 km. Golf 10 km. Family entertainment and activities organised. Telephones. Tourist information. Laundry. Cooking facilities. Gas supplies. Chemical disposal. Motorcaravan services. Cabins for rent.

Charges 1999: Per unit Skr. 80 - 155, with electricity 110 - 185, with TV also 120 - 195, with water also 130 - 205. Weekend and weekly rates available. Credit cards accepted, but not Eurocheques.

Reservations: Essential for high season (mid June - mid Aug). Address: 386 95 Färjestaden, Öland. Tel: 0485/35700. FAX: 0485/35664. E-mail: saxnas@krono-camping.oland.se.

AR Discount
Less 10% (not cabins)

SWEDEN - South

2675 Lysingsbadet Camping, Västervik (Småland)

Large site with unrivalled views of the 'Pearl of the East Coast' – Västervik, its fjords and islands.

One of the largest sites in Scandinavia, Lysingsbadet has around 1,000 large, mostly marked and numbered pitches, spread over a vast area of rocky promontory and set on different plateau, terraces, in valleys and woodland, or beside the water. It is a very attractive site, and one which never really looks or feels crowded even when busy. There are 83 full service pitches with TV, water and electrical connections, 163 with TV and electricity and 540 with electricity only, the remainder for tents. Reception is smart, efficient and friendly with good English spoken. The 10 modern sanitary blocks of various ages and designs house a comprehensive mix of showers, basins and WCs. All contain good quality fittings and are kept very clean. There are several campers' kitchens with dishwashing sinks, cookers and hoods, also 4 laundry rooms. Free hot water throughout and all facilities free of charge. Campers are issued with key cards which not only operate the entrance barriers, but are used to gain access to sanitary blocks, pool complex and other facilities. A further sanitary block with showers, changing rooms, basins, lockers and British style WCs serves the swimming pools. An hourly bus service to Västervik runs from the site entrance from May-September. On site facilities include a full golf course, minigolf, heated outdoor swimming pool complex with water slide and poolside café, sauna and solarium, children's playgrounds, boat hire, tennis, basketball, volleyball and fishing. A licensed restaurant is supplemented by a café/takeaway and a range of on site shops. For children, Astrid Lindgren's World theme park at Vimmerby is an easy day trip away and for adults the delights of the old town of Västervik and its shopping.

How to find it: Turn off E22 for Västervik and keep straight on at all junctions until first campsite sign. Follow signs to site.

General Details: Open all year. Supermarket and shops (15/5-31/8). Restaurant and café/takeaway (1/6-15/8). Swimming pool complex (15/6-31/8). Golf. Minigolf. Tennis. Basketball. Volleyball. Bicycle and boat hire. Fishing. Entertainment and dances in high season. Children's playgrounds. Quick Stop service. Telephones. Laundries. Hairdresser. Tourist information. Bus service. Cooking facilities. Motorcaravan services. Hotel rooms, cabins and caravans for rent.

Charges 2000: Per unit Skr. 120 - 180; electricity 35. Credit cards accepted.

Reservations: Advisable for peak season (July/Aug). Write to site for details. Address: 593 53 Västervik. Tel: 0490/36795. FAX: 0490/36175.

2665 SweCamp Rosenlund, Jönköping (Småland)

Town site overlooking Lake Vättern, ideal for visiting the important city of Jönköping.

Rosenlunds is a good site, useful as a break in the journey across Sweden or visiting the city during a tour of the Lakes. It is on raised ground overlooking the lake, with some shelter in parts. There are 280 pitches on well kept grass which, on one side, slopes away from reception. Some pitches on the other side of reception are flat and there are 200 electrical (10A), 100 cable TV and 40 water connections available. The owners have refurbished and extended the sanitary facilities which include hot showers on payment (some in private cubicles), washbasins, British style WCs and sauna, plus provision for disabled visitors and for babies. There is a laundry, dishwashing facilities, a well stocked mini-market, restaurant and a TV room. Jönköping is one of Sweden's oldest trading centres with a Charter dating back to 1284 and several outstanding attractions. These must include the Calle Ornemark wood carving centre at Riddersberg Manor, the museums of the 'safety match', ceramics and weaponry and, particularly, the superb troll artistry of John Bauer.

How to find it: Site is well signed from the E4 road on eastern side of Jönköping. Watch carefully for exit on this fast road.

General Details: Open all year. Shop. Restaurant (May - Sept). Playground. TV room. Bicycle hire. Minigolf. Fishing 500 m. Riding 7 km. Telephone. Tourist information. Laundry facilities. Chemical disposal. Motorcaravan service point. Caravans, rooms and cabins for hire.

Charges 1999: Per unit incl. all persons Skr. 135; electricity/TV 30. Credit cards accepted.

Reservations: Recommended for July - write to site for details. Address: Villa Bjorkhagen, 55454 Jönköping. Tel: 036/122863. FAX: 036/126687. E-mail: villabjorkhagen@surpnet.se.

2670 Grännastrandens Familjecamp, Gränna (Småland)

Large, lakeside site with modern facilities and busy continental feel, below the old city of Gränna.
Flat fields separate Gränna from the shore, one of which is occupied by the 25 acres of Grännastrandens where there are 500 numbered pitches, including a tent area and some pitches which are seasonally reserved. The site is flat, spacious and very regularly laid out on open ground with only a row of poplars by the lake to provide shelter, so a windbreak may prove useful against any onshore breeze. About 260 pitches have electrical connections (6/10A) and there is a good internal road system. There is one large, sanitary block in the centre of the site with modern, well kept facilities which include British style WCs, some with external access, washbasins, and free hot showers, some in private cubicles. There are dish and clothes washing sinks, laundry facilities and provision for disabled people, with a further small, older block by reception. Part of the lake is walled off to form an attractive swimming area with sandy beaches, slides and islands. Obviously the great attraction here is the lake. It offers beaches, bathing, fishing, sailing and superb coastal walks. Outstanding, however, is the 30 minute ferry crossing from the tiny harbour next to the site to Visingsö, the beautiful island reputedly inhabited for over 6,000 years. It is this excursion, complete with its gentle tour by horse drawn `remmalag' which alone warrants Grännastrandens as your base. Gränna is also the home of the famous peppermint rock which you can watch being made before you sample. In the Hallska Gården in the old city centre you will also find potteries, paper makers, basket weavers and goldsmiths. Gränna is also the centre of hot air ballooning and on 11 July each year there are ascents from Sweden's only `balloon airport'.

How to find it: Take Gränna exit from E4 road (no camping sign) 40 km. north of Jönköping. Site is signed in the centre of the town, towards the harbour and ferry.

General Details: Open 1 May - 30 Sept. Shop. Café outside site (1/5-31/8) or town restaurants close. TV room. Children's playground. Lake swimming area. Boating and fishing. Telephone. Laundry and drying. Cooking facilities. Chemical disposal. Motorcaravan services. Cabins and rooms to let.

Charges 1999: Per unit Skr. 140, with electricity 170. Credit cards accepted.

Reservations: Write to site for details. Address: Grännastrandens Familjecamp, Box 14, 563 21 Gränna, Småland. Tel: 0390/10706. FAX: 0390/41260.

2700 Borås Camping, Borås (Västergotland)

Pleasant municipal site in a park setting 2 km. north of the city centre.
Borås Camping is within easy walking distance of a swimming pool complex, Djurpark and shopping centre, and is convenient for ferries to and from Göthenberg. Located on the outskirts of Borås, this tidy, well managed site provides 500 large, numbered, level pitches, carefully arranged in rows on well kept grass with good tarmac perimeter roads. Electricity (10A) provided to 300 pitches and there is some shade in parts. Six good, modern sanitary blocks are clean and heated, providing hot showers, washbasins, WCs and facilities for babies and the disabled, in various combinations (the largest block new in '99). Good campers' kitchens have hobs, extractor hoods, and dishwashing sinks (free of charge) with laundry facilities are provided. Many activities are available both on the site and nearby, many free to campers; the excellent outdoor heated swimming pool complex, Alidebergsbadet, is only 400 m. away. Canoes and pedaloes are available on the small canal running through the site. Small shop for necessities and fast food service. Also on site is a Youth Hostel and many cabins for rent. The shopping precinct at Knalleland is only 500 m, the Zoo (Djurpark) is 400 m. The site can issue the 'Boråscard' which gives free and discounted access to city car parks, transport, museums and attractions during your stay.

How to find it: Exit road no. 40 from Göthenberg for Borås Centrum and follow signs to Djurpark and road no. 42 to Trollhåtten through the town. Turn left to site.

General Details: Open all year. Shop. Cafeteria and takeaway (full services 6/6-9/8). Several children's playgrounds. Minigolf. Bicycle hire. Swimming, tennis, frisbee, badminton, football, croquet, table tennis, jogging tracks, basketball all nearby. Telephones. Laundry. Cooking facilities. Motorcaravan service point. Tourist information. Cabins for rent.

Charges 1999: Per unit Skr. 110 - 145; electricity 25. Credit cards accepted

Reservations: One should always find room here. Write to site: Address: 500 04 Borås. Tel: 033/121434. FAX: 033/140582.

SWEDEN - West

2705 Lisebergs Kärralund Camping, Göteborg

Busy site, well positioned for visiting the amusement park and the city.

A well maintained site with 200 marked pitches, 150 with electricity (10A) and cable TV, 42 hardstand-ings, and several areas for tents. Pitches do vary in size, some are fairly compact and there are no dividing hedges, consequently units can be rather close together. Additionally there are cabins for rent, a budget hotel and a youth hostel. All this makes for a very busy site in the main season, which in this case means June, July and August. An advance telephone call to check for space is advisable. There are two heated sanitary buildings, the larger one fairly new, and a smaller one which is older and has limited facilities. However, both are well maintained and cleaned. They provide all the usual facilities, with controllable hot showers, a good suite for small children, dishwashing sinks and a laundry, kitchens with cooking facili-ties, and a complete suite for disabled visitors. Free hot water throughout. A breakfast buffet is served in low season from 08.00-10.00 (not 15/6-30/8), and there is a restaurant 300 m. from the site entrance. Reception has a very good range of tourist information, can provide advice on travel in the city, the Liseberg Amusement Park, and sells the Göteborg Card. The nearby Delsjö Camping (also a Lisebergs campsite) is only open in July.

How to find it: Site is about 2.5 km. east of city centre. Follow signs to Kärralund and campsite symbol from E20, E6 or Rv 40.

General Details: Open all year. Shop. Children's playground. TV room. Telephone. Cooking facilities. Laundry. Chemical disposal. Motorcaravan services. Tourist information. Cabins for rent.

Charges 1999: Per caravan and car Skr. 130-195; tent/car incl. 4 persons 120-175; tent/bike incl. 2 persons 100-150; tent/walker incl. 2 persons 90-130; extra tent 80-120; electricity 35. Credit cards accepted.

Reservations: Recommended from mid-June to end of August. Address: Olbersgatan 1, S-416 55 Göteborg. Tel: (0)31 840 200. FAX: (0)31 840 500. Email: boende.lgab@liseberg.se.

2706 Lisebergs Askim Strand Camping, Askim, nr Göteborg

Good quality site adjacent to beach, within easy reach of city.

This is a very pleasantly located site, close to a long gently sloping beach which is very popular for bathing. As a result the area behind the campsite is populated by many holiday homes and cabins. A very open site with very little shade, it has 276 mostly level, grassy pitches all with 10A electricity, plus two areas for tents. Many pitches are fairly compact, although there are some larger ones. There are two heated sanitary buildings, the larger of which is fairly new, the smaller has been recently refitted. Both are main-tained to a high standard. They provide all the usual facilities, with controllable hot showers, a good suite for small children, dishwashing sinks, a laundry, kitchens with cooking facilities, and a complete unit for disabled visitors. Hot water is free throughout. The keycard entry system operates the entrance barrier and access to the buildings and there is a night security guard (June-Aug). Reception has a range of tourist information, and can provide details of reductions on bus and taxi fares to the city, also selling the Göteborg Card. A small shop (24/6-8/8, 0800-2100) is well stocked and is supplemented by a snack bar in July.

How to find it: From E6, about 10 km. south of Göteborg, take exit signed Mölndal S and ports (Hamnar). Take the Rv 159 towards Frolunda, and watch for a slip-road to the right, signed to Askim and follow signs to campsite.

General Details: Open 7 May -29 August. Shop. Snack bar (July). Children's playground. TV room. Tourist information. Telephone. Cooking facilities. Laundry. Chemical disposal. Motorcaravan services. Cabins for rent.

Charges 1999: Per caravan or motorcaravan Skr. 140 - 180, tent 135 - 165; bicycle and tent 105 - 125; electricity 35. Credit cards accepted.

Reservations: Advised June-Aug. Address: Marholmsvagen, 436 45 Askim. Tel: (0)31 286 261. FAX: (0)31 681 335. E-mail: boende.lgab@liseberg.se.

For a list of sites which are open all year - see page 257

2710 Krono Camping Lidköping, Lidköping - Lake Vänern (Västergotland)

High quality, attractive site with lake and leisure facilities.
This attractive site provides about 430 pitches on flat, well kept grass. It is surrounded by some mature trees, with the lake shore as one boundary and a number of tall pines have been left to provide shade and shelter. There are 274 pitches with electricity (10A) and TV connections and 91 with water and drainage also, together with 60 cabins for rent. A tour operator takes a few pitches and the site takes a fair number of seasonal units. Excellent, modern sanitary facilities are provided in two identical blocks with under-floor heating, attractive decor and lighting (and music), and there is free hot water throughout. They have controllable hot showers (in roomy private cubicles with divider, hooks and seat), partitioned washbasins, British style WCs, make up and hairdressing areas with mirrors, electric points and shelves, baby room and facilities for the disabled. Dishwashing sinks are available outside each block. Good kitchens with cookers and microwaves are also provided. There is a laundry, a small shop (a shopping centre is very close) and a coffee bar with conservatory seating area in the reception complex. Very good playgrounds are provided for the children, together with a play field, TV room (cartoon videos shown) and an amusement and games room. Solarium, bicycle hire, minigolf and volleyball. The lake is available for watersports, boating and fishing with bathing from the sandy beach or there is a swimming pool complex (free for campers) adjacent to the site.

How to find it: From Lidköping town junctions follow signs towards Läckö then pick up camping signs turning right at second roundabout. Continue to site on left (0.5-1 km).

General Details: Open 13 April - 15 Sept (full services 13/6-14/8). Small shop. Coffee bar with snacks. Minigolf. Volleyball. Solarium. Children's playgrounds. TV room. Games and amusements room. Bicycle hire. Play field. Swimming pool adjacent. Lake swimming, fishing and watersports. Telephone. Tourist information. Laundry facilities. Cooking room. Motorcaravan services.

Charges 1999: Per unit Skr. 130 -160; electricity/TV connection 40, water and drainage 20.

Reservations: Write to site for details. Address: Läckögatan, 531 54 Lidköping. Tel: 0510/26804. FAX: 0510/21135.

2720 Hökensås Holiday Village and Camp Site, Tidaholm (Västergotland)

Well run site and holiday complex in wild, unspoiled national park.
This pleasant site is part of a holiday complex including wooden cabins for rent. It is relaxed and informal, with over 200 pitches either under trees or on a more open area at the far end, divided into rows by wooden rails. These are numbered and electricity (10A) is available on 130. Tents can go on the large grassy open areas by reception. The original sanitary block near reception is supplemented by one in the wooded area. These provide free hot showers with communal changing area and some curtained cubicles, open washbasins with hooks and mirrors, and WCs. There are separate saunas for each sex and facilities for the disabled and babies. A campers' kitchen is provided at each block with cooking, dish-washing and laundry facilities (irons on loan from reception). A children's playground, tennis court and minigolf are provided near the entrance and there is a small, but well stocked shop with a comprehensive angling section. A café with tables on a terrace outside also serves takeaway snacks. Hökensås is located just west of Lake Vättern and south of Tidaholm, in a beautiful national park of wild, unspoiled scenery. The park is based on a 100 km. ridge, a glacier area with many impressive boulders and ice age debris but now thickly forested with majestic pines and silver birches, with a small, brilliant lake at every corner. The forests and lakes provide wonderful opportunities for walking, cycling (gravel tracks and marked walks) angling, swimming and when the snow falls, winter sports.

How to find it: Approach site from no. 195 western lake coast road. at Brandstorp, about 40 km. north of Jönköping, turn west at petrol station and camp sign signed Hökensås. Site is about 9 km. up this road.

General Details: Open all year. Shop. Café with takeaway. Children's playground. Tennis. Minigolf. Sauna. Lake swimming. Fishing. Telephone. Tourist information. Laundry. Cooking facilities. Cabins for hire.

Charges 1999: Per unit Skr. 110 (more for Midsummer celebrations); electricity 30 - 35. Credit cards accepted.

Reservations: Write to site for details. Address: Blåhult, 522 91 Tidaholm. Tel: 0502/23053.

SWEDEN - West

2730 Ekudden Camping, Mariestad - Lake Vänern (Västergotland)

Well established site on the eastern shore of Lake Vänern with swimming pools adjacent.

Ekudden occupies a long stretch of the lake shore to the south of the town, in a mixed woodland setting, and next door to the municipal complex of heated outdoor pools and sauna. The lake, of course, is also available for swimming or boating and there are bicycles, tandems and canoes for hire. The spacious site can take 350 units and there are 230 electrical hook-ups (10A). Most pitches are under the trees but some at the far end of the site are on more open ground with good views over the lake. Sanitary facilities are provided in three low wooden cabins all of which have been refurbished or renewed. These have free hot showers, some with curtains and communal changing, some in private cubicles, and both open and cubicled washbasins. In addition there are facilities for the disabled with good access ramps and baby changing rooms. All are clean and well maintained. There are kitchens with cooking and dining facilities, dishwashing (free hot water) and other covered sinks, outside in groups of four (cold water only) around the site. The site becomes very busy in high season.

How to find it: Site is northwest of the town and well signed at junctions on the ring road and from the E20 motorway.

General Details: Open 1 May - 30 Sept. (full services 15/6-16/8). Shop. Licensed bar. Takeaway (high season). Swimming pools adjacent. Canoes, bicycles and tandems for hire. Children's playground. Minigolf. TV room. Lake swimming, boating and fishing. Entertainment in high season. Telephone. Tourist information. Laundry facilities. Cooking facilities. Mobile homes for hire.

Charges 1999: Per unit Skr. 100 - 130; electricity 30. Credit cards accepted.

Reservations: Essential in high season. Write to site. Address: 542 01 Mariestad. Tel 0501/10637. FAX: 0501/18601.

2740 Laxsjöns Camping Och Friluftsgård, Dals Långed (Dalsland)

Lakeside site with swimming pool in beautiful Dalsland region.

Laxsjöns is an all year round site, catering for winter sports enthusiasts as well as summer tourists and groups. On the shores of the lake, the site is in two main areas - one flat, near the entrance, with hardstandings and the other on attractive, sloping, grassy areas adjoining. In total there are 300 places available for caravans or motorcaravans, all with electricity (10A), plus more for tents. Rooms and cabins are also available for rent. The main toilet block has hot showers on payment (communal changing area), open washbasins, WCs and a hairdressing cubicle. With a further small block at the top of the site, the provision should be adequate. Other services include a shop, laundry, clothes drying rooms for bad weather, cooking rooms for tenters and provision for disabled visitors. Outside there is a good swimming pool (10 am - 9 pm.) with paddling pool, minigolf, tennis, trampolines and a playground. There is a restaurant at the top of the site with a good range of dishes in high season. In addition, there is a lake for swimming, fishing and canoeing (boats available). The site is located in the centre of Dalsland, west of Lake Vänern, in an area of deep forests, endless lakes and river valleys, and is one of the loveliest and most interesting regions in this always peaceful and scenic country.

How to find it: From Åmål take road no. 164 to Bengtfors, then the 172 towards Dals Långed. Site is signed about 5 km. south of the town 1 km. down a good road.

General Details: Open all year. Restaurant (high season). Shop. Tennis. Minigolf. Sauna. Children's playground. Swimming pool. Lake for swimming, Fishing and boating. Telephone. Laundry and drying facilities. Cooking facilities.

Charges 1999: Per unit Skr. 110 - 130; electricity 20.

Reservations: Advisable in peak season. Write to site for details. Address: 660 10 Dals Långed, Dalsland. Tel: 0531/30010. FAX: 0531/30555.

**All the sites in this guide are regularly inspected by our team
of experienced site assessors, but we welcome your opinion too.**

See Readers' Reports - page 366

2750 Årjäng SweCamp Sommarvik Resort, Årjäng (West Värmland)

Good quality site in beautiful surroundings beside lake Västra Silen, for family holidays.

Sommarvik has some 250 large, separated and numbered pitches arranged in terraces on a pine wooded hillside, some overlooking the lake; 100 of these have electrical connections, 30 are all service pitches and there is an area for groups at one end. It offers much in the way of outdoor pursuits and peaceful countryside. The site is served by five sanitary units which house a good mix of private shower cubicles (hot water on payment), washbasins (free hot water), WCs, family bathrooms, and facilities for disabled people and baby changing. All are kept clean. In addition there are good campers' kitchens with cookers and sinks, and laundry facilities. The site has 56 cabins for rent, 45 long stay units, with a youth hostel and conference centre also on site. A very large and smart restaurant offers a full range of meals, soft drinks, beers and wines, and takeaway meals. On site activities include swimming in the lake from a sandy beach (safe for children), canoe hire, windsurfing, rowing boats, fishing, sauna, tennis courts, football field, organised Elk safaris, minigolf, quizzes, guided walks, and there are good children's playgrounds. The site also organises local folk music during the main season. You can ride trolleys around the area on disused railway tracks or take a day trip to go gold panning. The site is within easy reach of the Norwegian border and Oslo. Skiing is also available (when there is snow) and there is an indoor swimming pool complex 3 km. away in Årjäng. This is a very scenic region and one which makes an ideal base for a family holiday with lots of activities and sightseeing trips available.

How to find it: Site is signed from roads nos. 172 and E18. It is 3 km. south of Årjäng Centrum.

General Details: Open all year. Restaurant and takeaway (1/6-1/9). Shop (all year). Minigolf. Lake swimming. Canoe, row boat and windsurfer hire. Bicycle hire. Fishing. Tennis. Sauna. Football field. Children's playgrounds. Range of organised activities. Riding 5 km. Golf 9 km. Telephone. Tourist information. Cooking facilities. Laundry. Chemical disposal. Motorcaravan services. 'Quick stop' pitches for overnight stays. Cabins for hire.

Charges 2000: Per tent (no electricity) Skr. 100 - 120; caravan or motorcaravan 130 - 200; electricity included. Credit cards accepted, but not Eurocheques.

Reservations: Recommended for peak seasons (summer and winter). Contact site. Address: 672 00 Årjäng. Tel: 0573/12060. FAX: 0573/12048. E-mail: swecamp@sommarvik.se.

AR Discount *Less 10% for camping; 20% for canoe hire*

2760 Frykenbaden Camping, Kil (Värmland)

Quiet, friendly site on the shores of Lake Fryken.

Frykenbaden Camping is in a wooded area and takes 250 units on grassy meadows surrounded by trees. One area nearer the lake is gently sloping, the other is flat with numbered pitches arranged in rows, all with electricity (6/120A), and many with satellite TV and phone connections also. Reception, a good shop and takeaway are located in a traditional Swedish house surrounded by lawns sloping down to the shore, with minigolf, a children's play barn and playground, with pet area, also close by. The main sanitary block is adjacent. It is of good quality and heated in cool weather with showers on payment, open washbasins, a laundry room and room for families or disabled people. With a further small block with equally good facilities, the overall supply is better than average for Swedish sites. Well equipped camper's kitchen with ovens, hobs and sinks together with tables and benches near the lake, where swimming and canoeing are possible. There is a good value restaurant at the adjacent golf club which can be reached by a pleasant walk. Fryken is a long, narrow lake, said to be one of the deepest in Sweden, and it is a centre for angling. Frykenbadens Camping is on the southern shore, and is a quiet, relaxing place to stay away from the busier, more famous lakes. There are plenty of other activities in the area (golf, riding, ski-ing in winter) and Kil is not too far from the Norwegian border.

How to find it: Site is signed from the no. 61 Karlstad - Arvika road, then 4 km. towards lake following signs.

General Details: Open 15 May - 15 Sept. (full service 15/6-16/8). Small shop. Snack bar and takeaway. Minigolf. Children's play barn and playground. Lake swimming. Canoes and bicycles for hire. Telephone. Tourist information. Campers' kitchen. Cabins for rent.

Charges 1999: Per unit Skr. 100 - 120, electricity 35; TV connection 15. Credit cards accepted.

Reservations: Write to site. Address: Frykenbaden PL. 1405, 665 00 Kil. Tel: 0554/40940. FAX: 0554/40945.

SWEDEN - Central

2800 Glyttinge Camping, Linköping (Östergötland)

Top quality site with enthusiastic and friendly management.

Only five minutes by car from the Ikea Shopping Mall and adjacent to a good swimming pool complex, Glyttinge is a most attractive site with a mix of terrain – some flat, some sloping and some woodland. It is maintained to a very high standard and there are flowers, trees and shrubs everywhere giving it a cosy garden like atmosphere. There are 239 good size, mostly level pitches of which 125 have electricity (10A) and 28 are fully serviced. The main centrally located sanitary block (supplemented by additional smaller facilities at reception) is modern, well constructed and exceptionally well equipped and maintained. It provides showers in private cubicles with dividers, hooks and seat, washbasins, and WC suites with basins, soap dispensers, hand dryers, and soothing music! There are excellent separate facilities for the disabled, a solarium, laundry and baby changing rooms. The superb kitchen and dining/TV room is fully equipped with everything you could possibly need to prepare and enjoy a meal. Hot water is free throughout. Children are well catered for - the manager has laid out a wonderful, fenced and very safe children's play area and, in addition, parents can rent (minimal charge) tricycles, pedal cars, scooters and carts. There is also a wet weather playroom for children, shop with gifts, fresh bread, milk, soft drinks and ices are sold. Takeaway snacks include burgers, pizzas and chips. Also on site are minigolf, a football field, and bicycle hire. Adjacent to the site is a heated outdoor swimming pool complex with 3 pools (charged). There is a bus stop at the camp gate. Attractions nearby include the old town of Gamla Linköping, Aviation Museum, Land Museum and the Ikea Shopping Mall. Also ask at reception about canal tours.

How to find it: Exit E4 Helsingborg - Stockholm road north of Linköping at signs for Ikea and site. Turn right at traffic lights and camp sign and follow signs to site.

General Details: Open 28 April - 3 Oct. Shop and takeaway (28/6-15/8). Swimming pool complex adjacent (1/5-25/8). Minigolf. Football. Bicycle hire. Children's playground. Fishing 5 km. Riding and golf 3 km. Telephones. Tourist information. Cooking facilities and dining/TV room. Laundry. Motorcaravan services. Cabins for hire.

Charges 2000: Per unit Skr. 120 - 140; electricity 30. Credit cards accepted, but not Eurocheques.

Reservations: Recommended for July/Aug. Write to site for details. Address: Berggardsvagen, 582 49 Linköping. Tel: 013/174928. FAX: 013/175923. E-mail: glyttinge@swipnet.se.

2820 Skantzö Bad Camping, Hallstahammar (Västmanland)

Attractive, well maintained municipal site by Strömsholms Kanal between Örebro and Stockholm.

A very comfortable and pleasant site just off the main E18 motorway from Oslo to Stockholm, this has 180 large marked and numbered pitches, 165 of these with electricity (10A). The terrain is flat and grassy, there is good shade in parts and the site is well fenced and locked at night. There are 22 new alpine style cabins for rent with window boxes of colourful flowers. Reception is very friendly. One sanitary block serving the camping area is located in the reception area and is maintained and equipped to a high standard, providing free hot showers (now in private cubicles with washbasin), basins (free hot water) and WCs, facilities for disabled people and baby changing. A new unit to the same high standards has been added at the far end of the site and both are heated. In addition there are good campers' kitchen facilities, a good laundry with drying room and lines, washing machine and dryer. Barbecue grill area. Cafeteria, fresh bread and milk, etc sold. Very large, fenced, outdoor, heated swimming pool and waterslide (free), children's playground, tennis and minigolf (charged) and a games area complex. Direct access to the towpath of the Stromsholms Kanal and nearby is the Kanal Museum. The site provides hire and transportation of canoes for longer canal tours. There are good walks and cycle trails all around the area, and excellent tourist information is available.

How to find it: Turn off E18 at Hallstahammar and follow road no. 252 to west of town centre and signs to campsite.

General Details: Open 1 May - 31 August. Cafeteria and shop (12/5-20/8). Swimming pool and waterslide (20/5-20/8). Minigolf. Tennis. Children's playground. Bicycle hire. Fishing. Canoe hire. Golf 9 km. Telephone. Conference room. Tourist information. Cooking facilities. Laundry. Chemical disposal. Motorcaravan services. Cabins for hire.

Charges 2000: Per unit Skr. 110; electricity 35. Credit cards accepted, but not Eurocheques.

Reservations: Write to site for details. Address: Box 506, 734 27 Hallstahammar. Tel: 0220/24305. FAX: 0220/24187. E-mail: turism@hallstahammar.se.

2840 Stockholm SweCamp Flottsbro, Huddinge

Neat, quiet lakeside site with ski slope and good security 18 km. south of Stockholm.

Flottsbro is a small site with good quality facilities and very good security, located some 18 km. south of Stockholm. There are 100 large numbered pitches for caravans and motorhomes and a separate unmarked area for tents. Pitches are arranged on level terraces, 65 with electricity (10A), but the site itself is sloping and the reception and restaurant are at the bottom with all the ski facilities and further good sanitary facilities with sauna. The main site road is tarmac. There are two other small sanitary units on the camping area and the modern facilities include free hot showers, WCs and washbasins, a suite for disabled people, baby changing facilities and a family bathroom. An excellent campers' kitchen has electric cookers and sinks with hot water, all free of charge. Small laundry with washing machine, dryer (charged for) and sink. The reception area is remote from the entrance but a very good security system is in place, campers have keys to the barrier and sanitary installations, there is a night guard and an entry phone/camera surveillance system on the entrance for good measure. Once you have negotiated the entry phone you will find a friendly and more personal service at reception. Do not be tempted to walk to reception from the gate, it is a long way down and a steep climb back. Other facilities on site include the ski slope and lift, restaurant which serves a selection of simple meals and snacks, beer, tea, coffee and soft drinks. The site has a small lakeside beach and grassy lying out area with children's playground and plenty of room for ball games. There is also minigolf, volleyball, frisbee, jogging track, canoe hire. A large supermarket and the local rail station are 10 minutes by car from the site. The area is also good for walking, cycling and cross-country skiing.

How to find it: Turn off E4 at Vårby/Huddinge and turn left on road no.259. After 2 km. turn right and follow signs to Flottsbro.

General Details: Open all year. Restaurant. Sauna. Minigolf. Volleyball. Frisbee. Jogging track. Canoe hire. Children's playground. Telephone. Tourist information. Cooking facilities. Laundry. Chemical disposal. Cabins for rent.

Charges 2000: Per caravan or motorcaravan Skr. 140; tent 110; electricity 35. Credit cards accepted, but not Eurocheques.

Reservations: Advisable for both summer and winter peak times. Write to site for details. Address: Box 1216, 141 25 Huddinge. Tel: 08/7785860. FAX: 08/7785755. E-mail: info@flottsbro.com.

2842 Bredängs Camping, Stockholm

Busy city site, with easy access to city centre

Bredängs is a large, fairly level site with very little shade. In total there are 500 pitches, including 115 with hardstanding and 180 with electricity (10A), with a separate area for tents. Four heated sanitary units provide British style WCs, controllable hot showers, with some washbasins in cubicles. The latest (built '97) also has a baby changing room, a unit for disabled people and a first aid room. They are cleaned twice daily. Cooking and dishwashing facilities are provided in three units around the site, and there is a laundry with washing machines and dryers, and separate saunas (18.00-21.00). The well stocked shop (1/5-30/9) has fresh fruit and vegetables, bread, cards, stamps, etc. and there is a small cafe (1/5-12/9) next door serving fast food and providing a small seating area/patio. Reception is open from 07.00-23.00 in the main season (17/5-29/8), reduced hours in low season, and English is spoken. They can provide the Stockholm card, or a three-day public transport card. Stockholm has many events and activities all year round, you can take a circular tour on a free sightseeing bus, various boat and bus tours, or view the city from the Kaknäs Tower (155 m). The nearest Metro station is five minute walk, trains run about every ten minutes between 05.00 and 02.00, and the journey takes about twenty minutes. The local shopping centre is five minutes away and a two minute walk through the woods brings you to a very attractive lake and beach.

How to find it: Site is about 10 km. southwest of city centre. Turn off E3/4 at Bredängs signpost and follow clearly marked site signs.

General Details: Open 1 April - 31 October. Shop. Café. Sauna. Children's playground. Tourist information. Telephone. Cooking facilities. Laundry. Chemical disposal. Motorcaravan services and car wash. Youth hostel and rooms for rent.

Charges 1999: Per unit Skr. 160 - 170; electricity 25. Credit cards accepted, but not Eurocheques. Discounts for pensioners in low season.

Reservations: Advised for main season. Address: Stora Sällskapets väg, 127 31 Skärholmen. Tel: (0)8 977 071. FAX: (0)8 708 7262.

SWEDEN - East

2835 Orsa Grönklitt Camping, Orsa (Dalarna)

Quiet, budget priced site, adjacent to the Grönklitt Bear Park

Primarily designed for winter, with a ski slope adjacent, the site is a rather large and featureless, gravel hardstanding, providing room for more than 50 units with electricity (10A) available to all, but particularly good for larger motorcaravans. In summer, this quietly located site rarely has more than a dozen occupants, yet it is half the price of the crowded, often noisy sites in Orsa town 14 km. away. The excellent, very modern, small sanitary unit is heated. It has one unisex WC with external access and, inside for each sex, there is one cubicle with WC and washbasin, and two hot showers with curtains and communal changing area plus a seat and masses of hooks. There are also hairdryers and soap dispensers, a suite for the disabled, drying room and chemical disposal point. A well equipped kitchen has two hobs and two dishwashing sinks. All showers, hairdryers, hot water, drying and kitchen facilities are free of charge. Reception is located in the holiday centre with its rental cabins, inn, tourist information and other services, about 1 km. below the camping area, and one should book in here and obtain a key for the sanitary unit before proceeding to the site. The Grönklitt Bear Park, with bears, wolves, and lynx is within a short scramble up the hillside from the site and there are magnificent views over this scenic lakeland area.

How to find it: From Orsa town centre follow the signs to Grönklitt and `Björn Park'. Site is 14 km.

General Details: Open all year. Kitchen. Drying room.

Charges 1999: Per unit, incl. all persons Skr. 105 - 190; electricity 35 - 40. Credit cards accepted.

Reservations: Not necessary. Address: Box 23, 794 21 Orsa. Tel: 0250/462 00. FAX: 0250/461 11. E-mail: fritid@orsa-gronklitt.se.

2845 Svegs Camping, Sveg (Jamtland)

Neat, riverside municipal site, on the 'Inlandsvagen' route through Sweden.

The town centre is only a short walk from this friendly municipal site, with two supermarkets, café and tourist information office adjacent. The 160 pitches are in rows, on level grass, divided into bays by tall hedges, and with electricity (10/16A) available to 70. The sanitary facilities provide British style WCs, stainless steel washing troughs, controllable hot showers with communal changing areas, and a unit for disabled visitors. These are in the older style, functional rather than luxurious, and although a little short on numbers will probably suffice at most times as the site is rarely full. The kitchen and dining room with TV, has four full cookers and sinks, plus more dishwashing sinks outside under cover. Free hot water throughout. Laundry facilities include a washing machine and dryers, and an ironing board (iron on loan from reception). The site has boats, canoes, cycles and rickshaws for hire, and the river frontage has a barbecue area with covered seating and fishing platforms. Alongside the river with its fountain, and running through the site is a pleasant well lit riverside walk. Places to visit include the town with its lovely church and adjacent gardens, some interesting old churches in the surrounding villages, and 16th Century Remsgården, 14 km. to the west.

How to find it: Site is off road 45 behind the tourist information office in Sveg.

General Details: Open all year. Children's play area. TV room. Minigolf. Canoe, boat, rickshaw and bicycle hire. Fishing. Kitchen. Laundry. Chemical disposal.

Charges 1999: Per unit Skr. 110 - 160; tent 60 - 70; electricity 30 - 40. Credit cards accepted.

Reservations: Contact site. Address: Kyrkogränd 1, 842 32 Sveg. Tel: 0680/107 75 FAX: 0680/103 37.

For guidance on taking your dog on holiday to Europe, see page 348

For a list of sites where dogs are not accepted, see page 347

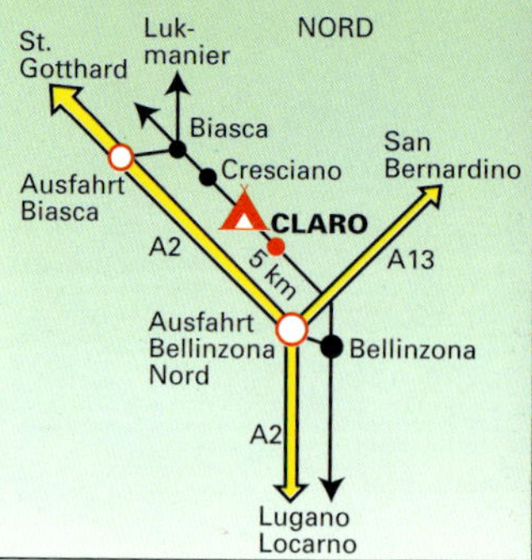

Select Site Reservations

The leading experts in organising continental travel for the independent camper, caravanner and motorcaravanner.

Friendly Personal Service

First Hand Knowledge of Sites

Expert Advice on Driving Abroad

Wide Choice of Ferry Route

Advance Book Any Number of Sites

Stay As Long As You Like

Comprehensive Holiday Insurance with Multi-Trip Option

Highly Competitive Ferry-Inclusive Rates

Free Travel Pack with Maps, Guides, GB Stickers etc

Excellent Low Season Prices

Tour As You Please at over 100 top sites.

For Colour Brochure contact:-
Select Site Reservations, Travel House, 34 Brecon Road, Abergavenny, Monmouthshire, NP7 5UG
Tel 01873 859876 (24 hrs service)
Web site www.select-site.com

2850 Östersunds Camping, Östersund (Jamtland)

Extensive, modern, woodland site, a good base for exploring central Sweden

Östersund lies on Lake Storsjön, which is Sweden's Loch Ness, with 200 sightings of the monster dating back to 1635, and more recently captured on video in 1996. Also worthy of a visit is the island of Frösön where settlements can be traced back to pre-historic times. This large site has 300 pitches, electricity (10A) and TV socket available on 120, all served by tarmac roadways. There are also 41 tarmac hardstandings available, and over 200 cottages, cabins and rooms for rent. The sanitary facilities are in three units, two providing British style WCs, washbasins and controllable hot showers (on payment) with communal changing areas, plus suites for the disabled and baby changing; the third has four family bathrooms each containing WC, basin and shower. There are two kitchens, each with full cookers, hobs, fridge/freezers and double sinks (all free of charge), and excellent dining rooms. Laundry facilities include three washing machines (charged) and dryers and drying cabinet (free). Also on site is a very good motorhome service point suitable for all types of unit including American RVs, and a children's playground. Adjacent to the site are the municipal swimming pool complex with cafeteria (indoor and outdoor pools), a Scandic hotel with restaurant, minigolf, and a Statoil filling station. A large supermarket and bank are just 500 m. from the site, and Ostersund town centre is 3 km.

How to find it: Site is to the south of the town off road 605 towards Torvalla, turn by Statoil station and site entrance is immediately on right. (well signed from around the town).

General Details: Open all year. Children's playground. Kitchen. Laundry. Motorcaravan service point. Cottages, cabins and rooms for rent.

Charges 1999: Per unit Skr. 125 - 150 (incl. electricity/TV), 90 - 150 (without). Credit cards accepted (not Amex).

Reservations: Contact site. Address: Krondikesvagen 95, 831 46 Östersund. Tel: 063/14.46.15. FAX: 063/14.43.23. E-mail: ostersundscamping@ostersund.se.

2855 Flogsta Camping, Kramfors (Västernorrland)

Delightful small municipal site, a good base to explore the 'High Coast'.

Kramfors lies just to the west of the E4, and travellers may well pass by over the new Höga Kusten bridge (one of the largest in Europe), and miss this friendly little site. The area of Ådalen and the High Coast, which reaches as far as Örnsköldsvik, is well worth a couple of days of your time, also Skuleskogen National Park, and Norfallsvikens, an old fishing village with many original buildings. The attractive garden-like campsite has around 50 pitches, 21 with electrical connections (10A), which are arranged on level grassy terraces, separated by shrubs and trees into bays of 2-4 units. All overlook the municipal swimming pool complex (one day free admission to campers), and attractive minigolf course. The non-electric pitches are on an open terrace nearer reception, and there are 16 rental cabins on site. Excellent sanitary facilities consist of nine well equipped family bathrooms, each with British style WC, basin with soap dispenser and hand dryer, shower (on payment), plus a laundry with washing machine and dryer. These are supplemented by more WCs and showers in the reception building with a free sauna facility. A separate building houses the kitchen, with hot-plates, fridge/freezer and TV/dining room (all free of charge). Also on-site is a small children's play area on a sandy base. The reception building has a small shop and snack-bar and is staffed 07.00-23.00 hours from 9/6-11/8. Outside these dates a warden calls daily. The town centre with supermarkets and restaurants is a 20 minute easy walk through a housing estate, and do use the excellent covered and elevated walkway to cross the main road and railway to the pedestrian shopping precinct with its floral arrangements and fountain.

How to find it: Well signed from road 90 in the centre of Kramfors, the site lies to the west in a rural location beyond a housing estate and by the Flogsta Bad, municipal swimming pool complex.

General Details: Open May - end Sept. Shop. Snack-bar. TV. Children's playground. Laundry. Kitchen. Cabins for rent.

Charges 1999: Per unit Skr. 85 - 100; cyclist/hiker and tent 55; electricity 25.

Reservations: Contact site. Address: 872 80 Kramfors. Tel: 0612/100 05. FAX: 0612/71.13.13.

SWEDEN - North

2860 Umeå Camping, Umeå (Västerbotten)

Good quality municipal site, on outskirts of university city.

An ideal stop-over for those travelling the E4 coastal route, or a good base from which to explore the area, this campsite lies 6 km. from the town centre, almost adjacent to the Nydalsjön lake, ideal for fishing, windsurfing and bathing. There are 320 grassy pitches arranged in bays of 10-20 units, divided by shrubs and small trees, all with electricity (10A), and some are fully serviced (electricity, water, waste water). The large, heated, central sanitary unit is modern and well equipped with British style WCs, open washbasins, controllable hot showers with communal changing areas, and a sauna. There is a well equipped kitchen with a large dining room adjacent, and a laundry with five washing machines (on payment), two dryers and ironing boards. The showers, kitchen facilities, hot water and dryers are all free of charge. These facilities are supplemented in high season by a basic smaller unit, plus a 'portacabin' style unit both with WCs and basins only. Outside the site adjacent to the lake, but with direct access, are football pitches, a small open-air pool with waterslide, minigolf, mini-car driving school, skateboard ramp, volleyball, a mini-farm and there are cycle and footpaths around the area. Umeå is also a port for ferries to Vasa in Finland (4 hrs).

How to find it: From the E4 on the northern outskirts of the town, turn at traffic lights, where site is signed.

General Details: Open all year. Shop and snack-bar (summer). Volleyball. Children's playgrounds. Bicycle hire. Boat hire. Fishing. Riding 15 km. Golf 18 km. Kitchen. Laundry. Car wash. Chemical disposal. Cabins for rent.

Charges 2000: Per unit Skr. 135; electricity 30; serviced pitch 170. Credit cards accepted, but not Eurocheques.

Reservations: Contact site. Address: Nydala Fritidsområde, 901 84 Umeå. Tel: 090/703600. FAX: 090/702610.

2865 Camp Gielas, Arvidsjaur (Norrbotten)

Modern site with excellent sporting facilities on outskirts of town.

This site is well shielded on all sides by trees, providing a very peaceful atmosphere. The 150 pitches, 80 with electricity (16A) and satellite TV connections, are level on sparse grass and accessed by tarmac roadways. There are two modern heated sanitary units with British style WCs, open washbasins and controllable hot showers with divider and seat (on payment), a unit for the disabled, well equipped kitchens (free of charge), also a laundry with washing machine and dryer. The unit by the tent area also has facilities for the disabled and baby changing. The sauna at the sports hall is free to campers, who may also use all the indoor sporting, gymnasium and solarium facilities at the usual rates. Also on site is a snack-bar. The lake on the site is suitable for boating, bathing and fishing and other amenities include tennis courts, minigolf, canoe and boat hire and children's playgrounds, There is a swimming pool and a 9-hole golf course nearby, and hunting trips can be arranged.

How to find it: Site is well signed from road 95 in the town.

General Details: Open all year. Snack bar. Minigolf. Children's playgrounds. Sauna. Solarium. Sporting facilities. Boat and canoe hire. Lake swimming. Fishing. Bicycle hire 2 km. Riding 500 m. Golf 200 m. Winter golf course on snow on site. Kitchen. Laundry. Car wash. Chemical disposal. Cottages, cabins and apartments for rent.

Charges 2000: Per unit Skr. 100; hiker's tent 70; electricity (incl. satellite TV connection) 40. Credit cards accepted, but not Eurocheques.

Reservations: Contact site. Address: Jarnvägsgatan 111, 933 22 Arvidsjaur. Tel: 0960/55600 FAX: 0960/10615.

2870 Jokkmokks Turistcenter, Jokkmokk (Norrbotten)

Attractive municipal site in a popular tourist area, 8 km. from Arctic Circle.

Large and well organised, this site is bordered on one side by the river and with woodland on the other, just 3 km. from the town centre. It has 170 level, grassy pitches, with an area for tents, plus 59 cabins and 26 rooms for rent. Electricity (10A) is available to all touring pitches. The heated sanitary buildings provide British style WCs, mostly open washbasins and controllable showers, a few in cubicles with divider and seat. A unit by reception has a baby bathroom, a fully equipped suite for disabled visitors, games room, plus a well appointed kitchen and launderette. A further unit with WCs, basins, showers plus a sauna, is adjacent to the heated open-air swimming pool complex (25 x 10 m. main pool with water slide, two smaller pools and a paddling pool with lifeguard). All facilities, hot water and the pools are free. There is a very smart restaurant and bar, plus takeaway. Free river fishing. Opportunities for snow-mobiling, cross-country skiing in spring, or ice fishing in winter. Nearby attractions include the first hydro-electric power station at Porjus, built 1910-15, with free tours 15/6-15/8, Vuollerim (40 km.) reconstructed 6,000 year old settlement, with excavations of the best preserved ice-age village, or try visiting for the famous Jokkmokk Winter Market (first Thurs-Sat February) or the less chilly Autumn Market (end of August).

How to find it: Site is 3 km. from the centre of Jokkmokk on road 97.

General Details: Open all year. Shop, restaurant and bar (in summer). Takeaway (high season). Swimming pools (summer). Sauna. Bicycle hire. New children's playground. Minigolf. Football field. Games machines. Fishing (licences sold). Riding 2 km. Kitchen. Laundrette. Chemical disposal.

Charges 1999: Per unit Skr. 120 - 150; car and small tent 90; electricity 30. Credit cards accepted (not Amex).

Reservations: Contact site. Address: Box 75, 962 22 Jokkmokk. Tel: 0971/123 70. FAX: 0971 124 76.

SWITZERLAND

This land locked country, with 22 independent Cantons sharing languages with its four neighbours, has some of the most outstanding scenery in Europe which, coupled with its cleanliness and commitment to the tourism industry, makes it a very attractive proposition. The Swiss are well known for their punctuality and hard work and have the highest standard of living of any country in Europe, which makes Switzerland one of the most expensive yet problem free countries to visit.

The Berner Oberland is probably the most visited area with a concentration of picturesque peaks and mountain villages, though the highest Alps are those of Valais in the southwest with the small busy resort of Zermatt giving access to the Matterhorn. Zurich in the north is a German speaking city with a wealth of sightseeing. Geneva, Montreux and Lausanne on the northern shores of Lake Geneva make up the bulk of French Switzerland, whilst the southernmost canton, Ticino, is home to the Italian speaking Swiss, with the resorts of Lugano and Locarno.

For further information contact:

Swiss National Tourist Office, Swiss Centre, Swiss Court, London W1V 8EE
Tel: 020 7734 1921   Fax: 020 7734 4577   E-mail: stlondon@switzerlandtourism.com

Population
6,800,000, density 165.5 per sq.km.

Capital
Bern.

Climate
No country in Europe combines within so small an area such marked climatic contrasts. In the northern plateau surrounded by mountains the climate is mild and refreshing. South of the Alps it is warmer, coming under the influence of the Mediterranean. The Valais is noted for its dryness.

Language
The national languages of Switzerland are German 65% (central and east), French 18% (west), Italian 10% (south), Romansh - a derivative of Latin 1% (south east), and others 6%. Many Swiss, especially those involved in the tourism industry speak English.

Currency
The unit of currency is the Swiss franc, divided into 100 centimes, coming in coins of 5, 10, and 20 centimes and Sfr 0.5, 1, 2, 5. Notes are Sfr 10, 20, 50, 100, 500, 1000.

Banks
Open Mon-Fri 08.30-16.30. Closed for lunch in Lausanne and Lucerne 12.30-13.30/14.00

Post Offices
Open Mon-Fri 07.30-12.00 and 13.45-18.30. Sat 07.30-11.00 or later in some major city offices.

Time
GMT plus 1 (summer BST +1).

Telephone
From the UK, the code is 00 41 followed by the area code (omitting the initial zero) followed by number. Phone cards are available.

Public Holidays
New Year; Good Fri; Easter Mon; Ascension; Whit Mon; Christmas, 25 Dec; Other holidays are observed in individual Cantons.

Shops
Generally open Mon-Fri 08.00- 12.00 and 14.00-18.00. Sat 08.00-16.00. Often closed Monday mornings.

Food: The cost of food in shops and restaurants can be expensive; it may be worthwhile to consider 'stocking-up' on basic food necessities purchased in the UK, or elsewhere in Europe. Note that, officially,only 2.5 kgs per head of foodstuffs may be imported into the country

The local specialities to try if there is money in the budget are 'Fondue' or 'Raclette' in French speaking Switzerland and 'Rösti' in German speaking areas.

Motoring
The road network is comprehensive and well planned. If the roads are narrow and circuitous in parts, it is worth it for the views. An annual road tax is levied on all cars using Swiss motorways and the 'Vignette' windscreen sticker must be purchased at the border (credit cards not accepted), or in advance from the Swiss National Tourist Office , plus a separate one for a towed caravan or trailer .

Fuel: On motorways, service stations are usually open from 0600- 2200/2400. On other roads it varies 0600/0800-1800/2000. Outside these hours petrol is widely available from 24 hr automatic pumps - Sfr 10/20. Credit cards generally accepted.

Speed Limits: Cars in built-up areas 31 mph (50 kph), other roads 50 mph (80 kph), and motorways 75 mph (120 kph). For towing vehicles on motorways 50 mph (80 kph).

Parking: Blue Zones are in operation in certain cities, discs obtainable from most petrol stations, restaurants and police stations.

Overnighting
Only permitted at a few motorway rest areas.

SWITZERLAND

905 Camping Bois du Couvent, La Chaux-de-Fonds

Hill-top site at 1,060 m. in the Swiss Jura.

The road from Lake Neuchatel to Chaux-de-Fonds, which stands just inside the Swiss border with France in the northwest of Switzerland, has been greatly improved with parts to motorway standard. La Chaux-de-Fonds is the biggest watch and clock-making centre in Switzerland and one of the largest agricultural centres. Completely destroyed by fire in 1794, it was rebuilt to a geometric plan. Postage stamps for Switzerland and many foreign countries are printed here. Camping Bois du Couvent is situated at the southern end of the town on a hill-top with splendid views. More than half the pitches are taken by static caravans but the 70 places for tourists, with 10A electrical connections, although not marked, are obvious, with an open lawn for tents. The site has a pleasant appearance and tarmac and gravel roads link the terraces, some of which have shade from tall trees. There is a good restaurant, but no shop as a supermarket is 1 km. away in town. Very little English is spoken but the warden has good tourist information available. Two sanitary blocks have British style WCs, free hot water in washbasins and on payment in sinks and showers. This is a good area for walking.

How to find it: Site is signed and is at south end of La Chaux-de-Fonds. Coming from Neuchatel, turn left at second roundabout after tunnel.

General Details: Open all year. 60,000 sq.m. Restaurant (open all year except Tues, 08.00 - midnight). Shop 1 km. Children's playground. Some entertainment for children in summer. Minigolf 300 m. Bicycle hire and tennis 100 m. Clock museum 1 km. Heated pool 500 m. Washing machine and dryer. Chemical disposal. Chalets, bungalows and caravans for hire.

Charges 2000: Per person Sfr. 3.50 - 4.50; child (4-16 yrs) 1.50 - 2.00; caravan 8.00 - 10.00; motorcaravan 12.00; family tent 7.00 - 9.00; small tent 6.00 - 7.00; car 3.00; m/cycle 2.00; dog 3.00; electricity 3.00 - 4.00 (8.00 in winter)l local tax 2.00.

Reservations: Write to site. Address: 2301 La Chaux-de-Fonds. Tel: 079/240 50 39. FAX: 032/914 48 77.

903 Camping Paradis Plage, Colombier, nr Neuchatel

Pleasant lakeside site with good facilities, near French border.

This area of Switzerland deserves to be better known as there is much of interest here near the French border. Paradis Plage is nicely situated on the shores of Lake Neuchatel, with access to the lake. The 160 pitches available to tourists are numbered and marked out on flat grass under a covering of tall, mature trees. All have electricity (10A) and some have gravel hardstanding for caravans and motorcaravans. There are separate areas of grass where pitches are not marked, including a small overflow section for individuals or groups. The 200 static pitches are occupied mainly at weekends and high season and are neatly set out together in rows. Although a motorway runs over the site near the entrance, we did not notice any undue noise as this seemed to be screened out by the trees. Access to the site is rather narrow but adequate. A very pleasant restaurant with a large terrace, well stocked shop and takeaway (all to end Sept) form the focal point in the centre with views through the trees to the lake. Three heated sanitary blocks, well sited around the site, have been refurbished and make a good provision with British style WCs and a baby room. Laundry rooms also have electric cooking rings for free use. Friendly, English speaking management. Well placed for walking in the Jura or touring the Bernese Oberland.

How to find it: Leave the short stretch of motorway at Colombier from where site is signed.

General Details: Open 1 March - 31 Oct. 40,000 sq.m. Restaurant and shop (1/3-25/9). Small children's pool (20/6-20/8). New children's play area. Table tennis. Bicycle hire. Fishing. Boating. Sports complex nearby with indoor and outdoor tennis courts, squash, bowls and football. Riding 3 km. Golf 12 km. Washing machines and dryers. Gas supplies. Chemical disposal. Motorcaravan services.

Charges 2000: Per person Sfr. 6.00; child (6-15 yrs) 3.00; tent or caravan 8.00 - 15.00; motorcaravan 9.00 - 15.00; car 1.00 - 2.00; m/cycle 1.00; electricity 3.50; local tax 2.00 per pitch. Discounts for stays over 17 days (10%) up to 30 days (23%). Credit cards accepted.

Reservations: Write to site. Address: 2013 Colombier. Tel: 032/841 24 46. FAX: as phone.

909 Camping Avenches Port-Plage, Avenches

Large site with good boating possibilities on Lake Murten.

This is a large site by Swiss standards, located in a quiet, open situation directly on Lake Murten with its own marina and excellent access to the water. The site is well cared for, with 200 out of the 700 pitches available for tourists. These are of reasonable size (80 sq.m.) with shade in parts from tall trees and electrical connections are available (6A). At the centre of the site is a large building which houses a general shop, butcher, baker and the main sanitary facilities. A separate restaurant is nearer the lake shore. The three toilet blocks are all of excellent quality with British style WCs. With its location directly on the shores of the lake, there are many leisure opportunities including watersports, fishing and sandy beaches for swimming or relaxing. Special events are organised for adults and children in July/Aug.

How to find it: Site is signed near Avenches on the Bern - Lausanne road no.1 (not the motorway).

General Details: Open 1 April - 30 Sept. 80,000 sq.m. Electrical connections most pitches. Restaurant. Shop, butcher and baker. First aid room. Children's playground. Watersports, boating and lake swimming. Pedaloes. Chemical disposal. Motorcaravan services.

Charges 1999: Per person Sfr. 7.00; child (4-16 yrs) 4.00; car 4.00; caravan 11.00; tent 7.00 - 11.00, acc. to size; motorcaravan 15.00; electricity 4.00; local tax 1.00.

Reservations: Write to site with Sfr. 20 fee. Address: Camping-Port-Plage, 1580 Avenches. Tel: 026/675 17 50. FAX: 026/675 44 69.

906 TCS Camping Caravaning Kappelenbrücke, Bern

Good site for overnight or longer stay, near city.

This well established site, being just outside the Federal Capital, is conveniently placed either for an overnight stop or for exploring the city and surrounds. A frequent bus service to the city passes the entrance. The 305 pitches (230 for touring) are numbered but not marked out and you choose your own place; cars are parked away from the pitches. All have electricity (4A or more) and there are special pitches for motorcaravans. There are some static units but there should always be room. Two new toilet blocks are of exceptional quality, with British WCs, enclosed washbasins with free hot water; also in the showers. One block is heated in cool weather. The sinks for laundry and dishwashing have free hot water and are under cover. There is a good children's playground, and the shop also serves drinks which can be taken to a pleasant rest room nearby or consumed on the terrace. This pleasant, well cared for site is near a small lake which is unsuitable for bathing, although there is now, however, a swimming pool and children's pool on site. It is probably the best site for visiting Bern.

How to find it: Take Bethlehem exit from N1 motorway on western side of Bern, towards Aarberg, and site will be seen on right before river.

General Details: Open all year except 11-31 January. 35,000 sq.m. Electrical connections throughout. Shop/bar. TV room. Day room. Children's playground. Table tennis. Fishing. Bicycle hire. Baby room. Washing machines and dryers. Chemical disposal.

Charges 1999: Per person Sfr. 4.50 - 6.50; child (6-16 yrs) 50%; tent or caravan 5.00 - 17.00, acc. to type; motorcaravan 19.00; electricity 3.00 or 4.00; local tax 1.40. Credit cards accepted.

Reservations: Write to site. Address: Wohlenstrasse 62c, 3032 Hinterkappelen (BE). Tel: 031/901 10 07. FAX: 031/901 25 91. E-mail: cpg@tcs.ch.

900 Camping Waldhort, Reinach, Basel/Basle

Satisfactory site for night halts or visits to Basel.

Although there are almost twice as many static caravan pitches as spaces for tourists, this is a quiet site on the edge of a residential district, within easy reach of Basel. The site is flat, with 220 level pitches on grass with access from the tarmac road which circles round inside the site. Trees are now maturing to give some shade. All pitches have electricity (6A) and are situated near the good quality, central sanitary block. This has British WCs, free hot water and facilities for disabled people. Owned and run by the Camping and Caravanning Club of Basel, it is a neat, tidy and orderly site and there is usually space available. An extra, separate camping area has been added behind the tennis club which has pleasant pitches and good sanitary facilities. Reinach is within walking distance from where there is a tram service into Basel.

How to find it: Take Basel - Delémont motorway spur, exit at `Reinach-Nord' and follow camp signs.

General Details: Open 18 March - 21 Oct. 23,000 sq.m. Small shop with terrace for drinks. Children's playground with 2 small pools. Table tennis. Swimming pool and tennis next to site. Washing machine and dryer. Chemical disposal. Motorcaravan services.

Charges 2000: Per person Sfr. 7.00; child (6-14 yrs) 4.50; car 3.50; tent 10.00; caravan or motorcaravan 15.00; electricity included. Credit cards accepted.

Reservations: made for main season; advance payment asked for single nights, otherwise no deposit. Address: Heideweg 16, 4153 Reinach bei Basel. Tel: 061/711 64 29. FAX: 061/711 48 33.

SWITZERLAND

912 Camping Lido Luzern, Lucerne/Luzern

Site in good touring area popular with the British.

Luzern is a traditional holiday resort of the British and this site has many British visitors. It lies near the shore of Lake Luzern, just outside the town itself. Next to the site (but not associated with it so you have to pay for entrance) is the Lido proper, which has a large sandy beach, bathing in the lake and sports fields. The town of Luzern has excellent shopping and sightseeing; one could walk there along the lake in about 20 minutes, or nearby buses run into town up to midnight. The site is divided into separate sections for caravans, motorcaravans and tents; the first two have hardstandings which, in effect, provide rather formal and small individual pitches. There are about 100 electrical connections (10A). Quiet in early season, from late June to late August it usually becomes full and, especially in the tent section, can at times seem rather crowded. The sanitary installations are in three sections, two being close to the reception area. A large and very modern block incorporates toilets, basins, showers, washing facilities, a rest room and cooking area with electric rings (pre-payment). British WCs: mostly individual basins, some in cabins for women, with hot water; hot water for showers and sinks is on payment. The blocks can be heated. Good English is spoken and the charges are reasonable.

How to find it: Follow Lido signs out of Luzern and a large sign to Lido is on right just outside of town.

General Details: Open 15 March - 31 Oct. 23,000 sq.m. Shade in parts. Smallish shop. Takeaway. Community room. Organised excursions. Doctor on call. Chemical disposal. Caravans to rent.

Charges 2000: Per person Sfr. 7.00; child (6-14 yrs) 3.50; local tax (over 11s) 1.20; car 5.00; tent 4.00; caravan 6.00 - 10.00; motorcaravan 12.00 - 17.00; m/cycle 3.00; dog 3.00; electricity by meter.

Reservations: Advised for 15/6-15/9; write to site. Address: Lidostr. 19, 6006 Luzern. Tel: 041/370 21 46. FAX: 041/370 21 45. E-mail: info@camping.ch.

913 Terrassencamping Vitznau, Vitznau, nr Lucerne/Luzern

Quiet site scenically positioned on shores of Lake Luzern.

Camping Vitznau is situated in the small village of the same name, above and overlooking the lake, with splendid views across the water to the mountains on the other side. It is a small, neat and tidy site very close to the delightful village on the narrow, winding, lakeside road. The 120 pitches for caravans or motorhomes (max length 7 m.) have electricity to most. They are on level, grassy terraces with hard wheel tracks for motorcaravans and separated by tarmac roads, and although of sufficient rather than large size, with single rows on each terrace, all places have views. However, larger units might have difficulty manoeuvring. There are separate places for tents. The single, well constructed sanitary block has British WCs, washbasins in flat vanity tops and free hot showers. Sinks for laundry and dishwashing are under cover with metered hot water. There is a general room for wet weather, a games room and a well stocked shop but no restaurant as village ones are five minutes walk. Trees provide shade in parts. This delightful site makes an excellent base for exploring around the lake, the town of Luzern and the nearby mountains.

How to find it: Site is signed from the centre of Vitznau.

General Details: Open 1 April - 3 Oct. 20,000 sq.m. Electricity connections (15A). 1,446 feet above sea level. Shop. Small swimming pool and children's splash pool (15/5-15/9). Fishing or bicycle hire within 1 km. Golf 15 km. Watersports near. Washing machines and dryers. Gas supplies. Chemical disposal. Motorcaravan services.

Charges 2000: Per person Sfr. 8.00 - 9.50; child under 6 yrs 2.50, 6-16 yrs 5.50; pitch 14.00 - 18.00; local tax 1.60; dog 3.00; electricity 4.00. Credit cards accepted.

Reservations: Write with deposit (Sfr 20). Address: 6354 Vitznau. Tel: 041/397 12 80. FAX: 041/397 24 57.

915 Camping Seebucht, Zürich

Busy lakeside site quite close to the city.

Being a smallish site only 4.5 km. from the centre of the important town of Zürich and in a pleasant situation with well kept lawns, Seebucht has more demands on space than it can meet. With 300 touring pitches (136 with 6/10A electricity), it may well pack units rather closely in season but there is much transit trade so there are usually plenty of vacancies each day if you are early (reservations not made). Caravans go on flat hardstandings (cars cannot always stand by them); tents, for which space may be easier to find, go on lawns. The grassy strip alongside the lake is kept free for recreational use. The single sanitary block has been improved and has British style toilets, with some Turkish style for men, individual washbasins (cubicles for women) with cold water and hot water on payment for the showers.

How to find it: Site is on southern side of the town and western side of the lake, at Wollishofen; well signed from most parts of town and at motorway exit.

General Details: Open 1 May - 30 Sept. 20,000 sq.m. Shop. Café for meals or drinks. Bathing possible into fairly deep water. Fishing. Jetty where small boats can be launched. Chemical disposal. Motorcaravan services.

Charges 2000: Per person Ffr. 7.00; child (4-16 yrs) 4.00; small tent (max. 3 persons) 12.00; large tent or caravan 14.00; motorcaravan 16.00 (plus 5.00 if over 6 m); car 3.00; electricity 3.00; plus local tax 1.20.

Reservations: not ma.de; for information only: Address: Seestrasse 559, 8038 Zürich-Wollishofen. Tel: 01/482 16 12. FAX: 01/482 16 60.

918 Campingplatz Buchhorn, Arbon

Small, well ordered site on Lake Bodensee in northeast Switzerland.

This small but clean and pleasant site is directly on Lake Bodensee and situated in the town's parkland. There is access for boats from the camp but powered craft must be under a certain h.p. and advice on this should be sought from the management. There are splendid views across this large inland sea and interesting boats ply up and down between Constance and Lindau and Bregenz. The town swimming lido in the lake, with a restaurant, is here, quite close to the camp. The site is well shaded with pitches for tourists by the water's edge and an overflow field for tents next door. There are a number of static caravans but said to be room for 100 tourists, pitches being on a mixture of gravel and grass, flat areas on either side of access roads, most with 6A electricity. A railway line runs directly along one side but one gets used to the noise from passing trains, and pitches near the lake should be requested if available. A single, well constructed set of buildings comprise reception, shop (small terrace for drinks), sanitary and washing arrangements. The sanitary facilities, which should just about suffice in high season, are clean and modern with free hot water in basins, showers and sinks. British WCs. This is a beautiful area and the site is well placed for touring around Lake Bodensee, the Vorarlberg province of Austria, Liechtenstein and northeast Switzerland. Watersports and steamer trips are available on the lake, walks and marked cycle tracks around it and a nature reserve is near. The weather can be unsettled in this region.

How to find it: On Arbon-Konstanz road 13, signed 'Strandbad' and 'Strandbad Camping' on leaving Arbon.

General Details: Open 14 April - 22 Oct. Well shaded. Shop (basic supplies, drinks and snacks - all season). General room. Children's playground. Town swimming lido 400 m. Tennis 150 m. Watersports and excursions on lake. Washing machine, dryer and drying area. Fridge. Chemical disposal. Gates closed 12-14.00 hrs daily.

Charges 2000: Per person Sfr. 6.65; child (6-16 yrs) 3.10; small tent 5.65; large tent, caravan or motorcaravan 11.35; car 3.10; m/cycle 1.05; electricity 2.05.

Reservations: Write to site. Address: 9320 Arbon. Tel: 071/446 65 45. FAX: 071/446 48 34.

Arbon *Camping Buchhorn*

One of the finest camping sites on the shores of Lake Constance
- 100 yards of own sandy beach
- idyllic site under old, high trees
- perfect, new sanitation equipment
- shop with Camping-Gaz
- free entrance to the Lido, 200 yds
- closed daily from 12 am to 2 pm

Edi+Lotty Hurter, CH-9320 Arbon
071 446 6545 Fax 071 446 4834

921 TCS Camping Pointe à la Bise, Vésenaz, nr Geneve/Geneva

Busy lakeside site within easy reach of Geneva.

Ideal for visiting Geneva, Pointe à la Bise is directly on the lake and has superb views of the lake and surrounding mountains which may well tempt you to stay longer. The 200 pitches for touring units, 70 with electricity are not marked so, although electricity boxes roughly determine where each unit goes, you do not have an exactly defined place which might make for crowding in high season. Tall trees provide some shade. It is possible to swim in the lake or the lido (5 km) and there is a children's pool. Windsurfing and small boats under 10 h.p. may be used from the site. Being away from the main road, this is a quiet site with a relaxed atmosphere – no disco, but occasional light, live music entertainment in high season and a programme of organised activities in July/Aug. The pleasant bar/restaurant is open all day and there is a separate hatch for takeaways. The raised restaurant terrace overlooks the pool and small children's playground. The friendly, English speaking manager will be pleased to advise on nearby attractions. He also leads a bicycle ride weekly in high season with lunch in a French restaurant. The single sanitary block, refurbished to a high standard, has British style WCs, free hot water in washbasins, sinks and showers and a baby room. There are a number of static caravans but these are grouped to one side.

How to find it: Follow lakeside road from city centre towards Thonon (lake on left) for 6.5 km. Site is signed.

General Details: Open Easter - 17 October. 32.000 sq.m. Electricity connections (4/10A). Shop. Bar (15/6-31/8 and weekends). Restaurant with takeaway. Community room with TV. Children's pool (15/5-15/9). Playground. Lake swimming and watersports. Fishing. Bicycle hire. Golf 3 km. Washing machines and dryers. Gas supplies. Chemical disposal. Motorcaravan services.

Charges 1999: Per person Sfr. 5.00 - 6.00; child (6-15 yrs) less 50%; pitch 7.00 - 19.00, acc. to size and season; motorcaravan 22.00; electricity 3.00; local tax 0.50. Credit cards accepted.

Reservations: Contact site. Address: 1222 Vésenaz. Tel: 022/7521296. FAX: 022/7523767. E-mail: cpg@tcs.ch.

SWITZERLAND

922 Camping Les Grangettes, Noville, nr Villeneuve

Lake-side campsite in quiet location at eastern end of Lake Geneva.

At first sight, Les Grangettes appears to be filled with static caravans and, indeed, 245 of the 315 pitches have these. However, to one side there is a separate section of 70 places for touring units. These are good sized level pitches, separated by saplings, and back to back in regular rows on either side of rolled stone roads backed by trees leading down to the lake. All have electricity (10A). This part has its own well built modern sanitary block with British style WCs, free hot water (pre-mixed from a single tap) in washbasins and sinks and on payment in the showers, facilities for disabled visitors and washing machines and dryers. There is an excellent bar/restaurant with terrace. Musical entertainment is provided in the restaurant in high season but this is a quiet site in a scenic location with views across Lake Geneva. It could make a useful night stop when travelling from Montreux to Martigny, the Rhone Valley and Simplon Pass but is, perhaps, better for a longer stay when exploring this part of Lake Geneva.

How to find: From N9 Montreux-Martigny, take Villeneuve exit, and follow signs to Noville and then the site.

General Details: Open all year. 30,000 sq.m. Restaurant. Basic food supplies. Motorcaravan services.

Charges 1999: Per person SFr. 6.00 - 7.50; child 2-6 yrs 2.50 - 3.00, 6-16 yrs 4.50 - 5.50; small tent 5.00 - 6.50; large tent 7.00 - 8.50; caravan 7.00 - 10.00; motorcaravan 8.00 - 11.00; car 2.00; electricity 4.00; local tax 1.00.

Reservations: Contact site. Address: 1845 Noville. Tel: 021/960.15.03. FAX: 021/960.20.30.

924 TCS Camping Le Petit Bois, Morges

Excellent site near Lausanne on Lake Geneva.

This attractive TCS campsite is on the edge of Morges, a wine-growing centre with a 13th century castle, on Lake Geneva about 8 km. west of Lausanne. Le Petit Bois is next to the municipal sports field complex with views across the lake to the mountains. A variety of flowers, shrubs and trees adorn the site and the neat lawns make a most pleasant place. The site has 170 grass pitches for tourists which are laid out in a regular pattern from wide hard access roads on which cars stand. There are 8 larger pitches for motorcaravans with electricity, water and drainage and 140 electricity connections in all. Two well built modern sanitary blocks with British style WCs, have free hot water in half the washbasins and sinks and on payment in the showers. These are in a separate block which also has an excellent baby room and cosmetics room. The first class restaurant, with terrace where heaters add warmth in cool weather, overlooks the good children's playground. Next to the site is the very good heated town swimming pool and an open space for ball games. The small harbour adjoining the site has some moorings for campers' boats. A fence separates the site from the lake with gates for access. As well as being good for a long stay to explore this scenic and interesting region, it also makes a night stop when passing this way. The town centre is within walking distance and the friendly managers, who speak good English, will advise on local attractions.

How to find it: On Rue de Lac (B1); coming from Lausanne, leave Lausanne - Geneva motorway at exit 'Morges-ouest', from Geneva exit 'Morges'. Turn towards town and signs for site.

General details: Open Easter - early October. 36,000 sq.m. Electricity connections (4A). Restaurant (with service) and takeaway. Well stocked shop. Washing machines, dryers and irons. Baby room. Small general room. Sports area. Children's playground. Some entertainment in high season. Treatment room, doctor will call. Chemical disposal. Motorcaravan services.

Charges 1999: Per person Sfr 5.00 - 6.50; child (6-16 yrs) less 50%; pitch 6.30 - 19.00, acc. to season and facilities; local tax 2.00. Credit cards accepted.

Reservations: Made for min. 1 week with deposit (Sfr. 80) and fee (20) Address: 1110 Morges. Tel: 021/801 12 70. FAX: 021/803 38 69.

930 Camping Le Bivouac, Les Paccots, Châtel St Denis, nr Lausanne

Pleasant, small site with swimming pool, in mountains north of Montreux.

A nice little mountain site, Le Bivouac has its own small swimming pool and children's pool. Most of the best places here are taken by seasonal caravans (130) and there are now only about 30 pitches for tourists. Electrical connections (10A) are available and there are five water points. The site is also open for winter sports caravanning and all the sanitary facilities are heated. These good facilities include British style toilets, pre-set free hot water in washbasins, showers and sinks for laundry and dishes, and a baby room. New facilities in the main building have more showers, free hot water and laundry facilities. Entertainment is organised for adults and children in high season. This is a good centre for walking and excursions.

How to find it: From N12/A12 Bern-Vevey motorway Châtel St Denis exit, turn towards Les Paccots (1 km).

General Details: Open all year. Shop (15/5-15/9). Café with takeaway (15/5-15/9, plus weekends). Swimming pool (1/6-15/9). Room for general use adjoining. Table tennis. Fishing. Bicycle hire 2 km. Riding 4 km. Laundry facilities. Gas supplies. Chemical disposal.

Charges 2000: Per person Sfr. 6.00 plus local tax (adults) 1.20; child (6-16 yrs) 4.00; pitch incl. car 15.00; electricity (10A) 4.00. 10% off with camping carnet. No credit cards.

Reservations: Advised for July/Aug. and made for 1 week with deposit (Sfr. 50) and fee (10). Address: 1618 Châtel St Denis. Tel: 021/948 78 49. FAX: as phone. E-Mail bivouac@swissonline.ch.

AR Discount
Less 10%
(excl. tax)

927 Camping de Vidy, Lausanne

Friendly site in popular city on Lake Geneva.

The interesting and ancient city of Lausanne - its first cathedral was built in the 6th century - spills down the hillside towards Lake Geneva until it meets the peaceful park in which this site is situated. The present owners took the site over from the City council in 1987 and have enhanced its appearance by planting many flowers and shrubs. Although only minutes from the city centre, only a gentle hum of traffic can be heard and the site exudes peace and tranquillity. A public footpath separates the site from the lakeside, but there is good access. The World HQ of the Olympic movement is adjacent in the pleasant park, which is also available for games and walking. Hard access roads separate the site into sections for tents, caravans and motorcaravans, with 10A electrical connections in all parts, except the tent areas. Pitches are on flat grass, numbered but not marked out, with 245 (of 350) available for tourists. A few apartments for hire. Two excellent sanitary blocks, one near reception (heated) and one on the opposite side of the site, have mostly British, some Turkish style WCs, free hot water in washbasins, sinks and showers with warm, pre-mixed water. Facilities for disabled people. A third small block of the same standard has been added. The lakeside bar/restaurant (also open to the public) provides entertainment in season in the various rooms so that the young and not so young can enjoy themselves without impinging on each other. The keen young couple who manage the site speak good English, whom they welcome. The site has a neat and tidy appearance. There is a frequent bus service into Lausanne and boat excursions on the lake.

How to find it: Left of the road to Geneva, 500 m. west of La Maladière. Take autobahn Lausanne-Süd, exit La Maladière, and follow signs to camp (very near). Care needed at motorway exit roundabout.

General Details: Open all year. Well stocked shop and self-service bar/restaurant (1/5-30/9). Takeaway in high season. Children's playground. Evening entertainment in high season. Lake swimming. Fishing. Gas supplies. Chemical disposal. Motorcaravan services (Euro-Relais; Sfr. 10 for overnight guests, 20 otherwise).

Charges 2000: Per person Sfr. 6.50; student 6.00; child (6-15 yrs) 5.00; car 3.00; m/cycle 2.00; tent, caravan or motorcaravan 10.00 - 12.00; 2 person tent 7.00; local tax 1.30 (caravan) 1.20 (tent). No credit cards.

Reservations: Write to site. Address: 1007 Lausanne-Vidy (Vaud). Tel: 021/622 50 00. FAX: 021/622 50 01.

963 Camping Sémiramis, Leysin

High level mountain site in well known winter and summer resort.

Leysin came to fame at the end of the last century when it was found that the pure mountain air was conducive to the cure of turberculosis. The discovery of antibiotic drugs in 1955 made the lengthy natural treatment redundant and Leysin turned to tourism as a summer and winter resort. At 4,500 feet above sea level in the Vaudois Alps, there are spectacular views over the Rhône valley. Reputably enjoying more hours of sunshine than anywhere in Switzerland, Leysin has become a well equipped resort with ski-ing facilities including a new cable way to a revolving restaurant. The village straggles up the mountain side and Sémiramis is at the start of this. With 120 pitches and on a slight slope with static caravans on the upper level, the meadow at the entrance provides 60 places for touring visitors. No places are marked out and long leads may be required for the electricity hook ups (6/15A). There is little shade but the views are breathtaking and mountains protect the campsite to the north. There are two sanitary blocks, heated in cool weather, one on the ground floor of the hotel and one next to the snack bar, shop and reception. British style WCs. Free hot water is dispensed through a single tap in washbasins, showers and sinks. Tennis courts and the town's large ice rink (open all year) are next to the site with restaurants and shops nearby. This neat, compact site has very friendly, English speaking management and provides an excellent base to enjoy the amenities of the region.

How to find it: Take Leysin road at Le Sepey on Aigle - Château-d'Oex road and turn left immediately after the town sign (just past Subaru garage).

General Details: Open all year. 12,000 sq.m. Shop (1/7-31/8). Bar and snack bar (cliosed May and Nov). Children's play area. TV room in bar. Boules. Sports centre. Table tennis. Badminton. Fishing 2 km. Bicycle hire or riding 1 km. Washing machine and dryer. Gas supplies. Chemical disposal. Motorcaravan services.

Charges 2000: Per person Sfr. 5.80; child (6-16 yrs) 3.00; tent 3.00 - 4.00; caravan 7.00; car 4.00; m/cycle 2.00; motorcaravan 12.00 - 15.00; electricity 2.70 plus meter; local tax 3.25 (child 1.70). Higher prices for winter. Credit cards accepted.

Reservations: Made with deposit (Sfr. 50). Address: 1854 Leysin. Tel: 024/494 18 29. FAX: 024/494 20 29.

AR Discount
Less 10% on camp fees

SWITZERLAND

933 Camping Bettlereiche, Gwatt-Thun

Small, lakeside site with good facilities, in popular area.

Bettlereiche is an ideal site for those who wish to explore this part of the Bernese Oberland and who would enjoy staying on a small site in a quiet area, away from the larger sites and town atmosphere of Interlaken. There are 90 numbered, but unmarked pitches for tourists, most with 4A electricity available, and about the same number of static units. There are hard access roads but cars must be parked away from the pitches. Although there are some trees, there is little shade in the main camping area. Direct access to the lake is available for swimming and boating. The single sanitary block is well constructed and modern with British style WCs and free hot water provided for the washbasins in cabins (cold otherwise) and in the showers controlled by a single tap. The facilities should be just adequate in high season. The site has a cared for air and the friendly management speak good English. Part of the restaurant is reserved for young people. Some animation is arranged in high season.

How to find it: From Berne-Thun-Interlaken autoroute, take exit Thun-Süd for Gwatt and follow signs for Gwatt and site.

General Details: Open Easter - 5 Oct. 15,000 sq.m. Well stocked shop. Restaurant (no alcohol). Room for disabled. Washing machine and dryer. Lake swimming. and boating. Chemical disposal. Motorcaravan services.

Charges 1999: Per person Sfr. 4.50 - 6.50; child 50%; pitch 6.50 - 19.00; local tax 2.60.

Reservations: Write to site. Address: 3645 Gwatt. Tel: 033/336 40 67. FAX: 033/336 40 17.

936 Camping Grassi, Frutigen, nr Spiez

Small, quiet site on the road to Kandersteg.

This is a small site with about half the pitches occupied by static caravans, used by their owners for week-ends and holidays. The 70 or so places available for tourists are not marked out but it is said that the site is not allowed to become overcrowded. Most places are on level grass with two small terraces at the end of the site. There is little shade but the site is set in a river valley with trees on the hills which enclose the area. It would make a useful overnight stop en-route for Kandersteg and the railway station where cars can join the train for transportation through the Lotschberg Tunnel to the Rhône Valley and Simplon Pass, or for a longer stay to explore the Bernese Oberland. Electricity is available for all pitches but long leads may be required in parts. The well constructed, heated sanitary block has good quality installations including British style WCs and also a rest room with TV. There is a kiosk for basic supplies, but shops and restaurants are only a 10 minute walk away in the village.

How to find it: Take Kandersteg road from Spiez and leave at Frutigen Dorf exit from where site is signed.

General Details: Open all year. 15,000 sq.m. Electricity connections (8 or 10A). Kiosk (1/7-31/8). Children's play area. Mountain bike hire and tours. Fishing. Bcycle hire. Riding 2 km. Outdoor and indoor pools, tennis and minigolf in Frutigen. Ski-ing and walking. Washing machine and dryer. Gas supplies. Chemical disposal. Motorcaravan services.

Charges 2000: Per person Sfr. 6.40; child 1-6 yrs 1.50, 6-16 yrs 3.20; pitch 6.00 - 12.00; local tax 0.80 (child 0.40); electricity (8/10A) 2.50. No credit cards.

Reservations: Write to site. Address: 3714 Frutigen. Tel: 033/671 11 49 or 671 37 98. FAX: 033/671 11 49.

 AR Discount
*Less 10-15%
for 14 nights;
free bike ride*

960 Camping Rive-Bleue, Le Bouveret, nr Lausanne

Site by Lake Geneva with good swimming pool and lakeside installations.
At the eastern end of Lac Léman, the main feature of this site is the very pleasant lakeside lido only a short walk of 300 m. from the site and with free entry for campers. It has a new 'Aquaparc' pool (100 sq.m), with a water toboggan and plenty of grassy lying-out areas, a bathing area in lake, boating facilities with storage for sailboards, canoes, inflatables etc, sailing school, pedaloes for hire. Also here and, like the lido, under same ownership as the campsite, is a quality hotel which at the rear has a café for food and drinks with access from the lido. The site itself has 200 marked pitches on well kept flat grass, half in the centre with 6A electricity, the other half round the perimeter. Two decent toilet blocks with British style WCs, washbasins with shelf, mirror and cold water in the old block, hot in the new, pre-set free hot showers with seat and screen, push-button operated but water runs on well.

How to find it: Approach site on Martigny-Evian road no. 21 and turn to Bouveret-Plage south of Le Bouveret.

General Details: Open 1 April - 30 Sept. Shop, restaurant by beach (both all season). Bicycle hire. Fishing. Covered area for cooking with electric rings and barbecue. Drying room. Chemical disposal. Motorcaravan services (Euro-relais; Sfr. 12).

Charges 2000: Per person Sfr. 7.20 - 8.70, plus local tax 0.80; child (6-16 yrs) 5.00 - 6.00, plus local tax 0.40; car 1.70; tent 6.30 - 9.90, acc. to season and size; caravan 7.90 - 10.80; motorcaravan 9.60 - 12.50; car 1.70; dog 2.00; electricity 3.20.

Reservations: are recommended and made for any length with Sfr. 20 non-refundable reservation fee. Address: Bouveret-Plage, 1897 Le Bouveret. Tel: 024/482 42 42 (reservation 481 21 61). FAX: 024/481 21 08.

RIVE-BLEUE, BOUVERET PLAGE
Lake Geneva Tel: (information) 024/482 42 42
(reservation) 024/481 21 61
Fax: 024/481 21 08

1st category international tourist site Natural beach, heated swimming pool, tennis, sailboarding, shop and restaurant. Modern toilet blocks with free hot water. New: AQUAPARK

939 Camping Vermeille, Zweisimmen, nr Gstaad

Attractive, small mountain site with good facilities, for families.
This small, well run campsite is about 1,000 m. above sea level, on a road followed by many tourists and can serve either as a night stop or as a holiday base for those who like a mountain site with many attractive excursion possibilities. In summer there are 40 pitches for tourists, in winter 25 (the remainder of the 125 total being seasonal lets), with 130 electrical connections available. There is a small free swimming pool which can be heated, open mid-May to late September if weather permits. The site is equipped for winter sports camping and a fair proportion of the available space, therefore, consists of hardstandings for caravans on stony ground. However, there are also lawns for tents. The sanitary installations have been upgraded and now include a baby room and facilities for disabled people. In the main building, they are fully enclosed and heated in winter. The facilities are kept extremely clean and include British WCs, troughs and washbasins for washing with a few private cabins, and hot water for washing up and showers on payment.

How to find it: Site is north of town on no. 11 road. Turn off where signed and go past a different site on left of access road. From N6 motorway take exit for Wimmis/Spiez (from Spiez before town, from Saanen after town).

General Details: Open all year. 9,000 sq.m. Electricity connections (from 6A). Limited shade. Shop for food and sports goods. New bistro. Two rooms for general use, one with sink and cooking facilities. Children's play area and trampoline. Mountain bike hire. Washing machine. Chemical disposal. Motorcaravan services.

Charges 2000: Per person Sfr. 6.90; child 6-12 yrs 3.80, under 6 yrs 2.20; local tax 0.80 (0.40); pitch 8.00 - 13.50; m/cycle 3.00; car 4.00; dog 2.00; electricity 2.00 (winter 2.00 - 9.00). Less 10% on person charge outside July/Aug.

Reservations: Made for min. 5 nights with deposit (Sfr. 40) and small fee (10). Address: 3770 Zweisimmen. Tel: 033/722 19 40. FAX: 033/722 36 25. E-mail: camping.vermeille@spectraweb.ch.

SWITZERLAND

969 Camping Swiss-Plage, Salgesch, Sierre

Large, well run site with natural lake, in the Rhône Valley.

This is a good site and is well run by its English speaking owner and, although about half is occupied by static caravans, there are still 250 pitches for visiting tourists. The site is also slightly unusual in that much of the terrain has been deliberately left in its natural state. The wooded section gives good shade and tree formations and access roads determine where units go. There is a central open meadow and some quiet spots are a little further from the amenities. Most pitches, although unmarked, have 10A electric points available. One part of the site may be reserved but some space is usually available. The centre of the site has a natural lake which is kept dredged and clean and is suitable for small boats (not windsurfers) and for bathing - the site say the water is tested weekly. It is possible to stroll along the banks of the Rhône and good walks are nearby. The main sanitary block in the centre has been refurbished to a high standard and can be heated in cool weather. Although the two other blocks are showing signs of age, the total provision should be sufficient. British style WCs, free hot water in basins in the new block, cold in some of the others, and hot showers on payment. Outside the excellent restaurant is a snack bar which offers good grill meals and 30 different pizzas which can be eaten on the terrace or taken away.

How to find it: From either direction on road no. 9 or more recent bypasses, follow signs for Salgesch which should bring you past site entrance 3 km. northeast of Sierre. Care is required to spot the first sign in Sierre at a multi-road junction; site is well signed from here.

General Details: Open 8 April - 1 Nov. 11,000 sq.m. Self-service shop. Bar/restaurant with terrace. Takeaway. Lake. Paddling pool. Children's playground. Table tennis. Fishing (on payment). Volleyball. Badminton. Some entertainment in high season. Washing machine and dryer. Chemical disposal. Motorcaravan services.

Charges 2000: Per person Sfr. 6.60, plus local tax 0.60; child (4-16 yrs) 3.30 plus tax 0.30; pitch 15.00; electricity 2.50; dog 3.00. Less 10% in low season. No credit cards.

Reservations: necessary and made for any length with deposit. Address: 3960 Sierre-Salgesch (Valais). Tel: 027/455 66 08 or 481 60 23. FAX: 027/481 32 15.

Camping Swiss-Plage, Sierre-Salgesch (Valais) Switzerland

★ ★ ★ ★

The only camp in the Valais region with its own natural bathing lake (entry free for campers), with temperature around 18oC. Part sunny, part shaded pitches. Well maintained sanitary facilities. Restaurant. Self-service shop. Starting point for innumerable excursions (Val d'Anniviers, etc). Sports centre (tennis, badminton, beach volleyball, sauna, climbing wall, fitness centre, etc) 800 m.

971 TCS Camping Les Iles, Sion

Pleasant, well organised campsite in the Rhône Valley.

Sion is an ancient and interesting town on the main route from Martigny to Brig and the Simplon Pass into Italy. Les Iles is an excellent, well organised and pretty site, useful for a night stop when passing through or for a longer stay to explore the region or relax in a pleasant area. Although it is near a small airport, it is understood that no planes fly at night. The rectangular site has 440 level pitches for tourists, 340 with 4A electricity and 22 serviced with water and waste water also. Well laid out, a profusion of flowers, shrubs and trees lead to a lake which supplements the pool for swimming and may be used by inflatable boats. There is a good area of grass for sunbathing and two playgrounds for children. Six good sanitary blocks are spaced around the site with British style WCs, free hot water in washbasins, showers and sinks, as well as baby rooms and provision for disabled people. The site has a popular restaurant with terrace and a well stocked shop (both open all year) with others in the town about 4 km. away. A very varied entertainment programme for both children and adults is offered in July/Aug. with organised excursions (extra cost) and a wealth of interesting activities near including watersports, mountain biking, para-gliding, etc from Swissraft. Good English is spoken and the warden is pleased to give advice on places to visit.

How to find it: Site is about 4 km. west of Sion and is signed from road 9 and the motorway exit.

General Details: Open all year excl. 1 Nov - 19 Dec. 80,000 sq.m. Electrical connections (4A). Shop. Restaurant. Swimming pool (12 x 10 m. mid May - mid Sept). Children's play areas. Football field. Table tennis. Tennis 100 m. Golf and horse riding 6 km. Good animation programme in July/Aug. and many sporting opportunities nearby. Bicycle hire. Washing machines and dryers. Chemical disposal. Motorcaravan services.

Charges 1999: Per person Sfr. 5.50 - 7.00; child (6-16) 50%; pitch 6.20 - 22.00; electricity 4.00; local tax 0.80.

Reservations: Write to site. Address: 1951 Sion. Tel: 027/346 43 47. FAX: 027/346 68 47. E-mail: cpg@tcs.ch.

966 Camping des Glaciers, La Fouly, nr Martigny

Mountain site with first-class facilities and spectacular views.

Situated at 1,600 m. above sea level, Des Glaciers is set amidst magnificent mountain scenery in a very quiet, peaceful location in the beautiful Ferret Valley. Being just off the main Martigny - Grand St Bernard route, it could make a night stop when travelling along this road but as this would entail a 13 km. detour along a minor road, it is more convenient for a longer stay. Those seeking peace, quiet and fresh mountain air or an opportunity for mountain walking would be well suited here. Marked tracks bring Grand St Bernard and the path around Mont Blanc within range, among many other possibilities with an abundance of flora and fauna for added interest. Guides are available if required. The site offers two types of pitches, about half in an open, undulating meadow with campers choosing where to go and the proprietor advising if numbers require this and the rest being level, individual plots of varying size in small clearings either between bushes and shrubs or under tall pines. Equally suitable for all units from small tents to large caravans. Torches may be useful. A small stream runs through the site. Of the 170 places, 150 have 15A electricity so a small heater can be used if evenings become chilly. There are three sanitary units, all of exceptional quality and heated when necessary. The smallest is under reception, there is another in the centre of the open area and a block in the centre of the site. Hot water is free in all washbasins (some in private cabins), showers and sinks. British style WCs. Each block has washing machines and dryers, one block has a drying room, another a baby room. A large wooden chalet which can be heated in cool weather has been added. There are sports facilities and swimming pools at 18 and 25 km. but this is, above all, a campsite for those who wish to enjoy the mountain atmosphere, get close to nature or walk in the mountains where there are also refreshment stops at mountain huts. The charming lady owner, fluent in six languages, is always ready not only to welcome you to this peaceful haven but also to give information on the locality. The site has a small shop for basic supplies with restaurants and village shop about 5 minutes walk away.

How to find it: Leave Martigny-Gd St Bernard road (no. 21) at Orsieres and follow signs to La Fouly. Site is signed on right at end of La Fouly village.

General Details: Open 15 May - 30 Sept. 70,000 sq.m. Shade in parts. Shop and restaurant 500 m. Recreation room with TV. Children's playground. Bicycle hire 500 m. Riding 8 km. Washing machines and dryers. Gas supplies. Chemical disposal. Motorcaravan services.

Charges 2000: Per person Sfr. 6.00; child (2-12 yrs) 3.50; baby 2.00; pitch 10.00 - 16.00; electricity 3.00; dog 1.00. Less 10% in June and Sept. Credit cards accepted.

Reservations: Made without deposit; write to site. Address: 1944 La Fouly (VS). Tel: 027/783 17 35. FAX: 027/783 36 05.

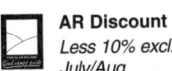

AR Discount
Less 10% excl. July/Aug,

967 Camping de Molignon, Les Haudères-Evolène

Mountain site with stunning views in the Herens Valley.

The uphill drive from Sion in the Rhône Valley is enhanced by the Pyramids of Euseigne, through which the road passes via a short tunnel. These unusual structures, cut out by erosion from masses of morainic debris, have been saved from destruction by their unstable rocky crowns. De Molignon, surrounded by mountains, is a quiet, peaceful place where, although there may be some road noise, the rushing stream and the sound of cow bells are likely to be the only disturbing factor in summer. The 100 pitches for tourists are on well tended, level terraces leading down to the river. Some 72 have electricity and are marked by numbered posts. They have a small shop for basic supplies and a pleasant restaurant with a good menu at reasonable prices. Although this is essentially a place for mountain walking (guided tours available), climbing and relaxing, there is a geological museum in Les Haudères, which has links with a British University, cheese making and interesting flora and fauna. Skiing and langlauf in winter. The two sanitary blocks, heated in cool weather, have British style WCs, free hot water in sinks and washbasins and on payment in the showers. Good English is spoken by the owner's son who is now running the site, who will be pleased to give information on all that is available from the campsite.

How to find it: Follow signs southwards from Sion for the Val d'Herens through Evolène to Les Haudères where site is signed on the right.

General Details: Open all year. 15,000 sq.m. 1,450 m above sea level. Electrical connections (10A). Shop (20/6-10/9). Restaurant (all year). Small playground. Guided walks, climbing, geological museum, winter skiing. Fishing. Bicycle hire 3 km. Riding 15 km. Tennis and hang-gliding near. Washing machines and dryer. Gas supplies. Chemical disposal. Motorcaravan services.

Charges 2000: Per person Sfr. 4.50 - 4.80; child (4-16 yrs) 2.00 - 2.50; pitch 8.00 - 13.00; dog 2.00; electricity 2.00; local tax 1.10 (child 0.55). Credit cards accepted.

Reservations: Contact site. Address: 1984 Les Haudères-Evolène. Tel: 027/283 12 40. FAX: 027/283 13 31. E-mail: camping.molignan@bluewin.ch.

AR Discount
Less 5% on camping fees

SWITZERLAND

972 Camping Bella Tola, Susten, nr Sion

Site with good facilities, swimming pool and individual pitches.

An attractive site with good standards, Bella Tola is on the hillside above Susten (east of Sierre) with good views over the Rhône valley. It boasts a good sized heated swimming pool and children's pool (both free to campers) which, like the restaurant and bar overlooking them, are also open to non-campers and so more crowded at weekends and holidays. In the low rain climate of the Valais the pool is naturally much used. Pitches are nearly all on sloping ground which varies in steepness, but extensive terracing is being carried out and about 50 plots had been completed when seen. Some 200 of the 260 individually numbered pitches have electricity connections. The fullest season is 10/7-10/8, but they say that there is usually room somewhere. The three good quality modern sanitary blocks should provide quite sufficient coverage and have British style toilets, individual washbasins (some in cabins), with free hot water in some ladies' basins, showers and sinks for clothes and dishes, plus baby rooms. Further improvements are underway including facilities for disabled visitors. Used by tour operators (20%). Torches are advised. Guests are requested to comply with environmental rules by sorting rubbish as directed.

How to find it: Turn south from main road at Susten where site is well signed.

General Details: Open May - Oct. (as are shop and restaurant/bar). 200 electrical connections (16A, long leads may be needed). Swimming pool (22/5-19/9). Tennis. General room with TV. Films, organised sports, activities, guided walks etc. in July/Aug. Riding near. Washing machines, dryers and irons. Car wash. Motorcaravan services.

Charges 2000: Per person Sfr. 9.50; child 2-6 yrs 4.50, 6-16 yrs 6.50; pitch 12.00 - 25.00, acc. to type and season; electricity 3.50; dog 2.50; local tax 0.80 (child 0.40). Less 40% on person and pitch fees outside July/Aug. Credit cards accepted.
Euro: per person 5.95; child 2-6 yrs 2.80, 6-16 yrs 4.05; pitch 7.50 - 15.60, acc. to type and season; electricity 2.20; dog 1.55; local tax 0.50 (child 0.25).

Reservations: will be made with deposit and fee (Sfr. 25). Address: 3952 Susten. Tel: 027/473 14 91. FAX: 027/473 36 41. E-mail: bellatolla@rhone.ch.

973 Camping Gemmi, Susten, nr Sion

Small, friendly, family site in Rhône Valley.

The Rhône Valley is a popular through route to Italy via the Simplon Pass and a holiday region in its own right. Enjoying some of the best climatic conditions in Switzerland, this valley, between two mountain regions, has less rainfall and more hours of sunshine than most of the country. It is an area of vines and fruit trees with mountain walks and the majestic Matterhorn nearby. Gemmi is a delightful small camp in a scenic location with 65 level pitches, all with 16A electricity, on well tended grass amidst a variety of trees, some of which offer shade. There are some pitches for motorcaravans with water and drainage. The modern, central sanitary block, part of which is heated, is of excellent quality and kept very clean. It has British WCs and free hot water in washbasins (some in private cabins), showers and sinks. Private bathrooms are available for hire on a weekly basis. The pleasant, friendly owner speaks fluent English, maintains high standards and has bucked current trends by establishing a camp for tourists with no resident static units. An attractive wooden building at the entrance includes a well stocked shop and small bar/restaurant where snacks and a limited range of local specialities are served.

How to find it: From east (Visp), turn left 1 km. after sign for Agarn Feithieren. From west (Sierre), turn right 2 km. after Susten by Hotel Auug, then after 300 m. right at sign for Camping Torrent.

General Details: Open 20 April - 14 Oct. 10,000 sq.m. Shop. Terrace bar and snack restaurant. Children's playground. Tennis, swimming and walking near. Fishing 6 km. Riding 2 km. Washing machines and dryers. Gas supplies. Chemical disposal. Motorcaravan services.

Charges 2000: Per adult Sfr 6.50 - 7.50; child 1-6 yrs 3.50 - 4.50, 6-16 yrs 4.50 - 5.50; pitch 10.00 - 14.00; pitch with drainage 14.00 - 18.00; electricity 3.00; private sanitary facility 150.00 per week; local tax 0.80 (0.40, under 16); dog 2.00. Credit cards accepted (Visa, Eurocard).

Reservations: Necessary for high season - no charge. Address: Briannenstrasse, 3952 Susten-Leuk. Tel: 027/473 11 54. FAX: 027/473 42 95.

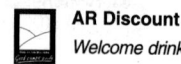
AR Discount
Welcome drink

977 Camping Santa Monica, Raron

Neat and compact all year campsite in the Rhône Valley.
We offer several different styles of campsite in the Rhône Valley and now add this pleasant, well tended site which stays open all year. The Simplon Pass is the only main route from Switzerland to Italy which avoids motorways and the need to buy the Swiss motorway vignette. It is also an easy pass for caravans which is only closed occasionally in winter and, even then, this way is possible by using the Brig-Iselle train ferry through the mountain. About half the site is occupied by static caravans and the site's own accommodation, but these are to one side leaving two flat, open meadows, bisected by the hard access road, so do not intrude on the tourist camping area. The 200 level pitches (100 for touring units) all have electricity (16A) and are roughly defined by saplings and electrical connection boxes. There is a small (12 x 4 m) swimming pool with another smaller one for children and a shop/bar/snack bar (open in high season) in the reception building, with other shops and restaurants near. Being right beside the main road 9, one does not have to deviate to find a night stop but it would also make a good base for exploring the area. It has an air of peace although, being so near the road, there is some traffic noise. Mountain views, close on south side, distant across interesting valley. The single, heated sanitary block is towards the entrance, has British style WCs, free hot water in washbasins and sinks and on payment in the showers, and facilities for disabled visitors. Tennis courts are next door to the site. Two cable ways start near the site entrance for winter skiers and summer mountain walkers.

How to find it: On the south side of road 9 between Visp and Susten, signed.

General Details: Open all year. 40,000 sq.m. Electricity (16A). Bar, restaurant and shop (1/6-15/10). Small pool and child's pool (15/6-31/8). Children's playground. Table tennis. Bicycle hire. Walking country, cable cars near. Riding 10 km. Gas supplies. Chemical disposal. Motorcaravan services (Euro-Relais).

Charges 1999: Per person Sfr. 5.00 - 6.00; child (6-16 yrs) 3.00 - 4.00; tent (max 3 persons) 7.00 - 8.50; caravan 9.50 - 12.00; electricity 3.00 (winter 5.00); local tax 0.50 (child 0.25); dog 3.00. Special offers in low season. Credit cards accepted.

Reservations: Write to site. Address: 3942 Raron (VS). Tel: 027/934 24 24. FAX: 027/934 24 50.

946 Camping Jungfrau, Lauterbrunnen, nr Interlaken
see colour advert between pages 320/321

Friendly site with good quality installations, in attractive mountain surroundings.
This site has a very imposing situation in a steep valley with a fine view of the Jungfrau at the end. You can laze here amid real mountain scenery, though it does lose the sun a little early. There are naturally many more active things to do - mountain walks or climbing, trips up the Jungfrau railway or one of the mountain lifts or excursions by car. The site itself is quite extensive and is grassy with hard surfaced access roads. It is a popular site and, although you should usually find space, in season do not arrive too late. All 391 pitches (250 for touring) have electrical connections (10-15A) and 50 have water and drainage also. There are three sanitary blocks, the new one at the far end of the site being a good modern one with hot water in all basins and showers, and the others having been thoroughly renewed and modernised. All have British style toilets, individual washbasins, free hot showers and dishwashing sinks, all with hot water. There are facilities for disabled visitors, baby baths and footbaths. Water taps on site. It is also open for winter camping and the installations are heated in cool weather. The site is owned and run by the von Allmen family who provide a warm welcome (English spoken). Improvements over the last few years have made this an excellent and most recommendable site. About 30% of the pitches are taken by seasonal caravans. The site is used by a tour operator and by groups of youngsters from many different countries - pitches at the top of the site may be quieter. Bungalows and caravans to let, plus hostel accommodation in winter only. Free bus to ski station (winter only).

How to find it: Go through Lauterbrunnen and fork right at far end before road bends left, 100 m. before church. The final approach is not very wide.

General Details: Open all year, including shop. 50,000 sq.m. Good shade in parts. Supermarket. Self-service restaurant with takeaway. Good general room with wooden tables and chairs, TV, jukebox, drink vending machines, amusements, with second one elsewhere. Well equipped and cared for children's playgrounds and covered area for children also. Washing machine, spin dryer and ironing. Hair dryer. Excursions and some entertainment in high season. Mountain bike hire. Doctor very close, will call. Chemical disposal. Motorcaravan services.

Charges 2000: Per person Sfr. 6.20 - 7.60, plus local tax 2.40; child (6-15 yrs) 3.10 - 3.80, plus 1.00; car 3.50; caravan or motorcaravan 12.00 - 18.00; tent 6.00 - 15.00; hiker's tent 4.00; electricity 2.50 + meter. Discounts for camping carnet and for stays over 3 nights outside high season.

Reservations: made for any period with deposit; write for details. Address: 3822 Lauterbrunnen. Tel: 033/856 20 10. FAX: 033/856 20 20. E-mail: camping-jungfrau@bluewin.ch.

SWITZERLAND

948 Camping Gletscherdorf, Grindelwald, nr Interlaken

Small campsite close to town with splendid mountain views.

Set in a flat river valley on the edge of Grindelwald, one of Switzerland's well known winter and summer resorts, Gletscherdorf enjoys wonderful mountain views, particularly of the nearby north face of the Eiger. The site has 120 pitches, 80 for touring units. Most are marked and have electricity, with a few others in an overflow field. A torch would be useful. The small, heated sanitary block is excellent and provides British style WCs and free hot water in washbasins, sinks and showers. There is a good community room with tables and chairs and a small shop provides basic food items. The town shops and restaurants are within walking distance. This is, above all, a very quiet, friendly site for those who wish to enjoy the peaceful mountain air, walking, climbing and exploring with a mountain climbing school in Grindelwald.

How to find it: To reach site, go into town and turn right at camp signs after town centre; approach road is quite narrow and steep down hill but there is an easier departure road.

General Details: Open 1 May - 20 Oct. for touring units (in winter for seasonal lets only). 10,000 sq.m. Electricity connections (10A). Small shop. Bicycle hire or golf 1 km. Washing machines and dryer. Gas supplies. Chemical disposal. Motorcaravan services. No dogs are accepted.

Charges 2000: Per person Sfr. 6.90, plus local tax 2.30; child (6-16 yrs) 3.00; pitch 5.00 - 15.00, acc. to size and season; electricity 3.00 - 3.50. Credit cards accepted.

Reservations: Essential for July/Aug. - contact site. Address: 3818 Grindelwald. Tel: 033/853 14 29. FAX: 033/853 31 29. E-mail: gletscherdorf@bluewin.ch.

AR Discount
Small gift
after 2 weeks

951 Camping Aaregg, Brienz, nr Interlaken

Lakeside site east of Interlaken.

Brienz is a delightful little town on the lake of the same name and the centre of the Swiss wood carving industry. Nearby at Ballenberg is the fascinating Freilichtmuseum, a very large open-air park of old Swiss houses which have been brought from all over Switzerland and re-erected in groups. Traditional Swiss crafts are demonstrated in some of these. Camping Aaregg is a very good site situated on the southern shores of the lake with splendid views across the water to the mountains. There are 45 static caravans occupying their own area and 220 tourist pitches, all with electricity. Of these, 15 are larger with hard-standings, water and drainage also. Pitches fronting the lake have a surcharge. Well built sanitary blocks have been refurbished to a high standard with British style WCs, free hot water in washbasins (some private cabins) and on payment in the showers. There is a pleasant restaurant with terrace and takeaway and a children's play area. The trees and flowers around the site make it an attractive environment. It could be useful as a night stop when passing from Interlaken to Luzern but would also make a good base from which to explore the many attractions of this scenic region. Good English is spoken by the friendly owners who will advise on local attractions.

How to find it: Site is on road B6 on the east of Brienz with entrance road between BP and Esso filling stations, well signed. From the Interlaken-Luzern motorway, take Brienz exit and turn towards Brienz, site then on the left.

General Details: Open 1 April - 31 Oct. 40,000 sq. m. Electricity connections (10A). Shop. Café with terrace (takeaway in season). Enlarged children's play area. Laundry facilities. Chemical disposal. Motorcaravan services.

Charges 2000: Per person Sfr. 6.60 - 7.80; child 6-16 yrs 3.00 - 3.60, 1-6 yrs 1.00; local tax 1.60 (child 0.80); tent or caravan 10.00 - 13.00; car 3.50; motorcaravan 12.00 - 15.00; small tent pitch 6.00 - 7.00; m/cycle 2.00; electricity 3.00; pitch with services plus 8.00; lakeside pitch (high season) plus 10.00; dog 3.00.

Reservations: Made with deposit (Sfr. 20); min. 14 days in July/Aug. Address: 3855 Brienz. Tel: 033/951 18 43. FAX: 033/951 43 24. E-mail: camping-aaregg@bluewin.ch.

944 Camping Jungfraublick, Interlaken

Pleasant site on edge of town with splendid mountain views.

The Berner Oberland is one of the most scenic and well known areas of Switzerland with Interlaken probably the best known summer and winter resort. This second site is offered here as a contrast from the larger one on the opposite side of town. Situated in the district of Matten and within walking distance of the town centre, Jungfraublick is a delightful, medium sized site with splendid views up the Lauterbrunnen valley to the Jungfrau, Monc and Eiger mountains. The pink glow reflected from the rising sun at dawn is a sight to behold when weather conditions allow and this then changes to the pure white of the everlasting snow cap as the day wears on. The motorway which bypasses the town runs in a deep cutting along one side of the site so traffic noise is screened out and an earth bank has been constructed alongside the access road reducing noise from here. The 135 tourist pitches (60-75 sq.m. and with electricity connections) are in regular rows on level, well cut grass. A number of fruit trees adorn but do not offer much shade. The static caravans are to one side of the tourist area and do not intrude. The sanitary facilities are divided between two buildings near the entrance with British style WCs, free hot water in the washbasins and on payment in the sinks and showers. The small swimming pool (12 x 8 m.) is open mid-June - mid-Sept. according to the weather. There is a shop for basic food requirements and others and restaurants about 1 km. away in the town. This is a very pleasant, neat, tidy site with a friendly, English speaking owner who is pleased to advise on the attractions of the region. It is a site for those who prefer a quiet place without organised entertainment.

How to find it: Take the 'Wilderswil' exit from the motorway bypass, turn towards Interlaken and site is on the left hand side.

General Details: Open 1 May - 25 Sept. 13,000 sq.m. Electricity connections (2-6A). Shop (from 20/5). Small swimming pool. Heated rest room with TV and electronic games. Bicycle hire. Golf 4 km. Washing machines and dryers. Chemical disposal. Motorcaravan services.

Charges 1999: Per person Sfr. 5.60 - 6.50; child 3.30 - 4.00; pitch 14.00 - 28.00; local tax 1.60. Credit cards accepted.

Reservations: Write to site with deposit (Sfr. 30) and fee (10). Address: Gsteigstrasse 80, 3800 Matten Interlaken. Tel: 033/822 44 14. FAX: 033/822 16 19. E-mail: jungfraublick.ch.

942 Camping Manor Farm, Interlaken

see colour advert between pages 320/321

Lakeside site in the Bernese Oberland popular with the British.

Manor Farm has for many years had a large proportion of British guests, for whom this is one of the traditional touring areas. The site lies outside the town on the northern side of the Thuner See, with most of the site between road and lake but with one part on the far side of the road. Interlaken is rather a tourist town but the area is rich in scenery, with innumerable mountain excursions and walks available and the lakes and Jungfrau railway near at hand. The flat terrain is divided entirely into 580 individual, numbered pitches which vary considerably both in size (60-100 sq.m.) and price; 110 are equipped with electricity, water, drainage and 55 also have cable TV connections. Reservations are made, although you should find space except perhaps in late July/early August, but the best places may then be taken. The ground becomes a little muddy when wet. Around 30% of the pitches are taken by permanent or letting units. There are seven separate toilet blocks which are practical, heated and soundly constructed. They have British style toilets, washbasins and showers, with free hot water in all blocks for washbasins, showers and baths. Twenty private units are available for rent. Bathing is possible in the lake at two points and boats can be brought if a permit obtained. The area is good for cycling and walking. Manor Farm is efficiently and quite formally run, with good English spoken, and the site is used by tour operators.

How to find it: Site is about 3 km. west of Interlaken along the road running north of the Thuner See towards Thun. Follow signs for 'Camp 1'. From the motor road bypassing Interlaken (A8) take exit marked 'Gunten, Beatenberg', which is a spur road bringing you out close to site.

General Details: Open all year. 70,000 sq.m. Electricity connections (10A). Shade in some places. Shop (1/4-15/10). Site-owned restaurant adjoining (1/3-30/11). Snack bar with takeaway on site (1/6-31/8). TV room. Football field. Children's playground and paddling pool. Minigolf. Bicycle hire. Table tennis. Sailing and windsurfing school. Boat hire. Fishing. Riding 3 km. Golf 500 m (handicap pool). Daily activity and entertainment programme in high season. Excursions. Bureau de change. Tourist information. Washing machine, dryer, ironing. Car wash. Gas supplies. Chemical disposal. Motorcaravan services. Bungalows, caravans and tents to let.

Charges 2000: Per person Sfr. 5.70 - 9.10; local tax 1.60; child (6-15 yrs) 2.60 - 4.30 (under 6 free); pitch 7.00 - 34.00, acc. to season and type (see description above); boat 2.00 - 6.00; dog (max. 1) 3.00 - 4.00; electricity 0.80 - 4.00. acc. to amperage. (0.5, 4 or 6A). Various discounts for longer stays. Credit cards accepted.

Reservations: Taken for high season (min. 3 days) with booking fee (Sfr. 30). Address: 3800 Interlaken-Thunersee. Tel: 033/822 22 64. FAX: 033/822 22 79.

SWITZERLAND

949 Camping Eigernordwand, Grindelwald

Friendly, mountain site at the foot of the Eiger.

Grindelwald is a very popular summer and winter resort and Eigernordwand, at 950 m. above sea level, is dramatically situated very close to the north face of the famous mountain in a delightful situation. The slightly sloping pitches have gravel access roads but are not marked out. There are some trees around but little shade, although there are splendid views of surrounding mountain peaks. Being so high it can become cool when the sun goes down. Excursions to the Jungfrau and climbing or walking tours are organised. Some static caravans remain during the winter with about 140 places for tourists in summer. Electrical connections are available. There is a good quality restaurant and hotel at the entrance. The new sanitary block, heated in cool weather, is of excellent quality and has British style WCs, a drying room and facilities for disabled people.

How to find it: 800 m. before entering Grindelwald bear right past Grund railway station. Turn right over bridge, follow railway line for 500 m. and cross stream to camp on right.

General Details: Open all year. 12,000 sq.m. Electricity connections (6A). Restaurant. Hotel. Kiosk for basic supplies. Children's playground. Barbecue hut. Ski lifts, cable cars near. Washing machines. Drying room. Chemical disposal. Motorcaravan services.

Charges 2000: Per person Sfr. 8.00; child (3-12 yrs) 4.00; tent 7.00 - 9.00; caravan 9.00 - 11.00; motorcaravan 9.00 - 12.00; car 3.00; m/cycle 2.00; electricity 3.00 (summer); dog 5.00; local tax 2.90. After 10 days, 1 day free.

Reservations: Write to site. Address: 3818 Grindelwald. Tel: 033/853 42 27.

Grindelwald - Eigernordwand

- The ideal place for your summer or winter holiday • Peaceful and sunny • Picturesque views of the Eigernordwand mountains
- Heated swimming pool nearby
- New sanitary building with first class facilities
- Impeccable motorcaravan service station
- Free hot water • Hotel*** restaurant for campers' friends and family.

TURN OFF BEFORE VILLAGE TOWARDS GRUND
Tel: 033-853 42 27

954 Camping Lido Sarnen, Sarnen, nr Luzern

Good lakeside site in a popular area.

Sarnen is about 20 km. south of Luzern on the main road to Interlaken and is, therefore, ideally placed for ski-ing in winter and sightseeing in summer. The summit of the well known Mt. Pilatus can be reached by mountain railway (the steepest of its type in the world) from Stansstad, about halfway between Luzern and Sarnen, and steamer trips on Lake Luzern can also be made from here. The site is on flat ground directly on the lake with lovely views of near and distant mountains. Suitable for long or short stays, it makes an ideal base for this part of Switzerland or for a night stop if passing through. The 220 pitches, 80 for tourists with electricity, are of 80-90 sq.m. on grass with hard access roads (some narrow). There is shade in parts and the location is a quiet one on the edge of the small town. The exceptionally good sanitary arrangements, heated in cool weather and including a special baby room, are in the main reception building at the entrance to the site. Hot water is free to washbasins, on payment in the showers and sinks, there are British style WCs and facilities for disabled visitors. The site is part of the town Lido complex with a large, heated swimming pool and child's pool and facilities for non-powered boats. There is a pleasant walk along the lakeside. The restaurant, which has a large terrace, is self-service at lunch time and waiter service at night. Narrow roads on site might make manoeuvring difficult for large units.

How to find it: Follow signs from southern junction where town road meets the main road from Interlaken.

General Details: Open all year. 20,000 sq.m. Electricity connections (10A). Shop. Restaurant. Table tennis. Watersports. Swimming pools. Good children's playground. Tennis nearby. Washing machines and dryers. Chemical disposal.

Charges 1999: Per person Sfr. 6.00 - 7.50; child (6-11 yrs) 3.00 - 4.00; under 6 free; local tax 1.20; lakeside pitch 9.00 - 12.00; inner pitch 7.00 - 9.00; car by pitch 3.00; m/cycle 2.00; electricity 3.00.

Reservations: advised for high season and made with Sfr. 30 deposit. Address: 6060 Sarnen. Tel: 041/660 18 66. FAX: 041/662 08 66. E-mail: camping.sarnen@bluewin.ch.

957 Camping Eienwäldli, Engelberg, nr Lucerne/Luzern

*see colour advert
between pages 320/321*

All year quality site with indoor pool in scenic location.

This super site has facilities which must make it one of the best in Switzerland. It is situated in a beautiful location 3,500 feet above sea level and surrounded by mountains on the edge of the delightful village of Engelberg. Being about 35 km. from Luzern by road and with a rail link, it makes a quiet, peaceful base from which to explore the Vierwaldstattersee region, walk in the mountains or just enjoy the scenery. The area is famous as a winter sports region and summer tourist resort and Eienwaldli is open most of the year (except Nov). The indoor pool has recently been most imaginatively rebuilt as a Felsenbad spa bath with adventure pool, steam and relaxing grottoes, Kneipp's cure, children's pool with water slides, solarium, Finnish sauna and eucalyptus steam bath. There is an extra charge to use this. Half of the site is taken up by static caravans but these are grouped together at one side. The camping area is in two parts - nearest the entrance there are 57 hardstandings for caravans and motorcaravans, all with electricity and beyond this is a flat meadow for about 70 tents. The reception building, as well as housing the pool complex, has a well stocked shop, a café/bar where simple meals are served, and rooms and apartments to rent. There is also a Gasthof/restaurant opposite the entrance. The excellent toilet block, heated in cool weather, has British style WCs, free hot water in washbasins (in cabins) and sinks and on payment in the showers. Torches would be useful.

How to find it: From N2 Gotthard motorway, leave at exit `Stans-Sud' and follow signs to Engelberg. Turn right at T-junction on edge of town and follow signs to `Wasserfall' and site.

General Details: Open all year excl. Nov. 40,000 sq m. Electrical connections (10A). Shop. Restaurant. Café/bar. Small lounge. Indoor pool complex. Ski facilities. Children's playground. Golf driving range and 9-hole course near. Washing machines and dryers. Chemical disposal.

Charges 1999: Per person Sfr 6.50; child (6-15 yrs) 3.50; local tax 1.90; caravan 11.00; car or m/cycle 2.00; motorcaravan 13.00; tent 7.00 - 11.00; electricity 2.00 + meter; cable TV 2.50. Credit cards accepted (surcharge).

Reservations: necessary summer and winter high seasons. Made with Sfr 50 deposit. Address: 6390 Engelberg. Tel: 041/6371949. FAX: 041/6374423. E-mail: eienwaeldli.engelberg@bluewin.ch.

987 Camping Piccolo Paradiso, Avegno, nr Locarno

Pleasant, popular site in mountain valley setting.

Locarno, in the most southern of Swiss cantons, Ticino, is a very popular holiday area with activities associated with lakes and mountains. Being on the south of Locarno, Avegno is also a good base from which to visit Lake Maggiori and this part of northern Italy. There are a number of very good camps around to which we add this one to give as much choice as possible. During our stay we were impressed with the friendly, happy atmosphere, much of which is engendered by the owner who appears to know visitors who return year after year and greets them enthusiastically. The lively social life revolves around the central bar/restaurant and terrace. However, all noise has to cease at 11 pm. The 300 tourist pitches are on two level terraces in a river valley, marked by numbered stones set into the ground. Spaces are not over-large but seem to suffice. There are 200 electrical connections, in all areas except the areas set aside for small tents. Three sanitary blocks are well spaced around the site and, although not too large, should be enough. Hot showers are on payment. British style WCs. Children are welcomed and catered for with two playgrounds, a small pool and organised games in high season making this an ideal family site.

How to find it: From Locarno follow signs for Valle Maggia and then camp signs to site (6 km.).

General Details: Open 1 March - 31 Oct. 4.5 ha. Self-service bar/restaurant (mainly Italian type fast food) with terrace. Shade in parts. Children's pool. 2 children's play areas. River bathing (summer). Boating. Table tennis. Volleyball. Mountain bike hire. Entertainment in high season. Washing machines and dryers. Chemical disposal. Motorcaravan services.

Charges 2000: Per person Sfr. 7.00 - 8.00; child (4-14 yrs) 5.00 - 6.00; caravan, motorcaravan or large tent 12.00 - 18.00, acc. to unit and season; medium tent 11.00 - 15.00; dog 3.00; electricity (10A) 4.00.

Reservations: Write to site with Sfr. 50 deposit. Address: 6670 Avegno, Valle Maggia. Tel: 091/796 15 81. FAX: 091/796 31 70.

SWITZERLAND

988 Camping Lido Mappo, Tenero, nr Locarno

Orderly but friendly site with good installations on Lake Maggiore.

Lido Mappo lies on the lakeside at the northeast tip of Lake Maggiore, about 5 km. from Locarno, and has views of the surrounding mountains and hills across the lake. A variety of trips can be made from here by car, lake steamer or mountain lift. The site has its own narrow beach with a frontage of 400 m., mainly sandy, but the lake, shelving very gradually, has a stony floor. Boats can be brought and left on the shore or at moorings. The site is attractively laid out in rows of individual, numbered pitches, half for tents and half for caravans and mostly split up by access roads or hedges. The pitches (421 for touring) vary in size, those by the lake costing more, and most are shaded. Electricity (10A) is available on all pitches. Although reservations are only made for longer stays, there is always a fair chance of finding space. The five toilet blocks can be heated and are well kept, although some are newer than others. They have individual wash-basins, all in cabins for women and some for men, free hot water and British WCs. Facilities for disabled people and a baby room. With helpful staff who speak good English, it is a quiet site.

How to find it: On Locarno side of Tenero, on Bellinzona - Locarno road, site is signed to the south.

General Details: Open 31 March - 29 Oct. as are all amenities. 65,000 sq.m. Supermarket. Restaurant/bar. Takeaway (high season). Large children's playground. Bathing raft in lake. Fishing. Bicycle hire near. Riding 3 km. Golf 5 km. First-aid post. Washing machines and dryers. Cooking facilities. Refrigerated compartments for hire. Chemical disposal. Motorcaravan services. Dogs are not accepted.

Charges 1999: Per unit incl. 2 persons Sfr. 32.00 - 46.00, on lakeside 42.00 - 70.00, acc. to season; extra person (over 3 yrs) 6.00 - 7.00; extra car 5.00 - 6.00; m/cycle 3.00 - 4.00; trailer 4.00 - 5.00; electricity included. Less 5% for stays over 10 days. Credit cards accepted.

Reservations: Min. 1 week (2 weeks lakeside) July/Aug, or 2 weeks at other times. Large deposit and smaller fee. Address: 6598 Tenero (Ticino). Tel: 091/745 14 37. FAX: 091/745 48 08. E-mail: lidomappo@bluewin.ch.

990 Camping Delta, Locarno

Good lakeside site within walking distance of central Locarno.

Camping Delta is actually within the Locarno town limits, only some 800 m. from the centre, and it has a prime position right by the lake, with bathing direct from the site, and adjacent to the municipal lido and sports field. Boats can be put on the lake and the site also has moorings on an estuary at one side. It has 300 pitches on flat ground of 80-100 sq.m. of which 250 are for touring units. They are marked out at the rear but have nothing between them. The single central toilet block is kept very clean and should be about large enough though it could be hard pressed at the busiest times. Hot water is free in the washbasins (some cabins for women), controllable showers and sinks; WCs are British type. Delta is a well run and well situated site and Locarno hosts a Film Festival, classical and jazz concerts and exhibitions.

How to find it: From central Locarno follow signs to Camping Delta, Lido or Stadio along the lake. Beware that approaching from south there are also Delta signs which lead you to Albergo Delta in quite the wrong place.

General Details: Open 1 March - 31 Oct. 65,000 sq.m. Partly shaded. Electrical connections (10A) all parts. Small supermarket. Restaurant/bar with limited menu. Fitness room. Children's playgrounds with new equipment. Volleyball/badminton court. Table tennis and amusements. Entertainment and excursions. Fishing. Bicycle hire. Golf 200 m. Riding 4 km. Baby sitting service. Washing machine and dryer. Chemical disposal. Motorcaravan services. Caravans for hire. Dogs are not accepted.

Charges 1999: Per person Sfr. 10.00 - 17.00; child (3-15 yrs) 5.00; pitch 20.00 - 30.00 or 30.00 - 40.00; electricity 5.00; local tax 1.20. Credit cards accepted (most).

Reservations: made for any length with deposit (Sfr. 50) and booking fee (50). Address: Via G. Respini 7, 6600 Locarno. Tel: 091/751 60 81. FAX: 091/751 22 43. E-mail: info@campingdelta.com.

991 Park-Camping Riarena, Cugnasco, nr Bellinzona

Friendly site with swimming pool between Bellinzona and Locarno.

An agreeable site close to the route from the St Gotthard to the south, Riarena may appeal both to those who are looking for a convenient night stop and to those seeking a holiday site, as it has a medium sized swimming pool and children's pool. Most of the site is covered by tall trees and it is in a peaceful setting, far enough from the main road to be away from noise. The sanitary block is of good quality and has British toilets, individual washbasins with shelf and mirror (a few in private cabins) and free hot water in all facil-ities. It is however small for the size of the site, though showers have been increased to 16 and facilities for disabled visitors added. The 210 pitches (170 for touring units) are now all individually marked with 10A electricity available. July is busiest; there is usually space at other times. Under new management.

How to find it: From motorway exit Bellinzona south in the direction of Locarno. After 10 km. at large round-about turn to Gudo-Bellinzona for 2.5 km. and follow signs for Cugnasco from where site is well signed.

General Details: Open 1 April - 20 Oct. 38,000 sq.m. Well shaded. Electrical connections available. Shop (15/5-15/9). Restaurant. Takeaway. Play area. Swimming pools (25/5-15/9). Mountain bike hire. Fishing 1 km. Riding 2 km. Golf 10 km. Siesta time 12.00-14.00 hrs. Washing machines and dryers. Chemical disposal.

Charges 2000: Per unit incl. 2 persons and tax 27.00 - 35.00; extra adult 7.00 - 8.00; child under 6 yrs 3.00 - 4.00, 6-14 yrs 4.00 - 5.00; dog 3.00; electricity 3.50. Credit cards accepted.

Reservations: Made without charge. Tel: 091/859 16 88. FAX: 091/859 28 85. E-mail: campingriarina@gmx.de.

995 TCS Camping Piodella, Muzzano, nr Lugano

Excellent lakeside site with sandy beach.

This modernised site, on the edge of Lake Lugano facing south down the lake must rank as one of the best in Switzerland. There are 265 numbered pitches (212 for touring units) of good size, with shade in the older part nearest the lake and young trees in the new area. Cars must be parked in the car park. The former sanitary block has been refurbished and a splendid new one has been built. This includes a baby room, bathroom for disabled visitors, British style WCs and free hot water in the washbasins, sinks and good sized showers. These facilities are heated in cool weather. A good, large swimming pool and a child's pool have been added and one can also bathe from the sandy beach. The site is a short way from the end of Lugano's airport but there appears to be no night flying or movements by large aircraft. There is a new bar/restaurant with a pleasant terrace. Although the site is well placed for exploring Lugano, southern Switzerland and northern Italy, many will be content to stay put and enjoy the facilities of the site.

How to find it: Piodella is on Bellinzona-Ponte Tresa road; take motorway exit Lugano-Nord for Ponte Tresa and turn left at T-junction in Agno. Follow signs for Piodella or TCS. Site is at south end of the airport.

General Details: Open all year except 2 Nov - 11 Dec. Electricity connections in all areas (4/6A). Shop. Bar/restaurant. Swimming pools (May - mid Oct). Day and TV rooms. Children's playground. Tennis. Washing machines and dryers. Gas supplies. Chemical disposal. Motorcaravan services.

Charges 1999: (2000 plus c. 10%) Per person Sfr. 5.50 - 7.00; child (6-16 yrs) 50%; pitch 9.00 - 28.00, acc. to season and type; motorcaravan 23.50 - 28.00; local tax 1.25; electricity 3.00 - 4.00, acc. to amps.

Reservations: Contact site. Address: 6933 Muzzano. Tel: 091/994 77 88. FAX: 091/994 67 08.

993 Camping Al Censo, Claro, nr Bellinzona   *see colour advert between pages 320/321*

Tranquil site on old Gotthard - Bellinzona road.

Now that most traffic uses the N2 motorway, the B2 Gotthard - Bellinzona one is used mainly by local vehicles and is, therefore, much quieter. Al Censo is a very pretty campsite with an abundance of flowers and shrubs and backed by a mountain face. Although the site is on a slope and levellers may be needed in places, the 90 tourist pitches, 52 with electricity (6A), are level and amongst mature trees with an over-flow section just outside the entrance for tents. The swimming pool (18 x 9 m) is unheated and there is also a sauna and whirlpool in high season. Two small sanitary blocks, one enlarged to a good standard and with a baby room, provide British style WCs, warm pre-mixed water and free hot showers. Reception and a shop are in the entrance building which has a small covered terrace where drinks are served. This is a useful site for those wanting a peaceful night away from the motorway, it may tempt for a longer stay to explore the Ticino. The friendly, English speaking owners live on site and will help with local attractions.

How to find it: Site well signed at northern end of Claro on old St Gotthard-Bellinzona road. From motorway going south, leave at Biasco exit, go into village and then south on B2. Heading north, take Bellinzona-Nord exit and go north on old pass road.

General Details: Open 1 April - mid-October. 25,000 sq. m. Good shade in most parts. Self-service shop (limited), drinks served. Swimming pool, sauna and whirlpool (high season). Games room. Table tennis. Washing machines and dryers. Chemical disposal. No entry to site 12.00 - 14.00 hrs.

Charges 2000: Per person Sfr. 7.00; child (1-12 yrs) 5.20; pitch 9.00 - 18.00; dog 1.00; local tax 1.30; electricity 3.00.

Reservations: made without charge. Address: 6702 Claro. Tel: 091/863 17 53. FAX: 091/863 4022.

981 Camp Au, Chur

Satisfactory site on through route in attractive part of country.

This modern site has some 120 individual pitches, not very big (say 60 sq.m.) but all with electricity (10A), and about an equal number of unmarked ones on an open meadow, all on flat grass. The toilet block is also modern and of good quality but would frankly be too small if the site were full. It has British style toilets, washbasins with free hot water, hot showers on payment and is heated in cool weather. There are no water points outside the block. Despite this drawback Camp Au is a good site for a night stop or a few days exploring this attractive mountain region. It is rarely full and with much short-stay trade, usually has vacancies. About 400 m. walk is a sports centre including indoor and outdoor swimming pools, and the centre of Chur, said to be the oldest town in Switzerland is about 3 km. The main entrance to the site is reached by passing under a bridge with only 3.05 m. clearance - there is an alternative but only 3.30 m.

How to find it: Site is on south side of town; from motor road take `Chur N' exit from north and continue on obvious main road - signs do appear. From south `Chur S' exit and follow camp signs. Note height limits.

General Details: Open all year. Small shop. Restaurants at both swimming and tennis centres (next to site). General room where drinks served. Children's playground. Table tennis. Washing machine and dryer. Chemical disposal. Motorcaravan services.

Charges 2000: Per person Sfr. 6.20; child (6-12 yrs) 3.10; local tax 1.00; 1 or 2 person tent 6.20, 3 or 4 person 8.30 - 12.50; caravan 12.50; motorcaravan 14.50; car 4.00; m/cycle 2.50; electricity 3.30; dog 2.00.

Reservations: made if you write to site. Address: Felsenaustrasse 61, 7000 Chur. Tel: 081/284 22 83. FAX: 081/284 56 83. E-mail: info@camping-chur.ch.

SWITZERLAND

982 Campingplatz Pradafenz, Churwalden

Mountain site with excellent facilities and services.

In the heart of the village of Churwalden on the Chur - St Moritz road, Pradafenz makes a convenient night stop and being amidst the mountains, is also an excellent base for walking and exploring this scenic area. There are 38 ski lifts serving the district with one starting from the site entrance both for winter ski-ing and summer walking. The 'longest toboggan run in the world' is to planned to be opened next year. Being at 1,200 m. above sea level and surrounded by pine-clad mountains, the views are breathtaking and the air fresh and clean. The absence of entertainment on site makes this a quiet, peaceful place although a variety of entertainment is offered in the region. At first sight, this appears to be a site for static holiday caravans but three large rectangular terraces at the rear take 50 touring units. This area has a hardstanding of concrete frets with grass growing through and 'super-pitch' facilities of electricity (10A), water, drainage, gas and TV sockets. A flat meadow is also available for tents or as an over-flow for caravans. Although the gravel road which leads to the tourers' terrace is not very steep, the very friendly German speaking owner will tow caravans there with his tractor if required. Torches may be useful. The main sanitary block is half underground and is very well appointed with free hot water in all washbasins (some in private cabins), sinks and showers, and British style WCs. There is a baby room and another with hair dryers. A warm temperature is maintained all year. Another good, heated small block has been added in the tourist section. The site has a small new restaurant serving good, simple meals and selling basic provisions. A supermarket is about 300 m. in the village along with other shops and restaurants. The municipal open air swimming pool, surrounded by plenty of grassy space, is 500 m.

How to find it: Site is 300 m. from the main road, signed in the village centre.

General Details: Open all year except 30 April - 1 June. 13,000 sq.m. New restaurant. Shop. General room. Restaurants and shops 300 m. Outdoor pool 500 m. Walking. Skiing. Boot drying room with freezer for ice packs. Bicycle hire. Riding 3.5 km. Golf 5 km. Washing machines, dryers and separate drying room. Gas supplies. Chemical disposal. Motorcaravan services.

Charges 2000: Per person Sfr. 6.00 - 6.50; child (up to 12 yrs) 4.00 - 4.50; local tax 1.80 (child 0.80); caravan 10.00 - 13.00; car 3.00; tent small 4.00, large 8.00; motorcaravan 12.00 - 15.00; electricity 2.00 (metered in winter). Prices higher in winter. Credit cards accepted.

Reservations: Advisable for winter; write to site. Address: 7075 Churwalden. Tel: 081/382 19 39. FAX: 081/382 19 21. E-mail: camping@pradafenz.ch.

985 TCS Camping Farich, Davos

Small, pleasant site on road to the Fluela Pass.

Davos extends for about 4 km. between Davos-Dorf and Davos-Platz between the Fluela Pass and Klosters. A ski centre in winter, Davos has the largest ice rink in Europe and cable cars to nearby peaks. Farich is situated on the edge of Davos-Dorf, at the start of the Pass road and, as the road rises as it passes the campsite, there is some road noise particularly at weekends and public holidays when hoards of motor-cyclists race round two passes - Fluela and Julier - with scant regard for other road users. The 90 pitches, mainly under tall pines, are on either side of a fenced river with bridges between. These are not marked or numbered but the centre road and the 50 electricity points roughly determine where units go. A small shop provides basic food items and a pleasant bar serves good grill meals during the evenings. There is a small children's play area, table tennis and bicycle hire, with a swimming pool 1 km. away. The single sanitary block is at the rear of reception with British style WCs and free hot water in washbasins, sinks and showers.

How to find it: On the main road at eastern end of Davos-Dorf at the start of the Fluela Pass.

General Details: Open 16 May - 28 Sept. 13,000 sq.m. Electrical connections (4A). Shop. Bar with grill meals. Children's playground. Bicycle hire. Table tennis. Swimming pool 1 km. Chemical disposal. Motorcaravan services.

Charges 1999: Per person Sfr. 4.50 - 6.00; child (6-15 yrs) 50%; pitch 6.00 - 19.00; electricity 4.00.

Reservations: Write to site. Address: 7260 Davos-Dorf. Tel: 081/416 10 43. E-mail: cpg@tcs.ch.

984 Camping St Cassian, Lenz, nr Lenzerheide

Mountain site with good facilities in scenic area.

Although St Cassian caters mainly for static holiday caravans, it has room for 40 touring units and is suitable for a night stop travelling to or from St Moritz, or for a longer stay. The site is on a gentle slope but the 40 touring pitches (out of 200) are terraced between the statics under a cover of tall pines. Being 1,415 m. above sea level in a north-south valley, this is a peaceful location surrounded by scenic views and abundant sunshine; 140 signed walking paths of various degrees of difficulty start from the site. Although there is no organised entertainment on the site, there are many opportunities at the holiday resort of Lenzerheide Valbella 3 km. Tennis, an 18-hole golf course, bars and discos, heated swimming pool and a lake for fishing and watersports are near. Good bus services (with a stop outside the entrance) serve the region and many places of interest are accessible by car. The small, heated, good quality sanitary facility is in the main block that also houses reception and an excellent restaurant. It has free hot water in washing troughs and sinks and on payment in the showers, and British style WCs. Torches useful.

How to find it: Site is 20 km. from Chur on no. 3 Chur - St Moritz road, between Lenzerheide and Lantsch/Lenz.

General Details: Open all year. Restaurant. Shop for basics. Fishing 3 km. Bicycle hire 1 km. Riding 2 km. Golf 500 m. Fishing 3 km. Washing machine and dryer. Dishwasher. Gas supplies. Chemical disposal. Motorcaravan services.

Charges 2000: Per person Sfr. 6.50 - 7.00; child (6-16 yrs) 4.00 - 4.50; car 2.50; m/cycle 1.50; caravan 8.50; motorcaravan 11.00; tent large 8.50, small 5.50; electricity (10A) 2.50 - 3.00. Credit cards accepted.

Reservations: Made with Sfr. 20 deposit. Address: 7083 Lenz bei Lenzerheide. Tel: 081/384 24 72. FAX: 081/384 24 89.

980 Camping Silvaplana, Silvaplana, nr St Moritz

Family run site on edge of lake in the Engadine region.

Silvaplana is situated at the junction of the road from Italy over the Malojapass, the road from northern Switzerland via the Julierpass, and the road which continues through St Moritz to Austria. Camping Silvaplana, therefore, might be useful for a night stop if travelling this way. Although the surrounding scenery across the lake is very pleasant, there is nothing remarkable about the site except that a wind blows along the lake most afternoons which is used by windsurfing enthusiasts. However, it is probably the best campsite in the area, with facilities next to the site for volleyball or football, a windsurfing school and good walking possibilities. There is a shop for basic supplies and a restaurant just away from the entrance which is open all day June-Oct. The site is mainly level and the 160 pitches for tourists are numbered and marked by posts or tapes, with 120 electrical connections (10A). The sanitary accommodation is old, but acceptable and heated, with British style WCs and free hot water in washing troughs, sinks and showers. There are no washing machines for campers but staff provide a laundry service. A fenced river runs through but the lake shore is unprotected (with access for boats to the lake).

How to find it: If coming from the Julier Pass continue through Silvaplana to junction with road to St Moritz, turn right and look for camp signs on your right. From St Moritz, continue along lakeside passing the village - camp signs are on your right.

General Details: Open 15 May - 15 Oct. 50,000 sq.m. Restaurant outside site (June-Oct). Shop (15/5-15/9). Watersports, climbing, walking. Lake swimming (pool 4 km. in St Moritz). Sports centre near. Small children's play area. Bicycle hire 200 m. Riding 5 km. Golf 10 km. Tennis near. Laundry service. Gas supplies. Chemical disposal. Motorcaravan services.

Charges 2000: Per person Sfr. 8.00; child 5-12 yrs 4.50, 12-16 yrs 6.50; tent 5.00 - 7.00; caravan 9.00; motorcaravan 12.00; car 8.00; m/cycle 3.00; electricity 2.80. Credit cards accepted.

Reservations: Write to site. Address: 7513 Silvaplana. Tel: 081/828 84 92.

**All the sites in this guide are regularly inspected by our team
of experienced site assessors, but we welcome your opinion too.**

See Readers' Reports - page 366

SWITZERLAND

983 Camping Sur-En, Sur-En/Sent, nr Scuol

All year campsite with excellent facilities.

Sur-En is at the eastern end of the Engadine valley, about 10 km. from the Italian and Austrian borders. The area is, perhaps, better known as a skiing region, but has summer attractions as well. At nearby Scoul there is an ice-rink and thermal baths, plus a wide range of activities including mountain biking, white water rafting and excursion possibilities. As you approach on road 27 and spot the site way below under the shadow of a steeply rising, wooded mountain, the drop down may appear daunting. However, as you drive it becomes reasonable, although the site owner will provide assistance for nervous towers. A level site, it is in an open valley with little shade. They say there is room for 120 touring units on the meadows where pitches are neither marked nor numbered; there are 60 electricity connections. The modern, heated sanitary block near the restaurant, shop and reception building is of a high standard and there is a further small provision in the main building when required. British WCs and free hot water in washbasins and showers. The good restaurant with a covered terrace overlooks the children's play area so that adults can enjoy a drink and keep watch on their children whilst enjoying the mountain views. Entertainment for both adults and children is arranged in July/Aug. and a symposium for sculptors is held during the second week in July. Excursions are also arranged in high season. The friendly, English speaking owner seems to have created a very pleasant atmosphere and although the site might be used for a night stay during transit, it could well attract for a longer period.

How to find it: Site is clearly visible and also signed from main road 27 to the east of Scuol.

General Details: Open all year. 20,000 sq.m. Electrical connections (6A). Shop (all year). Restaurant (closed Nov. and April and on Tues. and Wed. in low season). Takeaway (high season). Swimming pool. Good children's playground. Bicycle hire. Animation in high season. Golf 8 km. Activities near - see text. Washing machine and dryer. Motorcaravan services. Chemical disposal. Bus service to Scuol for train to St Moritz.

Charges 2000: Per person Sfr. 5.80: child (6-16 yrs) 2.90; caravan 13.40 - 15.00; tent 9.90 - 13.40; motor-caravan 13.40 - 15.00. Credit cards accepted.

Reservations: not made. Address: 7554 Sur-En/Sent. Tel: 081/866 35 44. FAX: 081/866 32 37.

986 Camping Plauns, Morteratsch, Pontresina

Mountain site in splendid scenery near St Moritz.

Pontrasina is at the mouth of the Bernina Pass road (B29) which runs from Celerina in the Swiss Engadine to Titana in Italy. Camping Plauns, some 4 km. southeast of Pontresina, is situated in the floor of the valley between fir-clad mountains at 1,850 m. above sea level. A river runs through this long, narrow site with lovely views on each side and a small lake at one end. There are about 210 pitches for tourists in summer, some in small clearings amongst tall trees and some in a larger open space. During the winter the number is reduced to 40. They are neither numbered nor marked and size depends on the natural space between the trees. Being in a mountain valley, the grass is thin over a stony base with tarmac roads running through. Torches would be useful. There are three sanitary blocks, one old and two new, which are modern and excellent, can be heated in cool weather, with British style WCs and free hot water in washbasins (some in private cabins) and sinks and on payment in the showers. Washing machines and dryers are provided and facilities for disabled visitors. This is a quiet site in a peaceful location and although no entertainment is provided on the site, a programme is offered, winter and summer, at nearby Pontresina. It could make a useful night stop when travelling through or a base for exploring the region which is good walking country. There is a small, well stocked shop and grill-bar for drinks and simple meals with a restaurant 1 km away.

How to find it: Site is on B29 road about 4 km. southeast of Pontresina - well signed.

General Details: Open 1 June - 15 Oct. and 16 Dec - 15 April. 40,000 sq.m. Electrical connections to all pitches. Shop. Grill-snack bar. Children's playground.

Charges 1999: Per person Sfr. 7.50; child 6-11 yrs 4.00, 12-15 yrs 5.50; tent pitch 9.00 - 13.00; pitch for caravan and car 14.00.

Reservations: Contact site. Address: Morteratsch, 7504 Pontresina. Tel: 081/838 83 00. FAX: as phone. E-mail: pontresina@compunet.ch.

OPEN ALL YEAR

The following sites are understood to accept caravanners and campers all year round, *although the list also includes some sites open for at least 9 months.* For sites in italics, with an asterix, please check our report for dates and other restrictions. In any case, it is always wise to phone as, for example, facilities available may be reduced.

Andorra
9143 Xixerella

Liechtenstein
0758 Mittagspitze

Austria
003 *Holiday* *
004 Zugspitze
005 Kroll
006 Natterer See
007 Hofer
009 Zillertal-Hell
010 T-Brantlhof
011 Tirol Camp
012 *Aufenfeld* *
013 Schloß-Itter
014 Euro
015 *Riffler* *
016 Zell am See
017 Kranebitten
018 Woferlgut
019 Erlengrund
020 Tirol
022 Krismer
023 Feldkirch
026 *Hirschenw't* *
032 Kloster'burg
033 Central
036N Rutar Lido
044 Schluga
048 Burgstaller

Belgium
053 Waux-Hall
054 L'Orient
056 Lombarde
058 Memling
059 De Gavers
066 Baalse Hei
067 La Clusure
074 *Eau Rouge* *

Czech Republic
468 Druhy Mlyn
477 Dlouha
481 Kotva
487 Morava

Denmark
2020 Mogeltonder
2090 Krakær
2140 Jesperhus
2150 Solyst
2215 Odense
2235 Sakskobing

Finland
2903 Käyrälampi
2930 Koskenniemi

Germany
3000 *Wingst* *
3010 Röders Park
3020 Bremen
3025 Alfsee
3030 Truma
3035 DCC Kur
3040 Prahljust
3045 *Walkenried* *
3210 Biggesee

3212 Wirfttal
3215 G-Meile
3222 Gülser
3235 Mühlenteich
3242 Country
3260 B-Dürkheim
3264 Büttelwoog
3280 Teichmann
3402 Cannstatter
3405 B-Liebenzell
3410 Aichelberg
3415 Adam
3420 Oberrhein
3430 Alisehof
3440 Kirchzarten
3445 Belchenblick
3450 Munstertal
3452 Sagemuhle
3455 Gugel's
3610 Nürnberg
3615 Stadsteinach
3620 Romantische
3625 *Frickenh'n* *
3630 Donau-Lech
3650 Gitzenweiler
3665 *Brunnen* *
3670 *Hopfensee* *
3675 Richterbichl
3680 *Tennsee* *
3685 Allweglehen
3690 Wagnerhof
3700 Bayerwald
3705 *Lackenh'r* *
3715 *Viechtach* *
3720 Naabtal
3725 Bavaria
3830 Krossinee
3833 LuxOase
3842 Schlosspark
3847 Auensee
3850 Aga

Hungary
515 Fortuna
516 Zugligeti
526 Jonathermál

Northern Ireland
850 LoanEden

Irish Republic
870 Gateway
874 Cong
908 Forest Farm
910 Camac
916 Moat Farm
938 Parsons G'n
939 Carrick-Suir

Italy
6037 Giuliana
6060 Estense
6200 Olympia
6201 Antholz
6220 Mombarone
6250 Lac-Como
6401 Dei Fiori
6412 Valdeiva
6427 Tranquilla

6602 *Bologna* *
6610 Fiesole
6623 San Marino
6663 Amiata
6665 Soline
6808 Genziana
6811 Ipini
6815 Fondi
6850 Sea World

Luxembourg
767 Ardennes
770 Gaalgebierg
781 Martbusch

Netherlands
550 Pannensch'r
552 Breskens
556 Wijde Blick
560 Delftse Hout
561 Oude Maas
562 Duinrell
563 Koningshof
564 Kijkduinpark
567 *Gaasper* *
573 Sikkeler
576 Kuilart
579 Kuierpadtien
580 Flevo-Natuur
584 Pampel
589 KI-Canada
591 Hertenwei
596 Wilerbaan

Norway
2315 Ringoy
2385 Sandvik
2400 Jolstrah'men
2455 Ballangen
2460 Prinsen
2475 Saltstraumen
2480 Bjorkedal
2490 Skjerneset
2505 Magalaupe
2510 Håneset
2513 Gjelten Bru
2545 Rustberg
2550 Strandefjord
2555 Lom
2570 Fossheim
2590 Sandviken
2610 Neset
2615 Olberg

Poland
315 Wilamowek
317 Mazurski
319 Kruska
321 Astur
323 Olenka

Portugal
803 Rio Alto
809 Figueira-Foz
810 S Pedro-M'l
813 Guincho
814 Lisboa
815 Caparica
816 Porto Covo
818 Milfontes

819 Sitava
820 Valverde
821 Albufeira
822 Quarteira
823 Olhao
833 Arganil
834 Évora
835 Markádia
836 Idanho
837 Cerdeira
838 Vilar-Mouros
840 O Tamanco
841 Armacao
843 Sagres
844 Q-Carriços
845 *Colina-Sol* *
846 Vale Paraiso

Slovak Republic
491 Turiec
493 Tourist Club
494 Neresnica

Slovenia
410 Spik
415 Kamne
435 Jezica
440 Dolina

Spain
8072 Les Medes
8130 Calonge
8240 Bona Vista
8390 Vilanova
8483 Tamarit
8506 Serra-Prades
8535 Cala-Oques
8615 Kiko
8680 Armanello
8681 Villasol
8683 Benisol
8685 El Raco
8686 Excalibur
8687 Cap Blanch
8711 *Nerja* *
8741 Florantilles
8742 La Marina
8743 Mar-Jal
8750 Gallardos
8751 Cuevas Mar
8752N El Portus
8753 La Manga
8755 Moraira
8760 Mar Azul
8770 El Paraiso
8782 Laguna
8800 Marbella
8801 Rosaleda
8803 Buganvilla
8805 Los Jarales
8809 El Sur
8810 Tropical
8812 Chullera 2
8850 Paloma
8865 Las Dunas
8871 Giralda
8872 Fontanilla
8940 Los Cantiles

8941 Valdoviño
8964 Cabuerniga
8965 P-Europa
8980 Bellavista
9024 Cancelas
9025 Regio
9027 Monfrague
9028 Villueracas
9030 Igueldo
9035 Portuondo
9038 *Orio* *
9040 *Haro* *
9060 Montañesa
9070 Pirineos
9081 Villsom
9085 Carlos III
9087 Merida
9088 Fuencaliente
9089 Desp'perros
9090 El Greco
9091 S-Castillo
9121 Vall d'Ager
9123 El Solsones
9142 *Solana* *
9200 El Escorial
9210 Pico-Miel
9250 Costajan
9270 Suspiro-M

Sweden
2650 Skånes
2665 Rosenlund
2675 Lysingsb't
2700 Boras
2720 Hökensås
2740 Laxsjons
2750 Sommarvik
2835 Orsa
2840 Flottsbro
2845 Svegs
2850 Ostersunds
2860 Umeå
2865 Gielas
2870 Jokkmokks
2705 Karralund

Switzerland
905 B-Couvent
906 Kappelenb'e
922 Grangettes
927 De Vidy
930 Bivouac
936 Grassi
939 Vermeille
942 Manor Farm
946 Jungfrau
949 Eigernordw'
954 Lido Sarnen
957 *Eienwäldli* *
963 Sémiramis
967 Molignon
971 *Les Iles* *
977 Sa Monica
981 Camp Au
982 *Pradafenz* *
983 Sur En
984 St Cassian
995 *Piodella* *

SITE BROCHURE SERVICE

The following sites have supplied us with a quantity of their brochures. These leaflets are interesting and useful supplements to our reports and most contain colour photographs or other illustrations of the site which cannot be reproduced in this book. If you would like any of these simply cut out or copy this page, tick the relevant boxes and post it to us. Please enclose a large envelope (at least 9" x 6") addressed to yourself and stamped (on average, 5 brochures will weigh 100 gms). Send requests to:

Deneway Guides Ltd, Chesil Lodge, West Bexington, Dorchester, Dorset DT2 9DG

Luxemburg

764	Auf Kengert	☐

Spain

8012	Mas Nou	☐
8035	L'Amfora	☐
8040	Las Dunas	☐
8060	Ballena Alegre	☐
8071	Castell Montgri	☐
8072	Les Medes	☐
8080	El Defin Verde	☐
8090	Cypsela	☐
8100	Inter-Pals	☐
8102	Mas Patoxas	☐
8103	El Maset	☐
8107	Valldaro	☐
8120	Kim's Camping	☐
8130	Calonge	☐
8150	Palamos	☐
8160	Cala Gogo	☐
8200	Cala Llevado	☐
8230	El Pinar	☐
8390	Vilanova Park	☐
8392	El Garrofer	☐
8395	Arc de Bara	☐

8410	Playa Brava	☐
8470	La Siesta	☐
8480	Sanguli	☐
8481	Cambrils Park	☐
8482	Pineda de Salou	☐
8483	Tamarit	☐
8484	Gavina	☐
8530	Playa Montroig	☐
8535	Cala d'Oques	☐
8537N	Templo del Sol	☐
8540	Torre del Sol	☐
8560	Tropicana	☐
8580	Bonterra	☐
8755	Moraira	☐
8800	Marbella Playa	☐
8860	Fuente del Gallo	☐
8960	La Paz	☐
9000	Playa Joyel	☐
9024	As Cancelas	☐
9042	Extarri	☐
9060	Pena Montanesa	☐
9200	El Escorial	☐
9210	Pico de la Miel	☐
	Junta de Extremadura	☐

NO DOGS !

Following the recent change in legislation, for the benefit of those who want to take their dogs with them to France, we list here the sites which have indicated to us that they do not accept dogs. The sites shown in italics do not accept dogs at certain times. If you are planning to take your dog we do, however, advise that you phone the site first to check – there may be limits on numbers, breeds, or times of the year when they are excluded.

NEVER: these sites do not accept dogs at any time.

Austria		Ireland		Norway	
009	Zillertal-Hell	951	Eagle Point	2330	Eikhamrane
046	Ossiachersee	**Italy**		**Spain**	
Belgium		6000	Mare Pineta	8005	Cadaques
063	Grimbergen	6010	Capalonga	8072	Les Medes
		6015	Il Tridente	8090	Cypsela
Germany		6020	Union Lido	8101	Playa Brava
3005	Schnelsen Nord	6025	Residence	8103	El Maset
3260	Bad Dürkheim	6030	Dei Fiori	8481	Cambrils Park
3405	Bad Liebenzell	6032	Cavallino	8530	Playa Montroig
3440	Kirchzarten	6035	Mediterraneo	8540	Torre del Sol
Hungary		6042	Alba d'Oro	8560	Tropicana
509	Füred	6055	Isamar	8681	Villasol
		6065	Tahiti	8801	Rosaleda
Netherlands		6265	Ideal Molino	**Switzerland**	
556	Wijde Blick	6401	Dei Fiori	918	Buchorn
568	Nordduinen	6624	Rubicone	948	Gletscherdorf
574	Sint Maartenszee	6645	Delle Piscine	988	Lido Mappo
582	Hertshoorn	6803	Athena	989	Campofelice
585	Hooge Veluwe	6815	Fondi	990	Delta
598	De Roos	6820	Baia Domizia		

SOMETIMES: these sites do not accept dogs at certain times of the year.

Austria			Italy		
003	Holiday	not 24/12 - 3/1	6210	Steiner	not high season
006	Natterer See	not July-Aug	6653	Listro	not high season
023	Waldcamping	not July-Aug	6660	Maremma	not 16/6-31/8
040	Arneitz	not July-Aug	6661	Cieloverde	not July-Aug
Ireland			6842	S' Antonio	not August
910	Camac Valley	not July-Aug	6845	San Nicola	not high season
915	River Valley	not July-Aug	**Portugal**		
961	Mannix Point	not Jun/Jul/Aug	835	Markádia	not July-Aug
Germany			837	Cerdeira	not July-Aug
3442	Herbolzheim	not June-Aug	**Spain**		
3465	Wirthshof	not July-Aug	8075	Estartit	not 20/6 - 20/8
Netherlands			8080	Delfin Verde	not 8/7 - 12/8
576	Kuilart	not July-Aug	8160	Cala Gogo	not 1/7 - 26/8
			8235	Blanes	not July-Aug

DISCOUNT VOUCHERS

Between pages 192/193 you will find two Discount Vouchers which will provide you with potential savings of more than the cost of the Guide itself! (valid 1 Jan - 31 Dec 2000 only)

Voucher A - Campsite Discount Voucher

This voucher entitles the holder to the relevant discounts or special offers at the sites in this guide that have a small Alan Rogers' logo by their entry. Retain this voucher for inspection at the campsite.

Voucher B - Travel and Breakdown Insurance

This voucher entitles the holder to a discount of 10% on Travel & Breakdown Insurance arrangements made via this Guide, as advertised between pages 160/161. To arrange cover please follow the instructions on the voucher.

TAKING YOUR PET ON HOLIDAY

How many times have you wished you could take your dog, or even your cat, with you when you go camping or caravanning abroad? Well, in the year 2000, and subject to your meeting some understandably strict conditions, you can!

Not only are the conditions strict, the procedure is quite lengthy and complicated, although we suspect it may become more simple in future years. In the mean-time the information available (in the autumn of 1999) about the arrangements for the year 2000 seems to be something of a closely guarded secret, and we are grateful therefore to Rip Kirby, the Vet who looks after our own dogs' well-being, and to John Noulton, Director of Public Affairs at Euro-tunnel, who have both been very forthcoming, and whose advice we are happy to pass on to our readers; our only caveat being that the regulations still seem to be something of a moveable feast at the moment.

So, if you plan to take your dog or cat abroad in 2000 please check that these regulations haven't been superseded – you can check the current situation via the MAFF Web Site: http://www.maff/gov.uk/animalh/quarantine/default.htm.

There is also a help line: 0181 330 6835, or e-mail pets@ahvg.maff.gov.uk

In fact we are fairly confident that the main conditions and arrangements detailed below will indeed apply – we have even had our own dogs vaccinated, microchipped and tested already in anticipation of their first trip abroad in 2000 – inspecting facilities for dogs on French campsites of course! We were also pleased to discover that the fees charged by our local Vet in Dorchester were about 20% cheaper than those indicated by MAFF and Eurotunnel.

As we see it the procedure in respect of the vaccination, microchipping, testing and certification against rabies seems straightforward, it is the procedure for treatment against parasites and tapeworm required between 24 and 48 hours prior to re-entering the UK that looks like being something of a nightmare (and nothing whatever to do with rabies). Essentially you will need to find a Vet in the country from which you are returning who understands what is required, and is authorised to issue the necessary certificate.

The Pet Travel Scheme

by Rip Kirby B.V.Sc. MRCVS

After a century of quarantine regulations imposed to protect us from that most emotive of all animal diseases, Rabies, the dawn of a new era of freedom of movement for pet dogs and cats has arrived. Bowing to both political pressure and pressure from the pet-owning public, the government has instigated the 'Pet Travel Scheme' as a means to allow you and I to holiday abroad with our companion animals. This scheme will commence in a trial form as early as New Year 2000 from selected embarkation points (currently Portsmouth, Eurotunnel, some Dover routes, and Heathrow) and is expected to rapidly expand to cover the majority of sea routes to the continent from the UK.

For the dog-loving members of the camping and caravanning fraternity all this is exceptionally good news. No more tearful good-byes as you leave your best mate behind at a kennels to pine for you as you selfishly indulge your desire for a holiday. Now you can enjoy the delights of touring together. First, however, there is a strict regime of vaccination and identification by micro-chipping that you must arrange for your pet. This is to prevent smuggling of rabies suscep-

tible animals into the UK, and also to avoid the accidental importation of various parasite diseases not currently established here. Briefly, to take your dog or cat on holiday with you, this is what you need to do:

1. Ask your veterinary Surgeon to microchip your pet. This involves the insertion of a tiny rice-grain sized device into the animals scruff which, when scanned with a suitable scanner shows a number unique to that animal. The insertion procedure is very quick and safe and is done at a normal consultation.

2. The animal is then given a rabies vaccine. This is a very safe product which has been used widely in other parts of the world for many years.

3. Approximately 30 days later you will need to return to the Vet and a blood sample will be taken to confirm adequate response to the vaccine.

4. Finally, shortly before you leave for your holiday you will need to pop in to your veterinary surgery for a health certificate to say that the animal is fit to travel.

5. Do remember that after the initial microchipping and blood testing all that will be required to maintain the animals status will be booster vaccines annually or biannually and health certificates when you are due to travel.

No doubt short sea routes and the Eurotunnel will prove most popular with pet owners as at the moment it seems likely the ferry companies may insist the animals stay in the car for the crossings.

On your return from holiday you will need to seek veterinary advice and treatment 24 - 48 hours before re-entering the UK to carry out the appropriate treatment for the parasitic diseases (ticks and tapeworm) mentioned above. You will be required to produce a valid certificate from the overseas vet on your return to the UK Port, otherwise your dog will not be allowed back into the UK.

Once initial teething problems have been ironed out in the trial period, there is little doubt in the industry that the demand for the Pet Travel Scheme will be enormous. Our friends in other European countries consider it standard practice to holiday with their pets in other parts of the continent, and we will rapidly be joining them.

If you are considering taking advantage of the Pet Travel Scheme then my advice would be to contact your local Veterinary Practice as soon as possible. This will be very popular and will place great strain on the blood testing labs and the vaccine suppliers.

After you have completed the procedures required, then all that will be left to do is to teach 'Rover' to bark in French, German, Spanish, Italian, Dutch........

Our readers, Mr & Mrs Spooner, have a Border terrier that goes camping by motorcycle!

Quarantine Questions and Answers

John Noulton, Director of Public Affairs, Eurotunnel

CAN I BRING MY DOG/CAT INTO THE UK WITHOUT QUARANTINE?
Not yet. The British government has announced that it intends to bring in a new regime to replace quarantine for animals imported from certain countries and provided that certain pre-entry conditions are fulfilled.

WHEN WILL THE CHANGE TAKE PLACE?
Spring 2000. Initially, the government will designate certain ports/terminals as approved points of entry as part of a pilot scheme. Eurotunnel hopes to take part in this pilot scheme. The full scheme will start in April 2001.

WHAT IS THE NEXT STAGE?
The government needs to change the law to introduce the new regime. We have been told that the necessary Order will be made in October/November 1999.

WHAT ARE THE PRE-ENTRY REQUIRE-MENTS?
Before an animal can be imported into the UK from the approved countries, five conditions must be fulfilled:

1. the animal must be implanted with an identity microchip.

2. It must be vaccinated against rabies.

3. 30 days later it must be subject to a blood test at a MAFF-approved laboratory.

4. It must have a certificate from an approved veterinarian confirming compliance with conditions 1, 2 and 3. (the 'Pet's Passport').

5. At least 24 hours and no more than 48 hours before entry it must be treated (and certified by an approved vet) for certain types of exotic parasite.

Note that no animal can be admitted to the UK until 6 months have elapsed following the initial blood test. (This requirement does not, exceptionally, apply to UK-resident animals which are blood-tested between 3 August 1999 and the start of the pilot scheme).

IS A BLOOD TEST NECESSARY EVERY TIME?
Not if the animal has been re-vaccinated annually in subsequent years.

SHOULD I HAVE MY ANIMAL VACCINATED NOW TO SAVE TIME?
It is now possible for animals to be vacci-nated and blood-tested to take part in the scheme. You should consult your vet.

Quarantine Questions and Answers

CAN I BRING MY WARTHOG/AARDVARK/ DONKEY IN WITHOUT QUARANTINE UNDER THESE ARRANGEMENTS?
No. The initial scheme is confined to cats and dogs.

FROM WHICH COUNTRIES WILL I BE ABLE TO IMPORT AN ANIMAL WITHOUT QUARANTINE?
All European Union countries (plus Switzerland) and from certain rabies-free islands such as Australia and New Zealand. Entry will not be allowed from the USA and Canada, at least until the full scheme begins in 2001.

WHERE WILL THE ENTRY CHECKS BE DONE AND WHAT IS INVOLVED?
The checks for shuttle customers will be carried out in the UK control zone in Coquelles before you board the shuttle. (There are no checks on departure from the UK). Staff will scan the animal to read the identification number and check that the documentation is correct and related to the animal in question.

WHAT WILL IT COST TO IMPORT MY DOG?
Eurotunnel has no information about the cost of vaccinations, blood tests, certificates and treatment for parasites. MAFF estimates put the initial cost at up to £200, plus £30 for annual boosters. In due course, your vet should be able to advise you on this. Customers bringing animals in via Eurotunnel will be required to buy a pets' 'ticket'. The cost of the ticket has not yet been decided.

HOW WILL THE ANIMAL TRAVEL THROUGH THE SYSTEM?
We shall require the pet to stay in the car at all times, although you may be asked to bring it outside the car for scanning and checking.

WHAT ABOUT PETS'TOILETS?
Customers are expected to have made appropriate arrangements before passing through tolls. Should there be a disruption to the system an emergency exercise area will be opened.

WILL ANIMALS BE ALLOWED ON THE FREIGHT SHUTTLE?
Not during the pilot phase. No decision has been taken about the longer term.

WHAT HAPPENS IF MY ANIMAL DOES NOT HAVE THE NECESSARY MICROCHIP/ VACCINATION ETC.?
The animal will be refused entry to the Eurotunnel system. If the discrepancy is capable of being resolved quickly we can put the owner in touch with an approved carrier/quarantine specialist either in France or the UK who will look after the animal until it can be allowed entry. Otherwise the owner will either have to stay in France or make arrangements for quarantine. Under the proposed new laws, an undocumented animal discovered on the shuttle will be impounded and quarantined for six months.

Any or all such arrangements will be at the cost of the pet owner

WILL THERE BE ANY RESTRICTIONS ON THOSE WHO CAN IMPORT ANIMALS DURING THE PILOT SCHEME?
In principle, no, but the pre-entry ('ticking and worming') requirement will probably rule out very short-stay visitors to the Continent.

MY ANIMAL IS ALREADY VACCINATED AGAINST RABIES. DOES THIS MEAN THAT I DO NOT HAVE TO WAIT FOR SEVEN MONTHS BEFORE ENTERING THE UK?
No: you have to start again from scratch with a fresh vaccination, followed 30 days later by a blood test. Your animal will then not be admitted until 6 months after the blood test. MAFF have told us that they cannot accept pre-existing blood tests even if they have been carried out at a laboratory which they eventually approve. Now that eleven (so far) laboratories have been accepted by MAFF, blood tests carried out in these premises after 27 May 1999 are valid for entry, but the 6-month 'incubation' period still applies.

HOW CAN I BE SURE BEFORE LEAVING THE UK THAT MY PET WILL BE RE-ADMITTED?
Provided that your animal complies with the five pre-entry requirements, there should be no difficulty about re-entry. Make sure that you have the necessary documentation and ask your vet to confirm that the chip is still legible (occasionally chips migrate round an animal's body). It is probable that ET will have facilities in the UK terminal for you to check compliance before you leave the country.

DOES THE VACCINATION ETC. HAVE TO BE DONE BY A UK VET?
No. Treatment, blood testing, and documentation by a qualified Vet in the approved countries is equally acceptable.

CAR FERRY SERVICES

The number of different services from the UK to the Continent provides a wide choice of sailings to meet most needs. The actual choice is a matter of personal preference, influenced by factors such as where you live, your actual destination in Europe, cost and whether you see the channel crossing as a potentially enjoyable part of your holiday or, (if you are prone to sea-sickness) as something to be endured!

Below is a summary of the services likely to be operating in the year 2000, based on information available at the time of going to press (Oct 99), together with a number of reports on those services which we have used ourselves during the last two years. Detailed up-to-date information will be available from ferry operators themselves, the Alan Rogers Travel Service (01892 615141) and travel agents in the New Year when the schedules are finalised; the information produced here is intended only as a provisional guide.

Destination	Ferry Company	Routes	Time
FRANCE	Brittany Ferries	Portsmouth-St Malo	9/11 hrs
		Portsmouth-Caen	6/7 hrs
		Plymouth-St Malo	6/9 hrs
		Plymouth-Roscoff	6/8 hrs
		Cork-Roscoff/St Malo	13 hrs
	Hoverspeed	Dover-Calais	35 mins
		Folkestone-Boulogne	55 mins
		Newhaven-Dieppe	2 hrs
	P&O Line	Dover-Calais	75 mins
	P&O Portsmouth	Portsmouth-Le Havre	5½ hrs
		Portsmouth-Cherbourg	5/9 hrs
	SeaFrance	Dover-Calais	90 mins
	Condor Ferries	Weymouth-St Malo	5-5½ hrs
		Poole-St Malo	5-5½ hrs
	Irish Ferries	Rosslare-Cherbourg	18 hrs
		Rosslare-Roscoff	17 hrs
	Eurotunnel	Dover-Calais	30-45 mins
BELGIUM	P&O North Sea Ferries	Hull-Zeebrugge	14 hrs
	Hoverspeed	Dover-Ostend	110 mins
NETHERLANDS	P&O North Sea Ferries	Hull-Rotterdam	14 hrs
	P&O Stena Line	Harwich-Hook (FastCraft)	3½ hrs
		Harwich-Hook (ferry)	6-8 hrs
	DFDS Seaways	Newcastle-Ijmuiden	14 hrs
GERMANY	DFDS Seaways	Harwich/Newcastle-Hamburg	19-20 hrs
SPAIN	Brittany Ferries	Plymouth-Santander	24 hrs
	P&O European Ferries	Portsmouth-Bilbao	28½ hrs
DENMARK	DFDS Seaways	Harwich-Esbjerg	20 hrs
NORWAY	Fjord Line	Newcastle-Stavanger/Bergen	c. 24 hrs
	DFDS Seaways	Newcastle-Kristiansand	18 hrs
SWEDEN	DFDS Seaways	Harwich/Newcastle-Gothenburg	c.24 hrs

Ferry Reports

Even though we travel to Europe frequently in respect of our extensive Site Inspection Programme, we do not use all the various services summarised every year. Our reports, therefore, cover those services which we have used over the past two years and, as our France Guide features reports on many of the services to France, we have included in this Guide only those we have used to destinations other than France.

Brittany Ferries - Plymouth/Santander

This service is operated by Brittany Ferries flagship, the 'Val de Loire'. Although this is a long crossing, which on the face of it appears relatively expensive, if you are travelling to Spain, Portugal or even the Basque area of France, the higher ferry cost may well be offset by the saving in fuel, autoroute tolls or overnight accommodation en route, so it's well worth making a comparative calculation of the total cost of your journey! Facilities on the Val de Loire are almost up to cruise liner standards, and the 24 hour voyage itself can be very enjoyable indeed, with plenty to keep you occupied or pleasantly relaxed – a good choice of restaurants, cinema, sun-decks, etc. all add to the 'cruising' atmosphere.

North Sea Ferries - Hull/Rotterdam and Hull/Zeebrugge

We have used these services on several occasions during the last two or three years, and our opinion is generally favourable. The two ferries on which we have travelled recently (the 'Norstar' and 'Norsea') are designed as a 'floating hotels', with first class facilities, plenty of space and ample entertainment; unfortunately the ticket price no longer includes a five-course evening meal and full English breakfast! The cabins are situated towards the forward end of the ship, away from the public rooms, providing the opportunity of an undisturbed night's sleep. The decor is above average, and there are private facilities available; a nice touch was early morning tea served in your cabin, which helps soften the blow associated with an early start! Overall, North Sea Ferries provide an excellent service, neatly illustrated by their getting us and our car on-board at Europort (Rotterdam) even though we arrived at the terminal (after an horrendous drive) actually at the precise time that the vessel was due to sail! This route must be a particularly attractive proposition for those living in the north or in Scotland.

Fjord Line - Newcastle/Bergen

Having never previously travelled to Scandinavia by sea, we were quite excited at the prospect of this crossing, and we weren't disappointed, despite the irritation of a two hour check-in time! In fact the two hours are necessary, as vehicles have to be loaded according to their port of disembarkation, because, unlike most ferries, this service calls at several ports. Finally arriving on board, I must confess that we wished we'd booked a better cabin - the standard inside cabins are pretty small and somewhat claustrophobic, so next time we get the opportunity to travel on this service we'll opt for one of the much nicer (but somewhat more expensive) outside cabins. The views, despite some very indifferent weather, as the vessel nosed her way into Bergen were rather spectacular, and we regretted having to disembark at the first port of call instead of being able to enjoy the views as the voyage continued down the coast. All in all a thoroughly enjoyable way to get to Norway. We used the 'Venus' which operates the thrice weekly service on this route - although built in 1975, this vessel has been extensively and continuously upgraded and now provides a modern smart and comfortable service in keeping with the length of the crossing. Catering is now of a very high standard; particularly impressive are the good-value Norwegian breakfasts. The whole operation gives the impression of a well-run company. The decor and overall design on board is distinctly different from what we're used to on the cross-channel ferries, so we spent quite a lot of time exploring the ship, sampling the restaurants, etc, hence the time passed all too quickly. We were generally very impressed with everything about this service (even the more or less mandatory briefing about disembarkation arrangements was presented in a quite amusing fashion!) At first sight the fares might seem rather high, but it must be remembered that this is a crossing that takes the best part of 24 hours, and saves a drive of some 2,000 km! Fjord Line's policy is, therefore, to offer a service which is equivalent to a holiday cruise rather than a ferry; reference to the cabin accommodation has already been made, but to be fair there is actually a wide range of overnight accommodation on offer, including four different grades of cabin, bunk-type couchettes, and airline-type reclining seats (which are, by the way, equivalent to an airline's first class).

DFDS Seaways - Newcastle/Gothenburg and Harwich/Gothenburg

Travelling with DFDS Seaways (formerly Scandinavian Seaways) from Newcastle to Gothenburg on board the 'Princess of Scandinavia' line added 22 hours cruising time to our journey. This leisurely crossing provided the perfect opportunity to relax and unwind after a hectic, pre-travel rush. Once on board, we found all services to be efficiently run without fuss by a friendly crew. Our twin berth outside cabin with en-suite facilities was comfortable, airy and spacious. Catering facilities included an à la carte restaurant offering Scandinavian and German cuisine, the popular Smörgasbord/carvery, a traditional Scandinavian feast, or the cafeteria and bistro is another option. Discounts for children are a plus, with under fours eating free and under twelves getting 50% discount on buffet meals. The list of on board activities is equally extensive with live entertainment, disco, casino, cinema, sauna, solarium, swimming pool, etc. There are shops and a bureau de change; vouchers, received with our travel documents, meant discount on certain duty free items. A most important factor on any journey is the cost, but with fare structuring and book in advance deals, we believe Scandinavian Seaways offers excellent value for money. Arriving in Gothenburg thoroughly refreshed, we also had to agree that the top AA rating awarded to the Princess of Scandinavia is well deserved.

DFDS Seaways - Newcastle/Kristiansand

Once, a long while ago, there was a wide and powerful river flowing through the forested countryside of Northumbria, with here and there a settlement including The Venerable Bede's Monastery at Jarrow. Every now and then word would come of the approach of a fleet of proud longboats, with large aggressive carvings at the bow, at which time the terrified locals would disappear as quickly as they could! Nowadays, as we descend down a dual carriageway towards the Royal Quay at the port of Tyne our gaze is drawn to the huge bulk of a mighty liner towering above the dockside buildings, with its huge funnel strangely reminiscent of the carvings on the Viking longboats. After parking our vehicle in the cavernous car deck, we discover that the Scandinavian crew of this 'Viking invader' are really here on a peaceful

OUR FRANCE & SPAIN *Direct*

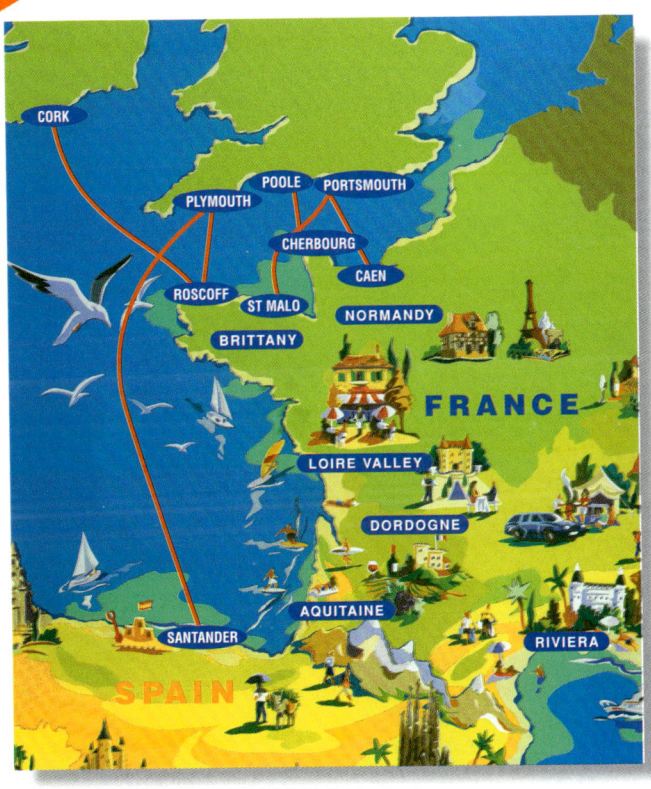

Travelling to Holiday France or Spain?
Why drive the long way round when you can sail direct?
We land you closer to where you'd like to be.

Brittany Ferries
The Holiday Fleet

BROCHURES 0990 143 554 (24HRS) RESERVATIONS 0990 360 360
OR SEE YOUR TRAVEL AGENT

ECONOMY DRIVE.

(P&O DIRECT FROM PORTSMOUTH TO FRANCE OR SPAIN.)

If you're going camping or caravanning this year, why not cut some corners? Avoid the busy Pas de Calais area and a long road journey down through France, by sailing most of the way instead.

Just get onboard at Portsmouth, sit back and relax while we do the driving. You'll not only arrive fully refreshed and nearer your destination, but you'll have saved a fortune in petrol too.

For more information on our routes, sailings, fares and timetables, call our reservations department on 0870 2424 999. For your free brochure, call 0870 9000 212 quoting AR.

Altogether more civilised.

www.poportsmouth.com

Caravans not carried on Fastcraft.

PORTSMOUTH TO BILBAO, CHERBOURG & LE HAVRE

P&O Stena
LINE

at your service

quality

choice

every
30
minutes

working together

Travel with P&O Stena Line ar you can enjoy the most extensive, up-to-date ferry service crossing the Channel from Dover to Calais.

All of our ships have experienced their share of a major £10 million refit, ready the millennium.

A completely revamped on board product features exciting shopping opportunities, restaurants, lounges and theme bars, designed for all tastes and purses. Ar with the arrival of our seventh ship – to give a crossi every 30 minutes at peak times – we know it's a servi that can't be beaten.

At P&O Stena Line we take the time to make your journey special.

reservations
087 0600 0600
07:30–22:30 7 days a week

where time sails by

Dover

Calais

FOR THE
LOWEST
FARES

FROM DOVER
TO CALAIS CALL
SEAFRANCE
FERRIES

08705 711 711

CRUISING COMFORT

EVERY NIGHT FROM

HULL TO THE

CONTINENT

Save yourself the tiring trek south,
P&O North Sea Ferries sail every evening
from Hull to Rotterdam and to Zeebrugge
which is less than an hour from France.
Enjoy a great night out with a five course
feast, entertainment, casino, cinema,
fantastic shops and fun for the kids.
With a comfortable bed in a cosy cabin
you'll wake up on the Continent with the
whole day ahead of you and excellent
road links to all parts of Europe.
Get the full picture in our Cruiseferries
Brochure – from your local Travel Agent
or direct from us on 01482 377177.

P&O North Sea Ferries

PHOTO COURTESY OF WHICH MOTORCARAVAN

motorhome
IRELAND

Motorhome Ireland offers you the freedom to tour Ireland in your own quality motorhome.

Rent in confidence from Ireland's only Motorhome centre.

MOTORHOME IRELAND LTD 8 Station Road, Saintfield, N Ireland BT24 7DU **TEL** (44) 01238 519519
FAX (44) 01238 519509 **E-MAIL** rental@motorhome-irl.co.uk **INTERNET** www.motorhome-irl.co.uk

France for beginners

NOT VENTURED ACROSS THE CHANNEL YET? FANCY THE CAMARADERIE AND FUN OF TRAVELLING IN AN ESCORTED GROUP?

At the Alan Rogers Travel Service we know that for many the first trip abroad can be a big step. That's why we invite you to join us on a fabulous escorted trip to a delightful hidden part of Northern France, less than an hour from Calais. We've put together an exciting 7 night programme, staying at the lovely Camping Château de Gandspette situated in the heart of the Audomarais National Park, twinned with the Norfolk Broads.

The Programme

Meeting at an Alan Rogers selected site in Kent for drinks, we'll take a morning Dover-Calais ferry next day, arriving at Château de Gandspette in time for lunch. There'll be plenty of time during the week to explore this fascinating area: delightful countryside, mediaeval cobbled towns like Arras and Cambrai, First World War battlefields, and of course St Omer with its pretty square, restaurants and colourful market. There's so much to see and your experienced escorts, both seasoned caravanners, will always be on hand for advice.

What's included

- 7 nights pitch fees
- Welcome drinks
- Return Dover-Calais crossing
- Farewell dinner
- Comprehensive Travel Pack
- Insurance for two people with car + caravan/motorhome

ALL THIS FOR JUST

£499

9th - 16th June

2 people with car + caravan/motorhome

Numbers are strictly limited - So call now for details or book today

01892 61 51 41

quoting **AR00**

THE ALAN ROGERS'
travel service

In association with

FOUR SEASONS TOURING

6-8 Garden Street, Tunbridge Wells. TN1 2XB email: travelservice@alanrogers.com website: www.alanrogers.com

mission to serve us and convey us in considerable comfort to their own beautiful lands! Our outside cabin, with en-suite shower and WC, and the many on-board facilities, including the Seven Seas restaurant serving an excellent Smorgasbord (£12-14) all contributed to making our crossing relaxing and enjoyable. A visit to the night club provided a fitting finale to a busy day, and it was only later during the night that we became conscious of the fact that this 22,000 ton floating hotel was speeding through the water at 25 knots to cover the 400 miles to our destination in just 18 hours. A civilised arrival time in Kristiansand enables one to enjoy a good breakfast before disembarking at around 10 am ready to face the drive to Oslo.

DFDS Seaways - Newcastle - Amsterdam (Ijmuiden)

This is an ideal route to the Netherlands for those living in the northern counties. It also offers a central disembarkation point. Having recently made this 14 hour crossing we found it to be a first class service. On board facilities were of a high quality, with an above average standard of cleanliness. There is an á la carte restaurant, smorgasbord/carvery, and café . On our crossing there was a special half-price offer in the Seven Seas restaurant for children up to 15 years, with under 4 years free and adults paying £14. The breakfast buffet had a similar good value offer, costing £5 per adult. Entertainment on board included live entertainment, disco, casino, cinema and children's play area, plus shops, bars and a bureau de change. We occupied a comfortable outside two-berth standard cabin with en-suite facilities.

P&O European Ferries - Portsmouth / Le Havre or Portsmouth / Cherbourg

The ferries which operate these services are most impressive and provide comfortable crossings. Travellers from the north will find Portsmouth a very easy port to use. There is little difference in mileage between Dover and Portsmouth, the motorway takes you directly into the port, and an added bonus is no M25 to give you hassle. We always find the P&O Ferries clean, with friendly and efficient staff. The meals we have had have always been excellent, and even on busy crossings the staff cope very efficiently. For a small extra charge Club Class allocates reclining seats, drinks and newspapers in a quiet comfortable lounge. Night services offer good cabins, ensuring that you arrive fresh for your journey into France (cabins are also available on day crossings) Embarkation and disembarkation are managed with little fuss. The drive out of Cherbourg is easy, and well signposted. However returning to Cherbourg involves driving through the town, and although we have never experienced any difficulties, you may encounter traffic queues down the hill into the centre. For hypermarket visits, our advice would be to use the large store on the outskirts of the town, before you descend the hill! Arrival and departure via Le Havre are also pretty straightforward, but beware of the height restrictions on the 'fast lane' into town which uses several tunnels under road junctions.

SeaFrance - Dover / Calais

Sea France operates up to thirty departures per day, using three ferries - The 'Cezanne' (550 cars), the 'Manet' and the 'Renoir', each 330 cars. We used the service in the peak season (mid August) and found the staff efficient and friendly. The vessels were clean, with modern decor, and quite comfortable, although not quite full, so movement around shops bars and restaurants was comparatively easy. With a distinctively French feel about them, each ship has a Relais Gourmet self-service restaurant, a Brasserie with waiter service, a Parisien Café and 'Le Pub' bars. The Cezanne and the Renoir both have private lounges (small supplement payable) and all have a bureau de change. One point worth noting was the fact that we had to park our motorhome on a sloping ramp/deck area, and although I was confident that my own vehicle wouldn't move, with the hand-brake on and in first gear, and with a chock provided by Sea France behind one wheel, some drivers still seemed nervous. We found Sea France to be quite flexible about bookings – on our outward journey we simply made a 'phone call (as it was peak season) and picked up the tickets on checking-in at Dover, and on returning to Calais earlier than expected we were offered a place on the very next crossing. We thoroughly enjoyed our crossings with Sea France.

P&O Stena Line - Dover / Calais

With 20 sailings each way from October to March and 25 each way from April to September, fares at a reasonable level, the use of 'super ferries' which make the crossing in 75 minutes and a check-in time of 20 minutes, P&O are taking on the Channel Tunnel head on to ensure a competitive alternative to the latest method of reaching mainland Europe. Although prior booking is advisable, the space on each vessel means that, except perhaps at peak times, one can just turn up and cross on the next sailing. The A20 extension to the M20 Folkestone to the Eastern Dock entrance at Dover and the direct access to the French Autoroute system at Calais with the pleasant 'cruise' across the channel in between, now make for a smooth start on the continental journey. This also helps the transition to driving on the right as, by the time one needs to use 'ordinary' roads, one has become used to overtaking on the left. Apart from these advantages, the ferries have been modernised to the highest standards with waiter and self-service restaurants, shops selling a wide range of duty-free and other goods, comfortable bars and lounges and Club Class at a small supplement for those who want peace and quiet away from the bustle on the decks below. Boarding and leaving the ships has been made simple by the use of double width ramps on two levels.

Understandably many caravanners are somewhat apprehensive at the thought of taking their caravan abroad for the first time – driving on and off the ferry, driving on the right-hand side of the road, road signs etc. in a foreign language, finding your way around, different customs, food and habits, all may seem fairly intimidating, but in fact the prospect is a good deal more frightening than the reality!

Nevertheless there is quite a bit to learn before you can claim to be a seasoned traveller abroad, and if the prospect still makes you apprehensive, why not consider making your first trip abroad with one of the specialist camping tour operators, such as Eurocamp Independent, Select Sites, Carefree Travel or the Caravan & Camping Service? Or why not take advantage of our own fully escorted 'First Time Abroad' trips (see advertisement opposite page 353). Booking through one of these experienced and reliable services takes care of a lot of the worry in terms of organising ferries, booking sites, insurance, etc. and can make life a lot easier, especially if you've not travelled abroad before.

On the other hand many of us prefer to do things for ourselves, be wholly independent and probably save ourselves some money at the same time, so, for the benefit of those of you who are contemplating 'going it alone' for the first time, the following tips will give you both an insight into what's involved and hopefully enable you to avoid most of the pitfalls!

The most important decisions are likely to be, where to go, how to get there and where to stay. Given that it is closest, that most of us learned at least a smattering of the language at school, that it has a wide variety of scenery and (normally) a wonderful climate, France seems an obvious destination for your first trip abroad. On the other hand, you don't actually need to travel far to reach some of the nicest holiday areas of Belgium or Holland for example, so driving need not necessarily be either long or tiring.

A good reliable campsite guide is a prerequisite, such as the Alan Rogers Good Camps Guide for France or Europe.

You will need to study the site descriptions in your guide of course, particularly in terms of meeting your needs, whether for a lively or a quiet site, a site in the countryside or near a beach or whatever, but remember many continental sites are unlike their British counterparts in so far as most southern European sites offer 'delimité' pitches (ie. pitches separated from each other, usually by hedges so you normally find a bit more privacy and shade than you would on an equivalent British site).

Having decided what part of Europe you want to visit, and chosen a site, the next logical steps are to book your ferry, or tunnel crossing, and to decide whether you need to make an advance reservation at your chosen site. If you're going in the high season (roughly mid July to mid August) advance booking is advisable, and if you're planning to go to one of the popular tourist areas it's more or less essential. If you are going out of that main season its not absolutely necessary to book in advance, although for peace of mind you may prefer to.

Although a number of well-publicised mergers have reduced the number of ferry operators to the Continent in recent years, there is still a wide choice of services in terms of both routes and fares, plus the opportunity to avoid a ferry altogether and go via the Tunnel. The choice is really a personal one, neither the ferries nor the tunnel involves any difficulty in terms of loading or unloading, so it's really a question of which you prefer and which is more convenient – you can't beat the tunnel for speed, but you may prefer to relax for an hour or two, enjoy a meal, and the often fairly luxurious ambience of one of the new super ferries. In either case booking by telephone, fax, or e-mail is simple, or you can of course book through your high street travel agent at no extra cost.

Once you have booked your ferry and perhaps also your campsite it is worth considering taking out travel insurance which will provide cancellation cover in the event of your having to cancel your bookings through illness, etc. In fact there are a number of insurance companies around offering special combined travel and breakdown policies for motoring holidays, and these are a very worth while consideration, but do shop around, the premiums vary enormously. Among the best in terms of cover and value is the Heritage Breakdown service operated in conjunction with Green Flag, featured between pages 160/161 of this guide

Before you go it is well worth making yourself a check list of things to do and what to pack – I've been travelling abroad several times a year for the past 25 years and I still don't rely on my memory for this, so here is shortlist of the essentials:

- Passport
- Tickets
- Motor Insurance Certificate, including Green Card or Continental cover clause
- Travel & Breakdown Insurance Certificate
- V5 Registration Document and/or (if not your vehicle) the owner's authority
- Driving Licence
- Form E1-11 (to extend National Health Insurance to European destinations)
- Foreign Currency and/or Travellers Cheques or Eurocheques and Card
- Credit Card(s)
- Campsite Guide(s)
- Tourist Guide(s)
- Maps/Road Atlas

First Time Abroad

- GB Stickers on both car and caravan
- Red warning triangle
- Spare car light bulbs
- Torch
- First-Aid kit (including Mosquito repellent and bite treatment!)
- Tools (even just a few basics – screwdrivers, pliers and an adjustable spanner)
- Continental Electric Mains Connector or Adapter – including a long cable
- Polarity tester
- Bottle/can opener
- Corkscrew!

It is also well worth having your car and caravan serviced before you go, especially if you're going to travel any distance – breakdown insurance is wonderful, but waiting for a replacement fan belt in an autoroute service area in the heat for a couple of hours is not my idea of what I prefer to do on holiday! Above all, before you set off, you should make sure that your caravan is not overloaded, that the recommended nose weight is not exceeded and that it is properly trimmed.

Once the great day dawns, it is a good idea to arrive at the terminal a good hour before your crossing time – as the driver of a 'high vehicle' you will probably be asked to board first – or last! Driving onto either a ferry or the tunnel is a piece of cake, just follow the instructions of the staff and since virtually all ferries (and trains) are now 'drive on – drive off' you won't be expected to make any fancy manoeuvres or turn round.

Once loaded on board, make sure your handbrake is on, that the car is in first gear, the car and caravan are both locked, and finally don't forget to take your tickets, boarding cards and passports (needed to get your duty free) with you when leaving the car deck, along with any overnight baggage, because once the vessel has sailed you won't be allowed back on the car deck until you are moored up at your destination.

Before you leave the car deck make a note of the door and staircase number or letter which you leave by. It is amazing how many passengers can't remember which deck they left their car on, and it can be very embarrassing to find that your car/caravan is blocking everyone else in when you finally find it. You won't be too popular!

If you have booked seats or a cabin on the ferry it's best to go straight to the Information Desk and claim them as soon as possible. Similarly, if you want to dine in the luxury of the main restaurant, rather than the self-service one, you may need to book a table early in the voyage. The same may apply to the cinema.

On arrival at your port of disembarkation, wait until the tannoy tells you before trying to get to the car deck, but it may be worthwhile actually locating the right staircase beforehand, as the stairways can become crowded, especially in the high season.

Once you have driven off the ferry or train, follow the signs through the immigration and customs controls, and have your passports handy, although the likelihood of your actually having to stop these days is becoming remote. At this stage it is quite helpful if you remember that you have just arrived in a foreign country, and that they drive on the right-hand side of the road. I don't think I've actually ever tried to drive down the wrong side when arriving on the continent, but I have driven some considerable distance through Poole on the wrong side of the road when arriving back in the UK in the middle of the night after six weeks driving on the continent – seriously embarrassing!

Remember that all speed limit signs are in KPH (not mph) and when you enter a town or village remember that, even if there is no actual 50 kph sign, the town sign itself is an indication that you have entered a 50 kph limit.

Ideally you should aim to arrive at your campsite before 7 pm, after which time you may find Reception has closed (in which case go straight to the bar – seriously, that is where you'll find a member of staff) and in any event you really must arrive before 10 pm. or you're likely to find the gate closed or the barrier down. Many continental caravanners don't bother to book in advance, and if you haven't either, why not take the opportunity to do as they do and ask to look around the site before deciding to stay or taking a particular pitch? This is a common practice, particularly among the Continentals, and far from being thought rude, you'll be respected for your experience and good sense if you do this.

Once you have agreed on your choice of pitch, check what you need by way of electricity – most European sites have a 220Volt supply, which is no problem, but the current provision can vary from as little as 2A up to 16A, although the norm is between 5-10A. Many sites offer a choice, and if you have any significant electrical equipment (eg. kettle, microwave or heater) you will need the maximum (remember 2A @ 220V produces only 440 Watts, ie. less than half a kilowatt.

Having established what you need, or what you can get, in terms of electricity connect up to the mains supply, using your continental adapter, and then check the polarity with your tester. If it indicates 'wrong or reverse polarity' you may perhaps be able to turn the adapter round to obtain the correct polarity; if not, consult the site operator and explain the problem.

Many people choose to ignore 'wrong polarity' as it doesn't seem to make any difference to the way most electrical appliances work (although it can affect some 'polarity sensitive' equipment such as TVs or computers) but the main problem is that it can be dangerous if you are using an appliance which has a single-pole switch – unfortunately many British appliances and most older caravans have this type of cheap switch, whereas most continental appliances are fitted with di-pole switches where polarity is not critical.. If you use an appliance with a single pole switch and the polarity is wrong (ie. reversed) when you switch the appliance off it will stop working, but the appliance itself will still be live, and hence potentially lethal.

Unless it is high season or particularly busy try to avoid committing yourself to, and maybe paying for, a long stay in advance, but give yourself a day or two to look around, see what the weather's like and so on before you decide exactly how long you intend to stay. If you don't like your pitch, or have any complaints, do take them up with the site owners there and then – the British have a rather sad reputation for moaning afterwards but not complaining at the time when something could have been done to put matters right.

Many European campsites have a wide range of amenities, sports facilities and activity programmes (animations) particularly in the main season, and most of these will be free. Most sites have shops, or at least a supply of essentials such as bread, milk and wine, but probably the best place to buy groceries, vegetables, fruit and cheeses is at the local market.

If you are planning to eat out, most restaurants offer a 'menu' or choice of menus – these consist of two, three or even more courses in the form of a set meal, but with several choices for each course, usually at prices significantly below the 'a la carte' prices for each individual item.

Hopefully what I have written will have reassured you that crossing the channel with your caravan is not the daunting experience you might have imagined, so all that remains is to wish you 'Bon Voyage'.

CE

Breakdown Experiences in Norway

by Mervyn Gwyn Jones

This is a tale of what happens when things don't go according to plan on a trip to the continent. Here we are just off the DFDS boat at Kristiansand, Norway at 10 am. facing urgent adaptation to right hand driving. Whilst we had definite long distance targets, we were not sure how to tackle Kristiansand itself, a pleasant and mildly congested town with its toll system.

So we made a cautious circuit of the town and still looking for parking stopped at the side of the bus station adjacent to the DFDS office. I thought a further move was necessary and tried to start the car - dead. Oh, does the worst dream come true.

The DFDS office was most helpful and a call was duly put through to Green Flag in London (Heritage Classic Insurance). It was not easy in the busy office as, by now, I was highly stressed and worried ... 'the bus station not the railway station.' Then an hour's wait. Nothing happened. More phoning at the DFDS office (very supportive) . My wife made short expeditions to the shops and I stood by the car getting cool with quite a cold breeze, pacing up and down, searching for a hopeful vehicle - none came, they all passed by.

About to go for call number three (two hours later), but joy at last. A yellow, well equipped Terrano appeared - NAF (Norges Automobil Forbund) - a sober, unsmiling man in a yellow waterproof. However, his quiet manner of approach to the problem inspired increasing confidence, although at that point a little tongue biting seemed best. His English slightly slow and halting but we were amazed at how well many Norwegians handle English. Battery condition flat, but chargeable. So alternator? The alternator is not charging the battery.

'Nothing for it' said the man, 'Autoelectrician'. I looked at my wife. The battery was being charged by the Terrano. 'Follow me. Don't turn your engine off'. So off we went through Kristiansand's flyover system, on out of the town taking a minor road up through the forest. Eventually we arrived at a group of neat factories. Again grave conversation and examination. Then a measured report: 'The control mechanism regulator in the alternator is not working. I will work on this, this afternoon. I hope it will be ready for 4 pm'. Joy, delight and relief that a reasonable diagnosis had been made.

The NAF man conveyed us back to the town centre leaving the heavily laden car. Our first visit was to the Information Konductor. Again a serious thoughtful approach and good English. As we were to find out, this lady made an inspired decision for us and sent us to Sjøløtt Hotel. There Mrs Helene Ranestad, Director, took great care of us. Her mother is English and Helene's English is impeccable. She was a wonderful listener and a great source of information on all things Norwegian.

After a short walk round this pleasant town we took a taxi back up to our Autoelectrician for 3.45 pm. The car was ready and the bill (carefully calculated, with a written account of what had been done) came to 769 Nkr (£61.52). Cash had been raised by changing emergency sterling at the bank. Always be prepared.

We drove back carefully to Hotel Sjøløtt and did relax in the cheerfully decorated and very comfortable room. Just a slight nag at the back of my mind - after a cold night, would it start? Well after breakfast with all sorts of lovely tastes we settled our B&B - 690 Nkr (£55.20). Yes, the car started fine and we were able to head off up the coast to our first stop, Holt Camping at Tvedestrand. The car is home now and has run well. Every credit to Green Flag/Heritage, the NAF man and Autoelectrician BILELELECTRIK.

First Time Abroad
INSURANCE

There is probably no subject which causes campers, caravanners and motorcaravanners venturing abroad more worries than insurance. The problem is that there is an overlap, so that sometimes one problem is apparently covered on two insurance policies. To avoid confusion let's cut through the hype and take a clear look at insurance.

If you are planning on camping, caravanning or motorcaravanning abroad, this is what you will need.

Road traffic insurance

Under European Law your ordinary car or motor-caravan road insurance will cover you anywhere in the EU. But many policies only provide minimum cover. So if you have an accident your insurance may only cover the cost of damage to the other person's property.

To maintain the same level of cover abroad as you enjoy at home you need to tell your vehicle insurer. Some will automatically cover you abroad with no extra cost and no extra paperwork. Some will say you need a Green Card - which is neither green or on card - but won't charge for it. Some will charge extra for the green card. Ideally you should contact your vehicle insurer 3 - 4 weeks before you set off, and confirm your conversation with them in writing.

A good insurance company will provide a European recognised accident report form. On this you mark details of damage to yours and the other party's property and draw a little diagram showing where the vehicles were in relation to each other. You give a copy of your form to the other motorist, he gives you a copy of his. It prevents all the shouting which often accompanies accidents in this country.

Holiday insurance

This is a multi-part insurance. One part covers your vehicles. If they breakdown or are involved in an accident they can be repaired or returned to this country. The best will even arrange to bring your vehicle home if the driver is unable to proceed.

Many new vehicles come with a free breakdown and recovery insurance which extends into Europe. Some professional motoring journalists have reported that the actual service this provides can be patchy and may not cover the recovery of a caravan or trailer. Our advice is to buy the motoring section of your holiday insurance.

The second section of holiday insurance covers people. It will include the cost of doctor, ambulance and hospital treatment if needed. If needed the better companies will even pay for English language speaking doctors and nurses and will bring a sick or injured holidaymaker home by air ambulance.

The third part of a good holiday insurance policy covers things. If someone breaks in to your motorhome and steals your passports and money, one phone call to the insurance company will have everything sorted out. If you manage to drive over your camera, it's covered.

One part of the insurance which is often ignored is the cancellation section. Few things are as heart-breaking as having to cancel a holiday because a member of the family falls ill. Cancellation insurance can't take away the disappointment, but it makes sure you don't suffer financially as well.

There are a number of good insurance policies available including those provided for their members by the two major clubs and those offered by the leading camping holiday agents mentioned and advertised in this guide. We recommend **Heritage Classic European Rescueline** (between pages 160/161) which is the insurance we use.

Ideally you should arrange your holiday insurance at least four weeks before you set off.

Which ever insurance you choose we would advise not picking any of the policies sold by the High Street travel trade. Whilst they may be good, they do not cover the specific needs of campers, caravanners and motorcaravanners.

Form E1-11

By arrangement between the British Government and the rest of the European Community Governments, British holidaymakers can enjoy the same health care as that Government offers its own citizens. The form which shows you are entitled to take advantage of this arrangement is called E1-11.

E1-11 doesn't replace holiday insurance, but is in addition to. The form is available from all main UK Post Offices. Fill out one for every member of your family. Get it stamped by the counter staff and take it on holiday with you. In theory one Form E1-11 lasts you for ever, but we have had reports that in some rural areas in Europe they may not under-stand that, so our advice is to get a new E1-11 every year. It is free.

And that is all you need to know about insurance. You know what they say about insurance, don't you? You'll only need it if you haven't got it.

Mike Cazelet

First Time Abroad
DRIVING IN EUROPE

Driving in Europe is really not the daunting experienced that those who've never done it imagine - honestly! For starters, generally speaking, there's a lot less traffic than we're used to in the UK. Traffic densities in most European countries are much lower than in the UK, with a few notable exceptions; do try to avoid driving in the Netherlands during the morning or evening rush hours for example (frustrating is a massive understatement) and try to avoid travelling south from Paris on Friday evenings and the weekends towards the end of July, early August.

Before setting out to drive on the Continent do make sure that you have read and understand the necessary requirements in terms of documentation, etc. which are summarised below, and that your car and caravan, or motorcaravan, have been recently serviced. Remember, in summer particularly temperatures are a lot higher on the Continent and if your radiator thermostat is stuck shut, or your alternator belt is worn, overheating is very likely resulting perhaps in a cooked engine and a very inauspicious start to your holiday.

At the other extreme, if you are travelling to the Alps or the Pyrenees in the winter, remember to adjust the level of your anti-freeze to cope with far lower temperatures than we are accustomed to in Britain, and don't forget that constant use of the heater, wipers, etc. coupled with trying to start the engine on often bitterly cold mornings is asking a lot of your battery

Similarly the use of 'all weather' or 'M&S' (mud and snow) tyres is advisable if you're venturing anywhere beyond the channel coast during winter. In certain mountainous parts you will even need special studded tyres or snow chains.

Documents

The most important documents you will need are your passport, your driving licence, and your motor insurance, followed by your vehicle registration documents, a Form E1-11 and Breakdown/Travel insurance.

Passports

Although routine passport checks have been largely abandoned in the EU countries (except in Britain) you are still required to provide proof of identity on demand, and the best way to do this is by means of a valid passport, added to which you will almost certainly encounter problems getting back into the UK without a passport.

Driving Licence

For most European countries the new style pink and green EU format British driving licence will suffice, but bear in mind that the minimum age at which one can drive a car in most European countries is EIGHTEEN years. For some countries, especially in Eastern Europe, an International

Driving Permit is required - these can be obtained from the AA or RAC.

Motor Insurance

Third party cover is a minimum requirement for all European countries. Many British motor insurance policies now provide European cover, but unless you notify your insurance company before you travel abroad your cover is likely to be reduced to 3rd part cover only! Some policies still require that you apply for, and in some cases pay extra for, a Green Card which extends your cover to the Continent. It is really essential that you check your exact situation with your motor insurer well before you set out. There's more about insurance in Mike Cazalet's article on the previous page.

Vehicle Registration Documents

(Vehicle log book/Form V5) You should always carry this with you when you travel abroad by road, and if you don't actually own the vehicle yourself you should also carry a letter of authority from the owner confirming that you are permitted to take it abroad.

Form E1-11

This document, from Post Offices, when stamped/signed by the Post Office, extends your NHS basic cover to those European countries within the European Economic Area, but the cover is very basic. You should have Medical Expenses insurance cover as well in order to be fully covered in the event of a serious accident or illness.

Travel/Breakdown Insurance

There are several reputable companies offering travel and breakdown cover, including cancellation and medical expenses cover. Among the best, and the one we use ourselves, is the Heritage Scheme, operated by Norton Insurance Brokers and Bishopsgate Insurance, in association with Green Flag breakdown/recovery services. We have negotiated special rates for our readers through this scheme, and special arrangements whereby there is no limit on the age of your vehicle. Full details are shown between pages 160/161.

In addition to the above documentation you are advised to carry, and in many European countries are required by law to carry, the following:

GB plates or stickers on the back of your car, and if towing, on the back of the caravan

'Beam Benders' - to ensure that your headlights dip towards the right hand side

Warning Triangle for use if you break down or have an accident

Set of spare vehicle light bulbs, and if appropriate, a set of caravan driving light bulbs

First-Aid kit

Fire Extinguisher

Snow Chains (or studded tyres) - a legal requirement in Alpine Countries during winter

First Time Abroad - Driving in Europe

There are many other 'local' rules and regulations applying to the various individual countries featured in this guide which we try to cover in the country introductions. Readers contemplateing any extensive travel by road in Europe to buy the RAC's handbook 'Motoring in Europe' which contains more detailed information on the national regulations applying in most of the countries featured in this guide, as well as details of toll roads, and tunnels, and the price of tolls, plus information on all the main mountain passes, including the dates when they are normally open, and any special restrictions as to the type of vehicles allowed to use them

Having obtained the necessary documentation, and the rest of the kit described above, you should now be in a position to consider where to go, and how best to cross the Channel - the choice is getting wider, with the Tunnel, Ferries, Hovercraft, the Seacat all competing for your custom, and with a good choice of routes as well.

If you haven't already made up your mind, and most likely you have, the question of where to go isn't easy - Italy, with its lakes, mountains and glorious Tuscan countryside, wonderful towns and cities such as Venice, Rome or Florence? Or maybe Spain with its beaches, wonderful climate, historic cities and festivals? What about Holland - only just the other side of the North Sea, good beaches, nice countryside, Amsterdam and friendly natives most of whom speak English? The choice is almost limitless, and with your accommodation in tow, its yours!

Obviously the choice of destination will influence your choice of channel crossing - not a lot of point in getting a good deal on the Poole-Cherbourg service if you live in East Anglia and intend going to Holland! Seriously though, it is worth careful thought - we have known people who have driven a hundred miles out of their way to save £10 on ferry fares. Similarly, if you are considering going to somewhere like Spain or Scandinavia, where there is a choice between a long-haul ferry direct to your destination country or a short sea crossing and a mighty long drive, do add up the 'hidden' costs (motorway tolls, fuel, overnight accommodation, wear and tear on vehicle(s) and driver/passengers, meals, etc. Long-haul ferries which at first sight look expensive aren't always as pricey when compared with the cost of driving overland.

Many of the ferry operators advertise in this guide, and a summary of the available services are provided on page 351. We have used most of the services ourselves in connection with inspecting all the sites featured in the guide, and we hope that the Ferry Reports that our Inspectors have compiled (on pages 351-3) will help you in making your choice.

It is worth keeping an eye open for special offers on the ferries, or of course you could take advantage of the 'package arrangements' provided by the camping tour operators such as Eurocamp Independent or Select Sites (both advertise in this guide) or use the services provided by the Caravan Club, Camping & Caravanning Club or the Motorcaravanners Club.

The most popular routes are of course the short-sea routes from Dover or Folkestone to Calais or Boulogne, and the Tunnel. There are several campsites featured (and fully described) in our Good Camps Guide for Britain & Ireland near to Folkestone and Dover for those who have a long journey to get to the port and want to have a night's rest before crossing the Channel. Amongst the most convenient sites featured in our Britain & Ireland Guide are: no. 304 Broadhembury Holiday Park at Kingsnorth, near Ashford (open all year, 01233 620859), no. 310 Hawthorn Farm, Martin Mill, near Dover (open 1 March-30 Nov, 01304 852658) and no. 309 Black Horse Farm, Densole near Folkestone, a Caravan Club Site (open all year, 01303 892665).

Alternatively you might prefer to cross the channel on an evening sailing and have a night's rest the other side - no. 6201 Camping La Bien Assise at Guines (open 25 April - 20 Sept, 0033 3.21.35.20.77) and 6203 Chateau de Gandespette at Eperlecques, near St Omer, (1 April - 30 Sept, 0033 3.21.93.43.93) and 6204 Caravaning du Chateau at Condette, near Boulogne (1 April - 31 Oct, tel 0033 3.21.87.59.59), all featured in the Alan Rogers Good Camps Guide for France and which are amongst several that are suitable for a night stop (or longer).

Landing at Calais or the Eurotunnel Terminal has the advantage of direct access to the wonderful (albeit quite expensive) French Autoroute system, which enables you to cross France with the minimum of delay, but of course you won't see quite so much of the French countryside from the Autoroute, although many of the most interesting attractions and views are indicated by brown tourist signs along the Autoroutes.

There are plenty of service areas (Aires de Service) on French Autoroutes for fuel and refreshments, and on some of these you can even stay overnight, but if you do stay do be careful about the lack of security on many of these, especially if there is no other vehicles around. We know plenty of motorcaravanners and caravanners who overnight at these Aires and when stuck for a proper campsite we have even used them ourselves, but for security reasons if nothing else we don't really recommend them for staying on. There are also Aires de Repos which are often very pleasant, with trees for shade, picnic tables and sometimes also 'loos (usually of the 'Turkish' type though).

One of our Inspectors, Gerry Ovenden, who is also a Travel Consultant for Motorcaravan & Motorhome Monthly, has kindly put together a few suggested itineraries (through routes) for crossing France to various popular destinations. For simplicity, these itineraries are based on Autoroutes, but if you prefer to travel on non-toll roads you can easily transfer the route to a map such as the Michelin Atlas; you can then find parallel 'free' roads (mainly Routes Nationale, N Roads) but still follow the general course of the suggested route.

We have included brief details of a few campsites suitable for night-stops along each of these routes, all of which are fully described in the 2000 edition of the Alan Rogers Good Camps Guide for France.

We hope you'll find these through routes useful in planning your journey through La Belle France, and wish you an enjoyable holiday wherever you're going!

First Time Abroad
ROUTES THROUGH FRANCE

TO SPAIN
From CHERBOURG - ST MALO

Not only may it be more convenient to cross from central southern England to Brittany rather than using the short Dover/Calais crossings, if travelling to Spain – particularly the Atlantic coast in the north – the driving distance is shorter. As the sea part of the journey takes longer, there is the opportunity, helpful if a long way from home to port, to book a cabin on a night ferry and arrive fresh to commence the continental drive.

From Cherbourg
Follow N13 for approx. 50 km, then via the N174 (St Lo) and N175 to the Rennes by-pass when you join up with the route from St Malo (as below).

From St Malo
Go south on N137 to Rennes. By-pass Rennes going south on N137 to Nantes, then south on A83 to its end near Niort. Join A10 south to Bordeaux.

To NORTHERN SPAIN

From Bordeaux continue south on A63/N10 to Bayonne and south west to enter Spain for the north Atlantic coast.

To EASTERN SPANISH MEDITERRANEAN COAST
Follow the above route to Bordeaux and then take A62 southeast to Toulouse, then A61 to Narbonne. Now south on A9 to the Spanish border.

SUGGESTED SITES ACROSS FRANCE
The following sites are fully described in the Alan Rogers Good Camps Guide for France:

Cherbourg: 1402M Municipal, Bayeux
5004M Ste Mere Eglise
Nantes: 4401M du Petit Port, Nantes
4402M Vieux Moulin

South of Bordeaux, route to northern Spain.
3320M de L'Eyre, Mios

East of Bordeaux, route to Mediterranean coast.
4710M Municipal, Tonniens
1104 Le Montinet Rouge, Brousses-Villaret
1111 Val d'Aleth, Alet les Bains

Narbonne: 1107 Les Mimosas, Narbonne

TO SPAIN or ITALY
via the South of France
From CALAIS

The routes to the Riviera, the Costa Brava and the Mediterranean coast of Spain are common to the city of Orange. One can drive either via the PARIS Bd. Péripherique, or avoid this crowded motorway ring around the French capital, or go a little further east via REIMS now that the A26 extends south to join the A5 near Troyes, A31 near Langres, A6 near Beaune and A7 at Lyon.

Continuing south to Orange; A9 southwest via Narbonne to the Spannish border.

For the Riviera, go south east from Orange on A8 for Marseille and Cannes. If then going on to the Mediterranean coast of ITALY, continue east from Monte Carlo.

At the time of writing, the Mont Blanc tunnel between France and Italy is still closed following the disastrous fire.

From Calais

Leaving the Eurotunnel, join autoroute A16 north towards Calais.

From Ferry terminal, take motorway feeder road at end of docks complex and follow signs for A26 'Paris péage'. Continue south east and:

Via PARIS: go south on A1, join Bd. Péripherique round the east of Paris. Leave the Péripherique on A6 southeast to Beaune.

Via REIMS: As above from Calais but continue on A26 through to Reims, short section of A4 and then A26 south to join A5 near Troyes. This links with the A31 near Langres and then the A6 near Beaune - route now as from Paris.

This links south to Lyon which is left on the A7, following the River Rhone to Orange from where it is southwest on A9 to the Spannish border or southeast on A8 for the Riviera.

The A8 continues to enter Italy at Ventimiglia for the Mediterranean coast of Italy.

TO ITALY

Milan, Veneto, Central and Coastal Italy via France and Switzerland

From CALAIS

This is the quickest and shortest but most expensive route if driving to Milan which makes a good starting point whether you are going to visit the Mediterranean coast (now the Mont Blanc tunnel is closed) Florence, Central Italy, Rome and Naples, as well as the Veneto.

From Calais

Join the motorway network at end of docks complex and follow 'Paris péage' to join A26 to Reims. At interchange with A4 (from Paris) continue towards Metz on A4 through the centre of Reims.

South of city, continue east on A4 through to Strasbourg, south through city and A35/N83 via Colmar to interchange just north of Mulhouse.

East on A36 to cross Rhine into Germany and south on A5 to enter Switzerland at Basel.

The A5 continues as the N2 as you follow to Luzern where the motorway tunnels under city, keep on the N2 with signs for Gotthard.

After skirting the lake comes the 6 miles long Seelisberg tunnel and, later, the 10.5 miles Gotthard tunnel. A series of small tunnels and viaducts continue the journey to the Swiss/Italian border near Como.

To MILAN

After wending one's way through the border post continue by motorway to Milan. There are two toll barriers en route where you pay cash and approaching Milan, motorways merge.

Take care to follow signs for correct lanes depending on whether you are going east (A4) to the Veneto or following the autostrada ring to the west of the city to join A1 south west for Florence and Rome or the A26 south to Genova on the Mediterranean coast.

SUGGESTED SITES ACROSS FRANCE

The following sites are fully described in the Alan Rogers Good Camps Guide for France:

St Quentin	0200 Vivier aux Carpes, Seraucourt
Laon	0201 de L'Ailette, Chamouille
Chalons	5102M Municipal
	5201M Presqu'ile de Champaubert, Braucourt
Metz	5705M Municipal Metz-Plage
Colmar	6806 Intercommunal, Riquewihr
	6804 Les Troix Chateaux
	6808 Clair Vacances
Dijon	2102M Les Cent Vignes, Beaune
	7107 Eperviere, Gigny-sur-Saone
Macon	7101M Camping Municipal

Lyon and south

6901 Porte de Lyon
2602 De Senaud, Albon, nr Tournon
2609 Les Truffieres, Grignan
8403M Bregoux en Provence,
    Aubignan, nr Carpentras

MOTORWAY SYSTEMS

France - French motorways (autoroutes) carry tolls, although there are some free sections in Northern France and through or near large towns like Reims and Strasbourg. The charging method used is that either a ticket is collected at the point of entry to the pay stage and pay at the end of the stage if continuing on the same road or when leaving at an exit between pay stages or, in a few places, you pay cash at each stage toll booth.

In 1999, the cost of driving a car from Calais to Strasbourg was approximately £25. The cost is greater if towing a caravan or if driving a motor caravan.

Service areas have a good range of facilities. Some sell bottles of wine as well. Wine is only pern-fitted with meals if accompanied by a hot food dish. There are often play areas for children. Excellent and frequent picnic rest areas.

Switzerland -The Swiss have a different method of charging to use their motorways. A tax disk - a vignette - must be purchased at a border and fixed in a specified place inside the front windscreen. This gives unlimited travel on all Swiss motorways and is valid until the following 31 Jan. An extra vignette is required if towing any form of trailer. The cost in 1999 was Sfr 40. Heavy fines are imposed if caught on motorways without the disk.

Service area buildings vary in size between small with bar service and shop selling a range of confectionery, souvenirs, biscuits etc to larger two-storey ones with a greater range of goods and a few much bigger ones which span across both carriageways. These have a variety of restaurants and full range of shops for groceries, fancy goods etc and a bakery. Bank or change facilities. Excellent picnic rest areas.

Italy - Tolls are charged, the majority paid by taking a ticket on entering a pay stage and paying either at exit or where toll boths barriers are across the road. There are toll free sections around large towns. Service areas are more frequent as many are small with refreshments taken standing at the bar but still have a range of other goods. Next in size are the round buildings with a larger range of food and other goods than in any other country and the exit from the bar is via the shop! The largest of all are those which span both carriageways where there are shops in the 'legs' and restaurants over. Notices in parking area give warnings about security. The picnic areas without services have now been sealed.

Motorbiking through Europe with an Alan Rogers' Guide

by Colin Walker

Over the last 10 years motorcycle ownership in Great Britain has been growing. Purchasers are, in the main, within the age range of mid 20's to 50+ and a lot of these bikes are bought as 'toys' maybe only clocking up 500 miles per year. So how are today's 'bikers' perceived and received? Last summer I decided to tour Europe on a Yamaha Virago XV535S and during this trip gauge the attitude of people both in campsites and in general to motorcyclists. Although I have travelled and camped extensively in Europe before this was my first touring trip by motorcycle and also my first solo trip. My route took me from my home in Scotland via Hull/Zeebrugge through Belgium, Germany, Czech Republic, Austria, Slovenia, Italy, France, back to Belgium returning home via Zeebrugge/Hull a distance of nearly 4000 miles.

My first concern arose on the ferry. On boarding a crew-member handed me some rope and it was my responsibility to secure my bike for the crossing. Speaking to other bikers I found out that this was standard practice. I wondered what the legal position would be if a bike was damaged in transit during a rough crossing. Would the shipping company deny liability because their employees had not secured the bike? Fortunately my concerns were not tested, as both crossings were dead flat calm.

I disembarked around 08.30. As I wanted my first stop to be just east of Frankfurt, leaving only a short hop to Heidelberg, where I intended to spend a few days, I headed for the autoroute and used it via Liege to just north of Bitburg then through Wittich to Kaiserslautern and into Bad Durkheim where I camped at Knaus Campingpark Bad Durkheim (AR no. 3260, DM 23.00). This is an excellent site with convenient access. A good overnight stop and probably worth staying for a few days. I was free to pitch where I liked within a specified area for tents. The toilet and washing facilities were excellent.

The next day it was only 36 miles to Heidelberg where I chose Camping Haide at Ziegelhausen (DM 16). This site is only a few miles from Heidelberg on the Eberbach road and is situated on a long strip of land running alongside the river Neckar. Again I was free to chose my own pitch which are not marked. The site has two toilet blocks and there is a charge for hot water in the showers. There is also a small bar/restaurant. This is a reasonable site with limited facilities. There is some traffic noise from the main road and also a railway line, which runs on the opposite side of the river. I stayed here for three nights sightseeing in

Heidelberg and surrounding area, which is very picturesque, and certainly worth a visit.

Now moving to the Czech Republic. My target was Plzen, which is famous for pils lager, for an overnight before moving on to Prague. My route took me via Eberbach to the autoroute A6 which I used to Amberg. Traffic was heavy with a constant convoy of mainly Eastern European trucks from Poland, Czech Republic, Slovenia, Hungary, etc. going east.

From Amberg I made my way to the E50 and crossed into the Czech Republic. I decided not to use the autoroute in the Czech Republic as I want to see the countryside. The route I decide to use seemed straightforward, the route 5 which goes straight to Plzen. However the main road signing directs traffic for Plzen onto the autoroute and as the minor signing is not always clear some care is required to stay on the 5 coupled with the fact that the road has been renumbered the 605. It took me a little time to get to grips with this, so take care. It would appear that a lot of the Czech road numbers have changed, at least from the road atlas I was using. The road is an excellent motorcycle run with very little traffic and long straight stretches running through some nice scenery and wooded sections. This area appears to be quite poor and mainly agricultural. The villages reflect this.

At Plzen I stayed at Camping Oestende which is in the Bl Hora area. This is not an easy site to find but once found you can pitch in a wooded setting beside a lake. On my approach into Plzen I started looking for campsite signs but did not see any. I got to the site only after seeking directions from a number of people and going up and down the same main road several times knowing that the site was just off this road. Again I was free to pitch anywhere within the tented area. Water points seemed few and far between and I had to walk a fair distance for water. Toilets, etc. are fine.

The next day it was on to Prague where I used the Caravancamp (AR no. 480, Ckc 345) which is on the road into Prague from Plzen. Once again I was given freedom to pitch anywhere. This site is ideally situated for trips into the city centre but a bit scruffy round the edges. It is listed as having a swimming pool. However I could not see any filtration of the water and it did not look particularly clean. Give the swimming pool a miss. The toilet block was OK and the food from the small bar was of a good basic quality, an excellent vegetable soup with bread followed by a tasty goulash washed down by three local beers all for under £4. There is a tramline right outside the site and it only costs 50p return. Prague is a wonderful city and would be on my highly recommended list.

I found the Czech roads, even on a Sunday, to be fairly quiet and very enjoyable to ride on but do use

> The price quoted after each campsite is the high season per night charge in local currency for one person, motorcycle and tent.

the public transport in the cities – it's so cheap.

From Prague my next destination was Lake Bled in Slovenia. My route took me, on the first day, to just south of Linz via Pisek and esk Budjovice, famous as the home of Budvar beer (Budweiser). Due to a mechanical problem I had an enforced stop at Traum where I had a very pleasant overnight in the excellent Gasthof Innviertlerhof. The next day, after a quick stop at the repair shop, I continued south and had an overnight at St Viet Camping Bad, St Viet (AS 140). Once again I was free to chose my own unmarked pitch but within a specific area that I was directed to. This is a small site that is conveniently situated close to the main route north/south. The facilities are adequate and clean.

The next morning it was off to Lake Bled. I went to Camping Zaka (AR no. 420, SIT 1,077) which is at the opposite end of the lake from the town of Bled. Again pitches are not marked and I am free to pitch anywhere. Zaka is a large site with excellent toilet and washing facilities in a beautiful location. There is a very good restaurant (soup, grilled chicken, side salad and French fries washed down with two local beers all for under £6) and shop at the camp entrance and it is only about a twenty minute lakeside walk to the Bled. Across the road from the entrance is Lake Bled which is lovely to swim in. This area is ideal if you love the mountains as there are plenty of mountain activities to get involved in. I spent four nights here then moved on to Italy.

Great roads from Slovenia through the mountains to Italy. This is obviously a winter sports area and some of the resorts on the Slovenian side of the border looked excellent. If you ski it might be worth checking it out.

Rimini was my destination. From Bled I went via Jesenice, Kranjska Gora and Udine on to Venice and then down the coast road to Rimini. I had not driven in Italy for a few years and I had forgotten just what Italian drivers were like. It took me a few miles to adjust but be aware Italian traffic laws are not observed so be very alert especially for the scooters.

In Rimini my first choice of site was full and I was directed to Camping Belvedere International (L. 30,500) where I was unlucky enough to get in. It was now around 20.00 and with a mileage from Bled of 310 in extremely hot weather conditions all I wanted was to pitch have a shower and eat. I booked in and was guided to my pitch, which was in a very dark, heavily wooded part of the site. Pitches were marked but they were squeezing two tents onto each pitch. I realised that this was not the site for me. This was reinforced when I could not find any showers. I was told that there were none (?). Also the toilets and washing areas were filthy. The clientele were mainly groups of teenagers and it was very very noisy. This is the worst site I have ever been on and if you are in this area and this site is the only one with space my advice is move on – sleep in you car if necessary but under no circumstances use this site. (*Editor's note: not an Alan Rogers' site!*)

The next morning I moved about 10 miles up the coast to Cesentico and got into Camping Cesentico (AR no. 6075, L. 32,400) an excellent site with a population, I believe, when full of about 5,000. The clientele is mainly Italian families and it is very well organised and geared to providing a good family holiday which includes an entertainment programme. It has it own section of private beach, private bike park at the beach and beach kiddies club. Also your pitch fee allows you free use of an umbrella on the beach. After five days of lying on the beach at Cesentico I moved to Tuscany.

My chosen site was Camping Villaggio Norcenni Girasle Club, Figline Valdarno (AR no. 6612, L. 27,100). This was the site of the trip and is a must for anybody visiting the area. But beware the ground is very hard and stony. Pegging is difficult and I had to watch for sharp stones cutting my groundsheet. This site is ideally placed for visits to Florence, Pisa and Siena with excellent motorcycling in the Tuscan hills. The rides to Pisa and Siena have some superb sections with stunning scenery. This was my first visit to Tuscany. I had often read about the colours of the area but nothing you read or see in photographs can properly portray the actuality. It is breathtaking.

Five days later I am off to the Mediterranean coast. I had chosen Imperia for my next few days before turning north and heading into France. From Figline Valdarno I headed for the autoroute which I took to the coast leaving it at Massa to continue on the coast road SS1 to Imperia. This was the biggest mistake of my trip. Traffic was horrendous and even on a motorbike the journey from Figline to Imperia, a distance of 182 miles took 9½ hours.

Genova was a nightmare to drive through. Signposting was horrendous as at most intersections there were no signs indicating any of the places in my direction and it was more by luck than judgement that I eventually came through Genova on the right road. The signing that I was looking for only seemed to start as I was leaving the city. Arriving in Imperia I drove through the city and made for the western outskirts to Camping De Wijnstok (L. 19,000). (*Editor's note: not featured in AR for 2000.*) The site is basic, as are the rather elderly toilet blocks. Flat marked pitches and again I was free to choose my own pitch. There is some shade provided by trees. Imperia is a large, not particularly attractive city. There is a large industrial zone, which incorporates the docks. The west end around the marina is probably the most attractive but it does not have that Mediterranean 'chic', so if that's what your looking for move along the coast to the principality of San Remo.

I left Imperia after three nights joining the SS1 again and heading for Ventimiglia where I turned into the mountains making for the border with France at Colle di Tenda. After weeks of hot sticky weather it was nice to experience the fresher air as I climbed into the mountains. This run can only be described as awe-inspiring. The grandeur of it all. Roads, sometimes very narrow, winding up to the top of a mountain, fantastic views, then all the way

down the other side. I have driven similar roads in a car but to experience it on a motorcycle is a whole new ball game. Just at the border there is a restaurant where I stopped for lunch. Although a bit on the expensive side its location is worth the stop. I entered France from Italy at the Colle di Tenda. The French part of my trip can be read in the Alan Rogers Good Camps Guide – France. I left France by picking up the autoroute to the north of Metz which took me all the way through Luxembourg and Belgium and then on to Zeebrugge and the ferry home.

Queues at the border crossings between east and west are common sometimes involving a wait of up to one hour. However it is common practice for motorcyclists to go to the head of the queue. So don't be shy.

There are a lot of bikers touring in Europe but I was surprised just how few were using campsites. My experience over the whole trip was that as a 'biker' I was treated no differently that anyone else, even in the gasthof in Austria where I arrived in full leathers and very hot and sweaty. However as somebody travelling with a small tent, where pitches were allocated, I was frequently given a very small pitch. Also many site shops do not carry stock suitable for the single traveller who does not have a fridge. Pre-packed goods, especially frozen or chilled, are in quantities for families therefore the available choice is very limited.

I would certainly recommend biking in Europe. Car drivers are more biker aware than in Britain and will, especially in Italy and France, where possible move over to allow for overtaking, even in the cities. There are lots of great roads, fantastic weather and parking is not a problem, even in the cities and it's free. So get over to Europe, stay off the autoroutes as much as possible, and enjoy the excellent byways.

REPORTS BY READERS

We always welcome reports from readers concerning sites which they have visited. Reports provide us with invaluable feedback on sites already featured in the Guide or, in the case of those not featured, they provide information which we can follow up with a view to adding them in future editions.

However, if you have a complaint about a site, this should be addressed to the campsite owner, preferably in person before you leave.

Please make your comments either on this form or on plain paper. It would be appreciated if you would indicate the approximate dates when you visited the site and, in the case of potential new sites, provide the correct name and address and, if possible, include a site brochure. We cannot always respond as quickly as we would wish, particularly during the summer and autumn months when we are working on the following year's guides. Please accept our apologies if your letter is not answered immediately - it does not mean we haven't followed up your comments. Send your reports to:

Deneway Guides & Travel Ltd, Chesil Lodge, West Bexington, Dorchester DT2 9DG

Name of Site and Ref. No. (or address for new recommendations):

....

....

Dates of Visit: ....

Comments:

Reader's Name and Address: ....

....

....

....

NATURIST SITES

We have had very favourable feedback from readers concerning our choice of naturist sites, which we first introduced in our 1992 editions. Over the last few years we have gradually added a few more.

Apart from the need to have a 'Naturist Licence' (see below), there is no need to be a practising naturist before visiting these sites. In fact, at least as far as British visitors are concerned, many are what might be described as 'holiday naturists' as distinct from the practice of naturism at other times. The emphasis in all the sites featured in this guide at least, is on naturism as 'life in harmony with nature', and respect for oneself and others and for the environment, rather than simply on nudity. In fact nudity is really only obligatory in the area of the swimming pools.

There are a number of rules, which amount to sensible and considerate guidelines designed to ensure that no-one invades someone else's privacy, creates any nuisance, or damages the environment. Whether as a result of these rules, the naturist philosophy generally, or the attitude of site owners and campers alike, we have been very impressed by all the naturist sites we have selected. Without exception they had a friendly and welcoming ambience, were all extremely clean and tidy and, in most cases, provided much larger than average pitches, with a wide range of activities both sporting and cultural.

The purpose of our including a number of naturist sites in our guide is to provide an introduction to naturist camping in Europe for British holidaymakers; we were actually surprised by the number of British campers we met on naturist sites, many of whom had `stumbled across naturism almost by accident' but had found, like us, that these sites were amongst the nicest they had encountered. We mentioned the Naturist Licence – French Law requires all campers over 16 years of age on naturist sites to have a `licence'. These can be obtained in advance from either the British or French national naturist associations, but are also available on arrival at any recognised naturist site (a passport type photograph is required).

The four naturist sites featured in this guide (the site numbers are prefixed with 'N'), together with the number of the page where they may be found, are:

Austria
N036   Rutar Lido FKK . . . . page 23

Netherlands
N580   Flevo-Natuur . . . . page 184

Spain
N8537   Templo del Sol . . . . . . .page 264
N8752   El Portus . . . . .page 275

Alan Rogers' Good Camps Guide - France features another fourteen naturist sites.

MAP - Austria

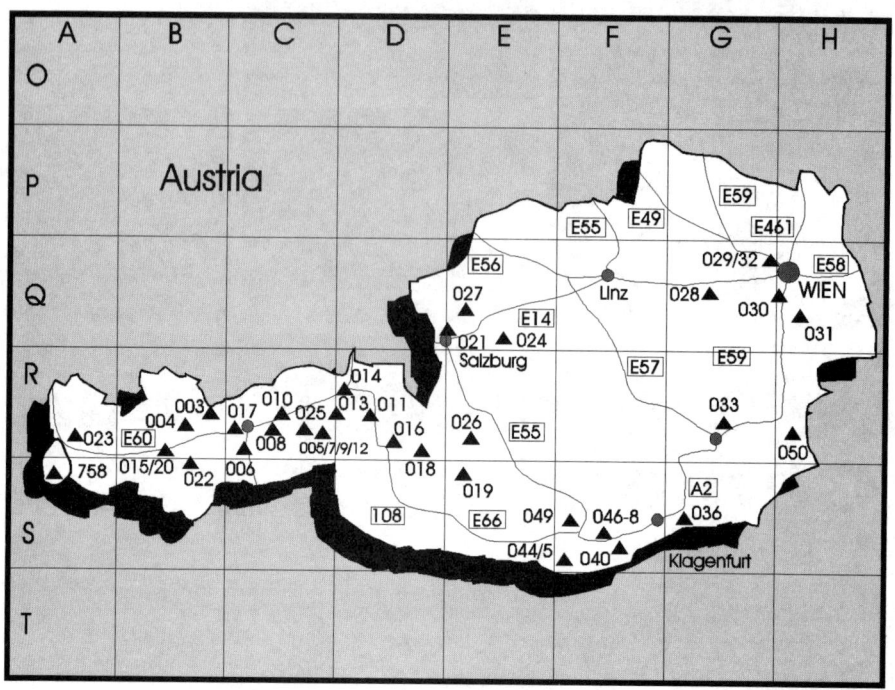

MAP - Hungary

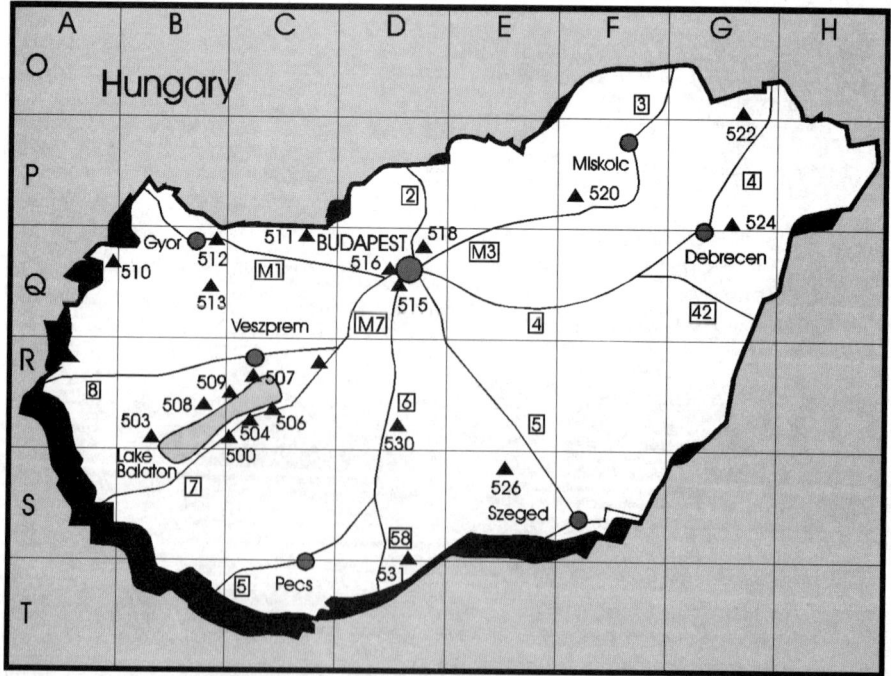

MAP - The BENELUX Countries

Belgium, Luxembourg and the Netherlands

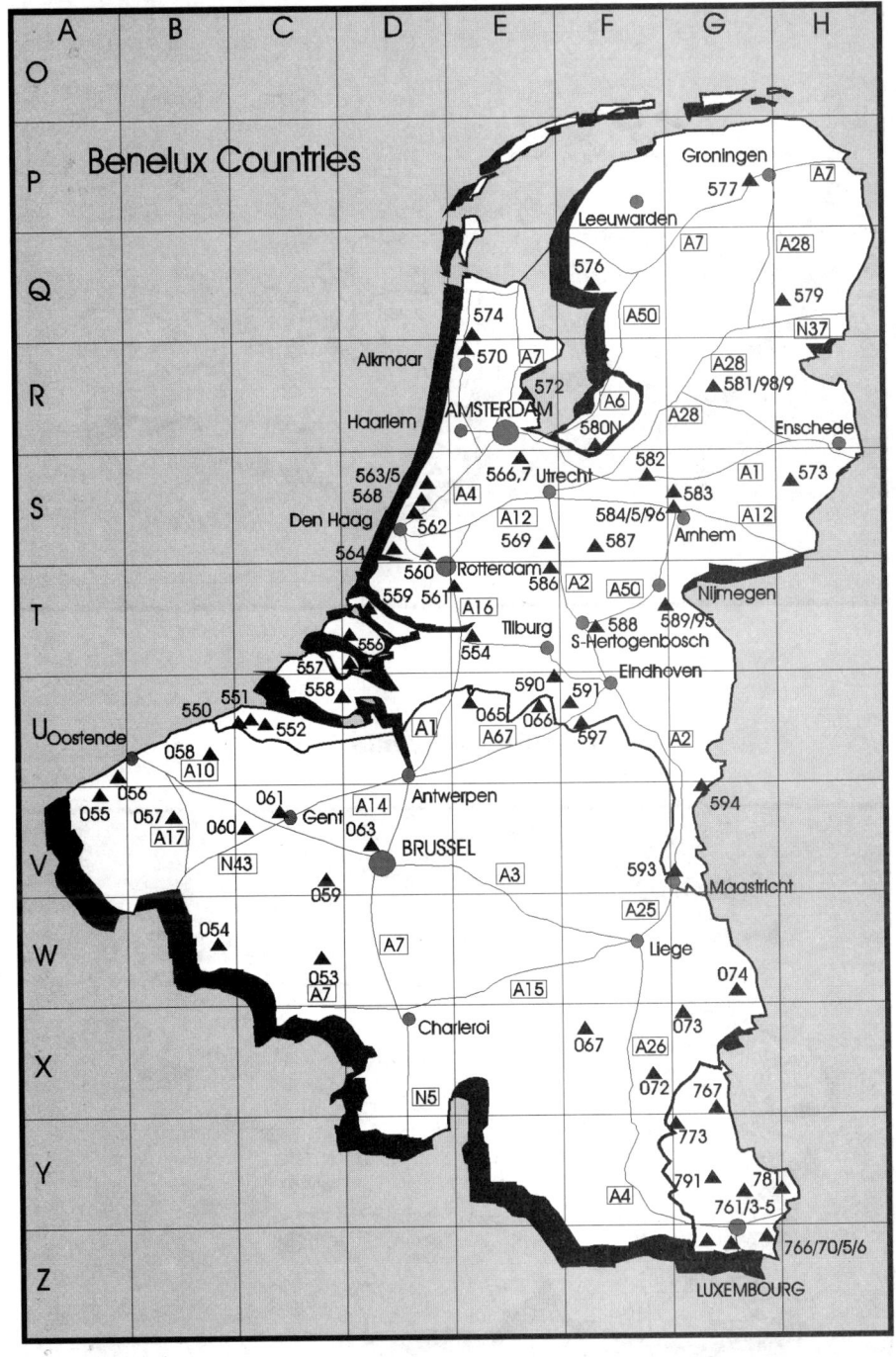

MAP - The Czech Republic and Slovakia

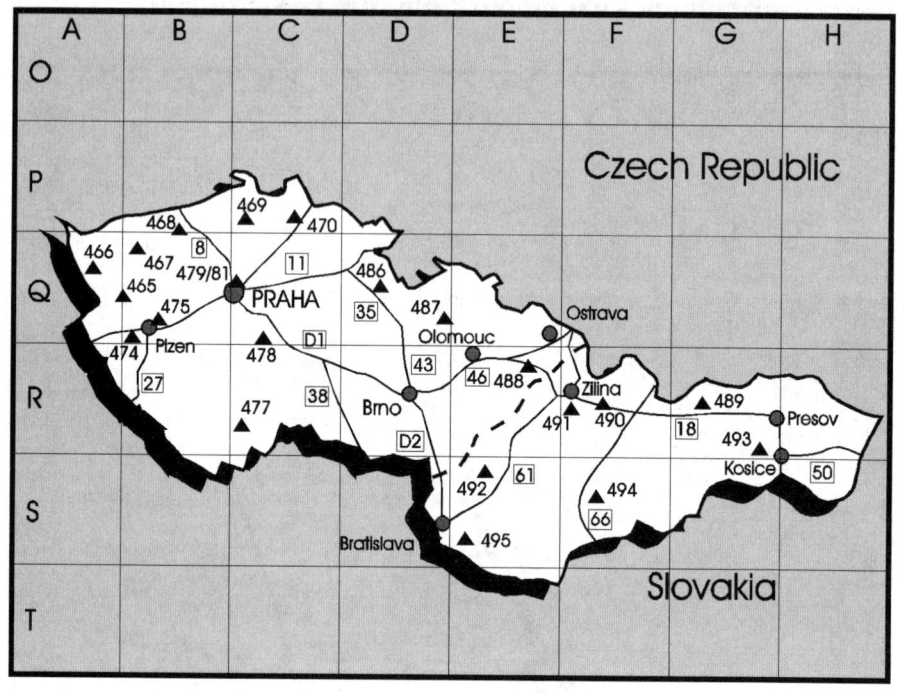

MAP - Slovenia

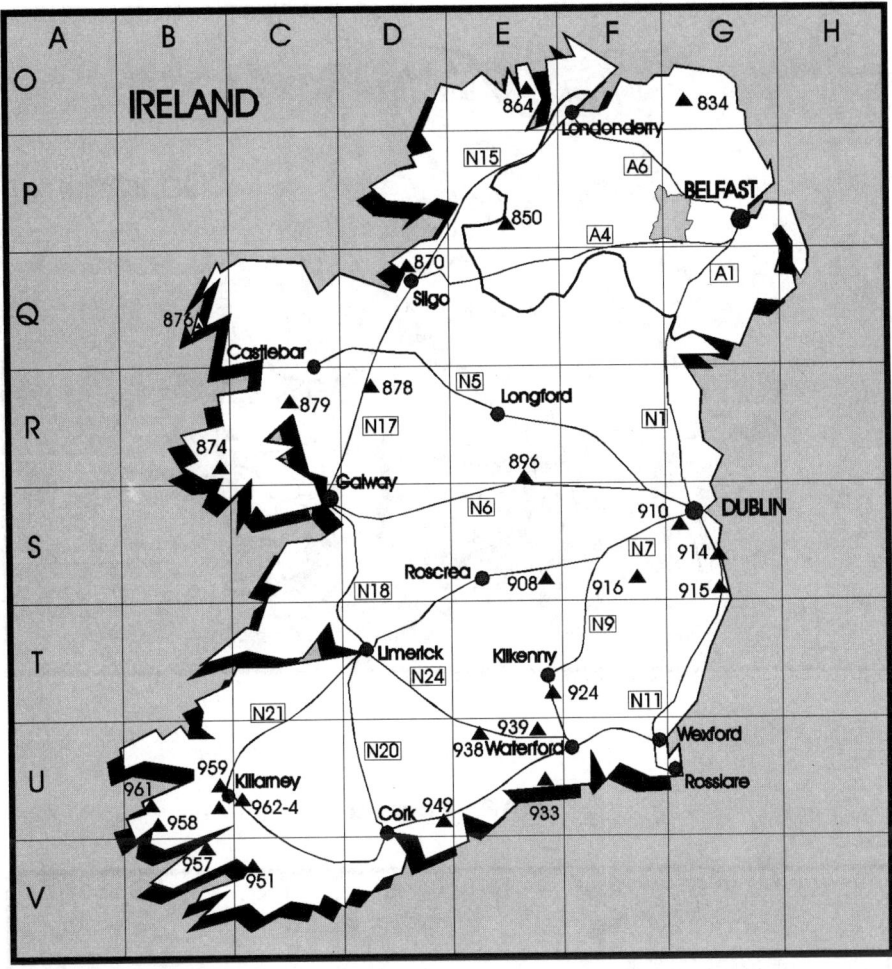

Maps and Index

The Site Index

The Site Index at the back of the guide (starting on page 381) comprises a listing of all the sites featured in this guide in the order in which they appear giving a page number together with a grid reference related to the appropriate country map - taking Spain, for example, site number 9250 is to be found in grid square FQ on page 292.

New sites: Sites that are new to the guide this year are highlighted in bold text in the index.

The Town Index

Comprises an alphabetical town name index to each country giving the names of all the towns where sites are featured. It starts on page 378.

The Maps

The maps are on pages 368 - 377. These may be used to identify the approximate location of sites; each site is identified on the appropriate map by reference to an individual site number and we include a grid system for each map. One can therefore identify the grid square (e.g. square BY) in which a particular site is situated.

MAP - Denmark

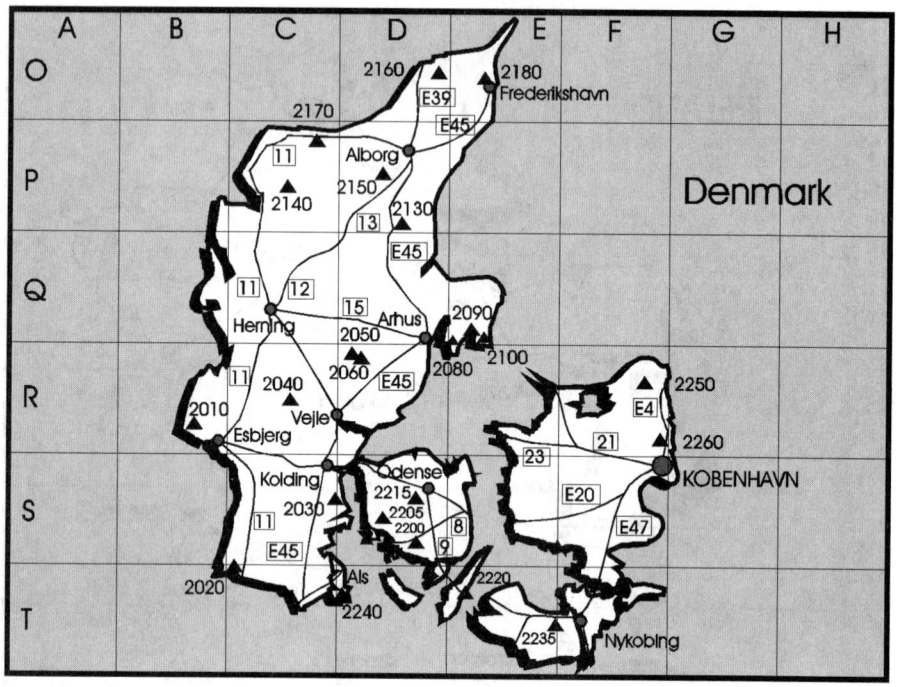

MAP - Finland

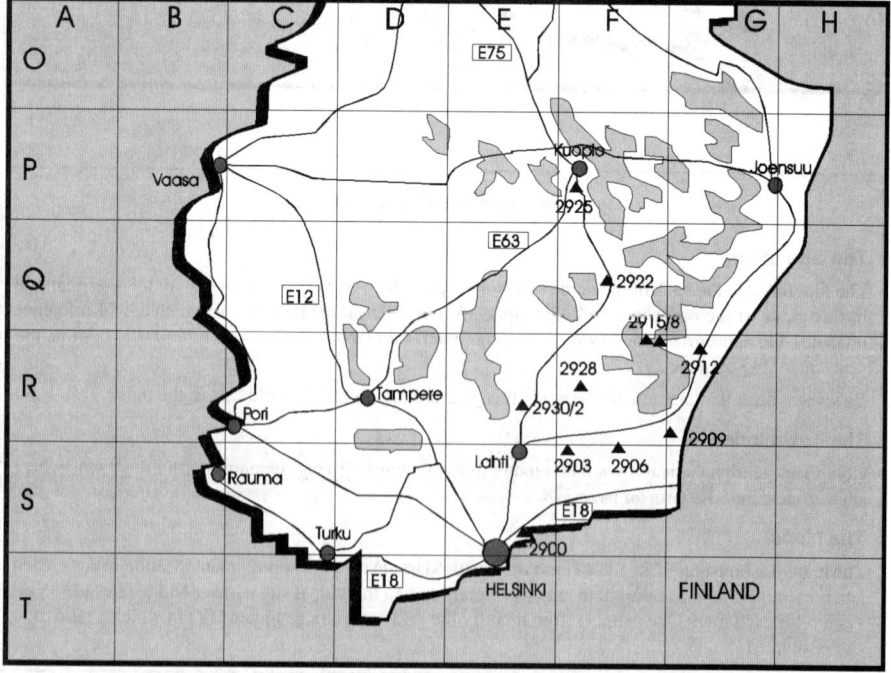

MAP - Germany

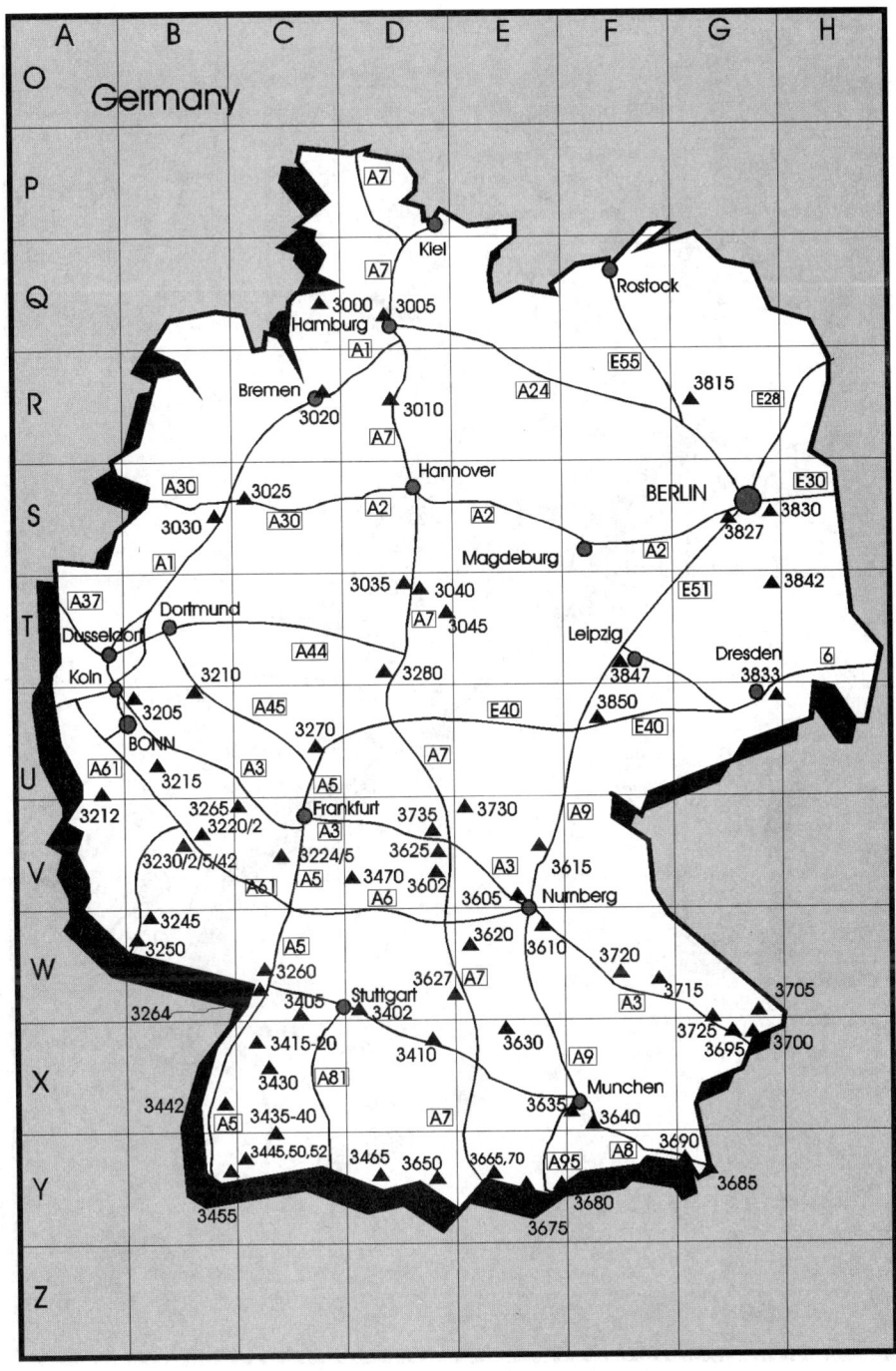

MAP - Italy

MAP - Spain and Portugal

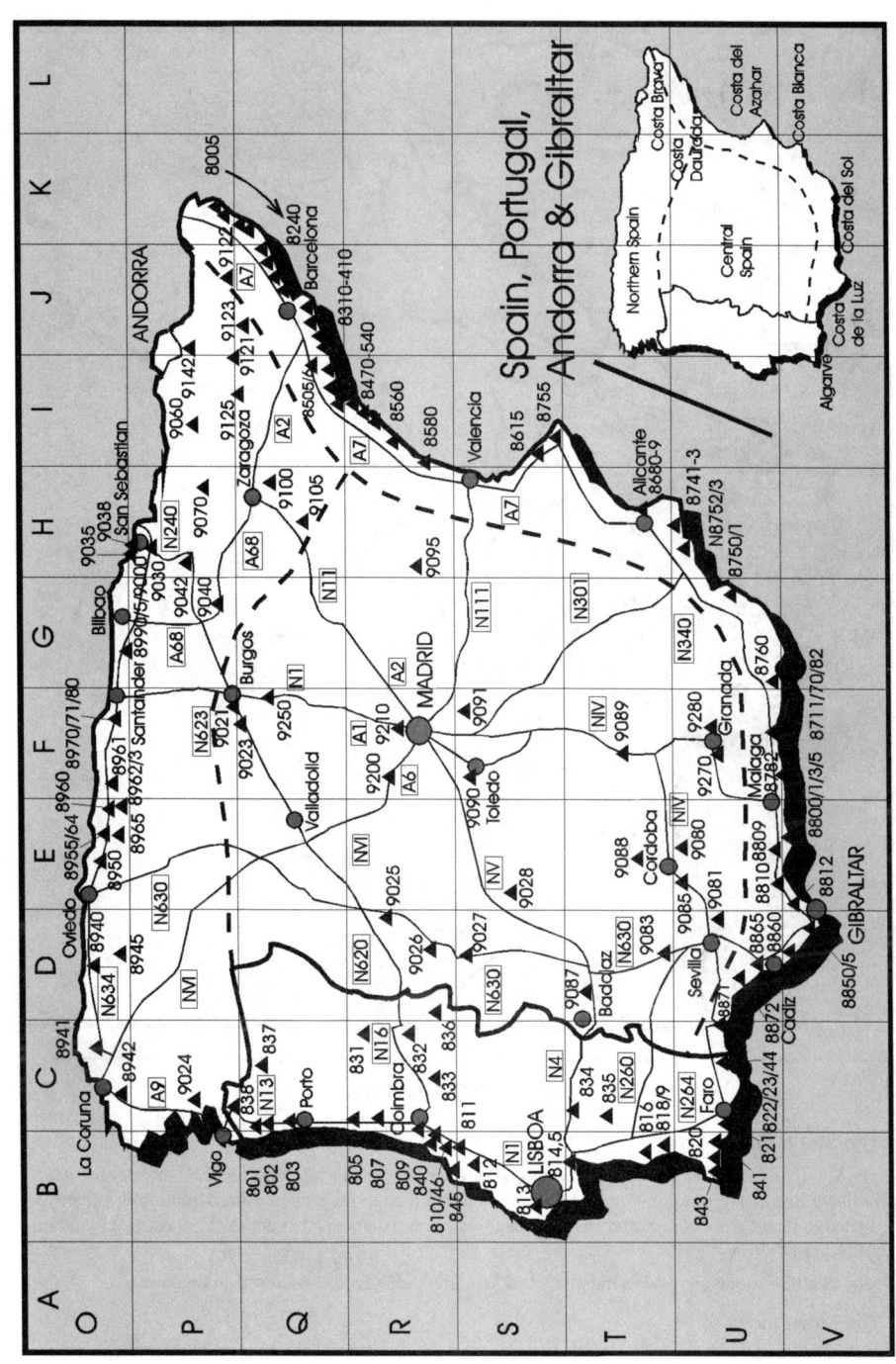

Spain, Portugal, Andorra & Gibraltar

MAP - Norway and Sweden

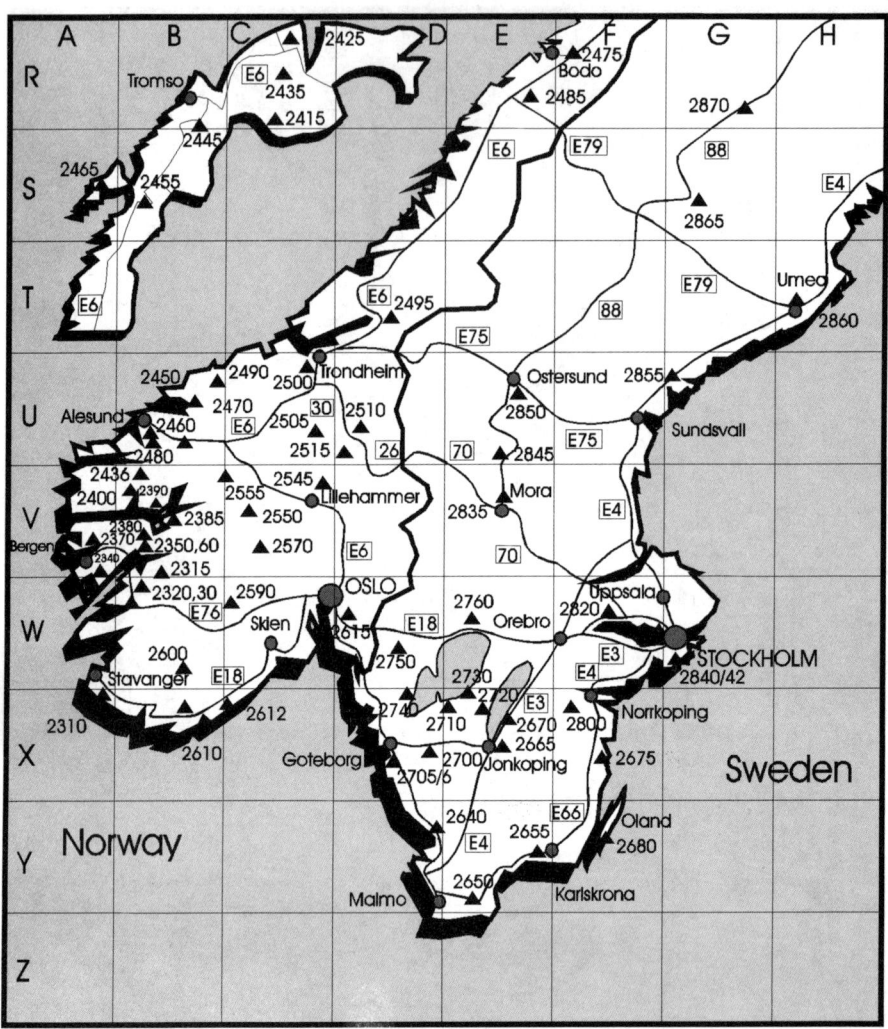

Maps and Index

The Site Index

The Site Index at the back of the guide (starting on page 381) comprises a listing of all the sites featured in this guide in the order in which they appear giving a page number together with a grid reference related to the appropriate country map - taking Spain, for example, site number 9250 is to be found in grid square FQ on page 292.

New sites: Sites that are new to the guide this year are highlighted in bold text in the index.

The Town Index

Comprises an alphabetical town name index to each country giving the names of all the towns where sites are featured. It starts on page 378.

The Maps

The maps are on pages 368 - 377. These may be used to identify the approximate location of sites; each site is identified on the appropriate map by reference to an individual site number and we include a grid system for each map. One can therefore identify the grid square (e.g. square BY) in which a particular site is situated.

MAP - Poland

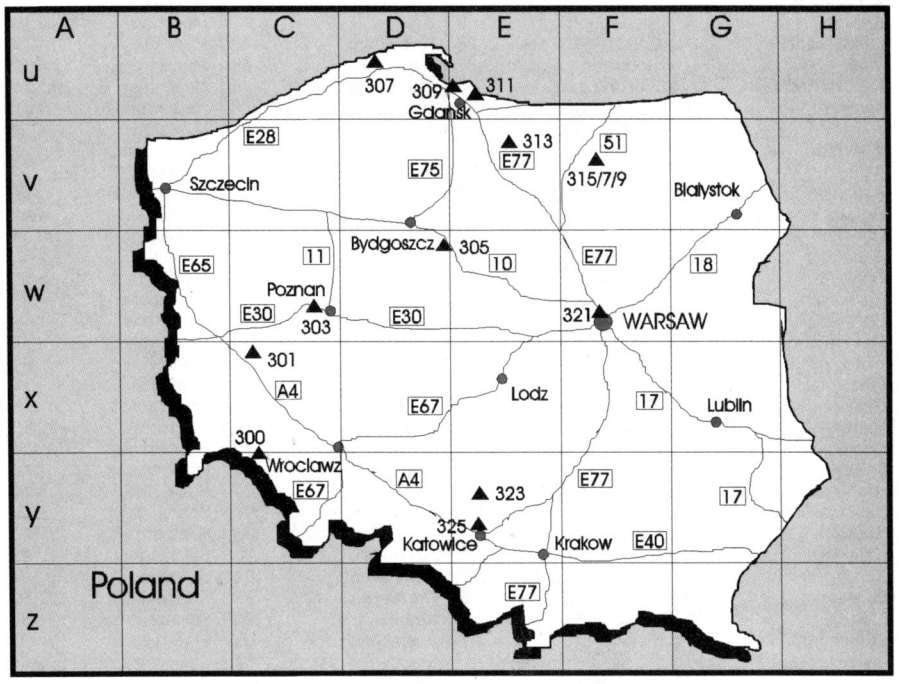

MAP - Switzerland

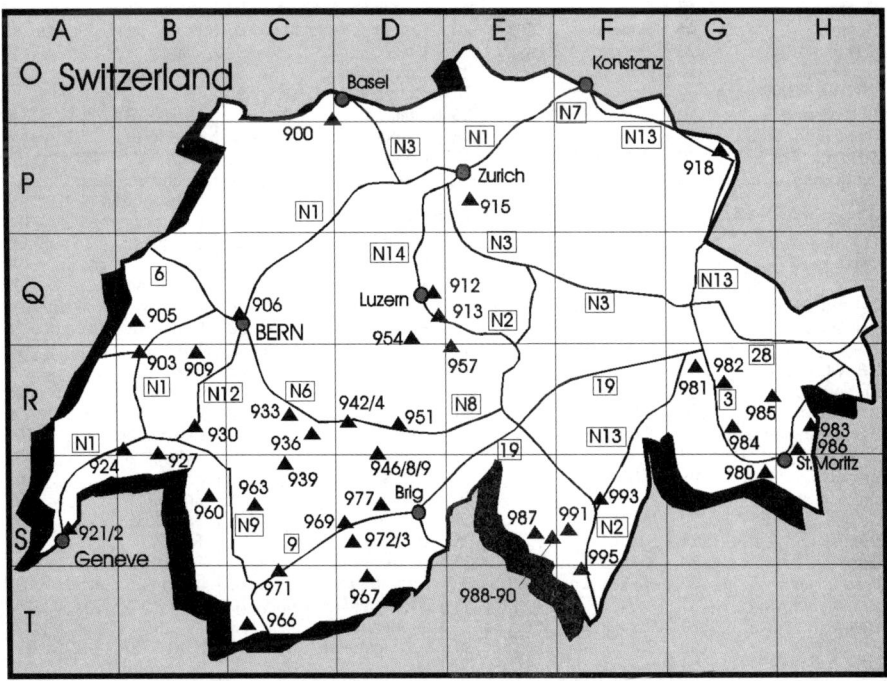

TOWN and VILLAGE INDEX

ANDORRA
Erts 7
La Massana 7

LIECHTENSTEIN
Triesen 7

AUSTRIA
Aschau 13
Badgastein 18
Bruck a.d. G'glockstr .17
Döbriach 24, 26
Eberndorf 23
Ehrwald 10
Faakersee 24
Feldkirch 9
Fieberbrunn 14
Fügen 15
Fürstenfeld 21
Graz 22
Hermagor 25, 26
Hopfgarten 15
Innsbruck ...12, 16, 17
Kitzbühel 14, 15
Klosterneuburg 20
Kössen 16
Kramsach 11
Kufstein 16
Landeck 9, 10
Laubühel 12
Laxenburg 22
Leutasch 10
Maltatal 25
Mayrhofen 12, 13
Millstättersee 24
Natters 16
Neumarkt-Wallersee .19
Ossiach 23
Rattenburg 11
Salzburg 18, 19
Schönbühel 21
Schwaz 14, 15
Seefeld 11
Spittal 26
St Johann 14
St Johann im Pongau 19
St Wolfgang 19
Styria 21
Tulln a.d. Donau 20
Umhausen 10
Vienna 20, 21, 22
Villach 23-26
Volders 17
Weer 14
Wien 20, 21, 22
Zell am Ziller 12
Zell am See 17, 18

BELGIUM
Amberloup 33
Antwerpen 32
Bachte-Maria-Leerne .30
Brugge 29
Brussels 29
Bure-Tellin 32
Deinze 30
Doornik 31
Gand 30
Gent 30
Geraardsbergen 31
Ghent 30
Grimbergen 29
Ieper 29
Lombardsijde 28
Manhay 33

Mons 31
Nieuwpoort 28
Ostend/Oostende ...28
Rochefort 32
Sint Job In't Goor ..32
Sint-Kruis 29
Ste Ode 33
Tournai 31
Turnhout 34
Ypres 29

CZECH REPUBLIC
Benesov 38
Ceské Lipy 37
Céske Budejovice ..39
Chomutov 37
Frantiskovy Lázné ...36
Franzensbad 36
Karlovy-Vary 36
Karlsbad 36
Kostelec 40
Liberec 37
Marianbad 36
Mariánské Lánzé 36
Mohelnice 40
Pilsen/Plzen 38
Prague 39
Praha 39
Roznov-Radhostem .40
Velká Hled'sebe ...36
Zandov 37

DENMARK
Blåvand 42
Copenhagen 52
Ebeltoft 45, 46
Esbjerg 42
Faaborg 50
Fjerritslev 48
Frederikshavn 49
Fuglsø 45
Give 43
Haderslev 43
Hillerød 53
Hirtshals 48
Hobro 47
Hårby 50
Klim 48
Krakær 45
Laven St 44
Lysabildskov 51
Møgeltønder 42
Nykøbing 47
Nærum 52
Odense 49
Rudkøbing 51
Ry 44
Sakskøbing 52
Silkeborg 44
Spodsbjerg 51
Sydals 51
Tønder 42

FINLAND
Hartola 60
Imatra 56
Kouvola 55
Kuopio 59
Mikkeli 59
Porvoo 55
Punkaharju 57
Savonlinna 58
Sysmä 60
Taavetti 56
Varkaus 58

GERMANY
Aga 91
Aichelberg 80
Augsburg 84
Bad Dürkheim 74
Bad Gandersheim ..66
Bad Kissingen 88
Bad Liebenzell 75
Baden-Baden ...75, 76
Bayreuth 86
Berchtesgaden 82
Bergen 82
Berlin 93
Bonn 68
Bremen 62
Bremerhaven 62
Brunnen 80
Bühl 75
Burgen 71
Cham 89
Clausthal-Zellerfeld .66
Cochem 72
Creglingen 86
Dahn 74
Dechsendorf 86
Dinkelsbühl 85
Donautal 90
Donauwörth 84
Dresden 92
Eberbach 74
Ebsmoor 63
Edersee 67
Eggelstetten 84
Eging am See 89
Ellwangen 85
Erlangen 86
Freiburg ...76, 77, 78
Freudenstadt 76
Frickenhausen 87
Friedrichsh'fen .65, 80-1
Füssen 80, 81
Garmisch-Part'hen ..81
Gemünden-Hofstet'n .87
Gera 91
Goppingen 80
Gottsdorf 90
Güls 72
Hamburg 62
Hausbay-Pfalzf'd 64, 72
Heidelberg 74
Herbolzheim 79
Irring 90
Karlstadt 87
Kempten 80, 81
Kirchzarten 77
Kirchzell 74
Kleinröhrsdorf 92
Koblenz 69-72
Köln 68
Krün 81
Lackenhäuser 90
Lahnstein 71
Laudert 70
Leeden 63
Leipzig 91
Leiwen 73
Limburg ad Lahn ...69
Lindau 65, 81
Lingerhahn 70
Lorch-bei-Rudesheim 70
Lübbenau 93
Ludwigshafen 74
Mainz 69
Marburg ad Lahn ...67
Markdorf 80

Mesenich 72
München/Munich .83, 84
Münster 86
Münstertal 64, 76
Neuenburg 65, 78
Neureichenau 90
Nürnberg 85
Oberbruch 75
Ochsenfurt 87
Olpe-Sondern 67
Osnabrück 63
Passau 89, 90
Peiting 82
Pforzheim 75
Pielenhofen 88
Pirmasens 74
Potsdam 92
Regensburg 88
Remagen 68
Rheinmünster 76
Rieste 63
Rosenheim 82
Rottenbuch 82
Rüdesheim 69
Saarbrücken 74
Saarburg 73
Salzburg 82
Schapbach 76
Schmockwitz 93
Soltau 63
Stadtkyll 69
Stadtsteinach 86
Staufen 78
Stuttgart 77
Sulzburg 79
Tecklenberg 63
Titisee 78
Trier 73
Untergriesbach 90
Viechtach 89
Vöhl-Herzhausen ...67
Walkenried 66
Waren am Müritzsee .93
Wingst 62
Würzburg 87

HUNGARY
Aszófö 101
Baja 101
Balatonalmádi 103
Balatonfüred .101, 104
Balatonszemes 103
Budapest 97, 98
Cserszegtomaj 96
Debrecen 99
Dömös 96
Dunaföldvár 100
Eger 98
Esztergom 98
Györ 95
Hévíz 96
Kiskunmajsa 100
Nyiregyhaza 99
Siófok 102
Sopron 95
Szeged 100
Tokaj 99
Törökbálint 97
Üröm 98
Zamárdi 102

NORTHERN IRELAND
Ballymoney 107
Kesh 106
Muckross Bay 106

Town and Village Index

REPUBLIC of IRELAND
Achill Island 109
Athlone 110
Athy 110
Ballinode 108
Ballycasheen 116
Ballykeeran 110
Ballylickey 115
Ballymacoda 114
Bantry Bay 115
Belcarra 109
Cahirciveen 117
Carrick-on-Suir 114
Castlebar 109
Clogheen.........113
Clonea 113
Cong 108
Connemara 108
Donard 112
Dublin 111
Dungarvan 113
Healy Pass 116
Kilkenny 112
Killarney 115-118
Kilmacanogue 110
Knock 109
Portsalon 107
Redcross Village ...111
Sligo 108
Waterville 117
Youghal 114

ITALY
Aglientu 160
Alassio 120
Albenga 120
Antholz-Obertal ...134
Assisi 153
Baia Domizia 157
Bari 159
Barrea 155
Baveno 123, 124
Bellaria 146
Bibione 129, 136
Bibione Pineda 129, 136
Bogliasco 120
Bologna 141
Bolzano 134
Bozen 134
Brescia 125, 130
Ca'Ballarin 135
Ca'Noghera 138
Campiglia Marittima .148
Cannobio 122, 123
Casciano di Murlo .150
Castagneto Carducci 144
Castelvecchio Preci 152
Castiglione Lago .149
Castigliόne Pescaia .151
Cavallino ...128, 135-8
Cecina 142
Chianciano 148
Cisano 126
Cortina d'Ampezzo .133
Deiva Marina 121
Dobbiaco 134
Donoratico 144
Ferrara 140
Fiano Romano 154
Fiesole 14
Figline Valdarno ...145
Firenze 141,145
Florence 141, 145
Follonica 147
Genoa 120
Grado 135

Grosseto 151
Iseo 125
Jesolo 128, 136
La Spezia 121
Laives 134
Lazise 127
Leifers 134
Levico Terme 133
Lido del Cavallino ..137
Lido delle Nazioni ..140
Manerba del Garda .126
Marina di Bibbona .144
Marina di Grosseto .152
Mestre 138
Mondragone 157
Moniga del Garda .132
Montescudaio 142
Naples/Napoli 157
Oriago 139
Paestum 158
Palau 160
Passignano 149
Pergine Valsugana .133
Pesaro 146
Pescara 153
Peschici 158
Piano di Sorrento ..157
Pineto 154
Piombino 148
Pisa 143
Pistoia 143
Ravenna 140
Rioveggio 156
Riva del Garda 132
Riviera Ligure 121
Rivoltella 127
Roma/Rome ..154, 155
Rossano 159
S. Anna di Chioggia 139
S Teresa di Gallura 160
Salô 125, 130-1
Salto di Fondi 156
San Baronto 143
San Felice Benaco .125
San Felice 130, 131
San Giorgio 159
San Marino 145
San Remo Beach ..121
Sarteano 148
Savignano Mare ...146
Seiano 159
Siena 147, 150
Silvi Marina 153
Sistiana 135
Sorico 124
Sovicille 147
Sperlonga 156
Toblach 134
Torre Daniele 122
Toscana Colliverdi .151
Trento 133
Treporti 136, 137
Trieste 135
Troghi 141
Venezia/Venice 128, 136
Verona 127
Vico Equense 159
Vignale Riototorto 147

LUXEMBOURG
Berdorf 162
Bettembourg 162
Consdorf 165
Esch-sur-Alzette ...161
Ettelbruck 165
Hosingen 165

Kockelscheuer 164
Larochette ..163, 164
Luxembourg 164
Reisdorf 164
Remich 162

NETHERLANDS
Aalsmeer 178
Afferden 190
Alkmaar 179
Amsterdam ..177, 178
Apeldoorn 186
Arnhem 185-7
Barendrecht 174
Beerze-Ommen ...182
Beesd 185
Bergeyk 192
Breskens ..168, 169
Delft 171
Den Haag 173-7
Den Helder 180
Eindhoven 192
Emmen 181
Erichem 189
Garderen 184
Goes 169
Groede 169
Groningen 181
Herkenbosch 191
Heumen 188
Hilvarenbeek 191
Hoenderloo 186
Kamperland 171
Katwijk 172
Kootwijk 185
Koudum 180
Lage Mierde 190
Leiden 176
Luttenberg 183
Maastricht 192
Meerkerk 174
Middelburg 171
Monickendam 179
Nieuwvliet 168
Nijmegen ...188, 190
Noord-Sharwoude ..179
Noordwijk 177
Oosterhout 172
Renesse 170
Rheeze-Hardenberg 182
Rijnsburg 176
Rockanje 170
Roermond 191
Rotterdam 174
Ruurlo 183
s'Hertogenbosch ..188
Sint Maartenszee ..180
The Hague 173-7
Tiel 189
Tilburg 190, 191
Uitdam 179
Utrecht 185
Vinkel 188
Wageningen-Hoog .186
Wassenaar 175
Wezuperbrug 181
Wolphaartsdijk 169
Zeewolde 184
Zierikzee 170
Zwolle 183

NORWAY
Alesund 200
Alta 203
Alvdal 206
Åndalsnes 201

Averoy 202
Ballangen 203
Brekke 197
Byglandsfjord 208
Byrkjelo 200
Fagernes 207
Gaupne 199
Gol 207
Hallingdal 207
Kautokeino 204
Leira 207
Lillehammer 206
Lofoten 202
Lom 206
Lyngvær 202
Malmefjorden 201
Mauranger 196
Nordkapp 204
Norheimsund 197
Nå 197
Odda 196
Oppdal 205
Orkanger 205
Oteren 204
Øyer 206
Ringoy 196
Roros 205
Saltstraumen 203
Sandane 200
Setesdal 208
Skarsvåg 204
Snåsa 201
Sogndal 199
Storforsheim 202
Suohpatjávri 204
Tinnsjo 207
Trøgstad 209
Tvedestrand 208
Ulvik 198
Valdres 207
Vangsnes 198
Vassenden 199
Viggja 205
Vik 198
Volda 200

POLAND
Cieplice 212
Czestochowa 215
Gdansk 214
Gdynia 213
Grabowo 214
Jelenia Góra 212
Jznota Bartlowo ...215
Katowice 216
Kretowiny 214
Leba 213
Morag 214
Poznan 212
Sopot 213
Stegna 214
Torun 213
Ukta 215
Warsaw/Warszawa .216
Wygryny 215
Zielona Góra 212

PORTUGAL
Albufeira 225
Alvito 227
Areia 222
Arganil 228
Armação de Pêra .224
Cabdelo 218
Campo do Gerês .228
Cascais 222

Town and Village Index

Castro Daire 228
Coimbra 219
Costa da Caparica .222
Estela 218
Evora 226
Faro 225, 226
Figueira da Foz ...219
Gala 219
Guarda 227
Idanha-a-Nova ...227
Lagos 224
Leira 221
Lisboa/Lisbon 222
Louriçal 220
Mata do Camarido .218
Mira 219
Nazaré 220, 221
Odivelas 227
Olhão 225
Pinheiros de Marim .225
Porto Covo 223
Povoa de Varzim ..218
Praia da Luz 224
Praia de Salema .226
Quarteira 226
Sagres 224
São Jacinto 219
São Martinho Porto 221
São Pedro de Moel .221
Sarzedo 228
Seixas 229
Sines 223
Viana do Castelo ..218
Vilar de Mouros ...229
Vila Nova-Milfontes 223

SLOVAKIA
Bratislava 231
Kosice 231
Martin 232
Trencin 232
Turany 230
Zvolen 231

SLOVENIA
Bled 234
Bohinj 235
Grad Otocec 237
Izola 236
Kamnik 237
Kobarid 235
Kransjska Gora ...234
Ljubljana 236
Mojstrana 234
Novo Mesto 237
Postojna 236
Prebold 237
Soca 235

SPAIN
Ager 306
Ainsa 305
Albarracin 292
Alcossebre 268
Alfaz del Pi 271
Algeciras 282
Alicante 273
Almeria 277
Almuñecar 277
Altea 272
Ametlla de Mar ...266
Aranda de Duero .292
Aranjuez 288
Avin-Onis 296
Barcelona ...256, 257
Bareyo 300

Begur 246
Bellver de Cerdanya 304
Benicasim 267
Benidorm 269-71
Blanes 255, 256
Burgos 292, 293
Caceres 289
Cadaqués 239
Cadiz 283
Calella de la Costa .256
Cangas de Onis ..296
Caravia Alta 296
Cartagena ..274, 275
Castelldefels 257
Castelló Empúries .241
Castellón/Castelló .267
Castrojeriz 292
Colunga 295
Conil de la Frontera .283
Cordoba 286
Creixell de Mar ...259
Cuevas-Almanzora .276
Cuidad Real 287
Dos Hermanas ...286
El Ejido 277
El Escorial 291
El Puerto-Sa Maria .283
Elche 274
Empuria Brava ...242
Escala 245
Estartit 248
Estepona 280
Etxarri-Aranatz ...302
Ferrol 294
Figueres 241-5
Fuencaliente 287
Fuengirola 279
Gerona/Girona ..240-55
Granada 285
Guadalupe 289
Guardamar-Segura 273
Hospitalet-Infant ..264
Huesca 304
Isla Cristina 284
Jaca 303
L'Estartit 240, 247
La Cabrera 290
La Carlota 286
La Coruña 293
La Escala 246
La Manga 274
La Marina 274
La Pineda 260
La Puebla de Castro 304
La Rioja 302
Labuerda 305
Linares 288
Llafranc 248
Llanes 298
Lleida 306
Los Boliches 279
Los Gallardos 276
Luarca 294
Madrid ..288, 290-1
Marbella 279, 281
Maro-Nerja 278
Mazagon 284
Mérida 287
Mijas-Costa 279
Miranda-Castañar .289
Monesterio 287
Montagut 306
Montroig 262-4
Moraira 267
Mundaka 301
Nerja 278

Noja 299, 300
Nuevalos 303
Orio 301
Oviedo 295
Oyambre 298
Palafrugell 248
Palamós 249
Palomares 276
Pals 249
Pamplona 302
Pechon 297
Platja d'Aro 252-4
Platja de Pals ...250-2
Playa del Albir 272
Playa de Oliva ...269
Potes 297
Prado 296
Puigcerda 304
Reus 307
Roda de Bara 258
Ronda 280
Ruiloba 299
Sa Riera 246
Sabinillas-Manilva .280
Salamanca ..289, 290
Salou 261, 262
San Sebastian ...301
S Vicente-Barquera 298
S Pere Pescador .243-5
Santa Cilia de Jaca .303
Santa Cruz 293
Santa Elena (Jaén) .288
Santander ...289, 300
Santiago-Comp'la .294
Santillana del Mar .299
Seville 286
Sitges 257, 265
Solsona 307
Somiedo 295
Son Bou 308
Sopeña 296
Tamarit 259
Tarifa 282
Tarragona 259-63
Teruel 292
Toledo 288
Torre del Mar 278
Torrevieja 273
Torroella de Montgri 247
Tossa de Mar ...255
Valdovino 294
Vidiago 298
Vilanova de Prades .307
Vilanova i la Geltru .257
Vildecans 257
Villajoyosa 272
Zaragoza 303

SWEDEN
Ärjäng 317
Arvidsjaur 322
Askim 314
Borås 313
Båstad 310
Dals Långed 316
Färjestaden 311
Flottsbro 319
Göteborg 314
Gränna 313
Hallstahammar ..318
Höör 310
Huddinge 319
Jokkmokk 322
Jönköping 312
Jularp 310
Kil 317

Kramfors 321
Lidköping 315
Linköping 318
Mariestad 316
Orsa 320
Östersund 321
Stockholm 319
Sveg 320
Tidaholm 315
Tingsryd 311
Torekov 310
Umeå 322
Västervik 312

SWITZERLAND
Arbon 327
Avegno 339
Avenches 325
Basel/Basle 325
Bellinzona 340
Bern/Berne 325
Brienz 336
Châtel St Denis ...328
Chur 341
Churwalden 342
Claro 341
Colombier 324
Cugnasco 340
Davos 342
Engelberg 339
Evolène 333
Frutigen 330
Geneve/Geneva ..327
Grindelwald ...336, 338
Gstaad 331
Gwatt-Thun 330
Interlaken 335-7
Kappelenbrücke ..325
La Chaux-de-Fonds 324
La Fouly 333
Lausanne 328-31
Lauterbrunnen 335
Le Bouveret 331
Lenz 343
Lenzerheide 343
Les Haudères 333
Les Paccots 328
Leysin 329
Locarno 339, 340
Lucerne/Luzern ..326-9
Lugano 341
Martigny 333
Morges 328
Morteratsch 344
Muzzano 341
Neuchatel 324
Noville 328
Pontresina 344
Raron 335
Reinach 325
Salgesch 332
Sarnen 338
Scuol 344
Sierre 332
Silvaplana 343
Sion 332, 334
Spiez 330
St Moritz 343
Sur-En/Sent 344
Susten 334
Tenero 340
Vésenaz 327
Villeneuve 328
Vitznau 326
Zürich 326
Zweisimmen 331

CAMPSITE INDEX

ANDORRA
9143 Xixerella 7

LIECHTENSTEIN
758 Mittagsspitze 7

AUSTRIA
023 Waldcamping AR . . . 9
020 Sport Tirol BR . . . 9
015 Riffler BR . . 10
022 Krismer BS . . 10
004 Zugspitzcamping BR . . 10
003 Leutasch BR . . 11
010 Toni-Brantlhof CR . . 11
017 Kranebitten CR . . 12
005 Kröll CR . . 12
007 Hofer CR . . 13
012 Aufenfeld CR . . 13
025 Alpencamping CR . . 14
011 Tirol Camp DR . . 14
009 Zillertal-Hell CR . . 15
013 Schlossberg Itter DR . . 15
006 Natterer See CR . . 16
014 Wilder Kaiser DR . . 16
008 Schloss-Volders CR . . 17
018 Woferlgut DR . . 17
016 Seecamp DR . . 18
019 Kur-Erlengrund ES . . 18
021 Nord-Sam EQ . . 18
026 Hirschenwirt ER . . 19
024 Appesbach EQ . . 19
027 Neumarkt EQ . . 19
029 Tulln GQ . . 20
032 Klosterneuburg GQ . . 20
028 Stumpfer GQ . . 21
030 Rodaun HQ . . 21
050 Fürstenfeld HR . . 21
031 Laxenburg HQ . . 22
033 Central GR . . 22
N036 Rutar Lido FKK GS . . 23
046 Ossiachersee FS . . 23
048 Burgstaller FS . . 24
040 Arneitz FS . . 24
049 Maltatal FS . . 25
044 Schluga 1 FS . . 25
045 Schluga 2 FS . . 26
047 Mössler FS . . 26

BELGIUM
055 IC-Nieuwpoort AV . . 28
056 De Lombarde AU . . 28
058 Memling BU . . 29
057 Jeugstadion BV . . 29
063 Grimbergen DV . . 29
060 Groeneveld CV . . 30
061 Blaarmeersen CV . . 30
053 Waux-Hall CW . 31
054 Orient BW . 31
059 De Gavers CV . . 31
067 La Clusure FX . . 32
065 Het Veen EU . . 32

072 Tonny FX . . 33
073 Malempré GX . . 33
074 Eau Rouge GW . 34
066 Baalse Hei EU . . 34

CZECH REPUBLIC
465 Luxor BQ . . 36
466 Amerika AQ . . 36
467 Karlovy Vary BQ . . 36
468 Druhy Mlyn BP . . 37
469 Slunce CP . . 37
470 Pavlovice CP . . 37
474 Lodni Doprava BQ . . 38
475 Bílá Hora BQ . . 38
478 Konopiste CQ . . 38
477 Dlouhá Louka CR . . 39
479 Sportcamp CQ . . 39
480 Caravancamp CQ . . 39
481 Kotva CQ . . 39
486 Orlice DQ . . 40
487 Morava DQ . . 40
488 Roznov ER . . 40

DENMARK
2020 Møgeltønder CT . . 42
2010 Hvidbjerg BR . . 42
2030 Sandersvig CS . . 43
2040 Riis CR . . 43
2060 Birkhede DR . . 44
2050 Terrassen DR . . 44
2080 Sølystgård DQ . . 45
2090 Krakær EQ . . 45
2100 Blushøj EQ . . 46
2150 Sølyst DP . . 46
2140 Jesperhus CP . . 47
2130 Hobro DP . . 47
2170 Klim Strand CP . . 48
2160 Hirtshals DO . . 48
2180 Nordstrand EO . . 49
2215 DCU Odense DS . . 49
2200 Bøjden DS . . 50
2205 Løgismosestrand DS . . 50
2220 Billevænge ET . . 51
2240 Lysabildskov DT . . 51
2235 *Sakskøbing* ET . . 52
2260 DCU Naerum FR . . 52
2250 Hillerød FR . . 53

FINLAND
2900 Kokonniemi ES . . 55
2903 Kayralampi FS . . 55
2906 Taavetti FS . . 56
2909 Ukonniemi GR . . 56
2912 Kultakivi GR . . 57
2915 Punkaharjun FR . . 57
2918 Vuohimaki FR . . 58
2922 Taipale FQ . . 58
2925 Rauhalahti FP . . 59
2928 Visulahti FR . . 59
2930 Koskenniemi ER . . 60
2932 Sysmä ER . . 60

GERMANY
3000 Knaus Wingst CQ . . 62
3005 Schnelsen Nord DQ . . 62
3020 Freie Hansestadt CR . . 62
3010 Kur-Röders' DR . . 63
3025 Alfsee CS . . 63
3030 DCC Truma BS . . 63
3242 Schinderhannes BV . . 64
3450 Münstertal CY . . 64
3455 Gugels BY . . 65
3650 Gitzenweiler DY . . 65
3035 Bad Gandersh'm DT . . 66
3040 Prahljust DT . . 66
3045 Walkenried DT . . 66
3280 Teichmann DT . . 67
3270 Lahnaue BU . . 67
3210 Biggesee-Sond'n BU . . 67
3215 Goldene Meile BU . . 68
3205 Stadt Köln BU . . 68
3212 Landal Wirfttal AU . . 69
3265 Limburg CV . . 69
3224 *Am Rhein* BV . . 69
3225 Suleika BV . . 70
3235 Mühlenteich BV . . 70
3220 Burg Lahneck BV . . 71
3230 Burgen BV . . 71
3222 *Gülser Mosel* BV . . 72
3232 *Family Club* BV . . 72
3242 Schinderhannes BV . . 72
3245 Sonnenberg BW . 73
3250 Warsberg BW . 73
3264 Büttelwoog CW . 74
3260 Bad Dürkheim CW . 74
3470 Odenwald DV . . 74
3405 Bad Liebenzell CW . 75
3415 Adam CX . . 75
3420 Oberrhein CX . . 76
3430 Alisehof CX . . 76
3450 Münstertal CY . . 76
3402 Cannstatter DW . 77
3440 Kirchzarten CY . . 77
3435 Sandbank CY . . 78
3445 Belchenblick CY . . 78
3455 Gugels BY . . 78
3442 Herbolzheim BX . . 79
3452 Alte Sägemühle CY . . 79
3410 Aichelberg DX . . 80
3465 Wirthshof DY . . 80
3665 Brunnen EY . . 80
3650 Gitzenweiler DY . . 81
3670 Hopfensee EY . . 81
3680 Tennsee EY . . 81
3675 Richterbichl EY . . 82
3685 Allweglehen GY . . 82
3690 Wagnerhof GY . . 82
3635 Obermenzing FX . . 83
3640 Thalkirchen FX . . 84
3630 Donau-Lech EX . . 84
3627 Azur Ellwangen EW . 85
3610 Knaus Nürnberg EY . . 85
3620 Romantische Str. EW . 85
3605 Rangau EV . . 86

Campsite Index - by Number

3615	Stadtsteinach	EV	86
3602	Romantische Str.	DV	86
3625	Frickenhausen	DW	87
3735	Schönrain	DV	87
3730	Bad Kissingen	EV	88
3720	Naabtal	FW	88
3715	Knaus Viechtach	FW	89
3725	Bavaria	GW	89
3695	Dreiflüsse	GX	90
3700	Bayerwald	GX	90
3705	Lackenhäuser	GW	90
3850	Strandbad Aga	FU	91
3847	Auensee	FT	91
3833	LuxOase	GU	92
3827	Gaisberg	GS	92
3842	Schlosspark	GT	93
3830	Am Krossinee	GS	93
3815	Ecktannen	GR	93

HUNGARY

510	Ózon	AQ	95
512	Pihenö	BQ	95
513	Panorama	BQ	96
511	Dömös	CQ	96
516	Zugligeti Niche	DQ	97
515	Fortuna	DQ	97
518	Jumbo	DQ	98
520	Autós Caraván	FP	98
522	Pelsöczy	GO	99
524	Dorcas Centre	GP	99
526	Jonathermal	CS	100
530	Kék-Duna	DR	100
531	Sugovica	DS	101
508	Diana	BR	101
504	Autós 1	CR	102
506	*Aranypart*	CR	102
500	*Vadvirág*	CS	103
503	Panorama	BR	103
507	Kristóf	CR	103
509	Füred	CR	104

NORTHERN IRELAND

850	LoanEden	EP	106
834	Drumaheglis	GO	107

REPUBLIC of IRELAND

864	Knockalla	EO	107
870	Gateway	DQ	108
874	Cong	BR	108
876	Sandybanks	BQ	109
878	Knock	DR	109
879	Carra	CR	109
896	Lough Ree East	ER	110
908	*Forest Farm*	ES	110
914	Valley Stopover	GS	110
910	Camac Valley	GS	111
915	River Valley	GS	111
916	Moat Farm	FS	112
924	Tree Grove	ET	112
933	Casey's	EU	113
938	Parsons Green	EU	113
939	Carrick-on-Suir	EU	114

949	Sonas	DU	114
964	Flesk Muckross	CU	115
951	Eagle Point	CV	115
962	Fleming's	CU	116
957	Creveen Lodge	BV	116
958	Waterville	BU	117
961	Mannix Point	BU	117
959	Fossa	BU	118

ITALY

6405	C'era una Volta	BS	120
6410	Genova Est	BR	120
6401	*Dei Fiori*	BS	121
6412	*Valdeiva*	BR	121
6220	Mombarone	BQ	122
6240	Valle Romantica	BQ	122
6245	Riviera	BQ	123
6247	*Tranquilla*	BQ	123
6248	*Parisi*	BQ	124
6250	Lac du Como	BQ	124
6259	Punta d'Oro	CQ	125
6260	Europa Silvella	CQ	125
6280	Week End	CQ	126
6285	Zocco	CQ	126
6252	San Francesco	DQ	127
6253	Piani di Clodia	DQ	127
6020	Union Lido	DQ	128
6010	Capalonga	EQ	129
6015	Il Tridente	EQ	129
6265	Ideal Molino	CQ	130
6270	*La Gardiola*	CQ	131
6275	*Fornella*	CQ	131
6277	*Fontanelle*	CQ	132
6235	Monte Brione	DQ	132
6230	San Cristoforo	DQ	133
6225	Due Laghi	DQ	133
6205	Dolomiti	EQ	133
6210	Steiner	DQ	134
6200	Olympia	EP	134
6201	Antholz	EP	134
6000	Marepineta	EQ	135
6005	Europa	EQ	135
6037	Giuliana	DQ	135
6010	Capalonga	EQ	136
6015	Il Tridente	EQ	136
6020	Union Lido	DQ	136
6035	Mediterraneo	DQ	136
6025	Residence	DQ	136
6030	Dei Fiori	DQ	137
6040	Garden Paradiso	DQ	137
6032	*Cavallino*	DQ	138
6042	*Alba d'Oro*	DQ	138
6050	Serenissima	DQ	139
6055	Isamar	DR	139
6065	Tahiti	DR	140
6060	Estense	DR	140
6602	Bologna	DR	141
6611	Il Poggetto	DS	141
6610	Panoramico	DS	142
6630	Montescudaio	CS	142
6600	Barco Reale	DS	143
6608	Torre Pendente	CS	143
6635	Le Pianacce	CS	144

6637	Il Gineprino	CS	144
6612	Norcenni	DS	145
6623	San Marino	DS	145
6624	Rubicone	DS	146
6620	Norina	ES	146
6625	Montagnola	DS	147
6640	Pappasole	DT	147
6641	*Blucamp*	DT	148
6645	Delle Piscine	DT	148
6653	Listro	DS	149
6650	Kursaal	DS	149
6654	Badiaccia	DS	150
6665	Le Soline	DS	150
6664	*Tos. Colliverdi*	DS	151
6660	Maremma-Souci	DT	151
6661	*Cieloverde*	DT	152
6656	Il Collaccio	ET	152
6655	Assisi	ET	153
6800	Europe Garden	FT	153
6805	Heliopolis	FT	154
6811	*Ipini*	GU	154
6808	Genziana	ET	155
6810	Seven Hills	EU	155
6813	*Porticciolo*	EU	156
6815	Fondi	EU	156
6820	Baia Domizia	EU	157
6832	*I Pini*	FU	157
6835	Riposo	FU	157
6845	San Nicola	GU	158
6803	Athena	GV	158
6842	Sant' Antonio	FV	159
6850	Sea World	GU	159
6852	Marina-Rossano	GV	159

Sardinia

6855	La Tortuga	BU	160
6860	Capo d'Orso	BU	160

LUXEMBOURG

770	Gaalgeberig	GZ	161
776	Europe	GZ	162
775	Bettembourg	GZ	162
781	Martbusch	HY	162
764	Auf Kengert	HY	163
766	*Kockelscheuer*	GZ	164
761	*Birkelt*	GY	164
765	La Sûre	HY	164
763	La Pinède	HY	165
791	Kalkesdelt	GY	165
767	Ardennes	GX	165

NETHERLANDS

550	Pannenschuur	CU	168
552	Zeebad	CU	168
551	Groede	CU	169
558	Veerhoeve	DU	169
556	Wijde Blick	DT	170
559	Rondeweibos	DT	170
557	Molenhoek	DT	171
560	Delftse Hout	DS	171
554	*Katjeskelder*	ET	172
568	*Noordduinen*	DS	172
564	Kijkduinpark	DS	173
561	Oude Maas	ET	174
569	Victorie	ES	174

Campsite Index - by Number

562	Duinrell	DS . 175	2510	Håneset	DU . 205	**SLOVAKIA**		
563	Koningshof	DS . 176	2515	Gjelten Bru	DU . 206	490	Trusalová	FR . 230
565	Club Soleil	DS . 177	2555	Lom	CV . 206	495	Zlaté piesky	ES . 231
567	Gaasper	ES . 177	2545	Rustberg	CV . 206	494	Neresnica	FS . 231
566	Het Amsterdams	ES . 178	2550	Strandefjord	CV . 207	493	Kosice Hamre	GR . 231
570	Molengroet	ER . 179	2570	Fossheim	CV . 207	492	Trencin	ES . 232
572	Uitdam	ER . 179	2590	Sandviken	CW 207	491	Turiec	FR . 232
574	St Maartenszee	EQ . 180	2600	Rysstad	BW 208			
576	Kuilart	FQ . 180	2610	Neset	BX . 208	**SLOVENIA**		
577	Groningen	GO . 181	2612	Holt	CX . 208	410	Spik Autocamp	BP . 234
579	Kuierpadtien	HQ . 181	2615	Olberg	DW 209	415	Kamne	BQ . 234
598	De Roos	GR . 182	Good ArctiCamps Guide		. . . 209	420	Zaka-Bled	CQ . 234
599	Vechtstreek	GR . 182				425	Danica Bohinj	BQ . 235
573	*Sikkeler*	HS . 183				423	Camp Soca	AQ . 235
581	Luttenberg	GR . 183	**POLAND**			427	Kamp Koren	BQ . 235
N580	Flevo-Natuur	FR . 184	*300*	*Stoneczna*	CY . 212	430	Belvedere	BS . 236
582	Hertshoorn	FS . 184	301	Lesny Nr. 52	CX . 212	433	Pivka Jama	CR . 236
583	Kerkendel	GS . 185	303	International 111	CW 212	435	Jezica	DR . 236
586	Betuwestrand	ET . 185	305	Tramp Nr. 33	DW 213	437	Resnik	DQ . 237
584	Pampel	GS . 186	307	Lesny Nr. 21	DU . 213	440	Dolina	EQ . 237
596	*Wielerbaan*	GS . 186	309	Mister Nr. 19	EU . 213	442	Grad Otocec	ER . 237
585	Hooge Veluwe	GS . 187	311	Stegna Nr. 180	EU . 214			
595	Heumens Bos	FT . 188	313	Kretowiny	EV . 214	**SPAIN**		
588	Vinkeloord	FT . 188	315	Wilamowek	FV . 214	**Costa Brava**		
587	Vergarde	FS . 189	317	Mazurski Eden	FV . 215	8005	Cadaqués	KP . 239
589	Klein Canada	GT . 190	319	Kruska	FV . 215	8007	Castell Montgri	KP . 240
591	Hertenwei	FU . 190	323	Olemka Nr. 76	EY . 215	8010	Castell Mar	KP . 241
590	Beekse Bergen	EU . 191	321	Astur Nr. 123	FW. 216	*8012*	*Mas Nou*	KP . 241
594	Elfenmeer	GV . 191	325	Auto Nr. 215	EY . 216	8015	La Laguna	KP . 242
597	De Paal	FU . 192				8020	Amberes	KP . 242
593	Dousberg	GV . 192	**PORTUGAL**			8030	Nautic Almata	KP . 243
			801	Caminha	BQ . 218	8035	Amfora	KP . 243
NORWAY			802	Viana-Castelo	BQ . 218	8050	Aquarius	KP . 244
At the Gateways		. . . 194	803	Rio Alto	BQ . 218	8040	Las Dunas	KP . 244
2315	Ringoy	BV . 196	805	São Jacinto	CR . 219	8060	Ballena Alegre 2	KP . 245
2325	Sundal	BW 196	807	Mira	CR . 219	8074	Paradis	KP . 245
2320	Odda	BW 196	809	Figueira da Foz	CR . 219	8070	La Escala	KP . 246
2330	Eikhamrane	BW 197	840	O Tamanco	BR . 220	8103	El Maset	KP . 246
2370	Botnen	AV . 197	846	Vale Paraiso	BR . 220	8072	Les Medes	KP . 247
2340	Mo	AV . 197	810	Sao Pedro-Moel	BR . 221	8080	El Delfin Verde	KP . 247
2350	Espelandsdalen	BV . 198	811	Valado	BS . 221	8075	Estartit	KP . 248
2360	Ulvik Fjord	BV . 198	845	Colina do Sol	BR . 221	8120	Kim's	KQ. 248
2380	Tveit	BV . 198	813	Guincho	BS . 222	8102	Mas Patoxas	KP . 249
2385	Sandvik	BV . 199	814	Lisboa	BT . 222	8150	Palamós	KQ. 249
2390	Kjornes	BV . 199	815	Caparica	BT . 222	8090	Cypsela	KP . 250
2400	Jolstraholmen	AV . 199	816	Porto Covo	BT . 223	8101	Playa Brava	KP . 250
2436	Byrkjelo	BV . 200	818	Milfontes	BT . 223	*8100*	*Inter-Pals*	KQ. 252
2480	Bjorkedal	BU . 200	819	Sitava	BT . 223	*8170*	*Valldaro*	KO . 252
2460	Prinsen	BU . 200	841	Armação-Pêra	BU . 224	8130	Calonge	KQ. 253
2470	Åndalsnes	BU . 201	843	Sagres	BU . 224	8140	Treumal	KQ. 253
2450	Bjølstad	BU . 201	820	Valverde	BU . 224	8160	Cala Gogo	KQ. 254
2495	Vegset	DT . 201	821	Albufeira	CU . 225	8200	Cala Llevadó	JQ . 255
2490	Skjerneset	BU . 202	823	Olhão	CU . 225	8230	El Pinar	JQ . 255
2485	Krokstrand	ER . 202	822	Quarteira	CU . 226	8235	Blanes	JQ . 256
2465	Lyngvær	AS . 202	844	Quintos-Carriços	CU . 226	8240	Bona Vista Kim	JQ . 256
2475	Saltstraumen	FR . 203	834	Evora	CT . 226	**Costa Daurada**		
2455	Ballangen	BS . 203	835	Markadia	CT . 227	8310	Ballena Alegre	JQ . 257
2435	Solvang	CR . 203	836	Idanha-a-Nova	DR . 227	8390	Vilanova Park	JQ . 257
2445	Slettnes	BR . 204	832	Guarda	CR . 227	*8395*	*Arc de Bara*	JQ . 258
2425	Kirkeporten	CR . 204	831	Castro Daire	CR . 228	8410	Playa Bara	JQ . 258
2415	Kautokeino	CR . 204	833	Arganil	CR . 228	8483	Tamarit-Park	IQ . 259
2500	Trasavika	CU . 205	837	Cerdeira	CQ. 228	8484	Gavina	IR. . 259
2505	Magalaupe	CU . 205	838	Vilar de Mouros	CP . 229			

Campsite Index - by Number

8482	Pineda de Salou	IQ . 260	*9028*	*Las Villuercas*	ES . 289	2740	Laxsjöns	DX . 316
8470	La Siesta	IQ . 261	*9027*	*Monfragüe*	DS . 289	2750	Sommarvik	DW 317
8480	Sanguli	IR . . 261	*9026*	*Burro Blanco*	DR . 289	2760	Frykenbaden	EW 317
8481	Cambrils Park	IQ . 262	9025	Regio	DR . 290	2800	Glyttinge	FX . 318
8520	Marius	IR . . 262	9210	Pico de la Miel	FR . 290	2820	Skantzö Bad	FW. 318
8530	Playa Montroig	IR . . 263	9200	El Escorial	FR . 291	2840	Flottsbro	GW 319
8540	Torre del Sol	IR . . 264	9095	Albarracin	HR . 292	*2842*	*Bredängs*	GW 319
N8537	Templo del Sol	IR . . 264	9250	Costajan	FQ . 292	2835	Orsa Grönklitt	EV . 320
8392	*El Garrofer*	JQ . 265	9023	Santiago	FQ . 292	2845	Svegs	EU . 320
8535	Cala d'Oques	IR . . 265	9021	Fuentes Blancas	FP . 293	2850	Östersunds	EU . 321
8536	Ametlla Platja	IR . . 266	**North**			2855	Flogsta	GU . 321
Costa del Azahar			8942	Los Manzanos	CO. 293	2860	Umeå	HT . 322
8580	Bonterra	IR . . 267	8941	Valdovino	CO. 294	2865	Gielas	GS . 322
8755	Moraira	IS . . 267	9024	As Cancelas	CP . 294	2870	Jokkmokks	GR . 322
8560	Tropicana	IR . . 268	8945	Lagos-Somiedo	DO. 295			
8615	Kiko Park	IS . . 269	8940	Los Cantiles	DO. 295	**SWITZERLAND**		
Costa Blanca			8950	Costa Verde	EO. 295	905	Bois-Couvent	BQ . 324
8680	Armanello	HT . 269	8955	Arenal de Moris	EO. 296	903	Paradis Plage	BR . 324
8681	Villasol	HT . 270	8965	Picos de Europa	EO. 296	909	Avenches	BR . 325
8685	El Raco	HT . 270	8964	Cabuérniga	EO. 296	906	Kappelenbrücke	CQ. 325
8683	Benisol	HT . 271	8962	La Isla	EO. 297	900	Waldhort	CO. 325
8686	*Excalibur*	HT . 271	8963	La Viorna	EO. 297	912	Lido Luzern	CQ. 326
8687	*Cap Blanch*	HT . 272	8970	Las Arenas	FO. 297	913	Vitznau	DQ. 326
8689	*Playa-Torres*	HT . 272	8960	La Paz	EO. 298	915	Seebucht	EP . 326
8741	Florantilles	HU . 273	8971	Playa-Oyambre	FO. 298	918	Buchhorn	GP . 327
8743	*Mar-jal*	HU . 273	8961	El Helguero	FO. 299	921	Pointe à la Bise	AS . 327
8742	La Marina	HU. 274	9000	Playa Joyel	GO. 299	*922*	*Grangettes*	AS . 328
N8752	El Portus	GU. 274	8980	Bella Vista	FO. 300	924	Le Petit Bois	BR . 328
8753	La Manga	HU. 275	8990	Cantabria	GO. 300	930	Le Bivouac	BR . 328
8751	Cuevas Mar	HU. 276	8995	Molinos	GO. 300	927	De Vidy	BR . 329
8750	Los Gallardos	HU. 276	9035	Portuondo	HP . 301	963	Sémiramis	CS . 329
Costa del Sol			9038	Orio	HP . 301	933	Bettlereiche	CR . 330
8760	Mar Azul	GU. 277	9030	Igueldo	HP . 301	936	Grassi	CR . 330
8770	El Paraiso	FU . 277	*9040*	*Haro*	GP . 302	960	Rive-Bleue	CS . 331
8711	Nerja	FU . 278	*9042*	*Etxarri*	HP . 302	939	Vermeille	CS . 331
8782	Laguna Playa	FU . 278	9070	Pirineos	HP . 303	969	Swiss-Plage	DS . 332
8801	La Rosaleda	EV . 279	9100	Casablanca	HQ. 303	971	Les Iles	CT . 332
8805	Los Jarales	EV . 279	9105	Lago Park	HQ. 303	966	Glaciers	CT . 333
8803	La Buganvilla	EV . 279	9125	Lago-Barasona	IQ . 304	967	Molignon	DT . 333
8809	El Sur	EV . 280	9142	Solana-Segre	JP . 304	972	Bella Tola	DS . 334
8810	*Parque Tropical*	EU . 280	9060	Peña Montañesa	IP . 305	973	Gemmi	DS . 334
8812	*Chullera 2*	EV . 280	*9122*	*Montagut*	JP . 306	977	Santa Monica	DS . 335
8800	Marbella Playa	EV . 281	9121	Vall d'Ager	IQ . 306	946	Jungfrau	DS . 335
Costa de la Luz			8506	Serra de Prades	IQ . 307	948	Gletscherdorf	DS . 336
8850	Paloma	DV . 282	9123	El Solsones	JQ . 307	951	Aaregg	DR . 336
8855	Tarifa	DV . 282	**Menorca**			944	Jungfrioublick	DR . 337
8865	*Playa Dunas*	DU . 283	*8000*	*Son Bou*	. . . 308	942	Manor Farm	DR . 337
8860	Fuente del Gallo	DV . 283				949	Eigernordwand	DS . 338
8872	*La Fontanilla*	DU . 284	**SWEDEN**			954	Lido Sarnen	DQ. 338
8871	Giralda	CU . 284	2640	Båstad-Torekov	DY . 310	957	Eienwäldli	ER . 339
Central			2650	Skånes	EY . 310	987	Piccolo Paradiso	ES . 339
9280	Sierra Nevada	FU . 285	2655	Tingsryds	EY . 311	988	Lido Mappo	ES . 340
9270	Suspiro Del Moro	FU . 285	2680	Saxnäs	FX . 311	990	Delta	ES . 340
9080	El Brillante	EU . 286	2675	Lysingsbadet	FX . 312	991	Riarena	FS . 340
9085	Carlos III	EU . 286	2665	Rosenlund	EX . 312	995	Piodella	FT . 341
9081	Villsom	DU . 286	2670	Grännastrandens	EX . 313	993	Al Censo	FS . 341
9083	Monesterio	DT . 287	2700	Borås	DX . 313	981	Camp Au	GR . 341
9087	Mérida	DT . 287	*2705*	*Kärralund*	DX . 314	982	Pradafenz	GR . 342
9088	Fuencaliente	ET . 287	*2706*	*Askim Strand*	DX . 314	985	Farich	GR . 342
9089	Despeñaperros	FT . 288	2710	Lidköping	EX . 315	984	St Cassian	GR . 343
9091	Soto del Castillo	FS . 288	2720	Hökensås	EX . 315	980	Silvaplana	GS . 343
9090	El Greco	FS . 288	2730	Ekudden	EX . 316	983	Sur-En	HR . 344
						986	*Plauns*	HR . 344